BLUE GUIDE

CENTRAL ITALY

Alta Macadam
with Ellen Grady

Somerset Books • London

LIGURIA

GENOA

Rapallo

Portofino
4

*Gulf of
Genoa*

LA SPEZIA

Carrara

Massa

*Ligurian
Sea*

Viareggio

Lucca

Pistoia

PRATO

FLORENCE

PISA

Arno

LIVORNO

I. di Gorgona

S. Gimignano

Volterra

TUSCANY

Siena

I. Capraia

Massa
Marittima

Piombino

Follonica

Montepulciano

Monte
Amiata
1738

I. Elba

Portoferraio

Grosseto

Ombrone

Bastia

Grosseto

Pitigliano

I. Pianosa

Orbetello

L. Bolsena

I. di Montecristo

I. del Giglio

Viterbo

Tarquinia

I. di Giannutri

FRANCE
Corsica

Civitavecchia

p.166

Porto-Vecchio

Fiumi
Lido di

p.1

Strait of Bonifacio

T y r r h e n i a n   S e a

Olbia

SARDINIA

BOLOGNA

RAVENN

Reno

EMILIA-ROMAGNA

Imola

FORLÌ

Monte Cimone
2165

A

P

E

Reno

pp.264–265

N

Sansepolc

Arno

Arezzo

Cortona

Lake
Trasimer

Orvieto

L. Bracci

pp.266–267

CROATIA

5

o Zadar

Dalmatia

pp.618–619

ena
RIMINI

o **S. Marino**
SAN MARINO

o Pesaro

o **Fano**

Urbino o

pp.486–487

Jesi o

✈ **ANCONA**

M A R C H E

Gubbio o

o Macerata

Civitanova
Marche

Tolentino o

ERUGIA

o **Fermo**

✈ o **Assisi**

Foligno o

o Ascoli
Piceno

San Benedetto
del Tronto

A d r i a t i c

Monte Vettore
2476

BRIA

Tronto

o Spoleto

Nera

S e a

Teramo o

TERNI

N

Gran Sasso d'Italia
2912.

o Rieti

L'Aquila o

✈ o **PESCARA**

Chieti o

Pescara

:ivita
stellana

Aterno

A B R U Z Z O

o Vasto

Tiber

Avezzano o

IO

o Sulmona

o Termoli

o Tivoli

Subiaco o

Liri

S

VATICAN CITY
ROME ✈

Fiuggi o

M O L I S E

P U G L I A

o Velletri

Anagni o

Sacco

San Severo o

o Anzio

LATINA

Cassino o

Isernia o

Campobasso o

FOGGIA

Liri

Gargliano

p.210

448
Monte Circeo

Terracina o

Minturno o

Gaeta o

Voltumo

o Benevento

Gulf of
Gaeta

Ponzian Islands
= Zannone

Caserta o

C A M P A N I A

Palmarola ƥ
ᴄ Ponza

Ventotene
ᴅᵒ

Pozzuoli o

✈ **NAPLES**

o Avellino

1277
Mt Vesuvius

First edition 2008

Published by Blue Guides Limited, a Somerset Books Company
Winchester House, Deane Gate Avenue, Taunton, Somerset TA1 2UH
www.blueguides.com
'Blue Guide' is a registered trademark

ISBN 978–1–905131–22–8

A CIP catalogue record of this book is available from the British Library.

Distributed in the United States of America by
WW Norton and Company, Inc.
500 Fifth Avenue, New York, NY 10110

The authors and the publishers have made reasonable efforts to ensure the accuracy of all the
information in *Blue Guide Central Italy*; however, they can accept no responsibility for any loss,
injury or inconvenience sustained by any traveller as a result of information
or advice contained in the guide.

Statement of editorial independence: Blue Guides, their authors and editors, are prohibited from
accepting any payment from any restaurant, hotel, gallery or other establishment for its inclusion
in this guide or on www.blueguides.com, or for a more favourable mention
than would otherwise have been made.

Your views on this book would be much appreciated. We welcome not only specific
comments, suggestions or corrections, but any more general views you may have: how
this book enhanced your holiday, how it could have been more helpful. Blue Guides
authors and editorial and production team work hard to bring you what we hope are the
best-researched and best-presented cultural, historical and academic guide books in the
English language. Please write to us by email (editorial@blueguides.com), via the comments page on our website (www.blueguides.com) or at the address given above. We will
be happy to acknowledge useful contributions in the next edition, and to offer a free copy
of one of our titles.

CONTENTS

The authors

Alta Macadam has been a writer of Blue Guides since 1970. She lives with her Italian family in Florence, where she has been associated with the Bargello museum, the Alinari photo archive, Harvard University at Villa I Tatti, and New York University at Villa La Pietra. Her *Americans in Florence* was published in 2003 (Giunti, Florence). As author of the Blue Guides to Florence, Rome, Tuscany, Umbria and Venice, she travels extensively every year to revise new editions. For this guide she wrote the chapters on Umbria, Tuscany, and northern Lazio.

Ellen Grady Journalist, interpreter and tour guide, Ellen Grady was born in London but has lived in Italy for many years. She is the author of *Blue Guide Sicily* and *Blue Guide The Marche & San Marino*. For this guide she wrote the chapters on the Marche and southern Lazio.

The contributors

Charles Freeman (C.F.) is a freelance academic historian with a long-standing interest in Italy and the Mediterranean. His *Egypt, Greece and Rome, Civilizations of the Ancient Mediterranean* (2nd edition, Oxford University Press, 2004) is widely used as an introductory textbook to the ancient world. His latest book, *AD 381, Heretics, Pagans and the Christian State* was published in the UK in February 2008. He leads study tours of Italy for the Historical Association and has recently been elected a Fellow of the Royal Society of Arts.

Nigel McGilchrist (N.McG.) is an art historian who has lived in the Mediterranean—Italy, Greece and Turkey—for over 25 years, working for a period for the Italian Ministry of Arts and then for six years as Director of the Anglo-Italian Institute in Rome. He has taught at the University of Rome, for the University of Massachusetts, and was for seven years Dean of European Studies for a consortium of American universities. He lectures widely in art and archaeology at museums and institutions in Europe and the United States, and lives near Orvieto. He is currently writing the new Blue Guide to the Aegean Islands of Greece.

Susan Jellis (S.J.) is a freelance writer, editor and lexicographer. She was one of the original editors of the Cambridge International Dictionary of English, and was Managing Editor of the Encarta dictionary series. She has a long-standing interest in garden history, with a qualification from Birkbeck College, London, and a special interest in the gardens of the ancient Roman world. For this guide she contributed to the entries on Villa Aldobrandini, Villa Buonaccorsi, the Boboli Gardens, Castello Ruspoli and Villa di Castello.

Annabel Barber (A.B.) is Editor-in-Chief of the Blue Guides.

EARLY HISTORY

by Charles Freeman

The western side of central Italy consists of the low-lying hills of Etruria, to the south of which is the plain of Latium. The soil is volcanic, enjoys good rainfall and so is always fertile. To the east the Apennines sweep down the peninsula. Although they are a formidable range, they are split by deep running gorges which allow the exploitation of pastures in valleys and in uplands. Communication routes run along the tops of ridges or through the valleys, but the earliest peoples of Italy lived in fragmented communities. Although they all, with the exception of the Etruscans, spoke languages from the Indo-European group, these had developed so as to be mutually unintelligible: Latin in central Latium, Faliscan to the immediate north of Rome, Volscian to the south, and Umbrian and Sabellian, each with many dialects, in the mountains. This was a diverse region, therefore, and difficult for any one people to dominate. Before the coming of the Romans, the only major civilisation was that of the Etruscans, whose lands reached between the Tiber and the Arno.

THE ETRUSCANS

Etruria, the homeland of the Etruscans, stretched across the western plains and hills of central Italy between the Arno and Tiber rivers. The peoples here had always been prosperous: the volcanic soil was fertile and there were metals—iron, copper and silver—in the hills. By 900 BC a growing population sustained by intensive farming was settling on hilltop sites. (Their culture is known as Villanovan.) The catalyst for further advance came in the 8th century with the arrival of Greek and Phoenician traders eager for metals. They based themselves in a cosmopolitan settlement on the island of Ischia, and began trading with the mainland. In return, the Etruscans received pottery and finished metalwork, and an Etruscan aristocracy emerged to enjoy it. Many features of their civilised life were borrowed from the Greeks, in particular banquets where they reclined on couches as the Greeks did and dined off Greek pottery. However, the Etruscans always controlled their own culture. While respectable women never attended Greek banquets, the Etruscan elite sat at theirs alongside their wives. The Etruscans even developed their own tastes in subjects for art. Hercules, for instance, was far more popular among the Etruscans than he was in Greece, and there is evidence that the Athenian potters created ware specifically for the Etruscan market. So popular were Greek vases that 80 per cent of all those known have been excavated in Italy.

There was never a distinct Etruscan nation; rather theirs was a society of clans whose chieftains asserted individual authority, often in single combat against their rivals. The tombs of the 8th century were furnished with the status symbols of a warrior aristocracy: helmets, swords and shields and chariots. The Etruscans had a common language, interesting for being non-Indo-European and thus distinct from its neighbours. Literacy seems to have been confined to the aristocracy, who adopted (and adapted) the Greek alphabet. The clans developed their own strongholds, usually on the same sites as earlier Villanovan villages. The local volcanic rock, tufa, was easy to quarry so that sites could be defended by fortifications. So evolved the major Etruscan cities, some of which can still be visited: Veio, Tarquinia, Vulci, Cerveteri, Volsinii (on the sites of the modern Orvieto and Bolsena). They were well defended and usually had a central square surrounded by monumental buildings, including temples. The largest towns may have had populations of up to 30,000. There are good stretches of surviving Etruscan walls in Cortona, Roselle and Volterra. The Etruscans spread southwards and many cities, among them Rome, came under their influence, often seen in monumental building projects. It was the Etruscans who built the first major temple in Rome, the Temple of Jupiter on the Capitoline Hill, and it was they who drained the marshy land at the foot of the Palatine Hill, paving the way for the Roman Forum.

The Romans always regarded the Etruscans as deeply religious, and certainly ritual pervaded their lives. There was a rich pantheon of gods, some local, some adopted from the Greeks. The Etruscan temples were based on Greek models but developed a much higher podium. It was from the podium that the augurs would watch the skies for portents. Each deity was assigned a portion of the sky. The augurs would watch how birds flew and make their forecasts accordingly. Another ritual required the minute examination of the entrails of sacrificed animals, especially the liver, which was seen as the seat of life. The anger of the gods was assuaged by votive offerings: a small warrior was a favourite choice.

It is difficult to know how the Etruscans viewed the afterlife, but their tombs were designed as if it was to be a continuation of life on earth. Typically, the tomb chamber would have carved recesses or stone benches for the sarcophagi. The painted tombs at Tarquinia are especially worth visiting as they show not only the skills of Etruscan artists, but also the aristocratic lifestyle that sustained them. It was a life based on banqueting, hunting and other sports, including boxing and wrestling. The earliest aristocratic burials are in scattered tombs, but with time the necropoleis became more formal, with streets of tombs and larger chambers, each probably reserved for a family or clan (see especially the Crocifisso del Tufo necropolis at Orvieto). This probably reflects the emergence of a more egalitarian society from the 6th century onwards.

By the 6th century, however, the Etruscans were under pressure. Greek expansion on the Italian mainland and the growing power of the Carthaginians were the first threats. The Carthaginian navy began forcing Etruscan shipping off the sea. Gold tablets found at Pyrgi, the port of Cerveteri (*see p. 189*), were dedicated to the shrine there by a Carthaginian ruler probably imposed on the Etruscans. In southern Etruria, the Samnites were raiding their cities from the hills, and Rome expelled its Etruscan kings, the Tarquins, about 510 BC. Gradually the Etruscans retreated from the coast, although some inland cites—Fiesole, Cortona, Volsinii (Bolsena) and Veio—continued to exploit their land successfully. Twelve of the leading cities maintained a common shrine to the goddess Voltumna (possibly discovered at Orvieto; *see p. 594*).

ETRUSCAN BRONZE & TERRACOTTA

The Etruscans had good supplies of copper, but it was always difficult to cast. Mixed with a little tin, however (imported from Bohemia, Gaul or Cornwall), its melting point fell and it solidified as bronze, which was stronger and more tensile.

As with most aspects of Etruscan culture, it was the Greeks who provided inspiration for designs and technical developments. Cauldrons for sacrificial banquets, the tripods on which they stand (a major votive offering at Greek shrines of the 8th century) and incense burners are common finds in Etruscan tombs. Some of the decoration of these and other vessels is especially fine: slim human figures are shaped as handles or ride on horseback around the rim. Particularly impressive are the mirrors, incised on the reverse with myths drawn from Greece.

Another important area was the creation of votive offerings for temples. Some of these were large, such as the *Chimaera* from Arezzo (now in the Archaeological Museum in Florence), which was an offering to Tinia, the Etruscan equivalent of Zeus, but the majority were smaller figurines. Some of the largest deposits have been found at healing shrines alongside casts of body parts, in a tradition which has continued through Roman times into Christianity. One of the most intriguing figures is the elongated bronze found at Volterra, the *Ombra della Sera*, now in the museum there (it was being used as a poker when discovered!). It proved an inspiration for the sculptor Giacometti.

As with the bronzes of other Mediterranean societies, most have disappeared. The metal was all too easy to recycle. When the Romans took the city of *Volsinii* they are said to have carted 2,000 bronze statues to be melted down for Roman coinage. The Romans were influenced by the later Etruscan penchant for portrait busts, of which the *Brutus* in the Capitoline Museum in Rome is a superb example. The style of the hair draws on Etruscan models; indeed it may have been made by Etruscan craftsmen for a Roman patron (date uncertain; perhaps c. 300 BC).

Etruscan terracotta

Etrurian tufa was ideal for building as it was easy to quarry and easy to carve. However, it also weathered easily and was unsuitable for decorative work. Neither could it take paint. This may be the main reason why the Etruscans developed terracotta, literally 'cooked earth', for so much of their sculpture. Terracotta was ideally suited to decorating temples. Fine examples come from the Portonaccio Temple at Veio (now in the Villa Giulia; *see p. 73*). The most moving creations of the terracotta sculptors, however, are the sarcophagi. They show either individuals or married couples reclining as they would do at banquets. Those of aristocratic couples from Cerveteri, of which there is a fine example in the Villa Giulia, are justly famous. Even though their clothing and the bed itself is of Greek design, the couples show a tenderness towards each other which is seldom found in Greek art.

As Rome began its inexorable expansion from the plain of Latium, it faced a society which was already in decline. The first major blow to the remaining city states came in 396, when after an epic ten-year war (as Roman historians later chronicled it) the city of Veio was taken. Veio was only 15km from Rome, but it marked the beginning of Roman supremacy. The collapse of Etruscan power came 100 years later (295) after a massive battle at Sentinum against a coalition of Etruscans and neighbouring tribes. In 27 BC, Etruria was classified as no more than the seventh region of Roman Italy. Nevertheless, the Romans retained great respect for the Etruscans. They absorbed their model of the temple with its high podium as well as the tradition of fine bronzework. The triumph, the parade of a victor with his spoils through the centre of Rome, appears to be Etruscan in origin, while Etruscan religious rituals were preserved in the so-called *disciplina*. The *fasces*, the bound rods which preceded Etruscan, and later, Roman magistrates, were to prove an all too enduring symbol of authority.

The Etruscans have always held a nostalgic appeal. Even the Romans surveyed their deserted sites and mourned their greatness. In the 1840s, the English scholar George Dennis toured the remaining citadels and in his *The Cities and Cemeteries of Etruria* produced one of the most beautifully written surveys of their civilisation. D.H. Lawrence (*Etruscan Places*, published posthumously 1932), talked of 'the true Etruscan quality: ease, naturalness and an abundance of life'. His romanticised view had taken hard knocks from archaeological research, but the Etruscans still remain one of the more attractive civilisations of the ancient Mediterranean world.

The finest Etruscan collections are those of the Villa Giulia in Rome, the Vatican Museums and the Archaeological Museum in Florence, but there are also good local collections at the main centres, particularly Tarquinia. An excellent introduction to Etruscan civilisation is the book of the same name by Sybille Haynes (paperback edition, 2005, British Museum Publications, London).

ROME: TEMPORAL & SPIRITUAL EMPIRE

Rome's rise to power in the face of such a sophisticated civilisation was remarkable and unexpected. The city owed much to its position on a crossing place on the Tiber, which exposed it to outside influences, notably Greek traders and Etruscan overlords. Rome's mythical founding date of 753 BC accords well with archaeological evidence of trade with Greece. In the 5th century BC the major threat to Rome lay in raids from the mountains, and Rome co-operated with other cities of Latium in seeing them off. Her victories allowed her to confront the Etruscan city of Veio (*see above*) and later expand towards the coast to incorporate the port of Ostia. The secret of Rome's success lay in a government where the leading magistrates (the consuls) were generals, backed by a highly effective infantry force (the legions); and in a brutal tenacity which was honed in tough struggles in the mountains. Many rival cities were razed to the ground, but others who submitted were given the right to trade with Rome and intermarry with her citizens, on condition that they provided their conqueror with troops. It was a flexible system which provided a continuously expanding army and so fuelled further expansion.

To consolidate her victories in central Italy, the Romans settled colonies of her own citizens. A notable colony in Etruscan territory was Cosa, settled on a hillside near modern Orbetello in 273 BC. It was a frontier town when built, manned by veteran soldiers and their families and defended by a wall. Inside there was a forum (the market place) and a chamber in the shape of an amphitheatre, where the town council met in debate. Other public buildings, a temple and a basilica, were added later. Later colonies did have to be so well protected. Florence, for instance, was founded as the Roman colony of *Florentia* in 82 BC in the open valley below the Etruscan town of Fiesole on the river Arno. (Its original plan can still be traced in the streets in the centre.)

Alongside the founding of colonies came the driving of roads through conquered territory. Perhaps the most important was the Via Flaminia, named after Gaius Flaminius, the magistrate who commissioned it in 220 BC. It ran north from Rome along the western side of the Tiber valley using the track of an earlier Etruscan road. It then reached the colony of *Spoletium* (modern Spoleto), and headed off on a twisting route over the Apennines. Some of the original bridges survive, and the tunnel the Romans cut through the Furlo Gorge is still used by the modern road (*see pp. 649–50*). The Via Flaminia ran down a valley to the Adriatic meeting the sea at another colony, *Fanum Fortunae* (modern Fano in the Marche), before running north along the coast to *Ariminum* (Rimini). It was a remarkable technical achievement, and it was primarily a route through which control could be maintained over defeated peoples and access gained to the fertile Po valley. Hardly had the road been put under construction than Rome suffered its greatest challenge when the Carthaginian general Hannibal swept through central Italy, destroying a Roman army (and killing Gaius Flaminius) at the battle of Lake Trasimene (217). The only consolation was that the cities of central Italy stayed loyal but it took many years of dogged fighting before Hannibal was driven from the peninsula.

With peace restored ancient cities close to the roads were drawn inexorably into Roman civilisation. Many were given the status of *municipium*, which meant that their autonomy was respected so long as they paid taxes and provided soldiers for the Roman armies. Gubbio, in a relatively remote setting in the Apennines, was an Umbrian city whose religious rituals are known from the Iguvine Tables, written in Umbrian using Latin and Etruscan script (and still in the museum in the city). It allied with the Romans as a *municipium* known as *Iguvium*, and its inhabitants retained their local culture and city government. Gradually, however, a typical Roman town with temples, planned streets and a fine theatre (which still stands) developed. Smaller Roman settlements appeared along the main routes as administrative and market centres.

As Roman power extended beyond central Italy to the Greek cities of the south and across the Mediterranean, vast amounts of plunder, including slaves, poured into the region. In Rome itself temples to the gods of war and the adoption of the triumph for victorious generals were symbols of her new status. The sanctuary to Fortuna at *Praeneste* (Palestrina) was rebuilt in grand style to reflect Rome's victories. In the countryside the smallholdings which had produced Rome's peasant farmers and soldiers were replaced by much larger estates run by the new wealthy on slave labour. This put enormous pressure on her subject cities, but a final explosion of discontent (the Social

War) was defeated in 90 BC. Rome rewarded those who stayed loyal with full citizen rights. Roman citizenship, extended to the whole of Italy by 49 BC, was an important sign that Italy, despite the survival of many local cultures, was now Roman. Roman political control coexisted with the survival of many local cults and ancient sanctuaries.

The 1st century BC saw almost continuous social unrest as rival politicians fought for control. The republican system collapsed and was replaced by a single dominant emperor. The first, Augustus (ruled 27 BC–14 AD), finally brought peace, and with that peace came the prosperity which was natural to a fertile area. Augustus lavished patronage on Italy. He improved the road network and commissioned new buildings, especially in the colonies. Although there were years of disruption, as in 69 AD when rival emperors contested the throne, Italy was much more settled after his reign. The smaller cities adorned themselves with market places, temples, majestic gateways and walls. In the countryside a villa economy became established, supplying the needs of the cities. Studies of even humble farms show that their owners used imported pottery and were able to roof their homes with tiles. Rome itself sucked in wealth from the empire, notably through the port of Ostia, which became a major city in its own right. The emperors glorified Rome still further with the lavish Imperial Fora and a sequence of vast public baths.

The increasing splendour of the city could not mask the fact that the emperors were spending less and less time there. The 3rd century was an unstable period as Rome's barbarian enemies began to gather. Public building in the cities of central Italy faltered and resources were now poured into defence. Villas were abandoned and many smaller towns atrophied. Some stability did return when the empire was reorganised under Diocletian (late 3rd century), but the most significant development was the patronage of Christianity by his successor Constantine (AD 312 onwards). Constantine followed pagan precedent in so far as he made opulent buildings, many of them modelled on the traditional Roman public hall (the basilica), the public expression of the new faith. At the beginning of the 4th century, churches were built on the edge of Rome: the first St Peter's on the Vatican Hill, and the major church of Christ the Redeemer (now St John Lateran) to the southeast. By the 5th century churches were beginning to intrude even into the ancient centre, and it was at this time that the senatorial aristocracy, many of whom had clung to their inherited wealth, began to convert in numbers. The Church also began to accumulate large estates throughout Italy (sometimes the gifts of converted aristocrats who had taken to asceticism), and the whole structure of landholding began to change.

The growth of the Church took place against a backdrop of social and economic breakdown. The first sack of Rome by Alaric and his Goths in 410 was a comparatively restrained affair (the Goths were also Christians and spared churches), but it sent a shock-wave throughout the Empire. Worse was to come, as the Empire disintegrated after the abdication of the last emperor, Romulus Augustulus, in 476. While the Ostrogoth ruler Theodoric (who seized power in Ravenna in 493) did restore Rome and use Roman administrators, with his death in 526 effective central government disappeared. An invasion by the Byzantine emperors, who hoped to regain Italy for the Empire, as well as wars between Gothic rulers, saw the dislocation of central

Italy. Rome shrank to just 30,000 inhabitants (from perhaps a million in Augustus' day). Pope Gregory the Great, whose administrative expertise did much to retain some power for the Church, recorded how '*towns are depopulated, fortified places destroyed, churches burnt, monasteries and nunneries destroyed; fields are deserted by men, and the earth, forsaken by the ploughman, gapes desolate. No farmer dwells here now; wild beasts have taken the place of throngs of men*'. The cities of the lowlands were abandoned in favour of hilltop settlements, and local warlords offered protection in return for service on the land or in the army. Trade with the rest of the Mediterranean had virtually ceased. The road from Ostia to Rome was reported to be covered in grass, and the great aqueducts were cut or left to fall into disrepair. This diminished world was further fragmented by the arrival of the Lombards from across the Alps. They successfully conquered northern Italy and penetrated as far south as Spoleto and Benevento, where they founded independent duchies.

Nevertheless, the Greek-speaking Byzantines managed to retain control over much of central Italy. They also collaborated with the Church in a period when the Eastern and Western Churches were still part of a single Christendom. Eight out of the eleven popes between 678 and 752 were Syrian or Greek. However, the Roman Church gradually distanced itself from its Greek overlords. It resented the intrusion of the Byzantine emperors, and the popes opposed the great 'iconoclastic' campaign against 'icons' which gripped the East in the 8th century.

This distancing put the Church in good stead when a further expansion of the Lombards in 751 saw the fall of Ravenna, capital of the Byzantine exarchate, and the collapse of Byzantine rule in Italy. Pope Stephen II (752–57) called to the Franks to help him thwart the Lombards. The most successful Frankish leader was Charlemagne, who defeated the Lombards and assumed the crown of Lombardy in 774. A contender for the papacy (later Leo III) then called on Charlemagne to help in his own struggle for election. It was a successful campaign, and on Christmas Day 800, Leo crowned Charlemagne as 'Roman Emperor'. Among the titles Charlemagne took was *augustus*, as if he could revive the lost glories of Rome. It marked a new beginning for Italy. For many centuries the relative powers of emperor and pope remained undefined, but the struggle between them was the context from which medieval Italy was to emerge.

POPES & HOLY ROMAN EMPERORS

by Annabel Barber

The Pope

The Pope, according to the tenets of the Catholic Church, is, in his capacity as Bishop of Rome, the spiritual successor to St Peter and vicar (representative on earth) of Christ. The claim is based on Christ's own words to his disciple: 'Thou art Peter, and upon this rock I will build my Church ... and I will give unto thee the keys of the kingdom of heaven'. Spiritually, these Petrine Claims were all that was needed. In temporal terms, they could be seen as flimsy. Hence the famous document known as the 'Donation of Constantine', a forgery from the 8th century asserting that Constantine, the first Christian emperor, had given the Bishop of Rome dominion over Rome and all parts of Italy. The popes clearly wanted this to be true. When Charlemagne's father, Pepin the Short, drove the Lombards out of Ravenna in 754, he presented the reconquered territory to Rome. Byzantium objected. The Lombards had taken Ravenna from Byzantium (*see p. 15 above*); to Byzantium it should be restored. Pepin replied that he had gone to war for St Peter, and to St Peter—ie Rome—the spoils would go. The Papal State, or Patrimony of St Peter as it was first known, was born.

Charlemagne was a very different man from his father. When he succeeded, he defeated the Lombard king altogether and became ruler of the Lombard lands himself. He also had grand ideas about his role, not only as temporal sovereign but as guardian of the faith. The weak pope Leo III was his perfect opportunity: Charlemagne persuaded Leo to crown him Emperor in the year 800.

Conflicting claims to authority between Pope and Emperor were present ever after. The papacy would claim that Leo had crowned Charlemagne, showing that the emperor owed his title to the pope, who was both a spiritual and a temporal prince, and whose sole authority it was to confer power. Charlemagne would argue that supreme power was his over Church and state, and that the pope was chief spiritual administrator. Charlemagne saw to it that his own son succeeded him before he died; he even crowned him with his own hands, so as to be indebted to Rome for nothing. But Charlemagne's heirs let the kingdom fall into disarray. The popes of the 9th century wrested back some power, not least the authority to confer the title of Emperor. But it remained a fact that the popes were not generals, and they were incompetent at wielding temporal power. Influential rival families made sure that their scions were elected: infighting, veniality and outright corruption were rife.

The Holy Roman Emperor

From its very inception the Holy Roman Empire was a symbolic creation. When Charlemagne was crowned in the year 800, he was crowned by the pope as a symbol of his role as defender of Christendom. He was also crowned in ancient Roman garb, harking back to the golden age of the Roman Empire, with all its unifying and civilising might. He was crowned in Rome, too, the ancient cradle of that empire, and the seat of the Western Church, as a way of demonstrating to the Byzantine emperor that his jurisdiction over Italy was gone forever.

When Charlemagne later conquered and christianised the Saxons, his empire acquired the Germanic element which in later centuries was to be its defining feature, in frequent conflict with the Roman and French popes. When Charlemagne died, the empire was divided among his heirs and became a broad federation of territories covering what is now most of France, Italy and Germany. Each dukedom or principality had its own ruler, and the symbolic nature of the Holy Roman Empire became more marked than ever, representing a European federal ideal which has exercised the imagination of the continent's leaders ever since. The relationship between Holy Roman Emperor and Pope also remained ambivalent. The Pope was the head of the Church, but the Emperor was its defender—against pagan barbarians, the Arab infidel and Byzantium. Frequent quarrels broke out over which of the two, Emperor or Pope, had the better right to consider himself God's representative on earth.

Emperors did not inherit the crown; they were chosen by election, and then crowned either at Rome (seat of the Church), at Aix-la-Chapelle (where Charlemagne died) or at Frankfurt ('stronghold of the Franks'). However, the empire's Frankish origins were swiftly diluted as the federation became more Germanic in its makeup, with first the Ottonian and then the Hohenstaufen dynasties. Though two Hohenstaufen emperors, Frederick I Barbarossa and Frederick II, fought numerous battles to conquer the heart of Italy, they both had to acknowledge the independence of the communes (*see below*). The emperors never managed to secure a power base in central Italy. By the 15th century theirs was no longer Charlemagne's 'Empire of the Romans and the Franks', but the 'Holy Roman Empire of the German Nation', a concept that put unholy ideas into the head of more than one modern despot. Napoleon wanted to reassert the empire's Frankishness, and saw himself as the natural heir of Charlemagne. In 1804 he declared himself Emperor of France, seizing the crown from Pope Pius VII's hands and placing it on his own head in conscious imitation of Charlemagne's gesture of a millennium before. In 1809 he annexed as much of Italy as he could to his empire. Though Napoleon was doomed to be defeated, the spectre of the Holy Roman Empire refused to rest. Fired up by the idea of that once-glorious German *Reich*, Adolf Hitler set the countries of Europe at each other's throats to try to recreate it—the ultimate revenge of the Saxon on the conquering Charlemagne.

Guelphs and Ghibellines

References to Guelphs and Ghibellines occur frequently in this book, and describe the partisan rivalries which dogged early medieval Italy. Both names are German in origin. 'Guelph' derives from the Welf family of Bavaria, enemies of the Hohenstaufen; 'Ghibelline' comes from the castle of Waiblingen in Baden-Württemburg, ancestral home of Frederick Barbarossa. The former is often taken to denote members of the merchant classes, propope in their sympathies; and the latter to describe the pro-imperial aristocracy. But it was never as simple as that. A string of weak emperors in the 11th century led to a power vacuum in Italy, and cities began to declare themselves free communes: the emerging merchant class was eager to take control of its own destiny. Many of these communes prospered, growing rich from trade. But they were always hotbeds of faction. And the leaders of the opposing sides, though they may have called themselves 'Guelph' or 'Ghibelline', were certainly not interested in more power for pope or emperor. Family rivalries were at the heart of most of the power struggles, with leaders fighting for more influence for their own clan. To secure this, they gave allegiance where they saw most advantage: shifting support between pope and emperor, and often seeking the protection of neither. The 'Guelph' and 'Ghibelline' squabbles which were such a feature of city life in medieval Italy eventually led to the collapse of the communes, as cities looked to a single powerful leader, a *signore*, or a *podestà*, a magistrate who was not a native, to lead them to prosperity and peace. The republican experiment did not survive its own turbulent age.

CHRONOLOGY

FROM THE DARK AGES TO THE ITALIAN REPUBLIC

compiled by Annabel Barber

The Dark Ages

When the last Emperor of the West, Romulus Augustulus, abdicates in 476, Italy enters the 'Dark Ages', as strife between Byzantines, Goths and Lombards plagues the peninsula. The Byzantines control the coast from Ravenna to Senigallia, maintaining a 'corridor' to Rome through Perugia. From the mid-6th century important coastal cities unite in the Maritime Pentapolis of Rimini, Ancona, Fano, Senigallia and Pesaro, governed by the Byzantines. Later invaders, the Franks, support the popes against the Lombards, and found the Carolingian dynasty.

480: St Benedict born at Norcia in Umbria

529: St Benedict founds the monastery at Monte Cassino

549: Totila the Ostrogoth holds the last games in the Circus Maximus in Rome

554: The important monastic centre of Farfa is founded near Rieti; the Byzantines under Narses defeat the Goths at Lucca. Narses is appointed prefect of Italy

568: The Lombards invade Italy. Two years later they set up an independent duchy in the centre of the peninsula, with its capital at Spoleto

578: Lombards take Ascoli Piceno

581: Lombards destroy Monte Cassino

590: Accession to the pontificate of Gregory the Great, who settles power disputes between Goths and Byzantines by asserting control himself, and founding the temporal power of the papacy

609: The Pantheon is consecrated as a church, the first pagan temple to be Christianised

728: The Lombard king Liutprand cedes Sutri to the papacy, reinforcing the temporal power of the popes

754: The Papal States are born, after the Frankish king Pepin captures Ravenna and its territory, which had been seized by the Lombards, and instead of restoring it to the Byzantines, presents it to the papacy

774: Franks oust the Lombards from Tuscany

781: Sant'Antimo abbey founded, allegedly by Charlemagne

789: The Lombard Duchy of Spoleto is absorbed by the Franks, though retains some autonomy for decades to come

800: Pepin's son Charlemagne is crowned Holy Roman Emperor

812: The Byzantine emperor recognises Charlemagne as Emperor of the West

951: Otto of Saxony takes central Italy after the collapse of the Carolingian dynasty

962: Otto is crowned as the Holy Roman Emperor Otto I, uniting the Italian and German empires

The Middle Ages

Against a backdrop of perpetual power struggles between popes and emperors, the first self-governing communes of Italy emerge, the earliest being merchant maritime states, where trade is allowed to develop to the common advantage. The maritime republic of Pisa is at the height of its power in the 12th century. The 12th–mid-14th centuries are the golden age of Siena. Florence develops as a centre of the wool trade in the 13th century, and greatly expands its territory over the course of the 14th and early 15th centuries. Government of the cities is always faction-riven, however, and gradually powerful local or foreign families begin to exert control as overlords.

1087: Genoa and Pisa oust the Arabs to gain control of the western Mediterranean

1138: Power struggles between Henry the

Proud of Bavaria and the Swabian Hohenstaufen clan are the first stirrings of what will become known as Guelph and

Ghibelline rivalry (*see p. 17*)

1152: Frederick Barbarossa becomes Holy Roman Emperor. His Hohenstaufen dynasty, powerful and overweening, spends much time in conflict with the papacy and the city states

1167: Barbarossa makes Viterbo a city. Popes and Holy Roman Emperors struggle to control it over the ensuing decades

1177: Barbarossa and Pope Alexander III sign a peace treaty between the Holy Roman Emperor and the 'Lombard League' of free communes

1181: St Francis of Assisi born

1194: The future Holy Roman Emperor Frederick II is born at Jesi in the Marche (*see p. 632*); baptised at Assisi in 1197

1209: Pope Innocent III verbally approves the Franciscan Order. His toughness as pope saves the power of the papacy, which had been much eroded by Barbarossa

1210: Order of the Friars Minor (Franciscans) founded. The first claimed example of a portrait from life (of St Francis of Assisi, at Subiaco in Lazio) dates from this time

1224: St Francis receives the Stigmata at La Verna in northern Tuscany

1247: Frederick II, now Holy Roman Emperor, rebuilds the castle at Castiglione on Lake Trasimene, making it one of the most impregnable strongholds in Europe

1260: Nicola Pisano: pulpit and baptistery at Pisa

1262: Pope Urban IV tries to end Hohenstaufen power by offering the kingdom of Naples to Charles of Anjou. Border areas around Amatrice come under Neapolitan control

1264: Urban IV institutes the festival of Corpus Christi, following a miracle at Bolsena (*see p. 180*)

1266/7: Birth of Giotto in Vespignano, north of Florence. His art becomes the springboard for the Italian Renaissance

1268: The last of the Hohenstaufen is defeated. He flees to Torre Astura in Lazio, is captured and beheaded by Charles of Anjou with the agreement of Clement V

1271: Pope Gregory X elected at Viterbo. The election lasts two years, and the new pope draws up revised rules for the electoral conclave. These rules are still largely followed

1275: Giovanni Malatesta of Gradara in the Marche marries Francesca da Polenta. Her fatal love affair with her brother-in-law Paolo has inspired poets and painters ever since

1276–81: Viterbo becomes the chief city of the popes, rivalling Rome

1284: Battle of Meloria. Pisa defeated by Genoa; its power comes to an end

1287–1355: Siena ruled by a Guelph oligarchy, the Council of Nine

1290: Cimabue: *Maestà*

1294: The house of Joseph of Nazareth, childhood home of Jesus, miraculously appears in a laurel grove in the Marche (*see p. 627*)

1300: First Holy Year proclaimed by Boniface VIII. Anyone making the pilgrimage to Rome in that year would obtain temporal absolution from their sins. Pilgrim numbers soar

c.1300: Giotto's *Maestà* (Uffizi)

1302: The *Neri* (Black Guelphs) of Florence drive out the *Bianchi* (Whites). Dante goes into exile; Pope Boniface VIII publishes his bull *Unam Sanctam*, stating the superiority of spiritual over temporal power, and claiming that no one who is not subject to the pope can obtain salvation

1308–11: Duccio's *Maestà* for Siena cathedral

1309: Clement V moves the seat of the papacy to Avignon

1310: Earliest known mining code drawn up at Massa Marittima in coastal Tuscany

1316–28: Lucca is the dominant power in western Tuscany

1343–69: Pisa dominates Lucca and western Tuscany

1347: St Catherine of Siena born

1348: Black death

1351: Giovanni Visconti of Milan tries to take control of Tuscany. Florence goes to war with him

1353: Cardinal Albornoz is sent to Italy by the popes in Avignon to prevent the city states from forming alliances with the Holy Roman Empire. He builds fortresses all over central Italy

1375: St Catherine of Siena receives the Stigmata at Pisa

1378: The papacy under Gregory XI returns

from Avignon to Rome and takes up residence in the Vatican. The Great Schism begins at Fondi, when dissident cardinals elect an antipope to challenge Urban VI. Popes and antipopes dispute claims to the papal chair for the next four decades
1380: St Bernardino of Siena, the great Franciscan preacher, born at Massa Marittima
1384: Florence takes control of Arezzo

1387: The Montefeltro, Counts of Urbino, take Gubbio, retaining it until 1508
1399: Siena allies itself with Milan against Florence
1402: Gian Galeazzo Visconti dies besieging Florence. Brunelleschi and Ghiberti: *Sacrifice of Isaac* panels
1406: Florence gains control of Pisa, and thus acquires access to the sea

The Renaissance

Spearheaded by economic and territorial expansion, art and learning flourish in Florence and Tuscany. During the 15th century, Italy leads the world in art and science. Rome is magnificently embellished when the popes return from Avignon, and the Papal States increase in size and influence. The 15th century is also the heyday of the Umbrian school of painting, whose greatest exponent is Perugino (c. 1446–1523), master of Raphael.

1417: The Great Schism ends with the accession of Pope Martin V
1420: Terracina becomes a frontier outpost of the Papal States, bordering the Kingdom of Naples
1421: Florence purchases Livorno to gain better access to the sea as Pisa's harbour silts up
1434: Cosimo il Vecchio comes to power in Florence. His family, the Medici, is to shape the city's—and much of central Italy's—fortunes for centuries to come. Cosimo is the patron of the architect Michelozzo
1436: Dome of Florence cathedral completed, the highest of its time (91m)
1439: Council of Florence. The Byzantine Emperor John Palaeologus comes with a delegation of Eastern Church leaders, aimed at healing the breach between East and West; Foligno and Trevi join the Papal States
1440: Battle of Anghiari. Florence defeats the Milanese Visconti
1441: Florence gains Sansepolcro
1444: Federico da Montefeltro becomes Duke of Urbino and ushers in the city's golden age; The Iguvine Tables, the most important record of the ancient language of the Umbri (3rd or 2nd century BC) discovered at Gubbio

1451: Leon Battista Alberti: Palazzo Rucellai
1452: Leonardo da Vinci born at Anchiano, near Florence
1453: Fall of Constantinople. Greek scholars are received as refugees in Florence
1464: The first printing press in Italy is set up at Subiaco. Its first two books are a volume of Cicero and a 4th-century Christian apologia
1469: Pope Paul II grants a plenary indulgence to all those who go to Loreto on pilgrimage
1471: The oldest public art collection in the world is inaugurated by Pope Sixtus IV (now part of the Capitoline Museums in Rome)
1472: Florence definitively (and brutally) subdues Volterra, and incorporates it into the Florentine republic
1475: Michelangelo born at Caprese Michelangelo in northern Tuscany
1483: Raphael born at Urbino
1489: First 'modern' archaeological dig takes place at Tarquinia
1490s: Discovery of Nero's Domus Aurea in Rome, with its painted walls and vaults, the design of which is to influence generations of Renaissance and Neoclassical artists and architects
1494: Charles VIII of France enters Italy

The 16th and 17th centuries

France and Spain begin their expansion into Italy, and spend the next 60 years fighting for territory in the peninsula, France under Charles VIII and Francis I, and Spain under Charles V and Philip II. This is also the age of the Counter-Reformation, in response to the perceived threat from

Protestant northern Europe. Italy is no longer the cultural or economic leader of Europe. Trade routes expand outside the Mediterranean (though Livorno prospers from trade with England).

1504: Michelangelo's *David*. The sculpture assumes importance for Florence as a symbol of the republican spirit prevailing against the Papal States

1508: The last of the Montefeltro dukes dies. Urbino passes to the della Rovere family

1508–12: Michelangelo: Sistine ceiling

1509: Florence takes control of Pisa

1513–21: Papacy of Leo X (Giovanni de' Medici of Florence), great patron of Raphael

1513: Machiavelli writes *The Prince*, at Sant'Andrea in Percussina, south of Florence

1516: Pope Leo X drives the della Rovere from Urbino, which he bestows upon his nephew Lorenzo (commemorated in a tomb by Michelangelo in Florence; *see p. 297*)

1527: Rome is sacked by the troops of Holy Roman Emperor Charles V, whose rival Francis I of France is supported by the Medici pope Clement VII. Pope Clement flees to Orvieto

1529: Charles V of Spain takes Amatrice on the Umbrian border

1532: Clement VII seizes Ancona and brings it under papal control

1534: The corsair Kheir ed-Din razes Collecchio in the Maremma, taking Margherita Marsili to the harem of Suleiman the Magnificent. She becomes the mother of Selim II

1535: The papacy under Paul III seizes Perugia and instals a papal governor

1549: The Adriatic city of Fermo turns itself over to the papacy during the reign of Paul V, who was born in the town

1550: Giorgio Vasari: *Lives of the Artists*. Though Florence's greatest hour is over, his work does much to inform our view of Tuscan supremacy in art and learning, and of the Medici as great patrons

1552: The corsair Dragut burns Scauri and enslaves the inhabitants, one of a series of pirate raids along the Lazio coast

1555: Siena conquered by a joint force of Florentine and Spanish soldiers. It comes under the control of the Medici

1557: In the aftermath of the victory over Siena, Philip II of Spain takes the coastal Maremma, constructing fortresses to create a garrison state, with its capital at Orbetello

1559: Treaty of Cateau-Cambrésis ends the wars between France and Spain, with the Spanish Habsburgs as the dominant power in Italy; the Papal States retain independence

1561: Cosimo I de' Medici founds the Knights of St Stephen to fight the Turks

1564: Galileo born in Pisa

1570: Cosimo I becomes Grand Duke of Tuscany, his title explicitly hereditary. He is the patron of Bronzino and Vasari

1571: Battle of Lepanto. The combined forces of Venice, Spain, Genoa, Naples and the Papal States defeat Ottoman Turkish naval power

1582: Pope Gregory XIII completes the reform of the calendar at Frascati

1592: The 21-year-old Caravaggio arrives in Rome and establishes his reputation

1623–44: Papacy of Urban VIII. His Inquisition condemns Galileo for upholding the Copernican theory. He is also a great patron of Bernini

1631: Urbino passes to the papacy with the death of the last della Rovere duke. Vittoria della Rovere marries Ferdinando II de' Medici. Many art treasures come to Florence as dowry

1667: Bernini completes St Peter's Square in Rome

The 18th century and Napoleon

Spanish hegemony in Italy leads in general to economic decline. Romantic ideals inspired by the revolution in France kindle sparks of hope for independence and unity in Italy. When Napoleon proves to have imperial and dynastic ambitions, such illusions are shattered.

1713: The end of the War of the Spanish succession results in the Spanish holdings in Italy passing to the Austrian Habsburgs

1737: The last of the Medici dies. Florence

passes to the house of Lorraine under Franz Stephan, husband of Maria Theresa of Austria

1765: Peter Leopold, son of Maria Theresa, becomes Grand Duke of Tuscany. He introduces many reforms, including drainage schemes in the coastal Maremma, malarial swamp since the Goths cut the Roman aqueducts in the 5th–6th centuries

1767: J.J. Winckelmann publishes his categories of ancient art, which influence all subsequent taste for the Antique

1776: Gibbon: *Decline and Fall of the Roman Empire*

1786: Goethe travels through Italy, hungry for first-hand experience of the world he had hitherto known only from his studies

1796: Napoleon's first Italy campaign

1797: Treaty of Tolentino signed in the Marche between Napoleon and the Papal States. Pope Pius VI surrenders territory and many valuable works of art to France

1798–1814: Napoleon creates a series of shifting republics and kingdoms in Italy, as he captures and reconfigures the territory to suit his aims. His placemen are often his siblings, for example his sister Elisa, whom he makes Grand Duchess of Tuscany in 1809, after annexing the Papal Sates to the French Empire. Pope Pius VI dies a captive in France

1812–18: Byron's *Childe Harold's Pilgrimage* describes his travels through Italy, and reflects also the disillusion of the Romantics with the Napoleonic age

1815: Napoleon defeated. The Congress of Vienna returns Tuscany to the Austrians, and the Papal States to the papacy. Canova retrieves many Italian artworks purloined by the French

Towards a republic

The mid-19th century is the age of the Risorgimento, a resurgence of nationalist, republican fervour, led on an intellectual level by Giuseppe Mazzini. Popular support is won by the guerrilla leader Giuseppe Garibaldi. A governable united Italy is made possible by the great statesman Camillo Cavour.

1837: An exhibition of antiquities in London brings Etruscan works before a wider public and sparks interest in the civilisation

1848: George Dennis publishes *Cities and Cemeteries of Etruria*

1860s: The Macchaioli School of painters (the 'Tuscan Impressionists') flourishes. They paint from nature, often *en plein-air*

1860: Papal forces suffer a defeat by the Italian army, which occupies Umbria and the Marche

1861: Gaeta, last stronghold of the Kingdom of Naples, falls to the Italian army. Florence becomes capital of the Kingdom of Italy, under Vittorio Emanuele II

1870: Pius IX meditates in Gaeta prior to pronouncing the dogma of Papal Infallibility; the Italian army enters Rome on 20th September (hence the many streets named XX Settembre in Italian cities). Pope Pius retreats to the Vatican, his temporal power at an end

1872: Giuseppe Mazzini dies at Pisa

1922: Mussolini becomes prime minister

1929: The Lateran Treaty creates the Vatican State, regularising relations between the papacy and the Italian government

1932: Mussolini founds Latina, the first of the new towns in the newly drained Pontine wetlands. It survives as an example of Rationalist urban planning

1939: Catherine of Siena and Francis of Assisi proclaimed patron saints of Italy

1940: Italy enters WWII on the Axis side; the burial place of St Peter is discovered beneath the Vatican Grottoes

1943: Allied bombs severely damage Frascati

1944: The Nazis' Gothic Line of defence stretches across the northern border of central Italy, from Versilia to Rimini. Allies land at Anzio and Nettuno, south of Rome, as part of a plan to advance on and capture the Alban Hills, and ultimately Rome. Coastal areas of southern Lazio suffer heavily from bombardments. The Abbey of Monte Cassino is destroyed by Allied bombs

1945: Mussolini is killed by partisans

1946: Abdication of King Vittorio Emanuele III. Italy votes to become a republic

LAZIO

Lazio is the region of Rome and the provinces around it, its most popular destination by far being the capital itself. The surrounding area receives far fewer visitors. However, both Hadrian's Villa at Tivoli and the Roman port of Ostia are both ancient Roman sites of exceptional importance.

The little towns of Lazio, where the the buildings are usually brown or rust-coloured, and the streets are often paved in the characteristic small cobblestones known as *sanpietrini*, and adorned with fountains, have a feel of Rome about them. In the distinctive countryside, with its outcrops of tufa, sheep are often to be seen grazing in the fields. The occasional palm tree provides a reminder that we are almost in the south—but also the slightly shabby and neglected atmosphere in some areas gives Lazio an atmosphere of its own which is very different from that of its close neighbour, Tuscany.

Although little trace remains of the beautiful classical landscape known as the *Campagna Romana*, which used to reach right up to the walls of Rome, the region today is the best place to study the Etruscan civilisation which preceded the birth of Rome: Tarquinia has the finest-known painted tombs of this period (and an excellent museum), and at the necropolis of Cerveteri the great variety of Etruscan sepulchral architecture can be appreciated. Vulci, where some of the most beautiful artefacts were found, still has a remarkably evocative landscape. Northern Lazio is especially known for its fine villas and gardens, the most beautiful of which is Villa Lante.

But Lazio also lends itself to the exploration of little-known places, where the restaurants serve simple, good and unpretentious food. In southern Lazio the Cistercian monasteries of Fossanova, Casamari and Trisulti are fascinating places to visit. Also in this area, both Subiaco and Monte Cassino are of fundamental importance to the history of monasticism. Beautiful medieval murals can be seen in the crypt of Anagni cathedral and at Castel Sant'Elia. In Ciociaria south of Rome there are a great number of small hill towns which preserve their mighty cyclopean walls, the like of which can be seen nowhere else in the country. Places well worth exploring for their extraordinary landscapes include Civita di Bagnoregio, Monterano, and the garden of Ninfa. Another feature of northern Lazio is its volcanic lakes, notably the beautiful, tranquil Lake Bolsena.

The province of Rieti, which borders with the mountainous Abruzzo, is a very remote area chiefly visited for its connections with St Francis; but it has numerous little towns well worth exploring in the district known as Sabina. Because of its vicinity to Rome, Lazio has also played an important role in the history of the papacy, and in particular in the late 13th century when the popes moved out to Viterbo. Today this town is the busy provincial capital of Tuscia, but a tiny part of the medieval city is exceptionally well preserved.

The place which perhaps sums up best both the Etruscan and medieval character of Lazio, and the distinctive countryside (and where there is a good place to stay and you can eat well) is Tuscania.

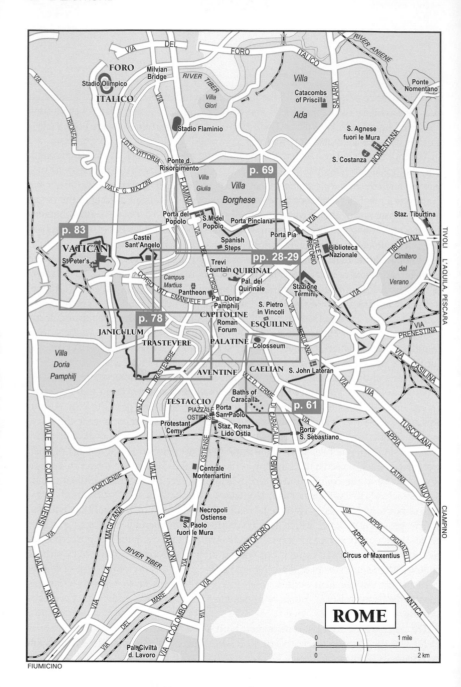

FIUMICINO

ROME

R ome is one of the most celebrated cities in the world, and ever since her greatest days as the centre of the Roman Empire, and later as the home of the Roman Catholic Church, has had a role of the first importance in European history. The Eternal City was the *Caput Mundi* (Head of the World) in the Roman era, and from it law and the liberal arts and sciences radiated throughout its vast Empire, which covered the whole of the known western world. The ancient Roman city, with a population of over one million, was built over the famous seven hills on the left bank of the Tiber. The walls built to defend it by the emperor Aurelian in the 3rd century AD still defined the urban limits of the city in the late 19th century, and it was only in the 1940s that the population began to equal (and then supersede) that of ancient Rome.

The city today preserves numerous magnificent ancient buildings side by side with palaces and churches from later centuries. Its squares are decorated with splendid fountains and Egyptian obelisks. The Vatican, in part of the district which from the 9th century onwards became the stronghold of the popes, has, since 1929, been the smallest independent state in the world.

For centuries Rome has been visited by pilgrims and travellers, but now mass tourism threatens the enjoyment of the individual visitor (over three million people see the Sistine Chapel every year, with up to 20,000 in a single day). For this reason visitors are strongly advised to see not only the most famous sights, but also to spend time exploring the quieter streets and the smaller museums and palaces. This chapter aims to cover both the major sights of the city and a few of its more hidden treasures.

NB: For full coverage of the city, see Blue Guide Rome.

HISTORY OF ROME

Rome was founded—in 753 BC according to legend and tradition, and probably much earlier—at the spot where the territories of the Latins, the Sabines and the Etruscans met. Favoured by its central position in the Italian peninsula, by the proximity of the sea, and by the enterprising character of its inhabitants, Rome grew rapidly in importance. Under its seven more or less legendary kings (Romulus, Numa Pompilius, Tullus Hostilius, Ancus Marcius, Tarquinius Priscus, Servius Tullius and Tarquinius Superbus) it conquered or formed alliances with the Latins and Etruscans. The last of the kings was in fact an Etruscan, who came to be hated for his lordly ways. He was brought down by a Latin plot, and in 510 BC Rome became a republic. Though dogged by the long and persistent struggle between the plebs and the patricians, it still managed to conquer the Etruscans of Veio and Tarquinia, the Latins and the Volscians. From almost total destruction by invading Gauls in 390 BC, Rome recovered to overthrow the Samnites in three campaigns, and then turned her arms against the Greek colonies in the south, including Sicily. The struggle against the Carthaginian leader Hannibal (the Punic Wars) was fought partly on Italian soil, and Hannibal and his elephants inflicted severe defeats on the Romans, most famously at Lake Trasimene (*see pp. 511–12*). It was not until the third Punic War that Carthage was utterly defeated (146 BC). The victory stimulated the ambition of the Romans, who now made themselves masters not only of all Italy, but also of Cisalpine Gaul, Illyria, Greece and Macedonia, and finally proceeded to the conquest of the world. Disaffection at home was not tolerated: the so-called Social War in 89 BC, an insurrection of the Italic peoples, was put down, and Rome went on to subjugate Asia Minor, Tauris, Syria and Palestine. Julius Caesar bore the Roman eagles to Transalpine Gaul and Britain.

Strife between the military commanders Marius and Sulla, leadership disputes between Caesar and Pompey, and the brief, vexed coalitions of the two triumvirates (Pompey, Caesar and Crassus; Antony, Lepidus and Octavian) resulted in the founding c. 27 BC of the Empire under Octavian (afterwards Augustus), marking the triumph of the democratic party over the old oligarchy. In spite of the incapacity and moral degeneracy of many of the later emperors, the dominion of Rome continued to extend, and reached its maximum expansion under Trajan (98–117). The language and the laws of Rome were accepted as standards by the world, and the solidity of the Roman state was still unbroken in the 3rd century AD, although barbarian pressure was beginning.

The decline of Rome began under Diocletian (AD 285–305), who divided the empire into western and eastern portions. The decline was confirmed when Constantine transferred the seat of government to Byzantium (AD 330). In the 5th century the barbarians descended upon Rome. The imperial city was sacked by Alaric the Goth in 410, by Genseric the Vandal in 455, and by Ricimer the Swabian in 472. Finally, in 476, the Germanic chieftain Odoacer compelled the emperor Romulus Augustulus to abdicate, and thus put an end to the Western Empire.

The Roman Church, persecuted until the reign of Constantine but finally triumphant, rescued Latin civilisation from ruin, and the supremacy of the bishop of Rome was gradually recognised by the Christianised world. At the beginning of the 7th century, Rome passed under the temporal protection of the popes, a protection which was later transformed into sovereignty. Pope Stephen II, threatened by the Lombards, appealed to Pepin the Frank, who defeated the enemy and bestowed upon the pope a portion of Lombardy (AD 754). Thus began the temporal power of the popes over the States of the Church. On Christmas Day 800, Charlemagne, son of Pepin, was crowned by Leo III in St Peter's as 'Augustus' and 'Emperor', and so began the 'Holy Roman Empire', which endured until Napoleon forced the abdication of Francis II of Austria in 1806.

On the death of Charlemagne a turbulent period ensued, which clouded the fortunes of the papacy. Gregory VII, however, reasserted papal authority, although he was unable to prevent the Normans under Robert Guiscard from devastating the city in 1084. Paschal II and Calixtus II did much to restore it. In 1309 Pope Clement V, former Archbishop of Bordeaux, was persuaded by King Philip the Fair of France to set up his court in Avignon. Political unrest in Italy made the move attractive to this French pope, who knew that in Avignon he could count on the protection of France. It was not until

1378, at the instance of St Catherine of Siena, that Gregory XI re-transferred the papal seat from Avignon to Rome. Rejoicing in the Eternal City was short-lived, for the Great Schism ensued, a period of uncertainty when popes and antipopes claimed authority simultaneously, and allegiances were divided. In 1420 Pope Martin V, scion of the Roman Colonna family, began to restore the city, which had deteriorated both physically and socially during its so-called 'Babylonian Captivity'. Under Julius II and Leo X Rome recovered brilliantly, and became the centre of the Italian Renaissance. This was the age of Bramante, Michelangelo and Raphael, the three greatest geniuses of their day.

In 1527, under Clement VII, who took the part of the King Francis I of France in his battles against the Holy Roman Emperor, Charles V of Spain, Rome was captured and ruthlessly sacked by Charles' mercenary troops. The restoration and further embellishment of the city occupied the attention of many succeeding popes, notably Sixtus V, who completed the dome of St Peter's, and ordered the siting of the Egyptian obelisks in the positions they occupy today.

In February 1798, the French entered Rome and proclaimed a republic. Pope Pius VI was carried as a prisoner to France, where he died in 1799. In 1809 Napoleon annexed the Papal States to the French Empire; in 1810 the French senate proclaimed Rome to be the second capital; and in 1811 Napoleon conferred the title of King of Rome on his new-born son. On the fall of Napoleon, Pius VII returned to Rome, to which were restored, also, almost all the works of art that had been removed by Bonaparte.

The city was keenly interested in the agitated period of the 'Risorgimento', when republican and nationalist sentiment coursed through the Italian peninsula. Pope Pius IX was no match for the radicals. He retired to Gaeta, and a republic was proclaimed at Rome, with the defence of the city entrusted to Garibaldi. The army dispatched by France to the aid of the pope entered Rome on 3rd July 1849, and Pius IX returned in the following April. In 1860, after the defeat of the papal forces at Castelfidardo, the Piedmontese general Enrico Cialdini occupied the Marche and Umbria; in September 1870, the Italian army under Raffaello Cadorna entered Rome by a breach in the walls to the northeast, beside the Porta Pia. Shortly afterwards, Rome was proclaimed the capital of united Italy. Pius IX was relieved of temporal power and confined to the Vatican.

After the First World War (which had little direct effect on Rome), the Fascist movement rapidly developed. The year 1922 saw the 'March on Rome' of Mussolini and his myrmidons, after which King Vittorio Emanuele III invited Mussolini to form a government. Italy entered the Second World War on the Axis side in 1940. In September 1943 the Allied invasion of the mainland began. The objective of the landings at Anzio and Nettuno (in January 1944) was at length achieved in June of the same year, when American troops entered Rome. In April 1945, Mussolini was killed after his capture by Italian partisans while attempting to escape into Switzerland. In May 1946, Vittorio Emanuele III abdicated. Less than a month later a general election, with a referendum on the form of government, was held. The referendum favoured the establishment of a republic. The royal family left the country a few days later, and a provisional President was elected. On 22nd December 1947, the Constituent Assembly approved the new republican constitution.

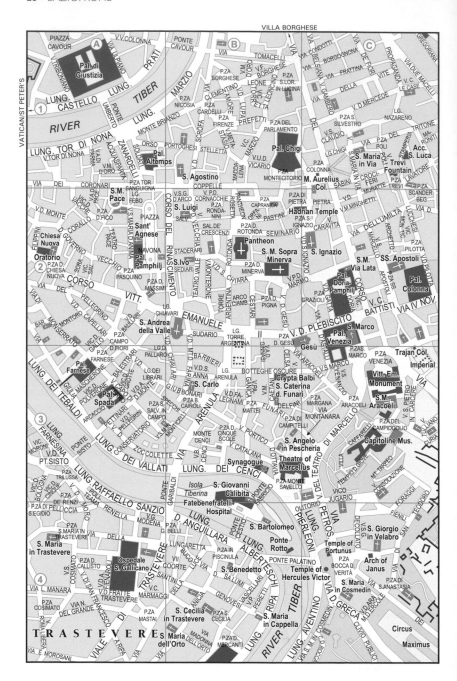

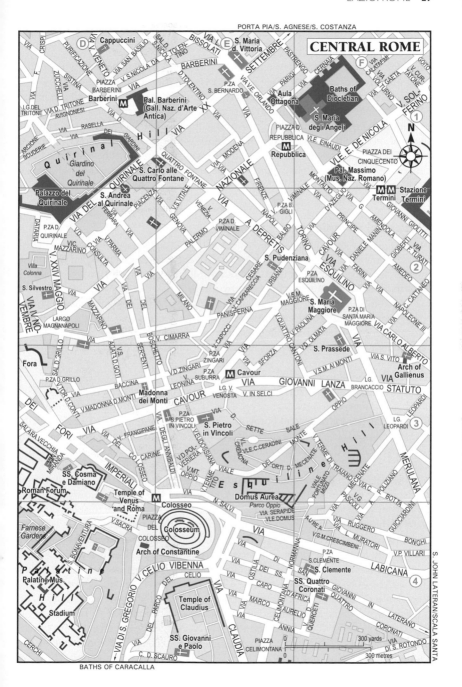

THE CAPITOLINE HILL

Although the smallest of the seven hills of Rome, the Capitoline (*map p. 28, C3*) is the most important, and the best place to start a visit to the city. It was the political and religious centre of ancient Rome, and its huge temple dedicated in the 6th century to Jupiter Optimus Maximus Capitolinus (remains of which survive) was the most venerated sanctuary. Sometime before AD 700 the church of Santa Maria in Aracoeli was founded on the hill, and since the 14th century the city government has had its seat here. There are wonderful views over the Roman Forum from the quiet road and peaceful gardens which encircle the summit near the site of the notorious Tarpeian Rock, from which traitors in the days of ancient Rome are said to have been flung to their deaths.

Piazza del Campidoglio

At the top of the great flight of steps known as the Cordonata, its balustrade decorated with huge statues of Castor and Pollux (*see p. 36*), is Piazza del Campidoglio. One of the most pleasing spaces in Rome, it was laid out by Michelangelo in 1538, when the equestrian statue of Marcus Aurelius (replaced by a copy in 1997) was moved here from the Lateran Hill. The original is now displayed in an interior courtyard (*see opposite*). Michelangelo provided the elegant base of the statue, and also drew up the designs for Palazzo Senatorio (seat of the municipality) and the two handsome buildings which now house the Capitoline Museums, Palazzo dei Conservatori and Palazzo Nuovo.

The Capitoline Museums

Incorporating the oldest public collection in the world, founded by Pope Sixtus IV in 1471, these museums (*open 9–8 except Mon; T: 06 3996 7800*) retain their old-fashioned, intimate arrangement and provide a wonderful introduction to Classical sculpture. The hospitable rooms are rarely over-crowded and have an atmosphere all their own, especially in the evening when they are illuminated solely by magnificent chandeliers.

Works of particular importance include fragments of a colossal seated **statue of Constantine the Great** (displayed in the courtyard of Palazzo dei Conservatori), and reliefs illustrating the life of Marcus Aurelius from a triumphal arch (displayed on the stairs of the same palace). The most celebrated masterpiece here (displayed in Room IV of the Appartamento dei Conservatori) is the bronze *She-wolf of Rome*, the symbol of the city and for centuries its most famous piece of sculpture. This has generally been taken to be an Etruscan work, although in 2006 it was seriously suggested that it may date instead from the medieval period. All that is definitely known is that the twins Romulus and Remus were added by Antonio Pollaiolo in the early 16th century. In an adjoining room is the *Spinario*, the marble statue of a boy plucking a thorn from his foot (probably dating from the 1st century BC), as well as the celebrated bronze head, known as '*Brutus*', of unknown date. An elaborate official marble **portrait of the emperor Commodus**, portrayed as Hercules, is a masterpiece of its period. The room where it is displayed (Room 10) connects to the glass-walled, covered courtyard, built to house the original statue of Marcus Aurelius, a Roman bronze masterpiece thought to date from the latter part of the philosopher-emperor's reign (AD 161–80). Palazzo dei Conservatori houses a picture gallery on its upper floor, particularly important for its 16th–18th-century Italian and foreign works, including two paintings by Caravaggio: the famous *Gipsy Fortune-teller*, and a *St John the Baptist*.

The **Capitoline Venus** (in Room III of Palazzo Nuovo), a Roman replica of a Hellenistic original, is one of the most famous nude female figures of Antiquity. Of the *Cnidian Aphrodite* type (the famous statue by Praxiteles), it shows the goddess taken by surprise while taking a bath, and attempting to cover her nudity with her hands. Two adjoining rooms have a wonderful display of marble portrait busts, produced during the Roman empire. Their spirit of realism was particularly popular with the Romans: you can get face to face with emperors and their wives and children, as well as with philosophers and poets, all displayed in serried ranks on marble shelves. A work particularly admired since the 19th century is the **Dying Gaul** (in Room VIII of Palazzo Nuovo), showing a mortally wounded moustached warrior, a copy of a Greek work made in the Roman period.

A further section of the museum is superbly displayed at the **Centrale Montemartini** (a former electrical plant near Porta San Paolo; *map p. 24*). Most of the 400 or so Roman and Greek sculptures here were found during excavations of ancient villas and gardens. They are of the first importance (including the *Esquiline Venus*, the 'Togato Barberini', and the reconstructed pediment from the Temple of Apollo Sosianus, which stood beside the Theatre of Marcellus (*see p. 74*).

Santa Maria in Aracoeli

The church of Santa Maria in Aracoeli, approached by a long flight of steps from the foot of the hill (but also by a side door from the piazza), has ancient Roman columns and a fine Cosmatesque pavement. It has interesting sepulchral monuments, and frescoes by Pietro Cavallini (late 13th century) and Pinturicchio (1486). Pinturicchio's frescoes of the life of St Bernardino of Siena are typical of his vivid narrative style (*see p. 537*). Placed against the west wall is Donatello's pavement tomb of Giovanni Crivelli (1432).

THE ROMAN FORUM

Map pp. 28–29, C3–D3. Open 8.30–dusk; free. Although there are a number of entrance gates, the best approach is from the Capitoline Hill. Numbers refer to the plan overleaf.

The marshy valley between the Capitoline and Palatine hills was drained and paved as a market-place by the Etruscan kings of Rome in the 6th century BC. During the Republican period (before 27 BC) the area became increasingly important as a political and religious centre, with the erection of huge assembly halls and numerous temples. The Emperors continued to erect important buildings here, but in the Middle Ages the area was used as a cattle pasture and the monuments were pillaged for their stone and precious marbles. Excavations begun at the end of the 18th century continue to this day.

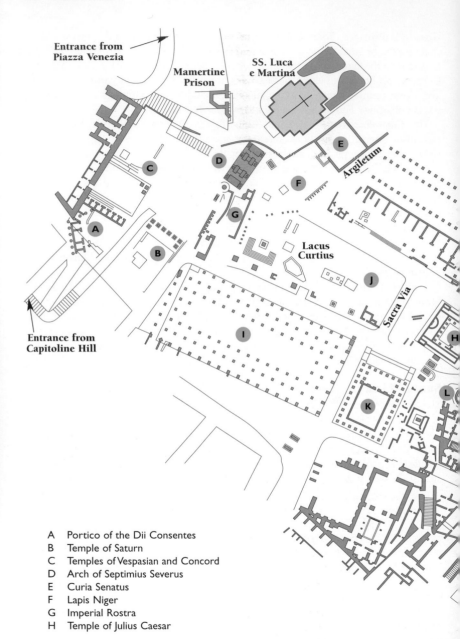

Entrance from
Piazza Venezia

Mamertine
Prison

SS. Luca
e Martina

Argiletum

Lacus
Curtius

Sacra Via

Entrance from
Capitoline Hill

A   Portico of the Dii Consentes
B   Temple of Saturn
C   Temples of Vespasian and Concord
D   Arch of Septimius Severus
E   Curia Senatus
F   Lapis Niger
G   Imperial Rostra
H   Temple of Julius Caesar

THE ROMAN FORUM

I   Basilica Julia
J   Area of original Forum
K   Temple of Castor
L   Temple of Vesta
M   Temple of Antoninus and Faustina
N   Temple of Romulus
O   Basilica of Maxentius
P   Arch of Titus

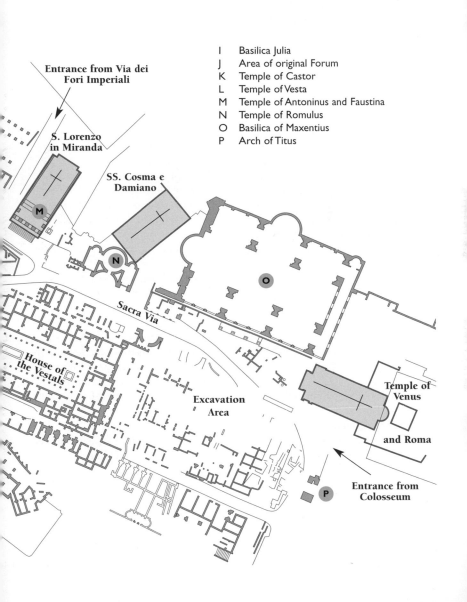

Entrance from Via dei
Fori Imperiali

S. Lorenzo
in Miranda

SS. Cosma e
Damiano

Sacra Via

House of
the Vestals

Excavation
Area

Temple of
Venus
and Roma

Entrance from
Colosseum

Today the Forum is a mass of ruins, with sometimes just one or two columns of a temple still standing, or only the pavement of a huge basilica, while elsewhere triumphal arches still stand majestically intact and a number of buildings retain their walls and roofs since they were adapted as churches when Christianity took over from paganism. In the absence of intrusive signposts and labels, the ruins are all the more romantic to visit, although without detailed plans and descriptions it can be hard to understand just what building stood where. Highlights are given below.

(A) Portico of the Dii Consentes: 12 white columns form an angle; the seven original columns are in marble, the restorations in limestone. Rebuilt in AD 367 by a prefect known for his opposition to Christianity, this was the last pagan monument in the Forum. It was decorated with statues Jupiter, Neptune, Mars, Apollo, Vulcan, Mercury, Juno, Minerva, Diana, Venus, Vesta and Ceres.

(B) Temple of Saturn: One of the oldest sanctuaries in the Forum, possibly inaugurated in 498 BC. Eight columns, and part of the entablature survive from a 1st-century BC rebuilding. The Ionic capitals were added in the 5th century. The *Saturnalia* (17th December) was the most important day of festivities in the Roman year, when temporary freedom was given to slaves and presents were exchanged.

(C) Temples of Vespasian and Concord: Three tall columns are all that remain of the Temple of Vespasian, erected by his sons Titus and Domitian in AD 79. Next to it is the site of the Temple of Concord, a reconstruction by Tiberius (7 BC–AD 10) of a 4th-century BC sanctuary built to commemorate the concordat between patricians and plebs.

(D) Arch of Septimius Severus: Erected in AD 203 and dedicated to Severus and his sons Caracalla and Geta, in memory of their military victories. The four large reliefs depict scenes from the two campaigns in Parthia (modern Iran): in the small friezes are symbolic Oriental figures paying homage to Rome, and at the bases of the columns are captive barbarians.

(E) Curia Senatus: The present senate house building dates from the time of Domitian and was restored by Diocletian after a fire in 283. It was originally preceded by a portico. The existing doors are copies of the originals, removed by Pope Alexander VII in the 17th century to St John Lateran where they still— incredibly enough—serve as the main entrance to the basilica.

The remarkable interior has a beautiful green-and-maroon pavement in *opus sectile*. The three marble-faced steps on the two long sides provided seats for some 300 senators. The porphyry statue of Hadrian or Trajan, dating from the 1st or 2nd century AD, was found in excavations behind the building.

Also exhibited here are the **Plutei of Trajan**, two finely-sculptured balustrades. Both their date and original location are uncertain. On both sides the statue of Marsyas is depicted beside the sacred fig tree (*see p. 36 below*).

(F) Lapis Niger: The *Lapis Niger* ('Black Stone') was a black marble pavement

Roman soldier in sandals and with short, tight curls, holds a Parthian prisoner in a cap, with long hair and beard. Detail of a relief on the Arch of Septimius Severus (3rd century AD).

laid to indicate a sacred spot. This was traditionally taken to be the site of the tomb of Romulus, or of Faustulus, the shepherd who found the infants, but is now identified as a sanctuary of Vulcan.

In front of some trees you can see the paved **Argiletum**, once one of the Forum's busiest streets, leading north to the Subura, a poor and unsavoury part of town, haunt of thieves and prostitutes.

G **Imperial Rostra:** These ruins are of the orators' tribune, from where magis-

trates' edicts and official communications were announced. The original structure, of very early date, was decorated with *rostra*, the iron prows of the ships captured at the Battle of Antium (modern Anzio) in 338 BC, when Rome subjugated the Volscians (*see p. 232*).

H **Temple of Julius Caesar:** Only a curved wall with a roof remains. The body of Caesar was brought to the Forum after his assassination in 44 BC, and it was probably here that it was cremated. The temple was dedicated by Augustus in 29 BC in honour of *Divus* (the 'Divine') *Julius*. The paved road in front of the temple is the **Sacra Via**, the oldest street in Rome, along which a victorious general awarded a Triumph passed in procession to the Capitol.

I **Basilica Julia:** Basilicas were used for public administration and as law courts, and were large, aisled halls ending in an apse. (Their plan was adopted in Christian architecture for the earliest churches.) All that remains of this huge building are the steps and some column bases. It was begun by Julius Caesar in 54 BC and finished by Augustus, and was the meeting place of the civil court of justice. Graffiti on the marble steps show that the Romans used to while away their time playing 'board' games.

J **Area of the original Forum:** This was where major religious festivals were held, where political offenders were executed, and where state funerals took place.

At a point where the low fence opens out on the right, you can see the covered, paved area of the **Lacus Curtius**. In 362 BC a great chasm is said to have opened here, which a soothsayer said could only be closed by throwing into it Rome's greatest treasure. A young man called Marcus Curtius, announcing that Rome possessed no greater treasure than a brave citizen, rode his horse into the abyss, which promptly closed. A bas-relief of a horse and rider was found here: a cast is shown *in situ*.

Behind and to the left of the Lacus Curtius is a small, unpaved space, which may be where a statue of Marsyas once stood next to the fig tree, the olive and the vine (all replanted here in 1956) recorded by Pliny the Elder as being in the centre of the Forum. All three were plants sacred to the ancient Romans, and the fig was a symbol of fertility.

K **Temple of Castor:** The Temple of the Dioscuri was built c. 484 BC in honour of Castor and Pollux, whose cult was adopted after the Battle of Lake Regillus (496 BC), where they led the cavalry charge that resulted in a Roman victory over the Etruscan Tarquins and their Latin allies. The twins are usually depicted as giants with white chargers: the most famous statues of them are on the Quirinal Hill (*see p. 54*).

L **Temple of Vesta:** The design of this circular edifice recalled the thatched huts of the original Latin settlers. Here the six Vestals, virgin priestesses of Vesta, goddess of the hearth, guarded the sacred fire which symbolised the perpetuity of the state. In the interior was the *Palladium*, a statue of Pallas Athena supposedly taken

from Troy by Aeneas. The safety of the city depended on its preservation.

After her election, a Vestal lived in the House of the Vestals (*see plan*) for 30 years: ten learning her duties, ten performing them and ten teaching novices. If a Vestal let the sacred fire go out, she was whipped by the *pontifex maximus*. If she broke her vow of chastity, she was immured alive, and the man was publicly flogged to death.

M **Temple of Antoninus and Faustina:** This well-preserved temple preserves its pronaos of ten huge columns above a flight of steps. It was dedicated to the empress Faustina after her death in AD 141. When her husband, the emperor Antoninus Pius, died 20 years later, the temple received its double dedication. It was converted into the church of San Lorenzo in Miranda (*closed to the public*) before the 12th century, and given a Baroque façade in 1602.

N **Temple of Romulus:** This 4th-century building (interior visible from the church of Santi Cosma e Damiano; *see p. 40*) still has its original bronze doors, a remarkable survival. This was formerly thought to be a temple to Romulus, son of Maxentius (d. AD 309), but it has now been suggested that it may have been a temple of Jupiter, or the audience hall of the city prefect. It was converted into a church in the 6th century.

O **Basilica of Maxentius:** The three vast barrel-vaulted niches are one of the largest and most impressive examples of Roman architecture to have survived anywhere. The design inspired many Renaissance builders, and it is said that

Michelangelo studied it when planning the dome of St Peter's. The niches formed the north aisle of a basilica begun by Maxentius (AD 306–10) and completed by Constantine after he defeated Maxentius at the Battle of the Milvian Bridge in 312. The basilica was used by the city prefects, and, in the 4th century AD, by the tribunal which heard cases against senators. In 1487 a colossal statue of Constantine was found in the west apse. Fragments of it are now in the courtyard of Palazzo dei Conservatori (*see p. 30*).

P **Arch of Titus:** This arch was presumably erected by Domitian just after the death of Titus in AD 81 in honour of the victories of Titus and Vespasian in the Judaean War, which ended with the sack of Jerusalem in AD 70. The reliefs inside show the goddess Roma guiding the Imperial quadriga with Titus and the winged figure of Victory; and the triumphal procession bringing war booty from Jerusalem. In the centre of the panelled vault is the *Apotheosis of Titus*, showing the deified emperor mounted on an eagle.

THE PALATINE HILL, COLOSSEUM & DOMUS AUREA

Map p. 29, D4–E3. Open 9–1hr before sunset; ticket includes admission to the Palatine Museum and Colosseum. Entrance from the Roman Forum or Via San Gregorio.

The Palatine Hill, which rises to the south of the Roman Forum, is a beautiful park with some impressive ruins of ancient buildings. It was here that the primitive city was founded in 754 or 753 BC, since according to legend the twins Romulus and Remus were discovered on the hill by a shepherd and famously nursed by a she-wolf, forever after the symbol of Rome. Excavations have confirmed that the area was occupied as early as the 9th century, and the northern slopes overlooking the Forum were from Republican times onwards considered a prestigious residential district: many prominent citizens lived here, including the great orator Cicero. Augustus also chose to have a house here, and successive emperors followed his example. The word Palatine came to be synonymous with the residence of the emperor (hence our word 'palace').

The approach from the Forum leads through the lovely **Farnese Gardens**, laid out in terraces in the mid-16th century for Cardinal Alessandro Farnese, grandson of Pope Paul III. On the edge of the hill there is a superb view of the Forum far below. The ruins in this area belong to part of Nero's Domus Aurea (*see overleaf*), reconstructed by later emperors. The central part of the hill has remains of the **Palace of Domitian**. Its huge 'stadium', probably in fact a garden sometimes used as a hippodrome, which occupies the eastern part of the hill, is the most impressive of all the ruins: although there is no admission to the ground level, there is a wonderful view of it from above. Also seen from above, but closer to the Palatine Museum building, are remains of the private residence of the emperor, with its numerous fountain courts.

The **Palatine Museum** (*open as the hill*) is beautifully displayed and well labelled. The exhibits include material from the earliest settlements here, as well as Roman wall-decorations and frescoes, stucco, marble intarsia, and important statues. Amongst the most precious items are a series of beautiful painted terracotta panels with reliefs of paired figures, and a memorable statuette of a satyr turning round to look at his tail, a Roman copy of a Hellenistic bronze.

A number of buildings with wall-paintings, including the so-called House of Livia, are sometimes shown on request (*T: 06 3996 7700*). Other important monuments, including the Temple of Cybele, the site of the Iron Age hut village, the House of Augustus and Temple of Apollo, all in the southwestern part of the hill, are closed for excavation and restoration.

The Colosseum

Map p. 29, E4. Open 9–dusk. Ticket includes same-day entrance to the Palatine; or, if you visit the Colosseum after 1.30, then entrance to the Palatine the following day.

The Colosseum is probably the most visited monument in Rome. It is the largest Roman amphitheatre ever built, and its design was copied in similar buildings all over the Empire. It preserves its remarkable grandeur even though its setting is unattractive, plagued by souvenir stalls and handcarts serving snacks and drinks.

It was begun by the emperor Vespasian in AD 70 and restored over the centuries. The mighty elliptical sustaining wall, built of travertine, has four storeys and today reaches a height of some 50m. The arches on the three lower storeys are decorated with the three orders (Tuscan Doric, Ionic and Corinthian). The projecting corbels at the top supported the wooden poles for the huge sun awning. More than two-thirds of the original masonry, including the tiers of seats, has gone, removed over time for newer buildings.

The interior of the amphitheatre, which could probably hold more than 50,000 spectators, is still magnificent. A wooden floor now covers part of the arena (the substructures visible beneath provided space for the mechanism which operated the scenery, cages for animals, and access passages). A wall, some 5m high, protected the spectators from the action on stage.

On the raised ground towards the Roman Forum are the ruins of the largest temple ever built in Rome, dedicated to Venus and Roma and designed probably by the emperor Hadrian himself. But the most conspicuous monument here is the triple **Arch of Constantine**, a finely proportioned triumphal arch erected in AD 315. Some of the sculptures and reliefs were reused from older monuments. Those contemporary with the arch include the decoration in the spandrels and oblong friezes above them on the long sides, and the roundels on the two short sides.

Domus Aurea

Map p. 29, E3. Open Tues–Fri 9–4; T: 06 8530 1758. Reservation essential.

The Domus Aurea was a huge palace built by Nero. It extended from here across the valley later occupied by the Colosseum all the way to the summit of the Palatine. Most of it was hastily demolished or covered up after the tyrant's death in AD 68, and it was not until the 1490s that some of its rooms, with their stuccoed and painted walls and vaults, were discovered underground: their delicate decorations characterised by fantastical motifs with intricate patterns of volutes, festoons, garlands, masques, griffins and sphinxes, normally on a light ground, at once became famous and widely copied by the artists of the High Renaissance: they were called 'grotesques' (from '*grotto*', meaning underground room). Today the visible remains (*shown on a guided tour*) are rather difficult to appreciate, but include a splendidly vaulted octagonal hall with a concrete dome lit by a central oculus and apertures in the side rooms. Other areas preserve vault mosaics and very worn frescoes and stuccoes.

THE IMPERIAL FORA

Map pp. 28–29, C3–D3. Forum and Markets of Trajan open Tues–Sun 9–dusk. Entrance by Trajan's Column.

It was Julius Caesar who decided that the Roman Forum had become over-crowded and should be extended. Towards the end of his life he laid out a new forum around a temple dedicated to Venus 'Genetrix', from whom he claimed descent. His example was followed by his successors, and the area soon filled up with temples and stately public buildings. The fora were excavated in 1924, when the area was cleared to make way for the Via dei Fori Imperiali, built to add dignity to Fascist military parades.

Detail from Trajan's Column (2nd century AD).

The most impressive monument, nearly 30m high, is **Trajan's Column**, still almost intact and generally considered to be the masterpiece of Roman sculptural art. It was dedicated to Trajan by Hadrian in memory of the former's conquest of the Dacians: the spiral frieze (some 200m long) depicts the emperor's military campaigns. The ashes of Trajan lie beneath the column: he was the first and probably the only emperor to be allowed burial in the centre of the city. The **Forum and Markets of Trajan** are entered from beside the column. They consisted of a covered basilica and an open forum (both now marked by just a few huge columns and fragments of the paving), as well as a splendid market building, which is, by contrast, very well preserved. Built into the slopes of the Quirinal hill, it was designed in a huge semicircle with some 150 shops.

The **Forum of Augustus**, adjoining that of Trajan, was built around the Temple of Mars Ultor (Mars the Avenger), one of the most honoured temples of the Empire: just three of its tall fluted columns supporting an architrave survive at the top of its broad, high steps. It commemorated the victory of Philippi, when Caesar's assassins, Cassius and Brutus, were defeated by Octavian, known to history by his title Augustus, 'the revered one'. After his death in AD 14 the Senate decreed that he should be ranked as a god; from then on Rome was ruled by emperors, deified after their deaths.

On the other side of Via dei Fori Imperiali are the remains of the **Forum of Caesar** mentioned above, with three re-erected columns of the Temple of Venus Genetrix. On this site in 2006, archaeologists found a necropolis dating back to the 10th century BC. The most exciting find has been the well-preserved skeleton of a woman, obviously of high rank, dubbed the 'Queen of the Latins'.

Close by is the **Mamertine Prison** (*open 9–5*), an ancient circular building which was used as a dungeon, most famously for St Peter. It is next to the handsome church of **Santi Luca e Martina**, an early masterpiece by Pietro da Cortona (1640).

The church of **Santi Cosma e Damiano** (*map p. 29, D3*) contains beautiful early mosaics (AD 527). The figure of Christ, bearded and carrying a scroll, dressed in a garment much like a toga, clearly borrows from Classical images of the orator/philosopher. Many other mosaic decorations in the early Christian churches of Rome took their inspiration from these works.

SAN PIETRO IN VINCOLI

Map p. 29, E3. Open 7.30–12.30 & 3.30–6. Entrance up the covered steps from Via Cavour. The church stands on the lower slopes of the Esquiline hill. The hill's four summits, together with the three of the Palatine, formed the early city of the *Septimontium*. In Antiquity most of the hill was considered an unhealthy place to live, though the area between the modern Via Cavour and the Parco Oppio (where the church stands) was fashionable. Pompey was one of its most illustrious inhabitants.

The church of San Pietro in Vincoli was restored in 1475 under Sixtus IV by Meo del Caprina, who was responsible for the façade, with its beautiful colonnaded portico. The splendid simplicity is echoed in the basilican interior, which preserves its 20 ancient fluted columns with Doric capitals.

To the left as you enter is the little tomb of Antonio and Piero Pollaiolo, with two expressive portrait busts attributed to Luigi Capponi. The ceiling painting in the nave shows the Chains of St Peter curing a man possessed by a demon. In the confessio below the high altar are the chains themselves, precious relics with which St Peter was supposedly fettered in the Mamertine Prison.

The most famous monument in the church is Michelangelo's unfinished **tomb of Julius II**, at the end of the south aisle. Some 40 statues were to have decorated the tomb, including the two *Slaves* now in the Louvre, and the four unfinished *Slaves* in

Florence (*see p. 292*). No idea of the original design can be gained from the current grouping, which is chiefly notable for the powerful figure of *Moses*. The satyr-like horns represent beams of light, a traditional attribute of the Prophet in medieval iconography, based on a mistranslation of the Hebrew word for radiance (it was confused with the Hebrew word for horns). The figures of *Leah* and *Rachel* on either side—symbols of the active and contemplative life—are also by Michelangelo. The rest is his pupils' work, although the effigy of the pope was attributed by some scholars to Michelangelo during restoration work in 1999. The pose is based on the reclining figures on Etruscan tombs.

PIAZZA VENEZIA & VIA DEL CORSO

Via del Corso (*map p. 28, C2–B1*) runs in a straight line for some 2km between Piazza Venezia and Piazza del Popolo. Piazza Venezia, a huge and busy square, is usually considered the centre of Rome. It is dominated by the colossal and rather ugly **monument to Vittorio Emanuele II**, inaugurated in 1911 to celebrate the achievement of Italian unity. Buildings were demolished to make way for it, and it even encroaches on the Capitoline hill itself. Built of incongruous white marble, it has allegorical sculptures typical of official Academic Italian art of the period. It also contains the grave of Italy's Unknown Soldier from the First World War, and official military ceremonies still take place here. Since it is one of the tallest buildings in the city, the views from the terraces are superb (*open daily except Mon, entrance on the Piazza*). In the interior is a museum dedicated to the Risorgimento and its heroes Giuseppe Garibaldi and Camillo Cavour.

The other important building which overlooks the piazza is **Palazzo di Venezia**, the first great Renaissance palace in Rome, begun in 1455 for a Venetian cardinal. During the Fascist regime Mussolini used it as his office, and some of his most famous speeches were made from the balcony. It now contains the city's museum of decorative arts (*open 9–7; closed Mon*). Although one of Rome's least visited museums, it has a very fine collection of works from all periods. The **basilica of San Marco** has a remarkable early mosaic in its apse, commissioned around 829. It shows Gregory IV with Christ and St Mark.

Palazzo Doria Pamphilj and Palazzo Colonna

The huge Palazzo Doria Pamphilj (*map p. 28, C2*), with a very fine Rococo façade, contains the **Galleria Doria Pamphilj** (*open 10–5 every day except public holidays; T: 06 679 7323*), the most important of the patrician art collections to have survived in the city. The beautifully kept period rooms retain an unforgettable old-world atmosphere of elegant living. The collection was begun by the Pamphilj pope Innocent X in 1651, and it is still hung as it was in the time of Prince Andrea Doria in 1760. Pope Innocent's portrait by Velázquez is the most famous piece, and there are also two early masterpieces by Caravaggio (*The Rest on the Flight into Egypt* and the *Penitent Magdalene*). Other artists well represented include Claude Lorrain, Quinten Massys,

Caravaggio: *Penitent Magdalene* (1598/99), part of the collection of the Galleria Doria-Pamphilj.

and Hans Memling, and there are busts of the Pamphilj family by Alessandro Algardi, the great 17th-century artist who—had it not been for the overpowering presence of Bernini—would have dominated Roman sculpture in his day.

Adjoining the palace, facing the Corso, is the small church of **Santa Maria in Via Lata** (*open 5–7*), famous for its façade by Pietro da Cortona. Close by, behind the Corso on the other side, is the church of **Santi Apostoli** (*open 7–12 & 4–7*). The huge Baroque interior contains the first important work in Rome by Antonio Canova: the mausoleum of Clement XIV (1783–87).

Adjacent to Santi Apostoli is the other most important private collection in Rome, the **Galleria Colonna** (*map p. 28, C2; open Sat only 9–1; closed Aug*), arranged in magnificent Baroque galleries. The atmosphere in the Great Hall or Gallery is even grander than that at the Galleria Doria Pamphilj. Oddone Colonna lived here as Pope Martin V in the 15th century. A later member of the family was Marcantonio, the victorious admiral at the Battle of Lepanto in 1571. This is still the Colonna family residence. The numerous interesting paintings include works from the Venetian school, and a *Madonna* by Stefano da Zevio in the International Gothic style.

The Trevi Fountain

The huge Trevi Fountain (*map p. 28, C1*) is perhaps the city's most exuberant and successful 18th-century monument, made all the more extraordinary by its confined setting in such a small square. The abundant waters are those of the Acqua Vergine Antica, an aqueduct which runs almost entirely underground, and was built by Agrippa in 19 BC from a spring some 20km east of the city to supply his public baths near the Pantheon.

The fountain is the work of the little-known Roman architect and poet Niccolò Salvi. His theatrical design incorporated, as a background, the entire Neoclassical façade of Palazzo Poli, which had been built in 1730. The fountain itself was completed in 1762, after Salvi's death. The figures in the niches are *Neptune* (centre), flanked by *Health* (right) and *Abundance* (left). The bas-reliefs above represent the legendary virgin—from whom the aqueduct took its name—pointing out the spring to the Roman soldiers, and Agrippa approving the plans for the aqueduct. The four statues above these represent the Seasons with their gifts. At the summit are the arms of the Corsini family, with two allegorical figures. On the enormous artificial rock, built out of tufa, two giant tritons, one blowing a conch, conduct the winged chariot of Neptune pulled by marine horses with webbed hooves.

There is a rooted tradition—which seems to have grown up only at the end of the 19th century—that if you throw a coin over your shoulder into the fountain before you leave the city it will bring good luck and ensure your return.

Piazza Colonna

In the centre of Piazza Colonna (*map p. 28, C1*) rises the majestic **Column of Marcus Aurelius**, erected between AD 180 and 196 in honour of Marcus Aurelius' victories over the Germans (169–73) and Sarmatians (174–76), and dedicated to him and his wife, Faustina the Younger. Statues of the imperial pair once crowned the top, but were replaced in 1589 by a statue of St Paul by Domenico Fontana. The philosopher-emperor Marcus Aurelius led his troops in all these important battles, which delayed the barbarian invasions of Italy for several centuries. The column was inspired by that of Trajan (*see p. 39*): around the shaft a bas-relief ascends in a spiral of 20 turns, interrupted halfway by a *Victory*; the lower part of the relief commemorates the war against the Germanic tribes, the upper that against the Sarmatians.

Piazza di Spagna

Piazza di Spagna (*map p. 69, B3*) takes its name from the residence of the Spanish ambassador to the Vatican, Palazzo di Spagna, at the northern end. For centuries it was the focus of the artistic and literary life of the city. John Evelyn, on his first visit to Rome in 1644, stayed nearby; Keats died in a house on the square. A delightful English 'tea-room', Babington's, still functions. In the centre of the square is the Fontana della Barcaccia, usually considered to be the work of Gian Lorenzo Bernini.

The theatrical **Spanish Steps** were built in 1723–26 to connect the piazza with the church of the Trinità dei Monti. A masterpiece of 18th-century town planning, they are the most famous (and almost the only) work of Francesco de Sanctis.

In the pink 18th-century house at the foot of the steps on the right, is the apartment where the poet John Keats spent the last three months of his life. This is now the **Keats-Shelley Memorial House** (*open Mon–Fri 9–1 & 3–6; Sat 11–2 & 3–6; closed Sun; T: 06 678 4235*) and retains the atmosphere of that time. Keats is buried in the Protestant Cemetery in the southern outskirts (*map p. 24*). His death mask and a sketch by Severn of the poet on his deathbed are preserved in the museum.

At no. 31 Piazza di Spagna is the **Casa Museo di Giorgio de Chirico** (*open first Sun of the month except in Aug; otherwise by appointment Tues–Sat 10–1; T: 06 679 6546*). The Metaphysical artist de Chirico (who was an important influence on the Surrealists) lived here from 1947 until his death, and his home and studio remain as they were furnished. Most of the works exhibited date from the 1960s and 1970s.

In the fashionable Via Condotti, named after the conduits of the Acqua Vergine, which feeds the Trevi fountain, is the renowned **Caffè Greco**, founded in 1760. It retains its delightful interior, with numerous little sitting-rooms with small, marble-topped tables. It is decorated with personal mementoes and self-portraits of some of its most famous patrons, who included Gogol, Baudelaire, Bertel Thorvaldsen and Goethe. Goethe stayed in Rome in 1786–88, and spent his time sightseeing and writing. The house where he stayed, **Casa di Goethe**, at no. 18 Via Fontanella (*map p. 69, A3*) is now a museum (*open 10–6; closed Mon; T: 06 3265 0412*).

Mausoleum of Augustus and the Ara Pacis

In the centre of Piazza Augusto Imperatore (*map p. 69, A3*), laid out in 1936–38, are the remains of the tomb of Augustus, one of the most sacred monuments of ancient Rome. Towards the Tiber is the **Ara Pacis**, cocooned in a building designed by Richard Meier (*open Tues–Sun 9–7; last tickets one hour before closing*). This monumental altar was reconstructed in 1937–38 from scattered remains and from reproductions of dispersed fragments. The carved decoration is a supreme achievement of Augustan art.

The altar was dedicated in 9 BC, in celebration of the peace that Augustus had established within the Empire. Built throughout of Luni marble, it takes the form of an almost square walled enclosure, with two open and two closed sides. Sacrifices took place in the interior. Between the jambs of the main (north) entrance are scenes illustrating the origins of Rome. The left panel (almost entirely lost) represented the *Lupercalia*; the right panel shows *Aeneas Sacrificing the White Sow*. The panels of the south entrance depict Tellus, the earth goddess (possibly an allegory of Peace) on the left, and a much-damaged Roma on the right. The side panels illustrate the actual consecration of the altar: the procession includes Augustus himself and members of his family.

PIAZZA DEL POPOLO

Piazza del Popolo (*map p. 69, A2*) was designed to provide a scenic northern entrance to the city. The monumental **Porta del Popolo** occupies almost the same site as the ancient *Porta Flaminia*. The piazza was created in 1538 for Paul III. In 1589, the obelisk was erected. Its hieroglyphs celebrate the glories of the pharaohs Rameses II and Merenptah (13th–12th centuries BC). After the conquest of Egypt, Augustus had the obelisk transported to Rome from Heliopolis, and it was dedicated to the Sun in the Circus Maximus. Domenico Fontana moved it here in 1589, as part of the urban plan of Sixtus V. The two twin-domed Baroque churches, **Santa Maria dei Miracoli** and **Santa Maria in Montesanto**, were added in the 17th century. The façades, designed by Carlo Rainaldi, were modified by Bernini and Carlo Fontana (1671–78).

Santa Maria del Popolo

In 1099 Pope Paschal II ceremoniously cut down a walnut tree which was thought to be giving shelter to a clutch of demons in the form of a group of black crows. On the site he founded a chapel. That chapel today is the church of Santa Maria del Popolo (*open 7–12 & 4–7*). Its present form dates from 1472–77.

High altar and apse: Over the high altar is the venerated *Madonna del Popolo*, a 14th-century painting. The apse, with its shell design, is one of the earliest works in Rome by Bramante, and was commissioned by Julius II (*there is a light on the left*). Here are the two splendid tombs of Cardinal Girolamo Basso della Rovere (1507) and Cardinal Ascanio Sforza (1505), signed by Andrea Sansovino. The vault frescoes of the *Coronation of the Virgin*, Evangelists, Sibyls and Four Fathers of the Church (1508–09) are fine works by Pinturicchio (*see p. 537*).

North transept: The first chapel to the left of the choir has two dramatic paintings by Caravaggio, the *Crucifixion of St Peter* and *Conversion of St Paul* (1600–01). The altarpiece of the *Assumption*, commissioned at the same time though markedly different in style, is by Annibale Carracci, who also designed the frescoes in the vault.

North aisle: To the left of the altar is a bust of Urbano Mellini by Alessandro Algardi, who also designed the tomb of Giovanni Garzia Mellini on the left wall.

The second chapel is the octagonal Chigi Chapel, founded by the Sienese banker Agostino Chigi (1465–1520). It is a fusion of architecture, sculpture, mosaic and painting designed by Raphael in 1513–16. The lovely mosaics in the dome were executed by a Venetian artist from cartoons by Raphael. Work on the chapel was interrupted in 1520 by the deaths of both Chigi and Raphael; it was completed by Bernini for Cardinal Fabio Chigi (Alexander VII) after 1652. The altar-piece of the *Nativity of the Virgin* (1530–34) is by Raphael's rival Sebastiano del Piombo; the bronze bas-relief in front, *Christ and the Woman of Samaria*, is by Raphael's disciple Lorenzetto. By the altar are statues of the prophets *Jonah* (left), designed by Raphael and executed by Lorenzetto, and the famous *Habakkuk* (right) by Bernini. By the entrance to the chapel are the prophets *Daniel*, also by Bernini, and *Elijah*, by Lorenzetto. The remarkable pyramidal form of the tombs of Agostino Chigi and of his brother Sigismondo (d. 1526), was dictated by Raphael's architectural scheme and derived from ancient Roman models.

THE PANTHEON & ITS DISTRICT

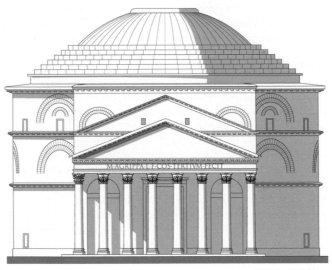

THE PANTHEON

The Pantheon (*map p. 28, B2; open Mon–Sat 8.30–7.30; Sun 9–6*) survives virtually intact as the most magnificent symbol of the Roman Empire. It was originally built in 27 BC to commemorate Augustus' victory over Antony and Cleopatra at Actium. The present temple was built and probably also designed by Hadrian. Begun in AD 118 or 119 and finished between AD 125 and 128, it received and retained the name of Pantheon, being dedicated to all the gods (*pan theon*). Hadrian set up the dedicatory inscription on the pediment—M. AGRIPPA L.F. COS. TERTIUM FECIT ('Marcus Agrippa, son of Lucius, consul for the third time, had [this building] made')—in honour of its original builder. It was consecrated as a church in 609, the first pagan temple to be Christianised. The monument was greatly admired during the Renaissance. The Barberini pope Urban VIII, however, employed Bernini to add two clumsy turrets in front, which became popularly known as the 'ass-ears of Bernini' until they were finally removed in 1883. Pope Urban also melted down the bronze ceiling of the portico to make the baldacchino for St Peter's and 80 cannon for Castel Sant'Angelo, an act of vandalism that prompted the stinging gibe, '*Quod non fecerunt barbari fecerunt Barberini*' ('What the barbarians did not do, the Barberini did').

The visual impact of the interior is extraordinary. The great concrete dome has five rows of coffers diminishing in size towards the circular opening in the centre, which measures almost 9m across. They were probably originally ornamented with gilded bronze rosettes. The height and diameter of the interior are the same—43.3m. The diameter of the dome, which until the 20th century remained the largest vault ever built, exceeds that of St Peter's by more than a metre.

Buried here are Vittorio Emanuele II, first king of Italy (d. 1878); and Raphael, his tomb usually honoured by a fresh red rose. The Latin couplet is by Pietro Bembo (buried in Santa Maria sopra Minerva; *see below*). Below the empty niche on the right is the short epitaph of Maria, niece of Cardinal Dovizi da Bibbiena, who was to have married Raphael but predeceased him.

Santa Maria sopra Minerva

Santa Maria sopra Minerva (*map p. 28, B2; open 7–7*) stands on the site of a former temple of Minerva. It was rebuilt in 1280 by the Dominicans, who modelled it on their church of Santa Maria Novella in Florence (according to Vasari, it was by the same architects). This explains its Gothic style, an extreme rarity in Rome. It was altered and over-restored in 1848–55, but nevertheless contains a wealth of monuments.

In the south transept is the **Cappella Carafa**, attributed to Giuliano da Maiano, with a beautiful balustrade. The chapel contains celebrated frescoes by Filippino Lippi, who had to interrupt work (temporarily) on his other great fresco cycle in the church of Santa Maria Novella in Florence when he received this commission in 1489.

In the choir, at the foot of the steps on the left, is a **statue of *the Risen Christ*** by Michelangelo (1514–21). Standing in marked *contrapposto*, Christ carries the instruments of the Passion (the rod and vinegar sponge, and Cross). Michelangelo's original figure was nude; the bronze drapery is a later addition. Under the 19th-century high altar lies the body of **St Catherine of Siena** (her head is in Siena; *see p. 436*). It was St Catherine who persuaded Gregory XI to return from Avignon to Rome. In the apse behind are the **tombs of the Medici popes** Leo X (left) and Clement VII, designed by

Elephant bearing an Egyptian obelisk (elephant by Bernini), outside Santa Maria sopra Minerva.

Antonio da Sangallo the Younger, with statues by Raffaello da Montelupo and Nanni di Baccio Bigio respectively. In the pavement is the slab-tomb of Cardinal Pietro Bembo (1547), secretary to Pope Leo X from 1512 to 1520, and friend of Michelangelo, Raphael and Ariosto.

To the left of the choir is the pavement **tomb of Fra' Angelico**, with an effigy taken from his death mask, attributed to Isaia da Pisa. Angelico died in the convent here in 1455. On the second nave pillar of the north side is the **monument to Maria Raggi**, a colourful early work by Bernini. Between the fourth and third chapels of the north aisle is the tomb of Giovanni Vigevano (d. 1630), with a bust by Bernini (c. 1617). In the second chapel, the tomb of Gregorio Naro has recently also been attributed to him.

The square in front of the church contains another work by Bernini (1667): a marble elephant supporting an obelisk from a former temple of Isis.

PIAZZA NAVONA & DISTRICT

The form of this famous piazza (*map p. 28, A2*) preserves the outline of the Stadium of Domitian, which could probably hold some 30,000 spectators. Its appearance, surrounded by stately palaces and churches, has remained almost totally unchanged since at least the beginning of the 18th century. It is the most animated square in Rome.

Of the three splendid fountains, the most famous is Bernini's **Fontana dei Quattro Fiumi** (Fountain of the Four Rivers). Four colossal allegorical figures are seated on a triangular base of travertine rock. They represent the Danube (Europe), Ganges (Asia), Nile (Africa) and Rio della Plata (the Americas): the four most famous rivers of the four continents then known, and were carved by Bernini's assistants. The head of Nile is covered, it is said, to indicate that the source of the river was as yet undiscovered. The figure of the Rio della Plata has coins by its side, symbolising the riches of the New World.

The Egyptian obelisk was brought to Rome by order of Domitian, who had Roman stonemasons carve hieroglyphics referring to himself as 'eternal pharaoh' and his predecessors Vespasian and Titus as gods. It was erected here by Innocent X, and is crowned with the dove, the Pamphilj (Pope Innocent's) family emblem.

Sant'Agnese and Sant'Ivo

The church of Sant'Agnese in Agone (*open 9–12 & 4–7 except Mon morning*) takes its name from the former stadium on which it stands (*agones* meaning athletic games). The striking concave façade is the work of Francesco Borromini, Innocent X's favourite architect and Bernini's rival. Borromini also completed the Palazzo Pamphilj next door (now the Brazilian Embassy) for the same pope. Palazzo della Sapienza nearby has a beautiful courtyard, also designed by Borromini, with the church of **Sant'Ivo** (*open 8.30–5; Sat and Sun 9–12*) at the far end. The dome is crowned by an ingenious spiral tower, unique in Rome. The remarkable light interior is painted white and entirely devoid of decoration. Begun for the Barberini pope Urban VIII, both the courtyard and the church incorporate his device (the bee) into their design, as well as Alexander VII's Chigi device of mounds.

San Luigi dei Francesi and Sant'Agostino

San Luigi dei Francesi (*map p. 28, B2; open 7.30–12.30 & 3.30–7; closed Thur afternoon*) is the French national church in Rome (1518–89). It contains, in the **Contarelli Chapel** (the fifth in the north aisle), three famous and very well-preserved paintings by Caravaggio of scenes from the life of St Matthew (1597–1603). The *Calling of St Matthew* shows Matthew the tax-collector surprised by a celestial ray of light. Facing it is *St Matthew's Martyrdom*. The altarpiece of *St Matthew and the Angel* shows the angel seeming to fall right out of the sky (a recurrent theme in Caravaggio's later works). These paintings date from the artist's early Classical and luminous period, and have none of the intense, sometimes overpowering atmosphere of his later works.

The church of **Sant'Agostino** (*map p. 28, B1; open 7.45–12 & 4.30–7.30*) contains Caravaggio's **Madonna di Loreto** (1604), one of his most beautiful paintings. The graceful figure of the Madonna appears at the door of her house to show the blessing Child to two kneeling pilgrims. According to legend, in 1294 the *Santa Casa* or House of the Virgin was miraculously transported by angels from Nazareth to a laurel wood in the Marche. This place became known as Loreto (from the word for a laurel grove) and is still one of the great pilgrimage shrines in the Catholic world (*see p. 626*). As in many of Caravaggio's works, the iconography is extremely unusual; in most other paintings of this subject the house itself is shown being transported through the sky. Caravaggio's contemporary detractors were critical of the pilgrims' dirty feet, but today the work appeals to us for its extraordinary humanity.

In the chapel to the left of the choir is the tomb of St Monica, mother of St Augustine (to whom the church is dedicated). Monica died suddenly in 387 in a hostel at Ostia, from where she was about to set sail to return to Africa with Augustine (a fragment of her tombstone is preserved in the church of Santa Aurea at Ostia Antica; see p. 122). Her relics were bought to this church in 1430.

Caravaggio (1571–1610)
Michelangelo Merisi da Caravaggio was the most important painter in Italy in the 17th century, and he made Rome the most influential centre of art in the country during his lifetime. He also had a profound influence on a large school of painters, who came to be known as the *Caravaggeschi*. The great number of extant copies of his works demonstrate how much he was appreciated. His works are characterised by a striking use of light and shadow, and for their dramatic realism and intensity of imagery.

Caravaggio came to Rome around 1592, and established himself rapidly as an artist of note. Among his patrons was Cardinal Scipione Borghese (a number of works painted for him are still in the Galleria Borghese). He had a violent temper, and in 1606 murdered a man. Condemned to death, he fled to Naples before setting sail for Malta, where he was caught and imprisoned. He escaped to Sicily in 1608. He still managed to paint, however, and several masterpieces of this period are preserved on both islands. One of the works he painted in Malta is now in Palazzo Pitti in Florence (*see p. 286*). Believing he would be able to obtain the pope's pardon he decided to return to Rome, but died on the way back, not yet 40 years old, of malaria contracted on the beach near Porto Ercole in Tuscany.

His works were largely ignored in the 18th century when the French school was in vogue, as he was considered too 'modern'. It was only in the 1950s that he was 'rediscovered', and his reputation has continued untarnished ever since.

Palazzo Altemps
Map p. 28, A1. Open 9–7.45; closed Mon; T: 06 3996 7700.
Palazzo Altemps houses the Ludovisi collection of ancient Roman sculptures from the Museo Nazionale Romano. The collection was begun in 1621 by Cardinal Ludovico Ludovisi, nephew of Pope Gregory XV. He acquired part of the Altemps collection of a century earlier, and other pieces from the Cesi and Mattei families. The collection was further enriched by finds from excavations, some of which were carried out in his own garden. He employed Bernini and Algardi to restore and integrate the statues. The collection is particularly interesting as a reflection of 17th-century taste for the Antique, and shows the skill with which many of the pieces were restored at that time.

One of the most famous pieces is a colossal **head of Marcus Aurelius**: the porphyry bust dates from the 4th century BC, but the bronze cloak and other additions were made in the 17th century. The celebrated Roman statue of a seated male, formerly known as the '*Resting Ares*', is now believed to be **Achilles**, and to have formed a pair with a statue of his mother, Thetis, which are both described by Pliny as adorning the Temple of Neptune in the Campus Martius. The statue of Achilles was restored by Bernini. The famous **Ludovisi Throne**, found at the end of the 19th century, is also displayed here. The central subject is apparently the birth of Aphrodite, who rises from the sea supported by two figures representing the Seasons. It is thought to have been intended for the statue of a divinity, and is usually considered to be a Greek original of the 5th century BC.

On one side of the *Ludovisi Throne* is the colossal head known as the *Ludovisi Juno*, three times natural size. Originally supposed to be a Greek work, it was greatly admired by Goethe. Its subject has now been identified as Antonia, mother of the Emperor Claudius. Another famous piece, the dramatic **Galatian Committing Suicide**, is a Roman copy of the time of Julius Caesar (46–44 BC) of an original Greek bronze. It formed part of the same group as the *Dying Gaul*, now in the Capitoline Museums (*see p. 31*).

Santa Maria della Pace

This beautiful church (*map p. 28, A2; often closed, though officially open Tues–Fri 10–12.45*) was partly rebuilt in the 17th century by order of Pope Alexander VII, under whose auspices the façade and lovely semicircular porch were erected by Pietro da Cortona. Inside, the first south chapel has superb though little-known **frescoes by Raphael** (c. 1511) showing the four Sibyls, to whom angels have descended to reveal the future. It was a common Renaissance conceit to portray the pagan Sibyls as forerunners of the Old Testament prophets (*cf Sistine Chapel, p. 95*). The four prophets above the Sibyls here are by a pupil of Raphael, Timoteo Viti. The bronze *Deposition* on the altar here is by Cosimo Fancelli.

The **cloisters**, where exhibitions are now held, commissioned in 1504, are among Bramante's finest works in Rome.

CAMPO DEI FIORI

Campo dei Fiori (*map p. 28, A2–3*) was once a meadow, but it became one of the most important *piazze* in Rome in the 15th century. Since 1869 it has been a market-place, and it is for its lively open-air stalls selling fresh produce and pungent dried herbs that it is chiefly known today. Executions occasionally took place here in the past: in 1600 the Neoplatonist thinker and philosopher Giordano Bruno was burned as a heretic, on the spot now marked by a dramatic monument by Ettore Ferrari (1889).

At the end of the square behind the statue is the little Piazza del Biscione, which was built over the ruins of the **Theatre of Pompey** (the impressive remains can be seen on request at the Pancrazio restaurant). The great rectangular Porticus of Pompey stood to the east of the theatre, off which opened the Curia. It was on this spot that Julius Caesar was murdered on 15th March 44 BC at the foot of a statue of Pompey—perhaps the very one now in Palazzo Spada (*see below*).

Palazzo Farnese and Palazzo Spada

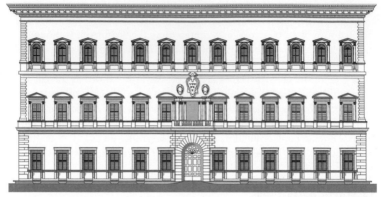

PALAZZO FARNESE

A few metres west of Campo dei Fiori is Piazza Farnese, created by the Farnese in front of their splendid palace. Here are two huge baths of Egyptian granite, brought from the Baths of Caracalla in the 16th century and used by members of the Farnese family as a type of 'royal box' for the spectacles which were held in the square. They were adapted as fountains (using the Farnese lilies) in 1626. **Palazzo Farnese**, the most magnificent Renaissance palace in Rome, is now the French Embassy (*not open to the public*); it was first used as such in 1635. It was designed by Antonio da Sangallo the Younger for Cardinal Alessandro Farnese, afterwards Paul III. After Sangallo's death in 1546, Michelangelo finished the upper storeys and added the superb entablature. In the 18th century the palace became, by marriage, the property of the Bourbons of Naples, who transferred the precious Farnese collection of antique sculpture (which included the *Farnese Bull* found in the Baths of Caracalla in 1545) to that city.

A few steps away from Piazza Farnese, on Via Capo di Ferro, is **Palazzo Spada** (*open 8.30–7; closed Mon; state rooms open by appointment first Sun of the month; T: 06 683 2409*) built in 1544 and acquired in 1632 by Cardinal Bernardino Spada, whose collection, augmented by successive generations, has survived almost totally intact, in rooms that retain their 17th-century furnishings. Highlights are two portraits of Cardinal Spada by Guido Reni and Guercino; an exquisite small *Visitation* by Andrea del Sarto; and a remarkable sketch by Baciccia for his famous frescoed vault of the church of the Gesù (*see opposite*). The General Council Chamber on the first floor (*for admission, see above*) preserves a colossal statue of Pompey, thought to be the one at the foot of which Caesar was murdered.

CHURCHES OF THE COUNTER-REFORMATION

The Gesù

The Gesù, or the Church of the Most Sacred Name of Jesus (*Santissimo Nome di Gesù; map p. 28, B2; open 6–12.30 & 4–7.15*), is the principal Jesuit church in Rome and the prototype of the sumptuous style to which the order has given its name. Both the façade by Giacomo della Porta and the interior by Vignola were important to the subsequent development of Baroque church design. It was built between 1568 and 1575 at the expense of Cardinal Alessandro Farnese. The cupola, planned by Vignola, was completed by della Porta.

The architecture of the interior perfectly serves the ideas of the Counter-Reformation: while Protestant Europe was destroying images and stripping churches, Rome was responding with ceremony as theatre, with emphasis on the high altar, where the mystery of the Mass was celebrated.

On the vault is a superb fresco of the *Triumph of the Name of Jesus*, the **masterpiece of Baciccia** (1672–83). In the north transept is one of the most elaborate Baroque altars in Rome: the **altar-tomb of St Ignatius**, founder of the Jesuit Order, by the Jesuit lay brother Andrea Pozzo and assistants (1695–1700). It is resplendent with marble and gilded bronze; the columns are encrusted with lapis lazuli and bronze decorations.

Sant'Andrea della Valle and Chiesa Nuova

The church of **Sant'Andrea della Valle** (*map p. 28, B2; open 7.30–12 & 4.30–7.30*) was begun in 1591, for the Order of the Theatines. Architects involved included Giacomo della Porta and Pier Paolo Olivieri. It was continued by Carlo Maderno, who crowned it with a fine dome, the highest in Rome after that of St Peter's. The façade was added in the following century (1665) by Carlo Rainaldi. The aisleless interior, inspired by the Gesù, gives the impression of a sumptuous reception hall rather than a house of prayer. In the dome, high up above the crossing, is the *Glory of Paradise* (1621–27), considered one of the best works of Giovanni Lanfranco, a painter from Parma who produced a number of early Baroque works in Rome. His more famous contemporary Domenichino added the Evangelists in the pendentives.

The **Chiesa Nuova** or Santa Maria in Vallicella (*map p. 28, A2; open 9–12 & 3–6*) was built under the inspiration of St Philip Neri, an outstanding figure of the Counter-Reformation, known affectionately as the 'Apostle of Rome'. Among the architects of this church were Martino Longhi the Elder (1575–1605), and the façade shows the influence of that of the Gesù. Inside, the vault, apse and dome were decorated by Pietro da Cortona (1664), and the whole church is brilliantly gilded. In the sanctuary are three very fine paintings by Rubens, commissioned before the artist left Rome in 1608. Resplendent with colour, they are *Sts Domitilla, Nereus and Achilleus* (to the right); and *Sts Gregory, Maurus and Papianus* (to the left). Over the altar itself is the *Madonna and Angels*. The central panel, painted on slate, can be moved aside to reveal the icon of *Santa Maria in Vallicella*, a miraculous image once seen to shed blood, which was placed in the church by order of St Philip Neri. Saint Philip is buried beneath the altar of the sumptuous chapel left of the high altar (1600–04), whose walls are adorned with gorgeous panels in *pietre dure*.

The adjoining **Oratorio dei Filippini** was rebuilt largely by Francesco Borromini (1637–52). St Philip Neri instituted the musical gatherings which became known as oratorios, and which have given their name to a form of musical composition. The dynamic, curvilinear front elevation sounds an unexpected note among a run of flat, static façades.

The piazza and church of Sant'Ignazio

Just off the left side of the Corso (reached by Via del Caravita) is the Rococo **Piazza di Sant'Ignazio** (*map p. 28, C2*), a theatrical masterpiece by Filippo Raguzzini (1728). The Jesuit **church of Sant'Ignazio** (*open 7.30–12.30 & 4–7.15*) rivals the Gesù in magnificence. It was begun in 1626 to celebrate the canonisation of St Ignatius Loyola, founder of the Jesuits, and was executed (to a design by Carlo Maderno and others) by Orazio Grassi, a Jesuit mathematician, who is also responsible for the fine façade, his only architectural work. In the **vaulting of the nave and apse** are remarkable paintings, the masterpiece of Andrea Pozzo, representing the missionary activity of the Jesuits and the triumph of St Ignatius. Pozzo, himself a Jesuit, was the greatest exponent of the *quadratura* technique, which used painted architectural elements to provide illusionistic decorations, and which became extremely popular in the Baroque period.

In Piazza di Pietra (reached by Via di Burro and Via di Pietra, in front of Sant'Ignazio) are the splendid remains of the huge **Temple of Hadrian**, built by Antoninus Pius in 145 and dedicated to his father. Now incorporated in the façade of the Chamber of Commerce building, the high wall of the cella survives, along with the peristyle of the right side with 11 disengaged fluted Corinthian columns (15m high). The houses in front follow the line of the portico which used to surround the temple. The square is filled with cafés and bars.

THE QUIRINAL HILL

The Quirinal (61m; *map p. 29, D1*) is one of the highest of the seven hills of Rome. In late Republican days and throughout the Empire, it was covered with gardens and summer villas. The spacious and dignified Piazza del Quirinale occupies the summit of the hill. It has a balustrade which opens onto a fine panorama across the rooftops to St Peter's in the distance. In the middle of the square are two famous colossal groups of Castor and Pollux, the Dioscuri (*see p. 36*), standing by their horses. They are Roman copies, dating from the Imperial era, of Greek originals of the 5th century BC, though not the work of Pheidias or Praxiteles as the inscriptions on the bases suggest. The statues have stood somewhere in the city ever since the fall of the Empire.

Palazzo del Quirinale

Palazzo del Quirinale (*open Sun 8.30–12; closed July and Aug and on major public holidays; T: 06 46991*) has been the official residence of the President of the Italian

Republic since 1948. The building was begun in 1574 by Flaminio Ponzio and Ottaviano Mascherino for Gregory XIII, and was continued by Domenico Fontana, Carlo Maderno, Bernini (who worked on the *manica lunga*, the 'long wing' in Via del Quirinale) and Ferdinando Fuga: it was not completed until the time of Clement XII (1730–40). The principal entrance is by Maderno.

From 1592 the Quirinal was the summer residence of the popes. Sixtus V died here in 1590. Pius VI was forced to leave the palace as a prisoner of Napoleon and was taken to France, where he died in 1799. From its balcony Pius IX blessed Italy on his election as pope in 1846, little knowing that his pontificate would see the end of the papal rule of the city: the Italian army seized Rome in 1870. From then until 1947 the palace was the residence of the kings of Italy, and the first king, Vittorio Emanuele II, died here in 1878. Most of the furniture, paintings and tapestries preserved in the interior belonged to the Italian royal family. The Oriental vases and Gobelins tapestries were the property of the papacy.

Sant'Andrea al Quirinale

This is often considered the most beautiful church by Bernini (*map p. 29, D2; open 8–12 & 4–7; closed Tues*). It was commissioned by Pope Alexander VII, and the great architect received the help of his pupil Mattia de' Rossi during building work (1658–70).

The façade is an enormous single aedicule with a convex, semi-circular portico. On either side of this Bernini placed segments of wall in the form of quarter circles, thus creating a charming and intimate urban forecourt. The concave-convex-concave contour of the façade is one of the most important guiding motifs in Bernini's work, appearing again in Ariccia (*see p. 126*). The forecourt, in the form of a half ellipse, anticipates the elliptical nave, and balances the repeated aedicule and half ellipse of the altar recess. Bernini chose to arrange the side-chapels radially, thus evoking the oblique axiality of the St Andrew's Cross.

The interior is very fine, with columns, pilasters and frames in pink and grey marble, and gilded and stuccoed decorations. A fisherman—another allusion to the titular saint Andrew—and numerous cherubim look down from the lantern and surmount the high altarpiece: these were executed by Bernini's assistant Antonio Raggi, who was particularly skilled in stucco-work.

San Carlo alle Quattro Fontane

This small oval church (*map p. 29, E1; usually open Mon–Fri 10–1 & 3–6; Sat 10–1; Sun 12–1 & 3–6*) is a masterpiece by Francesco Borromini, often considered his most innovative work. It is difficult to appreciate the structural richness of the façade, as the church stands in a cramped corner site, with traffic roaring mercilessly past. Borromini created a two-storey tripartite front with a concave-convex-concave rhythm behind the pilasters at ground level, a rhythm echoed—but not quite replicated—in the three concave bays on the upper façade. The interior, begun in 1638, has convex and concave surfaces in a complex geometric design using triangles in a unifying scheme: the symbolism throughout is of the Holy Trinity. The small cloister,

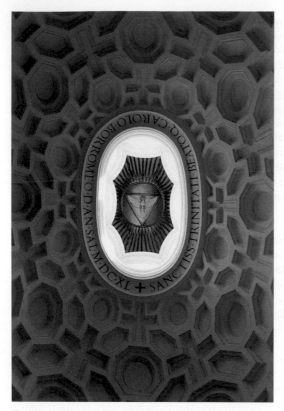

The triangle symbol of the Trinity decorates the lantern of San Carlo alle Quattro Fontane, while the dome itself is decorated with hexagonal, octagonal and cross-shaped coffers.

entered from the church, is one of the most original architectural spaces in Rome (every other pillar of the balustrades on the upper floor is turned upside down). Despite his manifold gifts, the irascible, introverted Borromini was never as fêted as his great contemporary and rival Bernini, nor did he receive such conspicuous papal support, except from Innocent X. He committed suicide in 1667.

Palazzo Barberini

Palazzo Barberini (*map p. 29, D1; open 9–7; closed Mon; T: 06 482 4184*), one of the grandest palaces in Rome, was begun by Carlo Maderno for the Barberini pope Urban VIII in 1624. Work was continued on the central block by Bernini, and Borromini designed the windows of the top storey, the stairs and some doorways.

The palace now houses part of the Galleria Nazionale d'Arte Antica (the remainder is in Palazzo Corsini; *see p. 80*). It is pre-eminent in Italian Baroque painting.

In the first-floor *Salone* is Pietro da Cortona's magnificent allegorical ceiling fresco of the *Triumph of Divine Providence* (1633–39), which shows Providence crowning with bays the arms of the Barberini family (three honey bees). Masterpieces of the painting collection include two important works by Caravaggio: *Narcissus*, and *Judith with the Head of Holofernes*. The *St Francis in Meditation* is also attributed to him. The *Portrait of a Lady* (or of a Sibyl) by Guido Reni was traditionally thought to be a portrait of Beatrice Cenci, a young girl of 22 who was executed in 1599 for having hired assassins to kill her father. Although Beatrice never confessed to parricide even under torture, she was beheaded. Her father was known to have been a violent man and was also accused of incest.

Probably the best-known work in the collection is the *Portrait of a Lady* by Raphael (also attributed to his pupil Giulio Romano), which became known as *'La Fornarina'* when the Romantics identified the sitter with Margherita, daughter of a Sienese baker (*fornaio*), and supposedly Raphael's mistress.

BATHS OF DIOCLETIAN & THE TERMINI DISTRICT

Begun in AD 299, the baths (*map p. 29, F1; open 9–7.45; closed Mon; T: 06 3996 7700*) were completed in less than eight years by Diocletian and Maximian. They were the largest of all the ancient Roman baths, and could accommodate over 3,000 people at once. The calidarium, which survived into the late 17th century, occupied part of Piazza della Repubblica. The tepidarium and the huge central hall of the baths are now occupied by the church of Santa Maria degli Angeli (*see below*). The frigidarium was an open-air bath behind this hall.

Much of the baths complex is closed, but the **Epigraphy Collection of the Museo Nazionale Romano** (about 10,000 Latin inscriptions) is one of the most important of its kind in the world, and is superbly displayed in modern halls. A beautiful domed octagonal bath hall, the **Aula Ottagona** on Via Parigi (*open 9–2; closed Mon; holidays 9–1; free entry*), provides a splendid setting for some magnificent Classical statues and busts found here and in other baths in the city. The hall is thought to have connected the open-air gymnasium and gardens of the baths with the heated calidarium. Roman foundations can be seen through the glass panel in the centre.

Santa Maria degli Angeli

Santa Maria degli Angeli (*open 7.30–12.30 & 4–6.30*) occupies the great central hall of the Baths of Diocletian, converted into the church of the Carthusian monastery that stood on this site. The original conversion was carried out in 1563–66 to a design by Michelangelo, who placed the entrance where the south transept is now, meaning that the doors opened onto a huge, long nave. The effect was spoiled by Vanvitelli, who constructed the current entrance, leading worshippers into a disproportionately long transept. To compensate for the loss of length, he built on an apsidal choir, which broke into the monumental southwest wall of the frigidarium.

In the disappointing interior, the circular vestibule stands on the site of the tepidarium. Here, on the right, is the tomb of Carlo Maratta (d. 1713), the most important painter in Rome in the late 17th century. By the entrance into the transept, on the right, stands a fine **colossal statue of *St Bruno***, the founder of the Carthusian Order, by the celebrated French sculptor Jean-Antoine Houdon, made when he was studying at the French Academy in Rome from 1764–68.

The vast transept is nearly 100m long. The eight monolithic columns of red granite are original; the others (almost indistinguishable), in brick, were added when the building was remodelled. The door to the sacristy in the left transept leads to a room with remains of the frigidarium of the Baths of Diocletian, and a display explaining the history of the building.

Palazzo Massimo alle Terme (Museo Nazionale Romano)

Map p. 29, F1. Open 9–7.45; closed Mon; T: 06 3996 7700.

The most important part of the vast state collections of ancient Roman art are kept here, in what is the finest museum of its kind in the world. The display is chronological, from Roman Republican sculpture from the time of Sulla (138–78 BC) to works from the 4th century AD. Of the many portraits of emperors and their consorts is a celebrated **statue of Augustus** portrayed as *pontifex maximus* or high priest, a demonstration of his piety. Some of the sculptures are Greek originals, for example the superb *Daughter of Niobe* (5th century BC) by the school of Kresilas; and *Aphrodite*, a copy of the *Aphrodite of Cnidos* by Praxiteles, signed by the Greek artist Menophantos. The so-called *Maiden of Antium*, from Nero's villa at Anzio (*see p. 231*), is a Greek masterpiece from the end of the 4th or beginning of the 3rd century BC, by a sculptor from the school of Lysippus, also showing the influence of Praxiteles. Also in the collection are two copies of the 5th-century BC *Discobolus* (Discus-thrower) by Myron.

On the second floor is the famous **room from the Villa of Livia** (wife of Augustus) at Prima Porta, its walls decorated with splendid murals of trees, an orchard and flower garden. Detached and restored in 1952–53, the works were saved just in time from complete decay, and are one of the most remarkable examples known of Roman art.

Santa Maria della Vittoria

The church of Santa Maria della Vittoria (*map p. 29, E1; open 7–12 & 4–7*) has a well-proportioned, relatively small, interior by Carlo Maderno, considered one of the most complete examples of Baroque decoration in Rome. The church is most famous for the Cornaro Chapel by Bernini (the fourth on the north side), a splendid architectural achievement, using the shallow space to great effect (c. 1647–50). To appreciate the composition fully, it is best not to stand too close. Over the altar is his famous marble group, the **Ecstasy of St Teresa**, showing the saint in an almost erotic swoon before an angel beneath golden rays of celestial light (lit, ingeniously, from a hidden side window). Bernini, a devout Catholic, vividly portrays the moment when the Angel of the Lord pierces the saint's heart, while members of the Cornaro family, in sculpted relief, look on from the sides, as if at the theatre. Bernini considered the chapel and this sculpture his best work.

Santa Maria Maggiore

Map p. 29, F2. Open 7–6/7. Museum open 9.30–6.30. The Loggia delle Benedizioni, with its 13th-century mosaics, is open twice a day (at 9.30 and 1). The church tends to be very crowded with tour groups; it is best to visit early.

The basilica of Santa Maria Maggiore is one of the great patriarchal basilicas of Rome. According to legend, the Virgin appeared one summer night to Pope Liberius (352–66) and to John, a patrician of Rome, telling them to build a church. She told them that in the morning they would find a patch of snow covering the exact area to be built over. The prediction fulfilled, Liberius drew up the plans and John built the church at his own expense. The present church dates from the 5th century; the apse and transepts are

13th-century additions. The fine campanile, the highest in Rome, was given its present form in 1377. The 18th-century main façade is by Ferdinando Fuga.

The vast, well-proportioned interior still preserves its basilican form. It is divided into nave and aisles by 36 columns of Hymettian marble and four of granite, all with Ionic capitals supporting an architrave. The coffered ceiling, attributed to Giuliano da Sangallo, was traditionally thought to have been gilded with the first gold brought from America by Columbus, presented to the Borgia pope Alexander VI by King Ferdinand of Aragon and his wife Isabella, Queen of Castile. The Borgia emblems of rosettes and bulls are prominent. The fine Cosmatesque pavement dates from c. 1150.

SANTA MARIA MAGGIORE

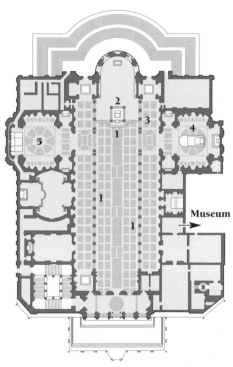

1	Mosaics	4	Cappella Sistina
2	Confessio	5	Cappella Borghese
3	Tomb of Bernini		

(1) The mosaics: The splendid 5th-century mosaics in the nave and over the triumphal arch are the most important Roman mosaic cycle of this period. On the left are scenes from the lives of Abraham, Jacob and Isaac; on the right, scenes from the lives of Moses and Joshua (restored, in part painted); over the triumphal arch, scenes from the early life of Christ.

The 13th-century apse mosaic is signed by Iacopo Torriti and represents the *Coronation of the Virgin*. She is seated on the same throne as Christ, a composition probably derived from the 12th-century mosaic in the apse of Santa Maria in Trastevere (*see p. 80*). Below, between the windows, are more mosaics by Torriti depicting the life of the Virgin.

(2) The confessio: Reconstructed in the 19th century by Virginio Vespignani, it contains a colossal kneeling statue of Pius IX by Ignazio Jacometti. A porphyry sarcophagus containing the relics of St Matthew and other martyrs serves as the high altar. A fragment of Jesus' crib is kept in a reliquary.

(3) Tomb of Bernini: By the sanctuary steps is the simple pavement tomb of the great architect and sculptor Gian Lorenzo Bernini (d. 1680).

(4) Cappella Sistina: This work of extraordinary magnificence was executed for Sixtus V by Domenico Fontana (1585). It is a veritable church in itself, decorated with statues, stuccoes, and Mannerist frescoes around the sumptuous tomb of the pontiff (and that of St Pius V on the left). The temple-like baldacchino, carried by four gilt-bronze angels by Sebastiano Torrigiani, covers the original little Cosmatesque Chapel of the Relics (*for admission, ask at the museum*), redesigned by Arnolfo di Cambio (late 13th century).

(5) Cappella Borghese: This splendid chapel was erected for Paul V by Flaminio Ponzio in 1611 as the pope's burial place. The frescoes by Cavaliere d'Arpino, the master of Caravaggio, are considered his masterpiece. To one side of the pope's tomb is that of Clement VIII, who has gone down in history as the pope who sent Beatrice Cenci (*see p. 56*) and Giordano Bruno (*see p. 51*) to their deaths.

Santa Prassede and Santa Pudenziana

The church of **Santa Prassede** (*map p. 29, F2; open 7–12 & 4–6.30*) is dedicated to Praxedes, daughter of a Roman senator. She and her sister Pudentiana are frequently depicted in the mosaics in the church, whose light interior is particularly inviting. To the left as you enter is the tiny Chapel of St Zeno, built by Paschal I, pope and saint, as a mausoleum for his mother, Theodora, in 817–24. This charming, perfectly preserved chapel is the most important work of its date to have survived intact in Rome. Above the entrance is a double row of mosaic busts: in the inner row, the Virgin and Child, St Praxedes and St Pudentiana, and other saints; in the outer, Christ and the Apostles, and four saints (the lowest two perhaps added in the 13th century). In the centre of the interior vault is Christ surrounded by four angels skilfully fitted into the angles of the ceiling. The mosaics show Byzantine influence, and demonstrate also how pagan symbolism became conflated with Christian. The figure of the general borne aloft on his circular shield by four winged Victories translates into Christ the victor over death portrayed in a roundel and borne aloft by angels.

Santa Pudenziana (*map p. 29, E2; open 8–12 & 4–6*) is thought to have been built c. 390 above a Roman thermal hall of the 2nd century. It was rebuilt several times later, notably in 1589. The church is dedicated to Pudentiana, sister of Praxedes (*see above*), and daughter of the Roman senator Pudens, who is supposed to have given hospitality to St Peter in his house on this site when the Apostle first arrived in Rome. The church contains an extremely interesting apse mosaic, the earliest of its kind in Rome, dating from 390. It shows Christ Enthroned between Sts Peter and Paul and the Apostles and two female figures presenting wreaths, representing the converted Jews and the converted pagans (or Gentiles). The Roman character of the figures is marked; the magisterial air of Christ recalls representations of Jupiter, and the Apostles, in their togas, resemble senators. It would appear that Imperial motifs were deliberately used in early Christian iconography to strengthen the position of the church in Rome. Paul is included to bring the number of Apostles to twelve, and this is one of the earliest instances in which we see him take pride of place with Peter beside Christ.

ST JOHN LATERAN & SAN CLEMENTE

The church of St John Lateran (San Giovanni in Laterano; *map p. 61, C2; open 7–6; 7–7 in summer*) is the cathedral of Rome and of the world (*Omnium urbis et orbis Ecclesiarum Mater et Caput*). It was the first Christian basilica to be constructed in Rome, probably between 314 and 318, and served as a model for all subsequent Christian churches. It has suffered ruin by the Vandals, fire and rebuilding, most notably by Borromini in 1646–49. Until 1870 the popes were crowned here. Under the Lateran Treaty of 1929 (*see p. 90*) it was accorded the privilege of extraterritoriality. After the ratification of the treaty the pope left the seclusion of the Vatican for the first time since 1870.

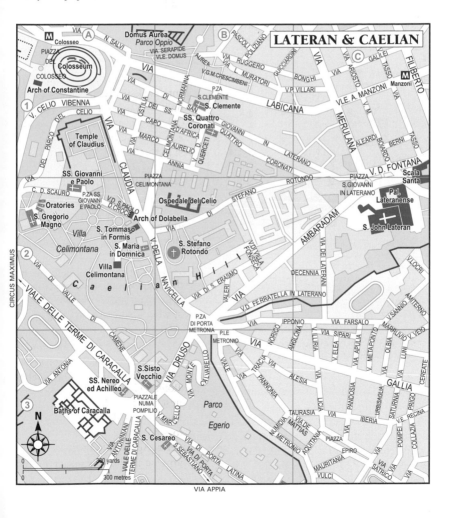

ST JOHN LATERAN

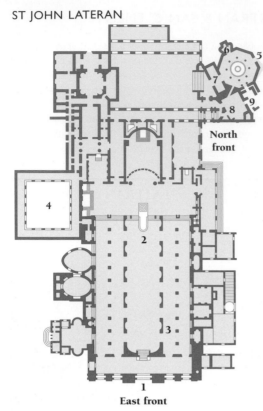

North front

East front

1 Bronze doors from the Curia
2 Confessio and baldacchino
3 Fresco by ?Giotto
4 Cloister
5 Baptistery
6 Chapel of St John the Baptist
7 Chapel of Sts Cyprian and Justina
8 Chapel of St Venantius
9 Chapel of St John the Evangelist

The **north front**, built by Domenico Fontana in 1586, has a portico of two tiers. The main **east front** is a theatrical early 18th-century composition by Alessandro Galilei. It consists of a two-storeyed portico surmounted by an attic with 16 colossal statues of Christ with the Apostles and saints. Beneath the portico, the central portal has the ancient **bronze doors of the Curia** in the Roman Forum (*see p. 34*) **(1)**, moved here in the 17th century by Alexander VII. On the left is a statue of Constantine, from his baths on the Quirinal.

The interior

A hundred and thirty metres long, with two aisles on either side of the nave, the church preserves in part its original 4th-century proportions, although it was entirely remodelled by Borromini in 1646–49. He designed the niches between the massive piers, each with two *verde antico* pillars, and Alessandro Algardi and his collaborators executed the scenes from the Old and New Testaments in stucco above them. Borromini also decorated the outer aisles, where he reconstructed the funerary monuments, enclosing them in elegant Baroque frames. The beautiful ceiling (dating from 1566) and the marble 15th-century Cosmatesque pavement have been retained.

The **confessio (2)** is modelled on that of St Peter's, with the beautiful bronze tomb-slab of Martin V (d. 1431) by the little-known Tuscan sculptor Simone Ghini. The elaborate Gothic baldacchino is by another Tuscan, Giovanni di Stefano (1367)—his best known work. It has frescoes which may also be by a 14th-century Tuscan master, but repainted in the following century by Antoniazzo Romano. The 19th-century gilded silver reliquaries are traditionally thought to contain the heads of St Peter and St Paul. The papal altar, reconstructed by Pius IX, encloses part of a wooden altar at which St Peter and his successors (up until the 4th century) are supposed to have celebrated Mass.

On the first nave pier in the inner south aisle there is an interesting **fresco fragment (3)** showing the elderly Boniface VIII proclaiming the Jubilee of 1300 (the first Holy Year). For a long time it was considered to be by the school of Giotto, but most scholars now consider it to be by the hand of the master himself.

The **cloister** (*entrance fee*) **(4)**, a magnificent example of Cosmatesque art, is the masterpiece of Iacopo and Pietro Vassalletto (c. 1222–32). The columns, some plain and some twisted, are adorned with mosaics and have fine capitals. The frieze is exquisite. In the centre is a well-head dating from the 9th century. Many fragments from the ancient basilica are displayed around the cloister walls. The most interesting is in the south walk: the tomb of Cardinal Riccardo Annibaldi, the first important work of Arnolfo di Cambio in Rome (c. 1276), reconstructed from fragments.

The baptistery

The baptistery (*open 7–12.30 & 4–7.30*) **(5)** was built by Constantine c. 315–24, but was not, as legend states, the scene of his baptism as the first Christian emperor (337). It is octagonal in design, although the original baptistery, designed for total immersion and derived from Classical models, may have been circular. It was remodelled in 432–40, and its design was copied in many subsequent baptisteries. The 17th-century decorations were added by Urban VIII, and the harsh frescoes of scenes from the life of St John the Baptist on the drum of the cupola are modern copies of works by Andrea Sacchi.

The interesting chapels are kept unlocked but you have to push the doors open. The **Chapel of St John the Baptist (6)** was founded by the martyred pope St Hilarius (461–68). It preserves its original doors. The **Chapel of Sts Cyprian and Justina (7)** was altered to its present form in 1154. High up on the wall can be seen a fragment of the original marble intarsia decoration. In the north apse is a beautiful 5th-century mosaic with vine tendrils on a brilliant blue ground.

The **Chapel of St Venantius (8)** contains 7th-century mosaics. Remains of 2nd-century Roman baths built above a 1st-century villa, with a mosaic pavement, can also be seen here. The **Chapel of St John the Evangelist (9)**, with bronze doors of 1196, is decorated with a lovely 5th-century vault mosaic of the Lamb surrounded by symbolic birds and flowers.

Scala Santa

The building that houses the **Scala Santa** (*open 6.15–12.15 & 3–6.30*), opposite the basilica's east front, was designed by Domenico Fontana in 1589. In the 15th century the staircase from the old Lateran Palace was declared to be that from Pilate's house which Christ descended after his condemnation: a legend related how it had been brought from Jerusalem to Rome by St Helen, mother of Constantine. The 28 Tyrian marble steps are protected by boards, and worshippers are only allowed to ascend them on their knees. At the top is the chapel of the **Sancta Sanctorum**, or Chapel of St Lawrence, the private chapel of the pope. It is never open, though partly visible through the grating. Protected by a silver tabernacle is the relic which gives the chapel its particular sanctity: an ancient painting on wood of Christ, which could date from as early as the 5th century, although it has been many times repainted and restored. It is said to have been begun by St Luke and an angel.

San Clemente

Map p. 61, B1. Open 9–12.30 & 3–6; Sun and holidays 10–12.30 & 3–6; entrance fee for lower church.

Dedicated to St Clement, the fourth pope (90–99?), this lovely basilica is one of the best-preserved and oldest in Rome. It consists of two churches superimposed, built above a large early Imperial building. The convent is home to a community of Irish Dominicans. The lower church, mentioned by St Jerome in 392, was destroyed when the Normans sacked Rome in 1084. It was rediscovered in 1857 by the prior of the convent, and was excavated four years later.

The upper church was begun in 1108 by Paschal II, who used the decorative marbles from the ruins of the old church. The schola cantorum, in the centre of the nave, comes from the lower church, and contains two ambones, a candelabrum and reading-desk, all characteristic elements of a basilican interior. The 12th-century apse mosaics are especially fine: in the apse-vault is the dome of Heaven with the hand of God above Christ on the Cross, with 12 doves representing the Apostles. Beside the Cross are the Madonna and St John.

The **Chapel of St Catherine**, to the left of the west door as you enter, is one of the most important early Renaissance works in Rome, entirely covered with beautiful frescoes by Masolino. Above the entrance arch is the *Annunciation*, and on the main wall, the *Crucifixion*. On the left wall are scenes from the life of St Catherine of Alexandria: at the top left she is shown discussing the merits of Christianity with the Emperor Maxentius. The next scene shows her being visited in prison by the emperor's wife, whom she converts and whom Maxentius therefore sentences to death. The three scenes below illustrate her converting a group of Roman orators in the presence of the emperor, who in anger has them burnt. In the centre, Catherine is about to be pulled apart by two wheels, but is saved by the intervention of an angel. The last scene shows her final martyrdom as she is beheaded. Outside the chapel, on the adjacent (north) wall, are two *sinopie* found during restoration: one for the *Beheading of St Catherine*, and one for the *Crucifixion*.

The lower church

Precious frescoes from the 9th–11th centuries show the legend of St Clement (narthex), scenes from the life of Christ, and the stories of St Alexius and Sisinius (all in the nave). The apse was built above a 2nd- or 3rd-century Mithraeum, which can be seen on the level below. Most impressive is the triclinium, with benches on either side and an altar in the centre showing Mithras sacrificing a bull to Apollo (*for more on the cult of Mithras, see p. 116*).

Also on this lower level are the remains of a 1st-century 'palazzo' constructed, after Nero's fire, on Republican foundations. The last two rooms are the best preserved, showing the original brick-work. There is also a spring: the sound of its gushing waters pervades the whole lower building.

Santi Quattro Coronati

Map p. 61, B1. Church usually open 6.15am–8pm; on holidays closed 12.30–3. Chapel of St Sylvester, cloister and crypt usually open 9.30–12 & 4.30–6; holidays 9.30–10.45 & 4–5.45, although—since it belongs to a convent—the opening hours are subject to change.
The present church was erected in 1110 by Paschal II and dedicated to the four crowned martyrs—Claudius,

Masolino: *The Virgin Annunciate* (detail) from the Chapel of St Catherine, in the upper church of San Clemente (1428–31).

Nicostratus, Symphorian and Castorius—who were a group of sculptors from the Roman province of Pannonia (present-day Hungary) martyred by Diocletian for refusing to make a statue of Aesculapius. The monastery is occupied by a closed order of Augustinian nuns. To visit the **Chapel of St Sylvester**, go in the door and ring the bell: ask through the grille for the key and collect it from the wooden turntable: you are asked to leave a donation. When the nuns are busy it is sometimes necessary to ring more than once; if there is no reply, wait and try again a little later. It is now rare in Italy to find a convent which still preserves this way of communicating with the outside world. The chapel was built in 1246, and contains a particularly well-preserved fresco cycle of the same date, illustrating the life of Constantine, his dream of Sts Peter and Paul and subsequent baptism, and the finding of the True Cross by his mother, St Helen.

THE CAELIAN HILL

The Caelian Hill (51m; *map p. 61, A2–B2*), is the most extensive of the Seven Hills after the Esquiline. The picturesque church of **Santi Giovanni e Paolo** covers Roman remains which are now open as a museum. The tall façade of a Roman house is incorporated into the church wall on Clivo di Scauro, where there is the entrance to the **Roman houses** beneath (*open 10–1 & 3–6; closed Tues and Wed; T: 06 7045 4544*). According to tradition this is where John (Giovanni) and Paul (Paolo), two court dignitaries under Constantine II, lived in the mid-4th century. They were martyred by Julian the Apostate and were buried here. At least four phases of habitation have been found from the 1st–5th centuries AD, including two Roman apartment houses with shops (2nd–3rd centuries AD), and a Christian house and an oratory founded before 410 by the senator Byzantius and his son Pammachius, a friend of St Jerome.

The remains are most interesting for their wall paintings: youths bearing garlands, a great variety of birds, architectural frescoes with painted imitation marble, and figures of philosophers, goats and masques. In the little medieval oratory (near the road) are 9th-century frescoes including a rare representation of the *Crucifixion* in which the figure of Christ is robed.

The church itself (*open 8.30–12 & 3.30–6; closed Fri and Sun morning*) stands beside the 12th-century convent built above remains of the Temple of Claudius. The travertine blocks of the temple are clearly visible in the base of the beautiful tall campanile (45m). The 12th-century Ionic portico has eight antique columns. Above it is a 13th-century gallery and the early Christian façade with five arches. The 13th-century Cosmatesque doorway is flanked by two lions and surmounted by an eagle with a rabbit in its talons. The interior, hung with chandeliers, with granite piers and columns, was restored in 1718. A tomb-slab in the nave, protected by a railing, commemorates the burial place of the two martyrs to whom the church is dedicated. Their relics are preserved in a porphyry urn under the high altar.

San Gregorio Magno

The church of San Gregorio Magno (*map p. 61, A2; open 9–12.30 & 3.30–6; closed Sat; oratories Tues, Thur, Sat and Sun 9.30–12.30*) is a medieval foundation dedicated to St Gregory the Great. From a wealthy patrician family, he founded a monastery on the site of his father's house, living as a monk here before (unwillingly) becoming pope in 590, the first monk ever to reach that position. At that time, the city was suffering from a long period in which its possession had been contested between Goths and Byzantines, but Gregory succeeded in establishing control and effectively asserted the temporal power of the papacy. From his time onwards the history of Rome became intricately connected with that of the Roman Church. St Augustine was prior in this monastery, and it was here in 596 that he received Gregory's blessing before setting out on his famous mission to convert the English to Christianity.

The staircase, façade and lovely atrium (1633) are by Giovanni Battista Soria (a Roman architect clearly influenced by both Carlo Maderno and Pietro da Cortona). The church itself was rebuilt in 1725–34. Of much greater interest are the oratories to the left of the church, once part of St Gregory's monastery. In the centre is the **chapel of Sant'Andrea**, which has a superb painting of the *Flagellation of St Andrew* by Domenichino, and on the left *St Andrew on the way to his Martyrdom* by Guido Reni. The chapel on the left, **Santa Barbara**, boasts a 3rd-century table believed to be the one at which St Gregory served twelve paupers daily, among whom an angel once appeared as a thirteenth. A fresco on the left, by Antonio Viviani (1602), commemorates the famous incident which culminated in St Augustine's mission: apparently Gregory saw some fair-haired children at a slave market in Rome, and upon hearing that they were English, declared '*non Angli sed Angeli*'. The chapel on the right, **Santa Silvia**, was built in 1603 and dedicated to St Sylvia, mother of Gregory. It contains a lovely fresco of an angel choir by Guido Reni (with the help of Sisto Badalocchio).

The Circus Maximus

Only the shape of the Circus Maximus (*map p. 28, C4*), the largest circus in ancient Rome, survives, but it is impressive for all that. Planted with grass and unenclosed, it can be enjoyed as a public park, from which there is a very fine view of the ruins at the southern end of the Palatine. According to Livy, it dates from the time of Tarquinius Priscus (c. 600 BC), who is said to have inaugurated a display of races and boxing match-es here after a victory over the Latins; but the first factual reference to it is in 329 BC.

Tiers of seats were provided all round except at the short straight end; here were the *carceres*, or stalls for horses and chariots. In the centre, running lengthwise, was the *spina*, a low wall terminating at either end in a *meta*, or conical pillar, denoting the turn-ings of the course. The length of a race was seven circuits of the spina. Though prima-rily adapted for chariot races, the circus was also used for athletic contests, wild-beast fights, and (by flooding the arena) for mock sea-battles.

The circus was destroyed by fire under Nero (AD 64) and again in the time of Domitian. A new circus was built by Trajan; Caracalla enlarged it and Constantine restored it. The last games were held under the Ostrogothic king Totila in AD 549.

The Baths of Caracalla

Map p. 61, A3. Open 9–dusk; Mon 9–1. Bus 628 runs from Largo Torre Argentina (map p. 28, B2) to the baths.

The huge Baths of Caracalla are the best-preserved and most splendid of the Imperial Roman baths. The romantic sun-baked ruins are on a vast scale and are an architectur-al masterpiece. Beneath ground level there is an intricate heating system and hydraulic plant, which may be restored and opened to the public. Of the elaborate decoration only a few architectural fragments and some floor-mosaics remain. The main buildings still maintain their romantic atmosphere, in places overgrown with vegetation, and with poppies and daisies growing in the grass.

The baths were begun by Antoninus Caracalla in 212, at a time when the construc-tion of vast concrete vaults had been perfected, allowing these to be truly monumental. It has been estimated that 9,000 workmen laboured for five years on the site. The baths opened in 217. They were fed by a branch of the Acqua Marcia, an aqueduct begun five years earlier specially for this purpose. After a restoration by Aurelian they remained in use until the 6th century, when the invading Goths damaged the aqueducts.

In the 16th–17th centuries, the *Belvedere Torso* (now in the Vatican museums; *see p. 100*), the *Farnese Hercules* and *Farnese Bull* (now in Naples), and many other statues were found among the ruins.

The baths are symmetrically arranged around the huge **central hall (1)**, with **dressing-rooms** (*apodyteria*) **(2)** on either side. The two *palaestrae* **(3)**, for sports and exercises, consisted of an open courtyard with porticoes on three sides and a huge hemicycle opposite five smaller rooms. The rooms to the south, which may have included a dry sweating room or **laconicum (4)**, led to the huge circular **calidarium (5)**, 34m across (only part of one side remains). It had high windows on two levels to admit the sun. From here bathers passed into the **tepidarium (6)** and the large vaulted central hall. Beyond it is the *natatio* or **swimming pool (7)** The open-air *piscina* had niches on two levels for statues.

The present entrance is through a hall on the south side which leads into one of the two *palaestrae*, where part of the polychrome pavement survives. From here you can walk straight through the central hall of the baths to the other *palaestra* where fragments of monochrome marine mosaics with dolphins, cupids, and sea-horses are propped against the walls. Also here are more fragments of the polychrome floor mosaic in peach, maroon, green and white.

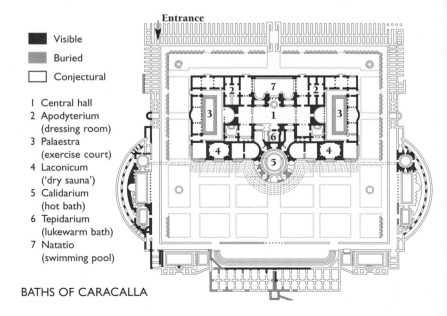

Visible
Buried
Conjectural

1 Central hall
2 Apodyterium (dressing room)
3 Palaestra (exercise court)
4 Laconicum ('dry sauna')
5 Calidarium (hot bath)
6 Tepidarium (lukewarm bath)
7 Natatio (swimming pool)

BATHS OF CARACALLA

From here you can visit one of the *apodyteria* and walk on the perfectly preserved monochrome floor mosaic, which has a pattern representing waves (or sails). Beyond a vestibule can be seen the huge swimming pool.

VILLA BORGHESE

The magnificent Villa Borghese is Rome's most famous public park, intersected in every direction by avenues and paths, with fine trees, statues, fountains and terraces.

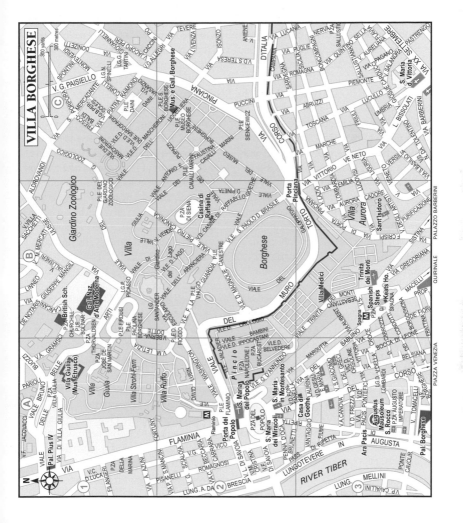

Museo and Galleria Borghese

Map p. 69, C2. NB: It is obligatory to book your visit in advance. (T: 06 328101; go to the entrance at least 15mins beforehand to pick up your ticket). Open 9–7.30; closed Mon. Entrance allowed only every two hours, at 9, 11, 1, 3 and 5. Ticket valid for two hours.

The Casino Borghese was begun for the Borghese family in 1608. Cardinal Scipione Borghese acquired numerous works of art through the good offices of his uncle Paul V, and it was Paul V's architect, Flaminio Ponzio, who was employed as architect here. The cardinal was also Bernini's first important patron, and the works Bernini made for him are still preserved here. He also owned no fewer than 12 paintings by Caravaggio, six of which still hang on the ground floor. The villa was altered for Marcantonio IV Borghese by Antonio Asprucci and Christopher Unterberger in 1775–90, when the splendid interior decoration was carried out. Later members of the family added to the collection, but much of the Antique sculpture was sold to Napoleon in 1807 by his brother-in-law Camillo Borghese (husband of Pauline Bonaparte). It is now in the Louvre.

Ground floor: the Sculpture Collection

Salone: Here you at once capture the atmosphere of the rest of the villa. Antique busts and sculptures are set side by side with 17th-century statues, the walls are covered with precious marbles and ancient reliefs, and the ceilings frescoed with elaborate scenes. An ancient Roman mosaic is set into the floor to add to the effect. On the wall in front of the entrance is a **high-relief of Curtius** throwing himself down into the room (the 'abyss'; *see p. 36*), a Roman work of the 2nd century AD re-elaborated by Bernini's father Pietro, who set it at this bizarre angle.

Room I: The sculpture of *Pauline Borghese* by Canova is justly one of his best-known works (1805–08). Napoleon's sister, who married Camillo Borghese, is daringly shown half nude, justified by the fact that she is holding an apple and therefore depicted in the guise of Venus Victrix.

Rooms II–IV: Here are some famous **works by Bernini**: *David*, *Apollo and Daphne* and the *Rape of Persephone*. The

David was made when the sculptor was 25 (1623–24) for Cardinal Scipione. The face, with its determined jaw set square, is a self-portrait. The ***Apollo and Daphne*** (1624) was also made for the Borghese cardinal, and is perhaps the most famous piece Bernini ever carved. The extraordinarily difficult subject, never before attempted in sculpture, is the dramatic moment when Daphne avoids capture by Apollo, because at his touch she is turned into a laurel tree. The group was designed to be exhibited against a wall (therefore only seen from sideways on). From the features of the face, the hairstyle and the sandals, it is evident that the figure of Apollo is modelled on the famous *Apollo Belvedere* (now in the Vatican). The ***Rape of Persephone*** was also designed to be seen from just one viewpoint. It shows Pluto at the door of Hades, seizing Persephone in his arms. His left hand clasping at her naked thigh is a masterpiece of carving.

Room VI: The group of *Aeneas and Anchises* was carved by Bernini when he was 20 years old (in 1618), with the help of his father, Pietro. Although the details of the carving reveal Bernini's precocious talent, it is a somewhat awkward group.

Room VIII: Six paintings by **Caravaggio** are shown here. The *Boy Crowned with Ivy*, also called *The Sick Bacchus*, and the *Boy with a Basket of Fruit* are both early works dating from around 1594. The former is apparently a self-portrait: although Caravaggio never painted his self-portrait as such, he often portrayed himself as a participant (especially in his religious paintings). The latter includes a superb still-life in the basket of fruit (familiar in several other works by Caravaggio). The *Madonna of the Palafrenieri*, painted in 1605, was commissioned for St Peter's but was deemed unsuitable for a church and was instead purchased by Cardinal Scipione Borghese. It shows St Anne (depicted as an elderly peasant woman) with the Madonna showing the young Christ Child (totally nude) how to crush a snake, symbolising evil. In his *St Jerome*, dating from the same year, the image has been reduced to its essentials by the skilled use of light. The *Young St John the Baptist* is Caravaggio's last known work, and it was sent by the artist to Scipione Borghese to try to obtain the pope's pardon for a murder (*see p. 50*). *David with the Head of Goliath*, dating from the same period, is one of several paintings by Caravaggio of this subject. It was also painted for Cardinal Scipione, and apparently includes Caravaggio's self-portrait in the head of Goliath.

Upper floor: the Gallery of Paintings

Room IX: Among the finest works displayed here is Raphael's famous **Deposition** (1507), painted for the Baglioni family of Perugia. It remained in Perugia until Paul V gave it to his nephew Cardinal Scipione. Critics have noted the influence of Michelangelo, notably in the pose of Christ, which is reminiscent of Michelangelo's *Pietà* in St Peter's, and in the woman with uplifted arms, who is much like the Madonna in the 'Tondo Doni' in the Uffizi.

Room X: Here is Correggio's superb **Danaë**, an overtly erotic scene showing Danaë on her bed receiving Jupiter transformed into a golden shower.

Room XIV: *The Goat Amalthea with the Infant Zeus* (c. 1615) is Bernini's earliest work. It was once taken to be a Hellenistic original, and may even have been made as a deliberate forgery. Bernini also carved the two marble portrait busts of his patron Cardinal Scipione Borghese (c. 1632).

Room XX: *Sacred and Profane Love* (1514) is a masterpiece by **Titian**, painted as a wedding gift. It depicts the bride beside an allegory of her eternal happiness in heaven in the form of a nude Venus.

Galleria Nazionale d'Arte Moderna

Map p. 69, B1. Open 8.30–7.30; closed Mon; T: 06 322981. Café and restaurant (T: 06 3229 8223).

This is the most important collection of Italian 19th- and early 20th-century art. The arrangement is chronological. The earliest works include Neoclassical sculptures by the greatest master of this school, **Antonio Canova**. Finest of all is the colossal statue (3.5m) of *Hercules and Lichas* (1815). Hercules is shown in agony, seizing the foot and hair of his herald Lichas, about to hurl him through the air. Lichas had unwittingly presented him with the poisoned shirt which corroded his flesh and killed him.

The **Macchiaioli School** (*see p. 288*) is well represented. Landscapes by **Giuseppe de Nittis**, who lived in Paris and absorbed much from the Impressionists, are shown alongside pieces (albeit minor ones) by Degas, Monet, Cézanne and other French Impressionists. Paintings by **Gaetano Previati** illustrate the movement which came to be known as Italian Divisionism. **Medardo Rosso**, whose work in some ways anticipated the Futurist movement, and who had a special skill in modelling wax, is well represented. Other sculptors of the period include **Ettore Ferrari**, who erected several monuments in Rome, notably *Giordano Bruno* in Campo dei Fiori.

Early 20th-century works are introduced by **Rodin**'s superb male nude entitled *Bronze Age* (1876; the first version is in the Tate in London). Because of its anatomical accuracy it was greeted by the critics with the accusation that he had made it by using a cast from a living model. Rodin is followed by **Klimt**, founder of the Vienna Secession. His *Three Ages of Woman* (1905) is one of his most important works. There follow fundamental works by Balla and Boccioni, leaders of the famous **Futurist movement**.

A room is devoted to the Metaphysical paintings of **Giorgio de Chirico**, and a large section displays works by the artists of the Italian **Novecento**: Morandi, Casorati, Gino Severini and others, who were opposed to the avant-garde art of the time, and promoted the values of form, while remaining interested in the development of Cubism.

There are also works by **Renato Guttuso**, a Realist painter of Communist sympathies, who owes much to Picasso. A collection of works illustrates the Dada movement, and includes historically important works by **Duchamp** (his mens' urinal entitled *Fountain*).

The second part of the 20th century collection has **non-representational works** from the '50s and '60s. Amongst many non-Italian artists represented are Jackson Pollock, Alberto Giacometti, Cy Twombly and Jannis Kounellis, Greek-born, but one of the founders of the Italian Arte Povera movement.

Museo Nazionale Etrusco di Villa Giulia

Map p. 69, A1. Open 8.30–7.30; closed Mon; T: 06 322 6571. Café. Tram 2 from Piazzale Flaminio (Belle Arti stop).
Villa Giulia is a charming 16th-century suburban villa, built in 1550–55 by Vignola, Vasari and Bartolomeo Ammannati, with some help from Michelangelo, for the pleasure-loving, nepotistic pope Julius III. It houses Italy's most important Etruscan museum. The principal find-sites are Vulci, Cerveteri, Veio, Palestrina, and Civita Castellana (all covered in later chapters). In the garden is a conjectural reconstruction (1891) of the Temple of Aletrium, using original terracottas found outside Alatri (*see p. 217*).

First floor

The hemicycle (Room 19) is devoted to the Castellani collection of vases, both Greek imports and local Etruscan-made pieces, including *bucchero* ware. Here also is the superb 6th-century BC terracotta **sarcophagus from Cerveteri**, representing a husband and wife on a couch at a feast. This remarkable and rare sculpture shows the extraordinary skill of this Etruscan artist, evident in the expressive rendering of the faces, hands and feet.

One of the most celebrated finds from Veio is the group of *Apollo* and *Hercules* from the Portonaccio temple (*see p. 190*). These colossal statues in polychrome terracotta formed part of a votive group representing the contest between Apollo and Hercules for the Sacred Hind (Hercules stands on the trussed animal), and are a splendid example of Etruscan sculpture of the late 6th or early 5th century BC. They were probably the work of Vulca, a sculptor born in Veio, who is said to have been summoned to Rome by Tarquinius Superbus to execute the statue for the great Temple of Jupiter Capitolinus.

VILLA GIULIA (MUSEO ETRUSCO)

Café and rear entrance

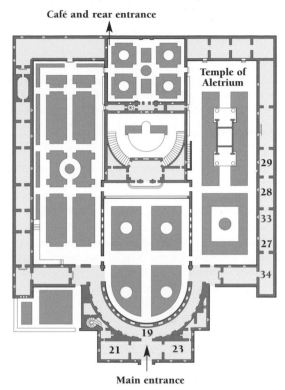

Lower floor rooms are shown in blue.

19	Castellani collection
23	Finds from Veio (including *Apollo* and *Hercules*)
21	Finds from Pyrgi
27–29	Finds from Falerii Veteres
34	Barberini and Bernardini tombs; Cista Ficoroni
33	Finds from Satricum

Finds from Pyrgi, the port of Etruscan Cerveteri, are also on this floor, including a reconstruction of Temple A, typically Etruscan with its deep porch and three-part cella. In front, at either side, was a hollow cylindrical altar for pouring libations to an underworld divinity. The remarkable pieced-together roof relief (470–460 BC) shows the *Seven Against Thebes*. In the same room are some of the terracotta antefixes that decorated the 'Twenty Cells' (small rooms thought to have housed the temple prostitutes who accounted for the enormous wealth of the sanctuary). Their iconography is unique: the devil in the form of a cockerel, interpreted as Lucifer, bringer of light, and a running Sun figure. In a small adjoining room are the gold *laminae* from the sanctuary of Astarte (*see p. 189*).

Civita Castellana (*Falerii Veteres*) was the main centre of the Falisci. Finds from its necropolis include a bronze urn in the shape of a hut (7th century BC); two kylices with Dionysus and Ariadne and a Faliscan inscription (resembling Latin, but written in Etruscan characters): 'Today I drink wine, tomorrow I shall have none'. The rhytons are masterpieces of Greek ceramic art of the first half of the 5th century BC. One in particular stands out: in the form of a domestic dog's head, with banqueting scenes on his collar, it is signed by the Brygos Painter.

Ground floor

Finds from Palestrina are grouped here, including the splendid **Cista Ficoroni**. This is the largest and most beautiful of these objects (known as *cistae*) to have survived. These were toilet boxes (or modern-day 'vanity cases'), and virtually unique to *Praeneste* (modern Palestrina). The *cistae* are usually cylindrical, with engraved decoration in repoussé, or pierced work, lids adorned with small figures, and feet and handles of cast metal. This one is named after Francesco Ficoroni, who bought it and gave it to the Kircher collection. On the body of the cista is a representation of the boxing match between Pollux and Amykos, king of the Bebryces, an elaborate design pure in its lines and evidently inspired by some large Greek composition, possibly a wall-painting contemporary with those by Mikon in the Stoa Poikile at Athens. The names of both the maker and the buyer of the cista are recorded in an archaic Latin inscription (*Novios Plautios med Romai fecit, dindia Macolmia fileai dedit*); it was no doubt a wedding present. By far the finest finds from Palestrina, however, are those from the **Barberini and Bernardini tombs**, two important examples of the Oriental period (7th century BC), in which objects in gold and silver, as well as bronzes and ivories, show the influence of Egyptian, Assyrian and Greek art.

On this floor also are **finds from *Satricum*** (*see p. 231*), which was famous for its temple of Mater Matuta in the 6th century BC.

THE GHETTO & VELABRUM

This area immediately west of the Capitoline Hill (*map p. 28, B3*), although in the very centre of the city, includes some peaceful narrow streets which preserve much of the character of old Rome. The small *piazze* are decorated with fountains, palaces and churches, and the characteristic *sanpietrini* cobbles and a few old-fashioned shops survive. In the area of the Ghetto are some Roman remains, including the **Theatre of Marcellus** (*open 9–6*). Planned by Julius Caesar, it was dedicated in 13 or 11 BC by Augustus to the memory of his nephew and son-in-law, Marcellus, who had died in 23

Ancient Roman family busts in the old ghetto surmount a wall collection box for money for local orphans.

BC at the age of 19. The building was fortified in the early Middle Ages and made into a stronghold by the Savelli and Orsini families. Renaissance architects frequently studied it. In the 16th century it was converted into a palace for the Savelli by Baldassare Peruzzi, who built the façade into the curved exterior. Beside the theatre are three tall columns from the Temple of Apollo Medico, built in 433 BC and restored by the consul Caius Sosius in 33 BC. Beyond are the ruins of the Temple of Bellona, built in 296 BC.

Beyond the archaeological area on the right is the **Porticus of Octavia**, once a huge colonnaded enclosure within which stood temples to Jupiter and Juno. Originally erected in 146 BC, it was reconstructed by Augustus in honour of his sister Octavia c. 23 BC, and restored by Septimius Severus in AD 203. The southwest entrance survives and serves as a monumental portal for the church of Sant'Angelo in Pescheria, founded in 755. The porticus was used from the 12th century as a fish market (hence the name of the church) up until the destruction of the Ghetto in 1888. From 1584 until the 19th-century papacy of Pius IX, Jews were forced to listen to a Christian sermon here every Saturday. On the wall of a house here, a plaque commemorates the 2,091 Roman Jews who died in concentration camps in the Second World War.

The old Ghetto

The area occupied by the old Ghetto stretched roughly from the Theatre of Marcellus to Via Arenula, and between Via del Portico d'Ottavia and the Tiber. From 1556 onwards, under Pope Paul IV, the Jews of Rome were segregated and lived subject to various restrictions on their personal freedom. The walls of the Ghetto were torn down only in 1848, and the houses demolished in 1888 before the area south of Via del Portico d'Ottavia was reconstructed around the new synagogue. This monumental temple was built by Vincenzo Costa and Osvaldo Armanni in 1899–1904. It contains a **Museum of Jewish Art** (open Mon–Thur 9–4.30, Fri 9–1.30, Sun 9–12; closed Sat; T: 06 6840 0661).

The unattractive **Piazza delle Cinque Scole** was laid out in the 19th century when the Ghetto was demolished, with a fountain from Piazza Giudea by Giacomo della Porta. The name of the piazza recalls the five synagogues which once occupied a building here. Palazzo Cenci at the far end belonged to the family of Beatrice Cenci who was beheaded for parricide in 1599 (see p. 56). Behind it is Monte dei Cenci, an artificial mound— probably on Roman remains—with a pretty little piazza where the restaurant Piperno (see p. 109) serves Jewish specialities.

Piazza della Bocca della Verità

Piazza della Bocca della Verità (map p. 28, C4) is now an open space dogged by traffic. It occupies part of the site of the Forum Boarium, the ancient cattle market. Two ancient Roman temples stand here, well preserved because they were transformed into churches in the early Middle Ages. The **Temple of Portunus** is dedicated to the god of harbours. Dating from the end of the 2nd century BC, four fluted Ionic columns in front of the portico and two at the sides survive, making it one of the most precious examples extant of the Graeco-Italian temples of the Republican age. The little round **Temple of Hercules Victor** was for long thought to be dedicated to Vesta, but an inscription from the base of a cult statue found here confirmed its dedication to Hercules Victor. It also dates from the end of the 2nd century BC and is the oldest marble edifice to survive in Rome. The roof is not original.

The church of **Santa Maria in Cosmedin** (*open 10–1 & 3–5 or 2.30–6.30; sung Mass on Sun at 10.30*) is a fine example of a Roman medieval church, preceded by a little gabled porch and arcaded narthex. Beneath the porch, to the left, is the so-called **Bocca della Verità**, a large cracked marble disc representing a human face, the open mouth of which was believed to close on the hand of any perjurer who faced the ordeal of placing it there. It is in fact an ancient drain cover, and was put here in 1632. It is much visited by tourists, who like to have their photographs taken with their hand in the mouth.

The church building incorporates the arcaded colonnade of the Imperial Roman *Statio Annonae* (market inspector's office), and the side walls of a porticoed hall, part of an early Christian welfare centre, or *diaconia* (c. 600). It was turned into a basilican church by Hadrian I (772–95), and was assigned to Greek refugees driven from Constantinople by the iconoclastic persecutions. The interior is very fine, and closely follows the 8th-century layout. In the first part of the nave, remains of the arcaded colonnade and side walls of the *Statio Annonae* and diaconia can be seen. High up on the walls are traces of 11th-century frescoes. The fine schola cantorum, screen, paschal candelabrum, episcopal throne and beautiful pavement (1123) all survive intact.

San Giorgio in Velabro

Via del Velabro (*map p. 28, C4*) perpetuates the name of this ancient district of Rome, the *Velabrum*, once a stagnant marsh between the river and the Palatine, which included the *Forum Boarium* cattle market. The massive four-sided **Arch of Janus** formed a covered passage at a crossroads and provided shelter for the cattle-dealers.

The steps on the left lead to the lovely church of **San Giorgio in Velabro** (*open 10–12.30 & 4–6.30*), thought to have been founded in the 9th century or earlier. The church was well restored to its medieval appearance in 1926, but was severely damaged in a Mafia bomb explosion in 1993, which destroyed the 9th–12th-century Ionic portico (now reconstructed). The basilican interior is beautiful in its plainness, with nave and aisles separated by 16 ancient columns of granite and pavonazzetto. In the apse is a fresco of *Christ with the Madonna and Sts Peter, Sebastian and George* attributed to Pietro Cavallini (c. 1296; repainted in the 16th century).

TRASTEVERE

The district of Trastevere (*map overleaf*), the area 'across the Tiber' (*trans Tiberim*), was the 'Etruscan side' of the river, and only after the destruction of Veio by Rome in 396 BC (*see p. 189*) did it come under Roman rule. In earliest Republican days, this bank of the Tiber was occupied by Lars Porsena in his attempt to replace the Tarquins on the Roman throne (*see p. 459*). From the Middle Ages it was essentially the popular district of Rome, distinguished by its artisans' houses and workshops. Today it has become a sought-after residential area.

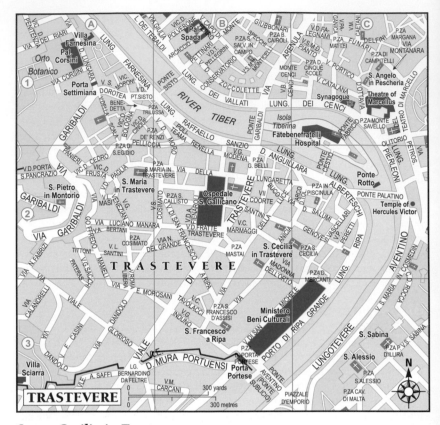

TRASTEVERE

Santa Cecilia in Trastevere

Map p. 78, C2. Open 9.30–1 & 4–6.15. Roman remains beneath the church open same hours; the convent can be seen 10.15–12.15; Sun 11.15–12.30.

Santa Cecilia in Trastevere is a lovely church, built on the site of the house of St Cecilia and her husband St Valerian, whom she converted to Christianity. St Cecilia, a patrician lady, was martyred in 230. She was shut up in the calidarium of her own baths (*see below*) to be scalded to death. Emerging unscathed, she was beheaded.

This building was adapted to Christian use probably in the 5th century, and in 820 the body of St Cecilia was transferred here and a basilica erected by Paschal I (817–24). As the reputed inventor of the organ, Cecilia is the patron saint of music: on her feast day on 22nd November churches hold musical services in her honour.

The present elaborate façade was provided by Ferdinando Fuga in the early 18th century. The interior was transformed at the same date into an aisled hall, when grilles were provided in the upper gallery for the nuns to attend services. In the south aisle, a corridor leads to the ancient calidarium, where St Cecilia was to be scalded to death.

In the sanctuary is a very fine baldacchino (1293), signed by Arnolfo di Cambio. The celebrated Parian marble **effigy of St Cecilia** is Stefano Maderno's masterpiece, carved in 1600 when he was only 23 years old: the body of the saint is represented lying as it was found when her tomb was opened in 1599, on which occasion the sculptor was present. The luminous 9th-century mosaic in the apse shows Christ blessing by the Greek rite, between St Peter, St Valerian and St Agatha on the right, and St Paul, St Cecilia and St Paschal (the last with a square nimbus indicating that he was still living at the time the mosaic was made) on the left. The long inscription records the finding of the relics of St Cecilia by Paschal I and the work he did to embellish the church.

The lower church and convent
One of the **Roman edifices** beneath the church is thought to be the house of St Cecilia. The Benedictine **convent** is entered to the left of the façade (*for opening times, see opposite*). From the nuns' choir above the west end of the church you can see the remains of a splendid fresco of the *Last Judgement* by Pietro Cavallini, which used to be on the inside façade of the old church (and was formerly much more extensive). This is a famous masterpiece of medieval Roman fresco painting (c. 1293), which clearly illustrates how Italian painting began to move forward, leaving Byzantine forms behind.

San Francesco a Ripa
The church of San Francesco a Ripa (*map p. 78, B3; open 7–12 & 4–7*) was built in 1231 to replace a hospice where St Francis stayed in 1219. The last chapel on the left has the famous effigy of the **Blessed Lodovica Albertoni**, a late work by Bernini, displayed effectively by concealed lighting. Although similar in some ways to the *St Teresa* (*see p. 58*), the work portrays agony rather than ecstasy. Lodovica is shown as a young woman in her death throes, clutching her constricted bosom and gasping her

Stefano Maderno: *St Cecilia* (1600).

last feverish breaths. Above the sacristy, lined with 17th-century wood cupboards, is the cell of St Francis (*usually shown on request*), which contains relics displayed in an ingenious reliquary, and a 13th-century painting of the saint.

Santa Maria in Trastevere

The large basilica of Santa Maria in Trastevere (*map p. 78, A2; open 7–7.30*) dates mainly from the 12th century and preserves some beautiful mosaics from that period. A long mosaic panel beneath the tympanum of the façade (12th–13th centuries) shows the Madonna surrounded by ten female figures with lamps (two of which are extinguished), of uncertain significance (recent scholarship suggests that they do not depict the Wise and Foolish Virgins). The three doorways incorporate Roman friezes. Lapidary fragments on the walls have Christian symbols, including the dove and olive branch.

In the splendid 12th-century interior are 21 vast ancient columns from various Roman buildings. The gilded wooden ceiling was designed by Domenichino (1617), who painted the central *Assumption*. The wonderful **mosaics of the triumphal arch and apse** (1140) are particularly fine: on the arch is the Cross with the symbolic Alpha and Omega between the seven candlesticks and the Evangelical emblems; at the sides, Isaiah and Jeremiah, beside two palm trees, and above them the rare and touching symbol of the caged bird, representing Christ imprisoned by the sins of man. In the semi-dome, Christ and the Virgin are shown enthroned beneath the hand of God bearing a wreath and the monogram of Constantine. Lower down in the apse and on the triumphal arch are six rectangles with more exquisite mosaic scenes from the life of Mary by Pietro Cavallini (c. 1291). Cavallini, a painter and mosaicist, was active almost entirely in Rome, though little of secure attribution now survives. The best examples of his work are here and in the church of Santa Cecilia (*see p. 79*).

Palazzo Corsini

Palazzo Corsini (*map p. 78, A1; open 9–1; closed Mon, admission on the hour; T: 06 6880 2323*) was the residence of the Florentine Corsini family in the 18th–19th centuries. Their library and art collection is preserved as part of the Galleria Nazionale d'Arte Antica, divided between this palace and Palazzo Barberini (*see p. 56*). It is richest in 17th- and 18th-century paintings of the Roman, Neapolitan and Bolognese schools, but also has important works by Fra' Angelico, Rubens, van Dyck, Murillo and Caravaggio. The original Corsini collection is identified by the inventory numbers 1–606.

The *Madonna and Child* by **Murillo** is one of his finest versions of the subject. The *Madonna and Child* by **van Dyck** was probably painted during the artist's stay in Italy. The *St Sebastian Tended by Angels* is considered to be by van Dyck's master **Rubens**, here clearly influenced by Michelangelo's Sistine ceiling, which Rubens saw when he first came to Rome. **Fra' Angelico**'s triptych with the *Last Judgement* flanked by the *Ascension* and *Pentecost* is thought to have been painted on one of the artist's two visits to Rome (either 1445 or c. 1450–55). Caravaggio is represented with a *St John the Baptist*.

Another celebrated piece is the marble *Corsini Throne* (2nd or 1st century BC), possibly a Roman copy of an Etruscan work, carved with scenes of hunting and sacrifice.

Villa Farnesina

The graceful Renaissance Villa Farnesina (*map p. 78, A1; open 9–1; closed Sun*) was built by Baldassare Peruzzi from Siena (1508–11; his most important early work) as the suburban residence of Agostino Chigi, a Sienese banker who controlled the markets of the East and became treasurer of the Papal States in 1510. Known as 'the Magnificent', he would entertain Pope Leo X, cardinals, ambassadors, artists and men of letters in grand style here. At a celebrated banquet, as a demonstration of Chigi's extravagance, silver plates and dishes were thrown into the Tiber after every course (it was later revealed that a net had been in position to recover them). Somehow even today the villa manages to retain something of a sumptuous atmosphere.

The painted decoration in the villa was carried out between 1510 and 1519. On the ground floor, the **Loggia of Galatea** has a ceiling frescoed by Peruzzi, with the constellations forming Chigi's horoscope. The lunettes, with scenes from Ovid's *Metamorphoses*, are by Sebastiano del Piombo, as is the giant Polyphemus above the entrance door, Next to it is Raphael's celebrated *Galatea*, a superb composition showing the sea-nymph in a deep red cloak riding over the waves on a scallop shell drawn by dolphins. *Trompe l'oeil* damask hangs below.

The famous frescoes in the **Loggia of Cupid and Psyche** were designed by Raphael and executed by his pupils, Giulio Romano, Francesco Penni, Giovanni da Udine and Raffaellino del Colle, in 1517. The story is taken from Apuleius' *The Golden Ass*, written in the 2nd century AD and the only Latin novel to have survived in its entirety. The young girl Psyche incites the jealousy of Venus because of her beauty: Venus therefore throws almost impossible obstacles in her way before she can finally drink the cup of immortality in order to marry Cupid.

On the upper floor (two flights up) is the **Sala delle Prospettive**, the drawing-room, with charming *trompe l'oeil* imaginary views of Rome and gods and goddesses (Vulcan above the fireplace) by Peruzzi. The bedroom, known as the **Sala delle Nozze di Alessandro e Rossana**, contains the *Marriage of Alexander the Great and Roxana*, a series of frescoes by Sodoma (*see p. 440*). The bedroom scene opposite the windows is particularly fine, with the shy Roxana in her diaphanous shift, and 24 playful cupids.

San Pietro in Montorio

The church of San Pietro in Montorio (*map p. 78, A2; open 7.30–12 & 4–6.30*) was built on a site wrongly presumed to have been the scene of St Peter's crucifixion, hence the dedication. It is traditionally taken to be the burial place of Beatrice Cenci, beheaded at Ponte Sant' Angelo in 1599 (*see p. 56*). The first south chapel contains a **Flagellation**, a superb work by Sebastiano del Piombo from designs by Michelangelo. Sebastiano trained in Venice with Giovanni Bellini and worked with Giorgione, the latter being his greatest influence. In 1511 he moved to Rome, where Raphael effectively blocked his progress to the most important commissions. Michelangelo befriended him, and made him to all intents and purposes his deputy in Rome. The composition of this work skilfully fits the curved wall of the chapel and the painted columns accentuate the motion of the torturers grouped around the central column, against which the twisted figure of Christ is superbly portrayed. Above is a *Transfiguration*, also by Sebastiano, though it lacks the force and drama of the *Flagellation* scene. The altar in the **Raymondi Chapel** (second north) is an early work (1640–47) by Bernini, showing his typical skill in dramatising the effect by hidden lighting. The relief itself, of the *Ecstasy of St Francis*, was executed by his pupils Francesco Baratta and Andrea Bolgi.

The Tempietto

The door on the right of the church gives access to a courtyard with the famous little Tempietto (*open 9.30–12.30 & 2–4; 4–6 in summer; closed Mon*), an extremely important Renaissance work by Donato Bramante (1499–1502 or 1508–12). Erected on what was thought to be the exact site of St Peter's martyrdom, it is a miniature circular building with 16 Doric columns of granite, and combines all the grace of the 15th century with the full splendour of the 16th. Perfectly proportioned and raised on three circular steps, it includes numerous Classical elements—columns, a frieze with triglyphs, scallop shell niches, and pilasters—but has a Mannerist balcony around the top. Bramante's original project envisaged a circular single-storeyed cloister, which would have made the effect even more remarkable.

CASTEL SANT'ANGELO & THE BORGO

The celebrated **Ponte Sant'Angelo** (*map p. 83, C2*), open only to pedestrians, was built by Hadrian in AD 134 as a fitting approach to his mausoleum, known since the Middle Ages as the Castel Sant'Angelo. The bridge was transformed by Bernini's ten statues of angels holding the symbols of the Passion, executed in 1688.

Castel Sant'Angelo

Open 9–7; closed Mon. Guided tours of parts of the castle not normally open to the public, including the prisons, are provided on certain days of the year (often on Sat and Sun): booking necessary; T: 06 681 9111.

Castel Sant'Angelo was begun by Hadrian as a mausoleum c. 128 and completed in 139, a year after his death, by Antoninus Pius. In the early Middle Ages the tomb became the citadel of Rome. The round tower is Hadrian's, without its marble facing and its statues. Above are additions of the Renaissance and later, such as the arcaded galleries. Inside the building, a spiral ramp (still extant) led to a straight passageway ending in the cella, in which was the Imperial tomb. Hadrian, his wife Sabina and his adopted son Aelius Caesar were buried in the mausoleum, as were succeeding emperors until Septimius Severus. According to legend, while crossing the bridge at the head of a procession to pray for the cessation of the plague of 590, St Gregory the Great saw an angel sheathing his sword on the top of the fortress. The vision accurately announced the end of the plague and from then onwards the castle bore its present name.

The castle is now a museum. Its 58 rooms, some of which have fine 16th-century stuccoes and frescoes, contain a collection of paintings, furniture and tapestries, as well as military artefacts. The views of Rome and the Tiber are superb.

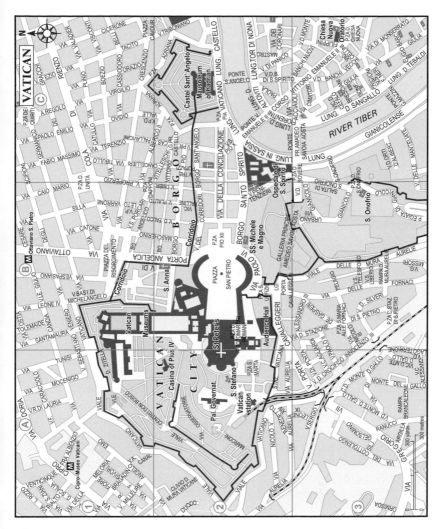

The Borgo

The Borgo district has always been associated with the Catholic Church. Just south of the present St Peter's basilica stood the Circus of Nero, in the gardens of which many Christians were martyred in AD 65, including St Peter, who was buried in a pagan cemetery nearby. Over his grave the first church of St Peter's was built (c. AD 90). During the 'Babylonian captivity' (1309–78), when the papacy was in Avignon (*see p. 26*), the Borgo fell into ruin, but when the popes returned they chose the Vatican as their residence in place of the Lateran. In 1586 the Borgo was incorporated into the city of Rome.

From Castel Sant'Angelo the broad, austere **Via della Conciliazione** leads towards St Peter's. The approach to the great basilica was transformed by this broad straight thoroughfare, typical of Fascist urban planning, which was completed in 1937 to celebrate the accord reached between Mussolini's government and the papacy (*see p. 90*).

ST PETER'S

The basilica of St Peter (*map p. 83, B2*) is the most important Roman Catholic church in the world, and one of the most visited places in Rome. It is the composite work of some of the greatest artists of the 16th century, and a masterpiece of the Italian High Renaissance.

Gian Lorenzo Bernini (1598–1680)

Bernini, one of the most famous architects and sculptors of all time, was born in Naples but came to Rome as a boy and remained here almost all his life. Though his father Pietro was himself an able sculptor, the boy Gian Lorenzo was considered a prodigy: in 1617 the Borghese pope Paul V ordered him to carve his bust, and the pope's nephew, Cardinal Scipione Borghese, commissioned Bernini's first important sculptures, which are still in the Galleria Borghese. He was at once recognised as the greatest artist working in Rome. His talent for theatrical effect was exceptional, and the development of the Baroque owes much to him.

The Barberini pope Urban VIII became an important patron as well as a close friend. The superb Fontana del Tritone in Piazza Barberini (*map p. 29, D1*) is arguably the sculptor's very best fountain in Rome. Many artists came to the city to benefit from Bernini's guidance, and his workshop was busy carrying out his numerous commissions. After the death of Urban VIII, however, Bernini fell temporarily out of favour with the papal court, even though in the end Urban's successor Innocent X did give him the commission for his great fountain in Piazza Navona. Bernini also carried out a great deal of work for Alexander VII: St Peter's Square, Sant'Andrea al Quirinale (*see p. 55*), the Chigi Chapel in Santa Maria del Popolo, and the Cappella del Voto in the duomo of Siena (*see p. 423*). The church of the Assumption at Ariccia (*see p. 126*) was built for the same pope's nephews. The great tomb of Alexander VII in St Peter's (*see p. 88*) is also Bernini's design.

Piazza San Pietro

Piazza San Pietro, the masterpiece of Gian Lorenzo Bernini (1656–67), is one of the most superb conceptions of its kind in civic architecture, and is a fitting approach to the world's greatest basilica. Partly enclosed by two semicircular colonnades, the piazza has the form of an ellipse adjoining an almost rectangular quadrilateral. Each of the two colonnades has a quadruple row of Doric columns, forming three parallel covered walks. There are in all 284 columns and 88 pilasters. On the Ionic entablature are 96 statues of saints and martyrs. In the centre of the piazza is an obelisk devoid of hiero-glyphics. It was brought from Alexandria (where it had been set up by the emperor Augustus) in AD 37. In 1586 Sixtus V ordered its removal here. The fountain on the right was designed by Carlo Maderno, and moved here and modified by Bernini in 1667. Between each fountain and the obelisk is a porphyry slab from which you have the illusion that the colonnades have only one row of columns, Covered galleries, also decorated with statues, unite the colonnades with the portico of St Peter's basilica.

St Peter's

Open 7–7; Oct–March 7–6. There can be queues except early in the morning and late in the evening. The dome can be climbed 8–5.45; Oct–Mar 8–4.45, although it is closed when the pope is in the basilica (often Wed morning). You are not allowed inside St Peter's or the Vatican City wearing shorts or mini-skirts, or with bare shoulders. Mass is held on Sun at 7, 8, 9 and 10, with Sung Mass at 10.30, and frequently during the week. Holy Communion can be taken in the Cappella del Santissimo Sacramento throughout the day on Sun.

A church dedicated to St Peter has stood on this site since the 1st century. In the mid-15th century it was decided to rebuild the old church on a grand scale: this herculean task, carried out by the leading architects of the time, was only completed in the early 17th century. Work was first entrusted to Bernardo Rossellino, Leon Battista Alberti and Giuliano da Sangallo. Julius II decided on a complete reconstruction and employed Bramante, who started work in 1506. The new basilica was on a Greek-cross plan surmounted by a gigantic central dome and flanked by four smaller cupolas. Bramante died in 1514, and Leo X employed Raphael to continue the building, now on a Latin-cross plan. On Raphael's death in 1520 Baldassare Peruzzi reverted to Bramante's design. Under Paul III the work received fresh impetus from Antonio da Sangallo the Younger. At Sangallo's death in 1546, Michelangelo, then 71 years old, was summoned. Michelangelo developed Bramante's idea with even greater audacity. He took as his model Brunelleschi's cupola of the duomo in Florence, and completed the dome as far as the drum. His plan for the façade was derived from the Pantheon. He continued to direct the work until his death in 1564. Vignola and Pirro Ligorio then took over, and were followed by Giacomo della Porta (assisted by Carlo Fontana), who completed the dome in 1590, adding the vault and lantern, and the two smaller domes. In 1605 Paul V directed Carlo Maderno to lengthen the nave towards the old Piazza San Pietro: thus the basilica was completed on a Latin-cross plan after all. The present façade and portico are Maderno's work. The statue of Constantine I to the right of the portico is by Bernini. On 18th November 1626, the 1300th anniversary of the original consecration, Urban VIII consecrated the new church. Bernini, who succeeded Maderno in 1629, was commissioned to decorate the interior. In 1940 the ancient cemetery in which St Peter was buried after his crucifixion was discovered beneath the Vatican Grottoes, and on 23rd December 1950, the pope announced that the tomb of St Peter had been identified. Despite its importance, St Peter's does not have cathedral status, nor is it the mother church of the Catholic faith (that position is held by St John Lateran).

The interior

The immensity of the interior (186m long and 137m wide across the transepts) is disguised by the symmetry of its proportions. The first part of the nave, with its aisles and three side chapels, is Carlo Maderno's extension, which transformed the plan of the church from a Greek to a Latin cross. The round slab of porphyry let into the pavement in front of the central door is that on which the Holy Roman Emperors used to kneel for their coronation in front of the altar of the old basilica. The gilded coffered ceiling was designed by Bramante. The coloured marble of the walls and pavement is the work of Giacomo della Porta and Bernini. The work of Bernini for this majestic church, which begins with the approach and is continued in the piazza outside, culminates in the magnificent baldacchino and exedra at the east end. There is much to see in St Peter's; only the finest highlights are given here.

The dome: Michelangelo's dome is an architectural masterpiece. Simple and dignified, and flooded with light, it rises immediately above the site of St Peter's tomb. In the pendentives are huge mosaics of the Evangelists: the pen held by St Mark is 1.5m long. On the frieze below the drum is inscribed in letters nearly 2m high: *Tu es petrus et super hanc petram aedificabo ecclesiam meam et tibi dabo claves regni caelorum* ('Thou art Peter, and upon this rock I will build my church; and I will give unto thee the keys of the kingdom of heaven').

Four pentagonal piers support the arches on which rests the drum of the cupola. They are decorated with balconies and niches designed by Bernini. Each balcony has two Solomonic columns taken from the saint's shrine in the old basilica. The niches are filled with colossal statues that give each of the piers its name: *St Longinus* **(1)** by Bernini; *St Helen* **(2)** by Andrea Bolgi; *St Veronica* **(3)** by Francesco Mochi; and *St Andrew* **(4)** by François Duquesnoy. On the balconies are reliefs referring to the *Reliquie Maggiori*; these precious relics, displayed in Holy Week, are preserved in the podium of the pier of St

Veronica. They are the lance of St Longinus, the Roman soldier who pierced the side of Christ on the Cross; a piece of the True Cross preserved by St Helen; and the cloth of St Veronica, with the miraculous image of Christ's face. The head of St Andrew, St Peter's brother, was presented to Pius II in 1462 by Thomas Palaeologus, despot of the Morea (the Peloponnese), who had saved it from the Turks in 1460. It has now been returned to Greece.

Against the pier of St Longinus is the **bronze statue of St Peter (5)**, seated on a marble throne. It is considered to be the work of Arnolfo di Cambio (c. 1296). The foot has been worn away by the touch of worshippers.

High altar: Over the high altar rises the great **baldacchino (6)**, designed by Bernini and unveiled in 1633. This colossal Baroque structure, a combination of architecture and decorative sculpture, is cast from bronze taken from the Pantheon. Four gilt-bronze Solomonic columns rise from their marble plinths, which are decorated with the Barberini bees (Urban VIII, Bernini's patron, was a Barberini). The columns support a canopy from which hang festoons and

ST PETER'S BASILICA

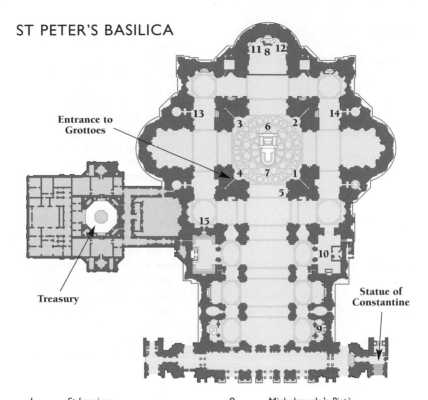

Entrance to
Grottoes

Treasury

Statue of
Constantine

1	St Longinus	9	Michelangelo's Pietà
2	St Helen	10	Cappella del SS. Sacramento
3	St Veronica	11	Monument to Paul III
4	St Andrew	12	Monument to Urban VIII
5	St Peter	13	Monument to Alexander VII
6	High altar and baldacchino	14	Monument to Clement XIII
7	Confessio	15	Monument to Pius VII
8	Cathedra of St Peter		

tassels and on which angels by
Duquesnoy alternate with children.
From the four corners of the canopy
ascend ornamental scrolls, which support the globe and cross. Inside the top
of the canopy the Holy Spirit is represented as a dove in an aureole.

The **high altar**, at which only the
pope may celebrate, is formed of a block
of Greek marble found in the Imperial
Fora. It covers the altar of Calixtus II (d.
1123), which in turn encloses an altar of
Gregory the Great (d. 604). It stands
over the space recognised as the tomb of
St Peter. In front is Maderno's **confessio
(7)**, encircled by perpetually burning
lamps. The mosaic niches and urn mark
the burial place of St Peter.

East end: At the east end of the church
two porphyry steps from the old basili-

ca lead to the tribune, the most conspicuous object in which is the **Cathedra of St Peter (8)**, an ambitious and theatrical composition by Bernini (1665). This enormous gilt-bronze throne is supported by statues of four Fathers of the Church: St Augustine and St Ambrose of the Latin Church (in mitres), and St Athanasius and St John Chrysostom of the Greek Church (bare-headed). It encloses an ancient wooden chair inlaid with ivory, said to have been the episcopal chair of St Peter. A circle of flying angels surrounds a great halo of gilt stucco in the centre of which, providing the focal point of the whole church, is the Dove, set in the window above the throne.

South aisle: Michelangelo made his exquisite *Pietà* **(9)** in 1499 at the age of 24. It is perhaps the most moving of all his sculptures and is the only one inscribed with his name (on the ribbon falling from the Virgin's shoulder). As an image, the *Pietà* possesses a symmetry with the *Madonna and Child* image: in both the Redeemer is in the lap of his mother, either dead or newly incarnate.

The **Cappella del Santissimo Sacramento** (*reserved for prayer*) **(10)** is protected by a grille designed by Borromini. The gilt bronze ciborium over the altar is by Bernini, modelled on Bramante's Tempietto (*see p. 82*).

Papal monuments: The great Farnese pope **Paul III** (d. 1549) **(11)** lies in a magnificent tomb by Guglielmo della Porta, later re-erected by Bernini.

Guglielmo began work on it just before the pope's death in 1549 and continued until he himself died in 1577. The present tomb comprises less than half the monument as planned. The figures of *Justice* (left) and *Prudence* (right) are both signed. Guglielmo's son Teodoro had to make imitation-marble clothes out of metal for the nude figure of Justice.

Bernini designed the fine monument to **Urban VIII (12)**, with statues of the pope and allegorical figures of *Charity* and *Justice*. The design of the tomb is clearly influenced by the Medici tombs in Florence by Michelangelo. The unusual curved lid of the sarcophagus is the same; the allegorical figures pose on top of it, while an effigy of the deceased sits above. The use of different materials in the sculpture gives an effective colour to the monument.

The monument to **Alexander VII (13)** shows the Chigi pope (d. 1667) kneeling above the allegorical figures of *Charity*, *Prudence*, *Justice* and *Truth*, all in white marble, while beneath is a huge carved shroud beneath which the gruesome figure of Death appears holding up an hour-glass, his feathered bones making him a macabre antithesis of the winged Victory.

The splendid monument to **Clement XIII (14)** is by Canova. Unveiled in 1792, it consolidated the young sculptor's reputation. Canova's influence can be seen in the monument to **Pius VII** (d. 1823) **(15)** by Bertel Thorvaldsen.

The Treasury

A large stone slab in the treasury vestibule has the names of all the popes buried in the basilica. The treasury contents were plundered in 846 by the Saracens, and again during the Sack of Rome in 1527, and it was impoverished by the provisions of the

Treaty of Tolentino (1797), which Pius VI was forced to conclude with Napoleon. It still, however, contains objects of great value and interest. The **Colonna Santa** is a 4th-century Byzantine spiral column, one of 12 from the old basilica. Eight now decorate the balconies of the great piers of the dome (the remaining three are lost). The column was once thought to be that against which Christ leaned when speaking with the Doctors in the Temple. The exquisite 6th-century *Vatican Cross*, made of bronze and set with jewels, is the most ancient possession of the treasury. It was the gift of the Emperor Justinian II. The beautiful **ciborium by Donatello** (c. 1432) comes from the old basilica; it encloses a painting of the *Madonna della Febbre* (protectress of victims of malaria—once rife in the Roman Campagna). The huge **monument of Sixtus IV** is a masterpiece in bronze by Antonio Pollaiolo (1493), seen to advantage from the raised platform. This pope is remembered as the builder of the Sistine Chapel (which is named after him). The superbly-carved **sarcophagus of Junius Bassus**, prefect of Rome in 359, was found near St Peter's in 1505. With scenes from the Old and New Testaments, it is an extremely important example of early Christian art.

The Vatican Grottoes

Open 7–6; Oct–Mar 7–5, except when the pope is in the basilica.

In the space (3m high) between the level of the existing basilica and that of the old one, the Renaissance architects built the so-called Sacred Grottoes and placed in them various monuments and architectural fragments from the former church. They have been used for the burial of numerous popes. The Old Grottoes have the form of a nave with aisles (corresponding to Maderno's nave but extending beyond it); on either side are the annexes discovered during the excavations. The New Grottoes are in the form of a horseshoe, with extensions. The centre is immediately below the high altar of St Peter's. On this spot, behind glass and marked by a mosaic, is the **tomb of St Peter** (*see below*). In a chapel to the side is the simple **tomb slab of John Paul II**, who was buried here in 2005. At the west end there is a very fine kneeling statue of Pius VI by Canova.

The tomb of St Peter

Group tours of the necropolis and tomb of St Peter are conducted most days 9–12 & 2–5; the visit takes about 1hr and groups are limited to 15 people. Apply in writing or in person to the Ufficio Scavi (beneath the Arco della Campana, left of St Peter's) Mon–Fri 9–5; T: 06 6988 5318.

In 1940 a double row of mausolea dating from the 1st century AD, running east–west below the level of the old basilica, was discovered. The extreme west series of these is on higher ground and adjoins a graveyard immediately beneath the high altar of the present church. Constantine significantly chose to erect his basilica above this necropolis, presumably knowing that it contained the tomb of St Peter.

The tomb was probably a mound of earth covered by brick slabs; what has been found and identified as such shows signs of the interference which history records. That this was a most revered grave is evident from the number of other graves which crowd in on it, without cutting across it. In front of a red wall, on which a Greek inscription is taken to name the saint, is a later wall, scratched with the names of pilgrims invoking the aid of Peter. Bones, obviously displaced, of an elderly, powerfully built man, were found in 1965 beneath this second wall and declared by Paul VI to be those of St Peter.

The Vatican City

Individual visitors are not admitted, but tours of part of the Vatican City and gardens, on foot (c. 2hrs), usually depart at 10am Tues, Thur, Sat. The tours are organised at the entrance to the Vatican Museums, T: 06 6988 4676. Tickets should be booked at least one day in advance.
The Vatican City covers an area of 43 hectares (less than half a square kilometre) and has a population of about 550; in size, it is the smallest independent state in existence. It has its own postal service and its own currency. It owns a radio station that was prominent in the Second World War, and its newspaper, the *Osservatore Romano*, has a worldwide circulation. Policing is carried out by the Swiss Guard, a corps founded in 1506, which retains the picturesque uniform said to have been designed by Michelangelo.

THE LATERAN TREATY

The temporal power of the popes ended with the breach of Porta Pia and the entrance of Italian troops into Rome in September 1870, signifying the unification of Italy. Until that time much of central Italy had been controlled by the papacy: the States of the Church had extended for 44,547km square. On the same day an agreement was made with the papacy that the Leonine City was excluded from the jurisdiction of Italian troops, and this led the way to the creation of the Vatican State in the Lateran Treaty (or Concordat), signed on 11th February 1929, which defined the limits of the Vatican City. The Treaty also granted the privilege of extraterritoriality to the basilicas of St John Lateran (with the Lateran Palace), Santa Maria Maggiore and San Paolo fuori le Mura, and to certain other buildings, including the pope's villa at Castel Gandolfo. Under the treaty, Italy accepted canon law on marriage and divorce and made religious teaching compulsory in secondary as well as primary schools. Italy also agreed to make a payment to settle the claims by the Holy See for the loss of papal property taken over by the Italian government. After the signing of the treaty, the pope came out of the Vatican for the first time since 1870. (A new concordat—which made religious instruction in schools optional, and contained modifications regarding marriage—was signed between the Italian government and the Vatican in 1984.)

Just inside the Arco delle Campane is Piazza dei Protomartiri Romani (*map p. 83, B2*), the site of the martyrdom of the early Christians near the Circus of Nero. Beyond, against the wall of the city, is the **Audience Hall** by Pier Luigi Nervi (1971). Designed in the shape of a shell, it has seating for 8,000 people.

The old Vatican radio station building was designed by Guglielmo Marconi and inaugurated in 1931.Vatican Radio now transmits from a station at Santa Maria di Galeria, 25km outside Rome. Nearer the huge buildings of the Vatican Museums is the **Casina of Pius IV**, two small garden buildings by Pirro Ligorio (1558–62), which are a masterpiece of Mannerist architecture. Here Pius IV (1559–65) held the *Notti Vaticane,* meetings during which learned discussions took place on poetry, philosophy and sacred subjects. Pius VIII and Gregory XVI used to give their audiences here.

To the south of St Peter's Colonnade is Palazzo del Sant'Uffizio. The Holy Office or tribunal, commonly known as the Inquisition, was established here in 1542 by Paul III to investigate charges of heresy, unbelief and other offences against the Catholic religion.

THE VATICAN MUSEUMS

The Vatican Museums contain some of the world's greatest art treasures, and are unique in their scope and quality. They include the largest collection in existence of ancient Greek and Roman sculpture, a picture gallery, Egyptian and Etruscan museums, collections of tapestries and early Christian art, as well as magnificently decorated halls and chapels. The palace also contains the famous Sistine Chapel, frescoed by Michelangelo, and the *Stanze* decorated by Raphael.

Tickets and opening times

Entrance on Viale Vaticano (map p. 83, B1). There is a costly admission fee (reduction for students under 24). All the museums are covered by one ticket, but only for a single visit. Museums open March–Oct Mon–Fri 10–3.30 (last exit at 4.45), Sat 10–1.30 (with last exit at 2.45); Nov–Feb Mon–Sat 10–12.30 (last exit at 1.45). Closed Sun except for the last Sun of the month (unless it is a holiday), when it is open free 9–12.30 (last exit at 1.45). Also closed on 1 Jan, 6 Jan, 11 Feb, Easter day and Easter Mon, 1 May, Ascension Day, Corpus Christi (both usually fall in May or June), 29 June, 15 Aug, 1 Nov, 8 Dec, Christmas Day and Boxing Day, and whenever special reasons make it necessary. Recorded opening times in Italian and English T: 06 6988 3333; to request specific information T: 06 6988 4947.

Planning a visit

The number of guided tours in the Vatican can seriously impede enjoyment. Well over three million people a year come here, and the Sistine Chapel is the exclusive goal of almost all the tour groups. Saturdays and Mondays, or days following holidays, are usually the most crowded days, and Easter is always the busiest time. Since there are usually long queues at the entrance well before the museums open, it is sometimes wise to plan a visit at the end of the session (at 12.20 or 3.20), though that allows only 90mins for the visit.

A number of galleries containing exceptional masterpieces can remain comparatively deserted (at least before 11am) simply because they are not 'on the way' to the Sistine

Chapel. These include the Picture Gallery, the Etruscan Museum, the Chiaramonti Museum, and the New Wing; however, when custodians are lacking these are the first galleries to be temporarily closed.

The 'Sistine Route' is a one-way itinerary imposed to regulate the flow of people to the Sistine Chapel. It is long and tiring, taking in Bramante's incredibly long west gallery, the Raphael Rooms, Borgia Rooms, Sistine Chapel and Museum of Christian Art; but at present it is the only way to reach the Sistine Chapel and Raphael Rooms. It is possible to leave after the Sistine Chapel, from where (except on Wed) there is an exit to St Peter's (this way, you miss the Museum of Christian Art and will not be able to return to the other Vatican museums on the same ticket). If you visit the other museums first, and leave after the Sistine Route, you will only miss the Museum of Christian Art.

Raphael Rooms

The Raphael Rooms (*Stanze di Raffaello*) were built by Nicholas V as papal audience chambers, a library and a hall for the papal tribunal. When in 1508, on Bramante's suggestion, Pope Julius II called Raphael from Urbino, he was so pleased with his work that he commissioned him to decorate the whole of this part of the Vatican. The *Stanze* are the painter's masterpiece: they show the extraordinary development of his art during the years between his coming to Rome in 1508 and his death at the age of 37 in 1520.

The new Medici pope, Leo X, appointed Raphael head of the building works in 1514. In 1518 Raphael painted his portrait, with two cardinals: this portrait is in the Uffizi. Leo made him commissioner of antiquities to ensure that everything possible was done to preserve the ancient buildings of Rome. Raphael left the huge altarpiece of the *Transfiguration*, now in the Vatican Picture Gallery (*see p. 103*) incomplete, and it was displayed above his coffin at his funeral in 1520. He is buried in the Pantheon.

Room IV (Sala di Costantino): This room was painted almost entirely in the time of Clement VII (1523–34), after Raphael's death, by Giulio Romano and assistants. The subjects are all related to the life of the emperor Constantine, including his baptism by St Sylvester (in fact a portrait of Clement VII). The **Chapel of Nicholas V** can be visited from here. It is entirely decorated with frescoes by Fra' Angelico (1448–50) of scenes from the lives of St Stephen (above) and St Lawrence (below).

Room III (Stanza d'Eliodoro): This was painted by Raphael in 1512–14, with subjects chosen by Julius II and Leo X. To the right is the *Expulsion of Heliodorus*

from the Temple at Jerusalem, alluding to Julius II's success in freeing the States of the Church from foreign powers. On the long wall is *Leo I Repulsing Attila*, executed partly by Raphael's assistants. The historic event is shown taking place in the environs of Rome, and the figure of the pope, on a white mule, alludes to the Battle of Ravenna in 1512, at which Leo X, then a cardinal, had been present, and which resulted in the expulsion of the French from Italy.

On the fourth wall is the *Liberation of St Peter*, alluding to the captivity of Leo X after the battle of Ravenna. Three night scenes, with remarkable light effects, illustrate three different episodes: in the

VATICAN MUSEUMS

LOWER FLOOR

UPPER FLOOR

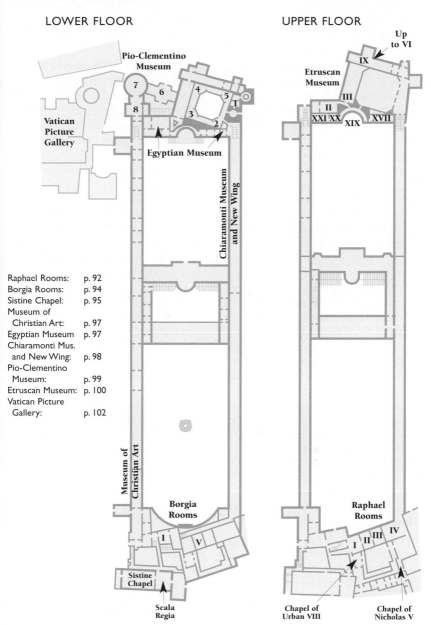

Pio-Clementino Museum

Vatican Picture Gallery

Egyptian Museum

Chiaramonti Museum and New Wing

Museum of Christian Art

Borgia Rooms

Sistine Chapel

Scala Regia

Up to VI

Etruscan Museum

Raphael Rooms

Chapel of Urban VIII

Chapel of Nicholas V

middle, the interior of the prison is seen through a high barred window, with St Peter waking up as the Angel frees him from his chains; on the left are the guards outside the prison; and on the right St Peter escaping with the Angel.

Room II (Stanza della Segnatura): This is where the pope signed bulls and briefs. It has the most beautiful and harmonious frescoes in the series, painted entirely by Raphael in 1508–11. On the wall opposite the entrance is the famous *Disputa*, representing a discussion on the Eucharist. On the wall nearest the Courtyard of the Belvedere is the equally famous *Parnassus* scene: Apollo plays the violin in the shade of laurels, surrounded by the Muses and the great poets.

On the wall facing the *Disputa* is the splendid *School of Athens*, symbolising the triumph of Philosophy, and forming a pendant to the *Triumph of Theology* opposite. The setting is a portico, a magnificent example of Renaissance architecture, inspired by Bramante. The remarkable vaulting, well depicted in light and shade, recalls the Baths of Caracalla. At the sides are statues of Apollo and Minerva. On the steps philosophers and scholars are gathered round the two supreme masters, Plato and Aristotle. The figure of Plato—probably intended as a portrait of Leonardo da Vinci—points towards heaven, symbolising his

system of speculative philosophy, while Aristotle's calm gesture indicates the vast field of nature as the realm of scientific research. Raphael's own self-portrait stands to one side.

Room I (Stanza dell'Incendio): On the ceiling is the *Glorification of the Holy Trinity* by Perugino, Raphael's master, the only work not destroyed when Raphael took over the decoration. The walls were painted in 1517 from Raphael's own designs by his pupils, including Giulio Romano. The subjects chosen mirror episodes in the life of Leo X.

Opposite the entrance is the *Coronation of Charlemagne by Leo III* (in 800), an obvious reference to the meeting of Leo X and Francis I at Bologna in 1516 (when the pope and French king drew up a famous alliance, and the pope's role as peacemaker between Christian rulers was confirmed). Leo and Charlemagne have the features of the later pope and king. Facing the window is the *Incendio di Borgo*, illustrating the fire that broke out in Rome in 847 and which was miraculously extinguished when Leo IV made the sign of the Cross from the loggia of St Peter's. This was probably intended as an allusion to the achievement of Leo X in restoring peace to Italy.

From the Stanza dell'Incendio a door leads into the **Chapel of Urban VIII**, its ceiling decorated by Pietro da Cortona.

Borgia Rooms

The first six Borgia Rooms (*Appartamento Borgia*) are named after Alexander VI, who adapted this suite for his personal use, and had it decorated with frescoes (1492–95) by Pinturicchio (*see p. 537*) and his school. The grotesques are inspired by the stucco and painted decorations discovered in the Domus Aurea (*see p. 38*) at this time, and include Christian, Jewish and pagan elements as well as Egyptian subjects. In **Room I (Room of the Sibyls)**, each of the lunettes has a Sibyl accompanied by a prophet. The juxtaposition of Sibyls and Prophets illustrates an ancient belief that the Sibyls foretold the coming of the Messiah. Cesare Borgia was imprisoned here by Julius II in 1503, in the very room where he had had his cousin Alfonso of Aragon murdered in 1500. Pinturicchio's masterpiece are the frescoes in **Room V (Room of the Saints)**. On the ceiling is the *Legend of Isis* and *Osiris and the Bull Apis* (a reference to the Borgia arms). The end wall shows the *Disputation between St Catherine of Alexandria and the Emperor Maximian*; the figure of the saint was once thought to be a portrait of Alexander VI's daughter, Lucrezia Borgia, or his mistress, Giulia Farnese. The figure behind the throne is a self-portrait by Pinturicchio, and in the background is the Arch of Constantine. The window wall shows the *Martyrdom of St Sebastian*, with a view of the Colosseum.

The Sistine Chapel

The Sistine Chapel, where the cardinals gather to elect each pope in secret conclave, is one of the most magnificently decorated spaces in the world. Its paintings are arranged in a complex programme illustrating Christian cosmology, and designed to reinforce the origins of papal authority. Three epochs of human existence are illustrated: *ante legem* (from the Creation up until the Law of Moses); *sub lege* (under the law of Moses) and *sub gratia* (the time 'of Grace' or Redemption following the teachings of Jesus Christ). The first of these periods is elaborated in images of the Creation and the life of Noah, painted on the vault by Michelangelo between 1508 and 1512; the second, a series of scenes from the life of Moses along the south wall, was painted three decades earlier by a group of Italy's greatest Quattrocento painters; the third, scenes from the life of Christ painted by the same group of artists, is on the north wall. The culmination is a depiction of the triumphal Second Coming on the Day of Judgement, painted by Michelangelo above the altar between 1536 and 1541. In the areas in between are images of those who bore witness: the Prophets and the Sibyls (interpreted as having foretold the redemption of mankind through a saviour); the ancestors of Jesus of Nazareth are in the lunettes; and the apostolic succession of popes in the spaces between the windows. Larger than almost any figure and directly above the altar, is the unusual *Jonah*, who in his self-sacrifice was seen to have foreshadowed the Saviour's life, and in his return to the world after three days in the whale's belly, prefigured the Resurrection.

The ceiling

Michelangelo was 33 years old in 1508 when he received the commission from Pope Julius II to paint the chapel's ceiling, an area of over 500m square. From the beginning, the project was beset with difficulties: the problem of painting on a curved horizontal surface over 20m above the viewing level; a cramped and insecure painting platform; insufficient illumination; and assistants whom Michelangelo considered a hindrance. He early on dispensed with all help, continuing the enormous project alone: he also designed a new kind of scaffolding, which spanned the whole width of the chapel, and kept him at a constant distance of about two metres from the surface he was painting. He worked from the east end, where his figures are noticeably too small, towards the altar end, where he soon masters the issue of scale. He worked constantly in very poor

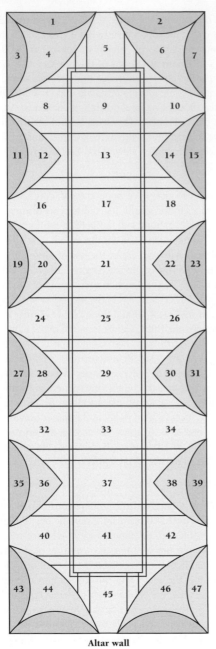

Altar wall

SISTINE CHAPEL CEILING

1	Jacob, Joseph
2	Eleazar, Mathan
3	Achim, Eliud
4	David and Goliath
5	Zechariah
6	Judith and Holofernes
7	Azor, Zadok
8	Joel
9	Drunkenness of Noah
10	Delphic Sibyl
11	Abiud, Elachim
12	Zerubbabel
13	The Flood
14	Josiah
15	Jechoniah, Salathiel
16	Eritrean Sibyl
17	Sacrifice of Noah
18	Isaiah
19	Jotham, Ahaz
20	Uzziah
21	Expulsion from Paradise
22	Hezekiah
23	Manasseh, Amon
24	Ezekiel
25	Creation of Eve
26	Cumaean Sibyl
27	Abijah
28	Rehoboam
29	Creation of Adam
30	Asa
31	Jehosaphat, Joram
32	Persian Sibyl
33	Separation of Land from Water
34	Daniel
35	Boaz, Obed
36	Salmon
37	Creation of Sun, Moon and Stars
38	Jesse
39	David, Solomon
40	Jeremiah
41	Separation of Light from Darkness
42	Libyan Sibyl
43	Aminadab
44	Death of Haman
45	Jonah
46	Moses and the Serpent of Brass
47	Nahshon

light, and without the possibility of seeing how his painting looked from below. He also had to contend with the impatience of Julius II.

The subject matter concentrates on the early chapters of Genesis. The exact programme would have not been of Michelangelo's devising; but the artist's own genius emerges in the clarity and dignity which he gives to the subjects, and in the way he encapsulates elusive concepts in simple and unforgettable images. Clear primary colour is used in the main narrative scenes, while neutral tints define the unifying architectural framework. Many of the nude male figures were inspired by the *Belvedere Torso* (in the Pio-Clementino Museum; *see p. 100 below*).

The *Last Judgement*

Where other artists in their *Last Judgements* had evoked contrasts of light and impenetrable dark, Michelangelo sets the whole against an intense lapis blue. Where many earlier painters had dwelt upon the multifarious punishments of the wicked, Michelangelo unifies the event into a vast, single, cyclical motion, radiating out from the magnificent gestures of Christ's arms. The eye is drawn into the movement of the whole work, passing from the central focus of Christ to the figure of his Mother beside him. Above, groups of angels and nude figures expand the scene outwards as they carry away the Cross and the column of the Flagellation to either side. In the depths of Hades below, the crazed glances and the floating figures seem to prefigure Goya by nearly 300 years.

The original nudity of the figures caused offence to some, and many of them were covered by Daniele da Volterra, at the request of Pope Pius IV, in 1565. The gigantic figure of St Bartholomew (below and to the viewer's right of Christ) holds up, as was traditional, the attribute of his martyrdom: the knife with which he was flayed and the flayed skin itself. The face in the limp, hanging skin is a self-portrait of the artist.

If you do not wish to continue the tour, you are often able to leave the chapel by the Scala Regia (usually open every day except Wed), a magnificent staircase by Bernini, which descends to the portico of St Peter's. To visit the other museums you leave the chapel by a small door in the north wall of the nave, which leads to the Museum of Christian Art.

Museum of Christian Art

The Museum of Christian Art (*Museo Sacro*) was founded by Benedict XIV in 1756, and enlarged in the 19th century, partly by the acquisitions of Pius IX but mainly by finds made during excavations in the catacombs. The exhibits include part of the treasury of the Sancta Sanctorum (*see p. 64*), once the pope's private chapel. The 9th–12th-century works include an exquisite enamelled Cross presented by St Paschal I (817–24), said to contain five pieces of the True Cross; and the reliquary of St Praxedes (*see p. 60*). Also notable is the wonderful collection of ivories including the *Ramboyna Diptych* (c. 900), with a representation of the Roman She-wolf.

Egyptian Museum

The Egyptian Museum was founded by Gregory XVI in 1839. Displays include the splendid sculptures from the Serapeum of the Canopus of the Egyptian Delta, built by Hadrian in his villa at Tivoli (*see p. 148*) after his journey to Egypt in 130–31, including Serapis, a colossal bust of Isis, and statues of Antinous. There is also a sandstone head of Mentuhotep II (reigned 2010–1998 BC), remarkable as the oldest portrait in the museum. The colossal statue of Queen Tuaa, mother of Rameses II, was brought to Rome by Caligula.

Chiaramonti Museum and New Wing

This superb collection of ancient sculpture was arranged for Pope Pius VII (Barnaba Chiaramonti) by Canova. The old-fashioned display includes numerous Roman works—sepulchral monuments, allegorical and mythological subjects and portrait sculpture—many of them copies of Greek originals of the 5th or 4th centuries BC.

The New Wing (*Braccio Nuovo*), an extension of the Chiaramonti Museum, contains some of the most valuable ancient sculptures in the Vatican. The **Augustus of Prima Porta** (14) is one of the most famous portraits of the Emperor, found in 1863 in his wife Livia's villa at Prima Porta, north of Rome on a hill above the Via Flaminia. The statue, in fine Parian marble, celebrates the Emperor as a general and orator, with a cuirass over his toga and his right hand raised showing that he is about to address his troops. The pose suggests the influence of Greek athletic statues of the 5th century BC, such as the *Doryphorus* of Polyclitus (*see below*). The small cupid riding a dolphin, placed as a support for the right leg, is an allusion to Venus, the goddess from whom Augustus' family, the Julii, claimed descent.

The **bust of Julius Caesar** is one of the best examples to have survived of a posthumous portrait, dating from the time of Augustus. The fine **statue of Demosthenes** is a replica of the original statue by Polyeuctus of Athens, set up in Athens in 280 BC to the memory of the great orator and statesman. The mouth plainly suggests the stutter from which Demosthenes suffered. The **Wounded Amazon** is a replica of one of the statues from the Temple of Diana at Ephesus, by Polyclitus. The arms and feet were restored by Thorvaldsen in the early 19th century.

The famous **Giustiniani Athena**, after a Greek original of the 4th century BC, portrays the goddess's twofold function as the divinity of the intellect and of arms. The delightful **Resting Satyr** (117) is one of several replicas of the famous statue by Praxiteles. The **Doryphorus** is one of numerous copies of the famous bronze statue of a young spear-bearer by Polyclitus, who made a careful study of the proportions of the human body.

Pio-Clementino Museum

The Pio-Clementino Museum, with a wonderful collection of Greek and Roman sculptures, was founded in the 18th century by Pius VI and is named after him and his predecessor, Clement XIV. It includes works collected by the Renaissance popes, in particular Julius II, as well as late 18th- and early 19th-century acquisitions.

The contents of the sculpture galleries are mainly Greek and Roman originals, or Roman copies of Greek originals of the 1st and 2nd centuries AD. In some cases the

Roman sculptor placed a contemporary portrait head on his copy; later restorers often made additions in marble, stone or plaster and also, in some cases, put heads on statues to which they do not belong. It was Paul IV, in the 16th century, who decided that the nudity of each male sculpture should be covered with a fig leaf.

(1) Gabinetto dell'Apoxyomenos: The statue of an athlete scraping oil from his body with a strigil is a copy from a Greek bronze original, the masterpiece of Lysippus' maturity (c. 330 BC), which illustrated his canon of proportions.

Through a glass door here can be seen the spiral **Bramante Staircase** (*open in summer*). The design is masterly; at each turn the order changes, from Tuscan at the bottom to Corinthian at the top.

(2) Gabinetto dell'Apollo: Here is the famous *Apollo Belvedere*, a 2nd-century Roman copy of a bronze original probably by Leochares (4th century BC). The statue was the centre of attention during the Grand Tour.

(3) Gabinetto del Laocoönte: This recess contains the famous marble group of *Laocoön* and his two sons in the coils of the serpents (*illustrated overleaf*), a vivid and striking illustration of the story related by Virgil in the *Aeneid*. Laocoön, priest of Apollo, warned his fellow Trojans against the trickery of the Greeks and entreated them not to admit the wooden horse into the city. In punishment Apollo or Athene sent serpents to crush him and his young sons to death. The violent realism of the conception as well as the extreme skill with which the agonised contortions of the bodies are rendered are typical of late Hellenistic sculpture. Ascribed to the Rhodian sculptors Agesander, Polydorus and Athenodorus (c. 50 BC), it was found on the Esquiline Hill in 1506, and was at once recognised as that described by

Pliny, though it is not carved from a single block, as he states, but from at least three pieces. It was purchased by Julius II and brought to the Vatican where it was greatly admired by the artists of the time: it has been suggested that one of the nudes in Michelangelo's 'Tondo Doni' (now in the Uffizi) may be a copy from the *Laocoön*. When the piece was found, it was felt appropriate to finish it, since Laocoön's arm was missing. An arm was created for the piece, and fixed on sticking straight upwards. Baccio Bandinelli's *Laocoön* in the Uffizi (*see p. 284*) shows how it would have looked. In 1905, however, an archaeologist called Ludwig Pollak found an arm in an antique shop in Rome, which he recognised to be possibly the original arm-fragment of the *Laocoön*. He could not persuade the authorities of his suspicion, and nothing happened until the 1950s, when the piece in the Vatican was cleaned and re-examined. By good luck, there was a bronze copy of the *Laocoön* in the Louvre, made from a cast taken before the erect right arm was added. The break on the Louvre copy corresponded with the break on Pollak's discovered arm, and it was attached forthwith.

(4) Gabinetto dell'Hermes: Named after the statue thought to represent *Hermes Psychopompos*, the conductor of souls to the Underworld, a copy of an original by Praxiteles. In the portico beyond (in a niche) is *Venus Felix and Cupid*: the body is copied from the *Aphrodite of Cnidos*.

(5) Gabinetto del Canova: Here are three Neoclassical statues: *Perseus* (inspired by the *Apollo Belvedere*) and *Creugas* and *Damoxenes* (both boxers) by Canova, placed here when most of the Classical masterpieces were taken to Paris by Napoleon in 1800.

(6) Hall of the Muses (*Sala delle Muse*): Seven of the statues of the Nine Muses in this room were found, together with the *Apollo*, in a villa near Tivoli, and are thought to be copies of originals, apparently of bronze, by Praxiteles or his school, but it is possible that they do not all belong to the same group. The statues alternate with herms which include portraits of Homer, Socrates, Plato, Euripides, Epicurus and Demosthenes.

In the centre is the famous **Belvedere Torso**, bearing the signature of Apollonius, an Athenian sculptor of the 1st century BC. The figure is sitting on a hide laid over the ground. There have been various identifications of the statue; recent studies have suggested that it may represent Ajax meditating suicide (in his right hand he probably held a sword with which he was about to kill himself). Found in the Campo dei Fiori at the time of Julius II, the torso was greatly admired by Michelangelo and Raphael. It was frequently drawn by Renaissance artists, and in the 16th and 17th centuries it was copied in small bronzes.

(7) Circular Hall (*Sala Rotonda*): In the pavement is a very well preserved polychrome mosaic from Otricoli (*see p. 576*), representing a battle between Greeks and Centaurs, with tritons and nereids in the outer circle. The huge monolithic porphyry vase was found in the Domus Aurea. Around the walls are displayed important colossal busts and statues (described from right of the entrance): **Jupiter of Ocriculum**, a colossal head of majestic beauty, attributed to Bryaxis (4th century BC); *Antinous as Bacchus*, from a Greek prototype of the 4th century, the drapery, originally of bronze, restored in the early 19th century by Thorvaldsen; bust of Faustina the Elder (d. 141), wife of Antoninus Pius; a beautiful statue of a female divinity, perhaps Demeter, wearing the *peplos*, after a Greek original of the late 5th century BC.

(8) Hall of the Greek Cross (*Sala a Croce Greca*): The room is dominated by two magnificent porphyry sarcophagi: that on the left belonged to St Helen, mother of Constantine, and that on the right to Constantia, daughter of Constantine, decorated with vine-branches and children bearing Christian symbols of grapes, peacocks and a ram.

Etruscan Museum

The Etruscan Museum is one of the most important collections of its kind. Although the focus is primarily Etruscan, there are also outstanding examples of Greek and Roman art. One of the most splendid exhibits is the **Regolini-Galassi Tomb**, in Room II, which was found in a necropolis south of Cerveteri in Lazio. Three important people were buried here in 650 BC, including a princess called Larthia, a warrior of high rank, and a priest-king who was cremated. Their funeral equipment includes gold jewellery (a superb gold clasp, with decorations in relief; necklaces and bracelets); ivories; cups; plates; silver ornaments of Graeco-Oriental provenance; a bronze libation bowl with six handles in the shape of animals; and a reconstructed throne.

Laocoön, priest of Troy, in the coils of serpents with his two sons (1st century BC).

Of the bronze objects in Room III, the finest is the **Mars of Todi** (found at Todi in Umbria; *see p. 596*), a superb statue of a man in armour dating from the beginning of the 4th century BC, but inspired by Greek art of the 5th century BC. The works in terracotta in Room VI include striking portrait heads. The bust of an elderly woman, dating from the 3rd century BC, is particularly remarkable. Some of the gold jewellery is truly magnificent. Much is from Vulci (*see pp. 206–07*), and includes a necklace with pomegranate drops; coronets and diadems used as funerary wreaths; and beautiful earrings. Room IX is home to the Guglielmi Collection, from Vulci, especially important for its **Attic black- and red-figure vases**, a number of them attributed pieces.

A valuable collection of **Greek, Italic and Etruscan vases** is in Rooms XVII–XXI. Most of them come from the tombs of southern Etruria. At the time of their discovery in the first half of the 19th century, the vases were all indiscriminately called Etruscan.

In fact many of them are Greek in origin, and illustrate the importance of the commercial relations between Greece and Etruria: from the end of the 7th to the late 5th century BC many Greek vases were imported. By the middle of the 4th century BC the Greek imports were largely replaced by the products of the Greek colonies of Italy.

The circular, domed Room of the Biga (*usually locked, but with a glass door*) was designed for the magnificent **Biga**, or two-horse chariot, reconstructed in 1788 from ancient fragments: only the body of the chariot and part of the offside horse are original. The chair was used as an episcopal throne in the church of San Marco during the Middle Ages. The bas-reliefs suggest that the *Biga* was a votive chariot dedicated to Ceres and that it dates from the 1st century AD. Also here are two statues of the famous **Discobolus**, one a copy of Myron's work with the head wrongly restored, and the other from a bronze original by Naucides, nephew and pupil of Polyclitus, a fine example of Peloponnesian sculpture of the 5th century BC.

Vatican Picture Gallery

The Vatican Picture Gallery (*Pinacoteca Vaticana*) owes its origin to Pius VI, but under the Treaty of Tolentino (1797; *see p. 680*) he was forced to surrender the best works to Napoleon. Of these, 77 were recovered in 1815. The collection is devoted mostly to Italian painters, and the arrangement is chronological and by schools.

Room II: One of the most important works in the collection is the ***Stefaneschi Altarpiece***, commissioned from Giotto for the confessio of Old St Peter's by Cardinal Jacopo Stefaneschi. The polyptych is painted on both sides so that it could be seen by the congregation and by the prelates celebrating the service: on one side the central panel shows *Christ Enthroned*, surrounded by angels, with the donor Stefaneschi kneeling, with his cardinal's hat at his feet. On either side are the *Crucifixion of St Peter* and the *Martyrdom of St Paul*. On the other side, the central panel depicts *St Peter Enthroned*, with St George presenting Stefaneschi to St Peter. Pope Celestine V is also shown kneeling making a gift of a codex. The side panels show Sts James, Paul, Andrew and John the Evangelist. The other Apostles are depicted in the predella.

The Sienese school is represented by some of its greatest painters—Pietro Lorenzetti, Simone Martini, Sano di Pietro, Sassetta (*Vision of St Thomas Aquinas* and *Madonna and Child*), and Giovanni di Paolo.

Room III: The Florentine school: **Fra' Angelico** (scenes from the life of St Nicholas of Bari, from a Perugian polyptych; *see p. 494*), Benozzo Gozzoli and Filippo Lippi.

Room VI: From the **Umbrian school** are a number of works by its most famous member, Perugino.

Room VIII: This room is devoted to **Raphael** and contains three of his most famous paintings. The lovely *Coronation of the Virgin* was his first large composition, painted in Perugia in 1503, when he was just 20 years old. The magnificent *Madonna of Foligno* (c. 1511) was a votive offering by Sigismondo Conti in gratitude for his escape when a cannon ball fell on his house during a siege. He is shown with St Jerome, and in the background is Foligno during the battle. The *Transfiguration* is Raphael's last work: the scene is shown above the dramatic episode of the healing of the young man possessed by a devil. It is not known how much of the painting had been finished by the time of Raphael's death in 1520; it seems likely that the lower part was completed by his pupils Giulio Romano and Francesco Penni.

Room IX: One of the least famous but most memorable works by **Leonardo da Vinci**—his *St Jerome*—hangs here. An early work, dating from around 1480, it was probably painted in Florence, but was left unfinished. It shows the aged saint, the pose and head owing much to Hellenistic sculpture, with his lion at his feet, in a shadowy 'desert', which gives an extraordinary sense of space to the painting. Another remarkable work here is **Giovanni Bellini's** *Pietà*, the cimasa of a monumental altarpiece of the *Coronation of the Virgin* painted for the

church of San Francesco in Pesaro (the altarpiece itself is preserved in Pesaro; *see p. 652*). Scholars have recently suggested that the subject is the embalming of the body of Christ.

Room XI: Here is an important group of works by Federico Barocci—born in the Marche but at work in Rome in 1561–63. The *Stoning of St Stephen* is by Vasari, whose famous patron, Cosimo I, is depicted in the marble bas-relief by Perino del Vaga in the centre of the room.

Room XII: The powerful and almost too dramatic *Descent from the Cross* (1602) by **Caravaggio**, which was copied by Rubens, is displayed in this room. The *Communion of St Jerome* by Domenichino (1614) was his first important work (there is a copy of it in mosaic in St Peter's).

Room XIII. The fine painting of *St Francis Xavier* was painted by van Dyck for the church of the Gesù c. 1622.

Room XVII: Clay models by **Bernini**, including a *bozzetto* for the tabernacle of the Holy Sacrament in St Peter's.

THE CATACOMBS & VIA APPIA

The catacombs

The catacombs are fascinating early Christian underground cemeteries that were established outside the walls, since burial within the city was forbidden. The most famous catacombs—San Callisto and San Sebastiano on the Via Appia, and Santa Domitilla close by—tend to be crowded with large groups, which can impair a visit. The catacombs of Sant'Agnese, entered from the church of Sant'Agnese fuori le Mura (*map p. 24; open Tues–Sat 9–12 & 4–6; Sun 4–6; Mon 9–12*) are much more peaceful and rewarding to visit. They are shown by a well-informed guide on a tour which normally takes about 40mins. They contain no paintings but there are numerous inscriptions, and many of the *loculi* are intact and closed with marble or terracotta slabs. They may date from before 258, but certainly not later than 305. The Catacombs of Priscilla on Via Salaria are also very interesting (*map p. 24; open for guided tour Tues–Sun 8.30–12.30 & 2.30–5; closed Jan; T: 06 8620 6272; bus no. 92 from Termini station or no. 63 from Piazza Venezia to Via di Priscilla*). Many early popes were buried here between 309 and 555, and there are some excellently-preserved 3rd-century paintings, including the oldest known representation of the *Madonna and Child*.

Santa Costanza

Close to the catacombs of Sant'Agnese is the round mausoleum of Constantia, known as the church of Santa Costanza since the 9th century (*map p. 24; open Tues–Sat 9–12 & 4–6; Sun 4–6; Mon 9–12*). It was built by Constantia as a mausoleum for herself and her sister Helena, daughters of the Emperor Constantine, probably before 354. It is remarkably well preserved and in a lovely peaceful spot. On the barrel vaulting of the ambulatory are remarkable very early Christian mosaics (4th century), pagan in character and designed in pairs on a white ground. Constantia's magnificent porphyry sarcophagus was removed to the Vatican in 1791 (*see p. 100*) and replaced here by a cast.

Via Appia

Map p. 24. Information office at Via Appia Antica 60; T: 06 5212 6314. The road is best seen on Sun, when cars do not use it. Also free guided Sunday visits (at other times these can be booked). Bus no. 118 runs every 20–40 mins from Piazzale Ostiense. On weekdays bus no. 218 runs from St John Lateran. There are a few cafés along the route.

This the most famous of the Roman consular roads, was built by the censor Appius Claudius in 312 BC. At its full extent it led all the way to *Brundisium* (Brindisi). For the first few miles it served as a patrician cemetery; some of the tombs can still be seen. The road is also noted for its early Christian catacombs (often crowded with tour groups). By far the pleasantest and most interesting stretches are those furthest from the city. As the area of the catacombs is left behind, the road becomes more attractive and interesting for its Roman remains. On the left, in a hollow at no. 153, are the extensive ruins of the Villa of Maxentius (*open 9–1; closed Mon; T: 06 780 1324*). Built in 309 by the Emperor Maxentius, it included a palace, a circus and a mausoleum built in honour of his son Romulus (d. 307). The **Circus of Maxentius** is one of the most romantic sites of ancient Rome. The main entrance was on the west side with the 12 *carceres* or stalls for the chariots and *quadrigae*. In the construction of the tiers of seats, amphorae were used to lighten the vaults, and these can still clearly be seen. In the centre of the left side is the conspicuous emperor's box, which was connected by a portico to his palace on the hill behind. At the far end was a triumphal arch where a fragment of a dedicatory inscription to Romulus, son of Maxentius, was found. In the centre is the round *meta* and the *spina*, the low wall which divided the area longitudinally and where the obelisk of Domitian, now in Piazza Navona, originally stood.

The **Tomb of Cecilia Metella** (*open 9–1 hour before sunset; closed Mon*), to which the Via Appia rises at the 3rd milestone, is a massive circular tower built in the Augustan period. A hundred Roman feet (29.5m) in diameter, on a square base, and extremely well preserved, this is the most famous landmark on the Appia, and numerous drawings of it were made over the centuries.

Parco degli Acquedotti

Accessible by car from the Via Tuscolana or Via Appia Nuova. To get there by public transport, take underground line A (Subaugusta stop), or buses 557, 451 and 503.
This beautiful protected area is traversed by seven aqueducts. Majestic long stretches survive, in open countryside where sheep are grazed. The aqueducts are supplied from springs in the upper valley of the Aniene beyond Tivoli, and in the Alban Hills. The most conspicuous aqueduct is the Acqua Claudia, long stretches of which survive.

THE AQUEDUCTS OF ROME

One of the most evocative sights of the Roman Campagna is the desolate line of an aqueduct running across the countryside. The aqueducts were one of the finest engineering achievements of the Roman Empire, developed to an extraordinary level of technical sophistication. The Anio Vetus, which ran from near Tivoli, was one of the earliest. It was begun in 272 BC.

As Rome expanded, the challenge lay in transporting fresh water across long distances, often over 50km, so that it arrived in the city in a constant stream. It was impossible for the water to flow uphill; if it was too level it risked becoming stagnant; and it needed to enter the city gently for filtering and distribution. So precision was vital. The surveyors would start by calculating the average fall from the original spring or river in the hills around Rome down to the city. Sometimes this was very small. The Acqua Vergine, built in 19 BC, fell only 20cm per kilometre over its 21-km length. Taking the eleven major aqueducts into Rome, the average fall was about 4m per kilometre.

To maintain the gradient there were times when the water had to cross a valley on a raised platform of arches, but the builders preferred to run the water underground in channels, perhaps a metre below the surface. This made the supply more secure. The channel was constructed as a vaulted chamber, to allow easy access for cleaning and unblocking. There was a continuous programme of maintenance and cleaning overseen by the water commissioner. He had to be vigilant. Unscrupulous landowners are reported as siphoning off the water, while others built tombs or planted trees too close to the water course. At least 5m had to be left clear on either side on pain of a 10,000 sesterces fine.

By the time the eleven Roman aqueducts were in full flow, they were feeding over a million cubic litres of water (over a thousand litres per head of population), into Rome each day, far more than a city would receive per head today. It was more than enough to meet the need for drinking water, industrial activities and to service the great public baths. The waste would be distributed down the sewers and hence into the Tiber. With the collapse of Rome in the 5th and 6th centuries, the aqueducts silted up and many were cut in the wars with the Goths. It was not until the 16th and 17th centuries that any were reconnected.   C.F.

PRACTICAL INFORMATION

GETTING AROUND

• **By air: Fiumicino** (T: 06 65951, www.adr.it): Non-stop trains run from Stazione Termini (*map p. 29, F2*) every half hour from about 7am–9.15pm (30mins) and underground trains every 15mins from Stazione Tiburtina (*map p. 24*) via Ostiense and Trastevere from about 5am–11pm (41mins). There are also night buses from/to Tiburtina. If you arrive late, however, it is usually best to take a taxi. Taxis cost standard meter charges plus an airport supplement. **Ciampino** (T: 06 794 941, www.adr.it): The easiest way to reach it is by taxi. By public transport take underground Line A from Stazione Termini to Anagnina, and from there by COTRAL airport bus from 6am–10pm (every 30mins).

• **By bus:** Free maps of the principal routes are usually available from the ATAC kiosk on the square in front of Stazione Termini (open Mon–Sat 8–8). Tickets are sold at tobacconists, bars and newsstands, at ATAC booths and by automatic machines at metro stations. They are valid for 75mins on any number of lines or for one journey on the metro. They have to be stamped on board.

• **By underground:** The service runs 5.30am–11.30pm; on Sat the last train is at half past midnight.

• **By taxi:** To call a taxi, T: 06 3570; T: 06 4994; or T: 06 8822: you will be given the approximate arrival time and the number of the taxi.

VISITOR INFORMATION

The official tourist agency for Rome is the APT (Azienda di Promozione Turistica di Roma), whose offices at Via Parigi 5 (*map p. 29, E1*) supply a list of hotels and up-to-date opening times:

The **Roma Archaeologia Card**, valid for 7 days, allows entrance to the main state-owned archaeological sites and museums. There is also a 7-day inclusive ticket for the four museums run by the Museo Nazionale Romano; for information T: 06 3996 7700. Up-to-date information on state museums is also available at www. beniculturali.it

HOTELS

€€€€ **Albergo del Sole al Pantheon.** ■ Possibly the oldest hotel in Rome, built in 1467. Guests have included Ariosto, who may have written his *Orlando Furioso* in what is now room 110, and Mascagni, who celebrated the première of *Cavalleria Rusticana* here (room 210). The breakfast buffet is one of the best in the city. *Piazza della Rotonda 63, T: 06 678 0441, www.hotelsolealpantheon.com. 31 rooms plus 5 additional suites in the building across the street. Map p. 28, B2.*

€€€€ **Hotel Art**. Contemporary hotel in a former church on tranquil Via Margutta. Each of the three floors has its own neon colour scheme: yellow, orange or blue. Rooms are not large, but well planned, with dark wood floors, polished concrete walls and excellent lighting. No restaurant. *Via Margutta 56, T: 06 360 03995, www.hotelart.it. 46 rooms. Map p. 69, A3.*

€€€€ **Hotel Forum**. ■ Relaxed and comfortable former convent in a superb location. The views of the Forum and

Capitoline Hill are spectacular. *Via Tor de' Conti 25–30, T: 06 679 2446. www. hotelforumrome.com. 80 rooms. Map p. 29, D3.*
€€€€ **Hassler Hotel** and €€ **Il Palazzetto**. ■ One of the most famous of Rome's luxury hotels, at the top of the Spanish Steps, with magnificent views. It has a delightful annexe in a tiny 15th-century palazzo on the other side of Piazza Trinità dei Monti, overlooking the Spanish Steps. Outdoor garden and restaurant. *Piazza Trinità dei Monti 6, T: 06 699 34730, www.hotelhassler.it. Hassler 99 rooms; Palazzetto 4 rooms. Map p. 69, B3.*
€€€€ **Hotel d'Inghilterra**. ■ A club atmosphere and a loyal following with many guests returning year after year. A former favourite of Gregory Peck during the filming of *Roman Holiday*. Though close to the Spanish Steps and the choicest shopping streets, its location is discreet and secluded. The small English-style bar is renowned for its excellent Martinis and Bloody Marys. *Via Bocca di Leone 14, T: 06 699 811. www.hoteldinghilterraroma.it. 98 rooms. Map p. 69, B3.*
€€€€ **Raphael**. ■ Ivy-clad 18th-century palazzo behind Piazza Navona, and one of the most charming hotels in Rome. The Bramante Bar is one of the finest spots in town for a glass of Prosecco. *Largo Febo 2 (Piazza Navona), T: 06 682831, www.raphaelhotel.com. 56 rooms. Map p. 28, A2.*
€€€€ **Hotel de Russie**. Part of the Rocco Forte Hotels Group, it attracts a glamorous crowd to its Jardin de Russie courtyard restaurant and extensive terraced gardens behind. *Via del Babuino 9. T: 06 32 88 81. www.roccofortehotels.com. 94 rooms. Map p. 69, A3.*
€€–€€€€ **Albergo del Senato**.

Rooms and a terrace overlooking the Pantheon, in a 19th-century building. Lovely roof terrace. *Piazza della Rotonda 73, T: 06 678 4343, www.albergodelsenato.it. 57 rooms. Map p. 28, B2.*
€€–€€€€ **The Inn at the Spanish Steps**. ■ One of Rome's most popular town-house hotels. Individual, distinctively styled rooms are by the Roman interior furnishings firm Tenco (whose work includes elements of the nearby Hotel de Russie). An evening glass of wine and canapés are included in the room rate. Advisable to book well in advance. *Via Condotti 85, T: 06 699 25657. www.atspanishsteps.com. 24 rooms. Map p. 69, B3.*
€€€ **Albergo Santa Chiara**. A welcoming place, with a loyal clientèle. Good value considering its excellent location on a quiet street close to the Pantheon. *Via Santa Chiara 21, T: 06 687 2979. www.albergosantachiara.com. 96 rooms. Map p. 28, B2.*
€€€ **Arco dei Tolomei**. ■ Lovely, tranquil B&B in an old house in a quiet part of Trastevere. Extremely helpful and attentive staff, cosy lounge, internet access for guests, and delicious breakfasts. Rooms are delightfully furnished, some with terraces. *Via Arco dei Tolomei 27, T: 06 5832 0189. www.inrome.info. 6 rooms. Map p. 78, C2.*
€€€ **Hotel Gregoriana**. ■ Originally a convent, a compact, bright, clean little hotel. Bedrooms are not large, but all have a feeling of space and light. No restaurant, breakfast delivered to the room. Excellent location near the top of the Spanish Steps, just far enough away to avoid the noise in the evening. *Via Gregoriana 18, T: 06 679 4269, www.hotelgregoriana.it. 19 rooms. Map p. 69, B3.*
€€€ **Intercontinental de la Ville**. A

fine Neoclassical building at the top of the Spanish Steps. Gracious rooms and panoramas across the rooftops. *Via Sistina 69, T: 06 67331, www.interconti.com. 192 rooms. Map p. 69, B3.*

€€–€€€ **Hotel Bramante.** ■ A small, beautifully decorated hotel adjacent to Borgo Pio, once the home of Domenico Fontana. Welcoming atmosphere, with stone floors, rich carpets, and beamed ceilings. No restaurant. *Vicolo d. Palline 24, T: 06 688 06426, www.hotelbramante.com. 16 rooms. Map p. 83, B2.*

€€–€€€ **Teatropace33**. Behind the Piazza Navona in the tiny Via del Teatro Pace. Designed by Onorio Longhi in 1585, and completely refurbished in 2004. The wonderful central oval stone staircase leads off to well-furnished rooms with polished wooden floors and high ceilings. Breakfast is served on a tray delivered to your room. Staff are friendly and helpful. *Via del Teatro Pace 33, T: 06 687 9075, www.hotelteatropace.com. 23 rooms. Map p. 28, A2.*

€€ **Albergo Cesari**. In a good location between the Trevi Fountain and the Pantheon. It opened as a hotel in 1787, and guests have included Stendhal and Giuseppe Mazzini. The rooms are classically simple. No restaurant. *Via di Pietra 89a. T: 06 674 9701. www.albergocesari.it. 47 rooms. Map p. 28, C2.*

€–€€ **Il Covo.** ■ In the charming Monti district, between Termini station and the Colosseum, with rooms in four buildings, two old and two more modern. There is a café with outside seating on the Piazza Madonna dei Monti. Breakfast is served on the ground floor, in a room which also operates as a restaurant. *Via del Boschetto 91, T: 06 481 5871, www.bbilcovo.it. 15 rooms. Map p. 29, E3.*

CONVENT ACCOMMODATION

The website of the American Catholic Church in Rome has a list (www.santasusanna.org/comingToRome/convents.html). Alternatively there is www.hospites.it, an Italian website for religious houses across the country, partially in English. You need to be aware of each establishment's curfew to avoid being locked out for the night.

RESTAURANTS

€€€ **Alberto Ciarla**. Well run old-established restaurant in Trastevere, serving mostly fish. Several set menus as well as à la carte, and a good wine selection. *Piazza San Cosimato 40, T: 06 581 8668. Open evenings only; closed Sun. Map p. 78, A2.*

€€€ **Dal Bolognese.** ■ In a wonderful position, with elegant clientèle and professional service. As the name suggests, the cuisine is from Bologna, with excellent fresh pasta. *Piazza del Popolo 1/2, T: 06 361 1426. Closed Mon. Map p. 69, A2.*

€€€ **Il Convivio Troiani**. A very good, small restaurant with cooking that begins with traditional ingredients but is particularly imaginative. It has an excellent *menù degustazione*—a many-course set menu—that changes weekly. *Vicolo dei Soldati 31, T: 06 686 9432. Closed Sun. Map p. 28, A1.*

€€€ **La Rosetta**. Handsome restaurant a few steps from the Pantheon, widely held to be the top fish restaurant in Rome. *Via della Rosetta 8, T: 06 686 1002. Closed Sun. Map p. 28, B2.*

€€€ **La Terrazza dell'Hotel Eden**. Having the best view in the city tends to distract attention from the food, but the modern interpretations of Italian classics are expertly prepared and beautifully presented. *Via Ludovisi 49, T: 06 478 121. Open every day. Map p. 69, B3.*

€€ **Checco er Carettiere**. Popular, noisy family-run restaurant in Trastevere, offering traditional Roman dishes, such as *coda alla vaccinara* (oxtail stewed in a tomato and celery sauce), as well as lighter food, such as simple grilled fish. Home-made desserts. *Via Benedetta 10, T: 06 581 7018. Closed Sun eve. Map p. 78, A1.*

€€ **Fortunato al Pantheon**. An efficiently run traditional Roman restaurant with particularly high-quality food. Frequented by politicians and businessmen. Seasonal fare and good fish. *Via del Pantheon 55, T: 06 679 2788. Closed Sun. Map p. 28, B2.*

€€ **Piperno**. ■ Small, cosy place in the old ghetto, serving home-cooked specialities. The Jewish-style artichokes are excellent, as is the light, refreshing house Frascati. *Monte dei Cenci 9, T: 06 6880 6629. Closed Sun evening and Mon. Map p. 28, B3.*

€€ **Settimio**. A simple restaurant with high quality traditional Roman cuisine. *Via del Pellegrino 117, T: 06 6880 1978. Closed Wed. Map p. 28, A2.*

€€ **Sora Lella**. Small, neat, family-run trattoria on Isola Tiberina. Traditional Roman cooking, such as oxtail, artichokes *alla romana* (stewed with mint) or *alla giudia* (deep-fried); home-made desserts. *Via di Ponte dei Quattro Capi 16, T: 06 686 1601. Closed Sun. Map p. 28, B4.*

€ **Cul de Sac 1**. The first wine bar in Rome. Long and narrow, warm and friendly, serving cheeses, cold meat, vegetable quiches, and hearty lentil soup in wintertime. There are over 700 wines to choose from. *Piazza Pasquino 73, T: 06 6880 1094. Closed Mon lunchtime. Map p. 28, A2.*

€ **Giggetto al Portico d'Ottavia**. Good pasta dishes, and traditional Roman fare including lamb (*abbacchio*) and *fritto di fiori di zucca* (courgette flowers stuffed with mozzarella cheese and salted anchovies, dipped in egg and fried). Tables outside in summer. *Via del Portico d'Ottavia 21, T: 06 686 1105. Closed Mon. Map p. 28, B3.*

€ **Montecarlo**. A good place for pizza or simple meal, with crowded old-fashioned tables, and a bustling atmosphere without any pretension. Good, simple local dishes (including desserts). No credit cards. *Vicolo Savelli 12, T: 06 686 1877. Closed Mon. Map p. 28, A2.*

BOOKSHOPS

English books are stocked at The Anglo-American Book Co, Via della Vite 102, near Piazza di Spagna (*map p. 28, C1*); The Corner Bookshop, Via del Moro 48. Closed Mon morning (*map p. 28, A4*); Feltrinelli International, Via Vittorio Emanuele Orlando 84 (*map p. 29, E1*); The Lion Bookshop, Via dei Greci 33. (*map p. 69, A3*).

FESTIVALS & EVENTS

Befana, Epiphany, celebrated at night in Piazza Navona, 5–6 Jan; Carnival is celebrated in the streets and squares on Shrove Tuesday; Anniversary of the birth of Rome, celebrated on the Capitoline Hill, 21 April; *Festa della Repubblica*, Military parade in the Via dei Fori Imperiali, first Sun in June; St Peter and St Paul, Festival of the patron saints of Rome, 29 June; *Festa di Noantri*, Celebrations in Trastevere for several weeks in July.

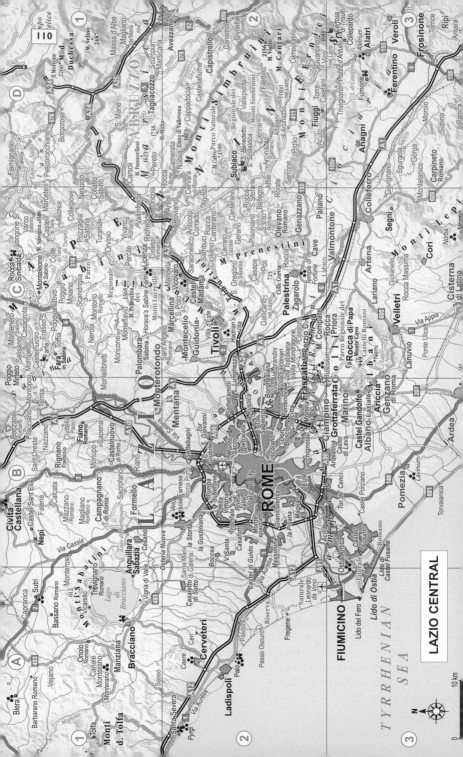

LAZIO CENTRAL

110

THE ROMAN CAMPAGNA

The Roman Campagna, literally 'countryside', is the land beyond Rome on all sides, bordered by the mouth of the Tiber on the sea and the Sabine hills to the east; the Castelli Romani in the volcanic hills to the south; and Lake Bracciano to the north. In the centre of Lazio, the name *Campania Romana* was used as early as Constantine's day to distinguish this area from the surroundings of Naples known as the *Campania felix* (and today called just Campania). It was once a most beautiful area of rolling farmland, where sheep would graze and the wide solitary views might be broken by the arches of an aqueduct, vividly recorded in numerous 18th- and 19th-century paintings. It was across this landscape that travellers rode in their carriages on their way to Rome, the great monuments of which would be visible for many miles before the walls were reached. Since the 1950s Rome has encroached on the countryside with high-rise buildings, and fast roads have spoilt acres of farmland. Only in a few places can the spirit of the Campagna still be felt, such as in the Parco della Caffarella on the Via Appia Antica close to Rome, in the distant view of Rome on clear days from the terraces of the Temple of Fortune in the little town of Palestrina, and around the Lago di Nemi in the Alban Hills. In ancient times the Campagna was a place where the wealthy would build country estates, the favourite places being Tivoli and the Alban Hills, and much of the land was used for growing wheat. In the Middle Ages the area was slowly abandoned, and became little more than malarial marsh. Today the most spectacular Roman remains are Hadrian's Villa at Tivoli, the excavations of the town of Ostia, and the Temple of Fortune at Palestrina. The borders of the Campagna coincide to a great extent with those of the present-day province of Rome.

OSTIA ANTICA

Map p. 110, B3. Open Tues–Sun Nov–Feb 8.30–4; March 8.30–5; April–Oct 8.30–6; closed Mon; T: 06 5635 2830. Museum open as site but closed 1.30–2.30 and open only 8.30–1.30 on Sun and holidays.
The excavations of the city of Ostia are one of the most interesting and beautiful sights near Rome; they well repay the (not terribly arduous) trip out of town. Many of the mosaics are covered with a thick layer of wind-blown sand.

The ruins, in a beautiful park of umbrella pines and cypresses, give a remarkable idea of the domestic and commercial life of the Empire in the late 1st and in the 2nd centuries AD. They are as important for the study of Roman urban architecture as those of the older cities of Pompeii and Herculaneum. The excavated area is now c. 34 hectares, or two-thirds of the area of the city at its greatest extent.

Ostia seems to have been divided into at least five districts or *regiones*. The description below groups the best-preserved and most interesting remains (or those open at the time of writing) into six geographically coherent sections. It takes time and stamina to visit the whole site in one day, but it is highly recommended.

HISTORY OF OSTIA ANTICA

According to legend, Ostia was founded by Ancus Marcius, fourth king of Rome, to guard the mouth (*ostium*) of the river Tiber. The surviving remains are not, however, older than the 4th century BC, and the city, which was probably the first colony of Rome, may have been founded about 335. Its first industry was the extraction of salt from the surrounding marshes, but it soon developed into the port of Rome, and shortly before the First Punic War (264 BC) it also became a naval base. The link between the port and the capital was the Via Ostiense: carrying as it did all Rome's overseas imports and exports, it must have been one of the busiest roads in the ancient world.

One of Ostia's main functions was the organisation of the *annona*, the supply of produce—mainly grain—to the capital. At its head was the *quaestor ostiensis*, who had to live at Ostia. He was appointed by lot and his office, according to Cicero, was burdensome and unpopular. By 44 BC the quaestor was replaced by the *procuratores annonae*, answerable to the *praefectus annonae* in Rome.

By the 1st century AD, the city had outgrown its harbour. A new port, *Portus*, planned by Augustus, was built by Claudius to the northwest. The decline of Ostia began in the time of Constantine, who favoured Portus. Even in the 4th century, however, though it had become a residential town instead of a commercial port, it was still used by people travelling abroad—in 387 St Augustine was about to embark for Africa with his mother, St Monica, when she was taken ill and died in a hostel in the city. In the following centuries, Ostia's decline was accelerated by loss of trade and by the increase of malaria. Its monuments were looted—items from the ruins have been found as far afield as Pisa, Orvieto, Amalfi and Salerno. An attempt to revive the city was made by Gregory IV, when he founded the *borgo* of Ostia Antica. By 1756 the city which at the height of its prosperity had a population of some 80,000, had 156 inhabitants; half a century later only a few convicts of the papal government lived here. Augustus Hare, writing in 1878, speaks of one human habitation breaking the utter solitude.

The upper decumanus maximus

The entrance to the excavations opens onto Via delle Tombe, the street of tombs, outside the walls, since Roman law forbade burials within the city limits. Terracotta and carved stone sarcophagi and sealed graves line the road.

The entrance to the city proper is by the Porta Romana, with remains of the gate in walls of the Republican period; some fragments of marble facing of the Imperial era have been found and placed on the inside of the gate. Piazzale della Vittoria is dominated by a colossal statue of Minerva Victoria, dating from the reign of Domitian and inspired by a Hellenistic original that may once have decorated the gate. On the right are the remains of *horrea* (warehouses), later converted into baths. In the **Baths of the Cisiarii** (Baths of the Charioteers) on the far side of the warehouses, is a large, well-preserved black and white mosaic (most mosaics in Ostia are black and white) with marine motifs and depictions of chariots and wagons.

The decumanus maximus, the main street of Ostia, runs right through the city for over a kilometre. On the right a flight of steps leads to a platform, on the second storey of the **Baths of Neptune**. You can see the tepidarium and calidarium, remains of columns, and the floor of the large entrance hall with a beautiful mosaic of Neptune driving four sea-horses and surrounded by tritons, nereids and dolphins. In an adjoining room is a mosaic of Amphitrite escorted by Hymen.

THE DOMESTIC ARCHITECTURE OF ANCIENT ROME

Research at Ostia Antica has led to an increased understanding of the types of house occupied by Romans of the middle and lower classes. It is unlikely that the domestic architecture of Ostia differed radically from that of the capital, and the examples of poorer dwelling here may be taken as typical of such buildings in Rome itself, though not of houses throughout the empire. The middle- and lower-class house at Ostia (*insula*) was in sharp contrast to the typical Pompeian residence (*domus*), with its atrium and peristyle, its few windows and its low elevation: houses of this type are rare at Ostia.

The ordinary Ostia *insula* usually had four storeys of apartments and reached a height of 15m, the maximum permitted by Roman law. It was built of brick, probably not covered with stucco, and had little ornamentation, although sometimes bricks of contrasting colours were used. The entranceways had pilasters or engaged columns supporting a simple pediment. There were numerous rooms, each with its own window. The arches over the windows were often painted in vermilion. Mica or selenite was used instead of glass in the windows. The façades were of three types: living-rooms with windows on all floors; an arcaded ground floor with shops and living-rooms above; and a ground floor with shops opening on the street, and living-rooms above. Many of the houses had balconies of various designs. The apartment houses contained numerous flats or sets of rooms designated by numbers on the stairs leading to them. They, too, were of different types; some were of simple design and others were built round a courtyard.

The rare *domus*, built for the richer inhabitants, was usually on one floor only and dates mostly from the 3rd and 4th centuries. They were decorated with apses, nymphaea and mosaic floors, and the rooms often had columns and loggias.

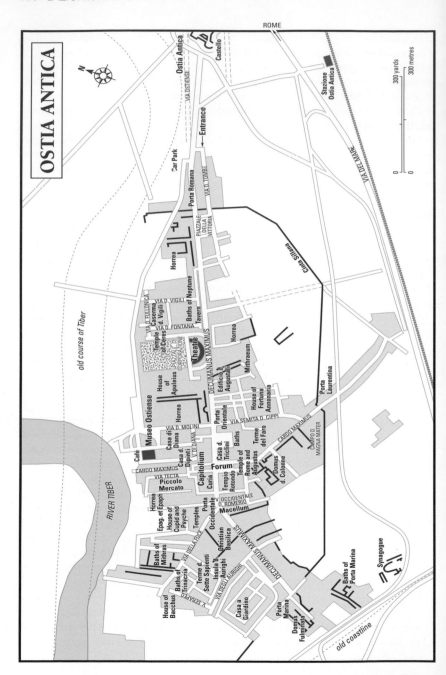

OSTIA ANTICA

ROME

Ostia Antica

Castello

Stazione
Ostia Antica

VIA OSTIENSE

Entrance

Car Park

Porta Romana

VIA D. TOMBE

PIAZZALE
DELLA
VITTORIA

Clivo Silfana

VIA DEL MARE

old course of Tiber

Horrea

VIA D. FULLONICA
Caserma
V. d. Vigili
VIA D. VIGILI
Temple
of Ceres
VIA D. FONTANA

Baths of Neptune
Tavern

Horrea

PIAZZALE
DELLA
CORPORAZIONE

Theatre

DECUMANUS MAXIMUS

House
of
Apuleius

Mithraeum

Edificio d.
Augustali

House of
Fortuna
Annonaria

Porta
Laurentina

Museo Ostiense

VIA D. MOLINI
Horrea

Casa di
Diana

Porta
Orientale

V. DI DIANA

VIA SEMITA D. CIPPI

Casa d.
Dipinti

Baths

Terme
del Faro

CARDO MAXIMUS

CAMPO D.
MAGNA MATER

Café

CARDO MAXIMUS

VIA TECTA

Casa d.
Triclini

Temple of
Rome and
Augustus

Domus
d. Colonne

Capitolium
Forum
Curia

Piccolo
Mercato

Tempio
Rotondo

Horrea
Epag. et Epaph

Porta
Occidentale

V. OCCIDENTALE
O. ROMERIO

House of
Cupid and
Psyche

Temples

Macellum

RIVER TIBER

Baths of
Mithras

DECUMANUS MAXIMUS

VIA DELLA FOCE

Baths of
Trinacria

Terme d.
Sette Sapienti

Christian
Basilica

Insula d.
Aurighi

V. SERAPEO

VIA DEGLI AURIGHI

Synagogue

Baths of
Porta Marina

House of
Bacchus

Casa a
Giardino

Porta
Marina

Domus
Fulminata

old coastline

300 yards

300 metres

N

Beyond the baths, on the corner of Via della Fontana, is a tavern which was owned by a certain Fortunatus, who wooed customers through the (now broken) inscription in the mosaic pavement: *Dicit Fortunatus: vinum cratera quod sitis bibe* ('Fortunatus says: drink wine from the bowl to quench your thirst').

Through the tavern you get to **Via della Fontana**, one of the best-preserved streets in Ostia, with typical apartment houses, with shops, and living quarters over them. About halfway along on the right is the old covered fountain. Just beyond it, a right turn leads to the Caserma dei Vigili (firemen's barracks), built in the 2nd century AD. It once had a large arcaded central courtyard. On the left are the remains of an Augusteum, or shrine for the cult of the emperors, with a mosaic of the sacrifice of a bull. Two huge curved water cisterns survive at the other end of the yard.

Via and Piazzale delle Corporazioni

The next street to the west is Via delle Corporazioni. At its entrance are the remains of a Christian oratory in honour of St Cyriacus and his fellow-martyrs of Ostia, built over a fountain. Beyond the oratory is the **Theatre**, built by Agrippa and enlarged by Septimius Severus in the 2nd century. It has two tiers of seats (originally there were three) divided by stairways into five sections or *cunei*. It could accommodate 2,700 people. A tufa wall with some marble fragments and three marble masks survive from the stage, behind which some *cipollino* columns that once decorated the third tier of the auditorium have been set up.

Behind the theatre extends the spacious **Piazzale delle Corporazioni** (Square of the Guilds). In this square were 70 offices of commercial associations ranging from workers' guilds to corporations of foreign representatives from all over the ancient world. Their fascinating trademarks are well preserved in the mosaic floors of the brick-built arcade running round the square. The trademarks of the foreigners tell where they came from (e.g. Carthage, Alexandria, Narbonne) and what their trade was (the elephant indicates ivory traders). Those of the citizens indicate their business, such as ship repair and construction, salvage crews, dockers or customs and excise officials. In the middle of the square are the stylobate and two columns of a small temple in antis known as the Temple of Ceres, and the bases of statues erected to the leading citizens of Ostia.

Beyond the theatre is the handsome **House of Apuleius** (*closed for restoration at the time of writing*) of the Pompeian type (rare at Ostia), with an atrium and rooms decorated with mosaics. Beside it is a Mithraeum, one of the best-preserved of the many temples dedicated to Mithras (*see box overleaf*) in the city. It has two benches for the initiated, on which are mosaics illustrating the cult of the god. In Ostia, as elsewhere in the Roman world, different religious cults flourished without disharmony. As well as temples dedicated to traditional deities such as Vulcan, Venus, Ceres and Fortuna, there was a popular cult of the emperors and a surprisingly large number of eastern cults too: Cybele, Egyptian and Syrian deities, and especially Mithras. Singularly few Christian places of worship have been found.

THE CULT OF MITHRAS

The cult of Mithras was one of the most popular foreign cults to spread in the Roman empire in the 2nd and 3rd centuries ad. Its origins were in Persia, where worship of the god is said to have been founded by the sage Zoroaster. Mithras was associated with the sun and with cattle-herding or stealing, and the most common representation of him, found in reliefs or statues in all Mithraic temples, shows him astride a large bull which he is stabbing in the neck. Other less common reliefs show a sequence in which Mithras appears to be born from a rock, pursues the bull and then, after he has killed it, strips it of its hide and enjoys a divine banquet on the skin with a sun-god (sometimes shown as Apollo in Roman settings). The violence shown to the bull is a dramatic contrast to Greek and Roman sacrifices, which maintain the pretence that the beast is willing to be sacrificed.

There is a great deal of unresolved debate on how and why Mithraism spread from Persia, and the extent to which the Romans developed the cult for their own ends. In the Western Empire, Mithraism was especially popular among soldiers, slaves and ex-slaves. Women were excluded. Members met in small groups, up to 35, in sanctuaries which were designed to resemble caves, the traditional haunt of the god. At the eastern end there would be a relief or statue of Mithras, surrounded by symbols of constellations and two deities carrying torches. This was the 'light' end of the sanctuary which contrasted with the 'dark' western end, and made the point that this was a saviour god who brought the initiate from darkness into light. During ceremonies the initiates would recline on platforms along the side walls of the sanctuary and enjoy a ritual meal. Some 400 sanctuaries are known, a high proportion of them in Rome (35) and Ostia (15), which shows that the cult must have been very popular here. They are also found in army camps along the northern border of the empire from Britain to the Danube.

In the Roman empire the most important feature of Mithraism was its series of graded initiations, each of them associated with a planet. The first was known as 'the Raven', under the protection of Mercury (ravens were always said to be able to communicate with the gods). The higher grades included 'Soldier' (Mars), 'Lion' (Jupiter), 'Persian' (Moon), 'Heliodromos' (Sun) and finally 'Father' (Saturn). Surviving inscriptions show that there might be one or two 'Fathers' in each group and the status of this grade was such that, unlike the lower ones, it could be recorded on an initiate's tombstone. It has been suggested that the disciplined ascent through the grades appealed especially to soldiers because their rise in status in the cult mirrored their own ascent through the ranks to officer; and to slaves hoping to make a similar transition into freedom.   C.F.

The horrea and Via di Diana

Horrea, large warehouses for the storage of corn, can be seen on the right of the decumanus maximus. They have over 60 small rooms, some of them arranged round a central colonnaded courtyard. Further along the decumanus, at the junction with Via dei Molini, stood the Porta Orientale, the east gate of the original fortified city.

A street on the west side of Via dei Molini, Via di Diana, takes its name from a house called the **Casa di Diana**. It has a characteristic façade with shops on the ground floor, rooms with windows on the first floor, and a projecting balcony on the second. The house is entered through a vaulted corridor. A room on the left has a ceiling and walls that have been restored with fragments of frescoes. The small interior courtyard has a fountain and a relief of Diana. At the back of the premises are two rooms converted into a Mithraeum.

On the left of Via di Diana (beyond the Casa di Diana on the other side), is the remarkable **thermopolium**. Just outside the entrance, under the alcove, are three brick-topped benches. On the threshold is a marble counter, on which is a small stone basin. Inside is another counter for the display of food; above are wall-paintings of fruit and vegetables. On the rear wall is a marble slab which once had hooks for hats and coats. Beyond is a delightful court and fountain.

At the end of Via di Diana on the right is an apartment house, originally of four storeys, called the **Casa dei Dipinti** (*largely closed for restoration*) A staircase leads up to the top floor from which there is a fine view of the excavations. The ground floor (entered around the corner from Via dei Dipinti) has traces of 'architectural' wall-paintings in many of its rooms. In a hall behind, a substantial piece of fine poly-chrome mosaic flooring has been set up. In the adjacent garden are numerous *dolii*, large terracotta jars for the storage of corn and oil. At the end of the street is the muse-um, which contains the principal finds from the excavations.

Museo Ostiense

The museum (*for opening times see p. 111; cafeteria and bookshop behind the museum*) is housed in a building dating from 1500 and originally used by the authorities con-cerned with the extraction of salt; it was given its Neoclassical façade in 1864. The most important exhibits are given below.

In one of the first rooms is a very fine statue of **Mithras Slaying the Bull**, from the Baths of Mithras (*see p. 119 below*), signed by Critios of Athens (1st century BC); next to it is displayed a copy made a few years later known as the *Giustiniani Torso*. This was owned by the Odescalchi family and they kept it in their villa garden at Bassano Romano, until it was stolen and found its way to the J. Paul Getty Museum in California where it was exhibited in 1980. It was retrieved by the Italian police in 1999.

Other important finds include **sculpture inspired by Greek art of the 5th–3rd cen-turies** BC, notably two copies of *Eros Drawing his Bow*, one a replica of an original by Lysippus. Inscribed bases testify to the presence of Greek artists. There are three heads of Athena, for example, from originals of the Pheidias type, the Kresilas type, and the Cephisodotus type (first half of the 4th century BC).

Roman sculpture ranges from the 1st century BC to the mid-2nd century AD. The headless male statue, nude except for the drapery over the left arm, is signed with the name of the donor Cartilius Poplicola, whose sarcophagus is near Porta Marina (*see p. 120 below*). It is regarded as the best extant copy of the type known as the *Hero in Repose*. Also here are portraits of Augustus; Trajan (including a statue of him wearing a cuirass); Hadrian; Sabina, his wife, as Venus Genetrix; and a group of portraits of members of the family of Marcus Aurelius.

The upper cardo maximus and forum

The wide cardo maximus, with remains of arcaded shops, runs to the forum. At the north end of the forum is the **Capitolium**. This was the city's most important temple, dedicated to Jupiter, Juno and Minerva. This prostyle hexastyle building, dating from the first half of the 2nd century, had six fluted white marble columns. In front of it is a reconstituted altar. The pronaos is reached by a wide flight of steps. In the cella are niches and a plinth for statues of the deities. During the early Middle Ages the temple was stripped of nearly all its marble facing, but a magnificent slab of African marble is still in place on the threshold and a few surviving marble fragments have been placed to the east behind a colonnade, which defined the sacred area.

On the south side of the forum, beyond the decumanus maximus, are the remains of the 1st-century **Temple of Roma and Augustus**. Like the Capitolium it had six fluted marble columns across the front, but with two side staircases. Fragments of the pediment have been placed on a modern wall to the east; the cult statue of Roma as Victory, dressed as an Amazon, has been placed inside the temple on a plinth, and a headless statue of Victory near the rearranged pediment fragments.

On the east side are the **Baths of the Forum**, built in the 2nd century and restored in the 4th, when they were decorated with mosaics and *cipollino* columns; some of the columns have been re-erected. The frigidarium survives, together with a series of rooms warmed by hot air. Off the north side is the town *forica* (public lavatory), its 22 seats almost perfectly preserved. Also on the east side, at the corner where the decumanus maximus enters the forum, is the **Casa dei Triclini**, so called from the couches in each of the three rooms on the east wing of the central courtyard.

Opposite, on the west side of the forum, are the scant remains of the **Basilica**. The façade towards the forum had a portico of marble arches with a decorated frieze. Fragments of this and of the columns survive. Next to it on the south side is the **Tempio Rotondo**, dating from the 3rd century and probably an Augusteum, or temple erected to the worship of the emperors. The peristyle was paved with mosaics and surrounded by marble-faced niches. It was reached by a flight of steps, which have been preserved: these led to the pronaos, which comprised a portico with brick piers faced with marble and with *cipollino* columns. In the cella are seven niches, three rectangular and four circular. Between the niches are column bases; to the right are the remains of a spiral staircase that led to the dome.

Opposite the basilica, on the other side of the decumanus maximus, is the Curia, or senate house. Next to it is the **Casa del Larario**, or House of the Shrine of the Lares, named from the pretty niche, with inlaid red and yellow brick, that would once have contained images of the household gods.

Leaving the Forum the decumanus maximus continues to the Porta Occidentale, the west gate of the original *castrum*. Square blocks of *opus quadratum*, remains of the ancient walls, can be seen in Via degli Horrea Epagathiana, a turning on the right. Just beyond the traces of wall are the **Horrea Epagathiana et Epaphroditiana**, warehouses in a remarkable state of preservation, including the bolt-holes in the doorways. They were built by two Eastern freedmen, Epagathus and Epaphroditus, whose names are preserved on a marble plaque above the entrance, a brick portal with two engaged columns supporting a pediment.

Back on the decumanus, the main street continues south (*see overleaf*), while the right fork is Via della Foce (Street of the River Mouth), described below.

Via della Foce

This is possibly the most interesting and rewarding (and least crowded) section of the site. Off to the left of Via della Foce, a long passageway leads to the **Mithraeum with Painted Walls** (*Mitreo delle Pareti Dipinti*), built in the 2nd century into a house of the Republican period. The Mithraeum is divided into two sections by partly projecting walls. In the rear wall is the brick-built altar, with a marble cippus on which once stood a bust of Mithras. On the north wall (sadly barely visible) are paintings of initiation rites.

Further up Via della Foce, to the right, is a sacred area of **three Republican temples**. The central and largest is the prostyle hexastyle Temple of Hercules Invictus. The pronaos, paved in black and white chequered mosaic, is reached by a flight of nine steps as wide as the façade. The temple, which may date from the time of Sulla, has an altar donated by Hostilius Antipater, *praefectus annonae*, in the 4th century AD. To the left as you descend the steps is the base of a tetrastyle temple of the same date, its dedication unknown. Between the Temple of Hercules and Via della Foce is the Temple of the Round Altar, named after the circular marble altar with winged cupids found there. It was built in the early Republican period and rebuilt under the Empire.

Behind the sacred area is a street leading to the **House of Cupid and Psyche**, an elegant *domus* dating from the end of the 3rd century: someone once lived a very gracious life here. In the centre is an atrium, with four rooms opening off to the left. One has a pavement of coloured marbles and a copy of the marble group of Cupid and Psyche found here on a pretty fluted pedestal. Opposite is an attractive nymphaeum in a courtyard with columns and brick arches. At the far end is a large room gorgeously paved with *opus sectile*, and preserving some marble mural facing.

Further along Via della Foce is Via delle Terme di Mitra to the right. The **Baths of Mithras** date from the time of Trajan and were rebuilt in the 2nd century. They had elaborate systems for heating and for pumping water. In the basement is a Mithraeum, in which was found the *Mithras Slaying the Bull* now in the museum.

On the left side of the main street are three blocks of small apartment houses; then follows a complex of two apartment blocks with baths between them. On the right is the **Hall of the Mensores** (grain measurers), with a fine mosaic floor. Opposite, the Insula di Serapide is named after a headless stucco figure of Serapis, an Egypto-Graeco-Roman grain deity, in an aedicule in the courtyard. The **Baths of the Seven Sages**

Mosaic in the Hall of the Grain Measurers (*mensores*). The *procuratores annonae*, the officials in charge of the grain supply to Rome, lived at Ostia.

(*Terme dei Sette Sapienti*) were so called from a satirical painting of the Seven Sages found in one of the rooms, formerly a tavern. The baths have a round central frigidarium that was once domed and is paved with a beautiful mosaic with hunting scenes, including a bear, a lion and a tiger. In the next room, with a marble plunge pool, is a painting of *Venus Anadyomene* (Venus 'arisen from the sea'). A covered passage leads to the extensive **Insula degli Aurighi** ('of the charioteers'), an apartment block which takes its name from two small paintings of rival charioteers in the arcade.

Further along Via della Foce, on the left, is a group of buildings of Hadrian's time. The **Baths of the Trinacria** preserve good mosaics and interesting installations for heating and conducting the water. On the other side of Via Serapeo is the **House of Bacchus and Ariadne**, with exceptionally fine mosaic floors.

The lower decumanus maximus

The **Porta Marina** (Sea Gate) was an opening in the walls built by Sulla, remains of which can be seen. Just inside the gate is a tavern (probably of ill-repute), the **Caupona of Alexander Helix**. The extension of the decumanus maximus beyond the gate, built in the time of Augustus, ran through an earlier cemetery. On this section on the left stood the **Santuario della Bona Dea**, a small prostyle tetrastyle temple dedicated to a goddess worshipped exclusively by women; four column bases survive. Further on, a turning to the left (Via di Cartilio Poplicola) leads to the Baths of Porta Marina past the tomb of L. Cartilius Poplicola, a prominent citizen. The surviving fragment of its decorative frieze shows a trireme with the helmeted head of a goddess. This and another tomb close by attest to the existence of a cemetery in the Republican era.

On the outskirts of the town towards the shore, and between the sea and the ancient Via Severiana (on the southwest side of this street), is the most ancient **synagogue** known from monumental remains. It was in continuous use from the 1st–5th centuries AD. Ritual carvings and poorly-preserved mosaics have been found; several Ionic columns have been re-erected. It was discovered in 1961–63 when the new road to Fiumicino airport was constructed. From here you can either walk across the fields to the lower cardo maximus (*see below*), or return to Porta Marina for the lower decumanus maximus.

The decumanus maximus returns past the charming Fontana a Lucerna. Further up on the other side is the School of the Shipwrights, with a temple. The arcade of the courtyard in front of the temple was evidently a marble store: unused and partly finished columns, bases and capitals have been found in it. The store appears to have belonged to Volusianus, a senator of the 4th century, as his name is carved on some of the column shafts. Adjoining is the **Christian basilica**, an unpretentious structure with two aisles divided by columns and ending in apses. At the end of the street on the right is the **Macellum**, or market; two fish shops with superbly-preserved marble counters, open onto the decumanus. Behind them is the market-place.

The lower cardo maximus

Via Occidentale del Pomerio and (left) Via del Tempio Rotondo lead to the south continuation of the cardo maximus. The area is rather overgrown and neglected, but has some points of interest. On the right is the **Domus di Giove Fulminatore**, a house of the Republican period remodelled in the 4th century, with a striking phallic 'doormat' mosaic. Symbols of Priapus was often put in entrances to ward off intruders. In his dual role as god of gardens and of fertility he also functioned as a kind of divine scarecrow. Further down on the same side is a well preserved nymphaeum, in which were found two copies of the *Eros* of Lysippus. The next building is the **Domus delle Colonne**. In the centre of the courtyard is a stone basin with a double apse and short white marble columns; beyond is the large tablinum with its entrance between two columns. On the next sidestreet to the right is the **House of the Fish** (*Domus dei Pesci*), evidently a Christian house (a far room has a polychrome mosaic showing a chalice and fish).

Further up the cardo, to the left, a ramp leads to the triangular Campo della Magna Mater, once an important sacred area. At the far end is the base of the prostyle hexastyle Temple of Cybele. On the near left-hand corner, the Sanctuary of Attis has an apse flanked by telamones in the shape of fauns.

Opposite the ramp, from the cardo maximus, the Semita dei Cippi (alley of the tombstones; a couple survive) leads to the right (north). A further right turn leads into a street named after the **House of Fortuna Annonaria** (on the right), which has a tranquil garden in its peristyle. On the right is a large room with three arches, columns and a nymphaeum. At the end of the street, on the right, is a **Mithraeum**, notable for its mosaic pavement showing the grades of the Mithraic cult (*see box on p. 116 above*). Heading back towards the decumanus maximus is a large fullonica (dyer's workshop). Next to it is the **Edificio degli Augustali**, the headquarters of the *Augustales*, priests in charge of the imperial cult. This building has another entrance in Via degli Augustali, which leads to the decumanus maximus and the main entrance.

MEDIEVAL OSTIA

Across the road from the entrance to the excavations are a few houses outside the *borgo* of Ostia Antica, a fortified village whose walls are still standing, founded by Gregory IV in 830 and given the name of *Gregoriopolis*. The walls enclose a tiny picturesque hamlet of russet-coloured houses beside the castle, bishop's palace and church. The castle (*open for guided tours daily except Mon at 10 & 12; Tues and Thur also at 3; T. 06 5635 8024*) is a splendid building erected in 1483–86 by Baccio Pontelli for Julius II while he was still a cardinal.

From the courtyard there is access to a remarkable spiral stone staircase used by the guards, an old oven, a bath-house, and a room from which cannon were fired. A spiral ramp (designed for use by horses) leads up to the residential area with traces of frescoes by the school of Baldassare Peruzzi. From the battlements and terrace there are views towards Fiumicino and the present site of the Tiber (which formerly flowed beneath the castle walls). An old fortified tower which predates the castle can be seen from here, and the site of a drawbridge which connected it to the main building.

The church of Santa Aurea, by Baccio Pontelli or Meo del Caprina, contains the body of the martyred St Aurea (d. 268) and, in a side chapel, a fragment of the gravestone of St Augustine's mother, St Monica (*see p. 50*), who died at Ostia in 387.

THE ROMAN LITTORAL

The nearest seaside resort to Rome is the Lido di Ostia (*map p. 110, A3*), which was first laid out in the 1920s and connected to the capital in 1928 by a fast road (parallel to the ancient Via Ostiense). It is now little more than a modern suburb of Rome. More fashionable resorts, but crowded in summer, are north of Fiumicino, and include Fregene, with its extensive pinewood, and Ladispoli.

Ladispoli and Palo

Ladispoli (*map p. 110, A2*) is a popular seaside resort founded by Prince Ladislao Odescalchi in the 19th century and greatly expanded in the 20th. At Palo nearby (ancient *Alsium*) there are remains of a large Roman villa with good polychrome mosaics. The garden of the picturesque 15th-century Odescalchi castle on the sea is now part of a nature reserve owned by the World Wildlife Fund. The garden was created by Prince Ladislao Odescalchi, and the vegetation includes turkey oaks, dwarf palms, cypresses, pine trees and ilexes. The sanctuary, which includes typical Mediterranean *maquis*, with myrtle and laurel bushes and cyclamens, violets and wild orchids, is inhabited by numerous marine birds and a large colony of great tits.

Riserva del Litorale Romano

South of Ostia and the Tiber delta, the pine forest of Castel Fusano stretches as far as the huge estate of Castel Porziano (59km square), which was once a royal chase and then became the property of the President of the Republic, who relinquished it in 1977.

The two areas have now been incorporated into a wildlife reserve known as the **Riserva Naturale del Litorale Romano** (*map p. 110, A3–B3; info: CEA, Via del Martin Pescatore 66, Castel Fusano; T: 06 5091 7817, www.parks.it*). It includes Capocotta, a lovely woodland close to the sea. The vegetation ranges from dunes and Mediterranean *maquis* to pine forests and woods of cork and holm oak, ash, poplar, elm and maple. The protected wildlife includes boar, roe deer, porcupine, green and great spotted woodpeckers, black kite, buzzard, and several owls. Rare Italian breeds of cattle and horses are also raised here. Threading its way through the park is the Via Severiana, built by Septimius Severus from 198–209 to connect Ostia with Terracina. The remains of several Imperial-age villas have come to light, together with the fascinating traces of many *vivaria*, pens and cages of various sizes (the largest capable of holding large numbers of elephants) for the wild beasts which were disembarked at the port of Ostia, destined for the spectacles to be held in the circuses and amphitheatres of Rome.

Lavinium and Ardea

Just 3km west of the modern industrial town of Pomezia (*map p. 110, B3*), built in 1939 to house the workers engaged in draining the Pontine Marshes, lie the ruins of **Lavinium** (*open only by appointment; for information call the archaeological museum in Pomezia–Pratica di Mare; T: 06 919 84744*). The settlement predates Rome, and was considered sacred by the Latins, who believed it had been founded by Aeneas himself after fleeing from Troy. Perhaps there is a grain of truth in the legend: several archaeologists today support the theory that it was founded by Trojan refugees. Excavations on the site, which are still in progress, have brought to light ample stretches of the city wall, a bathhouse, 13 altars and a necropolis, where a large tomb called the 'Heroön of Aeneas' has been found. There is an archaeological museum with finds from the site (*open Fri, Sat, Sun 10–1 & 3–8*), including a remarkable statue of Minerva.

South of Pomezia is **Ardea** (*map p. 110, B3*), ancient capital of the Rutulii, now a busy agricultural centre, in a splendid position on a piece of elevated ground (once the acropolis), commanding views over the countryside as far as the sea. For many years this was the home of the artist Giacomo Manzoni, known as Giacomo Manzù, who died here in 1991. Born in Bergamo, Manzù's early inspiration came from the time he spent in Milan, with artists of the Novecento. He admired the works in wax of Medardo Rosso, and wax and bronze were to become his preferred materials. He made one of the bronze doors of St Peter's in Rome (the 'Doorway of Death'; 1962). A collection of bronzes, jewels, medals, designs and theatre sets can be seen in a handsome white building just outside the town, the **Raccolta Amici di Manzù** (*open daily summer 10–9, Mon 2–9; winter 9–8, Mon 3–8; Via Laurentina; T: 06 913 5022*). The artist's tomb is in the garden.

THE CASTELLI ROMANI

The Castelli Romani is the name given to the 13 towns, most of them founded by popes or patrician Roman families, in the Alban Hills (Colli Albani; *map p. 110,*

B2–C3), an isolated volcanic group rising from the Roman Campagna, the foothills of which reach to within 12km of Rome itself. They enclose the two attractive crater lakes of Nemi and Albano. Castel Gandolfo is famous as the pope's summer residence, and the hills are an elegant residential area with numerous villas amidst the chestnut woods. Some of the towns have become cool summer resorts.

Castel Gandolfo

Approached by two roads bordered by ilex trees, whose branches are interlaced overhead to form arboreal tunnels, is Castel Gandolfo (*map p. 110, B3*), often called just 'Castello'. It is built on the lip of the crater of Lake Albano, and occupies the site of the citadel of *Alba Longa*.

HISTORY OF CASTEL GANDOLFO

The city of *Alba Longa* was founded, according to legend, by Ascanius, son of Aeneas. It was so called because it extended in a long line up the slopes of Mons Albanus. Head of the Latin League, Alba was the mother city of many of the Latin towns, and of Rome itself. Its war with Rome at the time of Tullus Hostilius, decided by the single combats of the three Roman Horatii and the three Latin Curiatii; the treachery of its dictator Metius Fufetius; and its destruction around the middle of the 7th century BC, are famous episodes in the legendary history of Rome. The town was never rebuilt, though its temples were respected and were still standing in the days of Augustus. Domitian built a villa here, ruins of which are visible (*see opposite*). There is no trace of the ancient town, but to the west of Castel Gandolfo there is an extensive necropolis of the early Iron Age (9th–7th centuries BC). Modern Castel Gandolfo derives its name from a castle of the Gandolfi, a Genoese family of the 12th century.

At the north end of the town, overlooking Lake Albano, stands the huge **papal palace** (*not normally open to the public*), designed by Carlo Maderno for Urban VIII in 1624 on the site of the Gandolfi castle. This castle passed first to the Savelli and, in 1596, to the Camera Apostolica. In 1604 it was declared an inalienable domain of the Holy See. After the papal palace was built here, it became the summer residence of the popes, and has been used as such ever since, except for the period from 1870–1929 when the pope was confined to the Vatican (*see p. 90*). Nothing remains of the original castle except some towers and sections of wall. The palace was enlarged by a succession of popes, most recently by Pius IX in the 19th century. Over the main entrance is a clock whose dial is divided into six sections: these are the 'Italian hours'. The hand begins in the segment numbered 1 at sunrise, and reaches number 6 at sunset; all the clock shows is how much daylight is left. The system was widely used in Italy until Napoleon introduced the European clock in 1815.

Joined to the palace is the **Villa Barberini**, built for the family of Urban VIII, whose coat of arms of three bees is everywhere to be seen. The villa stands on the site of the Villa of Domitian, of which traces of nymphaea, cisterns and a small theatre remain (*unfortunately not open to the public*). Since 1936 the villa has been home to the Vatican Observatory, when it moved here from the gardens of the Vatican City. The observatory is one of the most important in Europe which specialises in the study of variable stars.

A short alley to the right of the palace leads to a terrace with a fine view. In the piazza are an elegant fountain and the church of **San Tommaso da Villanova** (1661), with a good cupola designed by Bernini, with stuccoes by Antonio Raggi, similar in concept to those in Sant'Andrea al Quirinale in Rome (*see p. 55*), though the church overall is far inferior. The altarpiece of *St Thomas of Villanova* is by Pietro da Cortona. St Thomas, a Spanish Augustinian friar and bishop of Valencia, noted for his devotion to orphans and the sick, had been canonised in 1658 by Pope Alexander VII, who ordered this church to be built in the new saint's honour.

Below Castel Gandolfo, on the west shores of Lake Albano, is the *emissarium* or **outlet of the lake**, which maintains its waters at a constant level. It is a tunnel cut through the solid rock 1425m long and 1m wide, piercing the rim of the crater and emerging at Le Mole to the southwest. A very early Roman work, traditionally dated before 396 BC, it is said to have been constructed after the oracle of Delphi had declared that the Etruscan city of Veio (*see p. 189*) would not be conquered by Rome until the lake was drained.

Rocca di Papa and Monte Cavo

On the east shore of Lake Albano is **Rocca di Papa** (*map p. 110, C3*) the highest of the Castelli Romani, built up in picturesque terraces on the side of Monte Cavo (949m), the sacred *Mons Albanus* of the Latins, and surrounded by chestnut woods. The upper part of the town is medieval. Running south from the town, a road leads past the sanctuary of the Madonna del Tufo, just beyond which a road diverges left to wind up to the crater of Monte Cavo. A short way up, the perfectly preserved Via Sacra or Via Triumphalis climbs up the hillside to the left, and can be followed on foot for a considerable way. It was built to reach a famous temple sanctuary on the summit, the Temple of Jupiter Latiaris, sanctuary of the Latin League, whose religious festivals, the *feriae latinae*, were celebrated in spring and autumn by the 47 towns of the confederation. Excavations have failed to find any trace of the temple. On the presumed site Henry, Cardinal York built a Passionist convent in 1783, and this later became an observatory. The roadway was also used for the triumphal processions of generals whose feats of arms were not considered important enough for a Triumph along the Sacra Via in Rome.

Ariccia

On the right hand side of the road as you set off toward Ariccia from Albano Laziale is a majestic tomb in the Etruscan style, known as the **Tomb of the Horatii and Curiatii**. According to Livy's history of Rome, the Curiatii were three brothers from Alba Longa whose conflict with three brothers from Rome (the Horatii), would determine the future fate of the two cities. All three Curiatii and two of the Horatii were killed, leaving the remaining Horatius victorious. The tomb has a base, 15m square, made of *peperino* blocks, surmounted by two (originally five) truncated cones. The tomb in fact dates from the late Republican era.

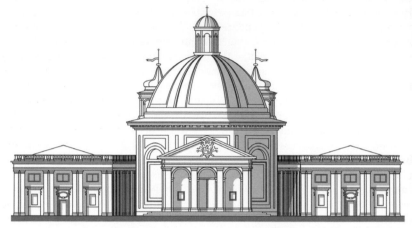

ARICCIA: SANTA MARIA DELL'ASSUNZIONE

Ariccia is in a charming position in wooded country with numerous villas. The town was acquired by the Sienese Chigi family in 1661, and they (chiefly the nephews of Pope Alexander VII) are responsible for the town's finest monuments: the round domed church of **Santa Maria dell'Assunzione** (1664), and Palazzo Chigi, both by Bernini. The church (1662–64) takes the Pantheon in Rome as the inspiration for its design, though everything is pared down to the barest minimum: a rotunda with a portico, but with simple lines, devoid of all decoration. On either side is a square flanking wing, providing an interesting contrast of curved and straight rhythms. Behind rear two bell-towers with squat onion domes, reminiscent of the two 'ass-ears' Bernini added to the Pantheon (*see p. 47*), and for which he was so lampooned.

Palazzo Chigi, in a delightful park, houses a museum of Baroque art formed by the collections of the art historian Maurizio Fagiolo dell'Arco and Fabrizio Lemme, who donated paintings by Cavaliere d'Arpino, Baciccia, Giacinto Brandi and others to the museum in 2007 (*museum open, together with the Stanze del Cardinale, Sat and Sun 10–1.30 & 3–6.30*). The *piano nobile* of the palace is shown on guided tours (*Tues–Fri at 11, 4 & 5.30, and more frequently at weekends: 10.30, 11.30, 12.30, 4, 5, 6 & 7; closed Mon*).

Nemi and Velletri

Nemi is an attractive, quiet little resort with a huge palace in a picturesque position above its beautiful lake, which is surrounded by delightful woods of ilex and manna-ash. There is a well-known painting by Turner of the lake, the ancient *Lacus*

Nemorensis, called also the 'Mirror of Diana', to whom were consecrated the grove and temple on its slopes. It was one of the most celebrated sanctuaries in central Italy, dating probably from the late 4th century BC. Diana was worshipped here with savage rites: only a runaway slave who succeeded in breaking off a branch ('the golden bough') from a certain tree in the grove could be a candidate for the priesthood of Diana, but before becoming the priest-king (*Rex Nemorensis*) he had to kill the reigning priest in single combat. This sinister rule of succession was described by Sir James Frazer in his famous book *The Golden Bough*, first published in 1890. On the lakeside is a vast pavilion erected in 1936 to house the Museo delle Navi Romane (*open daily 9–6.30; best approached by the road from Genzano*). It contains models of two huge Roman ships built by Caligula in AD 41 to convey visitors across the lake for the festival of Diana. The ships were sunk at the time of Claudius, and they were located at the bottom of the lake in 1446 by Leon Battista Alberti, but only salvaged in 1932 when the lake was partly drained. Conveyed to the museum, they were totally destroyed when German soldiers burnt them on 1st June 1944. Beneath the museum floor can be seen stretches of the Roman road which led to the Sanctuary of Diana.

The busy town of **Velletri** (*map p. 110, C3*) has a largely modern appearance, having been reconstructed after serious damage in the Second World War. Formerly the Volscian *Velester*, subjugated by Rome in 338 BC and called *Velitrae*, it was the home of the *gens* Octavia, of which Augustus was a member, and later became an independent commune from c. 1000–1549, when it was absorbed in the Papal States. It is worth visiting today for its good archaeological museum (*open 9–1 & 3–7 except Mon and major holidays*), with a splendid Roman sarcophagus complete with its lid. The cathedral (whose bishop is Dean of the Sacred College of Cardinals) has a Cosmatesque tabernacle surmounting the baldacchino over the high altar, and 14th-century frescoes on the lower walls of the apse. The cathedral museum preserves a number of important treasures, including Madonnas by Gentile da Fabriano and Antoniazzo Romano.

FRASCATI

Frascati (*map p. 110, B2–C2*), famed for its villas and gardens and for its wine, stands in a beautiful position on the northwest slopes of the Alban Hills. It was overshadowed by Tusculum (*see p. 130 below*) in Roman days. A small village in the Middle Ages, it expanded in 1191, when the inhabitants of Tusculum, after the destruction of their city, moved to the area around the ancient churches of Santa Maria and San Sebastiano in Frascata. Later it was a feudal holding, and at the beginning of the 16th century, it was taken by the Holy See, at which time it was adorned with the villas and gardens of powerful cardinals and prelates. Henry, Cardinal York, brother of Bonnie Prince Charlie, was bishop of Frascati, and died here in 1807. Over 80 per cent of its buildings were destroyed or damaged in the Second World War, when it was the army headquarters of the German field marshal Albrecht Kesselring, and was heavily bombed by the Allies early in September 1943.

Villa Aldobrandini

The huge Piazza Marconi is dominated by Villa Aldobrandini, the finest of Frascati's villas, splendidly sited on a hill above the square. It was designed on a vast scale by Giacomo della Porta and built by Carlo Maderno in 1598–1603 for Cardinal Pietro Aldobrandini, and is still owned by the family. The villa lies in the centre of its terraces and commands a view of distant Rome, where its owner's power and influence lay. Only the gardens are open to the public (*9–dusk except weekends*).

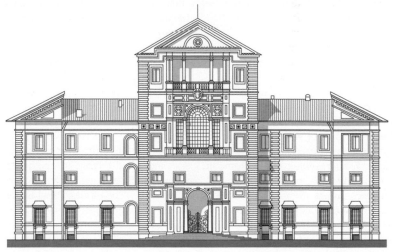

FRASCATI: VILLA ALDOBRANDINI

The gardens were completed in 1621, under the direction of Carlo Maderno, who was assisted in the creation of the waterworks by Giovanni Fontana and Orazio Olivieri (Olivieri had also worked at the Villa d'Este in Tivoli). It is an early Baroque garden; Edith Wharton described it as 'the first stage of the Baroque before that school had found its formula', and it illustrates the move towards spectacle and large-scale dramatic effects that characterise the style.

Gates lead from the original entrance into an avenue of clipped ilex. In front of the villa rise three terraces with symmetrically curving steps; two original fountains in the form of small ships (*barchette*) remain on the lowest level. The essential retaining wall behind the villa, which allows it to sit on a level terrace, is developed into the **Water Theatre**, an elaborate amphitheatre with five statues in niches fronted by water jets. Shaded by the villa, cooled by the fountains and with semi-subterranean rooms, this provided not only a magnificent display but also a delightful retreat in hot summer weather. The central figure of *Atlas* holding the globe is said to be a portrait of Pope Clement VIII, uncle of Pietro Aldobrandini. Below him is the head of *Tantalus*, who was punished for revealing the secrets of the gods by not being allowed to quench his thirst. The waterfall that washes over them drops off a steep water staircase (*scaletta d'acqua*) of eight steps, at the top of which are the **'Pillars of Hercules'**, decorated with mosaics incorporating symbols relating to the Cardinal, which perfectly frame the villa when viewed from the upper garden. Water runs down them in spiral grooves. The side niches of the theatre are occupied by Polyphemus playing pipes and a centaur playing a horn. Seeing the garden in a deteriorated state at the turn of the 20th century, Edith Wharton wasn't as impressed as John Evelyn had been in 1645. In common with other English visitors, he had delighted in the great variety and ingenuity of its waterworks (*giochi d'acqua*). The provision of water must have cost as much as building the villa, but Pope Clement received the aqueduct/pipeline which provided it as a gift.

ITALIAN RENAISSANCE GARDENS

The great gardens of the late 16th and early 17th centuries were about show and spectacle, rather than being places of retreat and contemplation. This may seem surprising given that many were commissioned by men of the Church. But it was a time when the Catholic Church was re-affirming its power, during the Counter-Reformation, and displays of wealth and grandeur were one way of demonstrating to the populace that the Roman Church was the door to the Kingdom of Heaven.

The typical site chosen for a garden was a sloping hillside with a commanding view, which also allowed the extensive estate to be seen rising impressively from below. Architects were involved in the design of the whole site, placing the house at its centre, and used terracing, perspective and illusion to achieve impressive effects. At Vignanello, for example (*see p. 175*), Ottavia Orsini had the entire hillside beyond her house banked up to the same level as the ground floor. On this bank she planted her formal garden, in such a way that it would be directly accessible from the house, and visible to stunning effect from the rooms of the *piano nobile*. When slopes were not banked up into a parterre in this way, practical solutions for levelling them were incorporated into decorative schemes, for example amphitheatres and terraces.

The garden was no longer kept enclosed within its boundaries, but reached out into the landscape, incorporating it by focusing avenues on outside viewpoints and bringing features such as wooded hillsides into the garden. The natural growth of these wooded hillsides was used as a backdrop to the more formal areas. Water was brought to the site where it did not exist, and was extravagantly used (*see box on p. 139*). Alongside the formal garden, where hedges were clipped into geometric forms and no flowering plants were permitted, a *giardino segreto* (secret or private garden), usually with a view, was included. This would be in a secluded site, and here the owner of the garden would arrange flowers in tubs (the flower bed as we know it did not exist), and hang cages full of songbirds. Nature was still confined, but not excluded altogether. The secret garden would become a favourite trysting place, somewhere to stroll and to enjoy the sunshine.　　S.J.

The garden above the water staircase contains two rustic fountains at different levels on the wooded slope. The whole watercourse gushes from the upper one, the **Fountain of the Shepherds** (it is not a natural spring but is fed instead by a reservoir). The further one gets from the house, the less formal the garden becomes. This is the part of the garden Edith Wharton liked: 'it merits all the attention that has been wasted on its pompous theatre'.

Many original features are now lost. The Hall of Apollo, at one end of the water theatre, remains but figures of the gods and the statue of Pegasus once on the huge Mount Parnassus water feature have gone, as have the effects of rain, birdsong, organ music and a ball balanced on a jet of water so enjoyed by 17th-century visitors, and which John Evelyn describes in detail, speaking of the cave next to the nymphaeum as an '*artificial grotto, wherein are curious rocks, hydraulic organs and all sorts of singing birds, moving and chirping by the force of the water, with several pageants and surprising inventions. In the centre of one of these rooms rises a copper ball that continually dances about three foot above the pavement by virtue of a wind conveyed secretly to a hole beneath it, with many devices to wet the unwary spectators...*' Several paintings on themes from Ovid that were once on the walls of the Hall of Apollo are now in the National Gallery, London. The garden was influential on later developments in garden design, both in Italy and further afield. The Villa Torlonia nearby (now a public park) had an even more monumental water staircase; and the 18th-century cascades at Chiswick and at Chatsworth in England both owe a debt to the Aldobrandini version.

The duomo and Gesù

The **duomo** preserves most of its façade (1697–1700) by Girolamo Fontana (nephew of Carlo Fontana), in a striking mix of travertine and local volcanic stone. The unattractive bell-towers are a later addition. The interior has an interesting plan by Mascherino, dating from 1598. To the left of the main door is the cenotaph of Prince Charles Edward, Bonnie Prince Charlie (d. 1788), who was buried here before his body was moved to the Vatican Grottoes. The **church of the Gesù**, attributed to Pietro da Cortona, has a magnificent *trompe l'oeil* dome by Andrea Pozzo.

Other villas surrounded by gardens on the outskirts of Frascati include the Villa Falconieri, enlarged by Borromini; Villa Tuscolana, also a hotel (*see p. 156*), and Villa Mondragone, built in 1573 for the Altemps family by Martino Longhi the Elder, who also built the Palazzo Altemps in Rome. Pope Gregory XIII often came to the villa as a guest of the Altemps: it was here that he set in motion the reform of the calendar. William Dean Howells, recording his visit to the villa in 1908, remarks that it was given 365 windows in honour of the number of days in the Gregorian year. All the villas can be visited by prior appointment (*T: 06 9454 9045*).

TUSCULUM & GROTTAFERRATA

Tusculum (*map p. 110, C2*) was an Etruscan centre and became famous in the Imperial period as a resort for wealthy Romans, who built numerous villas here. The most celebrated was Cicero's villa, called the *Tusculanum*, where his books of Stoic philosophy, the *Tusculan Disputations*, were supposed to have been written. The ruins include an elegant little theatre and an overgrown amphitheatre. In 1191 the Romans destroyed Tusculum in revenge for their defeat a quarter of a century before, in 1167, when Tusculum had allied itself with the Holy Roman Emperor Frederick Barbarossa against Rome and the papacy. The inhabitants of Tusculum founded a new centre at Frascati, originally, it is said, consisting of huts built of thin branches (*frasche*), hence 'Frascati'.

Grottaferrata (*map p. 110, B3*), south of Frascati, has an important abbey enclosed by massive walls. It was founded by St Nilus, a Greek abbot who died here in 1004, and built by his disciple St Bartholomew, who was a composer of Greek hymns and wrote a biography of the founder. Some 26 Basilian monks still live here: they are Roman Catholics who celebrate according to the Byzantine Greek rite. It has an interesting museum (*for admission, T: 9454 9045*) with a miscellany of works of art including a beautiful Classical Greek stele dating from c. 420 BC showing a seated male figure reading from a scroll; 13th-century detached frescoes; a 15th-century French statue of the *Madonna and Child*; and precious illuminated manuscripts. The church has a mosaic above the 11th-century wooden portal, and inside a Byzantine mosaic of the *Apostles* dating from the 13th century. Off the south aisle opens the Cappella Farnesiana, with frescoes (1609–10) of the lives of Sts Nilus and Bartholomew by Domenichino, masterpieces of his narrative style, and considered by many to be his finest works. They were commissioned by Odoardo Farnese and greatly admired by artists and travellers over the centuries. To the right of the entrance is *St Nilus Before the Crucifix*, and *St Nilus Averting a Tempest*. Inside the chapel to the left is *St Nilus with the Emperor Otho III* (the page holding the emperor's horse is Domenichino, and the figures on the right of the horse are Guido Reni and Guercino). On the right, St Bartholomew is shown averting the fall of a pillar during the building of the convent; on the end wall (left of the altar), is the *Exorcism of the Devil* and (right) the *Virgin Presenting a Golden Apple to Sts Nilus and Bartholomew*; in the lunette, *Death of St Nilus*; in the triumphal arch, *Annunciation*. The altarpiece of the *Madonna and Child*, with the two founders, is by Annibale Carracci, who had initially recommended Domenichino to Odoardo Farnese.

At the end of a long drive lined with pots of camellias, the **Villa Grazioli** is an interesting building of 1580 in a spectacular site with panoramic views. It has been beautifully restored as a 4-star hotel (*see p. 156; open to visitors on request from reception*), and retains its period furnishings and a frescoed *galleria* from 1736.

PALESTRINA

Palestrina (*map p. 110, C2*) is a small town (pop. 11,500) on the slopes of Monte Ginestro, a spur of the Monti Prenestini. It is famous for its huge Sanctuary of Fortune, a masterpiece of Roman architecture, which is still the dominant feature in the townscape. The very fine collection in the town's archaeological museum illustrates its ancient importance.

HISTORY OF PALESTRINA

One of the oldest towns of Lazio, ancient Palestrina was a thriving place from as early as the 7th century BC up until the Roman era. In the golden age of Rome 'cool Praeneste', as Horace called it, became a retreat of the patricians from the heat of the summer. The influence of its famous sanctuary survived until the 4th century AD. In the Middle Ages a town called Città Prenestina was built over the abandoned sanctuary. This town was occupied by the Lombards in 752, later passing to the counts of Tusculum and in 1043 to the Colonna. During the feuds between Guelphs and Ghibellines it was several times destroyed and rebuilt. In 1630 Francesco Colonna sold the town to Carlo Barberini, brother of Urban VIII. Its most famous native was Giovanni Pierluigi da Palestrina, the father of polyphonic music. Thomas Mann spent two summers here in 1878–98, with his brother Heinrich, during which he wrote most of I Buddenbrook.

Palazzo Colonna Barberini and the museum

The Archaeological Museum and the parts of the Sanctuary of Fortune open to the public (open daily 9–8) are entered from the top of the hill through Palazzo Colonna Barberini, built over the highest part of the sanctuary. The palace façade reflects the shape of the ancient theatre or hemicycle, and the approach steps are in fact the (restored) seats of the cavea (the scena would have been a temporary construction erected for each performance).

The palace interior incorporates the foundations of the round (reconstructed) temple which crowned the sanctuary. Although many antiquities from Praeneste are now in the Villa Giulia in Rome and other museums, the collection here offers as complete a picture as possible of local civilisation from the 8th century BC–4th century AD. The large **fragment of a statue of Fortune** in grey Oriental marble was found at the bottom of the well in front of the eastern hemicycle. Sculpture from the Augustan era includes an exquisitely carved curving relief (probably once part of a fountain) representing a wild boar with her litter, particularly interesting for the sculptor's skill in using high and very low relief to produce the effect of spatial depth. There is also a finely carved sarcophagus illustrating the myth of Endymion, and several good portrait heads. A room off the entrance displays the only known group of the **Capitoline Triad**: the three tutelary deities of Rome, Jupiter, Juno and Minerva seated together on a ceremonial throne. This dates from AD 160–180, but was only discovered in 1992 when it was confiscated by the Italian state from the hands of a private dealer. On the floor above are some magnificent examples of the numerous **cylindrical cistae** (bronze caskets used as 'vanity cases'), with incised decorations and small bronze statue groups on their lids, produced here by local craftsmen and of a type seldom found elsewhere. The bronze mirrors are also beautifully decorated. Another room has a display of very unusual stone tomb markers.

The Hellenistic 'Nile' mosaic (c. 100 BC) in the archaeological museum at Palestrina.

A room at the top of the building displays the museum's greatest treasure, the celebrated 'Barberini' or **'Nile' mosaic**, in muted polychrome, found in the town (near the
cathedral) at the end of the 16th or beginning of the 17th century: it is one of the largest
Hellenistic mosaics to have survived, and is one of the most extraordinary works of art
in all Italy, which engages you at once and invites you to pause at length to study the
details. Dated to c. 100 BC, it is thought to be the work of Alexandrian mosaicists. The
Nile is shown flowing in flood, from its source in the mountains of Ethiopia to the Delta,
through a mass of animal, bird and fish life, all of which is depicted in fine detail. The
upper part of the mosaic shows wild Egypt, a region of cataracts and deserts, with
hunters gathering exotic animals, possibly for the royal game park in Alexandria.
Further down is a sacred precinct, with pillars, towers and statues; to the left near a
building with obelisks is a well, perhaps that of Aswan which helped Eratosthenes to
calculate the meridian. In the foreground is the Canopus of Alexandria, with the
Serapeum to the right. The coming of the Macedonian Greeks is reflected in these
scenes, with a group of warriors in front of the Serapeum and another group of Greeks
enjoying their leisure at a banquet on a canal shaded with vines. The mosaic provides a
direct link to Hellenistic Egypt, and it has been argued that the choice of the Nile is to
stress a link between the Egyptian goddess Isis and the Roman goddess Fortuna (there
are Roman statues from the early centuries AD which show Isis arrayed as Fortuna). The

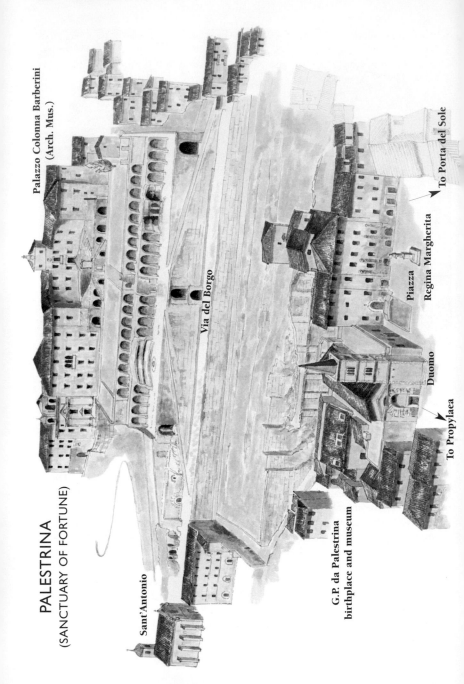

PALESTRINA
(SANCTUARY OF FORTUNE)

Palazzo Colonna Barberini
(Arch. Mus.)

Via del Borgo

Sant'Antonio

To Porta del Sole

Piazza
Regina Margherita

Duomo

To Propylaea

G.P. da Palestrina
birthplace and museum

scientific precision with which the river and its wildlife are portrayed appears to reflect the Alexandrian interest in geography and botany. It is assumed that the mosaic was an original commission of one of the Ptolemaic kings, perhaps to stress their involvement in the patronage of learning. Also in this room is a scale model of the sanctuary (*see below*).

THE CULT OF FORTUNA PRIMIGENIA

The sanctuary dedicated to Fortuna Primigenia at ancient Praeneste was the largest in Italy. Here Fortuna, the ancient goddess of Chance or Good Luck, the Greek Tyche, introduced to Rome by the Etruscan king Servius Tullius, had her oracle. Fortuna was associated with success in almost every sphere of life, from a good harvest to victory in war and the achievements of Rome itself. The Praeneste oracle was dedicated to the goddess in her role as First Bearer, able to direct the lives of the first-born towards achievement, but from the 2nd century it became linked to the victorious expansion of Rome into the Greek world of the East. The cult was connected with an oracle which claimed to foretell the future by delivering to enquirers *sortes*, or lots, which were pieces of wood with letters carved on them.

The original oracle site, a spring gushing from a grotto, was already enveloped in buildings, but in the late 2nd or early 1st century BC an ambitious construction programme began. It may have been initiated as late as 82 BC by the military dictator Sulla after he had captured the city from his rival, Marius. His destruction of much of the original city certainly cleared land for the expansion of the shrine, and the glorification of the site may be seen as an expression of his own 'good fortune'.

The project was to create, above the earlier sanctuary, a vast superstructure of terraces, ramps and colonnades crested by a columned exedra. This exploited Praeneste's magnificent setting so that, like the Greek temples of Sicily, it could be seen from a distance. The models were the vast building projects of the Hellenistic kings whose kingdoms the Romans had absorbed. The grandiose buildings of Alexandria, now long lost, may have been the inspiration, but much of the design was revolutionary. The Greek orders were broken up and reassembled in a style which can only be called 'baroque', while that quintessential Roman invention, the arch, was used with great effect to give further order to the whole. The complex is the earliest example of a Roman building with an overall plan, but is so vast that this is only gradually revealed to the onlooker as he ascends each terrace. The great imperial baths and the massive Forum of Trajan in Rome are its successors.

The idea of a series of terraces linked to each other became an important part of Renaissance garden design, as can be seen at the Villa d'Este in Tivoli (*see p. 138*). The 19th-century monument to Vittorio Emanuele II in the centre of Rome also drew on Praeneste as a model; but without an elevated position it overwhelms its setting.   C.F.

The sanctuary

The Sanctuary of Fortuna Primigenia, mentioned by Cicero, is a colossal monumental edifice laid out in a series of terraces conforming to the slope of the hill and connected by ramps and staircases converging towards a temple on the summit. With a quadrangular plan 118m square, and dedicated jointly to Fortuna and Juno, it is the most grandiose Hellenistic edifice in Italy, and has an important place in the history of architecture since it is one of the earliest instances in which concrete was used by the Romans as a building material in vaulting. Its unique concept and design did not, however, have a direct influence on later Roman buildings. It probably dates from around 130–100 BC.

The parts of the sanctuary at present open to the public are entered from a gate across the road from the museum, although it was designed to be approached from below (*a second entrance on Via Sant'Antonio is open Fri–Sun 10–dusk*). The top terrace was originally a courtyard with side porticoes in front of the cavea of the theatre. The central staircase descends to the next level, with a colonnade stretching the width of the sanctuary. The monumental staircase continues down to another terrace which is supported by a wall and divided into halves by a central staircase. Over the hemicycles was a coffered vault carried on Ionic columns, part of which is still in place. This was the shrine of the oracle, and the *sortes* (*see box on previous page*) were extracted from the well here. The view from the terrace is splendid: to the west is Rome, to the south the Monti Lepini and to the southwest the Roman Campagna can be seen stretching as far as the sea.

Two great ramps (formerly covered) constructed on rubble lead down to the great polygonal wall at the foot of the sanctuary (on Via del Borgo). When the town was bombed in 1944, the houses here were destroyed and so it was possible to clear this area. Below are two terraces and the level of the forum beside the duomo. Outside the Porta del Sole, where parts of cyclopean walls can be seen, excavations are in progress.

The town

A wall made with large blocks of tufa in the 2nd century BC supported the first terrace of the city, and remains of its monumental entrance, the propylaea, survive. The central Piazza Regina Margherita occupies the site of the ancient forum on another terrace above. On the square stands the duomo, built over a pagan Roman edifice in tufa in the 5th century and dedicated to St Agapitus, who was born here and martyred in 274. There are ancient remains in the crypt and piazza outside, where, in a sacred area there are fragments of a mosaic with fish (*open Fri, Sat and Sun 9–dusk*). In a small apsidal hall here the famous Nile Mosaic, now in the museum (*see p. 133 above*), was discovered.

The birthplace of Giovanni Pierluigi da Palestrina, near the church of Sant'Antonio to the northwest, is now a study centre with a small museum (*open 9.20–12.30 except Mon*).

TIVOLI

After Rome, Tivoli (*map p. 110, C2*) is probably the most visited place in all Lazio. A busy small town (pop. 52,000), surrounded by ugly high-rise buildings, and noisy with traffic, it is nevertheless justly famous for the gardens of the Villa d'Este in the town centre, and below the hill, protected by a beautiful park, for the magnificent ruins of Hadrian's Villa, one of the most important archaeological sites in Italy.

The Roman town of *Tibur* was built in this delightful cool position on the lower slopes of the Sabine Hills at the end of the valley of the Aniene, which narrows into a gorge and forms spectacular cascades. Its waters were carried to Rome by two aqueducts, the Anio Vetus (70km), begun in 273 BC, and the Anio Novus (95km) begun in AD 36. By the end of the 1st century BC numerous wealthy Romans came to live or pass the summer here. Temples were erected to Vesta, Hercules and other deities. Augustus and the poets Catullus, Propertius and Horace were frequent visitors. Trajan also favoured Tibur, but it reached its greatest fame when Hadrian chose it as his residence and built his remarkable villa on the outskirts. Tibur was sacred to the cult of the Sibyl Albunea. Later it was used for the confinement of state prisoners.

VILLA D'ESTE

HISTORY OF THE VILLA D'ESTE

Originally a Benedictine convent, the property was confiscated as a residence for the governor of Tivoli. The most famous of these was Cardinal Ippolito II d'Este. Son of Lucrezia Borgia and grandson of Pope Alexander VI, Ippolito had himself hoped for the papacy, and was disappointed when the Bishop of Palestrina was elected (Julius III). Nevertheless, Ippolito was wealthy and cultivated, a great collector and patron of the arts. When Pope Julius made him governor of Tivoli in 1550, he commissioned Pirro Ligorio to transform the convent into a sumptuous villa. The district of the town below the convent was destroyed and the hillside was levelled to provide space for the gardens. An underground conduit was constructed from the Aniene, to increase the water supply. The use of water as the main theme of the gardens may have been inspired by Hadrian's Villa, and the plan, based on a series of terraces, is similar to that of the Temple of Fortune at Palestrina (*see p. 135*). The work had not been completed by the time of the Cardinal's death in 1572, and it was continued by his successor, Cardinal Luigi d'Este, who employed Flaminio Ponzio after 1585.

Additions and restorations were carried out in the 17th century, in part by Bernini. In the 19th century the villa and gardens were neglected, and all the Roman statues were sold. It passed by bequest to Austria; and after 1918 to the Italian government, which undertook a general restoration. The top floor was the Italian home of Franz Liszt from 1865 to 1886, the year of his death; while here, he composed the third book of his *Années de Pèlerinage*, in which one of the most popular pieces is 'Les Jeux d'Eau à la Villa d'Este'. A fine Roman mosaic pavement was found beneath the villa in 1983.

The gardens

The famous gardens of the Villa d'Este (*open 8.30–dusk except Mon; T: 0774 312 070*) were largely created by Pirro Ligorio in the 1560s. Filled with the sound of water (and in spring and summer with the scent of orange and lemon blossom), they are built on terraces which descend from the villa, connected by steps and delightful paths which lead to numerous fountains and grottoes. The original vegetation (which included mostly plane trees and elms) was altered when evergreens (ilexes, pines and cypresses) were introduced in the 17th century, and sequoia and cedars were planted in the 19th century.

The entrance leads into a courtyard designed in 1567 on the site of the former cloister. The **Fountain of Venus** incorporates a Roman statue. In front of the garden-facing façade is a terrace, filled with the sound of water. In the centre is an elegant loggia (1567) on two storeys, connected to the terraced gardens by a double flight of steps.

In the centre of the gardens is the **Fontana del Bicchierone** (1661) by Bernini. From here a path leads down to the elaborate **Fontana di Roma**, designed by Pirro Ligorio and executed by Curzio Maccarone. This has numerous fountains and sculptures including a model of the Tiber with an islet (representing the Isola Tiberina) in the form of a boat, on which is an obelisk, a seated statue of *Rome*, the wolf suckling Romulus and Remus, and miniature reproductions of the principal buildings of ancient Rome. Originally it also sported a depiction of the Tivoli gorge and River Aniene, by Orazio Olivieri, but this is now sadly lost.

From here the **Viale delle Cento Fontane** leads right across the garden, parallel to the villa. It is skirted by a long narrow basin lined with hundreds of jets of water, surmounted by a frieze of obelisks, models of boats, the eagles and lilies of the Este coat of arms, overgrown with maidenhair fern and moss. At the far end, against the perimeter wall of the gardens, in a courtyard shaded by four splendid old trees, is the grandiose **Fontana di Tivoli** or *dell'Ovato*, by Pirro Ligorio, with the end of the conduit from the Aniene, which descends in an abundant cascade in the middle of a hemicycle which used to be decorated with statues of nymphs, by Giovanni Battista della Porta.

Beyond an archway, a path between two marble columns leads to the monumental **Fontana dell'Organo**, built around a water-operated organ (1568; later protected by a little temple). This was one of the most original and famous features of the garden. Its mechanism has been restored, and it is played at 12.30 every day.

Below here is the Viale del Drago, in the middle of which is the **Fontana del Drago** by Pirro Ligorio. This was probably intended as a homage to Gregory XIII (it reproduces the dragons in his coat of arms), who was a guest at the villa in 1572. Continuing straight along the Viale, crossing the Scala dei Bollori (an ingenious water staircase designed in 1567 but at present dry), you come to the other side of the gardens and the bizarre **Fontana della Civetta**, which once used water power to produce birdsong interrupted by the screech of an owl. It was begun in 1565 by Giovanni del Duca, and finished by Raffaello Sangallo in 1569. Next to it is the Fontana di Proserpina (1570), which was used as an outside dining room.

In the lower gardens are three fishponds, from where there is a splendid view of unspoilt countryside. In the centre of the perimeter wall, decorated with glorious climbing roses, is the **Fontana della Madre Natura**, with a statue of Diana of Ephesus, the great nature goddess. Nearby is the Rotonda dei Cipressi, surrounded by some of the mightiest cypresses in Italy (three survive, albeit propped up, from the 17th century).

WATER FEATURES IN ITALIAN RENAISSANCE GARDENS

Not content with a simple natural stream or spring, the Renaissance garden owners of Italy commissioned the development of a great range of splendid water effects—and those whose estates had no natural source of water went to the huge expense of bringing it in by pipeline or aqueduct. Sometimes the whole hillside was turned into a water park, as was the case here at the Villa d'Este, and many gardens contained a collection of different water features.

Cascades poured an impressive flow of water over a drop, as in the fountain of Tivoli (or the *Fontana dell'Ovato*), created at the Villa d'Este in the 1560s. Water staircases, where the water tumbled down a stepped watercourse, were created at, for example, Villa d'Este, Villa Lante (*see p. 173*) and Villa Aldobrandini (*see p. 128*). Water theatres, or nymphaea, were large structures with niches for statues, incorporating a theatrical display of water jets, fountains or cascades, as at the Villa Aldobrandini. The garden owners and visitors also loved their water tricks or jokes, the *giochi d'acqua*, which produced moving effects or even sound effects by the flow of water; artificial birds produced birdsong and organs played tunes; others were designed to surprise the unsuspecting visitor with a thorough drenching, and were hugely popular. Unfortunately—or perhaps fortunately—few of these remain today.

In addition to all these, there was the development of elaborate fountains. 'What pleases me… in these new fountains is the variety of ways with which they guide, divide, turn, lead, break, and at one movement cause water to descend and at another time to rise' said the writer Claudio Tolomei (1543). The novelty and excitement of 16th-century Italian fountains were created by the collaboration of a designer/sculptor, a hydraulic engineer who brought the water supply to the site, and a *fontaniero*, the man who made the fountain structure and constructed its plumbing. In complex and elaborate schemes of waterworks, many *fontanieri* might be employed at once. Other technicians specialised in water-powered automata and *giochi d'acqua*. The technology spread to the great gardens of France and elsewhere in Europe. In fact, the most famous water engineer working throughout Europe, including England, was a Frenchman, Salomon de Caus (1576–1626), who was influenced early in his career by Buontalenti. He wrote an influential treatise on hydraulics: *Les raisons des forces mouvantes* (*The Principles of Moving Forces*). S.J.

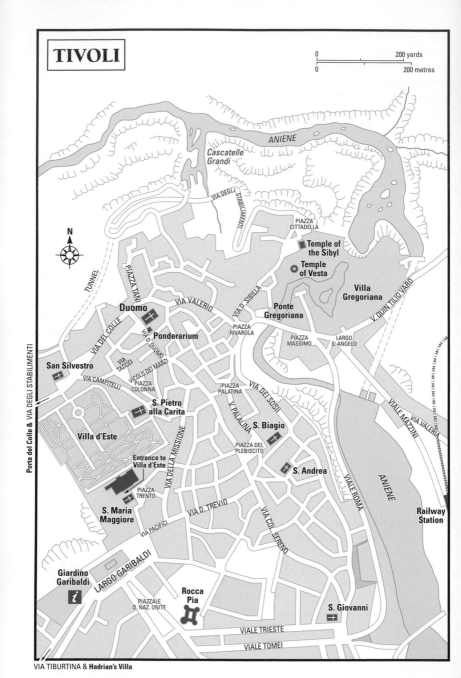

TIVOLI

0   200 yards

0   200 metres

ANIENE

Cascatelle Grandi

VIA DEGLI STABILIMENTI

PIAZZA CITTADELLA

Temple of the Sibyl

Temple of Vesta

Villa Gregoriana

N

TUNNEL

PIAZZA TANI

VIA VALERIO

VIA D. SIBILLA

Ponte Gregoriana

V. QUIN TILIO VARO

Duomo

VIA DEL COLLE

VIA D. DUOMO

Ponderarium

PIAZZA RIVAROLA

PIAZZA MASSIMO

LARGO S. ANGELO

San Silvestro

VIA TADDEI

VICOLO DEI MARZI

VIA CAMPITELLI

PIAZZA COLONNA

PIAZZA PALATINA

VIA DEI SOSII

S. Pietro alla Carita

V. PALATINA

S. Biagio

VIALE MAZZINI

VIA VALERIA

Villa d'Este

VIA DELLA MISSIONE

PIAZZA DEL PLEBISCITO

Entrance to Villa d'Este

S. Andrea

PIAZZA TRENTO

VIALE ROMA

ANIENE

S. Maria Maggiore

VIA D. TREVIO

VIA COL. SERENO

Railway Station

VIA PACIFICI

Giardino Garibaldi

LARGO GARIBALDI

Rocca Pia

S. Giovanni

PIAZZALE D. NAZ. UNITE

VIALE TRIESTE

VIALE TOMEI

Porta del Colle & VIA DEGLI STABILIMENTI

VIA TIBURTINA & Hadrian's Villa

The interior of the villa

The *Appartamento Nobile* on the ground floor is a series of rooms off a long corridor, overlooking the gardens. The largest room is the *Salone*, with the Fontana di Tivoli, a wall-fountain in mosaic, begun by Curzio Maccarone and completed in 1568 by Paolo Calandrino. The frescoes are by the school of Girolamo Muziano and Federico Zuccari. On the walls are views of the garden painted by Matteo Neroni in 1568. The two rooms behind the fountain were decorated by Cesare Nebbia and assistants, and the rooms on the other side of the *Salone* have frescoes by Federico Zuccari and assistants. The *Sala della Caccia* has 17th-century frescoes. Stairs lead up to a series of rooms, part of the *Appartamento Vecchio*, with ceiling frescoes by Livio Agresti, and a balcony overlooking the gardens. The chapel was frescoed in 1572 by the workshop of Federico Zuccari.

THE TOWN CENTRE

In the piazza outside the villa is the Romanesque church of **Santa Maria Maggiore**, with a handsome rose window attributed to Angelo da Tivoli above a later Gothic narthex (which contains a 13th-century fresco of the *Madonna and Child*, in a fine tabernacle). The interior contains remains of the original floor at the east end. In the presbytery are two triptychs: the one on the right dates from the 16th century, and the one on the left is signed by Bartolomeo Bulgarini of Siena (14th century). Above the latter is a *Madonna and Child* by Iacopo Torriti. Over the high altar is a Byzantine *Madonna* (perhaps dating from the 12th century); in the right aisle there is a Crucifix attributed to Baccio da Montelupo. Ippolito II d'Este was buried in the church.

The centre of town is Piazza del Plebiscito, with its daily market. Here is the church of **San Biagio**, founded in the 14th century. Rebuilt in 1887, the interior is a remarkable example of the neo-Gothic style, with three impressive stained-glass windows (replaced in 1950 after their destruction in the Second World War). On the second south altar is a good 15th-century painting of *St Vincent*. Behind the altar is a 15th-century detached fresco of the *Crucifixion*. Off the north side are interesting fresco fragments of the *Madonna Enthroned* and the *Glory of St Thomas*.

From Piazza del Plebiscito, Via Palatina leads down to **Piazza Palatina** with the fine Palazzo Bonfiglietti, incorporating numerous Roman fragments, including six columns low down on its façade. In the adjoining Piazza dell'Erbe is an old fountain and an ancient house which has part of a Roman statue supporting the masonry on the corner. Via Ponte Gregoriana, with a view of the hilly countryside outside the town, leads to Piazza Rivarola beside Ponte Gregoriana over the Aniene, with picturesque waterfalls and a fine view of the Temple of Vesta (*see overleaf*).

In Piazza Tani there is a huge sarcophagus serving as a wall fountain, and a side entrance to the **duomo** (San Lorenzo), rebuilt in 1650 but retaining a Romanesque campanile of the 12th century. In the interior, the fourth chapel in the south aisle (light on right) contains a beautiful 13th-century group of five carved wooden figures representing the *Descent from the Cross*. The third chapel in the north aisle has a superb mid-15th-century silver and gilt construction, called the '*Macchina del*

Salvatore', made by silversmiths from Lucca to enclose a precious 11th- or 12th-century triptych, painted in tempera (now exhibited only on high religious festivals on the adjoining altar).

From the little Piazza Duomo, the medieval Via del Duomo (partly stepped) leads past the entrance to the **Ponderarium** (no. 78; *at present closed to the public*), the office which controlled weights and measures, containing two tables with measures of capacity, used by the Roman inspectors. Via del Colle leads west past the Romanesque church of San Silvestro to Via degli Stabilimenti. A short way along it on the left is the entrance to the site of the **Sanctuary of Hercules Victor**, in a large area until recently occupied by a paper mill. It is being excavated and studied and there are long-term plans to open it to the public (*for information, T: 0774 330329*). This huge Hellenistic sanctuary is mentioned by Classical authors as being the most important in the city. There was an oracle here similar to the one in Palestrina (*see p. 135*). The buildings are thought to date from the end of the 2nd century BC. The most conspicuous remains are the Cyclopean substructures to the northwest where the hill descends to the Aniene valley. Above the mighty foundations are arches and vaults which supported a huge square, with a portico on three sides, a temple and a theatre. A market was connected to the sanctuary.

Temple of Vesta and Temple of the Sibyl

The picturesque Via della Sibilla, with interesting houses, leads to a little secluded piazza beside a restaurant, already famous in the 19th century (*see p. 157*). Here is an entrance to the Villa Gregoriana, beside the so-called **Temple of Vesta**, a circular Roman temple famous for its picturesque position above the Aniene valley, frequently drawn and painted by travellers in the 18th and 19th centuries. It is not known to whom the temple was actually dedicated; it is circular peripteral and dates from the last years of the Republic. It was converted in the Middle Ages into the church of Santa Maria della Rotonda. Ten of its 18 fluted Corinthian columns survive, and there is a frieze of bucrania, garlands, rosettes and *paterae*. The doors and windows of the well-preserved cella are trapezoidal. Close by is an earlier temple, known as the **Temple of the Sibyl**, also of uncertain attribution. Until 1884 it was the church of San Giorgio. The road ends in Piazza della Cittadella, the site of the Roman acropolis, and to the left a lane leads out to the edge of the cliff which dominates the valley.

Villa Gregoriana

Open daily except Monday 10–one hour before dusk (from Dec–Feb only by appointment); T: 06 3996 7701. If the main entrance on the far side of Ponte Gregoriano near the large Piazza Massimo and bus station is closed, it is entered from the gate by the Temple of the Sibyl.

The Villa Gregoriana is a park on a very steep hillside, with the cascades of the river Aniene extending all the way down to the floor of the valley. The name of the park commemorates Gregory XVI, who took decisive steps to put an end to the periodic local floods, which in 1826 had seriously damaged the town. On his accession to the papacy in 1831, he instructed the engineer Folchi to build a double tunnel under Monte Catillo, to ease the flow of the river. From this tunnel (300m and 270m), known as the Traforo Gregoriano, which bears inscriptions recording the visits of popes and kings, the water plunges down in another waterfall, known as the **Great Cascade**. From the park there are views of the Temples of Vesta and of the Sibyl across the valley. Steep paths cover the hillside, providing views of the various cascades, and from a terrace you can see the mouth of the tunnel where the Aniene emerges to make a leap of 108m. In other parts of the park there are also remains of a Roman villa, the fantastic **Grotto of the Siren**, a limestone cavern in which the water tumbles down a narrow ravine, and the **Grotto of Neptune**, through which the Aniene originally flowed.

Beside Villa Gregoriana, Via Quintilio Varo leads to Via delle Cascatelle (3km long), which winds above olive plantations and passes several times beneath the viaducts of the Rome–Tivoli railway. From the belvedere there is a fine view of the Great Cascade, and, after crossing beneath the railway for the last time, there is another very fine view of the waterfalls, as well as the town of Tivoli, and the countryside beyond

From Piazza Massimo, Viale Mazzini leads south to the station. Here, in a park, the ancient Roman tomb of a Vestal Virgin called Cossinia has been set up.

THE VILLA OF HADRIAN

About 5km below the town of Tivoli, beyond an olive grove on the hillside and reached off the Via Tiburtina, is Hadrian's Villa (*open daily 9–dusk; T: 0774 453 0203*), the largest and richest Imperial villa of the Roman Empire. Hadrian became emperor on the death of Trajan in 117, and began the villa the following year, completing it ten years later. It is known that he prided himself on his abilities as an architect, and it is therefore presumed that the remarkably original constructions, many of them inspired by famous buildings in Greece and Egypt, were directly designed by him. The villa seems to have been used as a residence for the emperor and his court, particularly in the summer months. Of all the splendid surviving buildings erected by Hadrian throughout the Empire, this is probably the most interesting. It is now one of the most evocative Classical sites to have survived in Italy, protected by a beautiful park.

Visiting the site

The general plan of the villa, which covers some 120 hectares, is capricious, although the buildings are grouped around four principal structures: the Pecile, the Imperial Palace, the Canopus and the Accademia (*shown on the plan overleaf*). Excavations and restorations are in progress on the hillside overlooking the Canopus. Recent studies suggest that the traditional interpretation of many of the buildings is probably wrong. All the ruins are labelled with explanatory diagrams (also in English). It is not easy to understand the connection between all the buildings, since the order of the visit does not begin at the main entrance to the villa (only recently identified). A whole day is needed for a detailed visit to this vast site.

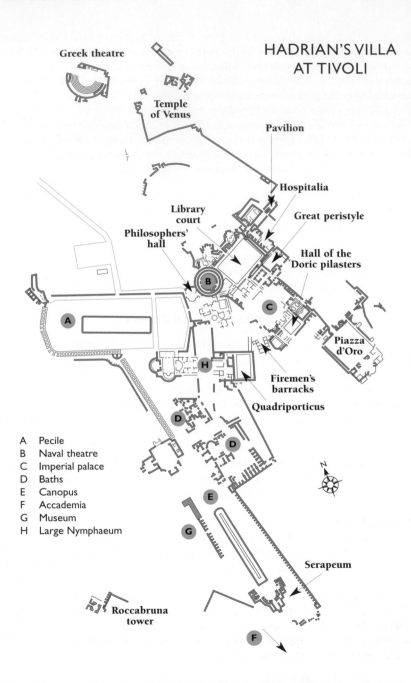

Greek theatre

HADRIAN'S VILLA AT TIVOLI

Temple of Venus

Pavilion

Hospitalia

Library court

Great peristyle

Philosophers' hall

Hall of the Doric pilasters

B

C

A

Piazza d'Oro

H

Firemen's barracks

Quadriporticus

D

D

A   Pecile
B   Naval theatre
C   Imperial palace
D   Baths
E   Canopus
F   Accademia
G   Museum
H   Large Nymphaeum

N

E

G

Serapeum

Roccabruna tower

F

HISTORY OF HADRIAN'S VILLA

It is difficult to understand why Hadrian, with all the resources of the Empire at his disposal, should have chosen such an unprepossessing site for his magnificent estate. Though little over 5km from the scenic Roman health resort of Tivoli, the low-lying surroundings of the villa have no particular attraction. In the emperor's day the flat plain was not even healthy. One reason for the choice was probably the fact that the owner of the land was the Empress Sabina; another reason may have been the emperor's desire to keep himself apart from his courtiers, many of whom owned villas on the hills around Tivoli.

Many buildings of the villa are derived from famous Classical monuments, some of which Hadrian saw during his prolonged travels in the Empire. These were the Lyceum, the Academy, the Prytaneion and the Stoa Poikile in Athens; the Canopus of the Egyptian Delta; and the Vale of Tempe in Thessaly. Hadrian also included a representation of Hades, as conceived by the Greek poets. An extensive system of underground passages (mostly now inaccessible), some mere corridors and others wide enough for a horse and carriage, exist beneath the villa; these were presumably service areas. Hadrian's successors enlarged the villa, and Constantine is supposed to have stolen some elements to decorate his new city of Constantinople. In the Middle Ages the site was plundered, and it later became a quarry for builders and lime-burners. Until the Renaissance the ruins continued to be neglected or abused.

The first excavations were ordered by Alexander VI and Cardinal Alessandro Farnese. Soon after he took up residence at the Villa d'Este in 1550, Cardinal Ippolito II d'Este employed Pirro Ligorio to continue excavations, taking many of the finds to decorate his villa. Further excavations were carried out from the 17th –19th centuries. Piranesi drew a plan of the site, and made engravings of the buildings and sculptures. In 1730 Count Fede planted cypresses and pines among the ruins. In 1870 the Italian government acquired most of the site, and systematic excavations were begun (still far from complete). The works of art discovered in the villa (more than 260) are scattered in museums all over Europe. Some are in Rome (the Museo Nazionale Romano, the Capitoline and Vatican Museums).

Ⓐ **The Pecile:** The entrance to the ruins is through the massive north wall of the **Pecile**, or portico, which seems to have been inspired by the Stoa Poikile (painted porch) in Athens, famous for its association with the Stoic philosophers. Hadrian's version is a rectangular peristyle (232m by 97m) with the ends slightly curved, similar to a Greek gymnasium. The huge north wall (9m high), running almost due east–west, still exists. The south wall is no longer standing, but there are remains of a pavilion with three exedrae and a fountain. This was probably a monumental atrium. On both sides ran roofed colonnades; sun or shade could be enjoyed at any hour of the day, and either warmth or coolness, depending on the season. In the middle of the rectangle, the fish pond has been restored. The free area around it was probably used for exercise. On the southwest was a huge sustaining wall with three rows of small chambers, now called the **Cento Camerelle**, or 'hundred small rooms', thought to have been used as accommodation for the imperial guard. Excavations are in progress.

At the northeast angle of the Pecile, a few steps lead up to the so-called **Philosophers' Hall** (17m by 9m), with an apse, seven niches and four side-doors. This is now thought to have been a large throne room, or auditorium, where the emperor held audiences, and met in council with court dignitaries.

Ⓑ Naval Theatre: This charming circular building, with an Ionic marble peristyle, was almost certainly a private retreat for the emperor, where he could be totally isolated. Unfortunately, it is now only possible to see it from outside. A circular moat (3.5m broad), lined with Luni marble, encloses an island on which stand an atrium with fluted Ionic columns in an intricate design, a series of living-rooms, and baths. It could only be reached by two small wooden (removable) bridges.

Ⓒ The Imperial Palace: The buildings belonging to the Imperial Palace are disposed parallel to the Vale of Tempe (*see below*); its elements are grouped round four peristyles. The so-called **Library Court** is now a secluded olive plantation. The 'Greek and Latin Libraries' on the northwest side have been identified by some scholars as the monumental entrance to the villa, with towers, on three floors. The third floor had a heating system and may have been used by the emperor before the villa had been completed. Behind, excavations have revealed part of a delightful walled garden with a long fountain basin.

To the north of the Library Court is the **Hospitalia**, a residential wing used by the high-ranking staff of the villa who were particularly close to the emperor. Here are ten well-preserved small rooms leading off either side of a wide corridor. Rectangular alcoves indicate space for the beds (three in each room). Lighting was provided by the high openings. The rooms are decorated with well-preserved mosaics. Steps lead down to a triclinium, with some capitals with a lotus motif, and a mosaic floor. To the right is a long corridor with oblique openings in the vault, to allow the light of midday to enter. This leads to the **Pavilion**, which overlooks a valley with a stream which is thought to have been landscaped by Hadrian to recreate the Vale of Tempe in Thessaly, famed for its beauty.

From here steps lead up to a path (south) which leads to the **Great Peristyle**, with a private library and other small rooms overlooking the Library Court. At the other end of this nucleus of the palace is the **Hall of the Doric Pilasters**, with a fine entablature, which connected the east and west parts of the villa. Beyond the so-called Firemen's Barracks (probably a storehouse near the kitchens) is a **Quadriporticus**, with a pool and a portico of fluted Composite columns. This is now considered to be at the centre of the most important part of the Imperial Palace and the residence of Hadrian. The upper floors were supplied with heating systems. Beneath it is a well-preserved extensive cryptoporticus. Beyond it, on a lower level, is the Large Nymphaeum (*see p. 149 below*).

Ruins of the Large Baths of Hadrian's Villa.

On the left is another nymphaeum, which had two round fountain basins, and from here a path leads to the **Piazza d'Oro**, a rectangular area at the southeast end of the palace. It was so named because excavations here yielded such rich finds. It is entered through the fine octagonal vestibule. The peristyle was formed of alternate columns of *cipollino* and granite in two rows. On the far side (southeast) is an intricate series of exedrae and nymphaea; the central one seems to have been a summer triclinium. This was an open courtyard with a remarkable Greek-cross plan, with alternate convex and concave sides. The plan of the portico recalls Greek gymnasia. It was formerly thought that this was used for banquets, but a recent interpretation is that it was in fact a stoa with libraries, similar to that which Hadrian had built in Athens in this period.

D **The baths:** The **Small Baths** are well preserved, with a large rectangular hall, perhaps the frigidarium, and an octagonal hall with a domed vault. They were particularly elegant and refined, and may have been reserved for the use of the emperor alone. The **Large Baths**, on a simpler design, were probably used by court dignitaries and visitors. They include a circular hall, with cupola and skylight. The huge hall has an apse and a superb cross-vault, now mostly collapsed. Opposite is another cross-vaulted room decorated with exquisite stucco reliefs. On the east is a swimming-pool, bounded on the northwest by a crypto-porticus with, on its ruined walls, numerous graffiti of the 16th and 17th centuries. This gives access to the so-called Praetorium, a tall edifice which was divided into three storeys by wooden floors. It may have been used as a warehouse, or as a service wing.

E **The Canopus:** Beyond a row of six huge ilexes is the celebrated Canopus, designed to imitate the famous Sanctuary of Serapis, which stood at the 15th milestone from Alexandria. Hadrian dug a hollow (185m by 75m), in which he constructed a basin, bordered on the east by a block of 20 rooms and a portico, and on the west by a heavy buttressed wall (238m long). Around the curved north end of the canal, reproductions of statues found on the site have been set up between marble columns surmounted by an epistyle arched over alternate pillars. Along the west side are reproductions of colossal caryatids and telamones (the originals were found in the basin in the 1950s). At the south end is the so-called **Serapeum**, a monumental triclinium in the form of a Temple of Isis, with a half-dome formerly covered with mosaics above a semicircular banqueting table (reconstructed) from which the diners had a scenic view of the Canopus. Some scholars think this may have been intended as a symbolic representation of the Nile: a series of fountains represent its source (in the niche behind), the cataracts, and its delta (in the piscina in front). The basin would then have represented the Mediterranean, with Athens to the west (represented by the caryatids), and Ephesus to the east (repre-sented by statues of Amazons). The Canopus may have been built by Hadrian in honour of his lover Antinous, a Bithynian boy born around AD 110, who was renowned for his graceful beauty. When he accompanied the Emperor on his trip up the Nile in 130 he was drowned in the river in mysterious circumstances. Hadrian founded a city in Egypt in his memory, and ordered his deification. Numerous statues of him survive in the museums of Rome and elsewhere, and his full lips and dreamy eyes are instantly recognisable.

F **The Accademia:** To the southeast, in an olive grove, is the so-called Accademia, a complex of buildings which some scholars identify as a secondary palace. The group includes a round hall, known as the **Temple of Apollo**, a peristyle, and the remains of three rooms with delicate stucco ornamentation. About 300m southeast are the remains of an **odeion**, or roofed theatre (45m in diameter), with the imperial box in the centre of the cavea. To the east a path descends to a hollow (150m long), hewn in the tufa and overshadowed by thick vegetation, which leads to a semicircular vestibule (once perhaps guarded by an image of Cerberus). This was the **entrance to Hades**, represented by a quadrangle of four subterranean corridors, 5.5m wide and 91m in total length, with 79 apertures for light.

G **The museum and Roccabruna Tower:** There is a fine view of most of the villa from the hill behind. On the northwest side of the hollow is the museum (*usually closed*), housing finds from excavations since 1950. The statues include a copy of the *Aphrodite of Cnidos* by Praxiteles; wounded Amazons, one a mutilated copy of a Polyclitan original, the other a fine replica of the famous original by Pheidias; *Athena* and *Mars*, both from mid-5th-century originals; a Crocodile; and four marble Caryatids, copies of the 5th-century originals on the Erechtheion at Athens.

A path leads west to the **Roccabruna Tower**, a belvedere which has square outer walls and is circular inside. This is possibly an imitation of the Tower of Timon, which stood near the Academy in Athens. It stands in an olive grove, famous for the size of its olive trees: one of them (the *Albero Bello*) is claimed to be the largest in the Tivoli district.

H **The Large Nymphaeum:** A broad main path returns towards the entrance. To the right, just before the Pecile, is the **Large Nymphaeum**. It was a decorative garden surrounded by porticoes, and a building with three exedrae. Between it and the Naval Theatre are remains of the first baths constructed in the villa, which had a large circular room with a heating system used for steam baths.

From here a fine avenue of cypresses leads north to the Greek Theatre, built over a semicircular portico. This frames a small **Temple of Venus**, a goddess particularly venerated by Hadrian. The temple was modelled on the Temple at Cnidos; the Cnidian-type *Aphrodite* discovered here has been replaced by a cast (original in the museum). Beyond, to the right, a walk leads to the modernised Fontana di Palazzo, near which are a few traces of the Gymnasium. Descending left through olives and cypresses, the path passes the **Greek Theatre**, c. 36m in diameter.

HORACE'S SABINE FARM

The lovely valley north of the little town of Vicovaro (*map p. 110, C2–C1*), which has an unusual and highly decorated octagonal Renaissance chapel, is now part of the Parco Regionale dei Monti Lucretili, where numerous wild flowers, including many orchids, grow. There are marked paths in the area. Just outside Licenza are the ruins of a simple Roman villa, which was almost certainly **Horace's Sabine farm** (*open 9–dusk except Mon; T: 0774 46031*) given to the poet in 33/32 BC and described in many of his letters. It was first excavated in 1911, and its beautiful, peaceful setting has been preserved.

> No gold or ivory gleams
> On panelled ceiling in my house … yet I am blessed
> With honesty and a streak
> Of golden talent, and, though poor, rich people seek
> Me out. I do not task
> The charity of the gods, nor from my patron ask
> Greater reward than this:
> My one dear Sabine farm is wealth enough and bliss.
> *Horace, Ode II: 18, Tr. James Michie*

ROMAN VILLA ECONOMY

'Happy is the man who remains far from the world of business, as did our puritan ances-
tors, and who cultivates the family farm with his own oxen … He trains the mature ten-
drils of his grapevines to the tall poplar trees; or he stands in a secluded valley and sur-
veys his herds of lowing cattle; or he shears the helpless sheep … How pleasant it is to lie
down, sometimes under an ancient oak, sometimes on the matted grass; meanwhile the
stream glides by between its high banks, and the birds warble in the trees.'
The romanticisation of rural life, here in one of Horace's Epodes, is a common
theme in Roman poetry. After the bustle of city life and the tensions of politics,
many Romans dreamt of their 'puritan ancestors', whose life was one of steady and
dignifying toil on the land. Such a life never existed, certainly not one with spare
time to sit by river banks! In any case, from the 2nd century BC onwards the small-
holders who had formed the backbone of the rural economy around Rome were
deposed by unscrupulous landowners, who ran their estates on slave labour
brought in from conquests overseas. Archaeological research suggests that a
landowner would accumulate a number of farms, with 250 hectares as a typical
size. By the end of the 1st century BC a prosperous villa economy emerged in central Italy, although it was still dependent on slaves, many of whom worked in
chained gangs. The aim was self-sufficiency, with sheep, cattle and pigs alongside
olives, vines, grain and fruits, all of which could be marketed locally. The owner
would normally delegate the day-to-day running of the estate to a farm manager.
A guide for the aspiring villa-owner was provided by the agricultural writer
Columella in c. AD 50, and gives a good picture of its household economy:
'The villa should be divided into three sections: one section resembling a city home,
one section like a real farmhouse, for workers and livestock, and the third section for
storing farm products. The landowner's section of the villa should be further subdivid-
ed into a winter apartment and a summer apartment … The baths should be turned
toward the northwest so that they may be lighted from midday until evening. The
promenades should have a southern exposure so that they may receive both the maxi-
mum of sun in the winter and the minimum in the summer … In the farmhouse part
of the villa there should be a large kitchen with a high ceiling … so that the wood beams
may be secure against the danger of fire, and so that household slaves may conve-
niently stop by here during every season of the year. The best plan will be to construct
the cells for unchained slaves facing south. For those in chains let there be an under-
ground prison … The third part of the villa is divided into rooms for oil, … for aged
wine and for wine not yet fermented, into lofts for hay and straw, and into areas for
warehouses and granaries. … It is also a good idea to enclose fruit trees and gardens
with a fence and to plant them close to the villa, in a place to which all the manure
seepage from the barnyard and the bathrooms can flow … For both vegetables and
trees thrive on fertilisers of this sort …'. (On Agriculture, Tr. Jo-Ann Shelton)   C.F.

Horace's farm had an oblong garden with a swimming pool in the centre. The excavations (where the American Academy in Rome and the University of California worked from 1997–2001) have been rather too tidied up, and the monochrome mosaics are usually covered for protection. There are also remains of Roman baths built here in the 1st or 2nd century AD, and traces of a little convent probably dating from the 8th century. But the most evocative sight is the spring, just 100m higher up the hillside, presumed to be the Bandusian Spring apostrophised in one of Horace's Epodes: 'O Bandusian spring, clearer than glass, worthy of sweet wine and flowers...' (*III: 13*). The Orsini constructed a nymphaeum here in the 17th century, and it still forms a charming waterfall in a natural setting which has been left as it always was, overgrown with wild celery and ferns and inhabited by numerous interesting insects. The hedgerows and fields here abound in a great variety of wild flowers in the spring, and the sound of the spring water in the countryside, as it runs down the hillside in rivulets, is extraordinarily evocative.

Licenza

This little hill-town, with streets too narrow for cars, has been known since Roman times for its *farro*, a species of grain called spelt, which has a very high nutritional content. Here it is made into *sagne*, a pasta in the form of *fettuccine* (celebrated in a festival in September), and it has recently been reintroduced into the cuisine of central Italy, eaten either hot as a broth, or cold as a salad. In a charming little piazza at the top of the town, an archaeological museum (*open 10–12 & 4–6 except Mon*) preserves the material found during excavations of Horace's villa. The Orsini castle above is now in an abandoned state. Just below the village there is a visitors' centre for the Parco Regionale dei Monti Lucretili.

SUBIACO

Subiaco (*map p. 110, D2*) is famous as the birthplace both of Western monasticism under the rule of its founder St Benedict; and of Luigina Lollobrigida, always known as Gina, the 1950s film star. St Benedict's legacy is more keenly felt, in the form of two monasteries reached by the same road, just outside the town. Subiaco derives from '*Sublaqueum*', meaning 'under the lakes', since Nero created three small lakes in the valley here by damming the Aniene, to provide a lovely setting for a huge villa (of which scant ruins survive, enclosed, to the left of the road to the monasteries). Towards the end of the 5th century Benedict of Nursia came here to live in prayer and contemplation in a cavern which became known as the *Sacro Speco*. The fame of his saintliness spread all over Italy, and many people came here to see him. His twin sister Scholastica later persuaded him to build a monastery near the ruins of Nero's villa. But having aroused the jealousy of a monk called Florentius, he left Subiaco and three tame ravens led him to Monte Cassino (*see p. 250*), where in 529 he founded a new monastery. Several convents survived here, however, and were of great importance in the 11th–12th centuries.

ST BENEDICT & THE BENEDICTINES

Benedict was born in the town of *Nursia* (modern Norcia; *see p. 562*) in AD 480, shortly after the abdication of Romulus Augustulus, the last Emperor of the West. We know something of his life from the reminiscences of his followers, which were collected by Pope Gregory the Great (pope 590–604) and which survive in Gregory's second book of *Dialogues*. His father was a city magistrate, and Benedict was torn between the life of a minor noble and commitment to the Church. Eventually giving up his studies and a woman who loved him in Rome he decided on the Church and set off with his old nurse to the mountains near Subiaco. After a period as a hermit, during which his faith matured, he was asked to become abbot of a neighbouring monastery. Here he came across the realities of a failed community. The monks tried to poison him, but each time he was saved by a miracle: a cup containing poison was shattered, a raven carried off a poisoned loaf (as shown in pictorial sequence here in Subiaco; *see illustration opposite*). Gregory believed strongly that the lives of holy men were linked to the miraculous, and he describes how Benedict's growing fame attracted would-be monks to Subiaco. He ended by setting up 12 monasteries in the valley, each with 12 monks, while he himself presided over a thirteenth. His most famous foundation was further south, at Monte Cassino (*see p. 250*), where he died in 547.

The practice of withdrawing from the world in the service of Christ had originated in Egypt, where large monastic communities existed alongside the cells of solitary hermits. There was no one rule. Some monks delighted in organising raids on pagan shrines; others lived lives of appalling austerity. A path of moderation was preached by one Cassian, a Scythian who had himself endured the rigours of the Egyptian desert. He had travelled west, reaching Rome in 405, and he founded his own monasteries here and in Marseilles. Cassian's *Institutes* and *Conferences* set out a pattern for monastic living in which balanced and purposeful life in the service of God can be lived without complete withdrawal from the world. This and another rule, the *Rule of the Master*, written at the beginning of the 6th century, were the main sources for Benedict's own Rule.

The core of his Rule is obedience to the abbot, an obedience which is set in the abbot's own responsibility to God for the way he uses his authority. 'Yet the abbot must not disturb the flock committed to him, nor by an arbitrary use of his power ordain anything unjustly; but let him always think of the account he will have to render to God for all his decisions and his deeds.' Within the community life is ordered, but there is a balanced mix of communal prayer, work (about six hours a day), and time for reflection and reading of the major Christian texts. No monk can own any property, but there is always enough food and drink, and the monastic habit, based on the clothes of a working labourer, is designed to fit the local climate. The monastery must accept guests and care for the sick and for the education of the young. 'As soon as a guest is announced, therefore, let the Superior or the brethren meet him with all charitable service. And first of all let them pray together, and then exchange the kiss of peace.' There are nice touches about the importance of moderation. A monk would get into trouble if he arrived for night service after the end of the first psalm. However, Benedict goes on, it must be said very slowly for that reason! An ancient saying sums up the attractions of the rule: 'A lamb can bathe in it without drowning, while an elephant can swim in it'. It is still used as the focus for life in Benedictine monasteries today.

The early monasteries were poor and usually set up on marginal land so that the prosperity of the local community was not undermined. They were not necessarily in remote regions, however. Monte Cassino, for instance, overlooked the main road from Rome to Naples, and some monasteries were founded in Rome itself, such as the town house on the Caelian Hill converted by Gregory the Great (*see p. 66*), who progressed from monasticism to the papacy, another piece of evidence that total withdrawal was not demanded (Benedict would have approved of Gregory's own moderation and administrative expertise).

Benedict is often described as the founder of western Christian monasticism. In 1964, Pope Paul VI declared him a patron saint of Europe.   C.F.

The friars Maurus and Placidus marvel as St Benedict's tame ravens make away with the loaves of poisoned bread. Fresco by Magister Consulus in the lower church of San Benedetto, Subiaco.

Santa Scolastica

The monastery of Santa Scolastica is still a Benedictine convent with 16 monks (*open 9–12 & 3–6; guided visits every half hour*). Although damaged in the war, three cloisters survive: off the first is a fresco of James II of England. The second, irregularly shaped, Gothic cloister has a good view of the beautiful campanile, which dates from 980. The well has two Roman columns from Nero's villa. There are interesting frescoes here by the 14th-century Sienese school. The third cloister is the most interesting, with remains of frescoes of the properties which belonged to the monastery, and little columns beautifully carved and designed, signed by Giacomo Cosmati (1210–43), without mosaic decoration. Inside the Gothic church (on 7th-century foundations) Giacomo Quarenghi built the present beautiful Neoclassical building in 1770 (the two columns at the west end also come from Nero's villa). The white interior is well lit by thermal windows and a window at the east end. This was the first and only work in Italy by this architect, who then went to live in Russia where he built much of St Petersburg. The Museo Ceselli outside the monastery has some archaeological material, but is often closed (*T: 0774 82421*).

Arnold Pannartz and Conrad Sweynheim, pupils of Gutenberg's partner, Johannes Fust from Mainz, set up the first printing press in Italy in the convent of St Scholastica in 1464, but when they quarrelled with the scribes in the monastery they transferred their press to Rome in 1467. Today the precious library and archives include the first two books they printed: Cicero's *De Oratore* and an incunabulum of 1465 of the 4th-century Christian apologist Lactantius (*library exhibition room open Mon–Fri 8.30–6.30, Sat 8.30–1.30*).

San Benedetto

The road ends at the convent of San Benedetto (also known as the *Sacro Speco*; *open 9–12 & 3–6*), reached in around 10mins by a path through woods of ancient ilexes. Four Benedictine monks still live here. There are two superimposed churches as well as chapels and grottoes carved out of the rocky hillside. A small Gothic door opens into a loggia, with a view of the wooded valley. In the last bay are 15th-century Umbrian frescoes of Benedictines, and above the door is a worn fresco of the *Madonna and Child*. Beyond is the old chapter house, with frescoes of the school of Perugino.

Three steps lead down into the **upper church** (c. 1350) with an aisleless nave and a chancel, and good cross-vaulting. The nave is decorated with 14th-century frescoes, mainly by the Sienese school. Outstanding among these are the *Kiss of Judas* and the *Way of the Cross* (left wall), the *Entry of Christ into Jerusalem* (right wall), and the *Crucifixion* (front wall). Steps lead down to the sanctuary, with more frescoes and a Cosmati altar. The frescoed transept has a stoup made from a Roman urn. The sacristy (*shown on request*) has a 15th-century fresco of the *Crucifixion*, two panels of the Sienese school, a painting showing the lake of Subiaco, and a fresco fragment of *St Benedict* by Consulus, a master of the Roman school of the second half of the 13th century.

Steps in front of the altar lead down to the **lower church**, with a series of chapels at different levels. Nearly all the frescoes here, of episodes in the life of St Benedict (as told by St Gregory the Great), are by Consulus, whose signature ('Magister Conxolus') can be seen in the niche at the top of the stairs on a fresco of the *Madonna and Child with Two Angels*. After a second flight of stairs, the level of the **Sacro Speco** is reached. The holy grotto is a small, dark natural cavern in the rock. Here is a marble statue of *St Benedict*, by Antonio Raggi (1657). The lower part of the grotto walls are lined with *cipollino* from Nero's villa. From the landing a little spiral staircase leads up to the Chapel of St Gregory (*usually closed*), with further frescoes by Consulus, and a portrait of St Francis, without halo or stigmata, painted at the time of his visit to the convent c. 1210, and claimed to be the first example in Italy of a genuine portrait. The *Scala Santa* was so called because it is on the line of the path taken by St Benedict on the way to and from his cavern. The stairway, decorated with macabre 15th-century Sienese frescoes depicting death, leads down past the 14th-century Chapel of the Madonna, covered with more 15th-century frescoes, and the **Grotta dei Pastori**, a small cave where St Benedict is said to have preached to the local shepherds. It contains the oldest fresco in the convent, an 8th- or 9th-century fragment representing the Madonna with St Luke and another saint. Outside the cave is a small terrace, from which can be seen the great columns and arches supporting the convent buildings. Here is another 15th-century fresco of the *Pietà*. The rose garden is on the site of a bramble where St Benedict was traditionally thought to have mortified his flesh, and which centuries later was turned into a rose tree by St Francis.

PRACTICAL INFORMATION

GETTING AROUND

• **By car:** Car parking is available in **Palestrina** in Piazza S. Maria degli Angeli or at the top of the hill near the museum; at **Tivoli** in Piazza Garibaldi opposite the tourist information office or next to the river on Viale Roma.
• **By train:** Trains to **Frascati and Castel Gandolfo** run from Rome's Termini station (*map p. 29, F2*). The service is infrequent (although many more trains run to Frascati) but takes a very scenic route. Trains to **Ostia** depart from Rome's Roma–Lido station beside Porta San Paolo (*map p. 24*). Services run every 30mins (journey time 30mins).

Ostia Antica station is only a few minutes' walk from the site entrance, across a footbridge. Trains to **Tivoli** leave from Rome's Tiburtina station (*map p. 24*) c. every hour (journey 1hr). Rome trains connect with buses for **Subiaco** from Mandela station.
• **By bus:** COTRAL buses (www.cotralspa.it) take a scenic route from Rome's Anagnina station (end of Metro line A) to the **Alban Hills**. A dayticket is useful for seeing a number of sights in the region. For **Hadrian's Villa** a local bus (no. 4) runs from the centre of Tivoli about every 30mins. Buses also run from Ponte Mammolo in Rome along Via Prenestina and stop c. 1.5km

from the site entrance (request stop). **Tivoli** can be reached from Rome from Ponte Mammolo (underground Line B) with COTRAL bus connections c. every 20mins (journey time c. 45mins).

INFORMATION OFFICES

Ardea Via del Tempio, T: 06 913 6464.
Castel Gandolfo Piazza Cavallotti 1, T: 0693 60134.
Frascati Piazza Marconi 1, T: 0694 20331.
Licenza (Parco Regionale Monti Lucretili) Località Fonte Macaruta, T: 348 743 3189.
Ostia Via Oletta 22a, T: 0656 324515.
Palestrina Via della Cortina, T: 0695 73176.
Subiaco Via Cadorna 59, T: 0774 822 013.
Tivoli Largo Garibaldi: T: 0774 334 522.
Vicovaro Via San Vito 29, T: 0774 498269.

HOTELS

Castel Gandolfo (*map p. 110, B3*)
€€ **Hotel La Culla del Lago**. Small, comfortable hotel set in pretty gardens with a view of the lake. Rooms are bright, with private balconies overlooking the pope's summer residence on the opposite shore. *Via Spiaggio del Lago 38, T: 0693 668231, www.culladellago.com. 15 rooms.*
Frascati (*map p. 110, B2–C2*)
€€€ **Villa Tuscolana**. Stunning views, a beautiful exterior and meticulously maintained gardens. The villa stands on a hill overlooking Frascati. A shuttle bus (small fee) runs from the town to the villa; useful after dark. *Via del Tuscolo, T: 0694 2900, www.villatuscolana.it. 110 rooms.*
€€ **Hotel Colonna**. An elegant hotel with good service and facilities, in a grand position on the main square, next to the duomo. *Piazza del Gesù 12, T: 0694 018088, www.hotelcolonna.it. 20 rooms.*
€€ **Hotel Flora**. A 19th-century villa tastefully restored by the family who own and manage the hotel. Individually designed bedrooms, a little on the small side, but with elegant furnishings. *Viale Vittorio Veneto 8, T: 0694 16110, www.hotel-flora.it. 37 rooms.*
Grottaferrata (*map p. 110, B3*)
€€€€ **Park Hotel Villa Grazioli**. On the road to Frascati, a grand 16th-century villa with wonderful views from its gardens, and impressive 17th-century frescoes throughout the interior. Free shuttle-bus service to Frascati station to connect with Rome trains. *Via Umberto Pavoni 19, T: 0694 54001, www.villa-grazioli.com. 58 rooms.*
Palestrina (*map p. 110, C2*)
€€ **La Meridienne**. Large, modern hotel with a pleasant swimming pool, situated in a private position 3km outside Palestrina. *Via Colle S. Agapito 1, T: 0695 36859, www.hotellameridienne.it. 200 rooms.*
€ **Hotel Stella**. Family-owned hotel in the centre of the town, close to the duomo, with simple but comfortable rooms. Restaurant open daily. *Piazzale della Liberazione 3, T: 06 953 8172, www.hotelstella.it. 30 rooms.*
Subiaco (*map p. 110, D2*)
€€ **Foresteria Monasteri Benedettini**. Simple rooms in part of the monastery which commands a beautiful position

above Subiaco, with cool, shady surroundings. B&B, half board and full board rates are available. *T: 0774 85569, www.benedettini-subiaco.it.*

Tivoli (*map p. 110, C2*)
€€ **Hotel Dimora Adriana**. Close to Hadrian's Villa, this is a modern, comfortable hotel with easy access to the A24 and A1 *autostrada* (the entrance is not clearly signed). *Via Maremmana Inferiore km 2,100, T: 0774 535955, www.dimoraadriana.it. 14 rooms.*

€€ **Hotel Sirene**. A 19th-century villa overlooking the Roman Temple of Vesta in a particularly picturesque position. Well situated for Villa Gregoriana and Villa d'Este. *Piazza Massimo 4, T: 0774 330605, www.hotelsirene.it. 38 rooms.*

€€ **Torre Sant'Angelo**. In a peaceful location just outside of the centre, at the top of a steep hill with quite exceptional views from some of the bedrooms. Restaurant. *Via Quintilio Varo, T: 0774 332533, www.hoteltorresangelo.it. 35 rooms.*

RESTAURANTS

Frascati (*map p. 110, B2–C2*)
€€€ **Ristorante Cacciani**. Long-established, large restaurant and hotel in the centre of Frascati, opposite the station. Wonderful views. Traditional dishes are served with Frascati wine. Closed Sun evening and Mon. *Via Armando Diaz 13, T: 06 942 0378.*

€€ **Nuova Enoteca Frascati**. The dining tables are set amongst stone archways in this small, relaxed restaurant. A trip to the cellars is worthwhile to view the best of the local wines on offer. Closed Sun. *Via Armando Diaz 42, T: 06 941 7449.*

€€ **Il Pinocchio**. Centrally located *trattoria* and pizzeria. The house speciality pizza, the *pinocchietti*, a rolled pizza with a variety of fillings. Friendly service and excellent value. Closed Tues. Hotel also with newly renovated rooms. *Piazza del Mercato 21, T: 06 941 7883.*

Grottaferrata (*map p. 110, B3*)
€€ **La Briciola di Adriana**. An informal dining room which belies the thoughtful preparation of the dishes. The owners are passionate about simple, delicious food sourced locally. Booking recommended. Closed Sun evening and Mon. *Via d'Annunzio 12, T: 06 945 9338.*

€€ **Taverna dello Spuntino**. Open since the 1960s, and now also an elegant hotel, Taverna dello Spuntino is wonderfully rustic in atmosphere with terracotta floors and stone walls, serving traditional dishes. Wine cellar. *Via Cicerone 20, T: 06 945 9366.*

Palestrina (*map p. 110, C2*)
€€€ **Il Piscarello**. Truffle and fish dishes are the speciality here. Closed Mon and Aug. *Via del Piscarello 2, T: 06 953 7751.*

Tivoli (*map p. 110, C2*)
€€€ **Antico Ristorante Sibilla**. A renowned restaurant whose service and quality of food is excellent. It has been patronised by the rich and famous since it first set up in business in the mid-18th century. The view from the terraces over the Aniene valley is unsurpassed. Closed Mon. *Via della Sibilla 50, T: 0774 335281.*

€€ **Antica Hostaria de' Carrettieri**. Good, medium-priced restaurant run by Sardinians. *Via Giuliani 55, T: 0774 330159.*

€€ La Ronda. In a pretty position beneath the Lucretili mountains, with a shaded outdoor terrace and a comfortable indoor dining room. The real draw are the excellent tasting menus. Closed Mon. *Via Domenico Giuliani 22, T: 0774 317243.*

€€ La Tenuta di Rocca Bruna. Large, modern restaurant ideal for lunch or dinner after visiting nearby Hadrian's Villa. It is set in picturesque gardens, with a number of spacious dining rooms. Aside from regional dishes, the restaurant serves pizzas from a wood-fired oven. *Strada Rocca Bruna 27, T: 0774 535985.*

LOCAL SPECIALITIES

Vineyards in the rich volcanic soil on the outer slopes of the Alban Hills produce the '**Vini dei Castelli**', of which the most famous is Frascati, a light white wine. Good cellars include the Cantine San Marco, at Via di Mola Cavona (T: 06 940 9403; www.sanmarcofrascati.it) and Carlo Micara, at Via di Salò 37a (T: 06 940 8585). Fuller-bodied wine, often of superior quality, is produced from Malvasia grapes grown on the well-exposed slopes of Lake Albano around Marino. For information, see www.collineromane.it

FESTIVALS & EVENTS

Castel Gandolfo The whole town turns out to celebrate the peach harvest, with open-air shows and food stalls. Representatives of the town go to the Vatican each year to present the pope with some of the year's crop, 3rd Sun in July.

Nemi To celebrate wild strawberry season, villagers dress in traditional strawberry-picking costume, and an abundance of the fruit is served with cream and sugar, 3rd Sun in June.

Tivoli Anniversary of the founding of the town, a month-long season of events including a special series of guided tours around Tivoli's museums and monuments, April.

NB: Until 1923 the province of Rieti was part of Umbria, of which it is a more natural geographical continuation. The northern part of the region is shown on the map on p. 487. The southern part is shown on p. 110.

Rieti (*map p. 487, C6*) stands on the Via Salaria, one of the oldest Roman roads (*see box below*). It claims to be in the exact centre of Italy.

ANCIENT ROMAN ROADS

Although the most famous of Rome's ancient roads is the Via Appia (*see p. 104*), the others, which led out of Rome in all directions, are still partly in use and most still carry their Roman names. Via Ostiense was one of the earliest, and dates from the victorious campaign of the Romans against Veio to secure their salt supply (5th century BC). It ran from Rome to Ostia, and from there, under the name of Via Severiana, it followed the coast to *Antium* (Anzio) and *Terracina*, where it joined the Via Appia.

The Via Aurelia, which leaves Rome to the southwest, was built before 109 BC but follows the line of an even older road which linked Rome with the Etruscan towns on the Tyrrhenian coast. It reached the shore at *Alsium* (Palo), a port of the Etruscan city of *Caere* (Cerveteri), and then followed the coastline to Pisa and Genoa. It ended in Gaul at *Forum Julii* (Fréjus) on the French Riviera.

The Via Cassia was originally a rough road running from Rome north to Etruria. When it was paved by Cassius Longinus, consul in 107 BC, it was named after him. The Via Flaminia, which also leaves Rome to the north, was begun in 220 BC and takes the name of Gaius Flaminius, censor and afterwards consul, who was killed at the Battle of Lake Trasimene in 217 BC (*see p. 512*) It leads across Umbria to Fano and Rimini on the Adriatic.

Via Salaria takes its name from its association with the salt trade between the Romans and the Sabines. Now the modern N4, it runs via Rieti and Ascoli Piceno to the Adriatic near San Benedetto del Tronto.

Via Latina, probably in use as early as the 7th or 6th century BC, ran south from Rome down the valley of the River Sacco in Latin territory and continued to the Campania around Naples. It was used by the armies of Pyrrhus and Hannibal.

The ancient Via Tuscolana ran to *Tusculum*, to the east of present-day Frascati. It was a short branch of the Via Latina, which left Rome by the Porta Capena, passed through *Ferentinum* (Ferentino), *Frusino* (Frosinone), *Aquinum* (Aquino) and *Casinum* (Cassino), eventually joining the Via Appia.

Rieti today is a provincial capital with a pleasant historical centre. It was the ancient *Reate*, chief town of the Sabines, an Italic tribe who occupied the hills between the Tiber and the Aniene and who came into conflict with the Latins and later the Romans. In 290 BC they were finally subjected to Rome. They are now mostly remembered for the famous legend of the Rape of the Sabine Women, depicted in numerous Roman sculptures. The story goes that Romulus, needing to populate his newly founded city, ordered each of his men to capture a Sabine woman, ravish her and then marry her and treat her well. The women, it is said, were reconciled to their lot by their Roman abductors' honeyed words.

The present-day Piazza Vittorio Emanuele is on the site of the Roman forum. The duomo, begun in 1109, has a beautiful exterior and contains a venerated fresco of the *Madonna del Popolo*, probably dating from the early 14th century. Some of the paintings are by the local 17th-century painter Vincenzo Manenti. The Museo del Duomo (*only open at weekends*) is arranged in the 14th-century baptistery and has a good collection of processional Crosses. Palazzo Vescovile preserves a loggia of 1288. The 13th-century church of Sant'Agostino contains ancient fresco fragments. The post office (1934) is the work of Cesare Bazzani, who also built the Galleria d'Arte Moderna in Rome.

THE PLAIN OF RIETI & ITS CONVENTS

The beautiful, fertile Plain of Rieti is traversed by the Velino. Cicero visited Rieti in 54 BC, and in a letter to Atticus speaks of the Reatines conducting him to 'their Tempe'— a strange comparison, as the Italian valley of the Velino is pastoral and quiet; the Greek Vale of Tempe a wild and steep-sided gorge. Dotting the plain are a few small lakes, relics of a much larger lake surrounded by marshes, which were drained in 271 BC. To the east rises a mountain range dominated by the peak of Monte Terminillo (2216m). Between 1209 and 1233 St Francis spent much time in this area, which still has four Franciscan sanctuaries. At the convent of **Fonte Colombo** (*map p. 487, C6; open 8–12 & 3.30–dusk*) in 1223 he dictated the last Rules of his Order before leaving for the East. He returned two years later to seek treatment for an eye disease.

In a beautiful peaceful position on the side of a steep wooded hill below the quiet little hamlet of **Greccio** is another convent (*open 9–12.45 & 3–dusk*) where St Francis also stayed in 1223. Here he is supposed to have assembled a crèche to celebrate Christmas, so beginning a tradition which survives to this day. A late 14th-century fresco shows a crèche and a scene of the Nativity. A corridor leads to the tiny rooms occupied by St Francis (the room where he ate, with a primitive little fireplace, and the cave where he slept). The tiny church dates from 1228 and preserves its stalls and lectern in the choir, and a carved 14th-century Crucifix. In a little adjoining room is a 14th-century copy of a contemporary portrait of St Francis wiping his eyes, an allusion to the eye complaint from which he suffered. It has been suggested that this was trachoma, an infection of the ocular tissue which causes excessive watering, photophobia and painful ingrowing of the lashes.

The convent of **La Foresta** (*open 8.30–12 & 2.30–7*), where St Francis stayed in 1225, has since 1989 been occupied by a community called Mondo X, founded to help young people in need. It is in a lovely setting beside a vineyard. A story relates how another vineyard here was trampled on by a crowd who had come to see St Francis, but when the grapes were harvested and pressed they produced more wine than in other years. The 13th-century church survives. The convent of San Giacomo at **Poggio Bustone** (*open as for Fonte Colombo*), also in a pretty setting, has a 15th-century church and a hermitage where St Francis stayed.

The Umbrian border

Labro (*map p. 487, C5*) is an exceptionally well-preserved stone-built village with numerous medieval streets. The Castello Nobili-Vitelleschi, privately owned, can be visited on guided tours (*usually open 10–12 & 3–7; T: 0746 636 020*). It contains paintings by the French Baroque master Simon Vouet, 16th- and 17th-century furniture, ceramics (including pieces of Pesaro ware), glass and firearms. The lake of Piediluco and the celebrated Marmore waterfall are just across the border in Umbria (*see p. 571*)

Leonessa, further to the northeast, is a pretty, small town with numerous fine palaces. The church of San Francesco contains a large *presepio* in terracotta dating from the early 16th century. Piazza del Municipio (dedicated to 51 victims of 'Nazifascism' who were killed here in 1944) has an attractive shape and a pretty fountain. On the Corso, beyond the ex-church of San Nicola, is the elaborate sanctuary (1746) of St Joseph of Leonessa, containing the body and relics of this local saint (1556–1612), who was a Capuchin friar (the Capuchins are a branch of the Franciscan order) and missionary in Turkey.

Along the Velino to Amatrice

Cittaducale (*map p. 487, C6*) was joined to the province of Rieti in 1923. Before that it had belonged to the Abruzzo, and as such formed the northernmost bulwark of the Kingdom of Naples. It was founded, in fact, in 1309 by Charles II of Anjou, and named after his son Robert the Wise, Duke of Calabria, who succeeded his father as King of Naples in the same year. It is laid out on a regular grid plan, but has suffered from earthquakes. Piazza del Popolo has a medley of buildings around a fountain and gardens. Santa Maria del Popolo, with a late Romanesque façade contains several 16th-century polychrome wood statues.

At **Terme di Cotilia**, due east along the N4 (the Via Salaria), is a spa which uses the sulphur springs of *Cutilia*, where the emperor Vespasian, born locally, died in AD 79. Further on is **Antrodoco** (*map p. 487, D6*), in an enclosed position at the junction of three gorges. The Romanesque church of Santa Maria extra Moenia and the baptistery of San Giovanni are of ancient foundation and contain 15th-century works of art.

On the border with Abruzzo and the Marche lies **Amatrice** (*map p. 487, D5*), a pleasant little town founded in the Middle Ages in a fine position overlooked by a mountain range which includes Monte Gorzano (2458m), the highest peak in Lazio. The mountains are famed for their numerous springs and luxuriant vegetation.

Amatrice was taken by Charles I of Anjou in 1274, and then conquered in 1529 by Charles V of Spain, after which it was reconstructed on a new plan traditionally attributed to Cola dell'Amatrice, the painter and architect born here in 1480, and who worked in the Marche, notably in Ascoli Piceno, where he succeeded Carlo Crivelli as principal artist. Here in his native town he is represented by a *Holy Family* (1527) in the ex-church of Sant'Emidio, now the Museo Civico d'Arte Sacra (*open July and Aug Tues–Sat 10.30–12.30 & 5–7; otherwise Sun only 10.30–12.30*). The museum's other great treasure is the *Madonna and Child* (c. 1280) from the church of Cossito, a little village further to the north.

Amatrice has given its name to *spaghetti all'amatriciana*, a well-known pasta dish with a spicy sauce made with bacon, onion and tomatoes served with grated pecorino cheese.

THE SABINE TOWNS

South of Rieti, on a wooded spur in a pretty valley, is the unspoilt hamlet of **Rocca Sinibalda** (*map p. 110, C1*) below its splendid castle. It was begun for Cardinal Alessandro Cesarini around 1530 by Baldassare Peruzzi and it has a hanging garden, but is not at present open to the public. **Monteleone Sabino**, 15km southwest, is a medieval village near the site of the Sabine town of *Trebula Mutuesca*, birthplace of Mummius, the Roman general who sacked Corinth in 146 BC. Outside the village is the 11th-century church of Santa Vittoria, with Roman fragments incorporated into its lovely Romanesque façade. The dedication of the church may be to St Victoria, an early martyr of Tivoli, or it may be a conflation with Vacuna, a Sabine goddess of the herd, later identified with Nike, or Victory, and honoured as a goddess of war. The small catacomb beneath the church bell-tower may possibly have been associated with her cult.

Southeast of Rieti is the wooded valley of the Salto with its artificial lake. Above the village of **Petrella Salto** (*map p. 487, D6*) is the Rocca Cenci, where the tyrant Francesco Cenci was murdered in 1598 at the instigation of his family, including his daughter Beatrice, who was beheaded for parricide a year later (*see p. 56*).

Farfa

Farfa (*map p. 110, C1*) lies in the district known as the **Sabina**, the land of the Sabines. The Sabina is today taken to refer to the pretty area of the Sabine Hills in the province of Rieti. The beautiful landscape is characterised by olive groves, and oak and chestnut woods between numerous little remote hill towns, many of which still have 'Sabina' or 'Sabino' attached to their names.

Farfa itself is a charming, well-preserved little *borgo* with two gates across the road, in a delightful setting on a wooded hillside. The houses have characteristic shops on the ground floor, which were let to the monks of the abbey during fairs. The **Abbey of Farfa** (*open for guided tours daily except Mon winter 10–1 & 3.30–6; summer 10–1 & 4–6.30; T: 0765 277315*) was one of the most important monastic centres in Italy in the Middle Ages. It is thought to have been founded in 554 by St Lawrence the Illuminator, a Syrian who had been Bishop of Spoleto. He was a peacemaker and is said to have had a gift of healing blindness. The monastery was rebuilt in 705 by St Thomas of Farfa, from Maurienne in Savoy, with the help of the Duke of Spoleto. It flourished after it was granted important privileges by Charlemagne in 775. After a period of decline in the 9th century, it recovered importance under Abbot Ugo (997–1038) who introduced Cluniac reforms. The chronicler Gregorio da Catino (1062–1133) worked at the abbey. Seven Benedictine monks still live here. The small cloister, dating from the 14th century, provides a good view of the campanile, which preserves its 9th-century base (the three upper stories date from the 12th–13th centuries). The large cloister was added in 1580. The apse of the crypt is part of the original 8th-century church. Here is kept a very well-preserved pagan sarcophagus carved in the 2nd century with battle scenes and found in the abbey orchard in the 1960s. The library of some 40,000 volumes displays some of its most precious contents, including a papal bull of 1286, an 11th-century breviary with illuminated letters in the unique style of Farfa, and the third book printed in Italy by Sweynheim and Pannartz at Subiaco (*see p. 154*) in 1467.

In the church the choir has 17th-century frescoes by the school of Zuccari. Beneath the ciborium is a 9th-century stone with fresco fragments, and in front of it is preserved the original antique altar. The ancient marble pavement is surrounded by a Cosmati floor. The nave has reused Roman columns, and a 9th-century bas-relief is carved with the symbols of the Evangelists. On the west wall is an interesting painting of the *Last Judgment* by a Flemish painter (1561), and the altarpieces on the north side are attributed to Orazio Gentileschi. On the second south altar is a venerated painting of the *Madonna of Farfa*, dating from the 13th century. The church has a good façade preceded by a courtyard paved with pebbles. The doorway has a lunette fresco of the *Madonna and Child*, with two Benedictine saints and donors (c. 1494), attributed to Cola dell'Amatrice.

Poggio Mirteto

Poggio Mirteto (*map p. 110, B1–C1*) has some medieval houses and an 18th-century district around its cathedral. The 13th-century church of San Paolo has frescoes by Lorenzo Torresani (1521), whose younger brother Bartolomeo painted the high altarpiece of the church of Santa Maria Assunta (1561) in **Roccantica** further north. The Torresani were very active in the Sabina, and were much patronised by the Dominicans. Further north still, outside Casperia on the road to Cottanello, the church of Santa Maria di Legarano has a fresco of the *Annunciation* by Bartolomeo Torresani. Also on the outskirts of Casperia, at the beginning of the road for Cantalupo to the southwest, the church of the Annunziata has an *Annunciation* by Sassoferrato (*see p. 634*).

Cottanello, in a beautiful position (*map p. 487, C6*), preserves its medieval walls, and the little church of San Cataldo, built into the rockface, with an interesting late 12th-century fresco of the *Redeemer*, with the Apostles and praying figures below. The church of **Santa Maria in Vescovio**, 17km southwest, contains an important fresco cycle of the early 14th century by Roman artists in the circle of Pietro Cavallini. The old district of **Contigliano**, east of Cottanello, sits on a hill dominated by the Collegiata of San Michele Arcangelo, begun in 1693, and which has good 17th- and 18th-century works in the interior.

PRACTICAL INFORMATION

GETTING AROUND

• **By car:** Free car parks in Rieti are situated in Via delle Palme, Via San Pietro, and Piazza Beata Colomba.
• **By train:** Rieti lies on the Rome–Terni line; the railway station is just to the north of the centre. Journey time from Rome is c. 2hrs.
• **By bus:** COTRAL buses run frequently from Tiburtina station in Rome to the railway station in Rieti, in c. 1hr 30mins.

INFORMATION OFFICES

Rieti Piazza Vittorio Emanuele 17, T: 0746 203220.

HOTELS

Labro (map p. 487, C5)
€ **Albergo Palazzo Crispolti**. An idyllic, rustic *albergo* in the centre of this hilltop village. The hotel has stone floors and open fireplaces, with the simplest of furnishings without skimping on comfort. Some rooms share a bathroom. *Via Vittorio Emanuele 16, T: 0746 636135, www.palazzocrispolti.com. 11 rooms.*
Poggio Catino (map p. 487, C6)
€€€€ **Borgo Paraelios**. Situated between Roccantica and Poggio Mirteto, this small hotel has been luxuriously converted from a 19th-century private country villa. The numerous common areas, such as the library and card room, are filled with family furniture and paintings, while the gardens surrounding the villa are immaculately kept. With beauty centre, golf course and restaurant. *Valle Collicchia di Poggio Catino, T: 0765 26267, www.borgoparaelios.it. 18 rooms.*
Rieti (map p. 487, C6)
€€ **Park Hotel Villa Potenziani**. A former 18th-century hunting villa, the residence now stands in its own vast grounds overlooking the town. Beautifully restored and renovated. *Via Colle San Mauro, T: 0746 202765, www.villapotenziani.it. 28 rooms.*
€ **Grande Albergo Quattro Stagioni**. A grand hotel situated in the centre of Rieti. The bedrooms are spacious and luxuriously furnished with chandeliers taking advantage of the high ceilings, and sumptuous bathrooms. Superb value. *Piazza Cesare Battisti 14, T: 0746 271071, www.hotelquattrostagionirieti.it. 43 rooms.*

RESTAURANTS

Fara in Sabina (map p. 110, C1)

€€ **La Badiola.** Pizzeria pleasantly situated among junipers, just 200m below the abbey of Farfa. *Via Porta Montopoli 1, T: 0765 277218.*
Greccio (*map p. 487, C6*)
€€ **Il Nido del Corvo.** In an unusual setting: a tower carved into the rocks (the name translates as 'crow's nest'). As you would expect, there are wonderful views, with a terrace that takes full advantage of them. Good local ingredients such as hare, crayfish and wild mushrooms. The tasting menu is very good. *Via del Forno 15, T: 0746 753181.*
Poggio Catino (*map p. 487, C6*)
€ **La Tancia.** Agriturismo serving extremely good food. *Via Giorgio Gioia, T: 0765 333330.*
Poggio Mirteto (*map p. 110, B1–C1*)
€€ **Il Caminetto.** Good value restaurant serving simple family cooking: polenta, bruschetta and grilled meats. *Via G. Mameli 51, T: 0765 441020.*
€€ **E Non Solo Carne.** Small restaurant serving superb meat dishes, sourced from the finest butcher in town. *Via Matteotti 23, T: 0756 22197.*
Rieti (*map p. 487, C6*)
€€€ **Bistrot.** In a pretty, peaceful piazza in the centre of Rieti, serving typical dishes from the region. Closed Sun and Mon lunch. *Piazza San Rufo 25, T: 0746 498798.*

FESTIVALS & EVENTS

Amatrice Festival in honour of the famous pasta dish *Spaghetti all'amatriciana*, also featuring other regional foods and crafts, last Sun in Aug.
Greccio Commemoration of the crèche of St Francis, which includes a re-enactment of St Francis building the Nativity scene, Christmas Eve.
Monteleone Sabino *Santa Vittoria*, Feast of the patron saint with live music, processions and fireworks, second Sun in May.
Rieti *Sant'Antonio*, Feast of the patron saint, 13 June.

LAZIO NORTH

VITERBO & NORTHERN LAZIO

The northern part of Lazio, also known as Tuscia, is a volcanic land of fertile fields and lovely lakes, scattered with the rock-hewn tombs of the ancient Etruscans. Bordered by Umbria to the east, Tuscany to the north and the Tyrrhenian sea to the west, it covers an area roughly equivalent to the modern province of Viterbo, its chief town.

VITERBO

Viterbo (*map p. 166, C2*) certainly had an Etruscan past, although the site of the ancient city is unknown. It rose to prominence again in the Middle Ages. After it was raised to the dignity of a city by Frederick Barbarossa in 1167, Viterbo was often disputed between the papacy and the Holy Roman Empire. Frederick II besieged it unsuccessfully in 1243. In 1257 Pope Alexander IV chose to come and live here, and after his death here in 1261, his three successors were elected in the town. Between 1276 and 1281 the conclaves for the election of three more popes were held here. During this short period Viterbo rivalled Rome in importance, and the struggle between the two cities lasted some three centuries. Today the old town within the walls is of great interest for its many medieval buildings built in the local grey stone called *peperino*, and it has numerous decorative fountains. The lion, the ancient symbol of the town, recurs frequently as a sculptural motif. Many of its streets are winding and narrow (and unfortunately still busy with cars). The town was seriously damaged in the Second World War, and when it became a provincial capital, it expanded in a disorderly way and now has extensive suburbs.

Palazzo Papale and the duomo

In the secluded Piazza San Lorenzo is the **Palazzo Papale** built around 1266, particularly memorable for its elegant Gothic loggia which frames the sky. It has been used as the episcopal palace since the 15th century, and beneath the arch can be seen Etruscan remains. The large hall (*for admission, ask at the cathedral museum*), at the top of the steps, witnessed the elections of Pope Gregory X in 1271; John XXI (1276), who died a year later of injuries when the ceiling of the new wing collapsed on his head; and Martin IV (1281). Intrigues protracted the first of these elections for two years, until Rainero Gatti, Captain of Viterbo, forced a decision (on the advice of St Bonaventure) by shutting the electors in the palace, then removing the roof of the hall, and finally reducing the food supply. The holes made in the floor for the cardinals' tent-pegs can still be seen. Pope Gregory's reign is best remembered for the set of rules he drew up to ensure that future conclaves would run more smoothly—rules that are still more or less in force today.

The Romanesque duomo of **San Lorenzo** (*open all day*) was built in 1192, although the façade was not erected until 1560. The fine campanile, striped on its four upper

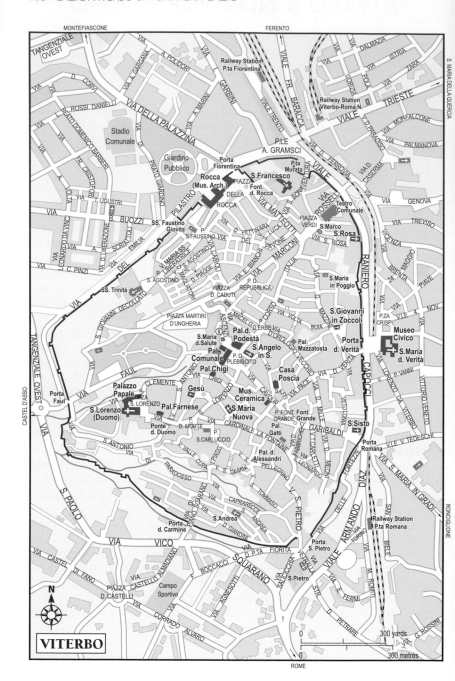

storeys, dates from the late 14th century. The nave arcades have good capitals, all of them different. The elaborately carved font dates from 1470. At the end of the north aisle is John XXI's tomb (d. 1277), with an effigy. The floor retains some 12th-century marble inlay. The Baroque choir is shown on a tour from the museum. The **Museo del Colle del Duomo** (*open 9–1 & 3–8; winter 10–1 & 3–6; closed Mon*) has a miscellany of ecclesiastical objects, but just one particularly precious work of art from the cathedral: a panel representing the *Madonna 'della Carbonara'*, which dates from the 12th century.

Via San Lorenzo passes the medieval Palazzo Farnese, supposed birthplace of Paul III, before crossing the old Ponte del Duomo, which has visible remains of its Etruscan origins beneath it, and a fountain in a charming little garden below. The shaded Piazza della Morte has another fountain and three bays of a 12th-century loggia.

The medieval district

In an attractive old market square with a medieval tower and pretty 17th-century fountain is the 11th-century church of the **Gesù** (*usually kept locked*). Prince Henry of Cornwall, nephew of Henry III of England, passed through Viterbo in 1272 on his return from the Crusades, and was murdered at the altar here by Simon and Guy de Montfort in revenge for the death of their father Simon (opponent of Henry III) at the battle of Evesham in 1265. The murder is mentioned by Dante (*Inferno XII: 118–20*).

From Via San Lorenzo, Via Santa Maria Nuova, with no less than four arches, leads to **Santa Maria Nuova** (*open 8–12.30 & 4–7*), one of the finest churches in the city, dating from the 12th century. St Thomas Aquinas preached from the tiny outdoor pulpit on the façade, and the marble head above the door is probably a Roman work representing Jupiter. The basilican interior has lovely capitals and a beautiful triptych of *Christ with Saints*, unusual for its iconography, which dates from the 13th century; the *Madonna and Child with Two Angels* dates instead from the 15th century. The Neoclassical tomb of a young poet called Orazio Carnevalini has a bust by Pietro Tenerani (1823). The cloister (entered from Via Santa Maria Nuova; *open 10–12 & 3 or 4–5/7*) with miniature, cigar-shaped columns and brick arches, probably dates from the Lombard period. Part of the ancient crypt is also shown.

The medieval district traversed by **Via San Pellegrino** provides an almost unspoilt picture of a 13th-century town (and it has often been used for film sets). Its narrow streets have huge old paving stones, and many of the houses (some of them now antique shops) have outside stairs and balconies. A little museum here documents the work of the men who transport the *macchina* on the feast day of Santa Rosa, the saint who helped the town and inspired its inhabitants to defend themselves against Frederick II in the mid-13th century. Via delle Piaggiarelle leads steeply down to a bridge above a garden inhabited by ducks and geese, across which is an old medieval walkway (Via Caprarecce) which provides a good view of the old houses and towers of San Pellegrino.

The town centre

Piazza del Plebiscito, in the centre of town, is unpleasantly busy with traffic which runs across it in a diagonal direction. **Palazzo Comunale**, begun in 1460, has a por-

Copy of a Roman sarcophagus on the church of Sant'Angelo in Spatha.

tico and picturesque garden courtyard with a 17th-century fountain. **Palazzo del Podestà** was first built in 1264, and its handsome central window has a balcony. The slender tower dates from 1487. On the corner is a column with a carved lion and a palm tree. The church of **Sant'Angelo in Spatha** has on its exterior a copy of a Roman sarcophagus with hunting scenes, which is supposed to be the sepulchre of the mythical 'Bella Galiana', a beautiful maiden killed by a Roman baron, whom she rejected as a lover, in the 12th century.

On the ground floor of the 16th-century Palazzo Brugiotti, at no. 67 Via Cavour, is the **Museo della Ceramica** (*open Oct–March Fri–Sun 10–1 & 3–7; April–Sept Thurs–Sun 10–1 & 4–7*) with a good collection of medieval and Renaissance ceramics from Viterbo and northern Lazio, most of them found in medieval wells used for rubbish. There is also a collection of pharmacy jars. **Piazza della Fontana Grande** has the finest and oldest fountain in the city, begun in 1206 and finished in 1279 (restored in 1424), but sadly at the time of writing it was dry. In the narrow Via Saffi the **Casa Poscia** is a picturesque 14th-century house, and **Palazzo Gatti** (in Via Cardinale La Fontaine), with elaborate tracery in the windows of its two upper floors, has a garden on its summit.

The little Piazza delle Erbe, where lots of streets converge, has a pretty fountain decorated with lions. On the long **Corso Italia**, the main shopping street of the town, the **Caffè Schenardi**, founded by Raffaele Schenardi in 1818, was decorated and superbly lit by Virginio Vespignani later in the 19th century. It survives intact as one of the most delightful cafés in Lazio.

The Rocca

From the end of Corso Italia a road leads to the sanctuary of **Sant Rosa**, which was built in 1850 to preserve the body of St Rose, a virgin saint famous in Viterbo for her ferocious opposition to the emperor Frederick II. The church contains a polyptych by the 15th-century artist Francesco d'Antonio, known as Il Balletta, a native of the town, who clung to the Late Gothic style.

San Francesco (*open 7–12 & 3.30–6.30*) is a Gothic church of 1237 which has a pulpit on the façade from which St Bernardino of Siena preached in 1426. In the lovely vaulted interior are a number of tombs of prelates, including two papal tombs in the transepts: that of Clement IV (d. 1268) by Pietro di Oderisio; and of Hadrian V

(d. 1276), a beautiful work, probably the first piece of carving by the great sculptor Arnolfo di Cambio.

In Piazza della Rocca, with a fountain by Raffaello da Montelupo (altered by Vignola), is the **Rocca**, built by Cardinal Albornoz in 1354, but later altered and enlarged, with a magnificent courtyard and staircases. It has been restored to house the **Museo Archeologico** (*open 8.30–7.30 except Mon*). On the ground floor are displayed finds made during excavations in 1956–78 at Acquarossa and San Giovenale by the Swedish Institute of Classical Studies in Rome. The material is particularly interesting for the light it throws on Etruscan domestic architecture in southern Etruria, and includes painted tiles, antefixes, panels with reliefs (6th century BC) and bronzes. On the first floor are displayed nine statues of the 1st century AD: eight Muses and *Pothos* (a male figure personifying yearning for a loved one), from originals by Skopas. These were found in 1902 in the Roman theatre of Ferento (*see p. 183*), where they formerly decorated niches in the scena. Another room has finds made in Lazio by the French school in Rome since 1983, including a hoard of coins and a pretty pavement from Roman baths. On the second floor is a display of material from sites in southern Etruria, including a pair of sphinxes in *peperino* stone (4th century BC); remains of two chariots from San Giuliano (Barbarano Romano); and lions in *nenfro* stone found in the rock tombs of Blera. Other finds are from Norchia and Lake Bolsena. A very well-preserved bronze statuette of *Jupiter Veiovis*, dating from the 1st century AD, was unearthed in Viterbo. From the loggia there is a fine view of the city and hills beyond. A small room displays a reconstructed ceremonial chariot dating from around 520 BC, dug up at Istria di Castro.

Around Porta della Verità

Santa Maria della Verità (*closed 12.30–5*), founded in the 12th century, contains good frescoes by Lorenzo da Viterbo (1469). The convent, with splendid Gothic cloisters, houses the **Museo Civico** (*partially closed for restoration at the time of writing*). The ground floor has a small archaeological collection with finds from Ferento, including a lovely marble panel with a relief of an olive tree (3rd century AD), and the original Bella Galiana sarcophagus (*see opposite*). Above is the Pinacoteca. Its main treasures are two masterpieces by Sebastiano del Piombo: a *Flagellation* painted in 1525, and a *Pietà* dating from about ten years earlier. They were commissioned by Monsignor Giovanni Botonti for churches in Viterbo. The *Flagellation* is derived from Sebastiano's fresco in San Pietro in Montorio in Rome (*see p. 81*). Some critics think it possible that Michelangelo had a hand in the *Pietà*. Both paintings have charcoal studies on the back, also by Sebastiano. Pastura, who was born in Viterbo, is represented by a number of paintings, including the *Nativity with Sts John the Baptist and Bartholomew*, dating from 1488. The collection also includes a precious *Madonna and Child Enthroned* by the 13th-century Roman school; an early work (the *Incredulity of St Thomas*) by Salvatore Rosa; works by the Viterbese Baroque artist Giovanni Francesco Romanelli (a pupil of Pietro da Cortona); and an unglazed terracotta bust of Giovanni Battista Almadiani by Andrea della Robbia.

The best preserved section of the medieval walls, with battlements and defensive towers can be seen along Viale Raniero Capocci. **San Sisto** retains its massive campanile, in part dating from the 9th century. In its fine basilican interior there is a splendid raised choir with massive pillars. The high altar is composed from 4th–5th-century architectural fragments. **San Giovanni in Zoccoli** is a much restored 11th-century church with a rose window in its fine façade, which is supported by two arches which extend across the road to the house opposite. In the handsome interior there is a beautiful polyptych by Balletta (1441), complete with its predella.

ENVIRONS OF VITERBO

Santa Maria della Quercia

The church of Santa Maria della Quercia (*open 6.30–12 & 3.30–7*), a few kilometres east of Viterbo (follow Viale Trieste), is one of the finest buildings of the High Renaissance. The façade, which dates from 1509, has three lunettes by Andrea della Robbia and a massive campanile by Ambrogio da Milano. The beautiful interior, designed by Antonio da Sangallo the Younger, contains a splendid tabernacle by Andrea Bregno (1490) behind the high altar, and altarpieces by the Tuscan artists Fra' Bartolomeo, Mariotto Albertinelli and Fra' Paolino da Pistoia. The conventual buildings include two lovely cloisters, and there is a museum of ex-votos (*open by appointment; T: 0761 303430*).

Blera, Castel d'Asso and Norchia

The environs of Viterbo (*map p. 166, C2*) are rich in Etruscan remains, many of them in particularly evocative settings. In the area around **Blera**, the *Phleva* of the Etruscans, numerous interesting excavations were carried out in the mid-20th century, when tombs and houses were unearthed. To see some of the tombs it is best to follow the signs to the car park at Ponte della Rocca near the necropolis at Pian del Vescovo, since the other marked paths follow a very long and circuitous route. The picturesque hill village of **Barbarano Romano** is near the site of an Etruscan township now known as San Giuliano, where the necropolis also has a great number of tombs interesting especially for the variety of their architecture. They are now in a beautiful protected area, where lovely walks can be taken, and a little church survives built out of numerous Roman fragments.

The Etruscan necropolis of **Castel d'Asso**, a romantic and remote-seeming spot, is reached from Viterbo down the splendid Strada Signorino, a road carved deep in the tufa in a way that recalls the famous *vie cave* near Pitigliano (*see p. 479*). The necropolis consists of tombs carved in a tufa cliff-face, fronting a beautiful wide and fertile valley. Most of the tombs have a rock façade with a false doorway. Below this was a room used for ritual banquets, often also with a false doorway. It would originally have been covered by a porch. The chamber where the sarcophagi were laid was accessed by a long, steep *dromos* cutting down into the rock beneath.

Norchia is another Etruscan necropolis (4th–2nd centuries BC), once again unenclosed in fertile farming country, again carved into a cliff-face beside a stream. To

Rock tomb at Castel d'Asso, showing the false door and cornice above, the ritual chamber below (also with a false door), and the narrow access *dromos* to the tomb chamber in front.

reach it, you have to leave your car by a stand of eucalyptus trees, from where a farm track leads to the edge of the cliff. A steep, narrow, rock-hewn path takes you down to the tombs (stout shoes essential). Unlike Castel d'Asso, the tombs were fashioned to look like temples rather than houses, with lateral flights of steps. Some still retain their pediments. In all cases the columns have disappeared, but it is still possible to see where they stood. Rockfalls threaten the site, and it is very little visited except by shepherds, who sing to their flocks from the clifftop opposite. It would be difficult to find somewhere which gives a more vivid sense of the vanished glory of Etruscan civilisation.

THE MONTI CIMINI

The lovely Lago di Vico (*map p. 166, C2*), used for sailing and swimming, is surrounded by a beautiful wooded nature reserve on the edge of the crater of Monte Venere, whose cone rises above the lake. The road above the western side of the lake passes through woods and offers only occasional glimpses of the water; the prettiest road is the one which descends beneath Monte Venere on the eastern and northern shores. Beyond rises the volcanic peak of Monte Cimino (1053m), thickly wooded with beech and chestnut.

Bagnaia and the Villa Lante

Bagnaia, northeast of Viterbo (*map p. 166, C2*), is a pretty little town with a medieval district around Piazza del Castello with several fountains, but it is mostly visited for its famous Villa Lante, with perhaps the most beautiful and best-preserved formal garden in Italy. Three attractive small 16th-century roads lead to the entrance to the property, which was owned by the Lante family from 1656 until 1973, when it was bought by the

Detail of the 16th-century formal gardens of Villa Lante.

Italian state (*the gardens are open Tues–Sun 8.30–dusk (in winter 4.30, in summer 7.30*). The park extends beyond the monumental Pegasus fountain, attributed to Giambologna, which has a hemicycle decorated with busts of the Muses. The Casinò di Caccia was built in the early 16th century by Cardinal Ottaviano Riario. The beautiful gardens, still very carefully tended, designed around a series of delightful fountains, were created by Cardinal Giovanni Francesco Gambara after 1566, almost certainly with the help of Vignola and Ammannati. The cardinal also planned the two symmetrical little garden pavilions or *palazzine*: he used one as his summer residence, but the second one was not built until 1590 when Cardinal Alessandro Montalto continued work on the gardens (and added fountains to the park). The vaulted *logge* have frescoes of other villas in Lazio, *grottesche*, and birds. The gardens were designed to be approached from above, rather than from the water parterre, which today is the first part to be seen and which has a French feel to it, with its box and yew hedges closely planted in intricate designs around square ponds and a large central fountain with four elegant statues (known as 'moors' since the *peperino* stone has darkened) holding up the Montalto arms. But the loveliest part of the garden is that laid out earlier on the little hillside above in five terraces connected by a central walk with a series of fountains, and planted with hydrangeas, camellias and rhododendrons beneath splendid old plane trees and ilexes. There is a long, stone dining table kept fresh by rivulets of running water, and a semicircular fountain with two reclining statues of river gods. Behind them is a water staircase in the form of a huge chain, which descends from an octagonal fountain decorated with dolphins. At the top of the garden is a grotto over-grown with mosses and maidenhair fern, where the spring water which supplies all the fountains in the garden issues from a monster's mouth. On either side are little *logge*, with the name and coat of arms of Cardinal Gambara, two gigantic herms, and fresco fragments of the Muses and birds. On the left, columns surround a rose garden laid out between box hedges near a venerable ilex grove. Near here was the original entrance, where visitors would pass through an area of incredibly lush vegetation before they emerged into the formal garden with its delightful fountains.

Soriano nel Cimino and Vignanello

Above the pleasant little restored medieval *borgo* in the highest part of **Soriano nel Cimino** (*map p. 166, D2*) is the imposing 13th-century Orsini castle (*open May and June 10.30–1 & 3–6.30 except Mon; July and Aug 4–7.30; otherwise only at weekends*) with some *grottesche* decorations and a chapel, but much of it transformed when it was in use as a prison from 1870–1989. The view of Monte Soratte and the open plain is superb. In the lower part of the town is Palazzo Albani Chigi, built in 1562 by Vignola, and once famous for its terraced garden with elaborate fountains and water-falls (the huge statue of a woman with a goat at her feet gave it its popular name, *Papacqua*, or 'the queen of water'). However, it is now sadly in a ruined state and has been closed for decades. The vineyards in the district of Soriano have been replaced since the 1960s by extensive plantations of hazelnut trees, which are now to be seen all over this area of northern Lazio, also to the south of the Lago di Vico (many of the nuts are turned into the famous 'chocolate' paste called Nutella).

The early 17th-century box parterre at Castello Ruspoli in Vignanello.

A by-road, signposted 'Faggeta' leads up past chestnut groves to end at a car park near the summit of the extinct volcano of **Monte Cimino** (1053m), covered with some 57 hectares of magnificent beechwoods, where the huge trees are over 200 years old and there are lovely woodland walks (and a café and refuge). Also here, right beside the car park, is the *Sasso Naticarello*, a massive rocking stone, mentioned by the Elder Pliny, a trachyte block weighing 250 tons, which was thrown up in an eruption and was caught by a projecting crag. It has remained thus poised ever since.

At **Vignanello** (*map p. 166, D2*) the huge Castello Ruspoli stands in the main piazza. The parterre garden (*open April–Oct Sun and holidays 10.30–1.30 & 3–6; or by appointment; T: 0761 755338*)—described by Georgina Masson as the best box parterre in Italy—survives intact from the 17th century. Low hedges of mixed shrubs surround the twelve dwarf-box parterres planted in 1610 with the initials of Ottavia Orsini (daughter of Vicino Orsini, who made the park at Bomarzo; *see below*) and her children, Sforza and Galeazzo; and later with those of Francesco Maria Ruspoli. The shapes are strictly geometric, and very Italian, with none of the swirls and curlicues of the later 17th century and the French style. There are lemon trees and roses in vases, and beyond the wall can be seen the park. The *giardino segreto* below of box and roses was replanted in the early 20th century. Visitors are also shown part of the castle, which retains the atmosphere of a private residence (it is still owned by the family), and from the windows of which there are wonderful views of the garden. Some decorations date from the early 18th century, when Handel stayed here as a guest of Prince Francesco Maria Ruspoli.

Bomarzo and Orte

Bomarzo (*map p. 166, D1*) is an interesting little town on a precipitous hill, built of dark grey stone which gives it rather a grim aspect, and recalls its Etruscan origins. It is particularly well preserved around the castle (*open at weekends*), built by the Orsini in 1523–83 and now partly occupied by the town hall. In an attractive secluded piazza is the 16th-century duomo, which has a campanile on Roman foundations with a Roman funerary monument with three busts incorporated into its masonry. The tiny Via Regina Elena leads through the attractive, well-kept old town with numerous outside stairs decorated with plants.

But Bomarzo is visited above all for its famous **Parco dei Mostri** (*open 8.30–sunset*) in the valley below the town. This was the *Sacro Bosco* created for his castle in the mid-16th century by Vicino Orsini, probably with the help of Pirro Ligorio or Vignola. Gigantic fantastic creatures and bizarre monsters were carved in the natural rocky outcrops and surrounded by thick woods of oak, pine and chestnuts, producing one of the strangest sights in Italy. Its original character was sadly altered at the end of the 20th century when it was to some extent 'tidied up'. The statues include a monster with a wide open mouth, two giants wrestling, a gigantic tortoise with a female statue of *Fame* on his back, a life-size Carthaginian elephant killing a Roman soldier, a dragon, exotic sea monsters, the three-headed Cerberus, and an ogre with a stone table in its open mouth. Beneath

Gaping-mouthed monster in the Parco dei Mostri at Bomarzo, created in the mid-16th century.

one of the sphinxes at the entrance, an inscribed stone asks 'Tell me, were such marvels wrought by enchantment or by art?' A miniature temple, with a pronaos derived from the Pantheon, was intended as a mausoleum to Vicino's wife, Giulia Farnese.

Orte (*map p. 166, D2*) stands on the site of the Etrusco-Roman *Horta*, perched on a tufa rock overlooking the Tiber. It has many handsome small palaces. A museum in the deconsecrated Romanesque church of San Silvestro has a rich collection of ecclesiastical objects, including an 8th-century mosaic *Madonna* from the old basilica of St Peter's in Rome, paintings (including a *Madonna* by Taddeo di Bartolo) and Church silver. On the other side of the Tiber are the ruins of Roman *Ocriculum* (*see p. 576*).

At **Vitorchiano** (*map p. 166, C1*) the Centro Botanico Moutan is a garden of Chinese peonies, at their best from mid-April–end May (*open 9.30–1 & 2.30–6*).

Caprarola

Palazzo Farnese, perhaps the most magnificent Mannerist villa in Italy, is in a splendid position dominating the little town of Caprarola. (*Map p. 166, D2. Admission 8.30–6.45 except Mon; guided visits every half hour except on holidays, when you can visit it on your own but when the upper gardens are kept closed.*)

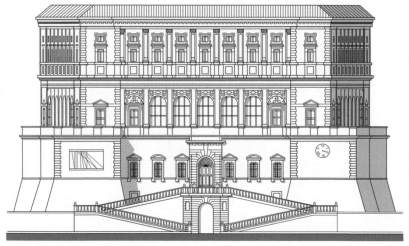

CAPRAROLA: PALAZZO FARNESE

The palace, designed by Vignola in 1559–73 for Cardinal Alessandro Farnese, was built on the foundations of a pentagonal fortress begun around 1515 by Antonio da Sangallo the Younger for the cardinal's uncle, Alessandro Farnese (later Paul III). The very fine exterior, approached by a series of monumental steps, ramps and terraces (the grey door was the entrance for carriages), was over restored at the end of the 20th century so that the local grey *peperino* stone now looks like white travertine.

In 1581, a few years after the villa had been built, Montaigne visited Caprarola, on the same day that he had seen the villa at Bagnaia, which he felt 'easily takes the prize for the use and service of water'. But of Caprarola he noted that it was already 'very greatly renowned in Italy. I have seen none in Italy that may be compared with it. It has a great moat around it, cut out of the tufa. The building is above, in the manner of a terrace: you do not see the tiles. The form is pentagonal, but to the eye it appears distinctly square. Inside, however, it is perfectly round, with wide corridors going around it, all vaulted and painted on all sides. The rooms are all square; the building, very large; very beautiful public rooms ... Outside there are many noteworthy and beautiful things, among others a grotto, which, spraying water artfully into a little lake, gives the appearance to the eye and the ear of the most natural rainfall.'

A splendid spiral staircase with a dome designed by Vignola leads up to the *piano nobile*, where a circular loggia overlooks the beautiful circular courtyard. The empty apartments here were richly decorated for the cardinal by Taddeo and Federico Zuccari, Antonio Tempesta and others, with stuccoes and frescoes on a scheme worked out by Annibale Caro celebrating the glorious history of the Farnese family from the time of Pope Paul III onwards. The most remarkable are the splendid **frescoes by Taddeo Zuccari** in the Sala dei Fasti Farnesiani (the scene of Francis I incorporates the self-portraits of the Zuccari brothers). Views from the windows take in the plain and Monte Soratte beyond the town's long main street. In the chapel the figure of St James the Great is supposed to be a portrait of Vignola. In the winter apartments the beautiful Sala degli Angeli has frescoes by the Mannerist artist Raffaellino da Reggio. The Sala del Mappamondo has extremely interesting and accurate maps of the world dating from 1574, and the vault decorated with the constellations.

The small **winter garden**, with two formal symmetrical beds edged with box and surrounded by holly and laurel hedges, is approached directly across bridges from the *piano nobile* high above the moat. The elaborate grotto here still rains down water from the vault as it did in Montaigne's day. The **upper garden** is a long way uphill beyond a chestnut wood and grove of silver firs: it is the most beautiful part of the gardens (not visible from the palace) approached from a circular fountain beside two grottoes and in front of a delightful water staircase, decorated with dolphins, which descends from a fountain with two river-gods in a hemicycle. This provides a splendid approach to the elegant Casinò di Caccia, a hunting lodge with a double loggia, designed by Vignola and completed by Jacopo del Duca. It is surrounded by another garden on a terrace with huge herms on the balustrade. Pretty stairways lined with more dolphins lead up to yet another garden which slopes gently down towards the lodge and has pebble mosaic paving. This was used for outdoor entertainments, and here is the aqueduct which supplies all the fountains in the garden. Thick woods of chestnuts, cypresses and pines extend over the hillside beyond.

Outside Caprarola, in a splendid position across the valley from Palazzo Farnese, is the huge church and convent of **Santa Teresa**, a very fine building by Girolamo Rainaldi (1623). **Ronciglione** (*map p. 166, C2*) has an impressive 15th-century campanile in dark grey *peperino* in front of a few remains of the church of Sant'Andrea, destroyed in the last war. In a piazza with a 16th-century fountain with unicorns' heads stands the duomo, rebuilt by Carlo Rainaldi (son of Girolamo) in 1695. Santa Maria di Provvidenza, with its 13th-century bell-tower, stands on a charming little terrace with a fountain and a loggia overlooking a gorge. The church of Santa Maria della Pace, attributed to Vignola or Rainaldi, has an interesting interior.

San Martino al Cimino

San Martino al Cimino (*map p. 166, C2*) is a village which was entirely rebuilt in the 17th century by Donna Olimpia Maidalchini-Pamphilj, when she was given the principate by her brother-in-law in gratitude for her help in having him elected Pope Innocent X. It has survived virtually intact, with its rows of simple little houses and wide streets, on a plan which recalls a Roman circus, a fascinating example of early town planning. In the centre the huge Palazzo Pamphilj (*being restored at the time of writing*) stands next to the splendid 13th-century Cistercian abbey church (*open every day except between around 12.30 and 3*), first mentioned in 838. The façade, which has a huge window which may date from the 13th century and bears the Pamphilj arms, is flanked by two high bell-towers which were added in 1654 for reasons of stability. The extremely fine uncluttered interior, with magnificent vaulting, retains all the characteristics of Cistercian architecture, with the exception of the polygonal (rather than rectangular) apse. A fragment of the Romanesque cloister survives, and a splendid vaulted hall, once part of the monastery, houses the Museo dell'Abate (*ring for the priest who lives close by*), a well-arranged collection of ecclesiastical art, including a magnificent standard of St Martin giving his cloak to the beggar, painted in 1649 by Mattia Preti (during its restoration in 1980 the striking painting of the *Saviour* on the reverse was discovered).

BOLSENA & ITS LAKE

Bolsena (*map p. 166, C1*) stands on or near the site of the Etruscan *Volsinii*, which seems to have been founded by the inhabitants of *Volsinii Veteres* (usually identified with Orvieto), after their city was destroyed in 265 BC. It became an important Roman town, especially after the opening of the Via Cassia here in 170–150 BC, and thrived up until the 3rd century AD. It was destroyed in the late 6th century by the Lombards. Today it is a pleasant, compact little town with an avenue leading down to the lakeside from its main square. Vases of hydrangeas decorate the streets, at their best in June.

Its most important church, **Santa Cristina** (*open 7.15–12.30 & 3/3.30–dusk*), was where a famous miracle is supposed to have taken place in 1263: a Bohemian priest who had doubts about the doctrine of Transubstantiation was convinced when he saw blood drop from the Host onto the altar during Mass. The pope of the day, Urban IV, commemorated the miracle by instituting the festival of Corpus Domini (Corpus Christi) and building Orvieto cathedral. In a chapel built in 1693, the altar stones supposed to be marked with blood are preserved. The altar cloth onto which the blood dripped is still preserved in Orvieto (*see pp. 585–86*).

The best work of Benedetto Buglioni can be seen on the façade and in the interior of the church: he was the only artist who succeeded in producing glazed polychrome terracotta sculptures of the same quality as the famous della Robbia family, after the death of Andrea at the end of the 15th century. His is the beautiful altarpiece of *Santa Cristina* with scenes of her martyrdom in a chapel off the south aisle (where there are also 15th-century frescoes), as well as her bust in the chapel to the right of the sanctuary. The nave has unusual cigar-shaped columns, numerous fresco fragments, and early 18th-century altarpieces by Francesco Trevisani. The lovely polyptych in the sanctuary is by the Sienese artist Sano di Pietro. At the entrance to the primitive Grotta di Santa Cristina an ancient baldacchino, which probably dates from the 8th century, protects a stone in which the footprints are meant to be those of the Saint: she is traditionally thought to be buried in the Roman sarcophagus above which is her beautiful effigy, also by Buglioni. Here is the entrance to extensive catacombs, probably in use from the end of the 3rd to the beginning of the 5th century AD.

A pretty medieval district at the top of the town surrounds the walls of the 12th-century **castle** (*open Tues–Sun 10–1 & 4–7*), seat of a museum which contains an extremely interesting archaeological collection illustrating the history of *Volsinii* and its territory from the Bronze Age up until the Middle Ages, beautifully displayed. Highlights include impasto ceramics from a Villanovan hut village, Etruscan altars, Roman pottery, and a terracotta throne dating from the 2nd century BC and used for Bacchic rites (the arms in the form of elegant seated panthers with putti on their backs). There is also a display illustrating the history of fishing in the lake, and you can go up onto the battlements for the view.

Reached from the road just outside are the **excavations of Volsinii** (*open Tues–Sun 8–1.30*), built in terraces on the hillside overlooking the lake, dating from both the Etruscan and Roman periods.

Lake Bolsena

The beautiful Lago di Bolsena (*map p. 166, C1*), with a circumference of 42km, is the largest of the three volcanic lakes in northern Lazio, and a delightful place to visit. Cultivated fields reach its shores, which are exceptionally well preserved—in particular on its southern and western sides, which can be explored on unsurfaced roads from Marta and Gradoli, and there are also places where you can swim. With a depth in places of nearly 150m, it abounds in fish, especially eels, and there is a great variety of birdlife in the reeds. There are two lovely little islands: the largest is the unusually shaped **Isola Bisentina**, named from the Etruscan town of *Bisentium* which stood opposite. It is privately owned (and at present closed to visitors). Its church has a cupola by Vignola. The uninhabited **Isola Martana** has remains of a castle and a 9th-century church amidst its olive, ilex and laurel groves (boat tours around both islands can be taken from Capodimonte).

On the east shore of the lake (on the Via Cassia between Bolsena and Montefiascone) the **Bolsena British Military Cemetery** contains the graves of 600 servicemen killed between the lake and Orvieto in June 1944 as the Allies advanced north through Italy.

At **Capodimonte** on a promontory on the southern shore of the lake (*map p. 166, C1*), boats can be hired or you can take a boat excursion to the islands. The conspicuous Palazzo Farnese (*no admission*) at the top of the town, approached by a bridge from its piazza, was built by Antonio da Sangallo the Younger, one of a number of buildings by him in this area (including the hexagonal church of Santa Maria in Monte d'Oro on the outskirts of Montefiascone, the Palazzo Ducale in Ischia di Castro and a Farnese palace in Gradoli). Giulia Farnese, the beautiful mistress of Pope Alexander VI, died here in 1524.

Montefiascone

The huge 17th-century dome of the cathedral (by Carlo Fontana) of Montefiascone (*map p. 166, C1*) is conspicuous on the skyline of its hill for miles around. James Stuart, the Old Pretender, married Clementina Sobieska here in 1719. They had two sons: the future Bonnie Prince Charlie, and Henry, Cardinal York. The town overlooks the southeastern edge of Lake Bolsena, in an area which still produces some good wines, the most famous of which is the white called Est! Est!! Est!!! (*see box below*). On the outskirts of town, on the Orvieto road (the Via Cassia) just below the historic centre, is the venerable basilica of **San Flaviano** (*open 7.30–8pm*). The façade dates from 1262, and the very unusual interior plan is on two levels. The lower church probably dates from 1032, and its architecture is particularly interesting at the east end, where through a huge square opening you can see the church above. Some splendid multiple capitals surround the clustered pilasters, some carved with monsters or abstract designs, while others are derived from Byzantine models. The third from the right has a caricature of the sculptor. Although in very poor condition, the frescoes all over the church dating from the 14th–16th centuries are of extreme interest for their iconography. In the third north chapel is the tomb slab of Bishop Fugger of Augsburg (d. 1114) with its famous epitaph: 'Est est est pr[opter] nim[ium] est hic Jo[annes] de Fourcris do[minus] meus mortuus est' ('Est est est, because of too much Est, here my lord John Fugger died').

EST! EST!! EST!!!

This famous wine takes its name from the story of a certain Bishop Fugger, who when he went travelling would send his servant in advance to mark with the word 'Est' ('here it is') the inns where good wine was to be found. At Montefiascone the servant found such exquisite wine that he wrote 'Est, est, est', with the result that the prelate overdrank and died. The date of his death and his exact name and title are often confused, but the story remains fixed in the popular imagination. The wine in question is a DOC-category light, easy-drinking dry white, usually a blend of *Malvasia bianca*, *Trebbiano giallo* and *Trebbiano toscano*. Wineries currently making good Est! Est!! Est!! di Montefiascone (to give the wine its full name) are Falesco and Mazziotti.

Civita di Bagnoregio

The most interesting place near the lake is Civita di Bagnoregio (*map p. 166, C1*). It is approached from the small town of Bagnoregio: where the road ends there is an extraordinary view of the village of Civita perched high up on a tufa rock, surrounded by a dramatic deserted landscape, with wooded valleys, and now reached only from here by a footpath carried on a long viaduct (built in 1965). Civita was the oldest district of Bagnoregio but became separated from it when the saddle of rock was eroded and damaged by earthquakes. It is now a peaceful little village without cars, and only about ten families have remained here (although many of the houses have been discreetly restored inside by the rich and famous for use in the summer), and there are one or two cafés and restaurants. There was probably an Etruscan and Roman settlement here, and it was occupied by the Lombards. The delightful medieval entrance gate has two lions in dark grey stone with the arch surmounted by an eagle. The church (*closed for restoration at the time of writing*) was the cathedral of Bagnoregio up until 1699, and the burial place of its 9th-century bishop St Hildebrand. It contains a Renaissance font and tabernacle and a revered wood Crucifix showing the influence of Donatello. It is worth taking the lane at the far end of the village past an old oil press to see the view across the valley to the *calanchi*, eroded rock formations where the friable tufa has produced frequent land falls: the walled mule path here used to follow the ridge.

Between Bagnoregio and Viterbo lie the ruins of **Ferento** (*map p. 166, C1; open Sun in spring and summer; T: 0761 325929*), founded by the Etruscans in the 4th century and a flourishing town in Roman times, as the very fine theatre attests. It was destroyed by Viterbo in 1172 for heretically representing Christ on the Cross with open eyes.

CIVITA CASTELLANA, NEPI & SUTRI

The attractive little town of Civita Castellana (*map p. 166, D2*) stands on a tufa hill surrounded by picturesque and precipitous ravines covered in wild vegetation and spanned by high bridges. It is on the site of the ancient *Falerii Veteres*, capital of the Falisci, a tribe belonging to the Etruscan Confederation but otherwise distinct and speaking its own language. In 241 BC it was destroyed by the Romans, who built *Falerii Novi*, 6km west (*see p. 184 below*). The new town prospered as an outpost on the Via Flaminia, the road that led from Rome to the Adriatic coast (*see p. 159*). In the 8th and 9th centuries, as the fortunes of Falerii Novi dwindled, the population returned to the ancient site, which acquired its present name of Civita Castellana. It is known for its ceramics.

The **duomo** (*open 9–12 & 3.30/4.30–6.30/7.30*) has a magnificent portico and west door by the Cosmati family (1210), of unique design and particularly delicate workmanship, considered the masterpiece of this Roman family of marble sculptors and extremely well preserved. Beneath the raised chancel (where a worn Roman sarcophagus serves as the high altar) is the charming crypt where the ancient columns have a great variety of capitals and there are two sculptured tabernacles. In an oratory reached by steps to the left of the high altar are two large *plutei* by the Cosmati from the choir-screen, and other sculptural fragments including a primitive hunting scene, and fragments of early 14th-century frescoes, interesting for the costumes of the female figures. It is known that the organ was played by Mozart when on a visit to the town in 1770.

The **Rocca** is a remarkable pentagonal fortress with two fine courtyards, begun by Alexander VI and completed for Julius II by Antonio da Sangallo the Elder. It contains the Museo Archeologico dell'Agro Falisco (*open 8–6 except Mon but only on the hour, when visitors are accompanied*), with material found in excavations in the *Ager Faliscus* (Falerii Veteres, Narce, Vignanello, Corchiano and Nepi) at the end of the 19th and beginning of the 20th centuries, including interesting tomb furniture.

A road from Civita Castellana which follows the branch railway line to Viterbo (signposted 'Fabbrica di Roma') passes close to the romantic site of the Roman town of **Falerii Novi**, which still has long stretches of its walls overgrown by vegetation and conspicuous in the open countryside. Triangular in plan and over 2km in length, they retain 50 of their original 80 towers and two of the nine gates, and are a unique survival. From the excellently preserved Porte di Giove, a pine avenue leads to the old abbey, now a farmhouse, built out of ancient masonry. Here is the large church of Santa Maria di Falleri, built in the 12th century but recently harshly restored (*open only Sat and Sun 9–1*). A path leads to excavations of the probable site of the forum and traces of two roads in a wood, and there are wonderful views over the fields.

Castel Sant'Elia and Nepi

Castel Sant'Elia (*map p. 166, D2*) has a rather abandoned atmosphere. A road leads steeply down to the wooded river valley past an old tufa tower pierced with a hole, to the Basilica di Sant'Elia (*open in summer Mon–Fri 5–7, Sat, Sun and holidays 10–12 & 5–7; winter Mon–Fri 3–5, Sat, Sun and holidays 10–12 & 3–5*), an 11th-century Benedictine foundation on the site of an ancient temple, in a magnificent isolated position below a tufa cliff in a wooded valley filled with the sound of the river. The simple façade incorporates ancient sculptural fragments. The interior has Roman columns and capitals and fragments of a Cosmatesque pavement, and is particularly interesting for its frescoes of scenes from the Apocalypse at the east end, signed by the brothers 'Giovanni' and 'Stefano' and a third master 'Nicola', and usually dated between 1080 and 1145. The bright colours and delightful costumes show Byzantine influence. Also here is a pulpit made up from ancient fragments, and a pretty ciborium.

Close by is **Nepi**, a small town surrounded by impenetrable wild ravines. An 18th-century aqueduct stands beside the huge ruined Rocca and the medieval walls on Etruscan foundations. The town hall was begun by Antonio da Sangallo, and has a bell-tower and fountain on its handsome façade. The duomo (*closed 12–3.30*) has an ancient crypt.

Sutri

Sutri (*map p. 166, C2*) is a pleasant and lively little town, well worth exploring. It was the ancient Etruscan *Sutrium* which was captured by Camillus in 389 BC. Marcus

Furius Camillus was often called the 'second founder of Rome'. He held various official posts (censor, military tribune and dictator), and was responsible for numerous victories over the tribes which occupied the territory close to Rome (notably the Etruscans at Veio; *see p. 189*). Though in later centuries his military prowess was perhaps exaggerated, it was undeniably through him that Rome greatly expanded its hold over central Italy. By 465 Sutri was the seat of a bishopric and its cession by the Lombard king Liutprand to Pope Gregory II in 728 is traditionally seen as marking the beginning of the temporal power of the popes. The rival popes Gregory VI and Sylvester III were deposed for simony by a synod held here in 1046.

The attractive central Piazza del Comune is entered by a Roman arch built of *peperino* blocks in the 2nd century BC beneath a clock-tower, which was probably the former entrance to the Roman forum. The pretty fountain dates from 1722. The duomo (*closed for restoration at the time of writing*), redesigned in 1745, retains its campanile of 1207, and the Cosmatesque pavement and beautiful crypt survive from the medieval church. On a side altar is an unusual early 13th-century icon of Christ blessing in the Byzantine style (in other words, with a finger forming a circle with the thumb). A large public fountain (once used for washing clothes), on the edge of the hillside overlooking a thickly wooded gorge, has been well restored. There is another pretty view from the terrace in front of the little church of Santa Croce, which has a fresco of the *Legend of the True Cross* by a painter close to Giulio Romano.

But Sutri is famous above all for its **Roman amphitheatre**, on the Via Cassia at the bottom of the hill in a little park and surrounded by trees (*open May–Sept 8.30–6.30 except Mon; Sun and holidays 8.30–2; Oct–April Sun and holidays, Tues, Wed and Fri 8–2; Thurs and Sat 8–5; when closed it can be partially seen from outside the gate*). Probably dating from the 1st century BC, this is a remarkable sight since it is carved entirely out of an outcrop of tufa rock. In a tufa cave close by there is a **Mithraeum**, converted into the church of the Madonna del Parto in the 13th–14th century. This is an extremely interesting building simply carved out of the rockface (with no façade), and contains fragmentary frescoes, some of which may date from the 9th century, and others from the 14th–15th centuries (*for admission ask at the amphitheatre; it is shown every hour on the hour*). A rectangular bas-relief of Mithras and the bull, which presumably came from here, can be seen embedded into the exterior of an old house on the Via Cassia near Vetralla, by a public park in the locality of La Botte (*map p. 166, C2; for the cult of Mithras, see p. 116*). Part of the interesting Roman necropolis of Sutri can be seen from a picturesque country lane near the Mithraeum which is lined with some 64 rock tombs. Farther uphill Villa Savorelli, built c. 1730, is privately owned but the fine garden and park are open to the public (*weekdays 8.30–4.30; weekends 8.30–1.30 & 3–6*).

LAKE BRACCIANO & ENVIRONS

The lovely Lago di Bracciano (*map p. 166, C3–D3*) occupies an almost circular crater in the volcanic Monti Sabatini. Reaching a maximum depth of 160m, the lake abounds in trout, tench and eels. Around AD 110 the emperor Trajan built an aqueduct from the lake to Rome, which was restored by Paul V in 1615 to supply some of the city's fountains. It is surrounded by wooded hills and cultivated fields and used for swimming, sailing and wind-surfing (motor boats are banned).

The small town of **Bracciano**, on the lake's southwestern shore, is dominated by the Castello Orsini, a magnificent and perfectly preserved example of a Renaissance baronial castle (*admission only by a guided tour of an hour, weekdays except Mon at 10, 11, 12, 3, 4 & 5; Sun and holidays every half hour 9–12.30 & 3–5.30*). It was begun c. 1470 by Napoleone Orsini and finished by his son c. 1485. It was the first place that Sir Walter Scott wanted to visit on his arrival in Rome. It now belongs to the Odescalchi family, who still use one wing. It is interesting above all for its architecture: it has five crenellated round towers supporting the superb pentagonal structure. The interior has coffered ceilings painted by Antoniazzo Romano, handsome fireplaces, and a collection of arms and armour. The loggia and ramparts provide splendid views of the lake.

The scenery on the lake is particularly beautiful near **Vicarello**, which has extensive olive plantations. **Trevignano Romano** is a picturesque village where the church of the Assunta (from which there is a magnificent view of the lake) has a striking fresco of the *Death and Coronation of the Virgin* by the school of Raphael (1517) and a precious 13th-century triptych. At **Anguillara Sabazia** another church dedicated to the Assunta also has a splendid position above the lake. At **Vigna di Valle** there is a museum of military aeroplanes, including some of the earliest examples used in the First World War. A by-road leads east from the lake to the beautiful little **Lago di Martignano**, also a lovely place to swim. The wild deserted landscape in this area recalls the Far West of the United States, and was indeed used as a setting for some Spaghetti Westerns.

Oriolo Romano and Monterano

Oriolo Romano (*map p. 166, C3*) still preserves its handsome spacious piazza laid out in the 16th century, with a fountain where three streets converge in front of Palazzo Altieri, built in 1578. Now owned by the state (*open daily except Mon 8.30–7*), the *piano nobile* has good frescoes by the Roman Mannerists (notably Giuseppe Barberi), and there is also a collection of portraits of the popes, commissioned in 1670.

From Canale Monterano (which has a church by Mattia de' Rossi perhaps designed by his master Gian Lorenzo Bernini, and an excellent bakery in the piazza), a country road (well signposted for 'Antica Monterano') leads in several kilometres to the romantic ruins of the ancient town of **Monterano** (*map p. 166, C3*), abandoned because of malaria in the 18th century and then destroyed by French troops in 1799. A path continues in 500m from the car park to a fountain beneath a ruined aqueduct beside the high walls of the ancient village. Inside is the ruined Palazzo Ducale with a monumental fountain against the façade, designed for the Altieri by Gian Lorenzo Bernini with a lion (a replica of the original) above an imitation rock. There are remains of several churches and the campanile of the cathedral. Just outside the gate, on a wide plateau, with magnificent views all around of thickly wooded hills without any sign of human habitation, is the crumbling façade of the **monastery church of St**

Bonaventure, also designed by Bernini, with a fountain on the grass in front. This constitutes one of the most striking and unexpected sights in all Italy. Beautiful walks can be taken along marked paths in this protected wooded area close to the Tolfa hills.

Tolfa

Tolfa (*map p. 166, C3*) sits on the peak of an extinct volcano commanding superb views: on a clear day from its ruined castle you can see the distant profile of the cupola of St Peter's in Rome. The hills of Tolfa were once famous for their alum mines (*see box below*).

THE ALUM OF TOLFA

The Tolfa hills were first quarried for iron by the Etruscans. The area's commercial importance was again realised in the 15th century when large deposits of alum were discovered by the agent of Pope Pius II, at just the moment when one of the west's principal sources of alum, Phocaea in Aegean Turkey, was cut off by the capture of Smyrna by the Turks. Alum (a complex, crystalline sulphate of potassium and aluminium) is not a commonly found substance in nature, but it is essential for the treatment of colour and fixing of dyes in textiles—an industry on which the wealth of Florence had been founded. The papacy was quick to exploit this valuable international commodity (of the best quality in Europe, furthermore). With the aid of Medici Bank financing, it secured a monopoly on its exploitation, and sought to constrain the entire Christian world to purchase solely the 'Alum of Rome', as it became known, justifying what was technically a sin (a commercial monopoly or cartel) by designating all revenues derived from the trade to the 'holy' end of financing the papal wars against the Turks. The Genoese and Venetians, who had previously dominated the alum trade, were no longer to purchase it from the Ottoman Empire, on pain of excommunication. Tolfa unexpectedly found itself at the centre of the Western world's financial and political stage. For a while the monopoly seemed an almost achievable aim, until the recalcitrance of the Venetians, and the concurrent discovery of other sources of alum, first in Castile and latterly in England (Alum Bay, on the Isle of Wight), caused its market price to collapse. The bubble burst, inflicting considerable damage on the Medici fortunes and on papal prestige. N.McG.

Tolfa still has the feel of a frontier settlement: for centuries cut off from the main routes of commerce and influence (the Via Aurelia on the coast, and the Via Cassia inland), the population lived from a mixture of banditry and cattle-raising. The wide-horned, ivory-grey *maremmano* cattle are still a feature of the area's wild and wooded landscapes, and cowboy lore is a predominant feature of its culture. In spring the southwestern slopes of the hills below Tolfa are a display of wild jonquils and flowering Judas trees; later in the year, at night, there are nightingales and fireflies in surprising numbers.

The area as a whole has a wide and varied appeal. The former quarries can be still seen, to the south of the main road from Tolfa to Allumiere. At Località Fontanaccia, 5km south of Allumiere along the road from La Bianca, are the remains of a panoramically sited Roman villa of the 1st century AD. The sulphurous fumaroles (the 'Solfatara', 9km southwest of Manziana, off the road to Sasso) were used by the Roman army for bathing and disinfecting the legionaries before their return to the city after campaigns in foreign lands. At Piantangeli, above the valley of the Mignone River (6km northeast of Tolfa, by the track which heads north from the first sharp turn in the road to Manziana, below the north side of the town), are the ruins of a 12th-century Romanesque church. It is a landscape ideal for exploring on foot or on horseback (for which there are local facilities). Tolfa has a long tradition of saddle-making and sturdy leatherwork; a kind of satchel made here and known as a '*tolfa*', was popular all over Italy in the 1970s.

CERVETERI & ITS ANCIENT PORT

The small town of Cerveteri (*map p. 166, C3*) preserves walls and towers from the medieval period, when it was the seat of a bishop and well fortified with an Orsini castle; but it is famous above all as the site of *Caere*, one of the largest cities in the Mediterranean and an important member of the Etruscan Confederation. It was always closely allied with Rome. Its **Etruscan necropolis** (*open 8.30–dusk except Mon*), on a tufa hill just outside the present town, is a beautifully planted site, where numerous tombs dating from the 7th–1st centuries BC can be seen. These are of all types, from the earliest shaft or trench graves, and those constructed in blocks with symmetrical doorways (interesting examples of 'urban' planning), to the later tumuli, with their typical conical grass-grown tops, some of them colossal with diameters exceeding 40m. These last are especially interesting for their architectural design: some of them contain numerous chambers modelled in the rock in the form of Etruscan dwellings (which were built in wood), and from these and their contents it has been possible to obtain the fullest picture known of Etruscan civilisation. Many of the tombs can be visited, including the 4th-century Tomb of the Stuccoes, which has a ceiling supported by two columns and the walls decorated with stuccoes and reliefs. Part of the old road which wound between the rocks from the city to the cemetery, with conspicuous cart ruts, also survives. The site was first excavated in 1834, and the most important finds are now in the Etruscan museums in Rome and the Vatican, but there is a well-displayed archaeological collection (*open 8.30–4.30 except Mon*), including splendid black- and red-figure vases, in the castle in the town.

Ceri, just inland from Cerveteri, is a superbly preserved inland village on a tufa hill in a beautiful setting. Beneath the medieval houses are numerous tunnels and grottoes which may date from the Etruscan era. In the church are interesting medieval frescoes with scenes from the life of St Sylvester, only discovered in 1971.

Pyrgi

The most important port of the Etruscan city of *Caere* was Pyrgi, near Santa Severa (*map p. 166, C3*), famous for its sanctuary—one of the largest known in all Etruria—with two temples built around 500–460 BC. The sanctuary was sacred to the Phoenician goddess Astarte. In 1964 archaeologists discovered three gold plaques (*laminae*) of c. 500 BC here, two inscribed in Etruscan and one in Punic (they are now preserved in the Villa Giulia in Rome). The text records the dedication of the temple by Thefarie Velianas, ruler of Caere. It has been suggested that either Caere had entered into an alliance with Carthage against the Greeks, or that Pyrgi had a sizeable population of Carthaginian traders, hence the dedication to a Punic goddess. Scholars had hoped that the texts would prove to be direct translations of each other. No substantial bilingual text such as the Rosetta Stone has ever been found that would help philologists fully to decode the Etruscan language. Though we can make sense of simple funerary inscriptions, the language as a whole is still largely a mystery.

Remains of the temples, as well as polygonal Roman walls, survive at the site, but are usually only visible in September, as at other times they are overgrown and flooded by seawater. However, there is a museum here (*open 9–dusk except Mon*), which is to be moved to the castle of Santa Severa when restoration work is finished. The castle ward, approached by an avenue of palms and umbrella pines, now encloses a picturesque little village and an imposing cylindrical tower survives near remains of the Roman *castrum* and port just offshore.

VEIO

The Parco Regionale di Veio is a protected area of some 15,000 hectares surrounding the site of the ancient city of Veio (*map p. 166, D3*), one of the most famous of the Etruscan cities, built on a triangular tufa plateau (124m) bounded by two streams. At the confluence the sides are precipitous; on the promontory above it was the citadel, now called the Piazza d'Armi. The city was directly accessible only from the northwest angle.

HISTORY OF VEIO

Veio was one of the 12 cities of the Etruscan Confederation, and apparently the largest of them all. Its walls had a circuit of 11km, and its territory was extensive, reaching to the Tiber on the south, east and southwest. It controlled the saltworks at the river mouth. On the west its neighbour was Caere (Cerveteri; *see above*). Veio reached the zenith of its power between the 8th and 6th centuries BC, and its position brought it into frequent conflict with Rome. In 396, after a historic siege of ten years, M. Furius Camillus tunnelled through the rock and at last captured the city. It was destroyed and remained in ruins until Julius Caesar established a colony here, which Augustus elevated into a *municipium*. But the new city did not prosper; it was in decline by the time of Hadrian, and soon disappeared from history.

Excavations on the site began in the 18th century. Many of the finds are in the Villa Giulia in Rome, among them the celebrated *Apollo of Veio* (*see p. 73*) found in the Portonaccio temple here in 1916. Today the ruins of the temple sanctuary can be visited (*open Nov–March 9–4, Sun and holidays 9–2; April–Oct 9–7, Sun and holidays 9–2*). From the Riserva Campetti bus stop at Isola Farnese, a rural road descends steeply downhill. At a cemetery, turn right. The road becomes a track. There is a car park just above the Mola torrent and its ruined mill. The torrent can be forded on foot above the waterfall. A path leads up to the right to the Portonaccio gate. The sanctuary is entered along a paved Roman road, laid over the Etruscan one. On a terrace, the base of the Temple of Apollo can be seen. It was distyle in antis with a tripartite cella. A modern metal superstructure gives an idea of its former height and shape. Adjoining it was a rectangular pool (piscina) for ritual ablutions. This pool was fed from the Mola stream by rock-hewn tunnels (their entrances can still be seen). Next to the piscina ran a road (overlain by a modern walkway), which leads past the remains of a cistern to the huge sacrificial altar.

To the north of Portonaccio is the Tomba Campana, a chamber-tomb of the late 7th century cut in the rock, and one of the earliest painted tombs ever discovered (*only open by appointment; T: 06 904 2774*). There is a museum at Formello, 10km north of Veio.

Remains of the large altar of Veio, which stands in front of the Portonaccio temple.

PRACTICAL INFORMATION

GETTING AROUND

• **By car:** There is a large free car park in Viterbo just inside Porta Faul. For Civita di Bagnoregio, park in Bagnoregio, and walk across the causeway.

• **By train:** For Veio from Rome, Metro line A to Valle Aurelia; then FM3 to Stazione Giustiniana; then bus 032 as below. Slow trains connect Rome with Formello (for Veio museum) in 1hr, and with Bracciano in 1–2hrs. Viterbo trains go on to Sutri. Trains on the Rome–Pisa line stop at Cerveteri and Santa Severa.

• **By bus:** Viterbo and Bagnoregio are on bus routes from Rome. The main bus station at Viterbo is at Piazza Martiri d'Ungheria. Buses run from Viterbo to Bagnaia every 30mins. For Veio, bus 301 from Piazzale Ponte Milvio in Rome to Tomba di Nerone; then bus 201 to Stazione La Storta; then bus 032 to Isola Farnese Riserva Campetti. All buses are reasonably frequent. Frequent buses link Rome with Cerveteri (from Via Lepanto in Rome, several blocks north of Castel Sant'Angelo).

• **By boat:** Lake Bolsena boats leave from Capodimonte for tours around the islands. T: 0761 870760 or 338 767 2849, www.navigabolsena.com

INFORMATION OFFICES

A useful website for the whole region is www.tusciaguide.it

Bagnaia Piazza XX Settembre 4, T: 0761 288125.

Bolsena Piazza Matteotti, T: 0761 7951.

Caprarola Via Filippo Nicolai 126, T: 0761 645038.

Cerveteri Piazza Risorgimento 19, T: 0699 551971.

San Martino al Cimino Piazza dell'Oratorio 2, T: 0761 3751.

Soriano nel Cimino Via Santa Maria 28, T: 0761 746001.

Sutri Piazza del Comune 31, T: 0761 600330

Viterbo Via Ascenzi 4, T: 0761 325992.

HOTELS

Bagnaia (*map p. 166, C2*)

€ **Casa per Ferie Domus La Quercia**. Converted 15th-century building in a lovely position, less than 1km from Villa Lante. Plain, simple rooms. *T: 0761 321322, www.domuslaquercia.com. 50 rooms.*

Civita Castellana (*map p. 166, D2*)

€€ **Palais Hotel Relais Falisco**. A sophisticated hotel converted from a 17th-century mansion, close to the duomo in the town centre. Rooms are individually sized and furnished, the larger suites are definitely worth the extra money. An interesting conversion of an Etruscan cave underneath the hotel has been made into a sauna and jacuzzi area. *Via Don Minzoni 19, T: 0761 5498, www.relaisfalisco.it. 43 rooms.*

Bolsena (*map p. 166, C1*)

€–€€ **Royal.** The oldest hotel in Bolsena, preserving some attractive public rooms. Bedrooms are spacious, with slightly dull modern furnishings, but comfortable. *Piazzale Dante Alighieri 8–10, T: 0761 797048, www.bolsenahotels.it. 37 rooms.*

San Martino al Cimino (*map p. 166, D2*)

€ **Albergo Doria**. A welcoming, small B&B with clean, spacious rooms and a large outdoor area, in the centre of San Martino. *Via Abate Lamberto 4, T: 0761 379924, www.albergodoria.it. 3 rooms.*

€ **Bed and Breakfast Widman**. A delightful B&B with elegant, bright rooms and a wonderful private garden. *Via Doria 5, T: 0761 379709, www.bedandbreakfastwidman.it. 3 rooms.*

Sutri (*map p. 166, C2*)

€ **Il Borgo di Sutri**. Situated just outside the town, this is a good-looking hotel with very comfortable accommodation. Set within the grounds of an aristocratic estate, the surrounding parkland is superb. A tiny, private chapel next to the hotel holds Mass on Sunday. *Località Mezzaroma Nuova, T: 0761 608690, www.ilborgodisutri.it. 21 rooms.*

€ **Sutrium**. Simple, recently renovated, pleasant hotel right in the centre of town. Excellent value. *Piazza San Francesco 1, T: 0761 600468, www.sutriumhotel.it*

Viterbo (*map p. 166, C2*)

€€ **Podere dell'Arco**. ■ Beautifully restored farmhouse B&B tucked away down the Etruscan, rock-carved Strada Signorino, 5mins drive from the centre of Viterbo. Delicious breakfasts (the homemade lavender cake is exceptional). Each apartment has self-catering facilities, and is well appointed in faultless taste. A first-class place to stay for exploring northern Lazio. *Strada Signorino 3, T: 0761 308688, www.poderedellarco.com. 7 apartments.*

€ **Al Cardinale**. B&B offering basic comfort in an old house in the medieval district. *Via Ottusa 8, T: 0761 092423, www.alcardinale.it. 3 rooms.*

€ **Hotel Nibbio**. A modern hotel in the centre of Viterbo, close to the train station. The rooms have simple wood furnishings and floors and are spotlessly clean. *Piazzale Gramsci 31, T: 0761 326514, www.hotelnibbio.it. 30 rooms.*

€ **San Pellegrino**. Splendid B&B in an atmospheric 17th-century house, in a peaceful medieval street right in the centre. *Via San Pellegrino 4, T: 0761 325082, www.bbsanpellegrino.com. 3 rooms.*

RESTAURANTS

Isola Farnese (*map p. 166, D3*)

€€ **Tempio di Apollo**. Restaurant attached to a hotel in the medieval centre of Isola Farnese, handy if you plan to spend a day exploring Veio. *Piazza Colonetta 8, T: 06 308 90595.*

Marta (*map p. 166, C1*)

€€ **Il Pirata**. ■ In a fabulous, peaceful position on an unsurfaced road right on the lakeside, just outside the town. Excellent and very reasonably priced food, including fish from the lake. Closed Wed. *Via della Spiaggi 3, T: 0761 871 515.*

Soriano nel Cimino (*map p. 166, D2*)

€€ **Ai Tre Scalini**. Simple, small-town restaurant and pizzeria. The *zuppa etrusca*, a thick broth with potatoes and beans, is excellent. On the main square. Closed Weds. *Via Vittorio Emanuele III 1, T: 0761 745970.*

Sutri (*map p. 166, C2*)

€€ **La Taverna**. Specialises in homemade pasta and grilled meats. Closed Mon. *Via San Francesco 1, T: 0761 600 131.*

€ **Il Buco**. Simple family restaurant with excellent homemade *fettucine*. Closed Wed and Sun evenings. *Vicolo Miscetti 4, T: 0761 600 598.*

Trevignano Romano (*map p. 166, D3*)

€€ **La Casina Bianca**. A well-established family restaurant with exceptional fish dishes, on the shores of Lake Bracciano. It has a large outdoor terrace which is generally packed at the weekends. Closed Fri. *Via della Rena 100, T: 0699 97231.*

Viterbo (*map p. 166, C2*)
€€ **Osteria San Pellegrino**. Cosy place in the medieval district, with typical Viterbese cuisine. Closed Mon, and Tues and Sun evening. *Via San Pellegrino 30, T: 0761 321632.*
€€ **Tre Re**. Small, old-fashioned restaurant right in the centre of town, serving good home cooking. The *acquacotta* (soup) is delicious. Plenty of mushroom dishes in season. Closed Thur. *Via Macel Gattesco 3, T: 0761 304619.*
€–€€ **Caffè Schenardi**. Founded in 1818 and retaining its decorations intact from that time. A delightful place to have coffee, and also a light lunch (daily set menu). Superb ice cream. *Corso Italia 11, T: 0761 323644.*
€ **Sub Rosa**. Wine bar serving light meals. Very agreeable on a sunny day, when you can sit outside with the sound of splashing water from the fountain. Closed Tues. *Piazza del Gesù 18, T: 328 377 1377.*

LOCAL SPECIALITIES

Bolsena The lake is known for its abundant eels. A live consignment is sent to the Vatican every Christmas.
Nepi The town is known for its mineral water, which has a slight natural effervescence, and is said to aid the digestion. It is bottled as Acqua di Nepi.
Tolfa The area as a whole is known for

its springs: geothermic springs at Bagnarello (two ancient, rock-cut baths in the open air, 2.5km south of Tolfa on the road to Santa Severa; 38°C), and at Stigliano (spa facilities, at the site of the ancient *Vicus Stiglianus*, 16km east along the road to Manziana; 35–70°C); cold springs of sparkling mineral water (below the *borgo* of Rota, 8km east of Tolfa).
Viterbo On the west side of the town (Strada Bagni 12) is a very well run and pleasant spa known as Le Terme dei Papi, with a thermal swimming pool.

FESTIVALS & EVENTS

Bolsena *Infiorata*, The streets of the town are decorated with floral carpets, a popular tradition throughout the Catholic world, but at its finest and most elaborate here, the town where the feast of Corpus Christi was first instituted, June; Festival of Santa Cristina, with a performance of tableaux illustrating her passion, 23–24 July.
Caprarola Hazelnut festival, with a parade and hazelnut biscuits, ice cream and liqueurs, last weekend in Aug.
Nepi Feast of St Anthony Abbot, with a bonfire and blessing of animals and crops, 16–18 Jan.
San Martino al Cimino Chestnut festival, third and fourth Sun in Oct.
Soriano nel Cimino Chestnut festival, with roast chestnuts and parades in historical costume, first and second weekends in Oct.
Viterbo *Santa Rosa*, Since 1663 the festival of the saint's translation has been celebrated with a splendid procession accompanying a great float, which requires some 80 men to carry it, 3 Sept.

TUSCANIA,
TARQUINIA & VULCI

Tuscania (*map p. 166, C2*) is a charming and peaceful little town in beautiful countryside, many of its streets decorated with fountains. Of all the little towns worth visiting in northern Lazio, it is perhaps the most pleasant. Its importance in the Middle Ages is testified by the two splendid Romanesque churches of Santa Maria Maggiore and San Pietro, which were left outside the town walls when the city expanded to the northwest in the 16th century. Numerous traces of its Etruscan origins have been found in the area since the end of the 19th century, and it was famous for its production of sarcophagi: the worn lids of some of these now present rather a bizarre sight on walls or inside churches.

HISTORY OF TUSCANIA

There are numerous Etruscan tombs just outside Tuscania, and evidence of an early Etruscan settlement has been found on the hill of San Pietro to the south. This bluff, defended by the river Marta and its tributaries, was at an important crossroads. Under the Romans the town was named *Tuscana*, and a bishopric was well established here by the 6th century. It became a free *comune* in the 13th century, and as a punishment for defection from papal control (imposed by Pope Boniface VIII) its name was changed to the diminutive Toscanella, a name it kept until it was finally able to resume its original title in 1911. Little sign remains of the earthquake here in 1971, which left 30 dead. The town has mostly been well reconstructed: some of the buildings have 'fortified' ground floors, the walls slightly protruding outwards in order to strengthen their stability.

The old town

Tuscania retains its impressive walls, and is decorated with a number of lovely 17th-century public fountains, the largest of which, set up in 1621 in front of the cathedral, fills the centre of the little town with its sound. Beneath its high basin four mermen ride dolphins. The façade of the **duomo** (*usually open only Thur–Sun for services*) was rebuilt in 1566–72. In the white interior, at the end of the north aisle, is an exquisite marble tabernacle with eight very beautiful angels (and the Crucifix in the scallop shell above), possibly by the school of Sansovino (also attributed to Isaia da Pisa). This was part of a large monument which has been dismantled: it included the six lovely carved reliefs of saints at the end of the south aisle. Here is a little chapel with

Cithara player from the 5th-century BC Tomba del Triclinio at Monterozzi, now preserved in the Museo Nazionale Tarquiniense.

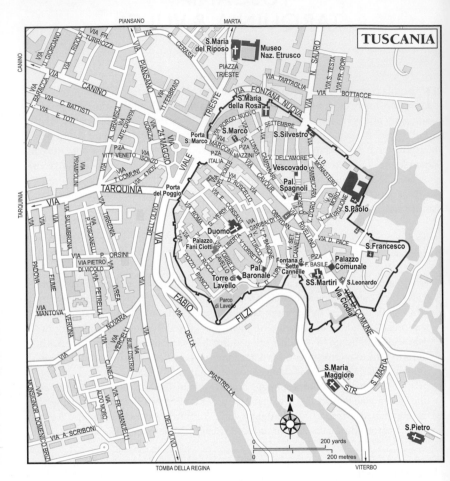

a fine collection of paintings and frescoes (*the gate is usually kept locked; ask the sacristan to turn on the light*). The large polyptych of the *Madonna and Child with Four Saints* by Taddeo di Bartolo (or the less well-known Andrea di Bartolo) has seven scenes of the Passion below. The striking 15th-century triptych of the *Redeemer*, painted on both sides and with folding doors, is by Francesco d'Antonio (called Il Balletta), who also painted the fresco of the *Madonna and Child*. The frescoes of the *Crucifixion* and *Assumption* are by the little-known painter called Domenico Velandi, a follower of Benozzo Gozzoli.

Beside the **Torre di Lavello**, named after Captain Angelo Broglio da Lavello (known as 'Il Tartaglia'), who ordered its construction after he had occupied the town in 1400, is a delightful public park above the walls, planted with pine trees, cypresses and olive trees, and with a particularly lovely simple fountain. There are lots of places to sit and enjoy the view over lovely countryside taking in the two great churches of Tuscania which now stand outside its walls: San Pietro next to a medieval tower on the skyline, and below, in a clump of trees, Santa Maria Maggiore. On the left can be seen a stretch of walls and the old Palazzo dei Priori on the hill of Rivellino. From the attractive little piazza the lovely old Via della Lupa leads downhill between high walls (with a view up left of the medieval Palazzo Baronale) past a public fountain with an excellent system of basins for laundering, to a monumental fountain with seven taps (Fontana delle Sette Cannelle), which has been functioning since 1309. It is immediately below the terrace of **Piazza Basile**, attractively laid out in the early 19th century, when the lantern of the closed church of the Santi Martiri was built. The Neoclassical Palazzo Comunale is decorated with two 17th-century statues, and has an outside stair and two protruding wings, one of which now forms the entrance to a theatre (with a typical painting by the contemporary local painter Giuseppe Cesetti in the foyer). A portal in a high wall surmounted by a row of Etruscan sarcophagus lids admits to steps up to the 12th-century ex-church of Santa Croce, now the municipal library, surrounded by a small raised garden with a fountain and cypresses. In the piazza a balustrade (decorated with more, head-less, sarcophagus covers) overlooks the valley.

San Pietro

The road which leads out of the piazza beneath the Palazzo Comunale passes a long stretch of the Roman Via Clodia (below the level of the present road) and continues to the little fortified hill of San Pietro, almost certainly the acropolis of ancient Tuscania. Excavations from the Etruscan, Roman and medieval periods can be seen behind a fence opposite the splendid apse of the great church of San Pietro. Founded in the early 8th century, this is Tuscania's most famous monument. Its setting is particularly memorable, with the beautiful façade facing a green with two huge medieval towers and the ruined remains of the 13th-century bishop's palace. It is made up of two wings in the 12th-century Lombard style, built in tufa and *peperino* (with two Roman marble lions' heads), and a projecting central portion built in the grey local stone called *nenfro*, with decorations in marble. The lovely main portal has refined geometrical decoration in polychrome marbles by Roman sculptors. Above is a loggia with little Ionic columns, flanked by two winged griffins. The splendid rose window is surrounded by symbols of the Evangelists and carved marble decorations, which include two extraordinary three-faced devils on the right, and a strange relief of a man (perhaps Etruscan) on the left. One of the most important churches of its date in Italy, the beautiful interior (*usually kept open by a kind volunteer custodian, 9.30–1 & 2.30–5 except Mon*) has low columns with massive capitals supporting arches decorated with an unusual toothed decoration. The slightly irregular trapezoidal plan which opens out at the east end means that its architectural features can all be seen from one vantage point. Beneath the arcades are benches. The fine Cosmatesque pavement survives. In the south aisle is a little ciborium (1093). On the right of the triumphal arch are three primitive little frescoes in black, white, green and yellow, and there are other fragments of the 12th-century frescoes which once covered the entire church. At the top of steps, 8th- and 9th-century carved panels divide the nave from the sanctuary,

Rose window of San Pietro, with the symbols of the Evangelists at each corner, two three-faced devils on the right, and a relief (possibly Etruscan) of a running man on the left.

and the arch which leads into the right apse is remarkable for its toothed stones which form the keystone and the central portion of the arch. In the north aisle are seven Etruscan sarcophagi. The splendid 11th-century crypt, approached by steps where the low columns have 11th-century capitals, has a forest of 28 Roman columns (all different), and an ancient fresco of the *Madonna Enthroned* in the Byzantine style, now sadly very worn. On the wall is a 14th-century fresco of the three patron saints of Tuscania, in their red robes.

Santa Maria Maggiore

On the road in the countryside just below San Pietro is Santa Maria Maggiore (*open 9–12.30 & 2.30–7; 2.30–5.30 in winter*), the oldest church of Tuscania, and the seat of the bishopric before it was transferred to San Pietro. Roman remains have been found beneath the church. The building was enlarged in the 12th century when the fine campanile was built and the sculptural decoration was added (using some earlier fragments). The very fine façade, similar to that of San Pietro, partly rebuilt in the mid-13th century, has numerous interesting sculptures. Above the central portal (with marble columns and capitals, the figures of Sts Peter and Paul, and an irregular group of sculptures in the lunette) is a loggia—another feature copied in San Pietro—with small columns flanked by two griffins. The beautiful rose window, with two circles of columns is surrounded by symbols of the Evangelists. The side portals are also richly decorated.

In the beautiful Romanesque interior, the octagonal font for total immersion survives from the 9th century. The pulpit is composed of 8th- and 9th-century panels, with primitive carvings. A fine Gothic ciborium, with frescoes, surmounts the high altar. On the east wall is a 14th-century fresco of the *Last Judgement* attributed to a certain Gregorio and Donato of Arezzo, which includes the humorous figure of the devil having difficulty digesting the wicked. In the apse below are late 13th-century figures of Apostles in the Byzantine style, and in the north aisle a beautiful detached fresco shows the Madonna holding the hand of the young Christ Child, just learning to walk.

Via Rivellino and Via Campanari

Via Rivellino, one of the two main streets of the town, leads north from Piazza Basile. Via della Pace, on the right, leads to **San Francesco** (*admission on request at the hotel in the convent*). Originally built in the 13th century, it was turned into a slaughter-house in the 19th century, and is now roofless. However, one of its chapels has survived, with beautiful frescoes dating from 1466, by Giovanni and Antonio Sparapane from Norcia.

Further up Via Rivellino is the 14th-century **Palazzo Spagnoli**, an interesting building, typical of the Viterbo area, with an outside stair and loggia below and fine windows. Beyond it is Piazza Matteotti, from which steps lead up to Largo Belvedere with a lovely fountain with two heads of lionesses and four human heads on the basin above. Here is the handsome **Vescovado**, a palace which dominates the town but is awaiting restoration inside (and its once famous garden is now in an abandoned state).

Back at the bottom of the steps, Via Campanari leads off to the right. It is named after the family of antiquarians who first brought the Etruscans to the attention of the English when they organised an exhibition of antiquities in Pall Mall in London in 1837. They lived at the palace at no. 5–13, and its garden—once decorated with Etruscan works—was mentioned by many British travellers to Etruria in the 19th century, including the great 'father of Etruscology' George Dennis. There are some interesting houses higher up the street: no. 26 has stone brackets very low down on its red façade, and no. 40 has a decorative portal leading into an old garden courtyard (opposite an overgrown walled garden with citrus trees).

Via Campanari ends opposite the church of **Santa Maria della Rosa** (*usually locked*), with a rose window on its handsome low façade and a short bell-tower. Inside is a fresco depicting the *Madonna Liberatrice* (the Virgin is said to have saved the town from a siege by Charles VIII of France in 1495, by sending a thunderstorm which scattered his troops). In Piazza Mazzini, with a pretty Baroque wall-fountain, is the church of **San Marco**, which has fine vaulting in its wide nave.

Santa Maria del Riposo and the Etruscan Museum

Just outside the well-preserved walls to the north is **Santa Maria del Riposo** (*ring at the door on the right in the piazza for the key*), rebuilt in 1495, and so named since it is on the site of a cemetery. In the lovely interior there are tall grey stone columns with capitals and even taller pilasters in the crossing. On the elaborate high altar is a small painting of the *Madonna and Child* by Pastura (1490), which is surrounded by a polyptych by Perino del Vaga (with an exquisite predella). Perin and his school also carried out the delightful frescoes in the chapel to the left, with scenes from the life of the Virgin (the altarpiece of the *Presentation in the Temple* is by Sermoneta). In the south aisle, the first and third altarpieces are by Scalabrino of Pistoia (who also painted the first altarpiece in the north aisle, now very ruined). The remains of 16th–17th-century frescoes include a fragment on the second south altar (of the *Madonna and Child*) attributed to the great Florentine artist Andrea del Sarto, who apparently stayed at the convent in 1501 when 15 years old. The walnut choir-stalls are dated 1534. In a niche in the north aisle is a *Nativity* by Lazzaro Vasari of Arezzo, great-grandfather of Giorgio Vasari the biographer, and uncle of Luca Signorelli. The Romanesque font is made from local *nenfro* stone.

The **Museo Nazionale Etrusco** (*open 8.30–7.30 except Mon*) is displayed in the adjoining convent. The rooms off the beautiful Renaissance cloister, with 17th-century frescoed lunettes, house the sarcophagi and finds (bronzes, red-figure ceramics) from the Curunas and Vipinana family tombs, found near Tuscania in 1839. On the upper floor, where some of the halls have splendid beamed ceilings, are artefacts from necropoleis in the Marta valley found as recently as 2006, including a pair of marine horses ridden by two youths, in *nenfro*, dating from the 6th–5th centuries BC, and terracotta tiles decorated with delicate reliefs. Another section displays finds from the Archaic period (7th–6th centuries BC), and architectural terracottas from the triangular cornice of the Ara del Tufo, with friezes of horsemen and chariots. The display of material from the late Archaic period up until the Hellenistic era (end of the 6th–beginning of the 2nd century BC) includes numerous terracotta sarcophagus lids, almost always portraying the deceased reclining and typically propped up on his or her elbow (an attitude which had also been used in previous centuries by the Etruscans for their stone sarcophagi). However, one of these is particularly notable since it shows the deceased lying more comfortably on his back, as if taking a quick nap. Since Tuscania was an important centre for the production of these lids, a display illustrates how they were made.

Tomba della Regina

The Etruscan tombs on the outskirts of Tuscania, most of them discovered since 1967, are not at present open except for the so-called 'Tomba della Regina', close to the sanctuary of the Madonna dell'Olivo south of the town, which has a particularly intricate plan, with a network of passages on different levels (*opened by a volunteer on Sat and Sun 10–1*). Four kilometres further south, along the road that follows the Marta river valley (*but at present closed*), is the lovely old ruined Abbey of San Giusto, founded by the Benedictines in the 10th century.

TARQUINIA

Tarquinia (*map p. 166, B2*) is famous for the many delightful painted tombs in the Etruscan necropolis on the outskirts of the town. A splendid museum houses finds from excavations in the vicinity, which brought to light some of the most important Etruscan antiquities known. The pleasant peaceful town on a hill, just 5km from the sea, has a medieval district which preserves numerous towers.

HISTORY OF TARQUINIA

Tarxuna (or *Tarxna*), cradle of the 'great house of Tarquin' was one of the 12 Etruscan regional capitals, and probably the head of the Etruscan Confederation. It is said to have been founded by Tarchon, son or brother of the Lydian prince Tyrrhenus, who is mentioned by Virgil as the person who helped Aeneas against the Latin warrior Turnus. According to a legend, Demaratus of Corinth settled here in c. 700 BC; his son, Lucius Tarquinius Priscus, became the fifth king of Rome. After the 3rd century BC the city became a Roman colony and *municipium*, and its power declined. In AD 181 the Roman colony of Gravisca was founded on the coast. After invasions by the Lombards and Saracens, in the 7th century it was deserted and the inhabitants founded *Corneto* closer to the sea on the western part of the hill of Monterozzi, site of the present town. In 1489 the first recorded archaeological 'dig' in modern times took place here, since the hill had been used by the Etruscans as their necropolis.

Museo Nazionale Tarquiniense

Above the Barriera di San Giusto, laid out in the 19th century as a monumental entrance to Tarquinia, in the west of town next to a stretch of the old walls, is the splendid **Palazzo Vitelleschi**, one of the best Renaissance buildings in all Lazio, built in 1436–39 by Cardinal Giovanni Vitelleschi, born in Tarquinia, who was a warrior as well as a churchman, and led a stormy life so that even before his death the palace was seized from him by the Church. It still has Gothic elements, and both the façade and courtyard are irregular in shape. The splendid stairways have ramps, but unfortunately some of the most interesting parts of the palace, such as the chapel, are today inaccessible. It contains the **Museo Nazionale Tarquiniese** (*open 8.30–7.30 except Mon*), one of the most important Etruscan museums in existence, founded in 1916.

Ground floor: In the beautiful courtyard and the rooms off it are displayed the remarkable collection of sarcophagi, most of them in the local *nenfro* stone, though two of the most important are in white marble. That of the so-called 'Priest' in fact belonged to Lars Parthunus, whose fine effigy in relief may be the work of a Parian Greek sculptor of the 4th century BC; on the sides are polychrome mythological scenes by a local painter. The limestone tomb of the 'Magnate', with a lid carved with lions and sphinxes, is thought to be that of Lars' son. The so-called 'Obesus' sarcophagus (marble), dating from the early 3rd century BC is surmounted by the splendid paunchy figure of the defunct, who may be the grandson of Lars (the Roman historian Livy was famously scornful of the 'fat Etruscans', gorging two fine repasts a day on their idle couches, completely lacking in Roman grit and sinew). The sarcophagus of the 'Magistrate' is that of Lars Pulenas, who is portrayed as a portly and pros-

Red-figure bell-krater (5th century BC) attributed to the Berlin Painter, showing Europa and the bull.

vases, including one by the Berlin Painter (*illustrated here*) and an amphora signed by Phintias (510–500 BC), with Apollo and Hercules fighting for the tripod. There is also a fine display of coins and jewellery, including a striking set of false teeth with gold bridgework.

Second floor: From the second floor loggia there is a splendid view of the sea. In the large hall is the famous polychrome group of two winged horses (4th–3rd century BC), of exquisite workmanship. They were found (in fragments) on the Pian di Civita, north of the necropolis, where the base of a temple, known as the Ara della Regina, is also situated, the largest Etruscan temple ever discovered. The horses had once adorned the façade, and had almost certainly pulled a chariot. It is not known to whom the temple was dedicated, though scholars have suggested Artemis. The horses were restored in 2004. There are also four painted tombs here, detached and removed from the necropolis, including the famous Tomba del Triclinio (*see illustration on p. 194*).

perous individual holding an unfurled scroll with a long Etruscan inscription, his *cursus honorum*. The front of the sarcophagus shows a scene familiar from much Etruscan funerary art: Charun, god of the underworld, cudgels the deceased with his mallet.

First floor: The rooms on the first floor display pottery and bronzes from the Villanovan period (9th century BC), jewellery, *bucchero* ware, bronzes, objects in bone and ivory, glass, terracottas, and a wonderful collection of Attic vases. The beautiful great hall, interesting for its architecture and fresco fragments, displays the most precious red-figure Attic

The duomo and Santa Maria di Castello

The **duomo** (*closed 12–4*) was rebuilt in 1656 and restored in the 19th century. In the sanctuary are very good frescoes (*lit on request*) among the best works of Antonio da Viterbo, known as Pastura, carried out in 1508. He was especially skilled at frescoes, and collaborated with Pinturicchio on the Borgia apartments in the Vatican. Most of the altarpieces date from the 19th century (many by the local painter Luigi Boccanera), and the last chapel on the south side has two paintings by Giacinto Brandi (1653). Brandi trained in the studio of the sculptor Alessandro Algardi, and it was Algardi who noted his talent for draughtsmanship and set him on his course as a painter.

Via di Porta Castello is named from the fine double gateway in the walls where there is a little public garden with a view of the unspoilt valley and fields below the town. Beyond can be seen the tallest and best-preserved tower in the city, standing beside the lovely Romanesque church of **Santa Maria di Castello** (*knock on the door at the house at the top of the steps on the left for the key*), in a peaceful corner of the town with simple little houses. The church was begun in 1121 and consecrated in 1208. On the façade is a Cosmatesque work signed by Pietro di Ranuccio (1143). High up on the north flank there is pretty arcading decorated with carving. The magnificent interior has an interesting plan with a rose window and a pretty dome in the nave. It contains Cosmatesque sculptural decoration, including part of its original pavement. Beyond an arch in the walls can be seen the pretty open countryside which has remains of a 12th-century public fountain.

Piazza Matteotti

The 13th-century church of **San Pancrazio** (now an auditorium) has a rose window, and impressive vaulting in the wide interior. Close by is the **Palazzo dei Priori**, with a fine arch and four towers (inside is a fresco cycle of 1429). Via delle Torri here is a characteristic medieval street. Nearby is the large **Piazza Matteotti**, scene of a weekly market, with an 18th-century fountain. Here the exuberant façade in the Baroque style of the church of the **Suffragio** (1761) stands next to the large town hall, built in a medley of styles. The road ends at a terrace above the walls built on outcrops of rock with a fine view of the valley below.

To the southwest, the church of **San Giovanni Battista** has a Roman sarcophagus over the left door and a fine Renaissance portal inside on the west wall. In a niche on the north wall the early 16th-century fresco fragment of the *Deposition* is an exquisite work attributed to Pastura. The apse has a good fan vault, and there are two lovely little Gothic chapels on either side, reminiscent of English church architecture.

East of here, in Via di Porta Tarquinia, is the 13th-century church and convent of **San**

Amphora of the 6th century BC, with racing athletes, by an Etruscan painter influenced by Greek prototypes.

CIVITAVECCHIA, ROME

Francesco, with a handsome interior with high Gothic arches. The chapel to the right of the sanctuary is entirely decorated with delicate stucco work. Nearby is a little gate in the walls with a charming simple scroll decorating its outer face and a little garden at the foot of the walls. A road continues from here past plain houses and shops (a walk of less than 10mins) to the entrance to the necropolis of Monterozzi.

The necropolis

The long hill of Monterozzi, parallel to the sea, was used by the Etruscans as a vast burial site: 5,735 tombs have been found here since the 19th century, making it the most important archaeological site of its kind in the Mediterranean. Many of the tombs are painted, and those dating from the 6th century BC are the most interesting and colourful (though the colours have much faded since they were first discovered), with banqueting scenes and depictions of human and animal figures, and often portraits of the defunct. Most of them are decorated as if they were rooms in a house, or pavilions, with decorated hangings on wooden supports.

The necropolis today takes the form of a pleasant park (*open Nov–March 8.30–1.30; otherwise 8.30–5.30; closed Mon*) covered with wild flowers in spring. At present 15 underground tombs can be visited, but the number open often varies and may be increased in the future. They have been protected by little houses with pretty tiled roofs and are excellently labelled, also in English. Steps lead steeply down to each burial chamber, seen through a glass door and lit by pushing a button.

On the paintings in an Etruscan tomb at Tarquinia

Can this be the resting place of the dead? Can these scenes of feasting and merriment, this dancing, this piping, this sporting appertain to a tomb? There on the inner wall is a banqueting scene—figures in richly embroidered garments recline on couches, feasting to the lyre and the pipes; attendants stand around, some replenishing the goblets from the wine-jars on a sideboard; a train of dancers, male and female, beat time with lively steps … Observe that fine and youthful pair on the central couch. The female of exquisite beauty, turns her back on the feast, and throws her arms passionately round the neck of her lover, who reclines behind her. The other guests quaff their wine without heeding them. The elegant forms of the couches and stools, the rich drapery, the embroidered cushions, show this to be a scene of high life, and give some idea of Etruscan luxury …

From George Dennis, Cities and Cemeteries of Etruria, 1848.

At the edge of the hill is the **Tomba della Pulcella**, the only one in this area which is still approached by its long access corridor (the *dromos*). It has a lovely ceiling. Above this tomb there is a view across to the hill called Pian di Civita, on a bluff above the Marta river valley, which was the site of the Etruscan acropolis of Tarquinia. The **Tomba dei Gioccolieri** shows a woman dancing in a diaphanous dress, with a seated man (probably the deceased) as her audience. The **Tomba Cardarelli** (510–500 BC) has some of the best paintings, with a prettily decorated ceiling with two pairs of lions attacking deer on the pediment. The particularly elegant figures on the walls include musicians holding vases, a man preceded by a double flute-player approaching a woman who is accompanied by a slave with a *flabellum* and a maid with a mirror. The scenes are enlivened by dancers and horsemen. **Tomb no. 5513** has banqueting scenes in which the particularly strong red and green colours have survived well. Don't miss the last two tombs, close to the road in a separate enclosure: the very well-preserved **Tomba dei Leopardi**, and the **Tomba dei Baccanti**, one of the smallest, with four graceful animals beneath the roof and flowers on the ceiling, and a drunken orgy of dancers on the walls. The same painter is thought to have worked here and in the Cardarelli tomb.

PAINTED ETRUSCAN TOMBS

The Etruscans had the idea that you lived on in the place where you were buried. The wealthier members of the community therefore took care to create a pleasant tomb for themselves, usually making them look like the rooms where they had once lived, and decorating the walls with portrayals of happy scenes of everyday life, including banquets, or activities in which the defunct had excelled, such as games or dancing. Tarquinia is the place where most of these have survived and where the styles over the centuries can best be studied, since the tombs found here date from the end of the 7th right up to the 3rd century BC. Each underground chamber or hypogeum was created by digging a sloping shaft (*dromos*) in the ground down to the level of the rock (on the Monterozzi hill this is a yellow tufa), which was then used to create the burial chamber. Some 200 painted tombs have been found in Tarquinia alone, although these represent only a very small proportion of the total number of sepulchres discovered, since it was only the aristocracy who could afford to have their tombs painted. Many of those now open to the public were unearthed in the 1960s. Although the human figure studies can be somewhat crude, the decorations and friezes truly catch the eye: ivy leaves, delicate trees, fish, birds, pairs of animals, colourful abstract panels, striped or chequered roofs. The technique used is similar to that of fresco painting, and scholars have suggested that some of the tombs may have been painted by artists from Greece. More than a third of D.H. Lawrence's well-known book *Etruscan Places* is devoted to Tarquinia's painted tombs. In his day the visit was the same as it is today: he describes walking out of the southwest gate of the city in 1927 along the level hill-crest (although it is now covered with many more buildings than the 'one or two forlorn new houses' he found there), and the first tomb he was shown was that of 'Hunting and Fishing', which is nowadays also close to the entrance to the enclosure, and still one of the most famous of all the tombs. He goes on to describe in precise detail each of the tombs, but his description of the first sums up the spirit of all the paintings: 'It is all small and gay and quick with life, spontaneous as only young life can be. If only it were not so much damaged, one would be happy, because here is the real Etruscan liveliness and naturalness. It is not impressive or grand. But if you are content with just a sense of the quick ripple of life, then here it is'.

VULCI

The site of the Etruscan Vulci, northwest of Tarquinia at Ponte dell'Abbadia, on the Tuscan border, is now in a totally deserted and beautiful landscape where the fertile open country has 'hedges' of olive trees and vineyards and is partially protected by the World Wildlife Fund. Although not mentioned in ancient literary sources (except for

its conquest by the Romans in 280 BC), Vulci must have been one of the most important Etruscan cities of southern Etruria from the 7th–4th centuries BC. Some 30,000
tombs have been discovered here since the 18th century: their incredibly rich contents, including bronzes of the 9th–8th centuries, stone sculptures, and superb vases,
are now dispersed in the great museums of the world.

Large-scale digging began here in the 1820s under Lucien Bonaparte, brother of
Napoleon, who had inveigled the title Prince of Canino from Pope Pius VII. He took
charge of the excavations of Vulci, which lay on his land. The result of the digging was
the largest haul of ancient vessels ever dragged from the soil in a single findspot, as
well as some superb gold jewellery, which his wife sported at official dinners, much
in the manner of Schliemann's wife with her Trojan finery. Landowners nearby were
infected with a similar zeal for spadework, though most were on the lookout for jewellery, and enormous quantities of pottery vessels were destroyed as being of no value.

The site

The archaeological area is now in a lovely park (*open daily 9–5; summer 10–6 except
Tues when it is open only 2.30–5.30; you can also visit the site on horseback by previous
appointment; T: 0766 89298*) where the vegetation has been left to grow wild, and
nightingales sing in the woods. There are signposted paths from the ticket office and
information centre, and it is a lovely place to spend a whole day. The ruins of the
ancient city of Vulci approached from its west gate include long stretches of Roman
road (the decumanus maximus), the forum, houses, a mithraeum, and storehouses
near remains of the Roman port. The most spectacular scenery (*reached in 15mins on
foot from the ticket office*) is that around the lovely little lake full of trout formed by a
waterfall on the river Fiora, remarkable for the colour of the sheer volcanic rockface
which rises above it. The immense necropolis on the other side of the river includes
the large tomb explored by Alessandro François dating from the 4th century BC (*usually open only by appointment at the ticket office, but sometimes open at 3 on weekends*),
and the Cuccumella, a gigantic hypogeum with a tumulus 75m in diameter.

The museum and Ponte dell'Abbadia

A short way beyond the turn for the park the main road leads to the **Archaeological
Museum** (*open 9–7 except on Mon*) in the Castello dell'Abbadia, a picturesque medieval
building constructed out of black trachyte, which has the appearance of a toy castle: its
moat is fed by a spring. It was originally built to guard the bridge over the Fiora river
(*see below*), and was appropriated by Lucien Bonaparte in 1808. The museum collection
includes finds from the site, including a beautiful terracotta head of a woman showing
the influence of Praxiteles. Beneath the castle's entrance portico are displayed the tools
confiscated from the *tombaroli*, the clandestine 'archaeologists' who carried out illegal
digs. The swifts and swallows who nest here are of the same species as those often
depicted in Etruscan wall paintings, distinguished by their thin red collar.

Beside the castle is the famous **Ponte dell'Abbadia**, a steeply hump-backed bridge
on tall piers, spanning the deep ravine of the Fiora. It is one of the best-preserved

ancient bridges to be seen in all Italy and an unforgettable sight. Built with Etruscan material but probably on Roman foundations, its splendid central arch, 30m high, also served as an aqueduct, and you can still walk across the medieval footpath on its summit. There is a good view of the bridge from the museum.

PRACTICAL INFORMATION

GETTING AROUND

• **By train:** The railway station at Tarquinia is 3km outside the town, and is served by trains to and from Rome and Pisa. Buses run between the station and the town.
• **By bus:** Tarquinia and Tuscania can be reached by bus from Viterbo, or from Rome with a change at Civitavecchia.

INFORMATION OFFICES

Tarquinia Piazza Cavour 1, T: 0766 856384.
Tuscania Piazzale Trieste, T: 0761 436371.

HOTELS

Tarquinia (*map p. 166, B2*)
€€ **Podere Giulio** and **Podere Gesso**. Run by the Serafini family and 500m apart, two farms offer excellent apartment accommodation in rolling countryside. A private lane leads to a quiet beach. The restaurant serves dishes using organic produce from the farms. *Pian de Spille, T: 328 986 7955, www.poderegiulio.it. Podere Giulio 10 apartments; Podere Gesso 9 apartments.*
€ **Al Corso**. Ideally situated for visiting the National Etruscan Museum, this is a comfortable B&B in the centre of town. *Via Giordano Bruno 1, T: 0766 856218, www.alcorsobedandbreakfast.com. 2 rooms.*
€ **Casale Farnesiana**. A farm B&B situated 5km from Tarquinia and the sea. All rooms are comfortably furnished, with bathrooms. A peaceful base from which to tour the area. Restaurant and bike hire. *Località Farnesiana, T: 0766 841224, www.casalefarnesiana.it. 5 rooms.*
Tuscania (*map p. 166, C2*)
€ **Hotel al Gallo**. ■ Small hotel in a lovely quiet position, extremely well run by the cordial owner, Perla Blanzieri, helped by a young and efficient staff. Comfortable, colourful rooms are heavily decorated with curtains and swags. Convenient for almost all the sites of northern Lazio. Restaurant. Half board available. *Via del Gallo 22, T: 0761 443388, www.algallo.it. 13 rooms.*
€ **Domus San Francesco**. A renovated 15th-century convent offers peaceful accommodation in the town centre. All rooms have their own bathroom, and breakfast is served in the ruins of the chapel. *Largo della Pace, T: 0761 444094, www.domuslaquercia.com. 31 rooms.*
€ **Locanda di Mirandolina**. Friendly B&B on a quiet road, with simple, bright (if small) bedrooms. *Via del Pozzo*

Bianco 40/42, T: 0761 436595,
www.mirandolina.it. 5 rooms.

RESTAURANTS

Tarquinia (*map p. 166, B2*)
€€€ **Re Tarquinio**. The best-known restaurant in Tarquinia, just off Piazza Matteotti. Beautifully presented regional dishes are served in atmospheric dining rooms—the best of which is the cellar dining room with the original decorated walls preserved behind glass screens. Closed Tues. *Alberata Dante Alighieri, T: 0766 842125.*

€€ **L'Ambaradam**. A well-patronised restaurant in the town centre, serving mainly fish, shellfish and beef. In season they prepare dishes with the local *ferlenghi* mushrooms. Closed Wed. *Piazza Matteotti 14, T: 0766 857073.*

€€ **Arcadia**. Ideally situated between the Museo Nazionale Tarquiniese and the duomo, Arcadia is a popular restaurant which specialises in seafood and fish cuisine, although meat and vegetable dishes also feature. Set menu available. Closed Mon. *Via Mazzini 6, T: 0766 855501.*

Tuscania (*map p. 166, C2*)
€–€€ **Trattoria Le Sette Cannelle**. Opposite the fountain of the same name, with seating outside in fine weather. The interior has a cosy, rustic feel. The menu features game (wild boar and rabbit), plenty of good pasta, and the signature dish, *fagioli con le fette* (beans on toast with a difference). *Largo Sette Cannelle, T: 0761 435739.*

€ **Al Gallo**. ■ Good, well-known restaurant where delicious and interesting dishes are prepared using local ingredients. Good wine list. Closed Mon. *Via del Gallo 22, T: 0761 443388, www.algallo.it. 13 rooms.*

€ **Locanda di Mirandolina**. Pleasant restaurant with a pretty covered terrace and views over the surrounding countryside. Homemade pasta and bread. Closed Mon. *Via del Pozzo Bianco 40/42, T: 0761 436595.*

Vulci (*map p. 166, B2*)
There is a pleasant *trattoria* called the **Casaletto del Parco** (*T: 0766 879729; closed Tues*) inside the archaeological park, with a large panoramic window overlooking the site. By the site entrance is the slightly more expensive **Casale dell'Osteria** (*T: 0766 898247; closed Mon*).

FESTIVALS & EVENTS

Tarquinia *Sagra del Fungo Ferlengho*, Wild mushroom festival, Oct/Nov.
Tuscania St Anthony Abbot and *Sagra della Frittella*, Celebrated with a bonfire, a parade of mounted *butteri* (herdsmen of the Maremma), and the famous cauliflower fritters, served either salted, or sweetened with sugar and cinnamon, Sun closest to 17 Jan; *Fiera di Maggio*, Two days of sports events, parades and market stalls in honour of the *Madonna Liberatrice*. In 1495, when Charles VIII of France was besieging the town, the Virgin is said to have sent a thunderstorm which rendered his efforts useless, first weekend in May; *Nitriti di Primavera*, National Italian horse fair, a huge event held every year in late spring; second weekend in May; *Festa dei Santi Martiri*, The whole of Tuscania turns out in honour of the patrons saints Secondianus, Marcellianus and Verianus; 7–9 Aug.

LAZIO SOUTH

— CIOCIARIA & THE MONTI LEPINI —

The district of Ciociaria is named after the *cioce*, the sandals with leather soles which used to be worn laced around the ankles by the peasants here (although this type of footwear was in fact diffused in other parts of the peninsula). It is the name given from the 18th century onwards to a vast area of southern Lazio, more or less coinciding with the present-day province of Frosinone, including the valley of the River Sacco and the Monti Ernici. But its borders have altered over the years depending on the extent of the Papal States to the south and the territories governed by the kings of Naples. Its name still conjures up a rather idyllic rural life based on the agriculture of smallholdings with fertile fields and orchards before the days of mechanised transport, where the peasants would wear distinctive costumes and the women were noted for their beauty and also their strength (up until a few years ago you could often see them walking back from the fields with huge baskets of produce perfectly balanced on their heads). One of Italy's most famous novelists, Alberto Moravia, published *La Ciociara* in 1957, which in 1960 was made into an extremely successful film by Vittorio de Sica, starring Sofia Loren as the peasant girl from Ciociaria.

The hill towns are especially interesting for their pre-Roman walls (*see box on p. 216*), although many of them have been rather spoilt since the last war by high-rise buildings, and a proliferation of factories built with funds from the 'Cassa di Mezzogiorno', which was set up to help the economy of southern Italy catch up with the rest of the country, but which found it convenient to concentrate much of its attention on the plain here rather than areas in the deeper south. The little towns are especially lively on market days: this is an area where you can find locally grown vegetables not available elsewhere in Italy (including *broccoletti di rapa*, and salad called *mesticanza*).

ANAGNI

Accelerated building in the 1950s and '60s was not kind to the southern suburbs of Anagni (*map. p. 210, B1*), but the old town preserves its lovely central street which runs uphill from the 18th-century Porta Cerere between numerous old medieval houses with arches on their ground floors, and many churches, through the piazza and past the old town hall to the venerable cathedral at the top of the town.

Many popes chose Anagni as their country residence, and the only English pope, Hadrian IV, happened to die here in 1159: according to one historian he swallowed a fly while on a walk below the walls, and died from choking. In the 13th century no less than four popes were natives of Anagni, including the great Innocent III. But the little town is best remembered by Italians as the birthplace of Boniface VIII. Boniface, a member of the Caetani family, was artistically inclined, but he also possessed a wily legal brain. His pontificate began amid a flurry of rumours that he had persuaded his predecessor, the simple hermit Celestine V, to resign the papacy, a step that no pope had ever taken before (nor has ever taken since). What is certain is that Boniface kept Celestine a close prisoner at Fumone, near Alatri, and that Celestine died a prisoner there. Boniface is most celebrated in Anagni for the infamous treatment he received here in 1303. After a quarrel with the French king Philip IV, who had taken it upon himself to tax the French clergy (and whom Boniface excommunicated), Philip sent an emissary together with soldiers and members of the Roman Colonna family (age-old rivals of the Caetani) to Anagni, and Boniface was held here for three days before his fellow citizens managed to rescue him. Although he returned to Rome, he died within a month. Whether or not he was physically assaulted (supposedly by a member of the Colonna family) during this humiliating incident is still hotly debated by historians, and the episode is mentioned by Dante (*Purgatorio XX: 85–93*). The fact that it is still discussed suggests there are grounds for considering that he did indeed receive the famous 'schiaffo', or slap in the face. The papacy of Boniface is also remembered for his papal bull 'Unam Sanctam', by which he established the political authority of the pope as Vicar of Christ, and for his idea of instituting the first Holy Year, in 1300: all pilgrims who visited Rome in the Holy Year would be granted remission from their sins.

The cathedral

The splendid cathedral (*open 9–1 & 3–7; Sun and holidays 9–10.30 & 3–6.30*), at the top of the hill, was built by a bishop-saint called Pietro, a Benedictine from Salerno, on the insistence of St Magnus (*see below*), who appeared to him in a vision. Pietro made two voyages to Constantinople, the second as a participant in the First Crusade of 1096, and he apparently brought back with him Byzantine craftsmen to help with the construction of the cathedral, which was probably consecrated the year before his death in 1105. The building is on several levels, and from its pretty lower piazza there is a view of its side flank: high up a baldacchino protects an imposing large statue of Boniface VIII, dating from the 15th century. The unusual little semicircular construction is the baptistery wall; at the end of the transept is a rose window; and then at the east end is the charming triple apse dating from 1104. The façade and entrance are reached by an inconspicuous staircase. The lovely campanile stands in front of the façade and from the terrace here there is a view over the unspoilt valley to the north.

The **interior** has a magnificent Cosmatesque pavement which dates from before 1227. The elegant ciborium, paschal candlestick and splendid bishop's throne in the apse, supported by two lions, are all the work of Vassalletto (1263), who also worked at St John Lateran (*see p. 63*). The Caetani chapel, dating from 1292, has a Cosmatesque Gothic tomb with a fresco of the *Madonna and Saints*. Just two other fresco fragments survive, a *Madonna and Saints* in a lunette above the west door, and a Byzantine *Madonna* on one of the pillars in the left aisle.

The **crypt** (*shown every half hour*) is entirely covered with extremely interesting frescoes, which are amongst the most important and extensive (and best preserved)

The crypt of Anagni cathedral.

medieval pictorial cycles in all Europe. Although their date has been much debated, they are usually now taken to have been executed in 1237 by three different (unknown) masters. They are remarkable for their narrative power, with each scene carefully fitted into the wall space and 21 little vaults, and they produce a highly decorative effect with stylised flowers and patterns even on the columns. The numerous angels are particularly graceful. Their iconography is complicated but includes (on the vaults) illustrations of medieval scientific doctrines such as the structure of the Macrocosm (the Zodiac) and the Microcosm (human life), and a diagram describing the theory of the elements; Biblical scenes illustrating the first book of Samuel, and episodes from the lives of Abraham, Elijah and the prophets. In the apsidal area are scenes from the Apocalpyse. On the walls the lives of saints particularly connected to Anagni are depicted, including, in the central apse, the story of St Magnus, a bishop from Trani in Puglia, who was martyred at Fondi during the persecutions of the emperor Decius in 250. In order to protect his body from Saracen raids, it was moved from Fondi to Veroli, probably sometime in the 9th century. But this did not daunt a group of pirates, who seized it in Veroli and had it with them when they reached Anagni, intent on destroying the town. The inhabitants decided to negotiate a peace with them and agreed to pay them off, but at the last moment the pirates decided to add the body of St Magnus to the deal in order to secure a better price. Ever since the saint has reposed here in the crypt and his cult became extremely popular in the Middle Ages, when he enjoyed a privileged position as protector and patron saint of the city. The ancient Cosmatesque pavement (c. 1235) is also preserved here intact and unrestored.

The **lapidarium** has Roman inscriptions and *cippi* and medieval architectural fragments. The **oratory of St Thomas Becket** (formerly a mithraeum) is sometimes shown on request: St Thomas, born in 1118 was at first a great favourite of King Henry II of England, who appointed him Chancellor, and made use of his diplomatic skills in support of his political, dynastic and military interests. After obtaining his appointment as Archbishop of Canterbury in 1162, expecting that what Thomas had done for him in the temporal sphere he would continue to do in the spiritual, Henry received a shock. Thomas found he could not reconcile royal interests with those of the Church, and opposed his monarch frequently. In 1170 he was murdered in Canterbury cathedral by four noblemen who understood themselves to be acting on the wishes of the king. Henry was obliged to do public penance, and at Segni, near Anagni, in 1173, Pope Alexander III promulgated Thomas's canonisation as a martyr. His cult spread quickly through the Papal States and especially in Anagni, and he was conveniently taken by the popes as a symbol of those who were faithful to the Church and opposed to the power of the Holy Roman Emperor. The primitive frescoes here (which probably date from around the same time as those in the crypt) are in rather poor condition. They represent the Creation, Old Testament scenes and saints, and in the sanctuary Christ and the Madonna and bishops, including Becket himself.

The **treasury** contains the pontifical ornaments of Boniface VIII, including his magnificent 14th-century cope, an exquisite example of *opus anglicanum*, with 30 medallions between 30 angels illustrating the lives of the Virgin and of Christ, made from silk and gold thread on a linen ground. Another splendid cope which belonged to Boniface, in red and gold silk decorated with parrots, was made in Sicily probably in the 9th or 10th century, and its symbolism is thought to derive from Syria. A Limoges casket with scenes from the life of St Thomas Becket dates from the 13th century. A chapel is also shown where the 12th-century wooden bishop's throne, in Arab style, formerly in the cathedral, is preserved, together with a painting of 1325 attributed to Pietro Cavallini; a late 14th-century wooden statue of St Anthony Abbot; and a 16th-century Crucifix. The perfectly preserved Greek vase here was donated to the cathedral along with an archaeological collection which will one day be on display. On request you can visit the sacristy and chapter house (with a collection of illuminated choir books) and another treasury with vestments and liturgical objects dating from the 15th century and later. The precious cathedral archives are kept on the floor above.

The Palace of Boniface VIII

The palace (*open 9–12.30 & 3–6; summer 9–1 & 3.30–6.30*), also in the cathedral square, was built in the early 13th century and acquired by Boniface's family, the Caetani, by the end of that century. A spiral staircase leads up to three rooms, two of them interesting for the remains of very unusual painted decoration contemporary with the building, probably in imitation of wall hangings, one with chessboard patterns and the other with a great variety of geese.

Around the main square

The main piazza has a terrace with a wide view over the Valle del Sacco. Steps beside the war memorial lead down to the public gardens, and more steps descend to a busy road where the best stretches of ancient walls, from the 4th century BC up to the Roman era, which defended the city from the south, can be seen (there are other well-preserved parts of the walls near the Porta Santa Maria at the top of the town). A magnificent wide, vaulted archway supports the **Palazzo Comunale**, erected c. 1160: its interesting façade faces north, and the hall above (*sometimes open to visitors*) is very fine.

Below a car park on the northern side of the hill are the **Arcazzi**, a series of arches some 15m high, named thus (instead of simply 'archi') because the central one bears a phallic symbol (*cazzo* is slang for penis). The ancient Romans often incorporated phallic symbols into buildings, as a talisman. The arches stand in front of a mighty wall thought to date from the 3rd or 2nd century BC. The Roman baths stood near here: all trace of them has vanished, though an inscription has been found commemorating Marcia, daughter of a local freedman, who became the mistress—and probably co-assassin—of the emperor Commodus. She is commemorated here for restoring the baths.

ALATRI, FERENTINO & VEROLI

Alatri

Alatri (*map p. 210, C1*), a picturesque little town on a hilltop which has been largely preserved from new building, has the most important example in Italy of the system of fortification using megaliths without mortar (*see box below*). The great **cyclopean wall** that surrounds the entire town can still be traced, in some places with medieval or later additions, and sometimes actually surmounted by old houses, their masonry fitting perfectly into the ancient stones.

THE CYCLOPEAN WALLS OF SOUTHERN LAZIO

Perhaps the most startling feature of many small towns in southern Lazio is the survival of mighty walls made out of huge polygonal blocks of calcareous rock or limestone, each fitting one against the other without any mortar between them. These are almost unique to this area of Italy and have a strong resemblance to the prehistoric walls and gates of Mycenae in Greece, which date from the Bronze Age, where they were known by the ancients as 'Cyclopean', because it was believed that none but giants (the Cyclopes) could have placed stone on stone. In fact the similarity between the Greek and Italian walls once led scholars to believe that the walls in Lazio were contemporary with those in Greece, and they were often termed Pelasgic, after the earliest tribes thought to have inhabited the Peloponnese and also this area of Italy. Since the 19th century there has been much debate amongst scholars about their date, but the discovery in 1901, during excavations at Norba (*see p. 221*), that the walls there must date from the 4th century BC, revealed that defensive walls of this type were built especially in that era by the local tribes called the Hernici (who subsequently came under the control of the Romans) and probably continued to be built up until the 1st century BC. However, it is still extremely difficult to date the walls with any accuracy as the method of building walls with huge, usually polygonally-shaped, megaliths of rock almost certainly existed for many centuries, and was widely diffused throughout the Mediterranean. There is still much research to be done both on the various periods involved and the techniques by which these mighty constructions were built. Alatri is the place where you can see the most remarkable of these walls, but there are other excellent examples in southern Lazio at Ferentino, Veroli, Anagni, Norba, Sora, Arpino, Segni, Cori and Sezze.

On the crest of the hill the **citadel** also has incredibly high walls of huge polygonal blocks without mortar, still perfectly preserved, with two mighty gateways, surmounted by immense monolithic architraves. Near the main gate there are three niches in the walls of uncertain significance, and the southeast corner of the defences, formed by huge perfectly cut stones, is perhaps the most impressive part of the entire circuit. The smaller gate is surmounted by phallic symbols (a common enough phenomenon; to the Romans the god Priapus was thought to ward off thieves, and his image, or a phallic symbol, was often placed at entranceways). The interior of the citadel now has gardens and the cathedral and episcopal palace.

In the main square below, with the 19th-century town hall and fountain, a sundial, and the 18th-century church of the Piarist fathers (*Padri Scolopi*), stands the Romanesque church of **Santa Maria Maggiore**, with a huge rose window. In the first chapel on the left there is a little collection of precious works of art: the wooden statue known as the *Madonna of Constantinople* is a very fine work dating from the 12th–13th century, flanked by two carved and painted wooden panels with scenes from the life of Christ and the Madonna; and the beautiful painted triptych of the *Redeemer between the Madonna and St Sebastian* is by a local painter named Antonio, who worked in the early 15th century.

The **Museo Civico** (*open 9–1 & 3–7 except Mon*), in the large medieval Palazzo Gottifredo, has a collection of scant interest; much better is the view from the top floor (which has a display of agricultural and artisans' tools). The narrow winding streets of the town are well worth exploring.

How local patronage worked

Lucius Betilienus Varus, son of Lucius, in accordance with a vote of the municipal senate, superintended the construction of the works which are recorded below: all the street paths in the town, the colonnade along which people walk to the citadel, a playing field, a sundial, a meat market, the stuccoing of the town hall, seats, a bathing pool; he constructed a reservoir by the gate, an aqueduct about 340 feet long leading into the city and to the hill of the citadel, also the arches and good sound water pipes. As reward for these works the senate made him censor twice and ordered that his son be exempt from military service; and the people bestowed the gift of a statue on him over the title of Censorinus.

Roman inscription found in the town of Aletrium (Alatri), c. 135–90 BC

A few miles to the north of Alatri is the site of the **Temple of Aletrium**, excavated in 1889. Well-preserved fragments of painted terracotta decoration were found, and the temple was 'reconstructed', along the lines of an account by Vitruvius, in the garden of the Villa Giulia in Rome (*see p. 72*). From here the road winds on northwards to the Certosa di Trisulti (*described on p. 219 below*).

Close by to the south, in a striking position against a low hillside, can be seen the extensive buildings of the **Grancia di Tecchiena**, built in the 18th century by the monks from Trisulti. The complex includes a barn and storerooms as well as a church. They retain their beautiful old red *intonaco*.

Ferentino

Ferentino (*map p. 210, B1*) suffered during the last war, and has been disfigured by much ill-advised building since then. Though its monuments are now rather neglected, like its neighbour Alatri, it is particularly interesting for its **cyclopean walls** and gates, the most impressive of which is the Porta Sanguinaria. It is from here also that the walls are best seen, even though, incredibly enough, unsightly houses and drainpipes have been allowed to mar the prospect. It is easy to distinguish the earliest masonry of huge polygonal blocks below, probably dating from the 4th century BC, from the later Roman defences above, and from the smaller medieval stone course on the summit. You can follow the path here to see another very ancient gate with a triangular pediment. In the other direction is the Porta Casamari, with its two Roman arches.

At the top of the town, the bishop's palace was built on the massive foundations of the ancient citadel. The old road tunnels beneath it (the other ancient structures here were once used as a prison) to reach the very fine cathedral (*usually kept locked*): if you do have a chance to see inside, note the 12th-century mosaic pavement, and beautiful transenna, ciborium and candelabrum dating from the following century.

Nearby can be seen the most impressive of the **Roman remains** in the town, dating from the 2nd century AD: the market building with a very high barrel-vaulted hall and five covered shops. Other Roman remains include the foundations of a Roman house beneath the tourist office, and, lower down the hillside, the ruined theatre, abandoned in the middle of a run-down *borgo*, and, just outside the walls, a very unusual monumental inscription carved in the rock identified as the last will and testament of a certain Aulus Quintilius Priscus. In this part of the town Santa Maria Maggiore (*also usually locked*) has a fine Gothic portal and a beautiful vaulted interior, dating from the 13th century, typical of Cistercian architecture.

Fiuggi and Fumone

Fiuggi (*map p. 210, B1*), in the Monti Ernici, is divided in two: the famous spa town and a medieval hill town. The spa is typical of such places in Italy, and its mineral water is bottled and now available throughout the country. Because of its altitude it is cool in summer, when it is particularly crowded. The curative properties of its springs have been known since the 13th century, and Boniface VIII and Michelangelo are known to have come here. The cold spring waters, filtered through an extensive layer of porous volcanic tufa, are tasteless, highly radioactive, and slightly mineral. Intended for drinking, they are use to treat kidney troubles.

Southeast of Fiuggi is the hilltop town of **Fumone** (800m; *map p. 210, C1*), famed for its medieval castle (now privately owned; *open 9–1 & 3–dusk*). It is here, in 1296, that Pope Celestine V, one of only six popes ever to renounce the pontificate, died, a prisoner of Boniface VIII (*see pp. 211–12*). The cell where he lived out the last months of his life is shown to visitors. The castle is also known for its hanging gardens.

Veroli

Veroli (*map p. 210, C1*) is a pleasant little town mostly with 18th–19th-century buildings and churches. The streets and *piazze* have recently been prettily repaved. The **duomo** dates from 1706, and preserves a rose window from the earlier church on this site in its elegant façade. A medieval tower serves as its campanile. In a chapel in the south aisle (*when locked, it can be seen through a grille*) is a little museum which contains the rich treasury from the monastery of Casamari (*see overleaf*), including a 13th-century processional Cross, ivory coffers, and reliquaries. In the courtyard of a medieval house nearby are the so-called *Fasti Verulani*, a Roman calendar inscribed on marble. The church of **Santa Maria Salomè** is dedicated to the town's patron saint, the mother of the apostles John and James. It has an elegant interior dating from 1773 with a tiny replica of the Scala Santa in Rome (*see p. 63*), 15th-century frescoes, a triptych in a pretty frame dated 1561, and a 13th-century crypt with frescoes. In the seminary is a library founded in 1773 by a local bishop. The Romanesque church of Sant'Erasmo has an 18th-century interior.

In the medieval *borgo* of San Leucio at the top of the town, with the ruins of a castle, a stretch of the **polygonal walls** can be seen.

Near Veroli to the northeast is **Prato di Campoli** (*map p. 210, C1*), a lovely wooded area in good walking country on the slopes of Mt Pedicino.

THE ABBEYS OF TRISULTI & CASAMARI

Certosa di Trisulti

In wonderful wooded countryside on the slopes of the Monti Ernici lies the huge Certosa di Trisulti (*map p. 210, C1; open every day 9.30–12 & 3.30–6; on Sun and feast days, unless you wish to attend a service, it is best visited in the afternoon*). In the 10th century a Benedictine monastery was built close by, the church of which now lies in ruins on the Veroli road. In 1204 the present monastery was founded, but its appearance today dates from a rebuilding in the 17th and 18th centuries. It can be approached from the southwest, along the road from Collepardo, where the landscape is the most beautiful, and where there is a strange carsic cavern in the ground called the **Pozzo d'Antullo** (*open at weekends*); but it is only from the Veroli road (from the southeast) that there is a spectacular view of the splendid monastery buildings from across the ravine. They have been occupied by the Cistercians from Casamari (*see below*) since 1947, and now just eight monks live here.

Above a charming little garden, beautifully planted with box topiary in eccentric designs, is the old **pharmacy**, which is the most memorable part of the monastery. The delightful waiting-room and corridor preserve their decorations intact from the 18th century, and have unusual oil paintings by the skilled but little-known Neapolitan painter Filippo Balbi (1806–90), who lived in the monastery from 1859–63. Although he also carried out some paintings for Roman churches and spent the last 30 years of his life in Alatri, his artistic output is perhaps best appreciated at Trisulti. He decorated the walls here with exotic plants (the palms are both painted and in relief), animals, still lifes, bizarre genre scenes and caricatures. The pharmacist of Balbi's day is also present in a painted *trompe l'oeil*. The original boxes and filters for various herbal infusions are still kept in the cupboards. The pharmacy itself, decorated in Pompeian style, retains its furnishings from 1763–70 and jars from the previous century (although Balbi provided some of them with their charming labels).

Trisulti abbey, nestling in woodland on the slopes of the Monti Ernici.

The **church** was given its handsome façade in 1768. Inside Giuseppe Caci carried out much of the painted decoration, including the vault, in 1683, and on the walls are more paintings by Balbi. The high altar in *pietre dure* dates from 1776. Outside there is an 18th-century fountain and portico, above which can be seen the Romanesque windows of the earliest part of the monastery to have survived, the Palace of Innocent III. Other parts of the monastery, including the cloister and refectory dating from the 17th–18th centuries, are shown by a monk. Liqueurs (including the unique Sarandrea; *see p. 229*), honey and other products made by the monks are on sale at the entrance.

Casamari

The famous abbey of Casamari (*map p. 210, C1; open 9–1 & 3–6*) lies, like the other Cistercian house in southern Lazio of Fossanova (*see p. 224 below*), on the river Amaseno, but is in a much less attractive position. Founded by the Benedictines in the 11th century, it was probably built on the site of a Roman *municipium* (remains of a bridge by a 14th-century aqueduct can be seen on the approach road, and a line of Roman columns survives in front of the church). In the 12th century the monastery was taken over by the Cistercians, and some 20 monks still live here. It is approached by an imposing gatehouse (once the abbot's residence), off which is the modernised library (80,000 volumes) in buildings once used as a mill and oil press.

The great **church**, completed by the early years of the 13th century, has a lovely carved main portal (the original doors were decorated with bronze reliefs in 1954 by

Pietro Canonica). The very beautiful vaulted interior, lit by alabaster windows, is typical of French Gothic churches, with half columns supported on brackets above the level of the pavement. It is unadorned except for a Baroque baldacchino over the high altar added in 1711, and which disturbs the architectural unity and vista of the east wall.

The **abbey buildings** are reached off the charming cloister with its coupled columns and well, with the walls in front of the cells above overhung with bright red geraniums. One of the little capitals on the south side may be a portrait of the Emperor Frederick II, carved to commemorate his visit here in 1222, when he was admitted to the brotherhood. The very fine chapter house has lovely vaulting supported by four pilasters of clustered columns and unusual large corbels around the walls. The present-day refectory is in a huge vaulted hall with massive columns, formerly a barn where the produce from the monastery's farm was stored. Part of the monks' walled orchard, with a vineyard, can be seen outside. In several rooms on the first floor there is a museum with Roman sculptural fragments found in the vicinity, including a delicately carved altar, remains of an elephant's tusk found on the bed of the river in 1923, and a detached fresco showing the martyrdom and beatification of St Thomas Becket. There is a painting by Annibale Carracci in the pinacoteca, but this is at present closed. The treasury of the monastery is now kept in the duomo of Veroli (*see p. 219 above*).

THE MONTI LEPINI

The Monti Lepini divide the wide valley of the Sacco from the Pontine plain, which extends to the sea. The saddle, which reaches a height of over 1000m, has no roads, but the lovely landscape, where the vegetation includes woods of chestnuts and oaks, can be seen on the peaceful road between Cori, Rocca Massima and Segni, where splendid cattle and horses are put out to pasture.

Segni, Cori and Norma

The little towns of **Segni** (*map p. 210, B1*) and **Cori** (*map p. 210, B2*) are now surrounded by many ugly new buildings, but both have important remains of their cyclopean walls (*see p. 216*): those at Cori form a threefold circuit of the hill, which also has Roman remains.

Just outside Norma (a rather unattractive, run-down village) are the impressive ruins of the Volscian city of **Norba** (*map p. 210, B2*), later occupied by the Romans. In a magnificent site overlooking the plain towards the sea, they are at present unenclosed, but a ticket office has been built. The main gate has remarkable cyclopean walls, rectangular to one side and rounded on the other. The walls, built of typical massive blocks of stone, can be explored from here, and there are other gates formed simply by megaliths. On the summit of the hill can be seen remains of a temple and baths and impressive stretches of Roman roads, complete with stepping stones and pavements. The regular plan of the streets is exceptionally well preserved. Goats often graze amongst the ruins, which are rendered even more romantic by the wild vegetation. Excavations appear to be in progress, and several edifices with mosaic pavements can also be seen. The cliff-edge is often used by hang-gliders.

Close by to the south, on the road to Sermoneta, is the **Abbazia di Valvisciolo** (*map p. 210, B2; open 8.30–12.30 & 3.30–6.30; T: 0773 30013*), an abbey founded in the 8th century by Greek monks of the order of St Basil, and dedicated to Sts Peter and Paul. The church, influenced by the style of Fossanova (*see p. 226 below*), was rebuilt in 1240 by the Templars, using the local limestone. On the simple façade is a large rose window with a Templar Cross in the centre. The abbey has been rather over-restored in recent years. It is chiefly interesting for its 13th-century cloister, on the west side of which, scratched into the plasterwork, can be seen the following inscription: SATOR AREPO TENET OPERA ROTAS. These are the words of the famous 'Sator Square', a fourfold palindrome: in other words when set in a square, one above the other, its words can be read top-to-bottom, bottom-to-top, left-to-right, and right-to-left. There are many Sator Squares in existence, notably on the duomo of Siena (*see p. 420*), and on the tomb of the Austrian composer Webern, who experimented with the palindrome in concerto form. The Valvisciolo version is not written as a square, but is circular, in the shape of a spider web. Magical, occult properties have been attributed to the palindrome. To rational minds it is vexing for the fact that it cannot be adequately translated: the word 'Arepo' has no known meaning, and interpreters maintain rather lamely that it is a man's name.

Sermoneta

The hill town of Sermoneta (*map p. 210, B2*) is one of the best-preserved on the slopes of the Lepini. Charming and quiet, its medieval centre is extremely well kept and efficiently designed to welcome visitors. Cars are excluded from the beautifully paved narrow streets, many of them stepped and decorated with pots of flowers, and there are numerous cafés, restaurants and little shops selling local handicrafts (almost too many of these). The 12th-century **Collegiata**, with a striking campanile, has a pretty corner portico. In the first chapel to the right is a painting of the Madonna holding a model of the little town surrounded by numerous angels, commissioned in 1457 by the inhabitants (after they had survived both a plague and earthquake the previous year) from the Tuscan artist Benozzo Gozzoli. At the east end is a remarkable little bishop's throne made out of a Roman altar.

The **Museo Diocesano** (*open Fri 3–7 or 4–8; Sat and Sun 9–1 & 3–7 or 4–8*) is arranged in an oratory next door, entirely frescoed in the 18th century. It contains a painting of *St Michael Archangel* (1595) by the Flemish artist Frans van de Kasteele, and early 17th-century works. The liturgical objects include a beautifully bound antiphonal of the 15th century. Close by, a passageway leads downhill to a delightful little garden of orange trees and palms. In the little piazza is the house where the painter Girolamo Sicciolante (known as 'Sermoneta') was born in 1521: his works can be seen in the church of San Giuseppe, and elsewhere in the little town. The Loggia dei Mercanti has a pretty portico on the first floor. Steps lead up to the well-preserved

Castello Caetani (*open daily except Thur summer 10–12 & 3–6, winter 10–12 & 2–4, but only on the hour with a guided tour*) which still dominates the skyline. The castle was bought in 1297 by the Caetani from the Annibaldi family (the great tower survives from their time). It was reconstructed by the Borgia pope Alexander VI, and in the 1920s restored by Gelasio Caetani (who first began the garden at Ninfa; *see below*). The rooms shown include the great hall built by the Caetani, the two *camere pinte*, with damaged frescoes dating from around 1470, as well as the towers and battlements.

On the main street of the town another Caetani residence now houses a well-displayed little museum (*open Fri 4–6, Sat and Sun 10–1 & 3–6 or 4–7*), which has excellent examples of ceramics from prehistoric and Roman times right up to the present day, with both Italian and European manufactories well represented.

Ninfa

On the plain close to the foot of the Monti Lepini is the famous Garden of Ninfa, created by the Caetani family. (*Open only April–Oct first Sat and Sun of the month; April, May, June, Oct, Nov also third Sun, opening hours April–June and Oct–Nov 9–12 & 2.30–6; April–June also third Sun. In addition open Easter Day, Easter Mon, 25 April, 1 May, 2 June and 15 Aug. Groups can book at other times, and you can sometimes join these by telephoning in advance, T: 0773 354241. Guided visits only, lasting c. 1hr. T: 0773 633935.*)

Wild iris in flower in the lovely English-style garden of Ninfa.

This romantic garden with a river and numerous rivulets of clear spring water amongst medieval ruins is famous for its great variety of plants and trees from all over the world and especially its some 800 species of roses (usually at their best around the second week in May), which thrive here in huge bushes or as climbers. The garden has a distinctly English feel to it, far different from the spirit of formal Italian gardens. Many of the plants are English too, a legacy of generations of Caetani marriages to British and Americans: Gelasio Caetani had an English mother; his sister-in-law Marguerite was a Bostonian; her daughter Lelia married a grandson of the Earl of Carlisle. In parts the garden is kept quite wild, but is never left to get out of hand by its five gardeners.

The lake of Ninfa was mentioned by Pliny (the name comes from 'nymphaeum'), and a medieval village grew up here which was donated to the papacy in 747. Since the Via Appia, which runs closer to the sea, traversed unhealthy marshes in this district, travellers would often chose to avoid that stretch of the famous road south from Rome and use instead the Via Pedemontana, which ran along the foot of the Lepini mountains. Because of this, Ninfa had already become a small town by the 11th century and an important outpost on the southern border of the Papal States. The Caetani family took possession of Ninfa at the end of the 13th century, but it was destroyed in 1382 in a war between rival factions of the family, and was never rebuilt because of the malaria caused by the stagnant waters of the lake. In the 1920s Gelasio Caetani decided to create a garden here amongst the ruins. It has thrived ever since in this mild and sheltered microclimate, where there is an abundance of water from the Monti Lepini. Planting was carried out from 1920 right up until 1990 by three generations of Caetani: Ada, Marguerite and Lelia, and many of the plants were supplied by Hillier & Sons of Winchester in England. Lelia's husband, Hubert Howard, continued to care for the garden after her death in 1977, and since his death in 1986 the garden has been owned by a foundation. The wonderful collection of roses is pruned every year by Peter Beales of Suffolk.

FOSSANOVA & PRIVERNO

In a lovely position in the fertile and well-watered valley of the Amaseno river, near a luxuriant wood of cork-oaks, lies the **Abbey of Fossanova** (*map p. 210, B2*) interesting above all for its plan, with numerous monastic buildings (including the cloister, chapter house, refectory, infirmary, and guest house; *see opposite*), which survive in an excellent state of preservation next to its extremely beautiful church. The complex is surrounded by a lovely hamlet of picturesque 19th-century buildings and cobbled lanes. It is entered beneath a little arched gatehouse, beside several buildings with deep rust-red *intonaco*, with exotic plants and bougainvillea growing against them, once the area of the monstery's farm buildings but transformed in the 15th century as a cardinal's residence. The atmosphere is reminiscent of a French village. It has one or two shops, a café, restaurant, and several places to stay.

A monastery was founded here by the Benedictines before 1089 on the site of a Roman villa (its peristyle has been identified beneath the present cloister, and the

FOSSANOVA: A TYPICAL CISTERCIAN MONASTERY

A: Church
B: Cloister
C: Lavabo
D: Refectory
E: Chapter house
F: Night stair to church from monks' dormitory

G: Lay brothers' refectory
H: Living quarters of lay brothers
I: Monks' infirmary
J: Pilgrims' guest house (Museo Medievale)
K: Lay brothers' infirmary

scant remains of its baths can be seen in the garden in front of the church façade). The abbey was conceded to the Cistercians in 1134, who dug a channel to drain the land: the *fossa nova*. The monastery became famous and wealthy, owning property as far away as Sicily. The buildings, in the Burgundian early Gothic style, date from that time. The church (*closed for restoration at the time of writing*), erected in 1187–1208 by monks from Clairvaux, is typical of Cistercian architecture, with wonderful vaulting and a square apse. It has a delightful octagonal bell-tower over the crossing (the lantern dates from the 19th century) and a rose window in its façade (the rough stone patches show that it was once preceded by an atrium).

Tour of the monastery

Visitors enter the monastery (*open 8–12 & 3–5.30; in summer 8–12 & 4–7.30*) to the right of the church façade. The charming **cloister** has coupled columns: the simplest walk is that erected by the Benedictines; the more elaborate columns date from the 13th–14th century. In the garden is preserved the typical monastic feature of a little covered porch or lavabo with a conical roof (redesigned in the 13th century). Here the monks would wash before entering the **refectory**, the splendid vaulting of which is well preserved. Also off the cloister is the **chapter house**, which has more elaborate vaulting supported by just two central columns. The monks' **dormitory** was above the east side of the cloister (with a night staircase which led directly down to the church), and above the west side of the cloister were the living quarters reserved for the *conversi* or lay brothers, who were usually artisans and peasants who helped the monks with menial tasks in return for their living, although they were also expected to take part in the spiritual life of the monastery.

Off another small cloister is a large hall which served as the **monks' infirmary**, again with lovely vaulting. An ancient little staircase leads up to a chapel with a simple coffered wooden ceiling where St Thomas Aquinas is supposed to have died in 1274 while staying here on his way from Naples to Lyon.

Just outside the main monastic buildings is the lovely vaulted pilgrims' guest house or *foresteria*, which was turned into a granary and stable block at the end of the 19th century (as can be seen from the double row of mangers along each side). It now houses an excellent museum, the **Museo Medievale di Fossanova** (*open Tues–Fri 9–1 & 2.30–6; summer Tues–Fri 4–8; Aug every day 4–8*), which documents life in the monastery, and contains architectural fragments, ceramic shards discarded by the monks in a well, and an unusual little headless statue of a seated cow in grey stone, perhaps once part of a 13th-century fountain in the cloister. A detached Byzantine-style fresco showing the Madonna with her hands raised in prayer between two saints in a niche flanked by two archangels, probably dates from the 9th century.

The **infirmary for the lay brethren** close by is another vaulted hall which is now used as an auditorium.

Priverno

Surrounded by fields of artichokes (for which it is renowned) is Priverno (*map p. 210,*

*B*2), ancient *Privernum*, a Roman colony founded in the 2nd century BC. The 19th-century bishop's palace in Piazza Tacconi, houses the **Museo Archeologico** (*open mid-Sept–May Tues–Fri 9–1, Sat and Sun also 3–6; June–mid-Sept Tues–Fri 4–8, Sat and Sun also 10–1, closed Mon; to visit the archaeological area of Privernum, T: 0773 905065*). It displays many of the objects in daily use in the wealthy homes of Privernum, including kitchen equipment, tableware, weaving weights and cosmetic articles, and the contents of a Bronze Age tomb found nearby. The centre of the museum is devoted to the *Soglia Nilotica*, an exquisite mosaic floor of Hellenistic workmanship, with a 5m-long Egyptian landscape, showing the Nile with many birds, plants and animals; ducks, storks, fish and hippos disport themselves in the water, while crocodiles try to eat them; here and there are groups of little pigmy-like people. Statues and sculptures found during excavations of the theatre are on display at the ex-church of Santa Chiara (*Piazza Santa Chiara; open as Museo Archeologico*). The art of bookbinding is still practiced here by some craftsmen; it was introduced by the monks of Fossanova, who were renowned for their production of fine books.

Just outside the town the square, red Castle of San Martino (16th century) houses a museum devoted to mathematics, the **Museo per la Matematica Giardino d'Archimede** (*open 16 Sept–31 May Tues–Sun 9–1, Sat and Sun also 3–6, closed Mon; 1 June–15 Sept Tues–Sun 4–8, Sat and Sun also 10–1, closed Mon; T: 0773 904601*), an up-to-date, fascinating series of exhibits, illustrating maths in a way to interest everybody, even those who thought they had no aptitude for it.

PRACTICAL INFORMATION

GETTING AROUND

• **By car:** Driving is the easiest way to get around this region, especially the Monti Lepini, where there is no railway line, and where local buses are infrequent.
• **By train:** For **Ninfa** trains from Rome stop at Latina Scalo (journey time 30mins), a short taxi ride (9km) from the gardens. Taxis are frequent, but also can be called on T: 0773 632292. Rome trains also stop at **Anagni-Fiuggi Terme** and at **Ferentino-Supino**, which are some way south of their respective towns. Buses provide a link.
• **By bus:** Buses run to **Anagni** from Rome Termini station. Much of this region is serviced infrequently by bus. For information on COTRAL local bus services, www.cotralspa.it.

INFORMATION OFFICES

Alatri Via Cesare Battisti, T: 0775 435318.
Anagni Piazza Innocenzo III, T: 0775 727852.
Cori Via della Libertà 36, T: 0696 78158.
Fiuggi Via Gorizia 4, T: 0775 515446.
Priverno Piazza Giovanni XXIII, T: 0773 904830.

Sermoneta Piazza del Comune 1, T: 0773 30312, www.sermoneta.it.
Veroli Via Giovanni Campano 9, T: 0775 238929.

HOTELS

Anagni (*map p. 210, B1*)
€ **Agriturismo Cisogna**. Simple, rustic farm accommodation in a picturesque setting above Anagni. *Via Cisogna, Locailtà S. Filippo, T: 0775 743017, www.cisogna.altervista.org. 6 rooms.*
Ferentino (*map p. 210, B1*)
€€ **Hotel Fontana Olente**. A large, modern hotel with good facilities including a spa. Set in pleasant gardens. *Via Casilina km 76, T: 0775 24181, www.hotelfontanaolente.it. 65 rooms.*
€–€€ **Agriturismo Punto Verde**. Well-equipped farm accommodation in picturesque surroundings. Swimming pool, tennis court and horseriding. *Via Casilina km 75, T: 0775 396596.*
Fiuggi (*map p. 210, B1*)
€€€ **Grand Hotel Palace della Fonte**. Now part of the Starwood group, this turn-of-the-century hotel offers elegant, quality accommodation. Swimming pool in picturesque grounds and beauty spa. *Via dei Villini, T: 0775 5081, www.starwoodhotels.com. 146 rooms.*
Fossanova (*map p. 210, B2*)
€€ **Agriturismo Agricola La Pisana**. Along a sweeping driveway, in beautiful grounds are three self-catering apartments beside a little lake. Simply furnished, all with direct access to the gardens, this is excellent value accommodation. *Via Abbazia 13, T: 0773 939054, www.agricolalapisana.it. 3 apartments.*
€ **Antico Borgo**. Pleasant, peaceful place to stay in part of the old abbey

buildings. *Via dei Guitti, T: 0773 939110, www.albergoanticoborgo.it. 10 rooms.*
Sermoneta (*map p. 210, B2*)
€ **Principe Serrone**. Interesting small hotel close to the castle, in an 11th-century watch-tower. No restaurant. *Via del Serrone 1, T: 0773 30342, www.hotel-principeserrone.it. 14 rooms.*
€ **Ostello San Nicola**. A 13th-century Benedictine priory with panoramic views offering comfortable rooms with breakfast. Helpful management (they will pick you up from Latina station). *Via Matteotti 1, T: 0773 30381, www.san-nicola-hostel.com. 7 rooms.*

RESTAURANTS

Collepardo (*map p. 210, C1*)
€ **Da Vittorio**. Whitewashed walls and stone floors dominate this typical Ciociaria restaurant, which serves good local dishes. The shaded garden is an added bonus. Closed Wed. *Via Municipio 30, T: 0775 47002.*
Ferentino (*map p. 210, B1*)
€€ **Hotel Bassetto**. Good value restaurant in a modern hotel, known throughout the area for its home-made pasta. *Via Casilina km 72, T: 0775 244931.*
Fossanova (*map p. 210, B2*)
€ **Il Forno del Procoio**. Part of the Agriturismo La Foresteria, this restaurant is set within an old bakehouse, in a lovely location on the village square. Pizzas, pies and tarts are baked in the wood-fired oven while lighter meals such as pasta and omelettes are served in summer. There are also six pretty apartments to let in the old stables and farm buildings. *Via dell'Abbazia 1, T: 0773 939073.*

Fumone (*map p. 210, C1*)

€€ **La Taverna del Barone**. La Taverna takes pride in its medieval heritage and retains its old cobbled floor and wooden beams. The menu changes daily, using local ingredients. Closed Mon. *Via del Ponte 4, T: 0775 49655.*

Priverno (*map p. 210, B2*)

€€ **Antica Osteria Fanti**. Close to the abbey of Fossanova, this inn is run by owners who take their food and wine very seriously. Try the country soup or home-made ravioli, followed by buffalo meat or rabbit; a good assortment of cheeses; splendid home-made desserts. Closed Thur. *Contrada Ceriara 26, T: 0773 924015.*

€ **Gliò Montano**. This simple restaurant specialises in the preparation of vegetables, freshly sourced from the surrounding farms. Attractive setting, good value. Closed Wed. *Via Majo 10, T: 0773 903838.*

Sermoneta (*map p. 210, B2*)

€€ **Il Mulino**. Popular restaurant near the castle, with a welcoming atmosphere and some excellent local dishes. *Piazza del Cauto 9, T: 0773 318303.*

€ **Trattoria Ghost**. At the entrance to the castle. A friendly trattoria serving generous portions of pasta at very reasonable prices. Closed Mon. *Via Sotto il Forte 2, T: 0773 30338.*

LOCAL SPECIALITIES

The **Ciociaria region** is known for excellent pasta (*fettuccine*), bread, and dry biscuits (*ciambelline al vino*), still made by hand and widely available in local shops and *trattorie*. The Cesanese del Piglio wine is renowned throughout Italy. Several monasteries in the area produce their own liqueurs made from herbs.

Anagni has a large market every Wed, which takes over the entire Corso from the cathedral all the way down to the north gate.

Trisulti produces a liqueur called Sarandrea, made from mountain herbs, and with an alcoholic content of 68%. It is recommended to be taken diluted with iced water, and the addition of sugar to taste.

Fiuggi is known for its mineral water (bottled as Acqua di Fiuggi), particularly effective for urinary tract disorders and kidney problems.

FESTIVALS & EVENTS

Anagni Traditional food fair, second Sun in May; Traditional music festival, July.

Ferentino Sausage and polenta festival, mid-Jan; Pecorino cheese festival, first Sun in June.

Fumone Festival honouring Pope Celestine V, who died in Fumone, second Sun in Aug.

Priverno *Processione del Cristo Morto*, Silent masked figures called *Spalloni* carry tableaux of the Passion in a nocturnal procession, while two men in chains carry a large Cross in front of the bier bearing the dead Christ, Good Friday.

THE TYRRHENIAN COAST

NB: This chapter is shown on the map on p. 210.

A lthough loved by Italians (who flock here in large numbers in July and August), the Tyrrhenian coast of Lazio is little known to foreign visitors. It offers varied scenery, sophisticated or simple resorts, a string of delightful off-shore islands, interesting cuisine, Roman remains, medieval fortress-villages and monumental Rationalist town planning from the days of the rise of Fascism. The economy is solidly based on tourism, mechanical and food industries, and agriculture: the kiwi fruit, white celery and artichokes are among the finest in the world, while the production of buffalo-milk mozzarella rivals that of Campania. Wines and olive oil are excellent.

ANZIO & ENVIRONS

HISTORY OF ANZIO

Anzio (*map p. 210, A2*), ancient *Antium*, is the oldest seaside resort in Lazio. It was a city of the Volscians, until it fell to Rome in the 4th century BC. The prows of the ships captured by Rome in the decisive battle of the conflict were the original rostra in the Roman Forum (*see p. 35*). Cicero had a villa here (although he owned 18, he said this was his favourite). As a consequence of being the birthplace of Nero, it was privileged in his lifetime with the construction of a fine port (west of the present harbour). As at *Praeneste* (Palestrina; *see p. 131*), the cult of the goddess Fortuna was very important. The city went into decline after Roman times and practically disappeared, until a new port was built in 1698; but with the advent of the railway in the late 19th century it acquired importance again as a bathing resort and for its fishing industry. On 22nd January 1944, the Allies landed here and at Nettuno, creating a bridgehead which resisted for four months (*see box opposite*).

In the central, 17th-century Villa Adele, built for Cardinal Bartolomeo Cesi and later owned by the Pamphilj and Borghese families, are the city museums. The **Museo Civico Archeologico** (*open daily 10.30–12.30 & 5.30–7.30; T: 06 984 99408*) shows finds from excavations in the area, especially from the Villa of Nero (however the famous Greek marble statues found here, the *Apollo Belvedere* and the *Maiden of Antium*, are in Rome, in the Vatican and Palazzo Massimo alle Terme respectively). There is also a large model of Nero's port, and an interesting section with objects from underwater explorations. The **Museo dello Sbarco** (Museum of the Landings; *open Tues, Thur, Sat and Sun 10.30–12.30 & 4–6; July–Aug afternoon times 5–7, T: 06 984 8059*) illustrates the dramatic days in January 1944, with displays of uniforms, weapons, battle plans, photographs of veterans and objects in daily use, in four sections: America, Britain, Germany and Italy. On the coast road (the old Via Severiana) at the entrance to the town is **Nero's Villa** (*open daily 9–1 & 5–8*); the sparse ruins, mainly a few walls in *opus reticulatum*, are surmounted by an arch.

Nettuno

Nettuno (*map p. 210, A2*), built at the foot of a legendary ancient temple dedicated to Neptune, now practically forms a conurbation with Anzio: it is hard to see where the dividing line might be between the two. Famous for its well-equipped yachting harbour, it still has a medieval centre, the *borgo medievale*, partly surrounded by walls and dominated by the fortress built from 1496–1503 for the Borgia pope Alexander VI. This, the **Forte Sangallo** (*open 9–12 & 3–7, closed Mon*), is a powerful square construction in sun-bleached, dusky pink brick, with four ponderous bulwarks. The work of Antonio da Sangallo the Elder, a great military architect, it was one of the first castles built to withstand cannon fire. It now houses the civic antiquarium (*open by appointment; T: 06 980 7114*) and the **Museo dello Sbarco** (Museum of the Landings; *open by appointment; T: 06 980 3620*), dedicated to the Allied landings in January 1944, with a collection of weapons, documents and explanatory panels. North of the town is the **American War Cemetery** (*open daily 9–5, except 25 Dec and 1 Jan*) with the graves of 7,861 men who gave their lives either in the 1943 Sicily campaign, or here at Nettuno and Anzio in 1944.

THE ALLIED LANDINGS

The landings at Anzio and Nettuno during the final stages of the Second World War were planned far in advance of the main battle line, and timed to follow an Allied attack on it. The design was to cut the German line of communications, to link up with the main Allied forces advancing from the south, and to seize the Alban Hills. The principal objective in all this was to draw off and contain German forces from northwest Europe, with the subsidiary hope of capturing Rome. Exploiting the initial surprise should have been a vital factor in the plan's success, but sadly this was not done, and four months of bitter fighting ensued, with much loss of life on both sides. Hostilities only ceased after the arrival of the troops in Rome, after the Battle of Monte Cassino (*see p. 251*).

Ancient Satricum

Inland from Nettuno, on the Astura river near the modern-day Le Ferriere (*map p. 210, A2*), lie the ruins of *Satricum*, once the foremost site of the worship of the great earth goddess Mater Matuta. Little is known about the ancient city: it appears to have allied itself with other Latin cities in the attempt to restore the Tarquins to the throne of Rome after 509 BC. It was conquered by Camillus (*see pp. 184–85*) in 386 BC, and after a series of skirmishes against Rome became the site of the last stand of the Volscians in 341 BC, before the decisive Battle of Antium three years later. After that it ceased to exist as a city, and became solely a place of pilgrimage. Excavations over the years—most recently by a team of Dutch archaeologists—have uncovered evidence of cult use of the site going back to the 9th century BC. The famous temple of Mater Matuta was built between 500 and 480 BC, and survived as a place of worship until the 1st century BC. The Romans adopted the worship of the goddess, and Livy recounts how when the temple at Satricum was struck by lightning in 207 BC, it was regarded as a dire portent. The collection of votive objects left here is the richest ever found in central Italy. Finds are kept in the Villa Giulia in Rome (*see p. 74*).

Torre Astura

At Torre Astura (*map p. 210, A3*) a picturesque 12th-century castle (*open Sun; July–Aug every day*) with a five-sided tower stands on an islet joined to the mainland by a bridge and dominating the Via Severiana. The name derives from *astore*, goshawk, which once nested on this spot. Cicero, after his proscription, embarked at Astura on the flight that ended with his death in *Formiae* (*see p. 246*). Conradin, last of the Hohenstaufen, sought refuge after the Battle of Tagliacozzo in 1268, only to be handed over by Giacomo Frangipane, lord of the castle, to his opponent Charles of Anjou, by whom he was beheaded. The magnificent view from the tower embraces the coast towards Nettuno and Anzio, with the Alban Hills to the north and the Monti Lepini and Ausoni to the northeast and east. In the sea on the east side of the building, at water level, are the ruins of what was a sumptuous Roman house, commonly called the Villa of Cicero, with a fish-pond in a good state of preservation. The Fosso Astura, which runs into the sea here, was the right flank of the Anzio beach-head in the Second World War.

LATINA

Latina (pop. 110,000; *map p. 210, B2*) is the second largest city in Lazio after Rome. Founded in 1932 and originally called *Littoria*, it was the first of the new towns of the *Agro Pontino*, the former Pontine Marshes, which were drained on the orders of Mussolini. Situated in the centre of the reclaimed wetland, it is a good example of Rationalist town planning. Its orderly buildings, restrained use of decorative detail, systematic street plan and large public spaces were intended to embody political principles dear to the Fascist regime, such as strength, authority and regimentation. Its overall design is the creation of the otherwise obscure Roman architect Oriolo Frezzotti (1888–1965).

The town centre

The spacious **Piazza del Popolo**, with its elegant porticoes and carefully trimmed trees, is the fulcrum of the town, at the centre of a spider's web design of the streets. The *Monument to Water* (1939) is a travertine sphere in a pool, compositionally balanced by the high clock-tower (32m) of the town hall. West of the square, at the end of the wide Viale Italia, is **Piazza del Quadrato**, where construction work for the new town began, on the site of a hamlet called *Quadrato*. The tufa sculptures of vases of fruit and groups of people symbolise the land reclamation which took place.

Further to the south is **Piazza San Marco**, with the church of St Mark (1933), patron saint of the city, chosen perhaps because most of the settlers came from Venice. The unusual façade is formed by a daringly high triple-arched portico in tufa and travertine, flanked by the statues of the Evangelists. On one side of the square is the curved façade of the ex-Opera Nazionale Balilla, now a museum dedicated to the Roman artist Duilio Cambellotti (1876–1960), an exponent of Italian Art Nouveau. The museum (*T: 0773 652635 or 0773 486916 to request visit*) has a vast collection of his works. His characteristic hand is unmistakable in the reliefs and other artwork he carried out for Latina.

Palazzo 'M'

Continuing south after Piazza San Marco, you will see on the right the huge Palazzo 'M', designed to honour the initial letter of Mussolini's name. It was to have formed part, together with the ex-barracks opposite, of a new 'forum', but work was discontinued in 1942. The barracks, now known as Palazzo della Cultura, house a beautiful theatre and two museums: the **Galleria d'Arte Moderna e Contemporanea** (*open Mon–Fri 9–1, Tues and Thur also 4–6; T: 0773 652600*) dedicated mainly to the designs of Oriolo Frezzotti; and the **Museo della Medaglia** (*open as above*), with interesting displays on the art of incision and the manufacture of coins and medals, together with a series of photographs documenting the birth of Littoria.

Piana delle Orme and Forum Appii

East of Latina, near the village of San Michele, is **Piana delle Orm**e (*map p. 210, B2; open 9–5, Sun and holidays 9–7; T: 0773 258 708, www.pianadelleorme.it*). Here is a large permanent exhibition devoted to the 20th century, with sections on aircraft, vintage tractors (over 350, all in working order), vintage toys, local agriculture and the battles of the Second World War which affected this area (the Sicily campaign, the Battle of Monte Cassino, and the Anzio-Nettuno landings), all with good explanatory panels and information in several languages; an absorbing way to spend an afternoon.

North of Latina, on the Via Appia, was the *Forum Appii*, where the Christian brethren from Rome went to meet St Paul (*Acts 28: 15*). In Antiquity, travellers from Rome who wished to continue their journey to Terracina by canal (thus avoiding the malarial stretch of Pontine marsh), started out from here. An amusing account of the rigours of the journey is left to us by Horace in his fifth Satire, where he grumbles about stomach upset, noisy bargemen, endless waiting around, plagues of mosquitoes and the boatman, soused in sour wine, singing of the girl he left behind him.

CIRCE'S SHORE

The coastal road to the promontory of Monte Circeo (*map p. 210, B3*) runs through sand dunes 12–15m high, separating a lagoon, the Lago di Fogliano, from the sea. This lagoon is 5km long, with a maximum width of 1.5km and a depth of 4–5m; it is joined to the much smaller Lago dei Monaci by a short canal called La Fossella. Further south is another lagoon, the Lago di Caprolace, which because of its brackish waters and relative inaccessibility is an excellent place for birdwatching in winter. It is connected by the Fossa Augusta, built by Nero, with the Lago di Sabaudia, former-ly Lago di Paola and in Antiquity *Lacus Circeus*. This is a long, narrow lagoon extend-ing for 8km with a maximum width of 505m, as far as the base of Monte Circeo. It is separated from the sea by dunes, through which the road runs. In places it is 15m deep. It has six branches or bays, called *bracci*, running inland, and is famed for its production of mussels. On the left are the dense woods of the Selva del Circeo. On the right, rising from the sea in the distance, are the Ponzian Islands: Ponza, Zannone and Palmarola.

Monte Circeo

The partly forested, colourful Monte Circeo (541m) rises abruptly from the south end of the plain. There is a lighthouse on the seaward side, and on its summit some remains of a temple, possibly sacred to Venus. On a natural terrace above San Felice Circeo can be seen some tracts of the cyclopean walls, made of great blocks of stone snugly fitted together, of the mysterious, all-but-vanished town of *Circeii*, thought to have flourished in the 5th century BC. So far 43 caves have been discovered; one of these, on the west coast and only accessible from the sea, is called the *Grotta della Maga Circe* (Circe's Cave). In fact, Monte Circeo was once an island identified with *Aeaea*, the home of Circe, notorious for her magic arts. Ulysses, who escaped the metamorphosis of his companions after they had been cast upon the island, and who forced Circe to restore them to human form, stayed for a year with the enchantress, who became by him the mother of Telegonus, reputed founder of *Tusculum* and *Praeneste*, now Palestrina

Sabaudia

Sabaudia (*map p. 210, B3*) is attractively situated between two arms of a lagoon. Founded in 1934, with its sleek Rationalist buildings, wide avenues and abundant vegetation, it is certainly the best designed of the new towns of the area. The compe-tition for its plan was won by four young architects, Alfredo Scalpelli, Gino Cancellotti, Eugenio Montuori and Luigi Piccinato; the town was completed in 253 days, to Mussolini's delight. It was described by the architect Le Corbusier (whose own bid to design the town had been turned down) as '…a sweet poem. Perhaps a little sentimental, but full of good taste, a true sign of love…'

Its centre is the Piazza del Comune, with a clock-tower (42m high), from which there is a fine view of the surrounding country. The tower now houses the **Museo Emilio Greco** (*open daily 6–9pm, closed Mon; T: 0773 515791*), with a collection of paintings, bronzes and drawings by Greco (1913–95), a Sicilian-born artist who lived in Sabaudia for many years. Initially inspired by the Dalmatian-born medieval master Francesco Laurana, he designed the bronze door for Orvieto cathedral (1964) which, however, was strongly opposed, and was only hung in 1970 amid bitter criticism. Six floors of the tower are occupied by the **Museo della Torre Civica** (*open as above*), with a collection of over 200 works inspired by Dante's *Divine Comedy*, mostly etchings, by the local contemporary artist Lorenzo Indrimi.

Largo Giulio Cesare leads to the **Annunziata**, a church with an imposing mosaic of the *Annunciation* (1935) on the façade; inside is the Cappella Sabauda (1901; transferred here from Rome), erected by Queen Margherita in honour of her husband King Umberto, assassinated in 1900.

At no. 13 Piazza Verbania, in the southeast part of town, is the **Museo del Mare Marcello Zei** (*open Tues and Thur 11–1 & 4–7, Wed and Fri 11–1, Sat 9–1, closed Mon, T: 0773 511340*), with a section dedicated to marine biology, another describing the coast of Sabaudia and the Roman remains, and an exhibit on the Villa of Domitian on the slopes of Monte Circeo, with some finds from the archaeological excavations there. The ruins of the villa can be seen on group tours; ask at the National Park office (*address overleaf*).

View of the Pontine Marshes near Lago dei Monaci.

PARCO NAZIONALE DEL CIRCEO

Visitor centre: Via Carlo Alberto 107, Sabaudia; T: 0773 511385, www.parcocirceo.it
This wild and beautiful nature reserve, created in 1934, is, with its various ecosystems, one of the most important in the Mediterranean. It preserves an area of great natural beauty together with its flora and fauna, and gives an idea of what the Pontine Marshes were like before they were drained for agriculture. Great flocks of birds once used the marshes either as a resting-place during migration or as a permanent abode, and many still come. Species include flamingo, spoonbill, various herons, ducks and cranes, and birds of prey such as the lesser kestrel, peregrine falcon, osprey, sea eagle and marsh harrier, besides green and great spotted woodpeckers.

Extended recently to an area of 8500 hectares, this vast reserve now includes the towns of Sabaudia and San Felice Circeo, as well as the four lagoons of Fogliano, Monaci, Caprolace and Sabaudia, and the little island of Zannone. Of particular interest, besides the lagoons, are the largest low-lying forest in Italy, with oaks, ash, hornbeams, elms, sorb-apples and black alders; over 20km of magnificent sand dunes; and the beautiful limestone outcrop of Monte Circeo, where the only palm native to the Mediterranean, the St Peter's or Dwarf palm, flourishes on its steep slopes; this is its northernmost limit in Italy.

San Felice Circeo

On the eastern flank of Monte Circeo is San Felice Circeo (*map p. 210, B3*). Inhabited since prehistory, it became a Roman colony in 393 BC, whereafter it flourished; many villas were built. Its attractiveness caught the eye of Alaric the Goth, who sacked it in 410; so did Totila in 546, and lastly the Saracens in 846. This destruction was so thorough that the town was rebuilt and fortified, becoming a castle of Terracina. The Templar knights acquired it as a base in 1250. The medieval centre, still partly surrounded by walls, survives in the upper part of town. San Felice changed hands frequently over the succeeding centuries, passing in turn to the Caetani, the Ruspoli, and the Orsini, and finally to the papacy. Pius VI sold it in 1808 to Prince Stanislaw Poniatowsky, (1754–1833), nephew of the last king of Poland. He came to San Felice in 1808, and lived a bucolic idyll here for 14 years, in the company of his mistress, a young local girl by whom he had several children.

On passing through the old gate of San Felice, Porta del Ponte, you enter the rectangular Piazza Vittorio Veneto, with the so-called **Casa dei Cavalieri** (House of the Knights), now the town hall. It incorporates the Torre dei Templari, seat of the civic museum: **Mostra Homo Sapiens et Habitat** (*admission by appointment at the tourist office; T: 0773 547770*), with a collection of prehistoric artefacts found locally, together with others from all over the world. In a nearby cave, the Grotta Guattari, the skull of a Neanderthal-type man was found (alas not in the museum); it showed deliberate mutilation leading some scholars to believe the person had been a victim of ritualistic cannibalism.

Continuing along Corso Vittorio Emanuele, you reach the panoramic Piazza Marconi, with views to the Ponzian Islands and to the Monti Lepini and Monti Ausoni. Many beautiful walks can be taken from San Felice Circeo, on the mountain and along the coast.

TERRACINA, FONDI & SPERLONGA

At the southeastern extremity of the Pontine plain, tucked neatly between the foot of the Ausonian mountains and the sea, is busy Terracina (pop. 43,000; *map p. 210, B3*). The new town lies close to the sea; the old town on the slopes above. It is an important seaside resort and fishing harbour, a point of embarkation for the Ponzian Islands, and is renowned for its wine production.

HISTORY OF TERRACINA

According to legend, the town was founded by Spartans who fled their city because they were in disagreement with the reforms proposed by Lycurgus. Taken by the Ausonians and later by the Etruscans, who named it *Tarcina*, it became the ancient Volscian town of *Anxur*. Because of its strategic position it was taken by the Romans in 406 BC, not without a strenuous rebellion. Terracina was an important stage on the Via Appia from Rome to Capua and Brundisium, and it became a favourite seaside resort of Roman patricians, who appreciated the splendid position of the town, dominated by the russet limestone acropolis, now Monte Sant'Angelo, with the famous temple of Jupiter Anxur. An important key to the success of Terracina was the presence of two copious thermal springs, used for health cures. Galba, Roman emperor from 68–69 AD, was born here in 4 BC.

Terracina was disputed for centuries between the papacy and the nobility, especially the Frangipane family. In 1420 it finally became a frontier station for the popes, on the border with the Kingdom of Naples. The progressive flooding of the plain brought malaria in its wake, and Terracina was almost abandoned, until Pius VI's land-reclamation programme in the 18th century gave it new life. The old city was severely damaged by bombing raids during the Second World War.

Santissimo Salvatore

Entering the city from the west along the main street, Via Appia then Via Roma (the old Appian Way), you reach an attractive semicircular garden called Piazza Garibaldi, planted with palms and cedars; facing the garden is the early 19th-century church of the **Santissimo Salvatore**, designed by Giuseppe Valadier and completed by Antonio

Sarti in 1830. The vast interior of three naves separated by columns and surmounted by a magnificent dome contains modern works of art; in the first south chapel is a dignified white marble *Pietà* designed by Antonio Canova and sculpted by his pupil Cincinnato Baruzzi.

The cathedral and Museo Archeologico

Via Annunziata, to the left of the Santissimo Salvatore, goes steeply up past a tall (6.5m high) Roman arch (1st century AD) to the Piazza del Municipio, a large square that occupies the site of the ancient forum. At the far end of the square stands the honey-coloured stone **cathedral** (1074 and 17th century), dedicated to St Caesareus, an African deacon martyred under Claudius by being tied up in a sack and thrown into the sea. He is patron saint of the town and of the diocese. An excellent example of recycling, the church was built amid the ruins of a preceding Roman temple, of which parts of the floor are well preserved. To the left is the beautiful Romanesque-

Detail of the mosaic frieze on the cathedral of Terracina.

Gothic brick bell-tower, dating from the 14th century, and decorated with a series of little blind arches, lancet windows, and bright majolica dishes. The church is approached by the original Roman stairway and a portico of antique columns, on medieval bases carved with lions, but notice the last one to the left, which shows four monkeys. Supported on beautifully carved Ionic capitals, the architrave is decorated with a 12th-century mosaic frieze, the work of Sicilian craftsmen. Only the right-hand section is preserved, and is embellished with a series of animals and monstrous creatures, the symbolic significance of which is now lost, as well as a depiction of armed knights flanking a Templar cross, and a man in a long galley. To the right of the entrance is a granite water-tank, used by the faithful in ancient times for their ablutions before entering the temple. In the interior is a fine mosaic floor dating from the 12th or 13th century; notice the lovely pulpit on the left, dated 1241, and the paschal candlestick made in the same year, a twisted column supported by two lions. The two ciboria and the high altar are composed of antique fragments.

Outside, along the right side and at the rear of the church, are vestiges of the temple dedicated to Roma and Augustus, which provided the foundation of the Christian building. The stones on the right flank bear a running acanthus-leaf pattern. Opposite are the remains of the temple dedicated to the Capitoline Triad, Jupiter, Juno and Minerva, dating from the 1st century BC. It was revealed accidentally during the war in 1944, and brought to light in 1948.

Back in the square, on the right rises the 14th-century Palazzo Venditti; on the left, the modern town hall, incorporating the sturdy 13th-century tower-house known as Torre Frumentaria, which contrasts strongly with the dainty campanile of the cathedral. This is the seat of the city museum, **Museo Archeologico Pio Capponi** (*open May–Sept Tues–Sat 9.30–1.30 & 3–9, Sun 10–1 & 5–9, Mon 9.30–1.30; Oct–April: Tues–Sat 9–1 & 3–7, Sun 9–1 & 3–6, Mon 9–1; T: 0773 707313*), illustrating the history of the territory from the Palaeolithic to the Roman period, with fossils, Roman statues and epigraphs from sites in and around the city.

Temple of Jupiter Anxurus

The walk along Via Anxur (from the right of the cathedral a Roman arch passes under Palazzo Venditti) and the Strada Panoramica up to the acropolis (227m) takes

30–45mins. Here are the ruins of the walls and of the **Temple of Jupiter Anxurus** (1st century BC; *Anxurus* = 'the Beardless One', or Jupiter as a boy), The powerful arches of its foundations (33m by 20m) dominate the surrounding landscape. Monte Circeo rises to the southwest and the view is superb. To the right, a rectangular base with a spur of rock pierced in the centre is all that remains of the point of communication with an oracle, which spoke from subterranean chambers under the terrace.

Pisco Montano and Borgo Marino

Below the acropolis is the **Pisco Montano**, a rocky promontory cut away by Trajan to a height of 36m, to make an easier path for the Via Appia, which originally climbed over the summit of the rock. The Roman poet Horace, who took the old road on his journey to Brundisium, refers to the three-mile uphill crawl in carriages to Anxur. The depth of the cutting is marked at intervals of ten Roman feet, starting from the top; the lowest mark, near the present roadway, shows the figure CXX.

   Borgo Marino is the name given to the new town south of the Via Appia. It incorporates many Roman remains, including several bath-houses and the sparse ruins of the amphitheatre; there is also a photogenic canal-port with fishing boats, occupying part of the Roman harbour. Borgo Marino is bordered by a fine sandy beach.

INLAND TO FONDI

The inland route to Formia, followed by the Via Appia, takes you past two lovely medieval hill-towns and through superb natural scenery. Beyond the citadel of Anxur, the Via Appia turns northeast with the foothills of the Monti Ausoni on the left; to the right is the outlet of the **Lago di Fondi**, the largest of the coastal lakes of Lazio (16km long; 30m deep), which you reach at Torre del Pesce. The lake now forms part of the Parco Naturale Regionale dei Monti Aurunci; with its brackish water it is a paradise for birds, and during migration you may see many kinds of ducks, the great white heron, spoonbill, wild geese and black kite, while the short-toed eagle and peregrine falcon nest here. The water-plants are abundant and form great clumps: perhaps this is why Pliny in his *Natural History* speaks of 'floating islands' on this lake. More than 1,900 plant species have been discovered in the park, including some rarities, and over 50 types of wild orchid. The Monti Aurunci were once notorious as a haunt of brigands, among whom was Fra' Diavolo, who fought for the kings of Naples against Napoleonic France, and was hanged by the French in 1806.

Fondi

Fondi (*map p. 210, C3*), the *Fundi* of Horace's satires, produced the highly-prized *caecubum*, a famous wine of Antiquity; it is still noted for wine, and even more so for the delicious oranges grown around the town, admired by Goethe. Midway between Rome and Naples, it is now one of the most important centres in Italy for the sorting, grading, packaging and distribution of agricultural produce, in direct contact with the major markets of Europe. The old town, much of which is in gleaming white limestone, is built along the traditional lines of the Roman battle camp. It is rectangular in plan, each side measuring about 400m. At the ends of the decumanus and cardo maximi are four gates; the forum stood at the centre of the grid, now Piazza della Repubblica. Here is the church of **Santa Maria Assunta**, its façade relieved from plainness by a lovely 15th-century portal. For centuries the church steps were the traditional meeting-place for the men of Fondi; badly worn, they have now been replaced. The steps continue down under the level of the present square, because the church was originally much higher, and probably replaces a Roman temple on the same spot; some authorities believe a Greek, or even an Etruscan, edifice. Although the town was sacked and burned by the Saracens in 866 and again destroyed by fire in 1222, its street plan still follows the ancient model, and the old walls, some of which go back to the 3rd century BC, are still perfectly visible.

Continuing east along the decumanus (Corso Appio Claudio), you reach Piazza Matteotti, with the imposing castle and the elegant 16th-century Palazzo Caetani, once the seat of the Caetani and later of the Colonna. The **castle** is noteworthy as the scene of the conclave of 1378, when the dissident cardinals, outraged by the refractory, unpredictable Urban VI, elected Clement VII as antipope, an act that marked the beginning of the Great Schism. It is now home to the **Museo Archeologico** (*open Mon-Fri 9.30–12.30, Sat 9.30–1 & 5–7, Sun 9.30–1, closed Wed; T: 0771 503775*), with an interesting collection of Roman sculptures found nearby; when complete, the museum will include sections on prehistory and the Middle Ages, and a picture gallery. In August 1534 the notorious corsair Kheir ed-Din Barbarossa, fired by the fame of the beauty of Giulia Colonna, attempted to abduct her from the palace here; he wanted to make a gift of her to Sultan Suleiman the Magnificent, to whom he was indebted; the lady, warned in time, fled to her mountain fief. In pique, Kheir ed-Din sacked the town. Close by (but outside the city walls, as was the custom of the Franciscans) is the convent and church of **San Francesco d'Assisi**, reputedly founded by the saint himself, and heavily restored from its original Gothic style. Looking back you get a good view of the palace, the castle and its tower. Inside the church are some beautiful stained-glass windows, of modern design. The convent, with its attractive cloister, is now the town hall.

South of Piazza Matteotti is Piazza Duomo, with the cathedral of Fondi, the early 12th-century church of **San Pietro**, built on top of the Temple of Jupiter. In the interior, in the chapel of the Cross at the end of the south aisle, is the 14th-century mosaic throne used by the antipope Clement VII, together with two remarkable 15th-century triptychs; there is also an elaborate Caetani family tomb. In the nave is a splendid 13th-century mosaic pulpit, with an image of *St Jerome* on the front, and the symbols of the Evangelists on the left face. Suspended over the main altar is a 12th-century Crucifix, with the emperor Constantine and his mother St Helen in the terminals. The floor in the baptistery, on the left on entering the church, is the original 12th-century mosaic, transferred here from the centre of the church during repairs.

Already by the 4th century Fondi had a flourishing Jewish community of dyers, who also traded linen and hemp. Their district was in the northern section of the town. Entering from no. 20 Via Manzoni, you can still see the old **Jewish Quarter**.

St Thomas Aquinas taught at the Dominican convent of Fondi, and the novelist Alberto Moravia lived here for many years. In 1957 he wrote his masterpiece *La Ciociara* here (*see p. 211*). Fondi was also the birthplace of the post-war neo-Realist film director Giuseppe de Santis.

Sperlonga

Sperlonga (*map p. 210, C3*), with its whitewashed houses clinging to the hillside, its narrow alleys and its steps leading under arches and through little tunnels from one tiny square to the next, is utterly charming, and well deserves its reputation as Italy's most beautiful village. It is also the only Italian resort to have won the Blue Banner for clean sea and beaches for ten consecutive years. For many years it was a simple fishing hamlet, but when the coast road was opened in 1958, it soon became a select resort, consisting of the old quarter on the rocky headland and a new district on the landward side. The name derives from the Latin word *spelunca*, cave, and it is here that Tiberius built one of his many villas, with the *pièce de résistance* being the sea-girt cavern fitted out as a dining hall. That cave, the **Grotta di Tiberio**, still exists, to the southeast of the town (*open daily 8.30–7.30; T: 0771 548028*). It was here that Sejanus, head of the Praetorian Guard, took the first step towards his pre-eminence by saving Tiberius from a fall of rocks.

> #### Sejanus gains the confidence of the emperor
>
> It came to pass at this time that a dangerous mishap which befell the emperor gave Tiberius reason to place more implicit trust in the loyal friendship of Sejanus. They were dining in a villa called *Spelunca*, between the bay of Amyclae and the hills of Fundi, in a natural grotto. The rocks at the cave entrance suddenly fell in and crushed some of the servants; the entire party was at once seized with panic and the guests all took to flight. Sejanus stayed beside the emperor, shielding him, and with his knee, head and hand parried the cascade of rocks. He was found thus by the soldiers who came to their relief. After this he rose higher than ever before, and fully gained the ear of the emperor, as if his thoughts were never for himself, though his advice did much harm.
>
> *Tacitus, Annals, 4:59*

Near the cave, surrounded by olive trees and carobs, is the **Museo Archeologico Statale** (*open as above*), which houses an *Odyssey* in marble: sculptures showing episodes from Homer's poem, in the Hellenistic style of Pergamon and Rhodes, found during excavations in the grotto (1957–60). In autumn 1957 the whole population blocked the road to stop the first statues found in the cave from going to Rome. An inscription with the names of the three Rhodian sculptors responsible for the *Laocoön* group in the Vatican (Agesander, Athenodorus and Polydorus) was found here, but scholars have not automatically concluded that the same three were responsible for the Sperlonga figures. Disputes continue about the date of the sculptures (it is not certain that they are even from Tiberius' time) and the proper reassemblage. One huge group, the *Struggle with Scylla*, has been pieced together, with Ulysses holding the *Palladium* (the wooden statue of Pallas Athena that was kept in the citadel at Troy) as protection against the monster: wild dogs springing from her loins are trying to devour six of the hero's men. Other notable works include *Ulysses Blinding Polyphemus*, *Zeus as an Eagle Kidnaps Ganymede*, and a bust of Aeneas as tutelary deity of the Julio-Claudian family group. It is assumed that the sculptures were arranged in the cave so as to provide pleasing and stimulating vistas for guests at the emperor's banquets. The triclinium was in the centre of a round pool, with the statues all around. It is thought that the statues, which were all found in a fragmentary state, were deliberately destroyed by Byzantine Christian monks. Many other extremely interesting items are on display in the museum, including the skull of a crocodile: besides fish, Tiberius raised crocodiles in the various pools of his villa.

GAETA & FORMIA

Gaeta (*map p. 210, C3*) is a beautiful town on the promontory of Monte Orlando, which divides into two parts the gulf of the same name. It was a popular seaside resort in Roman times, and the vestiges of many wealthy tombs have come to light. It later flourished as a Byzantine trading post. The first walls were constructed in the 9th century, but the city was fortified again several times in the course of the centuries, and it was an important military port; in fact the Christian fleet commanded by Marcantonio Colonna departed from Gaeta for the victorious battle over the Turks at Lepanto in 1571, and it is a NATO base even today. During the Unification of Italy, Gaeta was the last stronghold of Francis II of Naples, and it fell to the Italian forces only on 13th February 1861. After Unification, the castle lost its importance. During the Second World War the city was heavily bombarded, and the Germans deported many of the people. The claims of Gaeta rival those of Genoa as the birthplace of John Cabot, the great navigator. Today Gaeta is a popular resort for visitors attracted by the picturesque old centre, the lovely beaches, and by the gastronomy; it is also a busy fishing harbour and small industrial centre.

EN PASSANT

Charles Edward Stuart 'won his spurs' here, aged 13, against the Austrian garrison in 1734. During his voyage from Gaeta to Naples with Charles of Bourbon, the Young Pretender's hat blew into the sea: when it was proposed that a boat should be lowered to recover it, the young Charles told the crew not to trouble themselves, as 'he should be obliged before long to fetch himself a hat [the Crown] in England'.

Santissima Annunziata

Town life centres on the modern Piazza XIX Maggio, where the town hall is situated, on the harbour front. From here the Lungomare Caboto follows the shore around the north slope of Monte Orlando to the medieval quarter, passing two sets of defensive fortifications and the scanty remains of a 2nd-century Roman villa. The church of the **Santissima Annunziata**, midway along on the right, with a harmonious Baroque façade, dates from 1302, but was rebuilt in 1621. The elegant, single-nave interior houses a *Nativity* (on the right-hand wall) and a *Crucifixion* (opposite) by Luca Giordano. From the choir a corridor goes to the sacristy; on the left a door leads to the so-called *Grotta d'Oro*, or Golden Cave (*open 9–12 & 3–6; T: 0771 462265*), the dazzling Renaissance chapel of the Immaculate Virgin, where Pius IX meditated before pronouncing the dogma of Papal Infallibility in 1870. There is a marvellous carved and gilded coffered ceiling, but the walls are entirely covered with a masterpiece of art: 19 paintings (1531–36) by the local painter and sculptor Giovan Filippo Criscuolo, each with its original carved and gilded frame, depicting episodes from the lives of Christ and the Virgin. Criscuolo (1500–84) came from a family of artists; both his brother and his daughter were painters. According to Vasari, he wrote a biography of Neapolitan artists, unfortunately now lost.

The old town

Continuing to the heart of the old quarter, you soon reach the **duomo**, dedicated to the patron saint Erasmus. This suffered considerable damage in the Second World War. It was first built in 917 over an earlier, 7th-century, Byzantine construction, and consecrated in 1106, then rebuilt in the 17th and 18th centuries. The three-storey bell-tower (1148–1279), 57m high, incorporating architectural fragments from antique buildings, particularly the tomb of Sempronius Atratinus (*see p. 246 below*), is the finest building in Gaeta, and symbol of the city; it is surmounted by four little towers with domes, and brightened by majolica dishes. In the archway beneath the tower, steps lead to the interior of the cathedral. The passageway contains Roman sarcophagi and fragmentary 13th-century reliefs. The interior is divided into seven naves by columns recuperated from different pagan temples. The 13th-century paschal candlestick, 3.5m high, is decorated with 48 bas-reliefs depicting the lives of Christ and St Erasmus.

A doorway to the left of the façade provides access to the **Museo Diocesano** (*open Sun 10.30–12 and by appointment, T: 0771 462255*), which has a collection of sculptural and architectural fragments, detached frescoes of the the school of Giotto, fine 14th-century ceramics, and paintings, some (including two painted on copper) by the local 18th-century artist Sebastiano Conca, whose bold hand and sensitive use of colour helped him enjoy a successful career in Rome as a fresco painter; his brother Giovanni found popularity as a painter of altarpieces in the Marche region. A curiosity displayed in the museum is a sheet of paper measuring 80cm by 25cm, with the entire *Divine Comedy* by Dante written on it in minuscule handwriting.

More paintings, particularly of the Neapolitan school from the 16th–18th centuries, can be seen in a permanent exhibition at the library, **Centro Storico Culturale Gaeta**

Entry into Jerusalem, detail from the 13th-century paschal candlestick in Gaeta duomo.

(Piazza de Vio 9; *open daily except Sun 4.30–7.30; T: 0771 464293*); here also is a banner flown by the Christian fleet at Lepanto.

Further west is the little 10th-century church of San Giovanni a Mare, commonly called San Giuseppe, surrounded by the most picturesque of the area's narrow streets, vaulted passageways and winding steps, recently carefully and lovingly restored. The enormous **castle** (over 14,000m square; *temporarily closed*) is at the top of this district. Originally built in the 8th century, and reconstructed by that great castle-builder Frederick of Hohenstaufen in 1227, it was remodelled in later years; now the lower part dates from c. 1289, the upper from c. 1435. Giuseppe Mazzini, one of the architects of Italian unity, was imprisoned here in 1870.

Monte Orlando

On the summit of Monte Orlando stands the mausoleum of **Munatius Plancus** (*open Sat & Sun 9–1 & 2–6*), the founder of Lyon and one of Caesar's most noted generals (d.

after 22 BC). The monument, locally known as *Torre d'Orlando*, consists of a tower in *opus reticulatum* faced with travertine and crowned by a Doric frieze with battle scenes in the metopes. The hill itself is allegedly the grave of Caieta, Aeneas' nurse; Gaeta was named after her. At its southwest point the cliff, riven by three narrow chasms, is known as the *Montagna Spaccata* ('Split Mountain'): it is said to have cracked in this way at the moment of the Crucifixion of Christ. Dominating the headland, the sanctuary of the Santissima Trinità (*open 9–12.30 & 3–sunset*), entered through one of the cracks, was founded by the Benedictines in the 9th century. Steps lead down to a cave at sea-level known as the **Grotta del Turco** (*open as above, T: 0771 462068*).

Porto Salvo

From Piazza XIX Maggio, Via Indipendenza leads through the picturesque northern part of town, Porto Salvo, parallel to the sea. This is the oldest district, very animated, with a series of little shops and stalls, and washing hanging out from one side of the street to the other. More ancient tombs may be seen in the environs. Above the district stands the **Tomb of Sempronius Atratinus**, a Roman patrician tomb damaged by fighting in 1815. The marble facing was removed to build the cathedral's campanile.

FORMIA & ENVIRONS

The houses of Gaeta continue without interruption to Formia (*map p. 210, C3*), an attractive place, which bases its economy on market services. It is a very popular bathing resort (as it was in Antiquity), and the sea views are enchanting. It consists of two parts, both medieval: the centre of Castellone, on the hillside where there was a fortress, and Mola, near the coast, where the mills (*mole*) for grinding wheat were situated.

HISTORY OF FORMIA

The town is the ancient *Formiae*, the fabled abode of Lamus, King of the Laestrygones, notorious cannibals encountered by Ulysses. According to other sources, the town was founded by Spartans, and Aeneas stopped here on his way to Lavinium. Formia was the birthplace of the great architect Vitruvius. After the murder of Julius Caesar on 15th March 44 BC, Cicero placed himself at the head of the Republican Party and attacked Mark Antony in his 'Philippic' orations. On the formation of the triumvirate by Octavian, Antony and Lepidus, Cicero's name was put on the list of those proscribed. The orator fled to his villa at Formiae, but was caught by Antony's soldiers and killed on 7th December, aged 64. At the time, Formiae was second only to Baiae on the bay of Naples in terms of the number and opulence of its patrician villas. The area still contains numerous (though scanty) remains of ancient farms and villages. It was virtually destroyed in the Second World War, and has been rebuilt since.

The heart of the modern city today is the central Piazza Marconi (Piazza Municipio), with the **Museo Archeologico Nazionale** (*open daily 8.30–7.30; T: 0771 770382*) containing some fine statues and other sculptures, as well as wine jars, Roman coins and other material, dating from the 1st century BC–2nd century AD, brought to light in local excavations in the area of the forum, and also found in areas bombed during the Second World War. From the square a wide stairway leads down to Piazza della Vittoria, with trees and flowers, where some columns from a temple of Venus have been erected, and there are views over the Gulf of Gaeta and the port just below. The cult statue for the temple was a gift of the senate and the people of Rome to Formia for its loyalty during the Second Punic War.

The long, straight Via Vitruvio is the main street of Formia. From Piazza della Vittoria it leads westwards to the handsome Piazza Mattei, south of which is **Villa Rubino**, and the important remains (stuccoed vaults and fragments of wall-paintings) of a Roman villa of the 1st or 2nd century, commonly called Cicero's Villa. Here King Francis II of Naples signed the armistice which brought his struggle against the Unification of Italy to an end.

The picturesque district of Castellone is on the hillside to the north. Via del Castello passes through the district up to Torre Castellone, site of the Roman citadel; at no. 39, to the left, is the entrance to Vico Anfiteatro, where a whitewashed house stands on the remains of the **ancient theatre**, the structure of which is still clearly visible (the amphitheatre, after which the street is wrongly named, stands in an orange grove near the station and awaits excavation).

Itri

Northeast of Formia, the Via Appia winds away from the coast. At the point where it turns inland stands the so-called **Tomb of Cicero**, which has recently been restored. From here the road ascends, amid fabulous views, to **Itri** (*map p. 210, C3*), an important agricultural centre. Vittorio de Sica's film of Alberto Moravia's novel *La Ciociara* (*see p. 211*), starring Sofia Loren, was filmed here in 1960, and in 1966 John Huston chose it as the set for *The Bible*.

The town is divided in two by the Fosso Pontone stream: the spectacular upper town, with its medieval walls and castle still largely intact, in spite of heavy bombardments in 1944 (the people were awarded the bronze medal for valour); and the lower town, which fans out on more level land below. From Piazza Diaz in the modern quarter, steps go up to the lovely **Quartiere Medievale**. Along a narrow alley, passing under some arches, with ancient houses on each side, you reach Piazza Santa Maria Maggiore with its colourful 13th-century campanile and little Byzantine-style dome, which miraculously survived the bombs. Continuing up to the left, passing the house where Fra' Diavolo was born, you reach the 11th-century church of San Michele Arcangelo, with another lovely bell-tower, decorated with majolica dishes inside the arches. Still higher up, passing under some more arches, is the **castle**, a medieval complex badly damaged by the bombardments, recently restored and opened to the public (*request visit at town hall*).

Scauri

Scauri (*map p. 210, D3*) is a small bathing resort which has developed in recent years around the nucleus of a medieval village. A few wealthy Romans built their villas in this place, including Marcus Aemilius Scaurus, consul from 115 BC, after whom the town derives its name. From the Middle Ages a small community lived here, manufacturing textiles, pots and pans, and paper; they were sometimes attacked by pirates. The worst attack was in 1552, when the notorious corsair Dragut carried off all 200 inhabitants and sold them into slavery, after burning their village. In the tiny old centre of Scauri is a medieval tower, built to protect the water-mills on the Capodacqua stream, where most of the industries were concentrated. Beyond the tower is a stretch of the magnificent city walls of *Pirae*, formed of huge blocks of stone; Pirae, a city of the Ausonians, had already entered into decline in the days of the Romans. The remarkable gate is still intact. Close by are the imposing remains of Scaurus' villa and a small Roman harbour, the *Porticciolo di Gianola*. About 15mins away by boat, along a stretch of coast protected by the WWF, is a small **Grotta Azzurra** (*T: WWF 0771 683850; local boatmen will take you on request*) rather like the one on Capri. The rocky promontory of Scauri, the southernmost in Lazio, is also protected as a nature reserve, principally for the vegetation (cork-oaks and Mediterranean *maquis* of rosemary, cistus and asphodels); cormorants are often spotted here. To the south the River Garigliano, the ancient *Liris*, marks the boundary between Lazio and Campania.

MINTURNAE

On the west bank of the Garigliano, south of the modern town of Minturno, are the ruins of **Minturnae** (*map p. 210, D3*), once an important town in a strategic position for those using the river to reach the interior and Campania. The town's position at a river crossing has often made it a scene of conflict. French and Spanish soldiers clashed here in 1503; on the right bank of the river today, at **Minturno British Military Cemetery**, lie the graves of 2,038 men who fell in the Battle of the Garigliano in January 1944.

The site

The most distinct remains are located in the area of the Roman town (*open 9–7, T: 0771 680093*). Chief among these is the splendid **theatre**, built in the 1st century and later restored, of which the scena, orchestra and cavea survive. Behind it lies the **Republican forum**, originally surrounded by a colonnade and incorporating two fountains on the side that faced the Via Appia. To the west stood temples dedicated to the Capitoline Triad (Jupiter, Juno and Minerva) and, possibly, to Roma and Augustus; to the east another large temple extended over part of the Italic town. South of the Via Appia and separated from it by another arcade stood the **Imperial forum**, flanked by the basilica and public baths. Archaeologists have identified the site of an amphitheatre beyond. Along the riverbank are remains of the harbour and, 500m further on, part of a **Temple of Marica** (a fertility goddess; 6th century BC). Ruins of an aqueduct are also visible.

HISTORY OF MINTURNAE

The ancient Minturnae, the chief Tyrrhenian port of the Ausonians, became a major Roman colony in 295 BC. It is repeatedly described in the letters of Cicero, and a clue to its decline may be found in Ovid's *Metamorphoses* (*XV: 716*), where allusion is made to its malarial waters. The earliest settlement stood on the right bank of the *Liris* (Garigliano), roughly 3km from the river-mouth, and was enclosed within a rectangular wall of polygonal masonry, with gates on the north and south sides and bastions at the four corners.

The Roman town was built to the west within its own wall circuit in *opus reticulatum*, with square and polygonal towers. The Via Appia, which crossed it from end to end, passed between the Republican and Imperial fora, forming the main street. A road flanked by *tabernae* (shops) ran along the riverbank to the harbour, beyond which stood the chief sanctuary of the town, dedicated to Marica, the Italic goddess of fertility, to whom the waters of the river and its marshes were sacred.

Here the Roman consul Marius, proscribed in 88 BC, and who had been taken prisoner, daunted the would-be assassin sent by Sulla by shouting 'Would you dare kill Gaius Marius?'. The assassin fled, and Marius was allowed by the population to escape to Africa.

Excavations of ancient Minturnae, conducted jointly by the University of Pennsylvania and the Soprintendenza alle Antichità of Naples in 1931–33, brought to light numerous ex-voto offerings, with Archaic votive statues of Italic, Etruscan, and Greek workmanship, which were originally sent to the Museo Archeologico Nazionale in Naples. Now they are gradually being returned to the **Museo Archeologico di Minturno** (in the modern town at Via Appia 7; *open as the ruins*), where they are displayed together with sculpture, pottery and architectural fragments unearthed during the excavations.

MONTE CASSINO

The inland road for Monte Cassino passes Ausonia (*map p. 210, D3*), a village recalling the Samnite town of *Ausona* destroyed in the Second Samnite War. On a by-road just south of it is the 15th-century church of **Santa Maria del Piano**, noted for its frescoes, possibly of the 12th century, in its crypt. The surrounding ruins are probably those of Ausona.

The Abbey of Monte Cassino

Monte Cassino (*map p. 210, D2*) is perhaps the most famous abbey in the world. Unfortunately its fame today rests on the fact that it was totally destroyed in the final stages of the Second World War. There are several museums in the modern town of Cassino which illustrate the battle. The **Cassino British Military Cemetery** is the largest in Italy, with 4,267 graves of those who fell in battle in this district. In addition a memorial here commemorates over 4,000 soldiers from the Commonwealth who died in the Sicilian and Italian campaigns and who have no known grave. Many New Zealanders and Indian troops were killed in the fierce fighting at Monte Cassino, but it was in the final stages of the campaign that the Polish II Corps encountered the heaviest losses. Their military cemetery in the woods just below the abbey has over 1,000 graves.

Since its rebuilding, the abbey has become a famous pilgrimage shrine for visitors from Italy and the rest of the world: some 20 monks still live here.

Casinum

At the bottom of the hill on which the abbey stands (and on its approach road) are the very interesting remains of the Roman town of *Casinum*, which was in an important strategic position in the Liri valley where several roads, including the Via Latina, converged. The archaeological museum (*open 9–dusk every day*) illustrates its history, and the lapidarium has tombs and inscriptions. The amphitheatre could hold some 4,500 spectators, and the theatre, on the hillside just above, dates from the time of Augustus. Another Roman edifice here is designed on a Greek-cross plan with a cupola (later converted into a church). A long stretch of Roman road is also preserved, and remains of a nymphaeum with traces of painting.

HISTORY OF MONTE CASSINO

Monte Cassino was founded by St Benedict of Nursia in 529 after he had left Subiaco (*see p. 152*). It was renowned for its learning throughout the Middle Ages, and was considered a beacon of civilisation. On 15th February 1944 it was destroyed by Allied bombs, an action without any justification. The American general Mark W. Clark himself later recognised that this had been an error of judgement since there were no German troops in the abbey at the time (and indeed, the monks had given shelter to hundreds of civilians), and it also proved to be a tactical mistake as the ruins were immediately occupied by 80 German parachutists who held the hill for another three months, during which there were more heavy losses of life. The attack had been an attempt to break the formidable defences stretching all the way from the sea (the Gustav Line and the Hitler Line), which had been built by the Germans in 1943 on the bare and stony Monte Cairo, to block the Allied advance northwards to Rome.

The decision was at once taken to rebuild the abbey as it was and where it was, and the work took place mostly in the 1950s: today it stands again proudly in its magnificent site on a hilltop (517m) surrounded by a valley (now occupied by the modern city of Cassino), with a circle of higher mountains all around.

Visiting the Abbey

The cloisters and church (*open 9.30–12.30 & 3.30–6.30*) are entered to the right of the old entrance and the building which housed the papal apartments. The long wing which can be seen here above a little garden housed the monks' cells with the library below. Beyond a first cloister with a little garden inhabited by doves, is a replica of the cloister built in 1595 with a loggia opening out onto the valley, with the monks' vineyard immediately below and the Polish cemetery conspicuous on the hillside. A monumental flight of steps leads up to a portico, which leads into a rebuilt cloister designed at the beginning of the 16th century in front of the church, which preserves its splendid ancient bronze doors, cast in Constantinople in 1066, which were found damaged in the debris. It is covered with inscriptions inlaid with silver, which refer to the abbey's properties and to churches under its jurisdiction. The lowest right-hand panel bears the date. The interior is a reconstruction of the Baroque church designed in the early 17th century, and the paintings in the cupola and on the west wall (1979–80) are by Pietro Annigoni. The early 18th-century choir stalls were restored using the original woodwork as far as possible. The crypt, with mosaics, dates from 1913.

The museum (*open as above, except from Nov–March, when it is only open on Sun and holidays 3.30–5*) is approached through a little medieval reconstructed cloister off which is a chapel which preserves a damaged 13th-century fresco of *Christ Pantocrator*, the oldest painted decoration to survive in the abbey. The museum contains a few fragments of the 11th-century marble pavement salvaged from the ruins; book-bindings, illuminated choir books and vestments; and a painting attributed to Botticelli, which is a recent donation. There are also some exquisite liturgical objects from the abbey treasury. But the most precious contents are those from the famous library (which survived destruction in the last war since it had been moved to the Vatican). It has some 100,000 volumes and 500 incunabula, including a collection of works by Paulus Diaconus (Paul the Deacon), who wrote his famous history of the Lombards here in 790. The 11th-century *Biblia Hebraica* of St Gregory the Great, and the *Liber Moralium* with notes in the handwriting of St Thomas Aquinas are also among the library treasures.

PRACTICAL INFORMATION

GETTING AROUND

• **By train:** The main railway line from Rome to Naples follows the coast, linking **Latina**, **Sperlonga**, **Itri**, **Formia** and **Minturno-Scauri**. From Rome to Naples, trains run at least twice an hour 4am–11.30pm, and 4am–9.50pm in the opposite direction (additional, slower regional trains from Formia). Trains from Rome (Termini) serve **Anzio** and **Nettuno**.
• **By bus:** Express buses run from Rome to **Terracina**, with frequent connections to **Formia** and **Gaeta**, and between Terracina and points in the Parco Nazionale del Circeo. **Anzio** and **Nettuno** buses leave Rome from the Fermi underground stop.

INFORMATION OFFICES

Anzio Piazza Pia 19, T: 06 984 5147.
Fondi Via San Paolino da Nola, T: 0771 516 6501.
Formia Viale Unità d'Italia 30/34, T: 0771 771490.
Gaeta Corso Cavour 16, T: 0771 461165.

Latina Via Duca del Mare 19, T: 0773 695404; Piazza del Popolo, T: 0773 480672.
Minturno (Scauri) Via Lungomare 32 (corner of Via Impero), T: 0771 683788, www.minturnoscauri.it
Sabaudia Piazza del Comune 18/19, T: 0773 515046, www.sabaudia.net
San Felice Circeo Piazza Lanzuisi, T: 0773 547770.
Sperlonga Piazza della Rimembranza, T: 0771 54796.
Terracina Via Leopardi, T: 0773 727759, www.terracina.eu

HOTELS

Anzio (*map p. 210, A2*)
€ **Lido Garda**. 1920s building, close to the centre, with pool, garden and car park. Comfortable rooms with well-designed bathrooms; dependable service. Reputable restaurant. *Piazza Caboto 8, T: 06 987 0354, www.lidogarda.com. 42 rooms.*
Fondi (*map p. 210, C3*)
€€ **Villa dei Principi**. Comfortable hotel on the beach, open all year round and good value for money. The hotel is

especially known for its restaurant—creative cuisine and wonderful presentation. *Via Flacca km 1, Fondi Lido, T: 0771 57399, www.villadeiprincipi.com. 32 rooms.*

€ **Mblò**. An intriguing 13th-century house in the centre of Fondi, long famed as a restaurant, and now also offering comfortable B&B accommodation. *Corso Appio Claudio 11, T: 0771 502385, www.mblo.it. 8 rooms.*

Formia (*map p. 210, C3*)

€€ **Castello Miramare**. Alluring 19th-century castle-villa in a splendid garden, on the hill above Formia. Comfortable rooms, terrace with panoramic view, very good restaurant. *Via Balze di Pagnano, T: 0771 700138, www.hotelcastellomiramare.it. 10 rooms.*

€ **L'Olmo**. Comfortable rooms in the old city centre, close to the station, port and beach. *Via dell'Olmo 31, T: 329 842 9275, www.formiabedandbreakfast.it. 2 rooms.*

Gaeta (*map p. 210, C3*)

€€€ **Villa Irlanda**. In a magnificent position with fine views, this elegant hotel occupies three early 19th-century buildings and a Roman *domus*, in a large garden with pools. The lovely dining-room occupies an old church. Open all year. *Via Lungomare Caboto 6, T: 0771 712581, www.villairlanda.com. 40 rooms.*

€€ **Grand Hotel Le Rocce**. Seven kilometres west of the city centre on a cliff, immersed in vegetation; Moorish-style building offering garden terraces, two restaurants, car park, private beach and good views of the sea and coast. Open end April–start Oct. *Via Flacca km 23.3, T: 0771 740985, www.lerocce.com. 56 rooms.*

€€ **Hotel Serapo**. A large hotel on the beach, open all year round, with indoor pool, tennis, fitness centre, and a lovely open-air restaurant in the garden. *Via Firenze 11, Spiaggia di Serapo, T: 0771 450037, www.hotelserapo.com. 170 rooms.*

Itri (*map p. 210, C3*)

€€ **I Giardini di Margius**. Open all year round, this olive grove is on a hillside offering splendid views. Accommodation is in comfortable wooden bungalows, each sleeping two. Sheep and poultry are raised, and produce includes ricotta, eggs and milk. They will pick you up from the station. *Vico Scaliconte 3, T: 347 171 2604, www.igiardinidimargius.com. 6 bungalows.*

€ **Pennacchio Valle Itri**. Vineyards and olive groves on the hillside around a beautiful old farmhouse. The farm, open year round, provides self-catering apartments of various sizes. *Contrada Terragone, T: 0771 727641, www.valleitri.it.*

Sabaudia (*map p. 210, B3*)

€€€ **Il San Francesco Charming**. Luscious new villa on lakeside, with its own park, comfortable rooms, fitness centre, good restaurant which uses ingredients from local farms. Open March–Dec. *Via del Caterattino, T: 0773 515951, www.ilsanfrancescohotel.it. 27 rooms.*

€€ **Podere 1470**. Organically-grown vegetables and eucalyptus-blossom honey are produced on this farm, with charming rooms, a large pool, and a lovely garden. The delicious breakfasts are available year round, with home-made jam and cakes. Evening meals in summer only. *Via Migliara 51, T: 0773 531052, www.agriturismosabaudia.it. 8 rooms.*

€ **Marilà**. Farm in a panoramic position, a short distance from the sea. The land is partly wooded; vegetables and especially melons and watermelons are grown. Bikes are available; good area for birdwatching. English, French and German spoken. *Via Tenca 4, Località Sacramento, T: 0773 593012, www.agriturismomarila.com. 8 rooms.*

€ **Minihotel Saporetti**. Comfortable, small, family-run hotel in pleasant verdant location. The same family runs a renowned restaurant on the beach, where guests can take their meals. *Corso Vittorio Emanuele 2, T: 0773 515987, www.saporetti.com. 27 rooms.*

San Felice Circeo (*map p. 210, B3*)
€€€ **Maga Circe**. On the sea in a quiet location, very comfortable, with well-known restaurant. Sea-water pool, lush Mediterranean garden, diving. *Via Ammiraglio Bergamini 7, T: 0773 547821, www.hotelmagacirce.it. 46 rooms.*

€€€ **Relais Bed & Brunch 'Isola di Eéa'**. Exclusive accommodation in a lovely villa on the rocks. Delicious and abundant food available. *Via della Vasca Moresca 4, Località Quarto Caldo, T: 0773 548583 and 339 8211502, www.isoladieea.com. 6 rooms.*

€€ **Punta Rossa**. Beautiful and exclusive, the hotel offers rooms or apartments overlooking the sea in a secluded position 5km from the village centre, with luxuriant gardens, cliff-top pool, private beach, fitness centre and a good restaurant. Open all year. *Via delle Batterie 37, Località Quarto Caldo, T: 0773 548085, www.puntarossa.it. 38 rooms.*

€€ **Il Faro**. Small hotel 2km from centre with an enchanting cliffside position, restaurant and pizzeria. *Piazza Valente 3, T: 0773 548909, www.ilfarohotel.it. 19 rooms.*

Sperlonga (*map p. 210, C3*)
€€ **La Sirenella**. Ideal for family holidays, on the beach, with restaurant and car park. Open all year. *Via Cristoforo Colombo 25, T: 0771 549186, www.lasirenella.com. 40 rooms.*

€€ **Virgilio Grand Hotel**. Good modern hotel in the new town. Garage, restaurant, pool with hydro-massage. *Viale Prima Romita, T: 0771 557600, www.virgiliograndhotel.it. 72 rooms.*

Terracina (*map p. 210, B3*)
€€€ **L'Approdo**. On the beach, with restaurant and comfortable rooms. *Viale Circe, T: 0773 726221, www.approdograndhotel.it. 56 rooms.*

€€ **Cinque Pini**. Small hotel in a central position but not far from the sea, with a restaurant. *Viale Europa 201, T: 0773 732040, www.albergo5pini.it. 50 rooms.*

€€ **Mediterraneo**. Comfortable modern building in central position, close to the sea, with pool, garden and restaurant. *Via Veneto 2, T: 0773 733001, www.albergo-mediterraneo.it. 75 rooms.*

RESTAURANTS

Anzio (*map p. 210, A2*)
€€€€ **Alceste al Buon Gusto**. Anzio is famous for the exquisite flavour of its fish, and this restaurant is the best place to try it. The *antipasto* includes a wide range of raw and cooked seafood—the shrimps with orange and wild fennel seeds are irresistible. Imaginative pasta dishes are followed by fried or grilled fish of many kinds; leave room for the fantastic home-made ice cream for dessert. Good wine list. Tends to be

packed at weekends, but the highly professional staff handles the situation with ease. Beautiful views too. Closed Tues. *Piazza Sant'Antonio 6, T: 06 9846744.*

€€ **Flora**. Elegant restaurant with a garden for eating outside in summer. The menu changes every day, according to what fish is available at the market, but always includes plenty of seafood *antipasti*, both cooked and raw, and delicious pasta or fish soup. Meat-eaters and vegetarians are not forgotten either. Franca, the chef, serves her native Sicilian desserts. Closed Tues in winter. *Via Flora 9, T: 06 984 6001.*

€ **Del Gatto**. Tiny wine bar serving delicious hot snacks, cooked to perfection, making this an ideal place for a light supper. Closed Mon, Tues, Wed, except summer. *Via Mazzini 9, T: 06 984 6269.*

Fondi (*map p. 210, C3*)
€€ **Vicolo di Mblò**. Venerable establishment known for its traditional cuisine, and justly renowned for the pasta and the country soups (for example, the *zavardella*, a soup made of eight different vegetables, all cooked separately and then blended together). No written menu, let the chef tell you what he has prepared that day. Closed Tues in winter. *Corso Appio Claudio 11, T: 0771 502385.*

Formia (*map p. 210, C3*)
€€€ **Chinappi**. One of the best restaurants along the coast, with tasty and appetising local dishes, carefully prepared and served. Try, for example, the homemade tuna ravioli, or the fried baby squid. Nice desserts, good wine list; verdant garden for summer dinners under the orange trees. Closed Thurs.

Via Anfiteatro 8, T: 0771 790002.
€€ **Il Gatto e la Volpe**. Traditional trattoria in the old centre, where you can sample ancient recipes. The simple menu changes with the seasons. Pasta with shellfish is good, also the rich fish soup. Closed Wed and Christmas. *Via Abate Tosti 83, T: 0771 21354.*

€€ **Sirio**. Good value for money at this restaurant, founded by Sirio from Tuscany, and now run by his sons. Interesting and unusual *antipasti* include whitebait fritters, mussels stuffed with squid and shrimps, then perhaps fine noodles with squid-ink sauce; admirable cheese trolley; home-made desserts and ice cream; good wine list. You can eat outside in summer. Closed Mon evening and all day Tues (winter); Tues and Wed lunchtime (summer). *Viale Unità d'Italia, T: 0771 790047.*

Gaeta (*map p. 210, C3*)
€ **La Cianciola**. No frills in this true-to-life trattoria, but absolutely delicious food, starting with a series of seafood *antipasti*, then some interesting pasta dishes, followed by grilled fish or meat, and a wonderful home-made dessert called *delizia al limone*. Local wines. Closed Mon except in summer, and Nov. *Vico Buonomo 16, T: 0771 466190.*

Latina (*map p. 210, B2*)
€€€ **La Taberna dei Lari**. Charming little restaurant, offering mostly fish dishes in summer and meat in winter, preceded by delicious hot *antipasti*. Good assortment of cheeses and desserts. Open evenings only, closed Mon. *Via Leopardi 21, T: 0773 411061.*

€€ **Hosteria La Fenice**. Let Emiliano tell you about the various appetising dishes he has prepared: perhaps sheep's milk ricotta with truffles for *antipasto*, then unusual vegetable soups or pasta, followed by rabbit, stewed goat, snails or grilled meat; the desserts are delicious. Closed all day Wed and Sun evening (winter); all day Sun and Wed lunchtime (summer). *Via Bellini 8, T: 0773 240225.*

€ **Impero**. A family-run trattoria, well-known and loved by the local people, many of whom come back day after day. Central position. Closed Mon. *Piazza della Libertà 19, T: 0773 693140.*

Monte San Biagio (*map p. 210, C3*)
€€ **Hosteria della Piazzetta**. This well-known little restaurant specialises in interesting local dishes using ingredients from the lake and its surroundings, such as snails, eels, crayfish and frogs. Excellent home-made pasta, for example *linguine con gamberetti di lago* (noodles with lake shrimps). For dessert, biscuits or fruit tart accompanied by a series of deceptively innocent-looking liqueurs, also made by the owners. Closed Tues. *Viale Littoria 13, T: 0771 566793.*

Nettuno (*map p. 210, A2*)
€€€ **Antica Taverna Piazzetta**. Pasta, bread and cakes are home-made. Very good pasta and main courses, all using fish and local vegetables in a wide variety of ways. Extensive wine list. Closed Mon. *Largo Trafelli 5, T: 06 988 1440.*

Sabaudia (*map p. 210, B3*)
€€ **Clan Destino**. Central position for this little restaurant which serves inventive cuisine and unusual desserts. Well-chosen wine list. Closed Mon in winter. *Largo Giulio Cesare 6, T: 0773 511573.*

San Felice Circeo (*map p. 210, B3*)
€€€ **Miramare Le Tre Sorelle**. On the seafront, a classic restaurant offering classic food; meat or fish cooked to traditional recipes and well served. Dependable. Closed Mon in winter. *Lungomare Circe 40, T: 0773 546604.*

Sperlonga (*map p. 210, C3*)
€€€ **Archi**. A delightful place to eat outside in summer, in the square; the *antipasto*, both hot and cold, is very inviting, followed by simple pasta dishes, then lots of fresh fish. Attentive and courteous service, good wine list. Closed Wed in winter. *Via Ottaviano 17, T: 0771 548300.*

€€€ **Tramonto**. Right on the water's edge, this restaurant started out as a very good pizzeria, but since young Fausto has taken over the kitchen it is becoming a gourmet's paradise. Well-prepared, classic dishes such as spaghetti with clams, or the more unusual pearl spelt with tuna, followed by grilled swordfish, or tuna stewed with beans and onions. Excellent assortment of cheeses, delicious desserts, first-rate wine-list. All courses are accompanied by the tasty local white celery in some form or other—even the ice cream. Closed in winter all day Wed, and Thurs lunch. *Viale Colombo 53, T: 0771 549597.*

Terracina (*map p. 210, B3*)
€€€ **Rifugio Olmata**. If you don't like fish, this friendly little trattoria is just the place to find simple dishes prepared with the best vegetables, cheese, meat, and also wild mushrooms, all expertly prepared and served by the Di Bartolo family, who are from Ragusa in Sicily. You will find Sicilian wines and cheeses, besides the local specialities. Closed Wed. *Via Olmata 88, T: 0773 700821.*

€€ **Bottega Sarra 1932**. Small trattoria offering local cuisine, imaginative pasta dishes; good wine list. Closed Mon. *Via Villafranca 34, T: 0773 702045.*

LOCAL SPECIALITIES

Fondi is famous for its oranges, and for its buffalo-milk mozzarella. Good producers are Buonanno, at Via Mola della Corte 7–9; Casa Bianca, Via Arnale Rosso 30; Di Sarra on Via Sant'Anastasia; Paolella at Via Trento 34.

Itri is renowned for juicy black olives, usually called *olive di Gaeta.*

The **Sperlonga-Formia** area is known for delicious white celery, widely available from greengrocers.

For the wine of **Terracina**, a good producer is Cantina Sant'Andrea at Borgo Vodice (www.cantinasantandrea.it).

FESTIVALS & EVENTS

Cassino Feast of St Benedict, 21 March.

Itri *Infiorata del Corpus Domini,* The streets of town are liberally carpeted with freshflowers forming pictures of religious or historical subjects, Corpus Christi, May/June; *San Giuseppe,* Bonfires in the streets burn all night in the midst of singing, dancing and the immoderate consumption of *zeppole,* fritters made with flour, egg, sugar and honey. The ashes are carefully collected and kept indoors until the following year, to ward off the Evil Eye, 19 March.

Minturno *Festa di San Biagio,* Annual feast dedicated to the patron, St Blaise. Includes a fair of typical local products, 3 Feb; *Via Crucis,* Life-size theatrical representations of the Passion of Christ, Good Friday;

Sagra delle Regne, Pagan harvest festival absorbed into the Christian tradition and dedicated to the Virgin Mary, documented as far back as 1378. Bundles of grain are paraded on oxcarts to the main square where they are threshed by the men and the wheat is tossed high by the women, to separate it from the chaff. All dress in traditional costume, 2nd Sun in July.

Terracina *Festa del Mare,* Late-afternoon boat procession in honour of Our Lady of Carmel, followed by music, theatre, fireworks and a huge fish-fry on the beach, third Sat in July; *Festa di San Cesareo,* Feast of the patron saint, 4–6 Nov.

PONZA & ITS ARCHIPELAGO

NB: The Ponzian islands are shown on the overview map on p. 5.

The Ponzian Archipelago comprises two groups of islands, located approximately 35km apart and 32km from the coast of Lazio at Monte Circeo. The northwest group includes Ponza, the largest island and the chief centre of the archipelago; and the islets of Palmarola, Gavi and Zannone. The southeast group comprises Ventotene and Santo Stefano. All are of volcanic origin; the archipelago is linked geologically to the volcanic area of the Gulf of Naples; it was Mussolini who assigned them to Lazio, in order to increase the territory of Latina, the new city he had created (*see p. 232*). Through the ages these lovely islands, after being used by the Romans as places of exile, were practically uninhabited for long periods, even becoming the haunt of pirates, until Ponza was colonised by the Bourbons in 1734. As a result of careful farming, by 1822 it had become *'an enormous garden … shaded by hundreds of fruit trees … and protected from the winds by a series of vine-covered hills …'*, as a contemporary chronicler reports. The presence of the farmers attracted fishermen from the Naples area, who soon formed one of the best-known fishing fleets in the Tyrrhenian, happily exploiting the coral beds and the abundant lobsters. In 1768 King Ferdinand IV, inspired by Jean-Jacques Rousseau's theory of the 'noble savage', decided to send 200 convicts and 200 prostitutes to Ventotene, hoping to redeem them all, and create a viable population on the island at the same time. Sadly the place became so notorious as a den of iniquity, that three years later (after a tirade from the bishop of Gaeta) the king was forced to admit that his experiment had failed, and to return the 'colonists' to the prisons of Naples. Mussolini confined his political opponents on Ventotene, including Sandro Pertini (who would later become president of the Republic of Italy); he himself was interned for a short while on Ponza after his fall from power.

With their brilliant white rocks and pristine beaches, the islands are among the least spoilt in the Mediterranean, although their holiday popularity is slowly eroding their primitive beauty, and summer weekends are to be avoided. This development is most evident on Ponza, which nevertheless remains quiet and romantic out of season. The rocky coasts, especially around Ventotene, are a diver's paradise, and in fact are protected as a marine reserve. Boat trips around the islands will provide the opportunity to observe dolphins, flying fish and perhaps even a whale; they migrate along this route.

PONZA

Ponza (7.5km square; pop. 800), famous for its scenic beauty and its tiny rocky beaches dotted with Roman remains, is surmounted by Monte della Guardia (280m), offering views over the whole island. The coast is steep and irregular and in most areas cliffs fall 100m or more into the sea. The island is frequented by sophisticated, wealthy holidaymakers, including household names in the worlds of sport, fashion, cinema, politics and the media. The chief town is **Ponza**: with its brightly-coloured houses on the hillside, tumbling into the harbour at its foot, it is considered by many to be the most beautiful port in the Mediterranean. From here roads lead to (6km) Le Forna, a small village at the north end of the island, and Chiaia di Luna, a splendid beach 200m long on the west, which is reached from the sea or through a long tunnel dug by the Romans from the port. The beach is no more than a strip of white gravel, protected by a 130m cliff of volcanic rock, in varying tones of red, gold, yellow and silver, in front of the deep turquoise sea. Paths ascend to the Punta dell'Incenso and to Monte della Guardia, situated at the northern and southern tips of the island respectively. Boats may be rented at the harbour for visits to the beautiful caves called *Grotte di Pilato*, and to the outlying islands.

Palmarola, Gavi and Zannone

Palmarola, the ancient *Palmaria*, located 5 nautical miles from Ponza harbour, is the largest (1.3km square) of the islands that surround Ponza; with its jagged coastline and rich vegetation, it is also the one most similar to it. Protected as a nature reserve, many travellers maintain that this is one of the world's loveliest islands. It has one single permanent resident: Ernesto Prudente, historian and expert on the Ponzian Islands. It is an important nesting-place for several species of gull. The only landing-place is Cala del Porto, sometimes called Cala Circe, a spectacular little bay protected by a rocky promontory, with a pebbly beach. A simple restaurant with a few rooms to rent is open here in the summer.

Gavi is a brilliant white rock surmounted with a tuft of thick green vegetation, 7km from Ponza Harbour, but only 120m from Punta dell'Incenso. Now uninhabited, it was once exploited for its deposits of kaolin (china clay).

Zannone, about 11kms from Ponza Harbour, is a tiny (1.1km square), uninhabited triangular outcrop of dark red lava, barely covering the sedimentary rock beneath. With thick vegetation of Mediterranean *maquis*, it is the northernmost island of the archipelago. Of difficult access, it was however frequented during the Neolithic period because of its deposits of obsidian, much valued for the manufacture of sharp knives and axes before the age of metals. From the 13th century Christian monks sought the seclusion of this place, building a small convent, but they were so beleaguered by pirates that they soon left Zannone for the more secure Gaeta. The island enjoys special status as a wildlife reserve, instituted in 1979 to protect its unique flora (many of the plants are autochthonous) and as a resting-place for migratory birds. There is also a colony of mouflon, a rare wild sheep peculiar to southern Europe. It is not possible to spend the night here. (*Info: Parco Nazionale del Circeo, T: 0773 511385, www.parcocirceo.it*).

VENTOTENE

Ventotene (pop. 700), the larger of the two islands that make up the southeastern part of the archipelago, differs from Ponza both in the reddish-brown tone of its rock and in the nature of its vegetation, which in contrast to the lush vegetation of Ponza, is dominated by prickly-pear and low Mediterranean *maquis*. It was known to the ancient Romans as *Pandataria*, and Julia, the wayward daughter of Augustus, was the first of a series of unfortunate women to be exiled here. Remains of the **Imperial-age villa** built to house her may be seen near Punta Eolo, at the northern end of the island. Scholars think that the full extent of the original villa, together with its appendages, covered the entire island. Julia was followed by her daughter Agrippina, wife of Germanicus and mother of Caligula. Suetonius relates that after Germanicus' sudden death, Agrippina was ever after suspicious of the emperor Tiberius, widely rumoured to have poisoned him, and that when Tiberius handed her a piece of fruit at a banquet, she refused to touch it. Tiberius interpreted this as an accusation of attempted poisoning and banished her to this island. Her daughter Agrippina the Younger (mother of Nero) was also exiled here, as were Octavia (wife of Nero) and Flavia Domitilla (granddaughter of Domitian).

The town spreads southwest from Cala Rossano, where the ferry from the mainland moors, and the ramps of a yellow stairway lead to the upper town. Many of the houses are in fact rich golden yellow, with here and there some in cherry red, contrasting pleasantly with the deep blue of the sea. The atmosphere is relaxed: even in July and August (except at weekends) there is little to be seen of the crowds of holidaymakers and day-trippers which throng to Italy's offshore islands. The 18th-century Bourbon fortress in Piazza Castello houses the **Museo Archeologico** (*T: 0771 85345, open May–Oct daily 11–12.30, Sat also 5.30–7, it is possible to purchase a combined ticket allowing access to the museum, the various archaeological excavations and also Santo Stefano island*), with an interesting collection on the history of Ventotene, including finds from the excavations of the Roman villa at Punta Eolo. At one end of the harbour, the magnificent old lighthouse has now been transformed into the **Museo della Migrazione** (Via Olivi; *open May–Oct daily 6–7pm; at 7 there is a guided tour; T: 340 5412447*). First of its kind in Italy, it includes a very effective display illustrating the migration of birds from Asia and Africa to Europe and vice-versa. At Punta del Pertuso, the site of a Roman harbour, natural arches have formed in the tufa, due to the erosion of the sea.

The most impressively beautiful beach of Ventotene is **Cala Nave**, with sand of black basalt, guarded by two huge rocks in the bay. It is easy to reach from the town and there is a nice restaurant.

Santo Stefano

Near Ventotene lies Santo Stefano, a tiny, round island (300m square), crowned by the circular prison (innovative for the time) for convicts serving life imprisonment, erected by Ferdinand IV in 1794–95, and which closed in 1965. It was an Italian Alcatraz: prisoners disembarking knew they would never leave—when they died they were buried on the island. It soon became notorious: over a nine-year period in the mid-19th century, 1,250 prisoners died, but only 200 of them of natural causes. Gaetano Bresci, the anarchist who shot King Umberto I in 1900, was imprisoned here. Both Ventotene and Santo Stefano form part of a nature reserve created to protect the islands themselves and the rich marine habitats surrounding them.

PRACTICAL INFORMATION

GETTING AROUND

• **By car:** Cars are severely restricted (residents only in summer) and not advisable, given the size of the islands. At **Formia** you can leave your car on the dockside and the garage attendants will pick it up and return it when you come back. Info: Formia Servizi, T: 0771 85014; Sig. G. Bartolomeo, T: 0771 771 4931.

• **By bus:** There is a public bus service on Ponza during the day, connecting Ponza Porto and Le Forna.

• **By ferry:** Anzio to Ponza (motor-boat service in 1hr 45mins, April–Sept): CAREMAR, T: 06 986 0083, www.caremar.it; VETOR, T: 06 984 5083, www.vetor.it. Formia to Ponza (2hrs 30mins) and Ventotene: CAREMAR, T: 0771 22710. San Felice Circeo to Ponza (motor-boat service in 1hr, April–Sept): Società Pontina Navigazione, T: 0773 544157, www.circeoponza.it. Terracina to Ponza and Ventotene: daily (2hrs 30min, year-round), SNAP, T: 0771 820092, www.snapnavigazione.it.

• **By hydrofoil:** Anzio to Ponza (1hr 10mins) and Ventotene: VETOR, T: 06 984 5083, www.vetor.it. Fiumicino to Ponza (summer only): ALILAURO, T: 081 497 2222, www.alilauro.it. Formia to Ponza (1hr 10mins) and Ventotene: VETOR, T: 06 984 5083; CAREMAR, T: 0771 22710, www.caremar.it. Ponza to Ventotene and vice-versa, once weekly: ALILAURO.

INFORMATION OFFICES

Ponza Molo Musco 2, T: 0771 80031, www.ponza.com; Comunità Arcipelago delle Isole Ponziane, Via Roma 10, T: 0771 809893.
Ventotene Via Piazzetta 11, T: 0771 85257; Comunità Arcipelago delle Isole Ponziane, Piazza Castello 1, T: 0771 85265.

HOTELS

Palmarola
€ **O' Francese.** Very simple accommodation available May–Sept at this delightful trattoria on the beach of Palmarola, one of the most peaceful places in the archipelago. Book early. *T: 380 254 2553.*
Ponza
€€€€ **Grand Hotel Santa Domitilla.** Overlooking the harbour, with a beautiful pool, garden and tennis court. *Via Panoramica 10 (Porto), T: 0771 809951, www.santadomitilla.com. 47 rooms.*
€€€ **La Limonaia a Mare.** A picturesque old house set in the town rising above the harbour, with excellent views, and a garden full of lemon trees. *Via Dragonara, T: 0771 809886, www.ponza.com/limonaia. 3 rooms.*
€€€ **Torre dei Borboni.** The hotel occupies the old Bourbon fortress on the harbour; private lido on the rocks below. Very comfortable rooms with nice big beds. *Via Madonna 1 (Porto), T: 0771 80135, www.torredeiborboni.com. 48 rooms.*
€€ **La Corte di Ponza.** In a spectacular position overlooking Chiaia di Luna bay. Very comfortable accommodation with a lovely garden setting. *Via Chiaia di Luna, T: 334 848 3432, www.lacortediponza.it. 4 rooms.*
€€ **Grand Hotel Chiaia di Luna.** Superb panoramic position for this

unusual hotel, where the rooms are colourful little Mediterranean cottages. Very comfortable. Seawater pool. *Via Chiaia di Luna, T: 0771 80113, www.hotelchiaiadiluna.com. 66 rooms.*

€€ **Isola di Ponza**. Comfortable, beautiful house at Le Forna, with a lush garden, wonderful breakfast buffet, and helpful owner. *Le Forna, T: 0771 808383, www.infoponza.it. 6 rooms.*

€€ **Villaggio dei Pescatori**. Bright little local-style houses overlooking the lovely bay of Cala Feola, at Le Forna. Good restaurant. *Le Forna, T: 0771 809024, www.hotelvillaggiodeipescatori.it. 19 houses.*

Ventotene

€€€ **Agave e Ginestra**. Small hotel with breathtaking views, an excellent restaurant and a welcoming atmosphere. *Via Calabattaglia 10/12, T: 0771 85290, www.ventotene.net. 14 rooms.*

€€€ *Porto Azzurro*. Accommodation on a 1950s schooner, moored in the harbour. A decidedly pleasant experience, wonderfully in character with the island. Sleeps 8. Book early. *Goletta 'Porto Azzurro', T: 349 3269141 (Skipper Antonio Ancienna).*

RESTAURANTS

Ponza

€€€€ **Acqua Pazza**. Booking is essential at this renowned, deceptively simple restaurant, which reportedly refused access to a royal couple because they had not reserved a table. Exquisite *antipasti*, followed perhaps by their famous potato gnocchi with clams, shrimps and zucchini. Ask for a bottle of the locally-produced Pouchain Taffuri wine. Evenings only. *Piazza Pisacane 10, T: 0771 80643.*

€€€€ **Orèstorante**. Some surprising fish dishes invented by chef Oreste Romagnolo, who was a skipper for many years. Don't miss his squid couscous and sea-urchin mayonnaise, or the shrimps marinaded in rose petals. *Via Dietro la Chiesa 3, T: 0771 80338.*

€€ **Punta Incenso**. Simple but dependable trattoria presided over by Anna, on the north point of the island. Closed Tues (except in summer). *Località Le Forna, Via Calacaparra, T: 0771 808517.*

Ventotene

€€€ **Zi' Amalia**. Family-run trattoria, the oldest on the island. Sooner or later, practically all the inhabitants stop by for a chat with Giovanni (Amalia's grandson), or for a plate of the excellent lentil soup. *Via Roma 32, T: 0771 85129.*

€€ **Il Giardino**. The secret here is simplicity: the best local ingredients cooked to perfection. Vegetable or fish soups vary with the seasons; memorable fried fresh anchovies or wild asparagus omelette in spring. Try the grilled pink onions, grown only on Ventotene. *Via Olivi 43, T: 0771 85020.*

FESTIVALS & EVENTS

Ponza *Festa di San Silverio Papa*, Patron saint of Ponza and of fishermen, Sylverius was elected pope in 536. Theodora, wife of Justinian, had him exiled to Ponza, where he died of starvation. During the celebrations, his statue is carried out to sea in a boat procession. The festivities include food, music, dancing, games and fireworks, 9–20 June.

Ventotene Feast of St Candida, The saint is saluted by a firework display and the release of dozens of hot-air balloons that drift out over the sea, 10–20 Sept.

TUSCANY

Tuscany is the most famous of the 20 regions of Italy, home to the cities of Florence, Siena, and Pisa, as well as numerous beautiful and interesting small towns. It is well known for its splendid landscape, particularly that of the Chianti region between Florence and Siena, with its charming low hills covered with olive groves, vineyards, woods, and isolated cypress trees, and dotted with beautiful old farmhouses. The region also includes the Apuan Alps, white with snow and marble, which form a dramatic background to the coastal plain of Versilia. The high Monte Amiata is almost always prominent in the southern Tuscan landscape.

Tuscany derives its name from the inhabitants of ancient Etruria—the Etruscans—known in Latin as *Etrusci* or *Tusci*, who probably landed at Tarquinia (now in Lazio) in the 8th century BC. In Etruria Propria they formed themselves into a Confederation of 12 principal cities, of which Chiusi (*Clevsins*) was the most important in present-day Tuscany. There were also important Etruscan settlements in the Maremma (the coastal strip), and around Pitigliano and Saturnia. Numerous Etruscan remains can still be seen in these places, and finds from excavations are exhibited in museums all over the region.

In the Middle Ages Lucca was a powerful independent town, and Pisa, at the head of its Maritime Republic, was one of the most important cities in Europe in the 12th century. Siena reached the height of its power in the 12th–13th centuries, and is still one of the most beautiful medieval towns in Italy. Numerous small hill towns survive in Tuscany as testimony to the rise of independent communes in the Middle Ages, the most famous of which is San Gimignano. Siena, Lucca, and Pisa (as well as Florence) have some of the most beautiful Gothic and Romanesque buildings to be seen in Italy. The early 14th-century Sienese school of painting produced masters such as Duccio, Simone Martini and Pietro and Ambrogio Lorenzetti. In the 13th and early 14th centuries the great sculptors Nicola Pisano and his son Giovanni were active in Pisa.

Florence is famous for its Renaissance buildings, but other Renaissance monuments in Tuscany include the piazza in Pienza, Santa Maria del Calcinaio in Cortona, and Santa Maria delle Carceri in Prato. The great Florentine school of painting had a wide influence over local masters whose works are preserved in country churches and small towns. Luca Signorelli left some masterpieces in his native city of Cortona, and in Arezzo and Sansepolcro some of the best works of Piero della Francesca can be seen.

Apart from the fundamental importance to Western civilisation of the Florentine Renaissance, Tuscany also produced some of the greatest artists and writers of all time: Giotto, Masaccio, Brunelleschi, Donatello, Leonardo da Vinci, Michelangelo, Dante, Boccaccio, Politian and Petrarch.

The inhabitants of some of the larger towns in Tuscany retain notable individual characteristics, and often rivalry is strong between them. Pisa has traditionally been the enemy of Florence, and Lucca proudly independent of the two. Carrara has been an active centre of the Anarchist movement since the beginning of the 20th century.

Palazzo Pitti

FLORENCE

Florence is one of the most famous cities in Italy. As the birthplace of the Renaissance, it preserves some of the greatest works of art and most beautiful buildings in the world. From the 15th century onwards, it became a centre of learning in the arts and sciences unparalleled since Classical times. It is now a small city (pop. 380,000), the regional capital of Tuscany, with nearly all its finest buildings concentrated within a relatively small area. The major museums and sights of central Florence are covered here. For a fuller description, see *Blue Guide Florence*.

HISTORY OF FLORENCE

The Roman colony of *Florentia* was founded in 59 BC by Julius Caesar. The city was built on the Arno where the crossing is narrowest, and it flourished in the 2nd and 3rd centuries AD. The *comune* of Florence came into being in the first decades of the 12th century, and there followed a long struggle between Guelphs and Ghibellines. By the middle of the 13th century Florentine merchants, whose prosperity was largely based on the woollen cloth industry, were established in a privileged position in trade and commerce, and the florin, first minted in silver c. 1235, and soon after in gold, was used as the standard gold coin in Europe.

The city's greatest moment of splendour came in the 15th century, when a family of bankers of obscure north Tuscan origins emerged to lead the faction-riven medieval comune to political, intellectual, artistic and commercial pre-eminence. This family was the Medici (see p. 300); and though there were always staunch republican elements in Florence which disapproved of them and tried to unseat them, the three greatest members of that family, Cosimo il Vecchio, his son Piero (the Gouty), and his grandson Lorenzo the Magnificent, managed to steer a clever course between democracy and autocracy, 'ruling' as princes in a city which was proud of its freedoms and vocal in its detestation of tyranny.

Medici rule continued into the 16th century, becoming explicitly dynastic: the head of the family (Cosimo I) now styled himself Grand Duke of Tuscany. The last of the Medici died childless in 1737, and Florence passed to the house of Lorraine under Franz Stephan, husband of Maria Theresa of Austria. Napoleon briefly turned Tuscany into the Kingdom of Etruria, and installed his sister Elisa in Florence's Palazzo Pitti. The last of the Lorraine grand dukes left the city after a bloodless revolution in 1859. From 1861–75 Florence was the capital of the new Kingdom of Italy. All the bridges except Ponte Vecchio were blown up in the Second World War. In 1966 a disastrous flood of the Arno caused severe damage to the city and its works of art.

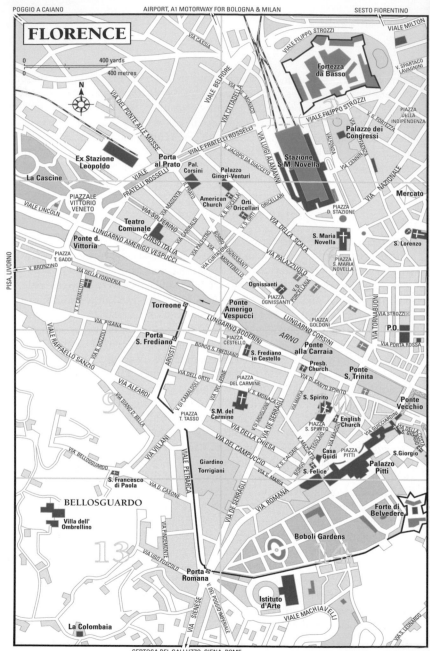

POGGIO A CAIANO   AIRPORT, A1 MOTORWAY FOR BOLOGNA & MILAN   SESTO FIORENTINO

FLORENCE

0   400 yards
0   400 metres

N

VIALE MILTON

VIA CASSIA

VIALE FILIPPO STROZZI

V. S. SPARTACO LAVAGNINI

Fortezza
da Basso

VIALE BELFIORE

VIA CITTADELLA

VIA MONACO

VIALE FILIPPO STROZZI

VALFONDA

PIAZZA
DELLA
INDIPENDENZA

V.G. FORTEZZA

Palazzo dei
Congressi

VIALE FRATELLI ROSSELLI

VIA LUIGI ALAMANNI

V. JACOPO DA DIACCETO

Stazione
S.M. Novella

VIA GIANNINI

VIA NAZIONALE

Ex Stazione
Leopoldo

Porta
al Prato

Pal.
Corsini

Palazzo
Ginori-Venturi

VIA DEL PONTE ALLE MOSSE

FRATELLI ROSSELLI

VIALE

La Cascine

PIAZZALE
VITTORIO
VENETO

American
Church

Orti
Oricellari

ORCELLARI

VIA DELLA SCALA

PIAZZA
D. STAZIONE

Mercato

S. Maria
Novella

S. Lorenzo

VIALE LINCOLN

VIA DELLA FONDERIA

VIA SOLFERINO

VIA MAGENTA

VIA B. ROCELLA

V.O. ORTI

Teatro
Comunale

Ponte d.
Vittoria

CORSO ITALIA

LUNGARNO AMERIGO VESPUCCI

VIA GARIBALDI

VIA PALESTRO

BORGO OGNISSANTI

VIA CURTATONE

VIA MONTEBELLO

Ognissanti

V. D. PORCELLANA

VIA PALAZZUOLO

PIAZZA
S. MARIA
NOVELLA

VIA TORNABUONI

PIAZZA
T. GADDI

V. BRONZINO

PISA LIVORNO

V.E. CAVALLOTTI

VIA DELLA FONDERIA

VIA PISANA

Torreone

Ponte
Amerigo
Vespucci

PIAZZA
OGNISSANTI

LUNGARNO SODERINI

ARNO

LUNGARNO CORSINI

PIAZZA
GOLDONI

VIA STROZZI

P.O.

VIA PORTA ROSSA

VIALE RAFFAELLO SANZIO

VIA B. BOZZOLI

ARIOSTI

Porta
S. Frediano

BORGO S. FREDIANO

PIAZZA
CESTELLO

S. Frediano
in Cestello

Ponte
alla Carraia

Presb.
Church

Ponte
S. Trinita

VIA GIANO D. BELA

VIA ALEARDI

VIA DELL'ORTO

VIA DEL LEONE

V. DI CAMALDOLI

PIAZZA
DEL CARMINE

V.S. MONACA

VIA DI SANTO SPIRITO

S. Spirito

Ponte
Vecchio

VIA DELLA COSTA S. GIORGIO

VIA GUICCIARDINI

S. Giorgio

VIA BELLOSGUARDO

VIA VILLANI

PIAZZA
T. TASSO

S.M. del
Carmine

VIA D'ARDIGLIONE

VIA DE' SERRAGLI

VIA MARIA

PIAZZA
S. SPIRITO

English
Church

PIAZZA
PITTI

Casa
Guidi

Palazzo
Pitti

S. Francesco
di Paola

VIA D. CASONE

Giardino
Torrigiani

VIA DEL CAMPUCCIO

VIA S. MARIA

BORGO TEGOLAIO

V. MAZZETTA

V.D. CALDAIE

S. Felice

BELLOSGUARDO

Villa dell'
Ombrellino

VIA PETRARCA

VIA DE' SERRAGLI

VIA ROMANA

Forte di
Belvedere

13

VIA PINCEMONTE

VIA UGO FOSCOLO

Boboli Gardens

Porta
Romana

VIA SIENESE

V. DEL POGGIO IMPERIALE

Istituto
d'Arte

VIALE MACHIAVELLI

VIA S. LEONARDO

La Colombaia

CERTOSA DEL GALLUZZO, SIENA, ROME

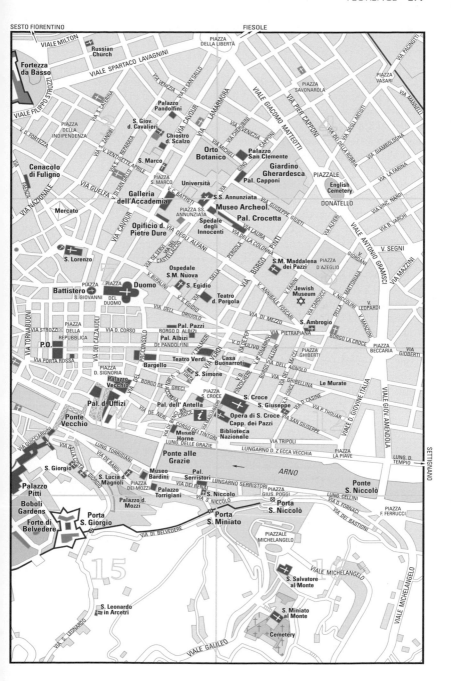

ART OF THE FLORENTINE RENAISSANCE

The idea of a picture realistically describing the world was re-born in Florence (for the first time since the end of the Roman Empire) in the early 1400s. The Renaissance was a conscious re-birth of the principles of ancient Roman and Greek thinking, and Florentine art cannot be understood except by reference to the emulation of, and desire to exceed, the achievements of Antiquity. We think of the Florentine Renaissance as principally an artistic revolution: but it was as much about science—about optics, geometry and anatomy, in particular—as it was about art, although that scientific thinking was linked to visual expression. This astonishing rebirth did not appear from nowhere, however; its roots are firmly embedded in the previous 150 years.

Cimabue (c. 1240–1302) is the first exponent of a style that we can begin to call distinctively Florentine. His unexpectedly moving (although much damaged) processional Crucifix in Santa Croce (*see p. 308*) is created in the Byzantine tradition. Yet although it is rhythmically stylised and icon-like in appearance, it nonetheless reveals an attention to modelling and a quality of pathos and drama which is essentially alien to the Byzantine spirit. This new and sculptural tendency was intently felt by Cimabue's greatest pupil, Giotto (1266/7–1337). If we compare Cimabue's *Maestà* with that attributed to Giotto (both in the Uffizi; *see p. 282*), we will see several things that distinguish Giotto's work from his master's: the pared-down simplicity; the coherence and unity of its design; the awakening humanity of the faces; and the new, weighty solidity of the figures. One of the things that most astonished contemporaries about Giotto's pictorial art, was this ability to give a convincing sense of human emotion and spatial reality. What they were observing was not only a change in artistic practice; it was a fundamental change in human thinking. Whereas Byzantine and medieval religious art aimed to take the gaze up and away from earthly life to an unchanging, golden eternity, suddenly, with Giotto, the direction was being reversed and the scenes of spiritual life were being brought down to the world of human reality, given physical depth and weight, and imbued with human feeling. Masaccio (1401–28) absorbed this lesson deeply, and many other artists—Donatello, Piero della Francesca and Michelangelo—studied his work. With Masaccio too, we get a genuine concern for convincing anatomy and physical presence, and for the accurate evocation of three-dimensional space and the grouping of figures. His paintings in the Brancacci Chapel (*see p. 311*) are amongst the most ground-breaking works in the history of Western art.

We know that Masaccio the painter, Donatello the sculptor, Brunelleschi the engineer, and Leon Battista Alberti the theorist were all close friends; all of them in turn were acquainted with Lorenzo Ghiberti, Luca della Robbia, Paolo Uccello and Piero della Francesca. Their closeness to one another gave rise not only to a cross-fertilisation of ideas and skills, but also to a powerful competitiveness. These two together were an irresistible force, increasing the critical mass and driving forward the achievements of Florentine art. No painter or sculptor or architect in Florence in the mid-15th century could remain wholly unaffected by this atmosphere. But perhaps no one assimilated all the lessons together so well as one painter, born in rural Tuscany, but who worked in Florence and who expresses almost better than any the quintessence of Florentine painting: Piero della Francesca (c. 1420–92). In him we find the gravity and clarity of Giotto, the limpid colour of Fra' Angelico, the sculptural weight of Masaccio, and the clear logical design of Brunelleschi.

The image of David, the young boy who slew the giant Goliath, had always been dear to the Florentine imagination as a symbol of their republic in its struggle against the monolithic forces at its borders—the Papal States of Rome, and the Duchy of Milan. For this reason, sculptures of David recur frequently throughout early Florentine art. In January of 1504, a committee was convened to decide where the latest and greatest *David* yet should be placed in the city. The *David* in question had been sculpted by the 29-year-old Michelangelo Buonarroti (1475–1564), whose genius dominated the art of Florence for the next six decades.

Michelangelo's death in 1564 left the artistic community of Florence in a stall. His presence had been so monumental, and his pre-eminence so total, that life without him was hard for Florentines to contemplate. But he had been directly involved in the crisis which was to bring Florence's artistic dominance to a close. He deliberately turned his back on a technical revolution which was to carry painting forward into the next four centuries: the development of oil, as against egg-tempera and fresco. This change was to transform both art and the artist: it liberated the artist from his studio of assistants, it freed him to paint in front of nature, it gave him new realms of possibility in the description of light and surface, and the creation of mood and colour, and, when combined with the canvas support currently being developed in Venice, it allowed works to travel easily and be seen in places they could never have reached before. The potential of oil as a medium had captivated the far-sighted Leonardo; Titian, a contemporary of Michelangelo had said he had no desire to emulate Michelangelo's greatness for fear of being judged by those high standards. But history has proven him to be a painter of a far greater influence, showing the way forward to later generations of artists.

The story ends, ironically, with the person who first wrote it down: Giorgio Vasari (1512–74), who came to Florence from his native Arezzo. His *Lives*, brimming as they are with urbanity and insight, are fundamentally autumnal works of profound nostalgia. By their very urge to look back and describe the greatness in words, they close the wide arc of time in which his city's greatness was incarnate instead in wondrous works of art.   N.McG.

THE DUOMO & BAPTISTERY

Map p. 268, 4. Open 10–5; Sun and holidays 1.30–5 (excavations of Santa Reparata closed Sun). Every year on 8 Sept the roof and galleries are opened to the public.

The Duomo is dedicated to the Madonna of Florence, Santa Maria del Fiore. An early Christian church stood on this site, considerable remains of which survive. By the 13th century, a new and larger cathedral was deemed necessary, and in 1294 Arnolfo di Cambio was appointed architect. In 1331 Giotto took over as director of works. The exterior is entirely covered with splendid white, green and pink marble. The majestic dome (1420–36), the greatest of all Brunelleschi's works, is a feat of supreme engineering skill. It was the the largest and highest of its time, and the first dome to be projected without the need for a wooden frame to sustain the vault during construction.

The most elaborate door is the Porta della Mandorla (north), with the *Assumption of the Virgin* by Nanni di Banco (c. 1418–20). The main façade is 19th-century.

The interior

South aisle: The bust of Brunelleschi (1) is by his adopted son Buggiano (1446). The bust of Giotto (2) (1490), similar to Brunelleschi's, is by Benedetto da Maiano, with an inscription by Politian. Steps lead to the excavations of the ancient cathedral of Santa Reparata (3). At the bottom to the left, beyond a grille, is the tombslab of Brunelleschi. The excavations (*admission fee*) include a fine mosaic pavement from the earliest church.

North aisle: Two famous frescoes of equestrian statues (4) commemorate two *condottieri*: Sir John Hawkwood, by Paolo Uccello (1436), and Niccolò da Tolentino (*see p. 681*), by Andrea del Castagno (1456).

Dome: The dome (5) soars to a height of 91m. The fresco of the *Last Judgement* (1572–79) is by Vasari and Federico Zuccari. The very fine stained-glass windows (1443–45) are by Paolo Uccello, Andrea del Castagno, Donatello and Ghiberti.

East end: Over the door of the north sacristy (6) is a fine relief of the *Resurrection* by Luca della Robbia (1442). The doors were Luca's only work in bronze (1446–67); he was assisted by Michelozzo and Maso di Bartolomeo. It was in this sacristy that Lorenzo the Magnificent took refuge on the day of the Pazzi Conspiracy in 1478 (*see p. 308*).

Inside the dome

The dome can be climbed 8.30–6.20; first Sat of the month 8.30–3; other Sats 8.30–5; closed Sun and holidays. NB: Not recommended if you suffer from claustrophobia. The climb (463 steps) follows a labyrinth of corridors, steps and spiral staircases (used by the builders of the cupola) as far as the lantern at the top. As you ascend, you can admire the dome's structure, as well as some of the original or reconstructed devices used to build it. The views of the Duomo interior from the two balconies around the drum, and of the city from the small windows and from the lantern, are stunning.

FLORENCE DUOMO

Porta della
Mandorla →

Campanile

1   Bust of Brunelleschi
2   Bust of Giotto
3   Entrance to Santa Reparata
4   *Condottieri* memorials
5   Dome
6   North sacristy

The campanile

The cathedral bell-tower (*open 8.30–6.50*), begun by Giotto in 1334 is one of the loveliest and most original in Italy. Its coloured marbles match the exterior of the Duomo. It was continued by Andrea Pisano, and completed by Francesco Talenti in 1348–59. The lower storeys have bas-reliefs by Andrea Pisano—some of them probably designed by Giotto—which illustrate the *Creation of Man*, and the *Arts* and *Industries*. Above are niches with statues of prophets and Sibyls (1415–36) by Donatello and his contemporaries. All are copies of originals moved to the Museo dell'Opera del Duomo (*see overleaf*).

The Baptistery

The octagonal Baptistery (*open 12–6.30; Sun and holidays 8.30–1.30*) is one of the oldest and most revered buildings in Florence, documented by 897. Its most famous feature is its gilded bronze doors. The **south door** (Andrea Pisano; 1336) has reliefs of the story of St John the Baptist and the Theological and Cardinal Virtues. The north and east doors are by Lorenzo Ghiberti. The **north door** (1403–24) depicts scenes from the life of Christ. Ghiberti's self-portrait appears as the fifth head from the top of the left door (middle band). The **east door** (1425–52) is Ghiberti's most celebrated work: Michelangelo is said to have called it the 'Gate of Paradise'. The ten panels (replaced by copies; originals in the Museo dell'Opera del Duomo) contain reliefs of scriptural subjects, with scenes in low relief extending far into the background. The use of perspective is typical of the new Renaissance concept of art. The subjects, from the top left panel downwards, are: 1. The Creation and Expulsion from Paradise; 2. Noah's Sacrifice and Drunkenness; 3. Esau and Jacob; 4. Moses Receiving the Tablets of Stone; 5. David and the Battle with the Philistines; 6. Cain and Abel; 7. Abraham and the Angels and the Sacrifice of Isaac; 8. Joseph Sold and Recognised by his Brothers; 9. Joshua and the Fall of Jericho; 10. Solomon and the Queen of Sheba.

Joshua and the Fall of Jericho: relief panel by Ghiberti from the south door of the Baptistery.

In the interior, the oldest part of the splendid **mosaic pavement** (begun in 1209) can be seen around the font. To the right is the **tomb of the antipope John XXIII** (d. 1419) by Donatello and Michelozzo, one of the earliest Renaissance tombs in the city, with exquisite carving. The **mosaics in the vault** are the only mosaic cycle in Florence. The earliest (c. 1225) are signed by the monk 'Iacopo', a contemporary of St Francis.

Museo dell'Opera del Duomo

The museum, at no. 9 Piazza del Duomo (*open 9.30–6.50, Sun and holidays 9–1; T: 055 230 2885*), contains masterpieces of sculpture from the Baptistery, Duomo and Campanile. Highlights are the original bronze panels by Lorenzo Ghiberti from the east door of the Baptistery; sculptures from the Duomo's old west façade, designed by Arnolfo di Cambio; and the beautiful *Pietà* by Michelangelo, carved when he was almost eighty years old. According to Vasari, the head of Nicodemus is a self-portrait.

On the first floor are two famous *cantorie*, made for the Duomo in the 1430s by Luca della Robbia and Donatello. Luca's was his first important commission, and is his masterpiece. Also in this room are the 16 statues from the Campanile, the most important being those by Donatello: *Jeremiah*, *Habakkuk*, *Abraham and Isaac* (a two-figure group), and probably also the head of *Jonah* (sometimes identified as St John the Baptist). An adjoining room displays the original bas-reliefs from the Campanile include some exquisite works by Andrea Pisano. Donatello's famous wooden statue of *Mary Magdalene* (c. 1454) stood formerly in the Baptistery.

PIAZZA DELLA SIGNORIA

This great square (*map p. 268, 6*) has been the political centre of Florence since the Middle Ages. It was the scene of public ceremonies, but also a gathering place in times of trouble. Here the Signoria (the magistrate and priors who ruled the city) would, in moments of crisis, call the citizens to a *parlamento*.

Sculptures in the Piazza

In front of Palazzo Vecchio stands a **replica of Michelangelo's** *David* (the original was removed to the Accademia in 1873; *see p. 292*). The huge statue was set up here in 1504 as a symbol of the victory of republicanism over tyranny. Much public sculpture in Florence takes this as its theme. Close by is a **copy of Donatello's** *Judith and Holofernes* (the original is inside). One of the sculptor's last works (c. 1455), it was commissioned by the Medici and used as a fountain in their palace garden. On their expulsion from the city in 1495, it was expropriated by the government and displayed publicly with an inscription warning against tyrants.

The **Neptune Fountain** (1560–75) has a colossal figure of Neptune, the work of Baccio Bandinelli, an ambitious sculptor who replaced Cellini in the favour of the Medici grand dukes. The porphyry disc in the pavement in front of the fountain marks the spot where Savonarola was burnt at the stake on 23rd May 1498 (*see p. 291*).

Giambologna's bronze **equestrian monument to Cosimo I** (1595) was commissioned by the grand duke's son Ferdinando I. On the base are scenes of Cosimo's coronation and his conquest of Siena, which he brought under Florentine rule in 1555.

Loggia della Signoria

The Loggia della Signoria, where the three semicircular arches break free from Gothic forms and anticipate the Renaissance, was used by government officials during public ceremonies. It was built in 1376–82, to a design probably by Orcagna. Cellini's magnificent bronze *Perseus*, in which Perseus exhibits the Medusa's severed head, was commissioned by Cosimo I in 1545; it is considered Cellini's masterpiece. Giambologna's three-figure group of the *Rape of the Sabines* was commissioned by Francesco I for this position in 1583. The elaborate serpentine composition is designed to be seen from every angle.

Palazzo Vecchio

Open 9–6; Thurs, Sun and holidays 9–2; T: 055 276 8224. Reduction for those aged 18–25 and over 65, and further reduction for children; family tickets also available. Combined ticket with the Brancacci Chapel valid 3 months. 'Secret' itineraries (percorsi segreti) are shown on guided tours (booking advised; T: 055 276 8224).

Palazzo Vecchio is an imposing fortress-palace built to a design traditionally attributed to Arnolfo di Cambio (1299–1302). It became the prototype of many other *palazzi comunali* in Tuscany. In the Middle Ages, the governing magistrates of the city lived here during their two-month term of office. In 1433, Cosimo il Vecchio was imprisoned in the tower before being (temporarily) exiled. The building became known as Palazzo della Signoria during the Republican governments of the 15th century. In 1540 Cosimo I moved here from the private Medici palace. It became known as 'Palazzo Ducale', and then—when the Medici grand dukes took up residence in Palazzo Pitti after 1549—as 'Palazzo Vecchio'. From 1865–71, when Florence was capital of the Kingdom of Italy (before the capitulation of Rome to Vittorio Emanuele's army), it housed the Foreign Ministry. Since 1872 it has been the seat of the municipal government.

Ground floor

In the interior it is still possible to trace successive rebuildings and redecorations: by Michelozzo, Giuliano and Bendedetto da Maiano and Ghirlandaio during the Republican days; and by Vasari and Buontalenti for the Medici dukes. The courtyard was reconstructed by Michelozzo in 1453, and the elaborate decorations were added in 1565 by Giorgio Vasari to celebrate the marriage between Francesco, son of Cosimo I, and Joanna of Austria. The columns were covered with stucco and the vaults and walls painted with grotesques and views of Austrian cities. The fountain, designed by Vasari, bears a copy of Verrocchio's *Putto Holding a Dolphin* (c. 1470), a bronze made for a fountain at the Medici villa at Careggi. The original is preserved inside the palace. The monumental grand staircase is also by Vasari.

First floor

The immense **Salone dei Cinquecento** was built in 1495 for the meetings of the new legislative body of the Republic, the Great Council. The room was transformed and heightened by Vasari in 1563–65, when the present decoration was carried out in celebration of Cosimo I. In the centre of the ceiling is the apotheosis of the duke surrounded by the coats of arms of the guilds. The other panels represent allegories of the cities of Tuscany under Florentine dominion; the foundation and early growth of Florence; and the victories over Pisa and Siena (1496–1509 and 1554–55 respectively). Michelangelo's *Victory*, against the east wall, was probably intended for a niche in the tomb of Julius II in Rome (*see p. 40*). It was set up here by Vasari as a symbol of Cosimo's victory over Siena. Opposite is Giambologna's original plaster model (the marble is in the Bargello) for *Virtue Overcoming Vice* (or *Florence Victorious over Pisa*), commissioned as a pendant to Michelangelo's *Victory*. At the far end of the hall is the **Udienza**, a raised chamber containing statues of distinguished members of the Medici family. Many of them, dressed as Romans, are by their favoured sculptor, Baccio Bandinelli.

The tiny **Studiolo** is a charming, windowless study created by Vasari and his workshop in 1570–75 for Cosimo's son Francesco I. Entirely decorated with paintings and bronze statuettes, it celebrates Francesco's interest in the natural sciences and alchemy, and is a masterpiece of Florentine Mannerist decoration. On the barrel vault are portraits by Bronzino of Francesco's parents, Cosimo I and Eleanor of Toledo. The four walls each symbolise one of the four elements, with paintings and bronzes by the leading artists of the day (including Vincenzo Danti, Santi di Tito, Alessandro Allori, Giambologna and Bartolomeo Ammannati).

Second floor
Here is preserved a suite of rooms forming part of the **apartments of Eleanor of Toledo**, daughter of the Spanish Viceroy of Naples, who married Cosimo I. The **chapel** was decorated by Bronzino in 1540–45, and is one of his most important and original works. On the vault, divided by festoons, are *St Francis Receiving the Stigmata*, *St Jerome*, *St John the Evangelist on Patmos*, and *St Michael the Archangel*. On the walls are episodes from the life of Moses.

The **audience chamber** has a superb gilded 15th-century ceiling by Giuliano da Maiano and assistants. The huge mural paintings illustrate stories from the life of the Roman hero Marcus Camillus (*see pp. 184–85*), and were added c. 1545–48 by Francesco Salviati; they are one of the major works by this typically Mannerist painter.

In the magnificent **Sala dei Gigli**, where Donatello's *Judith and Holofernes* is displayed (*see p. 277 above*), is a well-preserved fresco by Domenico Ghirlandaio (1482), intended as a celebration of the Florentine Republic.

The **Cancelleria** was used as an office by Machiavelli during his term as government secretary. He is commemorated here with a fine 16th-century bust and a painting by Santi di Tito.

Orsanmichele

The tall, rectangular Orsanmichele was built in 1337 by Francesco Talenti, one of the architects of the Duomo. This very tall, rectangular building, erected in 1337 by Francesco Talenti, was originally a market but then became a church. Inside (*open 10–5 except Mon*) is a superb Gothic tabernacle with sculptures by Andrea Orcagna, with a painting of the *Madonna* by Bernardo Daddi. The exterior is decorated with niches, which were filled with statues of the patron saints of the Florence guilds by the greatest sculptors of the time. All are now replaced by copies; the originals are kept inside in a museum on the upper floor (*closed at the time of writing*). Beginning on the side facing Via de' Calzaiuoli and going round to the right, the statues are:

Calimala (wholesale cloth importers): *St John the Baptist* (1413–16) by Lorenzo Ghiberti.

Tribunale di Mercanzia (merchants' court): *Incredulity of St Thomas* (1473–83) by Verrocchio. The tabernacle by Donatello formerly contained his *St Louis of Toulouse*, now in the Museo dell'Opera di Santa Croce (*see p. 308*).

Giudici e Notai (judges and notaries): *St Luke* (1583–1601) by Giambologna.

Beccai (butchers): *St Peter* (c. 1425), generally attributed to Bernardo Ciuffagni.

Conciapelli (tanners): *St Philip* (c. 1410–12) by Nanni di Banco.

Maestri di Pietrai e di Legname (stonemasons and carpenters): The *Quattro Santi Coronati* (*see p. 65*) by Nanni di Banco (c. 1409–16/17).

Armaiuoli (armourers): *St George* by Donatello (c. 1415–17). The marble statue was removed to the Bargello in 1891 and replaced by a bronze copy. **Cambio** (bankers): *St Matthew* (1419–22), by Lorenzo Ghiberti. **Lanaiuoli** (wool manufacturers and clothiers): *St Stephen* by Lorenzo Ghiberti (1427–28). **Maniscalchi** (farriers): *St Eligius* (c. 1417–21) by Nanni di Banco. **Linaiuoli e Rigattieri** (linen merchants and used-clothes' dealers): *St Mark*

(1411–13) by Donatello. **Pellicciai** (furriers): *St James the Great*, attributed to Niccolò di Pietro Lamberti (c. 1422). **Medici e Speziali** (physicians and apothecaries): *Madonna and Child* (c. 1400) attributed to Pietro di Giovanni Tedesco. **Setaiuoli e Orafi** (silk-weavers and goldsmiths): *St John the Evangelist* by Baccio da Montelupo (1515).

THE BARGELLO

Map p. 268, 6. Open 8.30–1.50; often extended to 5.50 in summer. Closed first, third and fifth Sun and second and fourth Mon of the month; T: 055 238 8606.
The massive, crenellated Palazzo del Bargello was built in 1255 as the Palazzo del Popolo, and is the oldest seat of government to survive in Florence. At first it was the seat of the *Capitano del Popolo*, who, during his one-year term of office, held supreme authority in the city government. From the end of the 13th century until 1502, it was the official residence of the *Podestà*, the governing magistrate. The building became known as the Bargello in the 16th century, when the police headquarters were moved here and prisons were installed. The museum it houses today is perhaps the best place in the city to understand the significance of the Florentine Renaissance—and is all the more appealing for hardly ever being overcrowded.

Ground floor
Pre-eminent here are some superb **works by Michelangelo**. The *Bacchus Drunk* is his first important sculpture, and shows the influence of Classical works. It was made c. 1497 for the banker Jacopo Galli, who also commissioned Michelangelo's famous *Pietà*, now in the Vatican. The 'Pitti Tondo' of the *Madonna and Child with the Infant St John* (c. 1503–05) is a fine example of the sculptor's *schiacciato* (very low relief) technique. The bust of *Brutus* is a much later work (probably from the 1540s), derived from Imperial Roman portrait busts, and is the only bust Michelangelo ever sculpted.

Also here is a group of **works by Benvenuto Cellini**, who was less influenced than his contemporaries by Michelangelo. The *Ganymede* consists of an antique marble torso, to which Cellini added the head, the arms and the eagle. The colossal bust of Cosimo I was Cellini's first work cast in bronze (1545–48). His talent can be seen in the delicate carved details of the armour. **Giambologna's *Mercury*** is his most successful and influential statue: it seems almost on the point of flying away.

First floor
The splendid Gothic hall contains masterpieces of Florentine *Quattrocento* sculpture,

including **eight works by Donatello**. His *St George* was made for Orsanmichele c. 1416. By endowing this remarkably well-composed statue with a sense of movement, Donatello's work represents a new departure from traditional Gothic sculpture, where the static figure was confined to its niche. His *David with the Head of Goliath* (c. 1430–40; *being restored in situ*), one of the earliest and most beautiful free-standing male statues of the Renaissance, was the first bronze nude since the Classical era.

The two **trial reliefs of the** *Sacrifice of Isaac* by Ghiberti and Brunelleschi were made for the competition in 1403 (won by Ghiberti) for the east doors of the Baptistery (*see p. 275*).

Donatello (c. 1386–1466)

The artist known as Donatello was the most important sculptor of the Quattrocento, and of fundamental importance to the development of Renaissance art; indeed, he is often considered the greatest sculptor of all time. He was born Donato di Niccolò di Betto Bardi around 1386, of humble parentage (his father was a wool-carder). Donatello first worked as assistant to Lorenzo Ghiberti, eight years his senior, and as a young man visited Rome with his friend Brunelleschi to study antique sculpture. He became a master of perspective, of high drama and of pictorial story-telling. All these qualities combine in his sculptures, and more particularly in his superb reliefs (for example the *Feast of Herod* in Siena; *see p. 428*). Cosimo il Vecchio recognised his exceptional talent and ordered that he be buried beside him in the Medici vaults below San Lorenzo.

Second floor

Chief among the exhibits here is **Verrocchio's** *David*, made for the Medici in 1469, and then acquired by the Signoria in 1476. It owes much to Donatello's earlier statue of the same subject. In the same room are charming marble works by Mino da Fiesole, including busts of Cosimo il Vecchio's two sons, Giovanni and Piero il Gottoso (1453; the first dated portrait bust of the Renaissance). On the wall opposite the windows is the *Bust of a Lady Holding Flowers*, one of the loveliest of all Renaissance portrait busts, once attributed to Verrocchio's pupil Leonardo da Vinci. It is particularly interesting as it is the first instance in a 15th-century portrait bust in which the hands are depicted. The marble **bust of Battista Sforza**, Duchess of Urbino, is by the Dalmatian-born Francesco Laurana, and is typical of his serene, beautifully stylised female portrait busts.

Other rooms contain part of a huge collection of Italian medals started by Lorenzo the Magnificent, with works by L'Antico, Pisanello and Matteo de' Pasti. Here also is Bernini's **bust of Costanza Bonarelli**, his mistress. There is also a superb display of small Renaissance bronzes, the most important collection in Italy. Artists represented include Giambologna, Cellini and Baccio Bandinelli.

GALLERIA DEGLI UFFIZI

Map p. 268, 8. Open Tues–Sat 8.15–6.35 (sometimes later in summer). To avoid the infamous queue the booking service (T: 055 294883; see p. 314) is highly recommended. The Corridoio Vasariano, a raised walkway which links the Uffizi to the Pitti via the Ponte Vecchio, contains a selection of self-portraits viewable by prior appointment. The gallery tends to be extremely crowded with tour groups, but is usually more peaceful in the early morning, over lunchtime, and in the late afternoon. Automatic signals provide information about expected waiting time (a maximum of 660 people are allowed into the gallery).

The massive Palazzo degli Uffizi extends from Piazza della Signoria to the Arno. Vasari was commissioned by Cosimo I to erect a building to serve as government offices (*uffici*, hence '*uffizi*'). It was begun in 1560 and completed after Vasari's death. The use of iron to reinforce the building allowed for the remarkably large number of apertures.

The building now houses the famous Galleria degli Uffizi, one of the great art collections of the world. The display is arranged chronologically by schools; the first rooms (up to Room 15) include the major works of the Florentine Renaissance. The following description isolates only some of the most important, though in fact all are of superlative interest.

East wing: Duecento to Renaissance

Duecento: The first room has three huge paintings of the Madonna enthroned (the *Maestà*). The one by Cimabue (c. 1285; *see p. 426*) marks a final development of the Byzantine style of painting, where a decorative sense still predominates; the *Rucellai Madonna* is by the Sienese master Duccio di Buoninsegna (1285); and the last, by Giotto, painted some 25 years later, projects a new sense of realism. Duccio's greatest follower, Simone Martini, is also represented, as are the brothers Pietro and Ambrogio Lorenzetti, also important protagonists of the Sienese school.

Trecento: The collection includes works by pupils of Giotto, by Bernardo Daddi, and by Orcagna and his brothers Nardo and Jacopo di Cione.

International Gothic: The monk known as Lorenzo Monaco was one of the greatest artists of this period (early 15th century). The other important exponent of this style was Gentile da Fabriano, whose *Adoration of the Magi* is also part of the collection.

Quattrocento: Paolo Uccello's *Battle of San Romano*, celebrating the battle in which the Florentines were victorious over the Sienese, is an amusing exercise in perspective. Also here is the famous diptych by Piero della Francesca, with the portraits of Federico da Montefeltro, Duke of Urbino (*see p. 659*) and his duchess, Battista Sforza, in profile against a superb detailed landscape.

Botticelli's tiny *Judith Returning from the Camp of Holofernes* and the *Discovery of the Decapitated Holofernes in his Tent* (c. 1470) are among the most exquisite works in the gallery. His famous *Birth of Venus* and *Primavera* were possibly inspired by the poetry of the great

Titian: *Venus of Urbino* (1538).

Humanist scholar Politian (*see p. 456*). His altarpieces are less familiar, and the Uffizi possesses an extremely fine collection. In the *Adoration of the Magi*, the interest lies in the portraits of the Medici courtiers who are depicted as the Kings and their entourage: Giuliano de' Medici (or possibly Lorenzo the Magnificent) is dressed in black and red on the right, and Botticelli himself is shown in a self-portrait (dressed in a yellow cloak) on the extreme right. The standing figure by the horse's head on the left may be Lorenzo the Magnificent next to the poets Politian and Pico della Mirandola (who were with Lorenzo on his deathbed). The kneeling 'Magus' in black represents Cosimo il Vecchio, and the one in red, his son Piero il Gottoso.

The early Florentine works of Leonardo da Vinci and paintings by his master, Verrocchio, are also in the collection. Leonardo da Vinci's *Annunciation* was painted in Verrocchio's studio. How much of the work is Leonardo's own is unclear: it is thought that he was responsible for the design, for the figure of the Madonna and for the classical sarcophagus. Verrocchio's *Baptism of Christ* was begun c. 1470. According to Vasari, the angel on the left was painted by the young Leonardo. **Classical sculpture:** The beautiful octagonal Tribune was designed by Bernardo Buontalenti for Francesco I (1584), as a showcase for his most valuable works of art. The octagonal table is a masterpiece of *pietre dure*, made in the Florence Opificio (*see p. 292*) between 1633 and 1649. The most famous of the sculptures is the *Medici Venus*, probably a Greek marble copy (made around the 1st century BC) of the *Aphrodite of Cnidos* by Praxiteles. Around the walls are court portraits, many of them of the family of Cosimo I, commissioned from Bronzino. The two idealised portraits of Cosimo's ancestors Lorenzo the Magnificent and Cosimo il Vecchio are by Vasari and Pontormo (Bronzino's master).

West wing: the High Renaissance and Mannerism

Cinquecento: The famous 'Tondo Doni' of the *Holy Family* by Michelangelo is his only finished tempera painting (1504–05). It breaks with traditional representations of this familiar subject and signals a new moment in High Renaissance painting, pointing the way to the Sistine Chapel frescoes.

Masterpieces by Raphael include *Leo X with Giulio de' Medici and Luigi de' Rossi*, one of his most powerful portrait groups: it was to have a great influence on Titian. The first Medici pope (son of Lorenzo the Magnificent) is shown with his two cousins, whom he created cardinals: Giulio later became Pope Clement VII. Raphael's self-portrait also hangs here.

Florentine Mannerism is well represented, with three of the few surviving Florentine works by Rosso Fiorentino, who went on to be court artist to Francis I of France. There are also good works by Pontormo, including the portrait of Maria Salviati, mother of Cosimo I.

Some of the finest works by Titian include the *Venus of Urbino*, commis-sioned by Guidubaldo della Rovere, later duke of Urbino, in 1538 (*see p. 647; illustrated on previous page*). It is one of the most beautiful nudes ever painted, and has had a profound influence on subsequent European painting.

17th–18th centuries: The collection ends with some fine works by Rubens, van Dyck and Rembrandt. There are also Venetian works by Piazzetta, Tiepolo, Guardi and Canaletto.

The last rooms: At the end of the west corridor is a copy by Baccio Bandinelli of the famous *Laocoön*, now in the Vatican. Bandinelli's version has Laocoön's arm upraised (*see p. 99*). Also in this part of the corridor is a sculpted boar (a copy of a Hellenistic original), the model for the *Porcellino* in the Mercato Nuovo (*see p. 316*). Stairs descend to the west corridor on the *piano nobile* and the huge marble *Medici Vase*, a neo-Attic work acquired by Lorenzo de' Medici. Beyond is a room with three famous works by Caravaggio: *The Sacrifice of Isaac*, *Young Bacchus* and *Medusa Head* (painted on a shield).

The Corridoio Vasariano and Contini-Bonacossi Collection

The **Corridoio Vasariano** (*visits by appointment; T: 055 265 4321*) was built by Vasari to celebrate the marriage—a deeply unhappy one as it turned out—of Francesco de' Medici and Joanna of Austria in 1565. Nearly a kilometre long, it functioned as a private, covered passageway connecting Palazzo Vecchio and the Uffizi with the new residence of the Medici dukes at Palazzo Pitti. The Uffizi's celebrated collection of self-portraits hangs here. Displayed chronologically (though only a selection is shown at any one time), it has self-portraits by artists from Agnolo Gaddi to Renato Guttuso.

The **Contini-Bonacossi Collection** is on the second floor of the Uffizi (*admission by appointment as above; entrance on Via Lambertesca*). Among the best works are a *Madonna and Child* by Duccio, and Sassetta's *Madonna of the Snow*, a lovely altarpiece painted for the Siena duomo. The predella (very ruined) shows the story of the miraculous fall of snow that traced the outline for the basilica of Santa Maria Maggiore in Rome (*see p. 58*). The sky is different in each scene, and in each is marvellously observed.

PALAZZO PITTI & THE BOBOLI GARDENS

Map p. 270, 10–14. Times and tickets vary for the different museums, and are attached to each museum description. A ticket for the Galleria Palatina includes admission to the Appartamenti Reali. There is a separate ticket for the Galleria d'Arte Moderna and the Galleria del Costume. A third ticket provides admission to the Museo degli Argenti and Boboli Gardens. It is well worth buying the combined ticket for all the museums and Boboli Gardens (valid for three consecutive days), although this is not available when exhibitions are on. Information and reservations, T: 055 294883 (Mon–Fri 8.30–6.30, Sat 8.30–12.30).

Palazzo Pitti was built by the merchant Luca Pitti as a demonstration of his wealth and power to his rivals the Medici. Built in huge, rough-hewn blocks of stone, its design is attributed to Brunelleschi, although building began c. 1457, after his death. The palace remained incomplete on the death of Luca Pitti in 1472; by then it consisted of the seven central bays with three doorways. Bartolomeo Ammannati took up work c. 1560 and converted the two side doors of the central elevation into elaborate ground-floor windows. These were then copied after 1616 by Giulio and Alfonso Parigi the Younger, when they enlarged the façade to its present colossal dimensions (possibly following an original design). The two wings were added later: the one on the right sometime after 1760, and the one on the left in the 19th century.

In 1549, the palace was bought by Eleanor of Toledo, wife of Cosimo I. It became the official seat of the Medici dynasty of grand dukes after Cosimo I moved here from Palazzo Vecchio. The various ruling families of Florence continued to occupy the palace, or part of it, until 1919, when Vittorio Emanuele III presented it to the state.

The courtyard

Ammannati's courtyard (1560–70) is a masterpiece of Florentine Mannerist architecture, with bold rustication in three orders. Nocturnal spectacles were held here from the 16th–18th centuries, and it is still sometimes used for summer concerts. The Grotto of Moses, beneath the terrace, was designed in 1635–42 around a porphyry statue of *Moses* (the torso is an antique Roman work). In the other niches and in the water are 17th-century statues. On either side of the grotto entrance are two Roman statues (copies of Hellenistic originals). At the end of the left colonnade is a restored Roman *Hercules*, and, beneath, a charming 16th-century bas-relief commemorating a mule who worked particularly hard during the construction of the courtyard.

First floor: Galleria Palatina

Open 8.30–6.50; closed Mon; T: 055 238 8611.

This splendid gallery of paintings acquired by the Medici and Lorraine grand dukes maintains the character of a private, princely collection of the 17th–18th centuries. Many of the ceilings are decorated with **frecoes by Pietro da Cortona**, painted in the 1640s. Most are elaborate allegories which include references to his patrons, Grand Duke Ferdinando II and his wife Vittoria della Rovere. The most refined of the frescoes are to be found in the so-called Sala di Giove, the throne-room of the Medici. They display the artist's skill in combining vivid colours in spectacular compositions based on complicated perspective devices and theatrical decorative schemes.

The collection includes some famous **masterpieces by Raphael**. The beautifully composed *Madonna della Seggiola* (named after the chair, *seggiola*, on which she sits), is one of his most mature works (c. 1514–15). It was purchased by the Medici shortly after the artist's death, and became one of the most popular paintings of the Madonna. The frame is by Giovanni Battista Foggini (*see p. 288*). In the same room (Sala di Saturno) is his *Madonna del Granduca*—named after Grand Duke Ferdinand III of Lorraine, who purchased it in 1800, while in exile during the Napoleonic period. It is probably an early work (c. 1504–05) and is painted in a very different style, showing the influence of Leonardo. Raphael's portraits of Agnolo Doni and Maddalena Strozzi (in the pose of Leonardo's *Mona Lisa*) were painted probably as a diptych about two years after their marriage in 1504. Both have splendid landscapes in the background, and monochrome scenes by another hand on the back, illustrating Ovid's account of the Flood. (Michelangelo's 'Tondo Doni', now in the Uffizi, was also painted for this young couple.) One of Raphael's most celebrated female portraits is his *Portrait of a Lady* (*La Velata* or 'Lady with a Veil'), purchased by Cosimo II de' Medici. The grace and dignity of the sitter are rendered with a skill which anticipates Titian.

No fewer than eleven **portraits by Titian** hang in these rooms, among them, in the Sala di Apollo, his *Portrait of a Gentleman*, probably dating from 1540–45 or perhaps much earlier. His *Portrait of a Lady* (*La Bella*) was commissioned by the Duke of Urbino in 1536, apparently an idealised portrait similar to the *Venus of Urbino* in the Uffizi. This superb work came to Florence as part of the dowry of Vittoria della Rovere in 1631, on her marriage to Ferdinando II.

Of the earlier works in the collection, one of the finest is a **tondo by Filippo Lippi** of the *Madonna and Child*. It is one of his best works, and had an important influence on his contemporaries. There are also good **paintings by Cigoli** (d. 1613), one of the best Florentine exponents of the transition from Mannerism to the Baroque, and a number of good **works by Salvatore Rosa**, a Neapolitan artist who was invited to Florence as court painter by Cardinal Gian Carlo de' Medici, brother of Ferdinando II. One of the most famous Florentine works of the 17th century is *Judith with the Head of Holofernes* by **Cristofano Allori** (the artist is said to have portrayed his mistress as Judith, her mother as the maidservant, and himself as Holofernes). It hangs in the Sala dell'Educazione di Giove, and on the opposite wall is another well-known painting, *Sleeping Cupid*, by **Caravaggio**, painted during his exile in Malta in 1608.

Giovanni Fattori: *La Maremma Toscana* (c. 1866).

The largest painting in the grand Sala di Marte is *The Consequences of War* by **Rubens**, one of his most important works. It is an allegory showing Venus trying to prevent Mars going to war, while both figures are surrounded by its destructive and tragic consequences. It was painted in 1638 and sent by the artist to his friend and fellow countryman Justus Suttermans. **Suttermans** (also well represented) was appointed to the Medici court in 1619 and remained in its service until his death in 1681.

Of the 19th-century works, possibly the most famous is the *Venus Italica* by **Canova**. It was presented to Florence by Napoleon in 1812 in exchange for the *Medici Venus*, which he had stolen from the Uffizi and transported to Paris. It is one of the masterpieces of Neoclassical art in Florence.

First floor: Appartamenti Reali

Open as Galleria Palatina, but usually closed for maintenance work in Jan.
These lavishly decorated rooms were used as state apartments from the 17th century onwards by the Medici and Lorraine grand dukes and later by the royal house of Savoy. They have been restored (as far as possible) to their appearance in 1880–1911, when they were first occupied by the House of Savoy. The contents reflect the eclectic taste of the Savoy rulers, as well as the neo-Baroque period of the 19th-century Lorraine grand dukes, and include splendid silks and furnishings; sumptuous gilded chandeliers; Neoclassical mirrors and candelabra; huge oriental vases; furniture decorated with *pietre dure*; and paintings and sculptures.

Second floor: Galleria d'Arte Moderna

Open 8.30–1.50; closed on second and fourth Sun, and first, third and fifth Mon of the month; T: 055 238 8616.
The works currently on show, arranged chronologically and by schools, cover the

period from the mid-18th century up to the First World War. The first rooms illustrate Neoclassicism and the influence of the Napoleonic French when they occupied Florence in the first decade of the 19th century. The most famous artist who worked for the French court was Antonio Canova, whose signed bust of the muse Calliope (1812) is displayed here. It is probably an idealised portrait of Elisa Bacciocchi, Napoleon's sister, whom Napoleon appointed Grand Duchess of Tuscany in 1809. Tuscan art of the 19th century is particularly well represented here, notably the Macchiaioli School, which was active before 1864. These artists took their inspiration directly from nature, and their paintings are characterised by *macchie*, or spots of colour. The most important Macchiaioli painters are Giovanni Fattori, Silvestro Lega and Telemaco Signorini.

Meridiana wing: Galleria del Costume
Entrance from Galleria d'Arte Moderna. Open at the same times.
The Galleria del Costume is the only museum of the history of fashion in Italy. The beautiful displays of clothes are changed about every two years and frequent exhibitions are held. There are also some clothes dating from the 16th century, including a number worn by Eleanor of Toledo, wife of Cosimo I de' Medici.

Ground floor: Museo degli Argenti
Open 8.30–dusk, closed on first and last Mon of the month; T: 055 238 8709. Entrance from the left side of the courtyard.
The Museo degli Argenti is arranged in the summer apartments of the grand dukes, whose main room contains exuberant and colourful frescoes by Giovanni da San Giovanni (17th century). The reception rooms are decorated with delightful *trompe l'oeil* frescoes by Angelo Michele Colonna and Agostino Mitelli.

The display includes the Medici family's eclectic collection of precious objects in silver, ivory, amber and *pietre dure*. Prize exhibits include 16 *pietre dure* vases which belonged to Lorenzo the Magnificent, most of which date from the late Imperial Roman era. There are also several examples of the craftsmanship of Giovanni Battista Foggini. One of the finest is a cabinet commissioned in 1709 by Cosimo III as a present for his favourite child, Anna Maria Luisa, when she married the Elector Palatine. When in 1719 she returned as a widow to Florence, she was careful to bring this beautiful piece back with her from Düsseldorf. It is the most famous of the many cabinets and table-tops designed in *pietre dure* by Foggini for the Medici. Foggini was a particularly versatile artist, who also worked as a painter and architect as well as producing small bronzes and reliquaries, and even perhaps the frame commissioned by Cosimo III for Raphael's famous tondo of the *Madonna della Seggiola* (*see p. 286 above*). Exquisite items in rock crystal, and one of the most important collections in the world of 17th-century ivories, are also on display.

On the mezzanine floor the wonderful jewellery collection of the electress Anna Maria Lodovica de' Medici is displayed.

The Boboli Gardens

Open 8.30–dusk, closed first and last Mon of month. There are four entrances (with ticket offices): one from the courtyard of Palazzo Pitti, one at the Annalena gate on Via Romana, one at Porta Romana and the other beside Forte di Belvedere. The Grotticina di Madama and Grotta Grande can be visited by appointment; T: 055 265 1838.

The magnificent Boboli Gardens, on the steep hillside behind the Pitti Palace, still retain the main outlines of the original Renaissance garden laid out for Duke Cosimo I and his wife Eleanor of Toledo from 1549. They were designed by Niccolò Tribolo, who had formerly worked for the Duke at Villa di Castello (*see p. 319*; the overall layout shows similarities). Known as the 'father of the Italian formal garden', Tribolo was also a talented hydraulic engineer, and he made creative use of his ability, planning monumental fountains of Oceanus (father of the river gods, representing Cosimo) in the hillside (a former quarry) behind the house, fed by a reservoir on the terrace above. The hills were planted symmetrically with evergreens, making a dark background for this proposed centrepiece. But Tribolo died in 1550 on his search for the piece of granite for the fountain basin, and the gardens were taken over first by his son-in-law Davide Fortini, and then by Vasari and Ammannati. After 1574, Francesco I employed Bernardo Buontalenti to direct the works. In the early 17th century the gardens were extended downhill by Giulio Parigi and his son Alfonso. The Parigi were especially known for their talents as set designers and architects: Giulio (1571–1635) became famous for his work as a stage designer and civil engineer (he produced spectacular celebrations for the wedding of Cosimo II and Maria Magdalena of Austria).

Highlights of the gardens include the **Amphitheatre**, close to the rear of the palace, which was laid out by Ammannati in 1599, and converted by the Parigi into an open-air theatre in 1630–35. Here lavish spectacles were held by the Medici to exalt the prestige of the family and offer public entertainment on a grand scale—sometimes there were elephants or horses combined with fantastic scenery and dramatic lighting. The obelisk of Rameses II, taken from Heliopolis by the Romans in 30 BC, found its way to the Villa Medici in Rome in the 17th century. It was set up here in 1789. The huge granite basin, from the Baths of Caracalla, also in Rome, was installed here in 1840.

About 170 **statues** decorate the garden walks. Many of them are restored Roman works, while others still remain unidentified. Two worn statues were recognised as works by Cellini (1500–71) only just before the last war (they are now in the Bargello museum). Other statues were added in the 16th and 17th centuries by Giambologna and others. Some of the statues have been restored *in situ*; others are replaced by casts.

On the left side of the terrace behind Palazzo Pitti, a wide gravel carriage-way descends past two pine trees (right) at the entrance to the narrow path which leads to the **Grotticina di Madama** (*admission by appointment; see above*). It was commissioned by Eleanor of Toledo in 1553–55, and is the work of Davide Fortini and Marco del Tasso. The sculptures are by Baccio Bandinelli and Giovanni Fancelli. It contains stalactites and bizarre goats. The frescoes are attributed to Bachiacca.

Against the wall of the palace near the exit from the gardens is a cast of the so-called **Fontana del Bacco**, an amusing statue of Pietro Barbino, the pot-bellied dwarf of

Cosimo I, seated on a turtle (1560). A flight of steps descends to the **Grotta Grande** (*admission by appointment; see above*). Begun in 1557 by Vasari, the upper part was finished by Ammannati and Buontalenti (1583–93). The two statues of *Apollo* (or David) and *Ceres* (or Cleopatra) in the niches on the façade (probably by Vasari) are by Baccio Bandinelli. The walls of the first inner chamber are covered with fantastic figures and animals carved in the limestone (to a design by Buontalenti). Francesco I installed Michelangelo's unfinished *Slaves* in the four corners in 1585 (replaced by casts after the originals were removed to the Accademia in 1908). The charming painted vault is by Bernardino Poccetti. Beyond is a sculptural group of *Paris Abducting Helen* by Vincenzo de' Rossi (a gift from the sculptor to Cosimo I). The innermost grotto contains a very beautiful statue above an antique fountain of *Venus Emerging From her Bath* (c. 1570) by Giambologna, designed to be seen from every point of view.

THE CONVENT OF SAN MARCO & DISTRICT

The **church of San Marco** (*map p. 268, 2*), founded in 1299 and rebuilt with the convent next door in 1442, assumed its present form in 1588 on a plan by Giambologna. On the north side are the tomb-slabs of the Humanist scholar and Neoplatonic philosopher Pico della Mirandola (1463–94) and the poet Politian (1454–94; *see p. 456*). Both men were members of the Platonic Academy in Florence, a body which saw the birth of the Humanist movement of the Renaissance. Both were with Lorenzo the Magnificent at his death. Also buried here is Prince Stanislaw Poniatowsky (d. 1833; *see p. 236*), in a tomb designed by Lorenzo Bartolini.

The Dominican convent contains the **Museo di San Marco** (*open 8.30–1.20; Sat–Sun 8.15–6.20; closed first, third and fifth Sun and second and fourth Mon of the month; T: 055 238 8608*), chiefly famed for its paintings and frescoes by Fra' Angelico, who was a friar here. Peaceful and beautifully maintained, this is one of the most delightful museums in Florence. Cosimo il Vecchio ordered Michelozzo to enlarge the buildings (1437–52), and founded a public library here, the first of its kind in Europe. Its most famous prior was Savonarola (*see opposite*).

Museum highlights

Cloister of St Antoninus: The attractive entrance cloister, was built by Michelozzo. It takes its name from the founding prior of the convent, who was canonised in 1523. In the corners are small frescoes by Fra' Angelico: *St Thomas Aquinas* (very worn); *St Dominic* and *St Peter Martyr*; a restored *Pietà*; and Christ as a pilgrim welcomed by two Dominicans.

Pilgrims' Hospice: The hospice (to the right as you enter the cloister) was built by Michelozzo. Its walls are now hung with superb paintings by Fra' Angelico, mostly from the 1430s.

Chapter House (opposite the hospice): The *Crucifixion and Saints* is by Fra' Angelico and assistants (1441–42).

Convent dormitory (on the upper floor): The first-floor dormitory consists

of 44 cells, each with a fresco by Fra'
Angelico and his assistants. It is uncertain how many of the frescoes are by the
master alone. At the head of the stairs is
Fra' Angelico's famous *Annunciation*.

Three rooms opening off each other
in the corridor furthest from the
entrance were occupied by Savonarola
in 1482–87 and 1490–98. There are
detached frescoes by Fra' Bartolomeo,
Savonarola's supporter and fellow friar,
and a portrait of Savonarola himself
(with the attributes of St Peter Martyr;
c. 1497).

Library: Outside the main entrance is a
plaque commemorating Savonarola's
arrest, which took place on this spot on
the night of 8th April, 1498. The library
itself, a light and delicate hall by
Michelozzo (1441), is one of the most
pleasing architectural works of the
Florentine Renaissance. It was famous
for its collection of Greek and Roman
authors; some that remain are usually
exhibited here, together with illuminated choirbooks, including a missal illuminated by Fra' Angelico.

Girolamo Savonarola (1452–98)
Savonarola, a Dominican friar born in Ferrara, came to Florence in 1489, where
he was appointed prior of San Marco. His eloquence was well known, and his
dramatic sermons—which he declared were divinely inspired—were full of apocalyptic fire, warning of perdition for those who strayed from Christian principles.
It was Cosimo il Vecchio who had claimed that 'you cannot govern a state with
paternosters'. Savonarola maintained that there was no other way for a state to be
governed. His advocation of theocracy and his puritan streak made him unpalatable to many, but he had a wide following as his congregations show (his sermons
had to be held in the Duomo as the only church large enough to hold them).

He was also a learned theologian, admired by the Florentine Humanists,
including Pico della Mirandola and Politian. Botticelli was one of the Renaissance
artists probably influenced by him, and Michelangelo is said to have commented
as an old man that he could still hear the friar's voice ringing in his ears. Although
Savonarola had been critical of Lorenzo the Magnificent, it seems Lorenzo called
him to his deathbed to receive his blessing. But Savonarola remained an enemy
of the Medici, and his address to the Great Council in 1496 did much to strengthen republican zeal. The Borgia pope Alexander VI excommunicated him, but he
contested the decree and continued to celebrate Mass. When he failed to accept
the challenge of an ordeal by fire (a gauntlet thrown down by a Franciscan opponent), his supporters began to desert him. Arraigned for heresy and treason, he
was burned in Piazza della Signoria, where, at his instigation only a few years earlier, bonfires had been lit to destroy profane books and works of art. Every year,
on 23rd May, a ceremony is held there in his memory by those who consider him
a martyr. As was the case with his 15th-century followers and opponents, he still
arouses strong feelings amongst historians today.   A.B.

Museo dell'Opificio delle Pietre Dure

Map p. 268, 2. Open daily except Sun 8.15–2; Thur until 7; T: 055 265111.

The Opificio was founded in 1588 by the Medici grand duke Ferdinando I, to produce mosaics in hard or semi-precious stones. This refined craft, perfected in Florence, is remarkable for its durability. Many of the best examples are preserved in Palazzo Pitti. Highlights here are Francesco Ferrucci del Tadda's portrait of Cosimo I, as well as works made for the Cappella dei Principi in San Lorenzo (*see p. 298*). There are also 17th-century works made for the Medici, including some by Giovanni Battista Foggini.

Galleria dell'Accademia

Map p. 268, 2. Open 8.15–6.50, closed Mon; usually later on summer weekends; T: 055 238 8609. The gallery can be crowded, and it is best to book a visit (T: 055 294883; booking charge). The least crowded time is late afternoon. The works are all labelled in English.

Most visitors to the gallery have the same aim in view: to see **Michelangelo's** *David*, perhaps the most famous single work of art in Western civilisation. It was commissioned by the city of Florence to stand outside Palazzo Vecchio, a monumental setting appropriate to its huge scale. A celebration of the male nude, it established Michelangelo as the foremost sculptor of his time, at the age of 29. Today it stands alone in a huge tribune, purpose built in 1882, when the statue was moved here.

Also on the ground floor are five other sculptures by Michelangelo. The four *Slaves* (variously dated 1521–23 or c. 1530) were begun for the tomb of Pope Julius II in Rome (*see p. 40*). They were presented to the Medici in 1564 by Michelangelo's nephew, Leonardo. In 1585, they were placed in the Grotta Grande in the Boboli Gardens (*see p. 290*), and were brought here in 1908. In the centre of the right side is the *St Matthew*

One of Michelangelo's unfinished *Slaves*: powerfully suggestive of the sculptor's belief that the finished work exists already within the unhewn stone.

(1504–08), one of the 12 Apostles commissioned from the sculptor for the Duomo, and the only one he ever began. These five sculptures, some of them barely blocked out, are magnificent examples of Michelangelo's unfinished works, the famous *non-finito*, evoking Michelangelo's idea that the sculpture already exists within the stone, and it is the sculptor's job merely to take away what is superfluous.

The other rooms on the ground floor contain Florentine paintings by Andrea Orcagna and his brothers Jacopo and Nardo di Cione; by followers of Giotto, including Taddeo Gaddi and Bernardo Daddi; and by Filippino Lippi, Domenico Ghirlandaio (an altarpiece of *Sts Stephen, James and Peter*, with a particularly striking St Stephen), and Botticelli. On the floor above are 14th- and early 15th-century paintings, including a splendid *Pietà* (1365) by Giovanni da Milano, one of the most interesting painters to succeed Giotto; and nine beautiful works by the monk Lorenzo Monaco.

PIAZZA SANTISSIMA ANNUNZIATA

Piazza Santissima Annunziata (*map p. 271, 7*) was designed by Brunelleschi. Surrounded on three sides by porticoes, it is the most beautiful square in Florence. In the centre is an equestrian statue of Grand Duke Ferdinando I, Giambologna's last work (and the first public monument to a Medici ruler in his own lifetime). It was cast by Giambologna's pupil Pietro Tacca in 1608, who also designed the two fountains with bizarre monsters and marine decorations. Both sculptors are buried in the church of the Annunziata here.

Spedale degli Innocenti

The Spedale degli Innocenti was opened in 1445 as a foundling hospital, the first institution of its kind in Europe. It operated as an orphanage up until 2000, and is now a research centre of UNICEF.

The Arte della Seta (silk-makers guild) commissioned Brunelleschi to begin work on the building in 1419. The arched colonnade (1419–26) is one of the first masterpieces of Renaissance architecture. (The last bays on the right and left were added in the 19th century.) In the spandrels are delightful medallions, perhaps the best-known work of Andrea della Robbia (1487), each with a baby in swaddling-clothes against a bright blue background (the two end ones on each side are mid-19th-century copies). Beneath the portico at the left end is the *rota* (turning-wheel), constructed in 1660 to receive abandoned babies, and only walled up in 1875.

The former convent houses the Museo dello Spedale degli Innocenti (*open 8.30–7; Sun and holidays 8.30–2*). There are two cloisters: the Chiostro degli Uomini (1422–45, reserved for the men who worked in the Institute); and the Chiostro delle Donne (1438; reserved for the women), another beautiful work by Brunelleschi. On the upper floor is a picture gallery. Notable among the display are the splendid *Adoration of the Magi* by Domenico Ghirlandaio, and the *Madonna and Child* in glazed terracotta by Luca della Robbia (c. 1445–50), one of his most beautiful works. There is also a touching series of 19th-century identification tags left by destitute mothers with their babies.

Santissima Annunziata

The church of the Santissima Annunziata (*open 9–12.30 & 4–6.30, daily except Weds*) was founded in 1250, and rebuilt by Michelozzo and others in 1444–81. Its famous painting of the *Annunciation*—held to be miraculous—made it one of the most important sanctuaries of the Madonna in Europe.

In the **atrium** are Mannerist frescoes painted in the second decade of the 16th century by artists including Andrea del Sarto, Pontormo, Rosso Fiorentino and Franciabigio. Andrea's *Coming of the Magi* (1) contains his self-portrait in the right-hand corner. The **shrine of the Madonna (2)** is highly venerated for its *Annunciation*, traditionally thought to have been painted by a friar who was miraculously assisted by an angel. Adjacent is a chapel that was formerly a private oratory for the Medici (3), containing an exquisite small painting of the *Redeemer* (1515) by Andrea del Sarto.

The **chapel off the south transept (4)** contains a sculpture of the *Dead Christ Supported by Nicodemus* by Baccio Bandinelli. This is the burial place of the artist, and the head of Nicodemus is a self-portrait. At the east end is the **tribune (5)**, begun by Michelozzo and completed by Leon Battista Alberti in 1477. It has a very unusual design: a rotonda preceded by a triumphal arch, derived from ancient Roman architecture. The high altar has a frontal by Giovanni Battista Foggini (1682). The **chapel at the far east end (6)** was reconstructed by Giambologna as his own tomb, and contains fine bronze reliefs and a bronze Crucifix by him, and statues by his pupils. His closest follower, Pietro Tacca, is also buried here.

Over the door into the church from the **cloister (7)** is Andrea del Sarto's *Madonna del Sacco* (which gets its name from the sack that St Joseph is leaning on), an original portrayal of

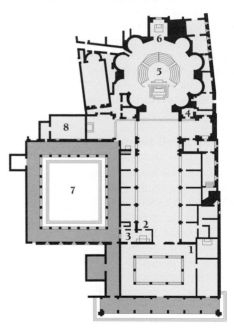

SANTISSIMA ANNUNZIATA

1   *Coming of the Magi* by Andrea del Sarto
2   Shrine of the Madonna
3   Medici oratory
4   *Dead Christ* by Baccio Bandinelli
5   Tribune
6   Tomb of Giambologna
7   Cloister
8   Chapel of St Luke

the Rest on the Flight into Egypt, and one of the artist's best works. The **Cappella di San Luca (8)** has belonged to the Accademia delle Arti del Disegno since 1565 (sadly it is open very rarely), and is dedicated to St Luke, the patron saint of artists. In the vault below are buried Cellini, Pontormo and many other artists. The altarpiece of *St Luke Painting the Madonna* is an interesting self-portrait by Vasari, a founder member of the Academy.

MUSEO ARCHEOLOGICO

Map p. 271, 7–8. Open Mon 2–7; Tues and Thur 8.30–7; Wed, Fri, Sat, Sun 8.30–2; in summer also Sat 9–midnight; T: 055 23575.

The Museo Archeologico contains many superb Etruscan and Roman works from the Medici collections, but for many years it seems to have been rather abandoned (and the second floor, with the most interesting exhibits, is not always open). The Egyptian Museum was founded by Grand Duke Leopold II. In 1845, Leopold II also acquired the famous *François Vase* (*see overleaf*).

Etruscan collections: Much of the Etruscan material, including a fabulous collection of gold jewellery, is still in the deposits, although some of it is shown in exhibitions which are held periodically on two storeys in the modern wing, which is the first area of the building to be visited. At present displayed near the entrance on the ground floor is the magnificent **tomb of the noblewoman Larthia Seianti**, shown adorned with jewels and reclining on her sarcophagus (*illustrated overleaf*). It was found near Chiusi in 1877 and is dated 150 BC.

On the first floor, in the long gallery, is the famous bronze *Chimaera*, which was found outside Arezzo in 1553 and acquired by Cosimo I. The work was incorrectly restored in 1785, and gives the mythical animal the body and head of a lion, the head of a goat on its back, and a serpent's tail. The myth relates that the chimaera was killed by Bellerophon, and it is here shown wounded. It is an Etruscan ex-voto probably dating from the end of the 5th or beginning of the 4th century BC, and it was made in southern Etruria (Chiusi, Arezzo or the Val di Chiana). The other two celebrated bronzes normally here, the *Minerva* and the *Arringatore* ('Orator') were removed some years ago for restoration. Etruscan funerary sculpture, including numerous urns, are displayed in two nearby rooms.

Egyptian Museum: The Egyptian Museum, founded by the Grand Duke Leopold II in 1845, is the most important of its kind in Italy after the museums in Turin and the Vatican. Of the very earliest exhibits, two of the finest are the two polychrome statuettes (restored) of a maidservant preparing yeast for beer and another kneading dough (c. 2480–2180 BC). The portrait of a young woman from the Fayum necropolis dates from the Roman period (1st–2nd centuries AD). The very rare Hittite chariot made of wood and bone, which was found in a Theban tomb, dates from the 14th century BC.

Etruscan tomb of Lartha Seianti (2nd century BC), inscribed with her name beneath the reclining effigy. (Note that Etruscan script reads from right to left.)

Second floor: On this floor (*admission usually on request*) is an outstanding collection of **Attic vases**, where you can study the development of black- and red-figure vases in the 6th and 5th centuries BC. They are decorated with numerous representations of the Greek myths as well as scenes of everyday life. The unique *François Vase* is displayed on its own. This huge, magnificent Attic krater is one of the earliest black-figure Attic vases known, made in Athens c. 570 BC. It was discovered in an Etruscan tomb at Fonte Rotella, Chiusi, in 1844. The decoration comprises six rows of more than 200 exquisite black-figure paintings of mythological scenes, identified by inscriptions.

Also on this floor are several rooms of Etruscan vases, and **Greek and Roman bronzes**. Highlights include a horse's head, probably from a Greek quadriga

group of the 2nd–1st century BC. Owned by Lorenzo the Magnificent, it is thought that both Verrocchio and Donatello saw it in the garden of the Palazzo Medici-Riccardi (where it was used as a fountain) before they began work on their own equestrian statues (Verrocchio's *Colleoni* in Venice, and Donatello's *Gattamelata* in Padua). The bronze torso of an athlete, found in the sea off Livorno, is thought to be a Greek original of c. 480–470 BC. Owned by Cosimo I, it is the earliest known example of a Greek bronze statue cast with the lost-wax technique. The display also includes a bronze head of Antinous, lover of Hadrian (*see p. 148*), the only bronze (as opposed to marble) head of Antinous to survive.

The *Idolino* is a remarkable bronze statue of a young man, thought to have been used as a lampstand at banquets.

Probably a Roman copy of a Greek original, it was found at Pesaro in the Marche in 1530 and donated to Francesco Maria della Rovere, Duke of Urbino. It passed to the Medici—as did so much else—when Ferdinando II married Vittoria della Rovere.

SAN LORENZO & PALAZZO MEDICI-RICCARDI

The church of San Lorenzo

The Medici commissioned Brunelleschi to rebuild San Lorenzo in 1425–46 (*map p. 268, 4; open 10–5 except Sun and holidays*). It is the burial place of all the principal members of the family from Cosimo il Vecchio (d. 1464) to Cosimo III (d. 1723). The west front remains in rough-hewn brick, as it has been since 1480. Pope Leo X held a competition for a façade, and in 1516 Michelangelo won the commission, though his design was never executed (the model survives in the Casa Buonarroti; *see p. 309*).

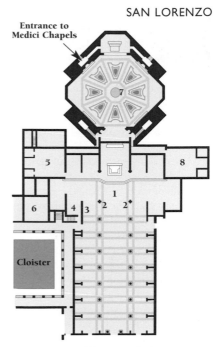

SAN LORENZO

The grey cruciform interior is one of the earliest and most harmonious architectural works of the Renaissance. Under the dome **(1)**, three grilles in the pavement mark the grave of Cosimo il Vecchio, named *Pater Patriae* by the Signoria. To either side are two bronze pulpits **(2)**, the last works of Donatello, made up of exquisitely sculptured panels (c. 1460), with scenes from the life of Christ and the martyrdom of saints. On the north wall is a huge fresco by Bronzino **(3)** of the *Martyrdom of St Lawrence*.

In the north transept is a monument to Donatello **(4)** (d. 1466; buried in the vault below) erected in neo-Renaissance style in 1896. The marble sarcophagus opposite of Niccolò and Fioretta Martelli (c. 1464) in the form of a wicker basket, is probably by Donatello. The *Annunciation* is a beautiful early work by Filippo Lippi.

1	Tomb of Cosimo il Vecchio
2	Pulpits by Donatello
3	Fresco by Bronzino
4	Monument to Donatello
5	Old Sacristy
6	Laurentian Library
7	Cappella dei Principi
8	New Sacristy

The Old Sacristy **(5)** is one of the earliest and purest monuments of the Renaissance by Brunelleschi (1422–28). It was erected at the expense of Giovanni di Bicci de' Medici, founder of the Medici dynasty, and father of Cosimo il Vecchio, who is buried here (d. 1429). The decorative details are mainly by Donatello: the *tondi* in the pendentives and lunettes depict the Evangelists and scenes from the life of St John the Evangelist, titular saint of Giovanni di Bicci. Over the two little doors are large reliefs of Sts Cosmas and Damian (patron saints of doctors, and thus of the Medici family) and Sts Lawrence and Stephen (the former may have been designed by Michelozzo). In the centre is the sarcophagus, by Brunelleschi's adopted son Buggiano (c. 1433), of Giovanni di Bicci de' Medici. Set into the wall is the magnificent porphyry and bronze sarcophagus of Giovanni and Piero de' Medici, the sons of Cosimo il Vecchio. It was commissioned from Verrocchio in 1472 by Lorenzo the Magnificent and his brother Giuliano.

The Laurentian Library
The Laurentian Library (Biblioteca Laurenziana; *open 9–1 except Sat; entrance through cloister*) **(6)** was begun by Michelangelo c. 1524 at the order of Clement VII (Giulio de' Medici) to house the collection of manuscripts made by Cosimo il Vecchio and Lorenzo the Magnificent. The solemn vestibule, with its blind windows and empty niches, is a remarkable monument of Mannerist architecture. It is filled with an elaborate free-standing staircase, a highly idiosyncratic work which clearly shows Michelangelo's sculptural conception of architecture. All the elements combine to provide a vertical emphasis, and the columns and volutes are set into the wall, producing strange shadow effects. As Vasari observed, this room did much to encourage Michelangelo's successors to explore new designs, and the subversion of architectural rules meant that later architects no longer felt obliged to conform to established styles. The peaceful reading room, a long hall, provides an unexpected contrast, fitted with reading desks. Exhibitions are held periodically of the precious library contents.

The Medici Chapels
Open 8.15–4.20; closed second and fourth Sun and first, third and fifth Mon of the month.
The **Cappella dei Principi (7)** is the opulent—if gloomy—mausoleum of the Medici grand dukes, begun in 1604 to a plan by Don Giovanni de' Medici, illegitimate son of Cosimo I. Its decoration is a *tour de force* of craftsmanship in *pietre dure*. In the sarcophagi around the walls, from right to left, are buried Ferdinando II, Cosimo II, Ferdinando I, Cosimo I, Francesco I and Cosimo III. The second and third are surmounted by statues in gilded bronze, by Pietro and Ferdinando Tacca (1626–42).

The so-called **New Sacristy (8)** may have been begun by Giuliano da Sangallo c. 1491. Work was continued by Michelangelo in 1520–24 and 1530–33, but was left unfinished when he left Florence for Rome in 1534. It is built in dark *pietra serena* and white marble in a severe style, which produces a strange, cold atmosphere. It was used as a funerary chapel for the Medici family, whose tombs were commissioned by the Medici pope Clement VII. To the left of the entrance is the tomb of Lorenzo, Duke of Urbino (1492–1519), grandson of Lorenzo the Magnificent. He was an unpopular ruler, who governed by force rather than by consensus. Machiavelli dedicated *The Prince* to him after he conquered Urbino in 1516–17. On the sarcophagus below are the reclining figures of *Dawn* (female) and *Dusk* (male). Opposite is the tomb of the third son of Lorenzo the Magnificent, Giuliano, Duke of Nemours (1479–1516). Well-liked for the brief year that he ruled in Florence, he famously exonerated Machiavelli from charges of having taken part in a plot against him. He counted Castiglione a personal friend (and is in fact one of the characters in *The Courtier*). On his sarcophagus are the figures of *Day* and *Night*. The massive male figure (*Day*) seems to have been influenced by the ancient *Belvedere Torso* in the Vatican (*see p. 100*). The head is hardly worked on at all.

The entrance wall was intended to contain a monument to Lorenzo the Magnificent and his brother Giuliano (murdered in the Pazzi Conspiracy; *see p. 308*); the only part carried out by Michelangelo is the *Madonna and Child*. It is his last statue of the Madonna, and one of his most beautiful. The figures on either side are St Cosmas and St Damian, the medical saints who were the patrons of the Medici.

Palazzo Medici-Riccardi

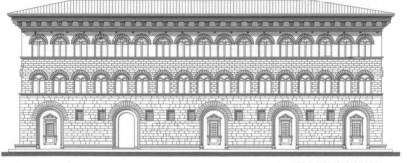

PALAZZO MEDICI-RICCARDI

Map p. 268, 4. Chapel and gallery open 9–7 except Wed. To book a visit, T: 055 276 0340.
Palazzo Medici-Riccardi was built for Cosimo il Vecchio by his favourite architect, Michelozzo, after 1444. This palace remained the residence of the Medici family until 1540, when Cosimo I moved into Palazzo Vecchio. The rusticated façade served as a model for other famous Florentine palaces, including those built by the Strozzi and Pitti.

The main staircase off the courtyard leads up to the **Chapel of the Magi** (*only 15 people admitted at a time*), the only unaltered part of Michelozzo's work. The walls are entirely covered with Benozzo Gozzoli's fresco masterpiece, *The Procession of the Magi to Bethlehem* (begun in 1459 and finished before 1463). It was probably commissioned by Cosimo il Vecchio, but it is known that his son Piero il Gottoso (the Gouty) also took an active interest in the work. The decorative cavalcade is shown in a charming landscape with hunting scenes, which seems to be inspired by Flemish tapestries.

Discussion continues about the identification of the various figures, some of which are vivid portrait studies. The two boys in red hats above a line of four horses' heads may have been intended to portray Lorenzo and Giuliano, sons of Piero il Gottoso, then around ten and six years old. Above them, the man looking out of the fresco is a self-portrait of Benozzo, with his signature on his red hat. In front, the man in a red beret on a mule is often taken as a portrait of Cosimo il Vecchio; the man just in front of him, dressed in green and gold brocade, on a grey horse with the Medici emblems on its bridle, may be his son, Piero il Gottoso. The young king, on a splendid grey charger, is usually considered to be an idealised portrait of Lorenzo the Magnificent.

On the second floor is the **Gallery**, an example of Baroque decoration unique in Florence (1670–88), covered by Luca Giordano's fresco of the *Apotheosis of the Second Medici Dynasty* (1683). The stucco was designed by Giovanni Battista Foggini.

THE MEDICI

The Medici first came to Florence from the Mugello valley. Their name suggests a medical ancestry, though by the 13th century they appear as money changers, and as bankers in the 14th. Giovanni di Bicci de' Medici (1360–1429), the founder of the family's great fortune, was in Florence by 1378, and worked his way up the family business until he was undisputed head of the bank. By 1401 he was well respected enough to be on the committee judging the competition for the Baptistery doors. But Giovanni never forgot that he was an outsider, and he carefully but quietly sided with popular feeling. It is said that he advised his son Cosimo (il Vecchio) never to go near the Piazza della Signoria unless summoned there, and never to make a show before the people or go against their will. Cosimo, already 40 when his father died in 1429, followed the advice.

And indeed, the Medici were never truly secure in their position. Even at the height of Lorenzo the Magnificent's power in the 1480s there were those who talked of Medici tyranny, and their rule collapsed quickly in 1494, with the inept behaviour of Lorenzo's son Piero. The Medici palace was sacked in an outburst of popular fury. Yet the family had an uncanny ability to reinvent itself. Few would have predicted that it would once again be a Medici, Cosimo I (1519–74), who would dominate the city again, and this time as a grand duke. The glorification of the dynasty began with Cosimo's symbolic move out of the family residence into the seat of government, Palazzo della Signoria.   C.F.

SANTA MARIA NOVELLA & OGNISSANTI

Santa Maria Novella (*map p. 268, 3. Open 9–5; Fri, Sun and holidays 1–5*) is the most important Gothic church in Tuscany. In 1221, the Dominicans were given the property, and building began in 1246 at the east end of the present church. The impressive nave was begun in 1279. Its architects are thought to have been the Dominican friars Sisto and Ristoro (also the architects of Santa Maria sopra Minerva in Rome). The church was completed under the direction of another friar, Jacopo Talenti, in the mid-14th century.

The lower part of the splendid marble façade above the Gothic arcaded recesses is typically Tuscan Romanesque in style and is also attributed to Fra' Jacopo Talenti. Its geometric design in white and dark green marble was inspired by the exteriors of the Baptistery and San Miniato al Monte. The upper part of the façade was completed together with the main doorway in 1456–70. It was commissioned by Giovanni Rucellai from the famous Renaissance architect Leon Battista Alberti, who also built Giovanni's town house, the Palazzo Rucellai (*see p. 304*). Major works of art in the church are highlighted below:

(1) Masaccio's *Trinity*: The *Trinity* (1427) shows God the Father supporting the Cross, with the Virgin and St John the Evangelist and donors beneath it. On the sarcophagus at the bottom is a skeleton representing Adam's grave. The symbol of Death is thus shown beneath the symbol of the Resurrection. This fresco is one of the earliest works to use accurately the system of linear perspective developed by Brunelleschi; indeed, it may be that Brunelleschi even intervened in the design of the shadowy niche. The perfect composition gives it an almost metaphysical quality.

(2) Giotto's Crucifix: The huge Crucifix hangs in the nave. Although painted well over a hundred years before Masaccio's fresco, it is interesting to confront these two great masters here at close range and see how both contributed in such a fundamental way to the development of Italian painting.

(3) The sanctuary: This is decorated with delightful frescoes, the masterpiece of Domenico

Ghirlandaio, who was buried in the church after his death (aged 45) from the plague. The frescoes were commissioned in 1485 by Giovanni Tornabuoni, who was for years manager

SANTA MARIA NOVELLA

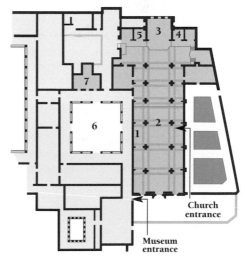

1 Masaccio's *Trinity*
2 Crucifix by Giotto
3 Sanctuary (frescoes by Ghirlandaio)
4 Strozzi Chapel (frescoes by Filippino Lippi
5 Gondi Chapel (Crucifix by Brunelleschi)
6 Chiostro Verde (frescoes by Paolo Uccello)
7 Spanish Chapel

of the Rome branch of the Medici bank and whose sister married Piero il Gottoso de' Medici. The scenes on the right wall are from the life of St John the Baptist; those on the left from the life of the Virgin. Many of the figures are portraits of the artist's contemporaries, including members of the Tornabuoni family. The altar has a bronze Crucifix by Giambologna.

(4) Chapel of Filippo Strozzi: The chapel is decorated with exuberant frescoes by Filippino Lippi. The chapel was acquired in 1486 by the great Florentine banker Filippo Strozzi, who built Palazzo Strozzi (*see opposite*) and was agent for the Medici in Naples. He commissioned the frescoes from Filippino as soon as the latter had finished work on the Brancacci Chapel (*see p. 311*), although the artist interrupted work here when he was called to Rome to work in Santa Maria sopra Minerva. Full of allusions to Antiquity and including grotesques, the design betrays Roman influence, and is quite different from other Florentine fresco cycles of this period.

(5) Gondi Chapel: Here is the famous Crucifix by Brunelleschi, his only sculpture to survive in wood (obviously made to wear a loin cloth, but this has since been removed). Vasari recounts the story that Brunelleschi carved this work after he had criticised Donatello for representing a mere 'peasant' on the Cross in his Crucifix (now in Santa Croce; *see p. 307*).

Museo di Santa Maria Novella

Open 9–5; Sun and holidays 9–5; closed Fri and Sun; T: 055 282187.

The Romanesque Chiostro Verde **(6)**, part of the Convent of Santa Maria Novella, remains an oasis of calm in this busy part of the city. It takes its name from the green colour of its famous decoration: the damaged frescoes by Paolo Uccello and assistants are painted in *terraverde*. They illustrate stories from Genesis, and the cycle begins at the far end of the east (entrance) walk, beside the door into the church. The numerous frescoes with animals are particularly charming. The following scenes are usually considered to be mostly by Paolo Uccello himself: the *Creation of Adam and the Animals*, the *Creation and Temptation of Eve* (c. 1425), the *Flood*, and the *Recession of the Flood* (with Noah's ark), and the *Sacrifice and Drunkenness of Noah* (c. 1446). The Spanish Chapel **(7)**, so named because it was assigned to Spanish members of Eleanor of Toledo's retinue, was built by Fra' Jacopo Talenti and is covered with splendid frescoes by Andrea di Bonaiuto (c. 1365), an artist influenced by the Sienese school.

Ognissanti

Map p. 270, 6. Open 7.45–12 & 5–6.30; Sun and holidays 8.45–1 & 5–7.30.

The frescoes of the *Pietà* and the *Madonna della Misericordia* on the south side, early works by Domenico Ghirlandaio, are interesting as the Madonna is shown protecting members of the Vespucci family, silk merchants who lived in Borgo Ognissanti. Amerigo (1454–1512) is supposed to be the boy whose head appears between the Madonna and the man in the dark cloak. He grew up to become a Medici agent in Seville, and gave his name to the continent of America, having made two voyages in 1499 and 1501–02 following the route charted by Columbus. Their neighbours in

Borgo Ognissanti were the Filipepi, the most famous of whom was Sandro, who became known as Botticelli, probably because he was apprenticed to a jeweller as a boy (*battigello* means silversmith), and who is buried here in the south transept. The Vespucci paid for Botticelli's fresco of *St Augustine* (between the third and fourth altars), which is the artist's most important work in Florence to survive in the church for which it was made (1480). The pendant of *St Jerome* opposite is by Domenico Ghirlandaio, dated (on the desk) 1480. The exquisite detail of the objects, including the saint's spectacles, recall contemporary Flemish works.

On the left of the church, at no. 42, is the entrance to the convent (*open Mon, Tues and Sat 9–12*), whose pretty refectory contains a *Last Supper* by Domenico Ghirlandaio (1480), the most beautiful of his several frescoes of this subject in Florence.

SANTA TRINITA & VIA TORNABUONI

The church of Santa Trinita (*map p. 268, 5; open 9–12 & 4–6*) has the austerity characteristic of all Cistercian churches. In the fourth south chapel are damaged but beautiful frescoes of the life of the Virgin by Lorenzo Monaco (1422). These are the most important frescoes, still Gothic in spirit, by this elegant painter. The altarpiece of the *Annunciation*, with a lovely predella, is also by him.

The Sassetti Chapel (to the right of the choir) is one of the best-preserved Renaissance chapels in Florence. Its delightful frescoes of the life of St Francis by Domenico Ghirlandaio (*coin-operated light*) were commissioned in 1483 by Francesco Sassetti, manager of the Medici bank. The scene in the lunette above the altar (*St Francis Receiving the Rule of the Order from Pope Honorius*) takes place in Piazza della Signoria, and those present include (in the foreground, right) Lorenzo the Magnificent with Sassetti and his son. On the stairs are Politian with Lorenzo's sons, Piero, Giovanni and Giuliano. In the *Miracle of the Boy Brought Back to Life* (beneath) is Piazza Santa Trinita (with the Romanesque façade of the church and the old Ponte Santa Trinita). The altarpiece shows the *Adoration of the Shepherds* (1485) and is also by Ghirlandaio. It is flanked by the kneeling figures of the donors, Francesco Sassetti and Nera Corsi, his wife.

Via Tornabuoni

In the little Piazza Santa Trinita stands the **Column of Justice**, a huge granite monolith transported from the Baths of Caracalla in Rome. It was presented by Pius IV to Cosimo I in 1560, and set up here in 1563 to commemorate his victory over an anti-Medici uprising led by Piero Strozzi in 1537. The porphyry figure of *Justice* that crowns it is by Francesco Ferrucci del Tadda.

Via Tornabuoni, Florence's most elegant shopping street, passes the huge **Palazzo Strozzi**, the last and grandest of the magnificent Renaissance palaces in Florence, built for Filippo Strozzi (grandfather of Piero the rebel). It is a typical 15th-century town mansion—half-fortress, half-palace—with three storeys of equal emphasis, constructed with large rough blocks of stone but left unfinished. It is thought that Strozzi himself took an active part in the design of the building, but it is uncertain who drew up the project, which was begun in 1489. The wrought-iron torch-holders and fantastic lanterns were designed by Benedetto da Maiano.

On Via della Vigna Nuova is **Palazzo Rucellai**, the town house of Giovanni Rucellai (1403–81), one of the most respected intellectual figures of Renaissance Florence, as well as one of the wealthiest businessmen in Europe. Scholars now agree that the palace must have been designed by Leon Battista Alberti, although it was built by Bernardo Rossellino (c. 1446–51). The dignified façade of the palace, with incised decoration, is in striking contrast to the heavy rustication of Palazzo Strozzi and the other Florentine palaces of the period, and its design had a lasting influence on Italian architecture.

In Via della Spada (no. 18) is the entrance (*usually open only on Sat at 5.30, but closed July–Sept*) to the remarkable **Cappella del Santo Sepolcro**, built by Alberti in 1467, also for Giovanni Rucellai. In the middle of the lovely barrel-vaulted oratory there is a perfectly preserved chapel by Alberti in inlaid marble with exquisite carving, the proportions of which recall the famous sanctuary of the Holy Sepulchre in Jerusalem.

THE DISTRICT OF SANTA CROCE

The church of Santa Croce

Santa Croce (*map p. 271, 12; open 9.30–5.30; Sun 1–5.30*) is the Franciscan church of Florence. It was rebuilt in 1294, possibly by Arnolfo di Cambio. The nave was still unfinished in 1375 and it was not consecrated until 1442. The bare stone front was covered with its neo-Gothic marble façade in 1857–63. The Gothic interior was rearranged by Vasari in 1560 when the choir and rood-screen were demolished and the side altars added. Some of the painted altarpieces are by Vasari himself; others are by his contemporaries. The church is the burial place of the great artists Lorenzo Ghiberti and Michelangelo, the statesman Machiavelli and the scientist Galileo. But the church is above all famous for its works by Giotto and his school.

Giotto (1266/7–1337)
Giotto di Bondone was born in the Mugello just north of Florence. A pupil of Cimabue and friend of Dante, he was appointed head of the Florence cathedral works and was the architect of the Campanile (1334). His most famous surviving frescoes (the only cycle of his which survives intact) are in the Cappella degli Scrovegni in Padua (1303–05). His finest works in central Italy are probably those in the church of St Francis in Assisi (*see p. 527*). The frescoes here in Santa Croce (probably dating from the 1320s) had a fundamental influence on Florentine painting: Michelangelo was later to make careful studies of them. Giotto's art had a new monumentality and sense of volume which had never been achieved in medieval painting. His remarkable figures are given an intensely human significance, which the art historian Bernard Berenson defined as 'tactile values'.

(1) Peruzzi Chapel: The badly damaged mural paintings are mature works by Giotto. The architectural settings contain references to Classical antiquity. In the archivolt, there are eight heads of prophets; in the vault, symbols of the Evangelists; on the right wall, scenes from the life of St John the Evangelist; and on the left wall, scenes from the life of St John the Baptist. The altarpiece of the *Madonna and Saints* is by Giotto's pupil Taddeo Gaddi.

(2) Bardi Chapel: The frescoes by Giotto were certainly designed by him, although it is possible that some parts were executed by his pupils. They illustrate scenes from the life of St Francis. On the altar is a panel painting of *St Francis*, with 20 scenes from his life, by a Florentine artist of the 13th century, now generally attributed to Coppo di Marcovaldo.

(3) Baroncelli Chapel: The frescoes of the life of the Virgin (1332–38) are by Taddeo Gaddi, Giotto's most faithful pupil. These are considered among his best works, and reveal his talent as an innovator within the Giottesque school (they include one of the earliest known night scenes in fresco painting). The altarpiece of the *Coronation of the Virgin* (restored) is by Giotto, perhaps with the intervention of his workshop.

(4) Castellani Chapel: Taddeo's son Agnolo Gaddi produced decorative frescoes for this chapel. They depict (right) the histories of St Nicholas of Bari and St John the Baptist, and (left) St Anthony Abbot and St John the Evangelist. Like his father, Agnolo was also known as a designer of stained glass, and he was responsible for the fine lancet windows.

(5) Sanctuary and High Altar: The vaulted space is entirely covered with Agnolo Gaddi's frescoes of *Christ*, the *Evangelists*, *St Francis*, and the *Legend of the Cross*. Above the altar is a large polyptych made up in 1869 from panels by various hands. The central predella panel is a very fine late 14th-century work by Lorenzo Monaco.

(6) Bardi di Libertà Chapel: Bernardo Daddi (another Giottesque painter) decorated this chapel with frescoes of the lives of St Lawrence and St Stephen.

(7) Bardi di Vernio Chapel: Perhaps the most original of all the followers of Giotto was Maso di Banco, whose colourful frescoes of the life of St Sylvester and the Emperor Constantine (after 1367) can be seen here. The first Gothic tomb contains a fresco, also attributed to Maso, of the kneeling figure of the patron of the chapel, with Christ receiving his soul (c. 1367).

(8) Tomb of Michelangelo: This rather disappointing monument was designed by Giorgio Vasari, who knew the great artist well. The paintings and sculptures are the work of artists of the Michelangelesque school, including Giovanni Battista Naldini.

(9) Dante's Cenotaph: Dante was exiled from Florence in 1302 as an opponent of the Guelph faction in the government. He died and was buried in Ravenna in 1321. This cenotaph is by Stefano Ricci (1829).

(10) Pulpit: This is perhaps the masterpiece of Benedetto da Maiano (1472–76), beautifully composed and with delicately carved scenes from the life of St Francis and five *Virtues*.

(11) Monument to Vittorio Alfieri: A very fine work by Canova to the tragic

SANTA CROCE

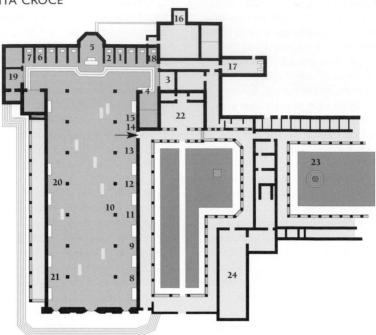

1	Peruzzi Chapel	13	Cavalcanti Tabernacle
2	Bardi Chapel	14	Tomb of Leonardo Bruni
3	Baroncelli Chapel	15	Tomb of Rossini
4	Castellani Chapel	16	Rinuccini Chapel
5	Sanctuary	17	Medici Chapel
6	Bardi di Libertà Chapel	18	Velluti Chapel
7	Bardi di Vernio Chapel	19	Donatello's Crucifix
8	Tomb of Michelangelo	20	Tomb of Ghiberti
9	Dante's Cenotaph	21	Monument to Galileo
10	Pulpit	22	Pazzi Chapel
11	Monument to Alfieri	23	Second Cloister
12	Tomb of Machiavelli	24	Refectory

poet who lived in Florence after 1787 with the Countess of Albany (previously married to Bonnie Prince Charlie). When Alfieri died, she commissioned Canova to erect this monument, in which the female figure of Italy is shown weeping at his tomb.

(12) Tomb of Machiavelli: The monument (1787) is the best work of the Neoclassical sculptor Innocenzo Spinazzi.

(13) Cavalcanti Tabernacle: An unusual monument with a beautiful high relief of the *Annunciation* in gilded limestone by Donatello. There is a remarkable spiritual bond between the figures of Mary and the Angel Gabriel, which makes this one of Donatello's most moving works.

(14) Tomb of Leonardo Bruni: The monument to this Florentine Humanist is by Bernardo Rossellino (c. 1446–47), and is one of the most harmonious and influential sepulchral monuments of the Renaissance. The architectural setting takes its inspiration from Brunelleschi.

(15) Tomb of Rossini: This memorial to the composer (1792–1868), by Giuseppe Cassioli, is a sad imitation of the Bruni tomb. Rossini was born in Pesaro (*see p. 651*) and died in Paris. His remains were moved here from Père Lachaise in 1887.

(16) Rinuccini Chapel: The Lombard Giovanni da Milano worked for a short time in Florence, and was one of the best and most sophisticated followers of Giotto. His frescoes entirely cover this chapel, with scenes from the life of the Virgin and St Mary Magdalene (c. 1365).

(17) Medici Chapel: This chapel, by Cosimo il Vecchio's favourite architect, Michelozzo (1434), contains a *Madonna with Saints* by Paolo Schiavo and *St John the Baptist* by Spinello Aretino, both dating from the early 15th century. The ter-racotta altarpiece of the *Madonna and Child with Angels* is by Andrea della Robbia (c. 1480; the saints were probably added by an assistant).

(18) Velluti Chapel: Here are some of the earliest frescoes in the church, damaged works by a follower of Cimabue (possibly Jacopo del Casentino), illustrating the life of St Michael Archangel.

(19) Donatello's Crucifix: When Donatello's friend Brunelleschi saw this Crucifix, he called it a mere 'peasant on the Cross', and vowed to show Donatello how the crucified Saviour should look. Brunelleschi's version is preserved in Santa Maria Novella (*see p. 302*).

(20) Tomb of Ghiberti: A handsome tomb-slab with niello decoration and the emblem of an eagle marks the burial place of Lorenzo Ghiberti and his son Vittorio, also a sculptor.

(21) Monument to Galileo: The great scientist (1564–1642) spent the latter part of his life in Florence. He was not permitted a Christian burial, having been condemned by the Inquisition under Pope Urban VIII for his defence of the Copernican theory. This monument was set up in 1737, to a design by Giovanni Battista Foggini, when Galileo's remains were finally allowed to be interred here.

The Pazzi Chapel

Open at the same time and with the same ticket as the church. Entrance from inside the church (marked with an arrow on the plan opposite).

The Pazzi Chapel **(22)** is one of the most famous works by Brunelleschi. It was commissioned as a chapter house by Andrea de' Pazzi in 1429 or 1430. Most of the work was carried out by Brunelleschi from 1442 until his death in 1446, but it was not finished until the 1470s. The portico may have been designed by Giuliano da Maiano. The terracotta frieze of cherubs' heads is attributed to the della Robbia workshop. In the centre of the barrel vault is a shallow cupola lined with delightful polychrome enamelled terracottas by Luca della Robbia, with a garland of fruit surrounding the Pazzi arms. Over the door is a medallion with *St Andrew*, also by Luca (c. 1461). The carved wooden door is by the Maiano brothers. The interior is one of the masterpieces of the early Renaissance, with carved *pietra serena* used to articulate the architectural features against a plain white ground. The 12 roundels in enamelled terracotta of the seated *Apostles* (c. 1442–52) are by Luca della Robbia. In the pendentives are four polychrome roundels of the *Evangelists* (c. 1460), possibly designed by Donatello and glazed by the della Robbia (although some scholars attribute them to Brunelleschi).

THE PAZZI CONSPIRACY

In 1478 Francesco de' Pazzi came close to bringing Medici power in Florence to a bloody end. The Pazzi were an old-established banking family whose fortunes took a turn for the better during the papacy of Sixtus IV. Sixtus distrusted the Medici, and transferred the financing of the papal alum mines at Tolfa from the Medici bank to the Pazzi bank. Supported by Rome, Francesco de' Pazzi and his fellow conspirators planned to assassinate Lorenzo the Magnificent and his brother Giuliano, at a moment when their attention was distracted by some kind of public spectacle. The event chosen was Mass in the Duomo. Giuliano's killers dealt him a mortal stab wound in the neck when he bowed his head in prayer. Lorenzo's assailants were less deft: Lorenzo parried the blow, and vaulted to safety over the Communion rail, taking refuge in the north sacristy.

Soon the hue and cry was raised all over town. The conspirators were apprehended, and vengeance was terrible. All those complicit in the plot—and, in the ensuing confusion, many who were not—were hounded out and killed. The ringleaders had ropes fastened to their necks and were tossed from the high windows of Palazzo della Signoria, to dangle to their deaths. A.B.

Museo dell'Opera di Santa Croce

Of the several works displayed here, the finest are in the **refectory (23)**, a fine Gothic hall with large windows. Cimabue's great Crucifix was the most important work of art destroyed in the 1966 Arno flood: a skilled restoration has recuperated the little original paint that survived. The end wall of the refectory is decorated with a huge fresco by Taddeo Gaddi of the *Last Supper* below the Tree of the Cross and four scenes showing *St Louis of Toulouse*, *St Francis*, *St Benedict* and *Mary Magdalene Anointing the Feet of Christ in the House of Simon the Pharisee*. On the two long walls (below roundels of saints) are detached fragments of a large fresco by Orcagna showing the *Triumph of Death* and *Inferno*, which used to decorate the nave of the church before Vasari's side altars were set up.

In a reconstructed tabernacle is Donatello's colossal gilded bronze *St Louis of Toulouse*, commissioned for a niche in Orsanmichele (but replaced there by Verrocchio's *St Thomas*). The original tabernacle of which this is a cast is still *in situ* there.

Museo Horne

Map p. 271, 11. Open 9–1 except Sun and holidays; T: 055 244661.

Palazzo Corsi (no. 6 Via de' Benci) is an attractive small palace (1495–1502) housing the Museo Horne. The English art historian and architect Herbert Percy Horne (1864–1916) purchased the palace in 1911 and carefully restored every detail to its late 15th-century appearance. Room I on the first floor has a **tiny work by Masaccio** (albeit in poor condition): *Scenes from the Legend of St Julian*. The saint is said to have killed his parents in their bed, believing them to be his wife with a lover. The scene showing Julian and his wife in despair after the event anticipates Masaccio's famous portrayal of Adam and Eve expelled from Paradise in the Brancacci Chapel. Room II contains the most precious piece in the collection, **Giotto's** *St Stephen*, one of the most important paintings known by the master. Horne purchased the work in London in 1904, believing it to be the work of Giotto. His attribution is now generally accepted. It has been suggested that it was part of a polyptych (the central panel of which is in the National Gallery of Washington). Room III has a very fine tondo of the *Holy Family* by the Sienese artist Beccafumi, in a beautiful contemporary frame.

Casa Buonarroti

Map p. 271, 12. Via Ghibellina 70; open 9.30–1.30 except Tues; T. 055 241752.

Three houses on this site were purchased in 1508 by Michelangelo. He left the property to his only descendant, his nephew Leonardo, who joined the houses together following a plan already drawn up. They now house a museum preserving **three of Michelangelo's sculptures** and some of his drawings and *bozzetti*.

The principal exhibits are on the first floor. The *Madonna of the Steps*, a marble bas-relief, is Michelangelo's earliest known work, carved at the age of 15 or 16. The low *schiacciato* relief shows the influence of Donatello. The relief showing a battle scene is also one of his earliest works, carved just before the death of Lorenzo the Magnificent in 1492, and then worked on a few years later, but left unfinished. Modelled on ancient sarcophagi, it represents a mythological battle between Greeks and centaurs.

The wooden model for the façade of San Lorenzo was designed by Michelangelo for Pope Leo X in 1516 but never carried out. The colossal torso, a model in clay and wood for a river god, was intended for the New Sacristy in San Lorenzo. In the room in front of the stairs are displayed (in rotation) five or six of Michelangelo's drawings.

PONTE VECCHIO, PONTE SANTA TRINITA & THE OLTRARNO

Standing near the site of the Roman crossing (which was a little farther upstream), **Ponte Vecchio** (*map p. 268, 7*) was the only bridge over the Arno until 1218. The present bridge was reconstructed after a flood in 1345, probably by Taddeo Gaddi, better known as a painter of the Giottesque school. In 1593, Grand Duke Ferdinando I decreed that the butchers' and grocery shops should be replaced by those of goldsmiths and silversmiths, who remain here to this day.

From the centre of the bridge there is a superb view of **Ponte Santa Trinita**. A bridge has spanned the Arno on that site since 1252, though the present Ponte Santa Trinita dates only from 1957. It is an exact replica of the bridge commissioned from Ammannati by Cosimo I. That graceful bridge (1567), linking the Medici residence with the centre of the city, was his masterpiece, and the finest of all the bridges across the Arno—it is probable that Ammannati submitted his project to Michelangelo for approval. The bridge was destroyed in 1944, when it was mined by the retreating German army. The replacement was financed by public subscription. Most of the original decorative details and the four statues from the parapet were salvaged from the bed of the river.

Santa Felicita

The church of Santa Felicita (*map p. 268, 7; opening times subject to change*) is probably the oldest church in the city after San Lorenzo. The first church on this site was built at the end of the 4th or the beginning of the 5th century, and dedicated to the Roman martyr St Felicity. The present church was erected in 1736–39 by Ferdinando Ruggieri. It is chiefly visited for its **superb works by Pontormo**, considered among the masterpieces of 16th-century Florentine painting. They were commissioned by Ludovico Capponi in 1525, for the chapel which bears his family name. The remarkable altarpiece of the *Deposition* is a triumph of Mannerism, where stylisation replaces naturalism and restraint gives way to virtuosity. The fresco of the *Annunciation* was detached when it was restored. The *tondi* of the Evangelists in the cupola are attributed to Pontormo and Bronzino. The 15th-century stained-glass window is by Guillaume de Marcillat, a French artist who lived in Arezzo, and was famous as a designer of stained glass.

Santo Spirito

Santo Spirito (*map p. 268, 7; open 9.30–12.30 & 4–5.30, closed Wed*) is an early Augustinian foundation, dating from 1250. In 1428 Brunelleschi was commissioned to design a new church, the project for which he had completed by 1434–35, though construction was not begun until 1444, just two years before the great architect's death. The interior is a superb creation of the Renaissance, remarkable for its harmonious proportions, its solemn colour, and the perspective of the colonnades and vaulted aisles.

South transept: The altarpiece of the *Madonna and Child with the Young St John, Saints and Donors* **(1)** is one of the best and most mature works of Filippino Lippi (after 1494). In the background is an early view of Florence. The 'dialogue' between the Young St John and the Christ Child is an interesting detail which was to be developed by later painters such as Leonardo da Vinci.

The original painting of the *Vision of St Bernard* by Perugino (now in Munich) was replaced in 1656 by a beautiful (and almost indistinguishable) copy by Felice Ficherelli **(2)**. This was often an accepted practice when a family wished to enjoy an important painting they had commissioned, and Ficherelli was known above all as a copyist.
Far east end: The polyptych of the

Madonna and Child with Saints **(3)** is the earliest painting in the church (c. 1340). It is by Maso di Banco, one of the most interesting followers of Giotto. The Pitti family chapel still contains the altarpiece of *Martyred Saints* **(4)** commissioned by the family from the best-known artist of the day, Alessandro Allori (1574). It is remarkable for its figure studies of the male nude, and incorporates a portrait of Allori's patron, Cosimo I, in the centre. The predella is especially interesting for the view of Palazzo Pitti before it was enlarged, with its owner Luca Pitti standing outside (in a red hat). The next-door chapel preserves another fine work by Allori, *Christ and the Adulteress* (1577) **(5)**.

North transept: In a chapel here is a wonderful altarpiece of *St Monica* **(6)** (mother of St Augustine), attributed by many to Verrocchio. Also here is the Cappella Corbinelli, with a beautiful altarpiece sculpted by Andrea Sansovino **(7)**.

Sacristy: The architecture of the octagonal sacristy **(8)** (*admission on request*) is inspired by Brunelleschi. Here is displayed a Crucifix in painted poplar wood attributed (with some uncertainty) to Michelangelo. Exquisitely carved, it shows the slight figure of

SANTO SPIRITO

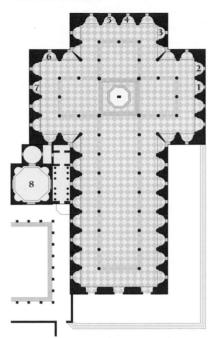

1	*Madonna and Child* by Filippino Lippi
2	Copy of Perugino's *St Bernard*
3	*Madonna and Child* by Maso di Banco
4	*Martyred Saints* by Allori
5	*Christ and the Adulteress* by Allori
6	*St Monica* by ?Verrocchio
7	Altarpiece by Andrea Sansovino
8	Sacristy with ?Michelangelo's Crucifix

Christ in an unusual *contrapposto* position, a design subsequently much copied.

Santa Maria del Carmine (Brancacci Chapel)

Map p. 270, 10. Open 10–4.30; Sun 1–4.30; closed Tues. Entrance through the cloisters. Combined ticket with Palazzo Vecchio. Visitors should book in advance (T: 055 276 8224 or 055 276 8558) but if you are on your own you can often go straight in.

A Carmelite convent was founded here in 1250, and the first church begun in 1268. The **Brancacci Chapel frescoes** of the *Life of St Peter* were commissioned c. 1424 by Felice Brancacci, a rich Florentine silk merchant and statesman. The design of the whole cycle may be Masolino's, and he worked on the frescoes together with his pupil Masaccio. Masaccio seems to have assumed full responsibility for the frescoes after Masolino departed for Rome in 1428. Later that year Masaccio also left for Rome, where, by the end of the year he was dead, aged only 27. Brancacci was exiled from Florence in 1436 as an enemy of the Medici, and the cycle was only completed some 50 years later by Filippino Lippi (c. 1480–85), who carefully integrated his style. Masaccio's frescoes combine a perfect application of the new rules of perspective with a remarkable use of chiaroscuro. They were at once recognised as a masterpiece, and profoundly influenced the Florentine Renaissance. All the major artists of the 15th century came here to study them.

The altarpiece of the **Madonna del Carmine** is the earliest of the huge *Maestà* altarpieces painted for churches in the city (*see p. 282*), and one of the very few works of this date not removed to a museum. It was probably made c. 1270 for the high altar of the original church, but was already in this chapel by 1460. Once thought to be by Coppo di Marcovaldo, it is now attributed to the anonymous Master of Sant'Agata.

Upper row

Entrance arch: Masolino, *Temptation of Adam and Eve*.

Right wall: Masolino, *St Peter Brings Tabitha to Life* and *St Peter Heals a Lame Man*. The figures on the left and some background details may be by Masaccio.

Right of the altar: Masaccio, *St Peter Baptising*.

Left of the altar: Masolino, *St Peter Preaching*.

Left wall: Masaccio, *The Tribute Money*.

Entrance arch: Masaccio, *Expulsion of Adam and Eve*.

Lower row

Entrance arch: Filippino Lippi, *Release of St Peter from Prison*.

Right wall: Filippino Lippi, *Sts Peter and Paul Before the Proconsul* and *The Crucifixion of St Peter*.

Right of the altar: Masaccio, *St Peter and St John Distributing Alms*.

Left of the altar: Masaccio, *St Peter Healing the Sick with his Shadow*.

Left wall: Masaccio, *St Peter Enthroned*, his last work; the next half of this panel, *St Peter Bringing to Life the Emperor's Nephew*, was begun by Masaccio and finished by Filippino.

Entrance arch: Filippino Lippi, *St Peter in Prison Visited by St Paul*.

San Miniato al Monte
Map p. 271, 16. Open winter 8–12 & 2.30–6; summer 8–12 & 2–7.

San Miniato is the finest of all Tuscan Romanesque basilicas. Together with the Baptistery and San Lorenzo, it was the most important church in 11th-century Florence. It takes its name from the deacon Minias, a member of the early Christian community from the East, martyred c. 250 and buried on this hillside. The present church stands on the site of a shrine protecting his tomb. The lovely **façade**, begun c. 1090, is built of white and dark-greenish marble in a geometric design reminiscent of the Baptistery. Above the exquisite little window in the form of an aedicule is a 13th-century mosaic (remade in 1861) of *Christ between the Virgin and St Minias*.

The superb interior, built in 1018–63, survives practically in its original state. Its design, with a raised choir above a large hall crypt, is unique in Florentine church architecture. In the centre of the nave are seven marble intarsia panels (1207), designed like a carpet, with signs of the Zodiac and animal motifs. At the end of the nave is the **Cappella del Crocifisso**, an exquisite tabernacle commissioned by Piero il Gottoso from Michelozzo in 1448. It was made to house a venerated Crucifix; the painted panels of the doors of the cupboard which protected it are by Agnolo Gaddi (1394–96). The enamelled terracotta roof and ceiling are the work of Luca della Robbia.

In the north aisle is a fine painted **Crucifix**, thought to date from c. 1285, showing *Christ Triumphant*. It is one of the most important works of its time, though the identity of the artist remains unknown.

Built onto the north wall of the church is the **Chapel of the Cardinal of Portugal**, who died in Florence. It was begun in 1460 by Antonio Manetti, Brunelleschi's pupil (who also worked on the church of Santo Spirito), and was finished after his death in the same year, probably under the direction of Antonio Rossellino (the exquisitely carved tomb of the cardinal is Rossellino's; 1461–66). The ceiling has five medallions (1461) by Luca della Robbia. The altarpiece of *Three Saints* by Antonio and Piero Pollaiolo (1466–67) was replaced by a copy when the original was moved to the Uffizi. The frescoed decoration of this wall is also by the Pollaiolo.

The apse mosaic represents *Christ Between the Virgin and St Minias* (1297; restored). To the right of the apse is an altarpiece by Jacopo del Casentino showing *St Minias*, and scenes from his life. The sacristy (1387) lies to the south of the apse. It is covered with frescoes by Spinello Aretino; in the vault are the Evangelists and in the lunettes the *Life of St Benedict*, one of Spinello's best works (restored in 1840).

The 11th-century crypt beneath the choir has beautiful slender columns, many of them with antique capitals. The original 11th-century altar contains the relics of St Minias. The small vaults are decorated with frescoes by Taddeo Gaddi of saints and prophets against a blue ground.

PRACTICAL INFORMATION

GETTING AROUND

• **By air:** The nearest international airport is at Pisa, 85km west of Florence.

Train or bus to Santa Maria Novella station in Florence in c. 1hr. Florence airport at Peretola, a few kilometres north, has a shuttle bus (Volainbus) every

30mins to Santa Maria Novella in about 20mins. Tickets can be bought on board. Taxis are also usually available.

• **By car:** The centre of Florence is closed to cars (except for residents and disabled drivers) for most of the day (and also usually at night around holidays and in summer). The limited traffic zone (ZTL) includes virtually all the area within the Viali and the Oltrarno and is electronically controlled. Access is allowed to hotels, but cars can only stay for 1hr (and must display a card from the hotel).

There are underground car parks beneath Piazza Stazione (*map p. 268, 6*) and the Parterre (north of Piazza della Libertà; *beyond map p. 271, 3–4*), and also under the Mercato Centrale (San Lorenzo; *map p. 268, 1*) and Sant'Ambrogio (*map p. 271, 12*). There is a large car park along the inside of the walls between Porta Romana and Piazza Tasso (entered from Piazza della Calza (*map p. 270, 13*). You can also park on the street outside the restricted zone, but only where there are blue lines (hourly tariff, pay and display). White lines indicate resident parking.

• **By bus:** Buses tend to be crowded and it is usually easier to walk, especially as the centre is so small. The town bus service (ATAF; www. ataf.net) has an information office under the bus shelter on the east (right) side of the Stazione Santa Maria Novella (*map p. 268, 1*) open daily 6.30am–8pm.

• **By taxi:** There are taxi ranks in the main *piazze*. Otherwise, T: 055 4242; 055 4390; 055 4499; 055 4798. A supplement is charged for night service and luggage.

VISITOR INFORMATION

Tourist office: Main tourist office at Via Cavour 1 (*map p. 268, 4*), T: 055 290 832 or 055 290 833, www.firenzeturismo.it
Museum tickets: There is an excellent telephone booking service for state museums (*T: 055 294 883; Mon–Fri 8.30–6.30, Sat 8.30–12.30*) which, for a small extra charge, allows you to avoid the queue (you collect and pay for the ticket at the museum just before the allotted time). Also free entry to these museums for EU citizens under 18 and over 65.
Street numbers: Numbers of private houses are written in blue or black, and those of shops in red; the same number often occurs twice in the same street.

HOTELS

€€€€ **Helvetia & Bristol**. Elegant but small enough to have an intimate feel. Beautifully furnished, with superbly appointed rooms and marble bathrooms. The small restaurant serves good snacks and full meals. *Via dei Pescioni 2, T: 055 26651, www.thecharminghotels.it. 67 rooms. Map p. 268, 5.*
€€€€ **J K Place**. Stylish boutique hotel on Piazza Santa Maria Novella, discreet yet friendly behind double wooden doors. The bedrooms could be a little larger, but they are beautifully furnished. *Piazza Santa Maria Novella 7, T: 055 264 5181, www.jkplace.com. 20 rooms. Map p. 268, 3.*
€€€ **Palazzo Magnani Feroni**. A sumptuous 16th-century *palazzo* offering suite-only accommodation. The deluxe suites on the upper floors are well worth the additional expense for their size and extra light. Drinks and dinner are served

on a wonderful roof-top terrace. *Borgo San Frediano 5, T: 055 239 9544, www.palazzomagnaniferoni.com. 12 suites. Map p. 270, 10.*

€€€–€€ **Loggiato dei Serviti**. In a lovely palace with vaulted rooms in the most beautiful square in Florence, converted with great taste into a small hotel. The simple furnishings and stone floors make it cool and pleasant, and the rooms have lovely city views. *Piazza Santissima Annunziata 3, T: 055 289592, www.loggiatodeiservitihotel.it. 38 rooms. Map p. 271, 7.*

€€ **Annalena**. Opened as a *pensione* in 1919 in an old convent. An attractive building with high ceilings and old-fashioned furnishings. Rooms are quiet, some on a long terrace overlooking a garden. *Via Romana 34, T: 055 222402, www.hotelannalena.it. 20 rooms. Map p. 270, 14.*

€€ **Berchielli**. Art Nouveau-style hotel in the town centre. Most of the rooms overlook the attractive Piazza del Limbo or interior courtyards: those on the Arno have the better views but are noisier. Breakfast is served outside in summer. No large groups. *Lungarno Acciaiuoli 14 and Piazza del Limbo, T: 055 264061, www.berchielli.it. 76 rooms. Map p. 268, 7.*

€€ **Hotel Davanzati**. A highly regarded, family-owned hotel. The bedrooms are spacious and comfortable, and a particularly good breakfast is served. Excellent central location. *Via Porta Rossa 5, T: 055 286666, www.hoteldavanzati.it. 21 rooms. Map p. 268, 6.*

€€ **Johanna and Johlea Residenze**. Elegant B&B accommodation in three converted *palazzi* in the city centre. The staff are discreet and each residence is very quiet. All make an excellent choice. *Antica Dimora Firenze, Via San Gallo 72, T: 055 462 7296; Antica Dimora Johlea, Via San Gallo 80, T: 055 463 3292; Residenza Johlea, Via San Gallo 76, T: 055 463 3292, www.johanna.it, www.anticadimorafirenze.it. Map p. 271, 3*

€€ **Porta Rossa**. Historic hotel retaining its Art Nouveau decoration. Spacious and old-fashioned, most of the rooms (not all with bathrooms) have high ceilings and are well furnished. No groups. Charming character. *Via Porta Rossa 19, T: 055 287551, www.hotelportarossa.com. 78 rooms. Map p. 268, 5.*

€€ **Residenza il Villino**. Friendly, family-run establishment. Bedrooms are immaculate with simple, wood furnishings and tiled floors, some with balconies, and there is a lovely courtyard where breakfast is served in warm weather. No lift. *Via della Pergola 53, T: 055 200 1116, www.ilvillino.it. 9 rooms. Map p. 271, 8.*

€€–€ **Beacci Tornabuoni**. Old-established hotel on Florence's smartest street. On the top floor of two adjoining palaces, it has an old-fashioned atmosphere, and a lovely roof terrace where breakfast and dinner are served. Some of the rooms are very spacious. Particularly friendly, courteous service. *Via de' Tornabuoni 3, T: 055 212645, www.hoteltornabuoni.it. 28 rooms. Map p. 268, 5.*

€ **Bretagna**. In a very fine position in the centre of Florence, it has a charming, old-fashioned living room and dining room overlooking the Arno, with echoes of E.M. Forster. The very simple rooms vary a great deal: some are more spacious than others; some are family rooms; not all have bathrooms. Only one room overlooks the Arno, but all the others are quiet. Takes small groups. *Lungarno Corsini 6, T: 055 289618, www.bretagna.it. 18 rooms. Map p. 268, 5.*

€ **Residence Michelangiolo**. Art Nouveau-style villa about 20mins walk from the centre in a peaceful part of the city. The family rooms with adjoining door are spacious with a tiny but useful kitchen (concealed behind a cupboard door), while the garden rooms are lovely in summer. *Viale Michelangiolo 21, T: 055 681 1748. 11 rooms. Map p. 271, 16.*

RESTAURANTS

€€€ **Cavallino**. A long-established and reliable restaurant in Piazza della Signoria, with tables outside. Its splendid setting is without equal. Closed Wed. *Piazza della Signoria 28, T: 055 215818. Map p. 268, 6.*

€€€ **Enoteca Pinchiorri**. One of the most famous restaurants in Italy, which opened in 1974 and has managed to retain its reputation for luxury and elegance, with an exceptional selection of wines, and creative cuisine. On the ground floor of a palace, it can seat about 80 people in two comfortable rooms, one with a balcony, and, in good weather, there are tables in the interior courtyard and in a loggia off it. Closed Sun and Mon. *Via Ghibellina 87, T: 055 242777. Map p. 271, 12.*

€€€ **Harry's Bar**. Elegant cocktail bar renowned for impeccable service and a formal, old-fashioned atmosphere. The cocktails are superb, but the food sometimes disappoints. A few tables are put out in the summer on the Lungarno. Closed Sun. *Lungarno Vespucci 22, T: 055 239 6700. Map p. 270, 5.*

€€€ **Taverna del Bronzino**. One of

the finest restaurants in Florence. Elegant and comfortable with impeccable service and creative cuisine: one of the best places for fish. Closed Sun. *Via delle Ruote 25–27, T: 055 495220. Map p. 271, 3.*

€€ **Borgo Antico**. A typical Florentine trattoria in one of the most attractive squares in Florence. It has tables outside in summer and is also a pizzeria. *Piazza Santo Spirito 6, T: 055 210437. Map p. 268, 7.*

€ **Da Nerbone**. A good cheap place to eat inside the busy central food market, where the stall-holders eat as well as locals. Closed Sun. *Inside the Mercato di San Lorenzo, T: 055 219949. Map p. 268, 1.*

€ **Sabatino**. One of the most typical cheap places to eat in Florence, run by an extremely friendly family and frequented by Florentines who live nearby and go there most days for lunch. Well worth a visit. Closed Sat and Sun. *Via Pisana 2, T: 055 225955. Map p. 270, 5.*

LOCAL SPECIALITIES

The **Mercato Nuovo** (*map p. 268, 6*) has been the site of a market since the beginning of the 11th century. The loggia was erected by Cosimo I in 1547–51 when it was used principally for the sale of silk and gold. It is still a busy market-place, and usually good value for leather goods and scarves. It is known to Florentines as 'Il Porcellino' (the piglet), after the statue of a seated wild boar, a bronze copied by Pietro Tacca c. 1612 from an antique statue (based on a Hellenistic original in the Uffizi). Coins thrown into the fountain are collected and given to charity. Another very popular street market (*closed Mon in Jan and Feb*) is that around the church and indoor produce **market of San Lorenzo** (*map p. 268, 1*). Here the stalls also sell leather goods, scarves, clothes, hats, and numerous trinkets for tourists. The **market at Sant'Ambrogio** (*map p. 271, 12*) is, instead, mostly frequented by Florentines, but here bargains can also often be found.

The shops on Ponte Vecchio and its immediate vicinity have superb displays of **jewellery**. Artisans who repair jewellery (or make it to order) have their workshops in the Casa dell'Orafo close by.

Trippai sell **tripe**, a Florentine speciality, in sandwiches from barrows on street corners. Good *trippai* include those in Via dell'Ariento (*map p. 268, 1*), Piazza de' Cimatori (Via Dante Alighieri; *map p. 268, 6*), Via dei Macci (corner of Borgo la Croce, *map p. 271, 8*) and Mercato Nuovo (*map p. 268, 6*).

For fine **marbled paper** the best known shop is Giulio Giannini, Piazza dei Pitti 37 (*map p. 270, 10*). A less well-known shop, which has excellent hand-made products made on the spot by a family of artisans (also to order) is Lo Scrittoio, Via Nazionale 126 (*map p. 271, 3*).

Vinai are traditional **wine bars** selling wine by the glass and good simple food. There are far fewer than there once were, but those that survive are well worth seeking out. The *vinaio* at Via Alfani 70 (*map p. 268, 2*), and the one in Via della Chiesa (corner of Via delle Caldaie; *map p. 270, 10*) both have seating; others are no more than 'holes in the wall'.

Procacci (Via Tornabuoni 64; *map p. 268, 5*) is famous for its truffle sandwiches.

FESTIVALS & EVENTS

Celebrations in honour of Anna Maria Luisa de' Medici, who left the Medici art treasures to the people of Florence in 1737: free entry to all state and municipal museums, 18 Feb;

Festa dell'Annunziata, Fair in Piazza SS. Annunziata, 25 March;

Scoppio del Carro, The most famous traditional religious festival in Florence, held in and around the Duomo at 11am. A wooden carriage covered with fireworks is drawn by oxen to the main door of the Duomo. Inside, a 'dove' (a rocket) is lit at the high altar and sent along a wire to ignite the fireworks. The dramatic explosion lasts several minutes, Easter Day;

Maggio Musicale, Music festival at the Teatro Comunale (Corso Italia 16; *map p. 270, 5*), May; Concerts by members of the Maggio Musicale orchestra in the courtyard of Palazzo Pitti and in the Boboli Gardens (*Info, T: 055 290838*), May–July;

St John's Day celebrations in honour of St John the Baptist, patron saint of Florence, with fireworks at Piazzale Michelangelo (*map p. 271, 16*) at 10pm, 24 June;

Calcio Storico Fiorentino, 'Football' game in 16th-century costume, usually in Piazza Santa Croce, late June;

Festa della Rificolona, Celebrated on the eve of the birth of the Virgin by children carrying paper lanterns through the streets (especially in Piazza SS. Annunziata), 7 Sept;

Fierucola del Pane, Organic produce market in Piazza SS. Annunziata, 8 Dec.

THE MUGELLO, PRATO & PISTOIA

The low hills which surround Florence offer beautiful unspoilt countryside, spectacular views of the city, and a number of lovely old walled roads, best explored on foot.

Fiesole and Settignano

Just below Fiesole (*map p. 265, D3*) is **San Domenico di Fiesole**, where the church (*open 8.30–12 & 4.30–6*) preserves a *Madonna Enthroned* by Fra' Angelico. The artist first entered the Dominican Order in the adjoining convent. From here the Via Vecchia Fiesolana, with a wonderful view of Florence, continues to the little hilltop town of **Fiesole**. Once a chief city of the Etruscan Confederation, it preserves sections of its Etruscan walls. Under the Romans it became the most important town in Etruria. Its theatre (1st century BC; *open 9.30–7; 9.30–5 in winter; closed Tues in winter*) is well preserved and still used for concerts and plays in summer. The Museo Bandini houses a collection of 13th–15th-century Florentine paintings. The cathedral has some very fine 15th-century works by the local sculptor Mino da Fiesole. At the top of the hill, on the site of the Etruscan and later Roman acropolis, are the convent buildings of San Francesco. The lanes near the village are particularly beautiful, and the wooded hillside has always been a fashionable residential district with lovely villas and gardens.

Settignano (*map p. 265, D3*) is a particularly peaceful little settlement close to Florence, where the lovely gardens of the **Villa Gamberaia** (laid out in 1717) can be visited (*open 9–6; 9–7 in summer; ring the bell for admittance*). The gardens have seen many changes over the centuries as owners and tastes have changed. Edith Wharton, visiting around 1900, commended their 'great effect on a small scale'. They spread to each side of the house as well as behind it, linked together by a long grassy walk, once the bowling alley. The villa may have begun life as a simple farm house, but subsequent owners built on or rebuilt. One owner, Andrea di Cosimo Lapi, brought water to the site and added fountains, statues and cypresses. Mid-18th-century records show the stone animals and urns which are on the terrace in front of the villa today. The vegetation is predominantly cypress; a cypress exedra clipped into blind arches encloses the far end of the parterre, outside which is a bay hedge with one arch open to the wonderful view.

The huge **Certosa del Galluzzo** (*open 9–11.30 & 3–5.30; 4.30 in winter; closed Mon*) retains its peaceful atmosphere and has very moving frescoes by Pontormo.

Villa La Petraia and Villa di Castello

Many of the Medici villas in the environs of Florence can be visited. Some of them, designed by Michelozzo and Buontalenti, were used by the family to entertain artists and poets and as summer retreats from the heat of Florence. **Villa La Petraia** (*map p. 265, D2; open 9–dusk; closes 1hr before dusk second and third Mon of the month*) and the Villa di Castello both have very fine gardens and are close together in the northern suburbs. The garden of **Villa di Castello** (*open 9–dusk; closed second and third Mon of the month*) in particular preserves its 16th-century appearance, and in fact became the prototype for all Italian gardens. The original conception was first elaborated by Tribolo, who later worked on the Boboli Gardens (*see p. 289*), commissioned by Duke Cosimo I in 1537–38, and completed after his death by Bernardo Buontalenti and sculptors including Bartolomeo Ammannati. The placing of significant features on an axis was an important departure from the medieval tradition of separate spaces—this is regarded as the first Renaissance garden to have a unified overall plan. Sculptures which were not part of fountains were commissioned for a garden for the first time, based on an allegorical scheme recognisable to people with a Renaissance education (although sadly little remains *in situ*, and the dense planting which gave them their setting has gone).

At the top of the slope water was brought from Villa La Petraia further up the hill to form a lake. It then descended through a lemon tree garden (the villa is still famous for its 100 or more varieties of citrus trees). In the lake is a bronze figure by Ammannati of a crouching, shivering old man. Sometimes called *January*, he represents the Apennine mountains. Built into the retaining wall of this garden terrace is a grotto full of life-size animals, including a unicorn (symbol of purity) made of coloured marbles above marble basins decorated with marine life, dating from c. 1568–80. The water flowed on through fountains with statues representing the rivers Arno and Mugnone, in reference to Cosimo's feat of bringing water not only to the site but to Florence (he built two aqueducts). Cosimo eventually retired here and devoted himself to growing jasmine.

Poggio a Caiano

Poggio a Caiano (*map p. 265, D3; open Nov–Feb 8.15–5; March, Oct 8.15–6; April, May, Sept 8.15–7; July, Aug 8.15–8; T: 055 877012*) is the most important of the Medici villas near Florence. It was rebuilt for Lorenzo the Magnificent in 1480 by Giuliano da Sangallo, and became his favourite country residence. The *salone* was designed by Lorenzo's son Giovanni (Pope Leo X) in 1513–21, with frescoes begun by Franciabigio, Andrea del Sarto and Pontormo (his is the remarkable lunette illustrating the story of Vertumnus and Pomona). It was in this villa that Francesco I and his second wife, his beautiful former mistress Bianca Cappello, died, allegedly the victims of arsenic poisoning. Forensic studies of Francesco's remains have since shown the rumour to be almost certainly untrue. A delightful museum of still-life paintings on the top floor includes a splendid series by Bartolomeo Bimbi, one of whose patrons was Cosimo III.

THE MUGELLO

The Mugello extends either side of the Sieve river. Its distinctive landscape of wooded hills rising above a cultivated valley seems far removed from Florence and its environs. Numerous churches and villas are dotted around the hills. The small towns of Borgo San Lorenzo, San Piero a Sieve and Scarperia contain interesting buildings, and Vespignano is famous as the birthplace of Giotto.

The Sieve Valley

The charming little convent of **Bosco ai Frati** (*map p. 265, D2*), in attractive wooded country, is shown to visitors by one of the friars. Founded before 1000, it was taken over by the Franciscans in 1212. When staying here in 1273, St Bonaventure was appointed Cardinal by Gregory X. The story is told that the saint was busy washing dishes in the scullery so he told the messenger to hang his cardinal's hat on a tree in the orchard. The convent was purchased by Cosimo il Vecchio in 1420 and he employed Michelozzo to restore it (and add the fine porch behind the church). Off the cloister a little museum contains a remarkable Crucifix, attributed to Donatello.

In the 1450s Cosimo commissioned Michelozzo to build two delightful fortified villas as country residences, and these can also be seen nearby. The **Castello di Trebbio** (*map p. 265, D2; privately owned, garden and ground floor sometimes shown by appointment; T: 055 845 6230*) is in a lovely elevated position, surrounded by a pretty little hamlet and a cypress wood. It has a pretty Italianate garden with a long pergola. The **Villa di Cafaggiolo** (*map p. 265, D2; open summer Wed–Fri 2.30–6.30, Sat 10–12 & 2.30–6.30, Sun 10–12.30 & 2.30–6.30; winter Sat and Sun only; T: 055 847 9293*) is really a huge battlemented castle, once surrounded by a moat. Cosimo's grandsons Lorenzo and Giuliano spent their childhoods at Cafaggiolo, which was sufficiently distant from Florence to be safe from plague.

San Piero a Sieve (*map p. 265, D2*) lies beneath a large fortress designed in the 16th century for the Medici by Bernardo Buontalenti, to guard Florence from the north. It is one of the most interesting examples of Renaissance military architecture left in Tuscany, and is to be restored and eventually opened to the public.

Borgo San Lorenzo (*map p. 265, E2*) is the main town of the region, with a pleasant old centre. The famous Chini ceramic factories, founded by Galileo and Chino Chini, were active here from 1906–44, producing very fine ceramic decoration and stained glass, much of it still to be found in churches and tabernacles of the town, and in the museum dedicated to their work in the Villa Pecori Giraldi, at the eastern edge of the old centre (*open Tues 10–1; Fri, Sat 3–6; Sun and holidays 10–1 & 3–6; T: 055 845 7197*). The large Pieve di San Lorenzo contains a *Madonna*, a ruined fragment of a *Maestà*, almost certainly a very early work by Giotto, thought to date from 1290–95.

Further down the valley is **Vicchio**, the birthplace of the painter Fra' Angelico. The museum dedicated to him (*open Sun 10–12 & 3–6; T: 055 844 8251*) has works of art from churches in the region, including a beautiful painting of the *Madonna and Child* by the Master of the Strauss Madonna. The hamlet of **Vespignano** (*map p. 265, E2*) was the birthplace of Giotto. The house where he is thought to have been born functions as a small museum (*open Sun 10–12 & 3–6; T: 055 843 9224*).

Rufina (*map p. 265, E2*) is well-known for its Chianti wines, and a museum in a 16th-century villa here illustrates the history of winemaking.

Scarperia and the Alto Mugello

Scarperia (*map p. 265, E2*) was founded by Florence in 1306, to protect her territories from invading armies from across the Apennines. The town preserves its interesting rectangular plan, laid out on either side of the main road which connected Florence to Bologna (now Via Roma). In 1415 it became the seat of a vicariate of the Florentine Republic, with jurisdiction over the whole of the Mugello. The splendid Palazzo dei Vicari (built in 1306, perhaps on a design by Arnolfo di Cambio), has a tall tower and numerous coats of arms all over its façade, some in enamelled terracotta by the della Robbia family. It now houses a museum of knife-making, which was a flourishing industry here from the 15th–early 20th centuries. The parish church contains a beautiful marble tondo of the *Madonna and Child* by Benedetto da Maiano.

Sant'Agata, a short way northwest of Scarperia, has a very old *pieve*, documented since 984. The interior is remarkable for its unusual columns on huge square bases which rise directly to the wooden roof beams. The baptismal font is enclosed by Romanesque marble intarsia panels (1165). In the oratory next door is a little museum of sacred art including a fine painting by Bicci di Lorenzo.

Firenzuola (*map p. 265, E1*), another colony founded by the Florentines in the 14th century, has a gateway at either end of its arcaded main street. The town was laid out on symmetrical lines within rectangular bastions, designed by Antonio da Sangallo the Elder. It was very badly damaged in the Second World War when in the autumn of 1944 the strongest German defences in the 'Gothic Line' (which stretched across the ridge of the Apennines between Versilia and Rimini) were established on the Passo della Futa (903m), one of the main Apennine passes (there is a British Military Cemetery at Moraduccio on the Emilian border). In the castle is a museum illustrating the traditional methods of quarrying *pietra serena*, found in the rock formations along the river valley just to the north. This fine-grained dark grey sandstone is particularly easy to carve, and although generally not sufficiently resistant for the exterior of buildings, it was used to decorate many Renaissance interiors in Florence.

SOUTH OF FLORENCE

The motorway south from Florence passes on the right the landscaped **U.S. Military Cemetery**, which has the graves of 4,403 American soldiers who died in service north of Rome in 1944–45. **San Casciano in Val di Pesa** (*map p. 265, D3*) is a small hill town which dominates a beautiful hilly landscape with extensive views all around. Its little museum contains 14th-century Madonnas by Lippo di Benivieni and Ambrogio Lorenzetti (one of the artist's earliest works, dated 1319), and the 'San Michele altarpiece', a rare 13th-century Florentine work, attributed to Coppo di Marcovaldo. The church of the Misericordia contains a painted Crucifix with the mourning Virgin and St John by Simone Martini (c. 1325).

Near Talente is **San Giovanni in Sugana** (*map p. 265, D3*), one of the oldest and most important Romanesque churches in the diocese of Florence. It was considerably restored and provided with a cupola and cloister in the 16th century. To the north of San Casciano, in woods, is the hamlet of **Sant'Andrea in Percussina** (*map p. 265, D3*), where Niccolò Machiavelli lived in exile from Florence in 1513 and wrote *The Prince*.

At **Impruneta** (*map p. 265, D3*), the clay has been used for centuries to produce terracotta for which the locality is famous. The kilns here still sell beautiful pottery. The Collegiata was severely damaged in the last war but preserves some lovely enamelled terracotta decorations by Luca della Robbia and his nephew Andrea.

The della Robbia family

The art of enamelled terracotta was invented in the 1440s by Luca della Robbia. The secret of the chemical composition he used for the enamelling (a lead glaze with the addition of oxides) was handed down through three generations of his family, and then lost. Tuscany is full of these colourful luminous works, usually blue and white, used in the decoration of buildings and for altarpieces and numerous half-length Madonna reliefs, which became popular for private devotion.

Luca started life as a marble sculptor (his earliest work and masterpiece is the cantoria now in the Museo dell'Opera del Duomo in Florence; *see p. 276*). He is generally recognised as one of the most important early Renaissance sculptors, and was clearly influenced by Classical art. His best enamelled terracotta works can be seen in Florence (in the Bargello Museum, the Duomo, and Pazzi Chapel), Pistoia (the *Visitation* in the church of San Giovanni Fuorcivitas), and here at Impruneta.

His nephew Andrea worked with him, and then went on to produce his own beautiful works at La Verna, the Spedale degli Innocenti in Florence, and in numerous churches in Tuscany. Of his five children, the most skilful was Giovanni, who made use of more colours. There was a revival of interest, particularly in England, in della Robbian works in the late 18th century, and they were imitated with some success in the 19th century.

PRATO

Prato (*map p. 265, D2*) was famous by the 13th century for the manufacture of wool, and its textile factories continue to flourish as the centre of the rag-trade in Europe. Now an industrial centre, its population is expanding faster than almost any other town in central Italy. It is surrounded by extensive suburbs and busy roads, but its peaceful historic centre preserves some beautiful monuments, all within its medieval walls.

The duomo and Museo dell'Opera

The duomo (*open Mon–Sat 7–12.30 & 3.30–7; Sun 7–12.30 & 3.30–8*) is a Romanesque building (1385–1457) with a beautiful exterior and a façade partly striped in green and white marble. The lunette above the main portal is by Andrea della Robbia. The external **Pulpit of the Sacred Girdle**, designed by Donatello and Michelozzo (1434–38), has a frieze of dancing putti by Donatello (replaced by casts). It was built for the public display of the Sacred Girdle, traditionally considered to be the sash which the Madonna gave to St Thomas at her Assumption. The relic came to Prato in 1141.

In the interior, the nave is supported by massive shiny green marble columns with good capitals, and the deep arcades are decorated with green and white striped marble. The pulpit is by Mino da Fiesole and Antonio Rossellino. The **Chapel of the Sacred Girdle**, under the first arch of the north aisle, was built in 1385–90 to house the greatly revered relic. It has a splendid bronze screen begun in 1438 by Maso di Bartolomeo.

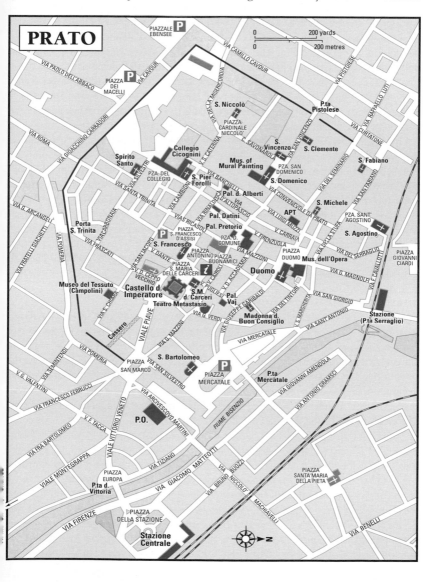

On the altar is a statuette of the *Madonna and Child*, one of the best works of Giovanni Pisano. The chapel is entirely frescoed by Agnolo Gaddi and his *bottega* (1392–95) with scenes from the life of the Virgin and the story of the Girdle.

The choir is decorated with **frescoes by Filippo Lippi** (helped by Fra' Diamante), one of the most beautiful fresco cycles of the early Renaissance (1452–66). On the right wall are scenes from the life of St John the Baptist (the Salome in the *Banquet of Herod* is supposed to be a portrait of Lucrezia Buti, the nun who was first Lippi's model and then his wife). On the left wall are scenes from the life of St Stephen. Filippo Lippi also designed the upper part of the beautiful stained-glass window. The **Cappella dell'Assunta** (first chapel right of the choir) is decorated with frescoes of the lives of the Virgin and St Stephen, begun in 1435 by Paolo Uccello, who painted the upper scenes (the vault, two lunettes with the *Birth of the Virgin*, *Birth of St Stephen*, and *Stoning of St Stephen*). When he left the following year to paint the monument to Hawkwood in the Duomo in Florence, the lower scenes were frescoed by Andrea di Giusto.

The **Museo dell'Opera del Duomo** (*open 9.30–12.30 & 3–6.30; Sun and holidays 9.30–12.30; closed Tues*) houses the seven original relief panels of dancing putti by Donatello and his *bottega* from the Pulpit of the Sacred Girdle. Dating from 1434–38, they have been irreparably damaged by exposure to the elements and by poor restorations. It is now thought that probably only the central panel is by Donatello's own hand, and possibly the panel to the left of that and the first one on the right. The gilded mosaic background was added after the crowd of chubby putti had been carved, in imitation of his more famous reliefs of putti made for the cantoria of the Florence Duomo at about the same time. The reliquary for the Sacred Girdle, an exquisite work by Maso di Bartolomeo (1446), is also preserved here.

South from Piazza del Comune

In the heart of the old centre is Piazza del Comune, with the splendid medieval **Palazzo Pretorio** (*closed for restoration*). The pretty fountain is by Pietro Tacca. To the east of here, in its own wide square (reached by Via Cairoli), is the church of **Santa Maria delle Carceri**, a masterpiece of the early Renaissance and one of the most important works by Giuliano da Sangallo, begun in 1485. The Greek-cross plan is derived from the architectural principles of Alberti and Brunelleschi. It was built on the site of a prison wall (hence 'Carceri'), on which a painted image of the Virgin was thought to work miracles. The green and white marble exterior recalls the Romanesque buildings of Florence. In the domed interior, *pietra serena* is used to emphasise the structural elements. The beautiful enamelled terracotta frieze and *tondi* of the Evangelists are by Andrea della Robbia. The stoup, with a bronze statuette of St John the Baptist, is by Francesco da Sangallo, son of the architect. The stained-glass windows date from the 15th century.

The impressive **Castello dell'Imperatore**, adjacent to the church, is an unusual sight for central Italy, being typical of the austere Hohenstaufen castles of the South: it was begun by the son of Emperor Frederick II to protect the route south from Germany, but left unfinished at the death of the Emperor in 1252. A fortified corridor built in 1351 to connect the castle to the city walls, with a walkway on its summit, can also be visited.

San Domenico

In the convent of San Domenico is the **Museum of Mural Painting** (*open 10–6; Sun and holidays 10–1; closed Tues*), with detached frescoes from buildings in the town and surrounding area. It also houses the most precious works from the Museo Civico (*closed since 1998*), including a predella by Bernardo Daddi illustrating the story of the Sacred Girdle; detached frescoes by Paolo Uccello; and works by Filippo Lippi.

PISTOIA

Pistoia (*map p. 264, C2*) is a lively old Tuscan town with an unusual number of beautiful churches, whose character reflects its position between Florence and Pisa, and many of which contain good sculptures. It is an important horticultural centre, and there are extensive nurseries on the surrounding plain. As an ironworking town in medieval times, it gave its name to the pistol (originally a dagger, afterwards a small firearm).

The duomo and baptistery

The duomo (*open daily 8.30–12.30 & 3.30–7; chapel 10–12 & 4–5.45*) has an arcaded Pisan Romanesque façade. The porch was added in 1311, and the high arch in the barrel vault is beautifully decorated by Andrea della Robbia, as is the lunette above the central door. The separate campanile (originally a watch-tower) can be climbed, and on a clear day there is a splendid view as far as the Duomo of Florence.

A cathedral in Pistoia is documented as early as the 5th century. The present church, dedicated to the Lombard saint Zeno, and erected c. 1220, was drastically altered at the end of the 16th century, but in 1966 it was restored as far as possible to its Romanesque form, and the fine wooden ceiling, decorated in 1388, was exposed. The Benedictine bishop Atho (canonised after his death in 1153) brought the relics of the apostle St James the Greater from Santiago de Compostela to Pistoia in 1144, and St James was declared patron saint of the city. Atho is buried in the cathedral, and his monument on the west wall has reliefs showing him receiving the relics. In a chapel in the south aisle is displayed the famous **Altar of St James**, a masterpiece of medieval goldsmiths' work. It was commissioned in 1287, and remodelled and added to during successive generations (up to 1456). The panel on the left flank, with stories from the life of St James, includes two half-figures of prophets by Brunelleschi (who may also have executed the standing figure of *St Augustine*, and the seated figure of an *Evangelist* in 1400).

The font is on a design by Benedetto da Maiano. The beautiful tomb of Cino da Pistoia (1337) is in the south aisle. Cino (Guittone Sinibaldi) was a jurist and poet, greatly admired by his friend Dante. Close to the tomb is a beautiful painted Crucifix by Coppo di Marcovaldo (and his son Salerno, 1275).

In the **Chapel of the Sacrament** is the *Madonna di Piazza with Sts John the Baptist and Zeno*, an extremely beautiful painting commissioned from Verrocchio c. 1476, but probably painted by Lorenzo di Credi. Opposite is a half-length bust of Archbishop Donato de' Medici, variously attributed to Antonio Rossellino or Verrocchio. Verrocchio

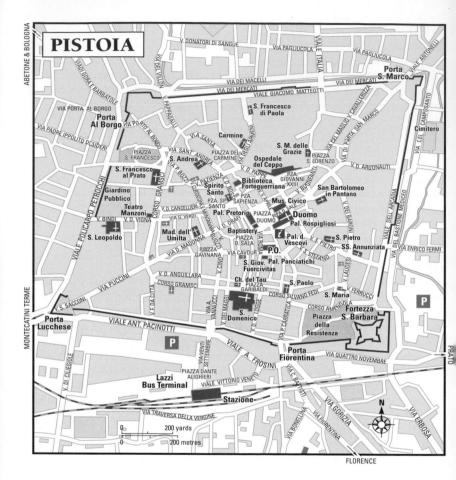

also designed the tomb of Cardinal Niccolò Forteguerri in the north aisle, with Christ in glory surrounded by angels and statues of *Faith* and *Hope*.

The beautiful octagonal **baptistery** is entirely decorated on the outside by bands of green and white marble. It was started in 1337 by Cellino di Nese, probably on a design by Andrea Pisano, and finished in 1359. The capitals and reliefs above the main entrance and the *Madonna* (attributed to Tommaso and Nino Pisano) in the tympanum are particularly fine. On the right is a tiny Gothic pulpit of 1399. In the bare brick interior is a font with fine intarsia panels made in 1226.

Piazza del Duomo and San Bartolomeo

Palazzo dei Vescovi, founded at the end of the 11th century, contains an archaeological display of finds from excavations beneath the building, dating from the Roman era and later, and the excellent cathedral museum (*open Mon, Wed, Fri 10–1 & 3.30–5*), which preserves the exquisite reliquary of St James, made in 1407 by Lorenzo Ghiberti and his *bottega*. The reliquary of St Zeno dates from 1369, and was made by a local goldsmith while in Aix-en-Provence. In a room upstairs are detached tempera murals by Giovanni Boldini (1868), with scenes of pastoral life and of the sea at Castiglioncello on the Tuscan coast. The young Boldini was influenced by the Macchiaioli painters (*see p. 288*), who spent much time at Castiglioncello, painting the beauties of its landscape.

Palazzo del Comune, a Gothic building of 1294, houses the **Museo Civico** (*open 10–7; Sun and holidays 9–12.30; closed Mon*), with a representative display of Tuscan paintings, including a fine 13th-century panel of *St Francis*, with stories from his life, and a lovely 14th-century painting attributed to Lippo di Benivieni (c. 1320). There are also drawings and models of works by the architect Giovanni Michelucci (who collaborated on the design of Santa Maria Novella station in Florence), born in Pistoia.

San Bartolomeo in Pantano and the Ospedale del Ceppo

The church of **San Bartolomeo in Pantano** was attached to a famous Benedictine monastery, founded c. 761. The church has a fine façade with a relief (1167) of *Christ and the Apostles* (late 12th century), probably by Gruamonte. This sculptor, active in Pistoia in the last years of the 12th century, produced reliefs of hieratic beauty, still to be seen in the churches of Sant'Andrea and San Giovanni Fuorcivitas. The beautiful basilican interior of San Bartolomeo, with its large capitals, has a 13th-century Tuscan fresco of *Christ in Majesty* in the apse. The lovely pulpit of 1250 is by Guido da Bigarelli (Guido da Como). Still Romanesque in spirit, it has one of its columns resting on a crouching figure thought to represent the sculptor. The four bas-reliefs show scenes in the life of Christ, and at the corners, symbols of the Evangelists.

The portico of the **Ospedale del Ceppo**, a hospital founded in 1277, is decorated with a colourful enamelled terracotta frieze (1514–25), excellently carved and very well preserved. It depicts the *Seven Acts of Mercy* and the Cardinal and Theological Virtues, by Giovanni della Robbia. Beneath are medallions with the *Annunciation*, *Visitation* and *Assumption*, and the arms of the hospital, of the city, and of the Medici.

Sant'Andrea, Spirito Santo and the Madonna dell'Umiltà

The church of **Sant'Andrea** has a fine 12th-century façade with polychrome marble decoration by Gruamonte and his brother Adeodato, who signed the relief of the *Journey and Adoration of the Magi* (1166). In the long, narrow interior (similar to San Bartolomeo in Pantano), the hexagonal pulpit is signed by Giovanni Pisano (1298–1301), and is usually considered his masterpiece. Slim porphyry columns, held up by lions, eagles and a crouching figure, support Gothic arches with reliefs and statuettes of prophets and Sibyls. Above, five dramatic reliefs show the *Annunciation* and *Nativity*; *Adoration of the Magi* and St Joseph being warned to leave Bethlehem; *Massacre of the Innocents*; *Crucifixion*; *Last Judgement*. Between the scenes are prophets, symbols of the Evangelists and the angels of the Apocalypse. It is probable that Tino di Camaino also worked on the carving. Giovanni Pisano also made the wooden Crucifix in the south aisle.

The church of the **Spirito Santo**, on Via Rossi further south, was founded by the Jesuits in 1647. It preserves a good Baroque interior. Cardinal Giulio Rospigliosi, on becoming Pope Clement IX in 1667, commissioned Bernini to design the high altar and Pietro da Cortona to paint the high altarpiece of the *Apparition of Christ to St Ignatius*.

The octagonal, centrally-planned sanctuary of the **Madonna dell'Umiltà**, built in 1495 by a pupil of Bramante, has a dome added by Vasari in 1562, a conspicuous feature of the city. The church of **San Francesco**, begun in 1289, has interesting 14th-century frescoes, including the *Allegory of the Triumph of St Augustine*, by the Sienese school.

San Domenico and the south

The church of **San Domenico**, built c. 1280, probably to the design of Fra' Sisto and Fra' Ristoro (architects of the Dominican church of Santa Maria Novella in Florence, and possibly also of Santa Maria sopra Minerva in Rome), is particularly interesting for its sculptured funerary monuments. In the sacristy are some beautiful detached frescoes. Benozzo Gozzoli died in the convent here in 1497 during the plague.

The church of **San Giovanni Fuorcivitas** has a handsome exterior and a portal with a relief of the *Last Supper* by Gruamonte (1162). The beautiful pulpit is by Fra' Guglielmo da Pisa, a follower of Nicola Pisano (1270), and the exquisite stoup in the middle of the church, with the *Theological and Cardinal Virtues*, is by Giovanni Pisano. The moving *Visitation* group in white glazed terracotta is by Luca della Robbia (c. 1445).

EMPOLI & VINCI

The pleasant little town of **Empoli** (*map p. 264, C3*) is famous for its glass manufacture, including the characteristic wine flask (protected by straw) which was first produced here in large quantities at the beginning of the 20th century. The Collegiata di Sant'Andrea, documented as early as 780 but begun in its present form in 1093, has a handsome black-and-white marble façade recalling that of San Miniato al Monte in Florence. Its museum (*open Tues–Sun 9–12 & 4–7*) of works from local churches includes a superb fresco of *Christ in Pietà* by Masolino; a polychrome wood statue of St Stephen (1403) by Francesco di Valdambrino; a *Madonna of Humility* (1404) by Lorenzo Monaco; a tabernacle (c. 1475) with lovely paintings of two angels by Francesco Botticini; and a beautiful statue of *St Sebastian* by Antonio Rossellino. The 14th-century church of Santo Stefano degli Agostiniani is important for its remains of frescoes and *sinopie* by Masolino, including a lunette of the *Madonna and Child with Two Angels*. It also has two beautiful statues of the *Annunciation* by Bernardo Rossellino (c. 1447).

East of Empoli is **Montelupo Fiorentino** (*map p. 265, D3*), an important centre of ceramic production in the 15th and early 16th centuries. In the Palazzo Pretorio is a museum with a chronological display, from the earliest 13th-century potteries, which produced green and brown ware mostly with geometric designs. By the late 14th century cobalt blue was also widely used. In the late 16th century the so-called 'harlequin' style was introduced, on a yellow ochre ground. In the church of San Giovanni Evangelista there is a *Madonna Enthroned with Saints*, by Botticelli and his workshop.

On the southwest slope of Monte Albano, in beautiful countryside, is the little village of **Vinci** (*map p. 264, C3*), where Leonardo was born in 1452. The restored 13th-century castle of the Guidi family houses a museum (*open daily 9.30–6*) containing numerous models based on his drawings, including a submarine, an underwater diving suit, a parachute, flying machine and a tank. The church of Santa Croce preserves the font in which Leonardo was supposedly baptised. In the hamlet of **Anchiano** on the hill above to the north (also approached on foot by an old path, c. 2km), amidst magnificent olive groves, is the house traditionally taken to be Leonardo's birthplace. It was restored in 1952 as a humble memorial to him (*open Thur–Tues 9.30–1 & 2.30–5*).

PRACTICAL INFORMATION

GETTING AROUND

• **By car:** Historic centres are usually closed to traffic. In **Fiesole** there are free car parks near the Roman theatre (the most convenient is off the main road to Pian del Mugnone, about 50m beyond the Museo Bandini); pay parking is available in the centre and on Piazza Garibaldi. In **Prato** there are pay car parks at Piazza Mercatale, Piazza S. Maria delle Carceri and Piazza San Francesco, and free parking in Piazza Macelli. In **Pistoia** there are car parks at the ex-Officine Meccaniche Breda, off Via Panciotti, or east of Fortezza Santa Barbara, between Via del Bastione Mediceo and Via Cellini.

• **By train:** The best way to approach the **Mugello** is by the pretty branch line from Florence (Campo di Marte station) to Borgo San Lorenzo in c. 45mins. Another line from Borgo to Florence passes through Vicchio and Rufina. Trains on the Pisa line link Florence and **Empoli** in c. 20mins. **Prato** is served by regular trains from Florence, Lucca and Viareggio. **Pistoia** is on the Florence–Viareggio line: trains from Florence in 35–45mins.

• **By bus:** A good network of local buses links Florence to most places in the environs. Lazzi (for **Empoli**): www.lazzi.it; SITA: www.sita-on-line.it; CAP (for **Prato** and **Pistoia**): www.capautolinee.it. ATAF bus no. 7 from Santa Maria Novella station and Piazza S. Marco in Florence goes to **Fiesole** via San Domenico in 30mins. Bus no. 37 from Piazza Santa Maria Novella goes to the **Certosa del Galluzzo** (request stop below the hill), also in 30mins. For the **Medici villas**: bus 14c from Via de' Martelli or Santa Maria Novella station (right side) to the Villa di Careggi (penultimate request stop). For Villa di Castello no. 28 from Santa Maria Novella station: the second 'Castello' request stop is for La Petraia; the last is for Villa di Castello. Buses from Florence to **Borgo San Lorenzo** take 1hr; from Borgo there are buses to Cafaggiolo.

INFORMATION OFFICES

Fiesole Via Portigiani 3, T: 055 598720.
Prato Via Cairoli 48, T: 0574 24112.
Pistoia Piazza Duomo, T: 0573 21622.
Vinci Via della Torre 11, T: 0571 568012.

HOTELS

Borgo San Lorenzo (*map p. 265, E2*)
€€ **Hotel Locanda degli Artisti**. Mid-19th-century *palazzo* in the centre of town, refurbished with both original and reproduction furnishings. *Piazza Romagnoli 2, T: 0558 455359, www.locandaartisti.it. 7 rooms.*

Empoli (*map p. 264, C3*)
€ **Tazza d'Oro**. Family-run central hotel, decorated in a clean, modern style. *Via Giuseppe del Papa 46, T: 0571 72129, www.hoteltazzadoro.it. 50 rooms.*

Fiesole (*map p. 265, D3*)
€€€€ **Villa San Michele**. One of the most famous hotels in Tuscany, a former monastery, now luxuriously appointed. In an incomparable position with extensive grounds. *Via Doccia 4, T: 055 567 8200, www.villasanmichele. orient-express.com. 46 rooms.*

€€ **Pensione Bencistà**. Charming villa on the hillside below Fiesole, set among olive groves, with sweeping views of the Arno valley. The high-ceilinged rooms are beautifully furnished with terracotta tiles and antique furniture. *Via Benedetto da Maiano 4, T: 055 59163, www.bencista.com. 44 rooms.*

€€ **Villa Aurora**. A former theatre, transformed into a hotel at the end of the 19th century. Rooms and suites are nicely furnished. Restaurant and bar. Glorious views. *Via Alamanni 5, T: 055 210 283, www.hotel-aurora-firenze.it. 12 rooms.*

Prato (*map p. 265, D2*)
€€ **Flora**. Friendly, family-owned hotel in a restored 19th-century palazzo. Rooms are cosy and comfortable. *Via Cairoli 31, T: 0574 33521, www.hotelflora.info. 31 rooms.*

€€ **Hotel Le Fontanelle**. South of the centre, below the *autostrada*, a 19th-century farm converted into a comfortable hotel. Garden, pool and restaurant. *Via Traversa del Crocifisso 7, T: 0574 730373, www.lefontanellehotel.it. 10 rooms.*

€€ **Giardino**. Family-owned hotel centrally located. The rooms have recently been redecorated; one is a loft conversion. Parking. *Via Magnolfi 2/4/6, T: 0574 26189, www.giardinohotel.com. 28 rooms.*

€ **San Marco**. On the edge of the walled town. Recently refurbished and comfortable. *Piazza San Marco 48, T: 0574 21321, www.hotelsanmarcoprato.com. 40 rooms.*

Pistoia (*map p. 264, C2*)
€€ **Il Convento**. Beautifully restored Franciscan monastery, nestling in the hills overlooking the city. Charmingly decorated in country-house style, with lovely views of the countryside. Restaurant. *Via San Quirico 33, T: 0573 452651, www.ilconventohotel.it. 32 rooms.*

€€ **Leon Bianco**. Centraly located, recently refurbished and comfortable. *Via Panciatichi 2, T: 0573 26675, www.hotelleonbianco.it. 30 rooms.*

€ **Firenze**. Nicely furnished, central hotel, a good choice in this price range. *Via Curtatone e Montanara 42, T: 0573 23141, www.hotel-firenze.it. 20 rooms.*

Settignano (*map p. 265, D3*)
€€€€ **Villa Gamberaia**. An exceptional place to stay; luxurious apartments in the grounds of the famous villa (*see p. 318*). Outstanding views of the Arno valley. *Via del Rossellino 72, T: 055 697205, www.villagamberaia.com. 4 apartments.*

RESTAURANTS

Pistoia (*map p. 264, C2*)
€€ **La Bottegaia**. Relaxed restaurant, close to the duomo. The choice of cheese and desserts is difficult to beat. Excellent wine list. *Via del Lastrone 17, T: 0573 365602.*
€€ **Corradossi**. Well-established restaurant, popular at lunchtime. In the evening it takes on a more formal tone. *Via Frosini 112, T: 0573 25683.*
€ **Trattoria dell'Abbondanza**. Unpretentious restaurant serving good regional cuisine. The *pappardelle sull'anatra* (pasta with duck), a dish which dates back to the Etruscans, is particularly good. Closed Wed and Thur lunch; most of May, and first two weeks Oct. *Via dell'Abbondanza 10–14, T: 0573 368037.*
Prato (*map p. 265, D2*)
€€€ **Baghino.** This is something of a Prato institution, good for Tuscan favourites and wines to complement the cooking. The *ravioli alla senese* (spinach sauce with pecorino cheese) is a favourite. *Via dell'Accademia 9, T: 0574 27920.*
€€€ **Il Borbottino**. Excellent seasonal food, sourced locally. Popular both at lunchtime, where the atmosphere is relaxed, and in the evenings, when it becomes more formal. *Via Fra' Bartolomeo 13, T: 0574 23810.*
€€€ **La Fontana**. Simple, scrumptious food in the hills overlooking Prato. *Località Filettole (follow Via Machiavelli), T: 0574 27282.*
€€€ **Il Piraña**. The 'Piranha', as its names suggests, serves fish with a bit of a bite; what the Michelin guide particularly recommends are the shrimps with valerian, pears and pecorino. It was recipes like this that earned it its Michelin rosette. *Via Valentini 110, T: 0574 25746. Closed Aug, Sat midday and Sun.*
€€ **Il Capriolo**. Popular place with good pizza and pasta. Booking essential on Sat. *Via Roma 306, T: 0574 633650.*
Sant'Andrea in Percussina (*map p. 265, D3*)
€ **Albergaccio di Machiavelli**. Once frequented by Machiavelli, this smart restaurant serves good Tuscan cuisine. Wines from the restaurant's own cellar. Closed Sun dinner, Mon and Tues. *Via della Scopeti 64, T: 055 828 471.*
Vicchio (*map p. 265, E2*)
€ **Casa del Prosciutto**. Excellent, popular, simple restaurant. You can also buy food here to eat outside in summer, on tables along the river. *Via Ponte a Vicchio 1, T: 055 844031.*

LOCAL SPECLIALITIES

Pistoia Pastry shops sell traditional hand-made *confetti* and *brigidini*, sweet-tasting wafers flavoured with anise. A good place to try them is Caffè Valiani, in the former oratory of Sant'Antonio Abate (del Tau).
Prato Prato is famous for its almond biscuits. A good source is Antonio Mattei, Via Ricasoli 20–22.

FESTIVALS & EVENTS

Pistoia *Giostra dell'Orso*, Medieval jousting tournament, 25 July (at 9.30pm).
Prato Presentation of the Sacred Girdle, Easter Sun, 1 May, 15 Aug, 8 Sept, 25 Dec.

LUCCA & VERSILIA

Lucca (pop. 80,000; *map p. 264, B2*) is one of the most beautiful small towns in Italy. It is surrounded by magnificently preserved 16th–17th-century ramparts: the broad avenues which surmount them, planted with trees, provide a spectacular walk of over 4km around the entire town. It is especially rich in Romanesque churches, with beautiful sculptural decoration on their façades, and the tradition of excellence in carving found its culmination in the work of Matteo Civitali, born in the town in 1435. Lucca conserves much of its Roman street plan, with most of its streets still paved or cobbled. Many of its palaces have walled gardens, and numerous handsome old shop-fronts survive. The inhabitants mostly use bicycles to get around, which means that the old city is especially peaceful. It has lots of good cake shops and pleasant restaurants.

HISTORY OF LUCCA

Stone implements discovered in the plain of Lucca show that it was inhabited some 50,000 years ago. The Roman colony of *Luca* was the scene in 56 BC of the meeting of Caesar, Pompey and Crassus which led to their political alliance two years later, known as the First Triumvirate. In 552 the Goths were besieged here by the Byzantine general Narses, who two years later, after their defeat, was appointed prefect of Italy by Justinian. In the Middle Ages Lucca was an important city under the Lombard marquesses of Tuscany, but thereafter was constantly at war with Pisa and Florence. Under the rule of Castruccio Castracani (1316–28), Lucca achieved supremacy in western Tuscany, but Castracani's death was followed by a period of subjection to Pisa (1343–69). Later in the century the Holy Roman Emperor Charles IV gave the Lucchesi a charter of independence, and it maintained its freedom, often under the suzerainty of noble families, until 1799. In 1805 Napoleon presented the city as a principality to his sister Elisa Bacciocchi, and in 1815, after Napoleon's exile, it was given to Maria Louisa of Bourbon as a duchy. The city was the birthplace of the great musician Giacomo Puccini (1858–1924).

San Michele in Foro

The delightful Piazza San Michele, on the site of the Roman forum, is still the centre of city life. The raised pavement and low columns, linked with chains resting on the ground, date from 1705. San Michele in Foro was mentioned as early as 795, but the present church was largely constructed in the 11th and 12th centuries, though work continued until the 14th century. The beautiful exterior has blind arcading and a loggia above, and carefully incorporates the rectangular campanile in its design.

LUCCA: SAN MICHELE IN FORO

The façade is a wonderful example of the richly decorated Pisan Romanesque style which developed in Lucca: the lower part, dressed in grey and white stone has geometric decoration with the central doorway surmounted by a tiny rose window, a classical architrave and an intricately carved panel with symbolic beasts. Above are four tiers of arcading remarkable for the variety of the little columns, some of them carved, some inlaid, and others in coloured marble, and all with elaborate capitals. Between each tier there is a frieze of grey and white marble inlay decorated with all kinds of animals. On the tympanum at the top is a huge statue of *St Michael*. The façade was often sketched by Ruskin. Puccini was a chorister here.

In the interior (*closed 12–3*) the marble columns have Corinthian capitals and the old grey-and-white pavement survives. In the apse hangs a very well-preserved Crucifix, with the mourning Madonna and St John and scenes in the terminals, painted for the church in the late 12th century by a local master. At the beginning of the south aisle is a beautiful statue of the *Madonna*, made for the façade by Matteo Civitali, and a white enamelled terracotta relief of the *Madonna and Child* attributed to Luca della Robbia. The most beautiful painting in the church is in the south transept: *Sts Helen, Jerome, Sebastian and Roch* by Filippino Lippi.

Piazza San Martino and the duomo

The attractive Piazza San Martino and the adjoining Piazza Antelminelli have two 16th-century palaces with walled gardens, and a circular fountain which dates from 1835. The cathedral of San Martino was consecrated in 1070 by Pope Alexander II, who had begun the rebuilding while bishop of Lucca. The very fine asymmetrical façade, with the right arch smaller to accommodate the splendid tall campanile with its Ghibelline battlements, is decorated with delightful sculptures in the Pisan Romanesque style peculiar to Lucca. Dating from 1204, it carries the signature of Guidetto (Guido) da Como, whose family name was Bigarelli and who worked elsewhere in Tuscany, including Pisa and Pistoia. Above the three wide arches are three tiers of arcades with beautifully designed little columns, all with different decorations (similar to those on the façade of San Michele). The statue of *St Martin* is a copy of the original, now inside the cathedral.

The beautiful sculptural decoration of the portico was begun in 1233, its exquisite details made out of pink, green and white marble. Above the central door is the *Ascension*, with the Virgin flanked by the Apostles below. Bas-reliefs depict the story of St Martin and the months of the year. Over the left doorway is a relief of the *Deposition*, and under it a very crowded *Annunciation*, *Nativity* and *Adoration of the Magi*, thought to be early works by Nicola Pisano. Over the right doorway is the *Meeting of St Martin with the Arians*. Martin's disputes against Arian heresy are one of the leitmotifs of his legend. In the lunette is the *Beheading of St Regulus*, an early bishop of Populonia executed by the Goths. The stone labyrinth inserted in the right pier of the portico, and symbolising the narrow, winding path to righteousness, dates from the 12th century.

The interior: nave and south side

The tall dark interior (*open March–Oct 9.30–5.45; otherwise 9.30–4.45*) was rebuilt in the 14th–15th century in a Gothic style, with a delicate clerestory. On the entrance wall is the moving sculpture, dating from the 13th or possibly the early 14th century, removed from the façade, of **St Martin sharing his cloak with the beggar** (the legend relates that he was converted to Christianity when he later had a vision of Christ as the same mendicant).

In his *Italian Hours*, Henry James recalled his visit to Lucca when '…*in the Cathedral [I] paid my respects at every turn to the greatest of Lucchesi, Matteo Civitale, wisest, sanest, homeliest, kindest of quattro-cento sculptors, to whose works the Duomo serves almost as a museum*'. **Works by Matteo Civitali**, dating from the late 15th century, include the beautiful inlaid pavement as well as the two stoups and the pulpit. His also are the two Renaissance tombs in the south transept: that of Pietro da Noceto, an exquisite work infused with the spirit of Humanism, and that of the papal secretary to Sixtus IV, Domenico Bertini, who commissioned the monument in 1479 before he became

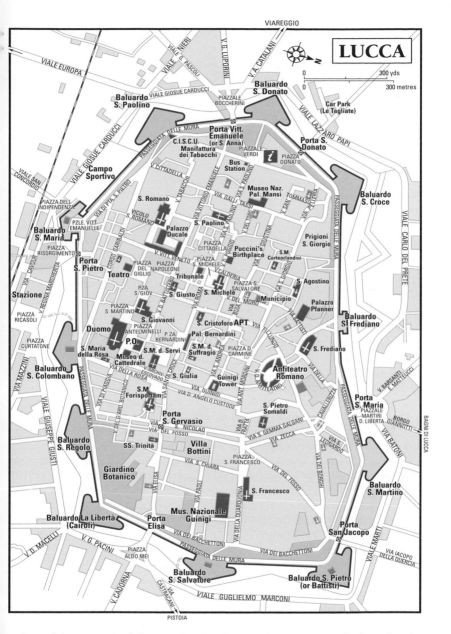

podestà of the city in the following decade. The two charming angels flanking the tabernacle in the chapel of the Holy Sacrament, and the altar of St Regulus (1484), right

of the sanctuary, are also by the hand of Civitali. The modern bronze high altar was installed in 1987, and part of the marble screen, by the school of Civitali moved to the side chapels, despite local protest. The stained glass in the apse and the choir stalls all dates from the late 15th century; on the high altar is a 14th-century Sienese trip-tych.

North side

In the north transept is an altar dating from 1579, with figures of the *Risen Christ* and *St Peter* and *St Paul* by Giambologna (the marble predella has a view of the skyline of Lucca). The very fine painting of the *Virgin and Child Enthroned with Saints* in the Cappella del Santuario is signed and dated 1509 by Fra' Bartolomeo; its composition had an important influence on the Lucchese school of painters. Matteo Civitali designed the charming octagonal gilded marble *tempietto* in the north aisle (and made the statue of St Sebastian for it), which was built to house the famous **Volto Santo** (the Holy Countenance), a cedarwood effigy of the crucified Christ, shown robed, supposed to have been begun by Nicodemus and miraculously completed. According to tradition, it was brought to Lucca in 782. It was greatly revered for centuries (and many copies made of it); the favourite oath of the English king William Rufus is said to have been 'Per Vultum de Lucca'. The effigy is usually assigned stylistically to the 13th century, proba-bly a copy of an 11th-century work (in its turn perhaps modelled on a Syrian image of the 8th century). Its air of mystery and sanctity is enhanced by the fact that it can only be seen by worshippers through a grating.

Sacristy

In the sacristy (*combined entrance ticket with the Museo della Cattedrale and SS. Giovanni e Reparata*) is the celebrated **tomb of Ilaria del Carretto Guinigi**. The serene effigy is the masterpiece of Jacopo della Quercia, and one of the most original works of the very early Renaissance in Italy (1407; it seems to be derived in part from French Gothic tomb sculpture). The sarcophagus may be the work of Francesco di Valdambrino. Ilaria (d. 1405) was the second wife of Paolo Guinigi (1376–1432), ruler of the city from 1400–30, who built Villa Guinigi (*see p. 340*). The tomb was sadly moved here in 1995 from the north transept where it had been placed in 1842, and it has not yet been decid-ed where it will be definitively installed.

The very fine painting of the *Madonna and Saints*, with a good predella, was painted for the church in 1479 by Domenico Ghirlandaio; the lunette of the *Dead Christ in the Arms of Nicodemus* is attributed to Filippino Lippi.

The cathedral museum

In the Museo della Cattedrale (*open daily 10–2; summer 10–6*) are preserved the elab-orate goldsmiths' work made to decorate the *Volto Santo*, including a frieze of 1382–84, a 17th-century crown, a huge jewel made in France in 1660, and a sceptre of 1852. Exquisite small treasures include a tiny wood pyx dating from 1174, a pre-cious Limoges reliquary coffer showing the martyrdom of St Thomas Becket, an ivory diptych carved in Constantinople in 506, and an elaborate Crucifix almost certainly commissioned by Paolo Guinigi in 1411. There are also works by the skilled silversmith Francesco Marti, who was at work in Lucca in the late 15th century, including a beautiful reliquary and a crozier. The sculpture displayed on the top floor includes a colossal statue of St John the Evangelist by Jacopo della Quercia, two statuettes of prophets by Francesco di Valdambrino, and two female heads from c. 1480.

Santi Giovanni e Reparata to Palazzo Ducale

The church of **Santi Giovanni e Reparata** (*open 10–5; Sat and Sun only in winter*) was built in 1160–87: the fine portal was preserved when the façade was erected in 1589. The interior has Roman columns with Romanesque capitals, and a 9th-century crypt. The baptistery has a remarkable roof from 1393. The 12th-century font is above a square 9th-century predecessor, which partially covers an even earlier one. Excavations below the church show five building levels, including a Roman house of the 1st century BC, traces of later Roman baths, and the remains of the huge geometric mosaic pavement of the first church on this site (4th–5th century), which was the cathedral of Lucca until 715. Its nave is occupied by conspicuous round kilns used during the construction of the present church.

Further west in Piazza del Giglio (also called Piazza Puccini) is the Neoclassical façade of the **Teatro del Giglio**, built in 1817 by the local architect Giovanni Lazzarini. It was one of the most important opera houses in Italy in the early 19th century, and here in 1831 was given the first performance of Rossini's *William Tell* (with Niccolò Paganini playing in the orchestra).

Piazza Napoleone, the largest square in Lucca, was laid out in 1806 in front of the Napoleonic residence, and planted with plane trees. The statue of Maria Louisa of Bourbon is by Lorenzo Bartolini—not one of the most successful statues by Tuscany's most famous 19th-century sculptor.

The huge **Palazzo Ducale**, with a courtyard designed by Bartolomeo Ammannati in 1578, was enlarged by Filippo Juvarra in 1728. The palace stands on the site of a much bigger castle (which occupied almost a fifth of the town) built for Castruccio Castracani, who as ruler of Lucca from 1316–28 lorded it over the whole of western Tuscany. However, after the Pisans seized power and occupied the castle, most of it was demolished by the angry populace in 1369. It then served as the seat of the Lords of Lucca, who ruled the city up until 1799. In 1805, when Napoleon presented the city as a principality to his sister Elisa Bacciocchi, she came to live here, and ten years later Maria Louisa of Bourbon took up residence in the palace when she became Duchess of Lucca. It is now the seat of the province.

San Paolino

The church of San Paolino, where Puccini used to play the organ, is dedicated to an obscure saint, Paulinus, who is said to have been sent from Antioch by St Peter as Lucca's first bishop, and who was martyred here together with a priest, a deacon and a soldier. If this tradition is correct, then Lucca must have been the first place in

Tuscany to have embraced the Christian religion. The church was designed in the early 16th century by Baccio da Montelupo, with a severe bright white façade, and dark grey columns and pilasters in the interior which carry an architrave all around the church. Small stained-glass windows provide the only colour. On the south side there is a 15th-century polychrome wooden statue of *St Ansanus*, by Francesco di Valdambrino; the wooden statues of the *Angel Gabriel* and *St Paulinus* in niches on either side of the presbytery date from the previous century. On the north side the very rare stone statuette of the *Madonna and Child*, dating from the end of the 13th century, was brought here from Paris in the Middle Ages by merchants of the city.

In a chapel in the south transept is the *Burial of St Paulinus and his Companions*, a very unusual painting attributed to Angelo Puccinelli, one of the most important artists at work in the city in the late 14th century. All four martyrs are laid out in a row side by side, while four saints attend to their burial. In the chapel to the left of the presbytery is another unusual painting (by Baldassare di Biagio, a collaborator of Matteo Civitali) of the *Coronation of the Virgin*, in the presence of St Paulinus and a crowd of onlookers. It is interesting especially for the view of Lucca beneath. Dating from around 1460, this is one of the earliest known representations of the city.

Museo Nazionale

The entrance to the Museo Nazionale di Palazzo Mansi is in Via Galli Tassi (*open 9–7; Sun and holidays 9–1; closed Mon*). The *piano nobile* of the 17th-century palace has period rooms, some also decorated in the 18th and 19th centuries. The pinacoteca, arranged in just four rooms, is especially interesting for its Medici portraits (in Room II) including a superb portrait of a boy (once thought to be Alessandro de' Medici) by Pontormo. His contemporary Bronzino painted Cosimo I in armour (one of several versions of this well-known portrait), Ferdinando de' Medici as a boy, and Don Garzia de' Medici as a child. There are also portraits by the court painter Suttermans. Important 17th-century paintings (many with good frames) include the *Triumph of David*, one of the best works of Rutilio Manetti. There are also works by Pompeo Batoni (1708–87), who was born in Lucca but who painted most of his fashionable portraits in Rome (many of his sitters were young men on the Grand Tour).

San Frediano and Palazzo Pfanner

The church of San Frediano, rebuilt in 1112–47, has a conspicuous tall campanile, with Ghibelline crenellations, restored in 1853. The upper part of the façade is occupied by a large gold-ground mosaic representing the *Ascension* (with the Apostles below) dating from the 13th century, and possibly the work of Berlinghiero Berlinghieri (also restored in the 19th century). In the splendid basilican interior the columns of the nave have handsome Classical capitals. The huge font (probably dating from the mid-12th century) is in the form of a covered fountain. The lower basin is sculpted with reliefs of the story of Moses, and with seven standing figures including the *Good Shepherd*, while the oddly-shaped cover, supported on small columns, has more carvings including representations of the Months. The huge marble monolith propped up against the left wall of the presbytery probably came from the Roman amphitheatre (*see overleaf*), but its 'sacred' significance is unclear. The greatest treasures are in the **north aisle**. The great Sienese sculptor Jacopo della Quercia was commissioned in 1412–22 by the Trenta family to carve the altarpiece and the two pavement tombs in a chapel here, a few years after his much more famous funerary monument of Ilaria del Carretto in the duomo. Opposite is a beautiful polychrome wooden statue of the *Virgin Annunciate* by Matteo Civitali. Another chapel in this aisle was entirely frescoed in 1508 by the eccentric artist Amico Aspertini: these frescoes are usually considered his best works in this medium. With interesting local details and Classical ruins in the landscapes, the scenes on the left wall show the *Volto Santo* arriving in Lucca, and St Ambrose baptising St Augustine (with a *Deposition* in the lunette above). On the right wall St Frediano is seen directing operations to divert the River Serchio on a new course to avoid future floods, next to a Nativity scene. In the lunette above, St Augustine is shown giving the rules of his new Order. The vault is decorated with *God the Father*, surrounded by prophets, angels and Sibyls, and there are strange monochrome scenes on the entrance arch. Aspertini also painted the two framed detached frescoes beneath the organ of the *Madonna and Child with Saints* and the *Visitation*.

Palazzo Pfanner, although privately owned, is open to visitors for much of the year (*generally March–Oct 10–6 every day, some variation possible; T: 0583 954029*). Built in 1667, it has a galleried outside staircase, and a little 18th-century garden, with a charming fountain and fine statuary. The *piano nobile* has 17th-century frescoes and is partly furnished, and an old kitchen survives.

The miniature campanile of the 14th-century church of **Sant'Agostino** rests on some arches of the Roman theatre. The dome belongs to a little Baroque chapel built in 1620 to house a venerated fresco of the Madonna.

The Guinigi Tower and nearby churches

San Salvatore, a 12th-century church, has a charming architrave over its south portal, showing a miracle of St Nicholas: the saint as a baby stands up in the bath in which he is being washed by two women. On either side are observers in towers and domed buildings. On the bath is the signature of the sculptor Biduino (late 12th century). The right door has another carved architrave with another story from the life of St Nicholas, showing a royal banquet. In the piazza is a pretty fountain (1842) by the local architect Lorenzo Nottolini, who designed a number of fountains in the town, as well as the monumental aqueduct on the plain to the south, to bring water from Monte Pisano.

The 13th-century church of **San Cristoforo**, with a fine interior (*now used for exhibitions*), is the burial place of the sculptor Matteo Civitali.

The **Guinigi Tower** (*open daily 9–7.30; winter 10–4.30; staircase to the top*) is famous for the seven ilex trees growing on its summit. During the rule of Castruccio Castracani in the 14th century, the Guinigi were one of the richest families in Lucca, many of them involved in the silk trade. They lived in the two large brick Gothic palaces nearby, and took an active part in the city government up until the 19th century. The church of **San Pietro Somaldi** was founded in 763. The grey-and-white banded façade (*being restored at the time of writing*) dates from 1248, although the relief above the central door by Guido da Como and assistants is a little earlier (1203), probably carried out at the same time as the work on the duomo façade. In the interior is a beautiful and highly venerated little *Madonna and Child* by Sebastiano Conca (second north altar).

The arena of the **Roman amphitheatre** now forms a delightful piazza, created in 1830–39 by Lorenzo Nottolini. The medieval houses which follow the ellipse of Via dell' Anfiteatro incorporate some of the amphitheatre's brick arches and masonry.

Museo Nazionale Guinigi

The unusual brick Villa Guinigi, an austere castellated suburban villa built in 1418, houses the Museo Nazionale Guinigi (*open 9–7; Sun and holidays 9–2; closed Mon*). The earliest exhibits from the archaeological collection date from the Bronze Age, and there are Villanovan finds from near Lucca, as well as Etruscan and Roman material found in the centre of Lucca, and gold jewellery from a 7th-century Lombard tomb. Medieval sculpture from churches in Lucca include a transenna with a relief of Samson and the lion. On the upper floor are paintings and later sculpture, mostly by artists born in Lucca or who worked here. Highlights from the 14th century include a *Madonna and Child* and *St John the Evangelist* by 'Ugolino Lorenzetti'; a painted Crucifix (from San Cerbone) by a certain Paolo da Siena; and a *Mystical Marriage of St Catherine and Saints* by Angelo Puccinelli. From the 15th century there are sculptures in wood and marble (including a beautiful relief of the *Annunciation*, and an *Ecce Homo* by Matteo Civitali), and some good works by Fra' Bartolomeo. Sixteenth- and 17th-century painters represented include Daniele da Volterra, Vasari, Aurelio Lomi, Ludovico Cigoli, Federico Zuccari, Pietro da Cortona, Guido Reni and Rutilio Manetti.

Santa Maria Forisportam

Santa Maria Forisportam is a fine church with a marble façade in the 13th-century Pisan style. Above the left door is a beautiful architrave with a lion and a griffin and a cast of a 12th-century high relief of the *Madonna Enthroned*. The pleasant grey interior was altered in 1516 when the nave and transepts were raised. On the west wall, an early Christian sarcophagus has been adapted as a font. On the fourth south altar is a beautiful painting of *St Lucy* by Guercino, who also painted the altarpiece of the *Assumption* in the north transept. The handsome high altar was designed by Vincenzo Civitali (grandson of Matteo). In the sacristy is a *Dormition and Assumption of the Virgin* by Angelo Puccinelli (1386) and a *Madonna and Child* by Pompeo Batoni. There is a charming small museum in some adjoining rooms with sculpture (including a 13th-century wooden statuette of the *Madonna and Child*), ecclesiastical objects and Roman material.

The city walls

A walk around the top of the 16th–17th-century ramparts (4195m in circumference) completes a visit to Lucca and provides delightful views of the town and of the Apuan

Alps. The broad walk on their summit is entirely closed to traffic, and is used by residents as a magnificent public park. The bastions have been planted with trees since the 16th century, including avenues of planes and ilex groves. The earliest circle of walls of which traces have survived dates from the Roman period; new walls were built in 1198. The present fortifications, extremely well preserved, were carried out in 1544–1650.

The walls are 12m high and 30m wide at the base. The grassy fields outside them are on the site of the moat. Many of the eleven bastions still have their guardhouses, complicated defence works, and ammunition stores. The walls were never put to use, but must have served as an effective deterrent to Lucca's enemies. They were built on a system afterwards developed by Louis XIV's great engineer Vauban, and recall the ramparts of Verona. The interior of the Baluardo di San Paolino, with a small museum, can be visited. In medieval times there were only three gates. The florid **Porta San Pietro**, built in 1566, is still the most important entrance to the town, and it preserves its original doors and portcullis (the side gates were added in 1846). The handsome Porta San Donato (1639) replaced the old gate of the same name, built in the medieval walls in 1591, and which is conspicuous nearby in Piazzale Verdi. This area of the town, formerly called Prato del Marchese, was used from the 18th century onwards for football games, horse races and other public spectacles.

ENVIRONS OF LUCCA

The environs of Lucca (*map p. 264, B2*) are noted for their fine villas and gardens built between the 16th and 19th centuries, although only a few of them are at present open to the public. At **San Pancrazio**, north of Lucca, is the 16th-century Villa Oliva Buonvisi, an example of the architecture of Matteo Civitali (*park open 15 March–15 Nov daily 9.30–6.30*). The proportions of the building are particularly pleasing: a high, two-storey loggia supported on slender columns occupies most of the front, with a single bay on either side, and one further storey above. At **Segromigno** is the 17th-century Villa Mansi (*open 10–12.30 & 3-5; summer 9.30–1 & 3–7; closed Mon*). Part of the garden, altered by Juvarra in 1742, survives near the house, with a fish pond, the 'Baths of Diana', and fine statues. The English park was created in the 19th century. The villa has late 18th-century decorations. The parish church has a tabernacle by Baccio da Montelupo showing the dying Saviour emptying blood from his own side into the Eucharistic chalice, thus symbolising his sacrifice to redeem mankind. Fifteen years earlier, in 1496–1501, Matteo Civitali had produced a similar tabernacle for the church of Santi Cristoforo e Filippo at **Lammari**.

The Lower Serchio Valley

In the lower Serchio valley north of Lucca is the interesting Romanesque church of **San Giorgio di Brancoli**, in beautiful countryside, and the **Ponte della Maddalena**, a remarkable ancient footbridge over the river. **Bagni di Lucca** (*map p. 264, B2*) is a little spa with warm sulphur and saline waters, somewhat off the main valley. It was particularly fashionable as a residence of the nobility of Lucca and foreigners from the 17th–19th centuries. Its visitors included Shelley, Byron, Browning (who advised Tennyson to stay here in 1851) and Walter Savage Landor. When its casino opened in 1837 it was the first licensed gaming house in Europe. The old English Chemist still has the royal coat of arms, and in the public gardens is the neo-Gothic English Church, built in 1839.

Barga (*map p. 264, B2*) is the most important place in the valley. It has expanded at the foot of its hill (410m) leaving the little old village remarkably peaceful. The narrow Via di Mezzo winds up and down through the centre of the village to Piazza del Comune with a picturesque loggia (once a market-place). From the grassy terrace in front of the duomo there is a splendid view which takes in the snow-capped Apuan Alps and the Apennines. The Romanesque cathedral has a fine exterior built in the local white stone (*alberese*), and an embattled campanile. It dates in part from the 9th century, but was altered in later centuries. The side of the earliest church serves as the façade, which has an interesting main door. The north doorway has a carved architrave. In the dark interior is a sculpted 13th-century pulpit attributed to Guido da Como, and in the main apse is a huge imposing *St Christopher* in polychrome wood, made in the early 12th century.

In the main valley above Barga is **Castelvecchio Pascoli** (*map p. 264, B2*). Nearby, on the hill of Caprona, is the house where one of the best-known Italian poets, Giovanni Pascoli (1855–1912), lived from 1895 until his death. The house has remained as it was at that time, with its original furnishings carefully preserved by his sister Maria, who survived him by many years. It contains mementoes and some of the poet's manuscripts. Pascoli and his sister are buried in the chapel in the garden.

The Upper Serchio: the Garfagnana

The beautiful upper valley of the Serchio (*map p. 264, B1*), well wooded and richly cultivated, is known as the Garfagnana. Lying between the Apennines and the Apuan Alps, the scenery is spectacular in the side valleys and on the higher ground. In the centre of the valley is **Castelnuovo di Garfagnana**. Its duomo has a beautiful enamelled terracotta of *St Joseph and Angels* (attributed to Verrocchio, or the della Robbia). Castelnuovo is the starting point for excursions in the **Parco Regionale delle Alpi Apuane**, a protected area between the Serchio valley and Versilia, interesting for its spectacular mountain scenery. On both sides of the mountain chain are marble quarries. The fauna include wild boar, deer and mountain goats. The highest peak is Monte Pisanino (1946m). On the other side of the valley is the Parco dell'Orecchiella in the Apennines, with meadows in the green upland plains and extensive woods. A mountain road leads north from Castelnuovo to **San Pellegrino in Alpe**, with an interesting local ethnographical museum (*open daily June–Sept 9.30–1 & 2.30–7; Oct–March Tues–Sat 9–1, Sun 9–12 & 2–5; April–May Tues–Sat 9–12 & 2–5*). It occupies part of a 12th-century hospice which served travellers crossing the Apennines, and illustrates peasant life in the area.

VERSILIA & MASSA CARRARA

Versilia, in the province of Lucca, is the name given to the narrow coastal plain at the foot of the Apuan Alps, famous for its beaches which stretch north from the resort of Viareggio all the way to Forte dei Marmi. In summer the coast is crowded with holiday-makers, many of them from Florence. The little inland town of Seravezza is attractive and has some buildings of interest.

Viareggio

Viareggio (pop. 60,000; *map p. 264, A2*) is the main town of Versilia, and the most popular seaside resort on the west coast of Italy. It first became fashionable in the early 19th century, and it retains an old-fashioned air with its esplanade planted with palm trees, its Art Nouveau houses, and huge, grand old hotels and cafés. The town retains its regular plan from the early 19th century, when it was laid out by Lorenzo Nottolini on a chessboard pattern, with long avenues parallel to the seafront and numerous parks. After Pauline Bonaparte built her villa on the edge of the sea in 1820, it became one of the first seaside resorts in Europe. The Villa Paolina itself is open to the public (*Sat 4–7; in summer also for exhibitions*), and it houses a small archaeological collection, a gallery of 19th- and 20th-century paintings, and a collection of musical instruments. Numerous decorative buildings survive from the Art Nouveau and Art Deco periods, many with frescoes and graffiti as well as external ceramic decoration (much of it by Galileo Chini). A splendid double promenade, with a road and a footway, leads along the shore, and some old bathing establishments survive here. Beautiful pinewoods extend along the shore in either direction from the town, and there is a distant view of the Apuan Alps. The outer harbour is busy with boatyards and a 16th-century tower guards the inner basins, where there is a port. The old fishmarket near the *darsena* is now a museum dedicated to seafaring (*open Fri, Sat and Sun 4–7*).

The coast to Marina di Carrara

Resorts (extremely crowded in summer) stretch north for some 30km all the way along the coast to Marina di Carrara. They are laid out on regular plans with long, straight roads parallel to the shore, and consist of elegant villas and hotels surrounded by gardens, all with spectacular views inland to the Apuan Alps and white marble quarries. The most elegant of the resorts are Forte dei Marmi and Marina dei Ronchi, with numerous villas and small hotels set in thick vegetation. In Forte dei Marmi Aldous Huxley wrote *Crome Yellow* in 1921, and two years later, *Antic Hay*.

Torre del Lago Puccini, on the Lago di Massaciuccoli (*map p. 264, A2*), is named after the composer who made his bohemian home on the lake here, where he enjoyed shooting waterfowl. On the waterfront, surrounded by a garden, is the villa which Puccini built (*guided tours every half hour, 10–12.30 & 2.30/3–dusk; closed Mon*). All his operas except the last, *Turandot*, were, to a great extent, written here. The house preserves mementoes, and his tomb is in the chapel. A summer opera festival is held on the lakeside in an open-air theatre (being replaced at the time of writing by a larger one, which has been criticised for its intrusiveness). On the other side of the lake, which is prettier, is the village of **Massaciuccoli**, with Roman remains, and a bird sanctuary.

Inland is **Seravezza** (*map p. 264, A2*), attractively situated in a narrow ravine, with numerous quarries and marble works. The tree-lined streets are built along the Versilia river (its waters white from marble). Some way upstream is the handsome Palazzo Mediceo built for Cosimo I in 1555 by Ammannati, and which now has a museum illustrating local crafts, including the extraction and working of marble. The courtyard has a well, charmingly decorated with a fish. Michelangelo stayed in Seravezza in 1517, while looking for marble suitable for his sculptures.

THE PROVINCE OF MASSA-CARRARA

Massa

Massa (*map p. 264, A2*) is built at the foot of the narrow Frigido valley in the Apuan foothills. It quickly expanded after the Second World War, and now has a largely modern appearance. Founded in the Middle Ages, it was the capital of the duchy of Massa-Carrara from 1442–1790, ruled by the Malaspina. Their huge palace, with a delightful red façade by the native architect Alessandro Bergamini (1701), stands in the central Piazza degli Aranci, planted with orange and lemon trees in the early 19th century.

In the duomo is the funerary chapel of the Cybo Malaspina, with the tomb of Eleonora Malaspina (d. 1515), influenced by the famous monument to Ilaria del Carretto by Jacopo della Quercia in the duomo of Lucca (*see p. 334*). There are a number of late 17th-century works by Giovanni Francesco Bergamini, member of a large family of local artists at work in the city in the 17th–18th centuries. In the left transept is a highly venerated wood Crucifix dating from the early 13th century.

High above the oldest part of the town is its most interesting building, the Rocca or **Castello Malaspina**, first built in the 11th–12th centuries. It is a building of the highest architectural interest (*open summer every day except Mon 9.30–12.30 & 4.30–7.30; otherwise only Sat 9.30–12.30 and Sun 3–6.30*). The 16th–17th-century Renaissance rooms are shown on guided tours every hour, as well as the medieval and defensive portions.

Carrara

The pleasant, flourishing town (*map p. 264, A2*) became part of the duchy of the Malaspina family, with Massa, in 1442. The most interesting part of Carrara today is around the fine Romanesque duomo, altered in the 13th century when the attractive Gothic storey was added to its façade, and the portal in the handsome south wall decorated. The charming apse and campanile can be seen in the courtyard of the priest's house, from which there is also a good view of the marble quarries in the mountains. The well-proportioned interior, with huge capitals, has rough marble walls. Over the high altar is a beautiful painted 14th-century Cross by Angelo Puccinelli. The two charming 14th-century statues of the *Annunciation* show French influence. The pulpit, decorated with local coloured marbles, dates from 1541. The baptistery contains a large

16th-century hexagonal font for total immersion, crowned by an unusual cupola in polychrome marble. The fountain in the piazza outside, with a statue of Andrea Doria, was left unfinished by Baccio Bandinelli. Also in the square is a red house (plaque) which is believed to have sheltered Michelangelo on his visits to buy marble.

A long straight avenue connects Carrara with Marina di Carrara, a marble shipping port and resort. It passes a modern building which houses a museum illustrating marble quarrying and craftsmanship (*open 9–dusk except Sun and holidays*).

CARRARA MARBLE

Carrara has been known for its white marble since Roman times. It is still one of the main centres in the world for marble production, from its famous quarries in the Apuan Alps, which have been worked for over 2,000 years. They are well worth a visit (*for information, T: 0585 844136; visits by bus are arranged in summer*). They produce about one and a half million tons of white marble a year, and over 95 quarries are now in use. They are situated in three valleys: Colonnata, Fantiscritti and Ravaccione, all accessible by road (signposted from Carrara). The quarries of Fantiscritti are perhaps the most interesting, since they are approached past the Ponte di Vara, the old railway bridge, and there is a good museum (*open daily; mornings only in winter*) which illustrates the history of marble quarrying by means of instruments and tools and remarkable life-size sculptures in marble.

Up until the end of the 19th century, marble was extracted by hand. Wooden wedges were inserted along the natural fissures in the rock: these were kept wet so that they would swell and eventually the block of marble would fracture. Another method was to use a handsaw operated by two workers, with the help of water and sand, but they could only cut into the marble at a rate of about 5cm a day. A radical change occurred at the end of the 19th century when steel wire, several hundred metres long, was introduced. This, still with the help of sand and water, can cut into the marble at a rate of c. 10–20cm an hour. Diamond wire and diamond-point saws are now also widely used. However, the dangerous quarrying techniques which have been in use since the end of the 20th century, which pay little attention to the geological structure of the mountains, have been criticised, and fatal accidents caused by landslides occur far too often.

In the past, once the blocks were extracted, they used to be sent down the mountainside on a slide using ropes and wooden rollers, and then transported by wagons drawn by up to ten bullocks in pairs. A railway was constructed between 1876 and 1891 from the quarries to Marina di Carrara. This is no longer used, but the track which traverses tunnels and the high Ponte di Vara has been converted into a road which is now used by the lorries which transport the marble either to Marina di Carrara for shipping, or to one of the sawmills in and around the town, which cut the marble into slabs and polish it before exportation.

PRACTICAL INFORMATION

GETTING AROUND

• **By air: Lucca** is 18km from Pisa airport. Buses run every hour from the airport to Lucca (Piazzale Verdi) from 6.45am–9.15pm, and from 5.48am–8.10pm in the opposite direction. The journey takes 1hr. www.lazzi.it. The train terminal at **Pisa** airport has frequent direct trains to Pisa Central, with connections every 30mins to Lucca, and infrequent connections to Florence.
• **By car:** Parking is restricted inside the walls of **Lucca** to less than 90mins. The most convenient free carpark is Le Tagliate, outside Porta San Donato.
• **By train:** Trains link **Lucca** with Florence in 70–90mins and with Viareggio. A magnificent railway line along the valley goes to Bagni di Lucca, Barga and Castelnuovo di Garfagnana (in c. 1hr). **Massa** and **Carrara** are on the Pisa line.
• **By bus:** Buses run by CLAP (www.clapspa.it) run from Piazzale Verdi in **Lucca** to Bagni di Lucca, Barga and Castelnuovo. Lazzi (www.lazzi.it) operates services to **Florence** and **Bagni di Lucca**. Buses from **Viareggio** (Viale Carducci) go to Forte dei Marmi and Torre del Lago, and from Piazza d'Azeglio go to Pisa, Lucca and Florence. Buses from **Carrara** (Via del Cavatore) operated by CAT go to Marina di Carrara and the railway station every 10mins, as well as to Massa and to the Fantiscritti quarries.

INFORMATION OFFICES

Lucca Piazza Santa Maria 35, T: 0583 919931, www.luccaturismo.it

Bagni di Lucca Via Umberto 1, T: 0583 888881.
Carrara Viale XX Settembre, Località Stadio, T: 0585 844403.
Castelnuovo di Garfagnana Via Cavalieri di Vitt. Veneto, T: 0583 641007.
Viareggio Viale Carducci 10, T: 0584 962233.

HOTELS

Lucca (*map p. 264, B2*)
€€€ **Locanda l'Elisa**. Gracious hotel in an early 19th-century country villa, 3.5km from the centre (just off the SS12 for Pisa). Highly polished furniture, festooned curtains and gleaming marble set the tone. Tuscan food is served in the English-style conservatory. *SS12r 1952, Località Massa Pisana, T: 0583 379737, www.locandalelisa.it. 10 rooms.*
€€€ **Villa La Principessa**. The magnificent home of Castruccio Castracani, tyrant of Lucca in the late 13th century, now a country-house hotel set in beautiful gardens, with swimming pool and restaurant. Rooms are spacious, elegant and comfortable. On the SS12 for Pisa. *SS12r 1616, Località Massa Pisana, T: 0583 370037, www.hotelprincipessa.com. 41 rooms.*
€€ **Alla Corte degli Angeli**. Tiny, pink-washed hotel inside the walls, close to the amphitheatre. Bright, well-decorated rooms. *Via degli Angeli 23, T: 0583 4694, www.allacortedegliangeli.com. 7 rooms.*
€€ **La Luna**. Welcoming place in the historic part of town. Recently refurbished rooms, well-appointed and comfortable. Bar and cosy reading room. *Via Fillungo-Corte Compagni 12, T: 0583*

493634, www.hotellaluna.com. 29 rooms.
€ **Ai Cipressi**. Nice little B&B just outside the city walls to the east. Simply furnished rooms and apartments with good bathrooms, air conditioning and parking. Bicycles for hire. Via di Tiglio 126, T: 0583 496571, www.aicipressi.it. 3 rooms.
€ **Piccolo Hotel Puccini**. Welcoming, family-run hotel. Though small, the rooms are neat and clean. Superbly located close to San Michele in Foro. Via di Poggio 9, T: 0583 55421, www.hotelpuccini.com. 14 rooms.

Bagni di Lucca (map p. 264, B2)
€ **Bridge**. Pleasant, family-run hotel. Piazza Ponte a Serraglio, T: 0583 805324. www.bridge-hotel.it. 12 rooms.

Carrara (map p. 264, A2)
€ **Michelangelo**. Attractive, well-located hotel, crammed with antiques and beautiful furnishings. The founder was an antiques dealer and the family still owns a shop in the Corso. Corso Fratelli Rosselli 3, T: 0585 777161. 30 rooms.

Castelnuovo di Garfagnana (map p. 264, B1)
€ **Da Carlino**. Charming-looking, plant-clad building in the centre of town. Somewhat old fashioned furnishings. Friendly service. A popular restaurant is attached. Via Garibaldi 13, T: 0583 644 270. www.dacarlino.it. 32 rooms.

Marina di Carrara (map p. 264, A2)
€€ **L'Hotel Maestrale**. With a fabulous seafront setting and two acres of parkland behind, this modern hotel is ideal for relaxed sight-seeing. Olympic-sized swimming pool and tennis courts. Via Fabbricotti 2, T: 0585 785371, www.hotel-maestrale.ms.it. 60 rooms.

Viareggio (map p. 264, A2)
€€€ **Plaza e de Russie**. Fine old belle époque establishment overlooking the passeggiata, purpose-built as a hotel in 1871. The high ceilings, plain walls and restrained furnishings give a slightly old-world feel. Many rooms face inwards; specify if you want a sea view. Piazza d'Azeglio 1, T: 0584 44449, www.plazaederussie.com. 52 rooms.
€€ **Hotel President**. Seafront hotel dating from 1949, recently refurbished. The rooms with balconies overlooking the sea are exceptionally pleasant. Rooftop restaurant and bar, swimming pool. Viale Carducci 5, T: 0584 962712, www.hotelpresident.it. 50 rooms.
€ **Hotel Arcangelo**. If you want to escape from the crowds on the seafront, this converted town house just off the promenade is perfect. The rooms are simply furnished and there is a courtyard garden. Via Carrara 22, T: 0584 47123, www.hotelarcangelo.com. 19 rooms.
€ **Bahia**. A modest hotel, clean and comfortable. Close to the beach and the fine promenade, as well as the famous pinewoods. Restaurant and bar. Via Carducci 53, T: 0584 48403, www.hotel-bahia.it. 14 rooms.

RESTAURANTS

Lucca (map p. 264, B2)
€€€ **Antico Caffè della Mura**. On the city walls, delightful in summer. Choose between wood-grilled meats and fish from the markets at Viareggio. Piazzale Vittorio Emanuele 2, T: 0583 47962.
€€€ **Giglio**. Elegant restaurant, in the 18th-century Palazzo Arnolfini, opposite the theatre. Varied and interesting menu; char-grilled salt cod with chickpeas is a signature dish. Dine indoors or out. Closed Tues afternoon and Wed. Piazza del Giglio 2, T: 0583 494058.

€€ **Buca di Sant'Antonio**. This claims to be one of the oldest restaurants in Lucca, and was once a staging-post for horses on the road to Florence. Well-prepared, hearty rustic food sourced from the Garfagnana area. Closed Sun evening and Mon. *Via della Cervia 3, T: 0583 55881.*

€€ **Gli Orti di Via Elisa**. Within the city walls, the restaurant offers an interesting take on traditional dishes, as well as the standard pizza and pasta. Closed Wed and Thur lunch. *Via Elisa 17, T: 0583 491241.*

€€ **Trattoria da Leo**. Lively, welcoming restaurant, serving simple but wonderful Tuscan food. Typical dishes include *zuppa di farro*, a filling white bean and spelt soup, and *tortelli lucchese*, pasta parcels filled with spiced meat and covered in a rich meat and tomato sauce. Booking advised. *Via Tegrimi 1, T: 0583 492236.*

Carrara (*map p. 264, A2*)

€€€ **Ninan**. A local-born chef has earned himself a Michelin rosette with his simple, delicious seafood. Space is limited; booking advisable. Closed Sun. *Via Lorenzo Bartolini 3, T: 0585 74741.*

€€ **La Tavernetta da Franco**. The décor in this small restaurant in the centre of town is plain and simple, but it serves excellent food. Its specialities include game and fish. Closed Mon. *Piazza Alberica 10, T: 0585 777782.*

€ **Pizzeria Il Castellaro**. Large place with magnificent mountain views, and both traditional Tuscan and international food. They are especially proud of their seafood, which includes ravioli stuffed with fish. Closed Tues. *Via Monteverde 24b, T: 0585 858908.*

Colonnata (*map p. 264, A2*)

€€ **Locanda Apuana**. A little out of town but worth the journey for good traditional Tuscan food and wines in a lovely rustic setting. *Via Comunale 1, T: 0585 768017.*

Viareggio (*map p. 264, A2*)

€€€ **Da Romano**. Well-established place with a Michelin rosette. The menu is focused confidently on seafood. Closed Mon, most of Jan, and midday Tues in July and Aug. *Via Mazzini 122, T: 0584 31382.*

€€ **Tito del Molo**. At the southern end of the promenade, this fish restaurant (a former fisherman's hut, transformed in 1928) is very popular with locals. There is outside dining in sun or in shade. *Viale Margherita (corner of L. del Greco), T: 0584 433577.*

LOCAL SPECIALITIES

In **Lucca** they make a delicious simple cake, *buccellato*, with fennel and raisins, particularly good at Taddeucci, in Piazza San Michele.

FESTIVALS & EVENTS

Lucca *Santa Zita*, Festival of the patron saint, and a week-long flower festival in the town, end April; *Palio della Balestra*, 12 July; Puccini Festival, July and Aug; *Luminara di Santa Croce*, Celebrates the arrival of the *Volto Santo*, with a huge procession through the streets, 13 Sept.

Lago di Massaciuccoli Opera festival, Puccini works performed on the lakeshore, entrance from Piazzale Belvedere, July and Aug.

Viareggio Carnival, held on four Sundays and Shrove Tuesday in the Lenten period, with a parade of allegorical floats (many of them topical). One of the most famous in Italy, late Jan or Feb.

PISA, LIVORNO & VOLTERRA

Pisa (pop. c. 104,000; *map p. 264, B3*) is one of the most famous places in all Italy because of its leaning tower, one of three beautiful Romanesque buildings which stand together in a magnificently sighted group at the northernmost limit of the old city. The rest of the town is much less interesting, and its general appearance suffers from the fact that it had to be rebuilt in the 1950s after considerable war damage. It has a slightly sleepy feel, although it has two flourishing universities.

HISTORY OF PISA

This site near the sea seems to have been settled by at least 1000 BC, and it became an Etruscan town which expanded in the 4th century BC. As a Roman colony from the 2nd century BC, when it was situated on a lagoon, it was a naval and commercial port (some ancient boats have been excavated near the station of San Rossore; *see p. 360*). It continued to flourish under the Lombards in the 7th and 8th centuries. By the 11th century Pisa had become an important maritime republic, rivalling only Genoa, Amalfi and Venice on the Italian peninsula. Constantly at war with the Saracens, Pisa captured from them Corsica, Sardinia and the Balearic Islands (1050–1100), and at the same time combined war and trade in the East. The wealth of the Pisans became proverbial. In 1135, assisting Pope Innocent II against Roger of Sicily, Pisa destroyed Amalfi. It subsequently joined the Ghibelline party, and remained proudly faithful to it, even though surrounded by Guelph republics such as Florence, Lucca and Genoa. The 12th century was the period of her greatest splendour, when she was one of the most important cities in Europe.

In 1284 Pisa was defeated by the Genoese in the naval battle of Meloria (a reef that rises 5km off Livorno). From then onwards the city had to submit to a succession of lordships, including those of the Gherardesca family (1316–41) and of Gian Galeazzo Visconti of Milan (1396–1405). After one or two unsuccessful efforts at rebellion it became a quiet refuge of scholars and artists, its university having been established in 1343. When Charles VIII of France entered Italy in 1494, he was expected to restore Pisa's liberty, but he broke his promise, and Florence took final possession of the city in 1509.

Piazza del Duomo

Map p. 350, 2. Admission to the duomo, baptistery and Leaning Tower is usually extremely well organised. All are open Jan and Feb 10–5; March 9–6; April–Sept 8–8; Oct 9–7; Nov and Dec 10–5; 25 Dec–6 Jan 9–6. There is a separate admission charge for the Leaning Tower and the time of the visit has to be booked. To avoid a wait, there is a booking service

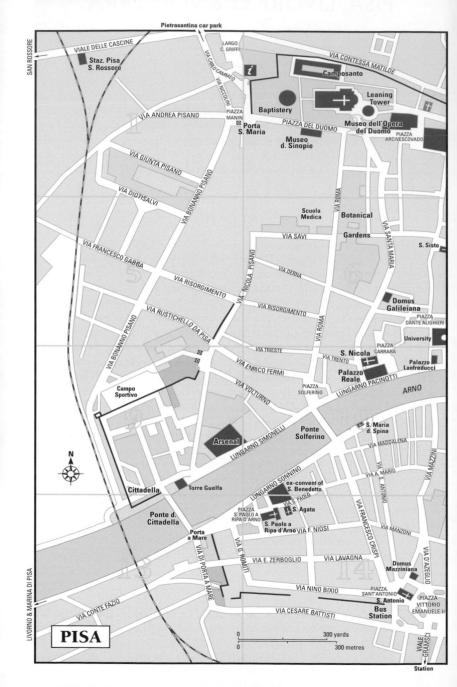

Pietrasantina car park

VIALE DELLE CASCINE

SAN ROSSORE

Staz. Pisa
S. Rossore

LARGO
C. GRIFFI

VIA CARD CAMMEO

VIA NICOLINI

VIA CONTESSA MATILDE

Camposanto

Leaning
Tower

Baptistery

PIAZZA
MANIN

Porta
S. Maria

PIAZZA DEL DUOMO

Museo dell'Opera
del Duomo

PIAZZA
ARCIVESCOVADO

VIA ANDREA PISANO

Museo
d. Sinopie

VIA GIUNTA PISANO

VIA DIOTISALVI

VIA BONANNO PISANO

VIA ROMA

Scuola
Medica

Botanical

VIA SAVI

Gardens

VIA SANTA MARIA

S. Sisto

VIA FRANCESCO GABBA

VIA NICOLA PISANO

VIA DERNA

VIA RISORGIMENTO

VIA RISORGIMENTO

Domus
Galileiana

VIA RUSTICHELLO DA PISA

VIA ROMA

PIAZZA
DANTE ALIGHIERI

University

VIA BONANNO PISANO

VIA TRIESTE

PIAZZA
CARRARA

S. Nicola

Palazzo
Lanfreducci

VIA ENRICO FERMI

VIA TRENTO

Palazzo
Reale

VIA VOLTURNO

PIAZZA
SOLFERINO

LUNGARNO PACINOTTI

ARNO

Campo
Sportivo

Ponte
Solferino

S. Maria
d. Spina

LUNGARNO SIMONELLI

Arsenal

VIA MADDALENA

VIA A. MARIO

VIA S. ANTONIO

VIA MAZZINI

N

Cittadella

Torre Guelfa

LUNGARNO SONNINO

ex-convent of
S. Benedetto

PIAZZA
S. PAOLO A
RIPA D'ARNO

VIA S. PAOLO

S. Agata

VIA FRANCESCO CRISPI

VIA MANZONI

VIA D'AZEGLIO

Ponte d.
Cittadella

Porta
a Mare

S. Paolo a
Ripa d'Arno

VIA F. NIOSI

VIA DI PORTA A MARE

VIA G. ROMITI

VIA E. ZERBOGLIO

VIA LAVAGNA

Domus
Mazziniana

LIVORNO & MARINA DI PISA

VIA NINO BIXIO

PIAZZA
SANT'ANTONIO

S. Antonio

PIAZZA
VITTORIO
EMANUELE II

VIA CONTE FAZIO

Bus
Station

VIA CESARE BATTISTI

VIALE
GRAMSCI

PISA

0   300 yards

0   300 metres

Station

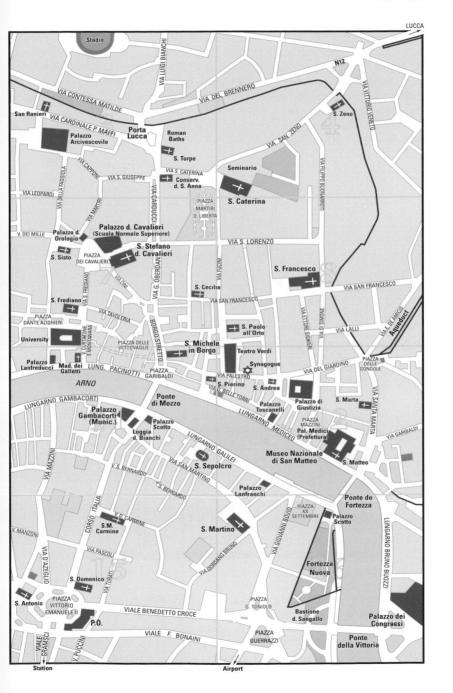

LUCCA

Stadio

VIA LUIGI BIANCHI

VIA CONTESSA MATILDE

VIA DEL BRENNERO

N12

VIA VITTORIO VENETO

San Ranieri

VIA CARDINALE P. MAFFI

Porta
Lucca

S. Zeno

Palazzo
Arcivescovile

Roman
Baths

VIA SAN ZENO

VIA CAPPONI

S. Torpe

VIA DELLA FAGGIOLA

VIA S. GIUSEPPE

VIA S. CATERINA

Conserv.
d. S. Anna

Seminario

VIA FILIPPO BUONARROTI

VIA LEOPARDI

VIA CARDUCCI

VIA MARTIRI

PIAZZA
MARTIRI
D. LIBERTA

S. Caterina

V. DEI MILLE

Palazzo d.
Orologio

Palazzo d. Cavalieri
(Scuola Normale Superiore)

VIA S. LORENZO

S. Sisto

PIAZZA
DEI CAVALIERI

S. Stefano
d. Cavalieri

VIA G. OBERDAN

VIA FUCINI

S. Francesco

VIA SAN FRANCESCO

VIALDINI

VIA S. FREDIANO

S. Frediano

S. Cecilia

VIA SAN FRANCESCO

VIA ETTORE SIGHIERI

VIA E. DE AMICIS

Aqueduct

PIAZZA
DANTE ALIGHIERI

VIA TAVOLERIA

VIA LALLI

University

V. CURTATONE
E MONTANARA

S. Paolo
all'Orto

BORGO STRETTO

PIAZZA DELLE
VETTOVAGLIE

S. Michele
in Borgo

Teatro Verdi

VIA DEL GIARDINO

PIAZZA
DELLE
GONDOLE

Palazzo
Lanfreducci

Mad. dei
Galletti

LUNG. PACINOTTI

PIAZZA
GARIBALDI

Synagogue

VIA PALESTRO

S. Pierino

VIA D. BELLE TORRI

S. Andrea

ARNO

Ponte
di Mezzo

Palazzo
Toscanelli

Palazzo di
Giustizia

S. Marta

VIA SANTA MARTA

LUNGARNO GAMBACORTI

Palazzo
Gambacorti
(Munic.)

Palazzo
Scotto

LUNGARNO MEDICEO

PIAZZA
MAZZINI

Pal. Medici
(Prefettura)

VIA GARIBALDI

VIA MAZZINI

Loggia
d. Bianchi

LUNGARNO GALILEI

VIA SAN MARTINO

V.S. BERNARDO

S. Sepolcro

Museo Nazionale
di San Matteo

S. Matteo

S. BERNARDO

Palazzo
Lanfranchi

Ponte de
Fortezza

CORSO ITALIA

V. D. CARMINE

S.M.
Carmine

S. Martino

VIA GIOVANNI BOVIO

PIAZZA
XX
SETTEMBRE

Palazzo
Scotto

LUNGARNO BRUNO BUOZZI

V. MANZONI

VIA PASCOLI

VIA GIORDANO BRUNO

Fortezza
Nuova

VIA D'AZEGLIO

S. Domenico

VIA TURATI

S. Antonio

PIAZZA
VITTORIO
EMANUELE II

VIALE BENEDETTO CROCE

PIAZZA
G. TONIOLO

Bastione
d. Sangallo

Palazzo dei
Congressi

VIALE GRAMSCI

P.O.

V. PUCCINI

VIALE F. BONAINI

PIAZZA
GUERRAZZI

Ponte
della Vittoria

Station

Airport

at www.opapisa.it; T: 050 387 2210. There are admission charges for all other monuments and museums (except for the duomo in Nov–Feb, when it is free, but when it closes between 12.30 and 2), and there are inclusive tickets for 5, 3 or 2 of them. Children under 10 are free. Tickets are bought at the offices of the Opera Primaziale Pisana (office just north of the Leaning Tower) or at the Museo delle Sinopie. You are asked to keep off the lawns except in the area behind the baptistery.

The duomo

PISA: DUOMO

The duomo is the prototype of the Pisan style of architecture, in which a strong Classicism survives. It was begun by a certain Buscheto in 1063, and continued by Rainaldo in the following century (both architects are known only from their work on this building). The effect of the building is heightened by the broad white marble pavement on which it stands. It is covered inside and out with black-and-white marble, toned on the exterior to a delicate grey and russet. There are four tiers of columns with open galleries on the façade, above a row of seven tall blind arches. The tomb of Buscheto is in the left-hand arch. The entrance is through the Portal of San Ranieri (south transept), which has superb bronze doors by Bonanno da Pisa (1180).

The huge cruciform interior has exceptionally deep transepts: it suffered from a serious fire in 1595, and the restorations undertaken a few years later still give it a slight feel that it is not as ancient as the exterior would lead one to expect. The nave has double aisles, and the 68 incredibly tall columns have 11th-century capitals made in imitation of Classical ones. The great bronze lamp hanging over the nave, supposed to have suggested to Galileo the principle of the pendulum, was in fact cast by Battista Lorenzi in 1587, six years after the discovery. Some of the small stained-glass windows are attributed to the 15th-century painter Alesso Baldovinetti. The clerestory is decorated with handsome geometric marble inlay in the arches, above which a wall of simple grey and white striped marble pierced by small windows with clear glass extends up to the gorgeous coffered and gilded ceiling, remodelled after the 1595 fire.

(1) Tomb of Henry VII: The Holy Roman Emperor Henry VII was much admired by Dante and is mentioned in his *Paradiso*. He died of fever at Pisa in 1313. The tomb, with a fine effigy, is by Tino di Camaino (1315; partly reassembled here; other statues are in the Museo dell'Opera del Duomo; *see p. 357 below*).

(2) Ranieri Chapel: Ranieri (1117–60), the patron saint of Pisa, came from a well-to-do family, but renounced riches and journeyed to the Holy Land, performing miracles on his return. The chapel honouring him has 17th-century sculptures by Francesco Mosca, and a marble and bronze coffer by Giovanni Battista Foggini, which contains the saint's remains.

(3) Choir: At the entrance to the choir are two bronze angels by Giambologna who, together with assistants, also made other bronze sculptures (less easy to see) in the sanctuary, including the Crucifix on the high altar. The beautiful paintings of saints below the cantoria are by Andrea del Sarto. The marble lectern and candelabra are by Matteo Civitali.

(4) Apse: The paintings in the apse, which can only be seen from afar, include works by Sodoma and Beccafumi. The huge mosaic of the *Redeemer Enthroned between the Madonna and St John the Evangelist* is a fine 13th-century work (except for the figure of St John, which dates from 1302, and is the last work of the great artist Cimabue).

(5) Painting of the Madonna: A much venerated 13th-century work, to which the Pisans have turned in times of trouble since 1225.

(6) Pulpit: The splendidly carved pulpit by Giovanni Pisano (1302–11; perhaps with the assistance of Tino di Camaino) is a masterpiece of Gothic sculpture. It broadly follows the design of his father Nicola's pulpit in the baptistery, but some of the carved details are rather gruesome. The columns have statues of Sibyls above the capitals, and florid architraves. Above, deeply carved relief panels representing crowded scenes from the New Testament are separated by figures of prophets.

PISA DUOMO

Entrance (Portal of St Ranieri)

I   Tomb of Henry VII
2   Chapel of St Ranieri
3   Choir
4   Apse
5   Painting of the *Madonna*
6   Pulpit
7   *Madonna delle Grazie*

(7) Madonna delle Grazie: This is the most interesting altarpiece in the church. It is by Andrea del Sarto and his much less well known assistant Giovanni Antonio Sogliani.

The Leaning Tower

The campanile (*for admission, see p. 349 above*) or celebrated Leaning Tower, is superbly sited at the east end of the duomo. This extraordinary monument has been admired for centuries by travellers since it is such a curious sight. Its famous lean has in part obscured the fact that it is also a very beautiful architectural work, and one of the most original bell-towers in Italy. Circular in plan, it has eight storeys of round arches, six open galleries, and a bell-chamber of smaller diameter. Over 54m high, its marked inclination is over 4m out of the perpendicular.

Begun in 1173, the tower was only 10.5m high when a subsidence of the soil threw it out of true. During the 13th century the architect in charge appears to have been the little-known Giovanni di Simone, who apparently only worked in Pisa, and who endeavoured, without success, to rectify the inclination as the building proceeded. Failure to halt the lean did not stop its completion: by 1301 it had risen as far as the bell-chamber, and by the late 14th century it was completed as it now stands. In the 1980s it was found that the lean was increasing by about 1mm a year, so in 1990 it was closed to the public, and in 1992 steel cables were inserted around the base and between the first and second galleries. Then from 1998–2001 the tower was 'anchored' with two steel cables, and a complicated operation on the subsoil was carried out to stabilise the foundations. The result of these measures was that by 2001 the lean had been reduced by some 40cm, thus returning the tower to the same position it had about 300 years ago, and it was reopened to the public. Remains of Etruscan and Roman buildings were found during excavations at the foot of the tower.

Galileo, according to his pupil Vincenzio Viviani, carried out experiments from the tower to provide a visual demonstration to members of Pisa university that all falling bodies, independent of their size, descend with equal velocity. The great physicist and astronomer was born in Pisa in 1564.

An easy spiral staircase with 294 old worn steps ascends past the windows on the various storeys to emerge on the highest little open gallery. Another flight of smaller steps continues up to the bell-chamber where the seven bells are hung. An even narrower, miniature flight of steps leads to the very top. There is a magnificent view of the roof of the duomo with a copy of the charming Islamic griffin on the summit at the east end. On clear days you can see the islands of Capraia and Gorgona (and sometimes even Elba), but the sea is mostly hidden behind the pinewoods on the shore. In the other direction rise the Apuan Alps.

The enduring charm of Pisa

Few of us can have had a childhood so unblessed by contact with the arts as that one of its occasional diversions shan't have been a puzzled scrutiny of some alabaster model of the Leaning Tower under a glass cover in a back-parlour. Pisa and its monuments have, in other words, been industriously vulgarised, but it is astonishing how well they have survived the process. The charm of the place is in fact of a high order and but partially foreshadowed by the famous crookedness of its campanile....

Henry James, Italian Hours (1909)

The baptistery

The baptistery (*for admission, see p. 349 above*) is a very fine circular building begun in 1152, the most important work of the Pisan architect Diotisalvi. The Gothic decoration was added to the Romanesque building in the 13th century by Nicola Pisano and his son Giovanni, including Giovanni's foliated columns and *Madonna* on the main portal facing the duomo (the originals are in the Museo dell'Opera del Duomo). The Gothic dome and cusped arches were added in the 14th century.

The interior, famous for its acoustics, has a two-storeyed ambulatory, and is decorated with bands of black-and-white marble. Perhaps because of the unadorned cupola

Detail of St Michael from the 14th-century *Last Judgement* frescoes in the Camposanto.

and the rather odd light effects, it is rather disappointing. The beautiful octagonal font of white marble, carved and inlaid in mosaic, is by Guido da Como (1246). The altar, which dates from the same time, stands on a raised mosaic pavement. The pulpit, by Nicola Pisano, is signed and dated 1260. Resting on slender pillars bearing figures of the *Virtues*, it is decorated with panels sculptured in bold relief (*Nativity*, *Adoration of the Magi*, *Presentation*, *Crucifixion*, and *Last Judgement*).

The Camposanto

The Camposanto, or cemetery (*for admission, see p. 349 above*), was begun in 1278 by the architect of the Leaning Tower, Giovanni di Simone, and completed in the 15th century. The bright marble exterior wall has handsome blind arcading and is spectacularly unadorned except for the Gothic tabernacle perched on the roof above a door.

The interior is in the form of an oblong cloister, lit by graceful traceried windows (never filled with glass), around a lawn which is supposed to be on the site of an earlier burial ground for which Archbishop Ubaldo Lanfranchi (1108–78) brought five shiploads of earth from the Holy Land. It was used as a cemetery for illustrious citizens up to 1779, and the names and deeds of important Pisans are still inscribed here.

The walls were decorated with frescoes in the 14th and 15th centuries by Taddeo Gaddi, Andrea Bonaiuti, Antonio Veneziano, Spinello Aretino, Piero di Puccio and Benozzo Gozzoli, but these were severely damaged in the Second World War. In an attempt to preserve them, they were all detached: the *sinopie* which were discovered beneath them are now preserved in the Museo delle Sinopie (*see below*). The frescoes are slowly being re-located on the walls, even though many were damaged irreparably.

From the 14th century onwards Roman sculptures were brought here to decorate the four walks, including a huge collection of sarcophagi, and these constituted one of the most important Classical collections in Europe in the early Renaissance. Many of these were destroyed or removed, and others severely damaged in the War, but a remarkable **series of 84 sarcophagi**, mostly from the 3rd century AD, has survived. Some were re-used by Pisan citizens in the Middle Ages for their own tombs. The huge **harbour chains of the ancient port of Pisa**, which were seized by the Genoese in 1342, were hung up here when they were finally returned to the city in 1860.

A huge room off the north walk houses some of the frescoes detached from the south walk, including the superb scenes of the *Triumph of Death*, *Last Judgement* and *Stories of the Anchorites*. These have been variously attributed to Orcagna, Francesco Traini, Vitale da Bologna and Buffalmacco, but are now generally held to be by an unknown 14th-century master named from these frescoes the Master of the Triumph of Death (1360–80). In 1839 Franz Liszt was inspired by these scenes to create his *Totentanz*.

The 12th-century castellated walls which enclose the north and west side of Piazza del Duomo were pierced in the 13th century by the Porta del Leone, named after the Romanesque lion which survives here (opposite the west end of the Camposanto). Through the closed wooden gates can be seen part of the **Jewish Cemetery**, which was moved here in the 16th century, and surrounded in 1801 by a high wall.

Museo delle Sinopie

On the south side of the lawn is the former Ospedale Nuovo di Misericordia (13th–14th century), which now houses the Museo delle Sinopie del Camposanto Monumentale (*temporarily closed at the time of writing; for normal admission, see p. 352 above*), with the restored *sinopie* detached from the walls of the Camposanto.

Museo dell'Opera del Duomo

The Museo dell'Opera del Duomo (*for admission, see p. 352 above*) is a very fine museum in the former chapter house. The collection includes works of art from the duomo, baptistery and Camposanto. Amongst the most interesting exhibits are the 11th–12th-century sculpture from the duomo, showing Islamic and French influences, including a splendid bronze griffin and basin brought from the East as war booty, and a polychrome wood figure of Christ descending from the Cross, attributed to a Burgundian artist. An exquisite late 12th-century capital from the Leaning Tower is displayed on its own. The **Gothic statues from the baptistery** include three very fine Madonnas by Giovanni Pisano. Works by his pupil Tino di Camaino include **St Ranieri's altar tomb** (1301–06), and statues from his important **tomb of Henry VII** (*see p. 353 above*), including two angels recently recognised as part of the monument but which somehow found their way onto the upper part of the cathedral façade. There are also two tombs by Nino Pisano. The treasury has exquisite works dating from the 12th–14th centuries, including Limoges enamel reliquary coffers, and a beautifully embroidered altar frontal.

The **ivory statuette of the** *Madonna and Child* is a superb work by Giovanni Pisano (1299–1300), originally over the main altar in the duomo.

On the first floor are engravings and watercolours by Carlo Lasinio (1759–1838), which provide a precious record of the frescoes in the Camposanto before their almost total destruction in the Second World War.

The exit from the museum is along the portico on the ground floor, where Nicola and Giovanni Pisano's colossal half-figures of Evangelists, prophets and the *Madonna and Child*, from the exterior of the baptistery (1269–79), are displayed.

Sculptors named Pisano (13th–14th centuries)
Nicola Pisano (c. 1200–78/84) had a profound influence on the development of sculpture in Italy. His works mark a break with medieval art, and contain a new Gothic realism and narrative style which point the way forward to the Renaissance. He was probably a native of Puglia in southern Italy, but lived most of his life in Pisa, where his first known work is the baptistery pulpit. The only other two sculptures certainly by his hand are the pulpit in Siena cathedral (1268; *see p. 422*) and the Fontana Maggiore in Perugia (1278; *see p. 496*).

For these last two commissions he was assisted by his son Giovanni Pisano (1245–1320), who later carved two more splendid pulpits of exquisite workmanship, one in the church of Sant'Andrea in Pistoia (1301; *see p. 327*), and the other, the most sumptuous of all, in the duomo of Pisa (1302–11). Giovanni, who worked for some ten years as a sculptor for Siena cathedral, is also recognised as having had a fundamental influence on Italian sculpture.

Later in the 14th century two more important sculptors, also called Pisano (but no relation to Nicola and Giovanni), were at work in Tuscany: Andrea Pisano (c. 1270–1348/49), who produced masterpieces for the Campanile and Baptistery of Florence, and his son Nino Pisano (d. 1368), who worked mostly in Pisa (see, for instance, his *Madonna and Child* in the church of San Nicola).

Piazza dei Cavalieri

Once the centre of the city (*map p. 351, 7*), this oddly-shaped piazza was named after the Knights of St Stephen, an order founded by Cosimo I de' Medici in 1561 to combat the Turkish infidel, in imitation of the Knights of Malta. Palazzo dei Cavalieri was modernised in 1562 by Cosimo's favourite architect, Vasari, with spectacular graffiti decoration, designed by him (much restored). It is now the seat of the **Scuola Normale Superiore**, a university college founded by Napoleon in 1810, and modelled on the Ecole Normale Supérieure in Paris. It incorporates a large medieval hall of the old Palazzo del Popolo, now used as a lecture hall. Concerts are given here from December to May. Outside is a statue of Cosimo I by Pietro Francavilla (1596).

The **Palazzo dell'Orologio**, closing the north side of the square, occupies the site of the old Torre dei Gualandi, also called the Torre della Mula when it was used as a mews for eagles (emblems of the city). The tower continued its function as a small prison when in 1288 Count Ugolino della Gherardesca, who was suspected of treachery at the Battle of Meloria (*see p. 349*), and his sons and grandsons were starved to death here. The episode is described by Dante (*Inferno XXXII*), who notes that from that time the tower came to be known as the 'Torre della Fame' (the Tower of Famine). The building is now used as a library by the Scuola Normale.

Santo Stefano dei Cavalieri (*open 9–12.30; also Sat and Sun pm*) has a handsome façade (1594–1606) by Giovanni de' Medici, illegitimate son of Cosimo I. Vasari provided the unusual campanile and decorated the fine interior in 1569 (and painted the first south altarpiece). The church is hung with banners captured from the Ottomans, and the 17th-century carved wooden ornaments and lanterns from the knights' galleys are displayed. The ceiling (1604–13) has six scenes showing Cosimo I as Grand Master of the Order; the return of the fleet after the battle of Lepanto; Maria de' Medici setting out to marry Henri IV of France; and three naval victories over the Turks. All are good works by the Florentine painters Cigoli, Jacopo Ligozzi, Cristofano Allori and Empoli. The high altar, with a statue of St Stephen, is by Giovanni Battista Foggini.

Along the Arno

At the foot of Ponte di Mezzo, rebuilt in 1950 but on the site of the Roman bridge, is the small but busy Piazza Garibaldi, now usually considered the centre of the city. **Borgo Stretto** (*map p. 351, 11–7*) is a pretty arcaded shopping street with wide pavements, off which are a number of narrow old streets. The church of **San Michele in Borgo** has a lovely 14th-century façade, typical of the Pisan Gothic style.

At no. 27 Lungarno Pacinotti, on the ground floor of Palazzo dell'Ussero (which has early 15th-century terracotta decoration on its façade), is the **Caffè dell'Ussero**, opened in 1794, and famous as the meeting place of writers during the Risorgimento. One of the most famous figures in this revolutionary movement was Giuseppe Mazzini, who died in Pisa in 1872 while visiting friends under the false name of John Brown. There is a small museum and library on the site of the house in the street now named after him (Domus Mazziniana, Via Mazzini 71; *map p. 350, 14; open mornings only; closed Sun*).

The tiny church of the **Madonna dei Galletti** has an attractive 17th–18th-century interior and a fresco of the *Madonna and Child* by Taddeo di Bartolo over the high altar.

In Piazza Carrara (*map p. 350, 6–10*) is a good statue of Grand Duke Ferdinando I by Pietro Francavilla (1594). The huge Palazzo Reale was built in 1583–87 by Bernardo Buontalenti for Francesco I de' Medici. On the site of a medieval building and incorporating an old tower house, it was severely damaged in the last war. It now houses the **Museo di Palazzo Reale** (*open 9–2, except Sun and holidays*), containing part of the city's art collections, illustrating the period of the Grand Dukes of Tuscany, as well as the Royal House of Savoy. The collection of the surgeon Antonio Ceci (1852–1920) includes a painting by Guido Reni of *Sacred and Profane Love*. A velvet dress which belonged to the grand duchess Eleanor of Toledo (wife of Cosimo I) is exhibited next to her very fine portrait (with her son Francesco) by Bronzino.

The church of **San Nicola**, founded c. 1000, has a 13th-century campanile. The interior contains a beautiful *Madonna and Child* by Francesco Traini, a polychrome wooden *Madonna Annunciate* by Francesco di Valdambrino, a Crucifix by Giovanni Pisano (c. 1300), and a beautiful statue of the *Madonna and Child* by Nino Pisano.

The Arsenal and Cittadella

Ponte Solferino (*map p. 350, 10*) was rebuilt in 1974 after its collapse in the Arno flood of 1966. Close to it on the far side of the river is the charming church of **Santa Maria della Spina** (named after a thorn of the Saviour's crown), which is an exquisite example of Pisan Gothic architecture (finished in 1323), commissioned by a Pisan merchant.

The **Arsenal** (*open 10–1 & 2–6*) is a boatyard built by the Medici grand dukes in 1548–88, and one of the splendid huge vaulted brick halls has been restored for an exhibition relating to the 16 ships dating from between the 5th century BC and the 5th century AD which, since 1999, have been unearthed near the station of San Rossore (*map p. 350, 1*), where traces of an old port have been discovered. Finds include remains of cargo such as amphorae, objects in glass, bronze, terracotta and leather, as well as ropes, baskets, and mats, and skeletons of sailors and animals. There are long-term plans to exhibit some of the boats themselves here.

The tall medieval **Cittadella** or Fortezza Vecchia (*map p. 350, 9*), with the Torre Guelfa, was enlarged in the 15th century. The tower can be climbed (200 steps; *open 10–2; summer 10/11–1 & 2.30–6/8*), and there is a very fine view from the top.

At the south end of Ponte della Cittadella is the 13th-century Porta a Mare, and abandoned ruins of a bastion in the walls. On the river can be seen the old gate of the Navicelli canal (now covered over), which was begun by Cosimo I in 1541 to connect Pisa with Livorno. In this quiet part of the city a spacious piazza with trees (and an excellent view of the tall Cittadella across the river) opens out in front of the church of **San Paolo a Ripa d'Arno** (*map p. 350, 14*), founded in 805. The splendid façade probably dates from the 13th century, and the north flank has fine blind arcading. Behind the east end, surrounded by a lawn with a few trees, is the unusual Romanesque chapel of Sant'Agata, a tiny octagonal brick building (after 1063).

Museo Nazionale di San Matteo

The museum (*map p. 351, 12; open 9–6; Sun and holidays 9–1; closed Mon*) contains works of art from Pisan churches and convents. The first room on the first floor has a fine collection of early Tuscan painted Crucifixes (13th century), including one signed by Giunta Pisano (believed to be the earliest painter whose name is inscribed on any extant Italian work). Fine polyptychs by Francesco Traini and Lippo Memmi are displayed near the splendid polyptych signed and dated 1319–21 by Simone Martini.

There is a good collection of 14th- and 15th-century Pisan wooden sculptures, including works by Francesco di Valdambrino. The very beautiful *Madonna del Latte*, a half-length polychrome marble gilded statue from Santa Maria della Spina, and the *Annunciatory Angel*, a wooden statue from San Matteo, are both by Andrea and Nino Pisano. Nino also made the *Christ in Pietà*, a wooden high relief and a marble statuette of the *Madonna and Child*. There are also sculptures by Tino di Camaino and Nicola Pisano. In Room 8 are some of the most precious works in the collection: *St Paul* by Masaccio; *Madonna of Humility* by Fra' Angelico; and a reliquary bust of St Rossore (St Luxorius), a splendid work in gilded bronze by Donatello (1424–27), from Santo Stefano dei Cavalieri. In the last long gallery, the lovely *Madonna of Humility* is by Gentile da Fabriano and the *Madonna in Adoration* by Andrea della Robbia.

LIVORNO

Livorno (pop. 169,000; *map p. 264, A3*) is a busy and lively town with a maritime air, which, since the 1970s has become one of the biggest container ports in Italy. It has a well-known street market where American goods are sold (Camp Darby, a US army base is nearby). In the 17th and 18th centuries the town, as a free port, was much frequented by British merchants and sailors, who called it Leghorn, the name by which it was called by English-speakers right up to the 20th century. With a long history as a free port and with a large Jewish community, the atmosphere of the town today is unlike anywhere else in Italy.

HISTORY OF LIVORNO

Ferdinando I de' Medici (1587–1609) continued work on the port begun by his father Cosimo I and employed the navigator and cartographer (and Catholic convert, son of the Earl of Leicester, favourite of Elizabeth I of England) Sir Robert Dudley to build warships, administer the port, and construct the great mole (1607–21) as a breakwater. Ferdinando, by his proclamation of religious liberty, made the town a refuge for persecuted Jews, Greeks who had fled from the Turks, converted Muslims expelled from Spain and Portugal under Philip III in 1609, and Roman Catholics driven from England under the penal laws against papists proclaimed by James I (1606). They were joined by many Italians fleeing from the oppression of their own states, and by exiles from Marseilles and Provence. During the 17th century the port was used to import herring from Great Yarmouth and wheat from King's Lynn in Britain. In the 18th century the 'British Factory' was established by a group of British merchants and factors to assist the numerous British families in the town.

As a neutral port, Livorno was able to supply numerous ships for the naval battles against Napoleon. In the mid-19th century the town became a well-known bathing resort. Robert Stephenson built the railway line from Pisa to Livorno, which was opened in 1844. A regular steam-ship service was introduced in 1872 between Livorno and Great Britain. During a congress of the Socialist Party in Livorno in 1921, a schism led to the founding of the Italian Communist Party.

Within the Fosso Reale

The port was laid out by Bernardo Buontalenti in 1576 for the Medici , who constructed the fortifications and surrounded it by a deep moat (the **Fosso Reale**). In 1984 two sculptures were dredged up from it and hailed by art critics as lost masterpieces by Modigliani, who was born in Livorno in 1884. They were soon proved to be fakes made with the help of an electric drill by a group of students, and the incident was recognised as one of the most successful hoaxes to fool the contemporary art world.

At the seaward end of the arterial Via Grande is the well-known **monument to Ferdinando I**, with a statue of him by Giovanni Bandini (1595), and four colossal Moorish slaves in bronze chained to the pedestal, the masterpieces of Pietro Tacca (1623–26). To the north near the **Fortezza Nuova**, built in 1590 on a design by Giovanni de' Medici, surrounded by a moat, and now enclosing a pleasant public park, there is an area of smaller canals known as 'Nuova Venezia' now used as moorings for boats. South of Via Grande, on Piazza Benamozegh, is the **Synagogue**, built in 1962 after the destruction of the previous one in the Second World War.

The British Cemetery

From the duomo, Via Cairoli leads down to Piazza Cavour, which spans the Fosso Reale. Off to the right after you cross it (third street), in Via Giuseppe Verdi, is the Old British Cemetery (*for the key to the gate apply at the offices of the Misericordia at the entrance*), probably opened in the 16th century, and for many years the only Protestant cemetery in Italy. Numerous British merchants, sea captains and Anglican clergymen and their families were buried here, as well as some Swiss and French Huguenots and Americans, including Elizabeth Seton, a Roman Catholic convert who became a missionary in America and was canonised in 1977 (the first American-born saint). Many of the monumental tombs, pyramidal in form, date from the 1660s. Tobias Smollett was buried here in 1773 (the tomb, with an obelisk and Latin inscription, is to the right of the centre). The cemetery was closed in 1840 when the new cemetery was opened in the northern suburbs. The Anglican church outside, with a classical temple façade, was built in 1840.

The southern parts of town

The spacious seaboard is particularly attractive. Viale Italia skirts the shore with a pleasant wide promenade passing ship-building yards, then gardens and elegant seaside houses, and 19th-century hotels and bathing establishments. In Via San Jacopo Acquaviva is Villa Mimbelli, a 19th-century building in a park, decorated in elaborate neo-Renaissance style and housing the **Museo Civico Giovanni Fattori** (*usually open 10–1 & 5–11; winter 10–7; closed Mon*) with a splendid collection of paintings by the excellent Macchiaioli painter Giovanni Fattori, born in Livorno in 1825.

Above the southern suburb of Antignano is **Montenero**, reached by a funicular railway. The little village, with fine views of the coast, is built round a sanctuary. The pilgrimage church (1676) contains a 14th-century painting of the *Madonna*, supposed to have sailed by itself in 1345 from the Greek island of Negroponte (Euboea) to the shore at Ardenza. In rooms near the sacristy is a huge collection of 19th- and 20th-century ex-votos, including some charming seascapes, and the Turkish costume of a little girl who was saved by her brother in 1800 after she had been carried off to a harem from Livorno by the Turks (the story was the inspiration for Rossini's opera *L'Italiana in Algeri*).

Shelley took up residence here in 1819, at Villa Valsovona, where he finished his tragedy *The Cenci*. While in Livorno he bought a little schooner, the *Ariel*, which sank off Viareggio in 1822. Shelley's body was washed ashore ten days later on the beach of Gombo, north of the mouth of the Arno, and was cremated there in the presence of Byron and Leigh Hunt. His ashes were collected and buried in the Protestant cemetery in Rome. He was 30 years old.

VOLTERRA

Volterra (pop. 12,600; *map p. 264, C4*) lies in a magnificent position on a hill, with open views in every direction across a yellow and grey landscape of rolling clay hills and white chalk hillocks known as *crete*. The scenery is at its best in the autumn and winter. The precipices all around, formed by the natural erosion of the Pleistocene clay, are known as *Le Balze*. Erosion, earthquakes and landslides engulfed the greater part of Volterra's earliest necropolis and subsequent buildings, and continue to be a threat.

The austere medieval walled town is the successor to an Etruscan city of much greater extent. Almost all the buildings are constructed from *panchina*, a kind of limestone which is the matrix of alabaster, and which is found here in abundance.

HISTORY OF VOLTERRA

Velathri was the northernmost of the 12 cities of the confederation of *Etruria Propria*, and one of the most prominent. In the 3rd century BC it became the Roman *Volaterrae*. In the late 2nd century BC it supported the cause of the democratic consul Marius against the dictator Sulla during the civil wars which preceded the collapse of the Roman Republic. Volterra was besieged for two years before falling to Sulla's troops. It gained some importance when for a time it was the residence of the Lombard kings.

After bitter struggles, it was subdued by Florence in 1361, and again in 1472 in the War of Volterra, waged by Lorenzo the Magnificent for control of its alum deposits, and which culminated in the sacking of the city by the Florentines under the command of Federico da Montefeltro. Lorenzo is said to have asked for forgiveness on his deathbed for this brutal act. Another rebellion was crushed by Francesco Ferrucci in 1530, and from then on Volterra remained under Florentine dominion, and later under the Grand Duchy of Tuscany, until the unification of Italy in 1860.

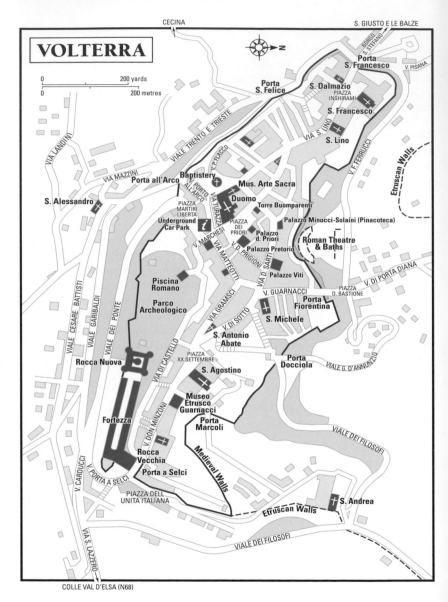

Piazza dei Priori

The central Piazza dei Priori is bordered by medieval and medieval style buildings. The austere **Palazzo dei Priori**, with its battlemented tower, is the oldest town hall in Tuscany. It was begun in 1208 and completed in 1257; the Sala del Consiglio Comunale has been the town council chamber ever since. **Palazzo Pretorio**, surmounted by the Torre del Porcellino, which derives its name from the sculpted boar on a bracket to the right of the top window, dates from the 13th century. The vertical emphasis of the building is underlined by the narrow windows flanking the tower. The adjacent Palazzo del Podestà is of the same date. The crenellated tower to the left, formerly a prison, has a variety of architectural elements in various different materials.

The duomo

The duomo (*open 8.30–12.30 & 3–5.30*) dates from the 12th century. The façade is in the 13th-century Pisan style. The tall, square campanile dates from 1493. In the interior (rebuilt in the late 16th century), the long nave and aisles are divided by columns of painted stucco and capitals, and there is a magnificent coffered ceiling both in the nave and the transepts. The altarpieces date mostly from the 16th century.

South side: The first altarpiece by Pieter de Witte (also known as Pietro Candido; 1578) shows the city of Volterra presented to the Madonna by Sts Justus and Octavianus. The second is a charming *Birth of the Virgin* by Francesco Curradi. In the south transept is a monumental *Deposition*, composed of life-size figures in wood, gilded and brightly painted, by a Pisan sculptor at work in 1228. In the adjoining chapel, to the right of the choir, a marble urn by Raffaello Cioli of Settignano (1522–25) preserves the body of St Octavianus, a 6th-century hermit and one of Volterra's patron saints.

Choir: Over the main altar is a magnificent tabernacle carved by Mino da Fiesole (1471) crowned by the Infant Christ standing above a chalice. The two angels holding candlesticks on the altar are by Andrea Ferrucci, also from Fiesole; the two other angels kneeling on two elegant Gothic columns, are by Mino. The fine choir stalls date from 1404. In the vault is a fresco of *God the Father* by Niccolò Circignani, known as Il Pomarancio after his birthplace of Pomarance, south of Volterra.

North side: The chapel of St Paul off the north transept has frescoes and paintings by Giovanni da San Giovanni in the vault and altarpieces by Domenichino (*Conversion of St Paul*), Francesco Curradi (*Beheading of St Paul*) and Matteo Rosselli (*Paul's Mission to Damascus*).

The 13th-century Pisan pulpit was assembled in 1584 using various sculptural fragments. In the north aisle, the third altar has an *Immaculate Conception* by Niccolò Circignani. The *Annunciation* by Fra' Bartolomeo (second altar; 1497) is a painting of great harmony and beauty, with a landscape extending far into the distance. The Chapel of Our Lady of Sorrows has two niches containing painted terracotta scenes of the *Adoration of the Magi* and the *Nativity* (c 1474), attributed to Luca and Andrea della Robbia, the latter with a charming frescoed background by Benozzo Gozzoli.

The baptistery and Museo d'Arte Sacra

The elegant, octagonal **baptistery** is built in the local stone with just the façade decorated with horizontal bands of black-and-white marble. Above the doorway the archi-

Krater (kelebe) with winged Victory, in the Museo Etrusco Guarnacci.

trave, carved with tiny heads of Christ, the Madonna and Apostles, is inscribed with the date 1283. The dome was added in the 16th century, when the walls had to be heightened to counteract the thrust. Inside, the holy water stoup is made from an Etruscan funerary urn, and the original baptismal font by Andrea Sansovino (1502) bears five carved panels. The altarpiece of the *Ascension*, by Niccolò Circignani, was damaged in the Second World War.

The Palazzo Vescovile (formerly the town granary) now houses the **Museo d'Arte Sacra** (*open 9–1 & 3–6; Nov–March only 9–1*), a charmingly displayed collection of works of art from the cathedral and other churches of the diocese. Some of the most precious possessions are a bust of St Linus, the reputed successor of St Peter in the papal chair, by Andrea (or Giovanni) della Robbia; and a silver reliquary bust of St Octavianus by Antonio Pollaiolo. The most important painting is a panel of the *Madonna and Child with St John the Baptist and St John the Evangelist* (1521) by Rosso Fiorentino.

Porta all'Arco and the west

The famous **Porta all'Arco**, the main gateway to the Etruscan town (4th–3rd centuries BC), was partly rebuilt by the Romans in the 1st century BC. The splendid round arch is decorated with three monumental heads, supposed to be of Etruscan divinities. A plaque records how the citizens of Volterra saved it from destruction in 1944 by undertaking to fill it with paving stones overnight. The inscription translates thus: 'Dear visitor, this arch, one of the greatest of our monuments, was preserved single-handed for your admiration from the threat of a barbarous war by ourselves, the citizens of Volterra'.

The oldest district of the town, with some lovely little streets, can be explored off Via Franceschini and Via San Lino. The church of **San Lino** has an unusual painted vault and lunettes by Cosimo Daddi (1618). At the bottom of the street, just before the 14th-century Porta San Francesco, one of the grandest and best-preserved gateways of the town, is the 13th-century church of **San Francesco** (*open 9–12 & 2.30–5.30*), which has a chapel entirely covered with frescoes by Cenni di Francesco in 1410, representing the *Legend of the True Cross* and the *Infancy of Christ*, commissioned by the Conti Guidi family. This is not only a rare and fascinating example of a narrative cycle, but it is also a description, in countless details, of the architecture and costumes of the period.

Museo Etrusco Guarnacci

A lovely building with a garden on Via Don Minzoni houses the Museo Etrusco Guarnacci, one of the most interesting Etruscan collections in Italy (*open 9–7; winter, 9–1.30*). The nucleus of the collection was donated in 1732 by Canon Pietro Franceschini, who was the first to discover Etruscan urns in the area. It was subsequently enriched by Monsignor Mario Guarnacci (1701–85), a wealthy prelate of Volterra who financed local excavations and bequeathed his archaeological collection and library to his native city.

The arrangement begins on the ground floor with a prehistoric section demonstrating the existence of primitive communities in this territory. Finds from the Roman period include portrait heads, reliefs, fragments of murals, and several mosaic floors from the theatre and baths.

The Etruscan civilisation, from the 10th century BC onwards, is magnificently documented. Entire finds from local tombs dating from the 8th–7th centuries BC are exhibited, with weapons, household objects, fibulae and bronzes. From the 6th century BC there are stelae and fragments with inscriptions. The collection is particularly famous for its Etruscan cinerary urns, in alabaster or terracotta, mostly dating from the 3rd century BC, found locally and numbering over 600. The terracotta urns are probably the oldest. Many are sculpted with fine reliefs, and the lids generally bear the recumbent figures of the dead, holding water vessels upturned or on their sides, symbols of the cup of life reversed. Particularly memorable is the terracotta tomb cover with strikingly realistic portraits of an elderly husband and wife (early 1st century BC). Perhaps the most famous piece in the collection is the elongated bronze votive figure known as the *Ombra della Sera* ('Evening Shadow'; *illustrated right*). It dates from the early 3rd century BC and is a superbly evocative example of the skill, artistry and inventiveness of Etruscan artists.

The Fortezza and Parco Archeologico

The Fortezza is a massive structure composed of the Rocca Vecchia, with a semicircular tower, built by Walter de Brienne in 1343, joined by a double rampart to the Rocca Nuova, which was added by Lorenzo the Magnificent in 1472–75 and is rectangular with circular towers at each corner, surrounding a battlemented tower. The Fortezza has always been a prison, and is still used as such; a prisoner rehabilitation programme includes an on-site restaurant open to outside guests and a renowned theatre company, which presents plays in the prison yard.

The celebrated *Ombra della Sera*, an Etruscan bronze of the 3rd century BC.

The **Parco Archeologico Fiumi** is a public garden on the site of the Etruscan and Roman acropolis (*open March–Oct 10.30–5.30; winter weekends only 10–4*). Here have been found the bases of two temples dating from the 3rd and 2nd centuries BC, as well as Roman cisterns and reservoirs.

Pinacoteca and Museo Civico

In the spacious Via Sarti are several handsome palaces, one of the most elegant of which is Palazzo Minucci-Solaini, traditionally attributed to Antonio da Sangallo the Elder, which houses the **Pinacoteca and Museo Civico** (*open 9–7; winter 8.30–1.30*). The collection consists mainly of paintings by Tuscan artists, arranged chronologically and well-labelled also in English. The gallery's most famous work, the *Deposition* by Rosso Fiorentino (1521), is usually considered one of the masterpieces of Florentine Mannerist art (although heavily restored). Other works include a magnificent polyptych (1411) and the *Madonna of the Rose*, both by Taddeo di Bartolo; an altarpiece of *Christ in Glory worshipped by Sts Benedict, Romuald, Attinia and Greciniana*, in a lovely landscape (1492), by Domenico del Ghirlandaio, and two works (both dated 1491) by Luca Signorelli: the *Annunciation* is particularly beautiful. The second floor has 16th-century paintings, and a detached fresco of *Justice* by Daniele da Volterra; a painting by Niccolò Circignani (Il Pomarancio); and a *Madonna with Saints* by Il Volterrano (Baldassare Franceschini).

The Roman theatre

The Roman theatre (*open March–Oct 10.30–5.30; in winter only at weekends 10–4*), built at the end of the 1st century BC, is one of the best preserved in Italy. Excavations, begun in 1952, revealed part of the cavea, but the most impressive part is the scena, with two tiers of Corinthian columns over 5m high. Many columns survive of the portico behind, which was added a century later. Inside it can be seen remains of Roman baths. If closed, the theatre can also be seen from Via Lungo le Mura del Mandorlo above.

PRACTICAL INFORMATION

GETTING AROUND

• **By air: Pisa** airport is 3km south of the centre. Town buses (no. 7; every 15mins) from the airport to the centre.
• **By car:** Free parking in **Pisa** is in Via Pietrasantina northwest of Piazza del Duomo (served by shuttle buses). Much of central **Livorno** is accessible to residents only. Free parking is off Viale Carducci; a pay car park can be found at Scali Bettarini 5. **Volterra** has a large underground car park just before Piazza Martiti della Libertà (hourly tariff), and other car parks (free) outside the walls.
• **By train:** Main-line trains from **Pisa** (Stazione Centrale; *beyond map p. 350, 14*) connect with Florence, Grosseto and Rome. Slow trains go to Lucca from San Rossore station (*map p. 350, 1*).

Livorno is served by frequent trains from Pisa and local trains to Florence (1hr 20mins). **Volterra** has a station (Volterra–Saline–Pomarance) 11km southwest, with a shuttle into town; a better approach is by bus (*see below*).
• **By bus:** Buses run by SITA (www.sitabus.it) link **Volterra** with Florence, Pisa, San Gimignano and Siena. **Livorno** services are opearated by Lazzi (www.lazzi.it).

INFORMATION OFFICES

Livorno Piazza Cavour 6, T: 0586 820288.
Pisa Via S. Pellico 6, T: 050 929777.
Volterra Piazza dei Priori 20, T: 0588 8725.

HOTELS

Livorno (*map p. 264, A3*)
€€ **Gran Duca**. Comfortable, elegantly furnished hotel built into the 16th-century Medici ramparts. *Piazza G. Micheli 16–18, T: 0586 891024, www.granduca.it. 80 rooms.*
€€ **La Vedetta**. Appealing, plain, simple hotel just above the town at Montenero. Built in 1700, the rooms have high ceilings and are bright and airy. Restaurant with panoramic views. The funicular will take you down into Livorno. *Via della Leccetta 5, T: 0586 579957, www.hotellavedetta.it. 31 rooms.*
Pisa (*map p. 264, B3*)
€€ **Royal Hotel Victoria**. Ancient building once owned by the guild of wine merchants. For centuries it served as an inn and was converted into a hotel in 1837, and is still family-run. It has a number of famous guests, among

them Charles Dickens and Charles Lindbergh. The rooms are beautifully decorated with antiques and frescoed ceilings. *Lungarno Pacinotti 12, T: 050 940111, www.royalvictoria.it. 48 rooms.*
€ **Hotel Francesco**. Very good 3-star hotel close to the Leaning Tower. All the rooms are bright and simply furnished. Restaurant and outdoor terrace. *Via Santa Maria 129, T: 050 555453, www.hotelfrancesco.com. 13 rooms.*
Volterra (*map p. 264, C4*)
€€€ **Relais dell'Orologio**. Boutique hotel in a 14th-century tower-house owned by the same family since the 16th century. Bedrooms are elegantly simple with stencilled walls and wood-beamed ceilings. Restaurant and bar. *Via della Faggiola 12/14, T: 050 830361, www.hotelrelaisorologio.com. 21 rooms.*
€ **San Lino**. Former convent retaining much of its tranquil atmosphere. Superior rooms have cherry-wood furniture and wall-to-wall carpets, while standard rooms are much simpler. Swimming pool. *Via San Lino 26, T: 0588 85250, www.hotelsanlino.com. 44 rooms.*
€ **Villa Nencini**. Just outside Volterra, a cosy country house hotel surrounded by a pleasant garden. Rooms are modest but comfortable. Swimming pool and restaurant. *Borgo Santo Stefano 55, T: 0588 86386, www.villanencini.it. 35 rooms.*

RESTAURANTS

Livorno (*map p. 264, A3*)
€€ **La Barcarola**. An acclaimed fish restaurant, famous for its traditional Livornese fish soup, *cacciucco*. Closed Sun. *Viale Carducci 39, T: 0586 402367.*
€€ **DOC Parole e Cibi**. Elegant restaurant with stylish food to match. Try the

raw scampi or *tagliolini* with lobster. It is also a wine shop, so the list is extensive and the recommendations are knowledgeably made. Closed Mon; July and Aug. *Via Carlo Goldoni 40–44, T: 0586 887583.*

€ **Antico Moro**. Classic seafood restaurant near the central market. Fish dishes only. Closed Wed and lunchtime except on Sun and holidays. *Via Bartelloni 59, T: 0586 884659.*

€ **Da Galileo**. Good place for the fish dishes, for which the town is famous. Off Via Garibaldi, east of Fortezza Nuova. *Via della Campana 20, T: 0586 889009.*

Pisa *(map p. 264, B3)*

€€ **Da Bruno**. Fashionable, sought-after restaurant serving seasonal cuisine. Hearty Pisan soup and salt cod with leeks are among the specialities. Closed Mon evening and Tues. *Via Luigi Bianchi 12, T: 050 560818.*

€€ **Ristorante Emilio**. Refined and elegant place. Meat and fish are served with great care and attention to detail. *Via Cammeo Carlo Salomone 44, T: 050 562141.*

€ **Osteria dei Cavalieri**. Typical Tuscan dishes creatively and inventively prepared, supported by a splendid wine cellar. Centrally located, in the lively university quarter. *Via San Frediano 16, T: 050 580858.*

Volterra *(map p. 264, C4)*

€€ **Il Sacco Fiorentino**. Warm atmosphere and welcoming staff. Good hearty food, including game when in season— the boar and *porcini* mushroom sauce is a classic. Closed Wed. *Piazza XX Settembre 18, T: 0588 88537.*

€ **Etruria**. An extremely popular place, some say the best in Volterra. Exellent value; dine on pasta with hare sauce beneath the beautifully frescoed ceiling.

Piazza dei Priori 6–8. T: 0588 86064.

€ **Il Rifugio**. Good down-to-earth restaurant serving traditional pizzas and pasta. *Piazza XX Settembre 9, T: 0588 86976.*

LOCAL SPECIALITIES

In **Pisa**, *torta co' bischeri* is traditionally eaten on Ascension Day. The round pastry tart is filled with a combination of rice, candied fruits, chocolate, strega liqueur and pine nuts. The characteristic *torta* of **Livorno**, made from chickpeas, is a delicious and cheap savoury snack, widely available. **Volterra** has for long been famous for its alabaster, and some 200 workshops here still produce *objets-d'art*.

FESTIVALS & EVENTS

Livorno *Risi'atori*, In the past, Livorno dockers would race each other to win the right to unload ships. That tradition is preserved in the traditional rowing race between *gozzi* (10-oar boats) and *gozzette* (4-oar boats), second Sun in June; *Palio Marinaro*, Another rowing race, this time only in *gozzi*, second Sun in July; *Effetto Venezia*, Festival in the Venezia Nuova quarter, with craft stalls and open-air performances, early Aug.

Pisa *Regata delle Repubbliche Marinare*, Traditional boat race between vessels representing Italy's ancient maritime republics: Genoa, Amalfi, Venice and Pisa, 16 June; *Festa di San Ranieri*, Feast of the patron saint, 16–17 June; *Gioco del Ponte*, A team of Pisans who live north of the Arno battle with those who live to the south to push a 7-ton cart over the Ponte di Mezzo, last Sun in June.

Volterra *Astiludio*, Flag-throwing and processions, first Sun in Sept.

THE CHIANTI &
SAN GIMIGNANO

The beautiful, hilly region between Florence and Siena is known as the Chianti district (*map p. 265, D3–E4*): properly speaking, this is the district of Chianti Classico, or *Gallo Nero*: the wines marked by a black cockerel on the label. Its characteristic landscape includes carefully tended vineyards, orchards and olive groves, as well as wilder wooded areas. It is particularly beautiful in autumn, when the leaves of the vines and deciduous trees turn to gold and stand out amidst the silver olives and dark green cypresses and pines. It is at this time that the harvest (*vendemmia*) takes place. Picturesque villages and medieval castles often dominate the hills and offer spectacular panoramas. The countryside is traversed by two winding roads, the Via Chiantigiana and the Via Cassia (following the route of one of the important consular roads which led north from Rome), but some of the most typical and beautiful parts of the countryside can be explored on white, unsurfaced roads. Also in this area are many old Romanesque country churches (*pievi*). Vineyards surround the typical, elegant farmhouses known as *case coloniche*. Many of them were built in the 18th century during the agricultural reforms carried out by Grand Duke Peter Leopold, and they are usually beautifully sited with characteristic towers (formerly dovecotes). Many are now second homes, often of non-Italians. Often the estates around the villas and castles produce their own wine, and their cellars are open to visitors.

Greve in Chianti

Greve in Chianti (*map p. 265, D3*), a pretty market town, has an attractive triangular piazza with porticoes along two sides. It is one of the centres of the wine trade. It has a small museum of diocesan art. Perched on a hill to the west, and still partly surrounded by its old walls, is the charming little medieval village of **Montefioralle**, the ancestral home of the Vespucci family. Amerigo Vespucci (1415–1512), a Medici agent in Seville, gave his name to America having made two voyages in 1494 and 1501–02 following the route charted by his Italian contemporary Columbus. **Panzano** to the south, originally a medieval castle in a strategic position, still preserves some of its old walls and towers. Its fine Romanesque *pieve*, San Leolino, is beautifully sited 1km south on a hill, and contains interesting works of art from the 13th–16th centuries, including a 15th-century triptych by an artist known as the Master of Panzano. All around Panzano are numerous villas and *case coloniche* in beautiful countryside.

Castellina in Chianti and the southern region

Castellina in Chianti (*map p. 265, D4*), with its 15th-century castle and town gate, is a small, well-kept medieval town which dominates the Arbia, Elsa and Pesa valleys, with spectacular views of woods, vineyards, olive groves, and scattered *case coloniche*. It has a modern suburb which meets the demands of the expanding wine trade, and smart shops which cater to its many visitors. A remarkable walkway (Via delle Volte) follows the eastern line of walls. There is a local archaeological museum in the castle, and just outside the town is the impressive Etruscan tomb of Montecalvario (7th century BC) surrounded by pine trees.

Radda in Chianti (*map p. 265, E4*), another major wine centre, was the principal castle of the Chianti League (a Florentine league against the Sienese) in the 13th century. On a hill to the north is the tiny fortified hamlet of **Castello di Volpaia**, in a splendid panoramic position. Wine has been produced here since the 11th century. The **Badia di Coltibuono** is a former abbey, surrounded by beautiful oak and pine woods, transformed into a villa, where wine is now produced. **Gaiole in Chianti** owes its importance as a market town to its position at the crossroads between the Chianti district and the upper Arno valley.

One of the most impressive castles in the Chianti which is open to the public is the **Castello di Brolio** (*map p. 265, E4*), the home of the Ricasoli family since the 12th century, and well known for its wine. Strategically placed at the south end of the Chianti hills, it was for centuries disputed between Florence and Siena. The impressive fortifications surrounding the castle date in part from the 16th century, but the villa was rebuilt in 1862–72 in Sienese Gothic style (with a dining room modelled on the medieval hall of an English castle) for Bettino Ricasoli, the eminent statesman and philanthropist, who died here in 1880. The magnificent view to the south stretches to Monte Amiata and Siena.

Further south is **San Gusmè**, one of the most picturesque villages in the area, surrounded by its original walls complete with two gateways. An excellent white wine (Val d'Arbia) is produced in this area.

CHIANTI CLASSICO

The Chianti Classico region includes the towns of San Casciano, Greve, Castellina, Radda, Gaiole, Castelnuovo Berardenga, Barberino Val d'Elsa, Tavarnelle and Poggibonsi. The 'recipe' for the wine itself is attributed to Baron Bettino Ricasoli (1809–80), second Prime Minister of united Italy, who recommended Sangiovese as the grape on which the wine should be based, with the addition of other native reds to temper it. Early Chianti broadly fell into two types: young, light, early-drinking wines, and slightly more robust wines with better ageing potential. Both were easy to drink table wines with no pretensions to top quality. But then something happened. During the dark ages of Italian wine-making in the 1960s and '70s, high yields per vine and poor fruit selection led to mass-market wines of indifferent quality, with Chianti a haphazard mix of red and white grapes. Regulations in the '80s limited the proportion of white grapes to between 10 and 30 percent; from 2006 white grapes were not permitted at all: Trebbiano and Malvasia have given place to Canaiolo and Colorino, other indigenous red varieties, or to noble varieties such as Cabernet Sauvignon and Merlot. Sangiovese must still provide the bulk of the wine (75–80 percent), and may indeed be the only grape used. The resulting wines are richly fruity and full-bodied. Chianti Classico Riserva is cask-aged for longer than simple Chianti Classico, making for a wine that can be cellared and left to mature longer in the bottle.

Barberino Val d'Elsa and Certaldo

The little village of **Barberino Val d'Elsa** (*map p. 265, D3*) preserves its medieval defensive walls and a gateway at either end of the main street, and several elegant palaces. At a crossroads on a by-road in beautiful countryside between Barberino Val d'Elsa and Certaldo there is a circular chapel surrounded by cypresses, known as **La Cupola** since it reproduces in miniature Brunelleschi's cupola of Florence cathedral. It was built in 1597 by Santi di Tito to commemorate the former stronghold of Semifonte, in a strategic position close to the Francigena and Volterrana roads, which became such a threat to Florence that in 1202, after a siege lasting four years, it was razed to the ground.

In the medieval walled upper town of **Certaldo** (*map p. 265, D3*; also reached by cablecar), built almost entirely of brick, Giovanni Boccaccio (*see box overleaf*) is known to have spent part of his later years, enjoying a peaceful and simple life. The rebuilt Casa del Boccaccio is now a museum (*closed at the time of writing*). The church of Santi Michele e Jacopo, where Boccaccio is buried, contains a charming fresco of the *Madonna and Child with Saints* by the 14th-century Sienese artist Memmo di Filippuccio. Next door is a museum with works from local churches, which include a monumental 13th-century Crucifix. At the top of the street, Palazzo Pretorio has its façade decorated with picturesque coats of arms in stone and glazed terracotta. The church of San Tommaso has frescoes by Benozzo Gozzoli.

Giovanni Boccaccio (1313–75)
Famous for his prose in the vernacular, Boccaccio, a great admirer of Dante (and friend of Petrarch), was of Florentine parentage, and it is his experience in the city during the great plague of 1348 which becomes—in his famous collection of short stories, the *Decameron*—an allegory of the moral decay of his time. Written in beautiful and articulate prose, it is a magnificent example of literary originality and of a 'Renaissance' sense of humour. In the *Decameron* Boccaccio imagines that three young men and seven young women, in order to escape a city devastated by greed and cupidity as well as the plague, find refuge for ten days in the lovely countryside near Fiesole where they recount stories to each other. Their tales create a world in which the bourgeois mercantile mentality is educated through the rediscovery of the values of *humanitas* and courtesy. Boccaccio is known to have had a great influence on European writers, including Chaucer.

At **Luiano** (*map p. 265, D3*) is one of the earliest churches in the Florentine diocese, which maintains its Romanesque structure and plan and exterior in white *alberese* stone. **Lucardo** is a hamlet with the remains of a castle, beautifully situated on a hill overlooking the Pesa and Elsa valleys. Its *pieve*, dating from the late 11th century, is a fine example of early Romanesque architecture, surrounded by medieval buildings. It is built entirely of sandstone and has a raised chancel terminating in three apses.

In a delightful setting east of the main road, enclosed by cypress trees and surrounded by vineyards and olive groves, is the monastery of **Badia a Passignano** (*map p. 265, D3*), founded in 1049. St Giovanni Gualberto, founder of the Vallombrosan Order, died here in 1073. The towers and battlements were added in the late 19th century. It contains a fresco of the *Last Supper* by Domenico and Davide Ghirlandaio (1476), and St Giovanni Gualberto's reliquary bust, made in Siena in 1324–32. In 1598–1602 Domenico Cresti, known as 'Il Passignano' since he was born in the village, remodelled the east end of the church and supplied it with frescoes and altarpieces. **San Donato in Poggio** nearby is a charming fortified medieval village in a beautiful setting, particularly well preserved. Just outside the village is a lovely Romanesque church of the late 12th century, built out of large blocks of cream-coloured *alberese* stone. Over the high altar is a Crucifix by a follower of Giotto, and the font is by Giovanni della Robbia.

SAN GIMIGNANO

San Gimignano (*map p. 265, D4*) is famous for its 13 tall towers, which have survived out of the many it—like numerous other small towns in central Italy—once had: they produce a wonderful sight from a distance, making the town look almost like a tiny modern city with so many skyscrapers in the middle of the wonderful Tuscan hills. San Gimignano is also remarkable for the fact that olive groves and orchards still reach right

Aerial view of the famous towers of San Gimignano.

up to its walls, and no new buildings have been allowed to alter its appearance. However, much has changed in the character of the place to accommodate the great number of tourists (an estimated 3 million a year) who flock here in spring and summer (mostly on day trips from Florence or Siena), making the little town almost always uncomfortably crowded. In the last few decades it has been supplied with a faster approach road, numerous car and coach parks, and new, rather over-bright brick paving in the old streets: most of the shops now cater to visitors rather than the local inhabitants. Only in the early morning in the depths of winter can you begin to feel what Edward Hutton found here in 1910: '*If we would know what a Tuscan hill town was like in the 14th century, we must go on foot or by carriage to San Gimignano delle belle Torri…there are few refuges in all Tuscany more secure from the rampant and sentimental materialism of our time than San Gimignano*'. There were reports at the time of writing of plans to build a new ring-road and two tunnels beneath the hill, with car parks for the 14,000 tour coaches which come here every year. Local inhabitants are battling to prevent these unwanted intrusions into the landscape.

On the credit side, San Gimignano has numerous artistic treasures, including important fresco cycles in the Collegiata, Palazzo del Popolo and Sant'Agostino, and some excellent little museums. The path at the foot of the 13th-century walls provides superb views of the town's wonderful setting in rich agricultural farmland which stretches for as far as the eye can see, and which is famous for its vineyards which produce the white Vernaccia wine, which was already renowned by the 14th century.

TOWERS

Towers were a characteristic feature of many medieval towns in central Italy (including Florence, Siena, Pisa and Lucca). They were first built by rich nobles for defence reasons: above strong stone foundations, the upper stories were usually faced with brick strengthened with an infill of cobbles and lime. They were usually around 50 or 60m high, but in some cases even higher. They would probably only have been inhabited in times of trouble, and sometimes they were built next to a nobleman's residence so that they could be connected to it when necessary by a flying bridge from a window on the upper storey. Others were constructed by members of one family or their associates in a group close together so they could dominate a particular area of a town.

During private disputes between feuding families a tower would sometimes be attacked from the street below, and perhaps toppled, while missiles were hurled from the upper storeys. When the first towers appeared in towns around the 11th century, they were modelled on the watch-towers which then existed in the countryside. They had become an extremely important feature of medieval towns by the 12th and 13th centuries. Only the wealthier inhabitants could afford to build these extremely tall 'houses', which also became status symbols: the higher the more impressive. At a certain stage, in order to lessen rivalry between their feuding inhabitants, many communes decided to fix a maximum height for them. In 1255 the town council of San Gimignano decreed that no tower was to exceed the height of the Torre della Rognosa (51m), which still stands in Piazza del Duomo. Over the centuries many towers were destroyed by order of the *comune* as a punishment against their owners and their retinues, since they were seen as tools which enabled certain families to become too powerful.

Today many central Italian towns still have one or two towers, often lowered in later centuries or incorporated into more comfortable town dwellings. Only San Gimignano still has enough of them grouped closely together to show us what a typical medieval skyline must have looked like.

The entrance to the town is through Porta San Giovanni (1262), the finest of the town gates. Via San Giovanni, with a good view of the tall tower of Palazzo del Popolo at the end (usually with large flocks of birds swirling around its summit), continues to the Arco dei Becci, another ancient gate beside several tall towers, forming part of the first circle of (12th-century) walls. Beyond is the triangular Piazza della Cisterna, built on a slight slope with a well dating from 1287, and surrounded by 13th–14th-century palaces, houses and towers. It is adjoined by Piazza del Duomo, another handsome medieval square with several spectacular towers.

HISTORY OF SAN GIMIGNANO

The town derives its name from St Jeminianus, a 4th-century bishop of Modena, traditionally venerated here. It has Etruscan origins and was later inhabited by the Romans. In medieval times it owed its prosperity to its position on the Via Francigena, an important road for commerce and the main pilgrim route to Rome from northern and central Europe (*see p. 448*), and it is reputed to have had 76 towers at that time. After the devastation caused by the Black Death in 1348, San Gimignano came under the protection of Florence and there was an artistic revival in the 15th century. However, the town declined commercially as a result of the deviation of the pilgrim route further northeast to the Elsa valley. The town now has around 7,000 inhabitants.

The Collegiata

Open 9.30–4.30; in summer 9.30–7. Ticket at the Museo d'Arte Sacra; a combined ticket gives admission to all the town's museums. The Museo d'Arte Sacra and Cappella di Santa Fina are closed in the last half of Jan and the last half of Nov.

The Romanesque Collegiata is the main church of San Gimignano, consecrated in 1148. Beneath an elegant loggia with 14th- and 15th-century frescoes is the baptismal font (1378). The interior is decorated with important fresco cycles, which were scarred by war damage but have been mainly well restored.

On the south wall the beautiful **New Testament cycle** is composed of 22 episodes on three levels, representing the life and Passion of Christ with a large Crucifixion scene in the fifth bay. It is one of the great works of Italian Gothic painting. For long attributed to Barna da Siena, it is now thought to have been executed some 50 years earlier, in 1333–41, by a master from the workshop of Simone Martini, possibly Lippo Memmi.

On the north wall the **Old Testament cycle**, again on three levels, comprises 26 episodes from the book of Genesis relating to Noah, Abraham, Joseph, Moses and Job. It is signed and dated 1367 by Bartolo di Fredi. On the west wall are the *Last Judgement*, *Paradise* and *Hell* by Taddeo di Bartolo (c. 1410). Flanking the west door are two fine wooden statues of the *Virgin Annunciate* and the *Angel Gabriel* by Jacopo della Quercia (1421; painted by another artist a few years later).

The beautifully preserved Renaissance **Cappella di Santa Fina**, decorated between 1468 and 1477, was commissioned from Giuliano da Maiano to honour Fina, a poor and devout girl who bore paralysis and severe bodily affliction with Christian fortitude. She is the patron saint of the town. The altar and marble shrine with exquisite bas-reliefs are by Benedetto da Maiano, and the rare reliquary bust of gilded and painted leather decorated with coloured glass inlay is thought to be an early 14th-century Sienese work. The frescoes decorating the vault and walls of the chapel are by Domenico Ghirlandaio: in the right lunette St Gregory is seen announcing to Santa Fina her imminent death (which was to occur on the day of his own feast), and a miraculous flowering of violets appears on her wooden bed; in the left lunette is shown the funeral of Santa Fina, accompanied by three miracles: the healing of her nurse's paralysed hand, the blind choir boy's sight regained, and the ringing of the church bells by angels. The saints and prophets are also by Ghirlandaio, possibly assisted by Sebastiano Mainardi.

The small **Museo d'Arte Sacra** (*open as Collegiata*) has mostly 15th–16th-century paintings, with works by Bartolo di Fredi and Benozzo Gozzoli. The sculpture includes busts by Pietro Torrigiani and Benedetto da Maiano (as well as a wooden Crucifix by him); a statue by Francesco di Valdambrino, and a wooden figure of Christ, similar to the *Volto Santo* of Lucca (*see p. 336*), probably an early 13th-century Sienese work.

Palazzo del Popolo

Palazzo del Popolo (1288–1323) contains the Museo Civico (*open 10–5; March–Oct 9.30–7*), and the splendid tower can be climbed. The **Sala del Consiglio** is where in 1299 Dante, as an ambassador of Florence, is supposed to have delivered his appeal to try to bring San Gimignano into the Guelph League. The superb large fresco of the *Maestà* is signed and dated 1317 by Lippo Memmi and his father, Memmo di Filippuccio. It shows the Madonna enthroned beneath a canopy surrounded by angels and saints, with the *podestà* Mino de' Tolomei kneeling in adoration. It recalls the famous work by Simone Martini (Memmo's son-in-law and pupil) in the Palazzo Pubblico in Siena, and it was subsequently enlarged in the mid-1350s by Bartolo di Fredi, who added two saints on each side. Benozzo Gozzoli is known to have repainted and restored parts of the fresco in 1466. The other walls were decorated in the late 13th century with Sienese frescoes of hunting and tournament scenes, and a depiction of the people of San Gimignano swearing allegiance to Charles of Anjou. In an adjoining room there are two busts by Pietro Torrigiani, one in painted marble of *Santa Fina* (c. 1498), and the other in painted terracotta of *St Gregory*.

At the top of the stairs is a little room with charming frescoes of domestic scenes warning against the wiles of women, including *Aristotle Ridden by Campaspe*, painted in the first years of the 14th century by Memmo di Filippuccio. The story goes that Aristotle, tutor to the young Alexander the Great, had warned his pupil to give up his lovely mistress, who was luring him away from affairs of state. Campaspe vowed to seduce the tutor herself, and succeeded: the riding scene symbolises Desire riding roughshod over Reason. The important collection of Sienese and Florentine paintings from the 13th–15th centuries includes a Crucifix with Passion scenes by Coppo di Marcovaldo, one of the masterpieces of 13th-century painting in Tuscany. The reliquary tabernacle of Santa Fina is a charming work painted around 1402 in brilliant colours on both sides, with stories of her life and miracles. Fourteenth-century works include the high altarpiece with *St Jeminianus* and stories from his life by Bartolo di Fredi. In the group of late 15th- and early 16th-century works are two altarpieces dating from 1466 by Benozzo Gozzoli, two large circular panels representing the *Annunciation*, early works of 1482 by Filippino Lippi, and a *Madonna in Glory with Sts Gregory and Benedict*, one of Pinturicchio's last works (1512).

Sant'Agostino

The church and convent of Sant'Agostino occupy the northernmost tip of the town, in a peaceful piazza which retains its ancient herring-bone paving. The church (*open 7–12 & 3–6 or ring at the convent*) was consecrated in 1298, and preserves some very fine works of art. The **Cappella di San Bartolo** contains the splendid tomb of the Blessed Bartolo (1228–1300), another patron of San Gimignano, made by Benedetto da Maiano in 1495. Set in a niche with a marble curtain drawn back on either side, it is composed of an urn with reliefs of two flying angels, above which are the three Theological Virtues seated in niches, and a roundel with a beautiful relief of the *Madonna and Child*. At the base of the shrine are three predella scenes with episodes from the saint's life. The frescoes of *Sts Jeminianus, Lucy and Nicholas of Bari* are by Sebastiano Mainardi, who also painted the four Doctors of the Church in the vault.

In the **nave** the striking large votive fresco of St Sebastian interceding for the citizens of San Gimignano after the 1464 plague is by Benozzo Gozzoli. On the same side there is a fragmentary fresco of the *Madonna and the Archangel Michael* by Lippo Memmi. There are also frescoes of c. 1374 by Bartolo di Fredi, and early 16th-century paintings by Vincenzo Tamagni. Mainardi painted the fresco of St Jeminianus blessing three dignitaries of the city (1487), above an effigy of Fra' Domenico Strambi, the patron who commissioned the painting for the high altar and the frescoes in the choir.

The large **high altarpiece** depicting the *Coronation of the Virgin worshipped by Sts Fina, Augustine, Bartolo, Jeminianus, Jerome and Nicholas of Tolentino* is signed and dated 1483 by Piero Pollaiolo. It has a wonderful azure-blue ground, and very unusual, elegant figures of *Christ* and the *Virgin*, both with blue cloaks, and a delightful glory of angels.

The **choir** is covered with charming frescoes by Benozzo Gozzoli and assistants (1464–65) illustrating the life of St Augustine. The sequence begins on the left wall:

Left wall, lower register: Augustine is sent to school in his native town of Thagaste; at 19 he goes to Carthage university.

Window wall: St Monica prays for her son; Augustine sails to Italy; his arrival in Italy. (The scenes were ruined by damp and repainted in the 18th century.)

Right wall: Augustine teaches Rhetoric and Philosophy in Rome; he departs for Milan (inscribed and dated 1465 by the artist, who included his self-portrait in this scene—last figure on the right).

Left wall, middle register: Augustine is received by St Ambrose and the Emperor Theodosius; (left) he listens to St Ambrose preaching; (centre) Monica implores the conversion of her son; (right) Augustine discusses Manichaeism with St Ambrose.

Window wall: Augustine reads the Epistles of St Paul; he is baptised by St Ambrose.

Right wall: (left) Augustine and the Infant Jesus on the seashore; (right) Augustine explains the rule to his monks; (centre) he visits the hermits at Montepisano; death of his mother St Monica.

Lunettes: Augustine, a consecrated bishop, blesses the people of Hippo; he converts the heretic Fortunatus; Augustine in ecstasy is inspired by St Jerome; Augustine's funeral.

The northern districts

The Romanesque church of **San Pietro** contains frescoes by Memmo di Filippuccio. In the large ex-convent of **Santa Chiara**, with a pretty garden, is part of the Musei Civici (the Museo Archeologico, the Spezeria di Santa Fina, and the Galleria d'Arte Moderna; *open 11–5.45; mid-June–mid-Nov 11–6*). The archaeological collection, well displayed in six rooms has Etruscan, Roman and medieval finds from the city and district. Ceramic jars and glass from the pharmacy of Santa Fina (1507) are arranged in 19th-century showcases. There is also a collection of good paintings by Raffaelle de Grada (1885–1957), who lived and worked here (his wife was a native of the town).

COLLE DI VAL D'ELSA

Close to San Gimignano is the little town of Colle di Val d'Elsa (*map p. 265, D4*), a town much less geared to tourism than San Gimignano. It is divided in two: the medieval upper town, preserved intact, is situated high up on a narrow rocky spur, and the lower town has spread out on the banks of the River Elsa. In the Middle Ages the town had flourishing wool and paper industries; today it has a number of glass factories. Colle was repeatedly disputed between Siena and Florence, notably in a battle here in 1269 in which the Florentines were victors. It finally came under Florentine dominion in 1333.

A splendid bridge (originally a drawbridge), with a fine panorama on either side, links Borgo Santa Caterina to Castello, the oldest district of the upper town, which has a sleepy atmosphere, and just three parallel streets. The very beautiful paving (carefully restored a few years ago) is made from large blocks of stone in different shades of grey and brown. An archway is incorporated in the stately Palazzo Campana, built in 1539 by Giuliano di Baccio d'Agnolo. The other handsome large 16th-century palaces here are all discreetly labelled and dated. In Piazza del Duomo, which retains its herring-bone brick paving, is Palazzo Pretorio (1335), which houses the **Museo Archeologico** (*open Tues–Fri 3.30–5.30; Sat and Sun 10.30–12.30 & 3.30–6.30; closed Mon*), which has Etruscan pottery and bronze objects excavated in the Elsa valley, and a collection of finds from an Etruscan necropolis. The **duomo** has a mainly 17th-century interior, though the pulpit is decorated with bas-reliefs dating from 1465, and in the south transept there is a pretty marble tabernacle attributed to Mino da Fiesole. The bronze lectern here is by Pietro Tacca. The **Museo Civico d'Arte Sacra** (*open 10–12 & 4–7 except Mon; weekends only in winter*) has good 16th–17th-century paintings, as well as a beautiful *Maestà* attributed to the Master of Badia a Isola, a late 13th- or early 14th-century artist very close to Duccio; and a *Madonna* by Segna di Bonaventura from the same period. The Treasury of Galognano, found in a field nearby in 1963, includes four rare silver chalices and a paten, thought to date from the late 6th century AD.

The Romanesque church of **Santa Maria in Canonica** has a simple interior with a lovely gold-ground altarpiece by Pier Francesco Fiorentino, complete with its predella. At the end of the street is the medieval tower-house taken to be the **birthplace of Arnolfo di Cambio**, the architect and sculptor who built Palazzo Vecchio in Florence. Just beyond it there is a good view from the top of a bastion, where a glass box contains a lift which descends to the lower town. The winding Via di Mezzo leads back to Piazza Duomo and from there Via delle Volte, a remarkable old covered alleyway, well lit, returns to emerge near the entrance bridge.

In the lower town, where the attractive main square is Piazza Arnolfo, is the fine church of **Sant'Agostino**, rebuilt in 1521 by Antonio da Sangallo the Elder, with good 16th-century altarpieces, including a *Pietà* by Cigoli.

PRACTICAL INFORMATION

GETTING AROUND

• **By car:** Free parking in **San Gimignano** is available on Via Roma, south of Piazza Martiri di Montemaggio. Near Porta San Giovanni is Montemaggio car park (limited space; hourly tariff). There are other pay car parks off the approach roads to north and south (signposted P3 and P4). **Colle di Val d'Elsa** has a car park beneath the walls (steps to the upper town).
• **By train:** Trains from Siena and Empoli and a few from Florence go direct to Certaldo and Poggibonsi, from where there is a bus service to **San Gimignano** (20mins) and to **Colle di Val d'Elsa**.
• **By bus:** Buses from most places to **San Gimignano** and **Colle di Val d'Elsa** require a change at Poggibonsi, from which there are frequent services. Buses from Florence (from Via S. Caterina da Siena, near Santa Maria Novella station), operated by SITA (www.sitabus.it), go to **Greve in Chianti** in 1hr. Less frequent services (one or two daily) link Florence with **Panzano**, **Radda** and **Gaiole** (2hrs).

INFORMATION OFFICES

Certaldo Via Giovanni Boccaccio 16, T: 0571 652730.
Colle di Val d'Elsa Via Campana 43, T: 0577 922791; Piazza Arnolfo in the lower town, T: 0577 920389.
Greve in Chianti Via Luca Cini, T; 055 854 5243.
San Gimignano Piazza Duomo 1, T: 0577 940008.

HOTELS

Greve in Chianti (*map p. 265, D3*)
€€ Castello di Lamole. Nine apartments converted from farm buildings, each nicely appointed. Rough-hewn walls and heavy wooden furniture make for rustic comfort. Restaurant. *Via di Lamole, Località Lamole, T: 055 630498. 9 apartments.*
Certaldo (*map p. 265, D3*)
€€ Il Castello. The historic, ivy-clad Palazzo Scoto di Semifonte has traditionally furnished rooms full of venerable antiques and oil paintings. A gracious, elegant place to stay (minimum three nights). Closed Nov. *Via Giovanni della Rena 6, T: 0571 668250, www.albergoilcastello.it. 12 rooms.*
Colle di Val d'Elsa (*map p. 265, D4*)
€€ Fattoria Belvedere. A lovely wine-producing *agriturismo*. The hotel is in an

18th-century villa and farmhouse. Other farm buildings have been converted into comfortable apartments, furnished in country-house style. Tastings are arranged of all the farm's produce (booking required). Cookery school and restaurant. *Colle di Val d'Elsa, T: 0577 920009, www.fattoriabelvedere.com. 57 rooms.*

Fiano (*map p. 265, D3*)

€€€ **Il Palchetto**. An ancient inn with large, comfortable rooms, all cosily decorated in warm terracotta colours and furnished with fine wooden furniture. The original medieval walls and brick arcading are retained in the restaurant. Garden and pool. *Strada Provinciale 79, Località Palchetto, T: 0571 669687, www.ilpalchetto.com. 11 rooms.*

Greve in Chianti (*map p. 265, D3*)

€€ **Albergo del Chianti**. In the main square, in an old town house tastefully decorated; the owner is a collector of old Tuscan furniture. Food and wine tastings by arrangement. *Piazza G. Matteotti 86, T: 0558 53763, www.albergodelchianti.it. 16 rooms.*

€€ **Albergo Giovanni da Verrazzano**. Medieval building in the town square, furnished in an unfussy, comfortable style—cool white walls, terracotta-tiled floors. Restaurant. *Piazza G. Matteotti 28, T: 0558 53189, www.albergoverrazzano.it. 10 rooms.*

€€ **Castello Vicchiomaggio**. Widely-praised complex of apartments in a 15th-century hilltop castle. Old-world charm combined with modern comfort and convenience. Cookery classes, and wine tasting by arrangement. *Via Vicchiomaggio 4, T: 0558 54079, www.vicchiomaggio.it. 7 rooms.*

Radda in Chianti (*map p. 265, E4*)

€€€ **Palazzo Leopoldo**. Originally a pilgrim's hostel, then the estate house managing 24 farms, Palazzo Leopoldo retains its original fresco decoration, terracotta-tiled floors and huge fireplaces. Breakfast is served on the terrace, or in the 18th-century kitchen. Restaurant and cookery school. *Via Roma 33, T: 0577 735605, www.palazzoleopoldo.it. 17 rooms.*

€€€ **Hotel San Niccolò**. Beautiful 15th-century palazzo, recently renovated, retaining many of the original structural and decorative features. Rooms are of a generous size, with marble bathrooms; showers and jacuzzis are modern conveniences discreetly accommodated. *Via Roma 16, T: 0577 735666, www.hotelsanniccolo.com. 15 rooms.*

San Gimignano (*map p. 265, D4*)

€€€ **Relais Santa Chiara**. Elegant hotel just below the city walls, set in private grounds with a garden, terraces and a pool. Sensitively decorated with nice attention to detail. Shady patio for dining and enjoying the views. *Via Matteotti 15, T: 0577 940701, www.rsc.it. 41 rooms.*

€€€ **Villa San Paolo**. Typical Tuscan villa in beautiful, terraced gardens. Rooms are bright and light and not over fussy; an informal and relaxed place to stay. Swimming pool and restaurant. *Strada per Certaldo-Casini-San Paolo, T: 0577 955100, www.villasanpaolo.com. 78 rooms.*

€€ **Apartamenti Rossi Carla**. Apartments within the historic centre, some with stone floors, beamed ceilings and antique furniture, and all with exceptional views. There is also a B&B outside the centre owned by the same mother-and-son partnership. *Via di Cellole 81, T: 0577 955041. www.accommodation-sangimignano.it. 8 apartments.*

€€ **L'Antico Pozzo**. A 15th-century building, now restored. Beautiful, clean rooms have high ceilings and frescoes.

Friendly, helpful staff. The place has a loyal following. *Via San Matteo 87, T: 0577 942014, www.anticopozzo.com. 18 rooms.*

RESTAURANTS

Castellina in Chianti (*map p. 265, D4*)
€€€ **Albergaccio di Castellina.** Intimate restaurant serving fresh, local dishes, with rabbit, Tuscan lamb, pigeon and *cinta senese* pork and salami featuring heavily. A carefully selected wine list accompanies the menu. Closed Sun. *Via Fiorentina 63, T: 0577 741042.*
€€€ **Al Gallopapa** Exquisitely presented dishes covering the whole range of Tuscan cuisine, served in a relaxed atmosphere. Booking recommended. Closed Mon. *Via delle Volte 14/16, T: 0577 742939.*
Colle di Val d'Elsa (*map p. 265, D4*)
€€€ **Antica Trattoria.** A superb restaurant, relaxed and welcoming. It prides itself on creative cooking while still paying homage to the great classics of the area. Closed Tues. *Piazza Arnolfo 23, T: 0577 923747.*
Radda in Chianti (*map p. 265, E4*)
€€ **La Perla del Palazzo.** Restaurant attached to the Palazzo Leopoldo. Good Tuscan food, thoughtfully presented and complemented by an excellent choice of local wines. *Via Roma 33, T: 0577 735605.*
San Gimignano (*map p. 265, D4*)
€€ **Ristorante Beppone.** Central restaurant in the cellar of a medieval building with brick arcading. Varied menu ranging from pizza to up-dated Tuscan recipes. Friendly owner and staff. *Via delle Romite 13, T: 0577 943135.*
€€ **Le Terrazze.** Part of La Cisterna hotel, this restaurant has magnificent views of the towers. The food is mainly traditional: try the *zuppa sangimignese.*

Piazza della Cisterna 23, T: 0577 940328.
€ **La Mangiatoia.** Quite an unusual place, near Porta San Matteo. There are several underground rooms with original 13th-century vaults, stuccoed walls and stained-glass panels, but very cosy and friendly. Outdoor seating also available. Try the rabbit with artichokes or pasta filled with pecorino and truffles. Closed Tues. *Via Mainardi 5. T: 0577 941528.*

LOCAL SPECIALITIES

The region's most famous product is its **wine**. For information on booking wine tours, and winery accommodation, see www.chianticlassico.net.
San Gimignano is known for its Vernaccia wine, and for its excellent saffron. The region as a whole produces excellent **olive oil**.

FESTIVALS & EVENTS

Chianti Festival, All over the region villages have pageants, outdoor theatre and concerts, July; Wine festival throughout the region on second weekend of Sept, beginning on the Friday.
Montefioralle *Festa delle Fritelle*, Rice fritters feast, Sun nearest St Joseph's Day (19 March).
Panzano *Festa della Stagion Bona*, The 'good season' is ushered in with a costume pageant, 25 April; Hazelnut festival 14 Aug.
San Gimignano Feast of St Jeminianus, 31 Jan; Feast of Santa Fina, 12 March; *Ferie delle Messi*, Harvest festival in medieval costume, with jousting and tilting at the quintain, late June; *Giallo come l'oro*, The 'yellow as gold' saffron festival, Oct.

THE CASENTINO &
UPPER TIBER VALLEY

The Casentino (*map p. 265, F3*) is the beautiful wooded upper valley of the Arno. The valley was dominated from the 10th until the middle of the 15th century by the Guidi counts, whose numerous castles are a feature of the region. Because of its position between Florence and Arezzo, it was long disputed between the two cities, but Florence remained the dominant force after its victory here on the plain of Campaldino in 1289. High up above the valley are the famous monasteries of La Verna and Camaldoli. Beautiful walks can be taken in the area, and in particular in the Parco Nazionale delle Foreste Casentinesi, Monte Falterona e Campigna.

The 11th-century **Castello di Romena** is the most important of the Guidi castles, where the exiled Dante sheltered after his expulsion from Florence. The impressive and well-kept remains are open by appointment (*T: 0575 582520*). Nearby is the **Pieve di Romena**, the most beautiful Romanesque church in the Casentino. It was built in 1152, although remains of its 9th-century foundations can still be seen. It has a splendid east end with blind arcading. The lovely interior (*only open by appointment; T: 0575 583725*) has a raised presbytery and fine capitals. **Stia** is a pretty little town where the Arno meets its first tributary, the Staggia, and there are fine walks to the river's source and from there to the summit of Monte Falterona (1654m), now part of a national park adjoining the Forest of Camaldoli.

Pratovecchio and Camaldoli

The large village of **Pratovecchio** was the birthplace of Paolo Uccello. The church of San Giovanni has a well-preserved painting of the *Assumption* attributed to an unknown 15th-century master called from this work the 'Master of Pratovecchio'. In a wooded valley above the village is the little **church of Valiana** (San Romolo), built in 1126, which contains a remarkable painting of *Christ in Pietà* with symbols of the Passion, dating from the late 14th or early 15th century.

In the splendid **forest of Camaldoli** silver firs and beech trees predominate. The forest is crossed by numerous streams and deer run wild here. It forms part of the Parco Nazionale delle Foreste Casentinesi-Monte Falterona-Campigna, one of the largest areas of forest left in Italy (36,000 hectares) The **Hermitage of Camaldoli** (Eremo di Camaldoli; 1100m) was founded in 1012 by St Romuald in this *campo amabile*, or 'charming field'; its present name is a corruption of these two words. The hermits of the Camaldolese order used to live in entire isolation: 12 monks now live here but they no longer choose to live a rigorous hermit's life, and meet for services, meals and work (*church and cell of St Romuald open 8.30–11.15 & 3–6; Sun and holidays 8.30–10.45 & 3–6*). Outside the church is the gateway into the enclosure (*no admission*) with the 20 hermits' cells, really a little village of tiny self-contained houses.

The **Monastery of Camaldoli** (Monastero di Camaldoli; 818m), founded in 1046, now houses about 40 Carthusian monks (*open daily 6.30–1 & 3–8*). The 16th-century pharmacy (*open 9–12.30 & 2.30–6.30; in winter closed on Wed*) preserves its lovely carved wooden cupboards and panelling. Products made by the monks are sold here. Another room is arranged as an apothecary's workshop.

St Romuald (c. 950–1027)

Romuald was born into a noble family in Ravenna in the 9th century. As a young man, he was involved in a family feud during which his father killed a relative, an episode which shocked Romuald deeply. Although innocent, he retired as a penitent to a Benedictine monastery. After a series of visions, he decided to become a monk himself, but found the behaviour of his brethren too lax. Instead he travelled as an itinerant priest, founding hermitages and small monastic communities. Emperor Otto III tried to persuade him to settle down as an abbot, but his strict adherence to the Rule of St Benedict made him unpopular with the monks; he left them to go to Monte Cassino. Even there he found plenty to criticise, and took to the road again, sometimes with like-minded companions, sometimes alone. In 1012 Count Maldolo of Arezzo gave him a piece of land at Camaldoli, where he founded his most famous monastery, renowned for the severity with which the monks applied the Benedictine rule to their daily lives. After his death in 1027, Romuald's body was stolen more than once by over-zealous monks and taken to various convents, until the 15th century when it was brought to San Biagio, the church of the Camaldolese order in Fabriano in the Marche, where it still lies.

Poppi and Bibbiena

At a fork on the main road between Pratovecchio and Poppi a column marks the **site of the Battle of Campaldino** on 11th June 1289. Here Dante fought as a young man in the Florentine Guelph army against the Ghibellines of Arezzo, who were defeated, and their leader, Bishop Guglielmino Ubertino, killed. It is estimated that some 2,400 mounted knights and 18,000 foot soldiers took part in the battle, which for centuries held almost mythical importance in the imagination of those who lived in the Casentino.

Poppi (*map p. 65, F3*) is a delightful little hill town, and its splendid castle (*open daily 10–6; in Nov and Dec only on Sat and Sun*) is the best preserved in the Casentino. It is thought to have been built for the Guidi counts by a certain Lapo, Arnolfo di Cambio's master, and the wing on the left was probably completed by Arnolfo di Cambio himself. The courtyard has a delightful staircase with old wooden balconies, and numerous coats of arms. Plans and models illustrate the famous Battle of Campaldino (*see above*). The library has a collection of 519 medieval manuscripts and 780 incunabula. On the top floor a chapel has good frescoes by Taddeo Gaddi (1330–40). At the end of the main street is the abbey church of San Fedele (*open 9–6.30*), built in 1185–95, one of the most important churches in the Casentino. On its high altar is a 14th-century painted Cross, and in the south transept is a *Madonna and Child* by the Maestro della Maddalena (late 13th century).

Bibbiena (*map p. 265, F3*) is one of the oldest towns in the Casentino: its name may be derived from *Vibia*, an Etruscan family. Built on a low hill, it is now the most important place in the valley, surrounded by small factories; in fact, the plain to the south has been disfigured by new buildings in recent years. Bernardo Dovizi, called Cardinal Bibbiena (1470–1520), famous statesman and man of letters, was born here. He was responsible for the election of Cardinal Giovanni de' Medici to the papal throne as Leo X, and was a friend and patron of Raphael, who painted his portrait (now in Palazzo Pitti in Florence). His daughter was to have married Raphael, but died before the wedding. She is commemorated together with Raphael in the Pantheon in Rome (*see p. 47*). The parish church of Bibbiena contains lovely paintings and a 13th-century Crucifix.

La Verna and Caprese Michelangelo

The monastery of **La Verna** (*map p. 265, F3; open 6.30–7.30 pm*) stands on a curiously shaped outcrop (1129m) visible for many miles around. The site was given to St Francis in 1213, and here in 1224 the Saint received the Stigmata. It is still a Franciscan convent (with about 30 friars) and a retreat. In 1433 Pope Eugenius IV commissioned a number of enamelled terracotta altars from Andrea della Robbia, today considered his masterpieces. There is a procession of the friars every day at 3pm from the monastery to the Chapel of the Stigmata, which contains a beautiful tondo of the *Madonna and Child* by Luca della Robbia and a large enamelled terracotta *Crucifixion* (1480–81) by Andrea della Robbia (in a delightful frame), one of the most monumental della Robbian works ever made. The Chiesa Maggiore is also filled with wonderful works by Andrea.

Caprese Michelangelo (*map p. 265, F3*) is a tiny isolated hamlet (pop. 200), with fine views. It is famous because this is where Michelangelo happened to have been born in 1475, since his father, Leonardo Buonarroti, was appointed *podestà* here in that year. A short time after Michelangelo's birth, the family moved back to Florence. Today the district is known for its delicious wild mushrooms (*porcini*).

SANSEPOLCRO & ENVIRONS

Sansepolcro (properly Borgo San Sepolcro; *map p. 267, F1*) is an attractive little town in a plain in the upper Tiber valley, in a tobacco-growing area on the Tuscan-Umbrian border. Most of its buildings date from the 15th century. It is famous as the birthplace of Piero della Francesca (1416–92), and preserves some beautiful works by him.

According to an ancient tradition, Sansepolcro is named in honour of relics brought back from the Holy Sepulchre in Jerusalem by two pilgrims named Arcanus and Egidius, who settled here on their return. An abbey built in the town in 1012 soon became very powerful, and Sansepolcro became seat of a bishopric in 1520. The town was contested between its powerful neighbours Perugia, Città di Castello, Rimini and the Papal States, as well as Milan, until it came under Florentine dominion in 1441. It was severely shaken by earthquake in 1351–52, and was again damaged in the Second World War. The Buitoni family began their pasta business here in 1827.

Museo Civico

The Museo Civico (*open every day 9.30–1 & 2.30–6; summer 9–1.30 & 2.30–7.30*) is famous for its masterpieces by Piero della Francesca. The beautiful polyptych of the *Madonna della Misericordia* was commissioned from him by the local confraternity. The **fresco of the *Resurrection*** was described by Aldous Huxley, in his *Notes and Essays of a Tourist* (*Along the Road*), as the best picture in the world. Huxley also has it described thus by the hero of *Antic Hay*, Theodore Gumbril. Justly one of Piero's most famous works, the remarkable figure of Christ is one of the most haunting images ever produced in Christian art. His head shows the influence of Masaccio, but the expression has a new spiritual intensity. The peaceful scene below, with the soldiers asleep, offers a striking contrast. Christ's foot is shown in perfect perspective. Also here are two more frescoes by Piero: the fragment of the bust of a saint (?St Julian), found in the former church of Santa Chiara, and *St Louis of Toulouse*. Piero also painted the central panel, with the *Baptism of Christ*, of the triptych by Matteo di Giovanni displayed here (that central panel is now in the National Gallery, London). Other works include a standard painted on both sides (*Crucifixion and Saints*) by Luca Signorelli, enamelled terracottas by Andrea della Robbia, and paintings by Santi di Tito.

The town of Sansepolcro

The **duomo** has an imposing Romanesque interior with Gothic elements. In the sanctuary, the polyptych with the *Resurrection of Christ*, attributed to Niccolò di Segna (son of Segna di Bonaventura), later influenced Piero della Francesca when he painted his own famous fresco of the *Resurrection* (*see above*). The date of the ancient *Volto Santo*, a huge wooden figure of Christ on the Cross, is still under discussion, but it seems that it may even predate the more famous work in Lucca (*see p. 336*). The other fine works include a fresco of the *Madonna with Sts Catherine of Alexandria and Thomas Becket* by the School of Rimini (1383), and 16th-century altarpieces.

In **Via Niccolò Aggiunti** is a large palace (no. 71) which was probably designed by Piero della Francesca, and where he may have lived for a time. It is now a study centre.

In the southern part of the town is the deconsecrated church of **San Lorenzo** (*open 9–1 & 3–7*), which contains a dark and crowded *Deposition* by Rosso Fiorentino (1528), painted while the artist was staying here after he had escaped from the Sack of Rome (*see p. 27*). Above is a lunette with *God the Father* by Raffaellino del Colle, whose works can also be seen in the museum and other churches in the town.

ANGHIARI & MONTERCHI

Anghiari (pop. 6,000; *map p. 267, E1*), in a spectacular position above a plain, has a well-preserved centre, typical of a medieval walled town. In 1440 it was the scene of a Florentine victory, under Francesco Sforza, over the Visconti of Milan (the subject of a fresco commissioned from Leonardo da Vinci for Palazzo Vecchio in Florence, the completed fragment of which has been lost). A museum in the town is dedicated to the battle. The local artisans are skilled cabinet-makers.

Major sights of Anghiari

In Piazza Baldaccio, the old market-place, a monumental arcade was erected in 1889. The unspoilt, walled medieval town lies on the other side of the square. Via Trieste ascends steeply to **Santa Maria delle Grazie**, which has an 18th-century Neoclassical interior and contains two charming early 16th-century paintings in their original frames by Giovanni Antonio Sogliani: the *Last Supper* and the *Washing of the Feet*.

The lower road from Piazza Baldaccio leads to Piazza Mameli, with the handsome Renaissance **Palazzo Taglieschi**, probably built in 1437. It contains a good local museum (*open 8.30–7; Sun and holidays 9–1; closed Mon*) whose treasures include a *Madonna* in polychrome wood. Made c. 1420, it is very well preserved, and one of the best works by the great Sienese sculptor Jacopo della Quercia. It is not known whether the *Child* was sculpted at the same time, nor whether it was intended as part of this group.

Left from Piazza Mameli, a road leads up to the inconspicuous church of the **Badia**, reconstructed in the 14th century, and with an unusual asymmetrical interior. A carved dossal attributed to Desiderio da Settignano surrounds a painted, wooden high relief of the seated *Madonna*, with the standing *Child* by Tino di Camaino. Dating from c. 1316, this beautiful work is the only wooden sculpture known by Tino. Opposite the church, in the former headquarters of the Confraternità della Misericordia, there is a delightful little museum (*for admission ring at Via Nenci 13, or T: 0575 789577*) illustrating the history of this charitable institution, one of many which are still active all over Tuscany.

Monterchi

Monterchi (*map p. 267, F1*) is a quiet little fortified village, damaged by earthquakes in the past. It was the birthplace of Piero della Francesca's mother, and the famous fresco of the **Madonna del Parto** by Piero was probably intended as a memorial to her. She is thought to have been buried in the cemetery at the foot of the hill just outside the village, where the fresco once decorated the church of Momentana, partially demolished in 1785. It was later included in a chapel in the cemetery, before being detached in 1910. Since its restoration in 1993, the Madonna has been displayed in an old school building in the village (*open April–Sept 9–1 & 2–6/7; closed Mon*). It now seems unlikely that it will be returned to the little chapel: its present display in a stark black glass case with harsh lighting has been justly criticised. The fresco was painted around 1460, and shows the pregnant Madonna revealed by two angels pulling back the curtains of a tent. It is perhaps one of the most moving works of art ever produced.

PRACTICAL INFORMATION

GETTING AROUND

• **By car**: Free parking in **Sansepolcro** in Via dei Molini, outside Porta del Castello, and in Via Alessandro Volta. A pay car park is outside Porta Fiorentina.

In **Anghiari** there is a car park off Via Matteotti below Piazza Baldacchio.
• **By train**: Bibbiena, **Poppi** and **Stia** are linked to Arezzo by rail.
• **By bus**: Several buses a day run between Florence and **Poppi** (2hrs) and **Bibbiena** (c. 2hrs 20mins). Buses also link Florence and **Stia** (1hr 45mins). Local buses from Arezzo serve **Caprese Michelangelo**; from Bibbiena there are buses to **Camaldoli** and **La Verna**. Sansepolcro, **Anghiari** and **Monterchi** are all accessible by bus from Arezzo and Florence.

INFORMATION OFFICES

Anghiari Corso Matteotti 103, T: 0575 749279, www.anghiari.it
Poppi Via Nazionale Badia Prataglia 14a, T: 0575 559054.
Sansepolcro Piazza Garibaldi 2, T: 0575 377678.

HOTELS

Anghiari (*map p. 267, E1*)
€ **La Meridiana**. In the old town, this hotel has been welcoming guests for more than 40 years. Modern and comfortable with a restaurant. *Piazza IV Novembre 8, T: 0575 788102, www.hotellameridiana.it. 23 rooms.*
Caprese Michelangelo (*map p. 265, F3*)
€ **Buca di Michelangelo**. A peaceful hotel with stunning views of the Tiber valley. Rooms are simply decorated with white walls, terracotta tiles, wooden beams and crisp cotton sheets. Close to Michelangelo's birthplace and the church where he was baptised. *Via Roma 51, T: 0575 793921, www.bucadimichelangelo.it. 20 rooms.*

Poppi (*map p. 265, F3*)
€ **Casentino**. Cosy and welcoming hotel in the town centre. Rooms are smartly decorated with cool-coloured walls and comfortable furnishings. Restaurant in the old castle stables. *Piazza della Repubblica 6, T: 0575 529090, www.albergocasentino.it. 30 rooms.*
€ **La Torricella**. Just outside the village, surrounded by lovely countryside. Rooms are traditionally furnished, with delightful patchwork quilts on the beds, beamed ceilings and creamy-white walls. There's a fine restaurant where the owner's daughter creates some superb cakes and desserts. *Località Torricella, T: 0575 527045/6, www.latorricella.com. 13 rooms.*
Sansepolcro (*map p. 267, F1*)
€€ **Borgo Palace**. Modern-looking from the outside, with lots of glass and marble, but the warm-coloured furnishings soften the edge. Rooms are plush and comfortable. There are splendid views of the wooded hills of the Tiber valley and a large garden. *Via Senese Aretina 80, T: 0575 736050, www.borgopalace.it. 74 rooms.*
€ **La Balestra**. A comfortable hotel which takes its name from the Palio della Balestra, a medieval cross-bow tournament in which the Tricca family (who own the hotel) have taken part for many years. The rooms are modern and well-furnished. Restaurant and parking. *Via dei Montefeltro 29, T: 0575 735151, www.labalestra.it. 51 rooms.*

RESTAURANTS

Anghiari (*map p. 267, F1*)
€ **Da Alighiero**. A lively, bustling place serving good, hearty Tuscan food. Closed Tues. *Via Garibaldi 8, T: 0575 788040.*

€ **La Nena**. Delicious home cooking. The game soufflé is excellent. Fine choice of wines. Good value. *Corso Giacomo Matteotti 10–14, T: 0575 789491.*

Caprese Michelangelo (*map p. 265, F3*)
€ **Buca di Michelangelo**. Attached to the hotel of the same name, this is a good place for spit-roasted meats and locally grown mushrooms. Friendly service. *Via Roma 51, T: 0575 793921.*
€ **Fonte della Galletta**. Simple hotel restaurant offering delicious, authentic Tuscan food and magnificent scenery. *Località Alpe Faggeta, T: 0575 793925.*

Monterchi (*map p. 267, F1*)
€ **Il Trovato**. A popular place with locals serving good, filling Tuscan food—veal, *porcini* mushrooms, truffles, and fish on Fridays. *Piazza Umberto I 20/21, T: 0575 70111.*
€ **La Vecchia Osteria**. Pretty little restaurant in a lovely old building well located for before or after a visit to Piero della Francesca's *Madonna del Parto.* White truffles, *porcini* mushrooms and chestnuts when in season all feature here, as well as good beef and game. *Via dell'Ospedale 16, T: 0575 70121.*

Sansepolcro (*map p. 267, F1*)
€ **La Balestra**. Hotel restaurant offering seasonal Tuscan food. In the summer barbecues feature strongly. Tasting menu also available. All food is locally produced. Closed Mon. *Via de' Montefeltro 29, T: 0575 735151.*
€ **Da Ventura**. Central, reliable, family-run restaurant with good Tuscan food. You'll be tempted to try the four-course menu, but if you want less you'll have to be firm about it. Accommodation also available. Closed Sun evenings and Mon. *Via Aggiunti 30, T: 0575 742560.*

€ **Enoteca Guidi**. Difficult to beat for a simple, unfussy lunch between sightseeing bouts. *Via Luca Paccioli 44, T: 0575 736587.*
€ **Il Fiorentino**. Lovely, honest food in a friendly atmosphere. Everything is fresh and seasonal, complemented by good wines. There are also four well-appointed rooms; don't let the lack of stars put you off. *Via Luca Pacioli 60, T: 0575 742033.*

LOCAL SPECIALITIES

Anghiari Weavers, potters and cabinet-makers are particularly skilled here, and artists' workshops can be visited throughout the historic centre.
Camaldoli Honey, liqueurs and soap are all produced by the monks and can be purchased at the monastery.
Caprese Michelangelo The woods are known for *porcini* mushrooms
Stia has long been noted for its small woollen manufactories. Traditional hand-made textiles are still produced here.

FESTIVALS & EVENTS

Anghiari Fair of artisans' work in the old town, late April–early May.
Bibbiena *Bello Ballo*, Shrove Tuesday celebrations, a tradition since the mid-14th century. People dance and sing around a juniper bush set up in the piazza.
Sansepolcro *Mezza Quaresima*, Large fair held after the fourth Sun in Lent; *Festa Popolare di San Rocco*, Festival in honour of St Roch, 16 Aug; *Palio della Balestra*, Crossbow contest in medieval costume against Gubbio, second Sun in Sept.

AREZZO & CORTONA

A rezzo (pop. 87,000; *map p. 267, E1*) is visited above all for Piero della Francesca's famous fresco cycle of the *Legend of the True Cross* in the church of San Francesco. The lively little town is an easy place to visit since all its historic monuments (including the *pieve*, one of the most beautiful Romanesque churches in all Tuscany) are very close together, just a short walk from its main-line railway station. Although it is in a low-lying position and was badly damaged in the last war, it does still have some pretty streets with picturesque old shop-fronts with shuttered windows (many of them selling antiques, curios and bric à brac). The pleasantest approach from the station is by Corso Italia, the main street of the medieval town, which leads gently uphill.

HISTORY OF AREZZO

Arretium was one of the more important of the 12 cities of the Etruscan Confederation, but from the 3rd century BC it became a faithful ally of Rome. It emerged as a free republic in the 10th century. Generally supporting the Ghibelline party, it was frequently at odds with Florence, and was defeated by that city at Campaldino in the Casentino in 1289, when the Aretine leader, Bishop Guglielmino, was killed. The town came under the control of Florence in 1384.

As a road junction, the town had tactical importance in the Second World War, and thus suffered heavily from bombing. Many unattractive new buildings were constructed in the 1950s, especially around the railway station. It is now a prosperous agricultural town and the capital of a province, surrounded to the south by industrial suburbs. It has long been famous for its goldsmiths. Apart from Petrarch and Vasari, whose houses can be visited, famous natives (all named from the town) include Guido d'Arezzo (c. 995–1050), the inventor of the musical scale; Spinello Aretino (d. 1410), the painter son of a Ghibelline refugee from Florence; and Pietro Aretino (1492–1566), the most outspoken writer of the late Renaissance.

San Francesco

San Francesco (*open 9–6; April–Oct 9–7; Sun and holidays 10–6/7*), built in 1322, houses the famous fresco cycle of the *Legend of the True Cross* by the great Renaissance painter Piero della Francesca, born at Sansepolcro further east (*see p. 386*). This is his masterpiece, and one of the highest achievements of Italian painting. A general view of the frescoes (which are kept permanently lit) can be had from the nave; to enter the sanctuary you need a ticket and booking time (*available from the office on the right of the church, or in advance at www.apt.arezzo.it or pierodellafrancesca@apt.arezzo.it; T: 0575 352727. Combined ticket available to include Vasari's house and the two Arezzo museums*).

The True Cross fresco cycle

In front of the sanctuary hangs a huge painted Crucifix, with St Francis at the foot of the Cross, attributed from this work to the Master of St Francis (1250). In 1447 the Bacci, a rich Aretine family, commissioned Bicci di Lorenzo to decorate the sanctuary: he had only painted the four Evangelists on the vault and part of the *Last Judgement* on the triumphal arch before he left Arezzo in 1448, and Piero della Francesca was called in to complete the frescoes. He may have interrupted work in the 1450s during absences in Rimini and Rome, but we know the cycle was finished by 1466. The frescoes underwent a complicated restoration programme from 1985–2000. They had deteriorated alarmingly for a number of reasons: the wall is particularly thin, the circulation of air in the church had been altered when the roof was rebuilt and central heating was installed, and the frescoes had been damaged by poor restorations in the past. During their restoration it was discovered that Piero, as well as using the technique of true fresco, had also painted parts of the scenes 'a secco', using tempera on the dry (or slightly humid) plaster, a technique he apparently learnt from Flemish painters, in order to provide even more colour, such as bright red and emerald green. However, these parts are those which have tended to fade over the centuries. It was discovered that all the preparatory drawings beneath the frescoes are by Piero's own hand (he made use of the 'spolvero' technique, by which the outlines were pricked with small holes over which a powder was dusted).

The frescoes illustrate the legend of the True Cross, taken from the Legenda Aurea written by Fra' Jacopo Varagine in the 13th century. The time span runs from the death of Adam to the battle against Chosroes, King of Persia, in the 7th century AD. An extraordinary calm and dignity pervades many of the figures, who are magnificently clothed and sport a remarkable variety of head-dresses. There is an atmosphere of detached spiritualism which suggests that we are witnessing events of the utmost importance, set in real time but of universal significance. The strong beautiful colours, especially the greens and reds, are unforgettable. The chronological order of the scenes is as follows:

Right wall (lunette): *Death of Adam.* On the right, Adam seated on the ground, announces his imminent death to his family; on the left is the dead figure of Adam, and Seth planting a fig tree on his grave (from which the Cross on which Christ is crucified will be made; the leaves added in tempera have lost their colour). Many of the figures in this scene are derived from Classical models, and a splendid mature tree spreads out its branches to fill the top of the lunette.

Right wall (middle band): *The Queen of Sheba recognises the Sacred Tree* (used as a bridge over the Siloam river) and kneels in adoration before it, and (on the right) she is received by Solomon (thought to be a portrait of Cardinal Bessarion; the Byzantine prelate and scholar came to Italy with the emperor John Palaeologus in 1439, as part of a delegation to the Council of Florence, aimed at reuniting the Eastern and Western churches). This is one of the best preserved scenes, with two lovely trees and gorgeously dressed courtiers and two horses in attendance.

Right of the window (middle panel): *The Tree is Buried.* On the orders of Solomon, the beam is dug deep underground.

Right of the window (lower panel): *Constantine's Dream.* This is perhaps the most dramatic scene of the whole cycle. The Emperor, asleep in his tent at dawn before the Battle of the Milvian Bridge in AD 312, dreams that an angel (depicted with remarkable foreshortening as it descends from the sky) presents him with the Cross declaring that: 'By this sign, you shall conquer'.

Right wall (lower band): *Constantine's Victory.* Constantine wins a bloodless victory over Maxentius early the next morning. Constantine, portrayed as the Byzantine Emperor John Palaeologus, leads his army holding aloft the tiny Cross. His soldiers' horses produce a sea of prancing hooves and the sky is filled with colourful lances and banners as they reach the translucent blue Tiber in the centre. The right-hand part, although very damaged, shows Maxentius and his army retreating without even attempting battle before such a vision.

Left of the window (middle panel): *Torture of a Jew named Judas* (the future St Cyriacus of Ancona; *see p. 623*). He is kept in a dry well until he reveals the secret hiding place of the Cross, stolen after the Crucifixion. This scene, illuminated from the left, instead of from the east window (as in all the other scenes) was carried out by an assistant.

Left wall (middle band): *Finding of the True Cross*. Judas digs up the Cross before St Helen and her courtiers (including a dwarf), with a walled town in the background. On the right, in a scene in front of a church decorated with precious marbles, its authenticity is demonstrated when it is held over a young man and he is raised from the dead (the Cross is shown in perfect perspective), while Helen kneels in wonder.

Left wall (lower band): *Victory of Heraclius over Chosroes*. The scene shows the battle in the 7th century AD, after Chosroes, king of the Persians, had seized the Cross and placed it near his throne (shown to the right). After his defeat he kneels, awaiting execution. Compared to the armies shown in the scene on the opposite wall, there are almost too many figures here.

Left wall (lunette): *Heraclius Restores the Cross to Jerusalem*.

Also by Piero is the figure of a prophet at the top of the window wall on the right (the prophet on the left seems to be by the hand of an assistant) and (on the lowest band left of the window) the *Annunciation* (thought by some scholars to be St Helen receiving the news of her death, and thus connected to the main cycle).

The chapels

The chapel to the right of the sanctuary has damaged frescoes, at least half a century earlier than those by Piero, by Spinello Aretino (who also painted the *Annunciation* on the nave wall). In his day he was one of the most famous painters of Arezzo, though he carried out much of his work elsewhere and returned to his native town only late in life. The lovely triptych here by Niccolò di Pietro Gerini dates from around the same time. The altarpiece of the *Annunciation* in the chapel to the left of the sanctuary is a fine 15th-century work by Neri di Bicci. The church also contains numerous other frescoes (mostly fragments) in the nave, many of them showing Piero's influence on the local school, notably his pupil Lorentino d'Andrea.

Around Piazza Grande

The **Pieve di Santa Maria** (*open 8–12 & 3–6.30/7*), dating from the 12th century, is a particularly lovely church, with a memorable interior, left uncluttered and simply furnished. The superbly conceived façade has a deep central portal decorated with reliefs flanked by blind arcades which support three tiers of colonnades, the intercolumnations of which diminish towards the top. The 68 diverse pillars include a human figure. The beautiful tall interior has clustered pillars with good capitals, and arches showing the transition to Gothic. The mullioned windows provide a diffused light on the mellow sandstone. The drum was to have supported a dome which was never built. In the raised presbytery is one of Pietro Lorenzetti's masterpieces: a polyptych of the *Virgin and Child with Saints* (the Virgin wears a magnificent ermine-lined robe), commissioned from this famous Sienese painter for the church by Bishop Guido Tarlati (*see overleaf*) in 1320. The painted Crucifix is attributed to the 13th-century painter Margaritone di Arezzo, who was born in the town. The crypt below has good capitals, and an exquisite reliquary bust of St Donatus, martyred in 361 and patron saint of the city, made in 1346 by a local goldsmith.

The arcaded apse of the *pieve* and its original campanile (1330) with its 40 windows are best seen from the delightful Piazza Grande behind the church, laid out around 1200 (some medieval houses and towers survive here; others were rebuilt in medieval style in the 19th century). It is still the centre of city life.

Beside the Palazzo del Tribunale (17th–18th century), with pretty circular steps, is the elaborate **Palazzo della Fraternità dei Laici** in a mixture of Gothic and Renaissance styles. The lower part dates from 1377 (with a detached fresco of *Christ in Pietà* by Spinello Aretino). In 1434 Bernardo Rossellino added the relief of the *Madonna della Misericordia* in the lunette above and two statues in niches on either side. The delicate cornice and loggia at the top were designed in 1460. The bellcote and clock date from 1552.

One whole side of the square is occupied by Vasari's handsome **Palazzo delle Logge** (1573). The long portico continues northwest back to Corso Italia, in which is the **Casa-Museo Ivan Bruschi** (*open 10–1 & 3–7 except Mon*), containing the extraordinary, eclectic collection of a native antiquarian who, after visiting the Portobello market in London in the 1960s, decided to promote the Arezzo antiques fair. After his death in 1996 his residence was opened as a museum, and the interior is a fascinating treasure-trove of some 6,000 works of art from all periods (unlabelled and so to be enjoyed for their curiosity as well as their value), including coins, ivories, ceramics, glass, Greek and Roman sculpture and ceramics, and sculpture. Visitors are shown the top floor also, where there is a splendid view of the *pieve* from the roof terrace .

Via dei Pileati winds uphill past the 14th-century Palazzo Pretorio, its façade decorated with the armorial bearings of many a *podestà*, and the **Casa Petrarca**, the supposed house of Petrarch, reconstructed (after its destruction in the Second World War) as an academy and library for Petrarchan studies. Visitors are shown the library, with MSS and an autograph letter of the poet (1370). In 1928 a huge monument to Petrarch was set up in the **Parco il Prato**, an attractive large park with pine trees, lawns and pretty views of the Tuscan countryside. The 14th–16th-century Fortezza, also in the park, was rebuilt by Antonio da Sangallo the Younger.

The duomo

The duomo (*open 7–12.30 & 3–6.30*) was begun in 1278, and building continued until 1510. The campanile was added at the east end in 1859 and the façade only completed in 1914. The handsome southern flank incorporates a good 14th-century portal. On the fine travertine steps which surround the exterior there is a statue of Ferdinando I de' Medici, by Pietro Francavilla, after a design by Giambologna. It was erected in 1594, in gratitude for his agricultural reforms and land reclamation in the Val di Chiana.

The beautiful Gothic interior has clustered columns and pointed arches. The splendid stained-glass windows are by Guillaume de Marcillat (William of Marseilles; 1519–23), a French artist who lived in Arezzo. They are the most important example of stained glass of this date in Italy. At the same time Marcillat painted the first three vaults of the nave and the first of the north aisle. He also made stained glass *tondi* for other churches in Arezzo (including San Francesco and Santissima Annunziata).

The funerary monuments in the **south aisle** include the tomb of Pope Gregory X who died at Arezzo in 1276 (the Gothic work dates from 1330), and that of a bishop-saint, with a 4th-century early Christian sarcophagus. In the **north aisle**, on the left of the sacristy door, is the unusual tomb of Bishop Guido Tarlati, with 16 panels representing the warlike life of this prelate, governor of Arezzo, patron of the arts and zealous Ghibelline (d. 1327). Here also is a beautiful fresco of *St Mary Magdalene* by Piero della Francesca (*inconspicuous light on the nave pillar*). The cantoria is Vasari's first architectural work (1535), made for the organ of the same date. Beneath it is a 13th-century wood statue of the *Madonna and Child* (thought to have been painted by Margaritone di Arezzo).

The large **Lady Chapel** contains enamelled terracotta works by Andrea della Robbia, including a lovely *Madonna and Child* on the entrance wall.

The **Museo Diocesano del Duomo** (*restricted opening hours*) has a collection of early Crucifixes, frescoes and Church silver.

San Domenico and Vasari's house

The church of San Domenico stands in a square of lime trees. It was founded in 1275 and contains a very fine Crucifix by Cimabue (1260–65), the only one by this great master to survive intact. It was used as a model for his later famous Crucifix in Santa Croce in Florence (*see p. 308*). The very beautiful fresco of the *Annunciation* by Spinello Aretino is one of a number of depictions by him of this subject. There are also fresco fragments by his son Parri di Spinello.

At no. 55 in the quiet Via XX Settembre is a charming house, with a little hanging garden, once the home of Vasari (*open 8.30–7.30; Sun and holidays 8.30–12.30; closed Tues; ring*). After he purchased it in 1540, he carried out the painted decorations on the ceilings, with the help of assistants (restored in the 19th century). It has a collection of 16th–17th-century paintings, many of them by the best artists in Vasari's circle. The precious family archives include letters to Vasari from Michelangelo.

Piero della Francesca: *Mary Magdalene* (c. 1460).

Giorgio Vasari (1511–74)
Giorgio Vasari, born in Arezzo, is well known as an art historian, painter and architect. His famous work *Le vite de' più eccellenti pittori, scultori e architettori*, first
published in 1550, and revised in 1568, has provided valuable information about
the lives of artists to generations of art historians. As a boy, Vasari worked in the
studio of Guillaume de Marcillat, but at 13 he was sent to Florence to study under
Michelangelo, Andrea del Sarto and others. He then worked as a painter for the
Medici, and in Rome received commissions from Cardinal Farnese and Pope Julius
III. But it was for Cosimo I in Florence that he carried out his most important
works, including the Uffizi building, the Corridoio Vasariano, and the decorations
of Palazzo Vecchio. In Florence he also founded the first art academy, the
Accademia delle Arti del Disegno.

Museo d'Arte Medioevale e Moderno

The Museo Statale d'Arte Medioevale e Moderno (*open 8.30–7.30*) has a great variety of
works of art from the medieval and later periods, housed in a fine 15th-century palazzo with a pretty courtyard. Four colourful 13th-century works by the native painter
Margaritone di Arezzo include *St Francis* and a *Madonna*, both signed by him. Spinello
Aretino's son Parri painted the beautiful *Madonna della Misericordia* in a variety of red
tones on a gold ground (1437), in the International Gothic style. The 'Madonna della
Misericordia' (Madonna of Mercy) was a favourite subject for painters in Arezzo since
the Confraternità dei Laici, founded in 1262, has always been active in the city as a char-
itable brotherhood. Another local painter well represented is Bartolomeo della Gatta, a
Camaldolensian abbot whose unusual style of painting shows Flemish influences: his
two votive paintings of *St Roch* were painted at a time of plague in 1478. The smaller
painting includes a view of medieval Arezzo, with the Piazza Grande and the seat of the
Confraternità dei Laici. Works by Vasari include his largest painting, the *Banquet of
Esther and Ahasuerus* (1548), and a standard, his last known work (1570). The collection also has a 16th-century chimneypiece, one of Simone Mosca's most important
works, and enamelled terracottas by Andrea della Robbia. The magnificent collection of
majolica is one of the most important in Italy, with examples from the famous Italian
manufactories of Faenza, Gubbio, Deruta, Casteldurante (Urbania) and Urbino.

Santissima Annunziata and the Badia

The Renaissance church of the **Santissima Annunziata** has an *Annunciation* by
Spinello Aretino on its exterior. The beautiful Renaissance grey-and-white interior is by
Bartolomeo della Gatta (1491) and Giuliano and the elder Antonio da Sangallo (1517).
The interesting plan includes a columned atrium and a dome over the crossing; the capitals of the columns and pilasters are superbly carved. In the chapel in the right transept,
the *Madonna and St Francis* is by Pietro da Cortona. The 17th-century high altar incorporates Renaissance statues in silver and a charming 15th-century statue of the

Madonna, attributed to Michele da Firenze. On the first north altar is a good *Deposition* painted by Vasari at the age of 18 on a cartoon by Rosso Fiorentino.

The interior of the **Badia di Santi Fiora e Lucilla** (*open 8–12 & 4–6*), first built by the Benedictines in 1278, is an interesting architectural work by Vasari (1565), who also supplied the good paintings on the high altar (including the *Calling of the Apostles*, intended for his own tomb) and in the choir. In the right transept is a large painted Crucifix by Segna di Bonaventura. On the west wall is a delightful fresco of *St Lawrence*, by Bartolomeo della Gatta (1476), showing the influence of Piero della Francesca.

The amphitheatre and Museo Archeologico

The rebuilt double *logge* of the Convento di San Bernardo follow the curve of the **Roman amphitheatre** (AD 117–138). The well-kept ruins (*open 8.30–7.30*) adjoin a public park. The old convent (*open as above*) now houses the **Museo Archeologico Mecenate**. Other parts of the amphitheatre are visible in the museum rooms. The collection includes Archaic and Hellenistic finds from Arezzo and the Val di Chiana, fine ceramics, and the famous Aretine vases, which were mass-produced in Arezzo for a period of some 100 years from 50 BC onwards, in a characteristic shiny red glaze, usually decorated with exquisite bas-reliefs. Moulds and instruments are displayed as well as the production of individual workshops, which numbered around 90. There are also Roman statues, portrait busts, mosaics, bronzes, and a very fine portrait of a man moulded in gold, made in Arezzo in the 1st century BC.

Santa Maria delle Grazie

Outside the historic centre stands the church of Santa Maria delle Grazie, built in the late Gothic style in 1449, and enclosed in a walled garden. The graceful early Renaissance loggia is a very fine work by Benedetto da Maiano. It contains a beautiful marble and terracotta high altar by Andrea della Robbia, which encloses a fresco of the *Madonna della Misericordia* by Parri di Spinello.

CORTONA

Cortona (pop. 22,600; *map p. 267, E2*) is a charming little town, with olive groves and vineyards reaching up to its walls. It is built on the slope of a long hillside, well preserved from new buildings, its summit also covered with fields and woods. The narrow, winding, well-kept medieval streets are mostly steep and often stepped, and many of the little houses are decorated with pots of flowers. It has two particularly fine museums: works of art include paintings by Luca Signorelli, the great precursor of Michelangelo, who was born here. It is one of the most delightful places to visit in all Tuscany, with magnificent views towards Lake Trasimene and over the wide agricultural plain below, where the town of Camucia has grown up around the railway station, leaving Cortona with a slight feeling of isolation (public transport up to the town is not very frequent).

HISTORY OF CORTONA

The hill on which Cortona stands was occupied by the Villanovan people in the 7th–6th centuries BC. It was in an excellent strategic and commercial position dominating the Val di Chiana, on the routes between Rome and southern Etruria, and northern Etruria and the Po valley, and midway between the Tyrrhenian and Adriatic coasts. It was one of the 12 cities of the Etruscan Confederation in the 4th century BC, and part of its walls and a gate survive from this period. On the plain at the foot of the hill are a number of exceptionally interesting Etruscan tombs. By the end of the century the town had come under Roman influence, and large villas were built on the plain, one of which is in the process of excavation. Although the marshes were abandoned in the Middle Ages because of malaria, Cortona was a flourishing commune by the 13th and 14th centuries, ruled after 1325 by the Casali family. From the 15th century onwards it was a dominion of the Florentine Republic. In 1996, Frances Mayes made Cortona the setting for her immensely popular *Under the Tuscan Sun*.

Piazza della Repubblica

Piazza Garibaldi, at the entrance to the town, has a superb view down to the Renaissance church of Santa Maria del Calcinaio (*see p. 405 below*). The hillside immediately below has recently been planted with gardens and pretty hedged walks beside the escalators which ascend from a car park. Via Nazionale, popularly known as *Rugapiana* ('level street'), because it is the only street without a gradient, ends at the central **Piazza della Repubblica**. This is one of the most idiosyncratic *piazze* in Tuscany, with a totally irregular shape where no fewer than nine streets end, and it has a miscellany of arches, balconies, flights of steps, *logge*, several busts decorating the buildings, a few shops, and one or two benches (with tables). The 13th-century Palazzo Comunale was enlarged in the 16th century and extends to Piazza Signorelli, where its façade has a worn *Marzocco* (the Florentine lion) of 1508. In this piazza is Palazzo Casali (or Palazzo Pretorio), the handsome 13th-century mansion of the Casali family, who became governors of the city. The Renaissance façade was added by the local architect Filippo Berrettini (uncle of Pietro da Cortona) in 1613. The 13th-century flank, on Via Casali, has numerous coats of arms of the governors of the city. The palace is the seat of the **Accademia Etrusca**, a learned society founded in 1727 for historical and archaeological research, and famous throughout Europe in the 18th century: Montesquieu and Voltaire were both early members. It houses the Academy's remarkable eclectic collection of precious works of art from all periods as well as the town's museum of Etruscan and Roman finds.

Museo dell'Accademia Etrusca e della Città di Cortona
Open April–Oct 10–7; winter 10–5 except Mon. Enquire at the museum or T: 0575 637235 about visiting the Etruscan tombs in the district, described on p. 406 below.

CITTÀ DI CASTELLO

CORTONA

0 _____ 200 yards
0 _____ 200 metres

Fortezza
Medicea

V. S. MARIA NUOVA

Porta
Montanina

Santuario
S. Margherita

S. Cristoforo

PIAZZALE
MAZZINI
P.ta Colonia

S. Antonio   Birthplace of
Pietro da   PIAZZA. D.
Cortona   PESCAIA

S. Niccolo   V. DELL'ORTO D. CERA

V. D. SANTUCCE

V. S. ANTONIO

P. ZA. POZZO
CAVIGLIA   Convent
S. Chiara

V. S. NICOLO

Museo
Diocesano   Duomo

P. ZA TRENTO
E. TRIESTE

VIA DARDANO

VIA BERRETTINI

V. S. MARCO

V. MONETI

Youth Hostel

VIA S. MARGHERITA

Accademia
P.ta S.   Etrusca
Maria

VIA ROMA

PIAZZA
SIGNORELLI

PIAZZA. D.
REPUBBLICA
Palazzo
Comunale

V. SANTUCCI

S. Francesco

V. MAFFEI

S. Marco

P.ta Beranda
S. Domenico

Public   V. LE GIARDINI PUBBLICI
Gardens

VIALE C. BATTISTI

Pretura   PIAZZA
GARIBALDI

VIA NAZIONALE

S. Filippo
S. Benedetto   Pal. Mancini

VIA GINO SEVERINI

Porta
Ghibellina

V. D. MURA D. MERCATO

VIA GHIBELLINA

S. Agostino

VIA GUELFA

VIA S. SEBASTIANO

VIALE CESARE BATTISTI

STRADA UMBRO CORTONESE

N

PIAZZALE DEL MERCATO

P.ta S.
Agostino

Spirito Santo

S. Maria
del Calcinaio

AREZZO, PERUGIA & STATION

The rooms on the second and third floors are those belonging to the Academy. The splendid main hall has a fine display in old showcases of small bronzes, including some in imitation of Antique works, Greek vases and votive statuettes, ivories, and glass. There are two *tondi* by Luca Signorelli and Pinturicchio, and Pietro da Cortona's last, unfinished work, a beautiful *Annunciation*. Displayed in a corner together are two 18th-century self-portraits by Zoffany and James Northcote. In a small room hangs a rare Etruscan chandelier, probably dating from the late 4th century BC. There is also a collection of gold-ground paintings and medieval works of art. The Galleria is decorated with busts and globes, and the huge Sala Medicea has a grand fireplace and panelled ceiling. There is a display relating to the military architect Francesco Laparelli (1521–70), born in Cortona, who designed La Valletta in Malta. A large and remarkably elaborate porcelain *tempietto* was presented by Carlo Ginori to the Academy in 1756, and it includes medallions of all the ruling members of the Medici family. The numismatic collection includes rare Etruscan coins. The famous 'Musa Polimnia', an encaustic painting for long thought to be a Roman work of the 1st–2nd century AD, is now usu-

Neck amphora showing lion hunt, in Museo dell'Accademia Etrusca in Cortona.

ally considered an excellent fake made c. 1740, although an air of mystery still surrounds it. There is a representative display of works by the painter Gino Severini (1883–1966), a native of Cortona, who spent long periods in Paris. He was one of the most important figures in the Italian political and artistic movement known as Futurism, which came into being at the beginning of the 20th century. On the third floor is an interesting and representative Egyptian collection made by Monsignor Corbelli, papal delegate in Egypt from 1891–96, including a rare wood model of a funerary boat (2060–1785 BC), and mummies. The 18th-century library can also be seen here.

The Etruscan and Roman museum is well displayed in 14 rooms in the basement, where Etruscan masonry in the foundations has been exposed. Much of the extremely interesting material, including numerous exquisite bronzes, comes from the Etruscan tombs found in the locality of Sodo (*see p. 406*) on the plain below the town, one of them discovered in the 16th century, and others since the 19th century (and where excavations are still being carried out). The dig of the Roman villa of La Tufa, in progress at Ossaia, 5km south of the town, is also very well documented.

The duomo and Museo Diocesano

Below Piazza Signorelli, where a terrace has a striking view of a bare hillside, are the duomo and Museo Diocesano. The **duomo** (*usually closed between 12.30/1 & 3/3.30*), on the site of an earlier church, was rebuilt in the 16th century probably by a local architect, a follower of Giuliano da Sangallo (but was later much modified). Remains of the Romanesque church can be seen in the façade (including a large capital with human heads). The campanile (1566) is by Francesco Laparelli. Beneath a pretty 16th-century portico is a delightful doorway by Cristofanello (1550), a local sculptor and architect who only seems to have worked in Cortona. The striking interior, unusually wide and with a barrel vault, has capitals similar to those in San Lorenzo in Florence. In the chapel to the right of the sanctuary there is a 13th-century terracotta *Pietà*. The high altar, with four carved angels, is a fine work by the local sculptor Francesco Mazzuoli (1664), and there are a number of good 16th- and 17th-century paintings, particularly in the choir. The *Adoration of the Shepherds* on the third south altar is by Pietro da Cortona.

The **Museo Diocesano** is one of the most important museums of its kind in Tuscany, with a small but extremely choice collection (*open daily 10–7; April–Oct 10–5; closed Mon*). In the first room there is a late 2nd-century Roman sarcophagus depicting the battle of the Amazons and Centaurs, known to have been admired by Donatello and Brunelleschi. The former church of the Gesù has a fine wooden ceiling, the only known work by the local artist Michelangelo Leggi (1536), with symbols of the Passion and the Eucharist. The two works by Fra' Angelico displayed here were painted for the church of San Domenico in Cortona: the *Madonna Enthroned with Saints* has an exquisite predella, and the *Annunciation* (1428–30) is one of his most beautiful works, with particularly luminous colours and abundant use of gold. The *Madonna and Child with Four Saints* by Sassetta was damaged when in storage during the last war, but the large painted Crucifix by Pietro Lorenzetti is, instead, very well preserved. The *Assumption of the Virgin* is one of the best works of Bartolomeo della Gatta, dating from the 1470s. In the figures in the foreground can be seen the influence of Piero della Francesca (including the dramatic stance of the saint seen from behind), as well as van Eyck. Another room displays a beautiful *Madonna and Child* attributed to Niccolò di Segna (son of Segna di Bonaventura) and a *Madonna Enthroned with Four Angels*, signed and dated 1320 by Pietro Lorenzetti. The very damaged painting of *St Margaret*, with stories from her life, by a 13th-century Aretine master is particularly interesting for the Saint's unusual dress which symbolises her poverty. The vault of the lower church was painted by Giorgio Vasari in 1545. The museum also displays a beautiful *Deposition* by Luca Signorelli, with superbly painted female figures and a fine predella. The early 16th-century Church vestments are the most important collection of their date in Italy, and include a velvet cope made for the Medici pope Leo X's visit to Cortona, embroidered in gold thread to designs by Andrea del Sarto and Raffaellino del Garbo.

Via del Gesù leads down to the ancient **Via Jannelli**, where a row of four little houses are a unique survival from the Middle Ages: built in stone on the ground floors, their protruding brick upper stories are supported on wooden *sporti*.

The Etruscan gate and San Filippo

From Piazza della Repubblica three narrow old roads, Via Roma, Via Guelfa and Via Ghibellina, all well worth exploring, lead steeply downhill to gates in the walls. In Via Guelfa is Palazzo Mancini-Sernini (no. 4) with an unusually tall façade incorporating a loggia on the top storey. It was designed by Cristofanello for the Laparelli family in 1533. Via Ghibellina ends at the remarkable remains of an **Etruscan double gate**, recently excavated in the walls, where the huge blocks dating from the Etruscan period are conspicuous below Roman and medieval masonry above. The charming lanes which follow the top of the walls are well worth exploring all the way to Porta Colonia. The church of **San Filippo** was built on a central plan with a dome by Antonio Jannelli in 1720 (approached through a side entrance on Via Roma). It contains altarpieces carried out around the same time by Camillo Sagrestani and Giovanni Battista Piazzetta.

The upper town

The stepped Via Santucci leads up beneath the Palazzo del Popolo in Piazza della Repubblica to the upper town past the church of **San Francesco** (*open 9–5.30*), with a worn Gothic portal. This was the first Franciscan church to be built outside Assisi after the death of St Francis, and the architect was Brother Elias, his friend and disciple, who died in the convent of the church in 1253 and is buried behind the altar. The interior has 14th-century fresco fragments and pretty 17th-century pews. On the north side is an *Annunciation* by Pietro da Cortona (1669) and a *Martyrdom of St Lucy* by Giovanni Camillo Sagrestani. Below the church steps, a 13th-century public fountain survives.

Via Berrettini, an exceptionally steep street, leads up through a delightful, quiet residential part of the town, with colourful gardens and plants around the well-kept houses, with a number of water cisterns and the sound of birdsong. It is named after Pietro Berrettini (1596–1669), who is always known as Pietro da Cortona, and whose birthplace at no. 33 is marked by a plaque. He was an outstanding painter as well as an architect, famous for the churches he built in Rome, as well as for the magnificent ceiling frescoes both there and in the Palazzo Pitti in Florence.

The 15th-century church of **San Niccolò** (*opened by the custodian who lives here; ring at the door on the left, 9–12 & 3–dusk*) is approached through a peaceful walled courtyard with cypresses. Over the altar is a standard painted on both sides by Luca Signorelli with a beautiful *Deposition* (in excellent condition) and a *Madonna and Child with Sts Peter and Paul* (*shown by the custodian*). Downhill in Via San Niccolò is the entrance to the church of the huge convent of **Santa Chiara**, built in 1555 by Vasari. The nuns can often be heard at services in the choir, and in the church is a *Deposition* attributed as an early work to Pietro da Cortona. Opposite is another large convent, **Santa Trinità**, occupied by Cistercian nuns, and in the church you can purchase little bottles of holy water. Uphill, beyond a charming little triangular public garden shaded by ilexes, is **San Cristoforo** with its little Romanesque bellcote, and on the edge of the hillside, planted with pine trees, is the picturesque Porta Montanina, decorated with four arches.

The hill of Santa Margherita

Via Santo Stefano, a stepped lane with gardens on either side continues uphill through cypress woods to reach the **sanctuary of Santa Margherita**, dedicated to St Margaret of Cortona (1247–97). Born at Laviano in Umbria, she became a Franciscan tertiary. Her name was associated with numerous miracles; a Gothic church, probably designed by Giovanni Pisano, was built on this site where she was buried. To celebrate her canonisation in 1728, Ferdinando Ruggeri built a neo-Gothic cupola over her tomb five years later, and then the whole church was rebuilt by Mariano Falcini in 1856–93 in Romanesque-Gothic style, retaining just a single rose window from the original church. It contains Margaret's lovely sarcophagus, thought to have been designed by the native artists Angiolo and Francesco di Pietro (1362), but also attributed to Giovanni Pisano.

In a splendid position on the hilltop dominating the town (651m) is the **Fortezza Medicea** or Girfalco (*interior open only for exhibitions in summer*), built by order of Cosimo I in 1556, and once thought to have been the work of Francesco Laparelli, but now considered to be by his friend Gabrio Serbelloni. There is a magnificent view of Lake Trasimene, and part of the outer circle of walls built by the Etruscans can also be seen from here.

Via Santa Margherita descends past a *Via Crucis* in mosaic by Gino Severini, set up in gratitude after Cortona was saved from severe war damage; and the church of **San Marco** with a mosaic (1961) of the Saint also by him, to the public gardens along the hillside. The early 15th-century church of **San Domenico** has a worn fresco over the portal by Fra' Angelico, who was a guest at the convent in 1438. The bright ancona of the *Coronation of the Virgin* on the high altar is a large, extremely well-preserved work in its original elaborate frame, signed by Lorenzo di Niccolò Gerini (1402). In the chapel to the left of the high altar is a *Madonna and Saints* by Luca Signorelli (1515).

Santa Maria del Calcinaio

Halfway up the hillside on which Cortona is built is the church of Santa Maria del Calcinaio, a masterpiece of Renaissance architecture (*open 3.30–6 or 7; Sun and holidays also 10.30–12.30*). It is difficult to reach without a car; but there is a request stop outside the church served by buses to Camucia. Otherwise it is a walk of several kilometres (partly on the main road) from Porta Sant'Agostino. Built on a Latin-cross plan with an octagonal cupola, it is one of the few works certainly by Francesco di Giorgio Martini to have survived—though he had completed it only as far as the drum of the cupola when he died in 1501. The building was finished under the direction of the otherwise unknown Pietro di Norbo in 1508–14, almost certainly following the original design.

Set into the hillside, its beautiful form can be fully appreciated as it is approached from above, along a short road with a few ancient cypresses. It was built on the site of a tannery (called a *calcinaio* from the use of lime), on the wall of which a miraculous image of the Madonna had appeared. It was Signorelli who advised the Arte dei Calzolai (Guild of Shoemakers) to commission Francesco di Giorgio to build the church to house the venerated icon. The beautiful light grey-and-white interior, with clean architectural lines, has a handsome high altar of 1519 which encloses the devotional image of the *Madonna del Calcinaio*, dating from the 14th or 15th century. The stained glass in the rose window is by Guillaume de Marcillat, and the two smaller windows are by his pupils. On the right side, the early 16th-century *Annunciation* and *Assumption* are by the local painter Tommaso Bernabei, called Papacello. The *Immaculate Conception* and *Epiphany* on the north side are also attributed to him.

OUTSKIRTS OF CORTONA

Outside Porta Colonia, in beautiful countryside on the hillside below the town to the north, is another centrally-planned church, that of **Santa Maria Nuova**. It is known that both Cristofanello (in 1550–54) and Vasari were involved in its construction, but it was not finished until 1600 when the (rather too small) cupola was built. Easily reached from here is the **Convento delle Celle**, in a beautiful position on the lower slopes of Monte Egidio. Its pretty stone buildings, grouped beside a river torrent, are immaculately kept. In 1226 St Francis is known to have visited a hermitage on this site, and since 1537 it has been occupied by the Capuchins, who welcome visitors. Above the convent a road leads along the wooded upper slopes of Monte Egidio, with particularly beautiful views of Cortona and Lake Trasimene, and a lovely road leads across the watershed to descend into the Tiber valley in Umbria.

On the plain below the town, in the locality of **Sodo** (*map p. 267, E2*), excavations have been in progress since 1990 on one of the largest tumuli so far found in Etruria, and the only Etruscan tomb known which conserves sculptural elements *in situ* (two large sphinxes with warriors carved in the early 6th century BC on either side of a monumental stairway). The tomb known as the 'Melone 2' (from its melon shape) can be visited (9–1.30); the other tombs, including that known as the Tanella di Pitagora can only be visited by appointment at the Museo dell'Accademia Etrusca (*see p. 400 above*).

PRACTICAL INFORMATION

GETTING AROUND

• **By car:** The centres of **Arezzo** and **Cortona** are closed to traffic, and parking is a challenge. There is free parking in Arezzo in Viale Mecenate. Most other car parks charge an hourly tariff. In Cortona there are free car parks in Piazzale del Mercato, Porta Colonia, Porta Santa Maria and Via Gino Severini.
• **By train:** **Arezzo** is on the main Rome–Florence line. Frequent slow trains go to Florence in c. 1hr. Less frequent Intercity services take 45mins. Camucia, 5km from **Cortona**, is the nearest station (a few trains a day to and from Florence and Rome). Buses run every half hour from Camucia station to Cortona's Piazza Garibaldi (10mins). A few Intercity trains on the Florence–Rome line also stop at Terontola, 11km from Cortona. Bus c. every hour to Piazza Garibaldi (25mins).

• **By bus:** Country bus services run by SITA (www.sitabus.it) link **Arezzo** (Piazza Stazione) to Florence in 90mins–2hrs; services run by LFI (www.lfi.it) link Arezzo with Siena (90mins) and **Cortona** at Piazza Garibaldi (c. 1hr).

INFORMATION OFFICES

Arezzo Piazza della Repubblica 28 (outside the railway station), T: 0575 377678.
Cortona Via Nazionale 42, T: 0575 630352.

HOTELS

Arezzo (*map p. 267, E1*)
€€€€ **Foresteria Il Giardino di Fontarronco**. Beautifully restored 18th-century farmhouse, surrounded by olive groves and orchards. The apartments have been converted from the original farm buildings, including the barn and

wine cellar. Each has been decorated and furnished with great care. There are open fires for chilly evenings and a pool in the summer. *Località Chiana 255, Alberoro di Monte San Savino, T: 0575 846044, www.foresteria.it. 10 apartments.*

€ **Le Capanne**. Small, comfortable hotel in beautiful countryside just 5km out of town. Once a farm house, the oldest parts of the building date from the 16th century. Also has a restaurant, gardens and swimming pool. *Località Il Matto 44, T: 0575 959634. 16 rooms.*

Cortona *(map p. 267, E2)*

€€ **Borgo Il Melone**. In a sensitively restored 19th-century *borgo*, with apartments converted from the original estate buildings, the names of which reflect their original purpose: Gardener's House, Groom's House, etc. In a beautiful setting, surrounded by gardens and orchards. Concerts are held here in the summer. The estate chapel has been retained, brightly frescoed, and is open for services. Minimum stay of three nights. *Località il Sodo Case Sparse 38, T: 0575 603330, www.ilmelone.it. 8 apartments.*

€€ **Villa Marsili**. Town house built in 1786 on the site of a church (some of its frescoes have been preserved in the Istituto delle Suore Serve di Maria Riparatrici opposite). Rooms are modern and comfortable, furnished with local antiques. There's a lovely garden with views across to Lake Trasimene. *Viale C. Battisti 13, T: 0575 605252, www.villamarsili.net. 27 rooms.*

€€ **Villa di Piazzano**. Welcoming country house hotel just outside town, dating back to the 15th century. Rooms are individually decorated with sumptuous fabrics and antiques; some have frescoes and four-poster beds. Lovely

garden with extensive views. The restaurant serves traditional seasonal Tuscan food. *Località Piazzano, T: 075 826226, www.villadipiazzano.com. 15 rooms.*

€ **San Michele**. In a building which forms part of the town's fortifications, now elegantly restored and gorgeously furnished with antiques and oil paintings. Rooms are bright and comfortable. *Via Guelfa 15, T: 0575 604348, www.hotelsanmichele.net. 50 rooms.*

San Giustino Valdarno *(map p. 267, D1)*

€€€€ **Villa Cassia di Baccano**. Extremely beautiful hotel, part villa, part mill. Rooms are elegantly furnished in sleek modern style, but original details of the buildings survive, including baronial fireplaces. Quiet, peaceful and stylish. *Via Setteponti Levante 132, T: 0559 772310, www.villacassiadibaccano.it. 12 rooms.*

CONVENT ACCOMMODATION

There is a good choice of convent accommodation in Cortona: € **Casa Betania**, *Via Gino Severini 50, T: 0575 630423, www.casaperferiebetania.com;* € **Istituto Santa Caterina** (with restaurant, but curfew at 10), *Via Santa Margherita 47, T: 0575 630343;* € **Santa Margherita**, *Viale Cesare Battisti 15, T: 0575 630336, comunitacortona@smr.it.*

RESTAURANTS

Arezzo *(map p. 267, E1)*

€ **L'Agania**. Long-established place popular with locals and visitors alike. Rustic Tuscan sauces accompany delicious pasta; traditional dishes such as tripe also on offer. Good choice of wines. Closed Mon. *Via Mazzini Giuseppe 10, T: 0575 295381.*

€ **Buca di San Francesco**. Basement restaurant in a building dating from the 1300s and run by the same family for 70 years. Specialities include succulent local beef. Very popular. Closed Mon evening and Tues. *Via San Francesco 1, T: 0575 23271.*

€ **Fiaschetteria de' Redi**. Simple, dependable wine bar serving hearty traditional food. The gnocchi are particularly recommended. Closed Mon. *Via de' Redi 10, T: 0575 355 012.*

€ **Il Saraceno**. A family-run place offering a variety of traditional Tuscan food, including fresh pasta with wild boar and *pappardelle* with a rich game sauce. Closed Wed. *Via Mazzini 6, T: 0575 27644.*

Cortona (*map p. 267, E2*)

€€ **Dardano**. Cosy, welcoming place owned by the Castelli family, who source all their ingredients either from their own or from local farms; Signor Castelli collects wild mushrooms and during the winter goes hunting for the game that is served in the restaurant. Closed Wed. *Via Dardano 24, T: 0575 601944.*

€€ **Osteria del Teatro**. Lovely, friendly, popular restaurant just off Piazza Signorelli. Black and white photographs of celebrity customers hang on the walls. The finale of the meal is the chocolate board, with a handsome selection on offer. Booking advised. Closed Wed. *Via Maffei 5, T: 0575 630556.*

€ **La Grotta**. In the back-streets off Piazza della Republica, this trattoria is, true to its name, cavernous and intimate, with stone walls and low ceilings. Wonderful seasonal food, including freshly-made pasta. The gnocchi with spinach and ricotta cheese in tomato sauce is famous; equally excellent are the grilled lamb and Tuscan sausage. Closed Tues. *Piazzetta Baldelli 3, T: 0575 630271.*

€ **Tacconi**. Simple, family-run trattoria. Very popular; best to book. Open midday only. Closed Mon. *Via Dardano 46, T: 0575 603588.*

LOCAL SPECIALITIES

Arezzo The town is noted for the skill of its gold- and silversmiths. The most famous culinary speciality is the bread soup, *acquacotta*, sometimes with porcini mushrooms or tomatoes, egg and cheese. **Cortona** The local sweet almond biscuits are known as *cantucci*, typically eaten with a glass of Vin Santo. Particularly good pottery and linens are on sale in the town.

FESTIVALS & EVENTS

Arezzo *Giostra del Saracino*, Tradition going back to the 13th century: local teams compete at tilting the quintain, which is in the form of a Saracen, an image probably originating with the Crusades. Tickets are available in advance (ask at the tourist office). Standing room only on the day, penultimate Sun in June and first Sun in Sept; *Concorso Polifonico Internazionale Guido d'Arezzo,* choral festival, late Aug; Antiques fair in Piazza Grande and surrounding streets, first Sun of every month.

Cortona Antiques fair in Sept; Street market every Sat in Piazza Signorelli.

SIENA & ITS TERRITORY

Siena (pop. 60,000; *map p. 266, C2*) is a brick-built medieval town of superlative beauty and interest. The Campo, the main square, is one of the most satisfying urban spaces ever built, remarkable above all for its scallop shape; it is here that both the Sienese and visitors come most often to meet, or rest or pass the time of day. The Sienese school of painting is one of the most colourful and joyous in all Italy, and its masterpieces are preserved in the great buildings of the town. Cars are not permitted in the old town, so most Sienese get around on foot—which means there is an industrious atmosphere in the streets and an air of a well-run, busy little place which can afford not to make a fuss of its tourists. The Sienese are proud of their city, and take care to preserve its beauty, from the paving of the streets to the old lanterns which illuminate them, and even, to a great extent, the immediate environs, where the lovely countryside reaches right up to many of the old gates in the town walls. The 17 *contrade*, or wards into which the town is divided (*see p. 430 below*), still play an active part in the life of the city, culminating in the famous Palio horse race, which has survived as perhaps the most spectacular annual festival in Italy.

Senus and Aschius, supposedly the twin sons of Remus, who shared an infancy similar to their father's, and founded the city of Siena. Inlaid marble floor in the duomo.

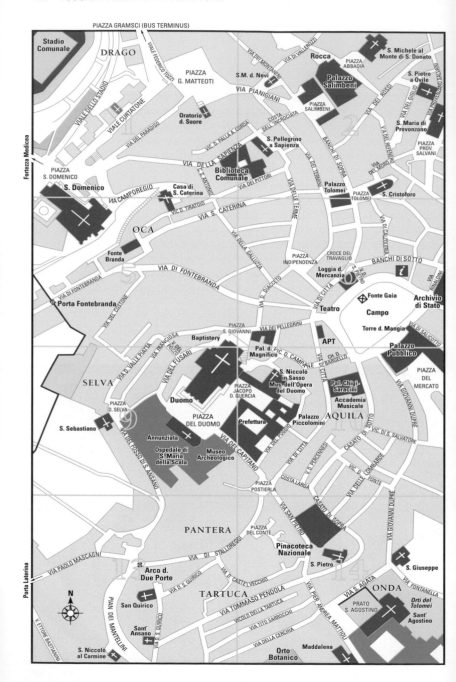

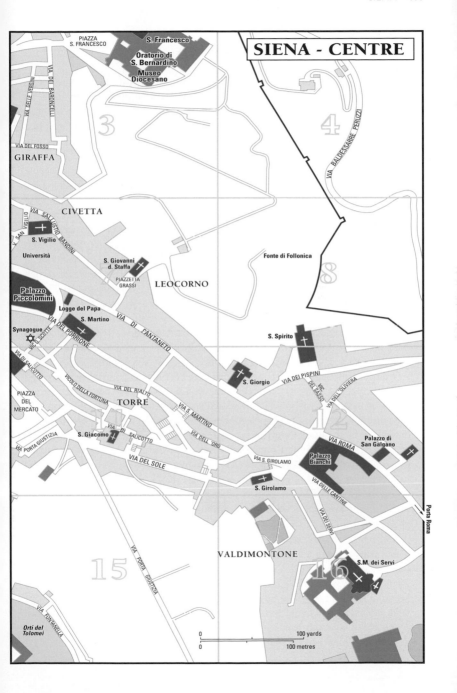

SIENA - CENTRE

PIAZZA S. FRANCESCO

S. Francesco

Oratorio di S. Bernardino

Museo Diocesano

VIA DE' BARONCELLI

VIA DELLE TERME DI DIANA

VIA DEL FOSSO

GIRAFFA

3

4

VIA BALDESSARRE PERUZZI

VIA SALLUSTIO BANDINI

CIVETTA

V. SAN VIGILIO

S. Vigilio

Università

S. Giovanni d. Staffa

PIAZZETTA GRASSI

LEOCORNO

Fonte di Follonica

8

Palazzo Piccolomini

Logge del Papa

S. Martino

VIA DEL PORRIONE

VIA DI FANTANETO

Synagogue

VIA D. SCOTTE

VIA DI SALICOTTO

S. Spirito

S. Giorgio

VIA DEI PISPINI

VIC. DEL SASSO

VIA DELL'OLIVIERA

VIA DEL RIALTO

VICOLO DELLA FORTUNA

TORRE

VIA S. MARTINO

PIAZZA DEL MERCATO

VIA PORTA GIUSTIZIA

S. Giacomo

VIA DI SALICOTTO

VIA DELL'ORO

12

VIA ROMA

Palazzo di San Galgano

Palazzo Bianchi

VIA DEL SOLE

VIA S. GIROLAMO

VIA DELLE CANTINE

S. Girolamo

VIA DE' SERVI

Porta Roma

15

VIA PORTA GIUSTIZIA

VALDIMONTONE

16

S.M. dei Servi

VIA FONTANELLA

Orti del Tolomei

0 ——— 100 yards

0 ——— 100 metres

HISTORY OF SIENA

Saena Julia was a Roman colony founded by Augustus. Although it was not an important centre, the Roman she-wolf feeding twin boys was adapted as an emblem of the city in the Middle Ages, when Siena's rulers wished to increase her prestige by emphasising her glorious past. (There is a tradition in Siena that the twins in question are not Romulus and Remus, but the next generation, namely Senus and Aschius, sons of Remus.) In the early Middle Ages the Lombards took control of the town, which was then on the the pilgrimage route from France to Rome (the Via Francigena; *see p. 448*). Under Charlemagne the town was governed by counts, but during the 12th century it became a self-governing commune and the noble families and bishops became less powerful. From this time began the rivalry with Florence which was to last for centuries.

In the 13th century Siena became an important banking centre. Rivalry with Florence reached a peak in 1260 when Siena, now head of the Tuscan Ghibellines, defeated Florence at the battle of Montaperti. However, when Manfred, son of the Holy Roman Emperor Frederick II, was defeated by Charles of Anjou in 1266, the merchant families and bankers of Siena decided it was now in their interest to side with the pope (since their support of the Ghibelline cause and subsequent excommunication had damaged their trade in Europe).

In 1287 a Guelph middle class oligarchy, ruled by a Council of Nine, was established in Siena. These councillors held office for only two months, and provided an exceptionally stable form of government for over half a century. They accepted the supremacy of Florence, and, deciding on a policy of peace with their neighbours, created a climate in which the town could prosper. It was at this time that the greatest Sienese works of art were executed. However, in 1348, the town was devastated by the Black Death and over three-quarters of the population died.

The government of the Council of Nine was overthrown by the Holy Roman Emperor Charles IV of Bohemia in 1355. Instability followed, with a revolt by the wool-workers in 1371. For a few years after 1399, Siena came under Gian Galeazzo Visconti of Milan (as part of an alliance against Florence). Unrest continued throughout the 15th century, although the *comune* survived—despite an attempt in 1487 by the nobleman Pandolfo Petrucci to seize autocratic control.

In the 16th century Siena made an alliance with the Habsburg Emperor Charles V, but when he sent a Spanish garrison to occupy the town, the Sienese switched their allegiance to France. As a result the Emperor combined forces with the Medici Duke Cosimo I of Florence, and Siena was taken in 1555 after a disastrous 18-month siege. Some 700 Sienese families, refusing to live beneath the Medici yoke, migrated to Montalcino, where they maintained a Sienese republic until 1559, when that too was handed over to Florence by the Treaty of Cateau-Cambrésis. From then on Siena shared the history of Florence and Tuscany.

ARCHITECTS & SCULPTORS OF SIENA

Siena is chiefly memorable for its superb Gothic buildings, including the Palazzo Pubblico, the duomo, and numerous palaces. The Renaissance period is represented by several fine palaces by Bernardo Rossellino and Giuliano da Maiano. The native architect Baldassare Peruzzi also worked here.

The sculptors Nicola Pisano and his son Giovanni (*see p. 358*) carried out numerous works for the duomo in the late 13th century: Nicola was involved in its design as well as carving the splendid pulpit, and Giovanni was responsible for the façade and its superb Gothic statues. Tino di Camaino also produced sculptures for the duomo. The most important Sienese sculptor of the early Renaissance was Jacopo della Quercia, although little is known about his early life and where he trained. His masterpiece in Siena was the monumental Fonte Gaia in the Campo (replaced by a copy in the 19th century), the damaged fragments of which are now exhibited in the Ospedale di Santa Maria della Scala. He also made an important contribution to the exquisite font in the Baptistery, and there are more works by him or his pupils in Palazzo Pubblico and the Museo dell'Opera del Duomo. From the 13th–15th centuries many Sienese sculptors, including Francesco di Valdambrino, produced delightful polychrome wooden statues, although many of these are now to be found outside Siena itself.

Other sculptors active in the town in the later 15th and early 16th centuries included Giacomo Cozzarelli (also an architect), Marrina and Il Riccio (also a painter). In the 19th century, the architectural movement known as *Purismo* took root here. Its finest exponent was Giuseppe Partini.

The Campo

Steep alleys lead down from the main streets of the town, Via di Città and Via Banchi di Sotto, to the Campo (*map p. 410, 6*), Siena's famous piazza, with its extraordinary shape in the form of a fan or scallop shell which slopes gently down to the magnificent Palazzo Pubblico on the flat southeast side. This has been the centre of civic life since it was laid out in the 12th century, and it was first paved in red brick and marble in 1327–49 (on quiet days in winter stonemasons can sometimes be seen sitting here carefully renewing by hand the herring-bone bricks or stone courses, with low basketwork screens in front of them to catch the splinters). The comparatively low picturesque buildings which follow its curve, mostly with restaurants or cafés on their ground floors, allow ample sunlight into the square, and its life moves in and out of the shadows at different times of day, according to the season. The huge Fonte Gaia is a free copy made in 1858 by Tito Sarrocchi of the famous original fountain by Jacopo della Quercia. (*see p. 429*). This was the main fountain in Siena, at the centre of the system of underground aqueducts, and it still has two little fountains which provide a constant stream of drinking water.

SIENESE ART

Unequalled in harmony of design and intensity of colour, and with the ethereal quality of deep, spiritual sentiment, Duccio's *Maestà* altarpiece for Siena cathedral (*see p. 425*), which typifies the highest traditions of the Sienese School, belongs to a different world from the masterpieces of Giotto, Duccio's contemporary, in Florence. Only a day's ride separated the two cities, but they espoused artistic visions that were worlds apart. Sienese art is the ripening of a long tradition, perfected in the works of Duccio di Buoninsegna (c. 1260–1319), which goes back to the greatest Byzantine icon painters. Fundamentally, it looks back. Florence, by contrast, reached forward into new areas and strove for new effects, in its scientific and experimental exploration of space and volume. Giotto's tableaux use colour to separate and distinguish elements of the composition, whereas the Sienese painters use it to unite the whole; they exalt its richness and tonal harmony, subtly exploiting the gamut of human and spiritual emotions which it evokes. At this, they were greater masters than the Florentine painters. The deep and luminous colours which Duccio uses show the influence of mediaeval stained glass and enamel-work—both high Gothic art-forms where material intensity of colour was foremost: yet there is nothing of the stilted or rhetorical style of late Byzantine art in the design of his works. His grouping of figures and narrative composition are natural and masterful. The *Maestà* remains one of the most beautiful works of Italian art—even though the course of painting in Europe was thereafter to take a new and different direction.

Duccio's greatest follower was Simone Martini (c. 1280–1344), whose own version of the *Maestà* of 1315 adorns the east wall of the council chamber of the Palazzo Pubblico (*see p. 418*); in it, his grasp of the depth of space is something new in Siena. Simone was also later commissioned to decorate the facing wall of the chamber, and although the equestrian figure of Guidoriccio da Fogliano may well be by his hand, the surrounding landscape is a much later addition, as can be seen from the type of military architecture it depicts. Simone worked in France, in Naples, and in the (Lower) Basilica at Assisi, where he felt the influence of works by early Florentine and Roman painters which he saw there; this gave his own work a greater concentration on volume and contrasting space—something which distinguishes it from the work of his talented brother-in-law, Lippo Memmi (active 1317–50), whose many elegant, but somewhat crowded paintings may be seen in various places in Tuscany and Umbria (such as Siena, San Gimignano and Orvieto).

The lessons of Simone Martini were keenly felt and absorbed by the Lorenzetti brothers, Pietro and Ambrogio (both active 1316–48), in the next generation. Ambrogio's justly famous frescoes of the *Effects of Good and Bad Government*, painted for the Sala della Pace in Siena's Palazzo Pubblico (*see p. 419*), represent the first coherent and convincing combination of narrative and landscape in art since ancient Roman painting of the 1st century. His naturalistic study of the Tuscan *campagna*, and his minute observation of people and pose create a series of unforgettable images. There is a grander simplicity and intensity to the works of his elder brother, Pietro, which can be sensed in his powerful frescoes in the Lower Basilica at Assisi (*see p. 525*). The careers of both brothers appear to have been cut short by the plague which devastated Siena in 1348. The severity of this epidemic may be one of the factors behind the decline of the city and its art in the later 14th century.

The next century saw a brief revival, especially in the works of artists in the circle of Stefano di Giovanni, called 'Sassetta' (1392–1450/1). The beauty of his paintings lies in the abstract play of his 'silhouette' forms—normally graceful and curving—together with a mastery of colour and texture which he absorbed from the work of Duccio: he experimented (not always successfully) with unusual techniques, such as painting tempera over gold-leaf and then partially scratching through the paint-layer so as to create the effect of satin. Unusually, he also did his own gilding, in a period when the gilder's art was strictly separate. Only a few of Sassetta's panels are preserved in Siena (in the Pinacoteca; *see p. 430*), since much of his best work is in London (National Gallery) and America (Metropolitan Museum, New York). In the 19th century Sassetta's paintings were sometimes confused with those of the anonymous painter, known now as the Master of the Osservanza, whose style is in fact very different. Quite apart from the latter's roughness of handling of figures and poses, and his, at times, almost expressionist rendering of background, he does not have the serene command of space which Sassetta possesses. Indeed, his paintings often have a suffocating anguish, because he leaves the viewer so little space. Once again, his finest works are in America, but his *Birth of the Virgin* can be seen in Asciano (*illustrated on p. 438*).

Sassetta's influence may more clearly be detected in his talented and individualistic contemporary Giovanni di Paolo (1399–1482), pupil of Taddeo di Bartolo. Gracefulness, idiosyncrasy, sensitive colour-harmony and technical mastery are all there in his works; yet he carries on serenely as if the artistic Renaissance of *quattrocento* Tuscany had never happened. In one sense, these two painters, Sassetta and Giovanni di Paolo, typify the story of Siena: rich expertise and imagination laid at the service of a great—but past—Gothic tradition, out of contact with the new and compelling direction taken by Italian and European painting. It was the way of the Renaissance to humanise the sacred by bringing it down to the level of the material and physical world we inhabit. The beauty and gift of Sienese art was to do the opposite: to raise our human gaze up to the level of the sacred, opening for us worlds of courtesy, romance, and often deeply contemplative spirituality.   N.McG.

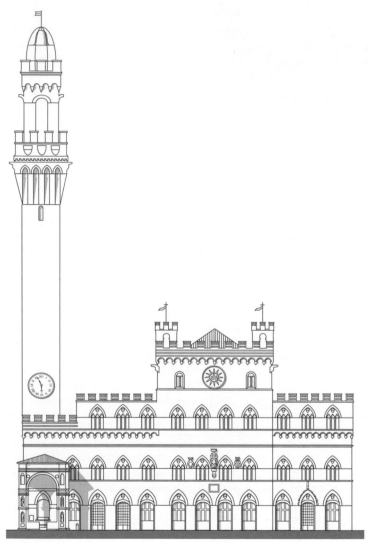

SIENA: PALAZZO PUBBLICO

Palazzo Pubblico: the Museo Civico

The Palazzo Pubblico (*map p. 410, 6–10*) is a very fine Gothic town hall built in 1297–1310 to house the Council of Nine, government offices and council chambers. The ground floor is still used as municipal offices, while the top floor, with its splendid frescoes, is open to the public.

The taller central block of four bays was the first to be built, with characteristic Sienese stone arches at ground level and brick upper storeys. The two wings on either side were heightened with a third, Gothic-style storey in 1681. At the foot of the left wing is the elegant Cappella di Piazza, an open loggia built to commemorate the deliverance of the city from the plague in 1348. Most of the statues are by Mariano d'Agnolo Romanelli (1376–80). The chapel was heightened above the four pilasters with arches and a beautiful carved architrave by Antonio Federighi in 1463–68. The frescoes in the interior are by Sodoma (*see p. 440*).

The most remarkable feature of the palace is its slim, tall tower (102m high), known as the Torre del Mangia, built in 1338–48 in ruddy brown brick. The beautiful stone cresting, probably designed by Lippo Memmi, is thought to have been constructed by Agostino di Giovanni. The tower may be climbed (*tickets for the tower only, or combined entry to the tower and Museo Civico from the ticket office in the tower, entered from the left of the inner palace courtyard*).

Museo Civico

The Museo Civico (*open 10–6.30/7; entrance from right of inner palace courtyard; tickets for museum only available here*) is remarkable for its superb frescoes by the Sienese school dating from the early 14th–16th centuries (by Simone Martini, Ambrogio Lorenzetti, Sodoma and others).

(1) Sala del Risorgimento: Designed in 1878–90, this apartment was decorated under the direction of Giuseppe Partini and Luigi Mussini to celebrate the life of the first king of Italy, Vittorio Emanuele II. Both Partini and Mussini were adherents of the artistic movement known as *Purismo* (Mussini's greatest formative influences were Raphael, and later, Ingres). Beyond this room is a corridor, with steps leading to a glass door onto the rear loggia (fine views).

(2) Sala di Balìa: The room is entirely frescoed with scenes from the life of Pope Alexander III by Spinello Aretino and his son Parri (1407–08). Pope Alexander (d. 1181) was a member of the Sienese Bandinelli family, and has gone down to posterity for forcing Henry II of England to do penance for the murder of Thomas Becket, as well as for forcing the emperor Frederick Barbarossa

to submit to him (Frederick had refused to acknowledge Alexander's pontificate, and had appointed a string of antipopes in his stead). The scene of submission forms part of this fresco cycle.

(3) Sala del Concistoro: The vault is beautifully frescoed by Beccafumi (1529–35), illustrating heroic deeds of ancient Greece and Rome.

(4) Vestibule: Here is the gilded bronze *She-wolf* (part of the coat of arms of Siena; *see p. 412*) by Giovanni di Turino (c. 1429), removed from the exterior of the palace.

(5/6) Antechapel and Chapel: Both were entirely covered with frescoes in the first years of the 15th century by Taddeo di Bartolo. The stalls in the chapel were decorated by Domenico di Niccolò dei Cori (he was nicknamed 'dei Cori' since choir stalls were his speciality).

SIENA: PALAZZO PUBBLICO

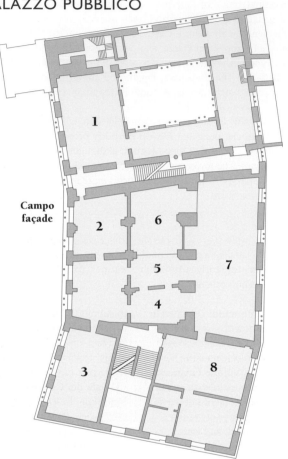

Campo
façade

1	Sala del Risorgimento	5	Antechapel
2	Sala di Balia	6	Chapel
3	Sala del Concistoro	7	Sala del Mappamondo
4	Vestibule	8	Sala della Pace

(7) Sala del Mappamondo: From the end of the 13th century this room was used for meetings of the Sienese Council, and it was they who commissioned Simone Martini's famous fresco of the *Maestà* here in 1315. It depicts a beauti-ful Madonna seated beneath a baldacchino borne by apostles and surrounded by angels and saints. The figure of the Christ Child is particularly charming. It was Simone's earliest work, although partly repainted by him in 1321.

On the opposite wall is the famous fresco (partly repainted) of Guidoriccio da Fogliano, Captain of the Sienese army, setting out for the victorious siege of Montemassi, a delightful work (cleaned in 1981), traditionally attributed to Simone Martini (1330). Since 1977 it has been the subject of heated debate. Some scholars suggest it may be a later 14th-century work, and therefore no longer attributable to Simone Martini. The fresco beneath, discovered in 1980, and thought to date from 1315–20, which represents the deliverance of a *borgo* (with the castle of Giuncarico) to a representative of the Sienese Republic, has been variously attributed to Duccio di Buoninsegna, Pietro Lorenzetti, or Memmo di Filippuccio (Simone Martini's master). The outline of a circular composition here is thought to mark the position of the lost fresco of a map of the Sienese territories, painted in 1345 by Ambrogio Lorenzetti, which gave its name to the room (Mappamondo).

On either side are two later additions by Sodoma, depicting patron saints of Siena, Victor and Ansanus (the two are also the outermost kneeling figures on Simone Martini's *Maestà*). Sodoma also painted the *Blessed Bernardo Tolomei* on the next wall (1530), where the two scenes above, of Sienese victories (one at the Val di Chiana, the other at Poggio Imperiale), are both painted predominantly in burnt sienna. The *St Catherine of Siena* (1460) is the work of Vecchietta; *St Bernardino* (1450) is by Sano di Pietro. **(8) Sala della Pace:** This was the room of the Council of Nine, who ruled Siena from 1287–1355. Benches allow you to sit and study the remarkable allegorical frescoes by Ambrogio Lorenzetti (1338), considered the most important cycle of medieval secular paintings remaining in Italy. On the wall opposite the window is the *Allegory of Wise Government*: the members of the Council of Nine would enter the chamber through the blocked-up door, directly (and symbolically) beneath the figure of Justice. On her left, on a sumptuously draped sofa, *Peace* reclines languidly, her armour discarded. Beside her sit *Fortitude* and *Prudence*. The huge bearded figure represents the common weal. Below him the twins Senus and Aschius suckle contentedly.

On the entrance wall is the *Allegory of Good Government*, with its effects in the town and countryside: shopkeepers plying their trade, women riding safe through the streets, young people making music, fine buildings in good repair, and man and beast working in harmony in fertile countryside. The city represents Siena. Opposite is the *Allegory of Evil Government* (very damaged), with its effects: murder and rapine prowl the streets, and in the fields all is desolation, while a village burns in the aftermath of war.

The duomo

Map p. 410, 9. The duomo, Museo dell'Opera del Duomo, baptistery and crypt are open 10.30–6.30 (7.30 in summer); Sun and holidays 1.30–5.30. The combined ticket allows a discount, and precedence in admission to the duomo at crowded times.

The Duomo of the Assumption is the earliest of the great Tuscan Gothic churches, despite certain Romanesque elements. It is known that Nicola Pisano (*see p. 358*) was involved as architect in the 13th century. The present cathedral was begun c. 1215, and the cupola was completed in 1263. After 1285 the façade, designed by Giovanni Pisano, was begun. The cupola was enlarged in 1316, under the direction of Camaino di Crescenzio (father of Tino di Camaino), and the apse was completed in 1382. The whole building was restored in 1865–69 under the direction of Giuseppe Partini.

In 1339 there was a scheme to build an even bigger cathedral: an immense nave was to be constructed south of the original church, which was to be turned into a transept (*see plan opposite*). The herculean task was begun, but plague and political misfortunes compelled its abandonment, although the huge unfinished nave remains.

The exterior

The entire exterior is beautifully decorated in white marble striped with black. Much of the statuary and carved decorations were replaced by copies in the 19th century, made in the workshop of Tito Sarrocchi. The originals are displayed in the Museo dell'Opera del Duomo. The lower part of the façade, with three richly decorated portals with triangular pediments, was designed by Giovanni Pisano in the last two decades of the 13th century, and he, together with his pupils, was responsible for the superb sculptures of prophets, philosophers and patriarchs (*described on p. 425*). The upper part, with a great rose window, was added in the second half of the 14th century, in the style of the cathedral of Orvieto, though the design is less harmonious.

The campanile, dating from 1313, has six storeys, banded in black and white, pierced by windows whose apertures increase in progression from single lights to hexaforae. Above the Porta del Perdono on the south flank is a copy of a beautiful tondo by Donatello (original in the museum; *see p. 425*). On the north flank, set into the wall, is a stone carved with the mysterious 'Sator Square' (*see p. 222*).

The interior

In the interior, the elaborate use of bands of black and white marble on the walls, columns, and pilasters provides a magnificent effect. The entire floor is ornamented with a series of over 50 exquisite marble inlaid designs. The iconographical scheme includes the Sibyls, symbolic references to Sienese history, and biblical scenes. The oldest (1373) are in simple graffiti, with black outlines on the white marble. Others are inlaid with black and white or coloured marble, or (in the 16th century) marbles of different tones. The most original and productive artist to work on the pavement was Domenico Beccafumi. From 1519–47 he executed many of the scenes in the central hexagon and at the east end. Some of these are kept covered, except from around 28th August until the end of October, when the entire pavement can be seen in all its glory. The pavement panels in the nave and central hexagon are as follows:

(**1**) *Hermes Trimegistus* (the 'thrice great'), an Egyptian sage renowned for his wisdom, from whom the term 'hermetic' is derived. By Giovanni di Stefano, son of Sassetta (1488).

(**2**) A mosaic tondo of 1373 (remade in 1864–65), showing the She-wolf of Siena and her allies: Arezzo (horse),

SIENA DUOMO

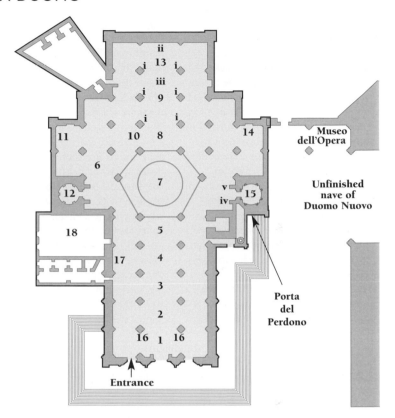

THE PAVEMENT

1 *Hermes Trimegistus*
2 She-wolf of Siena and her allies
3 Rose-window pavement design
4 The *Hill of Virtue* by Pinturicchio
5 The *Wheel of Fortune*
6 The *Massacre of the Innocents*
7 The *Story of Elijah*, some sections
   by Beccafumi
8 The *Story of Moses* by Beccafumi
9 The *Sacrifice of Isaac* by Beccafumi

THE MONUMENTS

10 Pulpit by Nicola Pisano
11 Tomb of Riccardo Petroni
12 Chapel of St John the Baptist
13 East end
    (i) candelabra by Beccafumi
    (ii) apse fresco by Beccafumi
    (iii) high altar
14 Statue of Alexander VII
15 Chigi Chapel
    (iv) *St Jerome* by Bernini
    (v) *St Mary Magdalene* by Bernini
16 Stoups
17 Piccolomini Altar
18 Piccolomini Library

Orvieto (goose), Rome (elephant), Perugia (stork), Viterbo (unicorn), Pisa (hare), Lucca (panther) and Florence (lion). In the corners are Massa Marittima (lion), Grosseto (griffin), Pistoia (dragon) and Volterra (eagle).

(3) A 14th-century rose-window design has the Imperial eagle at its centre, alluding to the Roman origins of Siena.

(4) The allegory of the *Hill of Virtue* is by Pinturicchio (1505). Fortune, depicted nude, is shown conducting a group of savants to the summit of a rock on which is seated a female figure symbolising Knowledge, with Socrates on her right. Crates, the Cynic philosopher, is emptying a basket of jewels (earthly riches) into the sea below. Notice the beautifully rendered plants and small creatures on the hillside.

(5) The *Wheel of Fortune* (1372) shows a king and four Greek philosophers. It is attributed to Domenico di Niccolò dei Cori, but was remade in 1864–65.

(6) The *Massacre of the Innocents* is presumed to be by Matteo di Giovanni (1482); there are analogies in style to his paintings of the same subject in Santa Maria dei Servi (*see p. 433*) and Santa Maria della Scala (*see p. 428*).

(7) Six lozenge-shaped scenes illustrate the *Story of Elijah*. The most beautiful (the central scene, and the three hexagons and two lozenges nearest to the altar) are by Beccafumi, who here introduced a new technique of marble inlay.

(8) Two splendid scenes beside the pulpit, also by Beccafumi (1525–31), illustrate the *Story of Moses*. A long, narrow panel shows Moses striking water from the rock, and the larger rectangle shows Moses on Mount Sinai.

(9) Between the two altars of the choir is the *Sacrifice of Isaac*, the last work Beccafumi made for the duomo pavement (1547).

Monuments

(10) Dome and pulpit: The hexagon of the dome was decorated at the end of the 15th century with gilded statues of saints, and painted figures of patriarchs and prophets in chiaroscuro high above. The dome itself is painted blue, with 100 golden stars in coffers. The octagonal pulpit, in Carrara marble, is a remarkable Gothic work by Nicola Pisano (1265–68), completed six years after his famous pulpit in the baptistery of Pisa (*see p. 356*). He was assisted by his son Giovanni, and by Arnolfo di Cambio. As at Pisa, the columns rest on the backs of alternating lions (with their prey) and lionesses (with their cubs). Around the base of the central column are the seated figures of *Philosophy* and the seven *Liberal Arts*, and at the top of the outer columns, the *Christian Virtues*, *Evangelists* and *Prophets*. The seven panels beautifully carved in high relief symbolise Redemption, with scenes from the life of Christ and two scenes of the *Last Judgement*. They are divided by another series of carved figures, including a *Madonna and Child*.

(11) Tomb of Riccardo Petroni: The tomb of this cardinal (d. 1313) is by Tino di Camaino. In front of it is the bronze pavement tomb of Bishop Giovanni Pecci, signed by Donatello (1426; *removed for restoration at the time of writing*).

(12) Chapel of St John the Baptist: This graceful Renaissance structure is probably by Giovanni di Stefano (1492), with a portal by Marrina (the column bases are by Antonio Federighi). The statue of *St John the Baptist* is unmistakably the work of Donatello (1457), reminiscent in its shaggy lines of his *St Mary Magdalene* in Florence (*see p. 276*). The interior frescoes, which include three scenes from the life of St John the Baptist, are by Pinturicchio.

(13) The east end: Against the pillars of the presbytery **(i)** are eight candelabra in the form of angels on brackets, fine works by Domenico Beccafumi (1551). This versatile artist also carried out the fresco of the *Ascension* in the apse **(ii)**, although it was altered in 1812. There are more fine bronzes (dating from the end of the 15th century) in the choir, above the high altar **(iii)**, including a bronze ciborium by Vecchietta and angels carrying candles by Giovanni di Stefano (the uppermost) and Francesco di Giorgio Martini (the lower two). The magnificent stained glass by Duccio in the oculus is now displayed in the Museo dell'Opera del Duomo and here replaced by a pale 'electronic' copy.

(14) Statue of Alexander VII: This Sienese pope, a member of the Chigi family, is commemorated with a monument by Bernini's pupil Antonio Raggi, though the design was by the master himself.

(15) Chigi Chapel: This circular Baroque chapel was built for Alexander VII (Fabio Chigi) in 1659–62. At the entrance are statues of *St Jerome* **(iv)** and *St Mary Magdalene* **(v)** by Bernini. The other statues, of the Sienese saints Bernardino and Crescentius, are by Bernini's pupils Antonio Raggi and Ercole Ferrata. The pavement of the chapel sports the Chigi device of mounds. The chapel was built to house the *Madonna del Voto*, a venerated icon of the Madonna and Child (once part of of a larger painting) by a follower of Guido da Siena. Still honoured with numerous ex-votos including, dramatically, a group of motorcycle helmets, it has been the traditional focus of entreaty for the Sienese in times of crisis. On six occasions in their history the inhabitants placed the keys of their threatened city before it and prayed for deliverance. The first was before the battle of Montaperti in 1260; the latest on 18th June 1944, a fortnight before the liberation of Siena.

(16) The stoups: Beautifully carved by Antonio Federighi. In recent years they have sadly had to be protected by glass.

(17) Piccolomini Altar: This is a magnificent work by Andrea Bregno (c. 1480). The statuettes in the four lower niches of *St Peter*, *St Pius*, *St Gregory* and *St Paul* are documented early works by Michelangelo (1501–04), who may also have worked on the figure of *St Francis* above, which was begun by Pietro Torrigiani (a fellow Florentine, who had famously broken Michelangelo's nose in a fight in the Brancacci Chapel). The beautiful *Madonna and Child* at the top is possibly Jacopo della Quercia's earliest work (c. 1397–1400).

(18) Piccolomini Library: This is one of the most delightful spaces in Italy, its walls and vault entirely covered with a decorative fresco cycle by Pinturicchio (*see p. 537*). The room was built in 1495 by Cardinal Francesco Piccolomini (after-

Aeneas Sylvius Piccolomini, as Bishop of Siena, witnesses the meeting between Holy Roman Emperor Frederick III and his betrothed, Eleanor of Portugal, outside the Porta Camollia in Siena. The fifth of the ten scenes by Pinturicchio in the Piccolomini Library (1502–07).

The episodes represented are (beginning at the right of the window): 1: Aeneas Sylvius sets out for the Council of Basel (as he looks back at us from his grey charger); 2: He is received as envoy at the court of James II of Scotland; 3: He is crowned as poet in 1442 by Frederick III; 4: He is sent by the Emperor to Pope Eugenius IV (1445); 5: As Bishop of Siena, he is present at the meeting in 1451 of the Emperor Frederick and his betrothed Eleanor of Portugal outside the Porta Camollia; 6: He is presented with the cardinal's hat by Calixtus III in 1456; 7: Elected pope in 1458, he is carried in state on the *sedia gestatoria*; 8: He proclaims a crusade at Mantua in 1459; 9: He canonises St Catherine of Siena (1461); 10: He arrives at Ancona to await in vain for the Venetian fleet before setting out on Crusade in 1464, again borne on the *sedia gestatoria*, but this time close to death.

The gilded vault is covered with colourful *grottesche* around the Piccolomini arms, and the ceramic floor has a beautiful design of blue and yellow Piccolomini moons. The celebrated group of the *Three Graces*, a Roman copy of an original by Praxiteles, was acquired in Rome by Cardinal Francesco Piccolomini. It was frequently copied and is known to have served as model to Pinturicchio, Raphael and Canova.

wards Pius III) for the library of his uncle Aeneas Sylvius Piccolomini (Pius II). It was painted in 1502–07 with ten large scenes from the life of Pius II, full of elegantly dressed spectators. In an excellent state of preservation, they are all by Pinturicchio with some help from his pupils (the young Raphael is also thought to have contributed).

Museo dell'Opera del Duomo

Map p. 410, 10. Open 10.30–6.30 (7.30 in summer); Sun and holidays 1.30–5.30.
Piazza Jacopo della Quercia occupies the site of the unfinished nave of the Duomo
Nuovo (*see p. 420*): the marble arcades survive as well as the façade and side portal,
which give some idea of the size of the projected building. Its south aisle has been converted into the Museo dell'Opera del Duomo.

Ground floor

The Sala delle Statue contains the original **statues from the façade of the duomo**, by
Giovanni Pisano and his school, constituting one of the most important groups of Italian
Gothic sculpture in existence. Even though very damaged, they are still memorable in
their dramatic attitudes. Their elongated necks made them more visible from the Piazza
below. They are *Solomon, Plato, Habakkuk, Simeon, Moses*, and his sister *Miriam* (who
was considered a prophet). The other figures, by Giovanni's assistants, are notably less
intense.

The splendid **stained-glass window** was designed by Duccio in 1288 for the east
end of the cathedral, and it is known that this great Sienese master also added some
details directly in paint. This is probably the oldest existing stained glass of Italian manufacture. It shows the *Burial, Assumption,* and *Coronation of the Virgin*, together with the
four patron saints of the town, and the four Evangelists. Since its recent restoration, it
has been replaced in the duomo itself by a copy. Also here are a bas-relief of the *Madonna
and Child with St Anthony Abbot and Cardinal Antonio Casini*, by Jacopo della Quercia,
and a **tondo of the *Madonna and Child***, almost certainly by Donatello (from the Porta
del Perdono of the Duomo; replaced *in situ* by a copy).

First floor

The museum is famous above all for the celebrated **Maestà by Duccio di
Buoninsegna**, one of the most beautiful and important works of art in Italy. It was commissioned in 1308 for the high altar of the duomo, where it remained until 1505. It was
dismantled in 1771, when the original frame was destroyed and a few of the panels from
the predella and cimasa were lost or dispersed (some of them are now in the
Washington and London National Galleries, and in the Frick Collection in New York).
It is still not known exactly how the great painting was composed. Although clearly
influenced by the Byzantine style, the panels are endowed with a new Gothic spirit and
extraordinary narrative power, which was to be developed from this work by the great
Sienese school of painters. It is sufficient to look at Duccio's *Madonna di Crevole*
(1270/1300), also displayed here, to compare the difference between its static, archaic
style, and the new approach of the *Maestà* panels.

The main *Maestà* panel depicts the *Virgin and Child*, surrounded by angels and saints
(the four patron saints of Siena, Ansanus, Savinus, Crescentius and Victor, are shown
kneeling in the foreground). On the throne is an invocation in Latin: 'Oh Holy Mother
of God bring peace to Siena and life to Duccio since he has painted you thus!' The Child
is particularly beautiful in a lilac-coloured shawl, which merges with that of the

Madonna, who is enveloped in a magnificent deep blue cloak. The most memorable figures in the crowd of angels and saints are perhaps the four angels leaning dreamily over the back of the throne, and St Agnes and St Catherine who stand at either side.

On the opposite wall are displayed 26 scenes with the story of Christ's Passion, formerly on the back of the main panel. Along the wall between them are panels from the predella and cimasa, with scenes from the life of Christ and the last days and death of the Virgin. Each tells a story, and some of the most striking details are the wonderful heavy catch of fish which is being drawn up by the apostles humped over the side of their little round boat as Peter walks on the water; the angel sitting on Christ's empty tomb; and the discarded black sandals in the *Washing of the Feet*. Duccio took some three years to paint this great work, and it was at once recognised as a masterpiece by the Sienese, who were so pleased with it that they declared a public holiday.

Also exhibited in this room is the **Birth of the Virgin** (1342), a beautiful painting full of marvellous detail, by Pietro Lorenzetti. The Master of the Osservanza's later rendering of the same subject in Asciano (*shown on p. 438*) seems to owe a debt to this work.

Duccio di Buoninsegna (c. 1260–1319)
Duccio di Buoninsegna was greatly admired by his contemporaries, although little else is known about his life, and very few works definitely by his hand have survived. His *bottega* was in Via di Stalloreggi just inside the Arco delle Due Porte (*map p. 410, 13*), where from 1313 he lived with his wife Taviana and their eight children. He is recorded as having worked as a young man for the *comune* of Siena decorating their statute-books and store chests. His first important commission was in 1285, when the Florentine Laudesi confraternity ordered a *Madonna* for their chapel in Santa Maria Novella. This work, known as the *Rucellai Madonna*, is now in the Uffizi (*see p. 282*). His masterpiece, however, was the Siena *Maestà*, which established him as the greatest painter of his time.

Another exquisite work preserved in Siena is his *Madonna 'dei Francescani'*, a tiny painting now in the Pinacoteca Nazionale. The cartoon for the round stained glass window in the duomo is also by his hand. Nothing is known of his life after 1313, and it seems that he never worked in fresco. There are works, mostly Madonnas, all over Tuscany attributed to his school. Simone Martini was his greatest follower. Although Lorenzo Ghiberti mentions him with great admiration, he was later forgotten and his importance ignored.

Top floor

In the room at the head of the stairs is the **Madonna dagli Occhi Grossi**, a rather forbidding icon, partly in relief, by a Sienese painter known as the Maestro di Tressa (1220–30). It used to adorn the high altar of the cathedral before Duccio's *Maestà*. The **St Bernardino of Siena** is by Sano di Pietro, flanked by two delightful paintings also credited to Sano showing the saint preaching in the Campo and in Piazza San Francesco.

The Marys at the Sepulchre, with an angel sitting on the empty tomb. Panel from Duccio's *Maestà* (1308–11).

In the room off to the right as you come upstairs there is a very fine painting of *St Paul* by Beccafumi. At the far end of the room is the **Scala del Facciatone**, a narrow stairway which winds up to the top of the unfinished nave façade of the Duomo Nuovo, from where there are extensive views of the city and countryside.

The crypt and baptistery

The side door of the Duomo Nuovo, between the incomplete nave and the cathedral, is a beautiful Gothic portal. From here steep steps, constructed in 1451, descend to the baptistery. Halfway down is the entrance to the crypt (*open 10.30–6.30; 7.30 in summer; Sun and holidays 1.30–5.30*), with remains of **extremely important frescoes of c. 1270**, some of the earliest known works of the Sienese school. They are variously attributed to masters working with Guido da Siena and Duccio. The largest composition (still being restored) depicts the *Crucifixion*, the *Descent from the Cross* and the *Burial of Christ*.

The baptistery, beneath part of the cathedral, has a lovely rectangular Gothic façade by Domenico di Agostino (1355), which was never finished. The interior (*open as crypt; see above*) is very well preserved with lovely 15th-century Sienese frescoes. The beautiful **hexagonal font** is one of the most interesting sculptural works by the Tuscan masters of the early Renaissance (1417–30). The gilded bronze panels in relief illustrate the life of St John the Baptist: the *Angel announcing the Birth of the Baptist to Zacharias* is by Jacopo della Quercia; the *Birth of the Baptist*, and his preaching, are by Turino di Sano and Giovanni di Turino (his son); the *Baptism of Christ* (recalling the south doors of the Florence Baptistery; *see p. 275*) and the *Baptist Before Herod*, are both by Lorenzo Ghiberti; and *Feast of Herod* is by Donatello, a work of enormous dramatic power capturing the moment when the Baptist's severed head is presented at table. Guests recoil in visible revulsion while the musicians in the next room play on obliviously. The marble tabernacle was designed by Jacopo della Quercia, who carved the five statues of prophets in niches and the crowning statue of the Baptist. The four bronze angels are by Donatello and Giovanni di Turino.

The best **frescoes** are those in the three vaults nearest the altar with the *Articles of the Creed*; the apsidal arch with the *Assumption of the Virgin* and a glory of angels; and the three scenes on the apse wall of the *Annunciation*, *Flagellation* and *Way to Calvary*, all by Vecchietta. In the large lunette to the left of the apse are scenes of the miracles of St Anthony of Padua by Benvenuto di Giovanni (c. 1460). The polyptych of the *Madonna and Child with Saints* is by Andrea Vanni (and in the predella are very unusual scenes from the lives of saints by Giovanni di Paolo).

Ospedale di Santa Maria della Scala

Opposite the duomo is the irregular Gothic façade of Santa Maria della Scala (*map p. 410, 9; open 10.30–4.30; mid-March–Oct 10–6*), a hospital founded in the 9th century for pilgrims travelling to Rome along the Via Francigena (*see p. 448*). Up until a few years ago it was still a hospital, but this has now moved, and the buildings are being restored as a cultural centre and museum (the Pinacoteca will one day be transferred here). The areas open at the time of writing are described below.

Sala del Pellegrinaio: The 14th-century pilgrims' hall has delightful frescoes (1440–44) illustrating the life of the hospital. Over the two doors is the *Story of the Blessed Sorore*, the mythical founder of the hospital, by Vecchietta, and, opposite, *Feeding the Poor in the Hospital* by Domenico di Bartolo. Domenico also painted the next two bays: *Reception and Education of Orphans in the Hospital* and the *Marriage of an Orphan*, and (opposite) *Building Work to Enlarge the Hospital*. The last two bays (16th-century), show Pope Celestine III granting rights to laymen for running the hospital, and the wet nurses of the hospital receiving payment.

Sagrestia Vecchia: The old sacristy was entirely decorated by Vecchietta in 1446–49, illustrating the articles of the Creed. The scenes are particularly interesting for their iconography (they are in the process of restoration). In the chapel is a very fine painting (1482) of the *Massacre of the Innocents* by Matteo di

Giovanni (originally from Sant'Agostino). **Oratorio di Santa Caterina della Notte and Fonte Gaia panels:** On the floor below, the 17th-century furnishings of a charming oratory survive virtually intact. Nearby are old storerooms, in which are exhibited parts of the damaged Fonte Gaia, one of the masterpieces of Jacopo della Quercia (*see p. 413*). This fountain was designed in 1414–19 for the centre of the Campo, with panels illustrating stories from Genesis, the Theological and Cardinal Virtues, a figure of *Justice*, and female allegorical statues. Made from a fragile local marble, it weathered very badly and was damaged by the water, so in 1844 it was decided to remove it from the Campo, and in 1869 it was replaced by a copy commissioned from Tito Sarrocchi. Casts of his works are dis-played with the casts he took of the original marble panels, and a few of the original (restored) panels and statues by della Quercia can also be seen here.

Museo Archeologico: On two more floors below, reached through the medieval 'labyrinths' connected by passageways in the tufa rock, this museum was rearranged in 2001. It contains Etruscan and Roman material from sites in Tuscany. Another exit was opened in 2007 along a remarkable old medieval road, vaulted in brick, leading downhill from the main entrance onto the Piazzetta della Selva.

Church of the Annunziata: The hospital church, dedicated to the Virgin Annunciate, contains a very fine bronze statue of the *Risen Christ* by Vecchietta (1476).

Pinacoteca Nazionale

Map p. 410, 14. Open Mon 8.30–1.30; Tues–Sat 8.15–7.15; Sun and holidays 8.15–1.15. This is the most important gallery for the study of the great Sienese masters. The display is chronological. There are plans to move the collection to Santa Maria della Scala, and the rooms are at present rather shabby, and the arrangement of works subject to change. The description below reflects the status quo at the time of writing.

Second floor

Rooms 1–2: The origins of Sienese painting. An altar frontal of Christ blessing between symbols of the Evangelists and scenes from the legend of the True Cross is the first securely dated work (1215) of the Sienese school, attributed to the Maestro di Tressa. Also here are three scenes from the life of Christ by Guido da Siena (late 13th century), one of the first works known on canvas.

Rooms 3–4: Here are two polyptychs by Duccio, as well as works by his followers. The tiny *Madonna 'dei Francescani'* (c. 1285), a work of great luminosity (though much ruined), is considered one of Duccio's masterpieces.

Room 5: Two important works by Simone Martini: *Madonna and Child* and the *Pala di Beato Agostino Novello*. Also here is a *Madonna* by his brother-in-law Lippo Memmi.

Room 7: Here are some very fine works by the famous brothers Pietro and Ambrogio Lorenzetti (first half of the 14th century). Ambrogio's last dated work is the *Annunciation* (commissioned in 1344).

Rooms 11–13: Early 15th-century painting, including good works by Domenico di Bartolo, Taddeo di Bartolo (the master of Giovanni di Paolo), Giovanni di Paolo and Sassetta. Room 12 has two charming small landscapes: *City by the Sea*, and *Castle by a Lake*, perhaps part of a larger decoration for a cupboard door, and tentatively attributed to Ambrogio Lorenzetti. The handful of Sassetta's works held by the Pinacoteca are in Room 13. All are from his *Pala dell'Arte della Lana* (1423–26), and include the famous scene of St Anthony being belaboured by devils.

Rooms 14–19: Later 15th-century paintings by Francesco di Giorgio Martini, Matteo di Giovanni, Sano di Pietro, Vecchietta, the Master of the Osservanza and Bernardino Fungai.

First floor

Rooms 27–37 display 16th- and 17th-century Sienese works, notably paintings by Beccafumi and Sodoma.

ITINERARIES THROUGH THE CONTRADE

Siena is divided into 17 administrative wards (*contrade*). Each has a headquarters, a small museum and an oratory. Children born in the *contrada* are baptised at an open-air font. The oratories and museums are only open on certain days of the year (*enquire at the APT office; map p. 410, 6*), or by appointment in advance. The noticeboards outside usually carry news about members of the *contrada*, or announce new births.

CONTRADA NAME	SYMBOL	ORATORY
Aquila	Eagle	Casato di Sotto
Bruco	Caterpillar	Via del Comune
Chiocciola	Snail	Via San Marco
Civetta	Owl	Via Cecco Angiolieri
Drago	Dragon	Piazza Matteotti
Giraffa	Giraffe	Via delle Vergini
Istrice	Porcupine	Via di Camollia
Leocorno	Unicorn	Piazzetta Grassi
Lupa	She-wolf	Via di Vallerozzi
Nicchio	Scallop shell	Via dei Pispini
Oca	Goose	Costa Sant'Antonio
Onda	Dolphin and water	Via di Fontanella
Pantera	Panther	Pian de' Mantellini
Selva	Rhinoceros	Valle Piatta
Tartuca	Tortoise	Via Tommaso Pendola
Torre	Elephant bearing a tower	Via di Salicotto
Valdimontone	Ram	Via Val di Montone

Contrada dell'Aquila

The lovely old Casato di Sotto (*map p. 410, 10*) winds gently uphill from the Campo. It is a street of grand palaces from various periods, all of different heights. The parallel street, Via di Città, is also bordered by handsome mansions. Chief of these is the 14th-century **Palazzo Chigi-Saracini**, which follows the curve of the street. This character-istic Sienese Gothic fortified palace, with its two lower storeys built in stone and the top one in brick, has splendid three-light windows. You can visit the charming courtyard with its well and busts and medallions beneath a frescoed loggia. Here the tiny bell-tower belongs to a chapel added in 1803, and the handsome windows bear the motto of the Chigi family (*Micat in Vertice*; 'resplendent at the summit'), now also that of the Accademia Musicale Chigiana, founded in 1932 by Count Guido Chigi-Saracini. The Accademia is still very active and gives excellent concerts in the lovely music room upstairs. Unfortunately the palace is otherwise closed to the public, although exhibi-tions are held periodically on the ground floor of parts of the famous Chigi-Saracini art collection, which is particularly important for its Sienese works, ranging from the 13th–17th centuries, including an *Adoration of the Magi* by Sassetta.

On the other side of the street is the Renaissance **Palazzo Piccolomini delle Papesse** (1460–95), built by Caterina Piccolomini, sister of Pius II, from the plans of Bernardo Rossellino (who designed Pienza for the same pope; *see p. 445*). It now houses a con-temporary art centre (due to move to Santa Maria della Scala; *see p. 428*).

Contrada della Civetta

From the Campo, Vicolo di San Pietro leads up to the Croce del Travaglio, where the three main streets of Siena, the Banchi di Sopra, the Banchi di Sotto, and Via di Città, meet. Here is the **Loggia della Mercanzia** (*map p. 410, 6*), where the merchants' guild held a commercial tribunal famous for its impartiality, to which even foreign states resorted. It was built in the 15th century and has statues of saints by Antonio Federighi and Vecchietta. From the southeast angle of the Campo, Via Rinaldini leads to Palazzo Piccolomini (*map p. 411, 7*), a handsome building facing Via Banchi di Sotto and a good example of Florentine Renaissance architecture, probably designed by Bernardo Rossellino but begun shortly after his death in 1469. The palace contains the **Archivio di Stato**, one of the finest extant collections of archives in Italy (well catalogued). It has a delightful little museum on the fourth floor (*open Mon–Sat at 9.30, 10.30 and 11.30*), with an inconspicuous entrance from the courtyard, reached by lift. The collection is famous for its unique series of little paintings known as the *Tavolette di Biccherna*. Dating from 1258, these were the painted covers of the municipal account-books, and give a fascinating picture of medieval life. The *Biccherna* was the name of the most important financial branch of government in Siena, and it was the first office which began the cus-tom of decorating the outside covers of their records; later other branches of Sienese government followed suit. In the rooms where the historic archives are shelved, the lit-tle paintings are arranged chronologically: they include works by the most famous Sienese artists of the day, including (in the 14th century) Ambrogio Lorenzetti, (in the 15th century) Giovanni di Paolo, Vecchietta, Sano di Pietro, Francesco di Giorgio

Martini and Bernardino Fungai, and (in the 16th century) Domenico Beccafumi. The important medieval documents (the oldest dated 736) in the archives include the contract between the *comune* and Jacopo della Quercia for the Fonte Gaia in the Campo, the contract drawn up by the Opera del Duomo for Duccio's *Maestà*, a pergamene signed by Frederick I Barbarossa, Boccaccio's will, and the imperial charter (with its seal intact) by which Montepulciano was ceded to Siena after their victory over the Florentines at Montaperti (20th November 1260).

Contrade della Tartuca and Chiocciola

The peaceful Via Tommaso Pendola (*map p. 410, 14–13*) runs straight through the Contrada della Tartuca. Parallel to the south is Vicolo della Tartuca, a medieval blind alley with a flying bridge, and Via Tito Sarrocchi, with the house (at no. 35) where the great Sienese artist Beccafumi lived from 1516. On the wide Pian dei Mantellini stands the Carmelite convent of **San Niccolò al Carmine** (*map p. 410, 13*), which was founded in the 13th century. At the beginning of Via San Marco, which leads down through the Contrada della Chiocciola (the snail; *just beyond map p. 410, 13*), a pretty little house, formerly a church, has a busy food shop on its ground floor. The relief of the lion of St Mark here was presented to the *contrada* by Venice in 1954.

Contrada della Pantera

The church of **San Niccolò al Carmine** (*map p. 410, 13*) doubles as the oratory for the *contrada* (by a peculiarity of Sienese geography, the convent is in the *contrada* of the snail and the church in that of the panther). It contains a memorable altarpiece of *St Michael*, a superb work by Domenico Beccafumi.

Piazza del Conte (*map p. 410, 14*), in an ancient, quiet medieval corner of the town, lies at the heart of the *contrada* of the panther. Here is the fountain where open-air baptisms of new-born panthers take place. Vicolo Contino winds up from the square to Via di Castelvecchio, which gives access to a miniature fortified piazza perched at the top of the little hill. Where Via di Castelvecchio emerges on Via di San Pietro, high up on the wall of a house there is a tablet which declares that no prostitute, even if married, and whether registered or not, may ever live in the street—at the risk of a fine of 10 *scudi*. Via di Castelvecchio leads down in the other direction into Via Stalloreggi. At the junction of the streets there is a pretty tabernacle (look up above head height) protecting a fresco of the *Pietà* by Sodoma. It is known as the **Madonna del Corvo**, supposedly because a crow afflicted by the plague dropped dead on this site in 1348. At the western end of Via Stalloreggi is the **Arco delle Due Porte**, just inside which a plaque records the house where Siena's greatest painter, Duccio di Buoninsegna, lived and had his studio. The 16th-century tabernacle here has a fresco attributed to Baldassare Peruzzi. High up on the wall of a house (no. 7) outside the gate is an early 14th-century fresco of the *Madonna and Child*, thought to be the oldest tabernacle in the town.

Contrada della Onda

From the Campo, the long Via Giovanni Dupré leads south. It ends at the little church of San Giuseppe, oratory of the *contrada*, with a pretty fountain decorated with dolphins in a garden outside. From here Via Sant'Agata leads uphill to the church of **Sant'Agostino** (*map p. 410, 14; open mid-March–end Oct 10.30–1.30 & 3–5.30*), which dates from 1258. The light, bright interior was remodelled in 1749 by Gaspare Vanvitelli. It has particularly interesting early 17th-century altarpieces, as well as a *Crucifixion* by Perugino (second south altar; c. 1504), showing the crucified Christ between the Marys and Sts Monica, Jerome, John the Baptist and Augustine. The Piccolomini Chapel (entrance off the south side) was founded in 1596 by Ascanio Piccolomini, Archbishop of Siena, in the chapter house of the Augustinian convent. It preserves an altarpiece of the *Epiphany* by Sodoma (c. 1530), and, on the opposite wall, a lunette fresco of the *Madonna and Saints* by Ambrogio Lorenzetti (1335–38). Outside the entrance to the chapel is a marble statue of an earlier Piccolomini, Pope Pius II (*see p. 424*) by the native Sienese sculptor Giovanni Dupré. Back in the main body of the church, the Cappella Bichi at the east end has two frescoes in grisaille of the *Birth of the Virgin* and the *Nativity*, attributed to Francesco di Giorgio Martini.

Contrada della Torre

The elegant **Logge del Papa** (*map p. 411, 7*) was built for Pius II by Antonio Federighi (1462). The decorations are attributed to Francesco di Giorgio Martini. Beside it the church of **San Martino**, mentioned in an 8th-century document, has a façade of 1613 and a pleasant 16th-century interior with two lovely side altarpieces: the *Circumcision* by Guido Reni, and a *Nativity* by Domenico Beccafumi.

The ancient old Vicolo delle Scotte leads under a passageway and down steps past the **Synagogue** (*open on holidays 10–1 & 2–4 or 5*), a Neoclassical building (1756). There was a Jewish community in Siena from 1229 onwards, and they were confined to a ghetto in this area by Cosimo de' Medici in 1571, the doors of which were burnt down by French troops in 1796. However, it was not until 1895 that the Jews were given complete freedom to reside in the city.

Contrada di Valdimontone

Solitary and little-visited, in a peaceful corner of town, is the large church of **Santa Maria dei Servi** (*map p. 411, 16*) with its massive brick campanile. The spacious interior, with lovely capitals, has numerous interesting works of art from different periods. In the second chapel in the south aisle, the *Madonna del Bordone* by Coppo di Marcovaldo, signed and dated 1261, was partly repainted by a pupil of Duccio (and is now in very poor condition). The fifth south chapel has a *Massacre of the Innocents* by Matteo di Giovanni (1491), one of several versions of this subject painted by him (*removed for restoration at the time of writing*). In the south transept, the *Madonna and Child* by Segna di Bonaventura dates from 1319, and the painted Cross is attributed to his son Niccolò. In the second chapel to the right of the sanctuary are especially interesting remains of frescoes (including the *Massacre of the Innocents*) by Pietro Lorenzetti and others; the same artists worked on the scenes from the life of St John the Baptist in the second chapel to the left of the sanctuary (where the altarpiece of the *Nativity* was painted in 1404 by Taddeo di Bartolo). In the adjacent north transept, the *Madonna della Misericordia* is signed and dated 1431 by Taddeo's pupil Giovanni di Paolo. On the high altar is a lovely large painting of the *Coronation of the Virgin* by Bernardino Fungai.

Contrada della Giraffa

The splendid exterior of **Santa Maria di Provenzano** (*map p. 410, 2*) is well seen from above, with its Mannerist façade (1604) and dome designed by Don Giovanni de' Medici (illegitimate son of Cosimo I). The interior has 17th-century altarpieces by Bernardino Mei and Rutilio Manetti, and on the high altar is a highly venerated little 15th-century terracotta bust of the *Madonna*, in honour of which the *Palio* of 2nd July is run. The prize banner is kept in the church before the race.

On the left side of the façade, Via Provenzano Salvani leads to the large Gothic church of **San Francesco** (*map p. 411, 3*), built in 1326–1475 but mostly destroyed by fire in 1655 and radically restored in neo-Gothic style by Giuseppe Partini. In the interior, high up on the west wall, are two detached frescoes from the Porta Romana by Sassetta (the artist died of a chill he caught while painting them) and Sano di Pietro, and from Porta Pispini by Sodoma. One of the choir chapels has two fine frescoes by Ambrogio Lorenzetti, one with the *Martyrdom of Franciscan Monks* and one with a scene of *St Louis of Toulouse before Pope Boniface VIII*. Louis, second son of the King of Naples, was a Franciscan friar before his appointment as bishop.

To the right of San Francesco, the 15th-century **Oratorio di San Bernardino** (*map p. 411, 3; only open mid-March–Oct 10.30–1.30 & 3–5.30*) stands on the spot where St Bernardino preached. The lower chapel has lunettes frescoed with scenes representing the Saint's life by 17th-century Sienese artists including Francesco Vanni and Rutilio Manetti. On a table is a charming little *Madonna and Child* by Sano di Pietro. The oratory, beautifully decorated by Ventura Turapilli (after 1496), contains fine frescoes of 1518 by Sodoma (*Presentation*, *Visitation*, *Assumption* and *Coronation of the Virgin*), Beccafumi (*Marriage of the Virgin*, *Transition of the Virgin*) and Girolamo del Pacchia. The 14th-century antiphonal is illuminated by Lippo Vanni.

The **Museo Diocesano di Arte Sacra**, a delightful little museum with works of art, mostly by Sienese masters, from churches in Siena or the diocese which have been closed, is exhibited in five small rooms. It has two interesting works by Vecchietta: one a fresco of the *Lamentation*, and the other a beautiful small polychrome wooden group of the *Pietà*, a very unusual work showing close stylistic similarities to the fresco. There is an exquisite *Madonna and Child* by Segna di Bonaventura, and the *Madonna del Latte* (from Lecceto) is considered one of the best works of Ambrogio Lorenzetti (a *Madonna Enthroned and Four Angels* is by his contemporary Bartolomeo Bulgarini). Matteo di Giovanni is particularly well represented, and the *Madonna and Child with Saints and Angels* here is one of his finest paintings.

Contrada del Drago

Via Banchi di Sopra (*map p. 410, 2–6*), Siena's busiest street, noisy until the small hours of the morning with human footsteps and human voices, leads north from the

Loggia della Mercanzia through Piazza Tolomei, where from the 11th century the Sienese parliament used to assemble. Here the splendid **Palazzo Tolomei**, with beautiful two-light windows, is one of the oldest Gothic palaces in Siena (now owned by a bank), begun around 1208 and restored some 50 years later. San Cristoforo, despite its early 19th-century façade in Palladian style, is one of the oldest churches in Siena dating from the 11th–12th century, where the magistrates of the Republic officiated.

On Siena

Our rooms were in a tower. From the window one looked across the brown tiled roofs to where, on its hill, stood the cathedral. A hundred feet below was the street, a narrow canyon between high walls, perennially sunless; the voices of the passers-by came up, reverberating, as out of a chasm. Down there they walked always in shadow; but in our tower we were the last to lose the sunlight… And at evening, when only the belfries and the domes and the highest roofs were still flushed by the declining sun, our windows were level with the flight of the swifts and swallows. Sunset after sunset all through the long summer, they wheeled and darted round our tower.

Aldous Huxley, Along the Road (1925)

Piazza Salimbeni (*map p. 410, 2*) was laid out in the late 19th century, when the statue of Sallustio Bandini by Tito Sarrocchi was installed, and the three fine palaces were enlarged or restored in neo-Gothic or neo-Renaissance style by Giuseppe Partini (Palazzo Spannocchi on the left preserves its façade by Giuliano da Maiano on Via Banchi di Sopra). These three palaces now form the seat of the Monte dei Paschi di Siena, a well-known bank founded in 1624.

Contrada dell'Oca

The **Casa di Santa Caterina** (*map p. 410, 1–5; open 9.30–7; winter 10–6*) is the house where St Catherine of Siena (*see box overleaf*) was born. It was converted into a sanctuary after its purchase by the *comune* in 1466. The present entrance is through a portico erected in 1941. The charming little loggia beyond was built in 1533. The Oratorio della Cucina, the family kitchen, was converted in the 16th century into an oratory and decorated at that time with wood stalls and a majolica pavement, as well as paintings including works by Riccio, Rutilio Manetti and Francesco Vanni (the altarpiece is by Bernardino Fungai). The Church of the Crocifisso was built in 1623 on the site of the saint's orchard, to house the *Crucifixion* (by the late 12th-century Pisan school) before which St Catherine received the Stigmata at Pisa in 1375. It is preserved over the high altar, in a cupboard decorated by Riccio. Stairs lead down to the Camera della Santa, St Catherine's cell, frescoed in 1896. It preserves a small early 15th-century painting of *St Catherine Receiving the Stigmata* by Girolamo di Benvenuto.

St Catherine of Siena (1347–80)

Caterina Benincasa, the daughter of a dyer, took the veil at the age of eight. Her visions of the Redeemer, from whom she received the Stigmata and—like her Alexandrian namesake—a marriage ring, have been the subject of countless paintings. Her eloquence persuaded Pope Gregory XI to return from Avignon to Rome, and her letters (preserved in Siena's municipal library) are models of style as well as of devotion. She died in Rome, where she is buried in Santa Maria sopra Minerva. Canonised in 1461, she was proclaimed a patron saint of Italy in 1939. She was made a Doctor of the Church in 1970, the first female saint, with St Teresa of Avila, to be given this distinction, and in 1999 was proclaimed a patron saint of Europe. The only authentic portrait of Catherine can be seen in the basilica of San Domenico, in the chapel in which she became a Dominican (*see below*). Another chapel in the same church was built in 1460 to preserve the relic of her head brought back to Siena from Rome in 1383.

The lovely **Fonte Branda** (*map p. 410, 5*) is the oldest and most abundant spring in Siena. It was mentioned as early as 1081 and covered over in 1248 with brick vaults by Giovanni di Stefano. The water from the large basins of the public fountain flows into small channels over the low wall once used for washing.

The **basilica of San Domenico** (*map p. 410, 5*) stands conspicuous on the hill of Camporegio. This austere Gothic building was begun in 1226, but enlarged, damaged, and altered in successive centuries. The interior (*open 9–6*) has the typical Dominican plan, with a wide aisleless nave, transepts, and a shallow choir with side chapels. A chapel at the raised west end, where St Catherine assumed the Dominican habit, contains the only authentic portrait known of the saint by her contemporary and friend, Andrea Vanni. The Cappella di Santa Caterina on the south side was decorated in 1526 with frescoes by Sodoma, with rather over-crowded scenes. On the back wall to right and left of the altar, the Saint is shown in ecstasy and swooning. And on the left wall, the Saint intercedes for the life of a young man brought to repentance. (The painting on the right wall, showing Catherine liberating a possessed man, is by Francesco Vanni.) The prettily carved tabernacle on the altar encloses a reliquary containing St Catherine's head. The beautiful 16th-century pavement is attributed to Giovanni di Stefano.

Over the high altar is a very fine tabernacle and two angels, all by Benedetto da Maiano (c. 1475; difficult to appreciate because of the incongruous stained glass inserted into the east windows in 1982). In the second chapel to the left of the high altar is a splendid huge painting of the *Maestà* by Guido da Siena (second half of the 13th century, but dated 1221). On the side walls 18th-century frescoes by Giuseppe Nasini surround *St Barbara Enthroned between Angels and Sts Mary Magdalene and Catherine*, a delightful altarpiece by Matteo di Giovanni, opposite a *Madonna and Child with four Saints* by Benvenuto di Giovanni, dating from the same period.

Contrada dell'Istrice

The huge **Fortezza Medicea** (*beyond map p. 410, 1*), or Forte di Santa Barbara, was built for Cosimo I in 1560. On the bastions are avenues with delightful views. In the vaults is a wine cellar specialising in Tuscan wines. When Cosimo's son Ferdinando I visited the city in 1604, an inscription was set up on the Porta Camollia, declaring '*Cor magis tibi sena pandit*'—'To you Siena opens her heart (wider than this gate)'. The walls of Siena are well preserved and one of its most splendid gates is the Porta Pispini (*beyond map p. 411, 12*), dating from c. 1326–28. which is near the only surviving bastion of the seven designed by Peruzzi in the 16th century to strengthen the earlier defences.

LE CRETE SENESI

The secondary road from Siena to Asciano and from there via Monte Oliveto Maggiore to Buonconvento is one of the most beautiful in Tuscany. It runs along ridges with exceptionally wide views through the remarkable landscape with outcrops of bare clay hills known as *Le Crete*. Beneath their deeply eroded slopes are clusters of trees. There are relatively few scattered farmhouses amidst open fields, and the crests of the hills are often marked by pines and rows of cypresses. It is wonderful walking country: some of the walks are signposted directly off the road.

Asciano

Asciano (*map p. 267, D2*) is a delightful and interesting small town in countryside which is particularly beautiful in spring, covered with yellow broom and red poppies. Surrounded by simple houses with orchards and vineyards (new building has taken place discreetly, some way from the town), it retains the slightly old-world atmosphere of a rural centre in Sienese territory.

On the main street is Palazzo Corboli, which houses the **Museo d'Arte Sacra** (*open Thur–Sun 10–1 & 3–6; sometimes also other days in summer*). Housed in an extremely interesting medieval building with delightful wall paintings, it has a very fine collection including several masterpieces of Sienese art. The unusual *Nativity*, with St Augustine and St Galganus, by Sassetta's pupil Pietro di Giovanni d'Ambrogio, is a somewhat *naïf* but charming rendition of the story, and the landscape in the background is clearly inspired by the *Crete*. Among the sculptural works are two polychrome wooden figures of the *Virgin Annunciate* and *Angel Gabriel* by Francesco di Valdambrino. There is also a large altarpiece by Ambrogio Lorenzetti representing St Michael slaying the dragon (*removed for restoration at the time of writing*). One of the most fascinating works is the triptych representing the *Birth of the Virgin*, by the Master of the Osservanza, an artist close to Sassetta (*illustrated overleaf*). The composition is strikingly similar to Pietro Lorenzetti's version of the same theme in Siena's Museo dell'Opera, painted a hundred years earlier: in both works we look into a vaulted chamber occupied by St Anne, the baby Virgin and her nursemaids, while to the left a pageboy informs Joachim of the safe delivery of a daughter. The style is very different, however: this later work, with its rich

Birth of the Virgin by the Master of the Osservanza (mid-15th century), in the museum at Asciano.

gold leaf and splendid brocaded costumes, is more refined, and much closer to the courtly world of Gentile da Fabriano and the International Gothic.

At the other end of the Corso is the collegiate church of **Sant'Agata**, rising above a flight of steps. The geometrical simplicity of the exterior enhances the beauty of the travertine stone. The façade probably dates from the later 14th century, at the time of the transition between the Romanesque and Gothic styles. It is composed of three slender blind arches, forming a triumphal arch, above which is a large oculus with blind arcading below the roof, separated by a string-course that creates the effect of a pediment. The decoration is confined to the inner arch surrounding the doorway and to the capitals of the pilasters. The interior is unique to the district: a Latin-cross plan with a single nave, with two side apses leading off the transept and a larger central apse. Above the crossing is a hemispherical dome resting on a drum, decorated with small columns and corbels, which is supported by four large arches springing from the piers. At the summit is an elegant lantern.

The **Museo Cassioli** contains paintings, oil sketches and drawings by Amos Cassioli (1832–91), who was born in Asciano. A romantic painter and a Purist (*see p. 413*), he is best known for his frescoes representing scenes of the Risorgimento in the Palazzo Pubblico in Siena.

Monte Oliveto Maggiore

The Abbey of Monte Oliveto Maggiore (*map p. 267, D2; open daily 9.15–12 & 3.15–5.45*), in a beautiful isolated position in a dense cypress wood, is one of the most important monasteries in Tuscany, famous for its frescoes by Luca Signorelli and Sodoma.

The monastery

The monastery was founded in 1313 by Giovanni Tolomei of Siena, a wealthy law professor who withdrew here at the age of 40, founding the Olivetan Order (a branch of the Benedictines). The order was approved by the bishop of Arezzo, Guido Tarlati, in 1319, and confirmed by Clement VI in 1344. Giovanni Tolomei, who assumed the name of Bernardo, was later beatified. By the early 15th century there were already 30 Olivetan houses in Tuscany and Umbria. Pope Pius II (Aeneas Sylvius Piccolomini; *see p. 424*) sojourned here, as did the Holy Roman Emperor Charles V, with 2,000 followers. The Olivetan Abbot General usually resides here, and a number of monks work on the restoration of rare books.

The entrance is past a drawbridge and through a fortified building with an arched passage, above which is a niche with a glazed terracotta statue of the *Madonna and Child*, by Giovanni della Robbia (the seated *St Benedict* on the other side is also by him). A path leads to the monastery through an avenue of cypress trees. In the surrounding woods are small 18th-century chapels, dedicated to saints and founder-members of the Order. The great cloister (1426–74) is famous for its **frescoes of the life of St Benedict**. Nine frescoes on the west wall are by Luca Signorelli (1497–98); the others are by Sodoma (1505–08). The cycle is a masterpiece, combining a lively, picturesque narrative style with charming naturalistic detail in a variety of landscapes and architectural settings. The scenes follow the account of Benedict's life taken from the *Dialogues* of St Gregory the Great (*see p. 152*).

East wall (frescoes by Sodoma): 1. Benedict goes to study in Rome; 2. Benedict leaves Rome; 3. Benedict miraculously mends a broken tray (here Sodoma painted his own portrait in the richly-clad young man with two tame badgers at his feet); 4. The monk Romanus gives Benedict a hermit's habit (Subiaco is represented in the background); 5. Benedict at prayer in front of his cave, with the Devil about to break the bell of his bread basket; 6. A priest is inspired by Christ to take a meal to Benedict on Easter Day; 7. Benedict instructs a group of peasants; 8. Benedict overcomes temptation by throwing himself naked into brambles; 9. Benedict accepts the request of a group of monks to become their abbot; 10. Benedict, with the Sign of the Cross, shatters a glass of poisoned wine prepared by the monks who found his rule too strict; 11. Benedict founds the first twelve communities.

South wall (frescoes by Sodoma): 12. Benedict welcomes Maurus and Placidus into the Order; 13. Benedict chastises a monk tempted by the Devil; 14. Benedict makes water spring from Monte Oliveto; 15. Benedict retrieves a scythe which has fallen into a lake; 16. Maurus is sent to save Placidus from drowning; 17. The miracle of the flask changed into a snake; 18. Florentius attempts to poison Benedict; 19. To tempt the monks, Florentius sends a group of prostitutes to the monastery.

Il Sodoma (Giovanni Antonio Bazzi; 1477–1549)

In Renaissance Italy artists were accustomed to move to other cities for short periods in search of commissions; but Giovanni Antonio Bazzi, known as 'Il Sodoma', is unusual in that he left his native Vercelli, below the foothills of the Alps in Piedmont, at the age of 24, moved to Siena, and appears never to have returned home. His dandyish image is familiar to us through the portrait of him, standing just to the right of Raphael's own self-portrait, at the edge of the *School of Athens* in the Stanza della Segnatura in the Vatican (*see p. 94*). Sodoma worked with Raphael on his important Roman commissions, and absorbed through him much of the character and style of Umbrian painting. Two clear influences can be traced in his development: the typically wistful landscapes and graceful figures of Perugino (Raphael's early master), and the shadowy *sfumatura* of Leonardo da Vinci's painting, which he had seen and studied in Milan.

Many of Sodoma's works are to be found in Siena and its hinterland. The frescoes at Monte Oliveto Maggiore show his considerable skill and narrative power; but in their management of space and focus they belong to the imaginative world of the previous century, the Umbrian quattrocento. In one of the most ambitious scenes (no. 12 in the list above), Sodoma has incorporated amongst the figures portraits of Raphael, Signorelli, Leonardo and Lorenzo the Magnificent. The landscapes owe much to Perugino, and the faces, especially of the women, are very Leonardesque. Sodoma seems to grow as an artist, however, in the more expressive medium of oil. His devotional works, for example the early *Christ at the Column* (Siena, Pinacoteca) or the late *St Sebastian* (Florence, Palazzo Pitti), show a real mastery of the sculptural depth given to the body by Leonardo's *sfumatura* combined with low and diffused lighting. His most famous work—and certainly the most richly decorative—remains the *Marriage of Alexander*, painted for the bedroom of the villa of the Sienese banker Agostino Chigi, beside the Tiber in Rome (*see p. 81*). Here he has shaken off any earlier timidity and his style looks forward to the grand decorative schemes of 16th- and 17th-century Rome.

Like his hero Leonardo, Sodoma was self-ironic, vain, and had a natural propensity to jokes. If Giorgio Vasari's testimony is to be believed, he appears not only to have merited his unflattering nickname, but also perversely to have relished using it to sign his paintings. Yet he was married and had a family. It appears he enjoyed teasing posterity, as much as his contemporaries, with the riddle of his sobriquet.

N.McG.

West wall (no. 20. by Il Riccio; nos. 21–28 by Signorelli; no. 30 by Sodoma): 20. Benedict sends Maurus to France and Placidus to Sicily; 21. Florentius' death; 22. Benedict converts the people of Monte Cassino; 23. Benedict defeats the Devil; 24. Benedict rescues a monk from beneath a collapsed wall; 25. Benedict tells two monks when and where they had dined outside the monastery; 26. Benedict reproaches Valerian's brother for breaking the fast; 27. Benedict unmasks Riggo disguised as Totila the Ostrogoth; 28. Benedict recognises and welcomes Totila; 30. Benedict foretells the destruction of Monte Cassino by the Lombards. **North wall** (frescoes by Sodoma): 31. Benedict miraculously obtains flour for his monks; 32. Benedict appears to two monks in their sleep and instructs them how to build a church; 33. Episode of two excommunicated nuns; 34. Miracle of the monk's burial; 35. Benedict forgives the monk who had escaped from the monastery; 36. Benedict releases a bound peasant by merely looking at him.

The church

In the passage leading to the church are two small frescoes of *Christ Carrying the Cross* and *Christ at the Column*, and *St Benedict giving the Rule to the founders of Monte Oliveto*, all by Sodoma. The church was renovated in 1772, but retains its magnificent choir stalls of inlaid wood by Fra' Giovanni da Verona (1505).

Buonconvento

Picturesque, brick-built Buonconvento (*map p. 267, D2*) retains its walls, decorated at the top with a little arcaded frieze. The charming main street is the old Via Cassia, which connected Rome to Siena. Next to the miniature Palazzo Pretorio, with a crenellated tower, is an Art Nouveau palace with a fine façade decorated with ceramics (1909). It houses the **Museo d'Arte Sacra della Val d'Arbia** (*open daily except Mon 10–12 & 4–7*), with works from local churches, including some attributed to Duccio; a 14th-century Crucifix assigned from this work to the Master of the Buonconvento Cross; and a luminous *Annunciation* by Benvenuto di Giovanni, with a charming landscape in the background. An old wine cellar in the walls houses an interesting **agricultural museum** (*open 10–1.30; Sat and Sun also 2–6; April–Sept 10–1 & 2–6; closed Mon*) which illustrates the *mezzadria* or crop-sharing system in the Sienese countryside. It provides a vivid documentation of the peasant life which survived here up until the 1960s.

Murlo

The tiny village of Murlo (*map p. 266, C2*) dominates the surrounding countryside, and although considerably restored, it preserves its medieval character: the 12th-century walls form a complete circle. The **Museo Civico Archeologico** (*open 9.30–12.30 & 3–5 or 7; closed Mon*) has an excellent small collection of finds from excavations at Poggio Civitate nearby. A palatial villa from the late 7th century BC was discovered here, as well as another Archaic building dating from c. 580 BC. These finds provide the best evidence we have of how the Etruscans used terracotta in a domestic setting. The site contains terracottas *in situ* in a workshop which was burned down at the end of the 7th century, and others from the later palace. The terracottas from the latter (now in the museum at Murlo) include a fine set of frieze plaques recording the ceremonial events of the residents' life, including carriage processions and a banquet. Equally remarkable are the statues from the roof, which included 23 male and female figures, the men in cowboy-style hats and the women in long skirts and laced-up boots. They were probably ancestors of the owners, whose presence ensured continuing protection.

PRACTICAL INFORMATION

GETTING AROUND

• **By car:** Central **Siena** is closed to cars. Parking areas are indicated at the entrances to town. Sometimes free spaces can be found near the Fortezza and La Lizza (*beyond map p. 410, 1*), except on market day (Weds) and on Sun, when football matches are held. Pay car parks are in Via Fontanella near Porta Tufi; near Porta San Marco; and in Viale dello Stadio (*map p. 410, 1*). From the Fontebranda car park (*map p. 410, 5*) there is a bus to the centre. Other free car parks with buses (every 15mins) are at Due Ponti, beyond Porta Pispini (*beyond map p. 411, 8*) and Coroncina, beyond Porta Romana (*beyond map p. 411, 16*).
• **By train:** Siena station is 1.5km north of the centre. Buses connect to Piazza Gramsci (*beyond map p. 410, 1*) in c. 7mins. The branch line from Siena to Chiusi stops at **Asciano**; another between Siena and Grosseto serves **Buonconvento**; and another line serves Florence.
• **By bus:** Frequent fast buses run by SITA (www.sitabus.it) link Florence and **Siena** in 1hr 15mins (NB: SITA also operates slow buses on the same route). Buses operated by TRA-IN run from Piazza San Domenico in Siena (*map p. 410, 1*) to

Asciano and **Buonconvento** (with a few services to **Monte Oliveto Maggiore**).

INFORMATION OFFICES

Asciano (open summer only) Corso Matteotti 18, T: 0577 719510.
Siena Via di Città (*map p. 410, 6*), and in the Campo (no. 56), T: 0577 280551.

HOTELS

Asciano (*map p. 267, D2*)
€ **Il Bersagliere**. Clean, simply-furnished hotel, in the hills of *Le Crete*, opened in 1989. Swimming pool and garden. *Via Roma 14, T: 0577 718629, www.albergoilbersagliere.it. 16 rooms.*
€ **Locanda del Ponte del Garbo**. Beautiful hotel in a 14th-century Palazzo. Rooms are simply and elegantly furnished in traditional Tuscan style. *Corso Matteotti 128, T: 0577 718011, www.locandadelgarbo.it. 5 rooms.*
Mt Oliveto Maggiore (*map p. 267, D2*)
€ **Agriturismo di Monte Oliveto Maggiore**. Typical Tuscan farmhouse owned by the abbey. There are five rooms and large living room with a cosy open fireplace and a communal kitchen. *Podere Le Piazze, Chiusure, T: 0577 707611,*

www.monteolivetomaggiore.it. 5 rooms.
To find out about accommodation at
the monastery itself, T: 0577 707017.
Pievescola (map p. 266, C2)
€€€€ **Relais La Suvera**. Magnificent
old papal villa and private patrician residence, converted into a hotel some 20
years ago. All rooms are exquisitely furnished with antiques. Pool, tennis,
restaurant. No children under 14.
Closed Nov–April. Località Pievescola, T:
0577 960300, www.lasuvera.it. 32 rooms.
San Giovanni d'Asso (map p. 267, D2)
€€ **La Locanda del Castello**. Fine old
building inside the castle, with rooms
decorated with family furniture. A place
of simple elegance. Restaurant. Piazza
Vittorio Emanuele 4, T: 0577 802939,
www.lalocandadelcastello.com. 7 rooms.
Siena (map p. 266, C2)
€€€€ **Grand Hotel Continental**. ■
Magnificent 17th-century palazzo converted into a luxury hotel. Rooms
exquisitely furnished, many with frescoed ceilings. Ample, excellent breakfasts in the glass-roofed central atrium.
NB: At night Banchi di Sopra is noisy;
ask for a room that doesn't overlook it.
Via Banchi di Sopra 85, T: 0577 56011,
www.hotelroyaldemeure.com. 51 rooms.
€€€–€ **Il Chiostro del Carmine**.
Former Carmelite convent of the church
of San Niccolò, now converted into a
guest house: a baroque experience in
both senses of the word. Rooms vary a
great deal (prices reflect this): some are
extremely pleasant, others have a more
boarding-house feel. No restaurant. Via
della Diana 4, T: 0577 223885,
www.chiostrodelcarmine.com. 18 rooms.
€€€ **Palazzo Ravizza**. ■ Beautiful,
uncluttered elegance in a former
Renaissance palace in the historic cen-

tre. The rooms are superbly appointed
(no luxury, just good taste), and the
garden commands vistas of the distant
hills. Good restaurant. Parking. Pian de'
Mantellini 34, T: 0577 280462,
www.palazzoravizza.it. 30 rooms.
€€ **Antica Torre**. In a 16th-century
tower tucked within the city walls, with
the original travertine staircase, wooden
beams and brick vaults. Rooms are small
and simply decorated. Good central
position. Via di Fiera Vecchia 7, T: 0577
222255, www.anticatorresiena.it. 8 rooms.
€€ **Arcobaleno**. Refurbished 19th-cen-
tury villa. Rooms are comfortably furnished in contemporary style. Restaurant.
Via Fiorentina 32/40, T: 0577 271092,
www.hotelarcobaleno.com. 19 rooms.
€€ **Duomo**. In one of Siena's oldest
streets, a completely refurbished hotel,
inside the shell of an 18th-century palace.
Rooms are plainly decorated; some have
views of the duomo and the surrounding
hills. Parking. Via Stalloreggi 38, T: 0577
289088, www.hotelduomo.it. 20 rooms.
€ **Alle Due Porte**. ■ Charming small
B&B with just three pretty rooms and a
tiny shared kitchen for making drinks
and preparing picnics. In an ancient
house in the old part of town. Via
Stalloreggi 51, T: 0577 287670, soldati-
ni@interfree.it. 3 rooms.

RESTAURANTS

Asciano (map p. 267, D2)
€€ **La Mencia**. Locals rate this as the
best restaurant in town, in a former olive
mill, serving local specialities. Quieter for
lunch than for dinner. Next to the Torre
Civico. Corso Matteotti 85, T: 0577 718227.
€€–€ **Locanda del Ponte del Garbo**.
Attractive restaurant-cum-pizzeria in

the centre of town offering a wide range of pasta, wild game and fish dishes in an atmospheric vaulted dining space. *Corso Matteotti 128, T: 0577 718011.*

€€–€ **Piccolo San Valentino**. Restaurant priding itself on its gourmet dishes, including tagliolini with Crete Senesi white truffles and fresh wild boar *alla cacciatore*. Closed Wed. *Strada Provinciale 451 di Monte Oliveto Maggiore, T: 0577 707153.*

Buonconvento *(map p. 267, D2)*

€ **Da Mario**. Experiences can vary here, though the prices are good value. Ted Kennedy ate here in 2006, and the place has slightly fallen victim to its reputation. Booking advised in high season. *Via Soccini 60, T: 0577 806157.*

San Giovanni d'Asso *(map p. 267, D2)*

€€ **La Locanda del Castello**. Pleasant place at the top of the hill, inside the castle. Two terraces overlook a pretty piazza and part of the town. Service is friendly and the cooking inventive, making use of the local white truffles. Superb value for money. *Closed Wed. Piazza Vittorio Emanuele 4, T: 0577 802939.*

Siena *(map p. 266, C2)*

€€€ **Tre Cristi**. First-class fish restaurant. The tuna tartare is magnificent. Not a place to come for a low-key lunch. They make a fuss of their customers here; you need to be in the mood. *Vicolo di Provenzano 1/7, T: 0577 280608.*

€€ **Le Logge**. ■ Excellent *osteria* serving fine local cuisine in delightful, old-fashioned surroundings. Elegantly relaxed atmosphere, and good service. Reservations recommended, especially on Saturday evening. Closed Sun. *Via del Porrione 33, T: 0577 48013.*

€ **Le Campane**. Pleasant local spot, serving good Tuscan standards. *Via delle Campane 6, T: 0577 284035.*

€ **L'Osteria**. Friendly place serving good, simple food. An excellent stop-off for lunch. *Via dei Rossi 79, T: 0577 287592.*

€ **La Torre**. Family-run trattoria serving good home cooking. Two steps from the Campo. *Via Salicotto 7, T: 0577 287548.*

LOCAL SPECIALITIES

Panforte, the rich, spiced cake of **Siena**, was first baked in the 12th century as a source of energy for residents following a seige. Depending on who you speak to, the cake also has aphrodisiac qualities as well as being a cure for marital strife.

Ricciarelli are diamond-shaped biscuits made from crushed almonds.

San Giovanni d'Asso holds a White Truffle Exhibit every Nov in the castle.

FESTIVALS & EVENTS

Siena, *Il Palio*, the famous horse race, consisting of three laps of the Campo. It is the horse that wins, not the jockey, so even if a horse comes in riderless, victory can be claimed. Victory celebrations last all night (the horse eats at the head of the table at the banquet). There has been criticism that the Palio is too dangerous for the horses: they can sometimes break a leg when they slip, 2 July and 16 Aug.

Asciano *Sagra della Ranocchia*, Just outside the town, in Castelnuovo Scalo, the annual frog festival is held: dishes with frog as the main ingredient are prepared and served, 1st Sun in June.

Buonconvento *Sagra della Val d'Arbia*, Harvest festival with a craft fair, street entertainment, and plenty of delicious food, Sept.

PIENZA, THE VAL D'ORCIA & MONTEPULCIANO

The landscape of the Val d'Orcia (*map p. 267, D3*) is perhaps one of the most beautiful in Tuscany. The Orcia river valley, with its characteristic eroded downs or clay hills, is in a majestic setting with Monte Cetona on one side, and Monte Amiata on the other. In the wooded foothills are interesting little towns and picturesque villages, often with medieval castles towering above. There are also hot springs, known since Roman times; and the old Roman road, the Via Cassia, in the stretch south of San Quirico, is still one of the prettiest roads in Italy (even though it has been widened and, sadly, raised on stilts in a few places). Since 2004 the area has been a UNESCO world heritage site.

PIENZA

Pienza (*map p. 267, D3*) is famous as an ideal Renaissance town, built in just five years from 1459–64. It was virtually created by Aeneas Sylvius Piccolomini, who, on becoming Pope Pius II in 1458, transformed the original fortified village of Corsignano (a Piccolomini fief and the place of his birth) and renamed it Pienza. The architect Bernardo Rossellino was commissioned to design the monumental piazza with its splendid cathedral and palaces. Retaining its beautiful paving and an elegant well, it is a remarkable example of Renaissance town planning, showing the influence of Leon Battista Alberti, Rossellino's master.

The duomo

The duomo has a superb façade in Istrian stone. The motif of the triumphal arch and the choice of details are evidently inspired by Classical Roman architecture. The proportions, the linear clarity and sober decoration, conform to the aspirations of dignity, harmony and beauty of the Humanist architect. At the centre of the great pediment are the papal arms of Pius II, on an awe-inspiring scale.

The interior (*open 7–12 & 2–7.30*) is unforgettable for the height of the huge clustered columns with tall dosserets which support the lofty vault. The elegant architecture is clearly influenced by northern European (and in particular French Gothic) models. The **five lovely altarpieces** were all painted for the church in 1461–63 by important Sienese masters: the *Madonna and Child with Sts Bernardino, Anthony Abbot, Francis and Sabina* (and a *Pietà* in the lunette) by Giovanni di Paolo; the *Madonna and Child with Sts Catherine of Alexandria, Matthew, Bartholomew and Lucy* (and the *Flagellation* in the lunette) by Matteo di Giovanni; the *Madonna and Child with Sts Jerome, Martin, Nicholas and Augustine*, also by Matteo di Giovanni; a triptych of the *Assumption with Sts Agatha, Calixtus, Pius I and Catherine of Siena* (with an *Ecce Homo* in the frame) by Vecchietta; and the *Madonna and Child with Sts Mary Magdalene, Philip, James, and Anne* (and an *Ecce Homo* in the gable and the *Annunciation* in the predella) by Sano di Pietro.

Palazzo Piccolomini

Palazzo Piccolomini was begun by Pius II and finished by his nephew Pius III (*the court-yard can be seen from the entrance; the main rooms are only shown on guided tours every half hour, also in English, 10–12.30 & 2–4; summer 10–12.30 & 2–6; closed Mon*). It is considered Rossellino's masterpiece, and shows the influence of Alberti's Palazzo Rucellai in Florence. The façade is built of sandstone with two elegant rows of arched mullioned windows alternating with pilasters, separated by horizontal cornices and simple doorways. The base becomes a projecting bench on three sides of the palace. The elegant courtyard is surrounded by a portico supported on a splendid Corinthian order, above which are two storeys of square mullioned windows with a glazed loggia on two sides. The hanging garden of box hedges and small trees (*not at present open, but visible from the first floor*) has remained unchanged. Seen against the backdrop of the Orcia valley, it is a supreme example of the Renaissance idea of the garden as the intermediary between architecture and nature.

The first-floor rooms were inhabited by the Piccolomini family up until 1962 (the atmosphere today is a little forlorn, with the smell of moth-balls lingering in the air). The Sala degli Antenati is hung with family portraits. In the music room is a rare *scagliola* table representing a map of the Sienese state, and hangings of Córdoba leather. The large Sala d'Armi has a display of arms and battle-paintings by Borgognone. From the Loggia is a view of the garden and beyond, in the distance, Radicofani with Monte Cetona on the left and Monte Amiata on the right.

Museo Diocesano

Palazzo Vescovile, on Corso Rossellino (*open Sat, Sun 10–1 & 3–6; April–Oct daily except Tues 10–1 & 3–7*), was modified and enlarged by Rodrigo Borgia, later Pope Alexander VI, whose arms it displays on the corner. On the top floor is the Museo Diocesano, which has some very fine works of art from local churches. Its treasures include two Crucifixes: one of the late 12th century, showing the influence of the Umbrian school, and another by Segna di Bonaventura. The **Madonna and Child** by **Pietro Lorenzetti** is one of his masterpieces (1310–20). A work of immense charm, its most memorable feature is the head of the Christ Child, thrown back as if on a sudden impulse. The *Madonna and Child* by the much less well-known Bartolomeo Bulgarini is also extremely fine. There is a lovely little portable triptych by the Master of the Osservanza, and a large portable altar with numerous scenes from the life of Christ, a rare work because of its dimensions and design, dating from the late 14th century. The two polychrome wood statues are by Domenico di Niccolò dei Cori, and the *Madonna della Misericordia* is by Bartolo di Fredi. Three fine Flemish tapestries from Brussels and Arras include a beautiful *Crucifixion* scene (c. 1460). A magnificent cope dates from the first half of the 14th century, with scenes from the life of the Virgin, saints and apostles; embroidered in silk and silver-gilt thread, it is one of the few surviving examples of medieval English ecclesiastical embroidery (known as *opus anglicanum*). There is a precious Byzantine Cross in golden filigree and rock crystal, and **Pius II's crozier** of gilded silver inlaid with enamels, a very fine example of Florentine goldsmiths' work (1460), with a charming

Annunciation scene above a small temple containing six angels holding shields with the papal arms. A 19th-century mitre incorporates ten enamelled plaquettes from Pius' original mitre. The large altarpiece by Vecchietta has a charming predella and an *Annunciation* which demonstrates the artist's interest in perspective.

Pieve di Corsignano

The rest of the pleasing, compact little town has some medieval houses from the days when it was still Corsignano. There is a delightful raised walkway along the walls on the south side of the village which overlooks the valley, and passes beneath the garden of Palazzo Piccolomini.

Just below the walls, a country lane leads to the beautiful Romanesque **Pieve di Corsignano**, in a clump of trees including a huge old olive, and beside a public fountain. The church is very ancient (10th–11th century) and has an unusual circular tower with eight large arched windows. The doorway is decorated with reliefs of stylised flowers and palmettes and a strange double-tailed siren; the window has a female caryatid at the centre. Beside a picturesque but abandoned old house can be seen the south doorway, where the delightful old carvings depict the Three Kings on huge chargers, the Nativity, and animals on the jambs. The lovely interior (*sadly usually locked*) still preserves the simple font in which Pius II was baptised.

THE VAL D'ORCIA

The Orcia valley (*map p. 267, D3*) has an interesting landscape of eroded clay slopes and small sharp ridges known as *calanchi*. Its wild aspect has been partly altered by the gravel works along the river bed, and the arable land created in the 1980s by levelling the hillocks. The fortified farm of Spedaletto belonged to the hospital of Santa Maria della Scala in Siena, and was once a hospice for pilgrims on their way to Rome.

San Quirico d'Orcia

The little medieval village of San Quirico d'Orcia takes its name from an ancient church, dedicated to the early martyr St Quiricus, which stood on the Via Francigena (*see box overleaf*). In the 13th century the town walls were enlarged and several hospices were built to accommodate pilgrims on their way to Rome. Today it is an extremely peaceful place, open in feel, partly perhaps because it is on flat ground, unlike many of the neighbouring towns and villages.

The Romanesque **Collegiata** (*open all day*) was built in the 12th century on the site of the ancient church. The exterior, built of travertine, has three elaborately decorated doorways, parts of which are in contrasting sandstone. The main entrance, beneath a large, late 12th-century rose window, is the finest and most elaborate example of a Lombard portal in Sienese territory. It incorporates a frieze of strange animal heads and an arch above four slender clustered columns, tied together with a loop at their centre. These in turn have Lombard lions at their base. A sequence of inner arches, surrounding the lunette with a little seated figure, said to be Pope St Damasus, are supported on five thin columns with unusual capitals. The sandstone architrave has two splendid dragons. The doorway on the south side, with a porch supported on telamones standing on lions, is slightly later in date and is attributed to the school of Giovanni Pisano. It has a fine architrave and is flanked by two elegant Gothic windows; the right window has a kneeling telamon and carved fantastic animals. The smaller doorway, at the end of the south transept, is dated 1298 (both were damaged by shell-fire in the last war). In the interior there is a fine polyptych by Sano di Pietro: the figure of St Quiricus and the red-and-white arms of the town prove that it was painted for this church. The marble pavement tombstone of Henry of Nassau, by Urbano da Cortona, is dated 1451. Count Henry died, aged 37, while on the pilgrim route.

THE VIA FRANCIGENA

The Via Francigena was the medieval pilgrims' way from France and northern Europe to Rome. Sigeric travelled along it from Canterbury to receive the pallium, symbol of his investiture as Archbishop of Canterbury, from the hands of Pope John XV. He described his return journey in 990, with its 80 stopping places. The manuscript of his chronicle is still preserved in the British Museum in London.

In the 8th century the road was used by the Lombards as a safe route to the south from their capital Pavia, avoiding Byzantine territory. The route across France started at Calais and traversed Picardy, Champagne and the Ardennes, then from Switzerland the Alps were crossed at the Great St Bernard Pass. From Aosta it passed through northern Italy (Ivrea, Vercelli, Pavia, Piacenza, Fidenza and Parma) and from the Passo della Cisa on the Emilian border it entered Tuscany. It continued south to Lucca, crossed the Arno at Fucecchio, and passed through San Gimignano, Siena, San Quirico d'Orcia, leaving Tuscany at Radicofani to cross Lazio (Bolsena, Montefiascone and Viterbo) before reaching Rome.

The journey from England to Rome took about ten weeks, and most pilgrims probably made the entire trip on foot, although prelates such as Sigeric may have travelled on horseback. The road was only sporadically paved, thus unsuitable for wheeled vehicles. Numerous *ospedali* grew up along the way, offering help and accommodation to travellers. The hospice of La Magione (*map p. 267, F2*) is one of the best preserved to have survived. Apart from pilgrims, the road was used by merchants and traders, and goods as well as works of art were transported along it. Castles and villages sprang up near the route, and towns such as Lucca and Siena prospered as a result of their proximity to it. Some of the Tuscan churches along the road show the influence of French Romanesque architecture, notably the abbey of Sant'Antimo.

The importance of the Via Francigena diminished after the 13th century, when other routes were opened over the Alps.

The huge **Palazzo Chigi** (1679) was built for Cardinal Flavio Chigi by Carlo Fontana. It now houses the town council chamber, library and offices, but the *piano nobile*—decorated with frescoes by late 17th-century Roman artists—may usually be visited in the mornings (*although closed at the time of writing; T: 0577 899724*).

On the main street are some well-preserved medieval houses and the Renaissance Palazzo Pretorio. The Chiesa di Santa Maria di Vitaleta (also known as San Francesco) contains a very beautiful white glazed enamel *Virgin Annunciate* by Andrea della Robbia (1510) on the high altar, and polychrome wood figures of the *Virgin* and *Angel Gabriel* by Francesco di Valdambrino. The *Preaching of the Baptist* is signed and dated 1597 by Empoli, who also painted the *Immaculate Conception* opposite.

Surrounded by the old ramparts, in an area once used as a resting place for pilgrims, are the beautiful 16th-century **Horti Leonini** gardens (*open all day*), named after their creator, Diomede Leoni. The layout follows the Renaissance pattern of box hedges in a geometric design, beside a *boschetto* or ilex wood on a slope. Giuseppe Mazzuoli's marble statue of Cosimo III de' Medici was set up in the centre in 1688. A gate leads into a little walled rose-garden behind the charming 11th-century church of Santa Maria Assunta, built of beautiful stone blocks. The apse is decorated on the outside with blind arches and zoömorphic heads.

Castiglione d'Orcia and Rocca d'Orcia

Castiglione d'Orcia (*map p. 267, D3*) is a picturesque village, built round a ruined castle. Just above the main square is an older piazza, paved in ancient brick and pebbles, named after the great 15th-century artist Vecchietta, who is traditionally believed to have been born here. Just above it is the Sala d'Arte San Giovanni (*open April–Oct Tues–Sun 10–1 & 3.30–6.30; in winter only at weekends*) with a little collection of early paintings. The *pieve* of Santi Stefano e Degna (the two saints are depicted in the stained-glass window at the east end) contains a charming little domed chapel, restored at the end of the 19th century, which houses a *Madonna and Child* by Pietro Lorenzetti (the *Madonna delle Grazie*). The painting, just restored, of the *Madonna of the Rosary* by Vincenzo Rustici (1557–1632) is a fine work and very unusual in that it incorporates a delightful series of little paintings in the lower part. It comes from the church of San Simeone in **Rocca d'Orcia**, which lies only a few hundred metres away, on another steep hill, dominated by the spectacular Rocca di Tentennano (*open in summer*), from which there is a good view. A lane leads round the hill to the little hamlet, a number of its houses now part of a pleasant hotel beside the church of San Simeone, which preserves a fresco of the *Madonna della Misericordia* by a follower of Bartolo di Fredi, and a charming popular statue of *St Anthony Abbot*, complete with his pig and staff and bell. Further downhill is the piazza, remarkable for its huge raised stone cistern around a large octagonal well. The views towards Bagno Vignoni and beyond are spectacular.

Bagno Vignoni

Of the several spas in this district, the best known is Bagno Vignoni (*map p. 267, D3*), a tiny medieval hamlet on a small plateau. The hot water spring, known since Roman times, bubbles up into a large *piscina*, constructed by the Medici, in the charming and perfectly preserved central piazza. It forms one of the most unusual and evocative sights in Tuscany, especially in winter when the condensation creates a mist. The water tumbles down the hillside into the river far below, and a path descends past a series of four old watermills. On another part of the hill (discreetly hidden from view), a huge spa hotel was opened in 2004. A white road climbs to Vignoni Alto, a tiny hamlet with one or two simple little houses, a truncated tower, and a little church with a delightful façade in carefully cut stone. Beyond a well-preserved arch, there is a grassy terrace with a stone bench looking over the lovely countryside. Delightful walks can be taken from here.

Radicofani

In a spectacular position on a basaltic hill (783m) at the southern end of the Orcia valley is Radicofani (*map p. 267, E3*), a remote, little-visited village approached by a pretty road with wonderful views in all directions. Dominating the hill is the huge **Fortezza**. Taken by the Sienese in 1469, it was forced to surrender to Cosimo de' Medici in 1559. New fortifications of impressive proportions were constructed by the Medici. The restored castle (*open at weekends*) has a spectacular view over the Orcia valley.

The church of **San Pietro** has a fine Gothic interior with two good della Robbia altars and a white glazed statue of the *Madonna*. The high altarpiece of the *Crucifixion* is by Benedetto and Santi Buglioni, the only artists outside the della Robbia family who came close to matching their skill. The polychrome wood statue of the *Madonna and Child* is by Francesco di Valdambrino. The simple little church of **Sant'Agata** has an enamelled terracotta high altarpiece of the *Madonna and Child with Saints*, with a charming *Annunciation* scene in the predella, a superb work by Andrea della Robbia.

A road descends south to the Via Cassia where there is a fountain erected by Ferdinando I dei Medici in 1603 with figures of *Justice* and *Abundance* flanking the Medici arms. **Palazzo La Posta**, a hunting lodge with arched porticoes on two levels, was built for the Grand Duke perhaps by Bernardo Buontalenti (1584). It later became an inn mentioned by Dickens (*see below*). Montaigne and Chateaubriand also stayed here. It is a remarkable survival (with the iron rings where the horses were tethered still decorating the arches).

The inn at Radicofani

We came to Radicofani, where there is a ghostly goblin inn; once a hunting-seat belonging to the Dukes of Tuscany. It is full of such rambling corridors, and gaunt rooms, that all the murdering and phantom tales that ever were written, might have originated in that one house ... there is a windy, creaking, wormy, rustling, door-opening, foot-on-staircase-falling character about this Radicofani Hotel such as I never saw anywhere else. The town, such as it is, hangs on a hill-side above...

Charles Dickens, Pictures from Italy, 1846

MONTALCINO & SANT'ANTIMO

Montalcino (*map p. 267, D3*) is a hill town in a beautiful position above vines and olive groves, with a wide panorama of the surrounding countryside. It is famed for its red wine, the remarkable Brunello (*see box below*). In the Middle Ages, Montalcino became a flourishing and independent town, but was repeatedly attacked by Siena and defended by Florence, finally succumbing to Sienese rule after the Battle of Montaperti in 1260. There followed a period of peace and prosperity, and in 1462 Montalcino received the title of city from Pius II. After successfully resisting two sieges in 1526 and 1553, the town was forced to capitulate to Florence, despite a heroic defence lasting four years. After Siena was defeated by the Medici in 1555, the displaced Sienese kept their republic alive here, for a few brief years until 1559. In 1559 it became part of the Grand Duchy of Tuscany.

The town has numerous medieval houses with gardens and orchards, and steep streets offering picturesque views. The 14th-century Sienese fortress (*open daily, except Mon 9–1 & 2–8; in winter 2–6*) was provided with its notable ramparts by Cosimo I de' Medici in 1571. Inside is a small garden with ilex trees, and a wine shop. There are magnificent views from the ramparts.

THE WINES OF MONTALCINO

Brunello di Montalcino, a luscious, full-bodied wine made exclusively from the Sangiovese grape (known locally as *Brunello*), was first developed in the second half of the 19th century. The thin, rocky soil of the hills south of Siena, and the warm, dry breezes blowing in from the sea, create an ideal climate for Sangiovese. Modern viticultural practice tends to keep yields low: when the vines put their all into fewer grapes, the results are memorably intense. Fruit is only harvested when fully ripe, and then fermented on the skins, to extract as much colour, flavour and aroma as possible. Lengthy cask- and bottle-ageing used to follow, which made the wine scarce and expensive. Regulations have been adjusted now to the demands of the market, with the ageing process reduced: even so, a Brunello won't reach the shelves before it is four years old. Alongside the Brunello, lighter, fruitier, earlier drinking wines are being produced too. Rosso di Montalcino is one such.

Adjoining the church of Sant'Agostino (Via Ricasoli; *closed for restoration at the time of writing*) is the **Museo Civico e Diocesano** (*open daily except Mon, Jan–March 10–1 & 2–4; April–Dec 10–6*) with an important collection of 13th–16th-century Sienese painting including a magnificent polyptych, signed and dated 1388, by Bartolo di Fredi, with a central panel of the *Coronation of the Virgin*, considered to be the artist's masterpiece. There is also a triptych by a close follower of Duccio; Madonnas by Luca di Tommè, Giovanni di Paolo, Vecchietta, Sano di Pietro and Guidoccio Cozzarelli;

and a unique group of polychrome, wooden life-size figures. On the upper floor are displayed two of the earliest works in the museum (12th century), from the Abbey of Sant'Antimo: a *Madonna and Child* and a Crucifix, painted in tempera on wood, showing Christ with open eyes.

A steep street leads down from Sant'Agostino to the triangular Piazza del Popolo, above which looms the incredibly tall, narrow tower of Palazzo dei Priori (1292), decorated with numerous coats of arms. Nearby there is a grandiose loggia (finished in the 15th century) and an attractive, old-fashioned café. The cathedral of San Salvatore is at the highest point of the town. It was rebuilt in 1818–32 with a grand brick portico and a spacious Neoclassical interior with Ionic columns. Downhill are pretty streets leading to an old mill and public fountain and wash-house.

Sant'Antimo

A beautiful country road leads south from Montalcino to the abbey church of Sant'Antimo (*map p. 267, D3; open all day, but visitors are asked to come 10.30–12.30 & 3–6; Sun 9.15–10.45 & 3–6. The times of the offices with Gregorian chant are indicated in the church; T: 0577 835659*). This is one of the finest Romanesque religious buildings in all Italy, and particularly memorable for the luminous colour of its stone and its beautiful valley setting, surrounded by ancient olive trees and hills covered with ilex woods and vineyards. The original abbey is said to have been founded by Charlemagne in 781. As a Benedictine foundation, it continued to enjoy the protection of the Holy Roman Emperor, as well as receiving papal privileges. After a period of decline in the 13th century, the abbey was suppressed by Pius II in 1462 and placed under the jurisdiction of the bishop of Montalcino. Ten monks now live here.

The present church probably dates from the early 12th century (the date 1118 is inscribed on a column of the ambulatory), and its style combines both French and Lombard elements. The exterior is of monumental simplicity, its forms outlined by sequences of pilasters, corbels and pierced openings. It is built of light travertine quarried locally, as well as some beautifully veined blocks of onyx and alabaster. The prow-like choir has three beautiful apses. A splendid tall cypress stands proudly beside the bell-tower which is divided into four storeys by a cornice and blind arches.

In the interior, the luminous honey-coloured stone and the numerous windows combine to create a wonderful, tranquil atmosphere. There is great harmony in the play of light, and some of the stones often take on a translucent glow. The nave is supported on columns and four cruciform piers, with an upper gallery and a clerestory above. The aisles become narrower towards the east end, leading into an elegant ambulatory, with three radiating chapels, a feature which may have been borrowed from French prototypes. The sculptural decoration is of exceptionally high quality: the capitals of the nave present a variety of geometrical and leaf motifs. The finest is that of the second column on the right, representing Daniel in the lions' den, which is now attributed to the Master of Cabestany, an itinerant 12th-century Pyrenean sculptor of French or Spanish origin (his works are found in northern Catalonia, in Languedoc-Roussillon, and in Tuscany). Columns surround the high altar, above which hangs a 13th-century carved and paint-

View of the abbey church of Sant'Antimo.

ed Crucifix. The sacristy occupies the primitive little rectangular church with an apse, the so-called Carolingian chapel, which has a 15th-century cycle of grisaille frescoes of the life of St Benedict, in a rather *naïf* style, by Giovanni di Asciano. The polychrome wood statue of the *Madonna del Carmine* in the nave is an Umbrian work (c. 1260). Practically nothing remains of the monastic buildings or cloister, except for the well.

MONTE AMIATA

Monte Amiata (*map p. 267, D3*), the highest mountain in Tuscany (1738m), was originally a volcano. This explains its interesting geological formation, its rocky spurs and ravines, mineral deposits and sulphurous springs. The rich mercury (cinnabar) deposits were known to the Etruscans, and they were systematically mined after 1860.

The mountain is encircled by a road which runs through woods of chestnuts, beeches, oaks and fir trees. On its southern slopes, approached from Arcidosso, is a wildlife reserve which extends over the northeast slopes of Monte Labbro. The view from the summit (1193m) embraces the Orcia, Fiora and Paglia valleys, and, on a fine day, it is possible to see the Tyrrhenian coast and the islands of Elba and Corsica. The ruins here are of the tower and church built by Davide Lazzaretti, the 'Messiah of Monte Amiata', who founded a Christian community on Monte Labbro in 1868. Condemned by the Church and regarded with suspicion by the local authorities, he was shot by *carabinieri* in 1878 as he led a throng of followers down the mountain to Arcidosso.

Castel del Piano and Santa Fiora

The small towns on the slopes of Monte Amiata are unexpectedly busy and not particularly attractive: **Castel del Piano**, in a beautiful position overlooking the Orcia and Ombrone valleys on the west side of the mountain, is perhaps the most pleasant. It was the birthplace of the Nasini family, which produced three generations of painters, the most important being Francesco (1621–95) and his son Giuseppe Nicola (1657–1736); their works can be seen in two of the churches here. The Corso, which is named after them, divides the medieval town—typical of the grey stone-built medieval districts of some of the other settlements on the mountain—from the spacious modern suburb on the south side.

The most interesting place on Monte Amiata—though it has a slightly abandoned feel—is the quiet little town of **Santa Fiora**. The town hall now occupies the huge Palazzo Sforza Cesarini, a late Renaissance palace bearing the family arms of a lion rampant and a quince tree. There is a museum which illustrates the mining of mercury (*usually open in summer 10–1 & 5–7*). Via Carolina leads to the Pieve delle Sante Fiora e Lucilla (*open all day*), dedicated to the two saints whose relics were brought here in the 11th century. It has a Romanesque rose-window in its façade, and the unusual interior, more or less square, contains beautiful altarpieces and a lovely pulpit all in enamelled terracotta and made between 1480 and 1490 by Andrea della Robbia and his workshop. The little Crucifix in a niche is decorated with a delightful frieze of della Robbian quinces.

A steep road leads down past Sant'Agostino, through a gateway, to the foot of the hill, where the large public fountain (still sometimes used for laundering clothes) is fed from the Fiora spring (the Fiora river provides water for much of the large province of

Grosseto). Behind it is a large rectangular fishpond beside a little oratory with a della Robbian relief representing Fiora and Lucilla built over the spring, which can be seen beneath its floor. Next to the chapel is the entrance to La Peschiera (*open weekends June–1 Sept 3.30–6, or by appointment; T: 0564 953134*), a delightful Renaissance garden restored in 1851. Wonderfully cool in summer, the garden surrounds the pond and bubbling rivulets which collect the spring waters.

Abbadia San Salvatore and Piancastagnaio

The largest town on Monte Amiata is Abbadia San Salvatore (pop. 8,500; *map p. 267, D3*). Largely modern in aspect and feel, it nevertheless has an old medieval district. From Piazza XX Settembre, an archway leads into the picturesque medieval *borgo*, which preserves numerous streets of houses in the local grey trachyte stone. Off Via Cavour, just 200m away, another arch leads to the **Benedictine abbey**. Only three Cistercian monks live here today, though once it was immensely rich and powerful, enjoying numerous privileges under the protection of popes and emperors, and exercising feudal jurisdiction over much of southern Tuscany. An important station in the Middle Ages on the Via Francigena (*see p. 448*), it was founded, according to tradition, in 743 by the Lombard king Ratchis. At the peak of its temporal and spiritual powers, in 1035, the abbey was rebuilt and reconsecrated. The monastery was suppressed by Grand Duke Peter Leopold in 1783, but a Benedictine community was reinstalled here in 1939. The unusual narrow façade, with its three-light window over the arched entrance, is flanked by two towers. The church was restored several times in the 20th century in an attempt to reconstruct its 11th-century appearance. The interior (*open all day*) has an elevated choir framed by three rounded arches spanning its entire width. The late 12th-century carved wooden Crucifix over the high altar shows *Christ Triumphant* (with open eyes). At the east end are frescoes by Francesco Nasini. But the most interesting feature of the church is its large crypt, which probably dates from the 10th–11th century. The 32 columns which support the stone vault are a remarkable sight, some of them beautifully carved, and their capitals with a variety of leaf, figure and animal motifs. The 16th-century cloister is being restored. The precious monastic treasury (*open in summer 10–12 & 4–7, or on request*) contains a tiny 8th-century Irish reliquary and a copper-gilt reliquary bust of Pope St Mark, dated 1381 and attributed to Mariano d'Agnolo Romanelli. The unique 8th–9th-century red silk cope, probably of Persian origin, is woven with a pattern of simurghs (legendary birds) in roundels. During its restoration an inscription was discovered relating to Pope John VIII (872–82). The hem was lined with strips of silk which are extraordinarily rare 8th-century Byzantine textiles, woven in four colours, with pairs of dancers in roundels.

The road northwest to the summit of Monte Amiata passes a deer park on the right and on the left the former **mercury mine**, now a museum (*open in summer 9–1 & 3–8*). **Piancastagnaio**, which overlooks the Paglia valley further to the southeast, is a village with narrow picturesque streets beyond a fortified gateway beside the impressive Aldobrandeschi fortress, one of the best preserved examples of 14th-century military architecture in the district.

MONTEPULCIANO & CHIUSI

Montepulciano (*map p. 267, E2*), in a lovely position near the Umbrian border, is one of the largest hilltop towns in the southeast part of Tuscany. It is well preserved and has many handsome 16th-century palaces built when it came under Florentine rule, including some by Antonio da Sangallo the Elder, who also erected the spectacular Tempio di San Biagio here. The area is noted for its red wines, the most famous being the Vino Nobile di Montepulciano (*see box opposite*).

Politian (1454–94)

Montepulciano was the birthplace of Agnolo Ambrogini, the great Classical scholar, who adopted the town's late Latin name, *Mons Politianus*, as his own: Politian (in Italian, Poliziano). He moved to Florence as a youth in 1468, and his erudition became such that Lorenzo the Magnificent appointed him both as personal secretary, and as tutor to his two sons, Piero and Giovanni (the future Pope Leo X). His famous *Stanze* (1475–78) were composed in honour of Lorenzo's brother Giuliano. These poems, written in the vernacular, are clearly influenced by Petrarch. Their main theme could be summarised by Lorenzo's own verses: 'Chi vuol esser lieto, sia; di doman non c'è certezza' (let him be glad who will be: there is no certainty in tomorrow). Botticelli's *Birth of Venus*, and possibly also his *Primavera* were inspired by poems by Politian.

Piazza Grande and the duomo

At the highest point of town is the beautiful Piazza Grande, with the crenellated 14th-century Palazzo Comunale surmounted by an impressive clock-tower (*open April–Nov 10–5*), which recalls that of Palazzo Vecchio in Florence. Opposite is Palazzo Contucci, begun by Antonio da Sangallo the Elder. The fine stone façade (*covered for restoration at the time of writing*) has five windows on the *piano nobile* with pediments supported on Ionic columns; the top floor was added later. The elegant well in the piazza is also attributed to Sangallo, and he probably also built the grandiose travertine façade of Palazzo Tarugi opposite the duomo steps, with its triple arched arcade on the ground floor and Ionic half-columns on high pedestals supporting a balustrade above the pedimented windows of the main floor.

The duomo was designed by Ippolito Scalza in 1592–1630, and is perhaps more impressive outside than in. Nevertheless, it boasts a very large and beautiful high altarpiece of the **Assumption** by **Taddeo di Bartolo** (1401). In the cimasa the Virgin is shown being crowned. Flanking this, amid tall, tapering pinnacles, are the *Angel Gabriel* and the *Virgin Annunciate*. The central panel of the triptych below has the Apostles around the Virgin's empty tomb, while the Virgin herself ascends placidly, eyes uplifted, surrounded by trumpeting angels. The Apostle Jude (Thaddeus) is depicted looking self-consciously out of the painting behind the tomb to the right. It has been interpreted as a self-portrait of the artist. In various other parts of the church are dismembered fragments of the lovely tomb of Bartolomeo Aragazzi, secretary to Pope Martin V, by Michelozzo (1427–36). The baptistery has a font by Giovanni di Agostino (c. 1340), and a tabernacle by Andrea della Robbia.

Just out of the piazza, on Via Ricci, the Gothic Palazzo Neri-Orselli (modified in later centuries), houses the **Museo Civico e Pinacoteca Crociani** (*open Sat, Sun 10–1 & 3–6; other times by appointment; T: 0578 757341*). It has an archaeological section with interesting Etruscan finds from the district, and paintings, including *St Francis* by Margaritone di Arezzo, and a *Holy Family* by Sodoma.

VINO NOBILE DI MONTEPULCIANO

Montepulciano wine is a sort of marriage between Chianti Classico and Brunello di Montalcino. In aroma it leans more towards the former; in taste to the latter. The Sangiovese that is cultivated around these parts, along the banks of the Chiana, is known as *Prugnolo gentile*. The best vineyards can be as much as 400m above sea-level. The soil is sandy and loose, and the resulting wine is aromatic and light in texture. Gone are the acidic, nothing-tasting wines of before the 1970s wine-making revolution. Maturation in small casks now means that acids are rounded, structure is tighter and flavours more concentrated. The *Riserva* wines are the fullest bodied. But all wines, regardless of their category, are aged only for a single year. Often there is little difference between a Vino Nobile di Montepulciano and the junior wine, the Rosso di Montepulciano.

Outskirts of Montepulciano

On the northern outskirts is the sanctuary of **Santa Maria delle Grazie**, designed by the architect of the duomo, Ippolito Scalza, with a porticoed façade (1605). The interior has elegant mid-18th-century stuccowork and a late 16th-century organ, the only example of its kind in Italy (there is a comparable one at Innsbruck). Its pipes are of cypress wood and produce a particularly soft and gentle sound, which was recommended by Monteverdi for the accompaniment of his *Orfeo*. Since the organ's restoration in 1983, it has been played by organists from all over the world.

To the west, off the road to Pienza, and approached by a beautiful cypress avenue, is the **Tempio di San Biagio** (*usually open 9–1 & 3–7*), one of the great church buildings of the High Renaissance. It was built by Antonio da Sangallo the Elder (1518–34) for the Ricci family on the site of an earlier church. It has a Greek-cross plan with a central dome. The exterior of travertine is of classical sobriety, and the beautifully proportioned design of the façade is repeated on the two sides. Only one of the towers was finished, and actually completed in 1545 by Baccio d'Agnolo, who also built the lantern of the dome. The interior (*being restored at the time of writing*), which is also very beautiful, repeats and elaborates the classical features of the exterior, with sculptural decoration carved in high relief in the yellow sandstone. Behind, in the area corresponding to the apse, is the sacristy, from which a staircase leads to the outside balcony. The canons' house nearby, with open loggias on both floors, was built after Sangallo's death.

THE VAL DI CHIANA

North of Montepulciano stretches the beautiful countryside of the Val di Chiana Senese (*map p. 267, E2*), with wooded hills (ilexes and oaks), cultivated fields, and a group of interesting, well preserved small villages.

Montefollonico and Torrita

The quiet, little fortified village of **Montefollonico** with its small medieval houses, is Sienese in atmosphere, and inhabited by numerous doves and pigeons. It has charming little churches including San Leonardo, with a pretty 13th-century exterior built of square blocks of local yellow-and-white stone. The Chiesa della Compagnia del Corpus Domini, preceded by a tiny courtyard with the bell-tower at one corner, has a *Deposition* by the school of Luca Signorelli, and 18th-century frescoed lunettes with amusing details.

The lovely little red-brick village of **Torrita di Siena** was an important stronghold of the Sienese Republic until it became part of the Medici Grand Duchy of Tuscany in 1554. It preserves parts of its walls. In the piazza, with a well, is Palazzo Comunale and the Romanesque church of Sante Fiora e Lucilla. In the pleasant brick interior, is an exquisite small **lunette by Donatello** of the *Blood of the Redeemer* (it once decorated a hospice in the town). Donatello's typical *schiacciato* technique is here used to portray the figure of Christ surrounded by eleven cherubim in the clouds and the busts of the two donors in a very small space. The triptych with the *Nativity and Sts Anthony Abbot and Augustine* is a charming work by Bartolo di Fredi.

Trequanda, Montisi and Castelmuzio

Trequanda (*map p. 267, D2*) is a medieval village which was once under the dominion of Siena. The parish church of Santi Pietro e Andrea has a delightful façade chequered in brown-and-white stone. The interior contains frescoes by Sodoma and a seated wooden statue of the *Madonna and Child*, attributed to Jacopo Sansovino.

Montisi, south of Trequanda, has a castle and, at the top of the hill, the Romanesque church of the Annunziata with a beautiful large polyptych of the *Madonna and Child with Sts Peter, Louis, James and Paul*, signed and dated 1496 by Neroccio di Bartolomeo Landi.

The village of **Castelmuzio** (*map p. 267, D2*), of Etruscan and Roman foundations, is first mentioned in the 9th century. It is built on a circular plan, so that all the streets are curving. In the piazza is a very unusual tower-house, reconstructed in the 18th century. Next to a hostel for pilgrims on the Via Francigena, a charming little museum contains a *Madonna and Child* by the school of Duccio, and a painting of *St Bernardino* by the saint's friend Giovanni di Paolo.

Petroio

Petroio (*map p. 267, D2*) has a very interesting circular plan, with its road forming a spiral leading up to the tower of the impressive 13th-century brick castle, high above its clustered medieval houses. In the choir of the parish church there is a large (damaged) fresco of the *Crucifixion*, attributed to Andrea di Niccolò. Petroio was the birthplace of an ascetic, Bartolomeo Carosi, known as Brandano (1483–1554), whose famous mottoes and prophesies have been handed down to this day. (The Palazzo Brandano hotel—see p. 463—is named in his honour.) The locality has been known since the 18th century for its ceramic vases and pots, made with the local ochre-coloured calcareous rock, and there is still a large terracotta works in the woods on the outskirts.

The large ex-Olivetan monastery of **Sant'Anna in Camprena** (*map p. 267, D2*), approached by a long cypress avenue, is beautifully sited on a peaceful hill which dominates the surrounding countryside. It was founded by Bernardo Tolomei (*see p. 439*) in 1324, rebuilt in the 15th century, and enlarged in the 17th. It is now used as a language centre and residence, but can be visited at weekends. The refectory has very well-preserved **frescoes by Sodoma** (*see p. 440*), his earliest works, painted in 1503–05, when he was 25. The colours are extraordinarily vivid, and the landscapes and use of perspective, as well as the expressive figure studies, show remarkable ability. The splendid old kitchen survives, and a charming walled garden with a pond.

CHIUSI

The hilltop town of Chiusi (pop. 8,700; *map p. 267, E3*), was an Etruscan town of great importance, as can be seen from the finds in its museum, and the vast Etruscan necropolis which surrounds the town. Under the streets runs a labyrinth of Etruscan tunnels.

HISTORY OF CHIUSI

Called *Clevsins*, ancient Chiusi was one of the 12 cities of the Etruscan Confederation, which reached its greatest splendour around the 7th or 6th century BC. The Latin authors often referred to the fertility of the surrounding countryside, which produced oil, wine and wheat in abundance. Strabo described how the Lago di Chiusi could be reached by river from Rome up the Tiber and Chiana. Lars Porsena, the legendary *lucumo*, or king of Chiusi, attacked Rome in 507–506 BC, after the fall of the Etruscan ruler Tarquinius Superbus and the declaration of the Republic. After 296 BC Clevsins became subject to Rome and took the Roman name of *Clusium*. It continued to flourish in the Augustan era, and was then occupied by the Goths from 540 probably up until the 10th century, when it became part of the Lombard duchy. The unhealthy marshes of the Val di Chiana caused malaria and brought about the decline of Chiusi, although the drainage works begun by Cosimo de' Medici did restore some degree of prosperity.

The duomo and Etruscan tunnel

The duomo (San Secondiano), in a pleasant little piazza with good paving, was founded in the 6th century and the interior retains its basilican plan from that time. It was restored in 1887–94, when the porch was reconstructed and the nave and apses were painted by Arturo Viligiardi in imitation of antique mosaics. The splendid columns and capitals, including one in breccia marble at the west end, come from local Roman edifices. Highlights of the **Museo della Cattedrale** (*open 10–8*) include 21 antiphonals from the abbey of Monte Oliveto Maggiore (second half of the 15th century), illuminated by Liberale da Verona, Sano di Pietro and others; and a remarkable late 14th-century polychrome wood figure of Christ (probably part of a *Deposition* group).

From the garden is the entrance to a very long Etruscan tunnel, known as the **Labirinto di Porsenna**, which may have served as a water channel, or as part of a defence system (it was not part of Porsena's tomb, allegedly in the area, but never certainly located). The iron staircase in the garden provides a view of three lines of fortification, dating from the Etruscan (3rd century BC), Roman and medieval periods. The tunnel is very narrow and low, and side tunnels can also be seen, as it winds its way beneath the piazza and duomo to emerge in a huge cistern with an impressive double vault and central pilaster, dating from the end of the 2nd or early 1st century BC. Beside it is a tall fortified tower dating from the 12th century, which was transformed into a campanile for the duomo in 1585. It can be climbed (up modern stairs), and the view on a clear day takes in the rock of Orvieto, as well as Monte Amiata, and the lakes of Trasimene, Chiusi and Montepulciano.

The mid-3rd-century **Catacombs of Santa Caterina**, near the station, can be seen on a guided tour (*daily at 11, request visit at the museum*).

Museo Nazionale Etrusco and the Etruscan tombs

The Museo Nazionale Etrusco (*open 10–8*) is one of the most important Etruscan museums in Italy. Chiusi was one of the first Etruscan cities to be explored, as early as the 15th century, but unsystematic excavations, especially in the 19th century, led to the dispersal of much of the material, and most of the objects in the museum are of unknown provenance (and some have been poorly or incorrectly restored). A great number of inscriptions were found in and near Chiusi, but they are now in other museums.

The ground floor illustrates the history of archaeological research in the area. The extremely fine **prehistoric and Villanovan material** includes finds dating from the 9th–8th centuries BC, and canopic vases of the 7th–6th centuries BC. Beautiful Archaic reliefs (late 6th century BC) show Greek influence. There are cases of *bucchero* ware, 5th-century Attic black- and red-figure vases, terracotta architectural fragments, and 5th–4th-century bronzes, as well as Etruscan vases and sarcophagi and cinerary urns (4th–2nd century BC) in alabaster and terracotta. The Roman material includes a head of Augustus, architectural and votive terracottas (3rd–2nd century BC) and Hellenistic bronzes, ceramics and sarcophagi.

In the basement the material is arranged topographically from excavations since 1930 in the centre of the city, in the necropoleis on the outskirts, and in the sites discovered

Etruscan tomb of Lars Sentinates (3rd century BC).

in the vicinity. The earliest finds date from the late Bronze Age. The remarkable alabaster **tomb of Lars Sentinates** is also displayed here.

At present just three of the many Etruscan tombs in the countryside around the town, a few kilometres outside the centre, can be visited. The **Tomba della Pellegrina** and **Tomba del Leone** can be visited (*by appointment; T: 0578 20177*) at the same times as the Museo Nazionale Etrusco (and with the same ticket). The **Tomba della Scimmia** is the most interesting since it preserves its wall paintings (*only open Tues, Thur, and Sat 11–12 & 4–5*). At some place under or near Chiusi must lie the foundations of the famous tomb of Lars Porsena, the only Etruscan tomb described by ancient sources, but which was destroyed by Sulla in 89 BC. No trace of it has ever been found.

Cetona

South of Chiusi is Cetona (*map p. 267, E3*), a beautifully preserved medieval village, and today a fashionable place to have a country house. The **Museo Civico per la Preistoria del Monte Cetona** (*open 9.30–12.30; Sat also 4–6; closed Mon*) is a delightful little museum documenting the presence of man on Monte Cetona (which was an island in the Pleiocene era) from the Palaeolithic era to the Bronze Age. The remains of a huge bear were found in a cave inhabited by Neanderthal man some 50,000 years ago.

Outside Cetona is the **Belverde archaeological park** (*for admission enquire at the museum in Cetona*), the most important Bronze Age site in central Italy, where, for the first time, various phases of Bronze Age habitation were found in one place, untouched by later constructions. It is on the side of Monte Cetona (1148m), a beautiful wooded mountain, with its summit often hidden by clouds, and visible, like Monte Amiata, for miles around. The calcareous rock with marine deposits (sea-shells, etc) is covered with interesting vegetation. A cavern where evidence of Neanderthal habitation was found, and which seems to have been used as a store in the Bronze Age, was formed by the collapse of travertine outcrops. Today it is lit by solar power and can be visited.

PRACTICAL INFORMATION

GETTING AROUND

•**By car:** Cars can be parked in **Montalcino** outside the fortress or outside the walls. There are car parks in **Chiusi** off Via Pietriccia and Via dei Longobardi.

•**By train:** The branch line between Siena and Chiusi stops at **Torrita di Siena** and Montepulciano Scalo, 11km north of **Montepulciano**. Main-line trains link Montepulciano with Rome and Florence. Some trains also stop at **Chiusi** (the railway station is 3km south of town).

•**By bus:** Buses operated by TRA-IN (www.trainspa.it) run from Siena (Piazza San Domenico) to Montalcino, Sant'Antimo, Montepulciano (not Sun), Pienza and San Quirico d'Orcia. Buses also link Pienza and Montepulciano. Buses run c. every hour between Montepulciano and Chiusi railway station, and every 30mins between Chiusi station and the town centre.

INFORMATION OFFICES

Chiusi Piazza Duomo, T: 0578 227667.
Montalcino Costa del Municipio 8, T: 0577 849331.
Montepulciano Via di Gracciano nel Corso 59, T: 0578 757341.
Pienza Corso il Rossellino 59, T: 0578 749071.
San Quirico d'Orcia Via Dante Alighieri 33, T: 0577 897211.

HOTELS

Bagno Vignoni (*map p. 267, D3*)
€€ **Albergo Le Terme**. Pleasant, traditional hotel, once the home of Pope Pius II. Run by the same family for over 30 years, it overlooks the remarkable 'piazza' with its hot thermal pool. Guests can use the thermal pool of the nearby Hotel Marcucci. *Piazza delle Sorgenti 13, T: 0577 887150, www.albergoleterme.it*

Chiusi (*map p. 267, E3*)
€€ **Albergo La Sfinge**. Small central hotel, with simple, slightly rustic furnishings of some charm. *Via Marconi 2, T: 0578 20157, www.albergolasfinge.com. 15 rooms*

€€ **Villa Il Patriarca**. A patrician villa carefully converted into a fine hotel. Spacious rooms, and outdoor swimming pool with an unsurpassed view. Attentive service. *Località Querce al Pino, T: 0578 274407 www.ilpatriarca.it. 23 rooms.*

Montalcino (*map p. 267, D3*)
€€€ **Castello di Velona**. Converted 11th-century castle and fortified villa, set on a small hilltop once the scene of encounters between the rival republics of Florence and Siena. Simply furnished, comfortable rooms have a peaceful feel. Restaurant and helipad, should you wish to arrive in style. *Località Velona, T: 0577 800101, www.castellodivelona.it. 24 rooms.*

€ **Le Camere di Bacco**. A charming bed and breakfast on the first floor of an old property in the centre of Montalcino, with rooms filled with elegant Tuscan furnishings. A pleasant kitchen area is useful for making snacks or a picnic. *Via Mazzini 65, T: 0577 849356, www.lecameredibacco.com. 4 rooms.*

Montepulciano (*map p. 267, E2*)
€€€ **Sant'Antonio**. Individual cottages and apartments are arranged within the beautiful grounds of the Sant'Antonio estate, 3km outside of Montepulciano (on the road to Chianciano Terme). Attentive service. *Via della Montagna 6/8, T: 0578 799365, www.santantonio.it. 14 apartments.*

€ **Meublè Il Riccio**. ■ Excellent place, with rooms on the first floor of a tiny cloister, just out of Piazza Grande. Very peaceful. *Via di Talosa 21, T: 0578 757713, www.ilriccio.net. 6 rooms.*

Petroio (*map p. 267, D2*)
€€€€ **Palazzo Brandano**. Recently-opened hotel in this small village north of Siena. Rooms are named after famous artists, and the walls decorated with pastiches of their works. It sounds—and is—twee, but don't be put off. The setting is superb and the accommodation peaceful and comfortable. Restaurant. *Via di Val Gelata 18, T: 0577 665169, www.palazzobrandano.com. 9 rooms.*

Pienza (*map p. 267, D3*)
€€ **Piccolo Hotel La Valle**. Pleasant, well-designed hotel, with parking and good bathrooms. The situation, with its view of the valley, could hardly be bettered (though the band in an old tower nearby disturbs the silence on certain nights). Pleasant garden. Slightly disappointing breakfasts. *Via Circonvallazione 7, T: 0578 749402, www.piccolo-hotellavalle.it. 15 rooms.*

Rocca d'Orcia (*map p. 267, D3*)
€€ **San Simeone**. Hotel occupying the houses of a tiny *borgo*, just below the Rocca and above the village in a very quiet position. A choice of rooms or apartments. Swimming pool. *Via della*

Chiesa 11, T: 0577 888984, www.hotelsan-simeone.com. 14 rooms.

San Quirico d'Orcia (*map p. 267, D3*)
€€€ **Relais Palazzo del Capitano**. Charming place in a restored 15th-century palazzo in the heart of the town. Rooms are simply and traditionally furnished—terracotta floor tiles, cool-painted walls, canopy beds and exposed beams. *Via Poliziano 18, T: 0577 899028, www.palazzocapitano.com. 16 rooms.*

Torrita di Siena (*map p. 267, E2*)
€€ **Valcelle**. ■ Delightful *agriturismo* in a beautiful, quiet position, run by a friendly, welcoming couple, who also farm. Apartments in the old farmhouse, dating from the late 19th century, or a villa to rent, complete with its original furnishings. Swimming pool. *Località Valcelle 74, T: 3292 256774, www.val-celle.it.*

RESTAURANTS

Bettolle (*map p. 267, E2*)
€€€–€€ **Walter Redaelli-La Bandita**. Booking is essential for an evening out here: the food and atmosphere make it worth it. Specify when booking if you want a table outside. Closed Tues. *Via Bandita 72, T: 0577 623447*

Cetona (*map p. 267, E3*)
€€€ **Osteria del Merlo**. A place to eat in calm and elegant surroundings, and to sample exquisitely prepared fish. Closed Mon. *Via Sobborgo 1, T: 0578 238299.*

€€€ **Osteria Vecchia**. Familiarly known as Nilo's, this is one of the classiest places in the area, a haunt of locals and of well-heeled visitors. The cooking is exemplary. Closed Tues. *Via Cherubini 11, T: 0578 239040.*

Chiusi (*map p. 267, E3*)
€ **Osteria La Solita Zuppa**. Friendly place with good cooking. The soups are a speciality (and genuinely unusual—in a good way). Closed Tues. *Via Porsenna 21, T: 0578 21006.*

Lago di Chiusi (*map p. 267, E3*)
There are two restaurants here, both serving the local speciality of *fagiolina*, small beans that grow wild in the surrounding wetlands. Useful to book on Sun or holidays, as both are popular:
€ **Da Gino**. Don't be put off by first appearances: this is an excellent place for fish caught on the lake—try the perch grilled on reeds from the lake or the fish stew, *tegamaccio*, cooked slowly for 24hrs. Simple Tuscan food at its delicious best. Closed Wed. *Via Cabina Lago 42, T: 0578 21408*; € **Pesce d'Oro**. Unpretentious, excellent lakeside restaurant serving freshwater fish, established for over 40 years and extremely popular with locals. Closed Tues. *Via Sbarchino 36, T: 0578 21403.*

Montefollonico (*map p. 267, E2*)
€ **La Botte Piena**. Authentic local place, and quite different from the other restaurants in town, which tend to be geared towards visitors. Wide variety of *antipasti* and first courses; the choice of main courses is smaller, but good. Carefully chosen wines. There are some tables outside in the pretty little square; be sure to ask for one when you book. Closed Wed. *Piazza Dionisia Cinughi 12, T: 0577 669481.*

Pienza (*map p. 267, D3*)
€€ **Latte di Luna**. This *trattoria* has been a favourite for many years, close to Piazza Pio II. Delicious hand-made pasta with traditional sauces, followed by wild boar in the winter, grilled steak

or duck with olives. Lovely friendly atmosphere. Closed Tues and July. *Via S. Carlo 2/4, T: 0578 748606.*
€€ **Il Rossellino**. Tiny place with just five tables, but fight for one if you can. The owners are welcoming and helpful, and the food is lovingly prepared from local produce. *Piazza di Spagna 4, T: 0578 749064.*
€ **Osteria Sette di Vino**. Simple, inexpensive, good home cooking. Tables spill out onto the piazza in warm weather. *Piazza di Spagna 1, T: 0578 749092.*

Rocca d'Orcia (*map p. 267, D3*)
€€ **Cantina il Borgo**. Extremely atmospheric place, part of an old inn. Open evenings only except weekends. Closed Mon. *Via Borgo Maestro 37, T: 0578 887280.*

San Quirico d'Orcia (*map p. 267, D3*)
€ **Al Vecchio Forno**. Cosy place serving traditional Tuscan food, well prepared from local ingredients—the roasts are particularly recommended. Sit outside in the lovely, herb-filled garden in summer. There's also an impressive wine list. *Via della Piazzola 8, T: 0577 897380.*

Sant'Angelo in Colle (*map p. 267, D3*)
€ **Il Pozzo**. West of the Abbey of Sant'Antimo, on a dirt road. Not the closely guarded secret it once was, but still good, and full of rustic charm, with honest, local cooking—the pasta with wild boar sauce is an enduring favourite. Closed Tues. *Piazza del Popolo 2, T: 0577 844015.*

Torrita di Siena (*map p. 267, E2*)
€€€–€€ **Ristorante Asso**. Elegant restaurant serving good fresh fish, some say the best in the area (it arrives on Tues, Thur and Sat). Closed Mon. *Via*

Pantanelli 116 (signed left off the road to Montepulciano), T: 0577 686343.
€ **Il Belvedere**. Simple, inexpensive and popular with locals and visitors alike. Service can be a bit slow at peak times. Tables outside in fine weather. Closed Tues. *Via Traversa Valdichiana Ovest 31, T: 0577 686442, www.belvedere-online.it.*
€ **Le Macine**. Good food, excellent prices and superlative views. After the Belvedere, turn right (signed) onto a dirt road; then keep left. Closed Wed. *Località Palazzetto 2, T: 0577 669690.*
Trequanda *(map p. 267, D2)*
€€ **Il Conte Matto**. Friendly place just outside the walls, serving excellent, creative cuisine. Popular with visitors and local residents. Lovely outdoor terrace. Closed midday Tues. *Via Taverne 40, T: 0577 662079.*

LOCAL SPECIALITIES

Montalcino Although particularly famous for its Brunello, other excellent wines produced around Montalcino include the Rosso di Montalcino, and Moscadello, a sweet fizzy wine. The town is also known for its traditional white-and-turquoise coloured pottery, and for its honey.
Petroio is known for its pottery. The terracotta museum in the town has interesting exhibits.
Pienza There are plenty of shops specialising in the particularly good sheep's cheese (*pecorino* or *cacio*) made in the district.
Sant'Antimo CDs of plainsong sung by the monks are on sale in the abbey church.

FESTIVALS & EVENTS

Montalcino Theatre festival, July; *Sagra del Tordo*, Archery competition, dancing and regional gastronomy, last Sun in Oct.
Montepulciano *Festa di Sant'Agnese,* Feast of the patron saint, 1 May; *Cantiere Internazionale d'Arte,* Classical and modern music, theatre, dance and art festival, last week July–first week Aug;
Mostra Interregionale dell'Artigianato, Regional craft fair, throughout Aug; *Bravio delle Botti,* Two men from each of the eight districts of the town compete in rolling a barrel (*botte*) weighing 80kg uphill, from Piazza Marzocco to Piazza Grande. The prize is a painted banner (*bravio*) and the privilege of offering a candle to the patron saint of the town, St Agnes, last Sun in Aug.
Petroio Pottery festival and market, third Sun in May; pig-racing on last Sun in June.
Sant'Antimo Organ concerts in the abbey church, July–Aug.
Torrita di Siena *Palio dei Somari,* Mule race, flag-throwing and other festivities, Sun following 19 March.

This chapter takes in the large province of Grosseto which extends all the way to the border with Lazio. The marshy coastal area, known as the Maremma, has some pretty resorts and remote beaches, as well as extensive protected areas of natural beauty and bird sanctuaries. There are numerous Etruscan sites in this area, including Populonia, Roselle and Vetulonia. One of the loveliest inland towns is Massa Marittima, and further north are the evocative ruins of the once powerful abbey church of San Galgano.

MASSA MARITTIMA

Mining has taken place in the hills around Massa Marittima (*map p. 266, B3*) since Etruscan times. It was a flourishing industry in the Middle Ages (when the earliest known Mining Code was drawn up here—one of the most important legislative documents to have survived from this time in Italy), and again in the 19th century. The town's period of greatest glory was from 1225–1335, when it was an independent republic: its splendid duomo, with its remarkable sculptural works, dates from this time. From 1317 it minted its own silver coin, the *grosso*.

The town is divided into two distinct parts, the Città Vecchia around the cathedral, and the Città Nuova on a hill above. Both districts were enclosed in the 13th-century circuit of walls, the extent of which reflects the prosperity of the medieval town prior to Sienese dominion in 1335. The Città Nuova and the Città Vecchia were then divided by the Sienese, who erected an immense fortified wall which incorporated Porta alle Silici.

St Bernardino of Siena (1380–1444) was born in Massa, and it was here that he preached his last Lenten Sermons. His family, the Albizzeschi, were nobles. He became a Franciscan friar and was famous as a preacher throughout northern and central Italy. Many of his sermons and writings have survived. He had a particular devotion to the Name of Jesus, and he is always represented as an old, ascetic friar holding a tablet with rays surrounding the letters IHS and a Cross.

The duomo

The memorable main square in the Città Vecchia is triangular in shape. The duomo (*open 8–12 & 3–6; summer 8–12 & 2–7*) was begun in the early 13th century and is magnificently positioned at an angle above an irregular flight of steps with the north side creating a monumental perspective, counterbalanced by the bishop's palace, and the towering campanile at the centre. Dedicated to St Cerbonius, whose relics were transferred to Massa from Populonia in the 9th century, the cathedral has a splendid Romanesque exterior in travertine with blind arcading. The upper part of the façade, with exquisitely carved arches and capitals, symbols of the Evangelists, and a kneeling telamon (some replaced by copies), was added in the Pisan Gothic style in 1287–1314.

Bas-reliefs sculpted above the main doorway in a single marble block, probably by a 12th-century Pisan sculptor, illustrate stories from the life of St Cerbonius: probably born in Africa in 493, he escaped from vandals to the Maremma, where he was condemned by Totila to be devoured by bears for giving shelter to enemy soldiers, but instead the bears only licked his feet. He succeeded Regulus (patron saint of Lucca; *see p. 334*) as Bishop of Populonia.

The interior, which has a basilican ground-plan, has **14th-century stained glass** in the rose window, representing St Cerbonius before Pope Vigilius. The apse was lengthened and given slender Gothic windows in the late 13th century, and the octagonal dome was added in the 15th century. The travertine columns have magnificent capitals. The huge **rectangular font** is most unusual: carved in a single square block of travertine, it rests on three lions and a lioness, with reliefs dating from 1267 of the life of the Baptist and Christ Blessing, and a 15th-century tabernacle rises from its centre, with carved figures of prophets in niches. To the right of the sanctuary is a painted Crucifix, attributed to Segna di Bonaventura. Behind the high altar (with a wooden Crucifix by Giovanni Pisano) is the **Arca di San Cerbone**, a marble urn signed and dated 1324 by Goro di Gregorio, a masterpiece of Sienese Gothic sculpture. The sculptor reveals great gifts as a storyteller and his reliefs are full of charming details, spontaneity and poetry.

In the chapel to the left of the high altar is the **Madonna delle Grazie**, a majestic icon (1316) by a close follower of Duccio, and probably executed in his workshop, but which has been attributed also to the young Simone Martini. The panel, which has been cut down, also has scenes of the *Crucifixion* and *Passion* painted on the back by the same hand.

Palazzo del Podestà

Opposite the duomo to the left of the piazza is the 13th-century Palazzo del Podestà, with an austere façade in travertine and numerous coats of arms recording the governors of the town from 1426–1633. It houses the **Museo Archeologico** (*open 10–12.30 & 3–5; in summer 10–12.30 & 3.30–7; closed Mon*). The collection documents the various settlements in the district from prehistoric times to the Roman era and has a particularly rich Etruscan section.

Città Nuova

Via Moncini, a beautiful street which becomes stepped, leads up to Piazza Matteotti and the Città Nuova. **Porta alle Silici**, part of the vast and impressive fortifications erected by the Sienese after their conquest of Massa in 1335, is connected to the older Torre del Candeliere by an immense flying arch. The clock-tower, which was reduced to two-thirds of its original height by the Sienese, may be climbed (*open 11–1 & 2.30–6.30; summer 10–1 & 3–6; closed Mon*).

On the north side of the piazza is **Palazzo delle Armi**, with a museum (*only open April–Oct 3–5.30 except Mon*) which documents excavations in the district, with reliefs, diagrams and photographs illustrating the development of mining from Etruscan to modern times. The Mining Code document of 1310 (*see p. 466 above*) is also kept here.

Corso Diaz leads from Piazza Matteotti to the church of **Sant'Agostino**, founded in 1299. The polygonal apse, pierced by arched Gothic windows (with modern glass), was designed by Domenico di Agostino (1348), who completed the cathedral of Siena. The interior has mostly 17th-century altarpieces. Beside the ex-church of San Pietro all'Orto is the **Museo di Arte Sacra** (*11–1 & 3–5; summer 10–1 & 3–6; closed Mon*) which has sculpture from the cathedral including a rare series of reliefs in grey alabaster, thought to be pre-Romanesque, representing Christ with angels, the Apostles, and the *Massacre of the Innocents*, and eleven small marble statues of the Apostles by an early 14th-century Sienese sculptor. The most precious painting is the *Maestà* by Ambrogio Lorenzetti, dating from around 1330, showing the Madonna and Child enthroned and surrounded by saints, angels, and the Theological Virtues (Faith, Hope and Charity).

Museo della Miniera

On the edge of the hill just below the old town, in Via Corridoni, is an abandoned mine which houses a museum (*guided visits every half hour, 10–12 & 3–4.30/5.30; closed Mon*) which demonstrates mining techniques and exhibits equipment, machinery and mineral specimens.

ENVIRONS OF MASSA MARITTIMA

Bolgheri

This little village close to the Tyrrhenian coast (*map p. 266, A2*) is approached by a splendid avenue of some 3,000 cypresses, nearly 5km long, planted in 1801 by Camillo della Gherardesca, whose family had been feudal lords in this area since the early 13th century (their castle dominated the town of Castagneto Carducci further south). Here the poet Giosuè Carducci spent his childhood (1838–49), and the cypress avenue is the subject of a famous poem by him (some of the diseased trees are being replanted with adult plants). The white and rosé wines of Bolgheri are particularly good, though the area is more famous today for its so-called Supertuscans (*see box opposite*).

On the coast there is a wildlife sanctuary, administered by the WWF (*open by appointment only 15 Oct–15 April; T: 0565 777125*). The landscape, typical of the Maremma, of which this is a northern extension, includes umbrella pines, ilexes, cork trees, and dunes covered with *macchia*. The marshland attracts a great variety of migratory birds.

Populonia

This ancient Etruscan town (*map p. 266, A3*) is situated high on the Massoncello promontory, originally an island, from which there is a magnificent view stretching from the Apuan Hills to Punt'Ala and the islands of Elba, Corsica and Capraia. It has a beautiful beach, backed by pine trees.

Populonia was one of the most important ports of ancient Etruria. Iron from Elba and perfumes, amulets and objects from Syria, Egypt and Greece were traded here as early as the 8th century BC in exchange for tin and copper mined in the nearby hills. Its importance was also due to its furnaces for smelting metals. The necropolis of Populonia and the archaeological sites document settlements in the area from the Iron Age to Roman times. They were reopened in 2007 as the Parco di Baratti e Populonia (*open 10–dusk except Mon; July and Aug every day; Nov and Dec weekends only 10–4; T: 0565 226445*). There are several interesting large tumulus tombs dating from the 7th–5th centuries BC, as well as one in the form of an aedicule, and grottoes. In the early Christian period, until its destruction by the Lombards in the late 6th century, Populonia was the seat of a bishop, a position held by the patron saint of Lucca (Regulus) and that of Massa Marittima (Cerbonius). Today, Populonia is a typical medieval hilltop town, encircled by its walls and dominated by its castle (*open 9.30–12.30 & 2.30–dusk, except Mon*).

BOLGHERI & THE SUPERTUSCANS

It was the Etruscans, here as elsewhere in Tuscany, who first introduced viticulture to Bolgheri. The terroir and microclimate of the region have probably changed little since then: the proximity of the sea means that almost constant breezes temper the heat of summer and the winter's cold. Rainfall is scarce and sunshine plentiful. The climate is perfect for winemaking. But for Bolgheri to become the wine Mecca of Italy, more was needed than what nature had given. The human factor has been important too: in this case in the shape of Mario Incisa della Rochetta, who planted new vineyards in the late 1960s, revolutionary because they grew Bordeaux vines (Cabernet Sauvignon and Cabernet Franc). The resulting wine, created by strictly limited yields, a long ageing process, and the exclusive use of oak casks, was known as Bolgheri Sassicaia, and soon became world-renowned, gaining DOC status in 1984.

The next stage of the revolution was Tignanello, a wine first produced by Antinori in 1971. A blend of noble French varieties with Sangiovese, it has never been admitted to the the DOC category, and is sold as IGT (indicazione geografica tipica). Robert Parker's coining of the term 'Supertuscan', however, has contributed to its standing as one of the most prestigious red wines in Italy.

SAN GALGANO & ENVIRONS

The ruined Abbey of San Galgano (*map p. 266, C2*) is one of the most spectacular sights in all Italy (*open all day; in order not to disturb the extraordinary atmosphere, visitors are asked to use the large car park, discreetly hidden from sight a few hundred metres away*). It has survived, abandoned and roofless, for centuries in majestic isolation in the middle of beautiful farming country—in some ways one has the impression of coming unexpectedly on a ruined Greek temple. It was once the church of a powerful monastery, built by the Cistercians of Casamari (*see p. 220*) around 1224–88, in honour of St Galganus (*see below*). Its monks often ruled over disputes between cities such as Siena and Volterra, and they also supervised the building of Siena cathedral.

The 'Excalibur' of San Galgano.

In the 16th century, after a period of decline and corrupt administration, the abbot sold the lead from the church roof, which later collapsed. The buildings were subsequently abandoned and the church deconsecrated. Nevertheless, it has survived extraordinarily well, the walls built of beautifully cut regular stones reaching right up to the roofline, now open to the sky. It recalls numerous other such romantic ruins depicted in prints and paintings of the 18th and 19th centuries; but very few of those survive today in Italy. Its majestic proportions are modelled on the French Cistercian mother-house of Cîteaux in Burgundy (*Cistervium* in Latin), with a characteristic flat east end (rather than an apse). The hanging half-columns which reach up to the arches above windows framing the sky in the upper storey are particularly beautiful. The simple capitals have stylised leaves or flowers, and numerous birds inhabit the nooks and crannies. The quaint altar survives.

The chapter house has a fine vaulted ceiling divided into two parts by low columns. Above it can be seen the windows of the 16 little cells where the monks lived, next to their chapel. Only a fragment of the cloister survives. The little rectangular detached cemetery chapel also dates from the 13th century.

Chapel of San Galgano

Close by, on the little hill of Monte Siepi, is the Chapel of San Galgano (*approached by a short path from the abbey; open all day; the custodian lives next door*). It was built in 1182 over the tomb of St Galganus (Galgano Guidotti, 1148–81, canonised in 1185). Galgano was born of noble parentage in Chiusdino, but a vision of the Archangel Michael persuaded him to abandon a life of ease to become a Cistercian monk. He spent his last years living as a hermit on this hill, where he built a chapel. The little circular edifice is unique since the exterior is built in stone to a height of 4m and then in alternate bands of stone and brick. This decoration is repeated to greater effect in the interior, where the concentric rings of red brick and white travertine cover the conical cupola. They produce a curious effect of spaciousness, and the slightly irregular rings near the centre make it all the more impressive. A sword dramatically piercing a stone (now protected) commemorates St Galganus' renunciation of knightly pursuits in favour of a life of prayer before the Cross. He is said to have been found dead on his knees before this very sword, about which much controversy has grown up. Historians have claimed that King Arthur and his sword *Excalibur* had a Tuscan, and not a British, origin

The adjoining chapel (*door unlocked; coin-operated light essential*) was added around 1344, when it was frescoed by Ambrogio Lorenzetti and his workshop. In the central lunette is the *Virgin in Majesty*, adored by saints and angels (one holding a huge basket, apparently full of flowers), with the unusual figure of Eve reclining in the foreground. Below, divided by the window, are the *Virgin* and *Angel Gabriel*; it is interesting to note the differences in composition between the frescoes and *sinopie*, which have been detached and hung on the adjacent wall. On the left wall are scenes from the life of St Galganus: the *Saint Conducted to Heaven* and his *Vision of St Michael in Rome* (including a depiction of the sword in the stone).

Chiusdino and Bagni di Petriolo

West of San Galgano, in beautiful countryside, is **Chiusdino** (*map p. 266, C2*), birthplace of St Galganus. It is a typical hilltop village, with a cluster of grey stone houses on narrow, steep and winding streets. In a picturesque little piazza is the Chapel of the Compagnia, with a relief of *St Galganus* by Urbano da Cortona (dated 1466) over the door. Nearby is St Galganus' house, with horizontal bands of brick decorating the façade, and the copy of another relief by Giovanni di Agostino showing the Saint in a wood. The original relief and a *Madonna and Child* by Niccolò di Segna (1336), together with 12th–13th-century liturgical objects, are kept in the nearby Casa Parocchiale. At no. 2 Via Mascagni is a small museum dedicated to the Cetine mines, with photographs, implements and objects relating to the mining industry in the surrounding hills.

Bagni di Petriolo to the southeast on the River Farma (*map p. 266, C2*) is a rare example of a medieval fortified spa. A little loggia on the edge of the river, a chapel and parts of peripheral 15th-century walls still survive from the time when Pope Pius II came here to benefit from the sulphurous spring water. The modern baths are open in summer on weekdays (*6.30–1.30 & 3.30–8*).

THE MAREMMA

The name Maremma was originally given to the marshy coastal plain which stretched all the way from Pisa to Grosseto and beyond and included the metalliferous hills inland, but is now usually confined to the area around Grosseto (*map p. 266, C4*).

HISTORY OF THE MAREMMA

The numerous rivers and streams attracted settlements long before the Etruscans, who arrived in the 8th century BC and founded the cities of Vetulonia, Populonia, Marsiliana and Roselle. Necropoleis, traces of houses and remains of walls are a constant and evocative presence. Following the destruction of the Etruscan settlements and their colonisation by the Romans, the population declined and canals and land were neglected. The few inhabitants withdrew to the towns and villages in the hills. In the early Middle Ages, the area came under the dominion of the Aldobrandeschi family and other feudal lords, who erected strongholds in defence against attacks, mostly from Siena and Orvieto.

From the 13th century onwards, sieges, conflicts, pirate raids and malaria caused destruction and depopulation, until the final capitulation to Sienese rule. In 1555, Siena in turn fell to the Medici of Florence, becoming part of the Grand Duchy of Tuscany. The Florentines had won the battle with help from the imperial Spanish forces in the command of Charles V. Two years later, his son, Philip II of Spain, gave Siena in fief to Florence, retaining for Spain only the coastal areas, which he provided with impressive fortifications (these can still be seen at Orbetello and Porto Ercole). The poverty was such that many villages were all but totally abandoned. Reforms did not begin until the 19th century under the Lorraine grand duke Leopold II, who drained the marshes, promoted an agricultural programme and introduced a few industries. However, it was only in the 20th century, after the First World War, with the introduction of industries along the railway and the building of the aqueduct which supplied water from the Fiora river to the Argentario, that modernisation was achieved. Since the late 20th century, there has been a real transformation in the standard of living.

GROSSETO & ENVIRONS

Grosseto is the lively chief town (pop. 72,000; *map p. 266, C4*) and provincial capital of the Tuscan Maremma, in a rich agricultural zone. Although a lot of new building has taken place on the surrounding plain, the old centre has been repaved and reserved for pedestrians, and is still surrounded by the ramparts built by the Medici in the late 16th century (today surmounted by a pleasant broad path and gardens). The rebuilt cathedral retains some 14th-century sculptures on the exterior, and in the church of San Francesco there is a large painted Crucifix attributed to Duccio, an early work strongly influenced by Cimabue. The **museum** (*open Tues–Fri 8.30–2; Sat and Sun 9.30–1 & 4.30–7; closed Mon and sometimes Sun*) is extremely well displayed with a large archaeological collection founded in 1860, with objects ranging from prehistoric to the Etruscan and Roman eras. The exhibits which document the history of the Etruscan and Roman city of Roselle include monumental statues of Claudius and his family. The

diocesan museum on the top floor is interesting for its early Sienese paintings, including a *Last Judgement* by Guido da Siena.

Northeast of Grosseto are the excavations of **Roselle** (*map p. 266, C3; open 8.30–dusk*), which was one of the most important Etruscan cities in northern Etruria. Probably founded in the 7th century BC on the southeastern side of Lake Prile, it came under Roman dominion in 294 BC, and most of its major buildings were erected in the Imperial era. A bishopric was founded here in the Middle Ages, but in 935 it was pillaged by the Saracens, and abandoned after 1138, when it became a quarry for the nearby villages. Near the site entrance is a stretch of impressive cyclopean walls (6th century BC), reaching 5m in height, which once had a circumference of 3km. The ruins include the area of the Roman forum, a house with mosaic floors, paved streets, and the amphitheatre, 37m by 27m, with four entrances, in *opus reticulatum* dating from the 1st century AD.

Vetulonia

The little hill-top town of Vetulonia, northwest of Grosseto (*map p. 266, B3*), with splendid views, is built on the site of one of the richest and most flourishing of Etruscan cities. It has several necropoleis, with the earliest tombs dating from the late 9th century BC. The period of greatest prosperity was from the 8th–7th centuries BC, and the numerous tombs excavated at the end of the last century, some of them outstanding in size, were particularly rich in terracotta vases and objects in bronze, silver and gold (*archaeological areas and tombs open daily 8–5; summer 10–7*). There is also an excellent museum (*open daily except Mon 10–1 & 3–6*) with finds from the area.

The Romans defeated the Gauls here in 224 BC, and are said to have borrowed from Vetulonia the insignia of their magistrates—the fasces, curule chair, and toga praetexta—and the use of the brazen trumpet in war.

Resorts of the Maremma

Castiglione della Pescaia (*map p. 266, B4*) is the best known and most attractive resort on the Maremma coast. It is very crowded in summer, but extremely pleasant in other seasons. Its small harbour, which was strategically important in Etruscan and Roman times, is now crowded with yachts. The Medici grand duke Ferdinando I rebuilt its walls, still well-preserved, in 1608 around the earlier Spanish fort overlooking the harbour. The Pineta del Tombolo to the south is an extensive wood of umbrella pines, totally preserved from buildings, which skirts the low dunes along an extensive sandy beach, accessible only by footpaths (in less than 10mins) off the road.

The most beautiful stretch of coastline, and the best places to bathe, are just north of the Alma river in the sandy bays of **Cala Martina** and **Cala Violina** (*map p. 266, B3*). They can only be reached on foot by paths (in about 30mins) through beautiful woods, from a car park approached off the coast road. There is a **nature reserve** (Diaccia Botrona) with exceptionally interesting birdlife and lovely walks in the marshes on the site of the Lake Prile, the salt lake of Etruscan and Roman times which gave access to the harbours of Vetulonia and Roselle. There is a visitors' centre and museum—excellent on the local fauna and flora—at the restored Casa Rossa (approached from the bridge over the Bruna river at Castiglione; *open at weekends*). This interesting building in brick and travertine, with three arched sluices, was designed in 1767 by Leonardo Ximenes, a Spanish Jesuit and an expert in hydraulics, for Grand Duke Peter Leopold. It was part of one of the earliest projects to reclaim the Grosseto plain, and it served as a dam to control the waters between the Ombrone and Bruna rivers. The bridge was added in the 1830s. The marshes here are on migratory routes, and from November to February birdwatchers can often see geese, spoonbills, waders, widgeon, teal, shellduck, pintails and numerous other birds. There are marked walks from here and also from Ponte di Badia (off the road between Castiglione and Grosseto) near a hillock, formerly a small island in the lake, and still known as the **Isola Clodia**, which has the crumbling ruins of two walls of a Benedictine monastery, built on the site of a Roman villa.

ALBERESE & THE COAST

Alberese (*map p. 266, C4*) is a small, pleasant village built on a spacious plan in 1951 near the northern entrance to the Parco Naturale della Maremma (*see box opposite*). North of the village, a road leads to the coast past farms where the Maremma white long-horned cattle are grazed, and then through pinewoods to **Marina di Alberese**, a beach with a car park. This unspoilt stretch of coast (although suffering from erosion) with sand dunes, and backed by thick pinewoods planted in the mid-19th century, begins at the estuary of the Ombrone river (the Classical *Umbro*, one of the chief rivers of Etruria). This marks the northern limit of the park, which stretches south across the beautiful wooded and roadless Monti dell'Uccellina (417m) to Talamone. The 15km of coastline here are perhaps the best preserved in all Italy.

On the right bank of the Ombrone is the remarkably well preserved **Palude della Trappola**, a marsh area and bird sanctuary. The beach extends south as far as Cala di Forno, at the foot of the Monti dell'Uccellina, where there are natural grottoes. Farther on, the rocky slopes of the Uccellina plunge straight into the sea: here the beautiful coastline and distinctive vegetation, which includes dwarf palm trees, can only be seen from the sea.

Talamone (*map p. 266, C4*) is a now a summer resort. The original Etruscan city and port, said to have been founded c. 1300 BC by the Argonaut Telamon, stood on the south side of the bay, but was abandoned for its present position by the Romans in the Imperial era. The medieval town developed on the rocky promontory overlooking the bay, and in the 14th century Talamone became the port for Siena. Garibaldi and the Thousand put in here on their way to Sicily in 1860, to collect arms and ammunition and to land a party for a feigned attack on the Papal States.

The picturesque harbour, with yachts and fishing boats at their moorings, lies at the foot of the steep village. Although damaged in the Second World War, Talamone retains its charm, and the walk up along the walls to the Rocca offers splendid views of the Argentario peninsula and the island of Giglio. The 15th-century Rocca, an impressive block-like construction with tower, was rebuilt by the Sienese on the site of an Aldobrandeschi family castle.

PARCO NATURALE DELLA MAREMMA

Tickets must be purchased at the information office in Alberese. A bus leaves on the hour every hour (9–dusk) on Wed, Sat, and Sun (numbers are limited during the summer months) for the park entrance (10mins), from which various itineraries are indicated along marked footpaths (most of them require a minimum of 3hrs; children welcome).

The Parco Naturale della Maremma, a coastal area of some 70km square just south of Grosseto, was designated a national park in 1975. Its vegetation varies from woods of pine trees, ilexes, elms, and oaks to marshlands, and the typical Mediterranean *macchia* of myrtle and juniper. Wild animals include the famous white long-horned cattle, deer, foxes, goats, wild cats, horses, and wild boar. The cattle and horses are herded by cowboys known as *butteri* (rodeo at Alberese in August). Migratory birds and numerous aquatic species abound.

Behind the church of Alberese is the entrance (*pedestrians only; open daily*) to the Itinerario Faunistico, a beautiful walk of less than an hour through a protected area, where deer and other wild animals can usually be seen.

The Monti dell'Uccellina offer splendid views and walks through a natural setting of great variety and beauty, with a few towers and romantic ruins. The Torre della Bella Marsilia is the lonely remnant of the castle of Collecchio, home of the Marsili family of Siena. In 1543 the castle was destroyed by the corsair Kheir ed-Din Barbarossa, and the entire household was murdered except for the lovely Margherita, who was carried off to the harem of Sultan Suleiman the Magnificent. She became his legitimate sultana and the mother of Selim II. Nearby are the ruins of San Rabano, an 11th-century Benedictine abbey later occupied by the Knights of St John of Jerusalem. The apse of the Romanesque church survives in part with some of its original decoration. The octagonal dome was probably a 14th-century addition and the tall tower is still standing. The towers of Castelmarino and Collelungo are near some natural caves, facing onto the beach. The walk to Cala di Forno and its tower, at the far end of the beach, ends in a charming little bay.

There is another entrance to the park at Fonteblanda, near Talamone on its southern boundary, where the walks are especially beautiful towards sunset.

Monte Argentario and Isola del Giglio

The Monte Argentario peninsula (*map p. 166, A2*) is mostly an exclusive residential area with numerous elegant holiday villas hidden in luxuriant vegetation, owned by some of the wealthiest Italians in the public eye. There are also two ports: Porto Santo Stefano, where a great many new, undistinguished buildings were erected in the 20th century, and the smaller and more attractive **Porto Ercole**, where Caravaggio landed on his way back from exile in Malta (*see p. 50*), and where he caught the malaria which killed him. Both are inhabited all year round but are particularly busy in summer, when their harbours are filled with yachts. They have impressive remains of their Spanish fortifications.

Parts of the hilly promontory are still thickly wooded with ilexes and oaks, and the luxuriant and unusual flora, including wild orchids and dwarf palm trees, includes a great variety of wild flowers in spring. The scenery is best seen from the sea, however, as there are few paths and very few beaches, and the narrow roads are busy in summer. The road which climbs to the top of Monte Telegrafo (635m) passes the mother-house of the Passionist Order, founded by St Paul of the Cross (Paolo Danei, 1694–1775).

The promontory is connected to the mainland by three narrow sand bars (or *tomboli*) which enclose a lagoon which is a bird sanctuary for some 200 species, since the mild climate of the promontory is ideal for the winter quarters of numerous migratory birds. It is protected by the World Wide Fund for Nature (*guided tours in winter*). The Tombolo di Giannella (where there are some campsites) and the Tombolo di Feniglia both have extensive beaches. The **Bosco di Patanella** is a beautiful pinewood on the lagoon, and pines were also planted in the 20th century on Feniglia, which is now one of the most beautiful wooded stretches along this coast, and a protected area with a lovely footpath.

The pretty **Isola del Giglio** (*map p. 4*) is reached by regular boat service from Porto Santo Stefano. It has an area of 21km square and a little grey granite fortess-village, vineyards, and a sandy beach. The island is crowded at weekends in summer, and new buildings are spoiling its natural beauty, although about half of the island has been protected since 1996 as part of the Parco Nazionale dell'Arcipelago Toscano.

Orbetello and Ansedonia

Orbetello (*map p. 166, A2*), in the centre of the lagoon, was once the most important harbour south of Livorno and it became the capital of the *Stato dei Presidi* (or garrison state), comprising Ansedonia, Porto Ercole, Porto Santo Stefano and Talamone along the Maremma coast, which came under the control of Philip II of Spain (*see p. 472 above*). After the War of the Spanish Succession in the early 18th century, the area passed to the Empire of Austria, and was part of Napoleon's Kingdom of Etruria in the early 19th century. All these coastal towns were incorporated into the Grand Duchy of Tuscany after the Congress of Vienna (1815). Orbetello is now a slightly old-fashioned resort with some remains of the Spanish period in its fortifications and cathedral, and an archaeological museum in a 17th-century ammunition store.

At the southern end of the Orbetello lagoon is the modern, fashionable resort of **Ansedonia** (*map p. 166, A2*), with elegant villas surrounded by pines and oak trees on the slopes of a beautiful promontory. Extending south was a lagoon rich in fish, separated from the sea by sand dunes, with a canal leading to a deep natural passage, 260m long, linking it to the sea. This passage provided for the ebb and flow of the tides and prevented the harbour from silting up. When parts of the passage collapsed in Roman times causing it to block up, another shorter passage, the *Tagliata*, was cut through the cliffs nearer the harbour. The hewing out of this passage, with walls some 15–20m high and other parts tunnelled through the rock, was an amazing feat, and it was also engineered to control the waters and the catching and farming of fish. There are steps and a walkway on the cliffs from which you can see it. Some remains of the Roman harbour are still visible in the little bay.

On the top of the hill are the excavated ruins of the **Roman town of** *Cosa*, which extend over a considerable area amidst magnificent olive trees and ilexes (*open daily 9–sunset*). The area was first settled in prehistoric times, and then by the Etruscans, and by the 2nd century Cosa was a flourishing Roman town: its capitol and two temples in the forum, as well as the city gates and walls, are still partially preserved. The little archaeological museum contains interesting pieces of sculpture, terracotta ornaments from the temples, pottery, oil jars, glass, bronze objects and coins.

The lovely bird sanctuary of the **Lago di Burano** is a marshy lagoon administered by the Word Wide Fund for Nature (*open Sept–April for guided tours of 2–3hrs on Sun at 10 and 2.30*). There is a fine beach at Chiarone.

Capalbio and Pescia Fiorentina

Inland, at the southernmost end of Tuscany, is **Capalbio** (*map p. 166, A1*), a charming little medieval village, now fashionable amongst wealthy Italians as an exclusive summer resort. It is in a beautiful position on a low hill above thick ilex, cork and oak woods, in the centre of a game reserve. The area is famous for its wild boar. The double circle of medieval walls and the entrance gateway and tower are well preserved. The castle has a tall tower which dominates the village. The streets are picturesque and there are charming views from the walkways above the walls overlooking houses and gardens. Domenico Tiburzi, the most famous brigand of the Maremma, died here.

At **Pescia Fiorentina**, to the east, on the border with Lazio (*map p. 166, B2*), an old iron foundry survives, of great interest to industrial archaeologists. It also has a modern sculpture garden known as the Giardino dei Tarocchi (*open April–mid-Oct 2.30–7.30; otherwise T: 0564 895122*) containing gigantic compositions of glass, ceramics and coloured enamels by Niki de Saint-Phalle.

PITIGLIANO & THE SOUTHEAST

In the southeastern corner of Tuscany, near the border with Lazio, the area around Pitigliano and Saturnia (*map p. 267, D4*) is of great natural beauty. The landscape is immensely varied: at times dramatic and austere, at others inviting and serene. Dense woods and coppices alternate with rolling hills and fertile valleys scattered with farmhouses. Characteristic are the ruined castles and hilltop villages, built out of the underlying rock or stone, many of them still enclosed in their medieval walls. Important Etruscan necropoleis have been found in the area, and excavations continue. The finds are exhibited in the local museums of Pitigliano, Manciano and Scansano. The area is known for its excellent wines.

PITIGLIANO

Pitigliano is spectacularly sited on a rocky spur overlooking a gorge on all sides, excavated by three torrents. The approach across the plateau from the west is the most dramatic: the town comes into view unexpectedly at a turn, spread out along a ridge parallel to the road, its houses more or less the same colour as the tufa rock on which it is built, and the fields at its foot untouched by new buildings. It is especially dramatic in the morning light. The town is still a lively place, and the inhabitants make use of the tufa rock (once used for storing produce) for garages and workshops.

Etruscan in origin, Pitigliano later came under Roman rule and was subsequently a feud of the Aldobrandeschi family of Sovana. In 1293 it passed by marriage to the Orsini. It became part of the Grand Duchy of Tuscany in 1608, and the Lorraine grand duke Peter Leopold restored the town in the late 18th century and built the bridge over the Meleta. It suffered damage from an air raid in June 1944.

At the entrance to the town is the impressive arched aqueduct, built in 1545 by Gian Francesco Orsini, who also commissioned Giuliano da Sangallo to enlarge the 13th-century castle in order to provide him with a suitable Renaissance palace. Sangallo added the fine entrance doorway and the unusual little paved courtyard with some pretty columns in the centre of the building, with a well bearing the family arms. It now houses a **museum** (*open 10–1 & 3–5/7; closed Mon*) with a miscellany of works of art including two altarpieces by Francesco Zuccarelli (1702–88), who was born here. Fragments of a frescoed frieze show members of the Orsini family together with famous historical figures. There is also a small archaeological museum (*at present closed*) with some fine Etruscan pottery from the nearby necropoleis of Poggio Buco. The palace faces Piazza della Repubblica, where the aqueduct has a pretty arch framing the view. A terrace overlooks the remarkable landscape, rich in water, with its torrents and waterfalls.

Via Zuccarelli and the duomo

Of the three peaceful parallel medieval streets of the town, the prettiest is **Via Zuccarelli**, which has many old houses with outside staircases decorated with plants (all the little shops are concentrated in Via Roma). It runs past an old low archway which descends to the entrance to the old **Jewish enclave**, now preserved as a museum (*open 10–12.30 & 3–5.30/6; summer 10–12.30 & 3.30–6.30; closed Sat*). Under the protection of the Medici, a Jewish colony was established here as early as 1570, and the synagogue had been built by the end of the next decade: there were still 424 Jewish residents registered in the town in the mid-19th century. A ritual bath, an oven used at Passover for baking unleavened bread, a Kosher wine cellar and slaughter-house, all carved out of the tufa rock, can be seen, as well as the synagogue, which was carefully rebuilt after it collapsed in the 1960s.

A remarkable old stepped passageway leads up from here to the **duomo**, which has a rather primitive Baroque facade and massive bell-tower. In the piazza there is a quaint monument erected in 1490 to celebrate the Orsini family (the bear, or *orso* is the family emblem). Via Roma and Via Zuccarelli converge at the charming little Renaissance church of **Santa Maria**, which was given its very unusual trapezoidal ground-plan in order to fit the site. It has a pretty façade above a little wall fountain. The houses in this peaceful corner of the little town are particularly attractive, and the terrace on the edge of the rock has another wonderful view.

Poggio Sterzoni

Outside the town, near the ruins of the monastery of San Francesco, on the road to Sorano, is a gateway which formed the entrance to Poggio Sterzoni (*map p. 267, D4*), once a famous park, similar to that of Bomarzo in Lazio (*see p. 176*), with gigantic sculptures of monsters and animals. It is now a wilderness containing remains of carved statues, steps and niches carved out of the tufa rock.

SOVANA & SORANO

Sovana (*map p. 267, D4*) is a village with just a single brick-paved street running from the castle ruins to the cathedral. It is in a beautiful position on a ridge overlooking a wide panorama. An important Etruscan settlement and later a Roman *municipium*, its period of greatest importance was in the 13th century, when it was the seat of the Sovana branch of the Aldobrandeschi family. Attempts to repopulate the village when under Medici rule were doomed on account of malaria. Today it is mainly given over to the reception of tourists, but nonetheless has several monuments of interest.

Near the ruins of the Aldobrandeschi castle (13th–14th century) are remains of the **Etruscan walls**. The street, with herring-bone paving, runs through the little piazza. In the pretty interior of the church of **Santa Maria Maggiore** there is a beautiful marble ciborium dating from the 9th century, unique in Tuscany. Four slender columns with elaborate capitals support the baldacchino with an octagonal pointed roof.

At the end of the village is the Romanesque **cathedral** (*open 10–1 & 2.30–6/7; in summer open all day*). The original church was probably begun during the papacy of Gregory VII, but its present structure is thought to date from the 12th–13th century. The doorway on the south side, probably removed from the façade and put together with pre-Romanesque fragments, is decorated with stylised figures, animals and plants. The interior is extremely beautiful, with exceptionally wide arches and a lovely east end with a semicircular apse and polygonal dome, all of which give it a remarkable sense of space. Compound piers divide the nave from the aisles and some of the capitals are finely carved, several of them with biblical scenes. In the right aisle a 15th-century urn, possibly Sienese, has a carved image of St Mamilianus, whose body it contains. He was long venerated as the evangeliser of the district in the 6th century. The small crypt (11th century), with six simple columns, preserves his charmingly displayed relics.

Just outside Sovana are many interesting **Etruscan necropoleis** (*well signposted; maps obtainable locally*), mostly rock tombs of the 3rd–2nd centuries BC, which were first excavated by George Dennis in 1844. Some, of impressive dimensions among thick vegetation, are easily accessible from the road, such as the arched niche of the Tomba della Sirena (*map p. 267, D4; open 10–5; until 7 in summer*). From the small car park, you cross a stream to reach the area of the tombs, carved into the tufa in a manner similar to those at Norchia and Castel d'Asso (*see p. 172*). The major tombs have sign-boards. A little further on, on the other side of the road, is the entrance to the temple-shaped Tomb of Hildebrand (Tomba Ildebranda; *open as above*), magnificent-

ly preserved, with the sepulchral chamber intact under the temple superstructure. Both this and the other complex of tombs were accessed in ancient times by the famous *Vie Cave*, narrow roadways carved deep into the rock, still preserved, and extraordinarily atmospheric. Debate continues as to whether these were drovers' routes or sacred ways linking the cities of the dead.

Sorano

Sorano (*map p. 267, D4*) has a similar site to Pitigliano, and the approach from Sovana, passing the Etruscan rock tombs, is particularly spectacular. From its spacious main piazza, an archway leads into the little medieval town, with picturesque old houses built on the ridge, a few of which have been abandoned and left to crumble into ruins. There are lovely little terraces with splendid views over the unspoilt countryside. Most of the streets are too narrow for cars, and all of them are worth exploring. Above the

Worn figure and Etruscan inscription at the Tomba della Sirena outside Sovana.

town towers the old Orsini fortress (*at present closed*). Another Orsini castle, built in 1552, and a fine example of Renaissance military architecture, on a higher hill on the south side of the town, now partly used as a hotel, can be visited from the outside.

SATURNIA & ENVIRONS

The village of **Saturnia** (*map p. 267, D4*), west of Pitigliano and Sovana, is built on a travertine spur overlooking the Albegna valley. It was an Etruscan town of some importance. In the 3rd century BC it became a Roman colony. The Porta Romana (through which ran the Via Clodia) and the adjacent walls are well preserved (the arch is medieval). There are remains of foundations and floors in the village from the

2nd–1st centuries BC. In 1299 Saturnia was sacked by the Sienese, who later built the fortifications.

The **Terme di Saturnia** is a spa of sulphurous water (37°C), known since Roman times. Nearby are the Cascate del Gorello next to an old mill, where hot water falls in cascades over whitened rocks, creating natural pools. This uniquely beautiful spot has unfortunately suffered from neglect, and the waters have been partially diverted.

Montemerano and Scansano

Montemerano (*map p. 267, D4*) is a picturesque walled village on a hill of ancient olive trees, with charming vistas. On the north side of the hill is a gateway, opening onto a beautiful view, and part of the old walls enclosing a small piazza with the church of San Giorgio with a simple late 14th-century stone façade. It contains a monumental polyptych by Sano di Pietro of 1458, complete with its predella and pinnacles; a painted wooden statue of *St Peter* by Vecchietta; a *Virgin of the Annunciation* by the Master of Montemerano; and a carved relief of the *Assumption* attributed to Vecchietta.

Scansano (*map p. 266, C4*) is an agricultural town with a well-preserved medieval district at its centre. Today it is well-known for its red wine, Morellino di Scansano. From the path which skirts the outside of the walls, overlooking the countryside, there is a striking view of the tower and apse of the church of San Giovanni Battista, soaring high above the walls. There is a small archaeological museum, with a section devoted to the history of wine-making.

Magliano in Toscana

Magliano in Toscana (*map p. 266, C4*) has splendid 14th- and 15th-century fortifications with seven semicircular towers and three gates. Outside the walls is the church of the Annunziata, in which there is a charming *Madonna and Child* by Neroccio, unfortunately cut out of a larger altarpiece. In the olive grove beyond the church is the ancient, gnarled 'witch's olive tree', alleged to be well over a thousand years old.

Outside the town, just past the cemetery, a by-road (signposted for Sant' Andrea) leads to the imposing ruins of the 11th-century church of **San Bruzio** (*map p. 266, C4*), among olive trees. Originally the church of a Benedictine monastery, now only the apse and the great arches opening towards the transepts and nave survive. There are beautifully carved capitals supporting the arches, on which rests an octagonal drum with squinches, open to the sky. The force conveyed by the structure and the luminous quality of the stone enhance the romantic effect of this extraordinarily beautiful ruin.

THE ISLAND OF ELBA

Elba (*map p. 266, inset; for its position relative to the mainland, see overview map on p. 4*) is the largest island (223km square) in the Tuscan archipelago, and is only 10km from Piombino on the mainland. It has 29,000 inhabitants, and becomes very crowded with holidaymakers in the summer. It has a particularly interesting geological formation, with numerous varieties of minerals; and iron ore was mined here up until the last century. The inhabited part of the island has pretty hills covered with *macchia mediterranea*, while other parts are barren and deserted. The island became famous in 1814–15 as Napoleon's place of exile, and the two villas where he passed his time can be visited: one is in Portoferraio, but Villa San Martino nearby is more interesting. The most attractive place on the island is the little fishing port of Marciana Marina near the scenic Monte Capanne (1019m), covered with chestnut, oak and ilex woods. The resort of Porto Azzurro overlooks a beautiful bay in the eastern part of the island. Some of the loveliest scenery can be seen on the road from Bagnaia (east of Portoferraio) to Rio nell'Elba, where there is a mineral museum. Another scenic road, the Volterraio, leads from Ottone to Rio nell'Elba.

The Parco Nazionale dell'Arcipelago Toscano includes the small islands of Gorgona, Pianosa, Montecristo and Giannutri, half of Elba and Giglio, and most of Capraia (for detail on all these, see *Blue Guide Tuscany*). Migratory birds (including shearwaters, shags, Adouin's gulls and herring gulls) visit the islands, and many nest here.

PRACTICAL INFORMATION

GETTING AROUND

• **By car:** Car parking in **Massa Marittima** is only possible outside the old town. In **Grosseto** you can park outside the ramparts.
• **By train:** **Grosseto** is on the main Pisa–Rome line (services to and from Pisa in 90mins). Slow trains from Grosseto and Pisa go to Follonica, 17km southwest of **Massa Marittima**. Slow trains on the same Pisa–Rome line also stop at **Orbetello** Scalo.
• **By bus:** Buses link Follonica, where there is a railway station, with **Massa Marittima** and **Orbetello**. Massa Marittima is also on bus routes from Grosseto and Volterra. **Grosseto** has good local bus networks to most places in the region, including Alberese, Saturnia and Pitigliano. It is also on a route from Siena.
• **By sea:** The main port for **Elba** is

Piombino, with offices of the two main shipping companies (Mobylines and Torremar) at Piazzale Premuda 13, www.mobylines.it and www.torremar.it. On Elba the offices are in Portoferraio (Calata Italia 22). Most car ferries and hydrofoils serve Portoferraio. Ferries make the journey in 1hr, hydrofoils in 30mins.

INFORMATION OFFICES

Alberese (for Parco Naturale della Maremma) Centro Visite di Alberese, Via del Bersagliere 7–9, T: 0564 407098, www.parks.it
Castiglione della Pescaia Piazza Garibaldi, T: 0564 933678, www.castiglionepescaia.it
Grosseto Viale Monterosa 206, T: 0564 462611.
Massa Marittima Via Norma Parenti 22, T: 0566 902756.

Orbetello Piazza della Repubblica, T: 0564 860447.

HOTELS

Castiglione della Pescaia (*map p. 266, B4*)
€ **Piccolo**. ■ Family-run hotel by the sea offering warm hospitality, splendid food, and an ideal environment to relax. Open May–Oct. *Via Montecristo 7, T: 0564 937081, www.hotel-castiglione.com*
Massa Marittima (*map p. 266, B3*)
€ **La Fenice Park Hotel**. Very pleasant small hotel in a 19th-century house. Nicely decorated rooms. Swimming pool. *Corso Diaz 63, T: 0566 903941, www.lafeniceparkhotel.it. 18 rooms.*
San Galgano (*map p. 266, C2*)
€ **Cooperativa Agricola San Galgano**. A pleasant *agriturismo* close to the abbey; there are lovely views across to the ruins. The rooms are simple yet comfortable and there is also a restaurant for breakfast and lunch. *San Galgano Chiusdino, T: 0577 751041 or 0577 756292, www.sangalgano.it. 12 rooms.*
Sorano (*map p. 267, D4*)
€€ **Hotel della Fortezza**. The hotel occupies part of the Castello Orsini, with high-ceilinged rooms commanding magnificent views down into town. Closed 8 Jan–1 March. *Piazza Cairoli 5, T: 0564 632010, www.hoteldellafortezza.it. 15 rooms.*
€€ **Terme di Sorano**. Spa resort well located for the lovely hill towns and Etruscan and Roman sites in the area. A luxurious place to stay (two nights minimum). Closed Jan. *Località S. Maria dell'Aquila, T: 0564 633306, www.termedisorano.it. 6 apartments.*
Sovana (*map p. 267, D4*)
€€ **Sovana Romantik Hotel &**

Resort. Despite the soppy name, this is a stylish hotel: a converted farmhouse situated in a large olive grove with a wide range of sporting and leisure activities on offer. It has a beautiful view of the Romanesque cathedral and is in an ideal situation to explore the nearby Etruscan and Roman sites. Good restaurant. *Via del Duomo 65, T: 0564 617030, www.sovanahotel.it. 18 rooms.*
€ **Hotel Scilla**. A newly renovated hotel which is very comfortable with open fires, traditional furnishings and a cosy feel. There is a pretty garden and restaurant. *Via del Duomo 5, T: 0564 616531, www.scilla-sovana.it. 15 rooms.*

RESTAURANTS

Grosseto (*map p. 266, C4*)
€€ **Gli Attortellati**. ■ On the road between Grosseto and Principina a Mare, it takes perseverance to find but is well worth it. Run by a farming family, serving superbly imaginative succulent dishes (not vegetarian), this self-styled *ristorante rurale* is a great culinary experience, and is reassuringly packed with locals. All is extremely good value, and you will be offered at least ten courses. Be sure to book. *Strada Provinciale Trappola 39, T: 0564 400059.*
€ **Casotto dei Pescatori**. Large restaurant and pizzeria, reasonably priced and popular with locals, specialising in fish. Situated at a group of houses on one of the secondary roads from Grosseto to Marina di Grosseto. Closed Mon. *Località Casotto dei Pescatori, T: 0564 404025.*
Massa Marittima (*map p. 266, B3*)
€ **Osteria San Cerbone**. ■ Excellent, friendly place serving high quality local

fare at unbeatable prices. Very close to the duomo. Closed Mon and Tues in winter. *Via Butigni 6, T: 0566 902335.*

€ **Osteria da Tronco**. A lively *osteria*, on two levels, in an old building with natural stone walls and brick arcades. Local cooking: try the huntsman's stew—hearty and filling. Closed Wed. *Vicola Porte 5, T: 0566 901991.*

€ **Taverna del Vecchio Borgo**. A husband and wife team run this lovely restaurant in, as the name suggests, the old town. The traditional soup (onions, tomatoes, celery simmered in chicken stock and poured over stale bread) is delicious. Booking advised. *Closed Mon. Via Parenti 12, T: 0566 903950.*

Montemerano (*map p. 267, D4*)

€€€€ **Da Caino**. An outstanding restaurant. Chef Valeria Piccini uses only the finest ingredients, from the seasonal vegetables to the hand-raised lamb, which she roasts with a confit of garlic. The wine cellar is under the supervision of Valeria's husband, and he will guide your choice. There's a relaxed atmosphere and it well deserves its Michelin rosettes. *Via Chiesa 4, T: 0564 602817.*

San Vincenzo (*map p. 266, A2*)

€€€€ **Gambero Rosso**. Situated on the sea in this resort town, this restaurant, with its two Michelin rosettes and innovative fish cuisine, is famed as one of the greatest restaurants in all Italy. Closed Mon, Tues and Nov–mid-Jan. *Piazza della Vittoria 13, T: 0565 701021.*

Sorano (*map p. 267, D4*)

€ **Fidalma**. Always very busy but the friendly owners make you feel welcome. The menu focuses on traditional Tuscan food, with plenty of game, *porcini* mushrooms and local truffles. Closed Wed. *Piazza Busatti 5, T: 0564 633056.*

Sovana (*map p. 267, D4*)

€€ **Dei Merli**. Restaurant attached to the Scilla hotel. Two large rooms, one with a view of the duomo, the other looking over the garden. Serves typical cuisine of the Maremma region. Opening times can be capricious; best to phone ahead. *Via del Duomo 5, T: 0564 616531.*

€€ **Locanda della Taverna Etrusca**. Small, elegant restaurant serving imaginative and delicate fare. The *zuppa dell' ortiche,* vegetable and herb (nettle) soup is particularly recommended. There's a small garden for summer dining. Closed Wed. *Piazza del Pretorio 16. T: 0564 616183.*

LOCAL SPECIALITIES

Grosseto A good fish market is open every day and a huge weekly street market is held on Thurs.

Scansano This town is renowned for its Morellino di Scansano, an aromatic Sangiovese wine, while Pitigliano and Sorano are known for their white wines.

Capalbio The speciality here is wild boar.

FESTIVALS & EVENTS

Alberese A livestock rodeo is held every summer, with cattle and horses herded into the village, Aug.

Capalbio Wild boar (*cinghiale*) festival, Sept.

Massa Marittima *Il Girifalco,* Crossbow contest in traditional costume between the various districts of town. Held twice a year, on the feast of St Bernardino (20 May or the following Sun) and second Sun in Aug.

UMBRIA

Umbria lies at the very heart of Italy. It is the only region on the peninsula without a sea coast. Although less well known than its famous neighbour Tuscany, it has some of the most beautiful landscape to be found in the country, as well as some of its most interesting towns. Its capital, Perugia, is a city of great antiquity which has numerous works of art. Gubbio, Spello, Todi and Spoleto remain among the most attractive and best preserved small medieval towns in Italy. Orvieto, with its magnificent cathedral, has perhaps the most spectacular position of all the hill towns. Assisi is world famous not only as the birthplace of St Francis, but as home to some of the finest frescoes of the 13th–14th centuries, by the Florentine artists Cimabue and Giotto, and the Sienese masters Simone Martini and Pietro Lorenzetti.

With an area of 8,456km square, Umbria has a population of only 850,000. The landscape is characterised by hills covered with small silver olive trees, chestnut woods and vineyards. The soil is not particularly rich, and so for centuries the farmers had to cultivate the fields of their smallholdings with extra care. A special feature of Umbria is Lake Trasimene, the fourth largest lake in Italy, with its reedy shores and lovely islands. The River Tiber traverses most of the region: in its upper reaches tobacco is cultivated, while south of Perugia its valley widens out and passes beneath the town of Todi, often covered by a bluish mist off the river.

Umbria takes its name from the Umbri, called *gens antiquissima Italiae* by Pliny the Elder. Of Indo-European origin, they inhabited an area considerably larger than present-day Umbria (including Romagna and part of the Marche). They settled here in prehistoric times and reached their moment of greatest cultural importance around the 5th–4th centuries BC. The seven bronze 'Iguvine Tables' still preserved in Gubbio include the most important known examples of the Umbrian language.

Umbria has a great variety of monuments from all periods of Italian history, including impressive Etruscan remains in Perugia. Prehistoric, Etruscan and Roman finds are displayed in the archaeological museums of Perugia and Orvieto. Indeed, some of the most remarkable Roman monuments north of Rome are to be found in Umbria. These can be seen at Assisi (Temple of Minerva), Narni (the Ponte d'Augusto), Bevagna (a mosaic, a temple and part of a theatre), Spello (several gateways and an amphitheatre), Todi and Spoleto. The ruined Roman towns of *Carsulae* and *Ocriculum* are archaeological sites of the greatest interest.

The Renaissance produced only isolated masterpieces in Umbria, such as the frescoes by Filippo Lippi in the duomo of Spoleto, and those by Luca Signorelli in Orvieto cathedral. The Umbrian school of painting flourished in the 15th–16th centuries. Its greatest exponent was Perugino (c. 1446–1523), whose works can be seen in Perugia (notably in the Collegio del Cambio), Città della Pieve, and other towns. His pupils included Pinturicchio, whose greatest work in the region is in Spello. The best comprehensive view of Umbrian painting is provided by the Pinacoteca Nazionale in Perugia.

PERUGIA

Perugia (pop. 129,000; *map p. 486, B3*), capital of a province which comprises well over half of Umbria, has a booming economy. Disorderly, unattractive suburbs (especially prominent on the approach from Florence and Siena) have spilled onto the hills below the old town since the 1960s. The historic centre, however, keeps its character, and numerous tortuous streets climb up and down the oddly shaped hilly spurs of land on which the town is built. The dark, steep streets of tall houses, some of them provided with characteristic brick and stone steps, provide a striking contrast to the magnificent wide Corso, always full of pedestrians. Perugia has a number of interesting monuments, including the Palazzo dei Priori, where the pinacoteca has a magnificent display of Umbrian art. The famous painter Pietro Vannucci was called 'Perugino' due to his long association with the town, and many works by him survive here, notably in the Collegio del Cambio. Students from all over the world come to Perugia to attend its Università per Stranieri (University for Foreigners); the presence of so many students makes for a particularly lively atmosphere.

HISTORY OF PERUGIA

Perusia was one of the 12 cities of the Etruscan Confederation and its ancient walls of irregular blocks of travertine with seven gates were built probably at the end of the 2nd century BC. It submitted to the Romans under Quintus Fabius in 310 BC. In the civil war between Octavian (Augustus) and Mark Antony, the city burnt to the ground during a siege. Augustus rebuilt it and called it *Augusta Perusia*. In 592 it passed to the Byzantines, and given to the Papal States by Pepin the Short (*see p. 16*). After this, its history is one of obscure and intricate wars with neighbouring towns, in which it generally took the Guelph side.

The first despot was Biordo Michelotti (1393), who murdered two of the noble family of the Baglioni, became leader of the Florentine army, and allied himself with Gian Galeazzo Visconti. The city passed to the latter family, and afterwards to the *condottiere* Braccio Fortebraccio (1416–24), who proved a wise governor. Perugia subsequently suffered from infighting between rival families, until Pope Paul III seized the town in 1535 and built the Rocca Paolina. From then onwards Perugia was ruled by a papal governor.

In 1809 it was annexed to the French Empire, and it was called *Pérouse* by the French; in 1815 it was restored to the Church. In 1859, during the struggle between the Papal States and the Italian nationalists, the papal Swiss Guard occupied the city after an indiscriminate massacre, but a year later they were expelled, and a popular insurrection all but destroyed the Rocca Paolina.

The Rocca Paolina and Corso Vannucci

The fortress known as **Rocca Paolina** (*map p. 491, 7*) was built by Antonio Sangallo the Younger at the command of Paul III to dominate the Perugians who had rebelled against his salt tax. A whole medieval district, including the ruins of the old Baglioni family mansions, was vaulted over to make way for it, but much of it was destroyed by the Perugians in their revolt against papal rule in 1859–60.

The escalators from Piazza Partigiani emerge at a crossing where the subterranean Via Baglioni, an ancient road, descends past remains of medieval and Renaissance dwellings (some built on Etruscan foundations), and the huge brick vaults built by Sangallo to sustain the fortress above. Only some of the buildings, including the 13th-century towers and houses of the Baglioni family, are identified, but the succession of tall scenic vaults and huge shadowy rooms produces a remarkable atmosphere. The area to the right of the road formed part of the defence works of the fortress, with cannon embrasures in the bastions, and huge cisterns for water. The Rocca, used as a daily thoroughfare, has survived well and remains a remarkable sight, reminiscent of a stage set.

Via Baglioni emerges on Via Marzia, beneath the splendid Etruscan **Porta Marzia** (3rd–2nd centuries BC), carefully re-erected in its present position by Sangallo. It is decorated on the external façade by a few worn sculptures in dark stone.

The last flight of escalators ends at the top of the hill by a charming little garden which has a view extending from Monte Amiata to the summits of the central Apennines, with Montefalco, Assisi, Spello, Foligno and Spoleto in the distance. Here begins the exceptionally wide and undulating **Corso Vannucci**, the magnificent centre of the old city, always animated. Its spacious atmosphere is increased by the vista at one end which is open to the sky. Towards the far end of the street, beyond Piazza della Repubblica, is the long curving façade of Palazzo dei Priori.

PALAZZO DEI PRIORI

Palazzo dei Priori (*map p. 490, 6*) is one of the largest and most magnificent town halls in Italy, begun in the late 13th century and finished in 1443. Beneath a high archway runs Via dei Priori, and two old glass doorways on either side of this street give admission to the Collegio del Cambio and the Collegio della Mercanzia, both housed on the ground floor. On the first floor are municipal offices and the council chamber, and on the two upper floors the Galleria Nazionale dell'Umbria. The front on the Corso has castellations above two rows of Gothic three-light windows placed unusually close together.

Collegio del Cambio

The Collegio del Cambio (*open Tues–Sat 9–12.30 & 2.30–5.30; Sun and holidays 9–1*) is the former guildhall of the money-changers, who played an important part in the public administration of the city, and passed judgement in lawsuits concerning financial disputes. It was founded before 1259 and still functions as a charitable institution. Since 1457 it has been housed in these rooms in Palazzo dei Priori.

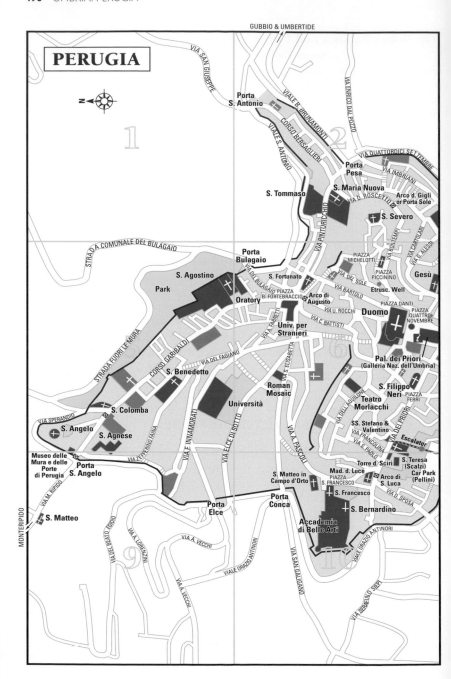

GUBBIO & UMBERTIDE

PERUGIA

N

VIA SAN GIUSEPPE

VIALE B. BRUNAMONTI

VIA ENRICO DAL POZZO

Porta
S. Antonio

CORSO BERSAGLIERI

VIALE S. ANTONIO

VIA QUATTORDICI SETTEMBRE

Porta
Pesa

VIA IMBRIANI

S. Maria Nuova

VIA D. ROSCETTO

Arco d. Gigli
or Porta Sole

S. Tommaso

VIA PINTURICCHIO

VIA BONTEMPI

VIA S. ALESSI

VIA CARTOLARI

S. Severo

STRADA COMUNALE DEL BULAGAIO

PIAZZA
MICHELOTTI

Porta
Bulagaio

VIA DEZ SOLE

PIAZZA
PICCININO

Gesù

S. Agostino

VIA DEL BULAGAIO

S. Fortunato

VIA BARTOLO

Park

PIAZZA
B. FORTEBRACCIO

Arco di
Augusto

Etrusc. Well

STRADA FUORI LE MURA

Oratory

VIA A. FABRETTI

VIA U. ROCCHI

PIAZZA DANTI

Duomo

PIAZZA
QUATTRO
NOVEMBRE

Univ. per
Stranieri

VIA C. BATTISTI

CORSO GARIBALDI

VIA DEL FAGIANO

VIA S. ELISABETTA

Pal. dei Priori
(Galleria Naz. dell'Umbria)

S. Benedetto

Roman
Mosaic

S. Filippo
Neri

PIAZZA
FERRI

S. Colomba

Università

VIA DELL'AQUILONE

Teatro
Morlacchi

VIA SPERANDIO

VIA ZEFFERINO FAINA

VIA INNAMORATI

VIA ELCE DI SOTTO

VIA A. PASCOLI

SS. Stefano &
Valentino

VIA FRANCOLINA

VIA DEI PRIORI

S. Angelo

S. Agnese

VIA S. PAOLO

Escalator

Museo delle
Mura e delle
Porte
di Perugia

Porta
S. Angelo

VIA M. RIPIDO

Torre d. Sciri

Mad. d. Luce

S. Teresa
(Scalzi)
Car Park
(Pellini)

MONTERIPIDO

S. Matteo

S. Matteo in
Campo d'Orto

PIAZZA
S. FRANCESCO

Arco di
S. Luca

VIA D. SPOSA

Porta
Elce

Porta
Conca

S. Francesco

VIA DEL BEATO EGIDIO

VIA A. LORENZINI

VIA A. VECCHI

VIALE ORAZIO ANTINORI

VIA SAN GALIGANO

S. Bernardino

Accademia
di Belle Arti

VIALE ORAZIO ANTINORI

VIA A. VECCHI

VIA SEGRETO D. SIERI

1 2 3 4 5 6 7 8 9 10

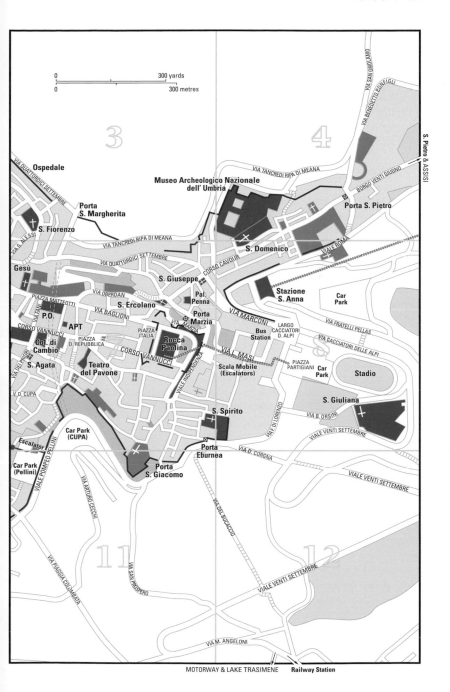

0 | 300 yards
0 | 300 metres

3

4

S. Pietro & ASSISI

Ospedale

VIA QUATTORDICI SETTEMBRE

VIA SAN GIROLAMO

VIA BENEDETTO BONFIGLI

VIA TANCREDI RIPA DI MEANA

Porta S. Pietro

BORGO VENTI GIUGNO

Museo Archeologico Nazionale dell' Umbria

Porta S. Margherita

S. Fiorenzo

VIA G. ALESSI

VIA TANCREDI RIPA DI MEANA

S. Domenico

VIALE ROMA

Gesù

VIA QUATTORDICI SETTEMBRE

PIAZZA MATTEOTTI

S. Giuseppe

CORSO CAVOUR

VIA FANI

P.O.

VIA OBERDAN

S. Ercolano

Pal. Penna

Stazione S. Anna

Car Park

APT

VIA BAGLIONI

Porta Marzia

VIA MARCONI

VIA FRATELLI PELLAS

CORSO VANNUCCI

PIAZZA ITALIA

VIA MARZIA

LARGO CACCIATORI D. ALPI

VIA CACCIATORI DELLE ALPI

Col. di Cambio

PIAZZA D. REPUBBLICA

Rocca Paolina

Bus Station

VIA DEI PRIORI

S. Agata

CORSO VANNUCCI

VIA L. MASI

Stadio

Teatro del Pavone

VIALE INDIPENDENZA

Scala Mobile (Escalators)

PIAZZA PARTIGIANI

Car Park

V. D. CUPA

S. Giuliana

S. Spirito

VIALE F. DI LORENZO

VIA B. ORSINI

Escalator

Car Park (CUPA)

VIA POMPEO PELLINI

Porta Eburnea

VIA D. CORGNA

VIALE VENTI SETTEMBRE

Car Park (Pellini)

Porta S. Giacomo

VIALE VENTI SETTEMBRE

VIA ARTURO CECCHI

VIA DEL BULAGAIO

11

12

VIA PIAGGIA COLOMBATA

VIA SAN PROSPERO

VIALE VENTI SETTEMBRE

VIA M. ANGELONI

MOTORWAY & LAKE TRASIMENE   **Railway Station**

The entrance to the Collegio del Cambio is through a room which became the property of the Collegio dei Legisti in 1613, and the fine carved walnut benches date from that time. The beautifully decorated **Sala di Udienza del Collegio del Cambio** is one of the best preserved rooms of the Renaissance in Italy, famous for its frescoes by Perugino, perhaps his masterpiece. The work was carried out, with the help of pupils, including Andrea d'Assisi (L'Ingegno), and possibly also Raphael, in 1498–1500 (although a final payment was made to Perugino in 1507).

Perugino (c. 1446–1523)

Perugino's frescoes in the Collegio del Cambio include a portrait, showing a man with small eyes and stubby fingers. This unprepossessing figure is the first great Umbrian painter himself, Pietro Vannucci, born in Città della Pieve c. 1448. He was called Perugino by his Florentine contemporaries because of his Umbrian background, but may not have visited Perugia until 1475. If Vasari is to be believed, he had no interest in God, and an obsession with making money. He spent his formative years in Florence in the workshop of Verrocchio with Leonardo da Vinci, and his work shows the influence of Botticelli and Piero della Francesca. Famous in his lifetime, he was called to Rome in the 1480s to paint *Christ Giving the Keys to St Peter* in the Sistine Chapel. His elegant, graceful figures and spacious, luminous landscapes greatly influenced his famous pupil Raphael. There are numerous paintings by him in the Galleria Nazionale dell'Umbria, and altarpieces by him in the city in the churches of San Pietro, Sant'Agnese, and San Severo. Other works by him can be seen all over Umbria, from his earliest dated work in the parish church of Cerqueto near Lake Trasimene, to works in churches in Assisi, Spello, Foligno, Montefalco, Trevi, Panicale and in the museum at Bettona.

The Sala di Udienza frescoes illustrate the ideal combination of Christian virtues with Classical culture, in a scheme drawn up by the Perugian Humanist Francesco Maturanzio. On the right of the portal is the figure of Cato, symbol of Wisdom. On the left wall is a lunette with *Prudence* and *Justice*, two of the Cardinal Virtues, seated above six standing figures of Classical heroes (all named). On the pilaster is Perugino's self-portrait. The second lunette, a pendant to the first, has the figures of the other two Cardinal Virtues, *Fortitude* and *Temperance*, seated above more Classical heroes; the figure of *Fortitude* has been attributed to Raphael, then only 17 years old. On the end wall are the *Transfiguration* and *Nativity*, and on the right wall, the Eternal Father in glory above 12 figures of prophets and Sibyls, perhaps the most successful composition in the room. The remarkable figure studies here include *Daniel*, thought to be a portrait of Raphael. The beautiful carved and inlaid woodwork both here and in the chapel is by Domenico del Tasso (1492) and Antonio Bencivenni da Mercatello (1508). In the niche is a gilded statue of *Justice* attributed to Benedetto da Maiano.

The Eternal Father in glory, with prophets and Sibyls below. Fresco by Perugino in the Collegio del Cambio (1498–1500).

The **Cappella di San Giovanni Battista** is entirely frescoed with stories from the life of St John the Baptist by Perugino's pupil Giannicola di Paolo (1515–18), who also painted the altarpiece.

The **Sala di Udienza del Collegio della Mercanzia** (*open 9–1 & 2.30–5.30, Sun and holidays 9–1; Nov–Feb 8–2 except on Wed and Sat when it is open 8–4.30*) has belonged to the merchants' guild (still a charitable institution) since 1390. Founded before the 13th century, it was the most important guild in Perugia in the 14th century. The vault and walls are entirely panelled with splendid carving and intarsia work, carried out during the early 15th century by unknown craftsmen, showing Northern European influence.

Galleria Nazionale dell'Umbria

The main portal of Palazzo dei Priori (*map p. 490, 6*) was erected in the 14th century and is beautifully carved. The outer pilasters, borne by lions, display the Perugian griffin, and in the lunette there are copies of statues of Perugia's patron saints. The doors are original. The entrance hall has fine vaulting. The Galleria Nazionale dell'Umbria, founded in 1863 and moved here in 1879, is the most important surviving collection of Umbrian paintings, and one of the finest galleries of paintings in Italy (*open every day 8.30–7.30 except Mon*). It was excellently restored in 2006 and the magnificent display is chronological.

The Umbrian school of painting was formed in the 12th century. By the 15th century it had became independent of Siena and Florence, and produced such masters as Gentile da Fabriano, Ottaviano Nelli, Niccolò di Liberatore (L'Alunno), Matteo da Gualdo and Bartolomeo Caporali. The first truly great Perugian painters were Benedetto Bonfigli (c. 1420–96) and his immediate follower Fiorenzo di Lorenzo (1445–1522). Works by both are preserved here. The greatest of all, however, was Perugino (c. 1446–1523; *see box on previous page*). He had a profound influence on numerous subsequent painters, including Pinturicchio (*see p. 537*).

Room 1: The Sala Maggiore, dating from 1317–26, used to be the hall of the Consiglio Generale del Comune. Here are displayed 13th-century dossals, a tabernacle with painted doors, and a moving polychrome wood *Deposition* (c. 1236).

The **Master of St Francis** is represented by a number of works, including a large painted Crucifix with St Francis in adoration (1272). The bronze group of three nymphs (or water-carriers) comes from the Fontana Maggiore (*see overleaf*). The group of griffins and winged lions, which after 1519 was installed above the nymphs at the top of the Fontana Maggiore, was originally made for another fountain. The sculptural fragments by Arnolfo di Cambio (1278–81) also come from a public fountain in Perugia. Here too are displayed the splendid original **Guelph lion and Perugian griffin**, from the façade of the palazzo. They were carried off from the gates of Siena by the Perugians after a victory at Torrita in 1358: their date is still not certain, but some scholars believe that the wings of the griffin were added before 1281 to an Etruscan body.

Room 2: The display here illustrates Umbrian art in the late 13th and early 14th centuries. The *Madonna and Child* with *Angels and Saints* is by the little-known Marino di Elemosina, and there are works by Meo di Guido da Siena. The exquisite *Madonna and Child* by Duccio was part of a polyptych.

Room 4: This large room displays 14th-century works, including the original statues from the main entrance to the palazzo, attributed to Ambrogio Maitani, and paintings which show Sienese influence. There is an exquisite small *Madonna and Child* in the Byzantine style.

Room 6: Here are early 15th-century works in the International Gothic style, including a polyptych by Ottaviano Nelli, a painter born in Gubbio, and an exquisite small *Madonna* by Gentile da Fabriano.

Room 8: The Guidalotti polyptych by Fra' Angelico was commissioned for a family chapel in San Domenico in Perugia in 1448. The frame dates from 1915. Two of the predella scenes (the one on the left and the one in the centre) are copies of the originals removed to the Vatican in 1817 (*see p. 102*).

Room 9: Madonnas by Giovanni Boccati from Camerino (his finest work is in Belforte del Chienti; *see p. 683*) and a *Pietà* by Perugino.

Room 10: Here is displayed the *Pala della Sapienza Nuova* (signed and dated 1456) by Benozzo Gozzoli, painted for the Collegio di San Gerolamo, where foreign students who attended Perugia university stayed.

Room 11: The famous *Polyptych of St Anthony* is a splendid Renaissance work by **Piero della Francesca** (painted for the monastery of Sant'Antonio in Perugia, probably c. 1459). On either side of the Madonna and Child are Sts Anthony of Padua and John the Baptist, and Sts Francis and Elizabeth of Hungary. Above is an exquisitely painted *Annunciation* and, in the predella, miracles of St Anthony, St Francis and St Elizabeth. Also here is a terracotta high relief of the *Madonna and Child* by Agostino di Duccio.

Room 14: Here are shown very fine works by Benedetto Bonfigli, the most important painter in Perugia between 1450 and 1470, including the beautiful banner of St Bernardino of Siena (1465); a *Madonna and Angel Musicians* from the church of San Domenico; and a charming *Annunciation with St Luke*. **Room 15:** Works by Bonfigli's contemporary Bartolomeo Caporali include a *Madonna and Child with Six Angels*, his earliest known work, and an *Adoration of the Shepherds*. Also here are the **Miracles of St Bernardino of Siena**, eight exquisite small panels painted in 1473 for the Oratorio di San Bernardino, with remarkable architectural details. They almost certainly decorated two sides of a niche which may have housed a statue of St Bernardino. Their attribution is still uncertain: Perugino, Pinturicchio and Francesco di Giorgio Martini have all been suggested. Displayed here also is

an early *Adoration of the Magi* by Perugino.

Room 16: The display includes a charming *Annunciation* by Caporali, a *Madonna and Child* by Antoniazzo Romano, and works by Fiorenzo di Lorenzo.

Room 17: The **treasury** is exhibited here, with exquisite ivories, some of them French, and Limoges work. The chalice and paten which belonged to Benedict XI were made by Sienese craftsmen in 1298–1304.

Room 20: In this corridor is a display of Deruta ware dating from the 16th–18th centuries.

Room 22: Three good **works by Perugino** are shown here, all painted in his maturity, including a banner, and the *Madonna della Consolazione*, both dating from around 1496.

Room 23: Here are more works by Perugino: a frescoed lunette of the *Adoration of the Shepherds* painted in 1504 (possibly with the help of his young pupil Raphael); *St John the Baptist* with four other saints; and a predella.

Room 24: The fine altarpiece from Santa Maria dei Fossi is by Pinturicchio (1495), as is the banner of St Augustine.

Room 25: Five works by Perugino are displayed here, all once part of a huge polyptych of St Anthony, painted on both sides.

Room 26: Predella scenes from the same polyptych are shown here, and an exquisite small bronze bas-relief of the *Scourging of Christ* by Francesco di Giorgio Martini.

Room 27: The *Entombment* by Cavaliere d'Arpino is a copy of Raphael's *Deposition* (now in the Galleria Borghese in Rome; *see p. 71*).

PIAZZA QUATTRO NOVEMBRE

Corso Vannucci rises to end at the delightful Piazza IV Novembre (*map p. 490, 6*), on a slope, with the famous **Fontana Maggiore**. The fountain, one of the most important Romanesque monuments in Europe, was designed in 1278 by Fra' Bevignate, a Silvestrine monk who lived in Perugia. At the centre of the town, it is its main fountain, at the end of an aqueduct from Monte Pacciano, some 5km long and specially built by the Venetian hydraulic engineer Boninsegna. It has two polygonal marble basins decorated with exquisitely carved reliefs and statuettes by Nicola Pisano and his son Giovanni, which follow a carefully worked-out scheme celebrating the glory of Perugia (each of them explained by a Latin inscription).

Lower basin
This has 25 double reliefs, separated by columns. The first twelve illustrate the *Labours of the Months*, each with their sign of the Zodiac, as follows:

January: Two seated figures beside an open fire.
February: A fishing scene.
March: A traveller extracting a thorn from his foot (derived from the Roman *Spinario*; *see p. 30*) and a man pruning a tree.
April: Two garlanded Roman figures bearing branches and cornucopia.
May: A chivalric scene with a lady with a falcon pursued by a knight with a bunch of roses.

June: A harvest scene with peasants reaping and scything.
July: Peasants at threshing time.
August: A man and a woman with baskets picking figs.
September: The grape harvest.
October: A man pouring wine into a barrel, while another one is repairing a barrel.
November: Ploughing and sowing.
December: The butchering of a pig.

Beyond a relief of a lion and griffin (symbols of Perugia) are four double reliefs illustrating the Liberal Arts (Grammar and Dialectic; Rhetoric and Arithmetic; Geometry and Music; and Astronomy and Philosophy—as the two highest Arts, these are shown crowned and enthroned. Beyond a double relief with two eagles are scenes from the Old Testament (*Temptation* and *Expulsion from Paradise*; *Samson and the Lion*, and *Samson and Delilah*). The relief with a seated lion and a young lion (or puppy) being beaten is an allegory of the virtues of punishment. The next panel depicts *David and Goliath* (the giant is shown dead), and the next *Romulus and Remus*, both seated and holding falcons. The panels with the She-wolf feeding Romulus and Remus and their mother, the Vestal Virgin Rhea Sylvia holding a large basket, are both copies (the originals are preserved in the Galleria Nazionale).The last relief illustrates two fables of Aesop: the *Crane and the Wolf* (the crane is extracting a bone from the wolf's throat), and the *Wolf and the Lamb*, showing the wolf about to devour the lamb.

Upper basin
This is decorated with 24 statuettes (most of them by Giovanni Pisano) depicting personages from the Old Testament and cities, saints and figures from Perugia's history:

1–3: Looking straight down the Corso is the seated female figure of *Perugia*, holding a cornucopia, flanked by *Chiusi* presenting ears of corn, and *Trasimene* presenting fish;

4: *St Herculanus*, bishop of Perugia in 547 and later patron saint;

5: The *Traitor Cleric*, who opened the city gates to Totila and his Goths during the siege in 547;

6: *St Benedict* is shown with two angels and his disciple St Maurus kneeling;

7: *Salome* (with the splendid head of St John the Baptist);

8: *St John the Baptist* (holding a lamb);

9: *King Solomon*;

10: *David* (holding a psalter);

11: *Moses*;

12: A portrait of Matteo da Correggio, *podestà* in 1278 (the date of the construction of the fountain);

13: The *Archangel Michael*;

14: *Eulistes*, the legendary founder of Perugia, shown holding a scroll;

15: *Melchisedech*, substituted by a copy in 1858;

16: Ermanno da Sassoferrato, *Capitano del Popolo* in 1278;

17: *Victory*, represented by a female figure holding a palm;

18: *St Peter* (holding a key);

19: An allegorical female figure, personifying the Roman Church, holding a model of a church (the face is a modern substitute);

20: The seated crowned figure of *Rome*, a copy made in 1949;

21: *Theology*, a fine robed figure looking up to the sky;

22: *St Paul* (holding a sword and scroll);

23: The *Cleric of St Lawrence*;

24: *St Lawrence*, patron saint of the town, dressed as a deacon with a finely embroidered dalmatic.

The simple basin above supports three graceful bronze female figures holding an amphora, thought to represent the three Virtues or Nymphs.

Sala dei Notari

Overlooking the piazza is the main façade of Palazzo dei Priori, with copies of the griffin and lion holding chains now exhibited in the Galleria Nazionale (*see p. 494 above*). A charming flight of steps leads up to a Gothic portal, the entrance to the huge Sala dei Notari (*open 9–1 & 3–7 except Mon*), one of the most impressive rooms in Italy, with remarkable vaulting. It was originally used for popular assemblies, and later as an audience hall by notaries of the city. It is now used for concerts and lectures. After 1860, when the city threw off papal rule, Matteo Tassi covered the walls with the painted coats of arms of the *podestà* of the city from 1297–1424, but the most interesting decoration (difficult to see) is high up on the spandrels of the arches which bear frescoes of Old Testament scenes and fables by a close follower of Pietro Cavallini (1297). In Via delle Volte nearby is an exceptionally high Gothic arch beside a fountain.

The duomo and Etruscan well

The duomo of Perugia (*closed between 12.30 and 4*), is a Gothic building of the 15th century. The exterior of the south side, overlooking the Fontana Maggiore, has a pulpit built for St Bernardino in 1425 and a bronze statue of Pope Julius II by Vincenzo Danti (1555; the year of the pope's death). The steps here are a favourite place for visitors and residents to sit and rest in the sun. On the steps on the other side of the church, Deruta ceramics are sold on Tuesday and Saturday mornings.

The dark **interior**, with aisles equal in height to the nave, has columns painted in imitation of impossible marble. Surrounded by a little altar, on a pillar of the nave, is the highly venerated *Madonna delle Grazie*, a beautiful painting attributed to Giannicola di Paolo. A chapel in the south aisle contains a magnificent *Descent from the Cross*, one of the best works of Urbino-born artist Federico Barocci (1569). The bishop's throne (1520) and stalls of intarsia work by Giuliano da Maiano and Domenico del Tasso (1486–91) in the choir were exquisitely restored using the traditional intarsia technique after over a third of them were destroyed by fire in 1985.

The **Museo Capitolare** (*open 10–1 & 2.30–5.30; closed Mon*), founded in 1923, has over 20 rooms, now a little shabby, which display the church treasury: illuminated missals, sculpture and paintings including works by Meo di Guido da Siena, Agnolo Gaddi and Andrea Vanni, and the skilled early Umbrian artists Bartolomeo Caporali and Benedetto Bonfigli. The most precious work in the collection is the *Pala di Sant'Onofrio* (1484) by Luca Signorelli.

At no. 18 Piazza Danti is the entrance to an **Etruscan Well** (*open 10–1.30 & 3–6; Nov–March 11–1.30 & 2.30–5; closed Mon*), beneath Palazzo Sorbello. The well, at least 35m deep and some 5.6m in diameter, was constructed in the 3rd century BC and could contain about 430,000 litres of water, enough to supply all the inhabitants. From a window the remarkable vault constructed with blocks of travertine can be seen. Steps lead down past the seeping walls to a bridge over the well. Palazzo Sorbello (Piazza Piccinino 9) is now the seat of the Uguccione Ranieri di Sorbello Foundation with a library and art collection (17th-century prints, fabrics and porcelain; *open on Wed at 5.30*). The well-head in the piazza sports the Sorbello arms.

Via del Sole and San Severo

Via del Sole leads up into an ancient medieval part of the town, the Rione di Porta Sole, well worth exploring. In a secluded corner, with some old ilex trees and a view over the valley, is the church of **San Severo** (*map p. 490, 2*). Probably on the site of a temple to the Sun, a convent and church dedicated to Severus, Bishop of Ravenna, were built here in the 11th century by Camaldolensian monks. Both were rebuilt in the 15th century, and a chapel survives (*open March–Oct 10–1.30 & 3–6; Nov–Feb 11–1.30 & 2.30–4.30; closed Mon; T: 075 573 3864*) with the *Holy Trinity with Saints*, the earliest fresco known by Raphael (c. 1505). He left it unfinished when he was called to Rome to work on the *Stanze* in the Vatican, and in 1521 his master, Perugino, was commissioned to paint the six saints below, the year after his young pupil's premature death. Raphael's work is unfortunately damaged, but is memorable for its colour and the four white robed saints. The charming seated statue of the *Madonna and Child* is by an unknown master. Nearby is the Etruscan **Porta Sole**, or Arco dei Gigli, mentioned by Dante.

VIA DEI PRIORI

Via dei Priori (*map pp. 491, 7–490, 10*) is an attractive old medieval street which descends steeply from Corso Vannucci through Palazzo dei Priori. The church of **Sant'Agata**, built on a simple plan in 1290–1314, with two cross vaults and just six mighty columns, preserves remains of frescoes, the best preserved of which is a *Crucifixion* by the late 14th-century Umbrian school. The grandiose and heavily decorated interior of the Baroque church of **San Filippo Neri** offers a striking contrast. The high altarpiece of the *Immaculate Conception*, showing the Virgin as described in the Book of Revelation, with a dragon beneath her feet which her Son will cast out, was completed by Pietro da Cortona.

Via dei Priori continues down to another small piazza in which is the delightful miniature apse, surmounted by a bell-cote, of the church of **Santi Stefano e Valentino** (*closed for restoration at the time of writing*). A chapel was founded here in the 10th century, and the interior now has two aisles, one of the 12th and one of the 14th century. It contains early fresco fragments, a painting of the *Madonna and Saints* by Domenico Alfani, and a copy made in 1911 of a triptych by L'Alunno.

Next to the entrance to the escalators (with a view of the countryside) and the church of the Scalzi, built in 1718, rises the splendid **Torre degli Sciri** (46m), the only tall medieval tower left in Perugia (there used to be some 500 towers in the town; *for information on medieval tower-houses, see p. 376*).

The church of the **Madonna della Luce**, with an elegant façade of 1512–18, is in a delightful little piazzetta surrounded by a medley of medieval buildings. In the tiny interior, the ceiling has a lovely circular fresco of *God the Father*, with the Evangelists and angels, by Giovanni Battista Caporali (son of Bartolomeo), and a gilded wooden high altar with a fresco of the *Madonna and Saints* by Tiberio d'Assisi.

Oratorio di San Bernardino

The Porta Trasimena is a gate opened in Etruscan times, with a tall Gothic archway. The peaceful Piazza San Francesco is surrounded by green lawns. The **Oratorio di San Bernardino** (*map p. 490, 10*) was erected the year after the saint's canonisation in 1450, in commemoration of his numerous preachings in the piazza here between 1420 and 1440. The beautiful façade, rich in polychrome marbles, was decorated in 1457–61 with exquisite bas-reliefs by Agostino di Duccio; it is the most important 15th-century sculptural work in the town. Below the lunette with St Bernardino in glory surrounded by angels are bas-reliefs with scenes of the miracles of St Bernardino, but the best works are those on either side of the portal, flanked by green marble pilasters: six delicately carved panels illustrate Franciscan virtues: on the left, from top to bottom, *Charity*, *Poverty* and *Chastity*, and on the right from top to bottom, *Justice*, *Mortification* and *Obedience*. Six more panels on the outer face have beautiful pairs of angel musicians.

In the stark interior, with pretty vaulting, a 4th century early-Christian sarcophagus serves as high altar. It was the tomb of the Blessed Egidius of Assisi, the third companion of St Francis, who died in 1262. On the right are two more works from San Francesco: a good 16th-century copy by Orazio Alfani of Raphael's famous *Deposition* (now in the Galleria Borghese in Rome; *see p. 71*) which was commissioned for the Baglioni chapel in that church, and a banner of 1464 by Benedetto Bonfigli showing the Madonna protecting Perugia from the plague of the same year. The pavement tomb of the chapel's patron Fra' Angelo del Toscano (d. 1453) has been placed on the left wall, and it may also be by Agostino di Duccio.

The large 13th-century church of **San Francesco al Prato** has a façade of unusual design (rebuilt in 1927). The church, damaged by landslides from the 18th century onwards, is being restored as an auditorium. Beyond is the charming little 14th-century church of **San Matteo in Campo d'Orto** (*closed*) with a very tall façade, on top of which is a bellcote.

CORSO GARIBALDI & THE NORTH

The so-called **Arco d'Augusto** (*map p. 490, 6*), leading onto Piazza Fortebraccio, is a noble gateway in which three periods of civilisation are represented. The Etruscan lower part dates from the 3rd–2nd centuries BC; the upper part, with the inscription 'Augusta Perusia', was added after 40 BC when Augustus rebuilt the town and added his own name to it. It is flanked by two trapezoidal towers, one of which was decorated with a graceful Renaissance loggia in the 16th century.

In the busy piazza beyond, where numerous roads meet, is the colourful façade built in 1740–58 of the palace which is the now seat of the **Università per Stranieri**, founded in 1925 for the promotion of Italian language, literature and culture abroad. It is open to students of all nationalities, and is one of the best known places in Italy for studying Italian. Directly west of here, on Via Santa Elisabetta, a modern university building covers a monochrome **Roman mosaic** of Orpheus charming the wild beasts (*viewable 8–7, Sat 8–1, closed Sun and holidays*).

The long, narrow **Corso Garibaldi**, a peaceful medieval street, leads up out of the town along a spur towards Porta Sant'Angelo. It is lined with fine old houses and a number of convents. Narrow lanes lead right to a charming little park outside the walls. The church of **Sant'Agostino** has an attractive pink-and-white chequered façade. In the 18th-century interior, the choir is finely carved and inlaid by Baccio d'Agnolo (1502). There is a 17th-century oratory next door. Off the other side of the street is the former convent of San Benedetto: the campanile has a most unusual design.

Chastity by Agostino di Duccio, bas-relief on the Oratorio di San Bernardino (1457–61).

At the **Convent of Beata Colomba** (no. 191; *map p. 490, 5; open 8.30–12 & 3.30–5.30; ring for access*) one of the ten Dominican nuns shows the cell of the Blessed Colomba of Rieti (1467–1501), in which is a remarkable painting of *Christ Carrying the Cross*, delicately painted in tempera on a very thin cloth, attributed to Lo Spagna. Also here are a charming 15th-century painting of the saint, and mementoes, including her carefully preserved and labelled clothes. You can also visit the church by asking for the key at the *ruota* (turning wheel).

Beyond an arch is the delightful little church of **Sant'Angelo** preceded by a pretty lawn with cypresses. It is a remarkable circular building derived from Roman models, erected in the 5th century as a temple to St Michael Archangel. In the beautiful interior, the rotunda has a drum supported by a ring of 16 splendid Roman columns of different heights and varying materials. There were formerly four chapels forming a Greek-cross plan: only the semicircular Cappella del Crocifisso and one rectangular chapel survive. The drum was reduced in height in the 14th century and the building restored in 1948, and again in 2007. The altar is supported by a Roman column.

Steps lead down from the garden past orchards to **Porta Sant'Angelo**, the largest of the medieval city gates, rebuilt in 1326 by Lorenzo Maitani. It has been beautifully restored to house the **Museo delle Porte e delle Mura di Perugia** (*open 10.30/11–1.30 & 3–5/6; closed Mon*), which illustrates the history of the fortifications. From the top there is a splendid view, taking in Assisi on the slopes of Monte Subasio, and the hills surrounding Lake Trasimene. Outside the gate, beautiful countryside reaches up to the medieval walls, providing a remarkably unspoilt approach to the town.

Back on the inner side of the arch, on Corso Garibaldi, there is a tiny walled garden with a pergola open to the public. A lane leads up to the convent of **Sant'Agnese** (*ring for access, 9–11 & 3–6*). One of the sisters (who rings a bell to warn away the nuns of the closed order) shows visitors a chapel with a fresco by Perugino of the *Madonna and Sts Anthony Abbot and Anthony of Padua*.

THE SOUTH OF THE OLD TOWN

Palazzo della Penna at no. 11 Via Podiani (*map p. 491, 7; open 10.30–1 & 4–6.30; closed Mon*) has late 19th-century painted ceilings. It contains works from the Accademia delle Belle Arti, and a section devoted to the Futurist artist **Gerardo Dottori**, including his *Triptych of Speed* (1927). A modern spiral staircase designed by Franco Minissi leads down to a floor which houses a collection of Baroque works (including a fine model of *Christ Bound* by Gian Lorenzo Bernini), left to the city by the art historian Valentino Martinelli (d. 1999). In more underground rooms there is an exhibition dedicated to the Fluxus artist and ecologist **Joseph Beuys** (1921–86), with the sketches he made on six blackboards to describe his philosophy when he visited Perugia in 1980.

San Domenico

Map p. 491, 8–4; open 7–12 & 4–7/7.30. This is the largest church in Perugia, founded in 1305 and rebuilt by Carlo Maderno in 1632. In the interior, the huge stained-glass window (23m by 9m; *covered for restoration at the time of writing*) bears the signatures of Fra' Bartolomeo di Pietro da Perugia and Mariotto di Nardo, and the date 1411, but it is thought that the upper part is a later work. It is the largest stained-glass window in Italy after those in the duomo of Milan. A chapel contains a beautiful marble and terracotta dossal by Agostino di Duccio (1459) and his pupils, and there are various interesting funerary monuments from the Gothic period to the 17th century (that of Elisabetta Cantucci bears a bust by Alessandro Algardi). There are also some 14th-century fresco fragments, and a banner painted by Giannicola di Paolo in 1494, with a view of the town of Perugia.

Museo Archeologico

The convent of San Domenico now houses the Museo Archeologico Nazionale dell'Umbria (*open 8.30–7.30; Mon 10–7.30; T: 075 572 7141*). It is arranged around two cloisters. On the ground floor of the large cloister is an underground room with an excellent reconstruction of the **Cutu family tomb**, in use from the Etruscan to the Roman period; another room has three magnificent large Roman sarcophaghi with mythological scenes. In the four upper walks is an impressive display of Etruscan and Roman urns (including the charming little **cinerary urn of Annia Cassia** from the Augustan period) and *cippi*. Rooms off this cloister have exquisite bronze decorations from chariots made around 530 BC, and the unique **Bellucci collection of amulets**.

In the two upper walks of the small cloister is displayed a celebrated **cippus in travertine**, with an inscription of 151 words, one of the most important monuments of Etruscan epigraphy. A small room contains tombs from an Etruscan hypogeum, many of them still brightly coloured. The **Prehistoric collection**, charmingly displayed in the huge *Salone*, is one of the most important in Italy, and illustrates the development of civilisation in the centre of the Italian peninsula. In rooms off a corridor at the foot of the steps (with a wonderful view of Assisi and Monte Subasio from the window at the end) are a stele with the representation of two warriors; a large stone sarcophagus from the Sperandio necropolis, which was made in Chiusi around 500 BC and has an unusual scene which may represent a victorious return from battle (or perhaps a family moving to colonise a new part of the country); a circular cippus with delicate bas-reliefs; bronzes; vases; and a numismatic collection. In another corridor is displayed Cypriot material dating from the Bronze Age to the Roman period from a collection made in 1875.

San Pietro

Beyond Porta San Pietro (*map p. 491, 4*), which has a lovely outer façade by Agostino di Duccio (1473), is the Benedictine church of San Pietro, with its graceful polygonal Gothic tower (rebuilt in 1463) crowned with a spire, a characteristic feature of the city and visible for many miles around. The church belonged to a convent founded at the end of the 10th century by a monk called Pietro Vincioli, who became the first abbot. It is still entered through the cloister.

The dark basilican interior (*open 8–12.30 & 3–6*), with ancient marble and granite columns, was transformed in the early 16th century. It is entirely decorated with frescoes and has a carved and gilded ceiling. The paintings, all in attractive stone frames, are of particularly high quality. In the nave are 11 large canvases by L'Aliense (1594). The earliest artists represented are Eusebio da San Giorgio (*Adoration of the Magi*) and Fiorenzo di Lorenzo (*Pietà with Two Saints*; 1469). There are interesting 17th-century works, notably by Cesare Sermei, and an amusing depiction of *Samson* by François Perrier. A better-known artist of this period, Sassoferrato, is also well represented, in particular by a lovely painting of *Judith* in the north aisle. He also made the copy here of Raphael's *Deposition*.

Perugino painted the three small paintings above the sacristy door, the five paintings of saints inside, and the *Pietà* in the north aisle (one of his last works). The bronze Crucifix is by Alessandro Algardi. In the choir, the stone pulpits with reliefs, the bishops' thrones, and the high altar were all carved in the 16th century. The stalls, among the finest in Italy, were richly inlaid and carved in 1526.

The convent is now used by the Faculty of Agriculture of Perugia university, and they have here planted a charming little symbolic **medieval garden** around an ancient olive tree, decorated with rivulets of water (*open Mon–Fri 8–5*).

ENVIRONS OF PERUGIA

Tomb of the Volumnii

This hypogeum (Ipogeo dei Volumni; *open daily 9–12.30 & 4.30–7; winter 9–1 & 3.30–6.30*) is one of the finest Etruscan tombs known. Having said that, it is in a very disappointing setting, right beside a railway crossing and the Perugia bypass (*map p. 486, B3*). Discovered in 1840, it dates from somewhere between the second half of the 2nd and the mid-1st century BC. There is a splendid display of Etruscan urns, mostly in travertine, found in the nearby necropolis of Palazzone on either side of the very steep flight of steps down to the entrance to the tomb, beside which the huge travertine slab which served as a door survives. On the right-hand door-post is an Etruscan inscription relating to the construction of the tomb.

The tomb itself is in the form of a Roman house. The ceiling of the atrium imitates a wooden roof, and above the entrance are two dolphins and a shield in relief. At the end is the tablinum with a Medusa's head carved in the ceiling. Here are six cinerary urns in travertine covered with stucco, containing the ashes of the Volumnii family. In the centre is that of Arnth Volumnius, with the figure of the defunct on a bed resting on a plinth with two winged demons. The urn, in the form of a seated lady in the Roman style, is that of Arnth's daughter. The seventh urn, in marble, is later and imitates the form of a building. It bears an inscription in Latin and Etruscan of the early Imperial era. The side cells are empty, but two of them have coffered ceilings with Medusa heads hewn out of the rock, and one of the cells on the right has two owls in relief.

Torgiano

Torgiano (*map p. 486, B3*) is a pleasant small village situated between the Tiber and Chiascio rivers, in a district well known for its wine. Torgiano, in fact, was the first Umbrian wine to receive the DOC classification. The successor to Rubesco di Torgiano is the Torgiano Rosso, made mainly from Sangiovese and Canaiolo grapes; Torgiano Bianco is mainly Trebbiano and Grechetto. The Fondazione Lungarotti runs an excellent **wine museum** (Corso Vittorio Emanuele 31; *open every day 9–1 & 3–6/7*) in the cool cellars of the 17th-century Palazzo Baglioni. This particularly interesting collection illustrates the history of wine-making from the origins of viticulture right up to the present day, with archaeological material including an Attic kylix from Vulci, and Roman amphorae. There is also a museum dedicated to the cultivation of the olive in a medieval building once used as a press (*first admissions at 10am, otherwise open as wine museum*). Simple traditional pottery is still made and sold in a few potteries here.

Bettona

Bettona (*map p. 486, B3*) is a peaceful little village surrounded by thick olive groves, with a fine view from its low hill. It has remarkable golden-coloured Etruscan walls. In the attractive piazza with a fountain is Palazzo del Podestà, where the **Museo Civico** (*open every day 10.30–1 & 3–6/7; Nov–Feb closed Mon*) has two paintings by Perugino painted for the church of Sant'Antonio here, and an altarpiece of the *Adoration of the Shepherds* with a predella showing stories from the life of San Crispolto, Dono Doni's most important work. The church of San Crispolto (dedicated to the town's first bishop) has a pyramidal campanile. In the Oratory of Sant'Andrea, an interesting large fresco of the *Passion of Christ* is attributed to the school of Giotto (1394).

Deruta

Deruta (*map p. 487, B4*) is famed for its majolica, which is still made in great quantity in modern factories in the new town below and sold in numerous shops in the old town. The former convent of San Francesco houses the excellent **Museo Regionale della Ceramica** (*open every day July–Sept 10–1 & 3.30–7; April–June 10.30–1 & 3–6; Oct–March 10.30–1 & 2.30–5 except Tues*), which illustrates the history of the production of Deruta ceramics from the 14th–19th centuries. The Pinacoteca Comunale (*opening times as Museo della Ceramica, but only at weekends*) contains paintings by Umbrian artists, including a beautiful detached fresco dated c. 1478 by Fiorenzo di Lorenzo, which has a view of Deruta with Sts Roch and Romanus (the head is attributed to Perugino).

PRACTICAL INFORMATION

GETTING AROUND

• **By car:** The one-way system in Perugia is confusing and the signposting erratic. The historic centre is closed to traffic on weekdays from 7am–1.30pm and after 8pm, and from 5pm on Sun and holidays, but visitors can obtain permission to reach hotels. Car parks are clearly indicated on the approach roads: the most convenient is in Piazza Partigiani (*map p. 491, 8*). This huge two-storey underground car park has an hourly tariff (special reduced tariff for overnight periods). A series of escalators (and some steps) lead up from the car park to Rocca Paolina. Another convenient (less expensive) car park, also provided with escalators, is in Viale Pellini (*map p. 491, 11*). On the approach to it, off Via Arturo Cecchi, there is free car parking in Piazzale della Cupa (*map p. 491, 7*), and on the other side of Via Arturo Cecchi, although it is not always easy to find space. From Via Arturo Cecchi an escalator ascends to Viale Pellini, where more escalators continue up to emerge in Via dei Priori (*map p. 490, 6*). There is also a car park below the covered market (*map p. 490, 2*) with a lift up to Piazza Matteotti. NB: lifts and escalators operate from 7am–2am.

• **By train:** Perugia's main station is in a modern part of the town at Fontivegge (*beyond map p. 491, 12*). There are frequent services from Foligno (with connections from Rome) and from Cortona (sometimes with a change at Terontola). Bus nos 6, 7 and 9 for Piazza Italia (*map p. 490, 6*). There is also an elevated red 'metro' under construction from the station up to Piazza Matteotti. Stazione Sant'Anna (*map p. 491; 8*) and the Stazione Ponte San Giovanni (6km southeast) have services from Città di Castello and Sansepolcro, and from Terni via Deruta and Todi.

• **By bus:** Bus services are run by APM (www.apmperugia.it). For city buses from the railway station, see above. There is a wide network of country buses from Piazza Partigiani to the main towns of Umbria, with frequent daily services to Assisi (c. 1hr; slower services via Santa Maria degli Angeli); Spello (50mins) and Foligno (1hr 15mins); Gubbio (1hr 10mins); Deruta (30mins) and Todi (1hr 30mins); Lake Trasimene (Passignano 1hr, Tuoro 1hr 15mins, and Castiglione del Lago 1hr 15mins); Città della Pieve (1hr 30mins) and Chiusi (1hr 40mins); Torgiano (20mins) and Bettona (30mins). Services once a day to Norcia (2hrs 50mins).

Long-distance coach services operated by Sulga (www.sulga.it) link Perugia with Florence (2hrs) and Rome (2hrs 30mins), as well as Rome's Fiumicino airport.

INFORMATION OFFICES

Perugia Palazzo dei Priori, Corso Vannucci 19, T: 075 5771.
Deruta Piazza Benincasa 6, T: 075 972 8647.

HOTELS

Castel del Piano (*map p. 486, B3*) €€ **Villa Aureli**. Grand country villa *agriturismo* on the edge of a little town

c. 7km southwest of Perugia. Surrounded by a handsome formal garden, and a large estate with fine trees, where sheep are grazed. Two spacious flats available for rent by the week, preserving their original 18th-century furnishings and charming majolica floor tiles. Small swimming pool. Good red and white wine is produced in the cellars here. *Via Luigi Cirenei 70, T: 340 645 9061, www.villaaureli.it. 4 apartments.*

Civitella d'Arno (*map p. 486, B3*)
€ **Agricola Arna**. A 10min drive east from Perugia is a charming palazzo with ample grounds, a good place for cycling and walking. The bedrooms are simply and elegantly furnished. *SS 318, km 33, T: 075 602896, www.agricolarna.it. 11 rooms.*

Perugia (*map p. 486, B3*)
€€ **Brufani Palace**. Opened as a hotel in 1883, it has comfortable old-fashioned public rooms with a panorama of the valley. Most of the bedrooms, which include five luxurious suites, are very quiet. A swimming pool is to be opened. *Piazza Italia 12, T: 075 573 2541, www.brufanipalace.com. 94 rooms.*
€€ **Fortuna**. In a lovely old palace in a very quiet position just off Corso Vannucci. A special feature is the terrace overlooking the old town and the valley beyond. On the third floor six rooms have their own little terraces. *Via Bonazzi 19, T: 075 572 2845, 34 rooms.*
€€ **La Rosetta**. A solid, old-fashioned hotel in a magnificent position at the beginning of Corso Vannucci. Cordial, efficient staff. The bedrooms are quiet. It can be busy with groups. Good restaurant attached. *Piazza Italia 19, T: 075 572 0841. www.perugiaonline.com/larosetta. 96 rooms.*

€ **Priori**. On one of the most characteristic old streets in the city, with a splendid large terrace for breakfast. Very simple décor. *Via dei Priori, T: 075 572 3378, www.hotelpriori.it. 55 rooms.*

Ripa (*map p. 486, B3*)
€€ **Ripa Relais Colle del Sole**. Three beautifully restored farmhouses c. 8km east of Perugia. Restaurant, with cooking courses available. *Strada Aeroporto Sant'Egidio 5, T: 075 602 0131, www. riparelaiscolledelsole.it. 16 rooms.*

San Biagio della Valle (*map p. 487, B4*)
€ **Torre Colombaia**. Large estate with a 19th-century hunting lodge in splendid wooded countryside 1km from the village. Simple but well-furnished accommodation of varying size, some in the hunting lodge itself. Meals are provided. Ideal for large family holidays. *T: 075 878 7341, www.torrecolombaia.it. 4 lodges.*

RESTAURANTS

Perugia (*map p. 486, B3*)
€€ **Antica Trattoria San Lorenzo**. Small restaurant next to the duomo, with exceptional service and food. Booking advised. Closed Sun. *Piazza Dante 19a, T: 0755 721956.*
€€ **Il Falchetto**. Central, attractive, well-run restaurant with medieval stone walls. The spinach gnocchi (*falchetti*) are the house speciality. *Via Bartolo 20, T: 075 573 1775.*
€€ **Osteria del Bartolo**. One of the finest restaurants in Perugia, with an elegant, vaulted interior. Closed Sun. *Via Bartolo 30, T: 075 571 6027.*
€€ **La Piazzetta**. A popular restaurant which serves pleasingly simple Umbrian dishes in an atmospheric, vaulted din-

ing room. Good wine list. Closed Tues.*Via Deliziosa 3, T: 075 573 6012.*

€ La Bocca Mia. A simple restaurant in the historic centre, serving delicious regional dishes including *stringozzi al tartufo nero di Norcia* (pasta with Norcia black truffles). Closed Sun and Mon lunch. *Via Ulisse Rocchi 36, T: 075 572 3873.*

€ Enoteca Provinciale. This is the best place in Perugia to sample the wines of Umbria. Both locals and visitors flock here due to the extensive variety of wines on offer, including some regional wines rarely found outside Umbria. *Via Ulisse Rocchi 18, T: 075 572 4824.*

€ Da Giancarlo. On a steep street off Corso Vannucci, an authentic Umbrian restaurant serving dishes such as *pasta alla norcina*, with a black truffle and anchovy sauce, and delicious *bruschetta*. Closed Fri. *Via dei Priori 36, T: 075 572 4314.*

€ La Lumera. A busy local *osteria*. Excellent selection of cheeses and salami, together with a varied wine list. Closed midday and all day Tues. *Corso Bersaglieri 22, T: 075 572 6181.*

Torgiano (*map p. 486, B3*)
€€€ Le Melograne. Part of the Le Tre Vaselle hotel, a 17th-century villa with vineyard, this is a wonderful place to enjoy a fine meal in quiet surroundings. *Via Garibaldi 48, T: 075 988 0447.*

LOCAL SPECIALITIES

Deruta Majolica has been produced in Deruta since the Middle Ages and the town is still well known for its ceramics which are produced in factories in the new town. **Torgiano** is renowned for its wine (*see p. 505*).

FESTIVALS & EVENTS

Perugia *Umbria Jazz Festival*, A weeklong summer programme. For details, www.umbriajazz.com, early July. *Eurochocolate Festival*, Exhibitions, cooking classes and tastings. For details, www.eurochocolate.com, mid-Oct.

LAKE TRASIMENE

Trasimene (Lago Trasimeno; *map p. 486, A3*) is a lake which has preserved its natural beauty to a large extent. It is surrounded by low, fertile hills covered with olive groves and vineyards, and reeds on its shores. It has some picturesque lakeside villages, and three lovely islands. The colour of its waters changes constantly according to the weather, and it is subject to sudden storms in winter. From a distance it provides one of the most breathtaking views in Umbria (particularly from the hills around Cortona).

It is the largest lake on the Italian peninsula, and the fourth largest lake in Italy, with a circumference of about 53km—but an average depth of only about 5m. Its shores have been inhabited since the Palaeolithic era, and by 507 BC it was under the rule of Lars Porsena, king of Clusium. It is famous as the site of the resounding victory of Hannibal over the Romans in 217 BC on its northern shores (*see pp. 511–12 below*), and it was often used as a battlefield in the Middle Ages, when numerous castles and fortified villages were built on its shores or on the neighbouring hills. Attempts have been made to regulate the level of the lake since Roman times, when the first outlet was constructed: another was built next to it in 1896, which finally solved the problem of flooding. Since the 20th century work has had to be carried out to try to ensure that the lake will not dry out in years of drought, as its level is constantly diminishing because of the formation of peat.

View of Lake Trasimene.

FISHING IN LAKE TRASIMENE

The lake has long been famous for its eel (*anguilla*), carp (*carpa*), tench (*tinca*), perch (*persico*), shad (*agone*), pike (*luccio*) and grey mullet (*cefalo*). Some 30 per cent of the fresh water fish caught in Italy come from this lake.

In past centuries most of the fishermen worked for the owners of parts the lake's waters or of the land along its shores. The only exceptions were the *vallaioli* of San Feliciano, who were both proprietors and fishermen, and who would spend the summer in simple huts on the shore, harvesting the reeds. Eels were caught in cane mats (*arelle*) placed on the muddy lake-bottom. Up until the 17th century, unusual fish-traps known as *tori*, made out of stacks of sticks, were used: it may be that the name of Tuoro was taken from these. Certain parts of the shore known as *porti* were kept as reserves to attract the fish, and here fishing was limited.

As early as 1342 fishing rights on the lake were regulated, and in 1566 Pius V introduced strict fishing rules as well as taxes on the catch. The fish was sold to fishmongers and transported by horse and cart to various parts of Umbria (the farthest place they reached, since they had to be sold in a few hours, was Todi). An arrangement also grew up whereby the fishermen and peasants who cultivated the fields around the shore would exchange each other's produce several times a week (without payment passing hands).

The traditional fishing methods changed in the 1950s, when artificial fibre was introduced in the manufacture of nets, and the boats were first powered by outboard motors. For a short period many peasants left the surrounding countryside and set up as fishermen, hoping to make a better living. The lake boats still have a flat keel, and the characteristic nets (*tofi*) or fish-traps (used for eels) are designed in concentric circles and fixed to wooden piles which stick out of the water. The fishing industry has been given incentives recently, and the lake is being restocked with pike and eel. About 150 professional fishermen still work here.

THE WEST & NORTH SHORES

Castiglione del Lago

Situated on a small promontory planted with olive trees, and dominated by its magnificent castle, Castiglione (*map p. 486, A3*) is the most interesting place on the lake. It was inhabited in Etruscan and Roman times, and in the Middle Ages its fortress was contended by Perugia and Cortona, the inhabitants always taking the side of Cortona. The Baglioni family of Perugia ruled the town after 1490: Machiavelli was a guest here, as was Leonardo da Vinci, who drew the castle in 1503. In the 16th century Ascanio della Corgna married Giovanna Baglioni; his uncle Julius III made him Marquis of Castiglione. He was a famous *condottiere*, his military achievements culminating in the victory at the Battle of Lepanto in 1571.

The little village has an interesting plan, with two parallel main streets ending in the gardens in front of the castle at the edge of the promontory. **Palazzo della Corgna** (*open daily April–Oct 10–12.45 & 4.30–18.45; winter at weekends only*), approached by a double ramp, was given its L-shaped plan when it was rebuilt in 1560 by Ascanio della Corgna, who probably used Vignola as architect. It contains numerous 16th-century frescoes, many of them by Niccolò Circignani, known as Il Pomarancio. From the studio of della Corgna, a door leads out to steps which descend to a long, narrow, fortified passageway with an old wooden roof and stone floor, which leads to the impressive **castle**. It was largely rebuilt by Frederick II in 1247, when it became one of the most impregnable fortresses in Europe. Its interesting plan is an irregular pentagon, with walls following the slope of the hillside, and four angle towers and a triangular keep. From the battlements there are excellent views down to the lake.

The battlefield of Lake Trasimene

On a plain near Tuoro (*map p. 486, A3*), where at one time the lake reached further inland, is the site of the battlefield where Hannibal routed the Romans in 217 BC, during the Second Punic War. Hannibal had marched over the Alps into Italy with his army, which included some elephants and about 6,000 horses. In the early hours of the morning of 24th June, 217 BC, the Roman consul Flaminius (who built the road still named after him, the Via Flaminia, from Rome to Rimini), rashly marched through the fog along the lakeshore with some 25,000 soldiers, only to be ambushed by Hannibal and his posse of 40,000, who had encamped on the surrounding hills. The massacre lasted just a few hours. Flaminius died in the encounter, and about 15,000 of his men, trapped between the hills and the lake, died or were taken prisoner; the others fled. Hannibal is thought to have lost only about 1,500 soldiers. The dead were burned in *ustrina*, remains of which have been found in the area. Hannibal had all the Roman captives killed, but let those from other Italic tribes go free; but at this crucial point in the history of Rome, when her supremacy was severely threatened, the cities of Umbria decided to remain faithful to her. Some Romans escaped to Perugia, and Hannibal was later unable to take Spoleto in his attempt to reach Rome. Byron, in the fourth canto of *Childe Harold* evokes the terrible battle scene and then records the tranquillity of the lake, in a description which is still apt today:

> Far other scene is Thrasimene now;
> Her lake a sheet of silver, and her plain
> Rent by no ravage save the gentle plough;
> Her aged trees rise thick as once the slain
> Lay where their roots are…

There is an interesting **itinerary of the battle** (*Percorso Storico Archeologico della Battaglia; marked by white signposts*), which can also be followed by car. It is provided with maps and explanatory panels, as well as viewing platforms. The first platform (*sosta* no. 1) has an excellent view of the lake and its islands, but is only just above the *superstrada*. On the other side of the main road (left), a single-track road leads inland. At the beginning of a cypress avenue is *sosta* no. 3. Beyond *sosta* no. 4 the road climbs uphill past another stopping-place (near a necropolis where soldiers' tombs and the base of a funerary monument have been found) to the hamlet of Sanguineto, whose name commemorates the bloody battle. A road continues right (keep right) and descends to another stopping-place (*sosta* no. 6), where there is a platform which provides the best view of the battlefield in a natural amphitheatre.

The Battle of Lake Trasimene

'Hannibal,' Livy tells us, 'had now reached a place which nature itself had made a trap for the unwary. Between the mountains of Cortona, where they slope down to the lake, and the lake itself there is only a very narrow path, an opening just wide enough to get through ... Further on is a somewhat wider area of level ground, and at the eastern end rises the barrier of the mountains. Here, at the eastern end, Hannibal took up a position, in full view, with his African and Spanish veterans ... He concealed his cavalry among the mountains north of the lake, close to the narrow western entrance, so that they could block it the instant the Romans had passed on within...'

The Roman consul Flaminius led his men straight into the trap. The Carthaginian cavalry quickly closed off his escape and the battle began. After three hours of hard fighting, Flaminius himself was killed. Livy goes on: 'For a large part of the Roman army the consul's death was the beginning of the end. Panic ensued and neither lake nor mountain could stop the wild rush for safety. Men tried blindly to escape by any possible way, however steep, however, narrow; arms were flung away, men fell and others fell on top of them; many finding nowhere to turn to save their skins, plunged into the edge of the lake until the water was up to their neck, while a few in desperation tried to swim for it—forlorn hope indeed over that broad lake, and they were either drowned, or, struggling back exhausted into shallow water were butchered wholesale by the mounted troops who rode in to meet them ... Such was the famous fight at Lake Trasimene, one of the few memorable disasters to Roman arms...'

Livy, History of Rome, 29 BC–AD 17

Isola Maggiore

This charming island, with a circumference of c. 2km and some 100 inhabitants, mostly fishermen, is the only island on the lake connected to the shore by a regular boat service throughout the year (*boats from Tuoro and Passignano*). It has no cars. Near the landing-stage is its one delightful, brick-paved street, with some 15th-century houses, and several simple restaurants. Here, too, is a little **museum** (*open Easter–Oct 10–1 & 2.30–6*) which illustrates the craft of lace-making, which was introduced to the island in 1904 and still survives. The 14th-century **Casa del Capitano del**

Popolo has a small museum illustrating the history of the island. The 12th-century church of **San Salvatore** contains a painting by the Sienese artist Sano di Pietro.

A path continues round the shore, with beautiful views across the water. A 14th-century Franciscan church and convent (St Francis is known to have visited the island in 1211) were incorporated in the Castello Guglielmi, a Romantic mock-Gothic pile designed and built by the Roman senator Giacinto Guglielmi in 1885–91. It was abandoned in 1960 and fell into ruin, retaining a remarkable atmosphere of decadent splendour, but is now being restored (*not accessible to the public*). On the highest point of the island, surrounded by olive groves, is the church of **San Michele Arcangelo** (*open as Lace Museum above*). It was founded before 1200, and contains 14th–15th-century frescoes, some attributed to Bartolomeo Caporali, and a painted Cross also by him.

Isola Minore, once renowned for the skill of its fishermen, was abandoned by the 16th century and is now privately owned.

Isola Polvese

Isola Polvese (*reached by boat in summer from San Feliciano*) is the largest island on the lake and has the most beautiful vegetation. It had five churches and 200 inhabitants in the 14th century, when the castle was built, but was abandoned by the 17th century because of malaria. It is now a protected area, interesting for its birdlife. There is a little beach (*bar and restaurant open in summer*), and a path leads to a group of poplars, tamarisk and cypresses near the impressive remains of the 14th-century castle, which has fruit trees growing inside its walls.

A beautiful path leads round the shore of the island in c. 1hr. The sound of the birds which nest in the reeds is remarkable: they include grebes, coots, cormorants, bitterns, kites, kingfishers and ospreys. Another path runs across the centre of the island, near which are the ruins of a 12th-century Olivetan monastery.

EAST & SOUTH OF THE LAKE

San Feliciano (*map p. 486, A3*) is an attractive village with a harbour for fishing boats. Some of the inhabitants work the reeds, which abound here. There is an excellent little **museum** which illustrates the history of fishing (*open daily except Mon 10.30–12.30 & 3/4–5/6.30*). Here also is the subterranean **emissary from the lake** built by the Romans, some 7300m long, and other outlets which helped to stabilise the lake's water level. A walkway built above the reeds leads in about 10mins out to a hide on the water where a great number of birds can be seen, including kingfishers and herons, which nest here, and (in spring) numerous migratory birds from Africa. There are excursions on an electric boat along the shore of the lake at weekends.

Panicale

South of Lake Trasimene is Panicale (*map p. 486, A3*), a picturesque little medieval village on a hill, with one of the best views of the lake from its medieval walls. It was the birthplace of the great early Renaisssance painter Tommaso Fini, known as Masolino da Panicale (1383–c. 1440), famous as Masaccio's master. The attractive Piazza Umberto I was built on a slope so that the rainwater would be collected in the well, replaced since 1473 by the present lovely fountain. Here is the massive fortified flank of the 17th-century **Collegiata**, with a very dark interior containing a lovely painting of the *Adoration of the Shepherds* attributed to Giovanni Battista Caporali. A museum illustrates the traditional craft of embroidery, which has been carried out here since the beginning of the 19th century. At the top of the hill there is a tiny piazza in front of the charming little Palazzo del Podestà (partly 14th-century), with a bell-tower added in 1769.

Outside the walls is the church of San Sebastiano with two **frescoes by Perugino**: the *Martyrdom of St Sebastian* is particularly beautiful; the *Madonna and Child* was damaged when it was detached.

Paciano

Paciano (*map p. 487, A4*) is another well-preserved little medieval village in a fine position, with a 14th-century castle. The church of San Giuseppe (reconstructed in the 18th century) preserves a *Madonna della Misericordia* from c. 1460. The little parish museum (*open on summer mornings*) has an unusual 15th-century fresco of the *Crucifixion*, as well as 17th-century reliquaries and 18th-century statues of the *Madonna* (the clothes carefully restored by the local inhabitants).

CITTÀ DELLA PIEVE

Città della Pieve is in a beautiful position some way south of the lake (but still with a distant view of it; *map p. 487, A4*). It is a well-kept little town with attractive streets.

HISTORY OF CITTÀ DELLA PIEVE

The origins of Città della Pieve begin with the Etruscans, who had a settlement here controlled by *Clusium* (Chiusi). This was later absorbed by the Romans, and in the 7th century was fortified by the Lombards against the Byzantine stronghold of Perugia. The *pieve* from which the town's name derives was a baptismal chapel dedicated to Gervasius and Protasius, martyred in northern Italy and much venerated by the Lombards.

In the Middle Ages the town was controlled by Orvieto until 1198, when it was taken by Perugia, who wanted to make use of its fertile agricultural land. Città della Pieve never sympathised with the Guelph city, and allied themselves with the Holy Roman Emperor Frederick II. In 1228 it became a free *comune*. Since the 13th century, most of its buildings have been built in red brick, which give the town its characteristic appearance. In c. 1446 the great painter Pietro Vannucci, known as Perugino, was born here. Many of his works are conserved in the town.

Via Vannucci

The main brick-paved street is named after Perugino. At its northern end is a well, the Pozzo del Casalino, from where Via Santa Maria Maddalena leads north past the exceptionally narrow and charmingly named Vicolo Baciadonne ('kiss the ladies') to the church of **Santa Maria Maddalena** (c. 1780 by Andrea Vici), which contains a 14th-century fresco of the *Crucifixion* attributed to Jacopo di Mino del Pellicciaio, a Sienese artist and follower of Simone Martini, who was active in Umbria in the Lake Trasimene area.

Back on Via Vannucci is another building by Andrea Vici, the handsome Palazzo Vescovile (c. 1780). Next to it is the church of **Santa Maria dei Bianchi**, which contains 18th-century decorations, and, in the sacristy, a fresco of the *Presentation in the Temple* by Antonio Circignani, who was born here in 1568 and was often called—like his father Niccolò—Il Pomarancio. The **Oratorio di Santa Maria dei Bianchi**, beside the church (*open daily 9.30–1 & 4–7.30; winter 10–12.30 & 3.30–6*) preserves a fresco of the *Adoration of the Magi* by Perugino (1504) with Lake Trasimene in the background. It was painted in 29 days, and copies of two letters from Perugino, found here in 1835, are displayed on the walls: he at first proposes 200 florins as a suitable fee, but then suggests reducing it to 100 florins since he is a native of the town, but after discussions with the confraternity finally agrees to an even more modest sum. This would seem to give the lie to Vasari's claim that Perugino was mercantile to the core and 'would do anything for money'. The charitable institution, founded in the 13th century, still operates and the robes of the brothers are displayed here.

Piazza Plebiscito

At the end of Via Vannucci is Piazza Plebiscito, with the **duomo**, built on the site of the original Lombard chapel, and dedicated likewise to Sts Gervasius and Protasius. The present building was begun at the beginning of the 17th century, and its façade incorporates 9th–10th-century sculptural fragments. The campanile was constructed in 1738. The interior (*open all day*) contains some particularly fine works. Above the first altar on the south side is a 16th-century Crucifix attributed to Pietro Tacca; the second altarpiece is a beautiful *Madonna and Child with Saints* by Domenico Alfani (1521). In the apse is a *Madonna in Glory with Saints* by Perugino, and a painting of the *Madonna* by Giannicola di Paolo. The frescoes above are by Antonio Circignani (who also painted several altarpieces in the church). In the Chapel of the Holy Sacrament are early 18th-century frescoes and a painting of the *Blessed Giacomo Villa* by Giacinto Gemignani. In the Chapel of the Rosary, there is a wooden sculpture of the *Madonna* attributed to Giovanni Tedesco. The font dates from 1548. The first altarpiece on the north side, of the *Baptism of Christ*, is by Perugino.

Adjacent to Piazza Plebiscito to the west is Piazza Gramsci, with the splendid **Torre Civica**, erected in the 12th century reusing travertine from an older building, and heightened in the 1400s. The restored Palazzo dei Priori opposite dates from the 14th century. The large **Palazzo della Corgna** (open as for the Oratorio dei Bianchi; *see above*), probably designed by Galeazzo Alessi, was commissioned by Ascanio della

Corgna (a future hero of Lepanto; *see p. 510*) on his nomination as governor of the town in 1550. On the ground floor the Sala delle Muse has a fine ceiling frescoed by Niccolò Pomarancio. Other frescoes on the stairs and first floor are by Salvio Savini (1580). There is a pretty view from the terrace. At the foot of the stairs is a curious sandstone obelisk, thought to be a sundial of ancient origin.

On the east side of Piazza Plebiscito (where Via Vittorio Veneto leads out of it) is the so-called **Casa di Perugino**, a little house on the site of one which may have belonged to Perugino's family. Almost nothing remains of the original building.

The eastern part of town

On Piazza Matteotti stands the **Rocca**, erected in 1326 by Ambrogio and Lorenzo Maitani, with four angle towers. It is connected to Porta Romana by a stretch of 13th-century walls. Further east is the church of **San Francesco**, with a 13th-century brick front. It contains paintings by Domenico Alfani and Antonio Circignani. The **Oratorio di San Bartolomeo** next to it (*open all day*) has a large fresco of the *Crucifixion*, known as the *Pianto degli Angeli*, by Jacopo di Mino del Pelliccciaio (1384).

Santa Maria dei Servi and San Pietro

In the south of the town (at the end of Via Roma) lies the ancient church of **Santa Maria dei Servi** (*open in summer on a guided tour at 11.30 and 6; in winter at 11 and 4.30*), transformed in the 18th century when it was decorated with stuccoes. It preserves remains of a *Deposition* by Perugino, frescoed in 1517.

In the far west of the old centre (at the end of Viale Garibaldi), is the church of San Pietro (*open as for Santa Maria dei Servi*), founded in the 13th century and restored in 1667. It contains a fresco by Perugino, recently restored, depicting *St Anthony Abbot between Sts Paul the Hermit and Marcellus*. From the terrace there is a lovely view of the Val di Chiana.

PRACTICAL INFORMATION

GETTING AROUND

• **By car:** Car parking in **Città della Pieve** is available near Santa Maria dei Servi, and at other places outside the walls. Otherwise with an hourly tariff within the walls.
• **By train:** There is a railway station at **Castiglione del Lago** on the old Florence–Rome line (some slow trains from Florence in 1hr 40mins–2hrs). The stations at **Tuoro** and **Passignano** are on the branch line to Perugia and Foligno (slow trains from Perugia to Passignano in c. 30mins).
• **By bus:** Regular bus services run between Perugia and Lake Trasimene (stops at **Castiglione del Lago**, **Tuoro** and **Passignano**). Services also link **Città della Pieve** with Perugia.

• **By boat:** Services are run by APM (www.apmperugia.it). There is a regular service throughout the year (about nine times daily) from Passignano via Tuoro to **Isola Maggiore** (and vice versa) in c. 30mins. The last boats from the Isola Maggiore to Tuoro and Passignano leave at 6.45pm, 7.45pm or 8.20pm, according to the season. From 1 May–end Sept there are more services from Tuoro to Isola Maggiore (10mins) on public holidays. From 1 April–30 Sept services at least eight times a day also from Isola Maggiore to Castiglione del Lago (and vice versa) in 30mins. On public holidays in April and daily from May–end Sept, services from San Feliciano 12 times a day to **Isola Polvese** (and vice versa). From 1 July–end Sept there is a service between Isola Polvese and Isola Maggiore.

HOTELS

Castiglione del Lago (*map p. 486, A3*)
€ **Miralago**. A thoughtfully restored hotel in the centre of town. The tasteful bedrooms have high ceilings and simple furnishings. Restaurant. *Piazza Mazzini 6, T: 075 951 157, www.hotelmiralago.com. 19 rooms.*
Città della Pieve (*map p. 487, A4*)
€€ **Vannucci**. In a pleasant position close to the centre of the town, between the churches of San Francesco and Santa Lucia. It has a peaceful walled garden and a restaurant. *Viale Vanni, T: 0578 299572, www.hotel-vannucci.com. 30 rooms.*
Isola Maggiore (*map p. 486, A3*)
€ **Da Sauro**. A simple little house beyond the end of the only street on this beautiful peaceful island. This has

been a delightful place to stay, with a good restaurant, since it was opened in 1964 by Sauro, a fisherman on the lake (whose wife and son also work here). For the timetable of the boat service from Passignano or Tuoro, see above. *Via Guglielmi 1, T: 075 826168, www.hoteldasauro.it. 12 rooms.*
Paciano (*map p. 487, A4*)
€€ **Locanda della Rocca**. In a lovely old country house in the centre of the village, owned by the Buitoni (pasta) family, with bedrooms which are charmingly furnished with family heirlooms. Restaurant. *Via Rossini 4, T: 075 830569, www.locandadellaroccabuitoni.it. 5 rooms.*
Panicale (*map p. 486, A3*)
€ **Le Grotte di Boldrino**. A family-run hotel in a handsome 19th-century palace in the old town. The rooms, most of them with views over the countryside, are eccentrically furnished but comfortable with lovely bathrooms. The restaurant serves local specialities, in the restored medieval cellars below, or in the garden in summer. *Via Virgilio Ceppari 30, T: 075 837161, www.grottediboldrino.com. 11 rooms.*
San Feliciano (*map p. 486, A3*)
€ **Da Settimio**. On the lakeside in this quiet little village, Settimio, formerly a fisherman on the lake, and his wife have run this simple hotel with a good restaurant for many years. Their son and daughter-in-law now help to continue the family tradition. *Via Lungolago Alicata 1, T: 075 847 6000, dasettimio@tiscali.it.*
Sanfatucchio (*map p. 486, A3*)
€ **Poggio del Sole**. Three kilometres south of Castiglione del Lago, this is an extremely well-run *agriturismo* sur-

rounded by olive and oak groves. Swimming pool, barbecue area and solarium. *Località Ceraso, T: 075 968 0221, www.terreumbre.it. 7 apartments.*

RESTAURANTS

Castiglione del Lago (*map p. 486, A3*) €€ **L'Acquario**. Excellent restaurant just off the main square at the east end of the old centre. Closed Wed. *Via Vittorio Emanuele 69, T: 075 965 2432.*
€ **La Cantina**. A cosy dining room in an old storeroom, with vaulted ceiling and a central fireplace, or tables outside in the summer. Delicious pizzas. *Via Vittorio Emanuele 89, T: 075 965 2463.*
€ **Il Lido Solitario**. Below the town at the bottom of the hill, with views across to the lake. Very pleasant spot, offering simple food at honest prices. *Via Lungolago 16, T: 075 951892.*
Città della Pieve (*map p. 487, A4*) € **Serenella**. Excellent value for money, with friendly service and wholesome food at this family-run trattoria. *Via Fiorenzuola 28, T: 0578 299683.*
€ **La Silvana**. Close to the church of Santa Maria dei Bianchi, an attractive restaurant which serves wonderful homemade pasta and other regional dishes in an attractive dining room. Closed Mon. *Vicolo del Gesù, T: 0578 298311.*
San Feliciano (*map p. 486, A3*) € **Da Settimio**. Right on the lake, with

wide windows affording an excellent view. The *tegamaccio* (fish stew) is a speciality. Closed Thur out of season. No credit cards. *Via Lungolago Alicata 1, T: 075 847 6000.*
€ **Rosso di Sera**. Imaginative cuisine, with an excellent range of central Italian dishes and a superb wine list. Closed Tues and midday Weds. *Via Papini 79, T: 075 847 6277.*

LOCAL SPECIALITIES

Fish is served in numerous restaurants all round the lake, and typical dishes include *regina in porchetta* (carp stuffed with lard or ham, rosemary, fennel and garlic and cooked in the oven with a little olive oil) and *tegamaccio* (a fish stew cooked slowly in tomato and white wine). Eels are usually cut up and fried or baked in pieces, and tench and perch filleted and fried in breadcrumbs.

FESTIVALS & EVENTS

Castiglione del Lago *Coloriamo i cieli*, Festival of kites, held biennially (even years) for three days at the beginning of May.
Città della Pieve *L'Infiorata*, Flower festival, Sun nearest 21 June; *Palio dei Terzieri*, Archery contest preceded by a parade in period costume, held on 15 Aug and the following Sun.

ASSISI

Assisi, on a commanding spur of Monte Subasio, is a little medieval town (pop. 25,000; *map p. 486, B3*) which has retained its beautiful rural setting with olive trees and cultivated fields reaching right up to its walls. St Francis of Assisi, one of the most fascinating characters in history, founded his Order here. In the great basilica begun two years after his death, the story of his life provided inspiration to some of the greatest painters of his time, including Cimabue, Giotto, Simone Martini and Pietro Lorenzetti: their frescoes here are among the most important works of art in Italy. In the 20th century Assisi became one of the most famous religious shrines in the world; it is uncomfortably crowded in spring and summer (some six million people visit the basilica of St Francis every year). In the winter months the town, which is slowly becoming depopulated, retains its quiet medieval character: at this time its famous monuments and picturesque old streets can be appreciated to the full. But even on the most crowded days, many charming old streets can be explored away from the crowds. Assisi also has important Roman remains: apart from the superb Temple of Minerva, a *domus* with exceptionally interesting wall paintings is in the process of excavation.

HISTORY OF ASSISI

An Umbro-Etruscan settlement here was succeeded by the important Roman town of *Asisium*. The elegiac poet Propertius was probably a native; his house is supposed to have been discovered under the church of Santa Maria Maggiore. The town was evangelised by St Rufinus, who was martyred here in 238. It was a flourishing place by the 13th century, but from the end of the 14th century when it was captured by Perugia, until the 16th century, when it passed to the Church, it was involved in the perpetual skirmishes between Guelphs and Ghibellines. After the Council of Trent it lost much of its religious significance as the shrine of St Francis. In 1786 Goethe described his walk up to Assisi, when he 'turned away in distaste from the enormous substructure of the two churches on my left, which are built one on top of the other like a Babylonian tower, and are the resting-place of St Francis', in order to proceed directly to the temple of Minerva, the 'first complete Classical monument' he had ever seen. In 1818 the coffin of St Francis was rediscovered and a new interest in the saint developed. Assisi was one of the worst-hit towns in the earthquake in 1997 and the upper church of St Francis was the most seriously damaged monument of major importance in the whole region. Restoration of the town is now almost complete: at the time of writing work was in progress on the careful repaving of the streets, mostly using the lovely rose-coloured local stone from Subasio and terracotta bricks.

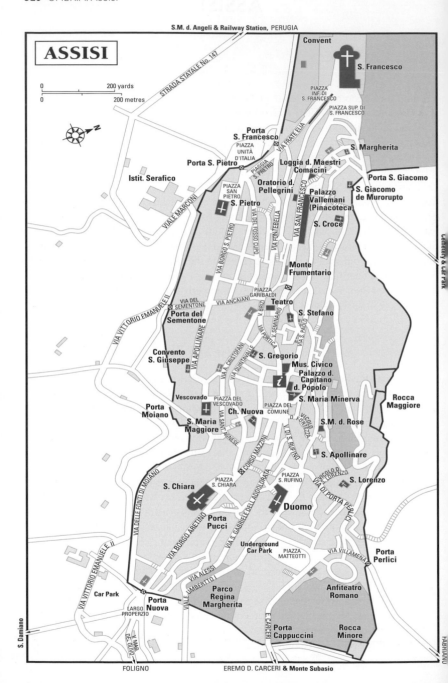

S.M. d. Angeli & Railway Station, PERUGIA

ASSISI

0   200 yards
0   200 metres

Z

STRADA STATALE No. 147

Convent

S. Francesco

PIAZZA INF. DI S. FRANCESCO

PIAZZA SUP DI S. FRANCESCO

Porta S. Francesco

PIAZZA UNITÀ D'ITALIA

Porta S. Pietro

PIAGGIA S. PIETRO

S. Margherita

Loggia d. Maestri Comacini

Porta S. Giacomo

Istit. Serafico

PIAZZA SAN PIETRO

Oratorio d. Pellegrini

S. Pietro

Palazzo Vallemani (Pinacoteca)

S. Giacomo de Murorupto

VIALE MARCONI

VIA DEL FOSSO CUPO

VIA BORGO S. PIETRO

VIA FONTEBELLA

VIA SAN FRANCESCO

S. Croce

Monte Frumentario

VIA VITTORIO EMANUELE II

VIA DEL SEMENTONE

PIAZZA GARIBALDI

VIA ANCAIANI

Teatro

V. BRIZI

S. Stefano

Porta del Sementone

VIA APOLLINARE

VIA A. CRISTOFANI

VIA FORTINI

V. SEMINARIO

VIA S. PAOLO

Convento S. Giuseppe

VIA QUINTAVALE

S. Gregorio

Mus. Civico

Palazzo d. Capitano d. Popolo

Vescovado

PIAZZA DEL VESCOVADO

Ch. Nuova

PIAZZA DEL COMUNE

S. Maria Minerva

Rocca Maggiore

Porta Moiano

VIA SANT'AGNESE

VICOLO D. FORTEZZA

S.M. d. Rose

S. Maria Maggiore

CORSO MAZZINI

V. DI S. RUFINO

S. Apollinare

VICOLO DI S. LORENZO

S. Lorenzo

VIA DI PORTA PERLICI

S. Chiara

PIAZZA S. CHIARA

VIA BORGO ARETINO

PIAZZA S. RUFINO

Duomo

Porta Pucci

VIA DELLE FONTI DI MOIANO

VIA S. GABRIELE DELL'ADDOLORATA

Underground Car Park

PIAZZA MATTEOTTI

VIA VILLAMENA

Porta Perlici

VIA VITTORIO EMANUELE II

Car Park

LARGO PROPERZIO

Porta Nuova

VIA ALESSI

VIALE UMBERTO I

Parco Regina Margherita

Anfiteatro Romano

E. CARCERI

Porta Cappuccini

Rocca Minore

S. Damiano

FOLIGNO

EREMO D. CARCERI & Monte Subasio

FABRIANO

Century & Car Park

St Francis of Assisi (1181–1226)

Francis was the son of a rich merchant, Pietro Bernardone, and of Pica (perhaps de Bourlemont, a Provençale). He was baptised Giovanni, but his father, who at the time was trading in France, called him Francesco. At the age of 24, after a year's imprisonment at Perugia, followed by an illness, he decided to give all he had to the poor, look after the sick, and lead a humble, exemplary life. He extended his devotion to animals and birds. As he was praying in San Damiano he heard a voice telling him to 'Rebuild my Church', and in the Chapel of the Portiuncula (Porziuncola; *see p. 533*) he heard the command 'Freely you have received, freely give'. He retreated with some followers to a stable in Rivotorto, and then settled in a hut around the Portiuncula.

In May 1209 he obtained from Pope Innocent III the verbal approval of his Order, founded on a rule of poverty, chastity and obedience. He preached his gospel in Italy, Spain, Morocco, Egypt (1219), where the Sultan Melek-el-Kamil received him kindly, and in the Holy Land. In 1221 the Franciscan Rule was sanctioned by Pope Honorius III, and three years later Francis himself retired to La Verna (*see p. 386*). On 14th September 1224, he had a vision of a seraph with six wings and found on his own body the stigmata or wounds of the Passion. He returned to Assisi and died at the Portiuncula on 3rd October 1226. St Francis was canonised in 1228 and became a patron saint of Italy in 1939. The Franciscan Order has various divisions: the first, a religious order divided into four families (Friars Minor, Conventuals, Capuchins and Tertiaries); the second, the Poor Clares, and the third, a secular order of Tertiary lay brothers. St Clare (Chiara), the daughter of a rich family, disciple of St Francis, and foundress of the Poor Clares, was born at Assisi in 1194, and died in her own convent in 1253.

THE BASILICA OF ST FRANCIS

Lower Church open 6.30–5.45; in summer 6.30am–6.45pm, but the east end is usually only illuminated from 9–4; otherwise the lighting is poor and it is difficult to study the frescoes in the other chapels in detail (binoculars are useful). Upper Church opens around 8.30, and closes at the same time as the Lower Church. Treasury of the Basilica and Mason Perkins collection of paintings open April–Oct Mon–Sat 9.30–5.

The two-storey basilica is the principal monument to the memory of St Francis. A fund for a memorial church was started in April 1228, and its foundation stone was laid by Pope Gregory IX the day following the canonisation ceremony. Friar Elias, close friend and follower of St Francis and Vicar-General of the Franciscans, took an active part in the construction of the church and it is thought that he may himself have been the architect. The Lower Church was soon ready, and on 25th May 1230 the tomb of St Francis was transferred there. The completed church was consecrated by Innocent IV in 1253. The beautiful tall campanile dates from 1239.

The colonnaded Piazza Inferiore di San Francesco was laid out in the 15th century, and rather unattractively repaved in 2000, with granite, stone and quartz from Brazil, Jerusalem, China and Namibia (trachyte from the Euganean hills, terracotta from Impruneta and stone from Puglia was also used). Here is the entrance to the Lower Church—which, because of the sloping terrain, has no façade—beside the huge convent (now a theological college), which is supported by massive tiered vaulting and buttresses built by Sixtus IV in the 15th century, conspicuous on the approach to the town from below.

Lower Church

The Lower Church of St Francis has a Renaissance entrance porch (1486–87) which protects its Gothic portal of 1271. The dark interior, lit by stained-glass windows, resembles a huge crypt with Gothic vaulting and low arches. Its form is that of a Tau cross (T); the narthex and side chapels were added at the end of the 13th century. It has a wonderful marble pavement, creamy white with rose-coloured patches.

Narthex: In this entrance transept is a 13th-century funerary monument **(1)** decorated, most unusually, with a huge porphyry vase (and no religious symbols). Also here is the tomb of John of Brienne **(2)**, King of Jerusalem and Emperor of Constantinople, friend of St Francis and a Franciscan tertiary, who was present at the saint's canonisation. The two carved angels are particularly fine. The stained-glass window dates from the early 14th century. The Chapel of St Catherine **(3)** was decorated in 1367 for Cardinal Albornoz (*see p. 550*), whose body found a temporary resting-place here before its transferral to Toledo. **Nave:** The floor slopes very slightly down towards the altar, and on the walls are the oldest frescoes (1253) in the basilica, attributed to a master known as the Master of St Francis, damaged when the side chapels were opened: on the right wall are Passion scenes, and on the left wall (with geometric decoration in the rib-vaulting), scenes from the life of St Francis. The lovely Cosmatesque tribune **(4)** has a 14th-century fresco by

Puccio Capanna (c. 1337). The two most important frescoed chapels are the first on the left and the last on the right. The Chapel of St Martin **(5)** contains a wonderful cycle of frescoes by Simone Martini (c. 1312–15) illustrating the story of St Martin. The chronological order of the scenes starts on the lower register (left side): *St Martin divides his cloak*; *Christ appears to the Saint in a dream*; (right side) *Investiture by the Emperor*; *the Saint renounces the sword*. Upper register: (left) *the Saint resuscitates a child*; *Meditation of the Saint*; (right) *Mass at Albenga*; *the Saint is honoured by the Emperor*. In the vault: two scenes of the *Death of the Saint*. Above the entrance arch Cardinal Gentile da Montefiore, who commissioned the frescoes, is shown kneeling before the Saint. On the intrados are paired saints in niches. Simone Martini may also have designed the beautiful stained glass in this chapel.

The Cappella della Maddalena **(6)**, with worn Cosmatesque panels, has frescoes (c. 1309) of the life of St Mary Magdalene, thought to be by Giotto,

ASSISI: ST FRANCIS, LOWER CHURCH

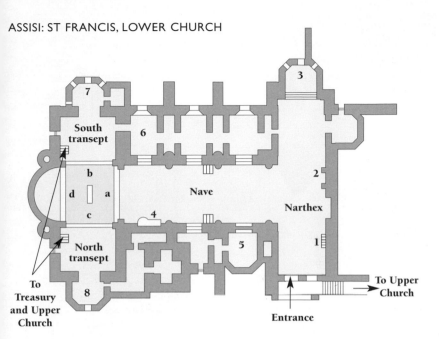

with the help of assistants including Palmerino di Guido. Left wall: *Supper in the House of the Pharisee, Raising of Lazarus*. Right wall: *Noli me Tangere, Journey of St Mary Magdalene to Marseilles* and the *Miracle of the Princess and her newborn child* (they are found alive on a rock in the middle of the sea). In the lunettes, the Saint is shown with angels, receiving the clothes of the hermit Zosimus, and kneeling before a priest. Her soul is also seen ascending to Heaven. In the vault, with stars on a blue ground, are *tondi* with figures of the Redeemer, St Mary Magdalene, Lazarus and St Martha. The rest of the decoration consists of figures of saints. The stained glass, with scenes of the life of the Saint, predates the frescoes.

Crypt: The crypt was opened in 1818, when the stone coffin of St Francis was rediscovered (it had been rendered inaccessible in the 15th century as a precaution against Perugian raids). In the side niches are the sarcophagi of the saint's four faithful companions: Fra' Leone, Fra' Angelo, Fra' Masseo and Fra' Rufino.

High altar: Consecrated in 1253, the altar is directly above the tomb of St Francis, which can be seen through a grille. The east end of the church is usually well illuminated (*for times see p. 521 above*) and has beautiful and well-preserved frescoes executed in a carefully worked-out scheme relating to St Francis. The cross-vault above the altar, known as the '*Quattro Vele*', contains four celebrated frescoes representing allegories of the three Virtues of St Francis: *Poverty* (**a**), *Chastity* (**b**) and *Obedience* (**c**); and his Triumph (**d**), richly decorated in gold, and probably the best 14th-

century frescoes in Italy. They are now usually recognised as by the hand of Giotto. The beautifully carved choir stalls date from 1471.The decoration, which replaces earlier frescoes by the Master of St Francis and Cimabue, was begun in the south transept and Cappella di San Nicola c. 1306, continued in the central cross vault (c. 1315) and terminated in the north transept (c. 1320).

South transept: In the vault and on the end wall are large scenes of the childhood of Christ, traditionally attributed to Giotto but now thought to be by assistants working under his direction, including an artist known as the St Nicholas Master. On the right wall, the *Crucifixion* may be by Giotto himself. Next to it is a *Madonna Enthroned with Four Angels and St Francis* by Cimabue. This survives from the earlier fresco decoration of c. 1280 in this part of the church, and the figure of St Francis is one of the most famous representations of the saint. The tomb of five companions of St Francis bears their portraits by Pietro Lorenzetti. To the left of the door, are half-length figures of the *Madonna* and *Child* with two king-saints, and (on the end wall), five saints including St Francis himself and one traditionally thought to be St Clare, all by Simone Martini.

The **Chapel of St Nicholas (7)** is decorated with frescoes of the life of St Nicholas, attributed by some scholars to Giotto, and with good stained glass dating from the same period. However, it is kept locked and is poorly illuminated. Steps lead down to the chapter house which has a fresco of the *Crucifixion* by Puccio Capanna (c. 1340) and exhibits reliquaries of St Francis including his chalice and paten, habit, and a horn and staff of office presented to him by Sultan Melek-el-Kamil, and the Rule of the Franciscan Order sent to the saint by Pope Honorius III in 1223.

North transept: The vault and walls are covered with moving frescoes of the *Passion* by Pietro Lorenzetti (c. 1320), including a large *Crucifixion* (damaged in the 17th century) and a *Descent from the Cross*. On the left wall is a charming *Madonna and Child with Sts Francis and John the Evangelist*. In the **Chapel of St John the Baptist (8)** there is a frescoed triptych of the *Madonna and Child with Sts John the Baptist and Francis*, also by Pietro Lorenzetti.

The Treasury and Mason Perkins Collection

Stairs lead up from both transepts to a terrace outside the apse of the Upper Church overlooking the cloister of Sixtus IV. Here is the entrance to the **Treasury of the Basilica** and the Mason Perkins collection of paintings (*for opening times, see p. 521 above*). From the windows of the Sala Gotica, where the precious church treasury is displayed, there are views of the lovely countryside. Amongst the most interesting exhibits is a magnificent Flemish tapestry; a Byzantine panel painting of *St Francis* dating from 1265; and an altar-frontal (1473–78) presented by Sixtus IV, with figures of the Pope kneeling before St Francis, designed by Antonio del Pollaiolo. The collection of paintings left to the convent by the art historian, collector and dealer Frederick

St Francis, one of five saints by Simone Martini in the south transept of the Lower Church.

Mason Perkins, is particularly interesting as an example of a private collection formed in Italy in the first half of the 20th century. Its most precious work is an exquisite *Madonna* by Pietro Lorenzetti.

Upper Church

Two more staircases continue up from the terrace to the transepts of the Upper Church of St Francis. This is a very fine 13th-century Gothic building which shows a close affinity to Northern Gothic churches, and may be the work of a French or even an English architect: it preserves its beautiful exterior with a fine rose window and portal, and a tall, light interior with the most important medieval stained glass in Italy. The earliest windows are those in the apse (c. 1253), probably by German artists, and the glass in the south transept and nave is attributed to the Master of St Francis, who is known to have worked between 1260 and 1280, and French masters.

The superb frescoes, carried out probably between 1277 and 1300, are by the greatest artists of the day, including Cimabue, Iacopo Torriti and probably Giotto, together with anonymous masters. They follow a careful scheme designed to illustrate the importance of St Francis in his role as an intermediary between man and God. Two bays of the vault and the arch at the west end, all of them covered with important frescoes, fell to the ground in the 1997 earthquake. They have been carefully recomposed as far as possible from the shattered fragments.

In the transept, crossing and apse are the **earliest frescoes** (c. 1277), with scenes from the lives of the Virgin and the Apostles, and the Apocalypse. They are very damaged and have lost their colour, taking on the appearance of negatives, for reasons still not fully explained. In the north transept are scenes from the *Apocalypse* by Cimabue, and a dramatic *Crucifixion*. In the crossing the vault is decorated with the four Evangelists, also by Cimabue (one of which, *St Matthew*, fell to the ground in the earthquake). In the apse are scenes from the life of the Virgin by an anonymous northern painter (finished by Cimabue). The papal throne also dates from the 13th century and is probably the work of Roman sculptors. The stalls date from 1501. In the south transept the frescoes, with scenes of the lives of Sts Peter and Paul, and another *Crucifixion*, were begun by an anonymous northern painter, and continued by Iacopo Torriti and assistants of Cimabue.

Nave frescoes: upper registers

In the two upper registers of the nave, between the windows, are frescoes of stories from the Old Testament (south wall) and New Testament (north wall), commissioned on the election of the first Franciscan pope, Nicholas IV, in 1288. Many of them have been damaged over the years. These were all ascribed by Vasari to Cimabue, but are now generally thought to be in part by pupils of Cimabue, and in part by painters of the Roman school, including Iacopo Torriti. Torriti also worked in Santa Maria Maggiore in Rome, whose decorative scheme was in part commissioned by the same pope. It is also now thought that Giotto may have been involved in some of the scenes; if this is so these would be his earliest works in the basilica.

The chronological order of the scenes follows the upper register, starting on the south side in the fourth bay with the *Creation of the World* and *Creation of Adam*, and continuing to the first bay, it then follows the middle register starting in the fourth bay with the *Creation of the Ark*. The two remarkable scenes in the second bay (with a striking use of a deep red colour) showing *Isaac Blessing Jacob* and *Esau Before Isaac*, for long attributed to an unknown 13th-century master called from these works the 'Isaac Master', are now usually identified with Giotto himself. They reveal an extraordinary new sense of volume and space, absent from painting before this time.

The New Testament scenes on the north side of the church start on the upper register of the fourth bay with the *Annunciation*, and continue to the first bay with the *Baptism of Christ*. The story continues in the middle register at the fourth bay with the *Marriage at Cana* and ends in the first bay with the *Marys at the Sepulchre*.

On the inner façade are two scenes of the *Pentecost* and *Ascension* and the heads of *St Peter* and *St Paul* in roundels. The frescoes of paired saints on the arch have been painstakingly recomposed since they were shattered in the earthquake, and the arch reconstructed. In the vault of the first bay of the nave are the four Doctors of the Church, now usually attributed to Giotto (the one nearest the rose window, with *St Jerome*, fell to the ground in the earthquake), and in the third bay, the *Redeemer*, the *Virgin*, *St John the Baptist* and *St Francis*.

The *St Francis* fresco cycle

The lower register of frescoes in the nave are the famous scenes from the life of St Francis, traditionally thought to be early works by Giotto and assistants (c. 1290–95), but not attributed to Giotto by all scholars. The story of the saint begins on the south wall, in the fourth bay, and the scenes are as follows:

1: The young saint is honoured in the piazza of Assisi by a poor man who lays down his cloak before him;

2: St Francis gives his cloak to a poor man (with a panorama of Assisi in the background);

3: The saint dreams of a palace full of arms;

4: The saint in prayer in San Damiano hears a voice exhorting him to 'Rebuild My Church';

5: The saint renounces his worldly goods in front of his father and the Bishop of Assisi;

6: Innocent III dreams of the saint sustaining the Church;

7: Innocent III approves the saint's order;

8: The saint appears to his companions in a Chariot of Fire;

9: Fra' Leone dreams of the throne reserved for the saint in Paradise;

10: The expulsion of the Demons from Arezzo;

11: The saint before the Sultan offers to undergo the Ordeal by Fire;

12: The saint in Ecstasy;

13: The saint celebrates Christmas at Greccio.

West wall

14: The saint causes a fountain to spring up to quench a man's thirst;

15: The saint preaches to the birds.

North wall

16: The Death of the Knight of Celano as foretold by the saint

17: The saint preaches before Honorius III;

18: The saint appears to the friars at Arles;

19: The saint receives the Stigmata;

20: Death and funeral of the saint;

21: The apparition of the saint to the Bishop of Assisi and Fra' Agostino;

22: Girolamo of Assisi accepts the truth of the Stigmata;

23: The Poor Clares mourn the dead saint at San Damiano;

24: Coronation of the saint;

25: The saint appears to Gregory IX in a dream;

26: The saint heals a man, mortally wounded, from Ilerda;

27: The saint revives a devout woman;

28: The saint releases Peter of Alife from prison.

Via San Francesco

Via San Francesco leads towards the centre of the town past many lovely old buildings, including the Loggia of the Maestri Comacini, where Vicolo di Sant'Andrea, a charming old stepped lane, leads up to a delightful quiet corner of the town with picturesque alleyways around the little churches of Sant'Andrea and Santa Margherita. A little terrace with two cypresses and a bench overlooks the upper church of St Francis and the countryside beyond.

On Via San Francesco, Palazzo Vallemani, with a long pale terracotta-coloured façade with handsome windows and an elaborate balcony houses the **Pinacoteca Comunale** (*open 10–1 & 2.30–5/7*). It is particularly interesting for its detached frescoes, including fragments from Palazzo del Capitano del Popolo, with 13th-century Gothic scenes with knights on horseback and representations of the seasons, and others from the city gates including a charming fragment of the *Child with St Francis* by Puccio Capanna, and others by Ottaviano Nelli.

The **Oratorio dei Pellegrini**, a relic of a 15th-century pilgrims' hospital, has delightful frescoes on the altar wall by Matteo da Gualdo; the vault and side walls were decorated in 1477 by Pierantonio Mezzastris with stories from the life of St James, including the miracle of the two hens resuscitated in order to proclaim the innocence of a young pilgrim who had been unjustly accused, and the miracle of a hanged man supported by the saint, and found alive by his parents. On the left wall are two stories from the life of St Anthony Abbot: the saint receiving some camels who have journeyed alone to bring provisions to the monks, and the saint distributing alms to the poor. The inner façade has figures of three saints, once thought to be early works by Perugino but now considered by some to be by his pupil Andrea, known as L'Ingegno, who was born in Assisi.

Next to a public fountain is a portico with seven columns, part of the huge **Monte Frumentario**, one of the first public hospitals in Italy. Founded in 1267, it was later used as a public storehouse and pawnshop for grain. The magnificent building which has a vaulted hall, remarkable for its huge dimensions, is being restored (it may one day be used for concerts). The road passes beneath an arch in the Roman walls, and continues steeply up, with a view ahead of the Torre del Popolo and dome of San Rufino.

Around Piazza del Comune

The beautifully shaped Piazza del Comune is the centre of the town. The **Museo Civico** (or Foro Romano and Archaeological Collection; *open daily 10.30–1 & 2/2.30–5/dusk; entrance in Via Portica*) is arranged in a crypt, and retains a delightfully old-fashioned atmosphere (*temporarily closed at the time of writing*). The collection consists of Umbrian and Roman material found in Assisi and environs. A corridor, with Roman paving stones and a drainage channel, lined with Roman inscriptions and funerary stelae, leads into a paved area first excavated in 1836, when it was thought to be the Roman forum. It is now usually interpreted as a sacred area in front of and below the so-called Temple of Minerva (*see below*).

On Piazza del Comune rises the tall **Torre del Popolo**, erected in the 13th century. At its base is a relief of 1348 showing various measures. Next to it is the 13th-century Palazzo del Capitano del Popolo, reconstructed in the 16th century. A neo-Gothic building (1927) has a 14th-century fresco of the *Madonna del Popolo*. The delightful fountain in the piazza was designed in 1762.

Beside the palace is the magnificent **Temple of Minerva**, with a perfectly preserved pronaos of six Corinthian columns on plinths which support a low tympanum, and a flight of travertine steps rising between the columns. The building dates from sometime between the 1st century BC and the Augustine age, and although always known as the Temple of Minerva, it may in fact have been dedicated to the Dioscuri, Castor and Pollux (*see p. 36*). The cella was transformed in 1539 into the church of Santa Maria sopra Minerva and given a Baroque interior by the local architect Giacomo Giorgetti in 1634. The church belongs to the friars of the Tertiary Order of the Franciscans.

Just out of the piazza is the **Chiesa Nuova**, built on the supposed site of the house which belonged to the parents of St Francis. The handsome, centrally-planned church dates from 1615, and contains contemporary frescoes, and stuccoes of 1769.

The Roman domus and Santa Maria Maggiore

In Via Sant'Agnese, beneath the 17th-century Palazzo Giampè, now the law courts, excavations have been in progress since 2001 of a Roman *domus*, where part of the peristyle and some of the rooms (with extremely beautiful frescoes) have come to light, dating from the 1st century AD. The structure appears to be exceptionally well preserved since it was filled with detritus and earth, rather than destroyed; but its excavation will be a long and complicated process since it now forms the foundations of the palace above. It is thought to be connected to the Roman house beneath the nearby church of **Santa Maria Maggiore**, where three rooms and a long corridor with more frescoes and lovely marble pavements were discovered in 1864, and traditionally taken to be the residence of the poet Sextus Propertius (c. 46 BC–c. AD 14). The church has a simple pink and white chequered façade with a good wheel window (1163), and above the doorway half a Roman marble fountain basin has been cleverly used to form a lunette. The interior has fresco fragments and a crypt dating from the 9th century. In **Piazza del Vescovado**, with a few trees and a 16th-century fountain, a delightful palazzo with a tall façade bears the name of its first proprietor Ignatio Vannola (*gonfaloniere* of the town in

1625), and a lion sleeps above the ingenious door. **Via Quintavalle** is one of the loveliest old streets in the town, and it leads from here towards Via Fontebella, named after a 16th-century public fountain, where the imposing exterior of the Monte Frumentario (*see p. 528 above*) is being restored.

In the northwest corner of town, the 12th-century abbey church of **San Pietro** (*open all day*) has a fine façade with a portal, guarded by two lions, and three large rose windows. The interior has interesting vaulting and a raised sanctuary beneath an unusual brick dome.

The duomo

The charming, secluded Piazza di San Rufino, with its wall fountain of 1532, is on the site of a Roman terrace which may have been the Roman forum (part of a Roman road was exposed in 2007 at the top of Via San Rufino). It provides a splendid setting for the duomo, dedicated to St Rufinus. Tradition relates that a chapel was built here c. 412 to house the relics of the saint, the first bishop of Assisi, martyred in 238. A church, which occupied the site of the present piazza, was built by Bishop Ugone around 1029. The campanile, which stands over a Roman cistern, the crypt, and the excavations in the nave, all survive from this building. The church was rebuilt in 1140 by Giovanni da Gubbio (who also raised the height of the campanile).

The **façade** has rectangular facing between its three doors, all guarded by lions. The main door has primitive pink stone sculptures in the lunette with *God the Father* enthroned between the moon and a star in a roundel, which recalls Byzantine iconography, flanked by the Madonna nursing the Child, and a male saint, perhaps Rufinus. This is surrounded by pink vine tendrils, and on either side of the door are six little columns with monsters in pairs at battle, and carved scenes above of uncertain significance. The outer arch is decorated with flowers, animals and birds. The side doors have pink stone lunettes with a pair of peacocks and two lions drinking at a fountain. White stone roundels enclose the *Agnus Dei* and symbols of the Evangelists, and animals, birds and fish. Above the doors is a frieze of animal and human heads, a gallery with blind arcading, and three lovely rose windows, the central one with good carved symbols of the Evangelists and telamones. The façade was heightened with a Gothic blind arch before the church was consecrated in 1253.

The **interior** (*open 7.30–12.30 & 2.30–6; weekends 7.30–6*) was transformed by Galeazzo Alessi in 1571, and large glass panels have been inserted into the nave floor to reveal the excavations of the earlier church. At the beginning of the north aisle can be seen a well-preserved Roman cistern with a barrel vault beneath the campanile. Both St Francis and St Clare were baptised in the font, and even the Emperor Frederick II in 1197 (at the age of three). St Rufinus is buried beneath the high altar. There are a number of altarpieces in the church by the local 16th-century artist Dono Doni.

In the piazza is the entrance to the **Museo Diocesano** and **Crypt of St Rufinus** (*open 10–1 & 2.30/3–5.30/6; closed Wed*). Here can be seen Roman capitals and part of the Carolingian cloister (still being excavated), with a well, and the crypt of the 11th-century church with primitive vaulting and Ionic capitals, where a handsome Roman sarcophagus (3rd century AD), with reliefs relating to the myth of Diana and Endymion, was once used as the tomb of St Rufinus. In other areas are exhibited a polyptych by L'Alunno, detached frecoes dating from 1334 from the oratory of San Rufinuccio by Puccio Capanna, and a standard with *St Francis Enthroned*, painted in 1378.

Further east, near Porta Perlici, the shape of the **Roman amphitheatre** (1st century AD) is perfectly preserved in the form of the wall and little houses, with a garden and a public fountain erected in 1736 next to the 13th-century Fonte di Perlici.

Santo Stefano, Santa Croce and the Rocca

Above Piazza del Comune is another lovely district. In a peaceful corner by a little garden with a view of the valley, is the simple little church of **Santo Stefano**, with a bellcote and pretty apse, and interesting old vaulting above the presbytery. Here in 1995 a tiny **medicinal herb garden** was created, with only those plants documented before the 15th century (all well labelled, also in English). Inspired by medieval monastic gardens, it contains aromatic herbs, and those used domestically (for dyes, preserves, condiments, moth repellants, etc.) or for curative purposes, or to decorate altars. Steps lead up to Via Capobove and Via Santa Croce, a pretty lane which follows the side of the hill at the top of the town, below orchards and olive groves. It ends at the convent of **Santa Croce**, occupied by German Capuchin nuns of the order of the Poor Clares. Steps lead down to the entrance to another convent (of the Franciscan Angelini) where you can ring to see the charming little cloister with two ancient low columns and the little Romanesque church of **San Giacomo di Murorupto**, with interesting vaulting.

From Via Santa Croce lanes climb the hillside to the **Rocca Maggiore** (*open daily 10–dusk*), which dominates the town. There are wonderful views towards the wooded Monte di San Rufino, and of the other citadel, known as the Rocchiciola, erected by Cardinal Albornoz (*see p. 550*) in 1367, with the walls enclosing the picturesque little *borgo* of Perlici. The hill was fortified in ancient times and its castle rebuilt in 1365 by Albornoz. The entrance is beside a circular tower added by Paul III in 1538. The inner keep is surrounded by a high wall with slits for marksmen. From the courtyard is access to the kitchen, storerooms and (on the floor above) the dormitory. A walkway leads to a polygonal tower, from which there is a remarkable view of the Basilica of St Francis.

Santa Chiara

Just outside the Portella di San Giorgio, a medieval gateway on the line of the Roman walls (but still within the present old town), is Piazza Santa Chiara, with a beautiful view of the valley and the Rocca on the skyline. The splendid red and white Gothic basilica of Santa Chiara (*open 6.30–12 & 2–6 /7*) was built in 1257–65. The simple façade has a portal flanked by high reliefs of two lions beneath a rose window and a tympanum. The great flying buttresses that span one side of the piazza were added in 1351; beneath them is a public fountain (originally medieval), with two large rectangular basins, recently reconstructed. The campanile is the tallest in Assisi. The present church was begun in 1257 as the shrine of St Clare. The lovely interior has a single nave with pretty vaulting supported by tall pilasters. The chapel on the south side preserves the famous late 12th-century painted **Crucifix that spoke to St Francis** at San Damiano (*see below*), as well as charming 14th-century frescoes by Puccio Capanna and Pace di Bartolo. Above the high altar hangs a painted Cross dating from before 1260, and in the transepts are frescoes and two paintings all by the 13th-century master known from these works as the Expressionist Master of St Clare, a close follower of Giotto.

The crypt, built in a neo-Gothic style in 1851–72, has the **tomb of St Clare**, and here (behind a modern grille) some of her relics—together with those of St Francis—are preserved. The triptych dates from around 1270.

In the huge Convent of Santa Chiara, enlarged in the 14th and again in the 16th century, live some 40 nuns belonging to the closed Order of the Poor Clares (they hold Matins and Vespers in the side chapel of the church).

ENVIRONS OF ASSISI

The Eremo delle Carceri and Monte Subasio

On the lower slopes of Monte Subasio is the entrance gate of the **Eremo delle Carceri**, (*map p. 486, C3; open 6.30–6; 7.15 in summer*), a forest hermitage in a remarkably secluded and peaceful spot, nestled in a wooded ravine. Here St Francis and his followers would come to dwell for a time in caves as hermits, and in 1426 St Bernardino founded a convent here. Beyond the entrance to the monastery is a triangular terrace (inhabited by doves) with two wells, overlooked by the little buildings of the convent with the refectory and dormitory, where a few friars still live. Various little chapels can be visited, and a cave where St Francis had his bed hollowed out of the rock. In the ravine iron bars support an ancient ilex tree on which birds are supposed to have perched to receive his blessing. Across the bridge there are lovely paths in the woods.

Monte Subasio (1289m) is part of a protected regional park with a number of marked paths. The mountain has a characteristic shape, with its gentle lower slopes covered with woods, and a bare summit. The views are magnificent and include, on a good day, the chain of the Apennines. This is a pleasant cool spot to picnic in summer, although many of the fields are fenced to provide pasture for animals. In spring cowslips and wild hellebores grow here, as well as the narcissus that is the symbol of the park.

San Damiano

San Damiano (*map p. 486, B3; open 10–12 & 2–4.30/6; Vespers at 5/7*) was where St Francis renounced the world in 1205, and St Clare died in 1253. It was a Benedictine priory documented in 1030, and it was restored in 1212. A chapel has a fine *Madonna and Saints* (1517) by Perugino's pupil Tiberio d'Assisi (born in the town), and the little church has a vaulted single nave with 14th-century frescoes showing *St Agnes, St Francis in Prayer before the Crucifix* (a damaged scene), *St Francis Throwing Away his Money in Front of the Priest*, and (on the west wall) the *Father of St Francis Threatening the Saint with a Stick*. The Crucifix is a copy of the famous original now kept in Santa Chiara in Assisi (*see above*), which, according to legend, spoke to St Francis here. From the choir, with its ancient stalls and an old fresco of the *Madonna and Child between Sts Rufinus and Damianus*, a door leads into the monastery, with another little choir once reserved for the Poor Clares, with more ancient stalls and a fresco of the *Crucifixion* by Pierantonio Mezzastris (1482). Steps lead up to an oratory with late 14th-century frescoes of the Poor Clares, and the old dormitory. A door leads out above the charming little 15th-century cloister, off which can be seen the refectory with its old tables and benches. Two frescoes in the cloister of *St Francis receiving the Stigmata* and the *Annunciation* are signed by Eusebio da San Giorgio (1507).

Rivotorto

The church of **Rivotorto** (*open 7–12 & 2.30–7*) stands out on the plain below the hill of Assisi, with its campanile crowned by a short spire. Next to another Franciscan convent, it is named after a stream which runs down from Monte Subasio and passes in front of the church, which was built in 1640 over a hovel where St Francis came to live in 1208. The interior, painted in brown, has little original character, but is busy with pilgrims who come to visit the two restored huts in the nave.

Santa Maria degli Angeli

The conspicuous domed basilica of Santa Maria degli Angeli (*map p. 486, B3; open 6–1 & 2.30–8; weekends 6.15am–7.30pm; Sat also at 9pm with a procession; July–Sept also 9–11 pm*). It is now surrounded by an unattractive small suburb. Visited by thousands of pilgrims because of its associations with St Francis, it has all the usual characteristics of a famous shrine (rather aesthetically unpleasing). The church is on the site of the Portiuncula where St Francis and his companions first came to live in simple huts and where, in a little chapel, he founded his Order. It was here that the saint met St Dominic, and here that he died.

The church was designed in 1569 by Galeazzo Alessi and finished in 1679, but except for the fine cupola and apse, it had to be rebuilt after an earthquake in 1832. Its architect was Luigi Poletti, and it was given its unattractive façade in 1928 by Cesare Bazzani. Beneath the cupola is the little **Chapel of the Portiuncula**, a simple rustic stone hut with pretty geometric decoration on the roof. Over the wide entrance is a fresco of the *Pardon of St Francis* by Nazareno Friedrich Overbeck (1829), and a neo-Gothic tabernacle. In the simple interior the splendid altarpiece of the *Life of St Francis*, the only known work by Ilario da Viterbo (1393), decorates the east wall. The tiny Cappella del Transito was built over the cell where St Francis died. Through the fine wrought-iron gate, frescoes of the first companions of St Francis by Lo Spagna can be seen, and a statue of the Saint by Andrea della Robbia. The **girdle of St Francis** is preserved in a glass case. The interesting decorations in the side chapels were mostly commissioned between 1590 and 1630, and there are also a number of 18th-century paintings by Francesco Appiani.

A portico leads past a statue of *St Francis*, where a dove nests, and a garden of thornless roses which bloom in May. The **Cappella delle Rose**, a barrel-vaulted chapel built by St Bonaventure over the cave of St Francis, has beautiful frescoes by Tiberio d'Assisi.

There is a museum (*open 9–12 & 3–6; closed Wed, Sun and holidays*) which contains a **portrait of St Francis**, apparently painted directly on a coffin lid, thought by most scholars to be by the hand of Cimabue (c. 1290).

PRACTICAL INFORMATION

GETTING AROUND

• **By car:** Driving and parking within the walls of Assisi are limited to certain times of day. Visitors are strongly advised to leave their cars outside the walls. The only large free car park is at the cemetery off Viale Albornoz (connected to the centre by minibus B). The three most central car parks (signposted 'A', 'B' and 'C', all with an hourly tariff) are in Piazza Unità d'Italia ('A'); outside Porta Nuova ('B'); and in Piazza Matteotti, partly underground ('C'), with minibus service A to Piazza del Comune.

• **By train:** Assisi's station is at Santa Maria degli Angeli, 5km southwest on the Terontola–Perugia–Foligno branch line (slow trains only); from Perugia the journey takes 25mins. Bus c. every 30mins from the station to Piazza Matteotti.

• **By bus:** Frequent buses link Assisi with Perugia (50mins), and with Santa Maria degli Angeli (20mins). Long-distance coaches come once a day from Florence, and three times a day from Rome. There are local services to and from Foligno and Spello. Timetables at the tourist office.

INFORMATION OFFICES

Assisi Piazza del Comune, T: 075 812534.

HOTELS

Armenzano di Assisi (*map p. 486, C3*) €€€ **Le Silve**. On a large, partly forested estate, 10km east of Assisi. Luxurious rooms and apartments in old stone farmhouses. The estate farm produces saffron, ham, salami, vegetables and cheese. Swimming pool and good restaurant. *T: 075 801 9000, www.lesilve.it. 19 rooms.*
Assisi (*map p. 486, B3*)
€€€ **Residence San Crispino**. A historic residence converted into hotel suites, offering spacious rooms, each with its own private balcony or terrace. In a quiet corner of Assisi, close to the basilica of Santa Chiara. *Via Sant'Agnese 11, T: 075 815 5124, www.sancrispinoresidence.com. 7 suites.*
€€ **Subasio**. The closest hotel to the basilica of St Francis. It has been thoughtfully run since its opening in 1868. Eccentrically furnished and decorated, the best rooms have a small patio with views. *Via Frate Elia 2, T: 075 812206, www.hotelsubasio.com. 70 rooms.*
€€ **Hotel Umbra**. Tucked down a quiet sidestreet off Piazza del Comune, this is an exceptionally friendly hotel which has been run by the same family for generations. Rooms have a small balcony with lovely views of Assisi and the valley. *Via degli Archi 6, T: 075 812240, www.hotelumbra.it. 25 rooms.*

€ **La Fortezza**. Small, central hotel with attractive, simple rooms. It is situated at the top of a steep flight of steps from the main piazza, so carrying luggage can be tiresome. Excellent value for its location. *Via Piazza del Comune, T: 075 812418, www.lafortezzahotel.com. 7 rooms.*

€ **Hotel Hermitage**. In an exceptionally pretty position in the centre of town, with a little terrace for guests. Rooms are small but well equipped. Extremely quiet. *Via Aromatari, T: 075 812080. 11 rooms.*

€ **Hotel Pallotta**. A pleasant, central hotel with helpful staff. Excellent restaurant (closed Tues). *Via San Rufino, T: 075 812307, www.pallottaassisi.it. 7 rooms.*

RESTAURANTS

Assisi (*map p. 486, B3*)
€€€ **Ristorante San Francesco**. Excellent regional cuisine combined with an unrivalled location in front of the basilica of St Francis. The view is breathtaking. *Via San Francesco 52, T: 075 812329.*

€ **Da Elide**. Conveniently located near the basilica of Santa Maria degli Angeli and Assisi railway station, this local trattoria serves flavoursome Umbrian food and is usually filled with locals due to its relaxed atmosphere and fair prices. A very good option. *Via Patrono d'Italia 48, T: 075 804 0867.*

€ **La Stalla**. A smoke-blackened former cowshed (the atmosphere here is marvellous) offering freshly cooked meat from a grill in the centre of the room. Delicious food at reasonable prices. A very popular and lively place, so reservations are highly recommended. Situated 2km outside the town centre. Closed Mon. *Via Eremo delle Carceri 8, T: 075 812317.*

€ **Trattoria da Erminio**. Simple, friendly and family-run. A good choice for lunch. Closed Thurs. *Via Montecavallo 19, T: 075 812506.*

Petrignano (*map p. 486, B3*)
€€€ **Ai Cavalieri**. A highly thought-of restaurant 10km northwest of Assisi. The bread rolls and pasta are homemade. Rooms available. *Via Matteotti 47, T: 075 803 0011.*

LOCAL SPECIALITIES

Monte Subasio is noted for its plant life. The pale yellow narcissus (*Narcissus poeticus*) is indigenous to the area, and is now a protected species. Culinary herbs grow plentifully, as do asparagus, juniper and chicory, all used in local cooking.

FESTIVALS & EVENTS

Assisi Festivals connected with St Francis are held throughout the year, with processions and liturgical ceremonies: Easter Week, Ascension Day, Corpus Christi, 22 June (*Festa del Voto*), 1–2 Aug (*Festa del Perdono*), 11 Aug (*Festa di Santa Chiara*), 12 Aug (*Festa di San Rufino*), 3–4 October (*Festa di San Francesco*), and at Christmas; *Calendimaggio*, Festival to mark the beginning of spring, celebrated with dancing, singing and processions through the streets. Traditionally, the participants separate into two factions, the rival Parte de Sotto and Parte de Sopra, based on two warring families in the 14th century, and prizes for the best performances are awarded on the last evening, in Piazza del Comune, first Thurs, Fri and Sat after 1 May; Peace March, An annual event, covering 23km, which begins in Perugia and ends at the Rocca Maggiore in Assisi, first week in Oct.

SPELLO, FOLIGNO & CENTRAL UMBRIA

Spello (*map p. 487, C4*) is a beautiful little medieval town, well preserved and charmingly situated on the southernmost slope of Monte Subasio, overlooking the wide alluvial plain known as the Valle Umbra, southeast of Perugia. The buildings are built of pink and white stone, quarried locally, and are well kept and decorated with colourful flowerpots. Many of the peaceful narrow streets retain their lovely old paving. The hillside is planted with olives. It has particularly important Roman remains: on the site of a settlement of the Umbri and then a Roman *municipium*, the *Splendidissima colonia Julia Hispellum* flourished here. Constantine named Hispellum the religious centre of Umbria. After destruction by the Lombards, it became part of the Duchy of Spoleto. In c. 1238 it was destroyed by Frederick II and then came under the dominion of Perugia. Today it is a small town with some 8,000 inhabitants.

The main entrance to the town is from the south, through the 14th-century Portonaccio. Beyond is **Porta Consolare**, a magnificent Roman gateway with three arches, beneath which can be seen the ancient paving of the Roman road. On the upper part of the façade, rebuilt in the Middle Ages, are three Republican statues found near the amphitheatre, and placed here at the end of the 17th century. The gate is flanked by medieval buildings, including a tower on Roman foundations. On the left, Via Roma follows a fine stretch of Augustan walls, built in pink and white stone from Monte Subasio, as far as Porta Urbica (or San Ventura), flush with the walls, also of the Augustan period. The steep and winding Via Consolare and Via Cavour, on the line of the ancient cardo maximus, climb to the centre of the town.

Santa Maria Maggiore

The Collegiata of Santa Maria Maggiore (*open 8.30–12.30 & 3–6/7*) was founded in the 12th century and reconsecrated in 1513. The façade (rebuilt 1644) incorporates Romanesque carving. At the foot of the campanile are two Roman columns of Luni marble.

The large interior was transformed in 1656–70, when it was decorated with fine stuccoes attributed to Agostino Silva (his best work is the altar of the Madonna of Loreto in the south transept). The **funerary altar of Caius Titienus Flaccus** (AD 60), one of the best pieces of Roman carving found in the city, is used as a stoup; an unfinished marble Corinthian capital serves as the other one.

The delightful frescoes in the **Cappella Baglioni** were commissioned from Pinturicchio by Troilo Baglioni, prior of the church, in 1500. They are among his most important works, and he may have been assisted by Giovanni Battista Caporali and perhaps also by Eusebio da San Giorgio. The three large lunettes, which incorporate numerous classical details, represent the *Annunciation*, the *Adoration of the Shepherds*, and *Christ among the Doctors*, and in the vault are four Sibyls. In the *Annunciation* scene, beneath a shelf, hangs a self-portrait of the artist. In the scene of *Christ among the Doctors*, the figure in a black habit on the left is a portrait of Troilo.

Pinturicchio (Bernardino di Betto; 1454–1513)

A masterful sense of the arrangement of figures and of the architecture of a painting's area, combined with a facility for conjuring a sense of airiness and freshness, make Pinturicchio's narrative paintings unforgettable and wholly individual. Neither by nature a profound nor particularly innovative painter, he nonetheless has few equals in his ability to lay out a pageant of figures in the illusion of open space. His most celebrated works are in the church of Santa Maggiore in Spello, and in the Piccolomini Library in the duomo of Siena (*see p. 423*). The rectangular hall of the library is not a special room in itself, but it has been transformed by Pinturicchio's skill into what feels like a protected loggia, opening on all sides into a clear and fantastic landscape, in which scenes from the life of Aeneas Sylvius Piccolomini, Pope Pius II, take place with naturalistic ease. In the same years as he was painting these scenes (1503–09), Leonardo was working on the *Mona Lisa*, and Michelangelo and Raphael were beginning their ground-breaking masterpieces in the Vatican; none of what was evolving in their experiments disturbed the serene surface of Pinturicchio's imaginative world. He is a master craftsman—a kind of pictorial perfectionist—the formal quality of whose works never drops.

One of the particularities of his method—rare in other painters—is the importance he gives to the relationship between separate scenes of a narrative cycle, helping to orchestrate their effect together as a group. A good example of this is his exquisite decoration of the Cappella Baglioni in Spello. There are single scenes on each of the three walls: an *Annunciation* (left), an *Adoration of the Shepherds* (back wall), and *Christ among the Doctors* (right). In the first, the solid architecture of a Renaissance palace beautifully frames a long, central view of open landscape; in *Christ among the Doctors*, the opposite is the case: open space surrounds the harmonious architecture of a central building; the *Adoration* synthesises these two themes in a broken collage of architecture, open space, landscape and figure groups. It is this natural thoughtfulness and symmetry of design that give Pinturicchio's works a sense of perfection. Nor are they without technical mastery on a smaller scale: the simulated panel picture with his own self-portrait, hanging on the wall in the *Annunciation*, is executed with perfect illusionism. This kind of 'conceit' was a frequent element of Pinturicchio's sophisticated taste.

Although he is justly famous for these two decorative cycles and for his earlier fresco works in Rome of the 1480s and 1490s (in the Vatican and in Santa Maria in Aracoeli), his output of devotional panels, painted in the very different medium of tempera and oil, is often overlooked. Here he is closer in style to his mentor, Perugino; there is the same love of placing minutely-executed detail against tranquil depths of space or landscape. More often than not, though, he reveals his identity by the inclusion of a 'conceit', some tiny, scattered domestic items, or a written note casually dropped in the foreground of a sacred scene.   N.McG.

The majolica floor dates from 1566 (perhaps manufactured in Deruta). In the rest of the church, the altarpieces on the south side date from the 17th century. The pulpit, font, choir stalls, and delightful baldacchino over the high altar all date from the 16th century. On the two pilasters flanking the apse are two very late **frescoes by Perugino** (1521), a *Pietà* and a *Madonna and Saints*.

Pinacoteca Civica and Sant'Andrea

Next to Santa Maria Maggiore is Palazzo dei Canonici, preceded by two Roman columns. It houses the **Pinacoteca Civica** (*open 10.30–12.30/1 & 3–5.30/6.30; closed Mon*), which contains some beautiful works of art displayed chronologically, including a fine wooden statue of the *Madonna and Child* dating from the end of the 12th or beginning of the 13th century. The 14th-century Crucifix has moveable arms. The precious enamelled silver Cross is by Paolo Vanni of Perugia, commissioned by the prior of Santa Maria Maggiore in 1398, and the little portable diptych, with the *Crucifixion* and *Coronation of the Virgin*, is signed by Cola Petruccioli (?1391). There are also painted panels dating from the 15th century, including some by L'Alunno. The bell from the campanile is signed and dated 1209. Sixteenth-century works include a polychrome wooden statue of the *Madonna and Child* and the banner of Santa Barbara. There are also five works by Marcantonio Grecchi, who died in Spello in 1651.

The church of **Sant'Andrea**, a little further north, was built in 1258. It contains 16th-century paintings, including one by Dono Doni of *Mary and Joseph* (unusual for its iconography), and in the right arm of the crossing there is a splendid large altarpiece by Pinturicchio and Eusebio da San Giorgio, and a tondo of the *Redeemer*, also by them (the *Resurrection* on the pulpit is also attributed to Pinturicchio). In front of the church, the picturesque Via Torri di Properzio, with charming little houses, descends to the remarkable **Porta Venere**, dating from Augustan times, the best-preserved of the Roman gateways in the town. It is flanked by two handsome pink 12-sided towers.

The northern part of town

Above Piazza della Repubblica is the Romanesque church of **San Lorenzo**, traditionally thought to have been founded in 1120. The interesting façade preserves Roman and medieval fragments. On the first pilaster on the south side is a well-carved 15th-century tabernacle. The altarpiece of *St Catherine of Alexandria with Christ and the Virgin* is by Frans van de Kasteele of Brussels (1599), who also painted the very unusual painting of *Christ and the Virgin receiving Souls from Purgatory*. The pulpit and baldacchino over the high altar date from the 17th century, and the choir stalls from the previous century.

Via di Torre Belvedere leads steeply up past the little Romanesque church of San Martino to a **Roman arch** which probably dates from the Republican era (part of it is underground). Remains of the Rocca are incorporated in the convent of the Cappuccini and the church of San Severino, one of the oldest in the town. In Piazza di Vallegloria are the church and monastery of Santa Maria, founded c. 1320. Via Giulia returns past the picturesque stepped **Via Fontanello**, and then a round tower of the Rocca, and (near the remains of a Roman gate) the characteristic Borgo dell'Arco d'Augusto.

FOLIGNO

Foligno (*map p. 487, C4*), on the River Topino, is one of the least visited towns in Umbria, but it has remarkable frescoes of secular subjects in Palazzo Trinci, as well as numerous interesting palaces dating from the Renaissance to the Neoclassical period, a fine duomo, and some churches with good 18th-century interiors. As the third largest town in Umbria (after Perugia and Terni; pop. 53,000), it was damaged in the last war and has industrial suburbs, but is an excellent shopping centre. It was one of the worst-hit towns in the earthquake of 1997–98, but restoration is almost complete.

HISTORY OF FOLIGNO

Foligno was the *Fulginia* of the Romans and absorbed the population of *Forum Flaminii*, another Roman town 3.5km west. Long a free commune, it came under the rule of the Trinci family in the 14th century until it passed to the States of the Church in 1439. Angela of Foligno (1248–1309), who became a Franciscan tertiary, was born here, and she became one of the most famous mystics of Europe. Foligno's school of painting was largely indebted to Nicolò da Foligno, or Nicolò di Liberatore, called L'Alunno (c. 1430–1502), who has a very unusual style. Printing was introduced to Foligno in 1470, only six years after the first book printed in Italy had appeared at Subiaco. The first edition of Dante's *Divine Comedy* was published here in 1472. Raphael's *Madonna of Foligno* is now in the Vatican.

The centre of the town is Piazza della Repubblica. The Neoclassical façade of Palazzo Comunale is by Antonio Mollari, and it has decorative bronze lamps. A medieval tower of the earlier town hall protrudes above the façade, but its lantern toppled down during the earthquake, and was being rebuilt at the time of writing. The Renaissance Palazzo Orfini (with traces of external painted decoration) may have been the seat of the first printing-house in the town. Next to it are remains of the Palazzo del Podestà with a large arch.

Palazzo Trinci

Palazzo Trinci, hidden behind a Neoclassical façade (1841–47), is a 14th-century Romanesque building reconstructed and enlarged in the Gothic style in 1407–11 as the palace of Ugolino III Trinci, who ruled the city from 1386–1415. Part of the exterior, dating from 1389, can be seen from Piazza del Grano. The beautiful brick courtyard has been restored. The interior (*open 10–7 except Mon*) is remarkable for its Gothic architecture as well as its early 15th-century frescoed decoration of secular subjects, in late Gothic style, most of them commissioned by Ugolino Trinci, and attributed to Gentile da Fabriano.

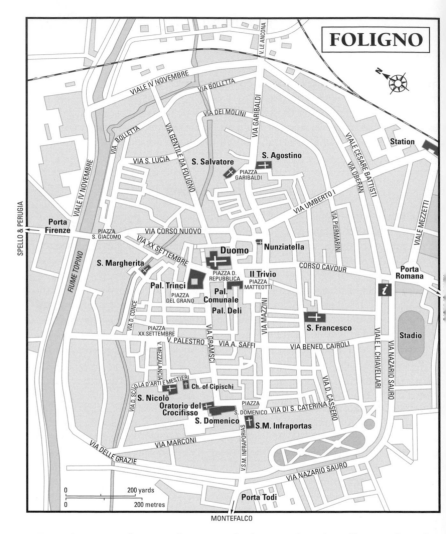

From the courtyard an outside staircase leads up to the ticket office. On the right, steps lead down into a series of Gothic vaulted halls (with some of their original wall decorations). The fine Gothic staircase, probably built 1390–1400, also preserves fragments of its original frescoed decoration with geometric designs. It leads steeply down to the ground floor where, beside the well, are some black-and-white mosaics found in a Roman house of the 2nd century AD Also on the ground floor is an archaeological section, with Roman sculpture including reliefs and a statue of a man in a toga dating from the 1st century AD found in Spello, and numerous inscriptions, all of them collected in Foligno between the 16th and 19th centuries. On the floor above are 14th–15th-century detached frescoes and a hall with an interesting old brick and marble floor and wood ceiling.

Top floor

The frescoes illustrating the legend of the founding of Rome, the Liberal Arts and Planets, the eleven heroes of Antiquity, the Seven Ages of Man, and the Emperors, were commissioned by the Trinci in the first three decades of the 15th century, and are among the most interesting secular works to survive in all Italy. After the discovery in 2000 of documents in the Trinci family archives, these are now thought to be by the hand of Gentile da Fabriano and his assistants. The epigrams and inscriptions were devised by the Humanist Francesco da Fiano.

Loggia and chapel: The loggia has very interesting frescoes illustrating the legend of the founding of Rome. A narrow staircase leads up to the chapel, where there are well-preserved frescoes of the life of the Virgin, commissioned in 1424 from Ottaviano Nelli by Corrado, son of Ugolino Trinci.

Room of the Liberal Arts and Planets: The Liberal Arts are represented by seated female figures in Gothic thrones: on the far wall (left of the chimney) are *Grammar*, *Dialectic* and *Music*; on the end (left) wall, *Geometry*, *Philosophy* (in the centre, but very ruined) and *Astronomy*. On the entrance wall, *Arithmetic* and *Rhetoric* are shown, both in the act of teaching pupils. The Planets are represented on the opposite wall, right of the fireplace: the *Moon* in a chariot drawn by grey chargers, and an allegory of *Decrepitude* in the tondo. Next to the standing figure of *Mars* in armour, a tondo depicts *Infancy*. On the next wall, is *Mercury* and *Youth* (in the tondo), and *Jupiter* (very ruined, with *Adolescence* represented in the corner tondo). On the last wall there was the representation of *Venus* and *Saturn* (very damaged) with a chariot drawn by red horses.

Corridor: This passage connected the palace to the duomo, and has fine frescoes of *Eleven Heroes of Antiquity* opposite the *Seven Ages of Man*.

Antique sculpture: Off the other side of the Sala delle Arti, this room displays pieces once owned by the Trinci family, including a relief of *Cupid and Psyche* (1st–2nd century AD), beneath which Ugolino Trinci added a long inscription in Gothic lettering recording the building of the palace; and seven Roman heads (2nd–3rd centuries AD), including Hadrian.

Room of the Emperors: The walls are decorated with a painted portico enclosing the gigantic figures of emperors standing in a meadow (c. 1415). More antique sculptures are displayed here, including a relief (3rd century AD) showing the games at the Circus Maximus in Rome; a sarcophagus front, also with circus reliefs; and a child's sarcophagus.

The room beyond displays detached frescoes, some by Giovanni di Corraduccio (c. 1428).

Sala Piermarini: This room is dedicated to the native architect Giuseppe Piermarini (1734–1808), including models of his works, and his bust.

Pinacoteca: Artists represented include L'Alunno, Bartolomeo di Tommaso (mid-15th century), Pierantonio Mezzastris, and Lattanzio di Nicolò, son of L'Alunno. **Room of Sixtus IV:** The wooden ceiling is the original. The damaged 16th-century frescoes are attributed to Lattanzio Pagani and Dono Doni.

Last room: Here are exhibited 16th-century works including an interesting view of Foligno by Il Fantino and works by Dono Doni, as well as a copy (painted in the 19th century by Enrico Bartolomei) of Raphael's famous *Madonna di Foligno*, now in the Vatican.

The duomo

On the east of the square is the magnificent north façade of the duomo (1133–1201), with a beautiful portal carved by Rodolfo and Binello. Between the north façade and west entrance is the pink and white Palazzo delle Canoniche with Gothic two-light windows (reconstructed in 1926). The main west façade of the duomo, also pink and white, with a rose window, was restored in 1904.

The huge, ornate interior (*closed 12.30–4*), reminiscent of St Peter's in Rome, although on a much smaller scale, was decorated by the native architect Giuseppe Piermarini in the 18th century on a design by Luigi Vanvitelli. There are 18th- and 19th-century altarpieces. There are long-term plans to open a museum here to exhibit a fine painting (in very good condition) of the *Madonna and St John* by L'Alunno, and two busts of Bartolomeo and Diana Roscioli by Gian Lorenzo Bernini. The church also owns a life-size 18th-century silver statue of *St Felicianus*, seated on a throne: although much of it was dismantled and stolen in 1982, some parts have been remade, and the scene of the Saint's martyrdom on the back of the throne was recovered. When the statue leaves the duomo in a procession on 24th January, it takes 16 men to bear its weight.

Northwest of the duomo, on a canal, is the picturesque **Via delle Conce** with old porticoed tanneries (a district particularly animated during the annual *Quintana* celebrations in September). In this area, near remains of a Roman bridge, is the church of Santa Margherita (or San Giuseppe), with a Rococo interior.

Via Gramsci

Via Gramsci has the finest *palazzi* in the town (all named and dated), including the graceful Palazzo Deli or Nuti (16th century), with a handsome portal and incorporating a medieval tower. The large Palazzo Alleori Ubaldi has a Neoclassical façade and contains contemporary painted decorations by Marcello Leopardi. Near the tiny church of San Tommaso dei Cipischi (1190), now deconsecrated, is **San Nicolò**, with a pink exterior. The charming bright interior with stucco altars, contains a fine polyptych of 1492 by L'Alunno (a *Coronation of the Virgin*, c. 1489, also by him, has been removed for restoration).

North façade of Foligno duomo.

BEVAGNA & MONTEFALCO

Bevagna (*map p. 487, B4*) is an attractive, ancient town on low ground surrounded by a fertile plain watered by numerous rivers. It has considerable Roman remains and a beautiful medieval central piazza. Its walls are well preserved: the medieval circuit in places incorporates Roman fortifications of the 1st century BC. An excellent red wine (including the strong Sagrantino) is produced in the district. The little town, which has a particularly friendly atmosphere, was badly shaken in the 1997–98 earthquake and San Michele Arcangelo is still closed for restoration. Bevagna was the Roman *Mevania* on the Via Flaminia to Narni, opened here in 220 BC. By 90 BC it was a Roman *municipium*, but lost importance in the 3rd century AD when the new Via Flaminia was diverted through Spoleto and Terni. Later, as part of the Duchy of Spoleto (*see p. 550*), Bevagna was ruled by the Trinci from 1371–1439. Hemp and flax were formerly cultivated in the surrounding countryside, and the craft of rope-making was still practised by a few inhabitants up until a few years ago. Today the town has a population of little more than 2,400.

Piazza Silvestri

The centre of the town is Piazza Filippo Silvestri, one of the most harmonious squares in all Umbria. The Roman column has a Corinthian capital, and the pretty fountain dates from 1896. The handsome 13th-century **Palazzo dei Consoli** has Gothic two-light windows and a wide external staircase. This was the seat of the government of the town until 1832, when it was severely damaged by earthquake. In 1872–86 the charming Teatro Torti (*combined ticket with the museum*) was built inside the Gothic shell, with painted decoration by Domenico Bruschi and Mariano Piervittori. The stage extends above three Gothic arches towards the restored two-light windows on Largo Gramsci next to the fine apse of San Silvestro. The ballroom, gaming room and foyer are all well preserved.

An arch (built in 1560) connects the palace to the church of **San Silvestro** (*open 9–12.30 & 3–7*), with an unfinished façade and no campanile. As recorded in the inscription on the right of the portal, it was constructed by Maestro Binello in 1195. It is built partly of travertine and partly of pink and grey stone from Subasio. The arch of the handsome portal is carved with a frieze with symbols of the Church and the devil in the form of a dragon. On either side is a comfortable stone bench. The three windows have pretty columns, and above is a cornice decorated with animal heads. The beautiful interior has a barrel vault in the nave, unusual flying buttresses in the aisles and a raised chancel. The handsome columns, with a slight convex curve (entasis), are crowned with double Corinthian capitals. The crypt can also be visited.

Opposite is **San Michele Arcangelo**, the parish church, built in the late 12th and early 13th century. The façade incorporates a fine 14th-century campanile and a central portal signed by Rodolfo and Binello beneath the relief of the dragon beside the bust of St Michael on the left impost. Opposite, on the right impost, is a flying angel. The door posts are made up of reworked Roman friezes. The wooden doors, with classical decoration and a relief of *St Michael*, date from the 16th century. The outer arch has Cosmatesque and marble decoration. Above is a frieze of human and animal heads and a large tondo, once filled with a rose window. The exterior of the beautiful apse, and the interesting flank, can be seen from Via Marconi. The lovely interior (*closed for restoration at the time of writing*) is similar to that of San Silvestro, with a raised chancel. In the sanctuary, beyond a glass door, a silver processional statue of *St Vincent* by Peter Ramoser (1785) can be seen. The crypt has ancient columns with Romanesque capitals and Roman bases (one of them an upturned Doric capital).

The church of **Santi Domenico e Giacomo** preserves some 18th-century scagliola altar frontals and paintings by the native artist Ascensidonio Spacca, known as Fantino (1557–1646). Above the 17th-century high altar is a bronze urn containing the body of the Blessed Giacomo Bianconi (1220–1301), who founded churches and convents in the town after its destruction by Frederick II in 1249 (and whose first tomb was the Roman sarcophagus still in the church). Via del Gonfalone leads past the side door of the church to the 18th-century church and oratory of the Gonfalone. Next to it are remains of a **Roman edifice** built in *opus reticulatum*, probably dating from the 2nd century AD, and thought to have been part of a port built on the River Clitunno.

Corso Matteotti

Corso Matteotti, on the line of the old Via Flaminia, is lined with some fine palaces, churches and convents. Palazzo Lepri, with a Neoclassical façade (1787), contains the **Museo della Città** (*open 10.30–1 & 2.30–5/6 except Mon*), a beautifully arranged small local collection with some interesting paintings. The archaeological material was put together in 1787 by the local historian Fabio Alberti, and first exhibited in this palace in the 19th century. The Roman material, all of it found in Bevagna or its vicinity, includes architectural fragments from the Roman theatre, inscriptions, sepulchral stelae, cinerary urns of Etruscan type, fragments of reliefs and statues from the Imperial era, and two fine portrait heads of the Republican era. The medieval section includes a bull of 1249 signed by Innocent IV. A Crucifix and statue of the *Madonna and Child* date from the 13th century. The Ciccoli altarpiece shows the *Madonna and Child*, with a boy of the Ciccoli family, who died at the age of ten. The work was commissioned in his memory by his uncle from Dono Doni around 1565. The native Bevagna painter Il Fantino is also well represented. The 18th-century *Adoration of the Magi* by Corrado Giacinto is one of the best works in the collection.

About halfway up the Corso, Via Santa Margherita leads right to the church of Santa Margherita, rebuilt in 1640. It has a 17th-century high altarpiece by Andrea Camassei, a painter who enjoyed the patronage of the Barberini. In a niche behind the altar (seen through a grille) is a good fresco of the *Madonna and Saints* by Fantino (1592).

Ancient Roman remains

Via dell'Anfiteatro, with pretty houses, leads left from the Corso along the curve of the Roman theatre, built on this site in the 1st century AD (the scena faced Via Flaminia). A yellow sign marks the entrance to part of the barrel-vaulted corridor which supported the cavea (later used as a wine-cellar). In Via Dante Alighieri a fine Roman frieze of bucrania has been set into the wall of a house. Standing on a high basement, is a Roman temple (thought to date from the 2nd century AD), later converted into a church. The exterior preserves some semi-columns and pilasters (with fragments of stucco fluting). In Via Porta Guelfa is the entrance to a building which protects a large **Roman mosaic** (*for admission ask at the museum*), depicting beautiful marine creatures, including octopus, lobsters and dolphins, in a symmetrical design. It was made of black and white tesserae at the beginning of the 2nd century AD. Discovered before the 17th century, it decorated part of a thermal building, more of which can be seen beneath the modern grid.

MONTEFALCO

Montefalco (*map p. 487, C4*) is a delightful little hill town with wonderful views. It is known as the 'Balcony of Umbria' because of its panoramic position. It has picturesque streets and numerous interesting frescoes in its churches. It is surrounded by extensive olive groves and its water-tower is visible from miles around. The area is known for its excellent wines including Sagrantino and Rosso di Montefalco which, together with other local specialities, are sold in a number of shops here.

Called *Coccorone* in the Middle Ages, the town was a free *comune* by the 12th century. In 1249 Montefalco adopted its new name, probably from the eagle (*falco*) of the arms of Frederick II, who visited the town in 1240. From 1383 until 1439 it was under the rule of the Trinci family. The medieval district, with the church of Santa Lucia, the 13th-century Porta Camiano decorated with the arms of the town, and Vicolo del Monte, are all worth exploring.

Museo Civico

From the charming, circular Piazza del Comune, with an attractive medley of buildings, Via Ringhiera Umbra leads downhill to the Museo Civico di San Francesco. It consists of a frescoed church, a pinacoteca and a lapidary collection (*open 10.30–1 & 2/3–6/7; closed Mon in winter*). The church was built in 1335–38 and contains 15th-century frescoes of the greatest interest. The main apse has a beautiful fresco cycle of the life of St Francis by **Benozzo Gozzoli**, one of his best works, showing the influence of the St Francis scenes in the upper church of Assisi. In the first south chapel, the Evangelists in the vault and a frescoed triptych with the *Madonna and Saints* (1452) are also by him. Gozzoli was a collaborator of Fra' Angelico, and worked with him in 1447 on the vault frescoes in the Cappella di San Brizio in the duomo of Orvieto. His most famous works are, however, in Tuscany, notably in Palazzo Medici-Riccardi in Florence and the duomo of San Gimignano. The frescoes he carried out in Montefalco, and at San Fortunato in 1450–52, had a wide influence on the Umbrian school of painters, including Benedetto Bonfigli and L'Alunno. His influence can also be seen in frescoes in the church of Sant'Agostino in Corso Mameli (which leads off Piazza del Comune).

Many of the other chapels have frescoes by Giovanni di Corraduccio of Foligno. In the sixth chapel is a fine painting of the *Madonna del Soccorso* by Tiberio d'Assisi (1510). It depicts the story of the Madonna saving a child from the devil (who has appeared after the mother's chastisement, threatening the child with the devil if he didn't behave). The square domed Cappella Bontadosi dates from 1589 with stuccoes and paintings by Fantino. On the west wall is a semicircular fresco of the *Nativity* (with Lake Trasimene in the background) by Perugino (1503).

The Pinacoteca includes paintings and frescoes by Francesco Melanzio (who was born in the town), a lovely *Madonna and Child* by the *bottega* of Melozzo da Forlì, and *Three Saints* by Antoniazzo Romano, a very fine but damaged painting. The Museo Lapidario is arranged in well-vaulted rooms downstairs. The sculptural fragments dating from the 9th–15th centuries include a stone lion (1270) and a beautiful 16th-century marble statuette of a river god.

Santa Chiara

Outside the walls to the south is the church and convent of **Santa Chiara**. This is the greatly venerated shrine of St Clare of Montefalco (1268–1308), who became a nun at a very early age and was abbess here from 1291. She was a Franciscan tertiary, but later followed the rule of St Augustine, and was famous for her devotion to the Passion of Christ. Her embalmed body is preserved here. She was canonised in 1881. The church has a fine 17th-century interior. The east end of the earlier church is now the Cappella di Santa Croce (*open 9.30–11.30 & 3.30–5/6; ring at the convent door at the end of the left aisle*). It has interesting Umbrian frescoes of 1333, including a crowded *Calvary* scene, the *Evangelists* (depicted with the heads of their symbols) in the vault, and scenes from the life of St Clare (as a child asking to be admitted to the convent; in her nun's habit, having a vision of Christ carrying the Cross; and her death, surrounded by nuns and friars). The convent has a 14th-century cloister, a collection of 16th-century marriage chests, a 14th-century Crucifix, the painted wooden chest (1430) where St Clare was interred, and a fresco of her by Benozzo Gozzoli.

Outside Porta Spoleto a road leads south (in the direction of Trevi) to the church of **San Fortunato** (*open all day; if closed ring at the monastery where three Franciscan monks live*), in a beautiful position surrounded by ancient ilex trees. A church was built here in the 5th century after the death of St Fortunatus, a parish priest known for his charity to the poor. The convent was founded in 1442. Off the 15th-century cloister, which incorporates four antique columns, is a chapel with frescoes (not in very good condition) of the life of St Francis (1512) by Tiberio d'Assisi, with a charming vault frescoed with *God the Father*. He also painted the fresco of *St Sebastian* in the cloister. In the lunette over the door into the church, there is a *Madonna with Saints and Angels*, frescoed by Benozzo Gozzoli, who also painted the beautiful fresco fragment inside the church of *St Fortunatus Enthroned*, in his priest's robes, a very striking work. His, too is the fragment with an *Adoration of the Child*, and three very worn frescoed *tondi* on a sarcophagus supposed to be that of St Severus.

TREVI & ENVIRONS

Trevi (*map p. 487, C4*) is a pretty, well-preserved little town (pop. 6,500) in an attractive position on a hill covered with olive groves. It has peaceful brick and cobbled lanes (mostly inaccessible to cars) and many of its old houses are decorated with pots of flowers. It suffered considerably in the 1997 earthquake.

Trevi became an important Roman town when the Via Flaminia was diverted through Spoleto and Terni. In the Middle Ages it was part of the Duchy of Spoleto (*see p. 550*) and seat of a bishopric. It later came under the rule of Perugia and of the Trinci of Foligno. After 1439, when it was incorporated in the Papal States, it became a commercial centre and in 1470 the fourth printing press in Italy was set up here.

The town centre

In the central Piazza Mazzini, Palazzo Comunale has a 15th-century portico, beneath which is a huge terracotta vase dating from the 2nd century AD, found in the vicinity. The tall 13th-century **Torre Civica**, lowered in the 14th century, is the emblem of the city. In front of Palazzo Comunale, the stepped Via Placido Riccardi leads up to the **duomo**, hemmed in among the old buildings of the town. It is dedicated to the city's patron saint Emilianus, a bishop martyred here in the 4th century AD. Founded in the 12th century, it preserves Romanesque elements on the exterior. The 15th-century portal has a charming relief of St Emilianus between two lions, and is flanked by two very worn Roman capitals. The three original apses survive, as does another door with a statue of St Emilianus. The centrally planned interior was reconstructed in 1775 and again in 1893. The altar of the Sacrament was beautifully carved by Rocco da Vicenza (1522). Beside the duomo is the fine old Palazzo Lucarini, seat of the **Flash Art Museum** (*open 4–7 except Mon*), a private museum of contemporary art.

Via Dogali, a pretty old street, leads to the medieval Portico del Mostaccio, once the main gate of the town. It continues up and back to Piazza Mazzini, out of which leads Via San Francesco, past the fine 16th-century Palazzo Valenti, to the Gothic church of **San Francesco**, the west end of which has been concealed. In the former convent are two museums (*open 10.30–1 & 2.30/3.30–6/7; closed Mon; winter only on Fri, Sat and Sun*), one of them dedicated to the history of the cultivation of the olive tree, and the production of olive oil. On the two upper floors is a collection of paintings (particularly important for its 14th- and 15th-century works). Lo Spagna is well represented. From the cloister there is access to the church of San Francesco, which contains two pretty *scagliola* altars, and a sarcophagus (3rd or 4th century), used as the tomb of St Ventura (d. 1310). The organ dates from 1509. Over the high altar is a fine 14th-century Crucifix. On the top floor are the earliest works in the collection: delightful small scenes from the life of Christ, and a very worn painted Crucifix dating from around 1310 (the head of Christ is particularly beautiful). Fifteenth-century works include the *Adoration of the Magi* by a Flemish master, and works attributed to the workshop of L'Alunno. The *Pietà* from the Madonna delle Lacrime (*see below*) is a good work of c. 1520–30.

View of the hilltop town of Trevi.

Madonna delle Lacrime

On the hillside below the town is the Renaissance church of the Madonna delle Lacrime, which contains an *Epiphany* by Perugino with a delightful background, some good 15th-century frescoes, and particularly fine 16th–17th-century funerary monuments, many with busts, of the Valenti family.

Tempietto del Clitunno

The little **Tempietto del Clitunno** (*open 8.45–5.45/7.45*) is on the Via Flaminia, the main road south from Trevi to Spoleto. It stands behind railings in a group of pine trees above the Clitunno river, surrounded by a little garden. Although adjacent to the road, it is easy to miss: it has to be approached from the old road which runs parallel to the fast road. The temple is thought to have been erected in the 4th or 5th century using Antique fragments from the pagan edifices which once lined the river here. It has a beautiful exterior with handsome Classical columns (two of them decorated to imitate the trunks of palm trees) and carved early Christian friezes in the pediments. The charming little interior also has lovely carved decoration around the apse and a tiny tabernacle. The very faded frescoes of *St Peter* and *St Paul* and *God the Father* are of the greatest interest since they are thought to date from as early as the 7th or 8th century. Further south are the **Fonti del Clitunno** (*open 9/10–dusk*), whose cool crystal clear waters were well known in Antiquity. The abundant spring was dedicated to the god Clitumnus, a famous oracle whose temple was erected here. Ovid tells of the white sacrificial oxen which were bred on the river banks. The beauty of this sacred spot was celebrated by Propertius, Virgil and Pliny the Younger, but soon after the Roman era the waters diminished considerably. In later centuries the little temple was sketched by Antonio da Sangallo the Younger, Piranesi and Palladio.

On the other side of the main road, surrounded by poplars, is a tiny chapel dedicated to **San Sebastiano**, which has lovely frescoes by Lo Spagna. A by-road leads up to **Campello Alto**, a well-preserved picturesque little hamlet, founded in the 10th century, on a mound in a beautiful position, with its walls intact.

SPOLETO

Spoleto (*map p. 487, C5*) is a beautiful old hilltop town (pop. 36,000) with Roman and medieval monuments of the highest interest, including the spectacular Ponte delle Torri. Many of the old streets are still cobbled, and in some of them charming details such as the old street lanterns and shopfronts have been retained.

The Umbrian *Spoletium* was colonised by the Romans in 241 BC, and survived an attack by Hannibal in 217. It suffered severely in the conflict between Marius and Sulla, but retained its importance since it was on the Via Flaminia.

THE DUCHY OF SPOLETO

The Duchy of Spoleto was established in 570–76 by the Lombards, a western Germanic people who settled near the River Elbe during the Roman Imperial era. At the end of the 5th century AD they moved south to the Danube, and their historian Paul the Deacon relates that they invaded Italy in 568. It seems that they established themselves with ease in the north, with Pavia as their capital, before descending into central Italy. By 603 they were in control of a large part of the peninsula. They chose the strongly defended site of Spoleto as the centre of a Duchy which ruled over a large area of Umbria and the Marche. Further south they created the Duchy of Benevento. However, the Byzantine Exarchate of Ravenna maintained power on the Adriatic coast, and a narrow corridor through Umbria was retained as a link with Rome (through Gubbio, Perugia, Todi and Amelia). In 774 the Franks took Pavia and conquered Spoleto and Benevento, and from 789 the Duchy of Spoleto was absorbed into the Carolingian (Frankish) empire, although it remained largely independent for nearly a century under a series of counts or dukes.

It was at this time that the temporal power of the papacy was established through the Papal States, and centuries later Spoleto was again to be important for its strategic position, when in 1353 Innocent VI made Gil Álvarez Albornoz, Archbishop of Toledo, a cardinal and sent him to Italy in an attempt to prevent towns from allying themselves with the Holy Roman Emperor.

The duomo

The duomo (*open 8.30–12.30 & 3.30–6/7*) was consecrated by Innocent III in 1198. The very beautiful façade is preceded by an elegant Renaissance portico (1491), incorporating two charming little pulpits. Above are eight rose windows, of varying design, and a splendid mosaic signed by a certain Solsternus (1207). The campanile (12th century, with additions from 1416 and 1518) incorporates Roman fragments. The main portal is a fine 12th-century Romanesque work. The interior was transformed in 1634–44 for Urban VIII whose **bust, by Bernini**, surmounts the central door. The frames of the rose windows are decorated with frescoes. The polychrome marble pavement dates in part from the 12th century. On the elaborate marble altar is a highly venerated icon of the *Madonna*, painted in Constantinople in the 11th or 12th century, traditionally thought to have been given to the church by Frederick Barbarossa in 1185. In the 12th-century apse are **frescoes by Fra' Filippo Lippi** of the life of the Virgin, perhaps the famous Florentine's best work, and one of the masterpieces of the Renaissance. The scenes, with monumental figures (larger than life-size), which cover the vast space of the semicircular walls are divided by painted columns and friezes, the Classical motifs of which are copied from buildings in Spoleto (including San Salvatore). In the central scene of the *Transition of the Virgin*, the group on the right includes Fra' Filippo's self-portrait (in a white monk's habit over a black tunic and with a black hat), a portrait of his son Filippino, who was to become an equally famous painter but was then just ten or twelve years old (the angel in front), and portraits of Fra' Diamante and Pier Matteo d'Amelia, who were his assistants and who painted the *Nativity*. In the half-dome is the wonderful *Coronation of the Virgin*, the best preserved fresco in the cycle, rich in blue and gold. The numerous figures include the Sibyls, Eve and other female personalities from the Old Testament, and angel musicians. Above, God the Father takes the place of Christ. No evidence of cartoons was found during restoration work on the figurative scenes. Many of the details (some of which have been lost) were added in tempera and highlighted with gilded wax roundels.

Filippo Lippi worked on these frescoes in the last two years of his life, and when he died here in 1469 he was buried in the **chapel in the south transept** in a tomb erected by Florentine artists at the order of Lorenzo the Magnificent, with a fine bust, and an inscription by Politian. In the same chapel is the recomposed funerary monument of Giovanni Francesco Orsini by Ambrogio da Milano (1499), who also worked on the portico of the church. The 16th-century altarpiece here is by Annibale Carracci.

The **Cappella Eroli** (first south), dating from 1497, has a frescoed altar niche by Pinturicchio. In a 16th-century chapel in the north aisle are displayed a 14th-century *Madonna and Child* in polychrome wood and an autograph letter of St Francis (to Fra' Leone), one of only two letters written by the Saint which have survived. The first north altar contains a brightly coloured Crucifix, signed and dated 1187 by Alberto Sotio, the earliest known Umbrian painter.

Museo Diocesano

The Museo Diocesano (*open March–Oct 10–1 & 3–6; weekends 10–6; closed on Mon in*

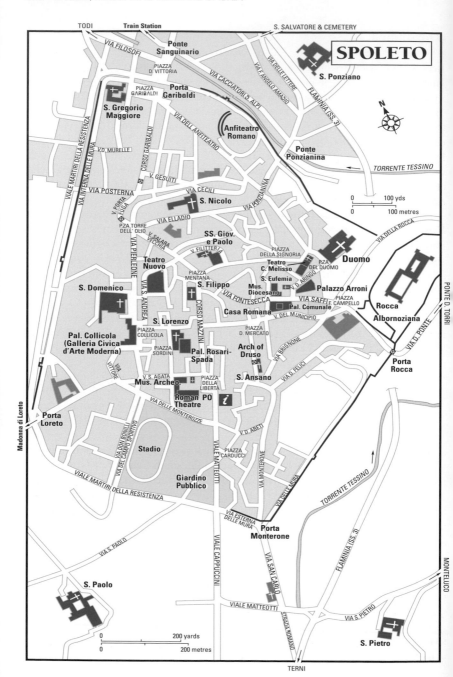

winter) is arranged in pleasant 18th-century rooms, with delightful views. It contains interesting 13th- and 14th-century paintings; a lovely *Adoration of the Child* by Domenico Beccafumi (in its original frame), a *Madonna and Child with Saints* by Filippino Lippi and hi s workshop, and a *Madonna of the Snow* by Neri di Bicci. Another room has 16th-century works by Giovanni Sparapane, an artist from Norcia. The collection of sculptures includes several fine 13th- and 14th-century statues of the *Madonna and Child* from the Valnerina. Early 17th-century works include a **bust of St Filippo Neri** by Alessandro Algardi, a **bust of Urban VIII** by Gian Lorenzo Bernini. Steps lead into the matroneum of the 12th-century church of Sant'Eufemia, with a beautiful plain Romanesque interior with some interesting capitals. The 13th-century Cosmatesque altar has exquisite carvings. Some of the columns are decorated with 15th-century frescoes.

Rocca Albornoziana

Near a splendid colossal 17th-century mask serving as a wall fountain (which marks the end of the Roman, and later medieval, aqueduct) is the entrance gate to the Rocca Albornoziana, erected in 1359–64 by Gattapone for Cardinal Albornoz, and which still dominates the town. It was used as a prison up until 1982, and since then has been undergoing a complicated restoration, but can now be visited (*open daily 10–12.30 & 2.30–5/7; weekends 10–5/7; guided tours on the hour every hour; the ticket includes the shuttle bus up the hill*). A museum with material relating to the medieval Duchy of Spoleto is to be arranged here. Albornoz used this castle as his headquarters, although he built many other fortresses, notably in Assisi and Viterbo. When he died in 1367 he was temporarily buried in the lower church of St Francis in Assisi (in a chapel designed by Gattapone), before his body was escorted back to Toledo.

A road leads up through several gates to the huge castle. There are superb views of the Ponte delle Torri, the unspoilt valley of the Via Flaminia, the walls which descend the hillside, and the plain towards Assisi. The Cortile delle Armi has been adapted as a huge open-air theatre. It adjoins the beautiful Cortile d'Onore, with a handsome well, which is thought to date in part from the time of Gattapone, but which was completed in the 15th century by Bernardo Rossellino, when Nicholas V enlarged the castle. The paving has been carefully renewed here (and new terracotta floors have been laid in all the main rooms). The most interesting frescoes to have survived from the early 15th century are in the Sala Pinta. Divided into two parts, they show charming scenes of courtly love and chivalrous deeds, including a tournament.

Ponte delle Torri

The peaceful Via del Ponte leads past the old wall of the castle. The wooded ravine here is spanned by the magnificent Ponte delle Torri, a bridge and aqueduct 250m long and 80m high, also probably built by Gattapone, but possibly on Roman foundations. In an incredibly peaceful spot, where the view is still unspoilt, the bridge can be crossed on foot and is one of the most remarkable sights in Italy (it was greatly admired by Goethe in 1786: his description of it is recorded here). Via del Ponte (*closed to cars*) continues round the castle hill, and steps lead down to the pretty hill-side below it.

Remains of Roman Spoletium

In Via Visiale is the entrance to the **Casa Romana** (*open daily 10–6/8*), the fascinating remains of a Roman house, supposed to have belonged to Vespasia Polla (1st century AD), Vespasian's mother, found and excavated in 1885–1912. It has very fine black-and-white geometric mosaic pavements. In the large atrium is a beautiful well-head (the sides apparently worn away by the iron chain used to draw up the water) and marble impluvium. The tablinum, triclinium and peristyle have been identified, and a fragment of red wall-painting survives. The walls and vaults are medieval or modern.

The central Piazza del Mercato is on the site of the Roman forum. A small daily market is still held here, with local farmers' produce. The monumental wall fountain (1746) incorporates a monument to Urban VIII by Carlo Maderno (1626).

Via Arco di Druso passes beneath the Roman **Arch of Drusus**, dedicated in AD 23 to Drusus and Germanicus (the lower part of the arch is buried). Beside the arch the foundations of the cella of a Roman temple and Roman shops can be seen. These are now part of the wall of the church of Sant'Ansano, which was built above it in the Middle Ages. The church was redesigned in the 18th century by Antonio Dotti, and contains a fresco fragment of the *Madonna and Child* by Lo Spagna, who was born in the town c. 1450. Remains of the Roman temple (1st century AD) have been exposed around the altar. The 11th-century crypt (*open 8.30–12 & 3.30–5.30/6.30*) has ancient columns with 8th–9th-century capitals, and very interesting primitive (11th–12th-century) frescoes (detached and restored). The 11th–12th-century sarcophagus of St Isacco, who died in 552, is a copy of the original now kept in the Rocca Albornoziana.

The Roman theatre and Museo Archeologico

In Piazza della Libertà there is a fine view of the **Roman theatre** (this, and the archaeological museum are entered down the passageway to the right; *open 8.30–7.30*). The theatre dates from the Imperial era; it was damaged by landslides and built over in the Middle Ages. The ruins were drawn in the 16th century by Baldassare Peruzzi, but were only rediscovered in 1891. After 1954 they were uncovered and heavily restored. A remarkable barrel-vaulted passageway survives beneath the cavea. The scena retains part of its lovely polychrome marble pavement (*covered in winter*), and behind it is the Romanesque apse of Sant'Agata.

In the conventual buildings is the **Museo Archeologico**. On the first floor are well-labelled finds from the town and surrounding territory, dating from the Bronze Age to the Middle Ages and including material from the tomb of a warrior found in the Piazza d'Armi of the Rocca Albornoziana, and jewellery and pottery (7th–4th centuries BC). The most recent excavations in various parts of the city have yielded more Bronze Age material. In the former refectory is a fine display of Roman busts and portrait heads (2nd–3rd century AD), the torso of a boy found in the theatre, and portraits of Augustus and Julius Caesar (1st century AD). Beyond is a section with beautifully carved epigraphs

(1st century AD) and, at the end, two remarkable inscriptions of the 3rd century BC forbidding the cutting of timber in a sacred grove. In a room off the staircase, diagrams explain the history of the occupation of the Colle Sant'Elia with Roman and medieval finds. On the second floor is a fine display of finds from the Valnerina, including a colossal marble head from Arrone (3rd–2nd century BC), and numerous works from the Santa Scolastica necropolis of Norcia (note the splendid carved bone decorations from a funerary bed, and two circular *cippi* with dancing figures).

The Galleria and Pinacoteca

The grand Palazzo Collicola (1737) now houses the **Galleria Civica d'Arte Moderna** (*open 10.30–1 & 3/3.30–5.30/7, except Tues*). Abstract artists represented include Alexander Calder, Anthony Caro, Lynn Chadwick and Pietro Consagra. The 13th-century church of **San Domenico** has a pleasant pink-and-white banded exterior. In the interior is a charming early 15th-century fresco of the *Triumph of St Thomas Aquinas*. Above the altar hangs a 14th-century painted Crucifix. In the centre of the nave is a striking polychrome wooden Crucifix.

On Corso Mazzini, the main shopping street of the town, particularly crowded with people taking their *passeggiata* on Sundays, Palazzo Rosari-Spada temporarily houses the **Pinacoteca Comunale** (*open 2.30–5; summer 4.30–7; closed Tues*), with paintings by the Maestro di Cesi (late 13th or early 14th century), Antonello da Saliba, L'Alunno, Bartholomeus Spranger, Livio Agresti, Sebastiano Conca and Guercino. Frescoes include a 14th-century *Crucifixion*; a lunette dating from the late 12th or early 13th century with scenes of the martyrdom of Sts John and Paul, attributed to Alberto Sotio; and works by Lo Spagna. There is also a collection of reliquaries, including an exquisite Cross painted on both sides and two small paintings of saints by the Maestro di Sant'Alò (late 13th or early 14th century), as well as a beautiful little 13th-century icon of the *Redeemer*, encrusted with jewels, showing Byzantine influence.

The former church of **Santi Giovanni e Paolo** (*only open by appointment; T: 0743 46434*), consecrated in 1174, has particularly interesting frescoes, which include a contemporary scene of the *Martyrdom of St Thomas Becket* (d. 1170) and a figure of *St Nicholas*, both attributed to Alberto (late 12th or early 13th century).

The busy **Via Cecili** follows the best section of walls. The polygonal masonry dates from the end of the 4th century BC; the walls were consolidated by the Romans and in subsequent centuries right up to the 15th century.

San Ponziano and San Salvatore

These important churches are close to each other but now on the far side of the Flaminia *superstrada*, and the approach on foot is not very pleasant.

The 12th-century church of **San Ponziano** is dedicated to the patron saint of Spoleto. It has a fine façade, with symbols of the Evangelists around the oculus, and a lovely Cosmatesque portal with delicate carving. The interior (*shown 8.30–5.30/6 by the custodian who lives at the house with a flight of outside steps on the right*) was remodelled by Giuseppe Valadier in 1788. Some huge old Corinthian columns embedded

Twelfth-century relief representing *Work* on the church of San Pietro, outside Spoleto.

into the later wall of the church can be seen in the corridor on the way to the crypt which leads past a sarcophagus from the Lombard period and a 15th-century terracotta sarcophagus. The crypt has two rare conical pillars, thought to be *metae* from a Roman circus. The 14th- and 15th-century fresco fragments include a fine *Trinity* beneath a little vault painted with four charming angels.

Via San Salvatore continues to the cemetery and the remarkable church of **San Salvatore** (or Il Crocifisso), an early Christian church almost certainly dating from the late 4th or early 5th century, and of the greatest interest for its numerous Classical elements. The damaged façade has three exquisitely carved portals with similar decorations: the architraves have volutes with flowers and rosettes on either side of a central Cross and delicate Classical friezes. Unfortunately only one of the beautiful curved brackets survives. Above a cornice are three windows, in the form of Classical aedicules. Here is preserved part of the marble panelling which used to decorate the entire upper part of the façade: it has very unusual Oriental motifs (repeated in the decoration of the doorways). Originally there was probably a portico on the lower part of the façade. The venerable interior (*open 7–dusk*) has numerous Classical columns and Roman architraves. The basilican nave has been altered, but at the extreme ends fragments survive of the Classical entablature and Doric columns which supported it. In the beautiful domed presbytery are 16 huge columns, mostly with Corinthian capitals (but some with Ionic and Doric ones) beneath an entablature (which continues that of the nave). Above the Classical cornice, part of the original decoration with pilasters between rectangles can be seen. The dome (apparently heightened in the 17th century) is supported by splendid acanthus-leaf capitals at the four corners of the presbytery. In a niche there is a very rare but damaged fresco showing a Cross with gems hanging from it, dated to the 8th century. The two chapels on either side, formerly closed sacristies, have remains of frescoes including the *Holy Father* and *Madonna and Saints* by a follower of Benozzo Gozzoli (1478).

San Pietro

Outside the town to the south is the ancient church of **San Pietro** (reached on foot from Piazza del Mercato by the steep old Via Monterone, Via San Carlo and then left across the Flaminia *superstrada*; or by a pretty walk across Ponte delle Torri by the Monteluco road). Reconstructed in the 13th century, it has a Lombard façade with a magnificent variety of large 12th-century reliefs, among the most important Romanesque sculptures in Umbria. On the upper part are high reliefs of Sts Peter and Andrew above two bulls looking down. Around the central Cosmatesque oculus are symbols of the Evangelists. The central door is surmounted by an Oriental lunette with Cosmatesque decoration and flanked by two eagles. On either side of the Classical decoration around the door, in between panels of blind arcading, are paired reliefs representing allegories of *Work* and *Eternal Life* (a farmer with two bullocks and a dog, a deer feeding its offspring and eating a serpent, and two peacocks pecking at grapes). The ten larger reliefs flanking the door represent (right) *Christ Washing St Peter's Feet*, the *Calling of Sts Peter and Andrew*, and three symbolic scenes relating to animal fables. On the left side: *Death and Judgement of the Just*, *Death and Judgement of Sinners*, and three scenes showing struggles between lions and men. The interior was remodelled in 1699. On the west wall are 16th-century votive frescoes. The font dates from 1487.

PRACTICAL INFORMATION

GETTING AROUND

• **By car:** In **Spello** there are two free car parks outside the walls: at the top of the hill outside Porta Montanara, in the south near Porta Consolare. Pay car parks are within the walls. In **Foligno**, there are car parks in Via Nazario Sauro, Via Chiavellati, and Via Oberdan; covered car park with hourly tariff at Porta Romana; limited space (with hourly tariff) in Piazza San Domenico, Piazza San Francesco, Piazza Garibaldi, Piazzetta Beata Angela, and Porta Todi. In **Bevagna** there are car parks outside the walls (Porta Todi). In **Montefalco** there are car parks outside Porta Sant'Agostino. Parking in **Trevi** is in Piazza Garibaldi. In **Spoleto** there is long-term (free) car parking off Viale Cappuccini and in Via Don Bonilli near the stadium.

• **By train:** **Spello** railway station, c. 1km from Porta Consolare, has services from Perugia (40 mins) and Foligno. **Spoleto** trains on the Ancona–Rome line connect with Terni (25mins), Foligno (25mins), and Perugia (1hr

15mins). Buses run from the station every 15mins to Piazza della Libertà. Town buses run from the station (Circolare A, B, C & D) every 10mins to Piazza Carducci.
• **By bus:** Services to **Spello**, run by Spoletina Trasporti (www.spoletina.com), from Perugia, Foligno and Assisi (except on holidays). Buses connect Perugia with Foligno, some via Assisi; other services from Rome, Spoleto, Spello, Trevi, Montefalco, Bevagna and Nocera Umbra. For **Trevi**, there are services from Foligno.

INFORMATION OFFICES

Bevagna Piazza Silvestri, T: 0742 361667.
Foligno Porta Romana 126, T: 0742 354459.
Spello Piazza Matteotti 3, T: 0742 301009.
Spoleto Piazza della Libertà 7, T: 0743 238920.
Trevi Piazza Mazzini 6, T: 0742 781150.

HOTELS

Bevagna (*map p. 487, B4*)
€€€€–€€€ **L'Orto degli Angeli**. A superb hotel in a 17th-century palace on Roman foundations. Each of the rooms is individually designed and carefully furnished. In winter, fires are lit in the rooms. *Via Dante Alighieri 1, T: 0742 360130, www.ortoangeli.com. 14 rooms.*
€€ **Palazzo Brunamonti**. In a delightful palace in the centre of town, with each room tastefully furnished. Some of the rooms are frescoed, while others have old brick vaulting and cool floors. Good value and friendly staff. No restaurant. *Corso Matteotti 79, T: 0742 361932, www.brunamonti.com. 16 rooms.*
€ **Il Chiostro di Bevagna**. In the Convent of San Domenico. Very pleasant, clean rooms with good bathrooms. Central. *Corso Matteotti, T: 0742 369231, www.ilchiostrodibevagna.com. 14 rooms.*
Foligno (*map p. 487, C4*)
€€ **Italia**. An elegant hotel, centrally located, with a restaurant in a characterful room with original brick walls and tiled floor. *Piazza Matteotti 12, T: 0742 350412, www.hotelitaliafoligno.com. 37 rooms.*
€€ **Poledrini**. A comfortable, central hotel with well-appointed rooms. *Viale Mezzetti 3, T: 0742 341041, www.poledriniumbria.com. 42 rooms.*
€ **Le Mura**. Excellent value accommodation inside the town walls, with restaurant. The rooms on the top floor have a lovely view across the Topino river. *Via Bolletta 27, T: 0742 357344, www.lemura.net. 31 rooms.*
Montefalco (*map p. 487, C4*)
€€€–€€ **Hotel Villa Zuccari**. A stunning family-run *palazzo* surrounded by vineyards within beautiful parkland with a swimming pool. Set in a tiny hamlet a couple of kilometres southeast of Montefalco. *Località San Luca, T: 0742 399402, www.villazuccari.com. 25 rooms.*
€€ **Villa Pambuffetti**. In a lovely villa outside the walls with beautifully furnished rooms and very professional service. Restaurant. *Viale della Vittoria 20, T: 0742 379417, www.villapambuffetti.com. 15 rooms.*
€ **Camiano Piccolo**. A 10-min walk from the centre of Montefalco, in a

16th-century villa with a swimming pool. Most rooms are inside the handsome manor house. *Via Camiano Piccolo 5, T: 0742 379492, www.camianopiccolo.com. 9 apartments, 10 rooms.*

€ **Ringhiera Umbra**. In a pretty house in the centre of town, a simple but very friendly family-run hotel, with good restaurant. *Il Verziere, T: 0742 379166, www.ringhieraumbra.com. 2 rooms.*

Pissignano (*map p. 487, C4*)

€€ **Vecchio Mulino**. Close to the Tempietto del Clitunno and the Fonti del Clitunno, this carefully restored old water-mill is a classified 'historic residence'. Traffic on the busy Via Flaminia nearby can be noisy. *Via del Tempio 34, T: 0743 521122, www.vecchio-molino.it. 13 rooms.*

Spello (*map p. 487, C4*)

€€ **Albergo del Teatro**. A 17th-century building in the centre of town. Carefully renovated with well-appointed rooms. *Via Giulia 24, T: 0742 011140, www.hoteldelteatro.it. 11 rooms.*

€€ **La Bastiglia**. In a former mill at the top of the town, with a pretty terrace. The rooms are heavily decorated and have fine views. Small swimming pool. Restaurant. Closed Jan. *Via dei Molini 7, T: 0742 651277, www.labastiglia.com. 33 rooms.*

€€ **Palazzo Bocci**. In a large 19th-century palace in a good central position. Frescoed drawing-room and pleasant garden terrace (where breakfast is served in warm weather). The hotel owns the Il Molino restaurant opposite. *Via Cavour 17, T: 0742 301021, www.palazzobocci.com. 23 rooms.*

€ **Il Cacciatore**. Run by the same proprietors as the Albergo del Teatro. Some of the rooms have wonderful views over the plain. Good restaurant. Central. *Via Giulia 42, T: 0742 651141, www.ilcacciatore hotel.com. 21 rooms.*

Spoleto (*map p. 487, C5*)

€€€ **Eremo delle Grazie**. 4km east of Spoleto on the road to Monteluco, a historic residence in a beautiful position with charming rooms and a restaurant. *Località Monteluco, T: 0743 49624, www.eremodellegrazie.it. 11 rooms.*

€€€ **Palazzo Dragoni**. A historic residence in a splendid, spacious 16th-century palace in a quiet position below Piazza del Duomo. Tastefully furnished. Many of the frescoed rooms have views over the valley. No restaurant. *Via del Duomo 13, T: 0743 222220, www.palazzodragoni.it. 18 rooms.*

€€€ **Villa Milani**. In a lovely wooded position just outside Spoleto, with spectacular views, especially from the panoramic Tower Room. *Località Colle Attivoli 4, T: 0743 225056, www.villamilani.com. 11 rooms.*

€€ **Aurora**. In a lovely, quiet position just off Corso Mazzini next to the Roman theatre, in a little cul-de-sac. The rooms are simply furnished, but comfortable, and some of them look out over the hills. Friendly atmosphere. Restaurant. *Via Apollinare 3, T: 0743 220315, www.hotelauroraspoleto.it. 23 rooms.*

€€ **Gattapone**. Charming little hotel in a peaceful spot, with panoramic views of the Ponte delle Torri. All rooms have large windows overlooking the valley. Rooms vary in size; all have fine wooden floors (those in the earlier wing are the best). Terrace and simple garden. Although five minutes' walk from the duomo, country walks can be taken directly from the hotel. No restaurant. *Via del Ponte 6, T: 0743 223447, www.hotelgattapone.it. 15 rooms.*

€ **Athena**. A new building just outside the historic centre. Well-run and pleasant. *Via Valadier, T: 0743 225218. 11 rooms.*

Trevi (*map p. 487, C4*)

€€ **Casa Giulia**. A country guest house in a lovely 17th-century building below the town on the Bovara road. There is a delightful, shady garden where breakfast is served in warm weather. *Località Corciano 1, T: 0742 78257, www.casagiulia.com. 7 rooms.*

€€ **Trevi Hotel**. A delightful hotel in an old house inside the walls. Some of the rooms have their old brick vaults, and all are beautifully furnished. Peaceful and friendly. *Via Fantosati 2, T: 0742 780922, www.trevihotel.net. 11 rooms.*

€ **Antica Dimora alla Rocca**. In the centre of town, rooms in two adjoining 17th-century *palazzi* (rooms in the newer annexe are larger). Restaurant. *Piazza della Rocca, T: 0742 38541, www.hotelallarocca.it. 34 rooms.*

€ **Hotel Terziere**. A modern hotel with a pleasant garden and swimming pool close to the historic centre. Some rooms with balcony. Restaurant. *Via Coste 1, T: 0742 78359, www.ilterziere.com. 9 rooms.*

RESTAURANTS

Bevagna (*map p. 487, B4*)

€€ **Ottavius**. A small, local restaurant with friendly service. The gnocchi are highly recommended. *Via Gonfalone 4, off Piazza Silvestri, T: 0742 360555.*

€ **Da Nina**. Traditional cooking at a well-established restaurant. Good value

lunches. Truffles feature heavily. Closed Tues. *Piazza Garibaldi 6, T: 0742 360161.*

Foligno (*map p. 487, C4*)

€€ **Hostaria Sparafucile**. Interesting dishes such as snails with wild fennel, as well as delicious home-made puddings. Closed Weds. *Piazzetta Duomo 30, T: 0742 342602.*

€€ **Marechiaro**. Their signature dish, *spaghetti marechiaro* (with clams and mussels) is worth making a lunchtime stop for. Good pizza also. *Via Piermarini 58, T: 0742 340551.*

€€ **Villa Roncalli**. 1km to the south of town, a restaurant in the best slow food tradition with fresh ingredients from the large garden. Excellent wine list. Rooms also available. *Viale Roma 25, T: 0742 391091.*

€ **Il Bacco Felice**. Once a well-kept secret, nowadays this is a much-frequented restaurant, but none the worse off for it. The menu changes daily, using organic produce. Easy, casual atmosphere. Booking recommended. Closed Mon, Easter and Christmas. *Via Garibaldi 73, T: 0742 341019.*

Montefalco (*map p. 487, C4*)

€€€ **Il Coccorone**. A restaurant renowned for its unrivalled choice of wines, including excellent local vintages. The house wine is also used in dishes such as *pappardelle al sagrantino* and *filetto al sagrantino*. Booking recommended. Closed Weds. *Largo Tempestivi, T: 0742 379535.*

€ **Il Falisco**. A good value bar and pizzeria. Pleasant outdoor terrace. *Via XX Settembre 14, T: 0742 379185.*

Spello (*map p. 487, C4*)

€€ **Il Molino**. Atmospheric dining room within a 14th-century cellar.

Traditional cuisine. Closed Tues. *Piazza Matteotti 6/7, T: 0742 651305.*

€ **Ristorante La Cantina**. Pigeon pâté, superb pasta and a famous wine list. A restaurant with a loyal following. *Via Cavour 2, T: 0742 651775.*

Spoleto *(map p. 487, C5)*

€€€ **Il Panciolle**. Acclaimed restaurant in a quiet road below the duomo, with a very pleasant atmosphere. Booking recommended. Rooms available next door. *Via Duomo 3, T: 0743 221241.*

€ **Ristorante degli Abeti**. Family-run restaurant close to the centre of town, but slightly off the beaten tourist path. Closed Tues. *Via Benedetto Egio 3, T: 0743 220025.*

Trevi *(map p. 487, C4)*

€€ **Maggiolini**. Homely, brick-vaulted restaurant. Grilled meats are Maggiolini's signature, as well as local Trevi sausages. Closed Tues. *Via San Francesco, T: 0742 381534.*

€€ **La Vecchia Posta**. In a lovely position on the piazza, with tables outside in summer. Well-prepared traditional dishes. Closed Thurs. *Piazza Mazzini 14, T: 0742 381690.*

LOCAL SPECIALITIES

Bevagna Iron is still wrought in workshops in the centre of Bevagna, and many residences feature beautiful wrought ironwork. Hemp has been cultivated throughout the region since ancient times, and Bevagna was once a centre for rope production. Basket-weaving is a vestige of that tradition; the craft can be seen throughout the town, especially on fair days.

Montefalco The area is known for its Sagrantino wine. The town opens its wine cellars for tastings and purchasing, on the last Sunday of May.

Trevi is one of the most important centres in Umbria for the production of olive oil. The oil produced here is typically bright green, with a particularly aromatic flavour.

FESTIVALS & EVENTS

Foligno San Feliciano market, 25 –26 Jan; San Manno market with typical local products, 14–15 Sept; *Giostra della Quintana*, Joust dating from 1613, held in the stadium at Porta Romana in two heats, second and third Suns in Sept; *Segni Barocchi*, Baroque music and theatre festival, Sept.

Spello *La Sagra della Bruschetta*, Festival to celebrate the end of the olive harvest, with music, dancing, food and processions, Feb; *Infiorata*, The streets are carpeted with fresh flowers in numerous different designs, and a procession is held at 11 o'clock, Sun after Corpus Christi (60 days after Easter, late May or June); .

Trevi *Palio dei Terzieri*, Festival culminating in a cart race, Oct; Annual fair of *sedano nero*, Trevi's distinctively strong flavoured celery, Oct.

Spoleto *Festival dei Due Mondi*, International arts festival, first two weeks in July.

NORCIA & THE VALNERINA

Norcia (*map p. 487, D4*) is a delightful little town, in a fertile basin surrounded by a wide amphitheatre of hills, on the borders of Umbria and the Marche. It has a notably cheerful atmosphere with numerous excellent food shops and restaurants, specialising in local delicacies (including black truffles and cured hams and salami, as well as lentils from Castelluccio). The town preserves a great many churches and a number of pretty fountains within its 14th-century walls, which survive intact.

On a site occupied in prehistoric times, Norcia came under Roman influence from 290 BC and was called *frigida Nursia* by Virgil. It was the birthplace of St Benedict (480–550; *see p. 152*) and his twin sister St Scholastica. It was a powerful free commune from the 13th–15th centuries. The town has suffered from earthquakes throughout its history. In 1859, the height of the buildings was limited to two storeys, and the lower walls of the palaces and churches are often buttressed for added solidity. The first public service of steam carriages in Italy was inaugurated from Spoleto to Norcia in 1926.

Piazza San Benedetto

The main entrance to the town is through the impressive 19th-century Porta Romana which leads into the Corso. Piazza San Benedetto, in the centre of town, is surrounded by handsome buildings. It has an attractive circular pavement and a monument to St Benedict (1880). The **Basilica of San Benedetto** has a fine 14th-century façade with statues of St Benedict and his sister Scholastica in two tabernacles, and in the lunette above the portal a good relief of the *Madonna and Child with two Angels*. The rose window is surrounded by the symbols of the Evangelists. Beneath the portico, added c. 1570, are interesting old stone measures for corn. The crypt, traditionally taken to be the birthplace of St Benedict and St Scholastica, has extensive remains of a late Roman building, and some late 14th-century frescoes.

The delightful **Palazzo Comunale** has a portico (1492) on the ground floor and a handsome enclosed loggia above. Inside, in the 18th-century Cappella dei Priori is a reliquary of St Benedict in gilded silver by a local goldsmith (1450). The **duomo** was built in 1560 by Lombard artists working with Vignola, and the interior was designed c. 1755. The Cappella della Madonna della Misericordia at the end of the north aisle is surrounded by a beautiful altar in coloured marbles and intarsia (1640–41), attributed to François Duquesnoy: the charming early 16th-century fresco fragment was detached from a miraculous shrine: it shows the *Madonna between St Scholastica and St Benedict* (who is holding a representation of the town of Norcia). In another chapel there is a wooden Crucifix of 1494 by Giovanni Tedesco.

The Museo Civico Diocesano

Also in Piazza San Benedetto is the handsome fortified palace, with four angle towers, called La Castellina, commissioned from Vignola by Julius III in 1554, and now the seat of the Museo Civico Diocesano (*open 10–1 & 3/4–5/6; closed Mon*). The rooms, some with pretty windows, have good views over the piazza and to the hills beyond. The precious works of art include a fine painted Cross from the late 12th or early 13th century: although in very poor condition it has an unusual *Ascension* in the cimasa at the top and two Marys on either side of Christ (there were originally four). The ropes have been installed to help it survive in case of an earthquake. A very beautiful *Deposition* group of five life-size wooden statues dates from the late 13th century. The beautiful painted Cross signed by 'Petrus pictor' is thought to be dated 1241. The beautifully painted head of Christ is the earliest instance known in Umbrian painting where He is shown dead (*Christus patiens*). The *Salone* displays 15th-century paintings, including Madonnas by the Sparapane and a *Risen Christ* by Nicola da Siena (c. 1460).

NORCINI & THE CURING OF PORK

Pork is the basis of local cuisine around Norcia, and in the Middle Ages herds of pigs fed off the acorns in the oak woods which used to cover the surrounding hills. The inhabitants of Norcia have been known for centuries for their skill in the butchering and curing of pork. It is said that before the surgeons of Preci (*see overleaf*) became famous in the 14th century, they first practised their skills on swine.

Pigs are traditionally butchered in winter, and up until the last war men from Norcia used to emigrate for the winter months to other parts of Italy, particularly Tuscany and Lazio, where they were employed on pig farms. Some of them (notably those from the village of Todiano in the lovely Valle Oblita) settled in Rome or towns in Tuscany, and started up successful food businesses. In Florence, the Spedale di San Giovanni Decollato in Via San Gallo was founded in 1317 to provide medical assistance and care for the *Norcini* staying in the city (it was suppressed only in 1751). Numerous Florentine works of art were brought back to Todiano and Abeto by their inhabitants, who had emigrated temporarily to Florence as pork butchers. In the early 17th century the *Norcini* of Rome had their own church in Via Torre Argentina. Pork butchers all over Italy came to be known as 'Norcini', and grocery shops selling ham and salami are still called 'Norcineria' in some Italian towns. The cured pork of Norcia retains its fame for its high quality, and there is still a local firm operating in a palace in Abeto.

THE VALLE CASTORIANA

The Valle Castoriana (*map p. 487, D4*) is a lovely solitary valley north of Norcia. The church of Santa Maria Bianca has a charming 15th-century loggia, with primitive capitals, and the church of Sant'Andrea at Campi Alto, and San Salvatore (with a delightful primitive façade) outside the lower hamlet of Campi are both worth visiting. Near Piedivalle is the former **Abbey of Sant'Eutizio** (*open April–Aug 10–12.30 & 3.30–7* *except Tues; Sun and holidays 10–6*), a Benedictine monastery which was particularly important from the 12th–14th centuries. Eutychius (Eutizio) was abbot of this monastery in the 6th century. He is mentioned in the *Dialogues* of Gregory the Great. The façade has a rose window (1236) with symbols of the Evangelists, and beside it, built on the top of an outcrop of rock, is the 17th-century campanile. The beautiful interior (1190) has a single nave with a raised and vaulted apse. On the high altar is a painted Crucifix by Nicola da Siena (c. 1460). Behind the altar is an unusual funerary monument to St Eutychius, a finely carved work of 1514. The ancient crypt has two huge sandstone columns. An archway leads into the former abbey, with good two-light windows and a fountain in the courtyard, from which steps lead up to the grottoes in the rockface. In the basement of the abbey buildings there is a small museum.

Numerous poplar trees grow along the river valley near **Preci** (*map p. 487, D4*), the old hamlet of which has attractive paving and many 16th-century houses with handsome carved inscriptions above the doors and windows. The little town was famous from the 14th–17th centuries for its school of surgeons, who attended patients as illustrious as Sixtus V, Elizabeth I of England, the Sultan Mehmet and Eleonora Gonzaga, when she was wife of the Holy Roman Emperor Ferdinand II.

Piano di Castelluccio

From Norcia a well-engineered road, with magnificent views back down to the plain, leads up through woods to a pass at 1521m from which there is an extraordinary view of the great **Piano Grande**, or **Piano di Castelluccio** (*map p. 487, D4*), a deserted

View of the village of Castelluccio.

upland plain beneath Monte Vettore (2476m) in a huge carsic basin which occupies the site of a glacial lake. It is one of the most beautiful spots in central Italy, surrounded on all sides by bare hills; and the well-watered pastureland where cattle are grazed is covered with wild flowers of great botanic interest in late May and June. The migratory birds which can sometimes be seen include a species of plover, the dotterel, which nests in the Arctic tundra. The only sign of habitation for miles around is the hill village of Castelluccio. Beyond stretches the lovely nature reserve of the Monti Sibillini (Sibylline Mountains), partly in Umbria and partly in the Marche. (*For full coverage, see pp. 687–90.*)

CASTELLUCCIO LENTILS

The fields on the plain at the foot of the hills around Castelluccio are cultivated with lentils, for which this area is famous throughout Italy. The crop is planted as soon as the snow melts, usually in March, and has bright yellow flowers in June. It is harvested at the end of July or in early August. The characteristic lentils are very small, and each bean differs slightly in colour. They are grown without the help of chemical fertilizers, and the success of the crop depends entirely on the weather conditions. The plants, which grow to a height of about 30cm, were picked by hand up until the 1950s (when women would walk here from neighbouring villages for the harvest). Lentils are recognised as a very nutritious healthy food (rich in iron). Traditionally they are cooked with celery.

SOUTH OF NORCIA

Beside the cemetery of Norcia is the church of **Santa Scolastica**. On the site of a very early church, the present building dates from the 17th–18th centuries, but an interesting fresco cycle dating from the late 14th and early 15th centuries, with scenes from the life of St Benedict, has been discovered beneath the whitewash.

In the lovely valley at the foot of the walls southwest of Norcia is an area of great interest and natural beauty known as the **Marcite**. The River Sordo and numerous springs and streams here were for centuries regulated by a complicated series of small dams and locks to provide abundant irrigation to the meadows, which were used exclusively to provide a maximum yield of fodder. Because of the optimum conditions and abundance of water, the crop in the marshes could be harvested up to seven or eight times a year (but due to the marshy terrain, this could only be done by hand). It is thought that this system of agriculture was introduced by Benedictine monks. Seven water-mills also operated here, one of which is again in working order, next to the simple house where the miller lived. The area has been partially reclaimed and the flora and fauna protected (the streams abound in trout), and there is a small museum (*for admission, contact the Comunità Montana; T: 0743 816938*).

Cascia

Cascia (*map p. 487, C5*) is famous for its sanctuary of St Rita, the Augustinian nun who died here in 1457: after her canonisation in 1900 her popularity was such that a huge new basilica dedicated to her was built at the top of the town in 1937–47, still visited by thousands of pilgrims every year. The little town has all the usual characteristics of an important pilgrimage shrine. Giovanni da Cascia, the composer of madrigals and great exponent of the Florentine style known as *Ars Nova*, was born here in the 14th century.

UMBRIAN WOMEN SAINTS

Apart from its two most famous saints, St Benedict of Nursia (480–550; *see p. 152*) and St Francis of Assisi (1181–1226), Umbria is interesting for the number of its women saints and mystics. Benedict's twin sister Scholastica is usually considered the first nun of the Benedictine Order (their story is illustrated in a fresco cycle in the church of Santa Scolastica in the cemetery of Norcia, traditionally supposed to be on the site of their mother's house). Clare of Assisi, follower of St Francis, was dedicated to relieving the suffering of the poor, and had a great influence on the spread of the Franciscan movement. Her order of the Poor Clares was approved by Innocent IV in 1253, two days before she died. She was canonised in 1255.

Perhaps the most popular woman saint in Umbria today is St Rita (or Margherita), born at Roccaporena, west of Cascia, in 1381 (*see opposite*). The story is told that after her marriage to a violent man who was killed by his enemies, she persuaded their two children not to take vengeance on his murderers, but they both soon died in an epidemic. Rita became an Augustinian nun for the last 40 years of her life but suffered terrible pain after receiving the Stigmata. She is considered the protectress of all those who are dogged by misfortune, particularly victims of domestic violence.

Clare of Montefalco (b. 1268) was also an Augustinian nun. On her death it is said that the symbols of the Passion of Christ were found engraved on her heart. Her embalmed body and relics are preserved at Montefalco (*see p. 547*). Beata Angela of Foligno (1248–1309) who, after having married and borne children, renounced the world and became a Franciscan tertiary aged 37, was famous for her mystical visions, and her cult was validated by Clement XI in 1701.

In Perugia, Dominican nuns preserve relics of the Blessed Colomba of Rieti (1467–1501), who lived in their convent. In Città di Castello there are still no fewer than three convents of the Poor Clares, all closed orders. St Veronica Giuliani (1660–1727) lived in one of them for 50 years (she was canonised in 1839): her possessions are all carefully preserved in a little museum shown by the nuns. There is also a convent of the Poor Clares next to the church of San Leonardo in Montefalco, where the nuns can be seen at worship in their adjoining church.

The **Collegiata of Santa Maria**, beside a little piazza where a Romanesque lion is used as a charming fountain, is the oldest church in Cascia, founded in 856. The façade has two doorways (1535 and 1620), and the other Romanesque lion rather uncomfortably inserted into a niche above. In the interior, at the west end, are interesting 14th-century fresco fragments. In the presbytery of the church of **Sant'Antonio Abate** (*open 10.30–1 & 3–6 usually only on Fri, Sat and Sun*) is a well-preserved late 14th- or early 15th-century fresco cycle with stories from the life of St Anthony Abbot, attributed to an Umbrian master known as the Master of the Terni Dormition. The charming scenes include numerous details of wild flowers which still grow in the district. The frescoes on the east wall show the *Annunciation* and a lovely little *Madonna and Child with Two Angels*. Behind is the monks' choir entirely decorated with more fine frescoes of the *Passion*, dated 1442. The beautiful wooden statue of the *Archangel Raphael with Tobias* is a very unusual late 15th-century work attributed to Antonio Rizzo.

At the top of the town (reached by steps, escalators, or lifts) is the overbearing, white **Basilica di Santa Rita**, built in 1937–47 on the site of an earlier church. The interior is lavishly decorated, though in a combination of styles that is not particularly successful. Rita's birthplace was at **Roccaporena** (*map p. 487, C5*). Above it towers a fantastic isolated rock, where a path leads up to a chapel, reconstructed in 1981. Her house was transformed into a chapel in 1630, and there is a large pilgrim centre here.

Monteleone di Spoleto

Near this remote little village south of Cascia (*map p. 487, C5;* on the N471 signposted for Leonessa), late Bronze Age tombs were found at the beginning of the 20th century, as well as a remarkable wooden chariot decorated with bronze reliefs, thought to be an Etruscan work (now in the Metropolitan Museum of New York). In the village itself is the huge church and convent of **San Francesco**, founded in the 1280s. The Gothic portal has fine carving. The interesting interior has an unusual painted wooden ceiling with symbols of the Madonna signed by an artist from Norcia and dated 1760. The handsome high altar has pretty carvings and marble intarsia. The carved stone tabernacle with two angels is a Renaissance work. The fresco fragments include a remarkable 15th-century *Christ as King*, fully robed, which recalls the *Volto Santo* at Lucca (*see p. 336*), and (at the west end) the charming little figure of a stonemason in his overalls. From the cloister, with sculptural fragments, there is access to the lower church, with well-preserved 14th–15th-century frescoes, including *St Anthony Abbot* near a frieze of animals.

THE VALNERINA

The Valnerina is a lovely wooded valley which follows the river Nera down through Terni from its source in the Sibylline Mountains . Its steep hillsides are dotted with little villages. Nearly all the monuments of interest are well signposted, but many churches in the more remote villages are kept locked for safety (*the key can sometimes be found by asking locally; otherwise they are open only for services*).

San Felice di Narco

San Felice di Narco (or Castel San Felice; *map p. 487, C5*) is a lovely 12th-century Romanesque church. A legend relates that Maurus, a holy man given to prayer, came to Italy from Palestine at the time of Theodoric. He settled with his son Felix in this valley, where the inhabitants asked him to liberate them from a dragon. With the help of God, Felix killed the dragon, and went on to perform other miracles. He died in 535, and Maurus built an oratory over his grave and named the nearby castle after him. He also founded a Benedictine monastery here. The lovely façade has a beautiful rose window surrounded by symbols of the Evangelists, beneath which is a frieze depicting the legend of Maurus and his son. It shows the fearsome dragon beside his cave, with an angel helping Felix to chop off his head. To the right is Maurus in prayer beside an angel protecting his son. The last scene shows Felix bringing a widow's son back to life.

The beautiful interior (*open all day*) has massive red and white paving stones. The raised sanctuary is flanked by two *transennae* with damaged Cosmati work. The 15th-century frescoes include an *Adoration of the Magi* (among the elongated figures is that of a falconer), and the *Redeemer* in the apse. The crypt preserves an ancient little sarcophagus, supposed to contain the remains of Maurus and Felix.

Vallo di Nera, Ponte and Cerreto

The carefully restored hilltop village of **Vallo di Nera** (*map p. 487, C5*) is particularly picturesque, with attractive roofs. The lower church of Santa Maria contains well-preserved frescoes in the sanctuary dating from 1383. The scenes include *St Francis Preaching to the Birds*, and stories from the life of Christ and the Virgin. On the walls of the nave, the votive frescoes include a charming frieze of pigs (the symbol of St Anthony Abbot). Lovely old red-and-white stone steps lead up past the impressive side of the church and the arches of Palazzo Comunale, past a little piazza with an open barrel-vaulted tower in the walls (used as a storeroom), and the apse of the 14th-century church of San Giovanni Battista at the top of the town, with frescoes by Jacopo Siculo (1536).

At **Ponte**, in a fine position between the valleys of the Nera and Tissino (*map p. 487, C4*), the church of Santa Maria Assunta (1201) has an unusually tall rectangular façade with a splendid rose window above a telamon surrounded by symbols of the Evangelists. The exterior of the apse is also decorated. The beautiful interior has a fine dome and crossing. Roman fragments include a beautiful small green granite font, and several capitals (one used as a step for the side door). Pretty red sandstone quarried locally was used for the pavement. In a charming little wooden cupboard is a statue of the *Madonna and Child*, fully dressed. On the south wall there is an incised sketch of part of the rose window, presumably made by the craftsmen to illustrate its design before they began work on it.

Cerreto di Spoleto is high up on a rockface above Borgo Cerreto (*map p. 487, C4*). The piazza has a pretty fountain and lamp-posts. The church of the Annunziata, and the 14th-century church of San Giacomo are of interest.

TRUFFLES

This is an area where numerous black truffles are found, particularly around Sant'Anatolia di Narco and Scheggino (*map p. 487, C5*). These rare tubers grow wild and can be found between 20cm and 50cm beneath the ground around the roots of trees, usually oak or beech. They are famous for their penetrating scent and very unusual taste. Despite their unappetising appearance, truffles have been considered an exotic delicacy since Greek and Roman times.

The white truffle (*tuber magnatum Pico*) is found mostly in Piedmont, but also sometimes in Umbria in October–December, and can cost up to €1500 a kilo. The only high-quality black truffle (*tuber melanosporum Vittadini*) is that found in the Valnerina and near Norcia and Spoleto, and at Périgord in France. It matures from late November–early March and usually costs around €700 a kilo (all other types of black truffle are much less highly prized and cost from €50–150 a kilo).

A truffle usually weighs between 30 and 100g, but the largest can weigh up to 1kg. For centuries their origins were a mystery: Aristotle's pupil Theophrastus mentions their excellent taste but, observing their lack of roots, he came to the conclusion that they were formed by a combination of rain and thunder. The first scientific study of them was made in 1831 by Carlo Vittadini, and although they are a type of fungus, they are still not precisely understood by botanists. They are known to have a high protein content.

Nowadays there are plans to protect the rare black truffle exclusive to this area, and, although truffles cannot be cultivated, experimental reafforestation is taking place and reserves are being established in an attempt to augment the number of truffles growing in the wild. Unfortunately, in the past few years it has become easier to produce false synthetic truffle aromas, and the fame of this black truffle has been damaged by the sale of inferior black truffles from North Africa and southern China.

Truffle-hunters usually work on their own with only a trowel, and sometimes a dog (usually a pointer or a setter) trained to detect the odour below the surface of the earth. Up until a short time ago truffles were often sold house to house. In the past pigs were used to help search for them, but are now rarely used as they also find them delicious and tend to gobble them up as soon as they find them!

Truffles have a particularly strong scent only when they are fully mature, and once extracted from the ground they lose their taste and perfume after a few days. They can be preserved in oil, but Umbrian cuisine uses them fresh, in countless different ways: as a spread on *crostini* as an hors-d'oeuvre, as a sauce for pasta, or in risotto, as well as a flavouring for meat, game, fish and egg dishes. An annual international gastronomy festival has been held in Norcia in February since 1951 in honour of the black truffle of Norcia and the Valnerina, and there is also a truffle festival at Città di Castello in November.

TERNI

Terni (*map p. 487, C5*), the Roman *Interamna* ('between rivers'), is the second largest town in Umbria (pop. 106,000) and capital of its second province. It faces the broad plain of the Nera river, and the presence of abundant water here has led to its expansion as a thriving industrial centre, particularly important for its steelworks, and the production of plastics and machinery. Its population has trebled since the beginning of the 20th century. Badly damaged in the Second World War, it was reconstructed with pleasant residential suburbs, particularly spacious and planted with trees, under the guidance of the architect Mario Ridolfi (1904–84), who lived here at the end of his life.

The town centre

The centre of the city is Piazza della Repubblica and the adjoining Piazza Europa. The huge Palazzo Spada (its main façade is on Via Roma) is an unusual fortress-like building of the late 16th century (later altered). Surrounded by a little garden is the church of **San Salvatore**. The 11th–12th-century façade and nave precede an interesting domed rotunda, with a central oculus, once thought to have been a Temple of the Sun. On the site of a Roman house, this was probably built as a little oratory in the 7th century.

The duomo and Roman theatre

The charming Piazza del Duomo is in a quiet corner to the south of Piazza Europa (follow Via Roma, the old main street, and turn right down Via dell'Arringo). The duomo, thought to have been founded in the 6th century, has a 17th-century portico crowned with a balcony and statues in 1933–37. The main portal has a fine frieze dating from the late 12th century, and another door was carved in 1439. The interior was reconstructed in the 12th century, and decorated in the 17th. On the west wall is a *Circumcision* painted in 1560 by Livio Agresti. The high altar and tabernacle in precious marbles are by Antonio Minelli (1762). The decorations of the organ are thought to have been designed by Bernini. The choir is by Domenico Corsi (1559). In the sacristy are fragments of sculptures and a 15th-century terracotta statue of the *Madonna and Child*. The crypt (*admission on request*) dates from c. 1000 and has four ancient columns, and a Roman altar with bucrania supports the little altar.

Just out of the piazza are the overgrown ruins of the **Roman amphitheatre**, built in AD 32 by a certain Faustus Titius Liberalis. Part of the wall in *opus reticulatum* survives.

The Pinacoteca Comunale and San Francesco

Via XI Febbraio leads north from Piazza del Duomo. In the first street on the right, Via Teatro Romano, is the Neoclassical Palazzo Gazzoli, which houses the **Pinacoteca Comunale** (*open 10–1 & 4–7 except Mon*). The paintings include the *Marriage of St Catherine*, an exquisite small work signed and dated 1466 by Benozzo Gozzoli; a large triptych by Pier Matteo d'Amelia (recently identified with the anonymous painter up to now known as the Master of the Gardner Annunciation) of the *Madonna with Four*

Saints, complete with predella and painted frame, dated 1485, a very fine work paint-ed for the church of San Francesco (*see below*); and a triptych of the *Madonna and Child between Sts Peter and Gregory the Great*, attributed to the Master of the Terni Dormition (late 14th century).

Further north, Via XI Febbraio crosses Via Cavour, from where Via Fratini leads to Via Nobili, and left to the church of **San Francesco**, first built in 1265. The interior has beautiful vaulting, and at the end of the south aisle (light on right) is the Paradisi Chapel, which was frescoed in the mid-15th century by Bartolomeo di Tommaso of Foligno, with unusual scenes of the *Last Judgement*, inspired by Dante's *Divine Comedy*. They are among the most interesting works of this period in Umbria.

ENVIRONS OF TERNI

The lower Valnerina near Terni is rather built-up, but still heavily wooded with a great variety of trees. It begins to become more attractive around the village of **Arrone** (*map p. 487, C5*). Here the church of Santa Maria (*open all day*) contains very fine early 16th-century frescoes, and, in a splendid frame a painting of the *Supper at Emmaus* by the school of Caravaggio.

San Pietro in Valle (*map p. 487, C5*), founded in the 8th century, is in a wonderful isolated position enclosed by woods and beautiful unspoilt countryside. The lovely campanile dates from the 12th century. Since 1998 the abbey buildings have been used as a hotel and restaurant. The church is opened by a custodian (*usually 10.30–1 & 2.30–5*). The domed interior preserves its triapsidal plan, and contains remark-able—though damaged—mural paintings of scriptural scenes (c. 1190). These are among the most important works of this date to have survived in Italy. On the left wall are Old Testament scenes and on the right wall New Testament scenes. There are a number of interesting Roman sarcophagi in the church. The high altar has a very unusual medieval Lombard altar with decorations in bas-relief signed by 'Ursus', and a panel behind decorated with floral motifs. The 15th-century apse frescoes include *Christ Blessing*, and, below, the *Madonna and Child with Angels*, and Benedictine saints by the Maestro di Eggi. In the right apse are frescoes by the school of Giotto.

The upper reaches of the Valnerina are steeply wooded and very beautiful. They are described earlier in this chapter (*see pp. 567–68*).

Cascata delle Marmore and Piediluco

The **Cascata delle Marmore** (*map p. 487, C5*) is the most famous waterfall in Italy (and in consequence much visited by tour groups). The falls are 165m high and on three levels, though the water has now been diverted entirely for industrial purposes, and is only released in its original channels on certain days, including public holidays, and every day in summer. (*NB: opening times tend to change, so it is best to check with the information office, T: 0744 62982.*) The falls are surrounded by poplars, elms, pine trees and ilex woods: a path leads to the best viewpoint. In recent years landslips have threatened the stability of the travertine rock.

In great measure the falls are the work of man, for Curius Dentatus, conqueror of the Sabines (271 BC), was the first to cut a channel by which the river *Velinus* (Velino) was thrown over a precipice into the river *Nar* (Nera), to prevent floods in the plain of *Reate* (Rieti). Another channel was cut in 1400, and a third (draining the plain of Rieti without flooding Terni) in 1785. Among the many travellers who have admired the falls are Galileo, Caroline of Brunswick (wife of King George IV of England), Corot and Byron (who describes the falls in *Childe Harold's Pilgrimage*).

Piediluco (*map p. 487, C5*) is a charming little resort on the beautiful lake of the same name, one of the largest in Umbria (with a perimeter of 17km). Its shores are very well preserved, and irregular fingers of water extend into pretty woods. The attractive long main street of Piediluco runs parallel to the lake past the side of the church of San Francesco (*open all day*), with a handsome exterior dating from 1293. Inside in a niche there is a very fine Roman statue of a lady, an unexpected sight in a church. The Rocca, built by Cardinal Albornoz in 1364, is now in ruins.

SAN GEMINI & ANCIENT CARSULAE

San Gemini (*map p. 487, B5*) is a small town famous for its mineral water. The church of San Francesco, with an attractive vaulted interior, has interesting frescoes (15th–17th centuries). The lovely, narrow old Via Casentino is worth exploring. It ends near the church of San Giovanni, which has two doorways: the one on the right looks onto an attractive little piazza, and the one on the left is near an old gate in the walls, which has a very worn Cosmatesque portal. The inscription above (now almost invisible) records the date (1199) and architects. The oddly-shaped interior has two octagonal pilasters and four gilded wooden altars. In a newer part of the town, outside a gate built in 1723, is the well-kept church of San Nicolò (privately owned; *opened on Fri, Sat and Sun 10–1 & 3–5*) with Roman and medieval remains and a fresco of 1295. The exterior is in very good condition, and there is Roman masonry in the lower part of the walls. The portal has an unusual carved frieze and two lions.

Ancient Carsulae

The extensive Roman remains of *Carsulae* stand in a beautiful peaceful setting in lovely countryside. The ruins are unenclosed and explained by maps and signs. This was an important Roman station on the Via Flaminia, on the site of the Umbrian town of *Carseoli*. It was abandoned after an earthquake.

The little medieval church of San Damiano was built from Roman materials. It faces the Via Flaminia, with its ancient paving stones, which formed the cardo maximus of the town. Near the church was the residential district of the Roman town and a basilica, beside which the decumanus maximus leads down towards the amphitheatre, connected to the theatre beyond. On the side opposite the church is a restored arch near shops, which gave access to the forum, once surrounded by public buildings including

The Cascata delle Marmore waterfall, near Terni.

two temples, the bases of which remain. The Via Flaminia leads uphill and winds round to the left to the limit of the town where a beautiful arch, known as the Arco di San Damiano, is well preserved. Outside the gate are remains of funerary monuments, one of them a large circular sepulchre and one with a conical roof.

THE ROMANS IN UMBRIA

For centuries the Tiber acted as a boundary line: to the west lay the Etruscan settlements of Perugia and Orvieto, while the district east of the river was inhabited by the Umbri (an Italic tribe of Indo-European origins) with centres round present-day Gualdo Tadino, Gubbio, Assisi, Spello, Todi, Terni and Narni. From the 4th century BC onwards the presence of the Romans in the area is attested, and they established control of central Italy definitively after the Battle of Sentinum in 295 BC (*see p. 633*) in which the combined forces of the Umbri, Etruscans, Samnites and Gauls were beaten. In 220 BC the Via Flaminia was built across Umbria, a road of great strategic importance to the Romans since it gave them direct access to the Adriatic across the Apennines. From *Ocriculum* in the south the road was carried over the valley of the *Nar* by an impressive bridge at Narni, which still survives in ruins. At Narni, where a colony had been founded in 299, and which still has important Roman remains, the road divided, one branch running though Terni and Spoleto (a Roman colony dating from 241 BC), and one (probably built later) through *Carsulae* and Bevagna. The two branches converged again beyond Foligno, where the stretch across the Apennines began.

Fine Roman remains are still to be found all over Umbria, including gateways, mosaics, temples, cisterns, amphitheatres, theatres and bridges. The Roman towns of *Carsulae*, *Ocriculum* and *Urbinum Hortense* have been excavated, and there are numerous archaeological collections which preserve finds from local digs.

NARNI & THE LOWER VALNERINA

Narni (*map p. 487, B5*) is a pleasant old town with many interesting medieval buildings along its attractively paved streets. It has extremely fine palaces, some of which have been restored, while others preserve a somewhat grim appearance. From its hill there are splendid views over the plain of Terni and the deep wooded gorge of the Nera river (the ancient *Nar*), which gave its name to the town when it became the Roman colony of *Narnia* in 299 BC.

Ponte d'Augusto

In order to carry the Via Flaminia across the river, the Romans built a monumental bridge here, famous for its height. Known as the Ponte d'Augusto, and probably built in

27 BC, it had a span of 160m, supported by three or four arches of different heights, and was built of concrete faced with blocks of white travertine. After it fell into ruins in the Middle Ages and came to be immersed in a wild landscape, it provided one of the famous 'views' of Classical ruins in Italy, sketched and painted numerous times by travellers on their way to Rome on the Grand Tour. Just one arch survives, 30m high—but it is extremely difficult to see as there is nowhere to stop on the modern road bridge, and from the road beyond it is lost to view. The only way it can be seen at closer range is by taking the rough road (signposted 'Molino Feroli') at Tre Ponti: the road descends and passes beneath the Roman arch, now in very unromantic surroundings (it can best be seen from the iron footbridge).

The duomo

Piazza Garibaldi, crossed by Via Roma and always busy with traffic, is the unusual main square of the town, with a quaint Neoclassical palace, a clock-tower and the side door of the duomo. The fountain, which has a bronze centrepiece with fantastic animal heads, dates from the 14th century (remade in the 17th century). Below it is an early medieval vaulted cistern on the site of a Roman piscina.

The main entrance of the duomo is preceded by a portico dating from 1490. The 12th-century portal has Classical carvings. The interior (*closed 12.30–3.30*), consecrated in 1145, has a very unusual nave with Corinthian columns supporting a wall with low arches. The two pretty pulpits, and the decorations in the third chapel in the south aisle all date from 1490. The remarkable old **Sacello di San Cassio**, where in 376 Narni's first bishop St Juvenal (Giovenale) was buried, is preceded by an old marble screen with Cosmatesque decoration and a relief above the door with two Lambs adoring the Cross. In the two niches are a terracotta *Pietà* and a statue of St Juvenal, both dating from the 13th century. High up on an inner wall (very difficult to see; *the sacristan turns on a light on request*) is a ruined 10th-century mosaic of the *Redeemer* and remains of Roman masonry. Inside the oratory, with its old pavement made out of Cosmatesque fragments, there is an interesting bas-relief and, in the inner cell, the open sarcophagus (6th century) of St Juvenal. On the last south pilaster of the nave is a beautiful painting of *St Juvenal* attributed to Vecchietta, the versatile Sienese artist who also signed the colossal wooden statue of *St Anthony Abbot Enthroned* in 1475.

The Cappella della Beata Lucia in the south transept was built in 1710 and decorated with paintings by Francesco Trevisani, and the high altar and presbytery were also elaborately decorated in coloured marbles at this time. In the apse, which retains its French Gothic form, are choir stalls of 1474.

Piazza dei Priori and the Pinacoteca

There are many traces of the Roman town in the masonry which was reused in later buildings, and the straight Via Garibaldi, with fine paving, leads north from Piazza Garibaldi on the line of the Roman cardo maximus. It ends in **Piazza dei Priori**, which has interesting medieval buildings, and a lovely circular fountain with a bronze basin made in 1303. The Loggia dei Priori, with two very tall arches and a Roman inscription, is attributed to the 14th-century architect Gattapone. Amongst the treasures in the **Pinacoteca** in Palazzo Eroli (*open daily except Mon summer 10.30–1 & 3.30/4.30–6/7.30; winter only on Fri, Sat and Sun*) are a beautiful altarpiece of the *Coronation of the Virgin* by Domenico Ghirlandaio and an *Annunciation* by Benozzo Gozzoli. An Egyptian mummy, dating from the 1st century BC (in a reused sarcophagus of the 5th–4th century BC), which was brought to Narni at the beginning of the 20th century by the local collector Edoardo Martinori, is also preserved here.

Further downhill, behind the former church of San Domenico, in the public garden, are remains of two sides of a very tall tower. There is a remarkable view over the deep Nera gorge to the wooded cliffs beyond, with the picturesque 12th-century Benedictine Abbey of San Cassiano.

On the north spur of the hill, Vicolo degli Orti (with steps) leads steeply down past orchards and a tall medieval tower to Porta della Fiera, in a picturesque spot in the walls. **Via Gattamelata**, with some old houses, leads uphill from the gate past no. 113 (plaque), traditionally supposed to be the birthplace in 1370 of Erasmo da Narni, the famous *condottiere*, always known as Gattamelata, who fought for the Venetian Republic and who is splendidly commemorated in Padua in an equestrian statue by Donatello. His father was a baker here.

Santa Margherita and the Rocca

From the south side of Piazza Garibaldi, Via del Monte leads up through another district of the town, which has a number of stepped medieval streets. The 17th-century church of Santa Margherita has a charming façade with twin doors. It contains frescoes of the life of St Margaret by the Zuccari. At the very top of the hill is the Rocca, a huge square-towered castle, very conspicuous above Narni from the plain of Terni. It was built for Cardinal Albornoz (*see p. 550*) in 1367 and is attributed to Gattapone. It is sometimes open to the public.

Ancient Ocriculum

The most interesting place in the environs of Narni is the old walled village of Otricoli (*map p. 487, B6*), on the site of the first settlement of the Roman *Ocriculum* (which later moved down to the banks of the Tiber). In the Middle Ages the inhabitants returned to this hilltop site to avoid the floods of the river. Many of its buildings still have Roman carvings inserted into their masonry. The church of Santa Maria, possibly founded as early as the 6th century, has a Neoclassical peach-coloured façade (1840) by Ireneo Aleandri, best known for his works in the Marche (*see p. 677*). The interesting interior has brickwork in the nave in *opus reticulatum*, an ancient crypt, and numerous sculptural fragments, some Roman, some early Christian, and others medieval.

About 1.5km below the town, signposted off the Rome road, is the **site of Ocriculum** (*unenclosed; usually guided visits at weekends at 10 and 5*), now semi-abandoned (it is dangerous to get too close to the ruins because of falling masonry). It is surrounded by fields, and the abandoned vineyard is full of birds. The important finds from the excavations carried out here in 1776–84 by order of Pius VI were taken to the Vatican Museums (*see p. 100*). The romantic overgrown ruins include those of baths with a circular hall, the theatre, a solitary tower in a field which was part of the entrance gate, a stretch of the old Via Flaminia and two funerary monuments (the circular one keeps part of its marble facing). Nearby are remains of the amphitheatre.

AMELIA & THE TEVERINA

Amelia (*map p. 487, B5*) is a beautifully situated hilltop town above the Tiber, surrounded by spectacular countryside. Its fine polygonal walls are a remarkable survival from around the 5th century BC. There are interesting buildings of several different periods, and numerous small orchards within the walls. This was the ancient *Ameria*, said by Pliny to have been founded three centuries before Rome. It became a Roman *municipium* in 90 BC on the Via Amerina from Nepi to Chiusi. Virgil and Cicero mention the fertile countryside surrounding the town, noted especially for its vineyards.

Via della Repubblica and the Museo Archeologico

The main entrance to the town is through the 16th-century Porta Romana, outside which the best stretches of the **ancient polygonal (Pelasgic) walls** can be seen. They are still some 8m high and 3.5m thick. Via della Repubblica leads up towards the centre of the old town: the Roman road beneath, with its large paving stones, is revealed in places. On the right opens Piazza Augusto Vera, with the church of San Francesco (with a rose window in its façade of 1401). In the chapel of Sant'Antonio on the south side are six beautifully carved funerary monuments, all of them with effigies of members of the Geraldini family. Alessandro Geraldini (1455–1525) is known to have helped obtain the approval at the court of Spain for Columbus' expedition, and later travelled as bishop to Santo Domingo.

Next door to the church is the **Museo Archeologico** (*open Oct–March Fri, Sat and Sun 10.30–1 & 3.30–6; otherwise daily except Mon 10.30–1 & 4.30–7.30*), which displays finds from the area including a superb colossal bronze statue of Germanicus, a member of the Julio-Claudian dynasty (he was the great-nephew of Augustus, nephew and adopted son of Tiberius, and father of Caligula). He died in Syria in AD 19, Suetonius says of poisoning at the hands of Tiberius, who had named him his heir and was jealous of his popularity. Germanicus' wife was exiled after his death to the prison island of Pandataria (*see p. 260*). The head is a remarkably fine posthumous portrait, and the elaborate armour includes a finely decorated breast-plate. It was found (in numerous fragments) outside the walls in 1963. Although it is beautifully displayed here, there is unfortunately a plan to move it to the archaeological museum in Perugia.

Palazzo Farrattini and the Arco di Piazza

Via della Repubblica continues uphill and, beyond a fork with Via Silvestri, a narrow stepped street leads left under an arch down to the handsome Palazzo Farrattini, with a long inscription dividing the first and second floors. It was built in 1520 by Antonio da Sangallo the Younger, who modelled it on his earlier design for Palazzo Farnese in Rome. In front of the palace, beneath a high arch, is a public fountain still in use on the site of Roman baths (part of the Roman wall in *opus reticulatum* can be seen here).

The main street (Via Farrattini) continues uphill, with its beautiful old paving now well preserved (relaid in 2001), beneath several flying arches. It then tunnels under the splendid Arco di Piazza, an impressive medieval gate made from Roman masonry, to emerge in the delightful old Piazza Marconi, once the centre of the city. There is a little medieval pulpit for public proclamations here, as well as several palaces.

The duomo and Sant'Agostino

The stepped Via del Duomo leads past the Vescovado, with Roman altars set into its façade. Here, at the top of the hill, in a very peaceful position, beside its fine 12-sided campanile, which incorporates Roman fragments, built as the Torre Civica in 1050, is the **duomo**, rebuilt in 1640–80. The interior (*open 10–12 & 4–6.30*) was decorated with frescoes and stuccoes in the 19th century by Luigi Fontana. An octagonal chapel (second south; attributed to Antonio da Sangallo the Younger) contains two Farrattini funerary monuments by Ippolito Scalza. In the first north chapel is the recomposed tomb of Bishop Giovanni Geraldini (1476) by Agostino di Duccio and assistants.

From outside the duomo, Via Geraldini curves north and then east to **Sant'Agostino**. The façade (1477) has a good portal and a lovely rose window. The interior, which retains its old terracotta pavement, was decorated in 1747 by Francesco Appiani. The first south altarpiece of the *Vision of St John at Patmos* is by Pomarancio. In the sacristy there are interesting *sinopie* thought to date from c. 1000 (left unfinished and never frescoed): in the vault there is a red star decoration and standing figures of saints, and unusual floral motifs on the walls.

The Roman cisterns and Teatro Sociale

Piazza Matteotti, in the north of town, is a pleasant square with a medley of buildings and an attractive clipped ilex tree surrounded by a circular hedge below the curving façade of the hospital. The **Roman cisterns** beneath the piazza can sometimes be visited at weekends (*for information, T: 0744 978436*). A very steep staircase leads down to ten remarkable vaulted reservoirs probably built between the 1st century BC and 1st century AD. These provided a huge collecting place for the rainwater channelled from the piazza above (sited in a declivity between two hills on which the duomo and the hospital now stand), capable of holding some 4,400 cubic metres of water, which provided the Roman town with an emergency drinking supply. The water, which filled the halls to a height of about 3m, was used by means of wells constructed through openings in the vaults. The room to the left of the stairs retains its original proportions and three large terracotta Roman floor tiles (it appears that there were plans to pave the whole room in this way). The vaults survive intact in six of the rooms together with their waterproof walls and original floors, although the four in the centre were altered when the palaces were built above. The entire floor slopes gradually down all the way to the tenth room, where the entrance to an underground channel can be seen; this ran for some 300m to emerge near Porta Posterula, and was used for flushing out the cisterns periodically so that the water would not stagnate.

Via Garibaldi (here beautifully paved) leads out of Piazza Matteotti. The first narrow lane on the right leads under a passageway down to the charming and well-preserved **Teatro Sociale**, where performances are held from November to May. It was built in wood in 1783 to a design by a local architect called Stefano Cansacchi (it bears a strong resemblance to the Fenice theatre in Venice, built ten years later). It can seat 92 in the stalls, 208 in the boxes, and 100 (seated and standing) in the 'gods'. It was restored in 1880, when Domenico Bruschi frescoed the foyer and the backcloth. In the entrance is a fire extinguisher made by the British firm of Bale and Edwards in Milan in 1816. The boxes are all preserved (some with their wooden cupboards for picnics during the performances) and the 'gods' (with a lovely view from a window), the stage apparatus, the artists' dressing-rooms and their kitchen, as well as an old projector used for silent movies, when the theatre was used as a cinema.

THE TEVERINA

Amelia is in the centre of this beautiful district between the Tiber and the Nera rivers, where little medieval villages and castles are dotted among low wooded hills (noted for their chestnuts) with vineyards and olive groves. This is ideal walking country. The two medieval *borghi* of Penna in Teverina and Giove, both of which have a huge palace, are worth a detour. Lugnano in Teverina and Alviano are the most interesting villages.

Lugnano in Teverina

Lugnano in Teverina (*map p. 487, B5*) is an old hill town with picturesque, well-paved streets, fine views, and a good bakery in Via Cavour. The splendid **Collegiata di Santa Maria Assunta** is a remarkable 12th-century church with important sculptural decoration. The delightful façade, with interesting carving, is preceded by a pronaos of 1230, with an unusual roof. The beautifully proportioned interior, with a Cosmatesque pavement, has a miscellany of carved capitals, including one with allegories of the Eucharist with a scene of the celebration of Mass according to Byzantine rites. The schola cantorum has been recomposed, and includes two interesting bas-reliefs showing two robed men greeting each other; *St Michael Archangel*, overcoming the devil in the form of a dragon; and a ciborium, restored in 1937 (with a rare stone hanging tabernacle in the form of a lantern for the Host). In the apse is a charming portable triptych with the *Assumption of the Virgin and Two Saints* by Foligno's most celebrated Renaissance artist, L'Alunno (Nicolò di Liberatore). The crypt has graceful columns. At the top of the left flight of steps is a painting of *St Jerome* by Leandro Bassano; at the top of the right flight of steps, a 13th-century Crucifix (a fresco transferred to canvas) and, in the chapel on the right, the *Beheading of the Baptist* (1571) by Livio Agresti.

Alviano

The impressive square castle of Alviano (*map p. 487, B5*) can be seen on a spur with the village behind it. The first castle on this site dated from 933; the present building (*usually open only at weekends*) was begun in 1495 by the *condottiere* Bartolomeo d'Alviano, and incorporates a cylindrical tower of the earlier castle (the three others were added at this time). The castle was bought by Donna Olimpia Maidalchini in 1651 and it remained in her family until 1920. The upper floor is now the town hall. Beside the bridge at the entrance is a lion with an iron collar, and on the round tower to the left a Medusa's head can be seen. Inside is a Renaissance courtyard, off which is a chapel with frescoes illustrating a miracle of St Francis, who in 1212 silenced the swallows who were disturbing his preaching outside the castle. The old herring-bone paving of the staircases survives. In underground vaulted rooms is a charming ethnographic museum, with exhibits illustrating the traditional agriculture of the area.

The parish church, built in 1506, has a pleasant interior with old columns and capitals and a wooden roof. Here is an early 16th-century fresco by Pordenone of the *Madonna and Saints*, with a striking portrait of Pentesilea Baglione, the elderly widow of Bartolomeo d'Alviano (on the right, protected by St Anthony), who commissioned the fresco. At the end of the south aisle is a lovely painting of the *Madonna in Glory* by L'Alunno (c. 1484), similar to the central panel of the triptych in the Collegiata of Lugnano (*see above*).

The Fossil Forest of Dunarobba

Leaving Amelia to the east, on the N205, you pass the huge, monumental gateway ('Le Colonne') of **Villa L'Aspreta**, seen at the end of a long cypress avenue, with a theatrical external staircase. The villa itself (*privately owned*) has been attributed to Antonio da Sangallo the Younger. Beside the gateway, to the left, is a turning signposted for Avigliano. The road leads on through **Dunarobba** (*map p. 487, B5*), with its massive 15th–16th-century castle. Just outside the village, on the Montecastrilli road, is the Fossil Forest, one of the most important palaeontological sites in central Italy (*for admission, T: 0744 933531 or ask at the town hall of Avigliano*). Here in 1983–87, during work in a clay quarry, a group of some 40 fossilised tree trunks were found, still in an upright position. They grew on the southwestern shores of the huge Lago Tiberino, which in the Pleistocene era occupied a large part of Umbria. Some of them are 1.5m in diameter and 8m high: they date from the Villafranchian or Pleiocene era (c. 3–4 million years ago), and are similar to the present-day sequoia. In the school next door is a research centre with exhibitions relating to the fossils.

PRACTICAL INFORMATION

GETTING AROUND

• **By car:** In **Amelia**, traffic is not

allowed inside the walls on weekdays from 9am–1pm and 5.30–7.30pm. It is best to park outside the walls and use

the frequent minibus service. Free car parks are on the right of Porta Romana beside the walls, and outside Porta Leone. The car park beside Porta Romana has an hourly tariff (inclusive of minibus ticket). In **Cascia**, there are several small car parks clearly signposted just below Piazza Garibaldi. A large car park on the side of the hill (mostly used by coaches) is connected to the church of Santa Maria by a series of escalators and a lift. At **Narni** the car park del Suffragio, off Via Roma, has lifts up to Via Roma and Piazza Cavour. **Norcia** has car parking outside Porta Romana. In **Terni** there are pay car parks opposite San Francesco, on Piazza Tacito, outside the Giardini Pubblici and on Corso del Popolo.
• **By train:** The Rome–Ancona and Rome–Florence lines serve this area (mostly slow trains). Terni is also served by the Rieti–Aquila line as well as the Ferrovia Centrale Umbra service from Perugia, Umbertide and Sansepolcro. The nearest stations to **Amelia** are Narni, 11km east and Orte, 15km south (bus services from both stations). For the **Cascata delle Marmore**, there is a train station at Marmore, on the Rieti line, with a path that leads directly to the falls. For **Narni**, there is a station at Narni Scalo at the foot of the hill.
• **By bus:** Services run by ATC (www.atcterni.it) link **Amelia**, **Narni** and **Terni** to Orte and Orvieto as well as the environs, including **Otricoli**. For the **Cascata delle Marmore** there are buses from Terni. **Cascia** and **Norcia** services are run by Società Spoletina (www.spoletina.it). A daily early morning bus leaves Rome via Terni and the Valnerina, or via Rieti, and vice versa.

INFORMATION OFFICES

Amelia Via Orvieto (outside Porta Romana), T: 0744 981453.
Cascia Via G. da Chiavano 2, T: 0743 71147.
Narni Piazza dei Priori 3, T: 0744 715362.
Norcia Information office of the Monti Sibillini national park at Piazza San Benedetto, T: 0743 817090.
Terni Via Cassian Bon 2/4, T: 0744 423047.

HOTELS

Castelluccio (*map p. 487, D4*)
€€ **Il Guerrin Meschino**. *Agriturismo* accommodation open all year. It has very simple but pleasant rooms, on the outskirts of the village, with a good restaurant run by the same family (who live on the first floor). *Via Monte Veletta 22, T: 0743 821125, www.guerrinmeschino.it. 5 rooms.*
Collicello (*map p. 487, B5*)
€€ **La Palombara Maison d'Hôtes**. Six kilometres north of Amelia in the hamlet of Collicello, a charming lodge run by an Italian-French couple, restored from a 17th-century farmhouse. Set in woodland and extremely peaceful. Rental is by the week although daily rates can be negotiated. *Via di Collicello 34, T: 335 613 7768, www.lapalombara-umbria.it. 2 apartments.*
Ferentillo (*map p. 487, C5*)
€€ **Abbazia San Pietro in Valle**. Three kilometres north of the village, a beautiful, well-restored former abbey in a lovely, isolated position. Family-run by the owners of the large estate. The

rooms in the spacious former monks' quarters are carefully furnished, some of them overlooking the cloister. Breakfast is served in the old vaulted refectory, and there is also a restaurant. *T: 0744 780129, www.sanpietroinvalle.com. 22 rooms.*

Lugnano in Teverina (*map p. 487, B5*)
€ **La Rocca**. Simple, family-run hotel in the old centre. Some of the rooms have views over the valley. Half- or full-board rates available. Restaurant. *Via Cavour 60, T: 0744 900064.*

Narni (*map p. 487, B5*)
€ **Dei Priori**. Hotel in a splendid position in the old centre, in a quiet, narrow alleyway just off Piazza dei Priori. The bedrooms are comfortable; some on the third floor have pretty balconies. Breakfast is served in a handsome room on the first floor. *Vicolo del Comune 4, T: 0744 726843, www.loggiadeipriori.it. 19 rooms.*

Norcia (*map p. 487, D4*)
€ **Hotel Garden**. A neat, modern hotel with a restaurant. *Viale XX Settembre 2, T: 0743 816687. 43 rooms.*
€ **Grotta Azzurra**. In an old palace close to Piazza San Benedetto, a hotel of some charm, with restaurant. There are two annexes attached. *Via Alfieri 12, T: 0743 816513, www.bianconi.com. 15 rooms.*

Preci (*map p. 487, D4*)
€ **Agli Scacchi**. Attractive little hotel at the top of a peaceful old village, with a good restaurant. Small swimming pool. *Quartiere Scacchi 12, T: 0743 99221, www.hotelagliscacchi.com. 26 rooms.*

San Gemini (*map p. 487, B5*)
€ **Duomo**. In a handsome, large late 18th-century palace with a frescoed *salone*, in a quiet position next to the

duomo. It was opened as a hotel at the beginning of this century and there are spacious public rooms and a terrace and small garden. Restaurant in summer. *Piazza Duomo 4, T: 0744 630015, www.gruppobacus.it/hotelduomo. 32 rooms.*

Scheggino (*map p. 487, C5*)
€€ **Del Ponte**. Pleasant hotel on the Nera below the picturesque village. The best rooms are in the annexe. Restaurant. *Via del Borgo 11, T: 0743 61253. 11 rooms.*

Vallo di Nera (*map p. 487, C5*)
€€ **La Locanda di Cacio Re**. In a pleasant restored farmhouse below the village overlooking the Nera valley. Restaurant. *Località I Casali, T: 0743 617003, www.caciore.com. 4 rooms.*

RESTAURANTS

Castelluccio (*map p. 487, D4*)
€ **Cantina Castelluccio**. Local wines, Norcia hams and truffles, and hearty Castelluccio lentil soup. *Piazzale della Fonte, T: 0743 821206.*

Narni (*map p. 487, B5*)
€€ **La Loggia**. Situated on the ground floor of the hotel Dei Priori in three vaulted rooms, it has a varied menu with local specialities. *Vicolo del Comune 4, T: 0744 726843.*

Norcia (*map p. 487, D4*)
€€ **Dal Francese**. A simple restaurant with a reputation for excellent truffle dishes. Also good local salamis and ham. *Via Reguardati, T: 0743 816290.*
€€ **Taverna de' Massari**. A pretty restaurant, well-known for its traditional dishes using the local pork and truffles. Closed Tues except summer. *Via Roma 13, T: 0743 816218.*

Otricoli (*map p. 487, B6*)
€€ **Locanda Casole**. In a fine building in the centre of the old town, open for lunch at weekends, and in the evenings during the week. *Via Vicolo dell'Olmo 6, T: 0744 719290.*

Terni (*map p. 487, C5*)
€€ **La Piazzetta**. Centrally located restaurant and bar in a 1930s *palazzo* with elegant interior. Classic interpretations of regional dishes. *Via Cavour 9, T: 0744 58188.*

€ **Caffè Pazzaglia**. A bakery, bar and restaurant with live jazz music in the evenings. Good for a light meal. *Corso Tacito 10, T: 0744 407102.*

LOCAL SPECIALITIES

Amelia The speciality here is candied figs with almonds and cocoa. **Norcia** is known for its hams and salamis, including *ciauscolo* (soft, creamy sausage), *lonza* (aromatic cured loin), and exceptional *prosciutto*. Excellent local suppliers include Fratelli Ansuini, at Via Anicia 105 (corner of Via Roma). **San Gemini** is famous throughout Italy for its mineral water. The mineral springs are located in a beautiful park, with ancient oak trees, just to the north of the town.

FESTIVALS & EVENTS

Amelia *Santa Fermina*, Annual festival of the 4th-century martyr, with a candlelit procession, 24 Nov.

Narni *Corsa all'Anello*, Medieval tournament preceeded by two weeks of festivities in honour of the patron saint, Giovenale (Juvenal). A torchlit procession takes place on the eve of the event, and the competition is held in Via Maggiore, where a ring is suspended across the street and the contestants from the three districts of town attempt to thrust a lance through it. The town is illuminated by candlelight during the festivities (iron candelabra have survived on all the palaces), second Sun in May.

Norcia Black truffle festival, with food stalls and live music, and a truffle auction on the final day, last week in Feb.

Piediluco *Festa delle Acque*, Festival with fireworks and a procession of illuminated boats after dark, end June/beginning July.

San Gemini *Giostra dell'Arme*, Local festival which includes parades through the town in 15th-century costume, exhibits of handicrafts, and the opening of town taverns, last two weeks of Sept and first two of Oct.

O rvieto (pop. 23,000, *map p. 487, A5*), famous for its magnificent position on a pre-cipitous tufa crag dominating the valley, is a city of great antiquity, with notable Etruscan remains, and today its numerous narrow streets preserve a medieval atmosphere. The oldest buildings are built in a rich golden-coloured tufa. It is renowned for the beauty of its cathedral which, at the highest point of the town, stands out on the skyline. New building has taken place around the station leaving the old town and the cultivated fields beneath its rock, some 315m high, remarkably unchanged. Lovely paths which circle the foot of the rock, but are approached from the town centre, were opened in 2006. Because of its position close to the A1 motorway and main railway line between Florence and Rome, and its proximity to the capital, Orvieto is one of the most visited towns in Umbria, well-equipped with hotels and restaurants, and can become very crowded. It is in the centre of a famous wine-growing area, and local crafts include lace-making and pottery. The hilly environs are particularly attractive, with many handsome old farmhouses.

HISTORY OF ORVIETO

The rock of Orvieto was already occupied in the Iron Age, and an important Etruscan city grew up here in the 9th century BC, usually identified as *Velzna* (later *Volsinii Veteres*), one of the chief cities of the Etruscan Confederation. The town was destroyed in 264 BC by the Romans, and the inhabitants resettled at a spot on the northeast side of Lake Bolsena, which developed into the town of Bolsena (*Volsinii Novi*). In the Middle Ages the commune of *Urbs Vetus* (from which the modern name is derived) was important, and it became especially powerful in the 13th century. The rivalries between the Guelph Monaldeschi and the Ghibelline Filippeschi dominated events during the 14th century, and later two popes, Alexander VI and Clement VII, were to take refuge here from revolts in Rome.

The duomo

Piazza del Duomo is dominated by the magnificent exterior of the cathedral. On the north side of the piazza beside a simple row of low houses is a clock-tower surmounted by a bronze figure known as *Maurizio* (1348) which strikes the hours.

The duomo is one of the most impressive buildings of its period in the country. It dominates the view of the city for miles around. The festival of Corpus Christi was instituted in Orvieto by Urban IV in 1264, to commemorate the miracle which took place in Bolsena (*see p. 180*) the previous year when a Bohemian priest who had doubts about the doctrine of Transubstantiation was convinced when he saw blood drop from the

Host onto the altar cloth during Mass. The first stone of the Orvieto duomo (where the stained cloth is still preserved), was laid on 3rd November 1290, when it was blessed by Pope Nicholas IV.

The exterior

The church was begun to a Romanesque plan, perhaps by Arnolfo di Cambio, but continued in the new Gothic style by Lorenzo Maitani of Siena, who took over in 1310. Other architects later involved in the building include Andrea Pisano (1347–48) and his son Nino, Andrea Orcagna (1359), and, in the early 16th century, Michele Sanmicheli. The church stands on a plinth of seven steps, alternately red and white. The two beautiful sides, built in horizontal bands of white travertine and grey basalt, are decorated with the exteriors of the tall semicircular side chapels and handsome Gothic windows. The huge façade, designed and begun by Lorenzo Maitani, is one of the finest Italian Gothic works, and has been compared in design to a painted triptych in an elaborate frame, since four elegant spires with high crocketed turrets divide it vertically. At the base of the pilasters are superb marble bas-reliefs (c. 1320–30) ascribed to Maitani and assistants. They are very well preserved, and the scenes are divided by delicately carved vine tendrils or acanthus branches. On the right pilaster, above crowded dramatic scenes of *Paradise* and *Hell*, is the *Last Judgement*: the next three pilasters illustrate the lives of Mary and of Christ; stories of Abraham and David, and the story of the Creation. The large bronze symbols of the Evangelists are also by Maitani. The great rose window, surrounded by statues in niches, is Orcagna's work. It has remarkable sculptural details. The harsh polychrome mosaics were mostly remade in the 17th–19th centuries. The bronze doors are by Emilio Greco (*see pp. 234–35*).

The interior

Open 7.30–12.45 & 2.30–dusk. Chapel with Signorelli frescoes open 9–12.45 & 2.30–dusk; on holidays only 2.30–5.45; 6.45 in summer. The ticket must be purchased at the ticket office in the piazza. Only 25 people are allowed into the chapel at any one time. T: 0763 342477. Binoculars are very useful. The interior is uncluttered and the fine architectural lines can be appreciated to the full above the lovely pavement in dark red local stone. The walls are lined with horizontal bands of white and grey. The nave columns, with fine capitals, carry round arches over which a graceful triforium, with a clerestory above it, runs all round the church, except in the transepts. The semicircular side chapels are particularly well designed (many have interesting 14th–15th-century fresco fragments). The lower panels of the stained-glass windows are made of alabaster.

Nave and north side: In the nave are a stoup by Antonio Federighi (1485) and a beautiful font of 1390–1407. At the beginning of the north side the fresco of the *Madonna and Child* is by Gentile da Fabriano (1425).

Chapel of the Corporal: Above the entrance to the chapel (at the east end, on the north side) is the huge colourful organ (1584, by Orvieto-born Ippolito Scalza). Inside, on the walls are restored frescoes (1357–64) by Ugolino di Prete

Ilario illustrating miracles of the Eucharist. In the Gothic recess the huge panel of the *Madonna dei Raccomandati* by Lippo Memmi (1320) is one of the loveliest paintings in Italy of this date. Over the altar, displayed in a large tabernacle designed by Nicola da Siena (1358) and continued by Orcagna, is the Corporal (linen cloth) of the miracle of Bolsena. It is taken in procession on Corpus Christi. Displayed in a showcase near the left wall of the chapel is the original Reliquary of the Corporal, a superb work in silver-gilt with translucent enamels, by the Sienese goldsmith Ugolino di Vieri (1337).

The tribune: This rectangular chapel at the east end is covered with frescoes by Ugolino di Prete Ilario and other Sienese artists. They were commissioned in 1370, and work continued until at least 1380: they represent one of the most important and largest fresco cycles in Italy of this date, remarkable also for their unusual iconography. They illustrate the life of the Madonna, with (on the vault) the *Madonna in Glory*. The beautiful stained glass of the great east window (1325–34) is by Giovanni di Bonino di Assisi. It has 22 panels illustrating the life of the Virgin and prophets, and is one of the most important Gothic stained-glass windows in Italy.

Chapel of San Brizio: The famous frescoes by Signorelli here constitute one of the most remarkable fresco cycles of the Italian Renaissance.

The wealthy local Monaldeschi family financed the building of the chapel in 1409–19. In 1447 Fra' Angelico, with the help of Benozzo Gozzoli, began the frescoes: he had completed just two sections of the vault over the altar before he was recalled to Rome. At the end of the century Luca Signorelli was commissioned to complete them (1499–1504). They represent the Day of Judgement and Life after Death, celebrating the importance of salvation through the Eucharist based on Dominican texts, as well as *De Civitate Dei* by St Augustine and the *Divine Comedy* by Dante. They are particularly interesting for their iconography, since there are very few other pictorial representations in Italy of these subjects. The beautiful nude figure studies are among the most important works of the Renaissance, and the chapel is Signorelli's masterpiece. Since the main scenes are very high up on the walls, the wonderful details are difficult to appreciate without the help of binoculars.

On the left wall (in the lunette nearest to the entrance) is the **Sermon of Antichrist**. Around the central figure of Antichrist (a false prophet), standing on a pedestal and being prompted by the Devil, is a crowd showing scenes of corruption and violence. The two solemn bystanders (dressed in black) are thought to represent Signorelli himself, and, behind, Fra' Angelico. To the right can be seen the figure of Dante (with his characteristic red hat). In the background is the splendid Temple of Solomon (which shows the influence of the architecture of Bramante), and the three groups of figures in front of it represent the execution of two penitents, a

Antichrist preaches a sermon, prompted by the Devil. Detail from the famous frescoes in the duomo of Orvieto by Luca Signorelli.

false miracle, and monks reasserting the authority of the Bible. In the sky St Michael is shown preventing the ascension into Heaven of Antichrist and causing a storm of fire to fall on the corrupt below.

On the entrance wall, above the arch on which a group of putti display the monogram of the Opera del Duomo and a cartouche with the signature of Signorelli, is the **Day of Judgement**. On the right is a group of figures around a man in a turban, presumably a prophet, and above various scenes which foreshadow the end of the world, including unnatural events such as the sea in flood, the red moon, and the black sun, and the stars falling out of the heavens, scenes of torture and buildings crashing to the ground. On the left is Judgement Day itself, with winged devils emitting a rain of fire which destroys the world.

On the right wall the first lunette shows the **Resurrection of the Body**, heralded by two angels in the sky above, and on the altar wall angels guide the elect to Paradise and drive the damned into Hell. Here the influence of Dante can be seen. Fragments of frescoes showing devils and a figure thought to represent Cain were discovered behind the altar during recent restoration work. The second lunette on the right wall, the **Casting out of the Wicked**, has three armoured Archangels repudiating the fallen angels above an extraordinary crowded scene of Hell. The nude studies are particularly famous, showing the influence of Antonio Pollaiolo, and the atmosphere of terror and suffering in this scene is remarkable. The second lunette on the left wall shows the **Blessed Entering**

Heaven and the crowning of the elect by a group of angel musicians.

The exquisite decoration on the lower part of the walls, framed with grisaille friezes and *grottesche*, includes medallion portraits of Dante and Classical authors. This was the last part of the chapel to be decorated by Signorelli. On the right of the entrance, with his back to us, is Empedocles, and on the left wall, Cicero, Dante and Statius (formerly believed to be Homer). On the right wall are Ovid, Virgil and Lucan. The *tondi* have scenes from mythology and from the *Divine Comedy*.

In the recess on the right wall, the **Mourning over the Dead Christ**, also by Signorelli, includes the figures of Pietro Parenzo who, when *podestà* of the town at the end of the 13th century, was killed by a group of heretics; and St Faustinus. Both were buried here.

In the two ceiling vaults the celestial host is depicted in a series of triangular compositions on a gold ground. Signorelli received the commission to complete the vault before he started the frescoes on the walls. In the first bay of the vault (nearest to the altar), the two cells by Fra' Angelico show the *Saviour in Glory* and (right) prophets. The other two cells by Signorelli show the Apostles, and the *Signs of the Passion of Christ displayed by Angels* (on either side of the Column of the Flagellation). In the second bay (nearest to the entrance) are martyred saints and virgins, and the two last cells show Doctors of the Church and Patriarchs.

The chapel received its present name when the charming altarpiece of the *Madonna di San Brizio*, by a local 14th-century painter, was moved here.

Luca Signorelli (c. 1441–1523)
Born in Cortona, just across the Umbrian border in Tuscany, around 1450, Signorelli was influenced by Piero della Francesca, with whom he worked as a young man, as well as by Florentine painters, notably Antonio Pollaiolo, from whom he learned how to convey movement and energy in his figure studies. Before carrying out this, his most important commission, he was called to Rome, with other leading artists of the day, to paint a fresco in the Sistine Chapel, and he also worked in Città di Castello (where he was proclaimed citizen of the town in 1488) and Cortona. But the frescoes in Orvieto were immediately recognised as his masterpiece and established his fame. They later had a profound influence on Michelangelo and Raphael, as can be seen in their famous works in the Vatican. Signorelli was also an extremely accomplished draughtsman, and his male nude figure studies are superb. He carried out other fresco cycles at Loreto (*see p. 628*) and in the cloister of Monte Oliveto Maggiore (*see p. 439*), and produced numerous panel paintings, including a number of charming *tondi* with the *Holy Family*. In the 19th century, British collectors became particularly interested in his work, and the first important exhibition of his paintings was held in London in 1893.

Piazza del Duomo

Beside the east end of the duomo are the 13th-century Palazzi dei Papi, built of yellow tufa and with lovely windows. Here in impressive and beautifully vaulted rooms are the archaeological museum and the cathedral museum.

The **Museo dell'Opera del Duomo** (*open daily except Tues 9.30–1 & 3–5/6; April–Sept 9.30–7; only partially open at time of writing; T: 0763 342477*) has an exceptionally fine collection of works of art. The first room has detached 14th–15th-century frescoes, mostly by local painters. An outside staircase leads up to a room where the seated marble statue of the *Madonna and Child* from the lunette of the central door of the duomo is displayed. It has a very unusual bronze canopy with emaciated bronze angels on either side. Dated to the early 14th century, it is usually attributed to the architect of the duomo, Lorenzo Maitani. In the next room is a beautiful reliquary of St Savinus by Ugolino di Vieri (who also made the reliquary of the Corporal in the duomo), and a tiny painting of the *Madonna and Child with Four Saints* attributed to Lippo Vanni. Sculptures include statuettes by Andrea Pisano and his son Nino (notably a *Madonna and Child*, a seated *Christ*, and an unfinished statue of *Fortitude*), a pear-wood statue of the seated *Redeemer* dating from around 1330, and two Madonnas in wood by French masters. A late 13th-century painting of the *Madonna and Child* thought to be by Coppo di Marcovaldo is displayed beside two other very early works, a Crucifix and a Byzantine-style *Madonna* decorated with two blue gems. A lectern and fragments from the choir stalls of the duomo have pretty intarsia decorations. Simone Martini is represented by beautiful fragments from two polyptychs painted for churches in Orvieto. The *Mary Magdalene* (1504) is by Luca Signorelli

Etruscan amphora with stylised animals, in the Museo Claudio Faina.

(although the landscape is by his workshop). The huge altarpieces painted for the side altars of the duomo in the mid-16th century by Girolamo Muziano, Cesare Nebbia and Pomarancio are also preserved here. The last room has ten extremely interesting *sinopie* for the frescoes by Ugolino di Prete Ilario in the Chapel of the Corporal; a marble statuette of *St Michael Archangel* by Raffaello da Montelupo (c. 1560) from the façade of the duomo; a self-portrait thought to be by Luca Signorelli; and a *Madonna and Child* in an elaborate tabernacle attributed to Pastura. The famous Baroque statues of the *Apostles* and *Annunciation* made for duomo nave are at present displayed in the ex-church of Sant'Agostino (*see p. 594*).

The **Museo Archeologico Nazionale** (*open 8.30–7.30; T: 0763 341039*), arranged in four huge rooms with fine barrel vaults on the ground floor of the Palazzi Papali, has a huge collection of objects from the two Etruscan necropoleis at the foot of the rock of Orvieto (Cannicella and Crocifisso del Tufo), dating mostly from the late 7th–early 6th centuries BC, and armour from the tomb of a warrior (4th century BC). There is also a good collection of Greek red- and black-figure vases (4th century BC), *bucchero* ware, bronze mirrors, and terracottas, as well as two very fine painted Etruscan tombs (*illuminated on request*).

The battlemented **Palazzo Soliano** was begun in 1297 for Boniface VIII. It is built in yellow tufa, typical of Orvieto, with arches and an external staircase. The ground floor at present houses sculptures left to the city in 1980 by Emilio Greco, who made the duomo doors. (*Since the opening hours are subject to change, check at the tourist office in the Piazza or T: 0763 344605.*)

Museo Archeologico and Museo Faina

Facing the façade of the duomo is a palace which houses the Museo Claudio Faina and **Museo Civico Archeologico** (*open 9.30–6; Oct–March 10–5; from Nov–Feb closed Mon*). This is one of the most charming museums in Umbria and the collections are beautifully displayed and well labelled (also in English). On the ground floor the archaeological collection includes the so-called *Venus of Cannicella*, a statue probably representing a female goddess of fertility made from Naxos marble and thought to be an Archaic Greek original of the 6th century BC; a colossal stone head of a warrior from the Crocifisso del Tufo necropolis (6th century BC); and polychrome terracotta decorations from the Belvedere Temple (4th century BC).

The **Museo Claudio Faina**, with finds from excavations in the necropoleis of Orvieto, and donated to the city by the Faina family in 1954, is arranged on the two upper floors, where some of the rooms still have their 19th-century painted decorations. The collection includes Etruscan gold jewellery; an important numismatic collection; Etruscan urns from Chiusi; black-figure amphorae and kraters; red- and black-figure vases from Orvieto; and three large black-figure amphorae dating from around 550 BC. The second floor has prehistoric finds, *bucchero* ware, Etruscan bronzes and ceramics, and the torso of a Greek marble statuette dating from the 4th century BC.

Parco delle Grotte

In a small park of pine trees in Piazza Duomo is the entrance gate to a path which leads downhill through a little garden provided with picnic benches, with wonderful views over the valley to the entrance to the Parco delle Grotte (or 'Orvieto Underground': *guided tours, also in English, are given every day: for information ask at the tourist office in the Piazza; T: 0763 340688*). There is a labyrinth of some 1,200 man-made caves in the tufa: it has been estimated that about 30 percent of the terrain below ground level has been excavated at one period or another (from Etruscan to medieval times) for wells, aqueducts, cisterns, wine cellars, tunnels, quarries, dovecotes, etc. In this part of the rock two grottoes can be visited. In the **first grotto** (where there is a constant temperature all year round of about 14–15°C) you can see a 16th-century olive-press which seems to have occupied an Etruscan cellar (with a typical carved ceiling imitating a wood roof). Beyond is a medieval *pozzolana* quarry (this friable rock was used for numerous buildings in the town), where two rectangular Etruscan shafts (40 other similar shafts have been found beneath the town) can be seen. One of them has been excavated to a depth of 42m, and they were presumably used as wells (since they pierce the tufa rock as far as the clay level).

Oil flask (askos) in the form of a duck, a popular Etruscan design, in the Museo Claudio Faina.

In the **second grotto** (which has some very steep, narrow and low stairs) there are numerous dovecotes, used since medieval times as nesting places for pigeons, which once provided the staple diet. Each of these, with many pigeon-holes carved out of the *pozzolana* rock, was connected by a staircase with the private dwelling above (and the pigeons would come and go

through the open rectangular windows in the rockface). There are spectacular views of the valley. In one of the dovecotes a pottery kiln was installed in the 18th century. On the upper floor another quarry can be seen and a very well preserved dovecote, with the staircase in the centre. The last room appears to have been constructed as a refuge connected to the hospital during the Second World War.

Piazza del Popolo and San Domenico

Corso Cavour is the main street of the town. The tall **Torre del Moro** (12th century) can be ascended by lift to the second floor and then by a long, modern wooden flight of stairs: an easy climb and well worth it (*open 10–7/8; Nov–Feb 10.30–1 & 2.30–5*). The clock dates from 1865, and the larger bell (which strikes every quarter) was cast in 1313. The remarkable view of the town and the countryside beyond is one of the best in Umbria.

The large peaceful Piazza del Popolo is dominated by the unusual **Palazzo del Popolo**, which is now a conference centre. The impressive exterior, built in tufa with decorated arches and windows, was probably begun in 1157. Excavations beneath the building have revealed Etruscan remains and a medieval well filled with ceramic shards (13th–16th centuries). A market is held in the surrounding *piazze* on Thursday and Saturday mornings. (*For the steps down to the path beneath the rock of Orvieto, and to the necropolis of the Crocifisso del Tufo, see p. 596.*)

Via della Pace leads towards the church of **San Domenico**, thought to be the first church dedicated to St Dominic, built in 1233–64. In its former convent St Thomas Aquinas taught theology. The church, of which only the transept remains, has a pretty exterior. In the interior the very beautiful tomb of Cardinal de Braye, who died in Orvieto in 1282, by Arnolfo di Cambio, has been reassembled. The Cappella Petrucci has an unusual design by Sanmicheli.

Piazza della Repubblica

Piazza della Repubblica is the central square of Orvieto. The 12th-century church of **Sant'Andrea** has a fine 12-sided campanile (over-restored in 1928). The beautiful interior has a nave with Composite capitals and fine vaulting at the east end. The pulpit is made up of Cosmati fragments, and there are remains of 14th- and 15th-century frescoes. In 1281, Martin IV was crowned here in the presence of Charles of Anjou (Charles I of Naples). Beneath the church, the 6th-century pavement from the early basilica overlies Etruscan and Roman remains. **Palazzo Comunale**, first built in 1216, has a façade (c. 1580) by Ippolito Scalza. Opposite is a Neoclassical palace by Virginio Vespignani.

Via Loggia dei Mercanti, with several towers, is characteristic of the old city: it leads past the former 14th-century church of the Carmine (now a theatre workshop) to Piazza de' Ranieri, where the escalators and moving walkway from the car park of Campo della Fiera, at the foot of the rock, emerge. The raised Via Ripa Serancia continues under a lovely old arch to an attractive piazza with two churches. San Giovanni Evangelista was founded in 916, and rebuilt in 1687 on an octagonal plan. In the apse is a framed fresco fragment of the *Madonna and Child* (1356). The pretty cloister dates

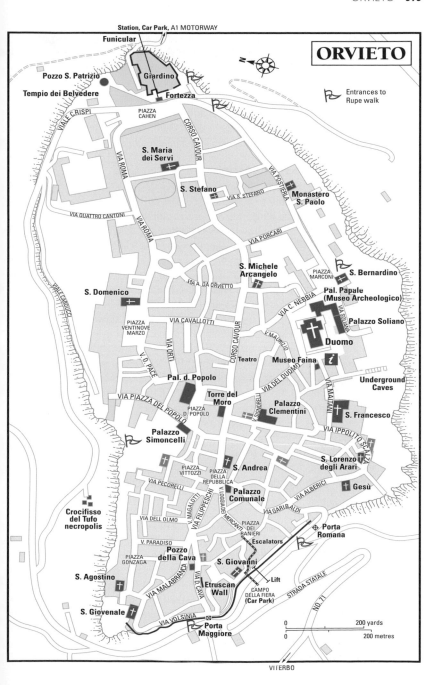

from 1513, with fine dark columns and a well-head of 1526. In the cellars of the old convent there is a wine cellar where Umbrian wines can be tasted and purchased. From the terrace in the piazza there is a lovely view of part of the old town and the countryside beyond. The sheer rockface drops abruptly to the car park at Campo della Fiera (reached by a lift just out of the piazza). It is well worth taking the lift in order to climb back up the rock by the escalators and moving walkway built into the tufa. Excavations are in progress near the Campo della Fiera, and it is thought that the site of the famous Etruscan sanctuary of *Fanum Voltumnae* may have been identified here.

San Giovenale and Sant'Agostino

Beside San Giovanni Evangelista a splendid old road (Via dei Malcorini; pedestrians only) can be followed downhill to a picturesque part of the town, well worth exploring. It crosses above the Porta Maggiore, one of the oldest city gates, and then ascends along the top of the walls to the church of **San Giovenale**, which stands in a beautiful position on the edge of the rock, with orchards below. The church, of ancient foundation, has a charming old interior with an unusual east end and little columns and lecterns in the sanctuary made up of old sculptural fragments. An early Christian carved panel serves as the altar frontal. There are numerous other sculptural fragments in the church including a little transenna decorated with peacocks, as well as 13th–16th-century frescoes. Close by is the ex-church of **Sant'Agostino** (*open as for the Museo dell'Opera del Duomo; see p. 589*) which provides a fit setting for the colossal statues of the Apostles, most of them made in the last years of the 16th century to decorate the nave of the duomo. They include works by Pietro Francavilla, Ippolito Scalza and Giovanni Battista Caccini. *St Philip* and *St Jude* (Thaddeus) were made in the early 17th century by Francesco Mochi, and show a new Baroque dynamism which typify his most famous works here, the two *Annunciation* figures. The Archangel is perhaps one of the greatest works of sculpture ever produced: it has incredible movement and is equally impressive when viewed from any angle. Exquisite details include the swirling tunic with its fringe and the delicate wings, and the soft cotton-wool cloud. The worried Madonna, reminiscent of a Roman muse, is instead wrapped in heavy drapery as she struggles up from her chair as it almost topples over.

Via della Cava

Via della Cava leads downhill to the **Pozzo della Cava** (*no. 26; open 8–8 except Mon*), a charming little private museum with a pleasant café, garden and simple restaurant (*only open at lunchtime*). An interesting Etruscan well excavated in the tufa rock (now some 25m deep) and used by Clement VII in 1527 (*see the Pozzo di San Patrizio opposite*) can be seen here. The underground grottoes also have remains of a pottery with several kilns, thought to have been active from the 13th–15th centuries, where numerous ceramic rejects were found. These have been carefully restored and are exhibited here.

Further downhill (entrance at no. 85), remarkable remains of the Etruscan walls of the city have been restored (*open by appointment; T: 076 334 1234 or 339 248 9666*). No fewer than eight courses of huge tufa rocks survive, built at the end of the 6th or beginning of the 5th century BC against the natural rock wall. At the upper end of Via della Cava (no. 8), beneath an antique shop, another underground medieval pottery and deep well may be visited on request. It was in operation from the late 14th to the mid-16th centuries, and has been carefully restored by the shop-owner. There is a delightful little museum exhibiting the ceramics found here and the kiln where they were made.

San Francesco and San Lorenzo de Arari

The large church of **San Francesco**, in Piazza dei Febei, has a 13th-century façade and a white interior (altered in 1773). Here, in the presence of Edward I of England, the funeral of Prince Henry of Cornwall took place, who was murdered at Viterbo in March 1271 (*see p. 169*). King Edward had been received in Orvieto by Pope Gregory X on his return from the Crusades. Here also Boniface VIII canonised St Louis of Toulouse: two statues of the pope made in 1297–1306 in honour of his visit to the town and set up on two of the town gates, have been displayed in the church since their restoration. The altarpieces are by Cesare Nebbia and Filippo Naldini. In a chapel to the left are interesting but very damaged late 14th-century frescoes attributed to Pietro di Puccio.

Via Ippolito Scalza leads south to the over-restored Romanesque church of **San Lorenzo de Arari** (or dell'Ara), which takes its name from an Etruscan altar (*ara*) beneath the altar-table. Above it is a pretty little 12th-century ciborium. The Byzantine-style apse fresco of *Christ Enthroned with Four Saints*, and the frescoes illustrating four episodes in the life of St Lawrence (1330) in the nave, have suffered from poor restorations in the past.

Pozzo di San Patrizio

At the easternmost part of the town is Piazza Cahen, with the funicular terminus. The grounds of the Fortezza (1364) here are now a pleasant public garden with views of the valley. An avenue to the left of the funicular station descends to the **Pozzo di San Patrizio** (*open daily 10–dusk*), a remarkable structure built by Antonio da Sangallo the Younger (1527–37) to provide an emergency water supply in the event of a siege, by order of Clement VII, who fled to Orvieto after the Sack of Rome. The ingeniously designed well, surmounted by a low tower, is 63m deep, and is encircled by two independent spiral staircases each with 248 wide steps and lit by 72 windows. It is called 'St Patrick's Well' because it is supposed to be similar to St Patrick's cavern in Ireland. You can climb all the way down to the bottom to the water level, and then up again by the other staircase. The steps were designed so that they could also be used by donkeys. In the public gardens above the well are conspicuous remains of an **Etruscan Temple**, known as the Tempio del Belvedere.

The Rupe Walk and Crocifisso del Tufo

In 2006 an excellent path was opened at the foot of the rock of Orvieto, approached from a series of steps, ramps, lanes or lifts (*not always well signposted; entrances are marked on the map on p. 593*). It is well worth exploring as it is only from this path that you can appreciate the mighty tufa rock on which the town is built. It makes a lovely, easy walk traversing little gardens, orchards and chestnut woods, and is a very pleasant place to picnic. At present the entrances are: Porta Vivaria (take Via del Popolo out of Piazza del Popolo, then Via Vivaria to Piazza Cimicchi, from where steps descend); Porta Maggiore (approached by Via della Cava); Porta Romana or Foro Boario near the car park of Campo della Fiera; Palazzo Crispo in Piazza Marconi (take the spiral staircase which descends past a grotto with remains of fossilised trees which grew here before the volcanic eruption of some 320,000 years ago which formed the rock of Orvieto); Porta Soliana or Porta Rocca at the Fortezza Albornoz in Piazza Cahen.

The Porta Vivaria entrance also provides an easy approach (in about 15mins) to the Etruscan necropolis of the **Crocifisso del Tufo** (*open 8.30–dusk*), laid out on a regular 'urban' plan probably in the mid-6th century BC. Many of the small rectangular chamber tombs constructed out of tufa blocks survive intact (and can be entered), with the names of their owners still inscribed above the entrance. Excavations began here at the end of the 18th century, and the important finds are now in the archaeological museums of Orvieto. There is a particularly good view of the site from the path above.

At the foot of the rock to the southwest of the town, next to a hotel and restaurant, is the Premonstratensian abbey of **Santi Severo e Martirio**, also known as La Badia, dating from the 12th century. Parts of the ruined abbey may be visited on request at the hotel: these include the abbot's house, the former refectory (now the Chiesa del Crocifisso), and the original church with its 12-sided campanile.

TODI

Todi is a beautiful old town (pop. 16,000; *map p. 487, B4*) in a delightful position on an isolated triangular hill. It retains many interesting medieval buildings and steep old streets. The surrounding countryside is particularly lovely. Todi was founded by the Umbri, and by 42 BC it had become the Roman colony of *Tuder*. One of the first free communes in the Middle Ages, it was at the height of its power (with Terni and Amelia under its rule) in the early 13th century, when the Palazzo del Popolo was built. In 1523 more than half the population died of the plague. In the 19th century numerous unsystematic excavations took place here, and nearly all the remarkable Etruscan and Roman finds made then, including a bronze statue of Mars dating from the beginning of the 4th century BC, are now in the archaeological museums of Florence and Rome.

The duomo

The central Piazza del Popolo, on the site of the Roman forum, is one of the finest in Italy, bordered by well-proportioned Gothic buildings. The battlemented Palazzo dei Priori dates from 1293–1337, when the bronze eagle (coat of arms of the town since 1267) was set up here.

The façade of the duomo (*open 8.30–12.30 & 2.30–6.30; winter 8.30–4.30*), above an imposing flight of 18th-century steps, was decorated in the early 16th century. The lovely interior has superb Corinthian capitals, a raised presbytery and a semi-dome in the

Façade of the duomo of Todi.

apse. On the west wall is a fresco of the *Last Judgement* (c. 1596), inspired by Michelangelo's famous work in the Sistine Chapel in Rome, by Ferraù Fenzoni. Beneath the pretty Gothic arcade on the south side (with 19th-century stained glass) is a detached fresco of *Mary Magdalene between two Angels*, and a fragment of the *Trinity* by Lo Spagna (1525). The beautiful font dates from 1507. At the end of this aisle, near an altarpiece by Giannicola di Paolo, is the entrance to the little Treasury museum. The two gilded wooden organs are particularly fine. Behind the high altar, with little Gothic columns, and above which hangs a late 13th-century Crucifix, can be seen the carved and inlaid stalls by Antonio Bencivenni da Mercatello. On either side of the presbytery are small paintings of *St Peter* and *St Paul* by Lo Spagna. To the left is the Cappella Cesi (1605): the tombs of Bishop Angelo and Giovanni Andrea Cesi have portraits attributed to Annibale Carracci. The Lapidary Museum and crypt can also be visited: off a long cor-

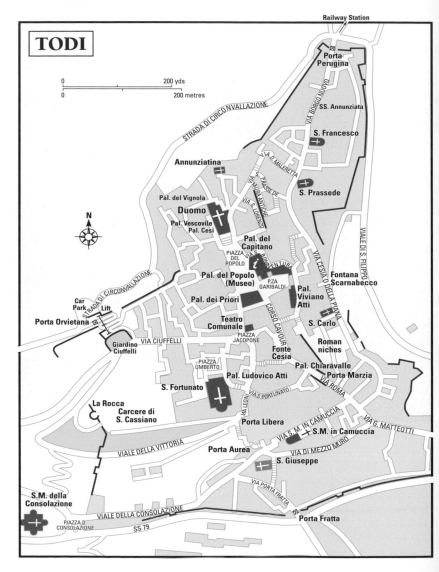

ridor in little cells (which were used as tombs until the 19th century) is a charming miscellany of objects including lanterns, bells and plaster reliefs, and in the crypt with fine vaulting are three mutilated statue groups attributed to the school of Giovanni Pisano.

Museo della Città

A monumental flight of steps (1267) provides an entrance to the Gothic Palazzo del Popolo (1213), one of the oldest town halls in Italy (the battlements were added in 1901), and the adjoining Palazzo del Capitano (c. 1290), which has two orders of elegant three-light windows (those on the first floor beneath pretty foliated triangular frames). They now house the **Museo della Città** (*open 10–1.30 & 3–6; winter 10.30–1 & 2.30–5; closed Mon*), where the history of the city is charmingly illustrated from the pre-Roman period through medieval times (with various representations of the patron saints of the city), right up to the Risorgimento. It preserves the comfortable saddle made for Anita Garibaldi when she passed through the town, heavily pregnant, in 1849. The archaeological section has finds from tombs in the district of Todi (5th–3rd century BC) including red-figure Attic vases and terracottas, and Roman fragments including a charming bronze weight in the shape of a pig. The well-labelled numismatic section has some 1,475 coins dating from pre-Roman to modern times, with a particularly important collection of Republican and Imperial Roman coins. The **Pinacoteca** is exhibited in a handsome large hall and includes works by Lo Spagna and Ferraù Fenzoni (1562–1645), an artist born in Faenza but mainly active in Todi.

At the upper end of Piazza del Popolo, on the left of the duomo façade, is **Palazzo Rolli**, attributed to Antonio da Sangallo the Younger (1547). Paolo Rolli (1687–1765), the Italian translator of Milton, was born in Todi. At the entrance to the courtyard of Palazzo Vescovile (1593) there is a portal by Vignola. Behind the duomo, in Via del Seminario, is the 16th-century Palazzo del Vignola, named after its architect, which ingeniously fits its corner site.

The northern part of town

The houses on the peaceful old Via Santa Prassede incorporate fragments of the earliest walls, and stretches of medieval fortifications can be seen nearby. Beyond a gate is the monastery of **San Francesco**, with its arch over the street. In the interior of the church, the 16th-century high altarpiece is by Livio Agresti. The interesting large 14th-century fresco represents an allegory of Salvation.

Via Borgo Nuovo continues out of the town through the double Porta Perugina, with its round tower in the medieval circle of walls (begun c. 1244), beyond which is beautiful countryside.

San Fortunato

San Fortunato (*open 10–1 & 2.30–5; summer 9–1 & 3–7; closed Mon*) has a portal with exquisite carving with saints beneath baldachins and curious figures entwined with leaves. On either side are statues of the *Annunciation*; the angel, with her robes flowing over her wings, is particularly fine and is attributed by some scholars to Jacopo della

Quercia. The campanile with its cusped top dates from 1460 and can be climbed (150 steps; *open 10–1 & 2.30/3–6.30/7 except Mon*) to enjoy the splendid view. The exceptionally light interior is typical of German late Gothic hall churches, with all three naves of equal height, clustered pilasters and a polygonal apse. It was begun in 1291 at the east end, but not completed until 1459. The attractive tiled brick floor dates from 1463. The grey stone brackets have been installed to counteract the outward lean of the pilasters. Many of the chapels have 14th–15th-century fresco fragments, and in the fourth south chapel is a lovely *Madonna and Child with Two Angels* by Masolino. The seventh chapel is a fine domed Baroque work, decorated with stuccoes. Another chapel preserves a reliquary with the arm of St Fortunatus, made in silver and copper in the late 14th century. The high altar has little Gothic columns (the figures of saints were painted in 1860). The choir stalls were carved in 1590.

In the crypt are preserved the remains of Jacopone da Todi (*see box below*), with a monument erected in the 16th century by Bishop Angelo Cesi (who built the Fonte Cesia in the centre of town, and is buried in the duomo). The third north chapel, with a dome, was well decorated by the local painter Andrea Polinori (1586–1648); other works in Todi by this artist can be seen in the churches of San Giuseppe (a *Holy Family*, considered one of his best works), the Annunziatina (a painting of Jacopone da Todi), and Santa Prassede.

From the church, a lane leads up to the top of the hill, where the large round tower of the ruined **Rocca** is surrounded by a delightful public garden with lovely views.

Jacopone da Todi (c. 1230–1306)
Todi was the birthplace of Jacopo Benedetti, always known as Jacopone da Todi, a poet whose fame was second only to that of Dante and is today considered one of the great figures in the development of Italian literature. Very little is known about his early life, but in 1278 he became a Franciscan. He is recorded as the first signatory in a document which proclaimed the papacy of Boniface VIII illegitimate (based on arguments invalidating his predecessor Celestine V's renunciation of the Papal Chair; *see also pp. 211–12*). For this he was excommunicated and imprisoned, but was released at the end of his life by Boniface's successor. He wrote numerous *Laudi* in the vernacular, and his works were widely diffused in Italy. Today he is best remembered as the reputed author of the *Stabat Mater*. At the bottom of the steps of San Fortunato is a monument to him, made of Antique fragments and with a bronze statue (1930).

Porta Marzia and the Roman niches

Porta Marzia, on Via Roma, is a medieval archway constructed with Roman material in the first circle of walls. Via Roma becomes Corso Cavour, off which the stepped Via del Mercato Vecchio leads right under a passageway to a piazza where there are four remarkable tall **Roman niches**, with semi-domes, from a Roman building. Nearby is the Romanesque church of San Carlo (or Sant'Ilario), with a charming façade and bell-cote, and a fountain dating from 1241, with a pretty portico.

Santa Maria della Consolazione

Outside the walls (best reached on foot from San Fortunato along Via Ciuffelli, or from a path which descends from the Rocca), unfortunately now on a busy road, stands the magnificent church of Santa Maria della Consolazione (*closed 1–3*), a masterpiece of the Renaissance. With an imposing domed Greek-cross plan, it clearly shows the influence of Bramante. Begun in 1508 and finished in 1607, its architect is thought to have been Cola da Caprarola, otherwise little known. The vault decoration in the interior dates from 1579–82.

PRACTICAL INFORMATION

GETTING AROUND

• **By car:** In **Orvieto** there is a large free car park beside the railway station. From there take the underpass to Piazza Stazione for the funicular. There is also a pay car park below the town at Campo della Fiera. There are free car parks in the centre of the town at Piazza Cahen, or off Via Roma. Car parking in **Todi** is best outside the walls at Porta Orvietana, Porta Romana, and in Piazzale G. Fabrizio Atti. In the centre (limited space) there is a car park with an hourly tariff in Foro Tempio di Marte (or Piazza del Mercato Vecchio).

• **By train:** **Orvieto Scalo** station is at the bottom of the hill on the line between Florence and Rome (only a few of the fastest trains stop here). ATC buses run to the station (except on Sun) from Bolsena, Narni, Terni, Amelia and Todi. **Todi** station is 2km north of Porta Perugina on the Ferrovia Centrale Umbra line from Perugia to Terni (buses connect).

• **By bus:** Orvieto services are run by ATC (www.atcterni.it) on weekdays from Todi, Narni and Terni. Services also to Civitella del Lago. **Todi** services run to Piazzale della Consolazione from Perugia and from Terni (both six times a day), and once a day to Piazza Jacopone from Rome (except Sun) and from Orvieto.

Town buses and funicular: In **Orvieto** minibus A (every 10mins) from Piazza Cahen via Via Postierla to Piazza Duomo. Minibus B (every 20mins) from Piazza Cahen via Piazza XXIX Marzo, Piazza della Repubblica, Via Alberici and Via Maitani to Piazza Duomo. The **Orvieto funicular** runs from the railway station to Piazza Cahen (in just over 2mins) every 10mins. You can buy a ticket to include the minibus service from Piazza Cahen direct to Piazza Duomo (line A) or via Piazza della Repubblica (line B).

INFORMATION OFFICES

Orvieto Piazza Duomo 24, T: 0763 341772. The **Carta Orvieto Unica** is available from the car park at the railway station or the tourist office and offers free funicular and bus trips as well as entrance to most museums and monuments.
Todi Piazza Umberto 1, T: 0758 943395; Piazza del Popolo 38, T: 0758 942526.

HOTELS

Orvieto (*map p. 487, A5*)
€€€–€€ **La Badia**. Below the town (a drive, not a walk away), in a 12th-century monastery beautifully positioned, with swimming pool. *Località La Badia 8, T: 0763 301959, www.labadiahotel.it. 27 rooms.*
€€ **Albergo Maitani**. A family-run hotel in a wonderful location in front of the duomo—the breakfast terrace looks directly onto the façade. *Via Lorenzo Maitani 5, T: 0763 342011, www.hotel-maitani.com. 39 rooms.*
€€ **Albergo Reale**. A beautiful old building in the lovely Piazza del Popolo. A very old-fashioned hotel which has never been renovated but retains a faded charm. The rooms have high frescoed ceilings and wonderful views. *Piazza del Popolo 27, T: 0763 341247, www.orvietohotels.it. 45 rooms.*
€€ **Duomo**. One of the first hotels to be opened in the town. A small house in a very peaceful position, just off the cathedral square, with a tiny garden where breakfast is served in summer. The pleasant rooms are particularly spacious, all of them different, and with

good bathrooms. Professionally run by a friendly couple. *Vicolo di Maurizio 7, T: 0763 341887, www.orvietohotel duomo.com. 18 rooms.*
€€ **Palazzo Piccolomini**. ■ In a beautiful 16th-century palace in the centre of the old town. Carefully restored and simply furnished with restrained taste, with cool stone floors. Breakfast is served in the vaulted cellars. Professional service. *Piazza Ranieri 36, T: 0763 341743, www.hotelpiccolomini.it. 34 rooms.*
€ **Posta**. In a fine house in the centre of town, with old-fashioned rooms. Simple and excellent value, with a welcoming atmosphere. *Via Luca Signorelli 18, T: 0763 341909. 20 rooms.*
Todi (*map p. 487, B4*)
€€€ **Bramante**. On the outskirts of Todi, near Santa Maria della Consolazione, a 12th-century convent converted into a lovely country hotel. Tennis court and swimming pool. *Via Orvietana 48, T: 0758 948381, www.hotelbramante.it. 50 rooms.*
€€ **Fonte Cesia**. Good, central location in a restored *palazzo*, this is an elegant hotel with professional service. *Via Lorenzo Leoni 3, T: 0758 943737, www.fontecesia.it. 42 rooms.*
€€ **San Lorenzo Tre**. A delightful small guesthouse in the centre of town, in an old palace which retains its elegant furnishings. Good value. *Via San Lorenzo 3, T: 0758 944555, www.todi.net/lorenzo. 8 rooms.*
€€ **Villa Luisa**. Two kilometres from the town centre, a relaxing hotel surrounded by immaculate grounds, with superb views and a lovely swimming pool. Modern and clean, with friendly staff. *Via A. Cortesi 147, T: 0758 948571,*

www.villaluisa.it. 40 rooms.
€ **Convento dei Frati Cappuccini (Sacro Cuore).** Excellent, simple place to stay, with apartments (all with private bathroom) in a part of the convent where three friars still live. Very clean. No breakfast. Parking in the interior courtyard. *Via Cesia 2, T: 0758 942358, padre.carlo@libero.it. 5 apartments.*

RESTAURANTS

Baschi (Civitella del Lago; *map p. 487, A5*)
€€€€ **Vissani.** For years this has been one of the most famous luxury-class restaurants in Italy, run by Gianfranco Vissani, a well-known chef who frequently appears on television. Gianfranco dominates the kitchen and dining room of his Michelin 2-star restaurant (converted from his parents' *trattoria*). Known for his passionate defence of traditional Italian ingredients, he creates dishes with flair and confidence. An outstanding dining experience. Closed Wed all day, Mon and Thur lunch, Sun evening, end July, end Aug, Christmas. *SS 448, km 66, Località Cannitello 294, T: 0744 950206.*
€€€ **Trippini.** A third of the price of Civitella del Lago's more famous restaurant, Vissani, yet the quality of the cuisine is still excellent. Lovely views over the lake. Closed Mon. *T: 0744 950316.*
Grutti (*map p. 487, B4*)
€ **Le Noci.** Ten minutes' drive from Todi, towards Montefalco. A splendid restaurant offering excellent Umbrian specialities, with views across the countryside. *Via Torino 6, T: 0742 98371.*
Orvieto (*map p. 487, A5*)
€€€ **Il Giglio d'Oro.** ■ Elegant restaurant serving excellent Umbrian cuisine, with tables on the cathedral square in summer. Closed Weds. *Piazza Duomo 8, T: 0763 341903.*
€€ **Osteria dell'Angelo.** A well-reputed restaurant in town serving fine, authentic Umbrian dishes. Closed Mon. *Piazza XXIX Marzo 8, T: 0763 341805.*
€€ **I Sette Consoli.** Smart gastronomy in this much-praised restaurant. Umbrian ingredients—*porcini* mushrooms, boar, truffles, pork and wonderful olive oil—are used at their best in a professional atmosphere. Closed Wed. *Piazza Sant'Angelo 1a, T: 0763 343911.*
€€ **La Palomba.** Simply delicious food and very good value. Dishes such as tagliatelle with a ragout of wild boar, and beef in red-wine sauce are superb. Closed Wed. *Via Cipriano Manente 16 (just off Piazza della Repubblica), T: 0763 343395.*
€€ **San Giovenale.** Newly opened, in a convent building in Piazzale San Giovenale. Good location and value for money. *Piazza San Giovenale 6, T: 0763 340641.*
€€ **Trattoria La Grotta.** A friendly place serving excellent local fare, just around the corner from the duomo. Arrive early to ensure a seat as the restaurant gets very busy, particularly at lunchtime. Closed Tues. *Via Luca Signorelli 5, T: 0763 341348.*
€€ **Trattoria dell'Orso.** ■ Excellent local home cooking in a cosy atmosphere, where the owner personally explains the daily specials in place of a printed menu. *Via della Misericordia 18–20, T: 0763 341642.*
€ **Bar Montanucci.** Good buffet food, ideal for a quick lunch between sights. *Corso Cavour 21, T: 0763 341261.*

€ **Enoteca Foresi**. A medieval wine cellar with a particularly varied selection of local wines. Served with good local hams and sausages, and pecorino cheese. *Piazza Duomo 2, T: 0763 341611.*

Todi (*map p. 487, B4*)

€€ **Pane e Vino**. In the historic centre, serving fresh dishes from a daily changing menu. A friendly establishment; tables outside in the courtyard in warm weather. Good wine list. Closed Weds. *Via Ciuffelli 33, T: 0758 945448.*

€€ **Umbria**. A pleasing selection of Umbrian dishes. Meat is cooked on the fireplace inside, which makes the restaurant very welcoming in winter, and there is a pretty terrace for the summer months. *Via San Bonaventura 13, T: 0758 942737.*

€ **Antica Hosteria de la Valle**. Very small *trattoria* in the centre of town, with just 6 or 7 tables, serving home-cooked dishes using local produce. Closed Mon. *Via Ciuffelli 19, T: 0758 944848.*

€ **Il Donatello**. Central restaurant serving excellent local food at reasonable prices. Closed Sun. *Via della Storta 29, T: 0758 942444.*

€ **Jacopone**. A traditional interior with maps and drawings on the walls and friendly owners, who have been running the business for five decades. Very tasty dishes, especially the truffle offerings. *Piazzetta Jacopone 3, T: 0758 942366.*

€ **La Scaletta**. Particularly good pasta dishes at this friendly restaurant. *Via Ciuffelli, T: 0758 94422.*

LOCAL SPECIALITIES

Orvieto Local wines can be tasted and purchased at the Enoteca Regionale at the Palazzo del Gusto (*open daily, Via Ripa Serancia 1, T: 0763 341818*). Information on wine-tasting and visits to the wine cellars in the locality from the information office.

FESTIVALS & EVENTS

Orvieto An Easter concert is held in the duomo each year; Open wine cellars in the region surrounding Orvieto for tastings and purchases, May; *Corpus Christi*, In 1264 Pope Urban IV instituted this festival in Orvieto and a procession in honour of the Holy Corporal (*see pp. 584–85*) has been held in the town since 1337. It now takes place in period costume on the Sun after Corpus Christi, starting in Piazza del Duomo, early June; *Palombella*, Pentecost festival with a dove and fireworks held at midday in front of the duomo, Whit Sunday; *Cittàslow*, Festival organised by SlowFood celebrating the best of the region's cuisine, Nov; A remarkable life-size crib (*presepio*) is set up in the Pozzo della Cava grottoes, taking a different theme each year, Advent; International Jazz festival, New Year.

Todi Antiques fair at the Palazzo delle Arti, Easter; Art festival held every year, with live music, theatre and exhibitions, July.

NORTHERN UMBRIA

Northern Umbria is a hilly land of thick forests and steep vales, with the fertile upper Tiber valley in the west, and the mountain passes of the Serra di Burano and Monte Cucco to the east. Its two most important towns are Città di Castello and Gubbio.

CITTÀ DI CASTELLO

Città di Castello (pop. 38,000; *map p. 486, A2–B2*) is a pleasant little town with two very fine museums. It flourished in the High Renaissance under the rule of the Vitelli, when it gave employment to many famous artists, among them Raphael, Luca Signorelli and the della Robbia. Its narrow old side streets preserve their lovely cobbled paving.

HISTORY OF CITTÀ DI CASTELLO

In the Pleistocene era the valley was submerged by the great Lago Tiberino, a lake which stretched as far as Terni and Spoleto. The region was later inhabited by elephants, hippopotami and rhinoceros. The presence of man here has been traced since the Stone Age. The inhabitants are still called *Tifernati*, after the Umbrian town of *Tifernum* on this site. The Roman municipality of Tifernum was mentioned by Pliny the Younger, who had a villa nearby, remains of which have been found in a locality called Colle Plinio. By the 6th century it was the seat of a bishopric, and in the Middle Ages, as a free commune, it was contested between Perugia and the Church. The Vitelli family held the lordship in the 15th and 16th centuries, and four of their palaces remain in the town. It has been noted for its printing industries since the 16th century. The firm of Scipione Lapi was famous for its book production here at the beginning of the 20th century.

The duomo

The duomo (*closed 12–5 on weekdays, and 1–3 on Sun and holidays*) has a bizarre exterior since its façade was left half-finished in the mid-17th century. It was rebuilt by St Floridus, who became bishop in 580, and again in the 11th and 14th centuries. The splendid round campanile (seen from Via del Modello) dates from the 11th century, and has a Gothic upper storey and a conical roof. The Gothic north portal has two beautifully carved panels dating from 1339–59 representing *Justice* and *Mercy*. In the interior the fine Corinthian pilasters were gilded in the 19th century. The panelled wood ceiling was made by local craftsmen in 1697, and incorporates two paintings of angels. Many of the altarpieces are by local 17th-century painters, and in the 18th century the crossing and dome were decorated, and a chapel built on the south side on a Greek-cross plan. In the lower church, on the site of the ancient crypt, the patron saints Bishop Floridus and Amantius are buried in a very old sarcophagus.

The **Museo del Duomo** (*open 10–1 & 2.30–6.30 except Mon*) has a very fine collection of liturgical objects and paintings beautifully arranged in fine 14th–15th-century vaulted rooms. Its most important works include the magnificent hoard of 25 silver plates and utensils used during the celebration of the Eucharist, found while ploughing a field near Canoscio. Made in the 6th century, they are a remarkable examples of early Christian art. In 1142, Pope Celestine II is supposed to have presented to the cathedral the very fine silver and gilded altar-frontal with carvings showing the figure of Christ blessing, surrounded by the symbols of the Evangelists and scenes from the life of Christ. In a splendid vaulted hall on the floor above are displayed a fine Tuscan wooden Crucifix from the late 15th century by the school of Giuliano da Sangallo, opposite a beautiful altarpiece by Rosso Fiorentino showing *Christ in Glory between the Madonna and Sts Anne, Mary Magdalene and Mary of Egypt*. The group of figures below represents the populace. Also here is a painting by Pinturicchio, and two well-painted putti (fragments) attributed to Giulio Romano.

Piazza Gabriotti and Corso Cavour

In Piazza Gabriotti (where a market is held on Thursday and Saturday) is Palazzo Comunale (or dei Priori), begun by Angelo da Orvieto in 1322 but left unfinished. It is constructed in sandstone with lovely two-light windows, and a well-designed vaulted entrance hall and stairway.

Corso Cavour has some interesting buildings and, above a covered market, the 18th-century printing works of Grifani-Donati, which retains its delightful old-fashioned premises where the original machines still operate (*open 9–12.30 & 3–7 except Sun and holidays*). Palazzo del Podestà was also designed by Angelo da Orvieto, and finished by 1368 (the façade was rebuilt by Nicola Barbioni in 1687). Corso Cavour leads to Piazza Costa, with the **Laboratorio della Tela Umbra** (*open 10–12 & 3.30–5.30 except Mon*), where you can see weavers at work on 17th-century looms, demonstrating this traditional Umbrian skill. A museum illustrates the history of Umbrian hand-weaving.

Piazza San Francesco and Piazza Garibaldi

Piazza San Francesco has the church of **San Francesco**, built in 1273, with a fine 18th-century interior. The Vitelli Chapel was built by Giorgio Vasari, and contains an altarpiece by him. Raphael's famous *Marriage of the Virgin* was commissioned for this church in 1504, but was removed by Napoleon in 1798 (and is now in the Brera Gallery in Milan): a copy is kept here. In a side chapel there is a carved wooden 15th-century group of the *Pietà*.

In Piazza Garibaldi is the large **Palazzo Vitelli a Porta Sant'Egidio**, now owned by a bank and used for concerts. It was built in 1540, perhaps on a design by Vasari, for Paolo Vitelli. It has a beautiful garden façade overlooking a large garden with a grotto. The 15th-century Palazzo Albizzini (*open 9–12.30 & 2.30–6; Sun and holidays*

10.30–12.30 & 3–6; closed Mon) houses a collection of works donated to the city in 1982 by the local artist Alberto Burri (1915–95). There is an even larger collection on the outskirts of the town, on the old road to Perugia. A warehouse once used for drying tobacco provides a superb gallery for huge works by Burri, donated by him to the city in 1990 (*open as above*).

Pinacoteca Comunale

In the southern part of the old town is the entrance to Palazzo Vitelli alla Cannoniera, seat of the Pinacoteca Comunale (*open 10–1 & 2.30/3–6/6.30; closed Mon*), the most important collection of paintings in Umbria after the Pinacoteca in Perugia. The palace was built for Alessandro Vitelli in 1521–32 by Antonio da Sangallo and assistants, and the frescoes on the stairs and vaults in some of the rooms, including the *salone*, are attributed to Cola dell'Amatrice and Cristofano Gherardi (called Il Doceno).

On the first floor, Room I is dominated by a beautiful painting of the *Madonna and Child Enthroned* (a *Maestà*) by an anonymous late 13th-century artist named from this work the Master of Città di Castello. The next rooms have early 15th-century paintings, including a *Madonna and Child*, by the Venetian artist Antonio Vivarini. The exquisite reliquary of St Andrew by the *bottega* of Lorenzo Ghiberti (1420) has two statuettes in gilded bronze by the master's own hand. In Room IV the striking *Head of Christ*, with signs of the Passion, is variously attributed to the Flemish school (?Joos van Ghent), to a follower of Piero della Francesca of the late 15th-century Umbrian school, or Cosimo Rosselli. In Room VI the standard with the *Creation of Eve* and the *Martyrdom of Sts Roch and Sebastian* is a beautiful but very damaged work by Raphael. In Room VII there are two paintings by the local artist Francesco Tifernate, and a sacristy cupboard in poplar wood with walnut inlay by Antonio Bencivenni (signed and dated 1501). On the ground floor, Room XII displays a beautiful painting of the *Martyrdom of St Sebastian* by Luca Signorelli, probably painted in the last years of the 15th century. Steps lead down to the loggia which has a small collection of sculpture, including a Sienese marble relief of the 14th century showing the *Baptism of Christ* and della Robbian works. From the garden the fine façade of the palace can be seen, with its remarkable graffiti decoration (1532–35) by Doceno, probably on a design by Vasari.

ENVIRONS OF CITTÀ DI CASTELLO

Citerna (*map p. 486, A2*) on the Tuscan border above the upper Tiber valley, is a delightful peaceful village with fine walls and brick buildings, well restored and well kept, on a wooded hilltop. Its origins go back to the Roman era. The church of San Francesco (1316; rebuilt 1508) contains a frescoed niche with the *Madonna and Child with Sts Michael and Francis and Two Angels*, thought to be a late work by Luca Signorelli. The two altars in the south transept have a della Robbian frieze with cherubs' heads, and *Christ in Glory with Sts Francis and Michael*, with six lovely angels in the frame, by Raffaellino del Colle. The choir has 16th-century stalls. Here are a *Madonna, Angels and Saints* by the 16th-century Umbrian school, a 14th-century statuette of the *Madonna* *and Child* in terracotta, and a crowded *Deposition* by a certain Alessandro Forzorio from Arezzo (1568). In the left transept is a *Deposition* by Pomarancio, and in an elaborate wooden altar, a *Madonna and St John the Evangelist* by Raffaellino del Colle, in a beautiful landscape on either side of a 14th-century wooden Crucifix. In a niche is a seated della Robbian statue of *St Anthony Abbot*.

Only 2km south of Citerna is Monterchi in Tuscany, where you can see Piero della Francesca's famous fresco of the *Madonna del Parto* (*see p. 388*).

The village of **Morra** (*map p. 486, A2*) lies in a valley of chestnut woods. Just beyond the village, on a little hill is the Oratorio di San Crescentino (*open 9.30–1 & 2.30–6.30; the custodian lives close by*). A confraternity was founded here c. 1264 and the church dates from 1420. The story goes that when Luca Signorelli first visited Morra sometime after 1507 on his way from Cortona to Città di Castello, he fell in love with a local girl and decided to stay and paint the oratory. Together with assistants he carried out the frescoes on the upper parts of the walls; those at the east end are the only ones well preserved, with the *Flagellation* and a crowded *Crucifixion* scene. In the niche behind the high altar (with a pretty carved stone arch) are frescoes of *Christ between Two Angels*, thought also to be by the hand of Signorelli, and *Sts Mary Magdalene and Anthony Abbot*. The frescoes of the *Madonna della Misericordia* and *Madonna of Loreto* (a particularly delightful work), in the two niches on the side walls, are by followers of Signorelli. The former oratory (now the sacristy) preserves some remarkable late Gothic frescoes, including St Crescentinus on horseback.

Montone

On the other side of the Tiber valley, the charming little well-kept hill town of Montone (*map p. 486, B2*) sits in a splendid position. Probably founded in the 11th century, this was the birthplace of one of the greatest of medieval Italy's *condottieri*, Andrea Braccio Fortebraccio (1368–1424), also known as Braccio da Montone. The church of San Francesco retains its carved wooden doors by Antonio Bencivenni from Mercatello (signed and dated 1519). In its convent is the **Museo Comunale** (*open Fri, Sat and Sun 10.30–1 & 3.30–6*), with a beautiful standard of the *Madonna del Soccorso* by Bartolomeo Caporali (1481) with a view of Montone below, and an *Immaculate Conception*, with saints and Sibyls and an extraordinary landscape and imaginary city by Vittorio Cirelli, who was born here. In the higher part of the village is the Collegiata with a *Last Supper* by Calvaert. The church of San Fedele has an unusual relief of two flagellants above its portal.

GUBBIO

Gubbio (pop. 31,000; *map p. 486, B2*), in an isolated position towards the border with the Marche, is one of the most beautiful and best-preserved small medieval towns in Italy; its handsome old buildings are built of the polished light grey stone which is quarried locally. Its peaceful main streets, most of which preserve their lovely old paving, run parallel with each other following the contours of the steep hillside, and between them towers the splendid Palazzo dei Consoli in Piazza Grande. The high green hillside (529m) which forms a background above the town, and the wide plain at its foot, are special features of Gubbio. Although lifts for Piazza Grande and the duomo were installed in 2000, discreetly hidden in old buildings, Gubbio is a town which lends itself to exploration on foot.

The town was founded by the Umbri in the 3rd century BC, and its political and religious importance is attested by the famous Iguvine Tables (preserved in Palazzo dei Consoli), which are fundamental documents for the study of the Umbrian language. The Roman city of *Iguvium*, at the foot of the hill, flourished in the Republican era when the theatre was built and its temple of Jupiter was celebrated. *Eugubium*, as it later came to be called, was sacked by the Goths but became a free commune in the 11th century. With the help of the bishop saint Ubaldo Baldassini, born here in 1100, the town was saved from Barbarossa in 1155, when it was granted numerous privileges. Although often at war with Perugia, Gubbio retained its independence, until from 1387–1508 it came under the peaceful rule of the Montefeltro, counts of Urbino.

THE ART OF GUBBIO

The frescoes and altarpieces in the churches of Gubbio are mostly by native artists. The miniaturist Oderisio (who was born here, and died c. 1299) is traditionally considered the founder of Gubbio's school of painting. In the 14th century local artists included Guido di Palmeruccio and Mello da Gubbio. Ottaviano Nelli (c. 1375–1444/50) was the most celebrated painter of Gubbio, and his beautiful frescoes survive in a number of churches in the town. His father Martino and brother Tommaso also worked here. In the 16th century Benedetto and Virgilio Nucci painted numerous altarpieces, and in the 17th century Francesco Allegrini and Felice Damiani were active here. The Maffei family of woodcarvers also produced fine work in the 16th century. The greatest architect of Gubbio was Matteo di Giovannelli, known as Gattapone (d. after 1376). The town has a number of churches with fine 17th- and 18th-century interiors.

Giorgio Andreoli (Mastro Giorgio; born c. 1470), spent most of his life in Gubbio, where he died in 1552. He discovered a particular ruby and golden lustre which reflects the light on majolica. Though hardly any examples of his work survive in the city itself, the tradition of producing fine ceramics is carried on by a number of firms here, including Rampini and Aiò.

Piazza Grande

The splendid Piazza Grande (or della Signoria) has a high balustrade overlooking the plain, and lovely herringbone paving. In 1322 the Consiglio del Popolo approved the construction of Palazzo dei Consoli and Palazzo del Podestà (now Palazzo Pretorio), with the Piazza Grande between them at the centre of the town. In 1841 Francesco Ranghiasci obtained permission from the *comune* to embellish the piazza further with the long Neoclassical façade of his palace, with its tall Ionic columns. **Palazzo Pretorio** (or dei Priori; now the town hall) was designed by Gattapone as a pair with Palazzo dei Consoli opposite, but left unfinished in 1350. Its interesting interior is constructed around a central pilaster which supports the Gothic vaulting on all floors. The L-shaped wing built in brick was added in the 17th century.

GUBBIO: PALAZZO DEI CONSOLI

The superb **Palazzo dei Consoli** is one of the most impressive medieval public buildings in Italy. It towers over the city, and the southwest side, which rests on massive vaulting, is 92m high to the top of the bell-tower. It is usually attributed to Gattapone. It is approached by a delightful outside staircase, and above the Gothic portal is a 15th-century lunette of the *Madonna and Child* with the patron saints of Gubbio, John the Baptist and Ubaldo.

In the huge barrel-vaulted Sala dell'Arengo, where assemblies of the *comune* were held, is displayed the **Museo Civico** (*open daily 10–1 & 2/3–5/6*). It preserves its crowded, old-fashioned arrangement of sculptural and architectural fragments, coats of arms, Roman inscriptions and sarcophagi. A small room displays part of Bishop Giacomo Ranghiasci-Brancaleoni's large numismatic collection, formed in 1816–38, including Roman coins and some minted in Gubbio. In the former chapel the seven celebrated

Iguvine Tables are still displayed in their quaint cases (which can be moved so that you can see both sides). These are bronze tablets found by a local inhabitant in 1444 near the city. Their inscriptions in the Umbrian language, five in Etruscan and two in Latin characters, record the rules of a college of priests, and probably date from 250–150 BC. They are the most important epigraphs in the Umbrian language known, and the most notable ritual texts to have survived from Antiquity.

Steep stairs (constructed in 1488) leads up past a loggia in which ceramics produced in Gubbio are displayed, including two plates by Mastro Giorgio Andreoli (*see box on p. 609*) showing the *Fall of Phaeton* (1527) and *Circe*. Purchased at a Sotheby's sale in 1991 and 1996, they are the only two works by him now in the city. In the main hall, which has a good brick vault, the symbolic 14th-century fountain and lavabo (now dry) are an unexpected sight. The picture gallery has 16th-century works by Benedetto Nucci.

The archaeological section is displayed on the ground floor in lovely barrel-vaulted rooms. The earliest finds from the area date from the 6th century BC, and there is Roman sculpture (including a so-called *Apollo* from the 1st century AD), a Byzantine sarcophagus complete with its lid, and medieval fragments.

Museo Diocesano, the duomo and Palazzo Ducale

Although there is a lift from Via XX Settembre to the Museo Diocesano and duomo, the prettiest approach is by the lane beneath a narrow archway in Piazza Grande, which ascends to the steep Via Federico da Montefeltro. Here the 14th-century Palazzo dei Canonici houses the **Museo Diocesano** (*open daily 10–6/7*). Amongst the 12th–16th-century sculptures and paintings is a 14th-century *Maestà* by Mello da Gubbio. On the upper floor, off the cloister, is the Refectory with the most precious object in the collection, a celebrated Flemish cope, designed by a disciple of Joos van Ghent and presented to the duomo by Pope Marcellus II in 1555.

The 13th-century **duomo** (*open all day*) has remarkable stone vaulting in the interior. In the centre of the nave is the unusual pavement tomb of Cardinal Federico Fregoso (d. 1541). The altarpieces are mostly by 16th- and 17th-century local painters, including Antonio Gherardi, Virgilio and Benedetto Nucci, and Dono Doni. In the eighth bay on the north side there is a *Madonna and Child with Saints*, signed and dated 1507 by Sinibaldo Ibi, a follower of Perugino. His best works are in Gubbio.

Opposite the façade of the duomo is the entrance to **Palazzo Ducale** (*open 8.30–7 except Mon*), built in 1476–80 by Francesco di Giorgio Martini (perhaps on a design by Francesco Laurana) for Federico da Montefeltro, Duke of Urbino, famous *condottiere* and man of learning (*see p. 659*), in imitation of his splendid residence in Urbino. The carved decorations in the courtyard and above the doors and windows include the inscription 'FD' (*Federico Duca*), and the ducal emblems of the black eagle of the Montefeltro, pairs of dolphins entwined in a trident, and the Order of the Garter (which the Duke received from King Edward IV of England). The Duke was born here in 1422.

The peaceful Renaissance courtyard, built in *pietra serena* and red brick, is one of the most beautiful 15th-century architectural works in Umbria. The architraves of the windows are exquisitely carved, all with different motifs. A charming spiral staircase in *pietra serena* leads down through a barrel-vaulted storeroom, to excavations which have revealed four different levels of habitation: from the earliest dwellings of the 10th century up to the 15th-century foundations of the palace with its plumbing. The medieval and Renaissance ceramics were all found here.

The ground-floor rooms are particularly interesting for their architecture, with beautifully carved doorways and windows in *pietra serena*. The fine terracotta floors with a simple flower motif also survive, and some good fireplaces. In the first room there is a painted cupboard dating from 1493. A door decorated with beautiful intarsia leads into a gallery with a delightful vault (probably once a library), off which was the Duke's *studiolo*; the little room is now totally bare since the exquisite intarsia panelling, carved by Giuliano da Maiano in 1478–82, was sold in 1874 to Prince Filippo Massimo Lancellotti for his Villa Lancellotti in Frascati, and in 1939 was acquired by the Metropolitan Museum of New York.

Sant'Ubaldo

A lovely walk can be taken by following Via Federico da Montefeltro uphill from the duomo through Porta di Sant'Ubaldo in the 13th-century walls, from where a path climbs the hillside planted with orchards and olive groves, and then traverses woods, to the basilica of Sant'Ubaldo, high up above the town on Monte Ingino (827m). The church was rebuilt in 1514, and St Ubaldo is buried above the high altar. The annual race of the *Festa dei Ceri* follows this path and the three *ceri* (floats in the form of wooden candlesticks) are kept here (*see p. 616*). Further up the hillside are remains of the 12th-century Rocca, where excavations are in progress.

GUALDO TADINO

Gualdo Tadino (*map p. 486, C3*) is a small town noted for its ceramic production, with a fine castle. The town was one of the worst-hit places in the 1997–98 earthquake, but life is now back to normal. In the central piazza is the duomo (San Benedetto), which has a lovely rose window. The Gothic building of 1256 was transformed by Virginio Vespignani at the end of the 19th century, when the pictorial decoration was carried out. On its exterior is a wall fountain attributed to Antonio da Sangallo the Elder.

Beyond a pretty Art Nouveau chemist's shop is the church of **San Francesco**. The exterior has a handsome north side with tall cylindrical towers. The beautiful light interior has a Gothic east end. The frescoes in the apse include a *Crucifixion* by the native artist Matteo da Gualdo, one of the most interesting painters active in Umbria in the later 15th century. The high altar and large pulpit both date from the 14th century. On the pilaster between the first and second arches, there is a *Madonna Enthroned* with the colossal figure of St Anne behind, interesting for its iconography. A painted Crucifix by a follower of the Master of St Francis has also been hung here.

The **Rocca Flea** is a splendid castle which may date from before 1000; its unusual name is derived from the river Flebeo (later called Fleo). It was restored, enlarged and surrounded by a wall by Frederick II around 1242. The interesting interior now contains the Museo Civico (*open June–Sept Tues–Sun 10.30–1 & 3.30–7; otherwise only at weekends*), with a representative selection of works, characterised by their delightful and unusual details, by Matteo da Gualdo. The altarpiece of the *Madonna Enthroned with Saints* (1462) is one of his earliest works, and the *Meeting at the Golden Gate* one of his last. The *Tree of Jesse* is another fine work. There are also paintings here by his son Girolamo and nephew Bernardo. The *Coronation of the Virgin* is a beautiful work signed by the Sienese painter Sano di Pietro. The masterpiece of the collection, a splendid polyptych by L'Alunno, commissioned for the high altar of San Francesco, is displayed on its own. There is also a display of ceramics made in Gualdo: the town was known for its production of ceramics, together with Gubbio and Deruta, as early as the 14th century, and became famous in the late 19th century for its lustreware.

Monte Cucco

Monte Cucco (1566m; *map p. 486, C2*), an area of natural beauty, is now protected as a regional park, and is good walking country. A calcareous mass of carsic origin planted with beechwoods, it has interesting birdlife, and wolves still live in the wild here. It has numerous large caves and grottoes of great interest to spelaeologists, including one 922m deep. Remains of huge bears from centuries past have been found here.

PRACTICAL INFORMATION

GETTING AROUND

• **By car:** Città di Castello has a large, free car park on Viale Nazario Sauro, with escalators to the duomo. In **Gubbio** there are free car parks off Viale del Teatro Romano; near San Domenico; and in Viale del Cavarello (near the cable-car station) outside Porta Romana; a car park with an hourly tariff is in Piazza 40 Martiri (except on Tues when the market is held).

• **By train:** Città di Castello is on the Ferrovia Centrale Umbra line from Perugia to Sansepolcro. From Rome, there are hourly trains with connections in Perugia or Terni (sometimes both), approx. 4hrs. The nearest station to

Gubbio, on the line between Ancona and Rome, is at Fossato di Vico (18km). There is a frequent bus service which takes 35mins, some buses connecting with trains. Perugia Fontivegge railway station (40km) is also connected to Gubbio by local bus.

• **By bus:** There are services to **Gubbio** run by APM (www.apmperugia.it) from Perugia (1hr 10mins), some with connections from Assisi, and from **Città di Castello** (1hr 30mins).

• **Lifts and cable car:** In **Gubbio**, from Via Baldassini to Piazza Grande and from Via XX Settembre to Via Federico da Montefeltro (for the Museo Diocesano and duomo) lifts are open 9/10am to 1/2pm, and 2/3pm to 5/6pm. The lift for the Museo

Diocesano is closed on Mon. The Gubbio cable car operates 10am–1.15pm, and 2.30–5pm; closed Wed in winter; July and Aug 8.30am–7.30pm, from outside Porta Romana to Sant'Ubaldo (827m) on Monte Ingino. It has open 'cages' for a maximum of two people, and takes 6mins to reach the top. From the upper station a short walk (less than 5mins) leads steeply up to the church.

INFORMATION OFFICES

Città di Castello Piazza Matteotti, T: 0758 554922.
Gubbio Piazza Oderisi 6 (Corso Garibaldi), T: 0759 220693.
Sigillo (for Monte Cucco) Villa Anita, Via Matteotti 52, T: 075 917 7326.

HOTELS

Camporeggiano (*map p. 486, B2*)
€ **Il Tamantino**. ■ A sheep farm on a hilltop 10km west of Gubbio on the road to Umbertide, with comfortable rooms, excellent home cooking, and a swimming pool. The owner is a tour guide, and can provide much useful information. Weekly rental only during the summer, Christmas and Easter. *Montelovasco 94, Camporeggiano di Gubbio, T: 075 925 2227, www.umbrian-hills.com. 6 apartments.*
Citerna (*map p. 486, A2*)
€ **Sobaria**. A modern hotel with a swimming pool set in woods on the outskirts of the hilltop village. Good facilities and helpful staff. *Via della Pineta 2, T: 338 194 9370. 25 rooms.*
Città di Castello (*map p. 486, A2–B2*)
€€ **Tiferno**. Comfortable, old-estab-

lished hotel (opened 1895) in a large palace, formerly a monastery, in the centre of town. No restaurant. *Piazza San Francesco 13, T: 0758 550331, www.hoteltiferno.it. 47 rooms.*
€ **Le Mura**. A fully refurbished hotel in a convenient location in the centre of town, just behind the walls. *Via Borgo Farinario 24, T: 0758 521070, www.hotellemura.it. 35 rooms.*
€ **Residenza Antica Canonica**. Charming, very reasonably priced place to stay in the old canonry attached to the cathedral. *Via San Florido 23, T: 0758 526550. 9 apartments.*
Gubbio (*map p. 486, B2*)
€€€ **Park Hotel ai Cappuccini**. Elegantly restored 17th-century monastery. Wonderful use has been made of the communal spaces to display the hotel's private collection of contemporary art. *Via Tifernate, T: 0759 234, www.parkhotelaicappuccini.it. 82 rooms.*
€€ **Relais Ducale**. Pleasant, peaceful hotel forming part of the palace of the Duke of Montefeltro. Rooms are in three adjoining buildings on different levels. Lovely gardens. *Via Galeotti 19, T: 0759 220157, www.mencarelligroup.com. 30 rooms.*
€ **Grotta dell'Angelo**. Good value, comfortable, central hotel. A popular restaurant is attached, with seating on the terrace outside. *Via Gioia 47 (off Via Cairoli), T: 0759 271747, www.grottadel-langelo.it. 8 rooms.*
Montone (*map p. 486, B2*)
€€ **La Locanda del Capitano**. In an old house in the centre of this beautiful, quiet hill town. The rooms are simply furnished with locally-made wrought-iron beds. Restaurant. *Via Roma 7, T:*

0759 306521, www.ilcapitano.com. 8 rooms.

RESTAURANTS

Città di Castello (map p. 486, A2–B2)
€€€ **Il Postale**. A Michelin-starred restaurant where the food is beautifully presented. An experience worth sampling. Closed Mon and midday Sat. Via Raffaele de Cesare 8 (100m up the Fano road), T: 0758 521356.
€€ **Il Bersaglio**. Wide menu and good choice of wines with excellent truffle dishes in season. Closed Wed. Via V.E. Orlando 14, T: 0758 555534.
€ **Amici Miei**. A quiet dining room in a pleasantly-lit underground vault. Small menu of well-prepared, delicious dishes. Closed Weds. Via del Monte 2, T: 0758 559904.
€ **Enoteca Altotiberina**. Easy, down-to-earth restaurant serving unfussy Umbrian food and pizza. In the centre of town close to the duomo. Closed Wed. Piazza Gabriotti, T: 0758 553089.
€ **Trattoria Lea**. Very good value place, typical of the many family-run trattorie that still exist in Italy. Via San Florido 38, T: 0758 521678.
Gubbio (map p. 486, B2)
€€€ **La Fornace di Mastro Giorgio**. Creative interpretations of classic regional dishes in a splendid converted ceramics factory. Closed Tues and midday Wed. Via Mastro Giorgio 2 (off Via Savelli della Porta), T: 0759 221836.
€€€ **Taverna del Lupo**. Forty years ago this restaurant opened in the vaulted rooms of a 14th-century palace as the first in the Mencarelli's growing profile of Umbrian hotels and restaurants. Highly regarded for its truffle recipes.

Closed Mon. Via Ansidei 21 (off Via XX Settembre), T: 0759 274368.
€€ **Fabiani**. Taking its name from a prominent local family, this is a well-established restaurant serving good regional dishes and making use of the local abundance of truffles. Piazza 40 Martiri 26, T: 0759 274639.
€ **Picchio Verde**. The set menus here are particularly good value for money. Excellent for a quick lunch. Via Savelli della Porta, T: 0759 276649.
Montone (map p. 486, B2)
€€ **Erba Luna**. Recently re-opened in a new location within the town walls. A small restaurant making creative use of the abundant local produce in a relaxing setting. Terrace dining in warmer months. Parco delle Rimembranze, T: 0759 306405.

LOCAL SPECIALITIES

Città di Castello Handwoven linens are particularly beautiful here, and can be bought at the Laboratorio della Tela Umbra in Piazza Costa and at Busatti on Piazza San Francesco. **Gubbio** is traditionally an important ceramics centre, famous for its lustre technique, with vibrant golds and reds. Today, two important family workshops remain in the centre of the town: Ceramiche Magnanelli and Bottega Artigiana Rampini. Both have shops.

FESTIVALS & EVENTS

Città di Castello Chamber Music Festival, with open-air concerts held within the town walls, end Aug–beginning Sept; Truffle festival, Stalls line Piazza Matteotti and its surrounding streets selling both black and the highly regarded white truffle, *trifola*, which grows in the upper Tiber valley, first or second weekend Nov.

Gubbio *Festa dei Ceri*, One of the most interesting annual festivals in Italy, thought to have pagan origins. It is held on the eve of the feast day of St Ubaldo, the town's patron saint. Three extremely heavy wooden floats, 4m high, crowned by the statues of St Ubaldo, St Anthony and St George, are raced through the streets. Each float has ten official bearers (who have to be replaced about every 10m without losing the pace). The first team to arrive at Sant'Ubaldo attempts to shut the church door, 15 May; *Palio della Balestra*, Crossbow contest of medieval origin, against the citizens of Sansepolcro, preceded by a procession from San Dominico into Piazza Grande. After a ceremony with flag-throwing and bands, four crossbowmen at a time aim at the targets set up in the piazza, last Sun in May; *Torneo dei Quartieri*, The best marksmen in town take part in another crossbow competition, 14 Aug; On Good Friday there is a traditional procession, and at Christmas the hillside is illuminated in the form of a gigantic Christmas tree.

Montone *Donazione della Santa Spina*, Week-long festival to commemorate the deeds of Count Carlo de' Fortebracci, whose legendary battles earned him the gift of a thorn from Christ's crown. Processions in medieval dress, an archery competition and medieval plays, mid-Aug; *Festa del Bosco*, Autumn fair held in the town streets, where local produce and home-made snacks are sold, 31 Oct–1/2 Nov.

THE MARCHE

L e Marche is the region known as the Marches in English, the frontier land between Umbria, Emilia Romagna and the Abruzzo. There are no big cities: tiny townships dot the countryside, usually perched on hilltops, and often little more than a castle (which is what they originally were), with small populations, particularly jealous of their traditions and way of life.

The first populations to leave traces of their presence were here in the Stone Age, about 100,000 years ago; tools and weapons made from pebbles have been found on Mt Conero. The Iron Age (9th century BC) saw the arrival from the west of the war-like Picenes, who traded with the Etruscans and the Greeks. In the late 6th century BC, with the rise of the Roman Republic, the Picenes and the Umbrians came under Roman sway, with the construction of the great highways, the Via Flaminia and Via Salaria. Under the Roman Empire, the territory of the Marche was divided into two administrative parts: the north became part of Roman Umbria, while the south was known as *Picenum*. With the decline of Rome, the Marche fell prey to Goths, Lombards and Franks, though the northern Marche remained governed from Ravenna, and so under the wing of Byzantium.

After the death of Charlemagne in 814, rivalry between Pope and Holy Roman Emperor was to become the norm, and the towns of the Marche found their overlords rallying behind one or the other—a situation that would eventually lead to the Guelph-Ghibelline strife (*see p. 17*). In 1356 the Avignon papacy sent the uncompromising Cardinal Albornoz to regain control over the Papal States; he built menacing fortresses which can still be seen in many towns of the Marche, but it was not until 1421, and the end of the Papal Schism, that a certain tranquillity returned to the area, thanks to the determination of Pope Martin V.

Christianity had come early to the Marche, brought by pilgrims travelling to Rome along the old roads from the coast. Monasteries following the rule of St Benedict sprang up along the routes in the 6th century. By the 10th century there was a net-work of flourishing religious institutions throughout the area. Romanesque architecture (11th–13th centuries), introduced by the Lombards, but often still showing traces of the old Byzantine traditions, is often to be seen here. The cathedral of San Ciriaco in Ancona is one of the finest of the period in Italy.

While it was a Marche-born painter, Gentile da Fabriano, who in the 14th century became the foremost exponent of the International Gothic school of art, so it was a Marche-born painter who became one of the greatest masters of the Renaissance: Raphael. One of the loveliest of all Renaissance cities is Urbino, scene of Castiglione's *The Courtier*. Under the auspices of Federico da Montefeltro it became the ideal city, and his palace was a meeting place of artists, architects, writers, poets and musicians.

From the 16th century onwards, following the peace treaty signed between France and Spain, the Marche's history follows that of the Papal States.

ANCONA &
CENTRAL MARCHE

A ncona (*map p. 618, D3*) is one of the ancient maritime powers of Italy. The heart of the city is still its port, where deep draft allows big ships to anchor. Ancona is in fact the busiest fishing and commercial port in the Adriatic.

HISTORY OF ANCONA

In 387 BC, Dionysius, tyrant of the Greek city of Syracuse in Sicily, chose the natural harbour where Ancona now stands as the site of a strategic outpost. The settlers built a Doric temple to Aphrodite on the acropolis (site of the present cathedral), and for centuries Ancona prospered from trade in amber, wool, purple dye, pottery from Greece, cosmetics and perfumes. Under the Romans the city became a *municipium* and a base for the fleet; Trajan improved the port, where he built a splendid arch of honour. Christianity arrived early, brought by travellers from the East. Under Byzantium, Ancona became the first city of the Maritime Pentapolis (the others were Rimini, Pesaro, Fano and Senigallia), governed by Ravenna, but with considerable autonomy. By the 10th century Ancona was an independent republic, rich from its commerce with Constantinople.

In 1348 the city was taken by the Malatesta, and forced to make act of submission to the pope's representative, Cardinal Albornoz. In the 15th century, Ancona formed an alliance with Venice against combined Milanese and Spanish forces. After the fall of Constantinople in 1453 Ancona's commercial fortunes waned. The Medici pope Clement VII seized the city in 1532, bringing it under papal control. In 1797 Ancona was occupied by the French, returning only to the Papal States in 1816, after the fall of Napoleon.

During the movement for the Unification of Italy, Ancona played an important role, and Piedmontese troops entered the city in 1860. Heavy bombing in the Second World War devastated the medieval and Renaissance quarters. An earthquake in 1972 caused serious damage to the cathedral, many ancient churches, and the Archaeological Museum.

The Arch of Trajan and port

At the heart of the busy port stands the **Arch of Trajan**, the symbol of the city. It was built in the year 115 in honour of the Emperor Trajan, as a token of appreciation from the populace for the remodelling of their harbour. The plinth is of local stone, but the archway itself is built of great blocks of Proconnesian marble (from Marmara, modern Turkey). The arch once sported bronze statues of Trajan, his wife Plotina, and his

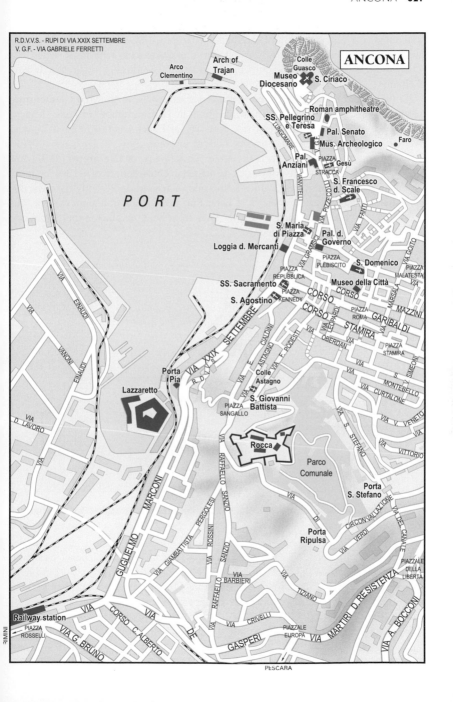

R.D.V.V.S. - RUPI DI VIA XXIX SETTEMBRE
V. G.F. - VIA GABRIELE FERRETTI

ANCONA

Arco Clementino

Arch of Trajan

Colle Guasco

Museo Diocesano

S. Ciriaco

Roman amphitheatre

SS. Pellegrino e Teresa

Pal. Senato

Mus. Archeologico

Faro

Pal. Anziani

PIAZZA Gesù

STRACCA

S. Francesco d. Scale

S. Maria di Piazza

Pal. d. Governo

Loggia d. Mercanti

PIAZZA PLEBISCITO

S. Domenico

PIAZZA MALATESTA

PIAZZA REPUBBLICA

Museo della Città

SS. Sacramento

PIAZZA KENNEDY

CORSO

CORSO

MAZZINI

S. Agostino

PIAZZA ROMA

GARIBALDI

STAMIRA

PIAZZA STAMIRA

OBERDAN

P O R T

Porta Pia

Colle Astagno

Lazzaretto

S. Giovanni Battista

PIAZZA SANGALLO

Rocca

Parco Comunale

Porta S. Stefano

Porta Ripulsa

PIAZZALE DELLA LIBERTÀ

Railway station

PIAZZA ROSSELLI

PIAZZALE EUROPA

PESCARA

sister Marciana, and the rostra of captured enemy ships—you can still see where they were attached. The architect was Apollodorus of Damascus, who also carried out many projects in Rome for the emperor, including the Markets of Trajan and Trajan's Column.

To the west of the arch, at the limit of the old city walls, is the **Arco Clementino**, clearly inspired by the Arch of Trajan, and built in 1738 in honour of Pope Clement XII, who had just made Ancona a free port. The architect was Luigi Vanvitelli, who worked on a number of papal projects, notably in Rome.

At the bottom of the harbour is the Mole Vanvitelliana, or **Lazzaretto** (*T: 071 222 5030/1 to request visit*), an enormous pentagonal construction of 1733, built by Vanvitelli as a quarantine hospital for sailors and merchandise. Recently restored, it is now used for cultural events. Nearby is **Porta Pia** (1789), built in honour of Pope Pius VI, in late Baroque style: there is a good view from here, embracing the whole city, from the Guasco Hill to the Astagno.

San Ciriaco

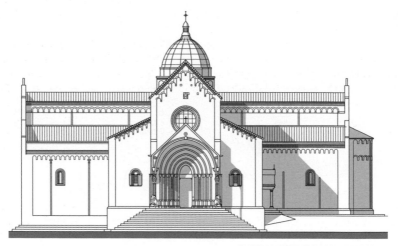

ANCONA: DUOMO DI SAN CIRIACO

The beautiful Duomo di San Ciriaco (*open 8–12 & 3–6; 7 in summer*) was built between the 11th and 13th centuries, on the site of the 4th-century BC Temple of Aphrodite. The beautiful, harmonious structure glimmers on high, and can be seen from the whole city, with its twelve-sided copper dome. The huge Romanesque portal (1228), in red and white stone from the Conero, has five orders of arches richly carved, and an elegant porch supported by pink granite lions.

The interior is a Greek cross, with nave and transepts divided by monolithic Roman columns surmounted by Byzantine capitals. The transepts are apsidal, with their altars raised over crypts. Parts of the floor are of glass, in order to reveal the outlines of the former temple. and the Palaeochristian basilica of St Lawrence which succeeded it. To the left on entering is the beautifully carved **sepulchre of Francesco Nobili**, warrior of Fermo (1530); according to legend, the knight will wake up in case of need. Also on the left is the Chapel of the Madonna, with a rich altar designed by Vanvitelli (1738); over the altar is a small, much venerated 17th-century **canvas of the Madonna**, by an unknown artist.

The **crypt** forms part of the old church, and contains urns with the remains of the saints of Ancona, notably St Cyriacus, to whom the present church is dedicated. Little is known about this saint, though local tradition claims him as St Judas Cyriacus or Quiriacus, a native of Jerusalem who is said to have shown St Helen, mother of Constantine, where the True Cross lay hidden.

The old city

Via Ferretti was the main street of old Ancona. At no. 6 is the **Museo Archeologico** (*open 8.30–7.30; closed Mon; T: 071 202602*), housed in the impressive rooms of Palazzo Ferretti (16th century; Pellegrino Tibaldi). It contains some superb Picene artefacts and a copy of the famous group of gilded bronze statues known as the *Bronzi di Cartoceto* (1st century BC). The originals are in the museum of Pergola (*see p. 636*).

On Piazza Stracca is the dramatic ex-church of the **Gesù** (1665), with a lovely curving façade preceded by a double stairway, designed by Vanvitelli in 1743. The old main street continues down from here to Piazza San Francesco and the 14th-century church of **San Francesco alle Scale**. Its outstanding Venetian-Gothic portal (1447) is by Giorgio Orsini (*see p. 624*). During the Napoleonic occupation the church was used as a barracks. Inside (in the apse) is a canvas by Lorenzo Lotto of the *Assumption of the Madonna*, signed and dated 1550. Over the first south altar is the *Baptism of Christ* by Pellegrino Tibaldi, while over the first north altar is a painting of the *Holy House of Loreto* by Ancona-born artist Andrea Lilli.

The Pinacoteca and Galleria Comunale

At no. 17 Via Pizzecolli is the **Pinacoteca Francesco Podesti** (*open 9–6.30; closed Mon afternoon; T: 071 222 5040*), the city gallery of beautifully displayed old masters. Outstanding is a tiny *Madonna with Christ Child* (1470) by Carlo Crivelli, full of the usual Crivelli symbolisms: the fruits and vegetables for resurrection, rebirth and the Passion, the goldfinch for the human soul, red and blue colours for the divine and the human nature of the mother and her Child. Also here is Lorenzo Lotto's *Pala dell'Alabarda* (1539), showing a charming Madonna accompanied by saints of Ancona; the lengthening shadows are those of sunset. The same building also houses the modern art collection, **Galleria Comunale di Arte Moderna** (*open as above*), with about 300 works by local and Italian artists.

Santa Maria di Piazza and the Loggia dei Mercanti

Behind Palazzo Bosdari, Vicolo Foschi leads down to the elegant church of **Santa**

Maria di Piazza (13th century), one of the most important monuments of the city. A frequently-seen feature of the buildings of Ancona, especially the churches, is the two-colour façade, ochre or brown brick for the upper part, and white plaster or stone for the lower. In this case, the generously wide lower section is of carved white marble, forming a triple series of little blind arches, some with figures of saints, angels, animals and birds, framing the exquisite portal, carved with a teeming *Tree of Life*.

Via della Loggia was the high street of the medieval and Renaissance city. It takes its name from the 15th-century Venetian Gothic **Loggia dei Mercanti**, once the merchants' trading hall. The superb façade is by Giorgio Orsini (1451–59); in the loggia are statues representing the Cardinal Virtues (Fortitude, Temperance, Prudence and Justice); over the doorway is a knight on horseback brandishing a sword, the emblem of Ancona.

Piazza del Plebiscito

The colourful Piazza del Plebiscito is also known as *Piazza del Papa*, from the statue of Pope Clement XII (1738), originally intended for the Arco Clementino in the port (*see p. 622 above*). The church of **San Domenico** (13th century and 1788) has an imposing—if unfinished—façade, the lower part in white stone, and the upper in hazelnut-coloured brick. In the single-nave interior are statues and medallions of Dominican saints by Gioacchino Varlé. This 18th-century sculptor was prized for his skill in stucco detail and wood carving, and was often hired by the religious orders to embellish their church interiors. There are two important paintings in this church: in the apse, an austere *Crucifixion* by Titian (1558); and over the first north altar, the *Annunciation* (1656) by the prolific Bolognese artist Guercino.

To the left of the church is the **Arco di Garola** (1221), or Porta San Pietro, one of the few surviving fragments of the 13th-century fortifications, which gives access to Via Matteotti. To the right of the stairs is the ex-hospital of St Thomas à Becket (1394), incorporating the old fish market (1817), and now seat of the excellent **Museo della Città** (*open 6pm–10pm, Sat & Sun also 10–1; closed Mon; T: 071 222 5037*), where four rooms illustrate the history of the city.

Colle Astagno

The church of **Sant'Agostino** was built by the Austin Fathers in 1338 as a gathering-place for travellers and pilgrims, and enlarged by Vanvitelli in 1764. The splendid Venetian Gothic portal (1475; Giorgio Orsini) has some of the finest carvings of the period to be seen along the Adriatic. Orsini, who was related to the patrician Roman family of the same name, is known on the other side of the Adriatic as George the Dalmatian (Juraj Dalmatinac). There are a number of works by his hand in Dubrovnik. His masterpiece here is the lunette, with *St Augustine Showing the Holy Scriptures to the Heretics*. The church, after being turned into a barracks in the 19th century, is now empty.

Via Cialdini climbs steeply up the Astagno hill; close to the top, on the left, you will see the little Romanesque church of **San Giovanni**, severely damaged in the 1972 earthquake, as was most of this district. Inside is a beautiful *Ecce Homo* by Federico Zuccari, a *Crucifixion* by Andrea Lilli, and a copy of the *Vision of the Blessed Gabriel Ferretti* by Carlo Crivelli (originally painted for this church, and now in the National Gallery, London).

At the top of the hill is the **Rocca**, built for Pope Clement VII in 1538 by Antonio da Sangallo the Younger. At no. 12 Via Astagno, which runs parallel to Via Cialdini, in what was once the Jewish quarter, are two **synagogues**, one of Italian rite, the other Levantine, with beautiful old furnishings. At its height in the mid-16th century, the Jewish community of Ancona numbered over 3,500.

Facing onto Piazza della Repubblica and the main entrance to the port, is the sumptuous opera house, **Teatro delle Muse** (*www.teatrodellemuse.org*), the pride of the city. From here two streets popular for strolling, Corso Mazzini and Corso Garibaldi, lead east to the public gardens of Piazza Cavour, where they join to become Viale della Vittoria, with enticing, expensive shops, and many charming Art Nouveau-style villas. The Viale terminates on the cliff-top at Passetto, the airy modern district: there are steps and an incredible old elevator going down to the sea below, a favourite spot for swimming.

THE CONERO PENINSULA

The limestone outcrop of Mount Conero (572m; *map p. 618, D3*), just south of Ancona, is an unmistakable landmark. It has been a nature reserve since 1988.

PARCO NATURALE DEL CONERO

Visitor centre: 30/a Via Peschiera, Sirolo; T: 071 933 1879, www.parcoconero.it
The park has many unique features: the lovely coastline with its typical vegetation and important wildlife; the rock formations (geologically the oldest in the region); its historical traces (people have been living on this mountain for at least 100,000 years); the traditions and occupations of the inhabitants; and the charming little towns. Eighteen nature trails of various degrees of difficulty have been laid out and signposted in the park, which covers over 600 hectares of Rosso Conero vineyards, olive groves, wheat, lavender, sunflowers, and rows of mulberry trees. The park also covers the only brackish-water coastal lakes remaining in the Marche, some breathtaking cliffs, and isolated beaches. This is just the place for birdwatchers, especially during the spring passage (Feb–April). The name derives from the Greek word for arbutus.

Sirolo and Numana

Sirolo, often declared 'the most beautiful village of the Adriatic', stands on a cliff, from where steep paths lead down through the *maquis* to sandy beaches below. A Picene burial ground has been discovered here, and finds include the unplundered tomb of a Picene queen (6th century BC), who was buried together with two chariots, a sumptuous bed inlaid with ivory and amber, fine vases and a gold and silver dish for ritual offerings. The queen's dress was richly decorated with glass and amber beads; so far almost 2,000 of her ornaments and jewellery have been recovered (*finds on display in Numana; see below*).

The hillside fishing village of **Numana** has colourful, picturesque little houses, and a bathing resort below, with lovely sandy beaches. It was an important base for the Greeks in the 8th century BC, and later became a Picene stronghold, and a Roman port. Nothing remains of the old city, which is thought to have disappeared under the sea after an earthquake in 558; although it was rebuilt, part of the town slipped into the sea again during the earthquake of 1292. In the central square is the modern Santuario del Crocifisso. Over the main altar is a life-size painted wooden Crucifix, thought by some scholars to be a 14th-century Byzantine carving, by others to be a Polish work. Local tradition says that this is the Crucifix carved by Luke and Nicodemus as Christ was dying, using a trunk of cedar of Lebanon. It shares this claim with the *Volto Santo* of Lucca (*see p. 336*).

The archaeological collections of Numana and the Conero area are housed at the **Antiquarium** (*Via La Fenice 4; open 8.30–1.30 & 2.30–7.30; T: 071 933 1162*), one of the most complete museums of the Picene era in the region. Numana has yielded more Picene tombs (over 2,000) than any other area in the Marche, and the well-displayed finds from the burials give an excellent idea of the evolution of these people from the 9th–3rd centuries BC. One of the most interesting sections is that dedicated to the rich contents of the 'Tomb of the Queen' at Sirolo (*see above*). A rare fragment of Picene sculpture, a 7th-century BC marble head known as the *Warrior of Numana*, is displayed together with drawings which seek to explain the unusual decorations on his helmet.

LORETO, RECANATI & OSIMO

Loreto (*map p. 619, D4*) is one of the most important Roman Catholic shrines in the world, receiving many thousands of pilgrims a year. In Europe, only Lourdes attracts more. The monumental Piazza della Madonna is dominated by its great fortress-church. In the centre of the square is a splendid Baroque fountain (1614), with bronze eagles, dragons and mermen riding dolphins. To the east of the piazza is the white marble façade (1571) of the sanctuary church of the Santa Casa, with Luigi Vanvitelli's bell-tower (1755) to the left. The beautiful octagonal dome of 1499 by Giuliano da Sangallo, visible from a great distance, is the third largest in Italy, with a diameter of 22m, and was completed in only nine months; the gilded copper statue of the *Madonna* on the top was added in 1894. The three bronze doors in the front were made for the Holy Year of 1600.

HISTORY OF LORETO

In the late 13th century Palestine was conquered by the Muslims, and Christians were obliged to flee, taking with them whatever relics they could. In 1291 the house where Jesus had lived with Mary and Joseph, scene of the Annunciation, disappeared from Nazareth, only to reappear, in 1294, in a clump of laurels (*laureto*—loreto) near Recanati, apparently transported there by angels. It is now believed that the house had been dismantled and shipped to Dalmatia by Crusaders, with the help of the powerful Byzantine Angelus ('angel') family. In 1294 Princess Thamar Angelus married Philip, son of Charles II of Naples, and the house formed part of her dowry. Bishop Salvus of Recanati ordered the ship transporting the stones to land at Porto Recanati, and had the house reconstructed within his territory. Recent scientific tests prove that the stones do indeed come from Nazareth, and correspond perfectly to the remaining part of the house which is still there, partially carved into the rock. In 1962 five crosses of red cloth, like those worn by the Crusaders, were found buried under one of the walls, and also two Byzantine coins minted at the time of Thamar's marriage.

Around the house a church was erected, which through the centuries became more and more magnificent; successive popes summoned the finest artists, craftsmen and architects to work on the building, especially after 1469, when Pope Paul II granted a plenary indulgence to all those who went there on pilgrimage, and gave the church the characteristics of a fortress, to protect it from pirate attacks. Lodges and a hospital were provided for the pilgrims, and later an aqueduct was built, bringing water into the heart of town, and providing drinking fountains along the access roads. Pope Sixtus V took particular interest in the sanctuary, declaring the town a city in 1586, thus raising it above Recanati.

In 1797 Napoleon arrived, hoping to take the priceless works of art to Paris—but Pope Pius VI had taken most of them to Rome, hidden in wine barrels; the French soldiers requisitioned everything that was left. Besides wheat and maize, they took 94 kg of gold, 17 quintals of silver, all the remaining paintings and carvings, even the Bohemian crystal wine glasses and the ancient cedarwood statue of the *Madonna*—the only object that was ever returned, in 1801 (it was destroyed by fire in 1921).

The Santa Casa and its church

Open April–Sept 6.30–8; Oct–March 6.45–7; closed for lunch 12.30–2.30 all year; T: 071 970104.

It is worth walking all the way around the outside of the church first, to see at the rear the massive brick apses (Baccio Pontelli), complete with the passage for patrolling sentries at the top. The interior of the building, designed to accommodate large numbers of worshippers, is somewhat overwhelming. Every part of the basilica is decorated with frescoes, carved marble, rich altars and bronze sculptures; many of the paintings over the altars have been replaced by mosaics, carried out in the Vatican studios.

(1) The Santa Casa: Under the dome is the Holy House itself, protected by an exquisite marble screen, designed by Bramante in 1509. Two grooves have been worn into the floor around the screen, by pilgrims going around it on their knees. The simple little Nazarene house, with its stones blackened by centuries of candle smoke, looks very humble. On the altar inside the house is the statue of the *Madonna and Child* (1922) a copy made to replace the Byzantine original, lost in a fire the previous year.

(2) Sacristy of St Mark: The little circular chapels dedicated to the Evangelists correspond to the four round towers of the original fortification of the church. That of St Mark was frescoed by Melozzo da Forlì from 1477–80, with angels and prophets in the vault, and on the side walls, *The Entry into Jerusalem*.

(3) Sacristy of St John: Decorated in 1479 by Luca Signorelli, it is thought with the assistance of Perugino, with angel musicians in the vault, and on the walls the *Conversion of Saul*, *Incredulity of St Thomas*, and ten Apostles.

(4) Sacristy of St Luke: Here is a terracotta image of *St Luke the Evangelist* in the lunette, by Benedetto da Maiano; inside are some beautiful inlaid wooden cupboards, made in Florence in 1516 to designs by Benedetto da Maiano and Andrea Sansovino.

(5) Cappella Tedesca: The neo-Gothic frescoes (1892–1908) on the theme of the life of Mary are by Ludovico Seitz; he used members of his own family as models.

(6) Cappella del Crocifisso: The impressively realistic wooden Crucifix is by the Sicilian friar Innocenzo da Petralia (1637).

(7) Sala del Pomarancio: This room, once the Treasury, is decorated with exquisite Mannerist-style frescoes by Pomarancio (1605–10), with ten stories of the life of the Madonna, six prophets, and six Sibyls. The Crucifix on the altar is also by Pomarancio. The wooden cupboards contain votive offerings.

LORETO: SANTA CASA

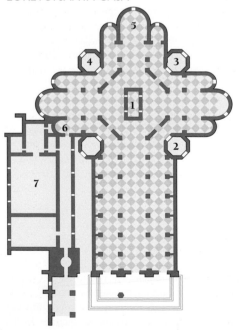

The Museo-Pinacoteca

The north and west sides of Piazza della Madonna are taken up by the L-shaped Palazzo Apostolico. Many artists were engaged in its construction, including Bramante (1509), Sangallo the Younger and Vanvitelli. The upper-floor **Museo-Pinacoteca** (*open April–Oct 9–1 & 4–7; Nov–March 10–1 & 3–6; closed Mon; T: 071 974 7198*) consists principally of the rich donations made to the sanctuary through the centuries. The paintings include works by Gian Domenico Tiepolo, Parmigianino and Palma Giovane; and nine works by Lorenzo Lotto, who spent the last years of his life in Loreto, poor and ill. These magnificent canvases represent his maturity, the conclusion of his search for an indefinable truth through religion. Unforgettable is the *Struggle between the Archangels Michael and Lucifer*, where the two angels divide the canvas diagonally, as if reflected in a mirror, their movement underlined by Michael's sword and Lucifer's newly-forming tail; between them is the torch of Knowledge, broken by Pride. A recent donation, *Fame defeats Time*, again uses the mirror-image device. The influence of Giorgione is clear in the *Baptism of Christ*, with the stormy sky forming the background. In *Christ and the Adulteress*, our attention is caught by the woman's beauty and the apparent detachment of Christ—on the right, a man in a red hat with his finger on his lips (probably a self-portrait of Lorenzo) warns us to make no comment. The *Presentation at the Temple*, almost Impressionistic, is Lotto's last work, and full of symbolic meaning; notice, for example, the human feet of the altar, an allusion to the sacrifice of Christ. The upper part of the painting, showing the Temple of Solomon, is in fact the interior of the Sanctuary of Loreto. The collections also include ten 17th-century Flemish tapestries, worked to designs by Raphael, of which four are usually on view.

RECANATI & OSIMO

Golden-brown Recanati (*map p. 619, D4*) is built along a winding crest, with an intricate web of narrow streets. Opposite the town hall is a museum to the great tenor Beniamino Gigli (d. 1957), and next to it is the church of **San Domenico** (11th–14th centuries), with a beautiful carved marble doorway (1481). Inside, over the second north altar, is a detached fresco by Lorenzo Lotto (1515), showing *St Vincent Ferrer in Glory*.

There are two excellent art collections in Recanati, both on Via Falleroni, northwest of the main square. The **Museo Diocesano** (*open Oct–May 9–12 & 3–6; June–Sept 9–1 & 3–7; T: 071 757 4278*) has a collection of magnificent paintings by Mantegna, Giacomo da Recanati, Guercino, Guglielmo da Venezia and Sassoferrato. There are also Etruscan and Roman vases and bronzes. Further along the street is Villa Colloredo-Mels, with a large park incorporating part of the old Jewish cemetery. It is home to the **Pinacoteca Comunale** (*open Tues–Fri 9–12 & 3–7, Sat, Sun 9–1 & 3–8; closed Mon T: 071 757 0410*), one of the most important galleries in the region, with a precious collection of paintings by Lorenzo Lotto. These include the first commission he carried out in the Marche, the polyptych for the church of San Domenico (1508), and perhaps his best-known work, the *Annunciation* (?1527), showing Mary strangely twisting her body as she turns to us for support, while God sternly marks her out as chosen, disrupting her orderly existence forever. Her startled tortoiseshell cat runs away from the Angel's shadow.

In the south of town is the 17th-century **Palazzo Leopardi** (Via Leopardi 14), where the poet Giacomo Leopardi used to live. It houses his library (*open summer 9–6; winter 9–12 & 3–6; T: 071 757 3380*), consisting of 20,000 books, documents and manuscripts, and the Centro Nazionale di Studi Leopardiani (*open Mon–Fri 10–1.30 & 4–7.30, Sat mornings only; T: 071 757 0604*), with a museum describing his life and times. Born in Recanati, Leopardi (1798–1837) died in Naples during a cholera epidemic, and was probably buried in a communal grave; his tomb, recently opened, was found to contain only a shoe. Behind Palazzo Leopardi is the summit of Monte Tabor, now called Colle dell'Infinito after one of the poet's most famous works, *The Infinite*, written when he was only 21. Steps give access to a pleasant walk along the hill, offering beautiful views.

Osimo

Osimo (*map p. 619, D4*) is a town of noble aspect, with harmonious streets and *piazze*, surrounded by a maze of steep, narrow alleys. It is one of the oldest towns in the Marche, founded in the 7th century BC by Greeks and Sicels (who had already established themselves on the coast at Ancona and Numana), on a hilltop once inhabited by the Picenes. It rose to importance under the Romans, and was bitterly fought over in 539 during the war against the Goths, when it capitulated out of hunger.

The main entrance to the city was originally through the northern gate, Porta San Giacomo, still protected by a massive tower. Via Baccio Pontelli leads to the main square. In the atrium of the imposing **Palazzo Municipale** are 12 headless marble statues found on the site of the Roman forum. Next to the town hall is the 13th-century clock-tower, with Guelph battlements (rectangular merlons) showing the town's traditional allegiance to the pope.

By going east through Piazza Boccolino you reach the 13th-century sanctuary church of **San Giuseppe di Copertino** (St Joseph of Cupertino). Over the second north altar is a large, splendidly proportioned panel painting by Antonio Solario (1503) of the *Madonna and Christ Child with Saints*, with the donor, Captain Boccolino Guzzoni of Osimo. This same church is visible in the background, behind the throne of the Madonna. In the modern crypt (1962) is the body of St Joseph of Cupertino, patron saint of students and aviators; students still come to invoke his aid when preparing for exams, and he is frequently called on for protection by American pilots. The apartment where he spent his last years is now the **Museo San Giuseppe** (*open 7–12 & 3–7; T: 071 714523*).

In the east of town, the Collegio Campana in Piazza Dante houses the **Civica Raccolta d'Arte** (*open Tues–Sat 5–7; Sun 10–12.30 & 5–8; T: 071 714621*), a collection of paintings by Giacinto Brandi, Andrea da Bologna, Claudio Ridolfi and Piranesi; a magnificent polyptych by Antonio and Bartolomeo Vivarini (1464) of the *Coronation of Mary*, with Sts Anthony of Padua, Peter, Francis and Louis, and above, Sts Catherine of Alexandria, John the Baptist, Jerome and Clare, together with an archaeological collection of objects found locally.

Along the northern walls, where traces of Roman fortifications can still be seen, is the **Fonte Magna**, a large Roman fountain. Under the nearby tourist office a labyrinth of man-made grottoes and tunnels has been discovered, extending for at least 9km, and is (in part) visible on request (Grotte del Cantinone, Via Fontemagna 12; *open 9–1 & 4–7, closed Mon; T: 071 724 9282, www.osimosotterranea.it*). Because of the mysterious carvings on the walls of the tunnels, it is thought that the Templars might have excavated the caves as a place for secret meetings and religious worship.

JESI & CUPRAMONTANA

The origin of Jesi (ancient *Aesis*; *map p. 618, C3*) is lost in legend: some say it was founded by Umbrians, led by a king who had a lion on his banner, his personal totem. The settlement certainly became an important Roman colony from 247 BC. Conquered and destroyed, first by the Goths and then by the Lombards, it was donated to the Church in 756, then taken by Charlemagne, and donated to the Church again in 999, finally becoming an independent commune in the 12th century. Jesi flourished under the Swabians, because Frederick II (*see box overleaf*) was born in the city; it supported the Ghibelline cause until 1305, when it returned to the Church. The following two centuries saw the city alternating between pope and emperor, passing from the Malatesta to Braccio da Montone (*see p. 608*), from the Sforza to the Malatesta once more; until 1512 when it was attacked and despoiled by the Duke of Urbino, Francesco Maria della Rovere. Rebuilt, the city was accorded of semi-independent government in 1586, but the *Respublica Aesina* came to an end in 1797, when Napoleon's troops entered the walls.

Other natives of Jesi include the musicians Pergolesi and Spontini. The spacious Piazza della Repubblica is dominated by the façade of the opera house, **Teatro Pergolesi** (*www.teatropergolesi.org*), one of the most important theatres in Italy, built in 1798. Inside the theatre is a gallery dedicated to Pergolesi and Spontini (*T: 0731 202944 or 0731 215643 to request visit; www.fondazionepergolesispontini.com*), with memorabilia concerning the two musicians.

Pinacoteca Civica

On the narrow Via XV Settembre stands the long façade (more than 100 windows) of Palazzo Pianetti (18th century), now the Pinacoteca Civica (*open 16 June–15 Sept 10–8; 16 Sept–15 June 10–1 & 5–7; holidays 10–1 & 5–8; closed Mon; T: 0731 538342*). The memorable and lovingly displayed collection includes a series of five paintings by **Lorenzo Lotto**: two panels of a triptych showing the *Annunciation* (1526; notice the almost mirrored images of St Francis and St Clare, founders of the mendicant orders of the Franciscans and Poor Clares, in the upper panel), with a recoiling Madonna dressed in red, a colour which gives her earthy substance, in contrast to the diaphanous blue garment of the Angel (the central panel was stolen by Napoleon); a sad *Madonna of the Roses* (1526), reluctant to relinquish her Son; a Giorgionesque *Deposition* (1512); a drastically over-cleaned *Visitation* (1531), and the plucky little

Lucy of the *Story of St Lucy* panel (1532), defying the Roman governor and accepting her martyrdom—certainly this painting alone would be worth a journey to the Marche to see.

STUPOR MUNDI

'The wonder of the world' is what his contemporaries called Frederick II of Hohenstaufen, for his many skills, ranging from languages (he could speak six), mathematics, astronomy, astrology, music, literature (he was the founder of the 'Sicilian School' which flourished at his court in Palermo; the first writers to use the Italian language in literature), the building of castles, hunting (his fundamental text on falconry, *De arti venandi cum avibus*, is still in the Vatican Library), to the intricacies of diplomacy. He was born quite by chance in Jesi, on 26th December 1194, because his mother, Constance de Hauteville, was travelling from Milan to Sicily to join her husband. She chose to give birth in the main square, under a canopy, so that the matrons of Jesi could witness the fact that the baby was really hers; gossip and speculation were rife; there was even a prophecy that the Antichrist was about to be born. Nine years earlier, Constance, as the last Norman princess of Sicily, had been brought out of a cloistered convent in order to marry the unpleasant, dissolute Henry IV of Swabia, eleven years her junior. Now she was 40, and this was her first child. Henry and Constance died soon after, so Frederick was brought up in Palermo, running free through the streets of the city, undoubtedly acquiring many of those accomplishments which would later stand him in good stead. Last of the medieval monarchs, first of the modern rulers, Frederick spent all his life trying to unite the Holy Roman Empire to the rich Kingdom of Sicily: unfortunately for him, the Papal States stood—both literally and metaphorically—between him and success. A colourful and fascinating figure in the history of Europe, defying the pope, even excommunicated, yet leader of the most successful and least bloody Crusade; the founder of modern diplomacy, and the first to draw up laws protecting the rights of women, and for the protection of wildlife; his body lies in the cathedral of Palermo.

Cupramontana

Southeast of Jesi, on a beautiful green and fertile hill (505m), stands **Cupramontana** (*map p. 618, C3*) on the site of a 5th-century BC temple to the Picene fertility goddess Cupra, known as *Bona* by the Romans. This is the most important centre of the Marche for the production of Verdicchio, a white wine perhaps of Etruscan origin.

The collegiate church of San Leonardo (1151 and 1760) was the first church built within the castle walls. Inside, over the first south altar, is a painting of the *Circumcision*, a masterpiece by Jesi-born Antonino Sarti (1615). The second south altar is lavish Baroque (1792); over it is an early 16th-century panel painting of the *Madonna Enthroned*, known as '*Madonna della Colonna*', by Andrea da Jesi. Over the main altar is a gilded wood carving by Andrea Scoccianti (1681). So famous was Scoccianti for his carvings with leaves and flowers, that he was often called the 'Raphael of Leaves'.

The church of San Lorenzo on Via Ferranti (1787; Mattia Capponi) is a refined example of Neoclassical architecture, listed as a national monument. From here you can walk round to the east side of the castle, where in Corso Cavour you will find the **Museo Internazionale dell'Etichetta** (*T: 0731 780199 to request visit; closed Mon*), a unique collection of over 90,000 wine labels, some of great historical interest.

VERDICCHIO

Praised by Pliny and by Varro, 'the most learned of all the Romans', and reputedly the favourite drink of Alaric the Goth, Verdicchio was first grown by the Etruscans, and passed into history on the banqueting tables of Charlemagne, the Malatesta, the Montefeltro dukes, the Sforza and the della Rovere. The Verdicchio grape is particular to the Marche, more specifically to the Esino valley near Jesi, and to the vineyards around Matelica. The breezy climate of the Esino valley keeps the air free from disease, and allows the vines to flourish. Classic Verdicchio is the wine known as Castelli di Jesi: strict rules mean that 85% of the fruit used must be from the Verdicchio grape, the rest can be made up of other native varieties. Verdicchio dei Castelli di Jesi comes in a number of categories: *Spumante* (sparkling), *Passito* (made from grapes that have been dried on straw to concentrate the sugars), *Classico* (minimum 11.5% alcohol), *Superiore* (minimum 12%) and *Riserva* (minimum 12.5%, and must have been aged for 2 years, with 6 months in the bottle). A light, straw-coloured wine with a delicate fruity perfume, the best Verdicchio always presents a hint of bitter almond on the palate, preventing it from being bland. It is an excellent accompaniment to salads, cold meats and fish.

SASSOFERRATO & ENVIRONS

The town of Sassoferrato (*map p. 618, B3*) is neatly divided into two parts: the modern town, known as *Borgo*, and the old centre, 2km above it, called *Castello*, dominated by the cube-like remains of the splendid old fortress. Close by, at the confluence of the Sentino and Marena rivers, stood the Roman city of *Sentinum*, the place where the Romans in 295 BC achieved a momentous victory, known as the Battle of Sentinum, over the Gauls, the Etruscans and the Samnites. The **Museo Civico Archeologico Sentinate** (*T: 0732 956231*) in the upper town has a collection of sculptures, epigraphs, bronzes, mosaics and other objects, from the site of Sentinum. Also in the upper town is the 13th-century **church and monastery of Santa Chiara**, where there are some paintings of the *Madonna* by the town's most celebrated native artist, Giovanni Battista Salvi, known as Il Sassoferrato (*see box below*). The 13th-century church of **San Francesco** has a magnificent 14th-century painted Crucifix over the high altar. It is the work of Giuliano da Rimini, a follower of Giotto.

Near Sassoferrato (2km, Località Santa Lucia) is the archaeological park of **Sentinum** (*map p. 618, B3; open 8–2, closed Sun and holidays; summer always open; T: 0732 956231*), with paved streets, ruined walls, and the remains of a Roman villa. Finds from the excavations are partly at the local archaeological museum, partly in Ancona, and partly in Munich.

Giovanni Battista Salvi: 'Il Sassoferrato' (1609–85)

Though he was born in the Marche, and though he takes his name from his native town, Giovanni Battista Salvi did not remain long in the provinces. He went early to Rome, where he was apprenticed to Domenichino, and where he made his name. His oeuvre consists almost entirely of religious works (chiefly tender and sweet-faced Madonnas), all attractive and easy on the eye, and all with a serene, static quality that entirely rejects the charged emotion and swirling sensual exuberance of the Baroque. His palate is rich but never violent or unexpected, and his style soft—even sentimental—harking back to the High Renaissance, particularly to Raphael. Sassoferrato was a very fine draughtsman, and this is reflected in his classical exactitude of line and accuracy of depiction. His finest works are scattered in churches and museums worldwide, though the city where he was born does conserve a few, in Santa Chiara (*see above*). As well as religious pieces, Sassoferrato also executed a number of portraits (it is thought that he took a great many private commissions). A particularly fine self-portrait is in the Uffizi.   A.B.

Genga and the Rossa-Frasassi region

Genga, in the heart of the Rossa-Frasassi Park (*map p. 618, B3*), is a perfectly intact, tiny medieval town set in the darkly forested hills. The ex-church of San Clemente now houses the civic museum, with a white marble statue of the *Madonna with Christ Child* from the Valadier chapel in the Frasassi Gorge (*see box opposite*), perhaps made by the great Neoclassical sculptor Antonio Canova. At the foot of the hill by the caves, a Roman bridge protected by a Gothic tower crosses the River Sentino to the splendid Romanesque church of **San Vittore alle Chiuse** (1007), once attached to a powerful Benedictine abbey. The old abbey buildings now house the **Museo Speleocarsico** (*T: 0732 90241*), a display of fossils and minerals from the area, including a fossilised ichthyosaurus, 150 million years old.

GOLA DELLA ROSSA-FRASASSI REGIONAL PARK

Visitor centre: Località La Cuna, San Vittore, Genga, T: 0732 97211, www.parcogo-larossa.it
Founded in 1997, and extending over 9,167 hectares, the park protects a unique environment of limestone mountains, forests, streams and caves. Breathtakingly beautiful, and rich in wildlife, it is the realm of the golden eagle, goshawk and peregrine falcon, as well as the edible dormouse and porcupine (symbol of the park), and unique flora.

The deep valleys in the park, Gola della Rossa, Gola di Frasassi, and Valle Scappuccia, have always been popular with cave explorers. In the **Grotta del Santuario**, Pope Leo XII built the little octagonal chapel, with a bronze roof, of Santa Maria Infrasaxa (1828; Giuseppe Valadier); at Christmas time the inhabitants of Genga mount a *tableau vivant* of the Nativity here. The best-known caves are the **Grotte di Frasassi** (*closed 1 and 10–30 Jan, 4 and 25 Dec; T: 0732 97211, call day before for opening times, which vary. July–Aug also night visits; tours of caves are professionally guided, from June–Sept also in German, English, French*). The cave system is the most extensive in Europe. New cavities are frequently discovered; at the time of writing their length is c. 26km. The Ancona Abyss, discovered in 1971, is 180m long, 120m wide and 200m high: one of the largest caves in the world. (*NB: Bring a jacket; the temperature is maintained at 14°C so as not to destroy the atmospheric conditions necessary to preserve the caves in their pristine state. Try to avoid summer weekends, and get there early.*)

Serra Sant'Abbondio
Serra Sant'Abbondio (*map p. 618, B3*) stands on the River Cesano, close to the border with Umbria, a spot inhabited since the Iron Age. The town was founded by the town of Gubbio in the 13th century, as an important checkpoint along the shortest—but most difficult—route from Umbria to the Adriatic. In 1384 the town became part of the Duchy of Urbino, and afterwards followed the destiny of that city. Two of the original four 13th-century gates are still standing, and the town retains its medieval aspect.

On the eastern flank of Monte Catria, in a peaceful wooded valley, stands the isolated monastery of the **Eremo di Santa Croce di Fonte Avellana** (*open 9–11 & 3–5; Sun and holidays 3–5*), founded by St Romuald (*see p. 385*) in 980, and which gave hospitality to saints, bishops, and Dante Alighieri (1310). It is still a functioning monastery, occupied by Camaldolensian monks (the order founded by Romuald). To the right of the church is the chapel of St Peter Damian, who spent some time here in 1035. Still further to the right is the entrance to the hermitage, and the room dedicated to the Saint, with 16th–17th-century furniture. The luminous scriptorium also functions as a solar clock, a meridian and a calendar, the rays of the sun arriving on different points of the floor and the walls, indicating times for prayers, equinoxes and solstices.

PERGOLA & CORINALDO

Pergola (*map p. 618, B3*) was founded by the Umbrian town of Gubbio in 1228, on the site of ancient *Pertia*, at the strategic confluence of the Cinisco and the Cesano, in order to facilitate trade between Umbria and the Adriatic. In its heyday it was renowned for the skill of its artisans and the beauty of its architecture: many Gothic doorways and medieval tower-houses can be seen in the centre.

Pergola is most renowned today for the group of statues known as the *Bronzi di Pergola*. They are housed in a special museum on Largo San Giacomo, the **Museo dei Bronzi Dorati e della Città di Pergola** (*open 2 Jan–30 June and 1 Sept–31 Dec 9.30–12.30 & 3.30–7.30; 1 July–31 Aug daily 10–12.30 & 3.30–6.30; closed Mon, T: 0721 734090, www.bronzidorati.com*).

THE PERGOLA BRONZES

Found by chance in 1946 near Cartoceto di Pergola, the group of life-size statues, partly fragmentary, is formed of two men on horseback and two ladies, in gilded bronze. Made by the lost-wax method, using bronze containing a high proportion of lead, they were covered with gold leaf, and therefore certainly represent members of a high-ranking family; a recent theory suggests they are Cicero, his wife Terentia, his brother Quintus and his sister-in-law Pomponia (second half of the 1st century BC). The artist was probably from *Sentinum* (Sassoferrato), where there was an atelier for the manufacture of bronze. As there is no trace of them having ever been fixed to a base, it is thought they were stolen by bandits when they were being transported from Sentinum to an unknown destination, and hastily broken up and hidden—the spot, of no particular archaeological context, was close to a busy road connecting the Metauro valley to the Chienti and the Tronto.

Corinaldo

Corinaldo (*map p. 618, C3*) is one of the best-preserved towns in the Central Marche. The name derives from *Cor in Altum* ('Heart on High'): on a hilltop (203m), it is almost perfectly symmetrical, and heart-shaped, divided in two by the long stairway called the *Piaggia*, and surrounded by magnificent fortifications; it is still possible to walk along the top of them, for almost their entire length. It was thanks to these walls, in 1517, that the town successfully repulsed an attack by Francesco Maria della Rovere. As a token of his appreciation, Pope Leo X declared Corinaldo a city—this status was endorsed by Pius VI in 1786.

The **Civica Raccolta d'Arte Claudio Ridolfi** (*open Sun only 10–12.30; July–Aug 10–12.30 & 4–7.30 & 8.30–11; T: 071 679047*) includes works by the Venetian artist Ridolfi (1570–1644), often called 'Il Veronese' after his birthplace, Verona. In the first years of the 17th century Ridolfi was invited to the court of Urbino by Barocci. It was there that he met the Augustine priest Bartolomeo Orlandi, who was from Corinaldo, and with whom he formed a lifelong friendship. Ridolfi even bought a house in Corinaldo, while maintaining another at Verona. He helped to strengthen the bond between the Veneto and the Marche, and thanks to his friendship with the priest, he was flooded with commissions to paint for churches. Two churches in Corinaldo preserve works by his hand: the little church of the **Suffragio** (in fact a medieval tower converted into a church in 1637), which has a *Madonna and Child in Glory* over the main altar; and the ancient Santa Maria del Piano, built over the remains of a pagan temple. The *Mary Magdalene at the Foot of the Cross* (1540) is considered by many to be Ridolfi's masterpiece.

Arcevia

Eternal rival of Pergola, the white stone town of Arcevia (*map p. 618, C3*) was the summer retreat of Duchess Livia della Rovere. The central church of San Medardo (rebuilt 1634) houses over the baptismal font the famous **Baptism of Christ by Luca Signorelli**, certainly worth a detour to see; while in the apse is a fine, luminous polyptych by the same artist, signed and dated 1507, in its original frame.

Senigallia

From Arcevia the main road leads to the coast and Senigallia (*map p. 618, C2*), the smartest resort on the Adriatic, with an enchanting historical centre, and some of the best restaurants in Italy. It is famous for its beach, 13km of velvety white sand, and for the romantic, circular Art Nouveau pier known as the Rotonda sul Mare.

PRACTICAL INFORMATION

GETTING AROUND

• **By train: Ancona** and **Senigallia** stations are on the Milan–Bologna–Pescara line; another line from Rome reaches Jesi and Fabriano. From Fabriano there is a line for **Sassoferrato** and **Pergola**.
• **By bus:** Conero bus (www.conerobus.it) runs services between Ancona and the Conero Peninsula, Senigallia,

Osimo, Jesi, Recanati and Loreto. Autolinee Binni connects Ancona with Loreto and Recanati. Services between Ancona and Senigallia, Jesi, Arcevia and Corinaldo are run by Autolinee Bucci (www.autolinee bucci.com). Crognaletti (www.autolineecrognaletti.it), also connects Ancona with Jesi. SACSA connects Ancona with Jesi and the other towns along the Esino Valley. For Jesi, Arcevia and Pergola, Autolinee Vitali (www.vitaliautolinee.it).

INFORMATION OFFICES

Ancona Via Thaon de Revel 4, T: 071 358991, www.provincia.ancona.it; Via Podesti 21, T: 071 222 5066/67.
Cupramontana Piazza Cavour 3, T: 0731 789746; Viale Vittoria 12.
Jesi Piazza della Repubblica, T: 0731 59788.
Loreto Via Solari 3, T: 071 970276; Corso Boccalini 67, T: 071 977748; for guided tours of the Sanctuary, T: 071 970104, www.santuarioloreto.it
Numana Via Venezia 59, T: 071 734 90179, www.turismonumana.it
Recanati Piazza Leopardi 31, T: 071 981471; Via Leopardi 26, T: 071 758 7218.
Sassoferrato Piazza Matteotti 3, T: 0732 956231.
Sirolo Piazza Vittorio Veneto, T: 071 933 0611.

HOTELS

Ancona (map p. 618, D3)
€€€€ **Grand Hotel Palace**. Situated between the port and the old centre, a comfortable and elegant hotel in a 16th-century building, with roof garden, car

park. No restaurant. Closed Christmas and New Year. *Lungomare Vanvitelli 24, T: 071 201813, www.hotelancona.it. 40 rooms.*
€€ **Gino**. Quite a find: small, old-fashioned, spotlessly clean, with a prize-winning restaurant (thanks to the chef Umberto), and right opposite the railway station. Car park next door. Fairly quiet (the rooms have been sound-proofed), excellent morning cappuccino. *Via Flaminia 4, T: 071 42179.*
€€ **Grand Hotel Passetto**. Luxurious hotel in splendid hillside position in the modern city. *Via Thaon de Revel 1, T: 071 31307, www.hotelpassetto.it. 40 rooms.*
Arcevia (map p. 618, C3)
€€ **Country House Paradiso del Re**. Seven kilometres north of Arcevia, a delightful hotel in one of the area's defensive fortresses, full of atmosphere: you can enjoy the bizarre experience of dressing up as medieval royalty and being suitably banqueted and serenaded. *Castello San Pietro in Musio, T: 0731 982162 and 982902, www.ilparadisodelre.it. 8 rooms.*
Corinaldo (map p. 618, C3)
€ **I Tigli** ■ A small hotel once a 17th-century monastery. Central, with a renowned restaurant. *Via del Teatro 31, T: 071 797 5849, www.hotelitigli.it. 13 rooms.*
Filottrano (map p. 619, C4)
€€ **Villa Centofinestre**. Centrally situated for Recanati, Loreto, Osimo and Jesi, an 18th-century country villa with a large park 2km east of Filottrano. Accommodation in the villa or in a cottage on the grounds; also self-catering. *Via di Centofinestre 4, T: 335 810 6514, www.villacentofinestre.com. 5 apartments.*
Genga (map p. 618, B3)

€ **Hotel Frasassi**. Convenient position in the Rossa-Frasassi park, walking distance from the caves, with a restaurant. *Via Marconi 33, T: 0732 905003, www.hotelfrasassi.com. 35 rooms.*

Jesi (*map p. 618, C3*)

€ **Mariani**. In the old town centre, a quiet and comfortable hotel, well run, in a medieval palace. Restaurant and garage next door. *Via dell'Orfanatrofio 10, T: 0731 207286, www.hotelmariani.com. 33 rooms.*

Loreto (*map p. 619, D4*)

€€ **Villa Tetlameya**. ■ Lovely old villa just outside town, with car park and excellent restaurant, run by the same family since 1785. Extremely helpful owner. *Via Villa Costantina 187, T: 071 977476 and 978863. 8 rooms.*

Massignano (*map p. 618, D3*)

€ **B&B Colle Lauro**. Situated in the Conero Park, in a comfortable, friendly home in the countryside; nice breakfasts with home-made food. English and French spoken. *Via Betelico 110, T: 071 731897, www.collelauro.com. 1 room.*

Osimo (*map p. 619, D4*)

€€ **La Commenda**. 15th-century stone-built villa charmingly furnished, with pool, gym and sauna, 4km west of Osimo. Very comfortable rooms, no restaurant. *Via della Commenda 1, Località Casenuove T: 071 710 3360, www.lacommenda.net. 8 rooms.*

Portonovo (*map p. 618, D3*)

€€€ **Fortino Napoleonico**. ■ Within Conero Park, this is undoubtedly one of the most unusual hotels in the region; it was once a fort (1810). Renowned restaurant, private beach, gym, tennis, garden, pool. Eco-friendly. *Via Poggio 166, T: 071 801450, www.hotelfortino.it. 33 rooms.*

€€€–€€ **Emilia**. ■ Lovely hotel immersed in the vegetation of the Conero Park, with a private beach, garden, tennis, parking and good restaurant. *Via Collina 149, Poggio di Portonovo, T: 071 801145, www.hotelemilia.com. 26 rooms.*

Recanati (*map p. 619, D4*)

€€ **Palazzo dalla Casapiccola**. Seventeenth-century palace built to accommodate Church dignitaries on their way to Loreto, this lovely building offers sumptuous rooms with frescoed ceilings, and a delightful Italian-style garden. *Piazzola Vincenzo Gioberti (Via Roma) 2, T: 071 757 4818, www.palazzodallacasapiccola.it. 4 apartments.*

€ **Gallery**. Near the cathedral, in a 17th-century palace, a new hotel offering attentive service, good breakfast buffet. *Via Falleroni 85, T: 071 981914, www.ghr.it. 68 rooms.*

Sassoferrato (*map p. 618, B3*)

€ **Il Miroccolo**. Cosy, comfortable rooms in the little houses of an ancient farming hamlet 6km north of Sassoferrato. Good restaurant. Organic wine, honey, hams and salami. Horses, pool with sauna, English spoken. *Località Monte 1, T: 0732 974510, www.ilmiroccolo.it. 4 rooms.*

Senigallia (*map p. 618, C2*)

€€ **Regina**. ■ A quaint little 1920s hotel right on the beach, with restaurant and car park, all rooms have air conditioning. *Lungomare Alighieri 5, T: 071 792 7400, www.albergoregina.it. 18 rooms.*

Sirolo (*map p. 619, D4*)

€€ **Locanda Rocco**. Tiny inn on the 14th-century walls, close to the path down to the beach. Good restaurant; eco-friendly. *Via Torrione 1, T: 071 933*

0558, www.locandarocco.it. 7 rooms.
€€ **Il Ritorno**. Three kilometres south-west of Sirolo, comfortable rooms in a traditional farmhouse, meals on request. The farm raises horses, for which it is famous. Via Piani d'Aspio 12, Località Coppo, T: 071 933 1544, www.ilritorno.com.

RESTAURANTS

Ancona (map p. 618, D3)
€€€€ **La Moretta**. Opened in 1897, and always with a good reputation for fish dishes. Lovely in the summer when you eat out in the square. Closed Sun. Piazza Plebiscito 52, T: 071 202317.
€€ **La Cantineta**. No-fuss restaurant dear to the hearts of the people of Ancona, close to the entrance to the port. Stoccafisso all'Anconetana (dried cod) and brodetto all'Anconetana (fish soup, made with 13 different kinds of Adriatic fish) are served every day. Finish off with a cup of turchetto, a mixture of coffee, rum and sugar. Booking advisable. Closed Mon. Via Gramsci 1/c, T: 071 201107.
€€ **Traiano**. ■ Perfect local tradition, fish soup Ancona-style, squid with peas, mixed fried fish, accompanied by well-chosen wines. Closed Wed. Via XXIX Settembre 6/a, T: 071 205540.
Arcevia (map p. 618, C3)
€€ **Pinocchio**. ■ Cosy little inn, especially in winter around the open fire. Traditional dishes, friendly atmosphere. Closed Wed. Via Ramazzani Vici 135, T: 0731 97288.
Cupramontana (map p. 618, C3)
€ **Anita**. An ancient tavern still called La Moretta by the local people, exactly the same for over 50 years. Traditional

food is served with a flask of Verdicchio. Closed Tues and Sun evenings. Via Filzi 7, T: 0731 780311.
Jesi (map p. 618, C3)
€ **Il Vegetariano**. At last, exciting vegetarian food! Even convinced carnivores will love this place, which is just outside the old city walls. Closed Mon evenings, Sat, Sun lunchtime in summer. Via Leopardi 1, T: 0731 208213.
Osimo (map p. 619, D4)
€€ **Ristorante di Palazzo Baldeschi**. Situated in the town centre, serving all the typical local dishes. The delicious bread and pasta are home-made. Closed Wed. Via Sacramento 3, T: 071 714566.
Portonovo (map p. 618, D3)
€€€ **Clandestino Susci Bar**. ■ Delightfully casual atmosphere at Moreno Cedroni's tiny open-air restaurant in the Conero Park, where you can sample Italian-style sushi. Extremely well-patronised so booking is essential. Closed when it rains, and Oct–April. On the beach, T: 071 801422.
Porto Recanati (map p. 619, D4)
€€ **L'Uomo del Brodetto**. Ten kilometres from Recanati and 4km from Loreto, this restaurant at the Bianchi Vincenzo hotel specialises in the local brodetto, fish soup, to which a little wild saffron is added; always available and really worth the journey. House Verdicchio from the flask. Book first, because the large dining room is often used for banquets. Closed Mon. Via Garibaldi 15, T: 071 759981.
Senigallia (map p. 618, C2)
€€€€ **Madonnina del Pescatore**. ■ Wonderfully inventive and innovative cuisine. Moreno Cedroni, justly proud of his two Michelin stars, uses fish as it has never been used before. An

absolutely unforgettable experience; it is worth coming all the way to the Marche just to eat here. 7km south along the coast from Senigallia. Closed Mon and Nov. *Lungomare Italia 11, Marzocca, T: 071 698484.*

€€€ **Al Cuoco di Bordo**. Pasta and fish, with a personal touch; no menu, the chef will tell you what he has prepared that day. Closed Tues in winter. *Lungomare Alighieri 4, T: 071 792 9661.*

LOCAL SPECIALITIES

Ancona People here have a taste for *stoccafisso*, dried cod, going back to the days when ships from Ancona went trading as far as Norway; every year there is a competition among the city restaurants for a coveted diploma, awarded to the best.

Pergola *Visciolata* is a drink made with wild cherries.

Porto Recanati In autumn the bakers prepare *pane nociato*, adding parmesan and pecorino cheese, walnuts, black pepper and currants before baking. Delicious eaten as a snack with a glass of wine.

FESTIVALS & EVENTS

Ancona Feast of St Cyriacus, 1–4 May.
Arcevia Feast of St Medardus, Traditional fair, fireworks, 8 June; *Festa dell'Uva*, Pageant to celebrate the grape harvest, Sept.

Corinaldo *Contesa del Pozzo della Polenta*, Commemorating Corinaldo's victory over Francesco Maria della Rovere in 1517, with pageants, contests, flag-tossing and archery, third Sun in July; *Festa della Streghe*, Hallowe'en witches flit through the streets after sunset, 25–31 Oct.

Cupramontana *Sagra dell'Uva*, Festivities and parades for the grape harvest, first weekend in Oct.

Jesi *Palio di San Floriano*, Jousting and crossbow contests, first week in May; Feast of St Septimius, 22–25 Sept; Pergolesi-Spontini Festival, Sept.

Loreto Feast of the Madonna of Loreto, 8 Sept; *Traslazione della Santa Casa*, Thousands of pilgrims arrive for the celebration of the transportation of the Holy House from Nazareth to Loreto; many people reach the church barefoot, or on their knees; bonfires are lit to light up the path for the angels who are said to have brought the house here, 9–10 Dec.

Osimo *Festa del Covo*, An enormous sculpture made of ears of wheat is taken by tractor to the Sanctuary of the Madonna, first Sun in Aug; Feast of St Joseph of Cupertino, 16–18 Sept.

Senigallia *Pane Nostrum*, Bread festival, Sept.

URBINO & THE NORTHERN MARCHE

U rbino (pop. 16,000; *map p. 618, B2*) is famed as one of the principal centres of the Italian Renaissance. It has one of Italy's most interesting and well-preserved historic centres, considered an 'ideal city' by many.

HISTORY OF URBINO

Little remains of Roman Urbino except perhaps for the street layout on the Poggio hill, where the duke's palace stands. The town was destroyed during the war between the Goths and the Byzantines, and suffered considerably during the Lombard invasion. Reconstruction began in the 12th–13th century, when it passed to the Montefeltro family. The 14th century saw rebuilding on the other hill, called Monte, but the 15th century was the 'Golden Century' for Urbino. Federico da Montefeltro summoned to his court the most illustrious and influential figures of the age, including architects Luciano Laurana and Francesco di Giorgio Martini, and the painter Piero della Francesca. After founding the university in 1506, Guidubaldo, the last of the Montefeltro (one of the speakers in Castiglione's *Courtier*), died without heirs, and the city passed to their kinsmen the della Rovere. Francesco Maria della Rovere held Urbino until 1516, when he was driven out by Pope Leo X, who wanted the duchy for his Medici nephew. The della Rovere only returned after Pope Leo's death, and remained lords of the city until 1631, when Urbino passed to the papacy. In 1797 Napoleon's troops occupied the city, including it in the Republic of Rome. In 1861 it became part of the new Kingdom of Italy.

Palazzo Ducale and Galleria Nazionale delle Marche
Open 8.30–7.15, last tickets 6.15; Mon 8.30–2, last tickets 1pm; T: 0722 322625.
The palace was built in the 15th century by a number of architects: the Florentines Maso di Bartolomeo and Luca della Robbia, and Luciano Laurana, Francesco di Giorgio Martini and Girolamo Genga. Described as a 'city in the form of a palace', it now houses the vast Galleria Nazionale delle Marche, one of the most important art galleries in Italy. The finest works are housed in the former apartments of the duke and duchess. Highlights are given below.

(1) Appartamento dei Melaranci: Contains 14th-century works, including a *Madonna* by Allegretto Nuzi from Fabriano, who served his apprentice-ship in Florence under the guidance of Bernardo Daddi, before returning to the Marche, where he spent the rest of his life as one of the most highly appreciat-

URBINO
PALAZZO DUCALE

1   App. dei Melaranci
2   App. degli Ospiti
3   App. del Duca Federico
4   App. della Duchessa
5   Sala del Trono

wood, where the refined perspective acquires an allegorical significance—the human figures, indifferent to the torture taking place behind them, seem less vital than the architectural lines of the city where the scene takes place. Also by Piero is the enigmatic *Senigallia Madonna*, where the solemn, colossal Christ Child appears to accept His future sacrifice, symbolised by the coral necklace and the white rose. Calm and silent, His mother supports Him as if she were an element of the architecture. The scene is imbued with impending tragedy; the only lighter touch is given by the basket of nappies on the shelf in the background.

The inlaid woodwork on the walls of the **Studiolo del Duca**, Duke Federico's study, is by Baccio Pontelli, using designs by Botticelli, Bramante and Francesco di Giorgio Martini. Joos van Ghent painted the portraits of 28 *Illustrious Men* for this room; 14 of them, now in the Louvre, have been replaced by reproductions.

Duke Federico's bedchamber, the **Camera da Letto del Duca**, has the famous portrait of *Federico da Montefeltro with his son Guidubaldo* by Pedro Berruguete; and a panel painting of the *Madonna* from the atelier of Andrea del Verrocchio. The **Sala degli Angeli** displays some well-known

ed painters of his time.

(2) Appartamento degli Ospiti: Includes a room stuccoed by Federico Brandani, representing the emblems of the Montefeltro and della Rovere families; there are paintings by Carlo and Vittore Crivelli, Giovanni Bellini and Alvise Vivarini.

(3) Appartamento del Duca Federico: In the **Sala delle Udienze**, with lavish decoration in carved and inlaid marble, where Duke Federico held his audiences, is the famous *Flagellation* by Piero della Francesca, painted on poplar

works, including the *Miracle of the Profaned Host* by Paolo Uccello, and the famous *View of the Ideal City*. Authorship is disputed between Luciano Laurana, Piero della Francesca, and Fra' Carnevale, though it is most usually attributed to Laurana. Apart from a couple of pigeons on the building on the right, no living creature is in sight, but the half-open door of the church in the centre seems to invite us to enter.
(4) Appartamento della Duchessa: Devoted to 16th-century works, including *La Muta* (1507) by Raphael, one of his finest (and most discussed) paintings, dating to the period when he had returned from his stay in Florence. Little is known about the sitter, but nowadays many scholars believe her to be Giovanna Feltria della Rovere, daughter of Duke Federico da Montefeltro, who lost her husband in 1501. Analysis of the work shows that the original drawing was of a younger version of the lady, made at the start of Raphael's career; he painted her later with a slightly different attire, before completing the portrait probably in about 1507, ageing her features each time. Her recent widowhood would explain her sad expression. Also by Raphael is the earlier *St Catherine of Alexandria*. The magnetic image of *Christ Blessing* is by Bramantino. More splendid works are in the **Duchess's bedroom**, including the *Last Supper* and the *Resurrection* by Titian.
(5) Sala del Trono: This imposing apartment, used by the duke as a setting for his parties, has another series of Flemish tapestries on the walls, the famous *Acts of the Apostles*, for which Raphael provided the designs.

The duomo and San Domenico

Next to the palace, in Piazza Federico, is Giuseppe Valadier's Neoclassical **duomo** (1802; *open 8–12 & 2.30–6.30*), which replaces Duke Federico's cathedral, destroyed by an earthquake in 1789. The only part of the building to survive the earthquake is the Chapel of the Sacrament, to the left; on the left-hand wall is a painting of the *Last Supper* by Federico Barocci. In the chapel to the right of the main altar, on the right-hand wall, is a painting of the *Madonna* by Carlo Maratta.

Opposite Palazzo Ducale, in Piazza Rinascimento, by the Egyptian obelisk brought here from Rome by Cardinal Albani in 1737, is the church of **San Domenico**. The superb stone portal of 1451 is by Maso di Bartolomeo, commissioned by Duke Federico. In the interior, in the apse, is a magnificent canvas of the *Madonna with Sts Dominic and Catherine of Siena* by Giovanni Conca. To the left of the church is Via San Domenico, leading east to the remains of the **Roman theatre** which came to light in 1943.

The enormous monastery of Santa Chiara was probably built by Francesco di Giorgio Martini for Duke Federico (or his daughter Elisabetta). It is now an applied arts institute. The round **church of Santa Chiara** was unfortunately spoilt in the early 19th century when it became the vestibule for the hospital; buried inside are Francesco Maria I della Rovere, his wife Eleonora Gonzaga, his son Cardinal Giulio and his niece Lavinia.

Bramantino: *Christ Blessing* (late 15th century), in the Galleria Nazionale delle Marche.

Piazza della Repubblica and the Casa di Raffaello

Piazza della Repubblica, with a graceful fountain, occupies the valley between the two hills of Urbino. To the left of it is the portico of the 14th-century church of **San Francesco** (*open 7–12.30 & 3–7*), with some finely-carved marble arches in the interior. In the apse is the *Pardon of St Francis* by Federico Barocci (1581).

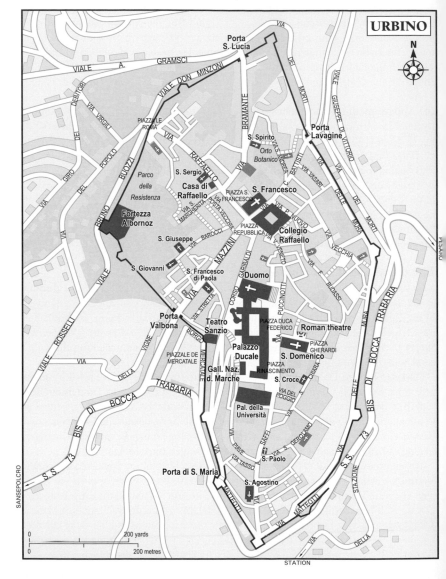

From the church, Via Raffaello leads up to the **Casa Natale di Raffaello** (*open Mon–Sat 9–1 & 3–7; Sun and holidays 10–1; T: 0722 320105*), Raphael's birthplace, where some of his early works can be seen, together with reproductions of his most famous paintings, and canvases by his father, Giovanni Santi. The house itself is interesting for its typical architecture of the times. Next door is the oldest church in Urbino, **San Sergio** (5th and 15th centuries). Traces of a Roman piscina came to light during repairs to the floor. The paintings are by Claudio Ridolfi and Girolamo Cialdieri.

Almost opposite Raphael's house is the picturesque Via Bramante: at no. 17 is Palazzo Albani, birthplace of Pope Clement XI (Giovanni Francesco Albani, reigned 1700–21). The road leads on, past the 16th-century church of **Santo Spirito**, with a beautiful portal, and a painting over the main altar of the *Pentecost* by Taddeo Zuccari.

THE DELLA ROVERE DUKES

The family, originally from Savona, gave two popes to the Church: Francesco, who ruled as Sixtus IV (1471–84), and Giuliano (Julius II, 1503–13). A nephew of Pope Sixtus, Giovanni, was made lord of Senigallia in 1474. He married a daughter of Federico da Montefeltro, and his son Francesco Maria I della Rovere (1490–1538), inherited the duchy of Urbino when the Montefeltro family died out in 1508; in 1513 he was awarded the city of Pesaro by the Church for his services as *condottiere*. Guidubaldo II (1514–74), his son, was no soldier. Patron of the arts, he turned Pesaro into a sumptuous Renaissance court, while preferring to live in Fossombrone because of the finer climate. In 1534 he married the ten-year-old Giulia da Varano of Camerino, commissioning from Titian the famous painting known as the *Venus of Urbino* (now in the Uffizi; *see p. 283*). The painting was hung in the little girl's boudoir, probably in the hope of awakening her senses before her husband died without an heir. Guidubaldo's son, Francesco Maria II (who was born 9 years later) preferred Urbania. After building a magnificent palace there, he took the intelligent Livia as his second wife, and, being of a studious turn of mind, hoped to pass the responsibilities of government to his young son Federico Ubaldo (1605–23), but the boy, after dutifully marrying and producing a daughter, died prematurely without a male heir. His father was forced therefore to resume his role as head of state. When he died in 1631, he was the last of the della Rovere dukes. His granddaughter Vittoria was the last of the family line. She married Ferdinando II de' Medici, Grand Duke of Tuscany, and many of the della Rovere treasures, including numerous famous works of art, were transferred from the Marche to Florence, where they still adorn Palazzo Pitti.

The old town

Via Barocci is named after the artist Federico Barocci, who was born at no. 18. The **Oratorio di San Giuseppe** (*open 10–12.30; weekdays also 3–5.30; T: 0722 2613*) is a

16th–17th-century church formed of two chapels, in one of which is the famous stucco **Presepio** (Christmas crib) by Federico Brandani. On 6th January, if the day is clear, a ray of sunlight comes through the window and alights upon the Infant Jesus. Further along the street is the 14th-century **Oratorio di San Giovanni** (*open 10–12.30; weekdays also 3–5.30; T: 0722 350025*), entirely decorated with a superb series of frescoes (1416) by Jacopo and Lorenzo Salimbeni, dedicated to the life of St John the Baptist; some authorities believe these to be among the best examples of the period to be seen in Italy; the fine details are incredible. The Salimbeni brothers, from San Severino Marche, were influential artists in their immediate area, although their work is virtually unknown outside the Marche. They were important exponents of the International Gothic style.

Turn right outside the church and take the alley called Via Scalette di San Giovanni, offering stupendous views over the Palazzo Ducale, down to Corso Mazzini: almost opposite is the 17th-century church of **San Francesco di Paola**, or Corpus Domini, built as an ex-voto by Francesco Maria II della Rovere, who wanted a son (his prayer was heard; the baby was Federico Ubaldo). The frescoes on the vault of the interior, of stories of the Saint, are the masterpiece of Antonio Viviani (1614).

ENVIRONS OF URBINO

Urbania

Urbania (*map p. 618, B2*) is surrounded on three sides by the Metauro, which literally washes the medieval walls, still in good condition, though the old centre was almost completely rebuilt after the destruction by bombing in 1944. This was the favourite city of Francesco Maria II della Rovere; he lived here, and this is where he died, in 1631. At his death, the duchy became extinct, and was taken over by the Papal States.

From the late 13th century until 1636, the town was known as *Casteldurante*. It takes its present name from Pope Urban VIII. During the Renaissance, Casteldurante was one of the most prestigious centres in Italy for the production of pottery, of which the decoration was inspired by Raphael; the tradition is still alive and flourishing.

In the 15th-century **oratorio del Carmine** is a fresco of the *Madonna*, thought to be by Giotto, and brought here from the castle when it was demolished in 1516. The church of the **Crocifisso** contains the tomb (1631) of Francesco Maria II della Rovere, last duke of Urbino. In the right-hand chapel is a splendid canvas by Federico Barocci of the *Madonna of the Clouds*.

The impressive brick **Palazzo Ducale**, built by the Brancaleoni family in the 13th century and later modified by Francesco di Giorgio Martini and by Girolamo Genga, houses the **Museo Civico** (*open 10–12 & 3–6; closed Mon; T: 0722 317175; entrance from Via Piccini*), with a rich collection of paintings and frescoes, including works by Palma Giovane, Federico Barocci and Giovanni Francesco Guerrieri.

Sant'Angelo in Vado and Piobbico

Sant'Angelo in Vado (*map p. 618, A2*) stands in a strategic position on the River Metauro, where the Romans built a settlement called *Tifernum Metaurense*, destroyed by the Goths in the 6th century. The survivors rebuilt their town, dedicating it to the Archangel Michael; 'in Vado' means a point where the river can be crossed by wading.

For many years Sant'Angelo was the capital of the Massa Trabaria Forest, a large tract of fir trees prized by the ancient Romans as an important source of straight, sturdy deal trunks, *trabes*, which were floated down the Tiber to Rome. At the entrance to the town (when coming from Urbania), at Pratello Santa Maria, just after the public gardens, is the Museo Archeologico Tifernum Metaurense (*open summer 9–12 & 3–7*), housing a collection of Roman epigraphs, statues, mosaics and coins, found locally.

Sant'Angelo is also an important truffle centre, especially for the prized white *Tuber magnatum*. Even more important for truffles is **Acqualagna** (*map p. 618, B2*), the most important centre in Italy for their production and sale.

Piobbico (*map p. 618, B2*) is a beautiful stone town, built in the 11th century on the ruins of a Roman settlement called *Publicum*, at the confluence of the Candigliano and Biscubio rivers. In the 12th century it was taken by the Brancaleoni family, who built the castle. In 1573 they called on the architect Girolamo Genga and his son Bartolomeo, to remodel it; the result is a magnificent building with graceful staircases, ornate stone fireplaces, and stuccoes by Federico Brandani. An unusual feature is the timepiece in the clock-tower: the face behind (inside the tower) has the hands going round in an anti-clockwise direction. The church of Santo Stefano (18th century) has an unusual ellipti-cal interior, striking works in stucco by Federico Brandani, and a lovely painting by Federico Barocci, representing the *Holy Family*, resting under a cherry tree. It is a gouache copy of an oil-on-canvas of the same subject, now in the Vatican. Painted at the request of Count Antonio Brancaleoni in 1574, Barocci held it to be his finest work.

Fermignano and the Gola del Furlo

Just south of Urbino is the picturesque grey stone town of **Fermignano** (*map p. 618, B2*), probably founded by the Romans because of its key position on the river and on the road to Urbino. Some historians believe that the historic battle between the Romans and the Carthaginians in 207 BC, took place here. Entering the city centre, you see the Roman three-arched bridge, and the medieval tower to protect it, over the Metauro, which forms a double waterfall. The wool mill, once a paper factory, near the tower, is a good example of industrial archaeology. The medieval heart of the town is a labyrinth of tiny streets called Pianello, surrounded by a curve of the river. From Fermignano you can walk (c. 3km) up the wooded hill of Serra Alta (400m), for magnificent views over Urbino and the Apennines.

Not far from Fermignano, just before joining the Metauro, the River Candigliano forms a gorge, now a wildlife reserve, **Riserva Naturale Gola del Furlo** (*visitor cen-tre at Via Flaminia 40, T: 0721 700041, www.riservagoladelfurlo.it*). It is spectacularly photogenic, and interesting both from the point of view of the wildlife (golden eagle, sparrowhawk, goshawk, peregrine falcon, lanner falcon, Montagu's harrier, pallid and alpine swifts, blue rock thrush, and chough—to mention only the birds) and for the tunnels built by the Romans to allow the passage of the Via Flaminia: the **Galleria del Furlo**, 38m long, just over 5m wide, and 6m high, was chiselled through the lime-

View of the beautiful Gola del Furlo.

stone by slaves for Vespasian, in AD 76–77. It has seen the passage of many kings, emperors and popes, with their carriages, cohorts and courtesans; many crucial battles; and, in 1502, Lucrezia Borgia, on her way to Ferrara. But the gorge gradually became infested with highwaymen and bandits, and was extremely dangerous for travellers until the 19th century. Close to the opening of the main tunnel is a smaller one carved by the consul Gaius Flaminius in 217 BC. Although only 8m long, it is an impressive achievement, deeply scarred by the wheels of chariots and carts.

The town of **Cagli** (*map p. 618, B3*), further south, goes back to pre-Roman times. It became a Roman town in 295 BC, and under the Byzantines, in the 5th century, its strategic importance along the Via Flaminia was such that it formed part of a pentapolis, or five-city alliance, together with Jesi, Fossombrone, Urbino and Gubbio. Cagli is dominated by the sturdy, elliptical Torrione, all that remains of the fortifications erected by Francesco di Giorgio Martini in 1481; it houses a collection of modern sculptures, including some by the local artist Eliseo Mattiacci (1940), a foremost exponent of Pop Art. The Museo Archeologico e della Via Flaminia (*open June–Sept 10–12 & 4–7; Oct–March Sat and Sun 10–12 & 3–6; T: 0721 78071*) illustrates the role of the Roman road in the history of the city, and how it affected trade. Just outside the town, on the Via Flaminia, is a Roman bridge, the **Ponte Mallio**, 2,000 years old, and in very good condition.

PESARO & ENVIRONS

Pesaro (pop. 92,000; *map p. 618, C1*) is a captivating seaside city. Its waterfront from Piazzale Libertà to the picturesque canal-port on the River Foglia is a favourite place for strolling. The main street, Viale della Repubblica, flanked by shady trees, corresponds to the principal Roman thoroughfare. The composer Rossini was born here.

HISTORY OF PESARO

Roman *Pisaurum* was founded in 184 BC on the Via Flaminia, at the mouth of the River Foglia, where the Picenes had a small settlement. Though the marshy area proved unhealthy, the thick, sticky clay was perfect for making bricks and tiles, and later it would prove to be the mainstay of the economy when the ceramics industry was introduced. Being on important trade routes, Pesaro was fought over by Goths, Byzantines, Lombards and Franks, until it was donated to the Church by Charlemagne in 774. Between the 6th and 7th centuries Pesaro, together with Rimini, Fano, Senigallia and Ancona, had formed part of the Maritime Pentapolis, under the protection of Ravenna. An independent commune in the 12th century, in the 13th it was taken by the Malatesta of Rimini, then by the Sforza (who built the castle and the Palazzo Ducale), and then by the della Rovere. These last fostered the ceramics industry, erected a new set of walls, and built the canal-port at the mouth of the Foglia river. The city remained in their hands until 1631, when on the death of the last duke, it returned to the Papal States. Under della Rovere rule Pesaro became the administrative and cultural centre of the Duchy of Urbino, attracting artists of the quality of Titian, and great writers, such as Torquato Tasso. In 1861 Pesaro became part of the Kingdom of Italy.

The cattedrale and Casa Rossini

Repairs to the cathedral floor in the 19th century brought to light two preceding mosaic floors, now partially visible thanks to an ingenious system of glass viewing panels and shifting blocks of mosaic. The artistic quality of both floors is exceptionally good, carried out using tiny coloured marble tesserae. The upper section was laid in the 6th century; the lower is from a 4th-century Palaeochristian basilica. Historians believe the first church was destroyed in 553 during the war between Goths and Byzantines, and rebuilt a few years later by Belisarius, Emperor Justinian's general. There are plans to remove both mosaics and place them in a purpose-built exhibition area. To the left of the main altar is a detached 15th-century fresco of the *Madonna with Saints*, recently attributed to Raphael—he would have been 15 when he painted it.

At no. 34 Via Rossini is the house where the composer was born, **Casa Rossini** (*opening times vary; T: 0721 387357*), a simple building where the Rossini family lived between 1790 and 1796, in two rooms on the first floor. It is now a museum.

Musei Civici

The 17th-century **Palazzo Toschi Mosca** houses the Musei Civici (*opening times vary; T: 0721 387541*). In the courtyard is Ferruccio Mengaroni's *Medusa* (1925), inspired by the famous painting by Caravaggio, with Mengaroni himself depicted as the gorgon. When the crate containing the work was being hoisted up to the first floor of the exhibition hall, the ropes broke, and Mengaroni, running to save it, was crushed under its weight.

The collection of paintings includes masterpieces by Paolo Veneziano, Jacobello del Fiore and Guido Reni, as well as a magnificent panel painting by **Giovanni Bellini**, the *Pala di Pesaro* or *Crowning of the Virgin* (1475), brought here by sea from Venice—a sign of the strong cultural relationship between the two cities under the Sforza. Depicting Christ crowning his Mother (the castle seen on the back of the throne is thought to be Gradara), with Sts Paul, Peter, Jerome and Francis of Assisi, the Holy Spirit and cherubim of different colours, the painting is contained within a frame consisting of smaller panels: saints on either side, and stories of saints at the bottom. The cimasa of the *Pietà* or *Embalming of Christ* was stolen by Napoleon. Returned to the Papal States thanks to the intervention of Antonio Canova, it is now in the Vatican Picture Gallery (*see p. 103*).

The **Ceramics Section** traces the history of the art, both in Pesaro and Casteldurante (Urbania). Casteldurante was renowned for love-cups known as 'beautiful women'. Gifts from a young man to his betrothed, they showed the face of a lady with a scroll giving her name and the word *bella*, beautiful. Pesaro acquired fame for richly-decorated, colourful majolica plaques and plates, and later for white china decorated with floral motifs, especially pink roses (the symbol of the city).

Piazza del Popolo and the Rocca

Piazza del Popolo, with a fine Baroque fountain (1685) in the centre, is on the site of the Roman forum. On the northwest side is **Palazzo Ducale**, now seat of the prefecture (*to request a visit, T: 0721 387393 or the Museum Service 0721 387474*). Most of the building goes back to the 14th century, but the elegant façade, with porticoes and battlements, and the magnificent *Salone Metaurense*, with its coffered ceiling, were added by Alessandro Sforza in 1465.

In Via San Francesco, opposite Palazzo Ducale, is the 13th-century sanctuary church of **Santa Maria delle Grazie**. In the south aisle is the lovely *Triptych of Montegranaro*, showing the Madonna with Sts James and Anthony Abbot, by Jacobello del Fiore (1407). In a room to the left of the main altar is a *St Ursula* by Palma Giovane.

The next turning on the left leads to Piazzale Matteotti and the **Rocca Costanza** (*to request a visit, T: 0721 387474*), built for Costanzo Sforza (son of Alessandro) in 1480 by Luciano Laurana. The massive structure, which once housed the prison, is one of the earliest examples in the region of a castle designed for flat terrain.

Sant'Agostino and the synagogue

The 14th-century church of **Sant'Agostino** has a splendid early 15th-century Venetian-Gothic portal. Over the second north altar is a canvas by Pomarancio showing *St Nicholas of Tolentino Pleading on Behalf of the Souls in Purgatory*—the city in the background is Pesaro. Over the third south altar a lovely *Annunciation* by Palma Giovane. In the little chapel to the left of the presbytery is a large *Crucifixion* in stucco, by Federico Brandani. The 15th-century carved and inlaid wooden choir is full of interesting details,

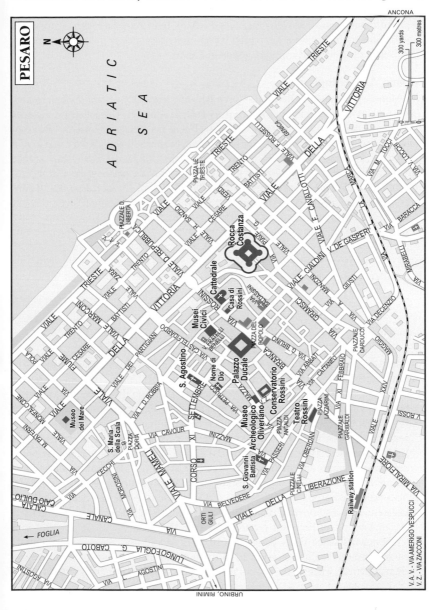

including views of Pesaro with Palazzo Ducale and the church of San Giovanni, the Rocca Costanza and the castle of Gradara. The two small dragons with human faces have been identified as Costanzo Sforza and Camilla of Aragon, who married in 1475.

At no. 25 Via delle Scuole (between Sant'Agostino and Via Castelfidardo), is the **Sephardic synagogue** (*open July–Aug Tues–Fri 5–8*), built in the late 16th century. The prayer room on the first floor has a high barrel vault, decorated with large rose motifs. This is now the only surviving synagogue in Pesaro.

Museo Archeologico

The **Museo Archeologico Oliveriano** (*open July–Aug Mon–Sat 4–7; Sept–June on request; T: 0721 33344*) is housed in the 17th-century Palazzo Almerici. The collection includes pieces found in excavations in Pesaro and at the Picene necropolis of Novilara. Of exceptional interest is the 7th-century BC tombstone from Novilara showing a sea battle fought between a Greek merchant vessel, helped by a Picene craft, and a pirate ship—pirate corpses are being thrown into the sea. On the first floor of the palace is the 18th-century **Biblioteca Oliveriana** (*open Mon–Fri 8.30–1.30 & 2.30–6.45; Sat 8.30–1.30*). It contains one of the oldest maps in the world, the Oliveriana World Map of 1508.

FANO

Fano (pop. 57,400; *map p. 618, C2*) is an attractive seaside town with an important fishing harbour and a colourful old centre.

HISTORY OF FANO

After the Roman victory over the Carthaginians in 207 BC, a votive altar was erected on this spot, dedicated to the goddess Fortuna, and a community grew around it. Vitruvius (1st century BC) erected a basilica on the forum. Destroyed by the Goths during their war against Byzantium in 538, Fano eventually joined Pesaro, Rimini, Senigallia and Ancona in the Maritime Pentapolis. In the 11th century, Fano declared herself an independent commune with allegiance to Venice. The late 12th century saw the rise of two opposing factions: the Guelph del Cassero family, against the Ghibelline da Carignano. Malatestino Malatesta murdered the heirs of both families, and Pope Benedict XI appointing Malatestino governor in 1304. In 1357 Cardinal Albornoz defeated the Malatesta and instituted the Parliament of the Marches at Fano. A constitution was drawn up, but Fano was given back to the Malatesta.

The town suffered heavy damage in the First World War, when it was bombarded from the sea, and again in 1944, both from Allied bombs and during the German retreat, when all the towers and bell-towers were deliberately destroyed.

The cattedrale and Santa Maria Nuova

The main entrance to the old city is the **Arco d'Augusto**, built of sandstone and travertine marble in the year AD 9, as part of the improvements made to the town by the Emperor Augustus. Via Arco d'Augusto corresponds to the Roman decumanus. On the right is the cathedral of Santa Maria Assunta, built in the 12th century to replace the original 10th-century church, and much modified since then. Inside is a magnificent pulpit, supported by four stone lions, made in 1941 from Romanesque elements found in the cathedral; on the back of some of them are pagan designs, indicating they had been recycled at least once before, and that there was probably a Roman temple on or near this spot. The third south chapel, the **Cappella Nolfi**, is richly decorated with frescoes illustrating episodes of the life of Christ and of the Virgin by Domenichino (1618). In the chapel to the right of the presbytery is a canvas by Ludovico Carracci (1613) of the *Virgin in Glory with Saints*.

By taking Via Alavolini behind the cathedral, you reach the church of Santa Maria Nuova (*open 10–12 & 4–6*) in Via de Tonsis, with a magnificent portal (1498). Over the third south altar is a **panel painting by Perugino** (1497) of the *Madonna with Christ Child and Sts Mary Magdalene, Paul, Peter, Francis and John the Baptist*, with a *Pietà* in the cimasa, where some scholars see the hand of Raphael (who was an apprentice in Perugino's *bottega*). The first north altar is surmounted by a panel painting of the *Visitation*, signed by Giovanni Santi (father of Raphael), while the second north altar has a memorable *Annunciation* by Perugino (1489).

Central Fano

The city centre is **Piazza XX Settembre**, the traditional market-place, with the magnificent terracotta façade of the Gothic **Palazzo del Podestà** (1299) dominating the north side. Once the council chamber, Cardinal Albornoz convened the Parliament of the Marches here in 1357. Next to the palace is the Arco Borgia-Cybo, an imposing Renaissance portal, giving access to the Corte Malatestiana, a lovely courtyard fronted by the **Case dei Malatesti**, once the homes of the powerful Malatesta family, now seat of a bank.

On the opposite side of the courtyard is the entrance to the **Museo Civico e Pinacoteca** (*open 9.30–12.30 & 4–7; Sun 10–1 & 4–7; closed Mon; T: 0721 839098*), housed in the 15th-century Palazzo Malatestiano. Under the portico is a 2nd-century mosaic known as *La pantera*, depicting a man (?Dionysus) riding a leopard. The archaeological collection displays an important group of Roman statues, epigraphs and mosaics, including a marvellous *Neptune on his Chariot* (2nd or early 3rd century). The numismatic section has an exceptional collection of Malatesta medals coined by Matteo de' Pasti (15th century). Among the numerous paintings is a polyptych of the *Madonna of the Rose with Christ Child and Saints*, by Michele Giambono (1420), a sumptuous *Guardian Angel* by Guercino, *David with the Head of Goliath* by Domenichino, and works by more recent artists such as Ettore Tito and Antonio Mancini.

South of Piazza XX Settembre, in Via San Francesco d'Assisi, next to the town hall (once the convent of St Francis, and thought to be by Luigi Vanvitelli), are the **Arche**

Malatestiane (Malatesta tombs), under the portico of the ex-church of San Francesco, brought here from the interior of the church in 1659. On the left is the elaborate tomb of Paola Bianca Malatesta (1398), the so-called 'great lady', first wife of Pandolfo III, whose lovely image can be seen on the lid, surmounted by statues, red marble arches, and a Crucifix, all Venetian workmanship. The tomb of Pandolfo III Malatesta was commissioned by his son Sigismondo in 1460, at least 30 years after his father's death. During recent repairs, Pandolfo's mummified body was found to be still inside.

ENVIRONS OF FANO & PESARO

The Metauro

The River Metauro, which enters the Adriatic just south of Fano, is historically the most important in the Marche; in 207 BC the Carthaginian general Hasdrubal was defeated by the Romans in an epic battle near Serrungarina (trying to interpret the description given by Livy, other historians say near Fermignano, or Montemaggiore, or Orciano), in which Hasdrubal was decapitated, and 56,400 of his troops and their allies were killed, against 8,000 Roman dead; in 271 AD, Roman forces exterminated here a huge, rag-tag army of Germanic tribes. At **Fossombrone**, once the most important trading centre in Italy for silk cocoons, the river is spanned by a stunning bridge, designed in 1780. The town was the birthplace of the Caravaggist painter Giovanni Francesco Guerrieri. From Fossombrone the river is flanked by the Via Flaminia.

Gradara

Gradara (*map p. 618, C1*) is a large, beautifully restored castle, surrounded by ancient olive trees, the setting for one of the most tragic love stories ever told (*see box below*). The castle is particularly attractive when approached from the sea, so that the walls, with their 17 towers, can be fully appreciated.

PAOLO & FRANCESCA

In 1275 Giovanni ('Gianciotto') Malatesta married the beautiful Francesca da Polenta, daughter of Guido da Polenta, lord of Ravenna, by proxy, sending his handsome brother Paolo to sign the marriage contract. Poor Francesca was horrified to discover that she had married a bad-natured and exceedingly ugly man. When Gianciotto was sent to Pesaro as governor, he closed his wife up in the fortress of Gradara, where the gallant Paolo kept her company, reading to her from romantic books. The two fell madly in love. One night Gianciotto returned to Gradara without warning, and caught them together—Paolo tried to escape, but his cloak caught on a nail (the guide will show you this), and the two lovers were stabbed to death by the outraged cuckold. The story has inspired many writers, poets, composers and painters, from Dante and Boccaccio to Byron and Ingres.

The castle was first built in 1150; in the 14th century the Malatesta enlarged it, surrounded it with a double defensive wall, and frescoed the salons. In 1464 it was taken by the Sforza, who gave it a Renaissance aspect, with an imposing stairway and a loggia. Lucrezia Borgia lived here for three of the five years of her marriage (1493–97) to Giovanni Sforza. In 1513 Francesco Maria della Rovere took Gradara, on behalf of the pope. On his death the castle reverted to the Papal States, and was practically abandoned. Ransacked by Napoleon's troops in the early 19th century, an earthquake in 1916 almost completely destroyed it. It was purchased as a private dwelling in 1920 by a wealthy engineer, who dedicated the rest of his life to restoring it. On the death of his widow in 1983, Gradara was donated to the Italian government.

Entrance to the town is through the only gate, Porta dell'Orologio—it is possible to walk along on top of the walls, for the entire length, from here (*open 9–1 & 2–7; also 8–midnight from 15 June–30 Sept; T: 0541 964115*), opening onto the steep main street, with medieval houses on either side. Another set of walls separates the township from the **Rocca** (*open 8.30–7; late closing Sat from 15 June–15 Sept; T: 0541 964181*), with a series of rooms decorated with paintings and frescoes. Among the most interesting are Lucrezia Borgia's room and Francesca's room. From the walls there is a splendid view over the surrounding countryside and the promontory of Gabicce.

Gabicce Mare (*map p. 618, C1*) is a small, delightful seaside resort, with a sandy beach, separated from Cattolica (in Emilia Romagna) by the River Tavollo. Just offshore, and now submerged, are the ruins of the Roman port of *Valbruna*.

SAN LEO & THE MONTEFELTRO

The name Montefeltro derives from *Mons Feretrus*, the rock on which San Leo (*map p. 618, B1*) stands, and it refers to a vast area in the northwest of the Marche region, between the Adriatic and the central Apennines; very hilly, and with several enormous limestone outcrops with castles on the top of them—of which San Leo is one—rising sharply and dramatically from among their more modest brethren. This characteristic landscape is the result of ancient subterranean upheaval, which forced to the surface a great plaque of limestone, the bed of a primeval sea, fracturing and tormenting it in the process.

Palazzo Municipale

Entering the town through the south gate, which is the only access, you reach Piazza Dante; on the left is the **Palazzo Municipale** (16th century), once the residence of the Montefeltro counts and of the dukes of Urbino; next to it is a beautiful church, the oldest in the town, the **Pieve** or Basilica (*open 9–1 & 3–6*), perhaps built in the 8th century, and modified in the 11th. Inside are some columns and capitals from Imperial Roman temples. In the presbytery, which is raised over the crypt, is a 9th-century ciborium supported by slender columns with medieval capitals. At the beginning of the south aisle is a narrow stair leading to an underground chamber, said to be the first church, founded here by St Leo in the 4th century. Further along, on the right, is Palazzo Nardini, where St Francis of Assisi stayed in 1213.

On the same square is the Palazzo Mediceo (1521), housing the **Museo di Arte Sacra** (*open 9–6; Aug 9–8.30; T: 0541 916306*), a collection of works of art from local churches, including a panel painting by Luca Frosino of the *Madonna and Child with Sts Leo and Marinus* (1487), and a *Deposition of Christ* by Guercino.

HISTORY OF SAN LEO & THE MONTEFELTRO

The wild character of this area made it attractive for prehistoric populations seeking the security of isolation, and they left many traces of their passage. Later came the Romans, who built a road through the mountains to Rimini. Then came the monastic communities of the early Middle Ages, followed by the powerful families who alternated in controlling this part of the region: the Montefeltro, the Malatesta, the della Rovere, and the grand dukes of Tuscany, who built the lonely fortresses and the magnificent castles. San Leo was once a rock worshipped as sacred by the primitive people of the area. It was chosen as a place of refuge by the runaway Christian Dalmatian slave St Leo, companion of St Marinus (after whom the republic of San Marino is named), in the late 3rd century. From here Christianity spread rapidly, and soon Montefeltro (the old name of the town) became an important diocese. The impregnable rock also made it an important military base; in 962 Berengarius II even declared it to be the capital of the Kingdom of Italy, and it was consequently besieged for months by Emperor Otto I. Later it became a key position during the struggles between Guelphs and Ghibellines. In the 13th century the counts of Montefeltro appeared—as dukes of Urbino, they would play a fundamental role in bringing the Renaissance to central Italy. With their extinction in 1631, San Leo passed to the Papal States, and its castle became a prison—the popes' preferred 'high security jail'. Among the famous visitors to San Leo are Dante (who commented on the stiff climb up), and St Francis of Assisi. In fact, in 1213 St Francis received here, as a gift from Count Orlando of Chiusi, the mountain of Verna, where he would build his convent (*see p. 386*).

The duomo

The duomo (12th century) is in the highest part of the town, built entirely of mellow ivory sandstone, with graceful apses decorated with little blind arches, lancet and double-lancet windows, revealing Lombard influence. The interior is solemn, a central nave and two side aisles, divided by pilasters; the date of construction (1173) is carved on the fourth south one. There are also two Roman columns, with 3rd-century capitals. Under the presbytery is the crypt, with the lid of St Leo's sarcophagus. At the back of the cathedral is the isolated, superb 12th-century bell-tower (*open 10–12*

& 3–7), 32m high, and a good viewpoint for the famous panorama over the Marecchia valley and the Marche, and to San Marino, Romagna, and sometimes even the mountains of Dalmatia. Between the bell-tower and the cathedral you will find a mysterious rectangular hole carved into the rock; it could be a prehistoric altar, or (when filled with water) an astronomical observatory; it may have been used as a baptismal pool by early Christians.

Federico da Montefeltro (1422–82)

A warrior who became a prince, Federico was born in Gubbio in 1422, the illegitimate son of Count Guidantonio of Montefeltro and Urbino. When he was five his father had a legitimate son, Oddantonio; to protect him from his stepmother, he was betrothed to Gentile Brancaleoni (aged 10), and sent to live with his future parents-in-law. It was an excellent turn of events for Federico. He was encouraged to study and to travel, and spent long periods in Venice, Mantua and other cities, learning the arts of diplomacy together with an appreciation of literature, painting, architecture and music. At the age of 16 he married Gentile and went to Milan to learn the art of soldiery. He soon became the *condottiere* of the Visconti, earning himself considerable respect—especially when he captured the Malatesta stronghold of San Leo in 1441, thought to be invulnerable. Even after becoming lord of Urbino and Montefeltro in 1444, when Oddantonio was assassinated, he never gave up his military campaigning on behalf of the great powers of the day—the Visconti, Francesco Sforza, the pope, Venice, the King of Aragon and Florence. In 1460, having lost his first wife, he married the 13-year-old Battista Sforza, a girl of character and learning. She convinced Federico to turn Urbino into a unique 'ideal city', where the palace became a meeting point for artists and intellectuals, and gave him six daughters, one after the other. At last, in 1472, she produced the much-desired son, Guidubaldo. She died not very long after; her distraught husband mourned her for the rest of his life. Their diptych portrait by Piero della Francesca hangs in the Uffizi (*see p. 282*).

The Rocca

The fort of San Leo or Rocca (*open 9–6; Aug 9–8.30; T: 0541 916302*), thought by many to be the most beautiful castle in Italy, is reached by taking Via Leopardi to the right, just after the south gate. It owes its present aspect to Francesco di Giorgio Martini, architect to Federico da Montefeltro, who adapted a medieval fortress (probably originally Roman); he devised the immense cylindrical towers, and the triangular fortification at one end, like the prow of a ship, ideal protection against cannon fire. In the castle is the **Museo della Città** (*open as above; T: 0541 916233*), with a collection covering the 3rd century BC to 1866, with particular information on Berengarius II, Otto I, St Francis, Dante, and the Montefeltro family. There is also an art gallery with old masters and contemporary paintings, and a section with pottery and furniture.

THE MARECCHIA VALLEY

Talamello and Maiolo

Talamello (*map p. 618, A1*) is opposite San Leo on the other side of the Marecchia, on a crest of Mt Aquilone, and protected by the high peak of Mt Pincio. The name of this delightful little town derives from *thalamos*, Greek for 'secluded room', a reference to the numerous caves carved into the limestone tufa. In the central Piazza Garibaldi, with its lovely fountain, is the church of San Lorenzo (17th century), with a remarkable painted wooden Crucifix (14th century), said to be the work of Giotto. It attracts many pilgrims.

The Museo Gualtieri in Piazza Saffi (*open April–Oct Wed–Sun 10.30–12.30 & 3.30–7; winter Sun and holidays only; T: 0541 920036; www.gualtierimuseum.com*) has a collection of paintings by the local artist Fernando Gualtieri (b. 1919), who now lives in Paris.

Southeast of Talamello is the conical hill of Maiolo (624m), with the ruins of a castle perched dramatically on the top, and the houses of the village of Maioletto on the steep hillside; the town of Maiolo on the northern slope was carried away by a landslide in 1700, and now the town centre is at nearby **Serra di Maiolo**. For centuries Maiolo was a rival to San Leo, and was bitterly contested by the Malatesta and the Montefeltro. This town is among the 21 places in Italy said to prepare the best bread: 50 wood-fired stone ovens are still in use—about one for every 12 inhabitants, but only about 10 are lit every day.

Sant'Agata Feltria

Under the imposing Monte Ercole (937m), sacred in the past to Hercules, is Sant'Agata Feltria (*map p. 618, A1*), instantly recognisable by its picturesque castle. Once inhabited by Umbrian tribes, then a Roman settlement in 206 BC, it became an important medieval fortress belonging to the Malatesta and the Montefeltro families. Just south of the town is the convent church of **San Girolamo**, built in 1568, with a superb *Madonna with Sts Jerome and Christina* by Pietro da Cortona (1640) over the main altar. In the central Piazza Garibaldi is the Palazzone, which encloses the oldest opera house in the region (and one of the oldest in Italy; 1660), **Teatro Mariani** (*T: 0541 929613*), still in regular use, built of wood, and exquisitely decorated. The castle (10th and 15th centuries; Francesco di Giorgio Martini), high on the rock, contains the civic museum, with some interesting collections: manuscripts dating from the 15th–19th centuries, antique furniture, 16th-century frescoes, and displays describing alchemy and tailoring.

Casteldelci

Casteldelci (*map p. 618, A1*), immersed in the forest, on the mountainside not far from the source of the Tiber, overlooks the Senatello stream, full of trout. This fortress-town was originally built for the bishops of the Montefeltro. In the course of time it passed to Cesare Borgia, Lorenzo de' Medici, and finally, in 1522, to the dukes of Urbino. A story is told here of Count Rapaché, paladin of Charlemagne, who once raped all the virgins in the village, an act which has never been forgotten; the local people still use the word *rapasceto* to indicate a disaster. In an old house in the centre is the Casa-Museo (*to request a visit, T: 0541 915423*), with a collection of archaeological finds. In the church of Santa Maria in Sasseto are some frescoes of the School of Rimini. There is a Roman bridge over the Senatello, and several tiny, enchanting hamlets in the surrounding woods, such as Campo, Gattara and Senatello.

BLACK DEATH & THE SCHOOL OF RIMINI

To this day very little is known about the identity of the artists who formed the so-called School of Rimini in the early 14th century. The foundation took place after a visit to Rimini by the great Florentine painter Giotto, who had been summoned there by the Malatesta, to decorate the church of St Francis. The school must have been quite numerous; its artists were soon carrying out commissions over a large area, spreading their fame and reputation. Apart from Giovanni, Giuliano and Pietro, who all signed themselves 'da Rimini', and Giovanni Baronzio, the other painters and their numerous apprentices remain frustratingly anonymous. Apparently not one was still living after 1348, when the Black Death swept through Europe, and a new theory suggests they all died in the epidemic, just as the artists of the Sienese school (notably the Lorenzetti brothers) are thought to have done. A ship arrived in Messina (Sicily) in 1347, on which everyone was dead; by 1348 the disease had reached Iceland, after killing 20 million Europeans (a third of the population), and about 75 million people worldwide. Highly pernicious, very few of the infected survived to tell the tale. A new theory suggests that bubonic plague alone was not responsible for the tragedy; plague requires rats (whose fleas bite humans after abandoning their infected hosts) and quite a long incubation period. The Black Death moved too fast, killing rapidly even in Iceland, where there were no rats at the time. Scientists have suggested instead that the outbreak might have been pulmonary anthrax, or a form of the Ebola virus (though it is also possible that the diseases were moving together).

PRACTICAL INFORMATION

GETTING AROUND

• **By air:** Rimini (25km; www.riminiairport.com), Ancona (45km; www.ancona-airport.com) and Forlì (60km; www.forli-airport.com) airports serve this area with connections for Pesaro and Gabicce Mare.
• **By car:** Useful car parks in **Urbino** are at Borgo Mercatale and outside Porta San Bartolo.

662 URBINO & THE NORTHERN MARCHE

• **By train:** Fano, Gabicce Mare (Cattolica) and **Pesaro** stations are on the main Milan–Bologna–Pescara line. Bus connections for Urbino, Urbania and Gradara are run by AMIBUS (www.amibus.it) and by SOGET.

• **By bus:** Autolinee Bucci (www.autolineebucci) has services connecting Urbino, Urbania, Fermignano, Pesaro, Fano and also Sansepolcro and Rome. Autolinee Reni (www.anconarenibus.it) runs services connecting Fano, Senigallia and Ancona. Autolinee Vitali (www.vitaliautolinee.it) links Pesaro and Fano to Ancona, Jesi and Pergola. SITA (www.sitabus.it) connects Arezzo and Sansepolcro with the Montefeltro. Salvatori connects Pesaro with most of the small towns of the Montefeltro. **Pesaro** central bus station is in Piazzale Matteotti. **Urbino** bus station is at Borgo Mercatale with a left-luggage service 8–8.

• **By sea: Pesaro** port runs summer daily excursions to Cattolica-Gabbice.

INFORMATION OFFICES

Fano Via Battisti 10, T: 0721 803534, www.turismofano.com
Fermignano Corso Bramante 3, T: 0722 330523.
Gradara Piazza V Novembre 1, T: 0541 964115, www.gradara.org
Pesaro Viale Trieste 164, T: 0721 69341, www.turismo.pesarourbino.it
San Leo Piazza Dante, T: 0541 916306.
Urbania Corso Vittorio Emanueler 21, T: 0722 313140.
Urbino Via Puccinotti 35, T: 0722 2613. It is possible to buy a combined ticket for all Urbino's museums.

HOTELS

Acqualagna (map p. 618, B2)
€ **Antico Furlo**. Five kilometres north of Acqualagna is an historic hotel (the oldest in the Marche) with an excellent restaurant. *Via Furlo 60, T: 0721 700096, www.anticofurlo.it. 6 rooms.*
Cagli (map p. 618, B3)
€€ **International Cagli**. In a lovely position, surrounded by woods on the outskirts of Cagli, good restaurant. *Strada Civita 5, T: 0721 782999, www.internationalcaglihotel.it. 22 rooms.*
Fano (map p. 618, C2)
€€€ **Castello Monte Giove**. Beautiful 19th-century country villa 4km from the centre, with large park, pool, golf course, restaurant and lovingly restored rooms and suites. Luxurious accommodation for those who want to spoil themselves. *Via Foscolo 28, T: 0721 864123, www.castellomontegiove.it. 21 rooms.*
€€ **Relais Villa Giulia**. ■ Panoramic villa set in luxuriant gardens, 3km from Fano railway station on the road to Pesaro, built for Eugène de Beauharnais, Napoleon's stepson, now belonging to Count and Countess Passi. Bed & breakfast or self-catering accommodation. *Via di Villa Giulia, T: 0721 823159, www.relaisvillagiulia.com.*
€€ **Spiaggia d'Oro**. On a particularly nice stretch of beach at Marotta di Fano, comfortable, with good restaurant. *Via Faà di Bruno 54, Marotta di Fano, T: 0721 96619, www.hotelspiaggiadoro.it. 40 rooms.*
€ **Amelia**. Small hotel in central position, with restaurant, run by the same family for over 50 years. *Viale Cairoli 80, T: 0721 824040, www.hotelamelia.it. 24 rooms.*

€ **Augustus**. Very pleasant hotel at Porta Giulia, with restaurant, gym and sauna. *Via Puccini 2, T: 0721 809781, www.hotelaugustus.it. 22 rooms.*

Fermignano (*map p. 618, B2*)
€€ **Serra Alta**. Panoramic position on a beautiful wooded hill overlooking the town, the hotel has comfortable rooms, pool, restaurant, pizzeria and car park. *Via Serra Alta 28, T: 0722 332525, www.serraalta.it. 13 rooms.*

Gabicce Mare (*map p. 618, C1*)
€€ **Posillipo**. ■ Charming old hotel in panoramic hillside position; garden, pool and excellent restaurant. Minimum 3-day stay. *Via Dell'Orizzonte 1, Gabicce Monte, T: 0541 953373, www.hotelposillipo.com. 35 rooms.*

Gradara (*map p. 618, C1*)
€ **Agricola della Serra**. Three kilometres west of Gradara, the farm raises animals and grows fruit and vegetables, cereals, olives and vineyards; strictly organic. Guests can help. Particularly good restaurant with home-made bread cooked in the wood-fired oven; cosy rooms. English spoken. *Via Serra 6/8, T: 0541 969856, www.agriturismogradara.it. 8 rooms.*

Pesaro (*map p. 618, C1*)
€€ **Des Bains**. ■ An elegant hotel with a good position close to sea and town centre. Restaurant. Parking available. *Viale Trieste 221, T: 0721 34957, www.innitalia.com. 70 rooms.*
€€ **Vittoria**. Romantic Art Nouveau building near the sea, with pool, renowned restaurant, garden, gym and car park. Previous guests range from Pirandello to Sting. *Via Vespucci 2, T: 0721 34343, www.viphotels.it. 28 rooms.*

Piobbico (*map p. 618, B2*)
€ **Vocabolo Ca' Bernardo**. Very comfortable house in the country c. 3km from Piobbico. *Via Ca' Bernardo 62/a, Località Piano, T: 0721 861333.*

San Leo (*map p. 618, B1*)
€ **Castello**. Small, family-run hotel on the main square with a restaurant in the old palace. *Piazza Dante 11/12, T: 0541 916214, www.hotelristorantecastello sanleo.com. 14 rooms.*
€ **La Rocca**. Comfortable inn with an excellent restaurant. *Via Leopardi 16, T: 0541 916241.*

Sant'Agata Feltria (*map p. 618, A1*)
€ **Borgo del Sole e della Luna**. Old house in a beautiful panoramic hamlet 3km from Sant'Agata towards Pennabilli. *Via Petrella Guidi 22, T: 0541 929814, www.borgodelsoleedellaluna.com. 1 apartment, 1 room.*

Sant'Angelo in Vado (*map p. 618, A2*)
€€ **Palazzo Baldani**. ■ Small hotel with excellent restaurant in an 18th-century palace in the historic centre. Elegantly furnished, gym and sauna. *Via Mancini 4, T: 0722 810101, www.palazzobaldani.it. 13 rooms.*

Serrungarina (*map p. 618, C2*)
€ **Casa Oliva**. ■ Beautiful little hotel entirely occupying a tiny medieval village. Excellent restaurant. *Via Castello 19, T: 0721 891500, www.casaoliva.it. 15 rooms.*

Urbania (*map p. 618, B2*)
€ **Mulino della Ricavata**. Ancient watermill and farm producing flowers for drying, vegetables and poultry; antique furniture, cooking courses. In a very peaceful position on the River Metauro, c. 2km from the centre, which once carried gold; interesting local food. Closed Jan–Feb. *Via Porta Celle 5, T: 0722 310326, www.mulinodellaricavata.com. 4 rooms.*

Urbino (*map p. 618, B2*)
€€ **Raffaello**. Comfortable little hotel in

the heart of the old city, with nice big beds. Shuttle-bus service to the car parks. *Vicolino Santa Margherita 40, T: 0722 4784, www.albergoraffaello.com. 14 rooms.*

€€ **San Domenico.** ■ Excellent position in front of Palazzo Ducale for this luxurious hotel in what was an old convent; you have breakfast in the cloister. *Piazza Rinascimento 3, T: 0722 2626, www.viphotels.it. 31 rooms.*

€ **Locanda La Brombolona.** ■ In a tiny village c. 6km from Urbino, with views over the city, a delightful inn situated in an ex-church; the friendly atmosphere and the marvellous home cooking make it a good choice. *Via Sant'Andrea in Primicilio 22, Località Canavaccio, T: 0722 53501. 12 rooms.*

RESTAURANTS

Acqualagna (*map p. 618, B2*)
€€€ **Antico Furlo.** ■ Mussolini loved this restaurant, where he always made a point of stopping, and cooking his own tagliatelle, followed by 12-egg omelettes with truffles. Nowadays, chef Alberto Melagrana prepares exquisite dishes using the local ingredients, including the world-famous truffles; the wine cellar (ask to see it) is a delight. 5km north of Acqualagna on the road to Fossombrone. Closed Mon evening. *Via Furlo 60, T: 0721 700096.*
Fano (*map p. 618, C2*)
€€ **Da Maria Ponte Rosso.** ■ Tiny *trattoria* where Maria serves only the fish brought to her daily by a local fisherman. Always crowded, book at least the day before. Try her delicate fish soup called *passatelli con brodo di pesce*, or the tagliatelle with sole. Simple desserts, all home-made, sponge cake

or jam tarts. Closed Sun in winter. *Via IV Novembre 86, T: 0721 808962.*
€€ **Ristorantino Da Giulio.** ■ Giulio is a fantastic cook; try his fresh sardines baked in the oven, or the delicious, spicy *guazzetto* fish soup (without tomato), tasty pasta and risotto, grilled fish. The desserts are superb; good local wines. Closed Tues. *Viale Adriatico 100, T: 0721 805680.*
€ **Al Pesce Azzurro.** A self-service restaurant run by fishermen; enormous so no need to book. Brown paper tablecloths, plastic cutlery, sublime food; fish soup and pasta, seafood salad and risotto, clams and mussels and lots of *pesce azzurro*, mackerel, sardines and anchovies; also cuttle-fish, all served with Bianchello del Metauro, and you finish up with a cup of *moretta*. Great fun. Closed Mon and Oct–April. *Viale Adriatico 48/a, T: 0721 803165.*
Gradara (*map p. 618, C1*)
€€ **Al Soldato di Ventura.** Old town restaurant, serving local dishes, both seafood and meat; the *tagliolini all'astice* (noodles with spiny lobster) are especially good. *Via IX Settembre 1, T: 0541 969810.*
€€ **Osteria La Botte.** A tavern and a restaurant combined, in the heart of the old town; snacks and a glass of wine, or a full meal—try the interesting combinations of pasta or ravioli with pit-matured cheese and chocolate. Closed Wed in winter. *Piazza V Novembre 11, T: 0541 964404.*
Pesaro (*map p. 618, C1*)
€€€ **Al Molo da Peppe.** Definitely for special occasions, the restaurant stands on stilts in the water, near the eastern pier; simple but beautifully prepared dishes, good choice of wines. Closed

Sun lunchtime in summer, Mon in winter. *Calata Caio Duilio, T: 0721 400395.*

€ **Osteria di Pinocchio**. Typical, central tavern serving delicious simple food. Closed lunchtime Sat and Sun. *Piazza Antaldi 12, T: 0721 34771.*

San Leo (*map p. 618, B1*)

€ **Il Bettolino**. ■ Friendly coffee bar and restaurant, also serving pizza in the evening; try the delicious ravioli with *formaggio di fossa* (pit-matured cheese), followed by *tagliata con lardo di Colonnata*, an unusual beef salad with pit-matured lard (scrumptious). They also make their own mascarpone. Closed Wed. *Via Montefeltro 4, T: 0541 916265.*

Sant'Agata Feltria (*map p. 618, A1*)

€€ **Trattoria Bossari**. Charming tavern where pensioners spend the afternoon playing cards; wonderful pasta; try *lombo al vapore*, steam-cooked pork which melts in the mouth, served with *funghi* and truffles. Closed Mon. *Via San Girolamo 2, T: 0541 929697.*

Urbania (*map p. 618, B2*)

€€ **Osteria del Cucco**. ■ Old tavern, no menu, brown paper tablecloths, marvellous food prepared with care by Donatella. Closed Sun evenings and Mon. *Via Betto dei Medici 9, T: 0722 317412.*

Urbino (*map p. 618, B2*)

€ **Buca San Francesco**. In the centre, home-made pasta, local wines, good value for money. *Piazzetta Feretrano 3, T: 0549 991462.*

LOCAL SPECIALITIES

Fano The fishermen's coffee called *moretta*, invented to keep themselves warm on chilly winter mornings, is unique. It is a stiff brew consisting of hot, sweet espresso, anisette liqueur, rum, brandy and lemon peel.

Sant'Angelo in Vado and **Acqualagna** are renowned for their truffles. In Oct and Nov the truffle-hunters can be seen sitting around in the coffee bars, showing off their finds—and their dogs.

Talamello is known for its pit-matured cheese, *Ambra di Talamello*.

Urbania is famed for ceramics in the traditional tin-glazed Casteldurante style.

FESTIVALS & EVENTS

Fano Carnival, Parade of enormous *papier-mâché* satirical figures and a 'Battle of the Sweets', which are thrown at the participants, Feb.

Fermignano *Palio della Rana*, To celebrate their independence from Urbino, declared in 1607, a race between representatives of the seven city districts, each with a frog in a wheelbarrow; the point is to reach the finish with the frog still there, first Sun after Easter.

Maiolo *Festa del Pane*, Bread festival, last weekend in June.

Pesaro *Mostra del Nuovo Cinema*, Film festival, www.pesarofilmfest.it, end June–July; *ROF—Rossini Opera Festival*, www.rossinioperafestival.it, Aug.

Talamello *Festa del Crocifisso di Giotto*, Perhaps the oldest and the most important celebration of the Montefeltro, Whit Monday; *Fiera del Formaggio di Fossa*, The famous cheese pits are opened among celebrations and gastronomic delights, first two Suns in Nov.

Urbania *La Befana*, Epiphany festival, 6 Jan.

Urbino *La Festa del Duca*, Tourney with jousting, costumes and horses, third Sun in Aug.

ASCOLI PICENO
& THE SOUTHERN MARCHE

One of Italy's loveliest cities, Ascoli Piceno (pop. 53,000; *map p. 619, C6*) lies in the extreme south of the Marche region, close to the border with Abruzzo, where the Castellano stream joins the River Tronto. The city is not visible from a great distance; you come across it suddenly, after a fold in the hills. Breathtaking, with a skyline positively bristling with towers, steeples and spires, Ascoli Piceno exceeds every expectation.

HISTORY OF ASCOLI PICENO

The strategic position at the confluence of two rivers, and the easy passage from the mountains to the sea, made this from the 9th century BC the most important centre of the Picenes. In 286 BC it was captured by the Romans, together with all the surrounding Picene territory, and named *Asculum*. In 578 it was taken by the Lombards and became part of the Duchy of Spoleto; then in 774 the city was donated to the Church. During the 9th century Asculum was attacked twice by the Muslims. In 1185 the city declared itself an independent commune; this was followed by a long period of financial prosperity and artistic vitality, which lasted throughout the Renaissance. In the Middle Ages Ascoli was called *Città turrita*—city of towers—because there were 200 of them, some even 40m high, though in 1242 Frederick II of Hohenstaufen destroyed 91. About 70 towers can still be traced in the fabric of the town, many of them in good condition. In 1799 Ascoli was invaded by the French, reverting to the Papal States in 1815. With the Unification of Italy in 1861, it became a provincial capital.

The duomo and baptistery

Piazza Arringo (or Arengo) stands on the site of the Roman forum, and throughout the Middle Ages it was the place for public meetings, hence the name, which translates as 'harangue'. To the east stands the austere **Duomo di Sant'Emidio**, with an unfinished façade (1529) by Cola dell'Amatrice. It is dedicated to St Emygdius of Trier, first bishop and patron saint of the city. Martyred in 303, his remains are kept in a Roman sarcophagus in the ornate crypt. Opening off the south aisle is the Chapel of the Sacrament (1798); the altarpiece is a masterpiece by Carlo Crivelli, the **Polyptych of St Emygdius**, or the *Madonna Enthroned with Christ Child and Saints* (1473), in a beautiful Gothic frame made in the artist's own workshop. Notice the characteristic Crivelli fruits and vegetables above the Madonna, each with a different symbolic meaning.

To the left of the cathedral, in an isolated position, stands the unusual **Baptistery** (4th century, rebuilt 12th century; *open after 3.30pm*), an octagonal construction on a square base, with a loggia on the top with three arches on each side (the rear has four) and a

St Catherine; detail from the Polyptych of St Emygdius by Carlo Crivelli (1473).

round dome. The symbolism of the numbers is deliberate; three for the Trinity, four for humanity, eight for resurrection and eternity achieved through baptism, and a circular dome representing perfection. Traces of the original baptismal pool can be seen inside, together with the more recent font, which stands on a 14th-century spiral column. It is thought that the building was originally the Temple of Mars.

Piazza Arringo museums

Close to the duomo stands the Palazzo dell'Episcopio, the Bishop's Palace, consisting of three different constructions built between the 15th and 18th centuries, housing the **Museo Diocesano** (*open daily 10–1; T: 0736 252883*), a rich collection of sacred art from churches and monasteries of the area. The paintings include works by Carlo Crivelli, Cola dell'Amatrice, Pietro Alemanno and Ludovico Trasi.

Next to the Bishop's Palace is the long façade of the Palazzo Comunale or Palazzo dell'Arengo, decorated with carved stone caryatids and telamones. It houses the magnificent **Pinacoteca Civica** (*open 9–1 & 3–7; T: 0736 298213*), with one of the most important collections of paintings and sculptures in the region. One of the most interesting rooms is the *Sala del Piviale*, on the first floor, where paintings by Carlo Crivelli and his follower Pietro Alemanno have been arranged together with the *piviale* itself, the cope of Pope Nicholas IV. Pope Nicholas (Girolamo da Lisciano), was a native of Ascoli. The cope is thought to have been made in England between 1266–68, and is embroidered with a series of roundels representing saints, popes, Doctors of the Church, the Crucifixion and the Madonna with the Child, worked with coloured silk and gold threads on thick, heavy silk, still in excellent condition. Tiny semi-precious stones and seed pearls form the outlines. The robe was originally encrusted with larger precious stones and pearls, which were removed and sold to pay for the construction of the Chapel of the Sacrament in the cathedral in 1798. In 1902 the cope was stolen, and reappeared two years later, in an exhibition held at London's South Kensington Museum (now the Victoria & Albert) as a loan from the American mil-

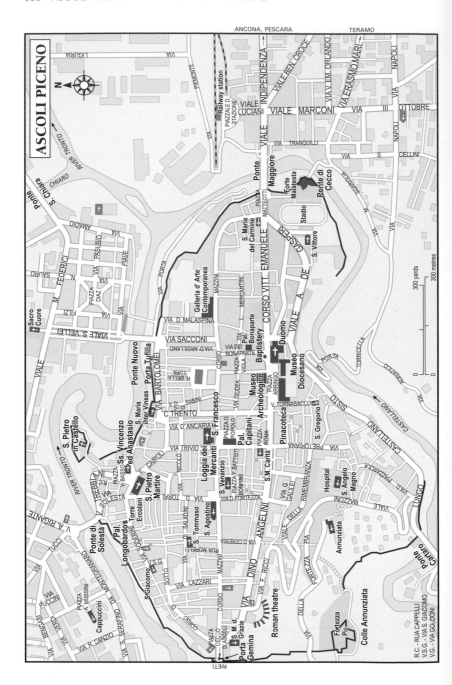

ASCOLI PICENO

N

ANCONA, PESCARA   TERAMO

RIVER TRONTO

S. Chiara

Ponte

Railway station

PIAZZALE D. STAZIONE

VIA LIGURIA

VIA PIEMONTE

VIALE INDIPENDENZA

VIALE BEN CROCE

VIA V. EM. ORLANDO

VIA V. ERASMO MARI

VIA NAPOLI

VIALE LUCIANI

VIALE MARCONI

VIA III OTTOBRE

VIA TRANQUILLI

VIA

VIA S. CELLINI

NAPOLI

Ponte Maggiore

Forte Malatesta

Ponte di Cecco

Stadio

PIAZZA MATTEOTTI

S. Maria del Carmine

VIA MERCANTINI

VIA MAZZINI

VIALE DE GASPERI

S. Vittore

Galleria d' Arte Contemporanea

VIA D. MALASPINA

VIA SACCONI

VIA D'ARGILLANO

CORSO

VIA DEI BONAPARTE

PIAZZA VIOLA

Pal. Bonaparte

Baptistery

Duomo

Museo Diocesano

PORTA

VIA TORRICELLA

CORSO VITT. EMANUELE

VIALE A. DE

VIA D. LUPA

PIAZZA SABINI

V. D.

Museo Archeologico

PIAZZA ARRINGO

VIA V. TORNASACCO

VIA ADRIATICO

Sacro Cuore

VIA S. VELLEI

VIALE

VIA AMADIO

VIA PASUBIO

VIA PIAVE

VIA FILZI

PIAZZA DIAZ

VIA FEDERICI

VIA M.

VIA SAURO

Ponte Nuovo

Porta Tufilla

VIA BARTOLOMEI

S. Maria inter Vineas

C. TRENTO

V. D. SABINI

S. Francesco

VIA GIUDEA

PIAZZA D. POPOLO

Pal. Capitani

PIAZZA ROMA

Pinacoteca

S. Gregorio

VIA PRETORIANA

VIA SISTO

VIA CASTELLANO

VIA CASTELLANO

S. Pietro in Castello

VIA D'ANCARIA

VIA TRIVIO

VIA NICOLO

Loggia dei Mercanti

S. Venanzio

PIAZZA V. BATTISTI

BONFINE

S.M. Carità

VIA G. GALLEI

Hospital

S. Angelo Magno

RIVER TRONTO

S. Pietro in Castello

Ss. Vincenzo ed Anastasio

V. BASSO

S. Pietro Martire

VIA CAIROLI

VIA D. TORRI

S. Agostino

VIA D. FORTEZZA

VIA G.

VIA DELLA RIMEMBRANZA

VIALE MAZZONI

Annunziata

V. A. RIGANTE

PIAZZA V. SOLESTA

Ponte di Solesta

Pal. Longobardo

Torre Ercolani

S. Tommaso

RUA MORELLI

VIA D CEREALE

VIA D. CEREALE

VIA DINO ANGELINI

VIALE DELLA PIA

LUNGO

Ponte Cartaro

VIA TUCCI

VIA SODERINI

S. Giacomo

V.S.G.

MAZZINI

CORSO

VIA LAZZARI

VIA F. RICCI

Roman theatre

VIA DELLA FORTEZZA

PIA

Fortezza Pia

Colle Annunziata

VIA PUCCINI

VIA VERDI

PIAZZA A. MUSSINI

Cappuccini

VIA BENGASI

VIA R. SANZIO

VIA S. SERAFINO DA

VIA S. GIACOMO

PIAZZA CECCO D. ASCOLI

S M. d. Grazie

Porta Gemina

R.C. - RUA CAPPELLI
V.S.G. - VIA S. GIACOMO
V.G. - VIA GOLDONI

300 yards

300 metres

lionaire J. Pierpont Morgan, who had bought it in Paris. The cope was recognised, and Morgan was obliged to return it to the Italian authorities.

Opposite the Pinacoteca is the **Museo Archeologico** (*open 8.30–7.30, closed Mon; T: 0736 253562*), with objects from the Bronze and Iron Ages with the Picene culture, through Roman domination to the arrival of the Lombards. An interesting exhibit is a funerary stele from Castignano with an inscription in the Picene language, written in the boustrophedon manner (where the lines read alternately left-to-right and right-to-left), containing the warning of a son not to violate the tomb of his parents. Some of the objects—gold and amber jewellery, ornamental plaques and fibulae—come from the nearby Lombard necropolis of Castel Trosino.

Piazza del Popolo

The square owes its present aspect to renovations carried out in the early 16th century, when all the shopkeepers were obliged to contribute to the construction of the arcade according to the dimensions of their shopfronts—which is why the arches surrounding most of the square are of different widths. The west side is dominated by the **Palazzo dei Capitani** (*open 9–1 & 4–7.30*), former residence of the *capitano del popolo*. First built in the 13th century, the palace was modified by Cola dell'Amatrice after 1520, and further modified many times after that. The tower, however, is still the original 13th-century one, and the massive portal with the monument to Pope Paul III is of 1549, with a wide arch on either side. The impressive façade includes a clock, added in 1543, and four statues representing the Virtues (1549), a token of the city's gratitude to Cardinal Alessandro Farnese, who as papal legate had obtained several concessions for Ascoli from his uncle, Pope Paul III. The courtyard is Renaissance in style, with a portico surmounted by a loggia. The building was seat of the *comune* from 1400 to 1564, then the residence of the governors and the papal legates. To the left of the Palazzo dei Capitani is one of the historic cafés of Italy, the **Caffè Meletti**, founded in 1907 and famous for its *anisetta* liqueur, made on the premises.

On the north side rises the church of **San Francesco**. Construction began in the 12th century, but was not completed until some 300 years later, so the lower five metres of the building are Romanesque, while the upper part is Gothic. The beautiful Venetian-style main portal, on Via del Trivio, is framed by elaborate, delicate carvings and by slender columns, five on each side, which are all very worn at the same height. In fact, when struck sharply with the palm of the hand they each emit a different musical note; few can resist the temptation to make a little music before going into church. Over the side door, on the square, is the **monument to Pope Julius II**, a member of the influential della Rovere family (*see p. 647*). The rear of the church is particularly theatrical; the magnificent apses appear to be nine instead of seven. The large stone phallus perched up on the balustrade of the second bell-tower is no optical illusion; for the ancient Romans, a large phallus was a symbol of fertility and happiness.

Close to the church is the Loggia dei Mercanti, erected by Cola dell'Amatrice for the influential Wool Corporation in the 16th century. The building still preserves the official measurements for bricks and tiles.

Santi Vincenzo e Anastastio and San Pietro Martire

The church of **Santi Vincenzo e Anastasio** in Piazza Ventidio Basso, is an 11th-century Romanesque construction, amplified in 1389. The façade is divided into 64 rectangles which probably once framed fresco paintings; the statues over the doorway (the *Madonna, St Vincent* and *St Anastasius*) were also originally painted. The interior has a central nave, pertaining to the old church, with two side aisles. Under the building is the 6th-century crypt, with recently restored frescoes.

Opposite is the large church of **San Pietro Martire** (late 13th–early 14th centuries); the left side portal is by Cola dell'Amatrice (1523). The lovely interior, full of golden light, has eight Baroque altars made by a local family, the Giosafatti, in 1674. That of the *Madonna of the Rosary* (fourth south) is very imposing, with different kinds of marble, gilded stucco, and two statues representing *Humility* and *Purity*. There are many paintings in this church by Ludovico Trasi (1634–94), a gifted local artist who studied in Rome with Andrea Sacchi.

Solestà and across the Tronto

From San Pietro Martire the attractive street called Via Solestà, with towers and medieval houses, leads north to Porta Solestà (1230) and the **Ponte di Solestà**, built in the early days of the Roman Empire, when Augustus decided to improve communications with this important city. The remarkable bridge is 62m long, 6.5m wide, 25m high, with a central span of 21m over the Tronto. It is hollow inside, and it is sometimes possible to visit the interior (*ask at the tourist office*). The bridge and the gate are particularly photogenic. There is a beautiful walk along the river, by the city walls, on old cobblestone streets, with enticing glimpses of houses and gardens. Also across the bridge is the little church of San Pietro in Castello, site of an ancient castle, which dominates a curve of the river.

Following Via Berardo Tucci, you reach the **Tempietto di Sant'Emidio Rosso**, a tiny red octagonal church built in 1623 over an ancient chapel containing the stone where St Emygdius was beheaded. Also in this district is the church of San Serafino di Montegranaro and **Convent of the Cappuccini**, founded in the Middle Ages and completely restructured in 1771. It was a Capuchin friar, Giovanni da Teramo, who set up a printing press here in 1477 and printed the first book to be published in Ascoli, *Le Storie di Sant'Isidoro*, and then the city statutes in 1496.

Piazza Sant'Agostino

Right in the centre of the city, the beautiful **Piazza Sant'Agostino** is dominated by the 12th-century twin towers on Via delle Torri, one of which leans noticeably. To the west is the church of **Sant'Agostino** (12th century, successively rebuilt). The simple rectangular façade is enriched by a splendid portal (1547). The altars in the interior are the work of the Giosafatti family. Among the many paintings, over the second south altar, behind a grille, is a lovely panel painting by Francescuccio di Cecco Ghissi of Fabriano (14th century) known as the *Madonna of Peace*. The July jousts are carried out in her honour. The convent now houses the **Galleria d'Arte Contemporanea** (*open 9–1 &*

3–7; closed Mon; T: 0736 248663), dedicated to the abstract painter Osvaldo Licini, who was born at nearby Monte Vidon Corrado. The fine collection includes many works by this artist, who lived in Paris for a while, and frequented the circles of Picasso and Modigliani. Other important contemporary Italian artists represented here include Severini, Fontana, Vedova and Capogrossi. Leading north from the square is the picturesque **Via delle Torri**, along which are some of the most beautiful houses of the city.

Roman Ascoli

Corso Mazzini was once the main street of Roman *Asculum*. It leads to **Porta Gemina**, which was built in the 1st century BC to span the Via Salaria, the Roman salt road which led from the coast to Rome. You can still see traces of the 3rd–2nd-century BC fortifications. Tucked away close by at the foot of the Colle dell'Annunziata hill, along Via Ricci, are the ruins of the **Roman theatre** of Asculum, built towards the end of the 1st century BC and modified in the 2nd century AD. It was pillaged through the centuries for building material, and not much of what remains has yet been brought to light, so there is little to see, although excavations are in progress.

Rua Morelli is a narrow little turning off Corso Mazzini, on the right if you are coming west from Piazza Sant'Agostino. After the arch is the old church of **San Tommaso**, built in 1064 using material from the Roman amphitheatre, which stood in front. The façade is modern, but the bell-tower, unfinished, is still the original. The cloister houses the Museo dell'Arte Ceramica (*open 9–1 & 3–7; closed Mon; T: 0736 240290*), with good examples of the decorative local ceramics; it is planned to open some ateliers here, to show the craftsmen at work.

The church of **San Gregorio**, on the other side of town, was once a Roman temple, perhaps dedicated to Isis, transformed into a Christian church in the 3rd century. Many traces remain of the original construction, visible both from outside and from the interior, which corresponds to the cella, and is in *opus reticulatum*. One of the 13th-century frescoes inside shows *St Francis preaching to the Birds*, thought to be the earliest-known representation of the episode.

Outskirts of the city

South of the city, on the far side of the Castellano, is the **Cartiera Papale**, rebuilt in 1512 by Pope Julius II on the site of medieval paper factories, which used the hydraulic energy of the river to work the machinery. Paper was made here until the end of the First World War; now the beautiful Renaissance buildings house the Museo di Storia Naturale Antonio Orsini (*open Fri, Sat, Sun 5–8, Sat also 10–12, or on request; T: 0736 252594 or 277554*), the collection of the dedicated 19th-century naturalist who gave his name to the meadow (or Orsini's) viper.

The characteristic little Baroque church of **Sant'Emidio alle Grotte** is to the north of the city, c. 30mins walk from Ponte Nuovo. This hill of tufa, with several caves, was the early Christian necropolis. After an earthquake spared Ascoli in 1703, it was decided to build the church as an ex-voto, and Giuseppe Giosafatti was chosen to carry out the project; it is considered to be his masterpiece.

THE PALM RIVIERA

The coast between Cupra Marittima and San Benedetto del Tronto (*map p. 619, D6*) is known as the *Riviera delle Palme*, for the elegant, palm-fringed promenades that characterise the resorts. Sandy beaches, summer crowds and good restaurants serving fish or pizza are all to be found here. At the same time the coastal centres are only minutes away from the unspoilt interior, with its intact farmland and tiny medieval cities, such as Offida, where you will see lace-makers at work, Ripatransone or Cossignano.

Cupra Marittima

Peaceful Cupra Marittima has 2km of white sands, bordered by tamarisks. This was the religious centre of the Picenes, who worshipped the goddess Cupra, an Etruscan divinity called *Bona* by the Romans, in a temple on Colle Morganti. More than 400 Picene tombs of the Iron Age have been found in the area, many containing chariots, weapons and jewellery. The picturesque old centre of Cupra Alta is still surrounded by defensive walls complete with towers, erected in the 15th century by Francesco Sforza. At no. 5 Via del Castello is Palazzo Cipolletti, housing the **Museo Archeologico del Territorio** (*request visit at tourist office*), with a selection of finds from the Picene necropolis; other items are at the museums of Ancona and Ascoli Piceno.

Just north of Cupra is the **Archaeological Park of Cupra Marittima** (*request visit at tourist office*), where the conspicuous remains of the Roman township can be seen, surrounded by olive trees; there is a nymphaeum with frescoes.

San Benedetto del Tronto

Probably founded in the early Middle Ages on the site of a Roman settlement called *Truentum*, San Benedetto del Tronto (*map p. 619, D6*) is both an elegant seaside resort and one of the most important fishing ports of the Adriatic, with a busy fish market (worth a visit at dawn to see the auction). Next to the fish market, at no. 28 Piazza del Pescatore, is the **Museo Ittico Augusto Capriotti** (*open summer 9–1; winter 9–12; closed Mon and holidays; T: 0735 588850*), a collection of 6,500 fish to be found in the Adriatic Sea. Nearby, in Viale de Gasperi, are the **Antiquarium Truentinum** and the **Museum of the Amphorae** (*open 9–12 & 4–7; closed Sun in winter; T: 0735 592177*) with archaeological finds, some from shipwrecks. The same building houses the **Museo della Pesca e della Civiltà Marinara**, a vivid description of fishing methods and techniques. The central Viale Secondo Moretti is a pedestrian area; part of it, called Isola dell'Arte, boasts contemporary sculptures by, among others, the American Mark Kostabi, Ugo Nespolo and the local artist Paolo Consorti.

FERMO

Fermo (pop. 36,000; *map p. 619, D5*), provincial capital, is a quiet town with strong traditions, perched on a hill only a stone's throw from the sea. It has a splendid main square, and an unusual cathedral surrounded by gardens, built on the summit. This is a particularly fertile part of the region, lovely in early spring when the fruit trees are in blossom—the peach orchards are renowned.

HISTORY OF FERMO

The strategic hill called *Sabulo* was a Picene stronghold from the 9th century BC. Taken by the Romans in 268 BC, a large group of perhaps 5,000 settlers arrived four years later to found *Firmum Picenum*. The city was further enlarged when space was assigned to veteran legionaries in 42 BC. In the 7th century, as part of the Duchy of Spoleto (*see p. 550*), Fermo controlled a large area, and in 825 a prestigious school was established by the Lombard emperor Lothair I. In the 14th century it became a university, functioning until 1826. The city became the seat of a powerful bishopric in the 9th century, and several religious communities came to Fermo to open monasteries and build new churches. Fermo became an independent commune in 1199. In the 13th century it was made part of the March of Ancona, and in 1275 formed an alliance with Venice. Besides guaranteeing a constant supply of wheat for the Venetians, this opened up new markets in the East. Venetian artists were welcomed, explaining the arrival of painters like Jacobello di Bonomo, Jacobello del Fiore, and the Crivelli brothers, Carlo and Vittore.

The most important statesman to lead Fermo was the *condottiere* Francesco Sforza, employed by the Pope Eugenius IV in the service of his league of Venice and Florence against the Milanese Visconti. Francesco turned Fermo into a beautiful, well-run Renaissance city. In 1549 the city council decided to turn over Fermo to the papacy, 'for the common weal' (Sixtus V was a local man and had obtained many privileges for the city). In the 18th and 19th centuries, Fermo was high on the list of places for travellers planning to embark on a Grand Tour.

Piazza del Popolo

Piazza del Popolo, a lovely square with high porticoes, has been the city centre since Roman times. The Palazzo dei Priori, to the north, was first built in the 14th century, then restructured and finally completed in 1525, with an attractive double staircase in the centre of the façade, surmounted by a bronze statue of Sixtus V (1590). The building now houses the **Pinacoteca Civica** (*open summer 10–1 & 3.30–7.30; winter 9.30–1 & 3.30–7; closed Mon; T: 0734 217140*), with a rich collection of paintings, including a glowing, nocturnal *Adoration of the Shepherds* by Rubens (1608), and eight panel paintings from a polyptych by Jacobello del Fiore with *Stories of St Lucy*.

Left of Palazzo dei Priori is the **Palazzo degli Studi** (16th–17th centuries), former seat of the university, which houses the important Biblioteca (*open Mon–Fri 8–2 & 3–7; Sat 8–2; closed Sun; T: 0734 217140*). The library boasts some rarities, such as a 14th-century prayer book, a first edition of Petrarch's *Triumphs*, and a 15th-century herbarium.

An old Roman building nearby in Largo Calzecchi Onesti houses the **Museo Archeologico** (*open June–Sept 10–1 & 4–8, winter on request; T: 0734 217140*), with an interesting collection of Roman and Etruscan funerary urns, and swords, buckles and vases of the Picene period.

East of Piazza del Popolo, accessible from Via Paccarone, is the stepped alley called Via degli Aceti; at no. 1 is the entrance to the underground **Cisterne Romane** (*open June–Sept 10–1 & 4–8, winter on request; T: 0734 217140*), 30 enormous water-storage cisterns, built between AD 40 and 60. Each one measures 9m by 6m, and is 6m high; six of them are still in use by the municipal water board.

Duomo della Madonna

The magnificent Duomo della Madonna, surrounded by cedars of Lebanon and other beautiful trees, was commissioned by Frederick II of Hohenstaufen in 1227 on what was once the acropolis of the Picene and the Roman cities. The white stone was brought from Istria. The portal dates from an earlier 9th-century church. A massive restructuring was completed by Cosimo Morelli in the 18th century.

The bell-tower, partly original, is enormous, occupying almost half of the façade. Notice the lovely rose window (1348), and above all the portal, with fine carvings in local stone representing the Tree of Life with birds, animals (notice the lobster with a snake writhing in its claw), people and demons. The architrave, with a series of superbly carved figures, is thought by some scholars to be an early work by Nicola Pisano. All the figures are holding rolls of parchment: they could represent Christ with the twelve Apostles, or Frederick with his *magna curia*. Part of the right side of the building is original, with a Romanesque portal surmounted by a 14th-century *Pietà*; to the right of it is an inscription dated 1227 giving the name of the mason (Giorgio da Como).

The interior is spacious and solemn. Along the sides are many statues and paintings, including a very rare 11th-century **Greek Byzantine icon** over the fourth south altar. In between the steps leading up to the presbytery can be seen the mosaic floor of the Palaeochristian basilica (5th century), discovered in 1934. The perimeter of the ancient church is shown by a strip of red marble. In the apse is a sculpture of the *Madonna* (Gioacchino Varlé, 18th century). The **Chapel of the Sacrament** in the north aisle has a canvas of the *Circumcision* by Andrea Boscoli, and a beautiful bronze tabernacle (1571), like a little Doric temple, with an elaborate support.

Around the duomo

Next to the cathedral is the **Museo Diocesano** (*open July–Aug 10–1 & 4–8; T: 0734 229350*), displaying works of art from the cathedral and local churches, including paintings by Crivelli, Barocci, Maratta, Pomarancio and Hayez. Pride of place is given to the **chasuble of St Thomas à Becket**, authenticated by the University of London, worked in gold thread on silk, with medallions, quotations from the Koran, and an inscription in Arabic saying it was made in Almeria (Mariyya) in the year 510 of the *Hegira* (corresponding to 1116). St Thomas gave this precious robe to a fellow student from Bologna University, Presbitero, who became Bishop of Fermo.

San Francesco and the Villa Vitali

The church of **San Francesco d'Assisi** (1240), at the far end of Via Perpenti, was completed in the 15th century, but the present façade was added in the 18th century, and the portal is of 1604. At the far end of the south aisle, a large Gothic arch gives access to the Cappella del Sacramento; on the right is a magnificent funerary monument to Lodovico Euffreducci (Andrea Sansovino; 1527). The 14th-century frescoes in the apse chapel are by Giuliano da Rimini, a member of the Giottesque school (*see p. 661*).

Beyond San Francesco, in Viale Trento, just outside the walls, is the 19th-century Villa Vitali, surrounded by wooded public gardens. The villa houses a museum of polar exploration and the **Museo di Scienze Naturali Tommaso Salvadori** (*open Mon–Fri 9–12.30 & 3.30–6.30; Sat, Sun and holidays 3.30–7*), with the famous meteorite of Fermo, found here on 25th September 1996, and weighing over 10kg.

MACERATA & THE
LOWER CHIENTI VALLEY

The dignified city of Macerata (*map p. 619, C4–D4*), set in rolling farmland, is the seat of one of Italy's oldest universities, has one of the finest libraries in the country, and boasts an unusual open-air theatre. Built on a crest between two valleys, the steep old centre, with its intricate web of narrow streets, is still almost completely surrounded by the 16th-century walls.

HISTORY OF MACERATA

Medieval Macerata was almost entirely constructed of material from the ruins of the Roman *Helvia Ricina*, 3km away in the locality now called Villa Potenza. Helvia Ricina was founded by the Umbri about 3,000 years ago, in a position dominating a series of important trade routes. The town was devastated by the Visigoths in 408, after which the site was abandoned, and Macerata was built.

In 1138 Macerata became an independent commune. During the struggles between Guelphs and Ghibellines, Macerata joined forces with the Guelphs (the papal faction). Pope John XXII declared Macerata a city in 1320, but powerful families still exerted their dominion over the territory, first the Mulucci (1326–55), followed by the da Varano (1385) and Francesco Sforza (1433). In 1455 the city again came under the influence of the Church when it was made the seat of the Legation of the March, the papal diplomatic representation in the region.

Macerata was pillaged by the French in 1799, who occupied it again in 1808. In 1849 the city played a leading role in the Republican movement. Fierce bombing raids in April 1944 meant that the city had to be extensively rebuilt; new housing went up outside the city walls, leaving the old centre repaired and intact.

The town centre

The central Piazza della Libertà is dominated on the west side by the portico of the **Palazzo dei Priori**, in the courtyard of which is a collection of archaeological fragments from the Roman city of *Helvia Ricina* (*see opposite*). Via Don Minzoni leads eastwards out of the square. On the right, at no. 11, is **Palazzo Compagnoni Marefoschi** (1771) with a particularly fine doorway surmounted by a balcony. In 1772 Charles Stuart, Bonnie Prince Charlie, married the Countess of Albany in this house. The street continues down to Piazza San Vincenzo Strambi, of which the **duomo**, dedicated to St Julian, occupies the east side. Building started in the 15th century (the bell-tower is of 1478) and continued from 1771–90 by Cosimo Morelli, but was never finished. The apse has a magnificent fresco of the *Assumption of the Virgin* (1930), and, beneath it, the panel painting of *St Julian Begs the Madonna to save Macerata from the Plague* (Christopher Unterberger; 1786). The organ, by Gaetano Callido (1790), is one of the largest he ever made. In the north transept is the Chapel of the Sacrament, with two beautiful stucco angels made by Gioacchino Varlé in 1790. Some of the finest works of art are in the **Sagrestia dei Canonici** (*open 3–6, but it is often closed*), where there is an outstanding panel painting by Vincenzo Pagani (16th century) of the *Madonna and Child with Sts Julian and Anthony of Padua*, with the tiny figures of the donors kneeling between the two saints, and a river—the Potenza?—winding its way to the sea in the background; a splendid triptych by Allegretto Nuzi (1369) of the *Madonna between St Julian and St Anthony Abbot*, still in its original frame, and two canvases by Giovanni Baglione (1600): *Crucifixion of St Peter* and the *Resurrection of Tabitha*.

Left of the cathedral, dominating the square with its curved façade, is the sanctuary church of the **Madonna della Misericordia**, built in 1736 on the site of a votive chapel and enlarged in the late 19th century. It is the smallest basilica in the world and a national monument. The oval interior by Luigi Vanvitelli, although small, is dazzling: richly decorated with stuccoes, precious marbles, paintings and wrought-iron work.

Museums of Macerata

In Piazza Vittorio Veneto, the former Jesuit college currently houses the civic museums and libraries (*at the time of writing there were plans to move them to Palazzo Buonaccorsi on Via Don Minzoni*). The **Pinacoteca Comunale** (*open Tues–Sat 9–1 & 4–7.30; Sun 9–1; Mon afternoons only; T: 0733 256361*), is divided into two sections, the first dedicated to works by artists from Umbria and the Marche from the 14th–19th centuries, including Sassoferrato, Federico Barocci and Carlo Maratta. Pride of place is occupied by a luminous but fragmentary *Madonna with the Christ Child* (1470) by Carlo Crivelli. Originally a part of a polyptych, it is thought that the *Pietà* now in the Fogg Art Museum of Cambridge, Massachusetts, was part of the same work. The second section of the gallery is dedicated to contemporary art.

The **Museo Civico** (*open as Pinactoeca, above*) contains archaeological finds from Helvia Ricina. There is also a **Museo delle Carrozze** (carriage museum; *closed Mon*) in the basement, with an interesting collection of vehicles, including an 'ambulance' and a tiny children's cart which was pulled by goats.

On the first floor is the magnificent Biblioteca Comunale, one of the finest in the region, comprising a public consultation section, and the historic **Mozzi Borgetti Library** (*open Mon–Fri 9–1 & 3–7; Sat and July–Aug mornings only; T: 0733 256360*) of which the Jesuit collection forms the nucleus. The beautiful rooms are the perfect setting for 300,000 rare manuscripts, incunabula, maps and medieval statutes. There is a reading room on the rooftop called the *Specola*, a long gallery with views over the city on one side, and as far as the Sibyllines on the other.

Leading northwest from Piazza Vittorio Veneto is Via Domenico Ricci; at no. 1 is the **Galleria d'Arte Contemporanea** (*open March–Dec Sat and Sun 10–1 & 4–8; July–Aug every day except Mon; T: 0733 261484, www.fondazionemacerata.it*). The collection was started in 1975 when a local bank intervened to save the painting *Treno in corsa* (*Racing Train*), by the local Futurist painter Ivo Pannaggi, from being sold abroad; there are now more than 400 paintings and sculptures, including works by Fontana, Morandi, de Chirico, Depero, Monachesi, Licini and Manzù.

The Sferisterio

The most unusual building in Macerata is in Piazza Nazario Sauro, in the southeast corner of the town. The Sferisterio (*T: 0733 234333 to request visit*) is a vast arena built in 1820–29 for a popular ball game, *pallone al bracciale* (*see box below*). Semi-elliptical, and capable of accommodating 7,000 spectators, it was designed by Ireneo Aleandri, inspired by Palladian models. When the game for which it was built lost favour, it was used for jousts and circuses until the early 1920s, when operas and concerts began to be organised in the summer. Thanks to the excellent acoustics, these are still very popular. The stage (90m wide) is the largest in Europe and has accommodated a performance of *Aida* with real elephants.

PALLONE AL BRACCIALE

One of the most ancient ball games in Europe, and one of the most exciting, *pallone al bracciale* goes back to Roman times, although some experts believe it to be a typical Spartan pastime. Two teams of three players try to keep a leather ball weighing 350g from touching the ground by bouncing it off a wall; they can make contact with the ball only with a heavy wooden arm guard, the *bracciale*, always made of sorb-apple wood. Very fast, the game can be quite violent. It was immensely popular in central Italy during the Renaissance, and again in the 19th century (the poet Giacomo Leopardi even dedicated an ode to it), but it has not been able to resist competition from football and is now seldom played. A national championship is nevertheless still held annually.

The ruins of Helvia Ricina

At Villa Potenza (*map p. 619, C4*), 3km from Macerata, the remains of *Helvia Ricina* with the vast Roman amphitheatre built by Trajan in the 2nd century AD can be seen (*visits by previous arrangement only; T: 0733 492937, but it is visible from outside the fence*), together with some architectural fragments found in the nearby River Potenza, where they had been used to strengthen the banks.

Villa Buonaccorsi

Potenza Picena (*map p. 619, D4*) is a honey-coloured town still surrounded by medieval walls, on a strategic hilltop close to the River Potenza. The imposing palaces in the central square belonged (or still belong) to the landowning families of the area. Between Potenza Picena and Porto Potenza Picena is **Villa Buonaccorsi**, an aristocratic villa with beautiful 18th-century Italian-style gardens (*open summer 9–1 & 3–7, gardens only; T: 0733 688189. To reach the villa from Porto Potenza Picena, follow the signs for Monte Canepino*). The Giardino Buonaccorsi is one of the few 18th-century Italian gardens preserved in its original form by the family who created it, as evidenced by comparison with an 18th-century drawing of the upper terraces. Here the writer Georgina Masson found 'that unique thing, an 18th-century garden perfect in every detail, right down to the furniture of its grottoes and the stars and diamonds of its original parterres'. The divisions of the parterres are bordered—uniquely in Italy—in stone. Five terraces drop down to the south behind the villa, giving a view of the sea. Near the house is a grotto with Baroque figures of friars surprised by a devil emerging from a niche, and a *giardino segreto*. Figures from the *Commedia dell'Arte* are on the second terrace, while the Roman 'emperors' on the third may be from a former garden. At the bottom of the stairs connecting the terraces is a room containing a remarkable survival of something that was once common in gardens: automatons, including a Harlequin, a Turk and a huntsman blowing a horn. Of the many *giochi d'acqua*, only a few remain in working order. The park was laid out in the English style in the 19th century, with a small lake and a mount for viewing the surroundings.

THE LOWER CHIENTI VALLEY

Santa Maria a piè di Chienti

According to legend, the abbey of Santa Maria a piè di Chienti (*map p. 619, D4*) was founded by Charlemagne to celebrate a victory over the Saracens which had taken place nearby. The church (*open 8–8; no visits during Mass*) was perhaps built a century later, in the 9th century, but the first written mention of it is dated 936. Attached to the church was a small monastic community, a dependency of the important abbey of Farfa, near Rieti (*see p. 162*). The monks drained the marshy land to cultivate it. Using the water from the drainage channels and also from the Chienti, they activated watermills and filled a series of moats, which together with high dykes, protected the community from attack. By the 11th century this monastery was one of the most important Farfa possessions, and probably a stop for pilgrims on their way to Rome and Jerusalem. The present church goes back to 1125. On two levels, built entirely of brick, the façade is plain, but the rounded lower apses jut out in the northern style, surmounted by the apse of the upper church, which was added in the 15th century. Further embellishments were added in the 16th century, when the church was at the centre of an important yearly market which attracted merchants from all central Italy and even from Dalmatia.

The interior is particularly atmospheric: the windows are of alabaster. The first part of the central nave is open to the roof; halfway along, it becomes a low presbytery, culminating in three chapels in the apses, while the upper church consists of another presbytery and the area reserved for the monks. The luminous frescoes, dominated by Christ in a mandorla, are dated 1447. The wooden Crucifix, which can be seen immediately on entering, in the centre, is 15th-century, as are the terracotta statuettes of the *Virgin Annunciate* and the *Angel Gabriel*.

Monte San Giusto

At 236m, Monte San Giusto (*map p. 619, D5*) enjoys a panoramic position facing the sea. In the little 14th-century church of **Santa Maria Telusiano** (*open 7.30–12.30 & 4.30–6.30; if closed ask in side alley for key*), in Via Tolomei, is one of Lorenzo Lotto's finest works, a large *Crucifixion* (1529–34), still in its magnificent original frame. Lorenzo probably painted most of it in Venice, completing the work in Monte San

Giusto when he added the portrait of the donor, Bishop Niccolò Bonafede, shown as a monk in the bottom left-hand corner. The scene is enacted on three distinct levels: in the foreground, the sorrow of the Mourners; in the middle, the cynical, jeering Soldiers, with the exception of Longinus, on horseback, who stretches out his arms to Christ; at the top, the crosses, against a lowering black sky. Power and movement are given to the scene by the diagonal position of the forest of lances and the outstretched arms. The dark, bearded man in the middle, gazing out at the onlooker, is perhaps the artist himself.

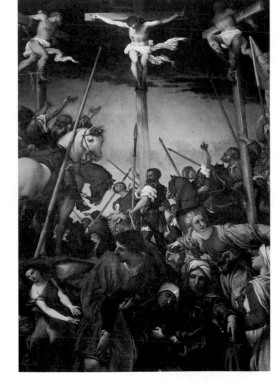

Lorenzo Lotto: *Crucifixion* (1529–34)

TOLENTINO & ENVIRONS

Standing on the left bank of the Chienti, against a background of green hills, is the ancient, largely unspoilt city of Tolentino (pop. 19,000; *map p. 619, C4*). One of Italy's great mystic saints, St Nicholas of Tolentino, lived and died here; the city has been an important destination for pilgrims ever since.

HISTORY OF TOLENTINO

Tolentino occupies a strategic position in the heart of the Marche, where the two rivers Chienti and Potenza flow closest together. It was a settlement of the Picenes and became the Roman *Tolentinum*, of which little trace remains. It played a vital role in the 10th century, assisting pilgrims and providing supplies for the monastic communities of the area, including Santa Maria a piè' di Chienti and Santa Maria di Chiaravalle di Fiastra. Craftsmanship flourished thanks to a dam on the Chienti which brought abundant water to the western side of town, where leather workers, brick-makers, millers and wool manufacturers plied their trade.

At the infamous Treaty of Tolentino in 1797, Napoleon forced Pope Pius VI to hand over lands, works of art and cash indemnities (*see below*).

Piazza Libertà and the Museo Napoleonico

Centre of the city is Piazza Libertà. On the north side is the unusual 16th-century **clock-tower** (the bell-tower of the church of San Francesco) with five quadrants: the top one indicates the phases of the moon, the second shows the hours for the principal prayers, the third gives the time, the fourth the days of the month and the week. Lastly, only just visible, is a small solar meridian, which was used to adjust the other dials. Leading north out of Piazza Libertà is Via Filelfo. A right turn at the end brings you into Via della Pace, where at no. 20 is **Palazzo Parisani Bezzi**, where the Treaty of Tolentino was signed on 19th February 1797 between the representatives of Pope Pius VI and Napoleon Bonaparte. It was a sad day for the pope: he was forced to renounce his treaty with Austria and to hand over Avignon, the legations of Bologna, Ferrara, Ravenna and Forlì, together with an enormous sum of money and many precious works of art. The palace now houses the Museo Napoleonico (*open Tues–Sun 10–1 & 3–7, T: 0733 969797*).

Basilica di San Nicola

Via San Nicola, probably the old cardo maximus, leads south from Piazza Libertà through a picturesque medieval district to the 13th-century Porta del Ponte and the River Chienti. A short way along, the street widens in front of the **Basilica di San Nicola** (*open 9.30–12 & 4–7*), where Nicholas of Tolentino, hermit, healer and great preacher (*see box opposite*), lived for 30 years. The church, originally dedicated to St Augustine and belonging to the Austin Fathers, is 13th-century, but was remodelled in the 14th century and also a century later when the magnificent late Gothic portal of 1432, by Nanni di Bartolo, surmounted by *St George and the Dragon*, was added. The doorway was commissioned by the local soldier-of-fortune Niccolò Mauruzi (1365–1435), as a token of devotion to St Nicholas; he wanted St George to appear on the portal because he was the patron saint of *condottieri*. Mauruzi is commemorated in the Duomo in Florence in a famous equestrian fresco by Andrea del Castagno (*see p. 274*).

The elegant façade in travertine marble with the star of St Nicholas was completed in the 18th century. The interior has an astonishing coffered ceiling of carved and gilded wood, with portraits of saints, completed in 1628. In the first chapel on the right is a canvas by Guercino of *St Anne with the Angel*, while the large canvases on the high altar, representing the *Amputation of the Holy Arms* and the *Madonna Appears to St Nicholas*, are the work of the local artist Giovan Battista Foschi (1628).

St Nicholas of Tolentino (1245–1305)

Born at Sant'Angelo in Pontano near San Ginesio, Nicholas joined the Augustinian order before being ordained as a priest at Cingoli in 1269, and from that moment wandered around the Marche, living a simple existence as a hermit and preacher. In 1275 he settled in Tolentino, where he remained until his death. People travelled long distances to listen to his sermons, or to invoke his intercession for the sick or dying; at his canonisation (1446) more than 300 miracles were reported. In paintings or sculptures, he is recognisable by the star on his chest or just above his head; it appeared a few months before he died, and was seen by many witnesses. Forty years after his death, a German pilgrim opened his coffin in order to remove part of the body to take home as a relic. He cut off the arms, which started to bleed copiously; the man fled in horror. For centuries the arms were carried in procession through Tolentino. To frustrate relic-seekers, the rest of the body had been hastily buried in a location lost to memory, until it was discovered under the oratory of the church in 1926, and finally laid to rest in the crypt together with the arms. It was Nicholas who instructed his followers to pray for the souls in Purgatory, now a regular practice in the Catholic rite; he is invoked against injustice and natural disasters, and protects young mothers and infants. In 1400 Pope Boniface IX conceded the plenary indulgence to all those who visited his tomb, thus encouraging the pilgrimage to Tolentino.

At the end of the church on the right is the entrance to the famous **Cappellone di San Nicola**, of which the walls and ceiling are entirely covered with a magnificent series of frescoes, carried out in the first years of the 14th century by Pietro da Rimini and his collaborators, known collectively as the School of Rimini (*see p. 661*), resulting in the most important expression of 14th-century painting in the Marche. The frescoes show scenes from the lives of the Madonna, Christ and St Nicholas, and are dominated by the *Crucifixion*, showing Mary Magdalene embracing the foot of the Cross, between the

Virgin and St John. The stone sarcophagus (1474) in the centre, made to replace the original wooden one, was never used for Nicholas's body, which had been hastily buried for fear of over-enthusiastic relic-seekers. The painted wooden effigy on top (15th century), is by a follower of Donatello.

From the Cappellone it is possible to reach the peaceful **cloister** (14th and 17th centuries), with a well in the centre, and an attractive loggia on one side. A small doorway leads into the saint's **oratory**, a tiny room decorated with frescoes, where it is thought Nicholas lived for 30 years, and where he died. Back in the church, you will find the richly decorated **Chapel of the Holy Arms** (*Cappella delle Santissime Braccia*); just outside the entrance is a tiny cell, the so-called 'prison of St Nicholas', and to the right of this, high up, is a niche in the wall covered with a coat-of-arms which holds the heart of Niccolò Mauruzi (*see previous page*). Behind the altar in the chapel is the wrought-iron coffer (1484) where St Nicholas's mutilated arms were kept for centuries, and carried in procession through the streets of Tolentino. The statues of the *Virtues*, the cupids and the angels, which look as if they are carved from white marble, are in fact made of plaster of which the composition was kept a secret, the work of Giambattista Latini (19th century). The two paintings on the walls were offered by two Italian marine republics, Venice and Genoa, and represent miracles performed by Nicholas to save the cities. On the left is the *Extinguishing of a Fire in the Doge's Palace* by Matthias Stomer (1650), while that on the right shows *Nicholas Ends the Plague in Genoa* by Giovanni Carboncino (1677).

To the right from the Chapel of the Holy Arms is a doorway to a wide staircase down to the **crypt**, completed in 1932, where the body of the saint (and his arms) repose in a silver urn. On coming up from the crypt, you will find the access to the **Museo dell'Opera**, which includes paintings by Simone de Magistris and Vittore Crivelli.

Ponte del Diavolo

If travelling from Tolentino to San Ginesio or Civitanova Marche, you will cross the Chienti on the Ponte del Diavolo (Devil's Bridge), built in 1276 in one night, according to legend, by the Devil in person. The constructor had been delayed in the work and was unable to fulfil his contract; he made a deal, promising Satan the first soul to cross the bridge—Nicholas of Tolentino sent a dog over, and all was well; but it is said that the dog could be heard howling in misery for many centuries afterwards.

ENVIRONS OF TOLENTINO

Belforte del Chienti

Perched on a ridge dominating the Chienti valley, Belforte del Chienti (*map p. 619, C5*) is still surrounded by its 14th-century walls. The steep, narrow medieval streets lead to the central church of Sant'Eustachio, where one of the most important paintings of the region can be seen: the **polyptych by Giovanni Boccati** of the *Madonna with Saints*, signed and dated 1468 (*if closed, ask at town hall or Pro Loco for the key*) The polyptych, the largest in Europe (4.83m by 3.25m), consists of 35 paintings set into a magnificent,

Detail of Giovanni Boccati's polyptych of the *Madonna with Saints* (1468).

intricate gilded frame, thought to come from San Severino Marche, where the craftsmen were renowned for this kind of workmanship. Although painted during the Renaissance, it is Gothic in style, and it was commissioned as an altarpiece for this very church, by a certain Taliano di Lippo da Belforte. The central panel shows the Madonna seated on a carved dais (on the front of the dais is the signature of the artist), with her feet on an Oriental rug. The Child on her lap is being teased by two cherubs, one of whom is offering Him a goldfinch to kiss, and the other is apparently about to tickle His feet. Beautifully portrayed angel musicians (it is known that Giovanni Boccati played the lute), seraphim and two guardian angels crowd around the Madonna. Symbolism abounds: the goldfinch represents the human soul; the eight-sided dais refers to resurrection and eternity; red and blue are the colours signifying the divine and the human nature of Christ and the Virgin; the acanthus, a frequent element in pagan temples, came to assume some of the characteristics of the Madonna for early Christians, hence the leaves on her robe; the coral around the neck of Jesus represents the blood of the Passion. It is thought to have provided inspiration for Raphael. High on the list of the masterpieces that Napoleon was anxious to take home to Paris in 1797, after the notorious Tolentino treaty (*see p. 680*), the priest was able to save it by dismantling all the various elements and hiding them in the roof, between the tiles and the ceiling.

San Severino Marche and Cingoli

The quietly prosperous San Severino Marche (*map p. 619, C4*), renowned for the skill of its goldsmiths, was the birthplace of the brothers Lorenzo and Jacopo Salimbeni, important exponents of the International Gothic style in the 15th century. The architect Pompeo Floriani, who designed the city of Loreto for Pope Sixtus V, was also a native, as was the 16th-century anatomist Bartolomeo Eustachio, famous for his studies of the ear (he gives his name to the Eustachian tube). The old town called Castello on the hilltop dominates the new town at its foot; the noticeably leaning medieval tower is the highest of its kind in the region (40m), it was also the first to have a clock installed in it, in the early 14th century.

North of San Severino Marche, in the heart of the central highlands, is the lovely, silent grey stone city of **Cingoli** (*map p. 619, C4*), universally known in Italy as the '*balcone delle Marche*', from where you can see the whole region and beyond. Inside the 14th-century church of San Domenico (*if closed, T: 0733 602877 to request visit*) is an exceptionally fine, well-composed painting by Lorenzo Lotto, the *Madonna of the Rosary*, showing the Virgin enthroned with saints. Each saint is a study of human character.

Santa Maria di Chiaravalle di Fiastra

Heading east from Tolentino along the SS 78, the Cistercian abbey of Santa Maria di Chiaravalle di Fiastra soon comes into sight (*map p. 619, C4; open 15 June–15 Sept 10–1 & 3–6.30; 16 Sept–14 June Sat, Sun and holidays 10–1 & 3–6; T: 0733 202190*). Founded by Cistercian monks from Chiaravalle Abbey in Milan in 1142, on the site of a preceding Benedictine convent between the Fiastra and Chienti rivers, it became one of the most powerful and influential religious communities of central Italy. For their church and monastery, the monks used material from *Urbs Salvia* (*see opposite*; notice the Roman columns in the refectory); they drained the marshy, unhealthy land and built roads and bridges, mills, oil presses and wineries. Devastated by Braccio da Montone in 1422, the abbey lost its splendour. Nevertheless, it is interesting to visit the farmland, created so painstakingly by the monks, and still perfectly functional.

Built during the period of transition between Romanesque and Gothic, with some typically Cistercian features, the red brick abbey church of Santa Maria Annunziata has a simple façade preceded by a narthex. The spacious interior has a single nave with truss-beam roof, and two side aisles, divided by four-lobed pilasters formed of half columns, characteristic of the churches of this Order. Many frescoes still survive, notably those of the square-sided apse, showing the *Crucifixion with Sts Benedict and Bernard*, dated 1473, by a follower of Giovanni Boccati; the altar stone comes from a Roman temple. Also typical of the Cistercians is the large square monastery (where the monks have now returned), built around an enormous cloister (15th century). From the cloister it is possible to reach the chapter house and the refectory, the roof of which is supported by seven Roman columns with beautiful capitals and bases, brought here from Urbs Salvia. In the little bell-tower is a bronze bell made in 1492.

Mogliano

Mogliano (*map p. 619, C5*) is an attractive little town on a ridge between the Cremone and Ete Morto rivers. It is of ancient origin, once inhabited by the Picenes, later a Roman settlement, then the property of the abbey of Farfa, near Rieti. In the central square, Piazza Garibaldi, is the church of **Santa Maria Assunta**. Over the main altar is a masterpiece by Lorenzo Lotto, a large panel painting signed and dated 1548, of the *Assumption of the Madonna with Sts John the Baptist, Anthony of Padua, Mary Magdalene and Joseph*, at last reassembled in its original frame, which was removed in 1720 and taken to another church. This painting is similar to the one Lorenzo painted two years later for the church of San Francesco alle Scale in Ancona (*see p. 623*), on the same subject; it has a melancholy air to it, and subdued colours. Nearing 70, he was probably still smarting from the criticism levelled at him by Pietro Aretino, who had called him 'outdated'. The theme of the work appears to be a Counter-Reformation invitation to reconsider the Sacraments: the figures in the foreground show from the left *John the Baptist* (Baptism), *Anthony of Padua* (Confirmation), *Mary Magdalene* (Last Rites), and *Joseph* (Matrimony).

Urbisaglia

In ancient times the town of Urbisaglia (*map p. 619, C5*) was an important settlement controlling a road crossing, later a branch of the Via Flaminia. The walls, which still partially surround the town, were built using stones from the ruins of the Roman *Urbs Salvia*, destroyed by Alaric the Goth in 410. In the **Museo Archeologico** (*open 8.30–1.30; Thurs, Fri, Sat also 3–7; Oct–March mornings only; closed Sun; ask here to visit the archaeological park if closed; T: 0733 50107*) are finds from Urbs Salvia, including marble statues from the theatre and monumental inscriptions from the amphitheatre, giving a good idea of what the ancient city was like.

The **archaeological park of Urbs Salvia** (*open as Museo Archeologico; T: 0733 506566*) covers about 40 hectares. It is in a beautiful setting, crowned by shady oaks. Not far away, a sacred area has been brought to light, dedicated to the goddess Salus Augusta, with a covered passage showing conspicuous traces of frescoes in the third

Female portrait head from the Roman town of Urbs Salvia.

Pompeian style (painted architectural elements with human and animal figures). By following a track which leads back towards Urbisaglia, you reach the theatre. This, thought to go back to AD 23, is the most important archaeological monument in the Marche region, and one of the finest Roman theatres in Italy. Judging by the size, and by the quantity of statues, inscriptions and decorative carvings recovered by the archaeologists (now in the Archaeological Museum), it was imposing and richly ornate; a providential landslide, which must have occurred soon after its construction, preserved it for posterity.

San Ginesio

Enticing when it comes into sight, San Ginesio (*map p. 619, C5*) does not disappoint on closer inspection. Forming part of the Italian association of beautiful villages (www.borghitalia.it), it offers spectacular views over the Sibylline Mountains. The defensive walls, built between the 14th and 15th centuries, are particularly impressive: the battlements, bulwarks and towers are still in excellent condition.

The main approach to the city is through Porta Picena (13th century), surmounted by battlements. Immediately on the right is the **Ospedale di San Paolo** (13th century), one of several pilgrim hospitals erected here. The town centre is Piazza Gentili. Occupying pride of place is the unusual **Collegiata**, a Romanesque church with a late Gothic façade, probably the work of German craftsmen. The richly-decorated portal and exceptional terracotta ornamentation at the top are by the otherwise unknown Enrico Alemanno (Henry the German), dated 1421. There is nothing like it elsewhere in the Marche, though similar examples are found in the Netherlands, Germany and Flanders. The chapels are all on the south side; in the third are three canvases by Simone de Magistris (1588): the *Last Supper*, *Christ Falls under the Cross*, and the *Crucifixion* over the altar. In the apse is a fresco of the *Crucifixion* (School of Rimini) behind the altar, while on the left is a lovely panel painting by Pietro Alemanno, signed and dated 1485, of the *Madonna of Mercy*. Inside the main altar is the body of the patron saint, Lucius Ginesius (284–305), actor and mimic dear to the emperor Diocletian for his mocking parodies of Christians. When Lucius converted, he was beheaded. Under the presbytery is the crypt, with frescoes by Lorenzo Salimbeni (1406).

Behind the Collegiata, at Via Merelle 14, is the ex-church of San Sebastiano, which now houses the **Museo Civico Scipione Gentili** (*open 9–12 & 3–4.30; Sat 3.30–4.30; T: 0733 656022*), with an archaeological section and a collection of paintings by Simone de Magistris, Vincenzo Pagani, Stefano Folchetti and others.

THE SIBYLLINE MOUNTAINS

This stretch of the Apennines, the watershed between the Tyrrhenian Sea and the Adriatic, is one of Italy's most beautiful national parks (*map p. 619, B5–C6*). Inhabited since the Neolithic era, these mountains offered refuge to the Sabines, the Umbri and the Picenes; they also constituted a barrier between east and west; were a source of timber, resin and furs; a place to pasture flocks and herds in security; while the woods supplied forage for pigs, resulting in excellent hams, salami and sausage. People thought of the Sibyllines as the dwelling place of witches, demons, necromancers and fairies, and in particular, of the Sibyl, who lived in a cave close to the summit of Mount Vettore. Some say she was the Sibyl of Cumae, condemned to live chained up in the cave till Judgement Day.

Visso

A handful of neat, pastel-coloured houses grouped around three lovely old churches, with its fortifications, gates and towers still intact and traditions and gastronomy proudly maintained, Visso (*map p. 619, B5*) is delightfully coherent with its past, but at the same time has a rather worldly air, deriving probably from its strategic position on the main route from Umbria to the Marche. It has seen many centuries of travellers, and commands the most important route over the Apennines from Rome. It houses the offices of the Sibylline Mountains National Park, and is the natural point of entry when arriving from Umbria.

Heart of the little town (one of Italy's 'beautiful villages') is Piazza Martiri Vissani. The collegiate church of **Santa Maria** dominates the square, with its 14th-century portal, above which is a striking *Annunciation* by the local artist Paolo da Visso (1444). In front of the beautiful 14th-century wooden door are two worn stone Romanesque lions. In front on entering, up some steps, is the Romanesque Cappella del Battistero with sculptures from the original 12th-century church, including two very unusual carved stone coffins. With two naves, this was the nucleus of the Romanesque church.

Left of the church is the simple 14th-century church of Sant'Agostino, now the **Pinacoteca Civica** (*T: 0737 95200*), with many paintings and sculptures, including the delightful 15th-century wooden *Madonna di Macereto*. On the opposite bank of the Ussita river is the interesting Gothic church of San Francesco (15th century), with a horizontally-styled façade of a type sometimes seen in Abruzzo.

Near Visso the Nera river forms the **Gola del Nera**, a beautiful gorge surrounded by woods of oak and beech, animated by the sudden flight of the sparrowhawk and the dipper. The Fiastra road leads north from Visso to the magnificent, isolated sanctuary church of the **Madonna di Macereto** at 998m. Built in 1528–38 of local limestone, eight-sided in Bramante style, the interior encloses a 14th-century oratory. The wooden image inside is a copy of the original, now in the museum of Visso. The architect was Giovanni Battista da Lugano, who fell from the scaffolding during the construction and was buried under the church. Next to the church is the so-called Palazzo delle Guaite (1583). The long arcade to the left was used in the 16th century for markets and fairs.

PARCO NAZIONALE DEI MONTI SIBILLINI

Park office: Piazza Capuzzi 55, Visso, T: 0737 95262, www.sibillini.net
At the heart of the mountain system are Mount Vettore (2476m), which is the highest peak; Cima del Redentore (2448m); Pizzo del Diavolo (2410m) and Cima del Lago (2422m), which form an amphitheatre enclosing Lake Pilato (1940m), the only glacier lake of the Apennines. The icy waters of this lake are home to a red shrimp called *Chirocephalus marchesoni*, found nowhere else in the world. Pizzo del Diavolo slopes steeply down to the three upland plateaux of Castelluccio (*see p. 564*), famous for wild flowers in June and July: swathes of red poppies, blue cornflowers, yellow mustard, and white lentils and narcissus. On Pian Perduto is a small lake called Stagno Rosso, which turns red periodically due to the presence of a tiny organism called *Euglena sanguinea*. More than 50 different varieties of wild orchid can be found, including *Dactylorhyza sambucina*, *Orchis mascula* and *Gymnadenia conopsea*. In the area of Madonna di Macereto varieties of *Ophrys* orchid are especially abundant. There are also some endemic species of flowers limited to the central Apennines, such as the *Viola magellensis* and the *Saxifraga italica*. This is the southernmost point for finding alpine plants such as the *Ranunculus alpestris*, the *Campanula alpestris*, and a rare local form of the edelweiss, *Leontopodium nivale*, and the dwarf willow. There are two very rare glacier plants, *Carex buxbaumii* and *Carex distica*, and a rare fern, *Ophioglossum pinnatum*.

Wolf packs are concentrated in the heights above Castelluccio, while there are so many wild boar that they constitute a problem. The lynx, once extinct, was reintroduced by an animal lover in the 1990s and the population is thought to be quite strong. Wildcats are frequent, and their number is increasing.

Birds include the short-toed lark, *Calandrella cinerea*, which nests on the plateaux of Castelluccio at a height of 1452m, while its normal maximum in Italy is 850m. In June and July its song fills the air. At the end of summer, the pallid harrier preys on the flocks of migrating birds, and it is planned to reintroduce the majestic Lammergeyer vulture.

Sarnano

An excellent base for exploring the park is Sarnano (*map p. 619, C5*), on the right bank of the Tennacola, and a perfect example of a brick-built, fortified medieval city. It is also a well-known spa centre. The town hall houses the **Pinacoteca** (*officially open summer 5–8; winter 4–7, but often closed; T: 0733 658126*), with a *Last Supper* by Giovanni Andrea de Magistris; a *Crucifixion* by Stefano Folchetti, signed and dated 1513; several panel paintings by Vincenzo Pagani; another panel painting by Vittore Crivelli, and a *Madonna and Child* attributed to L'Alunno.

Dominating the main square is **Santa Maria Assunta**, consecrated in 1280. The façade is adorned with a rich Gothic doorway, while the Romanesque bell-tower is of 1396. In the heavily restored interior is a fresco by Lorenzo d'Alessandro (1483) portraying the *Madonna and Child with Angel Musicians and Saints*. In the presbytery is a panel painting of the *Madonna of Mercy*, signed and dated 1494 by Pietro Alemanno, and elements of a polyptych by L'Alunno.

Right in front of the church is a mysterious, ancient white marble **menhir**, vaguely egg-shaped, with a basin hollowed out in the top. About one and a half metres high, its original purpose is unknown; there are conjectures that it was a tombstone, a sacrificial altar, or (by filling the basin with water to reflect the stars) an astronomical observatory. The priest has planted his geraniums in it for now.

Montefortino

The picturesque little stone and brick town of Montefortino (*map p. 619, C5*) clings to a steep, wooded hillside; there are still many 16th-century tower-houses (*see p. 376*). In the 16th-century Palazzo Leopardi is an important art gallery, the **Pinacoteca Civica Fortunato Duranti** (*T: 0736 859491 for opening times; closed Mon*), a collection including significant 15th–18th-century works, such as a *Madonna* by Perugino, three panel paintings by Pietro Alemanno (parts of a polyptych considered his masterpiece) and a lovely *Madonna with Christ Child* by Francesco Botticini.

The **Gola dell'Infernaccio**, a wild, magnificent gorge formed by the River Tenna, is c. 15km from Montefortino. It is reached from the Madonna dell'Ambro road, by turning left towards Rubbiano just before the bridge over the Tenna. Situated between the Sibilla and the Priora mountains, it is almost 4km long; in the first stretch it is not more than 2 or 3m wide, but it opens up further along, and passes through ancient beeches, before narrowing again between sheer rockfaces, until reaching a lake surrounded by woods and numerous springs. A further climb of c. 2 hours leads to the source of the Tenna, at 1178m.

Montemonaco

The road which leads south from Amandola to Arquata del Tronto (c. 40km) is tortuous but very scenic. One of the most attractive communities along the route, said to have been founded by Benedictine monks in the 6th century, is Montemonaco (*map p. 619, C6*). The village stands on **Monte Sibilla**, and is the ideal departure point for further exploration of this mythical mountain (2175m), with its strange rounded peak surrounded by enormous pink rocks: the view from the top (c. 5hrs on foot) is breathtaking. The cave close to the summit said to have been the dwelling of the Sybil-priestess is not accessible, due to rockfalls. Another excursion from Montemonaco leads to **Lago Pilato**, a glacier lake at 1949m, which periodically colours red due to the presence of a shrimp. This fact has given rise to local legends about Pilate and his bloodstained hands.

PRACTICAL INFORMATION

GETTING AROUND

• **By train:** the **Palm Riviera** towns of San Benedetto del Tronto and Cupra Marittima are on the main Milan–Bologna–Ancona–Pescara line; **Ascoli Piceno** can be reached from Porto d'Ascoli. The station for **Fermo** is Porto San Giorgio; there are frequent bus connections to the town centre.
• **By bus:** CONTRAM (www.contram.it), connects Ancona with Macerata and San Severino Marche. Autolinee START (www.startspa.it) has services between Ascoli Piceno and San Benedetto del Tronto, Fermo, the Sibylline Mountains and Rome. STEAT (www.steat.it, www.romamarchelinee.it) connects Fermo and San Benedetto del Tronto with Macerata, Ascoli Piceno, Amandola (Sibyllines), Rome and Florence.

INFORMATION OFFICES

Ascoli Piceno, Piazza Arringo 7, T: 0736 298204 and 298334. Cooperativa 'Pulchra', Museo Diocesano, T: 0736 252883, to visit a closed church.
Fermo Piazza del Popolo 6, T: 0734 228738.
Macerata Piazza Libertà 12, T: 0733 234807.
Tolentino Piazza Libertà 19, T: 0733 972937.

Visso Piazza Martiri Vissani, T: 0737 95421.

HOTELS

Amandola (*map p. 619, C5*)
€ **Paradiso**. At the highest point of the little town of Amandola, the ideal base for touring the Sibyllines, a comfortable family-run hotel with good restaurant. Helpful owner, tennis, children's playground. *Piazza Umberto 17, T: 0736 847726, www.sibillinihotels.it.*
Ascoli Piceno (*map p. 619, C6*)
€ **Conca d'Oro Villa Cicchi**. ▪ A farm producing organic food, while the farmhouse is a carefully restored aristocratic villa, open summer only. Very pleasant, and their Rosso Piceno wine is absolutely superb. *Via Salaria Superiore 137, Abbazia di Rosara, T: 0736 252272, www.villacicchi.it. 6 rooms.*
€ **B&B Musica e Danza**. A house with a musical history, right in the centre, run by a helpful tour guide. *Via Mariano Alvitreti 4, T: 0736 258721. 2 rooms.*
€ **Palazzo Guiderocchi**. Beautifully restored 15th-century palace, central, with restaurant. The bedrooms are lovely but the bathrooms could be bigger. *Via Cesare Battisti 3, T: 0736 244011, www.palazzoguiderocchi.com. 23 rooms.*
Cupra Marittima (*map p. 619, D6*)

€ **Anita**. Unpretentious small hotel, with private beach and car park. *Via Adriatica Nord 127, T: 0735 778155, www.hotelanita.it.*

€ **Castello**. Situated in the delightful medieval town (Marano) on the hilltop, this peaceful inn (closed winter) has a good restaurant. *Via Castello 67, T: 0735 778463.*

Fermo (*map p. 619, D5*)

€ **Astoria**. Central and panoramic, close to the cathedral, with restaurant and rooftop terrace, good value for money. *Via Vittorio Veneto 8, T: 0734 228601, www.hotelastoriafermo.it. 60 rooms.*

Macerata (*map p. 619, C4–D4*)

€ **Arena**. ■ Hidden away behind the Sferisterio, simple but very comfortable, an excellent choice. *Vicolo Sferisterio 16, T: 0733 230931, www.albergoarena.com. 27 rooms.*

Montemonaco (*map p. 619, C9*)

€ **Cittadella dei Sibillini**. ■ Lovely stone farmhouse, panoramic position, surrounded by forest c. 1.5km south of Montemonaco; horses raised. Has a renowned restaurant. *Località Cittadella, T: 0736 856361, www.cittadelladeisibillini.it. 15 rooms.*

San Benedetto del Tronto (*map p. 619, D6*)

€ **Haus Charlotte**. Clean, comfortable and excellent residence with a large terrace, private beach and inviting pool. *Via Giannina Milli 10, T: 0735 780738, www.hotelhauscharlotte.it. 39 rooms.*

€ **Pineta**. In a quiet position surrounded by trees, close to the beach, with garage and good restaurant. *Via dei Mille 103, T: 0735 659875, www.hotel-pineta.it. 40 rooms.*

San Severino Marche (*map p. 619, C4*)

€€ **Due Torri**. ■ Comfortable family-run hotel at Castello, in the old city, with a good restaurant, very peaceful. *Via San Francesco 21, T: 0733 645419, www.duetorri.it. 15 rooms.*

Serrapetrona (*map p. 619, C4*)

€ **Caravanserraglio**. Restored farm buildings 2km from the centre with panoramic views, horse-riding, pottery and cookery courses. They will pick you up from Tolentino station. Minimum two nights. *Contrada Colli 10, T: 0733 908284, www.caravanserraglio.com. 6 apartments.*

RESTAURANTS

Ascoli Piceno (*map p. 619, C6*)

€ **C'era una Volta**. By taking the panoramic road which leads from the city centre to Colle San Marco, you will find on the right this friendly restaurant specialising in Ascoli cuisine. In winter, interesting vegetable soups or polenta; all year, stuffed gnocchi are a great favourite; *crema ascolana* for dessert. Closed Tues. *Località Piagge 336, T: 0736 261780.*

Cingoli (*map p. 619, C4*)

€€ **La Taverna di Ro'**. ■ Lunch here on the veranda is worth the journey to Cingoli. Exceptional *calcioni* (pasta) and gnocchi. Good local wines. Closed Wed. *Via della Portella 13, T: 0733 604713.*

Macerata (*map p. 619, C4–D4*)

€€ **Osteria dei Fiori**. ■ Tiny, central *trattoria*, run by three dedicated and imaginative young people; it specialises in typical Macerata fare, such as *panzanella al ciauscolo* (soft bread with salami), and *coniglio* in porchetta (rabbit); absolutely superb desserts; only local DOC wines served. Closed Sun in win-

ter. *Via Lauro Rossi 61, T: 0733 260142.*
Potenza Picena (*map p. 619, D4*)
€ **Osteria del Vicolo**. This quiet little
restaurant offers local dishes with an
imaginative touch; choose between two
different menus according to your
appetite, various kinds of home-made
pasta, followed by meat dishes, all
superbly cooked. Central. Closed Mon.
Via Battisti 1, T: 0733 672340.
San Benedetto del Tronto (*map p.
619, D6*)
€€€ **Messer Chichibio**. Restaurant
with a high reputation, close to the
port, excellent fish and *antipasti*. Closed
Mon. *Via Tiepolo 5, T: 0735 584001.*
€€ **Papillon**. The best place for the
local fish soup *brodetto alla sam-
benedettese*, but call a few days before as
it is specially made, and quite complicated. Closed Mon. *Via Nazario Sauro
158, T: 0735 751902.*
Visso (*map p. 619, B5*)
€ **Richetta**. Marvellous *trattoria* very
popular with the locals, generous serv-
ings. Closed Mon. *Piazza Garibaldi 7, T:
0737 9339.*

LOCAL SPECIALITIES

Ascoli Piceno The famous liqueur
called *anisetta* was invented in Caffè
Meletti (Piazza del Popolo). If you order
it *con la mosca*, 'with the fly', you will
find some coffee beans in the bottom of
the glass.
Macerata Famous for *ciauscolo* (traditional soft, spreadable salami), biscuits
and bread.
Potenza Picena Hand-woven damask
brocade, in the tradition of the nuns at
the convent of the Addolorata.

FESTIVALS & EVENTS

Ascoli Piceno *Giostra della Quintana*,
Pageants and jousts in 14th-century
costumes based on the paintings of
Carlo Crivelli; competition between the
six *sestieri*, or city districts, July–Aug.
Cingoli *Cingoli 1848*, Everybody dresses
up in 19th-century costume to watch a
game of *pallone al bracciale* (*see p. 677*),
second week in Aug.
Fermo *Cavalcata dell'Assunta*, The *Palio,*
or banner, which goes back to 1182, is
contended by stalwarts representing ten
districts or *contrade*, 15 Aug.
Macerata Open-air opera festival at the
Sferisterio, www.macerataopera.org,
July-Aug; *Le Canestrelle*, Participants
carry baskets with offerings of wheat
and flowers to the sanctuary of the
Madonna della Misericordia, a tradition
going back to the ancient cult of
Cybele, first Sun in Sept.
San Severino Marche *Palio dei Castelli*,
Archery contests and races, June.
Tolentino *Tolentino 815*, Re-enactment
of the famous battle for Rancia Castle,
first Sun in May; *Dono dei Ceri a San
Nicola*, City corporations donate elaborate wax candles and a banner to their
saint, with archery contests and a tug-
of-war, end Aug–early Sept; *Sul Ponte
del Diavolo*, Folk dancing, archery and a
joust on the Devil's Bridge, end
Aug–mid-Sept; Feast of St Nicholas,
third Sun in July and 10 Sept.
Visso *Torneo delle Guaite*, Contests
between five *guaite* or districts, end
July–early Aug.

PLANNING YOUR TRIP

When to go

The countryside in central Italy is at its best in spring and autumn, although spring can be unexpectedly wet until well after Easter. Autumn is often warm throughout October and even in early November. Much of July and August is unbearably hot and humid; in fact Florence usually has the highest temperatures in the country. Of all the large cities in Italy, Rome has one of the best year-round climates. Easter is always very crowded, as are June and September. Although it is often bitterly cold, and the roads are sometimes icy, midwinter is always the best time to visit the most famous sights, since it is only then that places such as Assisi, Siena and San Gimignano are totally deserted. The best-known towns can be overrun from March–early May by Italian school parties. The coast of Versilia and the seaside resorts in the Maremma, and the island of Elba are extremely crowded with Italian holiday-makers in July and especially August (in particular in the weeks on either side of the national holiday on 15th August). The coastal resorts frequented by the Romans (such as Fregene and Ladispoli) also get very crowded in season. The Adriatic resorts in the Marche tend to be less crowded.

Maps

The best road maps, widely available in bookshops all over Italy, are published by the Touring Club Italiano. They are indispensable to anyone travelling by car. Their *Carta Stradale d'Italia*, on a scale of 1:200,000, is divided into 15 maps: the three which cover central Italy are *Toscana*, *Lazio*, and *Umbria e Marche*. There is also a handier three-volume atlas: the one entitled *Centro* covers the area of this guide.

Disabled travellers

Italy is fast applying current legislation, which obliges public buildings to provide disabled access and facilities within. However the numerous hilltop towns and villages often have very steep and narrow streets, some of them stepped. In the annual accommodation list published by the local tourist offices, places which can offer hospitality to the disabled are indicated. Airports and railway stations now provide assistance, and certain trains are equipped to transport wheelchairs. Access for cars is allowed to town centres otherwise closed to traffic, and parking places are provided. For all other information, contact the local tourist offices.

ACCOMMODATION

A selection of places to stay, chosen on the basis of character or location, is given at the end of each chapter: smaller hotels have been favoured (and those which are family run and do not take large groups), and those in quiet areas in the centre of towns, sometimes in historic buildings, and farmhouse accommodation (*agriturismo*) in particularly beautiful positions in the countryside. They have been classified as follows, for a double room per night in high season: €€€€ (over €300); €€€ (€200 or over); €€€ (100–200); € (under €100).

BLUE GUIDES RECOMMENDED

Hotels, restaurants and cafés that are particularly good choices in their category—in terms of excellence, location, charm, value for money or the quality of the experience they provide—carry the Blue Guides Recommended sign: ■. All these establishments have been visited and selected by our authors, editors or contributors as places they have particularly enjoyed and would be happy to recommend to others. To keep our entries up-to-date, reader feedback is essential: please do not hesitate to email us (editorial@blueguides.com) with any views, corrections or suggestions.

Farms which provide hospitality (*agriturismo*) are an excellent (and often cheap) way of visiting the Italy. In certain areas of Tuscany and Umbria almost every farm you pass now seems to have an 'agriturismo' sign up. These establishments, which should be working farms, are now officially classified by ears of corn (from the most expensive 3 ears to the cheapest 1 ear). Terms vary greatly from just bed-and-breakfast, to half- or full-board (the food is usually excellent with home-grown produce), or self-contained flats. There are a number of organisations, including Agriturist (www.agriturist.it), Terranostra (www.terranostra.it) and Turismo Verde (www.turismoverde.it).

Bed-and-breakfast accommodation is now often available both in towns and the countryside and can be a good choice (although the prices vary greatly). Religious institutions (usually listed as *case per ferie* or *case religiose di ospitalità*) also often provide simple hospitality at very reasonable prices. Another category of accommodation is the *residenza d'epoca*, in buildings of historic interest. Here you can usually stay for just a night or two, or rent a self-catering apartment. The category termed 'country house' operates in a similar way.

GETTING AROUND

By car

When driving in Italy, you must also keep a red triangle and a luminous jacket in the car in case of breakdown. You are required by law to keep your headlights on at all times on roads outside towns and cities. Pedestrians have the right of way at zebra crossings, although you're taking your life in your hands if you step into the street without looking. Unless otherwise indicated, cars entering a road from the right are given right of way. If an oncoming driver flashes his headlights, it means he is proceeding and not giving you precedence. In towns, Italian drivers frequently change lanes without warning.

Roads in Italy

Italy's motorways (*autostrade*) are indicated by green signs, and are toll roads. At the entrance to motorways, the two directions are indicated by the name of the most important town (and not by the nearest town), which can be momentarily confusing. Lorries are banned from motorways on Sundays, making that the best day to travel. Dual-carriageways are called *superstrade* (usually also indicated by green signs), but they are usually less well engineered with no emergency lanes. Secondary roads (*strade statali, regionali* or *provinciali*, indicated by blue signs marked SS, SR or SP; on maps simply by a number), normally carry less traffic.

Parking

Almost all cities and towns have now closed their historic centres to traffic (except for residents), and there are usually convenient, well sign-posted car parks on the outskirts. Access is allowed to hotels and for the disabled.

By rail

General information on rail links is given in individual chapters. Timetables are available at www.trenitalia.it. Tickets on the Eurostar-category trains must be booked in advance (up to 15mins before departure). All other tickets must be bought in advance to avoid paying a hefty supplement on the train. If you book online, you can either chose to collect your ticket from a machine on arrival at the station, or you can select the 'ticketless' system where you are given a code which you must show on the train. For all trains except Eurostar you must stamp your ticket in the meters on or near the platform before boarding.

By bus

There are local bus services between the main towns, especially those not on a railway line. The service varies greatly from region to region, but normally there is a bus stop very close to the centre of a town. Information is most reliably obtained from local tourist offices. Some services are direct, and others, much slower, stop everywhere on the way, so it is always worth asking more than once if you are on the right bus. Tickets are usually purchased before boarding (at tobacconists, bars, newsstands, information offices and so on), and must be stamped in a machine on board. Some services now only coincide with school hours—generally in the early morning and early afternoon. In the larger towns, the bus station is often close to the railway station. City buses are sometimes a good way of getting about in Rome and Florence, but most other towns are best visited on foot.

Cycling and walking

Cycling and walking have become more popular in Italy in recent years and more information is available locally. However many areas are not yet sufficiently mapped, and paths are often not consistently marked. The local tourist offices will supply information. The areas of Tuscany particularly suitable for walking are the Garfagnana, the Mugello, the Casentino and Monte Amiata. The Sibylline Mountains between Umbria and the Marche are good for hiking. In Umbria there are marked trails on Monte Subasio, Monte Cucco, near Castelluccio, above Lake Trasimene and in the Valnerina. In Umbria there is a path from Assisi via Valfabbrica to Gubbio, and a bicycle route from near Spoleto to Assisi. You can now take your bicycle on some trains.

Taxis

These are hired from ranks or by telephone; there are no cruising cabs. Before engaging a taxi, make sure it has a meter in working order. Only a very small tip is expected. Supplements are charged for late-night journeys and for luggage. There is a heavy surcharge when the destination is outside the town limits.

MUSEUMS & CHURCHES

The opening times of museums, sites and monuments have been given in the text, though they often change without warning, so care should be taken to allow enough time for variations. National museums, monuments, and archaeological sites are usually open daily 9am–dusk, and if they have a closing day it is usually Monday. Some museums are closed on the main public holidays. For museums, gardens, and other sites where admission is by appointment only, telephone numbers have been given in the text. Up-to-date information is always available at the local tourist offices.

Entrance fees vary according to age and nationality; British citizens under 18 and over 65 are entitled to free admission to national museums and monuments because of reciprocal arrangements in Britain, but you need to be able to prove your age. During the Settimana per i Beni Culturali e Ambientali (Cultural and Environmental Heritage Week), usually held in March or April, entrance to national museums is free for all.

Churches open quite early in the morning (at 7 or 8), and are normally closed during the middle of the day (12–3/4/5pm), although cathedrals and some of the most important churches are now often kept open without a break during daylight hours. The key for locked churches and oratories in villages can sometimes be found by enquiring locally. Some churches now ask that sightseers do not enter during a service, but normally visitors not in a tour group may do so, provided they are silent and do not approach the altar in use. At all times you are expected to dress with decorum and sometimes you are not allowed to enter important churches or religious sanctuaries wearing shorts or with bare shoulders. Churches are often unaligned: descriptions in the text always refer to liturgical (not compass) north, east, west and south; in other words, the high altar is always taken to be the 'east' end.

ADDITIONAL INFORMATION

Banking services

There are now ATM machines outside most banks throughout Italy. Money can also be changed at banks, post offices, travel agencies and some hotels, restaurants and shops, though the rate of exchange can vary considerably. Banks are open Mon–Fri 8.30–1.30 and for an hour in the afternoon, usually 2.30–3.30. A few banks now stay open on Saturday morning. They all close early (about 11) the day before a national holiday.

Crime and personal security

Pickpocketing is a widespread problem in Italy: it is always advisable to be particularly careful on public transport. Never wear conspicuous jewellery; women should carry their handbags on the side nearer the wall (never on the street side). Crime should be reported at once to the police or the local *carabinieri* office (found in every town and small village). A statement has to be given in order to get a document confirming loss or damage (essential for insurance claims). Interpreters are provided. **Emergency numbers:** Police: T: 113 (*Polizia di Stato*) or 112 (*Carabinieri*); Medical assistance: T: 118.

Pharmacies

Pharmacies (*farmacie*) are usually open Mon–Fri 9–1 & 4–7.30/8. A few are open also on Sat, Sun and holidays (listed on the door of every pharmacy). In all towns there is also at least one pharmacy open at night (also shown on every pharmacy door).

Public holidays

The Italian national holidays when offices, shops, and schools are closed are as follows:

1 January	1 November (All Saints' Day)
Easter Sunday and Easter Monday	8 December (Immaculate Conception)
25 April (Liberation Day)	25 December (Christmas Day)
1 May (Labour Day)	26 December (St Stephen)
15 August (Assumption)	

Each town keeps its patron saint's day as a holiday.

Sales tax rebates

If you're a non-European Union resident, you can claim tax back on purchases made in Italy, provided the total expenditure is more than €150. Ask the vendor for details.

Telephones

The country code for Italy is 39. To dial the UK from Italy (00 44) + number; dialling the US from Italy (001) + the number. Telephone numbers in Italy require the area code, even if you are calling from within the same area. With all numbers, including mobiles, you need to dial all the digits.

Tipping

Tipping is far less widespread in Italy than in North America. Most prices in restaurants include service: always check whether this has been added to the bill before leaving a tip. It is customary to leave just two or three euro on the table to convey appreciation. Even taxi-drivers rarely expect more than a euro or two added to the charge (which officially includes service). In hotels, porters who show you to your room and help with your luggage, or find you a taxi, usually expect a euro or two.

FOOD & DRINK

Restaurants

A selection of restaurants has been given at the end of each chapter. Prices are given as €€€ (€80 or more per head), €€ (€30–80) and € (under €30).

Prices on the menu do not include a cover charge (shown separately, usually at the bottom of the page), which is added to the bill. The service charge is now almost always automatically added; tipping is therefore not strictly necessary, but a few euros are appreciated. You should be given a receipt.

Bars and cafés

Bars and cafés are open from early morning to late at night and serve numerous types of refreshment, which most Italians take standing up. As a rule, you must pay the cashier first, then present your receipt to the barman in order to get served. If you sit at a table, the charge is usually higher, and you will be given waiter service (so don't pay first). However, some simple bars have a few tables that can be used with no extra charge, and it is always best to ask whether there is waiter service or not.

Coffee

Italy is considered to have the best coffee in Europe. *Espresso* (black coffee) can be ordered *lungo* (diluted), *corretto* (with a liquor), or *macchiato* (with a dash of milk). If you want milk with your coffee, order a *cappuccino* or a *latte macchiato*, which is hot milk with a dash of coffee in it. Iced coffee (*caffè freddo*) is served in summer.

FOOD IN CENTRAL ITALY

Tuscany, Umbria and the Marche are all famous for their excellent olive oil, the essential ingredient in Italian cooking. Some experts maintain that the oil from the olive groves at Cartoceto in the Marche is the finest in the world.

Pasta dishes

Italy is known above all for its pasta, which is served in countless ways, with a great variety of sauces. The best is usually home-made (*fatta in casa*). In central Italy this includes *tagliatelle* or *fettuccine*, ribbon noodles made with the addition of eggs, and *strangozzi* (also called *strozzapreti*, *bigoli*, *pici* and *umbricelli*), rustic thick spaghetti made with water and flour. These are served with a great variety of sauces including *ragù* (minced meat, onion and tomato) and mushrooms. In the Marche *tagliatelle alla papera* have a dressing of duck ragout, and in Tuscany *pappardelle alla lepre* are a short pasta served with a rich hare sauce. In Rome and Lazio menus often include *spaghetti alla carbonara*, with a light sauce of salt pork, beaten egg, pecorino cheese and black pepper. *Penne all'arrabbiata* is a short pasta with a hot (piquant) tomato sauce, and *bucatini* or *penne all'Amatriciana*, thick, hollow spaghetti or short pasta served in a light sauce of salt pork, tomatoes and pecorino cheese are often to be found in Lazio.

In Tuscany regional dishes include *tortelli di patate* (or *topini*), found especially in the Casentino and Mugello, which are ravioli filled with potatoes (sometimes spiced with sausage meat). *Tortelli maremmani* are filled with ricotta and spinach. In the Marche *vincisgrassi* is an exquisite version of *lasagna*.

In winter fresh *gnocchi* made from potatoes and flour are also ubiquitous, as well as *polenta*, a maize flour cake which can be a pasta dish (with a sauce of mushrooms, for example) or an accompaniment to sausages or game. *Gnocchi alla romana* are made from a dough of semolina flour, eggs and milk, covered in cheese and baked. *Timballo*, served in Lazio is an exceptionally rich pasta dish baked in the oven.

Soups and antipasti

Soups include the classic vegetable *minestrone*, often served in Tuscany. In winter this is made in a richer version called *ribollita* or *zuppa di pane*, with white beans, black cabbage and bread. A traditional peasant soup served all over central Italy is *acquacotta*, and there are numerous different versions of it: it is often made with onions, basil, celery, and greens (first lightly fried) with the addition of tomatoes, toasted bread, pecorino cheese, and eggs. In Lazio chicory, potatoes and dried cod are also sometimes added. *Stracciatella*, a meat broth with parmesan and a beaten egg, is often served in Rome.

Hors d'oeuvre (*antipasti*) can replace the pasta course: excellent cured pork meats including ham, sausages and salami are produced all over the region and especially around Norcia and the Valnerina in Umbria (*see p. ???*). A summer salad widely available in Tuscany is *panzanella* which dry bread, tomatoes, fresh onions, cucumber, basil, and capers. *Pappa al pomodoro* is also made mostly in summer, a thick tomato soup with bread, seasoned with basil, etc. In the autumn *bruschetta* is served all over central Italy: toasted bread with garlic and oil straight from the olive press; in Tuscany it is usually called *fettunta*, and, if it is topped with hot black cabbage it is called *cavolo con le fette*. *Crostini* are slices of bread or toast topped with grated truffles, mushrooms, tomatoes, or chicken liver paste. Olives can be very good, and they are particularly sweet and tender at Ascoli Piceno, where they are sometimes served stuffed and fried.

Meat and fish

Meat is often simply grilled or roasted on the spit, and the preference is for farmyard animals, such as rabbit, lamb, chicken, duck and pigeon. The famous *bistecca alla fiorentina*, a T-bone steak, is always cooked over charcoal, and *rosticciana* is grilled spare ribs. The best known meat dish in Rome is *abbacchio* suckling lamb usually roasted in the oven. In Tuscany, meat dishes are often stewed slowly in a tomato sauce, called *in umido* (*stracotto* is beef cooked in this way or in red wine). In the Maremma, and in Umbria wild boar (*cinghiale*) is sometimes prepared *alla cacciatore*, marinated in red wine, with parsley, bay, garlic, rosemary, onion, carrot, celery, sage and wild fennel. It is then cooked slowly at a low heat in a terracotta pot with oil, lard, hot spicy pepper, and a little tomato sauce. *Saltimbocca alla romana*, is veal escalope cooked with ham and sage, and *involtini*, are thin, rolled slices of meat in a sauce. *Porchetta*, roast suckling pig boned and stuffed with fennel, herbs, garlic, salt and pepper, is prepared all over Umbria. It is often sold from vans at local markets and makes a delicious sandwich.

Fish is particularly good in Livorno. The *cacciucco alla Livornese* is a rich stew made with a wide variety of fish in a spicy sauce. *Zuppa di pesce*, another version of *cacciucco*, is served along the coast in the Marche in a variety of ways. If the fish is really fresh it is often best simply roasted or grilled: among the most succulent Mediterranean fish cooked in this way are *dentice* (dentex), *orata* (bream) and *triglie* (red mullet).

Seafood, often served simply cooked in white wine with garlic and parsley, includes *cozze* (mussels) and *vongole* (clams): these are also sometimes served with spaghetti as a pasta course. *Gamberi* (prawns) are usually grilled. *Filetti di baccalà fritti*, fillets of salt cod fried in batter are an unexpected dish often served in Rome.

In Umbria, Lazio and Tuscany excellent fish (perch, eels and pike) is widely available in the lakeside restaurants of Trasimene, Bolsena and Chiusi. The rich fish soup typical of Trasimene, called *tegamaccio*, is prepared by lightly frying onions, garlic and parsley and then adding tomato purée. The fish are then cooked very slowly in the same pan with the lid on, in a little white wine. *Regina in porchetta* is carp stuffed with lard, rosemary, fennel and garlic and cooked in the oven in a little olive oil.

Vegetables

Carciofi, artichokes are especially important part of Roman cuisine. They may be *alla giudea* (deep fried) or *alla romana* (stuffed with wild mint and garlic and then stewed in olive oil and water). *Zucchini*, courgettes, are sometimes served *ripieni* (stuffed) or fried. *Fritto di fiori di zucca* are courgette flowers stuffed with mozzarella cheese and salted anchovies, dipped in batter and fried. *Insalata di puntarelle* is a typical Roman salad made from the shredded stalks of locally grown chicory, with an anchovy dressing. Particularly good cooked green vegetables in Lazio include *cicoria* (chicory) and *broccoletti* or *broccoletti di rapa* (broccoli). The rich green salad called *misticanza*, with a great variety of wild lettuce and herbs, is particularly good but only to be found in Ciociaria.

Lentils (*lenticchie*) are found in both Lazio and Umbria (where they are grown at Castelluccio; *see p. ???*). The classic *zuppa di lenticchie* is made with a lot of chopped celery and a clove of garlic, with fresh olive oil added when cooked. Spelt (*farro*) is a grain which has been cultivated in Umbria and Lazio since before the Roman era. It is a particularly nourishing food (usually organically grown). *Minestra di farro* is simply spelt boiled in water with whole cloves of garlic, with the addition of finely chopped garlic when cooked. Fresh wild mushrooms (*funghi*), especially *porcini*, are on menus all over the region in the autumn and sometimes around Easter. From April to June delicious *prataioli*, *sanguinacci*, *ovoli* and *prugnoli* are also sometimes served in Umbrian restaurants. Another speciality of Umbria and the Marche are truffles (*tartufi*), an expensive delicacy, often served on toasted bread as an hors d'oeuvre, or as a condiment for pasta or risotto, or as a flavouring for meat, game, egg or fish dishes.

Sweets

In the autumn in Tuscany *castagnaccio* is made, a chestnut cake with pine nuts and sultanas, as well as *schiacciata all'uva*, a bready dough filled and topped with black grapes and sugar and seasoned with fennel. In Umbria excellent cakes and biscuits are made with almonds, candied fruits, pine nuts, chestnuts and walnuts. The *torciglione* or *serpentone* is a delicious cake in the form of a snake made with almond paste. *Torcolo* is flavoured with pine nuts and candied fruits. The *crescionda* is a rich traditional cake, usually made with eggs, milk, almond biscuits, lemon rind, bitter chocolate and a little flour. It can also contain apples, cinnamon and raisins. A speciality of Amelia are the candied figs (*fichi*) prepared with almonds and cocoa. In Ciociaria the *ciambelline al vino*, dry biscuits made with white or red wine and flavoured with aniseed, are particularly good and always accompanied by a glass of wine.

Bread and cheese

In Livorno a delicious, thin pizza-like bread cooked with chick-peas, known as *torta*, is widely available. This is also found in Volterra, where it is called *cecina* (both are sweeter than normal bread). In and around Perugia, bread is sometimes made with the addition of cheese in the form of a cake. In various parts of Umbria *torta al testo* is made: this is a white pizza served with a great variety of fillings (lard and cheese, cooked greens, raw ham, salami). It is also very popular in the Marche where it is called *crescia*. *Pane nociato* is prepared near Città di Castello, when walnuts are added to the bread dough. Bread in the Marche is exceptionally good.

Cheeses in Tuscany include the ubiquitous *pecorino*, a strong, hard cheese made from sheeps' milk (the one from Pienza is particularly famous). In Lazio excellent *mozzarella di bufala* is often available. From the Marche comes the soft *caciotta d'Urbino*, as well as a pit-matured cheese from Talamello.

WINE

The finest Italian wines are marked DOC (*di origine controllata*) or DOCG (*di origine controllata e garantita*). This is Italy's *appellation controlée*, which specifies the maximum yields per vine, geographical boundaries within which grapes must be grown, permitted grape varieties and production techniques.

Lazio

Lazio, where the house wine served in Rome is almost always white, was famous for centuries for its Vini dei Castelli, and in particular the light white wine of Frascati with its clear amber tint: it is recorded that in 1450 there were over 1,000 taverns in Rome which were owned by wine-producers from Frascati. The volcanic soil around Bolsena is good wine-growing country, and here the famous white Est!Est!Est! DOC wine is produced near Montefiascone (*see p. 182*). Another DOC wine is the red Cesanese from Piglio in the Ernici mountains and Olevano Romano in southern Lazio. Aleatico is a good red wine made at Gradoli near Bolsena, which can also be sweet. Many monastic communities in Lazio still make their own herbal liqueurs (such as Sambuca, Nocino, Ralafia, and Sarandrea), but these are usually only sold at the monasteries themselves.

Marche

The best known red wine in the Marche is Rosso Conero, made from vineyards near Ancona, overlooking the sea. Verdicchio is a good white wine produced in the area around Jesi and at Matelica. Other good red wines of this region include Rosso Piceno Superiore, Lagrima di Morro d'Alba, Esino, Offida Rosso, and the distinctive, sparkling Vernaccia di Serrapetrona (the only wine in the Marche which has the DOCG appellation). In certain areas wine is also made with cherry juice: *visner* or *vino di visciole*. The most famous liqueur are the aniseed-flavoured *mistrà* and *anisetta*.

Tuscany

Tuscany produces the best known of all Italian red wines, Chianti. The name is protected by law and only those wines from a relatively small district which lies between Florence and Siena are entitled to the name Chianti Classico (*see p. 373*). Chianti Classico Gallo Nero (distinguished by a black cockerel on the bottle) is usually considered the best, but Chianti Putto and Chianti Grappolo are also very good.

Brunello di Montalcino and Vino Nobile di Montepulciano are premium-quality reds. From Bolgheri come the famous Supertuscans (*see p. 469*). Other good red wine is produced at Carmignano near Florence, and around Lucca. The most famous white wine of Tuscany is the Vernaccia di San Gimignano, but Pitigliano, Montecarlo, and the Val d'Arbia also have good whites.

Umbria

In Umbria the most famous white wine is produced around Orvieto. Another good white is the Torre di Giano from the vineyards of Torgiano. Among the best red wines are Montefalco (especially those produced by Caprai, Antonelli, Rocca di Fabbri, Adanti and Scaccia Diavoli) and Torgiano Rubesco. Other DOC wines in Umbria are Colli Altotiberini from the upper Tiber valley near Umbertide, the Colli Amerini from around Amelia, and the Colli del Trasimeno. One of the most exceptional wines in Umbria (documented in the 16th century but probably also produced by the Romans) is the deep red Sagrantino (which can be *passito* or *secco*) produced in a small hilly area between Montefalco and Bevagna. It is now one of the most expensive wines in all Italy. The Sagrantino di Montefalco from Arnaldo Caprai is particularly good (www.arnaldo-caprai.it). The Antinori family also makes a superb white wine: Castello della Sala, a blend of Chardonnay and the indigenous Grechetto.

GLOSSARY

Aedicule, small opening framed by two columns and a pediment, originally used in Classical architecture

Ambulatory, typically the section of a church beside and around the high altar; a walkway in a cloister

Ambo (pl. *ambones*), pulpit in a Christian basilica; two pulpits on opposite sides of a church from which the Gospel and Epistle are read

Amorino (pl. *amorini*), a small cupid or putto

Amphora, antique vase, usually of large dimensions, for oil and other liquids

Ancona, retable or large altarpiece (painted or sculpted) in an architectural frame

Annunciation, the appearance of the Angel Gabriel to Mary to tell her that she will bear the Son of God; an image of the 'Virgin Annunicate' shows her receiving the news

Antefix, an ornament at the eaves of a roof to hide the join between tiles

Antis, columns at the front of a temple are 'in antis' when placed between two projecting side piers

Archaic, period in Greek civilisation preceding the Classical era: c. 750 BC–480 BC

Architrave, the horizontal beam placed above supporting columns; lowest part of an entablature (*qv*), the horizontal frame above a door

Archivolt, moulded architrave carried around an arch

Arte (pl. *arti*), guild or corporation

Arte Povera, an Italian expression used to describe Conceptual or Minimalist art which deliberately uses materials of little worth

Assumption, the ascension of the Virgin to Heaven, 'assumed' by the power of God

Atlantis (or Telamon), supporting column in the form of a sculpted male figure

Attic, topmost storey of a Classical building, hiding the spring of the roof; of pottery, describing an ancient Greek style from Attica (fl. c. 650 BC–400 BC)

Baldacchino, canopy supported by columns, for example over an altar

Basilica, originally a Roman hall used for public administration; in Christian architecture an aisled church with a clerestory and apse and no transepts

Bas-relief, sculpture in low relief

Biga, a two-horse chariot

Biscuit (or bisque), fired but unglazed earthenware or pottery

Blind arch, an arch attached to a wall for purely decorative purposes

Borgo, a suburb; a district of town; street leading away from the centre of a town

Bottega, the studio of an artist; the pupils who worked under his direction

Bozzetto (pl. *bozzetti*), sketch, often used to describe a small model for a piece of sculpture

Bucchero ware, Etruscan black terracotta

Bucrania, a form of Classical decoration: skulls of oxen between flower garlands

Calidarium, room for hot or vapour baths in a Roman bath complex

Camaldolensian (or Camaldolese), pertaining to the monastic order founded at Camaldoli in Tuscany by St Romuald (*see p. 385*)

Campanile, bell-tower, often detached from the building to which it belongs

Canopic jar (or vase), ancient Egyptian urn used to preserve the internal organs, and placed in the tomb beside the mummy

Cantoria (pl. *cantorie*), singing-gallery in a church

Carolingian, pertaining to Charlemagne and the dynasty he founded in the 9th century

Cartoon, from *cartone*, meaning a large sheet of paper—a full-size preparatory drawing for a painting or fresco

Caryatid, sculpted female figure used as a supporting column

Cavea, the part of a theatre or amphitheatre occupied by the rows of seats

Cella, sanctuary of a temple, usually in the centre of the building

Cenotaph a symbolic tomb or funerary monument which does not contain the body of the deceased

Chiaroscuro, distribution of light and shade in a painting

Ciborium, casket or tabernacle containing the Host (Communion bread)

Cimasa, the topmost section of an altarpiece

Cinquecento, Italian term for the 'fifteen hundreds' ie the 16th century

Cipollino, onion marble; greyish marble with streaks of white or green

Cippus (pl. *cippi*), sepulchral monument in the form of an altar

Classical, in ancient Greece, the period from 480–323 BC; in general, when spelled with a capital C, denotes art etc from the ancient world as opposed to classical ('classicising') modern works

Clerestory, upper part of the nave wall of a church, above the side aisles, with windows

Condottiere (pl. *condottieri*), soldier of fortune, employed in Italy by popes and emperors, republics and duchies, to lead armies to fight their cause

Contrapposto, a pose in which the body is balanced on an S-shaped axis. First used in Classical statuary, it is characteristic of Michelangelo's sculpture

Corbel, a projecting block, usually of stone

Corinthian, ancient Greek and Roman order of architecture, a characteristic of which is a capital decorated with acanthus leaves

Cornice, topmost part of a temple entablature; any projecting ornamental moulding at the top of a building beneath the roof

Cosmatesque, Cosmati, medieval style of mosaic decoration or cladding consisting of geometric patterns made up of (often) ancient marble fragments

Crenellations, battlements, specifically the indented sections

Crocketed, ornamented with a foliage motif, typical of Gothic architecture

Cusped arch, an arch which has lobes on its inner side meeting in points (cusps); typical of Gothic and Moorish architecture

Cyclopean, masonry which uses enormous blocks, so large that they appeared to the ancients to have been built by the cyclopes

Decumanus, the main street of a Roman town running parallel to its longer axis

Diptych, painting or ivory tablet in two sections

Distyle, a temple or porch with two columns

Doric, ancient Greek order of architecture characterised by fluted columns standing close together on the stylobate (with no base)

Dossal, a cloth hung behind the altar or at the sides of the chancel

Dosseret block of stone placed above the capitals in an arcade to support the arch

Dromos, narrow external access corridor to a tomb, typically Mycenaean or Etruscan

Entablature, upper part of a temple above the columns, made up of an architrave, frieze and cornice

Epistyle, an architrave (*qv*)

Etruria, the territory of the ancient Etruscans, covering parts of present-day Tuscany, Lazio, Umbria and Emilia-Romagna

Evangelists, the authors of the gospels, Matthew, Mark, Luke and John, in Christian art often represented by their symbols: man or angel (Matthew), lion (Mark), bull (Luke), eagle (John)

Exedra, semicircular recess

Ex-voto, tablet or small painting expressing gratitude to a saint

Fibula (pl. *fibulae*), garment brooch or pin

Flavian, of the emperors Vespasian, Titus, Domitian, Nerva and Trajan; or the period of their rule

Foliated, decorated with a leaf motif

Fresco (in Italian, *affresco*), painting executed on wet plaster (*intonaco*), beneath which the artist had usually made a working sketch (*sinopia*)

Frigidarium, room for cold baths in a Roman bath complex

Ghibelline crenellations, fish-tail battlements on medieval towers, typically associated with Ghibelline allegiance

Gonfalone, banner of a medieval guild or commune

Gonfaloniere, chief magistrate or official of a medieval Italian Republic, the bearer of the Republic's *gonfalone*

Graffiti, design on a wall made with an iron tool on a prepared surface, the design visible in white. Also used loosely to describe scratched designs or words on walls

Greek cross, church plan based on a cross with arms of equal length

Grisaille, painting in various tones of grey

Grottesche (or grotesques), delicate ornamental decoration characterised by fantastical motifs, patterns of volutes, festoons and garlands, and borders of vegetation, flowers and animals or birds. This type of decoration, first discovered in Nero's Domus Aurea, became very fashionable and was widely copied by late Renaissance artists

Hellenistic, Greek culture of late 4th–late 1st centuries BC. Art from this period often displays more emotion than Classical works.

Hemicycle, a semicircular structure, room, arena or wall

Herm (pl. *hermae*), quadrangular pillar decreasing in girth towards the ground, surmounted by a head

Hymettian marble, from Mt Hymettus in Greece; blue-grey in colour

Hypocaust, ancient Roman heating system in which hot air circulated under the floor and between double walls

Hypogeum, underground chamber, typically of a tomb

Impluvium, a rainwater pool in the atrium of an ancient Roman house

Impost, a block placed above a capital from which an arch rises

Incunabulum (pl. *incunabula*) any book printed in the same century as the invention of movable type (ie between 1450 and 1500)

Intarsia, a decorative inlay made from wood, marble or metal

International Gothic, Painting style characterised by a poised elegance, still and static, but without the rigidity of pure Gothic. There is also a mingling of strong design with loving attention to detail, such as birds, animals and flowers. The style is often called 'courtly', because the natural and the stylised come together in images redolent of medieval courtliness

Intonaco, plaster

Intrados, underside of an arch, also known as the soffit

Ionic, an order of architecture developed in Ionia, a region of Asia Minor, in the late 6th century BC, and identified by its capitals with two opposed volutes (curls) supporting a moulded abacus. Columns are fluted, stand on a base, and have a shaft more slender than in the Doric order

Kouroi, from the Greek word for young man (*kouros*) used to describe standing, nude male statues in the Greek Archaic style

Krater, a large, open bowl used for mixing wines, especially in ancient Greece

Kylix (pl. *kylices*), a wide, shallow drinking vessel with two handles and a short stem

Lancet window, Gothic style with a pointed arched head, from the late 12th century

Lantern, a small circular or polygonal turret with windows all round, crowning a roof or a dome

Latin, Latins, pertaining to the people of ancient Latium (Lazio)

Latin cross, a cross where the vertical arm is longer than the transverse arm

Lavabo, hand-basin usually outside a refectory or in a sacristy

Lavatorium, the Latin name for a room with large hand-basins (*lavabi*) in stone or marble outside a convent refectory where the rites of purification were carried out before a meal

Lekythos, an ancient Greek vase, tall and narrow-necked with one handle, used as a vessel for oil

Loggia (pl. *logge*), covered gallery or balcony, usually preceding a larger building

Lunette, semicircular space in a vault or ceiling, or above a door or window, often decorated with a painting or relief

Maenad, female participant in the orgiastic rites of Dionysus (Bacchus)

Maestà, representation of the Madonna and Child enthroned in majesty

Majolica, a type of earthenware glazed with bright metallic oxides that was originally imported to Italy from Majorca and was extensively made in Italy during the Renaissance

Mandorla, tapered, almond-shaped aura around a holy figure (usually Christ or the Virgin)

Mannerist, a period of mainly Italian art between the High Renaissance and the Baroque (c. 1520–1600). Unnatural light, lurid colours, and elongated forms are characteristic of this style

Menhir, literally 'long stone', from the Celtic: a standing stone

Meta conical turning-post for chariot races in a circus or stadium

Metope, panel carved with decorative relief between two triglyphs (three vertical bands) on the frieze of a Doric temple

Mithraeum, a shrine of Mithras, a Persian sun-god worshipped in Imperial Rome

Monolith, single stone (usually a column)

Narthex, vestibule of a church or basilica, before the west door

Nenfro, grey stone found locally in Lazio, in particular around Tuscania

Nereid, sea-nymphs of Greek mythology; the 50 daughters of Nereus and Doris

Niello, black substance (usually a compound of sulphur and silver) used in an engraved design, or an object so decorated

Nimbus, luminous ring surrounding the heads of saints in paintings; a square nimbus denoted that the person was living at the time

Nymphaeum, a summer house in the gardens of baths and palaces, originally a temple of the Nymphs, decorated with statues of those goddesses, and often containing a fountain

Oculus, round window or aperture

Opus reticulatum, masonry arranged in squares or diamonds so that the mortar joints make a network pattern

Opus sectile, mosaic or paving of thin slabs of coloured marble cut in geometric shapes

Opus tessellatum, mosaic formed entirely of square *tesserae* (pieces of marble, stone or glass)

Pala, large altarpiece

Palaeochristian, from the earliest Christian times up to the 6th century

Palaestra, a public place devoted to training athletes in ancient Greece or Rome

Paschal, in the Christian Church, pertaining to Easter

Passion, the sufferings of Christ, ending with his death on the Cross. The Instruments of the Passion are symbols of these sufferings, and include the Cross, the crown of thorns and the column at which Jesus was flagellated

Patera (pl. *paterae*), small circular carved ornament, often Byzantine; a shallow ritual drinking dish

Pavonazzetto, yellow marble blotched with blue

Pax, sacred object used by a priest for the blessing of peace and offered for the kiss of the faithful; usually circular, engraved, enamelled, or painted in a rich gold or silver frame

Pediment, triangular gable above a portico

Pelasgic, pertaining to a pre-Hellenic people (the Pelasgians) variously regarded to have originated in the central and northern Greek mainland

Pendant, a painting or work which forms a companion or complement to another

Pendentive, concave spandrel beneath a dome

Peperino, a dark grey or bownish volcanic stone, common building material around Viterbo

Peripteral, of a temple, meaning surrounded on all sides by a colonnade

Peristyle, court or garden surrounded by a columned portico

Piano nobile, main floor of a palace

Picene, Picenes, pertaining to the ancient inhabitants of the Marche region, before the arrival of the Romans

Pietà, representation of the Virgin mourning the dead Christ (sometimes with other figures)

Pietre dure, hard or semi-precious stones, often used in the form of mosaics to decorate furniture such as cabinets and table-tops

Pietra forte, fine-grained limey sandstone used as a building material in Florence, and often for the rustication of palace façades

Pietra serena, fine-grained dark grey sandstone, easy to carve. Although generally not sufficiently resistant for the exterior of buildings, it was used to decorate many Renaissance interiors in Florence

Pieve, parish church; the main church in a parish, with one or more minor churches subject to its jurisdiction

Pilaster, a shallow pier or rectangular column projecting only slightly from the wall

Piscina, Roman tank; a pool for ablutions; a basin for an officiating priest to wash his hands before Mass

Pluteus (pl. *plutei*), marble panel, usually decorated; a series of them used to form a parapet to precede the altar of a church

Podestà, chief magistrate who ruled a medieval city with the help of a council and representatives from the corporations. He had to be someone who was not a Florentine, and was also a military leader

Polyptych, painting or panel in more than three sections

Porphyry, dark blue, purple or red-coloured igneous rock, much prized in the ancient world

Predella, small painting or panel, usually in sections, attached below a large altarpiece, illustrating scenes of a story such as the life of a saint, or of the Virgin.

Presbytery, the eastern part of a church chancel, beyond the choir

Presepio, literally crib or manger. A statuary group of which the central subject is the Infant Jesus in the manger

Pronaos, porch in front of a temple cella

Pulvin, cushion stone between the capital and the impost block

Putto (pl. *putti*), figure sculpted or painted, usually nude, of a child

Pyx, receptacle to hold the consecrated Communion bread in a church

Romanesque, architecture of the early Western Christian Empire, from the 7th–12th centuries, preceding the Gothic style

Quadratura, painted architectural perspectives; architectural *trompe l'oeil*

Quadriga, a two-wheeled chariot drawn by four horses abreast

Quadriporticus, rectangular court or atrium arcaded on all four sides, derived from the atria in front of palaeochristian basilicas

Quatrefoil, four-lobed design

Quattrocento, Italian term for the 'fourteen hundreds' ie the 15th century

Rhyton, drinking-horn usually ending in an animal's head

Rood-screen, a screen below the Rood or Crucifix dividing the nave from the chancel of a church

Rostra, orators' platform; ships' prows captured in battle, often used to decorate these platforms by the ancient Romans

Sabine, Sabines, an ancient people whose territory lay in the northeast of modern-day Lazio

Sarmatian, pertaining to the ancient Iranian nomadic peoples whose territory covered central Asia to eastern Europe

Scagliola, imitation marble or *pietre dure* made from selenite

Scarsella, the rectangular recess of the tribune of the Florence Baptistery. Now also sometimes used for the rectangular sanctuary in a church

Scena, the stage building of an ancient Roman theatre

Schiacciato, term used to describe very low relief in sculpture, where there is an emphasis on the delicate line rather than the depth of the panel (a technique perfected by Donatello)

Schola cantorum, enclosure for the choristers in the nave of an early Christian church, adjoining the sanctuary

Scriptorium, the room in a monastery where monks copied manuscripts

Seven Acts of Mercy, the Burial of the Dead; Visiting the Incarcerated; Feeding the Hungry; Clothing the Naked; Sheltering Pilgrims; Giving Drink to the Thirsty; and Tending the Sick

Sfumatura, in art, *sfumatura* or a *sfumato* technique denotes a smoky blending of colours and blurring of outline. It is typical of the painting of Leonardo da Vinci

Sibyls, the prophetesses of the pagan world; in Christian art they appear as precursors of the prophets of the Old Testament

Sinopia (pl. *sinopie*), large sketch for a fresco made on the rough wall in a red earth pigment called sinopia (because it originally came from Sinope, a town on the Black Sea). When a fresco is detached for restoration, it is possible to see the sinopia beneath, which can also be separated from the wall

Soffit, ceiling or underside of an arch or other element of architecture

Solomonic column, twisted column, so called from its supposed use in the Temple of Solomon

Spandrel, surface between two arches in an arcade or the triangular space on either side of an arch

Squinch, supporting block placed across the angles of a square area to allow a dome to be rested on top

Stele (pl. *stelae*), upright stone bearing a monumental inscription

Stemma (pl. *stemme*), coat of arms or heraldic device

Stigmata, marks appearing on a saint's body in the same places as the wounds of Christ (nail-holes in the feet and hands, and the sword-wound in the side)

Stoup, vessel for holy water, usually near the entrance door of a church

Stucco, plaster-work

Tablinum, the reception or family room in a Roman house

Telamon (*see Atlantis*)

Tempera, a painting medium of powdered pigment bound together, in its simplest form, by a mixture of egg yolk and water

Tepidarium, room for warm baths in a Roman bath

Term, pedestal topped by a human head and shoulders

Terraverde, green earth pigment, sometimes used in frescoes

Tessera (pl. *tesserae*), small cube of marble, stone or glass used in mosaic work

Thermae, originally simply Roman baths, later elaborate buildings fitted with libraries, assembly rooms, gymnasia and circuses

Thermal window, usually large, simcircular window, derived from those used in ancient Roman public baths (*thermae*)

Tondo (pl. *tondi*), circular painting or relief

Transenna, open grille or screen, usually of marble, in an early Christian church

Travertine, tufa quarried near Tivoli, used as a building material

Tribune, the apse of a Christian basilica that contains the bishop's throne or the throne itself

Triclinium, dining-room and reception-room of a Roman house

Triforium, upper-level arcaded aisle in a Romanesque or Gothic church, below the clerestory (*qv*)

Triglyph, small panel of a Doric frieze raised slightly and carved with three vertical channels

Triptych, painting or tablet in three sections

Triton, river god

Trompe l'œil, literally, a deception of the eye; used to describe illusionist decoration and painted architectural perspective

Truss-beam, system of roofing held together by trusses, that is beams tying the supporting structure together, mainly in a triangular form, to prevent it from splaying outwards

Tufa, volcanic rock, easy to work

Tuscan Doric, similar to the Doric order, but with columns unfluted and resting on a base, and without triglyphs in the frieze

Tympanum, the area between the top of a doorway and the arch above it; also the triangular space enclosed by the mouldings of a pediment

Umbri, the ancient inhabitants of the area now known as Umbria

Ustrinum, a square podium for a funeral pyre

Villanovan pertaining to early Iron Age Italian culture; the name derives from the town of Villanova near Bologna

Virtues, The Cardinal Virtues are Fortitude, Temperance, Justice and Prudence; the Theological Virtues are Faith, Hope and Charity

Volscians, ancient peoples who controlled southern Latium before being subjugated by the Romans in 338 BC

Volute, scroll-like decoration at the corners of an Ionic capital; also typically present console-style on the façades of Baroque churches

INDEX

More detailed or explanatory references (where there any many references listed), or references to an artist's masterpiece (in cases where it is not listed by name), are given in bold. Numbers in italics are picture references. Dates are given for all artists and sculptors. Conjectural or insecure attributions to artists and sculptors are not indexed.

Waterco...
Architectural line drawings:
Contributor (wine se...
Practical information sections con...

Photo editor: Róbert Szabó Benke, with Hau...
Photographs by Annabel Barber: pp. 35, 75, 79, 120, 173, 177, 190, 1...
Phil Robinson: pp. 39, 170, 174, 239, 249, 397, 501, 543, 549, .
Giacomo Mazza: pp. 356, 371, 470, 564, 650, 679, 686; Róbert Szabó Benke: pp...
Luca Bellincioni: p. 235; Julio Cid González: p. 101; Daniele Dalmasso: p. 453; Alinari Arc...
Florence: pp. 147, 153, 283, 292, 375, 493, 509, 524, 556; Alinari Archives, Florence (with the
permission of the Ministerio per i Beni e le Attività Culturali): pp. 287, 644; Bridgeman/Alinari
Archives, Florence: p. 427; The Bridgeman Art Library: pp. 133, 587; Red Dot/Alamy: pp. 220,
223, 572; Red Dot/Corbis: p. 245; © 1990 Photo Scala, Florence: p. 438; SEAT/Alinari Archives,
Florence: pp. 213, 683. Other images courtesy of Castello Ruspoli: p. 175; Collegio San Clemente:
p. 65; Comune di Pergola: p. 636; Galleria Doria: p. 42; Province of Ascoli Piceno: pp. 3, 667;
Soprintendenza Archeologica per La Toscana-Firenze: pp. 296, 367, 461.

Cover images
Top: Chapel on the Via Francigena near San Quirico d'Orcia (photo: Andrea Federici);
Bottom: Labyrinth on the portal of the duomo of Lucca (photo: András Jancsik);
Frontispiece: Detail from Carlo Crivelli's St Emygdius polyptych in Ascoli Piceno.

Authors' acknowledgements

The authors are particularly indebted to Françoise Pouncey Chiarini for her work in the past
on many parts of the Maremma and the Chianti area, which she first explored when
collaborating on *Blue Guide Tuscany*. As on previous occasions Alessandra Smith of the
Italian State Tourist Office was extremely kind and helpful. Particular thanks also to
Teresa Bellesi, Mario Giubbi, Maria Lunghi of the APT dell'Umbria, Anna Migliori,
Leila Pruneti of Toscana Promozione, Werner Rayé, the Touring Club Italiano,
as well as the staff in tourist offices throughout the region.

Printed in Hungary by Dürer Nyomda Kft, Gyula

ISBN 978–1–905131–22–8